DICTIONARY
OF
SCANDINAVIAN
LITERATURE

DICTIONARY OF **S**CANDINAVIA**N** LITERATURE

VIRPI ZUCK
Editor-in-Chief

NIELS INGWERSEN AND HARALD S. NAESS
Advisory Editors

GREENWOOD PRESS
New York • Westport, Connecticut • London

Library of Congress Cataloging-in-Publication Data

Dictionary of Scandinavian literature / Virpi Zuck, editor-in-chief ;
   Niels Ingwersen and Harald S. Naess, advisory editors.
      p. cm.
    Bibliography: p.
    Includes index.
    ISBN 0–313–21450–6 (lib. bdg. : alk. paper)
    1. Scandinavian literature—History and criticism—Dictionaries.
  I. Zuck, Virpi.
  PT7063.D5   1990
  839'.5'03—dc20   89–11970

British Library Cataloguing in Publication Data is available.

Library of Congress Catalog Card Number: 89–11970
ISBN: 0–313–21450–6

First published in 1990

Greenwood Press, 88 Post Road West, Westport, CT   06881
An imprint of Greenwood Publishing Group, Inc.

Printed in the United States of America

The paper used in this book complies with the
Permanent Paper Standard issued by the National
Information Standards Organization (Z39.48–1984).

10 9 8 7 6 5 4 3 2 1

Contents

Preface

"A country called Scandinavia . . . is a fairy tale written by Americans . . . Norden is reality, five countries whose distinctive aspects are fully as significant as their conceptual similarities and cooperative linkages."[1] That this literary handbook, which covers all five Nordic countries and more, is nevertheless called *Dictionary of Scandinavian Literature*, can be explained by its genesis. It was born out of the need in academic institutions that teach "Scandinavian" literature and its target audience consists of students and professors in the Scandinavian departments of universities as well as scholars in comparative literature and related disciplines. It is rare indeed in Scandinavia to find a literary history or even a survey article that would adopt such a synthetic view; most limit themselves to national literatures. One exception is *Nordens litteratur*, edited by Mogens Brøndsted. A good example of an American synthetic approach is Sven H. Rossel's recent *History of Scandinavian Literature* (Minneapolis, 1982). Viewing Scandinavia from a distance, similarities outweigh differences. For instance, already in 1875 when the first professorship in an American state university was established in Wisconsin, it was in Scandinavian studies rather than in Norwegian, although a majority of the Scandinavian immigrants in Wisconsin came from Norway. Later, after World War II, when a number of institutions added instruction in Finnish language and literature, it also found a home within the Scandinavian departments. Common history and culture have taken precedence over linguistic considerations. The same principle applies when we in the dictionary view Finland as a country with two literatures: one in Finnish and the other written in Swedish.

At times as editors we have asked ourselves whether a culture or a literature called Scandinavian is actually a mere fairy tale written by Americans. In re-

---

[1] Patricia Bliss McFate, "To See Everything in Another Light." *Daedalus* 113:1 (1984), 29.

cruiting contributors for the topical articles, such as autobiography, literary criticism, and women's literature, it soon became apparent that no single contributor was capable of covering all five countries, to say nothing of the smaller ethnic literatures like Sami, Inuit (Greenlandic), or Faroese. The best solution might have been a collage of contributions by experts on a particular topic from each country. But then the synthesized "Scandinavian" point of view would have been lost. As it is, some topical articles had to be left out entirely, and in others the coverage between the various countries is not always balanced: rather it is colored by the article writer's nationality or expertise.

The dictionary has been in production for a long time. We have learned a lot in the process and would have done many things differently had we had a chance to start from the beginning. Technology has changed. If computers had been available to us at the onset, it would have been, for instance, a routine task to update the entries instead of the cumbersome, one-time endeavor that it became, with many inherent problems. A reference work is by its very nature selective and the inclusion of one author versus another is always open to challenge. Seen from the present perspective, even the editors' choices might at times have been different. There are many writers that have risen to prominence during these years. However, a decision was made to keep to the original cut-off date of 1970. Thus, in order for an author to be included in the dictionary, his or her debut had to have taken place in or before 1970. To cover the literatures of five countries is not an easy task, particularly in view of the necessary space limitations. Our priorities could of course have been different. Less space could have been devoted to pre–1900 authors and a greater emphasis put on the very recent ones. A conscious English-language bias is also detectable. Our "ranking" of authors may deviate from the customary one in Scandinavia. If an author's works have been translated into English, it is more likely that the English-speaking readers need information about that author than about another whose works have remained essentially unknown in the English-speaking world. We can only hope that we will be given a second chance, an opportunity to issue a sequel volume in a few years.

Scandinavia consists of five small countries with a combined population of about 25 million people. Although the Scandinavian countries today belong to the most prosperous nations in the world with a high standard of living and an active cultural life, they have through much of their history been on the receiving end compared to the larger European nations in terms of intellectual ideas and literary movements. Early on, however, there have been notable exceptions. In the dictionary separate articles are devoted to each such outstanding period or prominent genre.

In the European letters of the 1200s the Icelandic Sagas were unique. When most of the literature in Europe was written in Latin under the tutelage of the Catholic church, the vernacular Icelandic sagas stand out as the early precursors of the novel. Skaldic poetry (see Old Norse Poetry), although less known outside Scandinavia than its contemporary Eddic poetry, owing to the difficulty of translation, merits more attention as it differs radically from all other kinds of Germanic verse. The Medieval Scandinavian ballads (see Scandinavian Folklore) represent a unique contribution to world literature and rival the Scottish ballads in originality and in scope. Within international folkloristics Nordic folklore research has long occupied a central position; the Finnish historic-geographic method of research and the Dane Axel Olrik's "epic laws" belong to the cardinal concepts of the discipline. *Kalevala*, the Finnish epic poem, compiled by E. Lönnrot from ancient oral poetry and published in 1849, has been translated into more than forty languages. It is often studied as the prototype of how other great epics might have been composed in earlier times. In as early as 1855 the American poet, H. W. Longfellow was inspired by *Kalevala* to write his *The Song of Hiawatha*, which both in its themes and in meter (trochaic tetrameter) emulates closely the Finnish epic. The seventeenth-century hymns of the Danish Thomas Kingo represent the culmination of Scandinavian Baroque and compare favorably with the English metaphysical poetry of the period. Ludvig Holberg, the first of the stellar figures of Scandinavian literature, "the Molière of the North," was the most important man of letters in eighteenth-century Scandinavia and, in the opinion of many, surpassed his French master. There is a tragic tinge to his comic characters and his milieu is that of the urban artisan or the country peasant, and as such, closer to the world of the viewers than Molière's courtly atmosphere. As a true man of the Enlightenment Holberg had an inherent trust in humanity. In his comedies even the fool is given a chance; he can be reformed. The Romantic writers of the Golden Age, Adam Oehlenschläger, Esaias Tegnér, J. L. Runeberg, Henrik Wergeland, and N.F.S. Grundtvig illustrate brilliantly how foreign cultural impulses can be transformed into genuine expressions of Nordic history and spirit. Søren Kierkegaard, the forerunner of existentialism, and a decisive influence on such American writers as John Updike, Walker Percy, and Woody Allen, is profiled not only as a philosopher but also as a writer of experimental fiction. Next to the Bible, H. C. Andersen's tales are the most translated pieces of writing in the world. But Andersen, a product—and a critic—of romanticism, was more than an heir to the traditions of the oral folktale or an amiable spinner of children's tales. He was a philosopher grappling with existential agonies and complexities akin to those of Kierkegaard. It was his expression of these ideas and, as a result, the composition of his audience, that so strikingly deviates from Kierkegaard's often highly theoretical discourse. J. P. Jacobsen, frequently characterized as the first naturalistic writer in Scandinavia, was also widely read and admired abroad, by Freud, Rilke, and Musil among others. And then there are the two acknowledged giants of Scandinavian literature: Henrik Ibsen and August Strindberg, without whom, we may safely claim, the drama of our times would not be what it is today. Neither of them ever received the Nobel prize, a comment on the judgment of the Nobel prize committee rather than on the caliber of the two writers. Nevertheless, Scandinavian authors have received their fair share of the eagerly coveted prizes. All fourteen of them are portrayed in the dictionary, from Bjørnstjerne Bjørnson to the Swedes

Eyvind Johnson and Harry Martinson, not to forget F. E. Sillanpää and Halldór Laxness, representatives of the two smaller languages. Perhaps not totally unexpectedly, Selma Lagerlöf and Sigrid Undset, two of only six women who have won the Nobel prize in literature, come from Scandinavia. The Nordic countries have produced a great number of excellent women writers, some of whom have enjoyed popularity and recognition all along. Others like the seventeenth-century Norwegian Dorothe Engelbretsdotter, Danish Thomasine Gyllembourg from the 1700s, or, closer to our days, the Swedish working-class writer Moa Martinson, have only in recent decades been accorded their due places in literary history. Appreciation for and indebtedness to the Finland-Swedish poet Edith Södergran has steadily grown through the years. Södergran, "the Rimbaud of Scandinavia," together with Hagar Olsson, Elmer Diktonius, Gunnar Björling, and Rabbe Enckell, spearheaded literary modernism in the Scandinavia of the 1920s. For once the tide of literary innovation flowed from the "periphery" toward the center. In recent years the international successes of Scandinavian film have enhanced interest in Scandinavian culture. Ingmar Bergman, with his Strindberg infatuation, is a given in any discussion of Scandinavian literature. It is to be hoped that the two strong Danish films, recipients of Oscars, *Babette's Feast* and *Pelle the Conqueror*, based on the works of Karen Blixen and Martin Andersen Nexø, respectively, will spark interest in the authors' other works and Scandinavian writing in general.

HOW TO USE THIS DICTIONARY

The dictionary contains two kinds of entries: author entries and articles of a more general nature. The author entries vary in length from 300 to 1,600 words and the topical articles, with a few notable exceptions, from 1,000 to 1,500 words. Each author entry opens with a brief paragraph of biographical data. In a few cases the statistical information is incomplete, owing to the problems of obtaining the facts. The initial paragraph is followed by an analysis of the author's major work(s), highlighting characteristic themes or stylistic features. A summary statement regarding the author's impact on the country's literature and his or her standing today concludes the entry. A few of the topical articles have been judged unique in that the subject has never previously been treated at any length in an English-language publication. In such cases, for example, Scandinavian Literary Criticism, or Inuit literature, entries exceed the customary length.

All entries are in alphabetical order. The Scandinavian initial letters å /æ,ö/ ø / ǫ, which come at the end of their respective alphabets, have been treated as *aa*, *ae*, and *oe* in accordance with the Library of Congress practice. If an author is better known by his or her pseudonym, this is the form used in the entry. The author's birth name in that case is given within parentheses following the pseudonym: for example, Sandel, Cora (pseud. of Sara Fabricius). Furthermore, in its place in the regular alphabetical progression the real name appears as a cross-reference to the entry under the pseudonym. If, however, an author is customarily known under his or her real name, a reverse practice is observed: Benedictsson, Victoria (pseud. Ernst Ahlgren). Within entries the asterisk (*) has been used as a cross-reference to indicate the presence of an entry under that term. It occurs only at the first mention of any one entry, regardless of how many times it may be repeated.

For the sake of uniformity, Icelandic personal names have been entered under the patronymic, contrary to Icelandic practice. Cross-references have been made from the given names and from toponyms, if part of the name. Icelandic has retained the old runic symbol Þ (thorn) for the voiceless *th*-sound and ð for voiced *th*. The Icelandic letters have been used in the dictionary except in cases when an author has chosen to transliterate them to *th* and *d*, respectively, in his or her personal name. Þ and ð have been alphabetized as *th* and *d*.

Each author entry is followed by a list of the author's works in chronological order. In the case of most pre-1900 authors only collected works have been listed. Titles that are already mentioned in the main entry have been omitted here. If a work has been translated into English, its English title and year of publication are given in parentheses. Individual poems or short stories that have appeared in English translation are listed under the subheading "Further Translations." To save space, only the title and the year of publication of an anthology or a periodical in which the poems or short stories appear are given, not the titles of individual items. For the same reason, regretfully, names of translators have in most cases been omitted. An anthology or a periodical issue has to contain at least three poems in order to be listed here.

Both the author and topical entries conclude with lists of reference sources. Each bibliographic citation includes the author of the work, title without a subtitle, and place and year of publication. Preference has been given to English-language items. Critical writings in English may extend to important periodical articles, whereas references in other languages have usually been restricted to books. Exceptions to this rule are chapters in books and instances when nothing is available in English. Every attempt has been made to limit the total number of references to ten. The volume concludes with an appendix section that includes a Table of Chronology, an article on Library Resources for Scandinavian Literature, extensive bibliographies for each country, an index, and a list of contributors. The country-specific bibliographies, that cover sources in English as well as in the Scandinavian languages, are further subdivided into listings of bibliographies, literary histories, English-language literary journals, anthologies in English, and biographies.

Acknowledgments

During these many years of working on the dictionary I have consulted and benefited from the advice and assistance of so many individuals that it is impossible to list them all. I owe the greatest gratitude to my coeditors, Professors Niels Ingwersen and Harald Naess, to all of our contributors, and to my colleagues, Ingrid Weatherhead and Jean Woods. Special thanks go to the Finnish Literature Information Service, especially to Marja-Leena Rautalin, who mediated most of the Finnish contributors, and the Norwegian Information Service. The grants from these institutes allowed me to do some field research and to contact contributors both in Finland and in Norway. Last but not least, I am deeply indebted to the secretarial staff both in Eugene and in Madison for doing much of the retyping occasioned by updating the entries. I would also like to commend Greenwood Press for its interest in the project and patience with its progress.

Virpi Zuck

DICTIONARY
OF
SCANDINAVIAN
LITERATURE

A

Åkesson, Sonja. Swedish poet and short story writer, b. 19 April 1926, Buttle, Gotland, d. 4 May 1977, Stockholm.

Åkesson's breakthrough as a poet came in 1963 with the collection *Husfrid* (Peace at Home), which portrays a housewife trapped at home, unhappy and frustrated. In a poetic style, in Sweden called the New Simplicity, Åkesson creates a sensualism that manifests itself in detailed descriptions of trivial, everyday objects and a concentration on the power of language to evoke sights and sounds. Her two most famous poems are included in this collection: "Vara vit mans slav" (Be White Man's Slave), which became the fighting song of the radical feminist movement in Sweden during the 1960s, and "Självbiografi" (Autobiography), a paraphrase of and reply to Lawrence Ferlinghetti's "Autobiography" (*A Coney Island of the Mind*, 1958). It is a deliberate attempt to show the other side, to create a dialogue between a male and a female point of view, to show the differences in the real-life situation of a man and a woman living in essentially the same kind of society during the same period of time.

In her later poetry, from the mid–1960s to her death, Åkesson continued to write in an even more openly confessional style, describing her own social problems of alcoholism, drug addiction, and nervous breakdowns.

Called the "National Poet of the Welfare State," Åkesson enjoyed great popularity during her lifetime. Because of her extraordinary ability to depict with humor and irony the life of a typical middle-class, middle-aged Swedish housewife, many women in Sweden easily identify themselves with her poems. But her importance goes beyond that. Her theme is more than the housewife's alienation in modern society: it shows the dilemma of both men and women coping with the contrasts between reality and an idyllic dream of society.

FURTHER WORKS

Situationer (1957); *Glasveranda* (1959); *Skvallerspegel* (1960); *Leva livet* (1961); *Efter balen* (1962); *Ute skiner solen* (1965); *Jag bor i Sverige* (1966); *Man får vara glad och tacka Gud* (1967); *Pris* (1968); *Slagdängor* (1969); *Ljuva sextiotal* (1970); *Hjärtat hamrar, lungorna smälter* (1972); *Dödens ungar* (1973); *Sagan om Siv* (1974); *En värk att anpassa. Dikter 1957–65* (1975); *Ett liv att avverka. Dikter 1966–74* (1976); *Hästens öga* (1976); *En tid att avliva. Prosa 1960–1970* (1978); *Sonja Åkessons dikter* (1986).

FURTHER TRANSLATIONS

Micromegas 6.1 (1969); *Lines Review* 51 (1974); *The Other Voice* (1976); *Modern Swedish Poetry in Translation* (1979); *Scandinavian Review* 67.3 (1979); *Swedish Books* 1.4 (1980); *Poetry East* 1 (1980).

REFERENCES

Claréus, Ingrid, "Sonja Åkesson." *Scandinavian Review* 61.3 (1973); Graves, Peter, "Sonja Åkesson." *Swedish Books* 1.4 (1980); Hammarberg-Åkesson, Jarl, *Mina kvinnor, min storfamilj* (Stockholm, 1979); Hammarberg-Åkesson, Jarl, *Kom Sonja! Kom strån* (Stockholm, 1979); Martin, Bengt, *Sonja Åkesson* (Stockholm, 1986).

Ingrid Claréus

Aakjær, Jeppe. Danish novelist, playwright and lyric poet, b. 10 September 1866, Aakjær, d. 22 April, 1930, Jebjerg.

Born of poor peasants in Western Jutland, Aakjær attended folk high school, studied history, worked as a schoolteacher and a journalist, and was a popular lecturer. From 1893 to 1900 he was married to author Marie Bregendahl, and from 1907 to his death he owned a farm in Jutland.

As a young man in Copenhagen Aakjær was a cultural radical follower of Georg Brandes.* His anti-clerical and social indignation, however, was more emotional than political. The controversial and critical tendency in his prose is repeatedly alternated by lyrical nostalgia for situations from the old Jutland countryside. In his novels about rustic life and culture, grotesque and distorted characters and episodes frequently disrupt the narrative until some lyrical passages provide for reconciliation with nature.

Aakjær's short stories are without such extenuating lyrical circumstances. The images of rural life are either totally dislocated from nature, or the connection is perverted and discrediting. On the other hand, in many of Aakjær's numerous lyrical poems and songs, the experience of harmonious concord between man and nature is almost religious and erotic. As his novel *Vredens Børn* (1904; Children of Wrath) was an ardent agitation against the oppression of farmhands, so are some of Aakjær's songs emotional propaganda. Nevertheless, the bulk of his occasionally moving but always singable poems—for example, from *Fri Felt* (1905; Free Field) and *Rugens Sange* (1906; Songs of Rye)—rely upon popular song tradition and upon an intimate sense of local milieu recalled from bittersweet memories. Aakjær tends to idealize his image of love, home, and female authority to the extent that their nuances evaporate.

Jutland as it was before capitalism definitely deformed its rural setting was Aajkær's fixation. It prevented him from transforming his harsh experiences and descriptions of the past into a viable utopia. But it offered, in his songs, generations of Danish workers and smallholders an opportunity to identify themselves with their past as something irreplaceably lost. In his book from 1903 to 1904 about the tragic life of Steen Steensen Blicher,* Jutland's first great lyric poet, the important traits of Aakjær's own life are discernible: the failure of his marriage to Bregendahl, an ambiguous attraction to outsiders, and a sense of history in which such characters find their place and meaning.

FURTHER WORKS

Missionen og dens Høvding (1897); *Bondens Søn* (1899); *Derude fra Kjærene* (1899); *Vadmelsfolk* (1900); *Fjandboer* (1901); *Steen Steensen Blichers Livs—Tragedie i Breve og Aktstykker* (1903–1904); *Fra Jul til Sanct Hans* (1905); *Livet paa Hegnsgaard* (1907); *Hvor Bønder bor* (1908); *Muld og Malm* (1909); *Ulvens Søn* (1909); *Den Sommer og den Eng* (1910); *Af Gammel Jehannes hans Bivelskistaarri* (1911); *Naar Bønder elsker* (1911); *Jævnt Humør* (1913); *Arbejdets Glæde* (1914); *Jens Langkniv* (1915); *Hvor der er gjærende Kræfter* (1916); *Vejr og Vind og Folkesind* (1916); *Af min Hjemstavns Saga* (1919); *Mit Regnebræt* (1919); *Hjærtegræs og Ærenpris* (1921); *Pigen fra Limfjorden* (1921); *Under Aftenstjærnen* (1927); *Fra min Bitte-Tid* (1928); *Drengeaar og Knøseaar* (1929); *Før det dages* (1929); *Studier fra Hjemstavnen* (1929–1932); *Efterladte Erindringer* (1934).

TRANSLATIONS

Contemporary Danish Prose, ed. Elias Bredsdorff (1958, 1974).

REFERENCES

Christensen, Hans Jørn, *Vredens Børn* (Grenå, 1979); Fuchs, Reinhard, *Der dänische Bauerndichter Jeppe Aakjær* (Gütersloh, 1940); Hjordt-Vetlesen, Inger Lise, *Flugtens Fængsel* (Odense, 1981); Nicolaisen, K. K., *Jeppe Aakjær* (Copenhagen, 1913); Nørgaard, Felix, *Jeppe Aakjær* (Copenhagen, 1941); Schmidt, August F., *Jeppe Aakjær* (Brabrand, 1933); Westergaard, W., "Jeppe Aakjær." *American Scandinavian Review* 12. 11 (1924).

Poul Houe

Aarestrup, Emil. Danish poet, b. 4 December 1800, Copenhagen, d. 21 July 1856, Odense.

Aarestrup took his medical examination in 1827, practiced medicine first in Nysted from 1827 to 1938, then in Sakskøbing from 1838 to 1849, and subsequently worked as a county medical officer at Fewnen and Odense until his death in 1856. His medical education and profession are significant for his poetry in which he worships the body and erotic sensuality in both a daring and artistic manner. Although a solid and respectable citizen of his time, he was exposed to a world of extravagant pleasure on the provincial manors where he was a beloved entertainer. Despite being only a provincial doctor, he was in frequent contact with the leading cultural milieu in Copenhagen, and was a close friend of the poet Christian Winther.

Aarestrup is primarily known as the great reviver of erotic poetry in Danish literature and a master of lyrical form. He developed the sonnet to a subtle and personal means of expression and transformed the influences of European Romanticism (Heine and Byron) into a lyrical tradition in Denmark. A special form of four-line stanza bears his name in the history of Danish prosody. Another personal form of his is the "ritournel," a three-line aphoristic stanza, using the description and nature of flowers as a metaphorical expression of an erotic situation.

During Aarestrup's lifetime few people were aware of his work, which eventually comprised six volumes. He published one single book, *Digte* (Poems), in 1838. A possible explanation for Aarestrup's late recognition could be his modern and revolutionary conception of sensual instincts that represents a break with the bourgeois morality and piety prevalent in his day. In Aarestrup's poems it is love and the sexual embrace that lead to "heaven." He worships wine, food, and women, and a worldly joy of life emanates from his serene image as father and civil servant. The spleen and depression that sometimes prevail over the joyous mood in his poetry are not expressions of repentance, but rather of anxiety and sadness in facing death, the ultimate final boundary of life and lust.

FURTHER WORKS

Efterladte Digte (1863); *Samlede Digte* (1877); *Samlede Skrifter, 5 vols.* (1922–1925).

TRANSLATIONS

A Little Book of Danish Verse (1950); *Book of Danish Verse*, comp. Oluf Friis (1922, 1976); *A Second Book of Danish Verse* (1947, 1968).

REFERENCES

Brix, Hans, *Emil Aarestrup* (Copenhagen, 1952); Zeruneith, Keld, *Den frigjorte. Emil Aarestrup i digtning og samtid.* (Copenhagen, 1981).

Ib Bondebjerg

Aasen, Ivar Andreas. Norwegian dialect scholar and poet, b. 5 August 1813, Ørsta, d. 23 September 1896, Kristiania.

Aasen, a farmer's son, grew up in poor circumstances in Northwestern Norway. Although his formal education was brief, he revealed a precocious talent and great interest in further learning. On his own he acquired an extensive knowledge of botany, grammar, language, and literature in private libraries. He worked as a teacher for many years. In the article "Om vaart Skriftsprog" (1836; About Our Written Language) he presented a program for the study and advancement of Norwegian dialects. After completing a grammar of the Sunnmøre dialect in 1839, he received a scholarship from the Royal Science Academy that enabled him to collect and study Norwegian dialects, first in western Norway and the mountain regions, and later in many other parts of the country. The work resulted in two publications, *Det norske Folkesprogs Grammatik* (1848; Grammar of Norwegian Folk Dialects) and *Ordbog over det norske Folkesprog* (1850; Dictionary of Norwegian Peasant Language). These two books constitute the basis for a new norm of written Norwegian based on dialects. Aasen presented the new written Norwegian as a national alternative to the Danish form of writing prevalent in Norway. With *Prøver af Landsmaalet i Norge* (1853; Specimens of Native Speech in Norway) Aasen laid the grounds for what was to become the standard for *landsmål* (later *nynorsk*, literally "New Norwegian"*).

Aasen also wanted to create a literature in the new language. Ever since his youth, he had tried to write poetry in the Dano-Norwegian language, but with little success. It was when he started writing poetry in the new *landsmål* that his talents surfaced. The musical *Ervingen* (1855; The Heir) derives its subject matter from village life and includes popular poems and songs. In 1863 Aasen collected the best poems that he had written over the years in a little book entitled *Symra*. The central lyrical themes that prevail in Aasen's poetry—nature and home, land and people, knowledge and faith, love and destiny—are often presented with an undertone of good-natured humor. In terms of form, his poems build on both Norwegian and European tradition; they are firm and clear in themes and in imagery. They are also popular and easy to sing; many of them have belonged to the national treasury of Norwegian songs for over 100 years. Aasen's poems have been one of the most important foundations for the further development of New Norwegian poetry.

FURTHER WORKS

Skrifter i Samling, 3 vols. (1911–1912); *Skrifter,* 2 vols. (1926); *Brev og dagbøker,* ed. Reidar Djupedal, 3 vols., (1957–1960).

REFERENCES

Dahl, Willy, "Ivar Aasen som lyriker," in his *Perspektiver* (Oslo, 1968); Eskeland, Lars, *Ivar Aasen* (Oslo, 1923); Garborg, Arne, *Ivar Aasen* (Oslo, 1902); Garborg, Arne, Anders Hovden, and Halvdan Koht, *Ivar Aasen. Granskaren, maalreisaren, diktaren* (Oslo, 1913); Handagard, Idar, *Ivar Aasen* (Oslo, 1944); Haugen, Einar, *The Origin and Early History of the New Norse Movement in Norway* (Menasha, Wis., 1933); Haugen, Einar, *Studies by Einar Haugen,* ed. Evelyn Scherabon Firchow et al. (The Hague, 1972); Hovden, Anders, *Ivar Aasen i kvardagslaget* (Oslo, 1913); Liestøl, Knut, *Ivar Aasen* (Oslo, 1963).

Leif Mæhle

Abell, Kjeld. Danish scenographer, dramatist, and essayist, b. 25 August 1901, Ribe, d. 5 March 1961, Copenhagen.

Abell was born into an upper-middle-class family and grew up in an intellectual milieu. In 1927 he received a master's degree in political science from the University of Copenhagen. In the same year he went to Paris, where he worked as a designer, and to a certain degree was influenced by the Russian ballet (Sergei Diaghilev) and "the poetical theater" of Louis Jouvet and Jean Giraudoux. His language and style, however, are poetic, rather in the manner of Hans Christian Andersen,* and uniquely Danish. Abell's first and most influential theater experience was Johan August Strindberg's* *Ghost Sonata,* and in his essays he defines theater as non-naturalistic, nonimitative, dependent only on theatrical possibilities.

Abell's first achievement in Danish theater was his cubistic and surrealistic scenography for a series of ballets at the Royal Theater, 1930–1931, with Balanchine as choreographer and music by Stravinskij, de Falla, and Richard Strauss. A few years later his own ballet was performed, *Enken i Spejlet* (1934; Widow in the Mirror), with choreographer Børge Ralow and composer Bernhard Christensen. His first play was a remarkable success: *Melodien der blev væk* (1935; The Lost Melody; songs by Sven Møller Kristensen, music by Bernhard Christensen). It is a revue-comedy with elements from European avant-garde theater and from the Danish vaudeville about 1830 (cf. J. L. Heiberg*). It provides a witty, sympathetic attack on the petty bourgeois and white-collar problems. The subtitle is "Larsen's comedy in 21 scenes," and in everyday speech "Larsen" has become *the* name for a white-collar proletarian. The main theme in *Anna Sophie Hedvig* (1939) is political apathy as a presupposition of fascism. The heroine is an elderly, mild-natured teacher who confesses that she, together with her pupils, has murdered the dictatorial principal of her school. In the final symbolic sequence of episodes, Anna Sophie Hedvig faces a fascist execution squad during the Spanish Civil War. Idealistic humanism has become defiant humanism. One of Abell's most ingenious and original plays is *Den blå Pekingeser* (1954; The Blue Pekingese), in which the color blue symbolizes poetry as a mode of intuitive knowledge or even as a mode of life. The theme is existential rather than political. Dramaturgically it is a monodrama; in other words, most of the action is not action (dramatic present) but memory (dramatic preteritum) or vision (dramatic future), and a combination of action and dialogue is only to be found in the visionary sequences. *Den blå Pekingeser* is a dramatic poem about human isolation and hope, a psychic progression made visible by theater.

Abell wrote several librettos for ballets including *Våren* (1942; Spring Time) and two original film manuscripts: *Tak fordi du kom, Nick* (1941; Thanks for Coming, Nick) and *Regnen holdt op* (1941; The Rain Has Ceased). Abell's most impressive prose work is *De tre fra Minikoi* (1957; *Three from Minikoi,* 1960), a novel based on experiences and reflections from visits to China in 1952 and 1956.

This great poet was obsessed by the problem of humanism. In drama and prose he was a master of the Danish language, which he used in a playful, often humorous, and always highly creative way to convey his convictions that the real danger to humanism is the tendency to praise ideals that are never translated into action.

Most of Abell's contemporary critics did not understand his later works, yet none of the more outstanding of them ever questioned his position as one of the innovators of theater in this century.

FURTHER WORKS

Eva aftjener sin barnepligt (1936); *Dyveke* (1940, pb. 1967); *Judith* (1940); *Dronning går igen* (1943); *Silkeborg* (1946); *Dage på en sky* (1947); *Teaterstrejf i påskevejr* (1948); *Miss Plinckby's kabale* (1949); *Vetsera blomstrer ikke for enhver* (1950); *Fodnoter i støvet* (1951); *Andersen eller Hans livs eventyr* (1955); *Fire skuespil* (1955); *Kamelia-damen* (1959); *Skriget* (1961); *Synskhedens gave*, ed. Elias Bredsdorff (1962).

REFERENCES

Bredsdorff, Elias, *Kjeld Abells billedkunst* (Copenhagen, 1979); Hind, Tage, *Dumas fils, Kjeld Abell og realismen* (Copenhagen, 1962); Kristensen, Sven Møller, ed., *En bog om Kjeld Abell* (Copenhagen, 1961); Madsen, Børge Gedsø, "Leading Motifs in the Dramas of Kjeld Abell." *Scandinavian Studies* 33.3 (1961); Marker, F. J., *Kjeld Abell* (New York, 1976).

Tage Hind

Aðalsteinn, Kristmundsson. *See* Steinarr, Stein.

Agnar, Þórðarson. *See* Þórðarson, Agnar.

Ahlgren, Ernst. *See* Benedictsson, Victoria.

Ahlin, Lars. Swedish novelist, short story writer, dramatist, and essayist, b. 4 April, 1915, Sundsvall.

Ahlin left school at the age of thirteen but obtained formal education later at a *folkhögskola*. In 1936 he went to Stockholm to work and write. He was awarded a house for life in 1957 and has received several other awards.

His first novel, *Tåbb med manifestet* (1943; Tåbb and the Manifesto) deals with issues to be explored further in later works: social value versus individual human value. Tåbb's belief in the Communist Manifesto leads to alienation from his self, since as unemployed he has no place in the social structure. Only through love can this destructive discrepancy between the two value systems be eliminated.

In *Fromma mord* (1952; Pious Murders) Ahlin investigates the complications inherent in interpersonal relationships and the difficulty to integrate social goals with personal desires and loyalties. Ideals (pieties) force his characters to violate (murder) personal integrity. Therefore, the main protagonist perishes without having accomplished any of his goals in life.

Failure or death is the focus of Ahlin's novels up to *Stora glömskan* (1954; The Great Amnesia), where love is explored as a power uniting social and universal forces. This is expressed in the word "glädje" (joy), indicating perfect harmony between inner and outer self.

Structurally most advanced is the novel *Om* (1946; If, About, Around), with three-part, subject-and-verb sequences intended to invite the reader to become co-creator of the final text by establishing a reading from the components.

In 1983 Ahlin made a powerful comeback with *Hannibal segraren* (Hannibal the Victor) in cooperation with his wife Gunnel Ahlin, investigating the role of the man who records the acts of the hero and thus shapes his image. Two years later Ahlin published an autobiographical novel, *Sjätte munnen* (1985; The Sixth Mouth) touchingly describing a boy's relationship with his father. It was followed by a much appreciated collection of his earlier short stories in *Vaktpojkens eld* (1986; The Fire of the Guard Boy).

Ahlin wrote many essays in the 1940s arguing for a more experimental form of the novel. Together with his novels they establish him as one of the most important writers in modern Swedish literature, both in terms of his aesthetics and in his philosophy of equality and love (agape).

FURTHER WORKS

Inga ögon väntar mig (1944); *Min död är min* (1945); *Jungfrun i det gröna* (1947); *Fångnas glädje* (1947); *Egen spis* (1948); *Husen har ingen filial* (1949); *Kanelbiten* (1953); *Kvinna, kvinna* (1955); *Natt i marknadstältet* (1957); *Gilla gång* (1958); *Nattens ögonsten* (1958); *Bark och löv* (1961).

TRANSLATIONS

Sweden Writes. ed Lars Bäckström and Göran Palm (1965); *Literary Review* 9.2 (1965–1966); *Art Drama Architecture Music International Review* 31 (1966).

REFERENCES

Augustsson, Lars-Åke, "Lars Ahlin: A Swedish Writer of European Status." *Cambridge Quarterly* 1.1. (1979); Ekman, Hans Göran, *Humor, grotesk och pikaresk* (Uppsala, 1975); Lundell, Torborg, "Lars Ahlin's Concept of the Writer as *Identificator* and *Förbedjare.*" *Scandinavica* 14.1 (1975); Lundell, Torborg, "Lars Ahlin's Concept of Equality." *Scandinavian Studies* 47.3 (1975); Lundell, Torborg, *Lars Ahlin* (Boston, 1977); Lundell, Torborg, "Lars Ahlin." *World Authors 1975–1980*, ed. Vineta Colby (New York, 1985); Melberg, Arne, *På väg från realismen* (Stockholm, 1973); Nielsen, Erik A., "Lars Ahlin and the New Swedish Novel." *Sweden Writes*, ed. Lars Bäckström and Göran Palm (Stockholm, 1965).

Torborg Lundell

Aho, Juhani (orig. Johannes Brofeldt). Finnish novelist, short story writer, dramatist, and journalist, b. 11 September 1861, Lapinlahti, d. 8 August 1921, Helsinki.

Aho, Finland's first professional writer, grew up as the son of a Lutheran minister in a country vicarage in the northern part of the Savo province. While attending high school in Kuopio, he befriended the author Minna Canth* and the cultivated Järnefelt* family. His finely honed literary style and liberal social views owe much to these early influences. As a journalist, Aho contributed throughout his career to a number of major dailies and in 1890 founded the paper *Päivälehti,* an organ for the Young Finland political faction. In 1907 Aho was granted a doctor's degree *honoris causa* by the University of Helsinki.

In his early realistic works Aho focused on the often perplexing encounter between the modern urban society with its technical advances and the traditional rural lifestyle. In *Rautatie* (1884; The Railroad) an elderly couple, Matti and Liisa, are driven by curiosity to undertake a daylong hike from their backwoods cabin to the railroad that has just reached the nearest village. Although the reader, being more knowledgeable than the fictional characters, may laugh at Matti's and Liisa's wild speculations about the looks of the railroad, the author's sympathies lie with the simple couple. Under the guise of a humorous exterior, Aho finds an opportunity to point at various social and human follies. "The first become the last, and the last become the first" in this story. Not only are the self-important and pompous members of the semi-urban station community rendered ridiculous compared to the unpretentious Matti and Liisa, but also between the two it is the man, Matti, who tries to assert his superiority and whose pride goes before a fall. During the short train ride Matti drinks himself into helplessness and it is Liisa who ends up leading him back home.

Among Aho's longer novels, the two most interesting ones are *Papin tytär* (1885; A Pastor's Daughter) and its sequel *Papin rouva* (1893; A Pastor's Wife). In the spirit of Minna Canth, Aho illustrates the waste of women's minds and bodies when their physical expression is curtailed by the rules of feminine behavior, their intellect stifled by the lack of educational opportunity, and their emotional life distorted by marriages forced upon them for economic reasons. Although the author lays the major blame on the authoritative fathers, the daughters can hardly expect support from the mothers either. For the sake of their own sanity and self-preservation, the women come in time to internalize their husbands' values and preach a doctrine of humility and sufferance to their daughters. The problem thus becomes generational. As always in Aho's works, nature plays a major role. Besides reflecting the protagonist's melancholy moods, it offers her a place of escape and the only source of solace in her otherwise joyless existence.

The novella *Helsinkiin* (1889; To Helsinki) provides an excellent period portrait as we follow a student's travel by boat and train from eastern Finland to Helsinki. But the journey marks also the young man's departure from the protective environment of a bourgeois home to the freedom of student life in the capital. At the time of publication, the book aroused anger because of its alleged immorality. Most fascinating to the modern reader are the descriptions of life on the boat and the impressionistic glimpses of the sights of Helsinki as the train approaches the town.

The influence of the new artistic trends of the 1890s, romanticism and nationalism, left their mark on Aho's works. His interest shifted from descriptions of contemporary society to the country's past and its geographic periphery,

Karelia. Events in *Juha* (1911), one of Aho's most popular works and the inspiration for operas and films, unfold in the Karelian wilderness in an unspecified past. It is a story of the self-denying love of the older, physically unattractive Juha for his young and beautiful wife, Marja, and Marja's passionate amour with a handsome Russian-Karelian trader, Shemeikka. While the charm of the story lies in its intensity of feeling and descriptions of the exotic nature and Russian-Karelian culture, it owes its lasting value to the author's sensitive probing of human emotions.

The two volumes of *Hajamietteitä kapinaviikoilta* (1918–1919; Stray Thoughts from the Weeks of the Rebellion) consist of diary notes written during the Finnish Civil War that lasted from the end of January to the middle of May, 1918. Besides furnishing an accurate recording of the day-to-day events and sentiments among the Whites in the Red-held capital, the notes provide an eloquent expression of Aho's agonizing struggle with his own inner convictions, for example, his pacifist renunciation of violence as a means to solve conflicts. Despite his white sympathies, he retained to the end an open mind for the justified causes of the Red rebellion, and warned the victorious Whites against indiscriminate revenge at the end of the war.

Throughout his writing career, Aho had composed short pieces of narrative prose, essays, and lyrical nature depictions that he called *lastuja* (shavings), which fell from his writing desk like the wooden shavings from the workbench of a carpenter. They were published in eight volumes between 1891 and 1921, and form perhaps the most unique part of Aho's production. In the shavings we encounter the newspaperman, social reformer, backwoods hunter, and philosophical brooder. Aho's longer prose may in the course of time have lost some of its freshness and appeal, but the best of his shavings belong securely among the living treasures of Finnish literature.

FURTHER WORKS

Sipolan Aapon kosioretki (1883); *Siihen aikaan kun isä lampun osti* (1883; *When Father Brought Home the Lamp*, 1893); *Muudan markkinamies* (1884); *Hellmannin herra* (1886; *Squire Hellman*, 1893); *Esimerkin vuoksi* (1886); *Yksin* (1890); *Heränneitä* (1894); *Maailman murjoma* (1894); *Panu* (1897); *Katajainen kansani*, 2 vols. (1899–1900); *Aatteiden mies* (1901); *Antti Ahlström* (1905); *Kevät ja takatalvi* (1906); *Tuomio* (1907); *Omatunto* (1914); *Rauhan erakko* (1916); *Kootut teokset* (1918; Supplement, 1961); *Muistatko—?* (1920); *Valitut teokset* (1953).

FURTHER TRANSLATIONS

Squire Hellman and Other Stories (1893); *Stories by Foreign Authors. Scandinavian* (1901); *Finnish Short Stories*, ed. Inkeri Väänänen-Jensen and K. Börje Vähämäki (1982).

REFERENCES

Aho, Antti J., *Juhani Aho*, 2 vols. (Helsinki, 1951); Castrén, Gunnar, *Juhani Aho*, 2 vols. (Stockholm, 1922); Havu, Ilmari, *Juhani Aho* (Helsinki, 1929); Koskimies, Rafael, *Kymmenen tutkielmaa Juhani Ahosta* (Helsinki, 1975); Kupiainen, Unto, *Juhani Ahon huumori* (Helsinki, 1937); Niemi, Juhani, *Juhani Aho* (Helsinki, 1985); Nieminen, Kaarlo, *Juhani Ahon sanataide* (Porvoo, 1934); Virtanen, N. P., *Ahon tuotanto sekä hänen teoksiansa ja elämäänsä käsittelevä kirjallisuus* (Porvoo, 1961).

Virpi Zuck

Ahrenberg, Johan Jakob (Jac.). Finland-Swedish novelist, memoirist, b. 30 April 1847, Viborg (Viipuri), d. 10 October 1914, Helsinki.

Ahrenberg's boyhood and youth were spent at Viipuri in extreme southeastern Finland (now Vyborg in the Soviet Union); there, four languages were employed—Finnish, German, Russian, and Swedish; this world of cultural mix and cultural conflict provided him with much of his material. Trained at the art academy of Helsinki and the school of architecture in Stockholm (where, interestingly enough, he became acquainted with the French theorist of ethnic supremacy and ethic degeneration, Arthur de Gobineau), Ahrenberg was appointed to Finland's Department of Public Buildings in 1877, and by 1910 had risen to its directorship. His literary production began with travel sketches (*Studieresor*, 1878; Study Journeys) and novellas in Ivan Turgenev's style (*På främmande botten*, 1880; On Foreign Soil); he then attempted novel-length depictions of town life in Karelia—*Hemma* (1887; At Home) and *Hihuliter* (1889; The Hihulites), a description of a religious sect not unlike America's Holy Rollers. The latter book also contains sharply autobiographical elements: Ahrenberg's mother had tormented her liberal-minded son with her stern pietism. (*Hihuliter*'s skeptical attitude toward religious extremism has a forerunner in Johan Ludvig Runeberg's* *Den gamle trädgårdsmästarens brev* [1836], and may be compared to such contemporary works from the North as the Norwegian Alexander Kielland's* *Skipper Worse*[1882].) Depictions of Ahrenberg's home region continued in *Österut* (1890; Eastward) and *Stockjunkarn* (1892; The Timber Baron), which is perhaps Ahrenberg's best work. Following Kielland's Stavanger masterpiece, *Garman & Worse* (1880) and preceding Thomas Mann's *Buddenbrooks* (1901), Stockjunkarn describes the decline of a merchant house. In the 1890s, as the new czar, Nicholas II, made ever-more overt attempts to deprive the grand duchy of its special status in the Russian Empire, Ahrenberg turned to themes concerning the Russification of upper-class Finland-Swedes in imperial service: the epistolary novella, *Anor* (1891; Forebears), and the novels *Familjen på Haapakoski* (1893; The Family at Haapakoski) and *Vår landsman* (1897; Our Countryman) all contain striking examples of Ahrenberg's ability to conjure up milieu and atmosphere. Ahrenberg's later historical novels are less satisfactory, showing the lack of self-discipline and self-criticism that sometimes pushed him over the line separating the serious craftsman from the entertainment novelist. His eye for personalities and moods, however, served him well as he wrote the six volumes of memoirs, *Människor jag kände* (1907–1914; People I Knew), a sometimes malicious masterpiece, sly and suggestive, although not to be used as a dependable historical document.

Ahrenberg was not a great literary artist, but nonetheless had a distinct voice in Finland's late nineteenth century. And, like Eduard von Keyserling (1855–1918), the classical portrayer of Baltic Germans, Ahrenberg has left behind a literary account of a culture that has wholly vanished. A certain tradition of denigrating Ahrenberg's work has existed in Finnish literary history, stemming from the days when the critic Werner Söderhjelm, and, then, Juhani Aho* and K. A. Tavaststjerna* condemned him as an ultraconservative; but he is, rather, a skeptical traditionalist, a fine observer, and, at his best, a splendid anecdotalist.

FURTHER WORKS

Med styrkans rätt (1891); *Rojalister och patrioter* (1901); *Kronofogdens pengar* (1917); *Samlade berättelser*, 10 vols. (1921–1922).

REFERENCES

Colliander, Börje, "Ett hundraårsminne: Bekantskapen mellan makarna Ahrenberg och Arthur de Gobineau." In *Från medeltid till 1900-tal* (Turku, 1977); Ekelund, Erik, *Johan Ahrenberg och östra Finland* (Helsinki, 1943).

George C. Schoolfield

Alfvén, Inger. Swedish novelist, b. 20 February 1940, Stockholm.

Alfvén made her literary debut in 1964 with a novel about a young girl who tries to break away from her family and her bourgeois surroundings.

The recurrent theme in Alfvén's writings is the scrutiny of the changing roles of women (and men) in Swedish society of today, the problems of changing attitudes in marriage and working life, and the struggle for self-realization against personal and societal obstacles.

In spite of their obvious emphasis on women's emancipation, Alfvén's novels are by no means simplistic descriptions of male villains and female saints, but rather studies of how external and internal forces exert almost irresistible pressure on both men and women. In her novels of the late 1970s she exposes the hollowness of society's claim to equality, and her women heroes grow weary in their efforts to corner their rightful place in a man's working world. She is very careful to point out that the barriers against progress are not only to be found on the outside. In reality, Alfvén's protagonists, men and women, often lack an understanding of the very concept of equality and mutual support; they are locked into outmoded sex-role patterns that squash opportunities for growth and fulfillment. Many of her women discover within themselves a self-destructive ambiguity toward career and marriage, and hidden behavior patterns from the past have left heavy imprints on their actions in the present.

In the novel, *Arvedelen* (1981; Inheritance) Alfvén moves further into explanations of the past as it influences contemporary woman. In this family chronicle about a line of women, daughters, and wives of domineering textile-factory owners, the central theme is the striving of these women to find outlets for their artistic talent in the face of male oppression and the incessant demands of domestic life.

All of Alfvén's works—but particularly her recent novel, *Ur kackerlackors levnad* (1984; Out of the Lives of Cockroaches), set on a decrepit boat in Guatemala, indescribably sordid in atmosphere and at times profoundly disturbing in the way the author dissects her characters and their hopes and dreams—explore the meaning of such concepts as dependence and freedom: freedom that is essentially equal to indifference toward oneself and others versus freedom as a dynamic force in growth and human development; dependence as submissive passivity or emotional exploitation versus dependence as a sense of communality through which each individual is ultimately enriched.

FURTHER WORKS

Vinbergssnäckan (1964); *Tusentals äpplen* (1969); *Lena Bell* (1971); *Ta ner månen* (1972); *Städpatrullen* (1976); *Dotter till en dotter* (1977); *S/y Glädjen* (1979); *Lyckans galosch* (1986).

REFERENCES

"Dotter till en dotter," a review, *World Literature Today* 53.1 (1979); "S/y Glädjen," a review, *World Literature Today* 54.2 (1980), "Arvedelen," a review, *World Literature Today* 56.4 (1982).

Rose-Marie G. Oster

Almqvist, Carl Jonas Love. Swedish author, teacher, philosopher, and journalist, b. 28 November 1793, Stockholm, d. 26 September 1866, Bremen.

When Almqvist was three years old, his father, Carl Gustaf, began a second career as a farmer and the family moved northwest of Stockholm. Here, among idyllic lakes, meadows, and forests, Almqvist and his mother, Birgitta Lovisa, shared an intimate relationship that remained the primary source of spiritual and artistic inspiration throughout the author's lifetime. A model for such strong female characters as Tintomara and Sara Videbeck was Almqvist's cherished friend Charlotte Hazelius (married name Södermark), who guided the development of his feminist consciousness. Almqvist's intellectual education began under the tutelage of his maternal grandfather, the publicist Carl Christoffer Gjörwell, and continued from 1808 to 1815 at Uppsala University, where he earned a master of arts degree.

From 1815 to 1923, Almqvist worked as a civil servant in Stockholm and devoted much of his spare time to theology, through both the written and the spoken word. In 1817, he founded Mannasamfundet (The Manna Society), a worship circle that identified the spiritual meaning of marriage with the purity of the natural countryside, setting itself in polemical opposition to the perceived dogma and corruption of the Lutheran establishment. Several members of the society, including Almqvist and his wife Maria Lundström, tested their ideals from 1824 to 1825, spending nineteen months with a utopian experiment in provincial Värmland.

From 1828 to 1840, Almqvist worked as a schoolteacher and rector at Stockholm's Nya elemetärskolan and wrote his popular *Törnrosens bok* (1833–1840, 1849–1951; The Book of the Wild Rose). This seventeen-volume opus ranges between romanticism and realism, including every possible genre: novels, essays, prose sketches, imitation folktales, dramas, poems, and musical songs.

The last era of Almqvist's life began in 1839 with the publication of his controversial novel *Det går an* (1839; *Sara Videbeck, The Chapel*, 1919, 1972). Bourgeois society was so profoundly shocked by this novel's rejection of conventional sex roles that Almqvist was forced in 1841 to resign from his pedagogical position, barred from employment elsewhere, and subjected to an ongoing heresy trial by the ecclesiastic authorities in Uppsala. Some relief from the economic hardship came in 1846, when Almqvist began writing steadily for the liberal newspaper *Aftonbladet*, often on the subject of women's rights. In June of 1851, accused of forging promissory notes and attempting to poison a moneylender, Almqvist fled suddenly to the United States. Formerly a dedicated traveler within Sweden and throughout Europe, Almqvist now journeyed as far as Texas and St. Louis before settling in a boarding house in Philadelphia. As "Professor Carl Westermann," he made a final voyage back across the ocean, hoping to return to Sweden, but getting no farther than the public hospital in Bremen, Germany, where he died on 26 September 1866.

Almqvist wrote a mythical sketch in 1824 entitled *Skönhetens tårar* (1839; Beauty's Tears), which he later identified as the sorrowful foundation for all of the higher happiness in *Törnrosens bok*. Beauty (Astarte) is a heavenly being who races away from a licentious pursuer, a nameless giant. When the desperate Astarte, whose name alludes to the pre-patriarchal Mother Goddess, is finally overcome, her tear mixes with a drop of her blood to create our planet. Our heritage from this primeval tragedy is an ironic home that simultaneously wants to rise toward spiritual purity (the tear) and fall in empty sensuality (the blood).

Ten years later, Almqvist wrote one of the greatest works in Scandinavian literature, the complex masterpiece *Drottningens juvelsmycke* (1834; The Queen's Diadem). This romantic novel is based upon the historic events surrounding the assassination of King Gustaf III by aristocrats at a masked ball in 1792. *Drottningens juvelsmycke* is rich with spiritual and political profundity, artistic heights, ironic tones, highly charged story lines, mysterious riddles, vivid imagery, and the unforgettable Azouras Lazuli Tintomara la Tournerose. The ever-more-popular classic has inspired six adaptations to other cultural media since 1953, including productions in film, radio, television, theater, and opera.

Almqvist's novel is structured by a contrast between the superficial and role-stereotyped "love" of aristocratic society and the natural genius for friendship radiating from Tintomara, a young, intuitive proletarian. This unbaptized heroine of Almqvist's anti-bourgeois *Bildungsroman* is a gifted dancer and musician whose discovery of self appears to follow a lesbian pathway. Tintomara's evolving consciousness brings her into personal and political conflict with a manipulative government official named Reuterholm, whose efforts to possess her as a court mistress eventually result in her accidental assassination.

Throughout his production, Almqvist incorporated the Swedenborgian belief that Divine Love is a balanced union between warmth, the feminine quality of goodness, and light, the masculine understanding. Earlier works separated the human reflection of God's warmth and light as sex-role differentiation, seeking synthesis through conventional marriage. With the character Tintomara, however, Almqvist discovered what was to become the modern feminist ideal of complete individuals who embody aspects from both feminine and masculine sex roles, and whose friendships therefore transcend economic, domestic, or emotional dependencies. Almqvist then believed that a happier society would not only offer ample educational and career opportunities to every citizen, but also assume collective responsibility for nurturing all of the children. The polemical novel *Det går an* and the utopian manifesto *Europeiska missnöjets grunder* (1850; Reasons for the European Dissatisfaction) present these potentially revolutionary insights as commonsense practicality.

Sara Videbeck, the independent heroine of *Det går an*, is a professional glazier whose windows serve to preserve warmth and admit light for the benefit of other human beings. While traveling to gather raw materials for her putty, Sara meets Albert and an innovative courtship begins. Sara helps the sensitive and open Albert learn that love thrives as freedom, not as sex-role conventions.

The novel ends with the hope that these two friends will invent a more natural, nonpossessive marriage based upon individual self-sufficiency that will remain outside the sanctions of the church and the state. The grace and joy with which these two lovers take up residence on separate floors of Sara's now-empty childhood home assume prophetic significance to a modern reader. Indeed, readers and scholars of recent decades are finding that Almqvist's powerful vision of a loving society is increasingly more comprehensible and realistic—perhaps even necessary for the survival of humankind.

FURTHER WORKS

Valda skrifter, ed. A. Th. Lysander (1874–1878); *Samlade skrifter*, ed. F. Böök, 17 vols. in 9 (1921–1938); *Valda skrifter*, ed. Ruben B:son Berg, 13 vols. (1902–1906); *Dikter i landsflykt* (1956); *Hvad är en tourist? Brev och korrespondenser*, ed. K. Aspelin (1961); *Källans dame*, ed. K. Aspelin (1966); *Brev 1803–1866*, ed. B. Romberg (1968); *Det går en åska genom tidevarvet* (1972); *Armodets son* (1972).

REFERENCES

Almqvist, Johan Axel, *Almqvistiana* (Uppsala, 1892); Balgård, Gunnar, *Carl Jonas Love Almqvist, samhällsvisionären* (Uddevalla, 1973); Blackwell, Marilyn, "Friedrich Schlegel and C. J. L. Almqvist: Romantic Irony and Textual Artifice." *Scandinavian Studies* 52.2 (1980); Blackwell, Marilyn Johns, *C. J. L. Almqvist and Romantic Irony* (Stockholm, 1983); Hellsten, Stig, *Kyrklig och radikal äktenskapsuppfattning i striden kring C. J. L. Almqvists 'Det går an'* (Stockholm, 1951); Holmberg, Olle, *C. J. L. Almqvist från 'Amorina' till 'Colombine'* (Stockholm, 1922); Jägerskiöld, Stig, *Från Jaktslottet till Landsflykten* (Helsingfors, 1970); Lagerroth, Ulla Britta, and Bertil, Romberg, eds., *Perspektiv på Almqvist* (Uddevalla, 1973); Olsson, Henry, *Törnrosdiktaren, den rike och den fattige* (Stockholm, 1966); Romberg, Bertil, *Carl Jonas Love Almqvist* (Boston, 1977); Werin, Algot, *C. J. L. Almqvist, Realisten och liberalen* (Stockholm, 1923); Westman Berg, Karin, *Studier i C. J. L. Almqvists kvinnouppfattning* (Göteborg, 1962).

Laura M. Desertrain

Alnæs, Finn. Norwegian novelist and essayist, b. 20 January 1932, Bærum.

The combination of cosmic perspectives, vitalism, and ecological values is the trademark of Alnæs's writing.

In his first novel he celebrates the display of masculine power and vitality. It is a story about a physical and intellectual superman, an outsider, whose human dimensions bring him close to the heroes of Greek tragedy. The novel's main theme is the question of personal guilt and the scope of individual responsibility reflected through the fate of the hero. His conflict is one between unrestrained vitalism and an ethical categoric imperative. The novel can also be read as a hymn to the spiritual and carnal love between man and woman, a theme that is repeated in later novels.

The novel was praised for its power of style and vivacity of language and won the first prize of a Scandinavian novel contest.

The same vivacity unfolds in *Gemini* (1968), where the decay of modern civilization is contrasted with a value system where the humanity of man is restored when man is replaced in nature and cosmos. The question of civil disobedience in a society where the rulers threaten to destroy their natural surroundings is discussed both here, in essays, and in his latest novel.

Musica. Ildfesten I (1978; Musica. The Feast of Fire) is the first novel in a planned eight-volume cycle that is to explore the conditions of modern civilization on the edge of an ecological disaster.

Alnæs combines a vivid realism with a metaphysical philosophy of nature. He rejects social realism and Marxism, but shares its criticism of modern capitalism and the growth philosophy of social democracy. In spite of his praise of the individual masculine hero, his novels are fairly populist and reflect popular, anti-technological environmentalist movements in Norway of the 1970s.

FURTHER WORKS

Koloss (1963); *Festningen faller* (1971); *På frihetens pinebenk* (1972); *Naturkatedral* (1976); *Svart snø* (1976); *Dynamis. Ildfesten II* (1982).

TRANSLATIONS

Literary Review 22.2 (1968–1969).

REFERENCES

Skagen, Kaj, "I opplysningens slagskygge. Dialog med en hovedlinje i Finn Alnæs' forfatterskap." *Arken* 3/4 (1982).

Øystein Rottem

Andersen, Astrid Hjertenæs. Norwegian lyric poet, b. 5 September 1915, Horten, d. 21 April 1985.

Andersen's greatest accomplishments are in poetry, but she is also a master of short prose and a talented translator from English and German. She has a strong interest in the visual arts, a fact that is reflected widely in her poetry, as far as both imagery and themes are concerned. In an introduction to an anthology of poetry she alludes to the fact that her poems come about in a dreamlike fashion:

Then all the visions come and set you free. Trees glide aside. Trees change into tigers which you fight and which you again transform into trees. Nothing is impossible. The white gate has opened up. . . . Everything comes to you and populates your landscape.

Many of the poems then are indeed "visions," and possess still-life character. They emphasize surprising, exquisite detail. The form is always free but the sounds, especially the vowels, have a conjuring quality. The movement, if any, is soft and sweeping like a dance.

However, not only is there gentleness and enchantment with the aesthetic, but there is also flintiness and backbone. One poem from her very first collection ends with the battle cry "Why don't you fight, woman?" The cry becomes fainter later on, but never dies down. Under the beautiful, often exotic surface—Andersen often seems inspired by her extensive journeys abroad—there is always a struggle of various forces. There is not only the battle of the sexes, but also the deeds of all the dark and light forces that rule human fate. These powers are innate in nature and reveal themselves in short glimpses of a detail, which acquires significance beyond itself.

Andersen's best poems seem to be the ones directly inspired by a work of art, be it a statue, a painting, a fairy tale or, in a much wider sense, a flower, a landscape.

WORKS

De ville traner (1945); *De unge søylene* (1948); *Skilpaddehagen* (1950); *Strandens kvinner* (1955); *Vandrersken* (1957); *Pastoraler* (1960); *Frokost i det grønne* (1964); *Dr. Gnomen* (1967); *Hyrdefløyten* (1968); *Som en vår* (1970); *Rosenbusken* (1972); *Svaner og nåtid* (1973); *Et Våroffer* (1976); *Samlede dikt* (1985).

TRANSLATION

König, Fritz H., "The Woman's Voice in Modern Norwegian Poetry." *North American Review* 257.1 (1972).

Fritz H. König

Andersen, Benny Allan. Danish poet, short story writer, and author of children's books, b. 7 November 1929, Copenhagen. Prior to his literary debut in 1960, while working as a pianist, Andersen traveled through Scandinavia with a group of musicians and began to write poems after encountering Swedish modernist poetry.

The fundamental theme, which Andersen varies with great virtuosity, no matter what genre he chooses to write in, is the complex problem of individual balance in a world dominated by one-sided norms and ever-mounting social and political pressures. As a social critic and moralist, Andersen explores the relationship between the individual and society in its dialectical processes by closely scrutinizing everyday life. Characteristic of his literary technique is his witty play with language, ranging stylistically from humor and irony to satire while complementing a serious thematic dimension. Andersen's portrayals of social outsiders often border the grotesque. Thus he creates an awareness of an individual's mistaken choice by depicting an often fatal pseudobalance; the tragicomic presentation serves to point out the high degree of individual alienation and thereby the profound lack of balance with which Andersen is concerned.

During the 1970s, Andersen's code of ethics begins to emerge more clearly in his works as a gradual shift in focus takes place from critically unbalanced existential situations to the genuine efforts necessary on the part of the individual if an authentic balance is to be achieved in everyday life. Andersen has always formulated this major concern quite clearly in his books for children in which he questions the restricted views of adults and has the children present a balancing perspective with a great deal of wit and charm. But in his poetry, fiction, and plays Andersen approaches his readers much more implicitly with the exception of his novel, *På broen* (1981; On the Bridge), in which he delineates the adolescent's intense search for a valid stance toward others and stresses the importance of authentic and continuous personal growth. In addition to employing a tragicomic strategy, Andersen has begun exploring new techniques by experimenting with the narrator's role in the collection of stories, *Over skulderen: Blå historier* (1983; Over the Shoulder: Blue Stories), in order to emphasize the complexity of his theme.

Despite visible affinities to the works of Albert Camus, Jean-Paul Sartre, and the Swedish author Gunnar Ekelöf,* it is the philosophy of Søren Kierkegaard* that forms the basis for Andersen's ethical concept and for his literary strategy. Andersen's strong humanistic commitment to society as an author is reflected in his universally significant contribution to a balanced stance of social criticism in literature.

FURTHER WORKS

Den musikalske ål (1960); *Kamera med køkkenadgang* (1962); *Den indre bowlerhat* (1964); *Puderne* (1965; *The Pillows*, 1983); *Snak* (1965); *Portrætgalleri* (1966); *Snøvsen og Eigil og katten i sækken* (1967); *Tykke-Olsen m. fl.* (1968); *Den hæse drage* (1969); *Det sidste øh* (1969); *Lejemorderen og andre spil* (1970); *Snøvsen på sommerferie* (1970); *Her i reservatet* (1971); *Snøvsen og Snøvsine* (1972); *Svantes viser* (1972); *Barnet der blev ældre og ældre* (1973); *Undskyld hr.—hvor ligger naturen?* (1973); *Personlige papirer* (1974); *Nomader med noder* (1976); *Orfeus i undergrunden* (1978); *Under begge øjne* (1978); *Himmelspræt eller kunsten at komme til verden* (1979); *Kolde fødder* (1979); *Oven visse vande* (1981); *Snøvsen hopper hjemmet* (1984); *Tiden og storken* (1985); *Hyddely-Hat* (1986); *Andre sider* (1987).

FURTHER TRANSLATIONS

The Devil's Instrument, and other Danish stories, comp. Sven Holm (1971); *Mundus Artium* 5.1/2 (1972); *Prism International* 12.1 (1972); his *Selected Poems* (1975); *Con-*

temporary Danish Poetry, ed. Line Jensen et al. (1977); *Scanorama* 6.4 (1977); *Scandinavian Review* 67.2 (1979); *Malahat Review* 52 (1979); *Scandinavian Review* 69.4 (1981); *Seventeen Danish Poets*, ed. Niels Ingwersen (1981); *Modern Scandinavian Poetry*, ed. Martin Allwood (1982); *Translation* 9 (1982).

REFERENCES

Marx, Leonie, *Benny Andersen: A Critical Study* (Westport, Conn., 1983); Marx, Leonie, "Exercises in Living: Benny Andersen's Literary Perspectives." *World Literature Today* 52.4 (1978).

Leonie Marx

Andersen, Hans Christian. Danish fairy tale writer, novelist, and poet, b. 2 April 1805, Odense, d. 4 August 1875, Copenhagen.

Andersen is the first Danish writer to achieve international fame who arrived not only from the lower classes but from the very bottom of society, the proletariat. His father, Hans Andersen, was a poor shoemaker but reputedly quite intelligent and well-read for his class, his mother an uneducated washerwoman who died in the poor house in Odense in 1833. The talented, imaginative boy Hans Christian soon realized that if he were to make his mark in the world, he would have to go to Copenhagen. Before he left (at only fourteen years old) for the Danish capital, he said to his anxious mother: "I want to be famous. First you suffer so terribly much, and *then* you become famous."

From 1819 to 1822 Andersen had a very difficult time in Copenhagen; at times he almost starved. But gradually, through his youthful writings, he attracted the attention of some influential men in the city, especially Jonas Collin, financial director of the Royal Theatre. Collin managed to secure funds that would enable Andersen to get a formal education. In 1822, with financial support from the state, Andersen entered the Latin school at Slagelse, under the leadership of Dr. Simon Meisling. After some miserable school years in Slagelse and later in Elsinore (still under Meisling), Andersen was tutored privately in Copenhagen, where he finally passed his "Studentereksamen" in 1828. In January 1829, he published a fantastic, humorous tale in the manner of E.T.A. Hoffmann. It was called "A Walk from Holmen's Canal to the East Point of Amager." This work might be said to form a transition to the later fairy tales. He was now launched on the career of a writer.

After some educational travels abroad (Germany, France, Italy) Andersen published his first major work, the novel *Improvisatoren* (1835; *The Improvisatore*, 1845). This autobiographical novel, which is set in Italy, was a success and made a name for Andersen, first in Scandinavia and later in translations in England and on the Continent. Its vivid, colorful descriptions of Italian folk life and scenes still make enjoyable reading today. That same year, 1835, Andersen started publishing a number of old Danish folk tales that he had retold in a new, original manner. The first booklets (*Hæfter*) of tales were subtitled "For Children," but after a few years Andersen removed the subtitle, as he became increasingly ambitious and began to realize how much he could accomplish in the "little" genre of the fairy tale. Gradually he made the little genre into the great genre, as he became the undisputed master of fairy tale writing in modern times. In the years that followed—almost until the end of his life in 1875—Andersen kept publishing tales and stories in booklets. His collected works in this genre number 156 plus a few posthumous ones. His friend, the physicist H. C. Ørsted, was the first person in Denmark to realize the importance and originality of the tales, especially their unique humor. He once said to Andersen: "Your novels have made you famous, your fairy tales will make you immortal."

The richness and variety of Andersen's oeuvre in the fairy tale are almost overwhelming. Here are tales and stories of every imaginable description and style: satirical tales ("The Emperor's New Clothes," "The Darning Needle," "The Rags"); moralizing Christian tales ("The Red Shoes," "The Evil Prince," "Anne Lisbeth"); profound allegories ("The Snow Queen," "The Bell," "The Marsh King's Daughter"); sentimental fantasies ("The Little Mermaid"); autobiographical allegories ("The Ugly Duckling," "The Fir Tree"); pessimistic, cynical tales ("The Shadow"); modern realistic short stories ("Under the Willow Tree," "What Old Johanne Told"); tales containing mild social criticism ("She Was No Good," "Everything in Its Right Place"); fireworks of pure, verbal wit ("The Hill of the Elves"). Very often in the tales Andersen contrasts the artificial with the natural (for example "The Swineherd," "The Nightingale"), always with a preference for the latter. Frequently he juxtaposes the heart and the intellect (for example "The Snow Queen"), always showing sympathy for the former. Andersen's advocacy of the natural and the heart (the emotions) places him squarely in the tradition of Danish romanticism. He was born at a propitious moment (1805): the older Danish romantics (Adam Oehlenschläger* and Bernhard Ingemann*) had paved the way for his acceptance. His poetic genius was greater than that of his predecessors, it is true, but they had nevertheless provided momentum for his literary career.

Andersen's tales and stories brought a fresh impulse to and a much-needed renewal of Danish prose in the nineteenth century. He revitalizes the academic prose of his time with elements from the spoken language, makes the style concrete and picturesque. In some tales he foreshadows the later impressionism of Herman Bang.* When he started publishing his first tales in the 1830s, fairy tales were not considered a respectable part of serious literature; therefore it took several years before his work in this genre gained the admiration that it deserved. But from 1840—when Andersen received his first public acclaim in Sweden—until his death in 1875, the fame of his fairy tales and stories kept rising. If anything, it has increased after his death. His tales have been translated into countless foreign languages and are read and loved everywhere. The fame that Andersen craved so fervently has indeed become his, and universally so.

What is the reason for this worldwide appeal of Andersen's tales? Most readers outside of Denmark are compelled to read them in translations that are often sadly inadequate. Nevertheless, the tales apparently contain some basic human qualities capable of transcending even the worst of translations. Most of the well-known tales deal with elemental human emotions that almost everybody can identify and empathize with: love, joy, fear, grief, pride, envy, happiness, sadness. All readers can sympathize with the heartrending grief of the bereaved mother in "The Story of a Mother." All readers can feel sorry for the ugly duckling in the tale of that name and join in its jubilation over its final triumph. All readers can empathize with the mermaid in "The Little Mermaid" who must see love and happiness elude her. She is an outcast like so many of Andersen's characters. Many of the tales, in fact, are permeated by a strong feeling of compassion for those who have been left out, whom life has passed by: old maids, lonely bachelors, social losers. Other qualities of Andersen's tales are appreciated fully only in the Danish original: his wit and tongue-in-cheek humor, the finesse and charm of his style. This man, who never learned to spell Danish correctly, is perhaps the greatest stylist in Danish literature.

Andersen is often thought of as only the writer of fairy tales, but he was prolific in several other genres: novel, travel book, drama, poetry, and auto-biography; he carried on an extensive correspondence. After *The Improvisatore* he published five other novels: *O.T.* (1836; *O.T.*, 1845); *Kun en Spillemand* (1837; *Only a Fiddler*, 1845); *De To Baronesser* (1848; *The Two Baronesses*, 1848); *At Være Eller Ikke Være* (1857; *To Be or Not to Be*, 1857); *Lykke-Peer* (1870; *Lucky Peer*, 1871). There are passages in the novels that reveal Andersen's droll sense of humor and occasional vivid descriptions of scenery and folk customs, but Andersen was not an outstanding novelist. The short form of the tale suited him better. The novels are rambling in composition, with Andersen taking off on all kinds of irrelevant digressions and causing his plots to meander in a most disconcerting way. He tends to side with or against his characters so that the novels become unconvincing psychologically. The two most readable of the novels are the first and the last: *The Improvisatore* and *Lucky Peer*, the shortest and best composed. Andersen's travel books contain some of his finest prose, especially the two most celebrated ones: *En Digters Bazar* (1842; *A Poet's Bazaar*, 1846; *A Visit to Germany, Italy and Malta, 1840–1841*, 1985) and *I Sverrig* (1851; *In Sweden*, 1852). Andersen is the most widely traveled of all Danish writers. He went almost everywhere in Europe, and on one occasion he even got to North Africa. "To travel is to live," he once observed, and he was an excellent, observant traveler. In Sweden he was warmly received on several visits, and in the panoramic *In Sweden* he pays off his debt of gratitude to his Swedish friends. The book is a homage to the natural beauty of Sweden and to the historical glories of its past—an exquisite work of art.

Andersen had an unhappy love for the theater and wanted desperately to win recognition as a dramatist. He submitted many plays to the Royal Theatre in Copenhagen, but most of these were only moderately successful; a few were failures. This part of his work has proved to be the least viable. As a lyrical poet he was more successful. Some of his *Fædrelandssange* (patriotic songs) are still popular in Denmark, especially "In Denmark I Was Born" and "Jutland.'' A few of his shorter poems—''The Mother with the Child'' and ''Study after Nature''—are perfect examples of bourgeois genre pieces.

Andersen wrote several autobiographies, but the most important one is *Mit Livs Eventyr* (1855, 1877; *The Story of My Life*, 1871, 1880). The most arresting pages in this work are those devoted to his childhood and youth. Later the book becomes a somewhat monotonous record of his triumphal tours through Europe, a proud account of all the princes and great literary figures who vied with one another to acclaim Andersen. In France he met Victor Hugo, Honoré de Balzac, Alexandre Dumas, the actress Rachel, Alfred de Vigny, and Heinrich Heine. In Weimar he became fast friends with the Grand Duke Carl Alexander, who even tried to persuade Andersen to settle in Weimar. In Sweden he became acquainted with the writer Fredrika Bremer,* and he fell in love—unhappily—with the ''Swedish nightingale,'' the famous singer Jenny Lind. In England, where his work was received with enthusiasm, he was for a while on friendly terms with Charles Dickens and corresponded with him.

On 15 November 1867, Andersen was made honorary citizen of his native city of Odense. This was undoubtedly the happiest day in his life, its apotheosis. His prophetic boyhood words to his mother had come true: ''First you suffer so terribly much, and *then* you become famous.''

Andersen's numerous letters and his voluminous diaries, which have recently been published in twelve volumes in Denmark, give a picture of the man that is different from the official portrait of the happy, feted poet presented in *Mit Livs Eventyr*. In reality Andersen was not at all the ''Lucky Peer'' that so many people assumed him to be. Much of his life he was a sick man. His nervous system was weak; he was a hypochondriac who struggled against a constant feeling of inadequacy; at times he was afraid of going mad, like his paternal grandfather. He often felt lonely and despondent; he badly missed a love life and a family life. It is true that in the first paragraph of *Mit Livs Eventyr* Andersen states his conviction that there is a loving God who has guided everything to the best for him. When the old Andersen looked back on his life, he felt that he had fulfilled his mission—he had become the one he was meant to be: Hans Christian Andersen, the great writer. But he had paid a heavy price for his literary fame in the loss of ordinary human happiness. This awareness is perhaps what accounts for the deep feeling of compassion that runs through his work for those who are unhappy and forsaken.

FURTHER WORKS

Kærlighed paa Nicolaj Taarn (1829); *Skyggebilleder af en Reise til Harzen* (1831; *Rambles in the Romantic Regions of the Hartz Mountains*, 1848); *Mulatten* (1840); *Maurerpigen* (1840); *Kongen Drømmer* (1844); *Den Nye Barselstue* (1845); *Das Märchen meines Lebens* (1847; *The True Story of My Life*, 1847); *I Spanien* (1863; In Spain, 1864); *Et Besøg i Portugal* (1866; *In Spain* and *A Visit to Portugal*, 1870); *H. C. Andersens Eventyr*, ed. Hans Brix and Anker Jensen, 5 vols. (1919); *Levnedsbogen* (1926); *Digte*, ed. Paul V. Rubow (1930); *H. C. Andersens Brevveksling med Jonas Collin den Aeldre og andre*

Medlemmer af det Collinske Hus, ed. H. Topsøe-Jensen, 3 vols.; *Samlede Eventyr*, ed. H. Fonsmark, 3 vols. (1958); *H. C. Andersen og Henriette Wulff*, ed. H. Topsøe-Jensen, 3 vols. (1959–1960); *H. C. Andersens Eventyr*, eds. Erik Dal and Erling Nielsen, 5 vols. (1963–1967); *H. C. Andersens Dagbøger*, 12 vols. (1971–1976).

FURTHER TRANSLATIONS

Fairy Tales, 4 vols. (1951–1960); *The Complete Andersen* (1952); *The Complete Fairy Tales and Stories* (1974); *Tales and Stories by Hans Christian Andersen* (1980); *The Shadow and Other Tales* (1983); *Hans Andersen's Fairy Tales* (1984).

REFERENCES

Böök, Fredrik, *Hans Christian Andersen. A Biography* (Norman, Okla., 1962); Bredsdorff, Elias, "A Critical Guide to the Literature on Hans Christian Andersen." *Scandinavica* 6.2 (1967); Bredsdorff, Elias, *Hans Christian Andersen, the Story of His Life and Work 1805–75* (New York, 1975); Dahl, Svend and H. Topsøe-Jensen, eds., *Hans Christian Andersen, His Life and Work* (Copenhagen, 1955); Grønbech, Bo, *Hans Christian Andersen* (Boston, 1980); Jørgensen, Aage, *H. C. Andersen litteraturen 1875–1968. En bibliografi* (Århus, 1970); Supplement, 1975–; Rubow, Paul V., *H. C. Andersens Eventyr* (Copenhagen, 1927).

Børge Gedsø Madsen

Andersen, Martin. *See* Nexø, Martin Andersen.

Andersen, Tryggve. Norwegian novelist, short story writer, essayist and translator, b. 27 September 1866, Ringsaker, d. 10 April 1920, Gran in Hadeland.

Born and raised in one of Norway's leading agricultural districts, Andersen had deep roots in two Norwegian cultural streams, that of freeholder and government official. Both folklore and aristocratic, Danish-inspired traditions gave impetus to his writing. Six years in Sunnhordland led to his great interest in the sea. Andersen also cultivated an early interest in German romanticism (Novalis, Adelbert von Chamisso and E.T.A. Hoffman) and Gotthold Ephraim Lessing while he rejected Georg Brandes* and John Stuart Mill, demigods of the 1880s radical movement. At the university Andersen studied German philology and Egyptology and became greatly involved in literary life and bohemian culture. He was a central figure in the new romantic movement of 1890. However, his promising academic future was ended abruptly in 1892 when the university expelled him on disciplinary grounds.

I Cancelliraadens Dage (1897; *In the Days of the Councillor*, 1969), Andersen's most important work, is a collective novel set in Ringsaker during the Napoleonic Wars and final years of Danish rule. Drawing on folklore and archive sources, it explores the conflict inherent in the lifestyle of freeholder and official, and the downfall from social refinement, to a wasted life of drinking and gambling. In *Mot Kvæld* (1900; Towards Evening) Andersen drew on his crisis following dismissal from university, his hallucinations and epileptic illness, to create Jørgen Holk. Holk's own destruction is paralleled by a natural catastrophe:

the sun does not rise, the sea burns. Andersen's short stories stem from a range of oral traditions and travel impressions, and often utilize death and the supernatural.

One of the founders of neoromanticism, Andersen occupies a central position in Norwegian arts and letters. His style is remarkably free of flowery, romantic language, and drawing on eastern dialects and cultivated sociolects, he is a major reviver of Dano-Norwegian literature. Andersen is considered one of the best Norwegian short story writers, with the surprise ending as his trademark. *Mod kvæld*, with its critique of middle-class narrow-mindedness and pessimistic ending, strikes familiar chords today and is a forerunner of absurd art.

FURTHER WORKS

Digte (1898); *Gamle folk* (1904); *Bispesønnen og andre fortællinger* (1907); *Hjemfærd* (1913); *Fabler og hændelser* (1915); *Samlede fortællinger*, 3 vols. (1916); *Ulykkeskatten* (1919); *Dagbok fra en sjøreise* (1920); *Fortellinger i utvalg* (1966).

FURTHER TRANSLATIONS

Slaves of Love and Other Norwegian Short Stories, ed. James McFarlane (1982).

REFERENCES

Gierløff, Christian, *Tryggve Andersen* (Oslo, 1942); Hougen, Frik, *Tryggve Andersens Opplandsfortellinger* (Oslo, 1953); Schiff, Timothy, ''Social Value and the Etiology of *Forkommenhet*. Towards an Understanding of Tryggve Andersen's Concept of Human Nature.'' *Scandinavian Studies* 53.3 (1981); Schiff, Timothy, ''Tryggve Andersen's novel 'Mot kvæld' and Its Motto.'' *Scandinavian Studies* 48.2 (1976); Villum, Asbjørn, *Tryggve Andersen og I Cancelliraadens dage* (Oslo, 1932).

Nancy L. Coleman

Andersson, Claes. Finland-Swedish poet, playwright, novelist, b. 30 May 1937, Helsinki.

Best known for his dozen books of lyric poetry, Andersson is a multitalented author appreciated for his diversity. Doctor of medicine and practicing psychiatrist, Andersson has also written three novels, translated two volumes of Finnish poetry into Swedish, authored or coauthored plays and reviews for the stage, radio, and cabaret. He frequently contributes debate articles to newspapers and occasionally performs as a jazz pianist.

Simultaneously a detached and impassioned observer of his surroundings, in all his writings Andersson is concerned with the relationship of the individual to society. As editor-in-chief of the temporarily avant-garde magazine *FBT* (1965–1968), Andersson was a vigorous leader of a writers' movement that sought to break free of what was perceived as the tyranny of the idyllic, politically unengaged, Finland-Swedish modernist lyric tradition. In all his collections of poems from the 1960s, Andersson creates his own ''impure'' poetic diction, one that skillfully combines scientific terminology with colloquial speech but still delights in wordplay, rhetorical devices, and strong rhythmic patterns. His particular talent for compiling macabre details—the technique might be termed premeditated surrealism—is calculated to startle, amuse, or shock the reader. Andersson's wry wit and black humor are those of a moralist gadfly.

A parallel, more personal line of development runs through his lyric production and becomes more pronounced in his books from the 1970s. Nature, human nature, the dark and light sides of love, Eros and Thanatos increasingly inform the poems. In his latest books, the novel *En mänska börjar likna sin själ* (1983; A Person Begins to Resemble His Soul), and the books of poems entitled *Tillkortakommanden* (1981; Shortcomings) and *Under* (1984; Under), the poet-psychiatrist turns his critical eye and wit more on himself than on society at large. In doing so he succeeds in describing what the suicides cannot: anomie in both the social and personal senses of the word.

Andersson is still rightly regarded as the leading Finland-Swedish poet of his generation, one who insists on discussing matters about which it is easier to remain silent.

FURTHER WORKS

Ventil (1962); *Som om ingenting hänt* (1964); *Staden heter Helsingfors* (1965); *Samhället vi dör i* (1967); *Det är inte lätt att vara villaägare i dessa tider* (1969); *Bli, tillsammans* (1970); *Bakom bilderna* (1972); *Rumskamrater* (1974); *Den fagraste vår* (1976); *Jag har mött dem—dikter 1962–74* (1976); *Genom sprickorna i vårt ansikte* (1977); *Trädens sånger* (1979); *Det som blev ord i mig* (1987); *Mina bästa dagar* (1987).

TRANSLATIONS

Books from Finland 13.3 (1979); *Grand Street* 1 (1981); *Poetry East* 6 (1981); *Seneca Review* 12 (1981); *Scandinavian Review* 69.4 (1981); *Territorial Song*, ed. Herbert Lomas (1982); *Books from Finland* 16.1 (1983); *Writ* 14 (1983). Andersson's translators are Lennart Bruce, Rika Lesser, and Herbert Lomas.

REFERENCES

Warburton, Thomas, "Claes Andersson: The Poet as a Progressive." *Books from Finland* 13.3 (1979).

Rika Lesser

Andersson, Dan. Swedish poet and novelist, b. 6 April 1988, Skattlösberg, d. 16 September 1920, Stockholm.

After his early death, a small cult grew up around Andersson's work, fueled by the so-called *kolarromantiken* (Charcoal-burner Romanticism) of his stories and poems of the isolated Finnskog of central Sweden. In much of his writing, the central problem is clearly the relationship of man to God, a prominent theme generally in twentieth-century Swedish literature and in Andersson's case a heritage from his strictly religious father. Though his father was a teacher, Andersson's formal education was fairly rudimentary, coming chiefly through the popular movement and culminating in a short stay at Brunnsviks folkhögskola in 1914–1915. Prior to that school term he had worked as a substitute teacher, a lumberjack, a free-lance journalist, and an organizer for the temperance movement. At the age of fourteen, he was sent to Minnesota to explore the possibilities for a family emigration. This resulted in a posthumous collection of short stories called *Chi-mo-ka-ma* (1920).

In 1914, through the aid of Martin Koch,* he published *Kolarhistorier* (Charcoal-Burner's Stories), tales of the lives and imaginations of those who tend the charcoal ovens, deep in the winter woods. Written with a combination of naturalism and mysticism, this collection has earned a high place in Swedish proletarian prose. These stories were followed in 1915 by *Kolvaktarens visor* (Coal-Watcher's Songs), a collection containing both songs and stories. Though these depict with sharp realism the arduous and monotonous life of the *kolare*, exploited as they were by forest and foundry interests, they are not primarily documents in the class struggle.

The realism of these early stories is transformed to expressionism in the tales of *Det kallas vidskepelse* (1916; It's Called Superstition). Here he suggests that what is called superstition really comes close to the meaning of life, Andersson's lifelong concern.

In 1917, he published his first collection of poems, *Svarta ballader* (Black Ballads). The simple song and ballad forms he employed here are invested with considerable fluidity. Often, he comes close to the dramatic monologue, as in "Omkring tiggarn från Luossa" (Around the Beggar from Luossa) or "Gillet på vinden" (The Party in the Attic). Though he occasionally approaches the sentimental, Andersson usually veers away in time. The innate musicality of his verse has attracted composers such as Gunnar Turesson.

Andersson's two autobiographical novels, *De tre hemlösa* (1918; The Three Homeless Ones) and *David Ramms arv* (1919; David Ramm's Inheritance), come out of the tradition of Johan August Strindberg's* *Tjensteqvinnans son* (1886), where the novel itself forms a kind of reckoning with the past. In his poetry and his last prose, Andersson brings a renewed intensity to his personal religious quest.

FURTHER WORKS

Efterskörd (1929); *Tryckt och otryckt* (1942); *Kulturjournalistik* (1971); *Valda brev, 1906–1913* (1972); *Nattvandrare: Okända dikter* (1972); *Brödkortsromantik: Reportage och artiklar publicerade i Ny tid 1917–1918* (1972); *Mot Mörkret: Okända kåserier* (1974); *Valda Brev, 1914–1920* (1976).

REFERENCES

Ågren Gösta, *Kärlek som i allting bor: Dan Anderssons liv och diktning 1916–1920* (Göteborg, 1971); Ågren, Gösta, *Dan Anderssons väg* (Göteborg, 1970); Holmqvist, Annie, "De svenska finnskogarnas diktare." *Finsk tidskrift* 195/196 (1974); Schleef,

Caroline, "Dan Andersson: Charcoal-Burner and Poet (1888–1920)." *American-Scandinavian Review* 42.3 (1954).

Alan Swanson

Anhava, Tuomas. Finnish poet, critic, essayist, and translator, b. 5 June 1927, Helsinki.

Anhava is a man of many literary roles, a master of style, an astute judge of literary taste, and the leading ideologue of Finnish modernism in the 1950s. He entered public life as a critic, essayist, and polemist whose frequently condemning and always severely critical statements paved the way for the acceptance and understanding of postwar modernism. As an editor in publishing houses and literary journals, Anhava held positions of great influence and could thus both support and reprimand authors. In the 1950s and 1960s he was the leading discoverer and mentor of new writers. His essays, characterized by a polished style and polemical attitude, heralded an era of new criticism in Finland.

Anhava published poetry only during a fifteen-year period. At the time of its publication his debut collection *Runoja* (1953; Poems) was regarded as arid and abstract and its language stiff and constrained. However, in the course of time people have come to appreciate the purity and clarity of its imagery. By concise and exacting stylistic means Anhava's poetry expresses old, classical, and romantic themes and feelings. In the works of his mid-period a more ample and colloquial diction gains ground while the later poetry again grows more ascetic. Before Anhava abandons poetry, he starts to compare words to silence, in favor of the latter. This preference reflects an influence from Eastern philosophies.

Next to poetry, translating has occupied center stage in Anhava's life. He has focused in particular on the modernists of Finno-Swedish poetry (Gunnar Björling,* Bo Carpelan,* Thomas Warburton, and Rabbe Enckell*) and classical Japanese poetry. Anhava has rendered into Finnish much "difficult" literature that otherwise would probably have remained untranslated. As a translator as well as a poet Anhava strives for total clarity and luminosity. His poetry translations are creative works in their own right.

Anhava's lasting significance lies in his contributions as a theoretician and polemist of the 1950s modernism. The conciseness, exactness, and clarity of his poetry render it resistant to the wear and tear of time.

FURTHER WORKS

Runoja (1953); *Runoja 1955* (1955); *36 runoa* (1958); *Runoja 1961* (1961); *Kuudes kirja* (1966); *Runot 1951–1966* (1967).

TRANSLATIONS

In the Dark Move Slowly (1969); *Books from Finland* 20.2 (1986).

Markku Envall

Arnér, Sivar. Swedish novelist, short story writer and dramatist, b. 13 March 1901, Arby.

Coming from a middle-class family, Arnér went to the university and worked as a teacher before his literary debut in 1943. He was a Bonnierstipendiat in 1943 and 1945 and received *Svenska Dagbladet's* literary award in 1945.

The typical Arnér protagonist is torn between extremes in a world where morals and justice must yield to brutality. This is reflected in the title story from his first collection *Skon som krigaren bar* (1943; The Shoe Worn by the Soldier), in which a pacifist shoemaker kills himself rather than make boots for an officer. His novel *Plånbok borttappad* (1943; Wallet Lost) explores the arrogance of power in the relationship between a hot dog peddler and his customer, an engineer whose wallet the peddler has found.

The cruel elements of existence are pursued also in Arnér's many novels dealing with the dynamics of marriage, which inevitably becomes a love-hate struggle for power between an aggressive, neurotic woman and a passive, weak man. This theme is explored in *Du själv* (1946; You Yourself), where the wife taunts her husband about her extramarital, sexually degrading affair and finally leaves him. The same lack of meaningful erotic relationship is found also in *Han Hon Ingen* (1951; He She Nobody), ending with murder. The interdependence between incompatible forces is masterfully brought out in "Luft och vatten" in *Mörkt och ljust* (1954; Dark and Light), a short story where a bird of prey and its victim both die locked in battle.

Arnér's greatest contribution lies in his brilliant exploration of interpersonal relationships and domestic dynamics, which also serve his political consciousness in their application to contemporary political dilemmas. Arnér tends to become somewhat repetitious in his many works but his style alone justifies his place in Swedish letters, characterized as it is by exquisite simplicity and freshness reflecting the spoken language.

FURTHER WORKS

Knekt och klerk (1945); *Verandan* (1947); *Egil* (1948); *Vackert väder* (1950); *Fyra som var bröder* (1955); *Som svalorna* (1956); *Fem hörspel* (1959); *Dag och natt. Hörspel* (1959); *Finnas till* (1961); *Nätet* (1962); *Tvärbalk* (1963); *ett ett ett* (1964); *Verkligheten* (1965); *Solgatan* (1967); *Vargkotletter* (1968); *Skön och god* (1969); *En satans person. Hon kommer ju. Två pjäser* (1970); *Det fanns en park* (1971); *Byta människor* (1972); *Vattenvägar* (1973); *Där är han* (1975); *Vilken kämpe* (1976); *Öppna dörrar* (1978); *När man är flera* (1982).

Torborg Lundell

Arrebo, Anders Christensen. Danish poet, b. 2 January 1587, Ærøskøbing, d. 12 March 1637, Vordingborg.

Arrebo, the son of a Lutheran pastor, studied theology at Copenhagen University. He became a favorite of Christian IV and, after taking orders, quickly rose through the clerical ranks and was appointed bishop of Trondheim in 1618. Arrebo was a zealous and effective administrator, but the king removed him from office in 1622 after several nobles unjustly accused him of immoral behavior. Arrebo then settled in Malmö, where he took consolation in the psalms and published a complete translation of them in 1623. The recognition that this edition aroused helped Arrebo to become pastor of Vordingborg in 1626. The psalter also betrayed Arrebo's interest in developing a Danish style equal to that of other European literatures, and in 1631 he was commissioned to translate Du Bartas' epic poem on the creation, *La première Sepmaine* (1578). This work, the *Hexaëmeron*, remained unfinished at his death, but its posthumous publication caused posterity to regard Arrebo as the father of Danish poetry.

Arrebo's fame rests on his introduction of Renaissance literary forms to Denmark. In his translations, Arrebo avoided a slavish imitation of his model so as to adapt the sense of the original for a Danish audience. In the psalms, Arrebo attempted to establish a metrical regularity by using the same number of stressed and unstressed syllables in corresponding lines. He also adapted his psalms to the melodies of traditional Danish hymns to counteract the popular Calvinist versions. Similarly, in the *Hexaëmeron*, Arrebo transformed Du Bartas' Huguenot presentation of a fearful and distant God into a Lutheran portrait of a forgiving deity. He also replaced Du Bartas' alexandrines with hexameters with an innovative caesure rhyme, but he later reverted to the alexandrine, for it best conveyed his encyclopedic knowledge of theology, classical literature, and natural science. Where Du Bartas had adorned his poem with novel conceits, Arrebo preferred to describe God's creation in exacting detail.

Although Arrebo was esteemed by seventeenth century writers as a talented artist, his works now appear repetitive and pedantic. Yet, despite stylistic weaknesses, Arrebo established a unique literary style to educate the common man in which Renaissance forms were combined with a personal and uncomplicated Lutheran faith.

FURTHER WORKS

Samlede Skrifter, 3 vols. (1965, 1968, 1975).

REFERENCES

Rørdam, Holger F., *Mester Anders Christensen Arrebos Levnet og Skrifter* (Copenhagen, 1857); Simonsen, Vagn L., *Kildehistoriske Studier i Anders Arrebos Forfatterskap* (Copenhagen, 1955).

James A. Parente, Jr.

Aspenström, Karl *Werner*. Swedish poet, dramatist and essayist, b. 13 November 1918, Norrbärke.

Aspenström took several menial jobs before attending high school as a mature student and proceeding to Stockholm University. He emerged as a poet in the mid–1940s, and was one of the editors of the influential journal *40-tal*. Aspenström has also written some thirty plays, many of them for radio. He espouses several social, political, and environmental causes, but lives quietly with his wife in Stockholm. Aspenström became a member of the Swedish Academy in 1981.

Skriket och tystnaden (1946; The Cry and the Silence) was very much in the spirit of the 1940s: imbued with angst, the poems are in rhythmical free verse, full of rich imagery and references to the current state of the world. Aspenström's real breakthrough, however, came with *Snölegend* (1949; Snow Legend), which forms a trilogy together with his next two collections of poems. Aspenström inquires about the nature of reality and links his conclusions with the symbol of snow, a transient substance that cannot be fixed or preserved. Typically, the snow image recurs in most of Aspenström's subsequent books of poetry—as do several others, for example, dogs, snails, a blue verandah. Death is a recurring theme in Aspenström's poetry, and also in his plays. His drama is lyrical in mood and often displays a whimsical sense of humor in surrealistic, almost absurd style. Here and in his polemical writings, Aspenström expresses concern about the future of mankind in a world obsessed by bombs and the space race.

Aspenström is primarily a poet, whose true quality has tended to be obscured by his modesty and retiring nature. Each new collection of poems seems to be a part of a whole life's work thanks to the constantly developing themes and symbols, and Aspenström grows in stature with the passage of time.

FURTHER WORKS

Oändligt är vårt äventyr (1945); *Litania* (1952); *Förebud* (1953); *Hundarna* (1954); *Dikter under träden* (1956); *Bäcken* (1958); *Teater I* (1959); *Om dagen om natten* (1961); *Motsägelser* (1961); *Teater II* (1963); *Trappan* (1964); *Teater III* (1966); *Sommar* (1968); *Skäl* (1970); *Stackars Job* (1971); *Under tiden* (1972); *Ordbok* (1976); *Tidigt en morgon sent på jorden* (1980); *Sorl* (1983).

TRANSLATIONS

Thirty-seven Poems from Four Books (1977); Burton, Nina, et al., "Werner Aspenström: An Introductory Note. Poems in Translation 1949–79." *Swedish Books* 2 (1979); *You and I and the World* (1980); *The Blue Whale and Other Pieces*, ed. Robin Fulton (1981); *Writ* 14 (1982); Green, Brita, "Death and the Tree." *Swedish Book Review* 2 (1983); *2 Plus 2* (Spring/Summer 1984); *Werner Aspenström. Poems 1946–1983*, ed. David Emblen (1987).

REFERENCES

Attius, Håkan, *Estetik och moral* (Stockholm, 1982); Burton, Nina, *Mellan eld och skugga* (Stockholm, 1984); Green, Brita, "Werner Aspenström: Making a Pillow from the Darkness." *Swedish Book Review* 2 (1983); Sjöberg, Leif, "Werner Aspenström: A Writer for All Seasons." *American-Scandinavian Review* 57 (1969); Törnqvist, Egil, "Poet in the Space Age: A Theme in Aspenström's Plays." *Scandinavian Studies* 39 (1967).

Laurie Thompson

Atterbom, Per Daniel Amadeus. Swedish poet, philosopher literary historian, b. 19 January 1790, Åsbo, d. 21 July 1855, Stockholm.

Atterbom, leader of the Swedish "neoromantic school," that is, romantics inspired by the Schelling-led stream of German romanticism, differed from his friend and fellow romantic Erik Gustaf Geijer* in his withdrawn life and delicate style. Intimately familiar with the philosophical orientation provided by Johann Gottlieb Fichte and Friedrich Schelling, in 1807 Atterbom founded the society "Musis Amici" renamed the "Aurora Society" (Auroraförbundet), but better known after the title of the society's journal *Phosphorus*. Among the "Phosphorists," one meets many of the phrases and motifs from the Schlegel-Tieck circle: exaltation of the Infinite, the poetic process and the quasi-religious faith in the ability of the poet to sense the transcendental coherence among man, nature, and God. As was the case with his mentors, however, Atterbom's way to the Infinite was less through faith in God than through faith in Schelling.

Atterbom's poetic talents appear clearly in his cycle *Blommorna* (The Flowers) from the *Poetisk Kalender* of 1811. The various flowers symbolize man's longing for the harmony and unity of Nature; while this thought was scarcely novel in romantic poetry, Atterbom's imagery was. Of particular interest in the *Kalender* is Atterbom's fragment *Fågel Blå* (Bird of Blue).

Atterbom shared with Geijer and the Gothic Society an interest in the Nordic past as a source of imagery for contemporary poetry, as can be seen in his programmatic poem "Skaldarmal" of 1811. In the *Kalender* for 1816, Atterbom published some folk ballads, "Nordmansharpan" (Harp of the Northman), but in contrast to Geijer, Atterbom's interest in the Nordic past remained largely theoretical, probably because the more abstract philosophical conjectures of Schelling remained his principal inspiration. In a series of articles in the *Svensk Literatur-Tidning*, Atterbom contended that Schelling's systematic philosophy was indeed compatible with Christian faith. Atterbom, however, had to confront this problem of the basis for art on a personal level in the 1820s, as he had to consider the subjectivity of his poetic vision. Geijer had suggested that the transcendental premises of Atterbom's poetry masked an essential egocentricity, in this echoing Goethe's criticism of romanticism.

One encounters the fruits of Atterbom's contemplations in *Lycksalighetens ö* (1824–1827; The Isle of the Blessed). This poetic drama constitutes Atterbom's most profound contribution to Swedish literature. Longing for the Infinite, King Astolf cannot live in the timeless world of the fairy Felicia without guilt, for the price of his dream is his forsaken kingdom and the faithful Svanhvit. Returning to his kingdom, Astolf finds it hopelessly materialistic. Having encountered the great enemy of the romantic moment, Time, Astolf tries to return to the Isle and Felicia, but only his body arrives.

Subsequently, Atterbom attempted in *Studier till filosofiens historia och system* (1835; Studies in Philosophy's History and System) to refine the philosophy of Schelling into a vision allowing for a personal, intervening God, but in a sense Atterbom lived too long; the questions changed before he found the answers. By mid-century, political and literary tastes had changed, and though his six-volume *Svenska siare och skalder* (1841; Swedish Visionaries and Poets) is excellent, Atterbom's place as a poet has only been secured in this century.

FURTHER WORKS

Samlade dikter (1837–1838); *Samlade skrifter i obunden stil*, 7 vols. (1859–1870); *Atterboms bref till sin fästmö 1823–26* (1911); *Valda skrifter*, ed. F. Böök, 6 vols. (1927–1929); *Samlade Dikter*, 6 vols. (1954–1963).

FURTHER TRANSLATIONS

The Mermaid: Cantata by Julian Edwards (1906); *Anthology of Swedish Lyrics from 1750 to 1925*, ed. C. W. Stork (1917; rev. ed., 1930).

REFERENCES

Santesson, Carl, *Atterbomstudier* (Stockholm, 1932); Frykenstedt, Holger, *Atterboms kunskapsuppfattning* (Lund, 1949); Frykenstedt, *Atterboms livs-och världsåskådning*, 2 vols. (Lund, 1951–1952); Frykenstedt, *Atterboms sagospel Lycksalighetens Ö* (Lund, 1951); Hellsten-Wallin, Elisabet, and Isak Hellsten-Wallin, *Den unge Atterbom och romantiken: genombrottsåren* (Stockholm, 1954); Kulling, Jacob, *Atterboms 'Svenska siare och skalder'* (Stockholm, 1931); Magnusson, Sigvard, *Det romantiska genombrottet i Auroraförbundet* (Stockholm, 1936); Santesson, Carl H., *Atterboms ungdomsdiktning* (Stockholm, 1920); Santesson, Carl H., *Mot Lycksalighetens Ö* (Stockholm, 1956); Vetterlund, Fredrik, *Atterboms sagospel 'Lycksalighetens Ö'* (Lund, 1902).

John L. Greenway

Aukrust, Olav. Norwegian lyric poet, b. 21 January 1883, Lom, Gudbrandsdalen, d. 3 November 1929, Lom.

Aukrust is very much a poet of synthesis; his work is characterized by an inherent unity, for which he continuously strives. His basic concern is "how can I gather the many rays?"

Although chronologically separated from the Age of Nordic Romanticism, Aukrust was still influenced by poets like Henrik Wergeland,* Erik Gustaf Geijer,* and Esaias Tegnér.* His religious outlook was formed by the principles of Nikolaj Grundtvig.* He knew Henri Bergson's and William James's psychological theories.

His poetry is a search for truth. He finds the foundation for this truth in a conscientious effort to study all literary, cultural, humanistic, theological, and scientific phenomena which are accessible to him. But this is only a preliminary step. Now enters the poet as catalyst: with spontaneous and intimate intuition he develops what he calls "the third view" (a new, immediate way of seeing and expressing nature). In Aukrust's opinion, poetry, via its technical resources, is the ideal means to let the human being feel a deeper unity of the self and the universe. He feels that he is closest to the truth when he sees objects as symbols.

Aukrust is able "to gather all the rays" only in a few of his poems. Many suffer from overly repetitive imagery, sound patterns, and a baroque wordiness. On the other hand, these traits have a conjuring quality that can almost transport us into a trance, a state of mind that is almost a necessity in order to understand Aukrust's mystic experiences.

As a patriotic poet Aukrust had many followers; as a mystic poet he stands alone. In literary histories he is frequently grouped with five other poets, his contemporaries Herman Theodor Wildenvey,* Olaf Bull,* Alf Larsen,* Tore Ørjasæter,* and Olav Nygard. Each of them with his own special poetic gift contributed to a renaissance of Norwegian verse in the second and third decades of this century, providing fertile ground for the prolific production of poetry in Norway up to our time.

WORKS

Himmelvarden (1916); *Hamar i Hellom* (1926); *Solrenning* (1930); *Norske terningar* (1931).

REFERENCES

Groth, Helge, *Olav Aukrust, Problematikk og utvikling* (Oslo, 1948); Krokann, Inge, *Olav Aukrust* (Oslo, 1933); Mæhle, Leif, *Skaldespor* (Oslo, 1965); Mæhle, Leif, *Vegen til varden* (Oslo, 1968).

Fritz H. König

Aurell, Tage. Swedish novelist, essayist, and translator, b. 2 March 1895, Kristiania (Oslo), d. 20 February 1976, Mangskog.

Aurell interrupted his formal education at age eighteen, abandoning his plans to study for the priesthood. For the next six years he worked as a journalist for a number of provincial newspapers. While in Norrköping (1917–1919), he reported on a court case, which a quarter of a century later was to provide the material for his novel *Skillingtryck,* a modern Woyzec story. Between 1919 and 1929 Aurell lived abroad, mainly in France. Concurrently with studies in literature at the Sorbonne, he contributed articles to Scandinavian newspapers and began his career as a translator with the translation into French of five one-act plays by Johan August Strindberg.* From his return to Sweden until his death, Aurell lived in Värmland, the native province of his mother.

Aurell's first three novels were largely neglected by readers and critics alike. In 1943 the influential critic Knut Jaensson wrote a highly appreciative essay on Aurell in *Bonniers Litterära Magasin*, alerting the public to Aurell's original talent and unique position in Swedish literature as a pioneer and major stylist.

Although Aurell's total production is quantitatively modest, consisting of five short novels (among them the basically autobiographical novel *Viktor* from 1956), two collections of short stories, and three collections of essays and travel sketches, it possesses a rare density and suggestive power, due mainly to the author's cultivation of a lapidary style of extreme economy. This style, in its diction close to poetry and characterized by unfinished sentences and fragmented dialogues or voices from an anonymous collective, may at times seem cryptic and places a major burden of interpretation on the reader. At the center of Aurell's novels and short stories are often socially insignificant, seemingly trivial characters placed in existential situations beyond their spiritual and intellectual powers. Despite the unemotional and often painfully comical narratives, a sense of pathos and dignity is conveyed to these basically pessimistic tales of quiet despair and unredeemed loneliness.

FURTHER WORKS

Tybergs gård (1932); *Till och från Högåsen* (1934); *Martina* (1937); *Skillingtryck* (1943); *Smärre berättelser* (1946); *Nya berättelser* (1949); *Bilderbok* (1950); *Liten fransk stad* (1954); *Vägar och möten* (1960); *Samtal önskas med sovvagnskonduktören* (1969).

FURTHER TRANSLATIONS

Rose of Jericho and Other Stories (1968); *Swedish Books* 2. 3–4 (1980).

REFERENCES

Jacobs, Alan, "Tage Aurell 1895–1976." *Swedish Books* 2. 3–4 (1980); Mattsson, Ragnar, *Berättaren i Mangskog* (Stockholm, 1970).

Lars G. Warme

Autere, Eeva. *See* Joenpelto, Eeva.

Autobiography and Memoir Literature. If you do not regard Egill Skallagrímsson's* *Sonatorrek* and the self-reflectory letters in Petri de Dacia, *Vit Christinæ Stumbelensis* (1269–1289), as autobiography, there is no such writing in Scandinavia in the Middle Ages. The earliest autobiography is probably the curriculum vitae of Jørgen Rosenkrantz (1523–1596), a Danish nobleman and distinguished statesmen of the period. In the seventeenth century there are among a heap of travelogues and diaries a few autobiographies in the true sense. The earliest work is probably the personal life story of Agneta Horn (1529–1672), *Agneta Horns lefverne*, written 1648 or 1656. Horn, the daughter of one of Gustavus Adolphus's generals, in the account of her sad, orphaned childhood and adolescence reveals her hysterical, stubborn, and passionate temperament. Her story, penned when she was nineteen, moves pointedly from the somber shadows of her early years into the bright sunny day of her amour and happy marriage, where the story comes to an end. Equally egocentric is the unfinished autobiography of Christina of Sweden (1626–1689), written in French in 1689 and covering only her first nine years. Though predominantly devoted to her royal position, it still gives an impression of the author's unusual personality and intellect. Another woman autobiographer, Leonora Christina* (Ulfeldt) (1621–1698), in the various accounts of her life makes the greatest contribution to the genre in the century. Though written in German, the *Memoires oder kurtze Erzählung meines Lebenslaufes* by Ditlev Ahlefeldt (1617–1686) may be considered as belonging to Danish literature. Ahlefeldt, who was an officer and diplomat in the service of Christian IV, writes about his life until 1659 with a sincerity and sobriety unusual for his epoch. Ahlefeldt's memoirs, where he expatiates on many subjects showing considerable learning, is a major source for our knowledge about the culture and manners of the times. Ahlefeldt's display of self-knowledge is not the forte of Jørgen Bielke (1621–1696), a Dano-Norwegian general, who wrote his life story after 1676 when he fell from grace. His self-glorifying account of his exploits as a hunter and warrior is more entertaining than credible, but his descriptions of court intrigues in the days of Frederik III of Denmark and Norway are of historical interest. The autobiography of Johan Monrad (1638–1709), in contrast to those of his contemporaries, is markedly idyllic and uneventful. It traces his progress from his happy childhood in the Danish provinces and his studies and career as a civil servant in the metropolis to his travels in Europe, and ends with an account of his romantic courtship and marriage at the age of forty-two. There is a disarming innocence about his smug self-admiration and a lyrical charm about the way he tells about the beauty of nature and falling in love. Urban Hiärne (1641–1724), the distinguished physician, dramatist, and scientist, in his autobiography, *Urban Hiernes Lefwernesbeskrifning* (1720), shows a similar complacency in the account of a truly remarkable career. Jesper Swedberg (1653–1735) was the author of the most voluminous autobiography of the period, *Jesper Swedbergs Lefwernes Beskrifning* (1729). The Swedish hymnist and churchman here gives a truthful picture of his righteous personality, visionary piety, pastoral zeal, and dynamic enterprise. The element of social rise found in the last three autobiographies mentioned is also a salient feature of the life story of Rasmus Aereboe (1685–1744). Aereboe's autobiography (written after 1736) vividly depicts its protagonist's poverty as a grammar school boy and student before his ability is noted and he is offered support. Its highlight is his description of his travels in Russia and sojourn at the court of Czar Peter the Great and the account of the heroic feat when as an emissary to Russia for the Danish king he crossed the Baltic in a rowing boat. (His adventures are parallel to those related in the notes and diaries of Swedish soldiers who fell into Russian captivity in the early decades of the eighteenth century. An example is the diary of Leonard Kagg.)

Ludvig Holberg* (1684–1754) published his autobiographical epistle, *Epistula de sua vita ad Vir Perillustrem*, in 1728 (followed by a second in 1737 and a third in 1743). The perillustrious addressee is a fiction; the epistle is meant for the reading public. This in itself ushers in a new era of autobiography. Those of the previous century were meant for family and friends and were generally not published until much later. But Holberg also introduces a new secular approach. In his account of his life and character there is no self-glorification or devoutness. His description of his youth in Norway and his years as an itinerant scholar in Europe presents him as almost a picaresque character, neither courageous nor virtuous, but with an eminent ability to survive in the adventures and vicissitudes in which he gets involved. Holberg views himself with humour and irony, but above all with a desire to understand. His first epistle concludes with an attempt at a self-portrait where he points out the contradictory features and irrational oddities of his enigmatic personality. In this Holberg stands out as an individual, but also as a true representative of the empirical and skeptical tradition of the Age of Reason. Holberg's only Scandinavian peer in his day,

Carl von Linné* (1709–1778), left an autobiography that records his life year by year until 1776. It is mainly devoted to the great Swede's academic progress, conflicts, and achievements, but has little to say about his personal life and temperament. The countercurrent to the enlightenment in the Scandinavian lands, pietism, is felt in the autobiography of Erik Pontoppidan (1698–1764), the Danish churchman, historian and topographer, but it also bears witness to the devout cleric's humour and tolerance. Holberg's would-be successor as a writer of comedies for the Danish stage, Charlotte Dorothea Biehl (1731–1788), in her autobiography (1771) makes an interesting account of the opposition a woman writer had to put up with in her day. In the Life and Opinions of Johannes Ewald* (*Levnet og Meeninger*) (1774–1775) a spate of feeling and sense of individuality breaks forth. Ewald uses the comic manner of Sterne to tell about his early years and youth, dwelling on the three themes that dominate his poetry and determine his fate, wine, heroism, and love. At the same time as Ewald confesses to the dispositions and weaknesses that cause his failure in life, he still proudly asserts his faith in the divine vocation of a poet. The digressionary manner of Sterne is used to handle three planes of time within his narrative structure: his adventures as a soldier of fortune at the age of sixteen, the circumstances in his upbringing and the passion that made him run away from home, and the moment of writing when he reviews the outcome of it all. Ewald's autobiography is wrought as a complex work of art. It borders on the autobiographical novel, which is realized by the Swedish parson Jakob Wallenberg (1746–1778) in his comic classic *Min son på galejan* (1781; My Son on the High Seas). The Rousseauism one might detect in Ewald is found in the poetry of Gustaf Fredrik Gyllenborg* (1731–1808), but hardly in the account of his personality and career *Mitt Lefverne 1731–1776* (My Life), which he wrote as an aging courtier and servant of the Swedish crown. The Gustavian period is well recorded in documentary writing as, for example, in the diaries of Princess Hedvig Elisabeth (1759–1818) and the memoirs of Carl Tersmeden (1715–1797). For the literature and culture of Denmark during the last decades of the eighteenth century, the *Erindringer af mit Liv* (5 vols., 1824–1829; Memoires of My Life), by Knud Lyhne Rahbek (1760–1830), is an important source. So is *Min Biografi fra min Fødsel til min Bortrejse fra København 1805* (My Biography from My Birth to My Departure from Copenhagen 1805), by Claus Pavels (1769–1822), a Norwegian bishop and politician, but it is also interesting for the sometimes unflattering picture it gives of the author's critical and sensitive self. For its human portrait the *Tanker og Bekjendelser* (Thoughts and Confessions) by Nikolai Wergeland (1780–1848), the melancholy father of the great Norwegian poet Henrik Wergeland,* is likewise noteworthy.

The romantic movement with the high value it sets on individuality and the experience of childhood strongly encourages and shapes autobiography in the nineteenth century. An example is *Oehlenschlägers Levnet fortalt af ham selv* (2 vols., 1830–1831; Oehlenschläger's Life Told by Himself) by the Danish poet Adam Oehlenschläger.* An augmented four-volume version *Erindringer* (Memoirs) appeared in 1850–1851. In this work Oehlenschläger attempts to show that the events of his life, particularly in childhood and youth, all led to what his innermost "poetic nature" always meant him to become, a poet. The idea of development toward a breakthrough of self-awareness and sense of destiny in 1846 is characteristic of *Meddelelser af mit Levnet* (1854; Reports about My Life), by Jakob Peter Mynster (1775–1854), the Danish bishop and theologian, and *Minder* (2 vols., 1867–1871; Memories), by Carsten Hauch. The memory of a childhood paradise is central to the life and work of Bernhard Severin Ingemann,* as is evident from his *Levnedsbogen* (1862; Book of My Life).

A presentation copy of Oehlenschläger's life gave Hans Christian Andersen* the impulse for his first autobiography *Levnetsbogen*, unpublished but written for a friend in 1833. Here Andersen gives an account of his life until his debut as a poet. Though indebted to both Oehlenschläger's life and Goethe's autobiography, and preoccupied with the idea of Providence at work in his destiny, Andersen here gives a more realistic and less self-pitying picture of himself and his surroundings than in the later autobiographies, *Mit eget Eventyr uden Digtning* (1847 in German translation) and *Mit Livs Eventyr* (1855; My Life's Adventure), which bring the story of his life closer to the *Bildungsroman* pattern that was so important to him and his contemporaries in their fiction. The most impressive attempt to make autobiography confirm a divine pattern in individual life and its integration in a universal design is *Livserindringer og Livsresultater* (2 vols., 1877; Memories and Accomplishments of Life), by Meïr Aron Goldschmidt.* The concluding words of the second philosophical volume are, "Man is there to apprehend order and to establish order in himself," which serves as the guiding principle for his account of his Jewish childhood, his career as a journalist and writer, and his return to his Jewish heritage. Goldschmidt's work appeared when the era of idealism it represents was running out. Two other works that likewise appear, so to speak, after their day are *Af mit Levned* (2 vols., 1882–1883; From My Vita), by Hans Lassen Martensen (1808–1884), the theologian and bishop who was Søren Kierkegaard's* pet aversion, and *Mit Liv genoplevet i Erindringen* (4 vols., 1891–1892; Life Recalled in Memory), by Johanne Luise Heiberg, the celebrated actress of the early half of the century.

Apart from Andersen and Mrs. Heiberg, all autobiographers of the century are middle-class. One exception to this is Ole Kollerød (1802–1840), a thief and convicted murderer, who wrote about his life and fate before his execution in 1840. In *Min Historie* (My History) Kollerød attempts to trace what went wrong in his life and led him on to the path of crime. Though Kollerød is far from trustworthy in the apology for himself, his description of the criminal underworld of Copenhagen and the brutality of prison life, where no taboo subject is avoided, is convincing, which also holds true of his response to kindness and his primitive groping for religious atonement.

Among the scant autobiographical writings in Norway in the early nineteenth century one finds the remarkable contributions of Camilla Collett* and Henrik Wergeland. As a young girl Collett, besides a diary, composed a moving account of her unhappy passion for Johann Welhaven* during the period 1833–1835, to which she added two books of published memoirs, *I de lange Nætter* (1862; During the Long Nights) and *Erindringer og Bekendelser* (2 vol., 1868–1872; Recollections and Confessions). In these she writes about her childhood and her relationship with her father and poet brother. Wergeland wrote autobiographical sketches, *Hasselnødder* (1845; Hazel Nuts), which due to their capricious humor and the pathos of the author's savoir-mourir bring to mind the life and opinions of Johannes Ewald. Interesting autobiographies about the same period are Conradine Dunker, *Gamle Dage* (1865; The Old Days), Gustava Kielland, *Erindringer fra mit Liv* (1882; Memories of My Life), and Wilhelmine Ullmann, *Fra Tyverne og lidt mere* (1880; From the 1820s and a Little More).

Of the major figures in Sweden in the early nineteenth century Franz Michael Franzén,* Erik Gustaf Geijer,* and Fredrika Bremer* produced notes and chapters for autobiographies in the 1830s where, in keeping with the spirit of the age, memories of childhood are given particular attention. That is also true of full-scale autobiographies by minor writers such as Samuel Ödmann's *Hågkomster från hembygden och skolan* (1828; Recollections of My Native Village and School), Bernhardt Beskow's *Levnadsminnen* (1870; Memoirs), and Carl Wilhelm Böttiger's *Självbiografiska Anteckningar* (1881; Autobiographical Notes), all of which have status as classics. Yet, the monumental works of the genre relating to the first five or six decades of the century are perhaps those of nonliterary men. Henrik Reuterdahl (1795–1870), theologian and bishop, in his *Memoarer* (completed 1865) draws an uncommonly candid portrait of himself in his account of the hardships of his early years and in the recollections of his academic and public career. Louis de Geer (1818–1896) in his *Minnen* (1892; Memoirs) writes with an exquisite pen about the unusual manor house milieu in which he grew up and of the aristocratic circles in which he moved as a young man, while accounting for his life as a major public figure of the century. Of no less proportions are the recollections of Paul Peter Waldenström (1838–1917) in which this outstanding free church leader reveals his powerful personality where puritanism and self-righteousness are mixed with humor and a robust sense of realism.

Sara Wacklin's (1790–1846) *Hundrade minnen från Österbotten* (1844–1845; Hundred Memories from Ostrobothnia) offers one of the earliest samples of autobiographical writing in Finland. A schoolteacher from Oulu, Wacklin moved to Sweden in 1843 and there, at the prompting of a relative, the author and pastor G. H. Melin, put in writing her recollections of life in the small coastal town in Finland. Although generally quite lighthearted in tone, some of the memories have, as G. C. Schoolfield aptly expresses it, "in their art of implication few rivals in pre-Strindberg Swedish prose fiction."

Another female writer, Fredrika Runeberg (1807–1879), wife of J. L. Runeberg,* concluded in 1869 her reflections over her own lifelong struggle as a writing woman and of woman's position in general. *Min pennas saga* (The Story of My Pen) wasn't published, however, until 1946. Also her *Brev till sonen*

Walter (1971; Letters to Son Walter), a collection of letters written between 1861 and 1879 to the sculptor Walter Runeberg during his years in France and Italy, reads like a political and cultural chronicle of the period in Finland as well as abroad.

Most of the nineteenth-century Finnish writers of memoirs were nationally prominent political or cultural figures rather than authors of fiction. One of the earliest, Johan Albrekt Ehrenström (1762–1847) worked as a private secretary to the Swedish King Gustaf III and later made a name for himself as the chairman of the committee for the reconstruction of Helsinki, the country's new capital. His *Historiska anteckningar* in two volumes came out in 1882–1883. Two other sets of memoirs, Anders Ramsay's *Från barnaår till silfverhår* (8 vols., 1905–1919; From Childhood Years to Silver Hairs) and Senator August Schauman's *Från sex årtionden i Finland: upptecknade lefnadsminnen* (2 vols., 1892–1893; Six Decades in Finland), merit a mention.

All of the above works, although published by Finlanders, had been written in Swedish. Agathon Meurman (1826–1909), an ardent champion of the Finnish cause, was the first to write his recollections, *Muistelmia* (1909), in Finnish.

An important subgenre within the Finnish autobiographical writing consists of the numerous travel accounts by nineteenth-century explorers, ethnologists, and linguists who undertook long journeys to the northernmost Siberia and the Near as well as Far East, for example, Matthis Alexander Castrén's *Nordiska resor och forskningar* (1852; Nordic Journeys and Research), Georg Wallin's *Bref och dagboksanteckningar jämte en lefnadsbeteckning* (1905; Letters and Diary Notes in Addition to a Biography) and his *Georg August Wallins reseanteckningar från Orienten åren 1843–1849* (14 vols., 1864–1866; Georg August Wallin's Travel Notes from the Orient) as well as Gustaf Ramstedt's *Seitsemän retkeä itään 1898–1912* (1944; Seven Journeys to the East). Carl Gustaf Mannerheim, better known as the commander in chief of the Finnish armed forces in 1918 and during World War II, and president of the republic from 1944 to 1946, published in 1940 a two-volume account of his travels as a young officer in the Russian Imperial Army in the Far East, entitled *Resa genom Asien* (Travel through Asia). Mannerheim represents also another category of memoir writers, that is, prominent statesmen and politicians. His two-volume *Minnen* came out in 1951–1952 (*Memoirs*, 1954). Another veteran statesman and later president, Juho Kusti Paasikivi, wrote a significant series of memoirs, *Paasikiven muistelmia sortovuosilta* (2 vols., 1957; Memoirs from the Years of Oppression) and *Toimintani Moskovassa ja Suomessa 1939–41* (2 vols., 1958; My Activities in Moscow and in Finland). Two volumes of diaries appeared in 1985–1986 covering the years 1944–1956.

Aino Kallas'* five volumes of diaries rank among the finest examples of the genre. In addition to their human interest, the diaries of this accomplished author offer valuable insights into the cultural life of Finland and Estonia during the first quarter of the twentieth century as well as give a vivid picture of her life in London as the wife of the Estonian ambassador, Oskar Kallas.

August Strindberg* inaugurates a new era of Scandinavian autobiography with his *Tjänstekvinnans son* (1886; *Son of a Servant*). Here he accounts for his early life with a ruthless frankness, unheard of since Rousseau, while as a naturalist he attempts to show himself as a product of biological heritage and environment. It is also unusual that Strindberg published his autobiography at the age of thirty-six. His contemporaries tended to turn to writing about themselves well into the next century. A case in point is Georg Brandes,* whose three-volume *Levned* (Life Story), covering his life until 1892, appeared 1905–1908. The first volume recording his childhood, as well as his intellectual formation and existential crisis before his emergence as a spokesman of radicalism in 1871, offers much insight into his personality, while the consecutive volumes tend to concentrate on his public role, his conflicts with the conservative establishment in Denmark, and his growing fame in Europe. Of his associates and contemporaries in the modern breakthrough in the 1970s and 1980s Sophus Schandorph, Erik Skram, Herman Bang,* Henrik Pontoppidan,* and Karl Gjellerup* have all produced memoirs, but none of them have written about the age of so-called naturalism in Scandinavia with such personal commitment as Nils Collett Vogt in *Fra gutt til mann* (1929), where he describes the enthusiasm for new ideas and the personal cost of pain and bitterness the break with family tradition and accepted values meant. An autobiography of the same epoch is *Erindringer* (1928; Memoirs) by Harald Høffding (1843–1931), where the philosopher offers a candid picture of his personal life and its crises and accounts for his role in the intellectual life of his day.

Johannes Jørgensen* in his *Mit Livs Legende* (7 vols., 1915–1928; Legend of My Life) seemingly reverts to the classical autobiographical pattern as he traces his development from a childhood paradise over lawless years as a poet and radical journalist to his conversion and reception into the Roman Catholic Church, but ultimately any idea of personal growth is repudiated as he shows the intervention of God both in his pagan youth and in the turns of his career after his conversion. It is, however, the fascination with his youth in spite of himself that makes the first book of his work so memorable. Johannes Jørgensen consciously relates to Saint Augustine's and Jean-Jacques Rousseau's *Confessions* and Goethe's *Dichtung und Wahrheit*. No such pretension with Martin Andersen Nexø,* whose autobiography comes closer to the level of the said great models. In the four volumes *Et lille Kræ* (1932; Urchin), *Under aaben Himmel* (1935; In the Open Air), *For Lud og koldt Vand* (1937; Roughing It), *Vejs Ende* (1939; End of the Road). Nexø deals with his life until the age of twenty-six. In the epic account of his struggle for survival in early childhood, of the crucial experience of Nature in boyhood and of the discovery of culture, society, and Eros in his youth, concluding in his realization of his calling as a writer of the working class, Nexø reads his individual self both as a being of nature and as a representative proletarian type. His sense of organic growth, meaningful destiny, and typicality makes his autobiography a parallel to the classical nineteenth-century ones. What makes Nexø different is his class consciousness and his intense body awareness. Nexø's account of his childhood among the common people has counterparts in the autobiographies of Carl Nielsen (1865–1931), *Min fynske Barndom* (1927; My Funen Childhood), and Jeppe Aakjær,* *Fra min Bettetid* (1928; From My Early Childhood), *Drengeaar og Knøseaar* (1929; Years as a Boy and a Youngster), and *Før det dages* (1929; Before Dawn).

The twentieth century sees an unprecedented flowering of autobiography. Politicians, theatricals, academics, journalists, writers—even writers of autobiographical novels (another growth industry) such as Ivar Lo-Johansson* and Jan Fridegård*—by their scores and dozens vie at writing about themselves, either on their own initiative or by invitation from the press or publishers. A general easing of taboos means that writers are prepared to be more open about their intimate life just as any reservation about writing about living contemporaries is abandoned. The interest in childhood traumas inspired by Freudianism tends to lay as much emphasis on that age as the romantics did; less and less, however, is it seen as a paradisiac state of innocence than as the time when unhealable wounds were inflicted and irredeemable conflicts started up. The parent-child relationship is bitterly laid open (Jan Myrdal*) and marital conflict and breaking up discussed in painful detail (Marika Stiernstedt, Tove Ditlevsen*). With all egocentricity, autobiographers, particularly after World War I, tend to relate their individual fate to the international political climate. The threat to freedom and the fear of war become existential problems (Elsa Gress). A feature of modern autobiography is that authors as often as not commit their life stories to paper when they are still comparatively young. As regards the structure of autobiography, one will find that the pattern of chronological development is not necessarily observed. The narrative may evolve on two levels of time, there may be offered a mosaic of biographical incidents (Hedenvind Eriksson), or the end may be in the beginning (Henrik Stangerup). Also, with all ruthless candor, the autobiographer may resort to provocative mythomania as an artistic device (Suzanne Brøgger*). It is part of the twentieth-century vogue in autobiography that a number of unpublished personal life stories have been brought to press, particularly by representatives of the social strata who are not usually articulate about themselves.

The four-volume *Mitt Liv* (1961–1964; My Life) by Herbert Tingsten (1896–1980), political theorist and writer, may be said to include some of the said features of modern autobiography. With merciless sincerity Tingsten draws a picture of his sensitive and disillusioned, irascible and insecure personality against the background of his extraordinary alertness to the intellectual currents of his age and his engagement in Swedish and international intellectual life and debate. The same proportions may be said to be found in the autobiography of Sven Lidman (1882–1960). With inexorable frankness the aging novelist, turned Pentecostal preacher, exposes the vanity and egoism of his erotic exploits in youth as well as the shallow aestheticism of his early career as a poet in the four volumes *Gossen i grottan* (1952; The Boy in the Grotto), *Lågan och lindansaren*

(1952; The Flame and the Rope Dancer), *Mandoms möda* (1954; The Toil of Manhood), *Vällust och vedergällning* (1957; Lust and Retribution). Sven Stolpe's three-volume *Memoarer* (1974–1976) is on the same scale.

The Freudian viewpoint is less prominent in *Rejsen til Kjørkelvik* (1954; The Journey to Kjørkelvik) by Aksel Sandemose* than one would expect. As Sandemose tells about his clash with the bigoted provincial milieu in which he grew up and the motley career of his youth, it is rather the author's sense of humor and the grotesque that attract attention. These qualities one also finds in *Foraaret saa sagte kommer* (1942; Slowly Spring Is Coming) by Kaj Munk*; Johan Borgen* in *Barndommens rike* (1961; Kingdom of Childhood) writes about the Oslo milieu he also deals with in his fiction. In two volumes *Mine mange hjem* (1965; My Many Homes) and Fuglefri og Fremmed (1971; Free and Foreign) Elsa Gress writes with frankness and affection about her childhood in a bourgeois family that was constantly moving, and accounts for her development into an anti-fascist intellectual and radical on hikes in prewar Germany and France and as a member of the resistance in occupied Denmark during her student days. The way her personal life and its crises are interwoven with the political events of the times lends to her book its special relevance. Her contemporary Tove Ditlevsen in *Det tidlige Forår* (1976; *Early Spring*, 1984) and *Gift* (1971; Married/Poison) writes about her childhood in a poor working-class district of Copenhagen, where against all odds she develops her precocious gift as a poet, and goes on to describe her life with poets and intellectuals in the forties when she goes through marriage crises and drug addiction, all related with merciless frankness. Ditlevsen achieves her effect by writing about her childhood milieu and herself as if observing through the all-seeing but uncomprehending eyes of the awkward girl unknowingly guarding her integrity as a poet. The account of the addict's inferno and the marital debacles reveals deep psychological insight that is strangely in contrast with Ditlevsen's lack of intellectual commitment and curiosity. The two last-mentioned autobiographies are representative of the many personal life stories by women appearing in the wake of the women's liberation movement. Of contemporary Scandinavian writers probably no one has used the confessional mode more poignantly than Jan Myrdal, particularly in *Confessions of a Disloyal European* (1965) and in the two volumes *Barndom* (1980; Childhood), and *En annan värld* (1984; Another World). His account of his Stockholm childhood is memorable, not primarily because of its intensely bitter attack on the author's famous parents, but thanks to his phenomenal recall of the boy's world and the poetic sharpness of Myrdal's style. The narcissist 1970s have valid exponents in Henrik Stangerup and Suzanne Brøgger. Stangerup in *Fjenden i forkøbet* (1978; Outwitting the Enemy) writes about himself as a misfit in a family of high social and cultural aspirations and describes the shipwreck of a marriage and the mixed success of his struggle for recognition as a writer and filmmaker in Denmark and Brazil. Brøgger in *Creme Fraiche* (1977) exposes a chaotic family background without the customary resentment and gaily records bisexual adventures on a worldwide scene from Bangkok to New York and

Copenhagen. The two writers, who share and flaunt a cosmopolitan outlook, employ a sophisticated narrative technique indebted to the idiom of the cinema and make provocative use of fantasies in the account of their lives. In the case of the work of Brøgger the shadows of Henry Miller and Anaïs Nin hover in the background.

Similarly characteristic of the confessional mode of the 1970s and 1980s are the family chronicles and autobiographical novels in several volumes by two Finland-Swedish writers, Christer Kihlman* and Henrik Tikkanen,* both among the leading novelists in Swedish today. Starting with the 1971 *Människan som skalv* (The Man Who Lost His Grip), Kihlman has dealt in an honest and often controversial manner with his family heritage and his own bisexuality. Tikkanen is best known for his self-ironic memoirs, the so-called address novels, named after some of the addresses in the author's life. In an artful, precise and aphoristic prose, Tikkanen paints a harrowing but also hilarious picture of his childhood and adolescence in a family belonging to the country's cultural elite. The later volumes of the series focus on his own bouts with alcoholism and his tumultuous sex life.

The welter of confessional literature of the last decade or so awaits its historian as does Scandinavian autobiography in general.

REFERENCES

Kondrup, Johnny, *Levned og tolkninger* (Odense, 1982); Mitchell, Stephen A., *Job in Female Garb: Studies on the Autobiography of Agneta Horn* (Göteborg, 1985); Platen, Magnus von, *Biktare och bedragare* (Stockholm, 1959).

Niels Lyhne Jensen

B

Baggesen, Jens. Danish poet, b. 15 February 1764, Korsør, d. 3 October 1826, Hamburg.

A sense of homelessness emanates from Baggesen's life and works, and it seems telling, after a seven-year long debate in which he had correctly, if in vain, questioned the quality of the later works of Adam Oehlenschläger that in 1820 Baggesen left his native country for the last time. Baggesen, who was a perennial traveler, was more European than Scandinavian. He was intimately familiar with various, but hardly congruous, philosophical and political movements, and his oeuvre offer a fascinating reflection of the often conflicting currents of a transitional age. He made his debut in 1785 with some clever satires written in the mode of Ludvig Holberg,* Christoph Martin Wieland, and Johann Wessel,* but Baggesen later became an admirer of Jean-Jacques Rousseau, and his travel chronicle from Germany, *Labyrinten* (1792–1793, The Labyrinth) signals a turn toward subjectivity and, at times, ecstatic emotionalism. *Labyrinten*, written in Laurence Sterne's manner, suggests the existential poles between which Baggesen's texts vacillate: a very mundane sensual delight in this material world and an ardent desire for a transcendence of this world. Although Baggesen might seem like a chameleon, it has been suggested that those restless fluctuations mirror his conviction that the very earthy as well as the spiritual spring from the same origin. Baggesen's works are uneven, but some of his poems offer a keen insight into the mind of someone who, split between two worlds, lives a tortured and homeless existence.

FURTHER WORKS

Komiske Fortællinger (1785); *Holger Danske* (1789); *Ungdomsarbejder*, 2 vols. (1791); *Samtlige Værker I* (1801); *Gedichte von Jens Baggesen* (1803); *Parthenais oder die Alpenreise* (1802); *Gengangeren og han selv eller Baggesen over Baggesen* (1806); *Skæmtsomme Rimbreve* (1807); *Blandede Digte* (1807–1808); *Heidenblume* (1808);

Taschenbuch für Liebende (1810); *Der Karfunkel—und Klingklingel—Almanach* (1810); *Per Vrøvlers yderst Grundige Kommentar* (1816); *Literaturblade* (1814); *Poetiske Epistler* (1814); *Danske Værker*, 12 vols. (1845–1847).

TRANSLATIONS

Extracts from *Labyrinten*, in *The Literature and Romance of Northern Europe*, ed. William Howitt and Mary Howitt (1852).

REFERENCES

Albertsen, L. L., *Odins mjød* (Aarhus, 1969); Bredsdorff, Thomas, "The Fox at Ploen." *Orbis Litterarum* 22 (1967); Henriksen, Aage, *Den rejsende* (Copenhagen, 1961); Henriksen, Aage, "Baggesen—The European." *Danish Foreign Office Journal* 48 (1964); Plesner, K. F., *Baggesen Bibliografi* (Copenhagen, 1943).

Niels Ingwersen

Bang, Herman. Danish novelist, short story writer, poet, and playwright, b. 21 April 1857, Adserballe, d. 28 January 1912, Ogden, Utah.

Degeneracy, dashed dreams, and decadence are predominant themes in Bang's works. After an unsuccessful career as an actor, Bang turned to journalism out of economic necessity. He began his career in journalism as a theater and literary critic. Later he became a controversial figure in Copenhagen for his feature articles in a major newspaper. Some of his best articles are found in *Realisme og Realister* (1879; Realism and Realists), *Kritiske Studier og Udkast* (1880; Critical Studies and Sketches), and *Herhjemme og Derude* (1881; Here at Home and Out There).

As a literary critic, Bang concentrated on the modern writers, Émile Zola, J. P. Jacobsen,* Vilhelm Topsøe, and Holger Drachmann* among others. Because of his literary activities, the Brandes brothers considered him a rival. In fact, Bang essentially wrote portraits of the men of the Modern Breakthrough before Georg Brandes* published his work in 1883.

His first novel, *Haabløse Slægter* (1880; Hopeless Generations), is a naturalistic novel that depicts the decline of a family. Although there are stylistic discords and youthful indulgences in the novel, Bang's use of dialogue and his scenic presentation make it a significant work. The novel was confiscated because of the depiction of sexual desire and decadence. The theme of sexual desire as a destructive force is found in his next novel *Fædra* (1883).

In 1884 Bang began his travels around Europe. During the next four years, Bang made his breakthrough as a writer with two collections of short stories: *Excentriske Noveller* (1885; Eccentric Short Stories) and *Stille Existenser* (1886; Quiet Existences). The latter collection contains the novella "Ved Vejen" (By the Wayside), which stylistically is a masterpiece of impressionism. In both collections, the lives of everyday people and outcasts are depicted in minute detail. Bang uses the stream-of-consciousness technique, giving only fragments of conversations, gestures, and stagelike directions.

Bang's scenic or filmatic technique shows the influence of Jonas Lie* and also bears the mark of Bang's career as both an actor and a stage director. Lie's influence is strongly felt in Bang's novel *Stuk* (1887; Stucco), which is a description of society's decay. The novel depicts a time of unhealthy speculation in Copenhagen. The false economic boom is like stucco covering underlying decay. Bang's scenic technique is taken to extremes as the narrative jumps back and forth between the many characters, capturing the life of the city. The tone of *Stuk*, though, is overwhelmingly pessimistic.

In the novel *Tine* (1889; *Tina*, 1984), Bang is able to portray the motive of ruin on both an individual and a national level. The frame of the story is Denmark's defeat by the Prussians in 1864. The happy portrayal of manor life on the island Als, where Tine serves as a maid, is replaced by the depiction of the terrors of war. War demoralizes, and as a consequence, Tine's master seduces her. She takes her own life when she realizes that his love was only sexual desire. The final scene stresses that life goes on even after such tragedies, a motive that recurs throughout Bang's work.

The short story collection *Under Aaget* (1890; Under the Yoke) depicts a bitter view of life that disregards human dreams. In the novel *Ludvigsbakke* (1896; *Ida Brandt*, 1928), Bang mocks society, which doesn't recognize good and generous people, but courts power and wealth.

The two novels *Det hvide Hus* (1898; The White House) and *Det graa Hus* (1901; The Gray House) are charming reminiscences of childhood all told in dramatic dialogue. Yet there is a deep tragic tone in the portrayal of the mother, whose ideal love turns into bitter jealousy.

The theme of jealousy is prevalent in Bang's last two novels, which are highly autobiographical. The novel *Mikaël* (1904) deals with the life of a famous painter, Claude Zoret, and his love for the young Mikaël, who deserts him for the sake of a woman. The deep-felt pain of this book distinguishes it from Bang's other works.

Bang's last novel, *De uden Fædreland* (1906; *Denied a Country*, 1927), again takes up the theme of outcasts and the desire for love. The main character, a Danish-Hungarian violin virtuoso, tries to establish himself in Denmark, but becomes disappointed with Danish pettiness.

Bang died while on a tour in the United States. His position as Denmark's most important literary impressionist was first obtained after his death. In fact, he is now one of Denmark's most read authors. During his lifetime, however, he never received due recognition and was openly persecuted by society, which despised his homosexuality and his mannerisms.

FURTHER WORKS

Værker i Mindeudgave, 6 vols. (1912, 1920–1921)

FURTHER TRANSLATIONS

"In Rosenborg Park" (1914); "The Pastor" (1927); *Four Devils* (1928); "The Last Evening" (1929); *A Play and Some Poems* (1943); "Irene Holm" (1972); "You Shall Remember Me!" (1973), "Expelled from Germany" (1977); "Franz Pander" (1977).

REFERENCES

Driver, Beverly R., "Herman Bang's Prose: The Narrative as Theater." *Mosaic* 4.2 (1970); Jacobsen, Harry, *Resignationens Digter* (Copenhagen, 1957); Lauterbach, Ulrich, *Herman Bang: Studien zum dänischen Impressionismus* (Breslau, 1937); Mogren, Jan, *Herman Bangs Haabløse Slægter* (Lund, 1957); Nilsson, Torbjörn, *Impressionisten Herman Bang* (Stockholm, 1965); Rubow, Paul V., *Herman Bang og flere kritiske Studier* (Copenhagen, 1958); Winge, Mette, ed., *Omkring Haabløse Slægter* (Copenhagen, 1972).
                                                                                    Janis E. Granger

Bellman, Carl Michael. Swedish lyric poet, b. 4 February 1740, Stockholm, d. 12 February 1795, Stockholm.

Born into a family of moderately good circumstances, Bellman was given excellent tutoring in languages and other subjects, ostensibly to prepare him for a career in the civil service or in banking. His lyric talent displayed itself early, however, along with a predilection for neglect of bookkeeping duties. As he rose rapidly in those social circles that demanded his drinking songs and satirical poetic scenes, he fell into such economic difficulty that he was forced for a short time (1763) to flee to Norway, to avoid debtors' prison. This was his only lengthy journey. Reestablished in Stockholm with the help of his parents, whose own economy was no longer stable, Bellman eked out a living from the time of their death (1765) for ten years. During this period, Bellman refined his musicianship, his imitative talent, and his poetic tools. He apparently never learned to read music, but used the cittra, a form of flat-bottomed lute, as an effective accompaniment to his poems, the majority of which were written to the melodies of popular table songs, dances, or theatrical airs. Although not active in party politics per se, he gave his unswerving support to Gustaf III, especially during the agitated period surrounding the coup d'état of 1772, and for this he was rewarded in 1775: Gustaf III, then at the height of his power and popularity, had Bellman appointed as secretary of the national lottery. The bureaucratic job itself meant nothing to Bellman, but the actual work was done by a stand-in, while Bellman was allowed to draw a major portion of the salary, while actually devoting his time to writing. Although his total income, including gratuities from the king and other sources, was never great, his economy had thus stabilized sufficiently that he could marry Lovisa Grönlund in 1777. The rich production of poetry of the 1760s and early 1770s gradually tapered off, however, and only long-delayed plans to publish his *Fredmans epistlar* (1790; Fredman's Epistles) and *Fredmans sånger* (1891; Fredman's Songs) stimulated him to add a few last poems to each of these collections. After the murder of Gustaf III in 1792, Bellman's foothold at the court was lost, and with it, all hope of further recognition or ultimate economic security. His health undermined by tuberculosis and his spirits depressed after a period in debtors' prison, Bellman died in 1795. He had already become something of a legend in Stockholm in his own lifetime; after his death, the legend continued to grow.

Bellman wrote in all over 1,500 poems, several plays and dramatic divertimenti, and satirical chapter meetings of the Knights of Bacchus (Bacchi Orden), the latter of which fall stylistically in between the one-man theater of his best poetry and the plays actually designed for theatrical performance. Only a few pieces of prose are preserved, most notably the short and anecdotal fragment of an autobiography that he wrote while in debtors prison. Bellman's early poetry is made up to a large degree of Bacchanalian songs and occasional verse written for the royalty or for friends and acquaintances, for birthdays, weddings, and funerals. But out of the drinking songs and the satirical dramatic scenes of the Bacchi Orden, Bellman fashioned the poems called *Fredmans epistlar*, upon which his fame chiefly rests. Originally conceived as satirical "letters" from a disciple of Bacchus (St. Fredman) to his "congregation" of drunkards, *Fredmans epistlar* expanded rapidly (late 1760s and early 1770s) to encompass scenes and anecdotes from a partially realistic, partially mythical Stockholm, populated by a collection of lower-class drifters, musicians, and tavern wenches, who try, with varying degrees of success, to follow their creed of carpe diem. Led by the raconteur Fredman, and alcoholic watchmaker whose real-life counterpart had died in 1767, Ulla Winblad (pseudonym for a known lady of easy virtue), the aggressive Corporal Mollberg, and the musician for all occasions, Mowitz, this half-satirized, half-idealized group is captured poetically in its wildest and most intimate moments, in a musical-poetic language that is elegant, drastic, concrete, moving, and sparklingly humorous. The collection is not a "cycle" in the sense of a consistent story, but it is nonetheless characterized by a single, sharply observant, nonmoralizing point of view. Eighty-two of a planned hundred epistles were eventually completed over a period of more than twenty years, during which marked changes in Bellman's style and attitude are also apparent. But its idiosyncrasies notwithstanding, the collection was quickly afforded a unique place in Swedish literature, and it has held that place to this day, despite its eighteenth-century language and occasional inscrutable local references.

Fredmans sånger, the well-known companion piece to the *Epistlar*, is actually quite different in intent and style. It comprises a set of drinking songs and lyrics ascribed to Fredman more as a publisher's convenience than as an indication of its contents. Here too, however, is evidence of the hand of a master: the songs are representative of Bellman's very best work, and many are often heard in private and public gatherings in Sweden today: "Fjäriln vingad syns på Haga," "Gubben Noach," "Så lunka vi så småningom," "Träd fram du Nattens gud," and others.

The fact that Bellman wrote in an extremely restricted form—that of the song lyric—and that his occasional forays outside that form produced work of unequal caliber, contributed to a certain disrespect for his special genius among the arbiters of literary taste at the court of Gustaf III. He was thus not elected to the Swedish Academy (he joined the Royal Musical Academy in 1791). Starting with the romantic period, however, Bellman attained a lasting position as the most brilliant of all the Gustavian poets. As standards for poetic beauty were liberalized, his popularity, which had never flagged among the general populace, widened to include critics and scholars as well.

FURTHER WORKS

Samlade Skrifter, ed. J. G. Carlén, 5 vols. (1861); *Samlade skrifter*, ed. C. Eichorn, 2 vols. (1877); *Skrifter*, ed. Bellmanssällskapet (B. Society), 13 vols. (1921–1980).

TRANSLATIONS

The Last of the Troubadours, ed. Hendrik Willem Van Loon (1939); *Fredmans Epistles: A Selection*, ed. Paul Britten Austin (1984).

REFERENCES

Afzelius, N., *Myt och bild i Bellmans dikt* (Stockholm, 1945); Austin, Paul Britten, *C. M. Bellman* (Malmö, 1967); *Bellmansstudier* ed. Bellmanssällskapet (B. Society), 18 vols. (Stockholm, 1924–1985); Byström, O., *Kring Fredmans epistlar* (Stockholm, 1945); Eriksson, L.-G., ed., *Kring Bellman* (Stockholm, 1964); Fehrman, C., *Vin och flickor och Fredmans stråke* (Stockholm, 1977); Larsson, C. and M. Hellquist, *Ordbok till Fredmans epistlar* (Lund, 1967); Ljunggren, G., *Bellman och Fredmans epistlar* (Lund, 1967); Massengale, J., *The Musical-Poetic Method of C. M. Bellman* (Uppsala, 1979); Sylwan, O., *Bellman och Fredmans epistlar* (Lund, 1943).

James Massengale

Benedictsson, Victoria. (pseud. Ernst Ahlgren). Swedish short story writer and novelist, b. 6 March 1850, Domme, d. 22 July 1888, Copenhagen.

Benedictsson was born into the strained and unhappy marriage of Thure Bruzelius and Helena Sophia Finérus. As a young girl, she had dreams of traveling to Stockholm to study at the art academy. When her father refused his permission for her to travel to Stockholm, Benedictsson married fifty-year-old Christian Benedictsson, a postmaster and widower with five children who lived in nearby Hörby. This marriage to a man almost thirty years her senior gave her time to write, but was an emotional catastrophe.

Benedictsson began her literary career in 1875 with a Gothic thriller she sent to the daily *Sydsvenska Dagbladet* in Malmö. In 1884, she met Axel Lundegård, a young writer, and they collaborated on and discussed literature. After her death, he was instrumental in editing her remaining literary material.

Benedictsson's first novel, *Pengar* (Money), was published in 1885. It is an indignation novel, a popular genre of the day, which depicts the life of a young girl who dreams of becoming an artist, but who instead marries a much older man. High-spirited and lively, it brought Benedictsson to the attention of other Modern Breakthrough writers in Scandinavia. While working on her second novel, *Fru Marianne* (1887; Mrs. Marianne), Benedictsson met Georg Brandes,* the renowned Danish literary critic. Her troubled relationship with this man is recorded in her moving journal, entitled *Stora boken* (1978–1982; The Big Book). When he broke off their relationship and criticized her second novel, Benedictsson thought her personal and professional life was at an end. She committed suicide by cutting her throat in a shabby hotel in Copenhagen.

Benedictsson is one of the most well known women writers from nineteenth-century Scandinavia. While her contemporaries, such as Alfhild Agrell and Anne Charlotte Leffler,* have largely been forgotten, Benedictsson has remained in favor with literary critics and the public for several reasons. Her tragic life and death and her relationship with Brandes have contributed to this interest. However, it is primarily her writings, especially her first novel and her short story collection *Folklif och småberättelser* (1887; Folklife and Little Tales), which have kept her from the neglect suffered by so many other women writers from the Modern Breakthrough. Both works offer a clean, lively prose and incisive and sympathetic portrayals of the people in her native province of Scania.

FURTHER WORKS

Bref från Victoria Benedictsson till Karl och Matti af Geijerstam (1909); *Samlade Skrifter*, ed. Axel Lundegård, 7 vols. (1918–1920); *Dagboksblad och brev*, ed. Axel Lundegård, 2 vols. (1928); *Skrifter i urval*, ed. F. Böök (1950).

TRANSLATIONS

Sweden's Best Stories, ed. H. A. Larsen (1928).

REFERENCES

Böök, Fredrik, *Victoria Benedictsson och Georg Brandes* (Stockholm, 1949); Borland, Harold, "Ernst Ahlgren: Novelist in Theory and Practice." *Scandinavica* 13.2 (1974); Linder, Sten, *Ernst Ahlgren i hennes romaner* (Stockholm, 1930); Lundbo Levy, Jette, *Dobbeltblikket: om att beskrive kvinder* (Copenhagen, 1980); Moberg, Verne, "Motherhood as Reality for Victoria Benedictsson." *Edda* 5 (1984); Moberg, Verne, "Truth against Syphilis: Victoria Benedictsson's Remedy for a Dreaded Disease." *Edda* 1 (1983); Schultén, Ingrid af, *Ernst Ahlgren* (Helsingfors, 1925); Sjögren, Margareta, *Rep utan knutar* (Stockholm, 1979).

Melissa Lowe Shogren

Benedikt Sveinbjarnarson. *See* Gröndal, Benedikt S.

Benediktsson, Einar. Icelandic poet and journalist, b. 31 October 1864, Elliðavatn, d. 12 January 1940, Herdísarvík.

Benediktsson's father was an important judge and politician who championed Iceland's independence, his mother an artistically gifted woman and sensitive poet. After studying law in Copenhagen, Benediktsson edited Sigurður Breiðfjörð's *rímur* (1894), published Iceland's first daily (*Dagskrá*, 1896–1898), translated *Peer Gynt* (1901), practiced law, served as district magistrate (1904–1907), and published five volumes of poetry. He argued for national independence and spiritual awakening, industrial harnessing of natural resources, and the reclamation of Greenland as a colony. Many of Benediktsson's poems are celebrations of Iceland and its potential. He spent many years abroad seeking support of European capitalists for his dreams of an industrialized Iceland. From such experience stem reflective poems which deftly capture the feel of a foreign place.

In the nineties Benediktsson shifted from the socialist doctrines of realism to symbolism. He is typically labeled a neoromantic, but his work, in which tensions abound, resists easy classification. He balances elevated metrical formalism with lyricism. His meters and diction, grounded in skaldic tradition, show a stunning inventiveness. A keen observer, Benediktsson moves from the particular to the universal. He loves contrasts and their delicate resolution in harmony. As a pantheist mystic, Benediktsson believed in the underlying unity of the world (e.g., "Í Slútnesi"[At Slútnes]) and suggests this through synesthesia and metaphoric transformations in which sky becomes ocean, its currents forest storms, sharks' teeth scythes biting grass, and macrocosm microcosm. As titles such as *Hafblik* (1906; Sea Calm), *Hrannir* (1913; Waves), and *Vogar* (1921; Billows) suggest, the ocean is a governing image in Benediktsson's poetry, the variety of its patterns representing for him energy, eternity, human life, soul, heartbeat, time, language, sorrow, the subconscious, and the unity and immensity of the world (e.g., "Utsær"[Mid-Ocean], "Öldulíf"[Wave Life]).

Benediktsson's intellectual poetry constitutes the high point of early twentieth-century Icelandic poetic craft.

FURTHER WORKS

Sögur og kvæði (1897); *Hrannir* (1913); *Thules beboere* (1918); *Hvammar* (1930). Benediktsson's collected poems appear in three editions with valuable essays: *Ljóðmæli*, ed. Pétur Sigurðsson, 3 vols. (1945); *Kvæðasafn*, ed. Pétur Sigurðsson (1964); *Ljóðasfn*, ed. Kristján Karlsson, 4 vols. (1979); his selected prose in two editions: *Laust mál*, ed. Steingrímur J.Þorsteinsson, 2 vols. (includes a biography) (1952); *Óbundið mál*, ed. Kristján Karlsson (1980–).

FURTHER TRANSLATIONS

Icelandic Lyrics, ed. Richard Beck (1930); *Odes and Echoes*, ed. Paul Bjarnason (1954); *Harp of the North: Poems by Einar Benediktsson*, ed. Frederic T. Wood (1955); *Northern Lights*, ed. Jakobina Johnson (1959); *An Anthology of Scandinavian Literature*, ed. Hallberg Hallmundsson (1965).

REFERENCES

Beck, Richard, "Iceland's Poet Laureate." *Books Abroad* 10 (1936); Beck, Richard, "The Dean of Icelandic Poets." *American-Scandinavian Review* 27.4 (1939); Beck, Richard, *History of Icelandic Poets 1800–1940* (Ithaca, 1950); Benediktsson, Valgerður, *Frásagnir um Einar Benediktsson* (Reykjavík, 1942); Nordal, Sigurður, *Einar Benediktsson* (Reykjavík, 1971).

George S. Tate

Bengtsson, Frans G. Swedish poet, essayist, and novelist, b. 4 October 1894, Rössjöholm, d. 19 December 1954, Ribbingsfors.

After intermittent studies in literature and philosophy throughout the 1920s,

Bengtsson received an advanced degree at the University of Lund. During this decade he published two collections of poetry and a first collection of essays. As a poet Bengtsson refused to conform to any modernist trends, striving instead for formal mastery of complex verse forms. In this cultivation of *l'art pour l'art* with Algernon Charles Swinburne and the French Parnassians as admired models, Bengtsson was deliberately anachronistic. A passionate interest in history and an impressive book learning made him equally at home in the world of antiquity, the French Middle Ages, and the Renaissance. His interests are reflected in his translations into Swedish of such works as *La Chanson de Roland*, John Milton's *Paradise Lost*, and Henry David Thoreau's *Walden*.

In his essays Bengtsson carries his erudition seemingly lightly and writes with formal elegance and Anglo-Saxon conversational ease and with that special irony and robust sense of humor associated with the literary circles at the University of Lund in the first decades of this century. Bengtsson's fascination with the heroical and with history's great men of action is evident in his two-volume biography of King Charles XII of Sweden. Steering clear of both the idolatry of Verner von Heidenstam* and the vituperations of August Strindberg,* Bengtsson presents a portrait of the controversial warrior king that is closer to Voltaire's views.

With *Röde Orm* (1941; *Red Orm*, 1943; *The Long Ships*, 1954), a novel set in Viking times, Bengtsson scored his greatest and most enduring popular success. In a personal adaptation of the Icelandic saga style, pithy, direct, and understated, Bengtsson presents an exuberant tale of Viking adventures. Lusty bouts of fighting and drinking and usually less-than-successful attempts by missionaries to Christianize the pagans are recorded with equal impartiality by the author. As in all his works, Bengtsson displays in this novel solid historical scholarship, a sure sense of style, and a judgment of men and their actions that is aesthetic rather than moral.

FURTHER WORKS

Tärningskast (1923); *Legenden on Babel* (1925); *Litteratörer och militärer* (1929); *Silversköldarna* (1931); *De långhåriga merovingerna* (1933); *Karl XII:s levnad* (1935–1936; *The Sword Does Not Jest: The Heroic Life of King Charles XII of Sweden*, 1960); *Sällskap för en eremit* (1938); *För nöjes skull* (1947); *Den lustgård som jag minns* (1953); *Folk som sjöng* (1955); *Breven till Tristan* (1986).

FURTHER TRANSLATIONS

A Walk to an Ant Hill and Other Essays (1950).

REFERENCES

Harrie, Ivar, *Legenden om Bengtsson* (Stockholm, 1971); Lindahl, M., on *The Sword Does Not Jest*, in *Saturday Review* 17 December (1960); Linklater, Eric, *A Year of Space*

(New York, 1953); Thompson, L. S., "Frans G. Bengtsson, 1894–1954." *Kentucky Foreign Language Quarterly* 2 (1955).

Lars G. Warme

Bergman, Bo. Swedish poet, short story writer, and essayist, b. 6 October 1869, Stockholm, d. 17 November 1967, Stockholm.

A postal official and theater critic most of his unpensioned life, Bergman was a prolific writer, but it is chiefly as a poet that he is known today. The first thing to strike one about his poetry is its extraordinary formal virtuosity, one could say musicality. His technical mastery reminds one of Gustaf Fröding* and Carl Michael Bellman,* two other musical poets. Unlike their energy, Bergman's tempos are slower, more atune with the pessimistic turn-of-the-century worldview that runs through his early work in *Marionetterna* (1903; Puppets). This determinism, clearly expressed in the title poem, eventually evolved through the bulk of his work into a more approachable humanism, as we can see in *En människa* (A Human Being) from 1908. His affirmation of the individual against the collective is clear in *Trots allt* (1931; In Spite of Everything), while in *Gamla gudar* (1939; Old Gods) and *Riket* (1944; The Nation), he protests openly and unabashedly, despite his aristocratic leanings, the repressive nature of the totalitarian moods then swirling over the world. The times made him into a "fighting humanist."

This philosophical persuasion in his poetry is not concentrated in indigestible rhetoric, however. The fluidity that carries one through the poem is sustained by a tangible world that constantly reaches out to the reader. For Bergman, like his friend Hjalmar Söderberg* (1869–1941), with whom he is often linked and compared, the reality of that world is Stockholm, as in "Stadsbarn" (City Child), for instance. In common with many Swedish poets, Bergman is essentially a poet of nature, even if that nature is limited to Stockholm.

Apart from his work as a theater critic, Bergman wrote short stories throughout most of his long career. *Drömmen och andra noveller* (The Dream and Other Stories) appeared in 1904, and four other collections followed at varying intervals until the last, *Inför rätta* (Before the Court), in 1965. His first novel, however, *Ett bokslut* (A Balancing of the Books), did not come until 1942, and his fifth and last, *Vi vandrare* (We Wanderers), was published in 1961. In 1963, he published four one-act plays, under the title *Det eviga spelet* (The Eternal Play/Game).

In 1925, he was elected to the Swedish Academy, and for them wrote two biographical sketches, one on Hjalmar Söderberg in 1951. There are also two essay collections; *Från den långa resan* (From the Long Journey) appeared in 1959, and *Predikare* (Preachers) in 1967.

FURTHER WORKS

Skeppet och andra noveller (1915); *Elden* (1917); *Livets ögon* (1922); *Min vän baronen och andra noveller* (1926); *Skyar* (1936); *Edvard Swartz* (1938); *Olof Ulrik Torsslow*

(1945); *Torsten Fogelkvist* (1946); *Epiloger* (1946); *Skulden* (1948); *Stunder* (1952); *Liv och läsning* (1953); *Den förrymda själen* (1955); *Väntan* (1957); *Så länge spelet varar* (1958); *Blott ett är ditt* (1960); *Makter* (1962); *Öden* (1963); *Trasmattan* (1964); *Kedjan* (1966); *Noaks ark* (1968); *Äventyret* (1969); *Brev från en gammal skald*, with Helena Klein (1971).

TRANSLATIONS

DAQ 17 (1983–1984).

REFERENCE

Asplund, Karl, *Bo Bergman: Människan och diktaren* (Stockholm, 1970).

Alan Swanson

Bergman, Hjalmar Fredrik Elgérus. Swedish novelist and playwright, b. 19 September 1883, Örebro, d. 1 January 1931, Berlin.

Bergman grew up in Örebro, the son of a well-situated banker. But middle-class security was little comfort to the sensitive Bergman, who suffered from shyness and being overweight, dreading the ridicule of his peers and the authority of the school environment and his domineering father. In later years, Bergman marked his childhood trauma as the beginning of a lifelong fear of the unpredictable in human existence, of insanity and ambivalent sexual identity. Bergman would accompany his father on business trips around the mining area of Bergslagen, where he readily absorbed the numerous stories that came to provide the setting and character portrayals for much of his writing. Following his matriculation examination in 1900, Bergman spent a year at Uppsala University, and then traveled to Italy, where Florence became his favorite city. Bergman's need for isolation, not lessened by his marriage in 1908, but increased rather by an uncontrollable jealousy, made his life one of restless movement, largely on the European continent. Summers spent on a small island in the Stockholm archipelago provided the only home of some permanence. Bergman received the Bonnier stipend in 1910 and 1915, and the award of Samfundet De Nio in 1926.

Bergman's early works are experiments in drama and fiction, directly influenced by the aesthetics of the 1890s, by the dream atmosphere of Maurice Maeterlinck and the post-Inferno plays of August Strindberg,* and with a preference for fin de siècle themes of decadence. In the novel *Blå blommor* (1907; Blue Flowers) is evident the symbolic representation of a realistic plot that was to become characteristic of Bergman's mode of expression.

There are two significant reasons for the public acclaim awaiting the novel *Hans nåds testamente* (1910; The Baron's Will). For the first time the setting is that of Bergman's childhood area of Bergslagen. The pessimism of the earlier works is here overshadowed by hilarious comedy in dialogue, plot, and character portrayal. But a closer look beneath the burlesque surface reveals the bigotry of the adult world, the sadistic elements of innocent love, and the disturbingly irrational behavior of old and young alike.

The next novel, *Vi Bookar, Krookar och Rothar* (1912; We Books, Krooks, and Rooths), is again set in Bergslagen, centered on the inhabitants of a town, modeled on Örebro, in later works the fictitious Wadköping. With a technique reminiscent of William Faulkner and Honoré de Balzac, Bergman also lets certain characters reappear, among them the heroine Blenda of *Hans nåds testamente*, whose wavering affection as a young girl has now grown into the whims and caprices of a disillusioned married woman. In the description of the town life is evident the recurrent tension between the strong and the weak, and Bergman's concern with the exploitation of the socially unprivileged.

A cat-and-mouse game, symbolic of the clash between wills and social classes, constitutes the opening scene of Bergman's immediate success, the novel *Markurells i Wadköping* (1919; *God's Orchid*, 1924). A newcomer in town, Markurell is looked down upon for his plebeian origin. Nevertheless, he becomes a threat to the aristocratic family de Lorche, and to the town as a whole, because of his cunning and ruthlessness in financial scheming. But Markurell has a weak spot: his son, Johan, the pride and joy of his life. His anguish when discovering that Johan is actually the illegitimate son of Carl-Magnus de Lorche shows Bergman's psychological insight and his ability to give tragic dimension to a primitive outburst of pain.

Together with the ludicrous and pretentious Herr von Hancken in the novel of the same name (1920; Herr von Hancken), and the strong-willed Agnes Borck in *Farmor och Vår Herre* (1921; *Thy Staff and Thy Rod*, 1937), Markurell is characteristic of Bergman's domineering personages. What unites these comical portrayals, caricatures that bring to mind both Charles Dickens and Fyodor Dostoyevski, is a deep-seated fear of relentless fate, an unknown power that eventually brings them to submission and self-awareness.

Bergman's fatalistic view of the human condition is emphasized in the novel *En döds memoarer* (2 vols., 1918–1919; The Memoirs of a Dead Man). In this story of how crimes in the past revisit later generations, the narrator is absolved from the family curse only by giving up his personal will, by becoming a living dead. The Freudian motif that underlies this narrative becomes the compelling force of presentation in the novel *Chefen fru Ingeborg* (1924; *The Head of the Firm*, 1936). Ingeborg's love for her son-in-law is the forbidden passion that must be denied at all costs. But through dreams and coincidence, repression gives way to unbearable recognition, and Ingeborg finally takes her life.

Bergman's health was seriously deteriorating, but he would still produce lighthearted comedy, as in the popular play *Swedenhielms* (1925; *The Swedenhielms*, 1951). He also wrote filmscripts and made successful dramatizations of several of his major novels. His last novel, *Clownen Jac* (1930; The Clown Jac), was serialized on the radio with Bergman himself reading the clown's monologue. In this testimony to his life and art, the clown represents Bergman's unique mingling of tragic and comic elements. Success for the clown is measured by a laughing audience, and laughter, in turn, depends on the clown's essential nearness to fear.

Immediate response was given to Bergman's effortless fantasy, bizarre characters, dramatic dialogue, and ingenious plots. But later research has come to focus on his symbolic language in an attempt to elucidate the relation of surface spectacle to the dark otherworld where terror reigns. With reverberations from late Strindberg and early Pär Lagerkvist,* Bergman is intricately part of Swedish expressionism and modernism.

FURTHER WORKS

Maria, Jesu moder (1905); *Solivro, Prins af Aeretanien* (1906); *Det underbara leendet* (1907); *Familjens renhet* (1907); *Fru Wendlas kedja* (1907, a play performed but not published); *Savonarola* (1909); *Amourer* (1910); *Loewenhistorier* (1913); *Komedier i Bergslagen* (1914); *Dansen på Frötjärn* (1915); *Parisina* (1915); *Knutsmässo marknad* (1915); *Sagor* (1916); *Marionettspel* (1917); *Ett experiment* (1918); *Vem dömer?* (1921); *Eros' begravning* (1922); *Jag, Ljung och Medardus; Spelhuset. Vävaren i Bagdad. Porten* (1923); *Nya sagor* (1924); *Flickan i frack* (1925); *Dollar* (1926); *Jonas och Helen* (1926); *Kerrmans i paradiset* (1927); *Lotten Brenners ferier* (1928); *Patrasket* (1928); *Kärlek genom ett fönster och andra berättelser* (1929); *Labyrinten* (1931); *Fästmansbreven*, ed. Erik Hjalmar Linder and Kerstin Dahlbäck (1983).

FURTHER TRANSLATIONS

Modern Swedish Short Stories (1934); *Scandinavian Plays of the Twentieth Century*, 1st ser. (1944); *Markurells of Wadköping. The Baron's Will. Mr. Sleemanm is Coming. Swedenhielms. Four Plays by Hjalmar Bergman* (1968).

REFERENCES

Axberger, Gunnar, *Den brinnande skogen* (Stockholm, 1960); Bergom-Larsson, Maria, *Diktarens demaskering* (Stockholm, 1970); Ek, Sverker, *Verklighet och vision* (Stockholm, 1964); Linder, Erik Hjalmar, *Hjalmar Bergman* (Stockholm, 1940); Linder, Erik, *Kärlek och fadershus farväl* (Stockholm, 1973); Mishler, William, *A Reading of Hjalmar Bergman's 'Markurells i Wadköping'* (Minneapolis, 1971); Mishler, William, "A Reading of Hjalmar Bergman's Story Konstapel Wiliam." *Scandinavica* 10 (1971); Petherick, Karin, *Parodi och stilimitation i tre av Hjalmar Bergmans romaner* (Uppsala, 1971); Quarnström, Gunnar, *I lejonets tecken* (Lund, 1959); Sprinchorn, Evert, "Hjalmar Bergman." *Tulane Drama Review* 6.2 (1961); Stevenson, Sarah A., " Comedy and Tragedy in 'Markurells i Wadköping'." *Edda* 3 (1974).

Monica Setterwall

Bergman, Ingmar Ernst. Swedish author of screenplays and stage dramas, b. 14 July 1918, Uppsala.

Born on Bastille Day, Bergman was destined to make a different nonpolitical kind of revolution: summing up, examining, and unmasking on the screen the bourgeois values on which Western middle-class society has been founded. After an early stage drama and screenplay production, Bergman became from the mid-fifties an *auteur du cinéma,* that is, a filmmaker expressing a consistent artistic vision through the cinematic medium, writing and directing his own films. During a forty-five-year career, Bergman has made some fifty films while at the same time maintaining a vital interest in the theater, directing remarkable productions of, above all, Henrik Ibsen,* August Strindberg,* and Molière.

Bergman's father was a Lutheran minister in a prestigious Stockholm parish. His mother came from a family of schoolteachers. Growing up in an authoritarian environment, Bergman has often explored in his work the struggles of individuals trying to cope with religious, parental, or social pressures. Most of his screenplays are vertical rather than horizontal in their conception, that is, exploring in psychological depth an individual's attempt to come to terms with his past rather than examining broadly the ramifications of current social or political issues. In the fifties and sixties in particular, Bergman's preoccupation with metaphysical issues gave him an international reputation. In his native Sweden his most popular works have been made for Swedish television such as *Scener ur ett äktenskap* (1973; *Scenes from a Marriage*, 1974) and *Trollflöjten* (1974; *The Magic Flute*).

A crucial dividing line in Bergman's life and career occurs in the early sixties. In a trilogy of films (1961; *Såsom i en spegel, Through a Glass Darkly*; 1962; *Nattvardsgästerna, Winter Light*; and 1962; *Tystnaden, The Silence*), Bergman breaks away from his religious heritage. This period is followed by three years (1963–1966) when Bergman is in charge of the Royal Dramatic Theatre in Stockholm. When he returns to writing and filmmaking in 1967 with *Persona*, his thematic focus is on the disintegrating artist and the failure of language to bridge the gap between people. Bergman has always seen the artist as a scapegoat, at the mercy of his public. Yet, as a creative person who can manipulate his *laterna magica*, Bergman has often felt himself in control of his viewers' emotions. This ambivalence has come to determine Bergman's whole conception of the film medium.

Bergman left his native Sweden in 1976 to settle in Munich, West Germany. The reason for his voluntary exile was his arrest by Swedish tax authorities in late January 1976. Charges of tax evasion were dropped, but Bergman remained abroad until 1982. Returning to Sweden he made *Fanny och Alexander*, a film that sums up his lifelong dedication to theater and film and evokes the two worlds he knew as a child: the restrictive realm of the Protestant church and the imaginative world of his grandmother's huge apartment in Uppsala, where he spent long periods of his childhood.

Bergman has received dozens of prizes for his films, including several Academy Awards. He was awarded the Dutch Erasmus Prize in 1965 and the Goethe Prize in 1976. He became the first recipient of the Alger H. Meadows Award for Excellence in the Arts in 1981. He has been awarded the Swedish Academy's gold medal and was made an honorary doctor at the University of Stockholm in 1975 and received a professor's title in 1985.

FURTHER WORKS

Hets (1944); *Moraliteter* (1948); *Fängelse* (1949); *Staden* (1950); *Mordet i Barjärna* (1952); *Kvinnors väntan* (1952); *Gycklarnas afton* (1953); *Trämålning* (1954); *En lektion i Kärlek* (1954); *Sommarnattens leende* (1955; *Smiles of a Summer Night*, in *Four Screen-*

plays of Ingmar Bergman, 1960); Det sjunde inseglet (1956; Seventh Seal, in Four Screenplays, 1960); Smultronstället (1957; Wild Strawberries, in Four Screenplays, 1960); Nära livet (1958); Ansiktet (1959; The Magician, in Four Screenplays, 1960); Jungfrukällan (1960); För att inte tala om alla dessa kvinnor, with Erland Josephson (1964); Vargtimmen (1967; Hour of the Wolf, in Four Stories of Ingmar Bergman, 1977); Skammen (1967–1968; Shame, in Persona and Shame, 1972); Riten (1969); En passion (1969; The Passion of Anna, in Four Stories, 1977); Beröringen (1970; The Touch, in Four Stories, 1977); Viskningar och rop (1971; Cries and Whispers, in Four Stories, 1977); Ansikte mot ansikte (1975; Face to Face, 1976); Ormens ägg (1977; The Serpent's Egg, 1977); Höstsonaten (1978; Autumn Sonata, 1978); Ur marionetternas liv (1980; From the Life of the Marionettes, 1980); Efter repetitionen (1984); Laterna magica (1987; Magic Lantern, 1988).

FURTHER TRANSLATIONS

"Wood Painting," in Tulane Drama Review 6.2 (1961); repr. in Focus on the Seventh Seal, comp. Birgitta Steene (1971).

REFERENCES

Cowie, Peter, Ingmar Bergman (New York, 1982); Donner, Jörn, The Personal Vision of Ingmar Bergman (Bloomington, Ind., 1962; new ed., The Films of Ingmar Bergman [New York, 1972]); Höök, Marianne, Ingmar Bergman (Stockholm, 1962); Livingston, Paisley, Ingmar Bergman and the Rituals of Art (Ithaca, N.Y., 1981); Mosley, Philip, Ingmar Bergman: The Cinema as Mistress (London, 1981); Simon, Johan, Ingmar Bergman Directs (New York, 1972); Steene, Birgitta, Ingmar Bergman (Boston, 1968); Steene, Birgitta, Ingmar Bergman: A Guide to References and Resources (Boston, 1987).

Birgitta Steene

Bergsson, Gürðbergur. Icelandic novelist and author of short stories, b. 16 October 1932, Grindavík, South Iceland.

After his examination as an elementary school teacher, Bergsson studied Spanish, literature, and history of art at the University of Barcelona and dwelt for long periods in Spain. He has translated Spanish literature into Icelandic, for instance, Don Quixote and novels by the Colombian author Gabríel García Márquez.

Along with Thor Vilhjálmsson,* Bergsson is a leading Icelandic prose writer in a modernist and experimental vein. But unlike his colleague he chooses typically Icelandic settings for his stories. An instance highly characteristic of his art is the novel Anna (1969). Its scene is a seaside village with a fishing industry; the model might well be his own birthplace on the south coast. The interest is focused on a family of three generations living together: the grandmother, her son and his wife, and their children. The relations between them are strenuous, as they live in worlds of their own, with different sets of values. The grandmother, who grew up in very primitive circumstances, is rather disoriented in the house with all its modern facilities. Brusque confrontations between the family members are frequent, and the conversation is tough, with plenty of irony and obscenities. Bergsson obtains many comic effects by mixing modern time with Icelandic tradition, on the thematic as well as linguistic level. In leisure hours the teenagers come together in the snack bar with its hamburgers, coke, and jukebox. They display a cynical attitude to life and sometimes a youthful spleen.

The narrative technique of this novel is intricate. One of the characters, the housewife Katrín, at long last turns out to be the author of the story—in that part by the name of Anna. Our impression of stalwart reality gradually begins to falter. The book ends with a series of apparently bizarre and incoherent remarks under the ironic heading "Answers." The last "answer" aptly runs as follows: "If the threads of the story are deranged, the system is shaken and turned into complicated fiction, got stuck in the addle-brained reader."

In his combination of intense and often coarse naturalism and a kind of burlesque surrealism Bergsson is an author of pronounced originality.

FURTHER WORKS

Endurtekin orð (1961); *Músin sem læðist* (1961); *Leikföng leiðans* (1964); *Tómas Jónsson, metsölubók* (1966); *Ástir samlyndra hjóna* (1967); *Hvað er eldi guds?* (1970); *það sefur í djúpinu* (1973); *Hermann og Dídí* (1974); *Það rís úr djúpinu* (1976); *Flateyrar-Freyr* (1978); *Saga af manni sem fékk flugu í höfuðið* (1979); *Sagan af Ara Fróðasyni og Hugborgu konu hans* (1980); *Tóta og táin á pabba* (1982); *Hjartað býr enn í helli sínum* (1982); *Hinsegin sögur* (1984); *Leitin að landinu fagra* (1985).

REFERENCES

Jónsson, Erlendur, *Íslenzk skáldsagnaritun 1940–1970* (Reykjavík, 1971); Magnússon, Sigurður A., "The Modern Icelandic Novel: From Isolation to Political Awareness." *Mosaic* 4.2 (1970).

                                                                                                    Peter Hallberg

Birgitta, Saint. Swedish mystic and religious reformer, b. c. 1303 (by tradition on 14 June), Finsta, Uppland, d. 23 July 1373, Rome.

Generally known in the English-speaking world as Saint Bridget of Sweden (canonized 7 October 1391), this redoubtable woman is medieval Scandinavia's most formidable religious and literary figure. Her *Revelationes celeste* (8 vols., Lübeck, 1492) has been translated into most European languages and into Arabic. The religious order that she believed herself divinely inspired to found came into existence in 1384 at Vadstena as a double cloister with nuns and monks sharing a common church but living in separate quarters. During its heyday, the Bridgettine order grew to include about seventy cloisters throughout Europe. It survives to the present in greatly diminished numbers and only as a woman's order; the last Bridgettine monks served in Bavaria in the early nineteenth century.

Of aristocratic background, Birgitta postponed her career as God's spokeswoman until the death of her husband in 1344. After receiving the church's certification of the divine source of her visions, she systematically monitored translation from their medieval Swedish origins to Latin. In 1349 she set out for Rome, hoping to get papal permission for her order during Holy Year, 1350.

No friend of the so-called Babylonian captivity of the papacy, Birgitta had to wait in Rome until Urban V's return in 1367 and then until a fiery confrontation at Montefiascone in 1370. His approval of her plan, albeit as a subdivision of the Augustinian order, was, for Birgitta, divine confirmation of her mission. One last pilgrimage remained, the journey to Bethlehem for a vision of the Nativity.

Not for their allegory, superb and deftly handled as it is, nor for their passionate intensity of spiritual experience, do Birgitta's revelations recommend themselves as literature to modern readers. Two matters do distinguish them: their drastic and unflinching realism and their rootedness at every point in *this* world's problems, concerns, and joys. As a writer, Birgitta is both heir to the nonabstract, nonsubjunctive, individualistic traditions established by the anonymous recorders of the Swedish provincial laws and forerunner of the visionary strain in the national literature exemplified by Emanuel Swedenborg,* Carl Jonas Love Almqvist,* and August Strindberg.*

FURTHER WORKS

G. E. Klemming, ed., *Heliga Birgittas uppenbarelser,* 5 vols. (1857–1884).

FURTHER TRANSLATIONS

Cumming, Patterson William, ed., *The Revelations of Saint Birgitta* (London, 1929).

REFERENCES

Fogelklou, Emilia, *Birgitta,* 2nd ed. (Stockholm, 1955); Flavigny, de C., *Sainte Birgitte de Suède* (Paris, 1892); Hammerich, Fr., *Den hellige Birgitta og Kirken* (Copenhagen, 1863); Jørgensen, Johannes, *Saint Bridget of Sweden,* 2 vols. (London and New York, 1954); Peacy, Edith, *Saint Birgitta of Sweden* (London, 1934); Redpath, Helen M.D., *God's Ambassadress* (Milwaukee, 1947); Stolpe, Sven, *Birgitta i Sverige* (Stockholm, 1973); Stolpe, Sven, *Birgitta i Rom* (Stockholm, 1973).

Raymond Jarvi

Bjarni Thorarensen. *See* Thorarensen, Bjarni.

Björling, Gunnar. Finnish poet writing in Swedish, b. 31 May 1887, Helsinki, d. 11 July 1960, Helsinki.

Björling was known as *brunnsparkspoeten,* having lived nearly his entire life on the southern shores of Helsinki, the scenery of much of his nature poetry. He studied philosophy, and was particularly influenced by the moral relativism of Edward Westermarck. During this period he began to conceive of the universe in ways that were to shape his radical poetry. Björling made his debut at thirty-five with *Vilande dag* (1922; Resting Day).

Björling's early production is heterogeneous and experimental. His contributions to the magazine *Quosego* (1928–1929) were intended to irritate and shock; they included the Scandinavian extreme in dadaist poetry, some of which can still be found in *Kiri-Ra* (1930). But with the collection *Solgrönt* (1933;

Sungreen), the mature poet begins to emerge as the angry overtones disappear. After *Solgrönt* Björling concentrates his vision and refines his diction. Two central themes crystallize, expressed in nature lyricism, and in what may be termed "you-poetry," sensuous odes to a mysterious and shifting "you." The nature lyrics, with their preoccupation with light, are hymns to the ever-expanding, partially observed universe. These pivotal themes are constantly reworked and refined in the collections *Fågel badar snart i vatten* (1934; Bird Soon Bathes in Water), *Men blåser violer på havet* (1936; But Blows Violets on the Sea), *Att syndens blåa nagel* (1936; That the Blue Nail of Sin), and reach their ultimate expression in *Där jag vet att du* (1939; Where I Know that You). Interspersed with the poetry are numerous aphorisms concerned with Björling's vision of language and his conception of a unity at the intersection of noncomplete events.

This unity is paradigmatic to all of Björling's poetry, having grown from his philosophical studies. There does exist a reality of the universe that, albeit in constant flux, can always be sensed and alluded to as the synthesis of partial experience. The essence of Björling's vision is reflected in the idiom he developed, a diction that can be described as the careful manipulation of metonymical relationships in language. The texts appear to have undergone extensive elision whereas in reality it operates on a system of contrapuntal oppositions that define semantic fields. Thus Björling avoids the delimiting expression that he feels anathematic to his message. Once so apprehended, the actual deviation from natural language is rather slight; even the grammatical function words that some commentators consider foregrounded have their ordinary properties.

Björling's collections are normally highly structured closed compositions, sometimes with a loose epic strand. Characteristically the works are divided into lengthy suites, each stanza in a different chord. The same practice is followed in the selections edited by Björling, for example, *Och leker med skuggorna i sanden* (1947; And Playing with the Shadows in the Sand) and *Du jord du dag* (1957; You Earth You Day). It is thus a clear misrepresentation to advance isolated stanzas, as frequently happens in anthologies.

For a long time Björling was ridiculed by the critics and rejected by the publishers. His influence upon younger poets, notably Henry Parland,* was enormous in Finland and significant in Sweden once *fyrtitalisterna* (poets of the 1940s) came to appreciate him. A brilliant essay by Bengt Holmqvist in *Prisma* (1949) marked the beginning of critical acceptance; since then Björling's reputation has made steady gains, to the point that today he is by many regarded as the most consequential of the Finno-Swedish modernists; his radicalism and absolute faith continue to provide inspiration for ever-new generations of poets.

FURTHER WORKS

Korset och löftet (1925); *Det oomvända anletet* (1939); *Angelägenhet* (1940); *Ohjälplig-heten* (1943); *O finns en dag* (1944); *Ord och att ej annat* (1945); *Luft är och ljus* (1946);

Ohört blott (1948); *Vårt kattliv timmar* (1949); *Ett blyertsstreck* (1951); *Som alla dar* (1953); *Att i sitt öga* (1954); *Du går de ord* (1955).

TRANSLATIONS

Books from Finland 14.2 (1985).

REFERENCES

Holmqvist, B., *Modern finlandssvensk litteratur* (Stockholm, 1951); Dickson, W., *En livslivets diktare* (Stockholm, 1956); Carpelan, Bo, "Gunnar Björling: The Universal Age." *Books from Finland* 14.2 (1985); Carpelan, Bo, *Studier i Gunnar Björlings diktning 1922–33* (Helsingfors, 1960); Nilsson, K., "Semantic Devices in Björling's Poetry." *Michigan Germanic Studies* 3 (1977); Wrede, J., "The Birth of Finland-Swedish Modernism." *Scandinavica* 15 (1965).

Kim Nilsson

Bjørneboe, Jens Ingvald. Norwegian novelist, dramatist, essayist, and lyric poet, b. 9 October 1920, Kristiansand, d. 9 May 1976, Oslo.

Bjørneboe received a good education and later studied to became a painter. During World War II he spent some time in Sweden, and after the war he became a teacher at the Steiner school in Oslo. Later on he was able to make a living as a writer.

Bjørneboe's first published book was a collection of poetry. His literary breakthrough, however, was the novel *Før hanen galer* (1952; Before the Cock Crows), which discussed medical experiments done by Nazi doctors in the German concentration camps during the war. This book is typical of Bjørneboe's authorship in that it deals with a highly controversial subject.

The next novel, *Jonas* (1955; *The Least of These*, 1959), is an attack on the Norwegian school system, while *Under en hårdere himmel* (1957; Under a Harder Sky) criticizes the treatment of Norwegian collaborators at the end of the war. *Den onde hyrde* (1960; The Bad Shepherd) expresses Bjørneboe's negative view of how the Norwegian criminal justice system deals with youthful offenders.

Bjørneboe's main theme is the problem of evil, which is given a comprehensive treatment in *Frihetens øyeblikk* (1966; *Moment of Freedom*, 1975). The novel portrays its protagonist's journey through time and space in an attempt to understand himself. As part of that process he gathers material for a literary project, the writing of a history of bestiality. Bjørneboe covers in nauseating detail many of the revolting acts that have been committed in the Western world. The result is a novel that might be so shocking that the reader will lose sight of its sophisticated narrative technique.

The American literary critic John M. Hoberman has termed Bjørneboe a gadfly (Hoberman, p. 52), and this evaluation is undoubtedly correct. Bjørneboe spent so much of his energy battling authorities of all kinds that he became a phenomenon in Norwegian cultural life and often antagonized both friend and foe. Since his suicide in 1976, however, his works have received a more balanced assessment, and he is now considered one of Norway's more important postwar writers.

FURTHER WORKS

Dikt (1951); *Ariadne* (1953); *Vinter i Bellapalma* (1958); *Den store by* (1958); *Blåmann* (1959); *Drømmen og hjulet* (1964); *Fugleelskerne* (1966); *Uten en tråd* (1966; *Without a Stitch*, 1969); *Norge, mitt Norge* (1968); *Aske, vind og jord* (1969); *Kruttårnet* (1969); *Semmelweis* (1969); *Vi som elsket Amerika* (1970); *Politi og anarki* (1972); *Hertug Hans* (1972); *Tilfellet Torgersen* (1972); *Stillheten* (1973); *Haiene* (1974); *Dongery* (1975); *Amputasjon* (1970).

REFERENCES

Garton, Janet, "A Vision of a Continual Battle: Jens Bjørneboe and the Theatre." *Scandinavica* 23.2 (1984); Gulbransen, Aud, and Jadwiga Theresa Kvadsheim, *Jens Bjørneboe. En bibliografi* (Oslo, 1978); Hoberman, John M., "The Political Imagination of Jens Bjørneboe: A Study of *Under en hårdere himmel.*" *Scandinavian Studies* 48.1 (1976); Wandrup, Fredrik, *Jens Bjørneboe: Mannen, myten og kunsten* (Oslo, 1984).

                                                                              Jan Sjåvik

Bjørnson, Bjørnstjerne Martinius. Norwegian journalist, poet, playwright, and novelist, b. 8 December 1832, Kvikne, d. 26 April 1910, Paris.

Bjørnson's father, a Lutheran minister, was transferred to Romsdalen when Bjørnson was five years old, and here among the fjords and mountains of western Norway, the younger Bjørnson gained the intimate understanding of nature and rural life from which his incomparable peasant stories are derived.

After Bjørnson graduated in 1852 from Hertzberg's "student factory," a college preparatory school in Kristiania (now Oslo), he worked as a private tutor for a year and then decided to try his hand as a journalist. In 1854–1856, Bjørnson was a literary critic at *Morgenbladet* (The Morning News). In 1856, he started *Illustreret Folkeblad* (Illustrated Popular Magazine), in which he published his first short stories. The same year Bjørnson led a group of students on a tour of Uppsala, where the many memorials to Sweden's heroic past inspired him to dramatize the history of his own country. In two weeks he composed *Mellem Slagene* (1857; Between Battles), the first Scandinavian saga play in prose.

In the autumn of 1857 Bjørnson traveled to Copenhagen and there he penned the short story *Thrond* (1857), which he considered his real breakthrough as a writer, and most of the novel-length story *Synnøve Solbakken* (1857; *Trust and Trial*, 1858), which made him the most popular writer of Norway almost overnight. During the next few years Bjørnson wrote alternately stories describing the rural life of contemporary Norway, and historical plays intended to show the cultural and spiritual continuity between the Viking ancestors of Norway and the people of the present. Combining features of the pastoral, the sentimental novel, and the *Bildungsroman*, Bjørnson's rural stories deal with the problem of fusing instinct with self-mastery, and spontaneity with responsibility to the community. The same general problem is portrayed in the plays, but in spite of noble struggle the heroes of pre-Christian Norway fail while their descendants succeed with the help of the Christian faith. The best of Bjørnson's saga plays from this period is no doubt *Sigurd Slembe* (1862; trans. 1888), a powerful trilogy influenced by Friedrich Schiller's *Wallenstein*.

His popular success notwithstanding, some critics accused Bjørnson of idealizing the rural folk. Bjørnson in fact did not shy away from depicting the shadowy side of the farmers' life, such as alcoholism, sexual abuse, illegitimacy, the exploitation of the poor, and even murder. But Bjørnson refused to accept the negative conclusions drawn, for example, by the sociologist Eilert Sundt on the basis of investigations of the living conditions among the rural lower classes (1850–1866). Like Henrik Wergeland,* Bjørnson believed in the importance of education in improving the lot of the common folk, and he saw himself as a teacher of his people.

Bjørnson's rural stories also contributed immeasurably to the development of a uniquely Norwegian literary language and style. Following the example set by Peter Christen Asbjørnsen and Jørgen Moe's collections of Norwegian tales and folk life descriptions, Bjørnson shaped his own style to reflect the syntactical patterns and idiom of folk speech, and the narrative perspective and tone of the ancient sagas.

Between 1857 and 1859, Bjørnson succeeded Henrik Ibsen* as theater director in Bergen and became editor of the paper *Bergenposten* (Bergen Mail). From 1865 to 1867 he directed the theater in Christiania, and from 1866 to 1871 he edited *Norsk Folkeblad* (Norwegian Popular News). Bjørnson became instrumental in establishing the Leftist party, and in his various roles as journalist, public speaker, theater director, and dramatist, made his voice heard in most of the literary, sociopolitical, and moral controversies of the day. But at the same time Bjørnson was productive as a lyrical poet during this period. He wrote lyrics patterned on folk song, as well as the poem "Ja, vi elsker dette landet" (Yes, we love this land), which was to become the Norwegian national anthem. Many of Bjørnson's songs, love poems, and romances based on folklore and saga motifs have been set to music. The volume *Digte og Sange* appeared in 1870 (*Poems and Songs*, 1915). The same year Bjørnson also published the lyric-epic cycle *Arnljot Gelline* (trans. 1917) based on a minor historical figure drawn from Snorri Sturluson's* saga of the missionary king Olav Trygvason.

In 1860–1862 Bjørnson had spent two formative years in Rome. He returned there in 1873 in order to escape the daily controversies and concentrate on his writings. The stay in Rome resulted in the publication of the first social play in Scandinavia, *En fallit* (1875; *The Bankrupt*, 1914), followed the same year by *Redaktøren* (*The Editor*, 1914). Social problems had been touched upon by other playwrights, Emile Augier among others, but they were central in Bjørnson's plays, and by virtue of these plays the author became widely known throughout Europe and the United States.

In his youth and early adulthood Bjørnson had considered himself a committed Christian in the liberal spirit of Nikolaj Grundtvig.* During the 1870s, however, exposure to the naturalistic philosophy of Hippolyte Taine, to John Stuart Mill, Viktor Rydberg's* and J. Ernest Renan's studies of the historical Christ, Georg Brandes'* book on Søren Kierkegaard* and, not least, Charles Darwin, caused Bjørnson to question Christian dogma. He eventually dissociated himself from the church, but he interpreted Darwin's theory of evolution theologically, believing the Divine to manifest itself in the ethical development of mankind. Bjørnson's religious crisis found expression in his greatest play, *Over Ævne I* (1883; *Pastor Sang*, 1893).

In 1880–1881 Bjørnson traveled and lectured in the United States. In autumn 1882 he moved to Paris where he lived for some five years, but even at a distance he remained involved in the battles at home, particularly the struggle for national independence. After 1890, Bjørnson was mostly concerned with social problems arising from the gradual transformation of Norway from an agrarian to an industrial society. He urged small nations to take a leading role in international politics for peace and the protection of minorities. During this time Bjørnson published a number of realistic novels and plays. An unquestioned masterpiece is *Paul Lange og Tora Parsberg* (1893; trans. 1899). The play has its background in Bjørnson's role in the political downfall and suicide of a former friend, Ole Richter.

Bjørnson received the Nobel Prize for Literature in 1903. During his lifetime his reputation eclipsed even that of Henrik Ibsen, while today the reverse is true. Besides the pivotal role he played in the political and cultural development of his people, Bjørnson is remembered today as an author who has made important contributions in every literary genre. His stories of rural life, some of his lyrical poetry and a handful of his plays have become permanent classics of Norwegian literature.

FURTHER WORKS

Aulestadbrev til Bergliot Ibsen (1911); *Gro-tid*, ed. H. Koht, 2 vols. (1912); *Artikler og taler*, 2 vols. (1912–1913); *Samlede digterverker,* crit. ed. by F. Bull, 9 vols. (1919); *Brytnings-år*, ed. H. Koht, 2 vols. (1921); *Breve til Alexander Kielland* (1930); *Kampliv*, ed. H. Koht, 2 vols. (1932); *Bjørnstjerne Bjørnsons og Christen Collins Brevveksling 1889–1909*, ed. Dagny Bjørnson Sautreau (1937); *Brevveksling med danske 1875–1910*, ed. Ø. Anker et al., 3 vols. (1953); *Din venn far*, ed. D. Bjørnson Sautreau (1956); *Brev til Karoline 1858–1907*, ed. D. Bjørnson Sautreau (1957); *Brevveksling med svenske 1858–1909*, ed. Ø. Anker et al., 3 vols. (1960–1961).

FURTHER TRANSLATIONS

Works, ed. Rasmus B. Anderson (1894–1899); *Poems and Songs* (1915); *Plays*, 2 vols. (1913–1916).

REFERENCES

Amdam, Per, *Bjørnstjerne Bjørnson: han som ville dikte et nytt og bedre Norge* (Oslo, 1979); Dahl, Willy, *Bjørnson* (Oslo, 1977); Downs, Brian, "Bjørnson and Tragedy." *Scandinavica* 1.1 (1962); Noreng, Harald, "Bjørnson Research: A Survey." *Scandinavica*

4.1 (1965); Noreng, Harald, *Bjørnsons dramatiske diktning* (Oslo, 1954); Øyslebø, Olaf, *Bjørnsons "bondefortellinger": kulturhistorie eller allmennmenneskelig diktning?* (Oslo, 1982); Sehmsdorf, Henning K., "Bjørnson's 'Trond' and Popular Tradition." *Scandinavian Studies* 41.1 (1969); Sehmsdorf, Henning K., "The Self in Isolation: A New Reading of Bjørnson's Arne." *Scandinavian Studies* 45.4 (1973); Thuesen, Arthur, *Bjørnson bibliografi*, 5 vols. (Oslo, 1948–1957).

Henning Sehmsdorf

Bjørnvig, Thorkild. Danish poet, literary critic, and researcher, b. 2 February 1918, Århus.

During his studies in comparative literature at the University of Århus, Bjørnvig acquired a wide literary horizon, which dominates his whole work. In 1946 he was awarded a gold medal for a dissertation on the German poet Rainer Maria Rilke, of whose poems he later was to make excellent translations. He was co-editor of the Danish periodical *Heretica*, which was of much importance to the Danish cultural debate in the postwar period. He has made several collections of poems and essays; in 1964 he wrote a doctoral thesis on the Danish writer Martin A. Hansen.* All his work relates to the question of modern existence.

The first collection *Stjærnen bag Gavlen* (1947; The Star Behind the Cable) describes love as a vital force, opening up the consciousness to the cosmos; only poetry is able to mediate this experience, which is similar to the fundamental openness to the world in childhood. Art, life, and consciousness are brought into relationship with death. Like nature, death is a factor to which man must bring himself into intimate and creative relation; through recognition and acceptance of the unknown and its strange beauty inherent in nature and death man will be regenerated.

Opposed to this creative strangeness, there is a destructive force: the alienation in the city. In his original philosophical essay "den aestetiske idiosynkrasi" (the aesthetic idiosyncrasy), Bjørnvig describes how the city environment provokes irrational and sudden violence. Environment and mentality cannot be separated, but must be interpreted together. In the collections *Anubis* (1955) and *Figur og Ild* (1959; Figura and Fire) he describes, in an intellectually and formally complex manner, our reduced cognition of reality, the problem of modern identity, the relations between intellect and emotion, and the competence of the arts to interpret life.

The environmental destruction of nature is a consequence of the way natural science understands the world: as dead material, the object of unlimited exploitation by man. But under these circumstances nature is no longer eternal. Living in a poisoned nature, man will also be poisoned, physically and mentally. As a consequence, in the latest collections *Delfinen* (1975; The Dolphin) and *Abeguder* (1981; Ape Gods), well documented poetical and political criticisms of contemporary culture, art is drawn into the struggle against this destruction.

Bjørnvig continually confronts his literary horizon with our modern situation. Through varied types of reflection and sensitive interpretation he synthesizes the conditions of modern existence, losing sight of neither the changing nor the eternal conditions of reality and existence. Hence he must be regarded as one of the most important Danish poets in the postwar era.

FURTHER WORKS

Rainer Maria Rilke og tysk Tradition (1945); *Evigt Foraar* (1954); *Begyndelsen* (1960); *Kains Alter. Martin A. Hansens digtning og tænkning* (1964); *Forsvar for Kains Alter* (1965); *Vibrationer* (1966); *Ravnen* (1968); *Oprør mod neonguden* (1970); *Virkeligheden er til* (1973); *Pagten* (1974; *The Pact* 1983); *Stoffets krystalhav* (1975); *Det religiøse menneskes ansigter* (1975); *Morgenmørke* (1977); *Også for naturens skyld* (1978); *Barnet og dyret i industrisamfundet* (1979); *Solens Have og Skolegården. Erindringer 1918–33* (1983); *Hjørnestuen og Månehavet. Erindringer 1934–38* (1984); *Jordens Hjerte. Erindringer 1938–46* (1986); *Gammelt og nyt under solen* (1986); *Gennem regnbuen* (1987).

TRANSLATIONS

Modern Danish Writers, special issue of *Adam—International Review* (1948); *Twentieth Century Scandinavian Poetry* ed. Martin S. Allwood (1950); *Literary Review* 8.1 (1964); *American-Scandinavian Review* 54.1 (1966); *Anthology of Danish Literature*, ed. P. M. Mitchell and F. J. Billeskov Jansen (1972); *Massachusetts Review* 64 (Autumn 1973); *Scandinavian Review* 64.4 (1976); *Orbis* 27/28 (1977); *Contemporary Danish Poetry*, ed. Line Jensen et al., (1977); *Scandinavian Review* 66.3 (1978); *Seventeen Danish Poets*, ed. Niels Ingwersen (1981).

REFERENCES

Brostrøm, Torben, "Thorkild Bjørnvig" in *Danske digtere i det 20. Århundrede*, vol. 3 (Copenhagen, 1981); Julén, Bjørn, "Thorkild Bjørnvig" in *Danske digtere i det 20. Århundrede*, vol. 3 (Copenhagen, 1965); Dahl, Per, *Thorkild Bjørnvigs tænkning* (Copenhagen, 1976); Nielsen, Erik A., *Ideologihistorie*, vol. 3 (Copenhagen, 1976).

Ole Wøide

Blicher, Steen Steensen. Danish short story writer and poet, b. 11 October 1782, Vium, d. 26 March 1848, Spentrup.

As a student Blicher was drawn to English literature; he translated James Macpherson's *Ossian* (1807–1809) and Oliver Goldsmith's *The Vicar of Wakefield* (1837). Not only did a late eighteenth-century mixture of rationalism and emotionalism set its mark on his early poetry and drama, but Ossianic moods continued to echo in his works. He made a living as a country minister in Jutland; hardly an enthusiastic clergyman, he engaged in a pursuit—similar to Nikolaj Grundtvig's,* but much less successful—to educate the farming populace. His respect for the ordinary people is evident in his works; he collected legends from his region, and like Robert Burns, he wrote some of his works in dialect. In *E Bindstouw* (1842, In the Spinning Room) both his poetry and prose demonstrate the power of dialect to capture tragic as well as comic situations.

Blicher was forty before he found the genre in which he was to excel. For economic reasons, he wrote some short stories for a provincial magazine, the readership of which demanded local color, exoticism, and melodrama. Blicher provided those ingredients in many stories, but in a handful of them he achieved small masterpieces. Amazingly enough, the very first story, "En Landsbydegns Dagbog" (1824; "The Diary of a Parish Clerk," 1945), is perfect artistically. Those "diary entries," supposedly from the early 1700s capture the impressions and moods of a gullible young servant at a manor house; during a few years he sees not only the death of his own youthful hopes, but the downfall of the wealthy family as well. His unreciprocated love for the daughter of the house marks him for life (Blicher's model for the young woman is Marie Grubbe, whom J. P. Jacobsen* later made the subject of a psychological novel). It is tempting to see the ending of this story, as well as those of many others, as an expression of fatalistic resignation, but that would hardly be correct, for Blicher quite consistently, if discreetly, suggests social reasons for the tragedies experienced by his characters. In "Hosekræmmeren" (1829; "The Hosier's Daughter," 1945), Blicher shows that it is not the inscrutable ways of the Lord or of fate, but a materialistic outlook that turns to ashes the dreams of the young lovers. Similarly, in "Præsten i Vejlby" (1829; "The Minister of Vejlby," 1945), the protagonist's diary indirectly reveals how the ideology of absolutism—the story takes place in the 1600s—blinds intelligent, moral people to the evil designs of a Machiavellian person.

Some modern readers may take exception to Blicher's use of melodramatic effects, but in his best stories, their attention is actually drawn away from the plot to the narrator, the perceiving mind, and thus Blicher's texts become not just melodramatic, but psychological studies of considerable depth. As in the works of Henry James, the reader may become aware that the narrator is unreliable and may then attempt to detect the reason for the narrator's limited perception. In "Sildig Opvaagnen" (1828; "Tardy Awakening," 1945), a minister describes how an adulterous woman destroyed the lives of two families, but as the reader analyzes the narrator's enraged statements, the minister's fury subtly reveals itself to be a cover, conscious or unconscious, for his own attraction to the woman whom he labels vampiric.

In the collection *Trækfuglene* (1837; Migratory Birds), Blicher also found his tone as a poet. With beautiful simplicity but without sorrow, the poems center on the theme of life's brevity.

During Blicher's life, he was a provincial outsider, and for many years following his death, he was considered to be a local color writer, the bard of the Danish heath. Of late, the subtlety of his point-of-view technique, as well as of his insight into the power exercised by the ideology of an age or a milieu, has been recognized. Blicher foreshadowed the rise of realism, but later developments have not overshadowed him as one of Scandinavia's finest short story writers.

FURTHER WORKS

Samlede Skrifter, 33 vols. (1920–1934); *Digte og Noveller*, 3 vols. (1967).

TRANSLATIONS

Twelve Stories (1945); *From the Danish Peninsula; Poems and a Tale by Steen Steensen Blicher* (1957); *The Journal of a Parish Clerk*, in *An Anthology of Danish Literature*, ed. F. J. Billeskov Jansen and P. M. Mitchell (1971).

REFERENCES

Aakjær, Jeppe, *St. St. Blichers Livs-Tragedie* (Copenhagen, 1903–1904); Baggesen, Søren, *Den blicherske novelle* (Copenhagen, 1965); Brask, Peter, *Om "En Landsbydegns Dagbog"* (Copenhagen, 1982); Brix, Hans, *Blicher-Studier* (Copenhagen, 1916); Nørgaard, Felix, ed., *Omkring Blicher* (Copenhagen, 1974); Nørvig, Johannes, *Steen Steensen Blicher, hans Liv og Værker* (Copenhagen, 1943); Olwig, Kenneth, *Nature's Ideological Landscape* (London, 1984); Sørensen, Knud, *St. St. Blicher. Digter og samfundsborger*; von Törne, Björn, *Zwischen Loyalität und Servilität* (Neumünster, 1980); Undset, Sigrid, *Steen Steensen Blicher* (Oslo, 1957).

Niels Ingwersen

Blixen, Karen. *See* Dinesen, Isak.

Blomberg, Erik. Swedish poet, essayist, and art historian, b. 17 August 1894, Stockholm, d. 8 April 1965.

Blomberg received his formal education in art history, and his research and criticism in this field, culminating in a three-volume study of Ernst Josephson, rank among his most influential works. His essays on literature and culture were also significant since Blomberg was one of only a very few Swedish critics articulating Marxist viewpoints during the 1920s and 1930s. Such viewpoints are strikingly absent, however, from the lyric poetry that formed the basis of his own art. Even so the ideal of social harmony—and its inherent political implications—prevails throughout his work.

His lyricism has its roots in expressionism, and in this regard he is most often associated with his contemporary Pär Lagerkvist,* although lacking the latter's stylistic virtuosity. Blomberg's poems retain a traditional, ballad-like form. In the collections published between the end of World War I and 1927, Blomberg formulated what was to become the central problematic of his poetry: how does one overcome the isolation and loneliness that are the terms of human existence? In his earlier volumes the problem formulated itself in religious terms—where is God, the spirit who encompasses and dissolves all isolation? In *Jorden* (1920; The Earth) Blomberg proclaims that earth is the proper home of this spirit and that only in the brotherhood of man can it find definition. Consumed by faith in humankind, one ceases to live alone, and the terms of existence are radically redefined. By the time Blomberg wrote *Den fångne guden* (1927; The Imprisoned God), however, his optimism had been tempered. Here it is made clear that if God does exist on earth then he is imprisoned and man must first struggle to achieve brotherhood before God can be released and man redeemed. In *Nattens ögon* (1943; Eyes of the Night), Blomberg's next collection, religious speculation has subsided, but the imagery of all-encompassing light, a dominant leitmotif in other collections, remains. Here as elsewhere it is coupled with equally powerful images of darkness. Again a major paradox in Blomberg's work emerges: to what extent are our dreams of salvation, freedom, and light not also dreams of self-annihilation—of denial and darkness?

The depth of Blomberg's commitment to Swedish literature and culture is reflected in the fact that he made important contributions in so many areas—literature, art, politics, etc. But it is perhaps this commitment itself that is his greatest contribution, for it was provocatively perceptive, vocally Marxist and consciously modern when modernism was new. Without it Swedish modernism, as well as later generations of Marxist writers, would have been robbed of an insistent, influential voice.

FURTHER WORKS

Ensamhetens sånger (1918); *Människan och guden* (1919); *Den nya svenska konsten* (1923); *Visor* (1924); *Tidens romantik* (1931); *Stadens fångar* (1933); *Efter stormen—före stormen* (1938); *Mosaik* (1940); *Demokratin och kriget* (1945); *Från Josephson till Picasso* (1946); *Från öst och väst* (1951); *Ernst Josephson. Hans liv* (1951); *Ernst Josephsons konst*, 2 vols. (1956–1959); *Bleknad konsthimmel* (1958); *Vem äventyrar freden?* (1962); *Öppna er, ögon* (1962).

REFERENCES

Björck, Staffan, "Smärtans ansikte. Erik Blomberg: Ansikten," in his *Lyriska läsövningar* (Stockholm, 1961); Stenkvist, Jan, *Den nya livskänslan* (Stockholm, 1968); Zetterström, Margareta, *Erik Blomberg: en kämpande intellektuell* (Stockholm, 1977).

Deborah Regula

Bodelsen, Anders. Danish novelist and short story writer, b. 11 February 1937, Copenhagen.

Bodelsen's mother was an art historian, his father a professor of English. Bodelsen was thus imbued at an early age with an appreciation for the arts and began writing as a child. He studied law, economics, and comparative literature at the University of Copenhagen but became increasingly convinced of his calling as a writer. His first novel, *De lyse nætters tid* (1959; The Time of the Light Nights), dates from his student years and reflects its author's search for direction. Bodelsen has written regularly for various Danish newspapers as well as for radio and television. He has received numerous literary prizes, among them the Grand Prix de la Littérature Policière in 1971. Many of his works have been translated into other languages.

A neorealist, Bodelsen accurately chronicles the evolution of the Danish middle-class milieu since World War II. He often weaves recent historical events into the framework of his narratives, providing a reference point for contemporary readers. Many of his writings share characters and motifs with one another, lending much of his oeuvre an internal consistency. Bodelsen's works deal primarily with two major themes: individual moral responsibility and the inauspicious fate of the welfare society.

Most representative of the former are the suspense novels *Tænk på et tal* (1968; *Think of a Number*, 1969, or *A Silent Partner*, 1978) *Hændeligt uheld* (1968; *One Down* or *Hit and Run Run Run*, 1970), and *Borte borte* (1980; Gone, Gone) and many of the short stories in the collections *Drivhuset* (1965; The Greenhouse) and *Lov og orden* (1973; Law and Order) in which otherwise law-abiding Danes resort to criminal acts to attain their goals, exhibiting little contrition in so doing. In these works particularly, Bodelsen demonstrates his consummate skill in psychological portraiture. The futuristic novel *Frysepunktet* (1969; *Freezing Down* or *Freezing Point*, 1971) best illustrates Bodelsen's thesis that the welfare state is disintegrating. The novel *Bevisets stilling* (1973; *Consider the Verdict*, 1976) combines these two themes and shows how society's institutions can destroy the individual. In several recent novels, *Over regnbuen* (1982; Over the Rainbow) and *Domino* (1984), Bodelsen expresses a more optimistic outlook for the future of Danish society, pinning his hopes for tomorrow on the promise of the youth of today.

Ever the moralist, Bodelsen reaffirms traditional standards of ethics and defends middle-class values. Frequently, Bodelsen poses questions but leaves their answers up to the reader. Bodelsen's ability to evoke the essence of his own time is unsurpassed in modern Danish literature, and his straightforward, often ironic style makes him one of today's most popular and accessible authors.

FURTHER WORKS

Villa Sunset (1964); *En hård dags nat* (1966); *Filmen nu* (1966); *Rama Sama* (1967); *Til døden os skiller* (1967); *Lørdag aften* (1969); *Ferie* (1970); *Hjælp* (1971); *Professor Mancinis hemmelighed* (1971); *Straus* (1971; *Straus*, 1974); *Pigerne på broen* (1972); *Skygger* (1972); *Uden for nummer* (1972); *Alt hvad du ønsker dig* (1974); *Fjernsynet flimrer* (1974); *Blæsten i alleen* (1975); *Operation Cobra* (1975; *Operation Cobra*, 1976); *Pengene og livet* (1976); *De gode tider* (1977); *År for år* (1978); *Overhøring* (1979); *Passageren* (1979); *Borte borte* (1980); *Revision* (1985); *Guldregn* (1986); *Jeg kommer til at løbe* (1987).

FURTHER TRANSLATIONS

The Devil's Instrument, and Other Danish Stories (1971), comp. S. Holm.

REFERENCES

Grefe, Eric, "Anders Bodelsen." *Scanorama* 7.5 (1978); Nielsen, Geert A., *Anders Bodelsens realisme* (Copenhagen, 1978).

Frank Hugus

Bødker, Cecil. Danish poet, playwright, and writer of short stories, plays, and children's books, b. 27 March 1927, Fredericia, daughter of H. P. Jacobsen.

Trained as a silversmith, Bødker published her first collection of poems,

Luseblomster (Dandelions), in 1955. In 1961 she received the critic's prize for her collection of novellas, *Øjet* (The Eye), in 1967 the Danish Academy's prize for the children's book *Silas og den sorte hoppe* (*Silas and the Black Mare*, 1978), and in 1976 the H. C. Andersen prize in recognition of her children's books.

Bødker is known primarily for her works for children, particularly for her Silas stories. Through 1975 she had written thirteen, several of which have been translated. Bødker has claimed that her children's stories (like those of Hans Christian Andersen*) can be read by adults as well as children.

The author's development in prose can be described as a movement from the abstract and mythical to the concrete and realistic. Her macabre collection of novellas, *Øjet*, first brought her to the attention of the literate public. A fairly recent novel, *En vrangmaske i vorherres strikketøj* (1974; A Purl in Our Lord's Knitting), concrete and detailed, describes a boy's experiences in a lower-class setting.

Her lyrics show the same general trend. *Anadyomene* (1959) deals in mythical terms (Adam and Eve, Cain, Aphrodite) with man's (and woman's) creation and fall. *I vædderens tegn* (1968; Under the Sign of the Ram) continues the emphasis on myth but in more concrete settings and in realistic detail.

FURTHER WORKS

Fygende heste (1955); *Lytteposter* (1960) *Latter* (1964); *Samlede digte* (1964); *Tilstanden Harley* (1965); *Pap* (1967); *Dukke min* (1968); *Silas og Ben-Godik* (1969; *Silas and Ben-Godik*, 1978); *Timmerlis* (1969); *Leoparden* (1970; *The Leopard*, 1972); *Dimma Gole* (1971); *Fortællinger omkring Tavs* (1971); *Kvinden som gik bort over vandet* (1971); *Tre fortællinger fra Ethiopien* (1971); *Salthandlerskens hus* (1972); *Skyld* (1972); *Silas fanger et firspand* (1973; *Silas and the Runaway Coach*, 1978); *Far, mor og børn* (1975); *Jerutte fra Ræverød* (1975); *Silas stifter familie* (1976); *Et udvalg* (1977); *Silas og Hestekrage mødes igen* (1978); *Evas ekko* (1980); *Tænk på Jolande* (1981); *Marias barn*, 2 vols. (1985); *Silas—Sebastians arv* (1986).

FURTHER TRANSLATIONS

Literary Review 8.1 (1964); *American-Scandinavian Review* 60.2 (1972); *Prism International* 13.2 (1973); *Contemporary Danish Poetry*, ed. Line Jensen et al. (1977).

REFERENCES

Gormsen, Jacob, *Cecil Bødker* (Copenhagen, 1976).

Otto M. Sorensen

Böðvarsson, Guðmundur. Icelandic poet and novelist, b. 1 September 1904, Kirkjuból, Mýra district, d. 3 April 1974, Kirkjuból.

The son of a farmer, Böðvarsson was himself a farmer all his life except for three years in his late fifties that he spent as a librarian in Hafnarfjörður. Having had little formal schooling, he yet acquired by himself a good education and was well read in the Scandinavian languages and in English. His translation of twelve cantos from Dante's *Divine Comedy* is a remarkable piece of work by a self-taught farmer. Böðvarsson's travels, all undertaken in the latter part of his life, took him to Scandinavia and as far as Central Asia in the Soviet Union. This is attested to in his poetry.

Böðvarsson was deeply embedded in the Icelandic tradition of alliterated and rhymed verse, although even his first book, *Kyssti mig sól* (1936; The Sun Kissed Me), showed some stirrings toward a freer mode of expression. As time went by, his form loosened, becoming lighter and less rigid, but he never abandoned alliteration though he would occasionally do without rhyme. Böðvarsson's first book also revealed most of the strands of which his poetry continued to be spun: a lyrical sensibility born of the landscape and culture of his native country; a cosmopolitan outlook, despite his small, rural surroundings; and a deep feeling of solidarity with the unfortunate and oppressed. In this, as in many other ways, he bore a close resemblance to another farmer-poet, Stephan G. Stephansson.*

Despite his roots in tradition, Böðvarsson was very much a product of his time, and the currents of world as well as national events found a ready course through his writings. From the mid–1930s on, he was concerned with the conflicts then going on in the world, foreboding the carnage of World War II, and during the war it remained his preoccupation. In the postwar period his attention shifted to the continued stationing in Iceland of U.S. troops, against which he fought with every stroke of his pen. He never, however, stooped to crude propaganda; rather, in giving his views poetic expression, he would use the symbols from the farmer's everyday life and chores—the elemental forces, the cycle of the seasons, the whetting of a scythe, the tilling of the earth—to draw up pictures and vignettes, the deeper meaning of which was obvious to any reader. Through all his writings shone his undivided love for his country, his sense of unity with its nature and people, and his pain over the actions of those he felt had betrayed its history. His innate kindness, however, prevented him from becoming bitter, and his outlook, despite many expressions of disappointment, was basically a sunny one. Böðvarsson's novel, *Dyr í vegginn* (1958; A Door Through the Wall), and his three volumes of short fiction do not measure up to his poetry.

FURTHER WORKS

Hin hvítu skip (1939); *Álfar Kvöldsins* (1941); *Undir óttunnar himni* (1944); *Krystallinn í hylnum* (1952); *Kvæðasafn* (1956); *Minn guð og þinn* (1960); *Saltkorn í mold*, vol. 1 (1962); *Landsvísur* (1963); *Saltkorn í mold*, vol. 2 (1965); *Hríðarspor* (1965); *Innan hringsins* (1969); *Atreifur og aðrir fuglar* (1971); *Safnrit*, 7 vols. (1971–1976); *Konan sem lá úti* (1972); " . . . og fjaðrirnar fjórar" (1973).

FURTHER TRANSLATIONS

Poems of Today from Twenty-five Modern Icelandic Poets, Comp. Alan Boucher (1971).

REFERENCE

Hallmundsson, Hallberg, "Guðmundur Böðvarsson." *American-Scandinavian Review* 53.1 (1965).

Hallberg Hallmundsson

Bojer, Johan. Norwegian novelist, short story writer, and dramatist, b. 6 March 1872, Orkdalsøyra, d. 3 July 1959, Oslo.

Bojer grew up in extreme poverty with a crofter's family to whom he had been put out to nurse. In spite of their humble position his foster-parents were able to give him human warmth and care, and through all his life Bojer maintained a deep respect for and loyalty to his family and the population of the coast.

Bojer's first novels are molded on certain fundamental ethical ideas, most of them related to morals in politics and man's struggle for power. Sometimes Bojer's eagerness to express a message leads him to neglect the drawing of his characters. During the decade of c. 1905–1915 there is an important change in Bojer's attitude toward life. His pessimistic view of human nature gives way to a strong belief in man's dignity. In the first of his really successful novels, *Den store hunger* (1916; *The Great Hunger*, 1918), the principal character devotes his life to modern technology, believing that it will save the world and replace God. In the end, however, he realizes that technology can never satisfy the human longing for a divine transcendental power.

At this stage of his career, Bojer's interest in subjects from recent Norwegian history and his own background was steadily growing. He developed a style more faceted than before, and like many other Norwegian novelists he enriched his language with elements of his own dialect.

Bojer's masterpieces were all published in the 1920s, *Den siste viking* (1921; *Last of the Vikings*, 1923), *Vor egen stamme* (1924; *The Emigrants*, 1925), and *Folk ved sjøen* (1929; *Folk by the Sea*, 1931). They are united by one common main subject: the heroic fight by the characters to survive spiritually and physically in harsh surroundings, in the fisheries of the Lofoten Island, at the poor seaside farm, on the endless American prairies.

Bojer's reputation in France and the English-speaking world was great, and he became one of the most widely translated Norwegian authors. In Norway he is recognized as an important neorealist. He is especially remembered for *Den siste viking*, which has won a place among the classics in Norwegian literature.

FURTHER WORKS

Gravholmen (1895); *Helga* (1895); *En moder* (1895); *Et folketog* (1896); *Olaf den Hellige* (1897); *Paa kirkevei* (1897); *Rørfløiterne* (1898); *Den evige krig* (1899); *Moder Lea* (1900); *Gamle historier* (1901); *En pilgrimsgang* (1902; *A Pilgrimage*, 1924); *Theodora* (1902); *Troens magt* (1903; *The Power of a Lie* 1908); *Brutus* (1904); *Hvide fugle* (1904); *Vort rige* (1908; *Treacherous Ground*, 1912); *Kjærlighetens øine* (1910); *Liv* (1911; *Life*, 1920); *Fangen som sang* (1913; *The Prisoner Who Sang*, 1924); *Marie Walewska* (1913); *Sigurd Braa* (1916); *Verdens ansigt* (1917; *The Face of the World*, 1919); *Dyrendal*

(1919; *God and Woman*, 1921); *Stille veir* (1920); *Det nye tempel* (1927; *The New Temple*, 1928); *Huset og havet* (1933; *The House and the Sea*, 1934); *Dagen og natten* (1935; *By Day and by Night*, 1937); *Kongens karer* (1938; *The King's Men*, 1940); *Gård og grend* (1939); *Hustruen* (1941); *Skyld* (1948); *Lov og liv* (1952); *Fjell og fjære* (1957).

FURTHER TRANSLATIONS

Told in Norway, ed. H. A. Larsen (1927); *The World's One Hundred Best Short Stories*, ed. G. M. Overton, vol. 9 (1927); *Short narratives*, ed. Paul M. Fulcher (1928).

REFERENCES

Johan Bojer, the Story of His Life, Mostly in His Own Words (New York, n.d.); Gad, Carl, *Johan Bojer: The Man and His Works* (Westport, Conn., 1974); La Chesnais, P. G., *Johan Bojer. Hans Liv og verker* (Oslo, 1932); Lødrup, Hans P., "Johan Bojer." *American-Scandinavian Review* 14.4 (1926); Ræder, Trygve, *Johan Bojer og heimbygda Rissa* (Oslo, 1972).

Jostein Fet

Bondestam, Anna. Finnish novelist writing in Swedish, b. 1 April 1907, Jakobstad (Pietarsaari).

Bondestam was a child in a family actively engaged on the socialist side during the class struggle in Finland around 1918. Events unfolding before her have clearly imprinted her production. She is not strictly a proletarian writer; rather her sympathies lie directly with those who by social circumstance or psychological forces can be seen as imprisoned.

Bondestam made her debut with *Panik i Rölleby* (1936; Panic in Rölleby), a historical novel with a whimsical tone. With *Klyftan* (1946; The Rift), Bondestam received recognition as she deftly juxtaposed the division between classes and between child and adolescent. The same interweaving of social and psychological pressures occurs in the attempted, still uncompleted epic of her native Ostrobothnia and its gradual industrialization, of which two volumes have appeared, *Vägen till staden* (1957; The Road to the City) and *Stadens bröd* (1960; City Bread). In short story format Bondestam presents penetrating but compassionate psychological portraits, as in *Enskilt område* (1952; Private Domain). A volume of poetry, *Jordnära* (1972; Close to Earth), and a detective story of insignificant merit also occur in her production.

Bondestam is generally overlooked in anthologies and literary surveys in Swedish Finland, despite hers being the most consistent voice of "the other side," and as a writer whose sensibilities today would clearly be labeled feminist. It is, in the end, the wisdom of women that allows the characters to break or tolerate their fetters. It is true that Bondestam's work is slim and uneven, still she is a rather unique phenomenon in Finno-Swedish letters.

FURTHER WORKS

Fröken Elna Johansson (1939); *Bergtagen* (1941); *Lågt i tak* (1943); *Sällboda frivilliga deckarkår* (1949); *Jakobstads svenska arbetarförening 60 år* (1964); *Arbetet* (1968); *Åland vintern 1918* (1972); *En stad förvandlas* (1978); *Som en stubbe i en stubbåker*, with Alf-Erik Helsing (1978).

Kim Nilsson

Borgen, Johan. Norwegian novelist, b. 28 April 1902, Oslo, d. 16 October 1979.

Borgen was the youngest of four sons in a comfortable, bourgeois Oslo family. In addition to being a significant writer of fiction and drama, he was an accomplished journalist, critic, and social commentator. In the 1930s he wrote plays in a manner later associated with Eugène Ionesco and the postwar avant-garde in France. Nevertheless, it is in his short stories and novels that Borgen truly excels. As a novelist he matured slowly. His breakthrough came with the first volume of the *Lillelord* (*Lillelord*, 1982) trilogy in 1955, a full thirty years after his debut as a prose writer. Between 1955 and 1972 Borgen published a series of extraordinary novels, and it is safe to say that these works will determine his place in the realm of Scandinavian letters. While many of the themes in the mature fiction appear in his earlier works, it is in the later novels that Borgen fully develops these themes and ultimately resolves the conflicts upon which his fiction is based.

Borgen's mature fiction is remarkably coherent. In fact, each of the novels essentially treats aspects of a single problem—that of the conflicting forces that pull the protagonist between a subjective quest for identity and an outward movement toward others. It is the conflict between psychological solitude and social solidarity. All of Borgen's important subthemes—the sense of lost identity, the fragmentation of the personality, and the quest for innocence and wholeness—are intimately related to the basic conflict within the protagonist's personality. While each novel represents an attempt at solving the conflict, the entire corpus unveils an evolutionary pattern—from mysticism, through faith in knowledge and artistic vision, through disenchantment, and finally toward resolution through concrete involvement in the world.

There exists in Borgen's work an interesting correlation between form and meaning. The form of the *Lillelord* trilogy (1955–1957) is diffuse and ambitious, the work of an author virtually overwhelmed by the richness of his own material. Nevertheless, it is a highly appropriate way of relating the torment of Wilfred Sagen, a protagonist literally ripped apart by conflicting inner drives. The aesthetically superior novels, *Jeg* (1959; I) and *Den røde tåken* (1967; *The Red Mist*, 1973), reflect varying degrees of faith in the artistic vocation and acceptance of a poetic solution to the problems of life. On the other hand *Blåtind* (1964; Blue Peak) betrays a sense of intense doubt, illustrated by agonized, fragmented dialogues among the main characters. Conversely, the simple, realistic structure of *Min arm, min tarm* (1972; My Arm, My Gut) nicely complements the way in which the protagonist, Frank Vegårdshei resolves his underlying problems.

Borgen's fiction reveals the author's struggle to liberate himself from a literary tradition he has inherited. What he seems to be saying with increasing urgency is that the novel has reached a stage in its development where it can no longer afford to lean wholly on tradition. In fact, by continuing to re-create the old myths in new dress, we risk degrading the originals. Moreover, the time has come to start reexamining the content of the myths upon which so many of our literary works are built. Do the patterns they force us into really respond to the need of our time? When Peter Holmgren in *Blåtind* starts to suspect that the map he is carrying does not match the landscape, he will instinctively trust the map more than he will trust his own eyes. He perishes because he decides to change his course too late. Borgen, then, proposes a reevaluation of our total literary heritage, so as to liberate us from the circles of the past and enable us to start mapping out a new, more realistic course for the future.

FURTHER WORKS

Mot mørket (1925); *Betrakninger og anfektelser* (1932); *Når alt kommer til alt* (1934); *Lille dommedag* (1935); *Kontorsjef Lie* (1936); *Seksti Mumle Gåsegg* (1936); *Barnesinn* (1937); *Høit var du elsket* (1937); *Mens vi venter* (1938); *Andersens* (1940); *Anes eventyr* (1941–1943); *Ingen sommer* (1944); *Det nytter* (1944); *Nordahl Grieg* (1944); *Dager på Grini* (1945); *Far, mor og oss* (1945); *Hvetebrødsdager* (1946); *Kjærlighetsstien* (1946); *Reidar Aulie* (1946); *Akvariet* (1947); *Jenny og påfuglen* (1949); *Vikinger og eventyr* (1949); *Kunsten i Oslo rådhus* (1950); *Noveller om kjærlighet* (1952); *Natt og dag* (1954); *De mørke kilder* (1956); *Vi har ham nå* (1957); *Danmark dejligst?* (1960); *Innbilningens verden* (1960); *Noveller i utvalg* (1960); *Frigjøringsdag* (1963); *Barndommens rike* (1965); *Nye noveller* (1965); *Ord gjennom år* (1966); *Innbilningen og kunsten* (1966); *Bagateller* (1967); *Alltid på en søndag* (1968); *Traer alene i skogen* (1969); *Elsk meg bort—* (1970); *Mitt hundeliv* (1971); *129 Mumle Gåsegg* (1971); *Den store havfrue* (1973); *Eksempler* (1974); *Lykke til!* (1974); *Dronningen nikker* (1974); *Notater fra hverdagen* (1975); *I dette rom* (1975); *Borgen om bøker, fremmed*, ed. Lone Klem (1977); *Borgen om bøker, norsk og nordisk*, ed. Erling Nielsen (1977).

REFERENCES

Birn, Randi, *Johan Borgen* (New York, 1974); Birn, Randi Marie, "The Quest for Authenticity in Three Novels by Johan Borgen." *Mosaic* 4.2 (1970); Birn, Randi Marie, "Dream and Reality in Johan Borgen's Short Stories." *Scandinavian Studies* 46.1 (1974); Borgen, Annemarta, *Deg* (Oslo, 1981); Johanssen, K. J., *Johan Borgen* (Oslo, 1980); Mawby, Janet, "The Norwegian Novel Today." *Scandinavica* 14.2 (1975); Mishler, William, "Metaphor and Metonymy in Johan Borgen's 'Eksempler.' " *Scandinavica* 16.1 (1977).

Randi Brox

Born, Heidi von. Swedish novelist and poet, b. 13 May 1936, Stockholm.

Born comes from a family of writers: both her parents were journalists and writers, and very early she felt herself predestined for writing. She made her debut in 1956 with a collection of poetry, a medium to which she has returned successfully in 1983 with *Jordväxling* (Landrotation). In her novels of the sixties, Born developed and fine-tuned the themes and style that characterize her major works of the last decade with which she has established herself as one of Sweden's most respected writers.

Born's protagonists are people who are alienated from society and by society—the economically and socially disadvantaged, the emotionally disturbed, and the elderly. Her novels are often journeys through interior landscapes where no additional information about background or circumstance is supplied to the reader. In a world distorted by fear and panic, disturbing and absurd happenings are common occurrences. The characters barricade themselves behind meaningless rituals or strike out beyond the acceptable limits of society. In *Hungerbarnen* (1981; Children of Hunger), the much acclaimed novel for which Born won *Svenska Dagbladet's* literature prize in 1981, the two "hunger children" exist precariously at the margin of society, totally without an emotional safety net, clinging desperately to each other and preying on the adult world in an effort to salvage a future in the face of overwhelming odds. The sequel, *Kungariket Atlas* (1984; The Kingdom of Atlas), finds the two siblings after the mother's final breakdown frantically trying to build an independent existence in a society that has already branded them "underclass." Caught in a web of terror from within and without, the mother and son can escape only in madness or death. Yet, in a hopeful ending, Ella, the sole survivor, is on her way from the dreary world of Atlasgatan in Stockholm to the South, to the Atlas mountains.

In spite of the author's obvious empathy with her characters, there is no room for indulgent reflection. Born's prose, lyrical and sensual, yet tightly reined to contain the tension within, cuts harshly through any leaning toward sentimentality on the part of the reader.

Born's novels do not intend to scrutinize the "normal" world outside the narrow confines of her heroes; yet they become, indirectly, commentaries on a society that finds itself unable to alleviate such suffering or establish contact with its most needy citizens. Born refrains from offering any solutions; the reader is left to ponder for him/herself the limits of individual and communal responsibility.

FURTHER WORKS

Det förtrollade huset (1956); *Leken är förbi* (1957); *Molnen kommer med morgonen* (1958); *Pavane* (1959); *Tre* (1960); *Martinas dagar* (1962); *Frigångare* (1964); *Insida* (1966); *Spårhunden* (1968); *Handen full* (1969); *Dagar som de faller* (1972); *Den tredje handen* (1974); *Aldrig mer tillbaka* (1975); *Simulantens liv* (1977); *Det japanska skriket* (1979); *Hummerkriget* (1983); *Kungariket Atlas* (1984); *Den vita öknen* (1986).

TRANSLATIONS

Malahat Review 67 (1984).

REFERENCES

"Pavane," a review *Books Abroad* 35 (1961)

Rose-Marie G. Oster

Boye, Karin Maria. Swedish poet, novelist, and critic, b. 26 October 1900, Gothenburg, d. 24 April 1941, near Alingsås.

Boye studied at Uppsala University from 1921 to 1926 (Master of Arts 1928).

She taught literature at many schools, the longest period 1936–1938, and wrote numerous essays and articles. After a Christian youth full of doubt and guilt, she joined the socialistic and pacifistic group Clarté in 1925 (Clarté was inspired by Henri Barbusse's writings and was influential in Scandinavian debate in the thirties) and helped start the modernistic journal *Spektrum* in 1931. Though Boye was married from 1929 to 1932 to a Clarté friend, she had been torn by sexual ambivalence since an early age. In 1932 she sought psychoanalytic help in Berlin. Boye committed suicide in April 1941. Hjalmar Gullberg* wrote one of his greatest poems about her death, "Död amazon" (Dead Amazon).

Boye's early collections of poems, *Moln* (1922; Clouds) and *Gömda land* (1924; Hidden Lands) are pleasing but vague and influenced by Vilhelm Ekelund.*

In all her work a tension exists between rigid moralism and spontaneous instinct. In *Härdarna* (1927; The Hearths) her disillusion with Christianity and embrace of "faith in life" together with a painful knowledge of being different are articulated.

In *För trädets skull* (1935; For the Sake of the Tree) form and point of view are influenced by psychoanalysis in the manner she postulates in the essay "Språket bortom logiken" (Language beyond Logic). The symbolic language both confesses and hides her tragic personal split. Boye reaches equally high in the posthumously published *De sju dödssynderna* (1941; The Seven Deadly Sins), particularly in the short, simple poems about love and death.

Boye's best prose fiction is the negative utopia *Kallocain* (1940; trans. 1966), inspired by fears of nazism and communism.

Boye's lyrical production was fastidious, but cut short. Her finest poems have an original rhythm and a religious seriousness that fully express her "faith in life" and assure her rank among the great.

FURTHER WORKS

Merit vaknar (1933); *Uppgörelser* (1934); *Kris* (1934); *För lite* (1936); *Ur funktion* (1940); *Samlade Skrifter*, II vols. (1948–1950).

FURTHER TRANSLATIONS

To a Friend (1985).

REFERENCES

Abenius, Margit, *Drabbad av renhet* (Stockholm, 1950); Tegen, Gunhild, "Karin Boye in Memoriam." *American-Scandinavian Review* 30.3 (1942); Vowles, Richard B., "Ripeness Is All: A Study in Karin Boye's Poetry." *Bulletin of the American-Swedish Institute* (Spring 1952).

Margareta Mattsson

Boyson, Emil. Norwegian poet, novelist, and translator, b. 4 September 1897, Larvik, d. 1979, Oslo.

In all his works, Boyson strives for the creation, awareness, and maintenance of self in a complicated modern society. His poetical prose is full of reflections, fantasy, and mood. *Yngre Herre på besøk* (1936; Young Gentleman on a Visit) deals with split personality and identity shifts; it is important technically for Boyson's use of stream of consciousness. In *Vandring mot havet* (1937; Journey to the Sea) an insignificant person turns inward to form a personality in a living relationship to his past.

Boyson began writing poetry as early as 1917, but since his work was years ahead of time for Norway—he was strongly influenced by the French symbolists, Charles Baudelaire, Paul Verlaine, and Stéphane Mallarmé, of whom he made several translations, and also by English metaphysical poetry and the German expressionists—he had difficulty getting it published. In his lyrical debut in 1934, *Varsler og Møter* (Signs and Meetings), he turned to more traditional forms, and only later did some of his earlier poems appear. This caused some confusion about his development, making some critics think that he developed a more modernistic style, when it had actually been there from the beginning.

Boyson sought timeless and universal values in poetry, using simple, concrete images to reveal fundamental human experience, to analyze consciousness, and to preserve individuality. His love poems are particularly well done.

Boyson hated and condemned the nazis, but in *Sjelen og Udyret* (1946; Soul and Monster) he offered some gripping poems about the psychological aftermath of the war and the ever-present danger of becoming like those we hate.

Although Boyson completed most of his slight production before World War II, he enjoyed renewed popularity with the coming of the modernist generation in the 1960s. To an ever-increasing degree, Boyson has awakened the interest of a younger generation of readers and has become a model for them.

FURTHER WORKS

Sommertørst (1927); *Tegn og Tydning* (1935); *Gjemt i Mørket* (1939); *Gjenkjennelse* (1957); *Udvalgte dikt* (1959); *Europeisk Poesi* (1965); *70 dikt* (1974).

REFERENCES

Aarnes, Asbjørn, et al., ed., *Poesi og virkelighet* (Oslo, 1967); Hultengreen, Rudolf, "Emil Boyson," in his *Nye profiler i norsk lyrik* (Oslo, 1944).

Walter D. Morris

Brandes, Georg. Danish literary critic, b. 4 February 1842, Copenhagen, d. 19 February 1927, Copenhagen.

Brandes was born in 1842 into an unorthodox, prosperous Jewish family in Copenhagen. After his "Studentereksamen" in 1859, he at first studied law but soon shifted over into comparative literature and philosophy. In 1864 he passed his magister's degree in comparative literature (æsthetics). He had been the most brilliant and promising student of the Danish professors Carsten Hauch, Hans Brøchner, and Rasmus Nielsen.

As a literary critic the young Brandes at first followed in the footsteps of Johan

Ludvig Heiberg* with his formalistic insistence on the strict separation of literary genres. But after a couple of educational journeys abroad (1866; 1870–1871), Brandes came in contact with modern French positivistic and psychological literary criticism (Hippolyte Taine and Charles-Augustin Sainte-Beuve). He became a personal friend of Taine's and in 1870 defended his doctoral dissertation on Taine's literary theories: *Den franske Æstetik i vore Dage* (French Aesthetics in Our Time). Brandes collection of essays, *Kritiker og Portrœter* (Critiques and Portraits), of 1870 shows clear influence from both Taine and Sainte-Beuve. In 1869 he had translated John Stuart Mill's *The Subjection of Women* into Danish.

On 3 November 1871, at the University of Copenhagen Brandes started a series of lectures on *Hovedstrømninger i det Nittende Aarhundredes Literatur* (6 vols., 1872–1890; *Main Currents in Nineteenth Century Literature*, 6 vols., 1901–1905). In the opening lecture Brandes stated some of his basic convictions and critical theories. He advocated the right to free research and free thought. He said that he considered it an honor and a duty to champion these ideas. He considered modern Danish (Scandinavian) literature conservative, not to say reactionary and pointed to liberal movements on the Continent and in England. "In Scandinavia we are as usual," he caustically observed, "forty years behind the times!" He called for more realism in Scandinavian literature and proclaimed: "A modern literature is only alive insofar as it takes problems up for debate," words that were to have a profound effect on Danish (Scandinavian) literature during the next two decades. The lectures on the *Main Currents* were on French, German, and English literary movements in the nineteenth century, but Brandes constantly draws (humiliating) comparisons between progressive Continental and English works and their stale Scandinavian counterparts. He goes out of his way to nettle his northern contemporaries.

Brandes lectures created a furor in Copenhagen. They antagonized conservative circles because of their defiantly anti-clerical tone and critical attitude toward Danish romanticism ("the Golden Age"). On the other hand, they aroused the enthusiasm of radical and liberal writers who flocked around Brandes in what came to be known as "The Modern Breakthrough" in Scandinavian literature. The Modern Breakthrough can be characterized briefly as a period of realism and naturalism, 1870–1890. It started in Denmark with Brandes and his activities but soon came to encompass all of Scandinavia. In the 1890s there developed a neoromantic or symbolistic reaction against it.

In 1872 the professorship in comparative literature at the University of Copenhagen became vacant through the death of Carsten Hauch. Brandes was the obvious candidate for the position, but it was denied him because of the radicalism of his views. In 1874–1877 he published, together with his brother Edvard B., the literary journal *Det Nittende Aarhundrede* (The Nineteenth Century). In 1877 this journal had to cease publication, and angered by all the opposition against him in Denmark, Brandes left for voluntary exile in Berlin. His five years in Germany were a productive period in his long productive life. He published, among other things, *Søren Kierkegaard* (1877) and *Esaias Tegnér* (1878). His studies in Berlin also enabled him to publish, a few years later, the monographs on *Disraëli* (1878; *Lord Beaconsfield*, 1880) and *Ferdinand Lassalle* (1884; *Ferdinand Lassalle*, 1911).

In 1882 a number of friends in Copenhagen succeeded in persuading Brandes to return to Denmark. They had managed to procure funds that would assure him the equivalent of a professor's salary. The first book he published after his return was *Det moderne Gennembruds Mænd* (1883; The Men of the Modern Breakthrough). In this work the general, as it has been said, reviews his troops. How loyal to the cause was the old guard? The Danish writers included in the book were: J. P. Jacobsen,* Holger Drachmann,* Sophus Schandorph, Erik Skram, Edvard Brandes, and the two famous Norwegians Henrik Ibsen* and Bjørnstjerne Bjørnson.*

After his launching of the Modern Breakthrough in 1871, Brandes's second major critical feat was his discovery of Friedrich Nietzsche in the late 1880s. Brandes himself had secretly been growing tired of the "program" of the 1870s ("taking problems up for debate"). Something different was indicated, and Friedrich Nietzsche's aristocratic philosophy was a welcome change. Brandes lectured on Nietzsche at the University of Copenhagen in the spring of 1888. He introduced August Strindberg,* who at this time was staying in Denmark, to the writings of Nietzsche, and a correspondence developed between the two famous misogynists. In 1889–1890 Brandes became involved in a polemic with Professor Harald Høffding over Nietzsche's philosophy. To Nietzsche's and Brandes's "Aristocratic Radicalism" Høffding opposed a more "Democratic Radicalism."

Brandes' capacity for work did not abate with the advent of old age. The last phase of his life was as productive as any of the earlier periods. He published a number of big monographs on some of history's greats: *William Shakespeare* (3 vols., 1895–1896; *William Shakespeare, A Critical Study*, 1898), *Wolfgang Goethe* (2 vols., 1915; *Wolfgang Goethe*, 1936), *Cajus Julius Caesar* (2 vols., 1918), and *Michelangelo Buonarotti* (2 vols., 1921; *Michelangelo, His Life, His Times, His Era*, 1963). Some of the old Brandes polemic writings against Christianity seem less important today, for example, *Sagnet om Jesus* (1925; *Jesus, a Myth*, 1927).

Brandes is the most important literary critic and historian that Denmark has produced over the last one hundred years. During the Modern Breakthrough his influence and authority were immense, not only in Denmark but in all of Scandinavia. Great writers like Ibsen and Strindberg, among many others, have expressed the debt they owed to him. But though Brandes lived until 1927, his influence in Scandinavia had culminated by 1890. Many of the young Danish writers of the 1890s turned against him, for example, Karl Gjellerup,* Johannes Jørgensen,* and Helge Rode.* Some of the older naturalists—J. P. Jacobsen and Herman Bang*—were too independent to follow him slavishly. Henrik

Pontoppidan,* also, went his own ways. Brandes is, however, still very much alive even in modern Denmark, as is testified by the many books that have been published on him there in recent years: he is still controversial.

FURTHER WORKS

Dualismen i vor nyeste Philosophie (1866); *Æsthetiske Studier* (1869); *Forklaring og Forsvar: En Antikritik* (1872); *Mennesker og Værker i nyere europæisk Litteratur* (1883); *Ludvig Holberg. Et Festskrift* (1884); *Berlin som tysk Rigshovedstad* (1885); *Indtryk fra Polen* (1888; *Poland. A Study of the Land, People and Literature*, 1903); *Indtryk fra Rusland* (1888; *Impressions of Russia*, 1889, 1966, 1968); *Essays. Danske Personligheder* (1889); *Essays. Fremmede Personligheder* (1889); *Undenlandske Egne og Personligheder* (1893); *Samlede Skrifter*, vols. 1–12 (1899–1902), vols. 13–18 (1903–1910); *Levned*, 3 vols. (1905–1908); *Armand Carrel* (1911); *Fugleperspektiv* (1913); *Verdenskrigen* (1916; *The World at War*, 1917); *François de Voltaire*, 2 vols. (1916–1917; trans. 1930, 1964); *Napoleon og Garibaldi* (1917); *Sønderjylland under prøjsisk Tryk* (1919); *Tragediens anden Del, Fredsslutningen* (1919); *Taler* (1920); *Hellas* (1925; *Hellas, Travels in Greece*, 1926, 1969); *Petrus* (1926); *Urkristendom* (1927).

FURTHER TRANSLATIONS

German Literature, in *Academy* 14 (1878); *New Danish and Norwegian Poetry*, in *Academy* 16 (1879); *Eminent Authors of the Nineteenth Century* (1886); *Henrik Ibsen, Bjørnstjerne Bjørnson* (1899, 1964); *Recollections of My Childhood and Youth* (1906); *On Reading* (1906); *Anatole France* (1908); *Friedrich Nietzsche* (1909, 1972); *Creative Spirits of the Nineteenth Century* (1924).

REFERENCES

Ahlström, Gunnar, *Georg Brandes' Hovedstrømninger* (Lund, 1937); Asmundsson, Doris R., "America Meets Georg Brandes." *Scandinavian Review* 65.1 (1977); Fenger, Henning, *Georg Brandes' læreår* (Copenhagen, 1955); Hertel, Hans and Sven Møller Kristensen, eds., *The Activist Critic* (Copenhagen, 1980); Kristensen, Sven Møller, "Georg Brandes Research: A Survey." *Scandinavica* 2 (1963); Larsen, Sven, "Georg Brandes' Views on American Literature." *Scandinavian Studies* 22.4 (1950); Moritzen, Julius, *Georg Brandes in Life and Letters* (Newark, N.J., 1922); Nolin, Bertil, *Georg Brandes* (Boston, 1976).

Børge Gedsø Madsen

Brandt, Jørgen Gustava. Danish poet, essayist, fiction writer, b. 13 March 1929 in Copenhagen.

In 1946 Brandt studied painting and lived in Marseille during 1947–1948. He has worked as a journalist for various magazines and papers and at present works for Danish Radio in the Cultural Department.

The author of over forty books, including poetry, novels, short stories, essays, and reminiscences, Brandt is best known for his steady production of the poetry of highest quality and his continual experimentations with language. His debut book was *Korn i Pelegs mark* (1949; Wheat in Peleg's Field). His work came

to its full power in *Fragment af imorgen* (1960; Fragment of Tomorrow), passionate and reflective lyrics written in the high style.

While his contemporaries have been interested in a literature of engagement
and confrontation, Brandt has written a poetry of introspection, openness, au-
dacity, and affirmation. He has long been an admirer of Zen, T. S. Eliot, and
Henry Miller.

Writing about the art of poetry in *Hvad angaar poesi* (1982; As Far As Poetry
Is Concerned), he best sums up his own aesthetic:

That Epicurus attracts me is probably due to two things I see in him: the sovereignty of
sensuality and the deepest tendency to believe in nothing. (Thus I admit that I "make
capital of him," he strengthens my immediate experience, or more correctly: a method
of experiencing!) There is nothing a priori with him, reality becomes autosymbolic. By
beginning with rejecting all "meaning" and thus all meanings in existence, it happened
that things themselves began to speak to him, everything flowed in from *outside,* from
that which isn't ourselves, and which thereby acquired meaning. Abandonment to this
experience was a pure enrichment of the senses and enlightening of thought.

Brandt is a mystical poet of the senses who emphasizes the intensity of the
ordinary. He is usually more interested in the rhythm of experience than grasping
for conclusions. His experimentation with language often leads to "difficult"
poetry. His poem "Bi lidt, du er ingen engel" (Settle Down, You're No Angel)
can perhaps be understood only in relation to the techniques of action painting.

A trip to Israel in 1977 led to an awakening of Brandt's interest in his roots
and to the book *Her kan samtale føres* (1978; Here Conversation Can Be Carried
On), and a number of his later poems deal with his experience in Israel.

Brandt is a poet's poet. His influence on the younger poets in Denmark is
enormous, and though his general audience is not large, he has a high reputation
among other poets and his books have been translated into Hebrew, Italian, and
English.

FURTHER WORKS

Tjørneengen (1953); *Dragespor* (1957); *Udflugter* (1961); *Janushoved* (1962); *Etablis-
sementet* (1965); *Der er æg i mit skæg* (1966); *Ateliers* (1967); *Stof* (1968); *Digt på min
fødselsdag* (1969); *Kvinden på Lüneburg Hede* (1969); *Vendinger* (1971); *De nødstedte
djævle er de værste* (1972); *Pink Champagne* (1973); *Den finske sømand* (1973); *Her
omkring* (1974); *M. A. Goldschmidt. En tekstmosaik* (1974); *Lyset i stenene* (1974); *Mit
hjerte i København* (1975); *Jatháram* (1976); *Regnansigt* (1976); *Almanak* (1977); *Ophold*
(1977); *Oh Israel* (1978); *Tidens fylde* (1979); *Ud af intet kommer du blødt gående* (1979);
Idiotes (1980); *Vente på et pindsvin* (1981); *Serie* (1981); *Hop* (1982); *Saften og døden*
(1985); *Emanation—23 besøg i billedhuggerens værksted* (1985); *Harlekinade* (1985);
Scala-Suite/lys (1986).

FURTHER TRANSLATIONS

Contemporary Danish Poetry, ed. Line Jensen et al. (1977); *Orbis* 27/28 (1977); *Tête à
Tête* (1978); *Selected Longer Poems* (1983).

REFERENCES

Holk, Iben, ed., *Livstegn: En bog om Jørgen Gustava Brandts Forfatterskab* (Copenhagen, 1979); Kromann, Jette, "Jørgen Gustava Brandt" in *Digtere på baand*, vol. 1 (Copenhagen, 1966); Larsen, Finn Stein, "Jørgen Gustava Brandt" in *Danske digtere i det 20. århundrede*, ed. Frederik Nielsen and Ole Restrup, vol. 4 (Copenhagen, 1966); Ørnsbo, Jess, "Jørgen Gustava Brandt" in *Danske digtere i det 20. århundrede*, ed. Frederik Nielsen and Ole Restrup, vol. 3 (Copenhagen, 1966).

Alexander Taylor

Branner, Hans Christian. Danish novelist and short story writer, b. 23 June 1903, Ordrup, d. 23 April 1966, Copenhagen.

For several decades after World War II Branner and Martin A. Hansen* were considered to be Denmark's foremost writers of fiction. Unlike Hansen, Branner was born into an academic milieu; he attempted to become an actor, worked briefly in the publishing business, but from his thirtieth year, he supported himself through his writing. Like other young writers of the 1930s, such as Hans Kirk,* William Heinesen,* and Hansen, he started with the collective novel, that is, *Legetøj* (1936; Toys). Besides embodying the social realism of the decade, the novel reads as an allegory directed against the fascist threat. The person who yearns for power and who delights in subjugating other human beings remained central to Branner's *oeuvre*. Branner's ensuing works suggest that his main interest lies in the probing of the mind rather than in depicting a social milieu: *Drømmen om en Kvinde* (1941; The Dream of a Woman) shows not only a strong influence from psychoanalysis, but also an inclination to put female figures on a pedestal. Susanne in Branner's best known novel, *Rytteren* (1947; *The Riding Master*, 1951, *The Mistress*, 1953), is attracted to a ruthless riding master, but she eventually finds that a seemingly weak humanist, a doctor named Clemens (Branner does not shy away from quite obvious symbolism), is the man who is able to provide her with hope for the future. Branner's themes place him among those many Scandinavian writers who, during the postwar decades, used existentialism as a frame of reference.

Branner's characters are often, albeit vaguely, seeking a better, more authentic existence and, at the same time, are tormented by guilt for having made others suffer. The long, dramatic novel *Ingen kender natten* (1955; *No One Knows the Night*, 1958), which takes place one night during the Nazi occupation of Denmark, depicts a quest for clearer moral guidelines in a world that Branner unfailingly finds to be complex and ambiguous. Branner has also tried his hand at drama, and his most successful play, *Søskende* (1952; *The Judge*, 1955), is an effective, if technically quite traditional, confrontation between three siblings, who are brought to investigate the reasons for their failures in life.

If Branner's longer fiction at times seems too marred by heavy-handed allegorical patterns, his short stories will surely withstand the passing of time. In *To minutters stilhed* (1944; *Two Minutes of Silence*, 1966, contains stories from other volumes as well) and other collections, he manages with remarkable sensitivity to capture the inner life of a child. Like Branner's mature characters, the child is in a state of crisis, and it becomes obvious that the crisis, if unresolved, may well result in crippling the person mentally. Like Ernest Hemingway, Branner is most successful if he need not work out an elaborate plot for his characters, but can merely give a glimpse of a person caught in a crisis. In some longer texts, for example, *Bjergene* (1953; The Mountains), Branner conducts the sort of experiments with narrative form that were nearly obligatory for serious writers in the 1950s, and these forays into modernism—which he also attempted to make in some plays written for the radio—show that he was constantly seeking new ways to express his ever-present sense of crisis.

FURTHER WORKS

Barnet leger ved stranden (1937); *Om lidt er vi borte* (1939); *Historien om Børge* (1942; The Story of Børge, 1973); *Humanismens krise* (1950; *Thermopylæ*, 1974); *Vandring langs floden* (1956); *Ariel* (1963); *Fem radiospil* (1965); *Tre Skuespil* (1968).

REFERENCES

Dinesen, Isak, "H. C. Branner, The Riding Master" in her *Daguerreotypes* (Chicago, 1979); Madsen, Børge Gedsø, "H. C. Branner: A Modern Humanist." *American-Scandinavian Review* 47.1 (1959); Markey, Thomas L., "H. C. Branner: An Encomium." *Scandinavica* 7.1 (1968); Markey, Thomas L., *H. C. Branner* (Boston, 1973); Mishler, William, "The Theme of Reflection in H. C. Branner's *Ariel.*" *Scandinavian Studies* 47.1 (1975); Vowles, Richard B., "Bergman, Branner and Off-stage Dying." *Scandinavian Studies* 33.1 (1961); Vosmar, Jørn, *H. C. Branner* (Copenhagen, 1959).

Niels Ingwersen

Brekke, Paal. Norwegian poet, novelist, critic, translator, b. 17 September 1923, Røros.

A student in Oslo at the outbreak of World War II, Brekke escaped to Sweden, where he made his debut as a writer. Although he experimented in several genres during this period, the most interesting work Brekke produced was a novel, *På flukt* (1942; In Flight), which incorporated many of his own experiences as a refugee. Perhaps the most important factor in Brekke's artistic development while in Sweden was his exposure to the movements of Swedish and European modernism, which had not yet reached Norway.

Upon returning to Norway in 1945 Brekke became the chief spokesperson for the new movement. In 1949 Brekke published a translation of T. S. Eliot's *The Waste Land* and a volume of poetry, *Skyggefektning* (Shadow Fencing). This collection exhibits all the characteristic forms of European modernism, and is widely recognized as a breakthrough for literary modernism in Norwegian literature. Two novels from the next decade, *Aldrende Orfeus* (1951; Aging Orpheus) and *Og hekken vokste kjempehøy* (1953; And the Hedge Grew Ever Higher), though not particularly successful at the time, are now recognized as forerunners of modern Norwegian prose, breaking with the tradition of realism.

En munnfull av Ganges (1963; A Mouthful of Ganges), marks a turning point in Brekke's work. Reporting on a trip to India, Brekke documents his first encounter with the poverty and repression of the Third World. His work reflects an increasing political engagement and his style becomes more direct and simpler in form. Brekke won the literary critics' prize for *Aftenen er stille* (1972; The Evening Is Quiet), poetry and prose texts about the lives of the elderly.

Brekke has earned a solid reputation as a poet, novelist, critic, and translator. He has edited a number of collections of Norwegian and foreign poetry. Perhaps his major contribution to Norwegian literature is the establishment of modernism as a viable literary movement in Norway.

FURTHER WORKS

Av din jord er vi til (1942); *Jeg gikk så lange veier* (1945); *Damen vil helst ikke brennes* (1950); *Cocktail selskapet* (1951); *Modernistisk lyrikk fra 8 land* (1955); *Den unge lyrikken 1939–1955* (1955); *Løft min krone, vind fra intet* (1957); *Amerikansk lyrikk, et utvalg i norsk gjendiktning* (ed. and trans.) (1957); *Roerne fra Itaka* (1960); *Nordisk poetisk aarbok* (1963–1967); *Det skjeve smil i rosa* (1965); *Det er alltid nå* (1967); *Fakkeltog* (1968); *Granatmannen kommer* (1968); *Norsk lyrikk nå* (1968); *Til sin tid. Journalistikk 1945–70* (1970); *Aftenen er stille* (1972); *Paal Brekke. Dikt 1949–1972* (1978).

Torild M. Homstad

Bremer, Fredrika. Swedish novelist, b. 17 August 1801, Åbo (Turku), Finland, d. 3 December 1865, Årsta, Sweden.

Bremer had an unhappy and lonely childhood and youth as one of six children of rather strict, eccentric parents. She published her first work, *Teckningar utur hvardagslifvet* (1828; *Scenes from Everyday Life*), in order to raise money for charity work on her family's estate. This collection of tales brought her almost instant fame and popularity. This was due in part to the growth of the middle class in Sweden, and this group's interest in reading works that were a reflection of their lives and concerns.

Bremer was also well known in the rest of Europe and the United States, due to the numerous translations of her works. In 1849–1851, she traveled to the United States and met with the leading cultural and literary figures of the day. This trip influenced her profoundly, especially in regard to her views on women. In the United States, she had been impressed by the active role of Quaker women in political issues, and the various institutions of higher learning for women that she visited. On her return to Sweden she wrote her most famous novel, *Hertha* (1856; *Hertha*, or *The Three Sisters*, 1856), which expresses her attitude toward the role of women in Sweden. In this novel, Bremer criticizes Swedish society for providing women with no education and training. Bremer believed that women should work for the betterment of society and its members. *Hertha* generated much discussion that eventually led to political and economic reforms for Swedish women.

Bremer was a prolific writer, and of great importance to the growth of the novel in Sweden. Her successful career, and the quality of her works, inspired many of the women, and men, prose writers who followed her.

FURTHER WORKS

Samlade skrifter i urval, 6 vols. (1868–1872); *Tvenne efterlemnade skrifter,* ed. A. Hierta (1902); *Fredrika Bremers brev,* 4 vols. (1915–1920); *Den unga Amerika,* ed. Klara Johanson (1927); *Fredrika Bremer i brev,* ed. Ellen Kleman (1944); *Livet i Gamla världen,* ed. G. Fredén (1961).

FURTHER TRANSLATIONS

Works, 4 vols. (1852–1853; 1909–1913); *Life, Letters, and Post-humous Works,* ed. Charlotte Bremer (1884); *America of the Fifties: Letters,* ed. A. B. Benson (1924).

REFERENCES

Axberger, Gunnar, *Jaget och skuggorna* (Stockholm, 1951); Bremer, Charlotte, ed., *Sjelfbiografiska anteckningar, bref och efterlemnade skrifter jemte en teckning af hennes lefnad och personlighet,* 2 vols. (Örebro, 1868); Holm, Birgitta, *Fredrika Bremer och den borgerliga romanens födelse* (Stockholm, 1981); Montén, Karin, *Fredrika Bremer in Deutschland* (Neumünster, 1981); Qvist, G., *Fredrika Bremer och kvinnans emancipation* (Göteborg, 1969); Wägner, Elin, *Fredrika Bremer* (Stockholm, 1949); Westman-Berg, Karin, and Birgitta Onsell, eds., *Fredrika Bremer* (Uppsala, 1979); Wieselgren, Greta, *Fredrika Bremer och verkligheten* (Stockholm, 1978).

Melissa Lowe Shogren

Bridget, Saint. *See* Birgitta, Saint.

Brøgger, Suzanne. Danish novelist and essayist, b. 18 November 1944, Copenhagen.

The writings of Suzanne Brøgger are created as a mixture of genres, both fiction and nonfiction. Her own life is the object of reflection in these books. Yet the public display of her private life does not necessarily lead to a lack of political commitment or existential insight. Relating everything to herself, she at the same time distinguishes herself from everything, thereby eliminating the border between the public and private spheres. She presents her own personal life as an alternative to the traditional life of women with its inherent contradictions. She works through this alternative in her writings, trying to dissolve the contradictions that are present in women's literature elsewhere, including the conflict between work and love. The character ''Suzanne Brøgger'' in her works has decided once and for all that she does not want to work, in the traditional sense of the word. This means that she does not look at writing as a kind of work. Writing is a way of life. As the title of her first novel, *Fri os fra kærligheden* (1973; *Deliver Us From Love,* 1976) indicates, the subject of her books is not personal love. Instead she describes a larger, expansive community of people whose relationships to one another are based on Eros. Her books express an attitude that fears stagnation and stasis and encourages change and creativity. The dynamics of change become an existential principle: "Now I will tell you the best way to live is like a fish in the water or a bird in the air. It is best to live in motion."

The reflective essay is her characteristic genre. This is a natural manifestation of the fact that she is expressing a personal attitude in her works. Her lifestyle is the result of a conscious moral choice. She reenacts her own life in fiction. Moments of weakness, anxiety, loneliness, and inadequacy, which permeate the more confessional writings in women's literature, are conspicuously absent in Brøgger's works. This means that the author's will to enact the alternative has become one with her literary intent.

Creme Fraiche (1978) is a kaleidoscopic journalistic description of the author's own international escapades, a gigantic world tour that includes visits to both Eastern and Western capitals, including Saigon, Bangkok, New York, and London. Her visit to New York includes conversations with Henry Miller, her much-admired "mentor" who, like herself, advocates an anti-bourgeois lifestyle. Again she depicts her frightening closeness to life, love, pain, and death. Her own words serve best to illustrate the style of *Creme Fraiche*: "I'm not a poet, but a choreographer. I choreograph the movement that already *is* in order to make it more obvious, illuminating, attractive and frightening. It is not the goal of this movement that is important, it is the dance itself."

Her most critically acclaimed work, the epic poem *Tone* (1981), is about characters from the street whose lives are intense and passionate, characters who break with habit and with the bureaucratic and patriarchal organization that we call society. The heroine, Tone, lives life in the streets, full of intense happiness and closeness to life and death. *Tone* is about life as creativity and desire. It is about choosing to live a life of risk by exposing one's soul, thus rejecting stagnation, which is synonymous with death. This is Brøgger's most complex work. It reveals many of the same images and themes found in her early works, but these are treated more seriously, less superficially, in a characteristic interplay of styles that break with and underscore each other.

FURTHER WORKS

Kærlighedens veje og vildveje (1975); *En gris som har været oppe at slås kan man ikke stege* (1979); *Brøg: 1965–1980* (1980); *Ja* (1984), *Den pebrede susen* (1986).

REFERENCES

Kistrup, Jens, "You Shouldn't Be Allowed to Put up with It," in *Out of Denmark,* ed. Bodil Wamberg (Copenhagen, 1985).

Jody Jensen

Brofeldt, Johannes. *See* Aho, Juhani.

Brorson, Hans Adolf. Danish poet, b. 20 June 1694, Randerup, d. 3 June 1764, Ribe.

Brorson, the son of a Lutheran pastor, spent his early years in hardship but, after his father's death in 1704, he studied at the Latin school in Ribe and in 1712 at Copenhagen university. There Brorson displayed an enthusiastic interest in theology, literature, and history, but overexertion and personal difficulties led to a physical collapse. During his recovery, Brorson's religious fervor was strengthened by his exposure to German pietism, which his brother and uncle were spreading in Denmark. In 1729, Brorson, now a minister in Tønder, translated several German pietist hymns into Danish, which, along with many original poems, appeared in the collection *Troens rare Klenodie* (1739; Rare Jewel of Faith). In 1741 Brorson became bishop of Ribe, where he was regarded as a kind and vigilant administrator. There Brorson continued to compose devotional poetry (often accompanying the songs on his lute), and the posthumous collection *Svane-Sang* (1765; Swan-Song) betrayed an aesthetic sophistication and an increasingly emotional religious passion.

Brorson's poetry was imbued with the personal and intense devotion of the pietists. Although many of the songs suggest the ecstasy and sensuality of mystical poetry, Brorson remained an orthodox Lutheran writer. He preferred to describe the spiritual yearnings of earthbound man who did not so much strive for a mystical union with God as he did for his love, grace, and forgiveness. In his presentation of the soul's progress from the world to heaven, Brorson employed a vivid, realistic vocabulary to appeal to his congregation for whom the hymns were composed. His poems also displayed his accomplished use of religious imagery from both the biblical and the mystical traditions as well as his sensitivity to rhythm and assonance. In *Svane-Sang*, Brorson continued his experimentation with meter and rhetorical figures and adapted popular musical forms (aria; cantata) for his religious lyric.

Brorson has been justly classified as one of the great Danish religious poets. His works recall the piety of Danish baroque lyric, but their unique personal religious sentiments continue to ensure them a major place in Danish devotional literature.

FURTHER WORKS

Samlede Skrifter, ed. L. J. Koch, 3 vols., (Copenhagen, 1951, 1953, 1956); *Visitationsberetninger og Breve*, ed. L. J. Koch (Copenhagen, 1960).

REFERENCES

Koch, L. J., *Salmedigteren Brorson* (Copenhagen, 1918); Koch, L. J., *Brorson-Studier* (Copenhagen, 1936).

James A. Parente, Jr.

Brú, Heðin (pseud. of Hans Jacob Jacobsen). Faroese novelist and short story writer, b. 17 August 1901, Skálavík.

As a boy Brú joined the Faroese fishing fleet, but in 1919 he turned to study, finally graduating from the Royal Veterinary and Agricultural High School in

Denmark in 1928. On returning to the Faroe Islands he worked as an agricultural consultant.

Brú's works reflect everyday life in the Faroes, normally in the villages, but occasionally in Tórshavn. The first, semi-autobiographical novels, *Lognbrá* (1930; *Mirage*) and its sequel *Fastatøkur* (1935; *Firm Grip*), portraying the childhood and youth of a village boy, contain the first realistic descriptions of the life of the Faroese fishermen. Alongside the realism goes a poetical element verging on the symbolical. Brú's principal work is the short novel *Feðgar á Ferð* (1940; *The Old Man and His Sons*, 1970), showing the generational conflict in the period of social transition in the 1930s. It is written with a keen sense of humor accompanied by a sensitive understanding of both generations as the father buys more whalemeat than he can afford and tries desperately to pay for it without resorting to the borrowing that the younger generation is now willing to accept.

Many would argue that Brú's greatest strength is in his short stories, where he shows a penetrating understanding of village life and mentality. His characters are often slightly larger than life, and his situations dramatic; humor and an awareness of the darker as well as the lighter sides of village life go hand in hand, often accompanied by nature descriptions of great beauty. Some of his stories are more like essays, poetic presentations of his own travels, showing a deep reverence for Faroese people, nature, and history.

Brú has an unfailing sense of style and has fashioned a Faroese literary tradition. He is generally considered the greatest writer of Faroese prose.

FURTHER WORKS

Fjallaskuggin (1936); *Flókatrøll* (1948); *Leikum fagert* (1963); *Purkhús* (1966); *Men livið lær* (1970); *Búravnurin* (1971); *Tað stóra takið* (1972); *Endurminningar* (1980).

FURTHER TRANSLATIONS

Faroese Short Stories. comp., Hedin Brønner (1972).

REFERENCES

Brønner, Hedin, "Heðin Brú, Faroese Novelist." *American-Scandinavian Review* 59.4 (1971); Brønner, Hedin, *Three Faroese Novelists* (New York, 1973); Jones, W. Glyn, "Fate and Fortune in the Work of Heðin Brú and Martin Joensen." *Northern Studies* 20 (1983); Jones, W. Glyn, "Types of Determinism in the Work of Heðin Brú and Martin Joensen." *Skandinavistik* 14.1 (1984).

W. Glyn Jones

Bull, Olaf. Norwegian lyric poet, b. 10 November 1883, Oslo, d. 23 June 1933, Oslo.

Bull, son of a successful regional novelist who was also a muscular Christian, rejected all his father stood for. Throughout his life he remained a bohemian and a nomad—"one of those whose cloak is his home" ("Sneen"[The Snow], 1913). Though he married three times, he never had a place of his own or a proper job, and he was constantly plagued by financial worry. Restless, he traveled ceaselessly, especially to France, which meant much to him long before his marriages, the last, to a Frenchwoman.

Poetry to Bull, as for the symbolists, was a means of subverting the tyranny of time, of seizing moments out of the flux of experience and perpetuating them in what William Butler Yeats called the "artifice of eternity." Having abandoned religion, Bull sought to redeem the loss through literary creation. Consequently, his lyricism is charged with a rare emotional intensity and intellectual passion. Several poems are the vehicles of a philosophical-religious quest à la Nietzsche, who had a profound impact on his mind. Whether his themes are love, nature, beauty, or the poet's self, the great nothingness, death, presents an ever-renewed challenge to his genius. Characteristic of his symbolist inspiration is also the rich vein of metapoetry in Bull's production; his meditations on the transmuting nature of the creative process elucidate the conditions of imaginative activity in a world stripped of transcendence.

Bull was a mature poet from the start. Already his first collection, *Digte* (1909; Poems), is profoundly personal, centered on the existential dialectic of life and death and dramatizing the violent tensions within the poet's conflicted psyche. Yet, Bull's poems are firmly lodged within sensory reality—observations of the seasons, of a familiar street, scenes and encounters from everyday life. Their main substance, however, is provided by a powerful, often visionary imagination, which sometimes creates a world of fable, fairy tale, or Wergelandian fantasy (e.g., "Gobelin," 1913), and by an intellect schooled in modern philosophy and science. Especially notable, both for its intellectual scope and its imaginative transmutation of scientific abstractions, is the grandiose cosmic fantasy "Ignis ardens" (wr. 1929, pub. 1932), an artistic synthesis of the evolution of life on a Bergsonian basis. Interestingly, the fragments of an *ars poetica* that Bull left behind work out a detailed parallel between the methods of scientific discovery and those of poetic creation (Brønsted, pp. 423–24).

Bull was not a facile poet; only by developing a cool mastery of his craft was he able to blend the often disparate elements that constituted his creative impulse—perception and memory, image and abstraction, reality and fantasy, picture and sound, spontaneous feeling and discursive thought. Nor does Bull make it easy for the reader, especially since he tends to eliminate transitions and uses abrupt juxtapositions in the modern manner. Sometimes his verse strains the very resources of poetic language. As Helge Krog* noted, "The rhythms are weighted down with compressed, intensely accentuated meaning, and at any moment the form seems about to break under the multitude and the rich variety of the themes" (*Ord och Bild* 27[1918]: 105). But if the reader collaborates with the poet, he will be rewarded—in such lyrics as "Fra Mezzaninvinduet" (1909; From the Mezzanine Window), "Bjærken" (1916; The Birch), "Metope" (1927), "Anima" (1930), and many others—by the production of a seamless web of verbal artistry.

Bull's poetic temperament was as manifold as his sense of form was exacting.

His poems express a kaleidoscope of contrary moods—devoutness and irreverence, gravity and whimsy, festiveness and the quotidian, ecstatic rapture and bleak despair. He is capable of the most lighthearted humor and tender pathos as well as irony and satire. In his conception of poetry as well as in his form, he is close to such twentieth-century greats as William Butler Yeats, Rainer Maria Rilke, Aleksandr Blok, Paul Valéry, and Wallace Stevens. The only reason he is not as well known is that he wrote in a so-called minor language.

FURTHER WORKS

Nye Digte (1913); *Digte og Noveller* (1916); *Kjærlighedens Farce*, with Helge Krog (1919); *Mitt Navn er Knoph* (1919); *Samlede digte* (1919); *Stjernerne* (1924); *Metope* (1927); *De hundrede aar* (1928); *Oinos og Eros* (1930); *Ignis ardens* (1932); *Samlede digte* (1934); *Dikt i utvalg*, ed. Jan Bull (1950).

REFERENCES

Bly, Robert, "A Note on Olaf Bull" (with six poems). *Sixties* 10 (Summer 1968); Brøndsted, Mogens, "Olaf Bull," in *Fremmede digtere i det 20. århundrede*, ed. Sven Møller Kristensen, vol. 1 (Copenhagen, 1957); Bull, Suzanne, *Ni år: Mitt liv med Olaf Bull* (Oslo, 1974); Elster, Kristian, "Three Lyric Poets of Norway: III. Olaf Bull." *American-Scandinavian Review* 13.11 (1925); Greiff, Trygve, *Olaf Bull: Taper og seirer* (Oslo, 1952); Lyngstad, Sverre, "Olaf Bull: A Passion for Poetry." *News of Norway* 41.1 (1984); Ofstad, Erna, *Olaf Bulls lyrikk: En analyse av konfliktene i et livssyn* (Oslo, 1955); Wyller, Egil A., *Tidsproblemet hos Olaf Bull: Et eksistens-filosofisk bidrag* (Oslo, 1959).

Sverre Lyngstad

C

Cajanello, duchessa di. *See* Leffler, Anne Charlotte.

Calamnius, Ilmari. *See* Kianto, Ilmari.

Canth, Minna. Finnish playwright and short story writer, b. 19 March 1844, Tampere, d. 12 May 1897, Kuopio.

Canth was a forty-year-old widow and a single parent with seven children when she began to write. At the same time, she began three years (1882–1884) of intensive study to familiarize herself with current literature and social theories. This experience transformed the former wife of a conservative teacher into a radical writer.

An acute social concern—a cry for improvement in the lives of women and workers—dominates Canth's early work. The play *Työmiehen vaimo* (1885; *A Workman's Wife*) presents the economic and moral dilemma of a woman at the end of the last century: her husband can legally, and with approval of society, drink up his wife's property and impregnate a young girl with no fear of the consequences. *Kovan onnen lapsia* (1888; Hardluck Children) examines the paradox of the poor: money is needed to survive, but when work is not available there is no money. In each play, there is no way out except to submit or to take the law in one's own hands, and each alternative leads to destruction.

The short story "Kauppa-Lopo" (1888; Thriftstore Lopo) sets off a respected but callous middle-class matron against a scorned peddler woman with a heart of gold.

In the play *Papin perhe* (1891; The Minister's Family), a psychological portrait of the main character replaces social concern as the main theme. The children of a clergyman champion new, independent thought and freedom of conscience against their conservative and dogmatic father. The result is a compromise between the old and the new. The Tolstoyan drama *Anna-Liisa* (1895) examines the development of a woman to acceptance of full responsibility for her actions. The title character is an exemplary young woman, respected by her neighbors, who as a teenager bore an illegitimate child, killed it, and succeeded in keeping the matter secret. As the play progresses, she moves toward a voluntary confession of her crime.

Canth had the courage and the talent to address the most important issues of her time. In her best works the structure is vigorous and her characterization powerful. "Kauppa-Lopo" is one of the better Finnish short stories. The plays *Papin perhe* and *Anna-Liisa* have been presented for almost a hundred years, and they remain part of the living literature of Finland.

FURTHER WORKS

Novelleja ja kertomuksia (1879); *Murtovarkaus* (1883); *Roinilan talossa* (1885); *Hanna* (1886); *Köyhää kansaa* (1886); *Salakari* (1887); *Lain mukaan* (1889); *Agnes* (1892); *Novelleja*, 2 vols. (1892); *Hän on Sysmästä* (1893); *Sylvi* (1893); *Spiritistinen istanto* (1894); *Kotoa pois* (1895); *Kauppaneuvos Toikka* (1897); *Agnes* (unfinished play, 1897); *Kootut teokset*, 4 vols. (1917–1920); *Kirjeitä vuosilta 1860–97* (1944); *Valitut teokset* (1953); *Suolavakka* (1945); *Minna Canthin kirjeet*, ed. Helle Kannila (1973).

FURTHER TRANSLATIONS

Finnish Short Stories, ed. Inkeri Väänänen-Jensen and K. Börje Vähämäki (1982); *Sanoi Minna Canth. Minna Canth—Pioneer Reformer. Extracts from Minna Canth's Works and Letters*, ed. Ritva Heikkilä (1987).

REFERENCE

Frenckell-Thesleff, Greta, *Minna Canth* (Helsinki, 1944).

Terttu Hummasti

Carpelan, Bo Gustaf Berelsson. Finland-Swedish poet, critic, novelist, translator, and writer of children's books, b. 25 October 1926, Helsinki.

Since Carpelan's first volume of verse, *Som en dunkel värme* (Like a Dark Warmth) appeared in 1946, he has published eleven volumes of poetry and several prose works. His early writings share similarities with the Finland-Swedish modernists of the 1920s—Edith Södergran,* Elmer Diktonius,* Rabbe Enckell*—who introduced expressionism and free verse into Swedish literature. Carpelan's early collections also reveal the influence of the heavy and profuse imagery of the Swedish poets of the 1940s.

Two major periods divide Carpelan's poetic oeuvre. The first one covers five collections published between 1946 and 1956. The second period begins with the collection *Landskapets förvandlingar* (1957; The Changing Landscape), which was followed by five more collections during the next twenty-two years. The last one of these, *Jag minns att jag drömde* (1979; I Remember Having a Dream) contains refined prose poems. In all of his poetry Carpelan presents life as a mystery but his approach to this mystery changes and develops. Although the language of his early works was deft, private, and intimate, it becomes sharp and simple later on.

Town and nature, sometimes the sea, and very often the poet's own recollections provide the setting for Carpelan's themes, which emphasize the infinite complexity of life. He extracts creative energy from uncertainty, doubt, and failure. The author's strength resides in freedom from any kind of prejudice and the lack of any sense of commitment.

In the collection *Gården* (1969; *The Courtyard*, 1982) Carpelan returns to his own childhood recollections from the depression of the 1930s. The first-person narrator tells about poverty and loneliness, asphalt streets, and a stunted tree growing in the backyard of a Helsinki apartment building, and of the echoing passages that connect one backyard to another. While everything is seen through the eyes of a child, Carpelan manages to weave into the poems a consciously meditative and analytical sense of perspective. Thus minor events and trivial details are raised to the level of significance: they become symbols of a way of life that has gone forever. Carpelan applies the same technique in his nature poems. Momentarily experienced feelings are allowed to grow in scale and depth until they become the bond between past and present.

The best known of Carpelan's prose works is *Rösterna i den sena timmen* (1971; *Voices at the Late Hour*, 1988). The novel, originally written as a radio play, describes the outbreak of nuclear war and the response of different people as death approaches.

Outside the Nordic countries Carpelan is mainly known for his outstanding books for young people, stories that display the same sensitivity as his poetry.

FURTHER WORKS

Du mörka overlevande (1947); *Variationer* (1950); *Minus sju* (1952); *Nicodemus, 19 år* (1952); *Moln* (1954); *Objekt för ord* (1954); *Ballad* (1957); *Sex tal ur samtiden* (1958); *Anders på ön* (1959); *Din gestalt bakom dörren* (1960); *Studier i Gunnar Björlings diktning 1922–1933* (1960); *Den svala dagen* (1961); *Anders i stan* (1962); *100 inhemska år* (1964); *En gammal mans dag* (1966); *Eva och/ja Erkki* (1966); *Krokodilen* (1966); *73 dikter* (1966); *Kuka teki murhan?* (1967); *Bågen* (1968; *The Wide Wings of Summer*, 1971, *The Bow Island*, 1971); *Janne*, with Carl Mesterton (1968); *Rösterna i den sena timmen* (1968); *Bonny och Clyde på Åland* (1969); *Lili*, with Henrik Tikkanen; *Paavo* (1969); *Tadd*, with Henrik Tikkanen (1969); *Paluu nuoruuteen* (1970); *André i människans lustgårdar* (1972); *Källan* (1973); *Paradiset* (1973; *Dolphins in the City*, 1976); *Rum vi engång levde i* (1974); *I de mörka rummen, i de ljusa* (1976); *Tre enhörningar dricker ur barndomens källa* (1976); *Vandrande skugga* (1977); *Det är kväll, det är mycket sent* (1978); *Slaktmånad* (1978); *Elämä jota elät* (1974, 1983); *Dikter från trettio år* (1980); *Julius Blom, ett huvud för sig* (1982); *Trösklar* (1982); *Dagen vänder* (1983); *Marginalia till grekisk o. romersk diktning* (1984); *Axel* (1986); *Armbandsuret* (1986).

FURTHER TRANSLATIONS

Scandinavian Review 68.4 (1980); *Books from Finland* 16.3 (1982); *Scandinavian Review* 70.4 (1982); *Swedish Book Review* 1 (1984).

REFERENCES

Ahokas, Jaakko A., "Two Poets of Finland: Paavo Haavikko and Bo Carpelan." *Books Abroad* 46.1 (1972); Huldén, Lars, "Swedish Poetry in Finland on the Threshold of the Eighties." *World Literature Today* 54.1 (1980); Laitinen, Kai, " Poems from 'Jag minns att jag drömde.' " *Books from Finland* 3 (1977).

Kai Laitinen

Children's Literature. Thanks to the international popularity of Hans Christian Andersen's* "fairy tales," as his *eventyr* are misnamed in English, and of Astrid Lindgren's* *Pippi Longstocking*, the Scandinavian countries are credited with having one of the richest bodies of children's literature in the world. Its richness is due in large part to the tensive co-existence of fantasies of this sort with a hearty strain of domestic realism. At times it seems that fantasy and realism vie for dominance, and the advocates of each must prove their case by striving for higher standards of quality.

The origins of Scandinavian children's literature were quite derivative and its development somewhat delayed, due to several nonliterary factors, such as a paper shortage, religious pietism that declared pleasure reading sinful, the employment of children in agricultural labor and early industry, and, in Norway, the lack of a common language. Literacy, however, was higher than elsewhere in Europe, thanks to Lutheranism, which encouraged the practice of reading Scripture in the vernacular. The requirement that those to be confirmed in the faith must "läsa för prästen," or read for the minister, had an unintended side effect: it created an audience of readers just literate enough to enjoy chapbooks, the predecessors of comic books. And comic books are still, in spite of their high-quality competition, the best-selling variety of children's reading.

Until the second decade of the nineteenth century, native literary works for children were rare and of limited appeal. The books read in upper-class families were translations or imitations of Continental literature. Children and adults both read Aesop's fables, translated first to Swedish in 1603. The earliest proponents of a literature especially for children were rationalist teachers and clergy. The objective of such a literature was to be moral education, following the principles of the Enlightenment, and didactic authors' prefaces made that purpose clear. The first two native children's books, *Den danske Skolelemester* (1766; The Danish Schoolmaster) and Johan Wellander's *Kronprinsens barnabok* (1780; The Crown Prince's Children's Book), as well as the first serial publication, C. G. Gjörwell's *Magazin for Swenska Ungdomen* (1777; Magazine for Swedish Youth) are good examples of literature in the service of education.

The Rousseauian romanticism that so deeply affected adult literature after the turn of the century also changed the nature of children's literature. The joint assumptions that children have a natural virtue unsullied by adult experience and that civilizations also have a childhood, the values of which are worth reclaiming, produced a national literature that drew on Norse myth and folktales. Erik Gustaf Geijer* and Arvid August Afzelius' *Svenska folkvisor* (1814–1817; Swedish Folk

Ballads), which included orally preserved nursery rhymes, was the first mani-festation of this. A Danish edition of the tales collected in Germany by the Brothers Grimm appeared in 1816 and won immense popularity. As a result, efforts were undertaken to publish the oral tales that had always been a prime form of entertainment for people of all ages. The Finnish national myth, the *Kalevala*,* was published in 1835, and stories based on Finnish folktales were collected and published by Eero Salmelainen in a four-volume work, *Suomen kansan satuja ja tarinoita* (1852–1866; Fairy Tales and Stories of the Finnish Nation). In Sweden George Stephens and G. O. Hyltén-Cavallius collected their *Svenska folksagor* (Swedish Folktales) in the 1840s. The most faithful followers of the meticulous Grimm method were P. C. Asbjørnsen and Jørgen Moe, whose first volume of Norwegian tales appeared in 1841. In the wake of Norway's independence from Denmark, Asbjørnsen and Moe sought to establish a truly Norwegian literature free of outside influence. This meant forging a new written language faithful to the idiom of the oral tales. These folktales, so significant to the development of a Norwegian national culture, have enjoyed an international readership as well, introducing trolls to the common pool of fantasy figures from which current writers for children draw.

Svend Grundtvig's collected Danish folktales have been overshadowed by the fanciful tales composed by Hans Christian Andersen (first volume 1835), who was inspired by the Brothers Grimm but chose to rely on his own fantasy and his previous familiarity with folktale elements rather than scholarly research. His well-deserved international fame is, unfortunately, based in large part on faulty, embellished translations from the German editions of his work and on Disney bowdlerizations. Eric Haugaard's complete edition of the Andersen tales (1974) has helped rectify that by retaining the stories' conversational simplicity, as well as their occasional horrors, which were often omitted to spare readers' emotions. The legacy Andersen left to his successors was an emphasis on en-tertainment rather than edification, reliance on fantasy and a natural storytelling capacity, empathy for characters, symbolic complexity, and an appreciation of the homely elements of everyday life.

Zacharias Topelius,* a Swedish-speaking Finn, was the first noted writer to stake his reputation on writing expressly for children. Even Andersen did not anticipate an exclusively young audience. Topelius's *Läsning för barn* (1847; Reading for Children) long held sway as the most popular work of the nineteenth century. Henrik Wergeland's* *Vinterblommer i Barnekammeret* (1840; Winter Flowers in the Nursery) also deserves mention as a classic intended for children, written by an already established author and political figure. Otherwise, much of the literature preserved from the mid–nineteenth century is of a borderline variety shared by children and adults: Esaias Tegnér's* *Frithiofs saga* (1825); Johan Ludvig Runeberg's* tales of Finnish patriotism, *Fänrik Ståls sägner* (1848–1860; *The Tales of Ensign Stål*, 1938); Fredrika Bremer's* domestic novels, and Bjørnstjerne Bjørnson's* *Bondefortællinger* (Farmer Stories). There were several periodicals for children, as well as annual Christmas collections, which, because of their physical format, could not be handed down intact. Selected items from these do appear from time to time in anthologies of older literature. A good deal of their content was, however, imported.

A major development about midcentury was the entrance of women into the field of children's literature, which offered fewer impediments than breaking into the "man's world" of adult literature. Drawing on familiarity with the British novel tradition and their own observations of family life, the female writers introduced as a subject appropriate to children's literature the ordinary experiences of Scandinavian children themselves, inaugurating a tradition of domestic realism that still prevails. Ironically, the book usually cited as the prototype was written and illustrated by two brothers, Johan and Pietro Krohn. *Peters Jul* (1866; Peter's Christmas) is most remarkable for its visual rendition of the bourgeois Danish home. Stories of family life apparently did not appeal to all readers. The bifurcation of children's literature into "girls' books" and "boys' books" can be traced back at least to 1870. Boys' reading consisted heavily of imported adventure stories, many from the American frontier.

With the exception of Norwegian *landsmål* writers such as Per Sivle and Rasmus Løland, the tendentious social criticism of the Modern Breakthrough of the 1880s had almost no effect on children's literature. It clung instead to a patriarchal, agrarian worldview despite industrialization and the rise of the labor movement. The authors writing for children at this time were predominantly women of upper-class origins with a more conservative, religious outlook than their counterparts in adult literary circles. Their books sought to provide moral uplift in the face of disruptive social change. Even the most widely renowned work of social consciousness, Laura Fitinghoff's *Barnen i Frostmofjället* (1907; *Children of the Moor*, 1927), has a pronounced moral tone. The Darwinian theory that underlay the notions of human behavior central to the adult naturalist novel was manifested in children's literature in stories based on the life cycles of plants and animals, notably those stories of the Danes Carl Ewald and Svend Fleuron.

The national romanticism of the 1890s found immediate response in children's books. In Norway, a native literature drawing on the richness of folk culture was vigorously encouraged by Nordahl Rolfsen, editor of *Illustreret Tidende for Børn* (1885–1892; Illustrated Newspaper for Children), whose *Lesebog for fol-keskolen* (1892–1895) received a stunning review from Ellen Key, who later won world renown for *The Century of the Child* (1900): "If, in the future, Norway's existence as a nation, its cultural significance as an independent people should be called into question, then Norway ought to need only a single accomplishment in its defense: its elementary reader." Following Rolfsen's example, the Swedish Public Elementary Teachers' Union started its own series, Barnbiblioteket Saga (The Saga Children's Library), in 1899, making high-quality literature available at low cost. They solicited illustrations from such talented artists as Jenny Nyström, Ottilia Adelborg, Carl Larsson, and Elsa Beskow. In 1901, the Teachers' Union issued a call for textbooks that "have a folkish

Swedish aura throughout, so that the children's best and most beautiful impressions of the Swedish home and Swedish nature can be the departure point for their spiritual growth.'' The result best known to English readers is Selma Lagerlöf's* *Nils Holgerssons underbara resa* (1906; *The Wonderful Adventures of Nils*, 1907), commissioned as a geography text. A more representative example is Anna Maria Roos's readers, *Sörgården* and *I Önnemo* (1913), where clean, blond children play in front of quaint red cottages in perpetual midsummer. The mention of ''Sörgården,'' like ''Dick and Jane'' for Americans, evokes for Swedes an image of family life that has prescriptive force even though its actuality is limited. The Roos readers were the obvious prototype for the American series *Flicka, Ricka and Dicka* and *Snipp, Snapp, Snurr*, published by Swedish immigrant Maj Lindman in the 1930s and 40s.

Coinciding as it did with major advances in printing technology, national romanticism attained its fullest expression in the picture book. The new possibility of multicolor, finely detailed illustrations was perfectly suited to the reigning pedagogical theory. The contributors to Barnbiblioteket Saga and *Illustreret Tidende* were noted for their meticulous attention to the details of Scandinavian nature and domestic life. The foremost works of the period have indeed become classics. Elsa Beskow's anthropomorphized flowers, berries, and mushrooms are still much loved, despite criticism in the 1960s of her patriarchal, class-structured worldview. Erik Werenskiold's drawings grace the preferred editions of the Norwegian folktales. Louis Moe's animated trees are still dear to Danish hearts.

While very young children were the prime audience for the new, improved picture book, their older sisters were treated to a somewhat revised version of the girls' book. Novelists such as Dikken Zwilgmeyer and Barbra Ring in Norway, Bertha Holst in Denmark and Jeanna Oterdahl in Sweden drew portraits of girls who experienced the joys of family life but also rebelled, at least temporarily, against its limitations by behaving as tomboys. Despite their implicit criticism of sex-role norms, these can be grouped together with readers of the Sörgården type under the heading of ''family idyll.'' Based on childhood reminiscences, this genre has until recently tended toward a nostalgic picture of family harmony. The fictional family took adventurous summer vacations, welcomed poor, orphaned children into the fold, and included a loving grandparent with a gift for storytelling. In Finland the most prominent writer of children's books during the first half of the century was Anni Swan (1875–1958), a talented author who successfully combined fantasy and realism in her works.

Remarkably, the bleakest moment in twentieth-century Scandinavian history—World War II and the Nazi occupation—produced a body of children's literature of special imaginative richness. A preschool seminar in Copenhagen run by Jens Sigsgaard, head of the children's literature section of the Danish Writers' Union, was the center for a new pedagogy that regarded children as actual, rather than potential, human beings with their own needs, experiences, and views of the world. The objective of education was not discipline but development. To carry out the dictum that children must be addressed on their own terms, the use of fantasy was stressed, and illustrators were encouraged to imitate the naive simplicity of children's own drawings. Author-illustrators Arne Ungermann, Egon Mathiessen, Poul Strøyer, and the somewhat younger Ib Spang Olsen are good examples of this approach. Sigsgaard's own most famous work is *Palle er alene i verden* (1941; *Paul Is Alone in the World*, 1964), a picture book based on a survey that asked more than one thousand children from three to eight what they would do if they were all alone in the world. The fantasy begins as pure, antisocial wish fulfillment, with a good bit of stealing and looting, but ends reinforcing the value of the social order, as Paul discovers he is lonely as well as alone. The book was made into a movie in 1946 but was not shown in Sweden for several years because the Svensk Filmindustri judged it immoral and frightening. In the English translation, Arne Ungermann's final drawing of a crying child was replaced by a happy playground scene.

In Sweden, meanwhile, the publishing arm of Kooperativa Förbundet, the cooperative movement, undertook a new effort to foster a good native literature. Kooperativa Förbundet launched the careers of Helga Henschen, Britt G. Hallqvist, and Lennart Hellsing, whose statement of philosophy is cleverly paradoxical: "All pedagogical art is bad art—and all good art is pedagogical." His own witty, irreverent nonsense rhymes are a case in point: they are excellent exercises in Swedish phonology. The fondness for child's-eye fantasies continues in the illustrations of Inger and Lasse Sandberg and Gunilla Bergström.

Torbjörn Egner, author of a consciously developmental series of readers for the Norwegian schools (1950–1972), was also the creator of Kardemommeby, Cardamom Town, where the only law requires that you not pester other people. Otherwise, you are free to do what you want. Egner's stated intention was antiauthoritarian: a child's fantasy must be freed from adult moral strictures in order to flourish. It is interesting to note that Hellsing and Egner were responsible for translating A. A. Milne's *Winnie-the-Pooh* into their respective languages. Egner was an early contributor to children's radio programming, as was Alf Prøysen,* best known abroad for his stories about *Teskjekjerringa* (1957–1967; *Mrs. Pepperpot*, 1959–), who keeps inadvertently breaking social norms. In Norway, Prøysen is greatly appreciated for portraying rural working-class children in a realistic, nonpatronizing manner.

It was into this fantasy-charged atmosphere that Astrid Lindgren's *Pippi Långstrump* was born in 1945. Lindgren has described her intention with Pippi, in retrospect, as, first of all, entertainment, and second, to give children a sense of power and to show them that power need not be abusive. Pippi's strength, wit, and independence have won her an enormous international following. Lindgren herself has gone on to write many highly respected works in a variety of genres and to exercise great influence during her twenty-four years as children's book editor at Rabén and Sjögren, which supports its adult publications on Pippi's income.

The year 1945 also marked the debut of Tove Jansson's* Mumintroll series, published in Swedish in Finland. These might be seen as quintessentially Scandinavian, playing on the dominant themes in the history of Scandinavian children's literature: it is outrageous fantasy that mirrors and parodies social reality. It is a family idyll, but the family members are supernatural beings and not all blood relatives. Jansson's illustrations pay close attention to natural detail, but embellish it with peculiar flora and fauna that resemble children's drawings.

By the late 1960s, even Pippi Longstocking had become a sacred cow subject to the barbs of a new generation of iconoclasts schooled in Marxist theory. They saw the fantasy of the supergirl as a safety valve for children's discontent with their inferior social position. A debate ensued in the public media and in academic institutions about how children's literature functions in teaching societal norms and inculcating political ideology. A new generation of novelists that debuted in the 1950s had already given the family idyll a psychological twist with themes such as parent-child conflict, loneliness, fear, and feelings of inferiority: Anne-Catharina. Vestly, Ebba Haslund,* and Finn Havrevold in Norway, Thøger Birkeland in Denmark, and Gunnel Linde in Sweden. Now they were challenged to reflect new social realities as well: single-parent families, chemical dependency, adolescent sexuality, racial injustice. Advocates of social change who were not primarily children's authors also went to work to produce an instructive, politically conscious literature for children that often fell victim to a moral didacticism rivaling that of the eighteenth century. While it claimed that children were capable of critical social consciousness, it often gave them finished analyses rather than problems to think about. It also tended heavily toward realism, overlooking the visionary capacity of fantasy.

At present, fantasy and realism seem to be forging a respectful coexistence. Two living writers, in addition to Astrid Lindgren and Tove Jansson, whose award-winning books are now routinely translated into English, are the Swedish novelist Maria Gripe and the Dane Cecil Bødker.* They combine realism, fantasy, magic, social consciousness, and depth psychology in works that show a keen sensitivity to the hazards of being a child in an adult world. They represent well another tendency in Scandinavian children's literature that has precedent in the folktales and Hans Christian Andersen: the desire to bridge the gap in experience and communication that separates children and adults.

REFERENCES

Ahola, Suvi, "Fantasy and Exploitation: Contemporary Finnish Children's Literature." *Books from Finland* 18.3 (1985); Hagemann, Sonja, *Barnelitteratur i Norge*, 3 vols. (Oslo, 1965, 1970, 1974); Helakisa, Kaarina, "Stories for the Young at Heart." *Books from Finland* 13.2 (1979); Lehtonen, Maija, "Teenage Fiction in Finland." *Books from Finland* 16.1 (1982); Lehtonen, Maija and Marita Rajalin, eds., *Barnboken i Finland förr och nu* (Stockholm, 1984); Ørjasæter, Tordis, *Den norske barnelitteraturen gjennom 200 år* (Oslo, 1981); Stybe, Vibeke, *Fra Askepot til Asterix: Børnebogen i kulturhistorisk perspektiv* (Copenhagen, 1974); Zweigbergk, Eva von, *Barnboken i Sverige, 1750–1950* (Stockholm, 1965).

Cheri Register

Chorell, Walentin. Finland-Swedish novelist and dramatist, b. 8 April 1912, Åbo (Turku), d. 18 November 1983, Helsinki.

Chorell, who had gone through emotional disturbances in his youth, evidently took to writing as therapy; this self-treatment was transformed, then, into a startling productivity, with novels, stage plays, and dramas for radio or television. However, he shied away from other genres; after two tyro collections of verse, he did not try the lyric again, and never ventured into the short story. Yet he also shunned the large and complex epic—his novels are all brief, and centered around a very small cast.

Directly after a detective novel, *Lektion för döden* (1947; Lesson for Death), Chorell made a name for himself with *Jörgen Hemmelincks stora augusti* (1947; Jörgen Hemmelinck's Great August), in which a middle-aged man tries to flee from a life of quiet desperation; the structure is varied in *Calibans dag* (1948; Caliban's Day), *Blindtrappan* (1949; Blind Stairs), and *Intim journal* (1949; Intimate Journal), where, respectively, the owner of a seedy café, a blind man, and a mentally disturbed youth are beset by a threatening world. Although without much specific social or political detail, these books capture the gray and anxious atmosphere of Finland in the immediate postwar years, and it could be that they will constitute Chorell's most enduring contribution to literature. The somewhat more hopeful tone of the 1950s—in *Sträv gryning* (1952; Harsh Dawn), with its unhappy young man who begins to find his way into society—and the trilogy about an independent girl (*Miriam*, 1952; Miriam; *Främlingen*, 1954; The Stranger; *Kvinnan*, 1958; The Woman) gave way, once again, to a darker view in the case studies of the next decade: the boastful psychopath of *De barmhärtiga* (1962; The Merciful Ones) and the religious fanatic of *Saltkaret* (1963; The Salt-cellar) are typically "Chorellian," wretched creatures trapped in small circumstances and cramped rooms. Next, Chorell interested himself in good intentions gone awry: sentimental guardians cannot understand a mildly handicapped girl in *Grodan* (1966; The Frog: the allusion is to the girl's physical defect), an aging man commits murder out of sympathy in *Agneta och lumpsamlaren* (1968; Agneta and the Ragman) and its sequel, *Sista leken* (1970; The Last Game). A decade before, in *Stölden* (1960; The Theft), Chorell had shown his unsentimental interest in the ways of modern young love (for many years, Chorell was a teacher in a Helsinki school); during the seventies, he wrote two trilogies on the same topic—the one, with a Helsinki milieu, about two young people from disparate social backgrounds who love, marry, and grow apart (*Äggskalet*, 1972; The Egg Shell; *Knappen*, 1974; The Button; *Livstycket*, 1976; The Bodice), the other about a love affair and disastrous marriage between a chronic liar and a victim of polio (*Dockorna*, 1978; The Dolls; *Rävsaxen*, 1980; The Fox-trap; *Lekhagen*, 1981; The

Play-yard). This final serial-work has two aspects of special interest: in it, Chorell returns to the poor quarters of Turku that, ever so lightly sketched, have been the setting of a number of his books; and, in its portrait of the prevaricating writer, Chorell presents the last and most carefully described of his social misfits. With *Kvarteret barmhärtighet* (1982; The Section Called Mercy), Chorell looks closely at what may have been his own childhood; the main figure remembers the game he played as a six-year-old: in another of Chorell's ambivalent mercy killings, the child pretended that his aunt was dead.

Abroad, Chorell has been best known for his plays, which deal with the same stifling little worlds and emotional cripples as do his novels: the trapped middle-aged man of *Fabian öppnar portarna* (1949; Fabian Opens the Gates), the aging actress of *Madam* (1952), the haunted couple in *Vandringsman* (1954; Wanderer), the rival siblings in *Systrarna* (1955; The Sisters, 1971), the lovers (who turn out to be brother and sister) in *Gräset* (1958; The Grass), and the women factory workers of *Kattorna* (1961; The Cats, 1978). However, the stage works of Chorell will probably age much more rapidly than the novels; their symbolism already seems heavy, and their psychology obvious. The best of Chorell's dramatic work has been done for broadcasting; here, amid portraits of degradation such as *Tomflaskan* (1952; The Empty Flask), a play bearing the nickname of an aging prostitute reduced to collecting bottles, and *Dialog vid ett fönster* (1952; Dialogue by a Window), about ugly envy between bedridden old men, Chorell has also revealed a gift for the comedy of errors, as in *Ariadne* (1965)—set in a business office closed for the night—or the black comedy of *Grå Eros* (1965; Gray Eros): lovers meet again half a century later.

FURTHER WORKS

Vinet och lägeln (1941); *Spegling* (1943); *Ensam sökan* (1948); *Åtta radiopjäser—Haman* (1952); *Fem spel* (1967); *Pizzamordet* (1977).

REFERENCES

Salminen, Johannes, "Walentin Chorell: An Appreciation." *American-Scandinavian Review* 56.2 (1968); Schoolfield, George C., Introduction to *The Sisters*, in *Five Modern Scandinavian Plays* (New York, 1971); Schoolfield, George C., "The Postwar Novel of Swedish Finland." *Scandinavian Studies* 34.2 (1962); Jones, W. Glyn, "Ethics and the Individual: The Drama of Walentin Chorell." *Books from Finland* 18.1 (1984); Warburton, Thomas, "Literary Portrait: Walentin Chorell." *Books from Finland* 3.3 (1969).

George C. Schoolfield

Christensen, Inger. Danish poet and novelist, b. 16 January 1935, Vejle. Christensen is without doubt Denmark's leading woman of letters. Her first two volumes of poetry, *Lys* (1962; Light) and *Græs* (1963; Grass) are treatises to her poetic progress and artistic growth. These volumes were followed by the novels *Evighedsmaskinen* (1964; The Eternity Machine) and *Azorno* (1967).

Christensen's breakthrough came with the collection of poems *Det* (1969; It), consisting of a prologue; three sections, "The Stage," "The Action," "The Text"; and an epilogue. Each section is further divided into eight subsections containing eight poems each, coined: symmetries, transitivities, continuities, connexities, variabilities, extensions, integrities, and universalities. It is a complex work that describes the modern world that is limited by "it," attempts to suggest a new order, and addresses deep political and social problems. Christensen leaves the work "open"; there is no final period. The collection opens and closes with "it." The text itself is printed in typewriter-like print that gives the impression that the manuscript is unfinished, encouraging the reader to continue to take "it" up for review and discussion.

Christensen's novel *Det malede værelse* (1976; The Painted Room) is influenced by the paintings of the Italian Andrea Mantegna (1431–1506). This novel was followed by the poetry collection *Brev i april* (1979; Letter in April).

Leonardo Fibonacci's sequence of numbers is the structure behind *Alfabet* (1981; Alphabet). Every section begins with a letter of the alphabet, while the number of lines of each section is determined by the total of the lines of the two previous sections. The poem builds, almost writing itself, from the simplest form to a symphony of words. The tone, as in all of Christensen's poetry and prose, is musical; Christensen's alphabet demands to be sung. The content reflects the structure, moving from simple observations of nature to a world that is threatened by pollution and death.

Christensen is a very private person who rarely appears in public. But in a collection of essays, *Del af labyrinten* (1982; Part of the Labyrinth), she gives a clue as to her way of thinking. She suggests that Descartes should have claimed: "I think; therefore, I am a part of the labyrinth," and she explains that the labyrinth is a symbol of the modern world, a Möbius strip between man and nature. In her essay on Dante and a piece on the baroque, she discusses how artistic creativity is a current through time, which moves toward unity and helps us to understand an unperceivable world.

Christensen's poetry, whether structured by grammatical or mathematical systems, stresses the discord between language and experience. Christensen imposes complex systems and order, which are foreign to life, while, paradoxically, preserving the singularity of life and thus opposing systematization. Christensen's art represents a many-sided complex in that she strives to give us immediate visions and sensual impressions, embracing the sum of modern experience.

FURTHER WORKS

Intriganterne (1972); *Det store ukendte rejse* (1982); *En vinteraften i Ufa* (1987).

TRANSLATIONS

Lines Review 46 (1973); *Mundus Artium* 7.2 (1974); *The International Portland Review 1980*, ed. Cindy Ragland (1980).

REFERENCES

Brostrøm, Torben, and Mette Winge, eds. *Danske digtere i det 20. Århundrede,* vol. 5 (Copenhagen, 1980); Wamberg, Bodil, ed., *Out of Denmark* (Copenhagen, 1985).

Janis E. Granger

Christiansen, Sigurd. Norwegian novelist and dramatist, b. 17 December 1891, Drammen, d. 23 October 1947, Drammen.

Christiansen was a postal worker who lived his whole life in Drammen. For the most part, his long, difficult, and introspective works deal with more or less anonymous members of the lower middle class who bear great burdens of inner conflict and face dilemmas concerning eternal ethical problems. Often these characters spend a great part of their lives trying to find a way to justify going on as they are. Christiansen avoids politics, milieu descriptions, and social problems, trying to keep more to universal themes such as guilt, responsibility, and freedom.

In 1931 Christiansen received the Norwegian and the Nordic prize in a novel competition for *To levende og en død (Two Living and One Dead,* 1932), a novel that is shorter and easier to read than his other works, but typical in its analysis of the characters' deeper motives. Its theme is justice. A post office in a small town is robbed; one man is killed, one resists the thieves, and one simply surrenders the money. The latter is condemned as a coward and seems finished in life, but he has suffered injustice and yearns for a restoration of his honor, which he achieves.

Although Christiansen is best known for *To levende og en død*, his greatest works are his double novel, *Vort eget liv* (1918; Our Own Life) and *Ved Golgata* (1920; At Calvary), and his two trilogies, 1925–1929 and 1935–1945. The double novel—about a father and his two sons—deals with guilt and justice and with the coolness that separates people caught in moral dilemmas. The first trilogy also deals with a family and treats the same basic motifs, but with a breadth and depth unparalleled in Norwegian literature. The second trilogy is about the artist, his dreams, calling, loneliness, and sensitivity, and his drive to give form to his experiences, to find a means of expression. It is the best Norwegian work on a writer's development. Christiansen says that it is the writer's task to understand life and to help people to live, bear their fate, and be themselves.

Although Christiansen's plays are not as important as his novels, *Edmund Jahr* (1924) is a good portrayal of post–World War I radical youth, and *En reise i natten* (1931; A Trip in the Night) shows how a fanatic ideology leads to the most extreme consequences.

Christiansen has been called Norway's Dostoyevski. He is the most important soul searcher in Norwegian literature. Like Henrik Ibsen,* he is a psychologist and moralist with a strong demand for self-knowledge and right action.

FURTHER WORKS

Seieren (1915); *Thomas Hergel* (1917); *Offerdøden* (1919); *Døperen* (1921); *Blodet* (1923); *Indgangen* (1925); *Sverdene* (1927); *Idyllen om Sander* (1928); *Riket* (1929); *Dydens have* (1932); *Agner i stormen* (1933; *Chaff before the Wind*, 1934); *Drømmen og livet* (1935); *Det ensomme hjerte* (1938); *Thorvald Erichsen* (1940); *Mannen fra bensinstasjonen* (1941); *Henrik Sørensen. Til sekstiårsdagen* (1942); *Menneskenes lodd* (1945); *Alexander Paulovitsj* (1947); *Samlede verker*, 9 vols. (1949–1950).

REFERENCES

Helliesen, Knud, "Skyld—soning—oppreisning i Sigurd Christiansens diktning," in *Norsk litterær årbok* (1967); Kielland, Eugenia, *Sigurd Christiansen i liv og diktning* (Oslo, 1952).

Walter D. Morris

Claussen, Sophus Niels Christen. Danish poet, b. 12 September 1865, Helletofte, d. 11 April 1931, Copenhagen.

Claussen was the son of a farmer and politician and early developed an interest in radical politics. He studied law at Copenhagen, but gave up law to become a journalist, working on various Danish provincial newspapers. He was financially independent and able to spend lengthy periods in Paris and Italy, living as a free-lance writer and painter.

In the 1890s Claussen was closely associated with Johannes Jørgensen* in the symbolist movement, though his poetry was of a more complex nature.

In his first book, *Naturbørn* (1887; Nature Children), later incorporated into *Pilefløjter* (1899; Wooden Whistles), Claussen wrote poems in the radical spirit of the time, betraying a satirical attitude to traditional morality. The love poems pre-echo the erotic nature of much of the later work. Best known is "Rejseminder" (Memories from a Journey) in which the poet surrenders himself to a fantasy about a young woman glimpsed on a railway station. *Pilefløjter* covers a wide range of moods, from the light and optimistic radiance of "Solskinnet" (Sunshine) to the hopeless resignation of "Buddha." In "I en Frugthave" (In an Orchard) Claussen shows a closer approximation to symbolism proper at the same time as freeing himself from his earlier models (e.g., Heinrich Heine) and establishing himself as a writer who can regenerate Danish as a poetic medium.

The element of tangible experience in Claussen's work was gradually reduced, as is seen in "Ekbatána" from *Valfart* (1896; Pilgrimage), where in imprecise terms he proclaims the power of poetry and dream as opposed to learning, and exploits the emotive effect of the sound of the word "Ekbátana."

From *Djævlerier* (1904; Demonisms) Claussen moves in the direction of the darker sides of Charles Baudelaire's poetry and into an examination of the more somber aspects of human nature. In "Trappen til Helvede" (The Staircase to Hell) he sketches a young man in love with a repulsive old hag, while "Sorte

Blomst'' (Black Flower) is a portrait of a prostitute. ''Il letto'' portrays the Queen of Sheba who, having been rejected by King Solomon, humiliates him by making her slaves her lovers.

In the 1890s Claussen published a number of prose fiction works reflecting his political and erotic preoccupations, together with a drama, *Arbejdersken* (1898; The Factory Girl), a mixture of symbolism and realism, which was poorly received. He had hoped through this drama to achieve a degree of popularity, and in his disappointment at its reception he gave up all pretense at writing in a way that could be understood by the uninitiated.

Fabler (1917; Fables) shows a critical attitude toward modern materialism, while in the later collection of poems, *Heroica* (1925), Claussen goes yet further along these lines, particularly in ''Atomernes Oprør'' (The Revolt of the Atoms), in which he prophetically foresees the world as being destroyed by liberated atoms.

In his bold imagery, the esoteric nature of much of his poetry, and the technique of a progression of images—seen already in ''Rejseminder''—Claussen is often seen as a forerunner of Danish modernism, and his influence on later writers has been considerable. His intellectualism prevented him from becoming a poet of the people, as he had hoped, but he now stands as one of the most important Danish poets of his age.

FURTHER WORKS

Unge Bander (1894); *Kitty* (1895); *Antonius i Paris* (1896); *Byen* (1900); *Junker Firkløver* (1900); *Trefoden* (1901); *Eroter og Fauner* (1910); *Foraar i Paris* (1911); *Løvetandsfnug* (1918); *Den danske Sommer* (1921); *Foraarstaler* (1927); *Titania holder Bryllup* (1927); *Fortællinger om Rosen* (1927); *Hvededynger* (1930).

FURTHER TRANSLATIONS

Contemporary Danish Poetry, ed. Line Jensen et al. (1977).

REFERENCES

Andersen, Harry, *Studier i Sophus Claussens lyrik* (Copenhagen, 1967); Frandsen, Ernst, *Sophus Claussen*, 2 vols. (Copenhagen, 1950); Hallar, Søren, *Sophus Claussen Studier* (Copenhagen, 1943); Jørgensen, Bo Hakon, *Maskinen, det heroiske og det gotiske* (Copenhagen, 1977); Modvig, Gunnar, *Eros, kunst og socialitet* (Copenhagen, 1974).

W. Glyn Jones

Collett, Camilla. Norwegian novelist and essayist, b. 23 January 1813, Kristiansand, d. 6 March 1895, Kristiania (Oslo).

The parsonage at Eidsvoll provided the backdrop for Collett's childhood. Here she grew up amid charming pastoral beauty but in marked isolation; and here, the course of her later rebellion was set. The forceful genius of older brother, poet Henrik Wergeland,* and father, pastor Nicolai Wergeland, stimulated her own creative thinking, yet also intimidated her. Whereas brother Henrik was allowed a Rousseauian free rein, Collett was introduced to the conventional code of female behavior and directed toward marriage as her goal in life. She received her early education at home. At the age of twelve she was sent to boarding school in the capital, Kristiania, and at fourteen left for two years at a girls' school in Denmark. She returned to Eidsvoll a much-admired, but restless, young woman, who through thoughtful correspondence and diary writing began to hone her descriptive and reflective powers.

Collett focused her attention on the poet Johan Sebastian Welhaven,* whom she loved intensely and despairingly. A heated, and very public, debate ongoing between Welhaven and Henrik Wergeland heightened the tension surrounding this ill-fated romance. The loss of Welhaven became one of the two great tragedies in her life, the other being the early death of husband Peter Jonas Collett, whom she married in 1841. Her husband's death in 1851 brought Collett into a precarious financial situation, with four sons to raise and only a meager widow's pension. Economic need thus became the practical impulse for her career as an author. The decades that followed were difficult ones, necessitating frequent moves and separation from her family; but toward the end of her life, Collett experienced increased recognition and appreciation for her writings, and for her strong stance on behalf of women.

The most famous work from Collett's hand is her earliest extensive narrative—*Amtmandens Døttre* (1854–1855; The Governor's Daughters). This book signaled a new wave of prose writing for Norwegian literature. Not only was it the first social novel to appear in Norway, but it was also the first literary work to examine closely the female situation and to present a heroine who questioned conventional patterns of education and marriage. The novel describes the fortunes of the daughters in a rural, upper-class family, contrasting the unhappy, loveless marriages of the older sisters with the hopes nurtured by Sofie for a union with the man she loves. Convention wins out over romance, however, and Sofie lands instead in a sedate, comfortable marriage to a widowed clergyman. The novel's implicit social criticism rises out of its documentation of the general disregard for women's feelings and the dependence of women upon male initiative (a marriage proposal) for economic security and social respectability. Viewed against the literature of the 1870s and 1880s, *Amtmandens Døttre* stands as a forerunner of the marriage novels fine-tuned by Jonas Lie* and foreshadows social themes central to the plays of Henrik Ibsen.*

With *Fortællinger* (1861; Stories), Collett offered a collection of her prose pieces, a number of them dating from the time of her literary debut in the 1840s. Her fascination with legends and folktales shines through these stories and reminds us that as a budding writer, Collett supplied the folklore collector P. C. Asbjørnsen with descriptive settings for his material. A more important literary effort is *I de lange Nætter* (1862; Through the Long Nights), where childhood memories have been selected and arranged as episodes to be shared with kindred souls who, like the insomniac narrator, pass the nights with book in hand. The scenes are carefully manipulated and the home at Eidsvoll and the Wergeland personalities come vividly alive. Capping the episodes is the poignant "The First and the Last Night" in which Collett re-creates the mood and scene of her two most painful blows—Welhaven's rejection and Collett's death.

The volumes that follow are for the most part compilations of essays, reflections, and travelogues. *Sidste Blade* (Latest Pages) appeared in three installments in 1868, 1872, and 1873. With the 1873 volume Collett finally relinquished her nominal anonymity and placed her name upon the title page. The topics in *Sidste Blade* cover a wide range. Best known is the article "Om Kvinden og hendes Stilling" (On Woman and her Position), in which Collett asks men to lead the feminist debate. Male voices are crucial, she argues, for many women have been so heavily repressed that they cannot speak on their own behalf. *Fra de Stummes Leir* (1877; From the Camp of the Mute) represents another landmark in Norwegian literary history. It focuses on the depiction of women in literature and offers a fascinating, if somewhat flawed, example of early feminist criticism. The work also provides interesting insight into Collett's personal view of literature as a mirror of life.

Collett anchored her writing in the events of her own life, which she then extended into the larger social realm. Anger, frustration, and tears lie close to the page, but moral indignation is mingled with a keen wit. Her life has been described as a long battle against hypocrisy and adversity. That she also viewed herself this way is shown by the title of the last essay collection. *Mod Strømmen* (Against the Stream) draws its inspiration from the tale of the woman who was so contrary that she floated upstream. The first installment from 1879 was joined by a second series in 1885. Her diaries and correspondence were left largely intact. These have been edited by Leiv Amundsen and published in four volumes (1926–1933).

Collett is remembered as Norway's pioneering agitator for women's rights. Her efforts were aimed not at practical reforms, but at the spiritual and moral elevation of women. The organized women's movement honored her for her contribution, and generations of women writers have looked to her as a role model. When Gustav Vigeland designed his masterful statue of Collett, he placed her facing into the wind, chilled but defiant.

FURTHER WORKS

Samlede Værker, 3 vols. (1912–1913); *Optegnelser fra Ungdomsaarene* (1926); *Breve fra Ungdomsaarene* (1930); *Frigjørelsens Aar* (1932); *Før Bryllupet* (1933).

TRANSLATIONS

Scandinavian Review 5.6 (1917); *An Everyday Story*, ed., Katherine Hanson (1984).

REFERENCES

Aarnes, Sigurd As, ed., *Søkelys på Amtmandens Døtre* (Oslo, 1977); Benterud, Aagot, *Camilla Collett* (Oslo, 1947); *Diktning og demokrati*, special issue of *Samtiden* 72.1

(1963); Steen, Ellisiv, *Diktning og virkelighet* (Oslo, 1947); Steen, Ellisiv, *Den lange strid* (Oslo, 1954); Steen, Ellisiv, *Camilla Collett om seg selv* (Oslo, 1985); Wergeland, Agnes M., "Camilla Collett" in her *Leaders in Norway* (Menasha, Wis., 1916; repr. Freeport, N.Y., 1966).

Janet Rasmussen

Colliander, Fritiof *Tito*. Finland-Swedish novelist, b. 10 February 1904, St. Petersburg.

Colliander spent his childhood in St. Petersburg where his father was an army officer, but the family fled to Finland after the revolution. Colliander studied painting in Helsinki and then worked for a time as an art teacher. In the 1930s he was received into the Russian Orthodox Church, and has since lived as a writer, artist, and teacher.

Colliander began writing in 1930, and his first books, like some of the later ones, reflect the lives of refugees from the Bolshevik Revolution living in Finland. It was, however, not until his novel *Korståget* (1937; The Procession) that he became acknowledged as a major writer. Ending with almost mystical intensity, this is a conversion novel, reflecting much of the author's own conversion, and dealing with the problems of guilt and personal weakness confronted with simple goodness. Two years later came *Förbarma dig* (1939; Have Mercy), perhaps Colliander's greatest novel, a shorter work, less emotional, though touching on related themes; it portrays a good but weak and incompetent father who is finally driven by narrow-mindedness and pettiness to commit murder. The pathos is heightened by everything being seen through the eyes of an incomprehending child.

Colliander's sympathy for and understanding of human weakness and suffering appear to have resulted from his witnessing a thief being lynched in St. Petersburg, an event mirrored in various works. The full account is found in his seven-volume autobiography, published between 1964 and 1973 and considered to be one of the most important Finland-Swedish prose works of recent years.

Recently Colliander has moved away from pure fiction to reflective works in which it is not always easy to distinguish between fiction and reality. Outstanding is *Början* (1979; The Beginning), describing the author's experiences in a Greek Orthodox monastery.

Colliander is now recognized as the most important Finland-Swedish prose writer in the present century. Because of his themes and his approach, he has often been compared with Fyodor Dostoyevski.

FURTHER WORKS

En vandrare (1930); *Småstad* (1931); *Huset där det dracks* (1932); *Bojorna* (1933); *Taina* (1935); *Direktör Brenner* (1936); *Ljuset* (1936); *Dagen är* (1940); *Grottan* (1942); *Ilja Repin* (1942); *Den femte juli* (1943); *Två timmar och andra noveller* (1944); *Bliv till* (1945); *Vart tog det lilla livet vägen* (1945); *Ilja Repins ungdomsår* (1946); *Träsnittet* (1946); *Riskmomentet* (1947); *Sallinen* (1948); *I åratal* (1949); *Samtal med smärtan*

(1956); *Glädjes möte* (1957); *Vi som är kvar* (1959); *Med öppna händer* (1960); *Bevarat* (1964); *Gripen* (1965); *Vidare* (1967); *Givet* (1968); *Vaka* (1969); *Nära* (1971); *Måltid* (1973); *Motiv* (1977).

REFERENCES

Jones, W. Glyn, "Tito Colliander: Glimpses into the Past and Present." *Books from Finland* 13.1 (1979); Warburton, Thomas, "Literary Portrait: Tito Colliander." *Books from Finland* 2.1 (1968).

W. Glyn Jones

Cour, Paul la. *See* La Cour, Paul.

Creutz, Gustaf Philip. Swedish poet, b. May 1731, on the family estate Malmgård in Swedish Finland, d. 30 October, 1785, Stockholm.

Count Creutz studied at the University of Åbo (1749–1751), became a government employee in Stockholm in 1751, was appointed Prince Fredrik Adolf's gentleman-in-waiting in 1756, and while in that role won the friendship of Crown Prince Gustaf (later Gustaf III). In 1763 he was appointed minister to Spain; two years later he was transferred to France, where he played an important role in Swedish-French relations and became a popular figure in French court and cultural life. In 1783 he was made head of the royal chancellery in Stockholm and in 1784 chancellor of the University of Uppsala. A friend of Benjamin Franklin's, Creutz helped arrange close ties between Sweden and the American revolutionists.

Interesting as his career as a diplomat and public servant is, his major impact came through his contributions to Swedish literature. When he came to Stockholm in 1751 he soon became the close friend of Gustaf Fredrik Gyllenborg* (1731–1808) and of Hedvig Charlotta Nordenflycht* (1718–1763), the key members of Tankebyggarorden, the literary group of gifted ambitious young writers that published much of what was best and most original in the literature of the time in *Våra försök* (1753, 1754, 1756; Our Attempts) and in revised and expanded form in *Witterhets arbeten* (1759, 1762; Literary Works). Much of the material in these five volumes consists of satires and didactic poems, appreciably influenced by classic and French models as well as by Alexander Pope's poetry. But in addition there are poems that reveal a remarkably great appreciation of external nature, an eighteenth-century "discovery" traceable to Carl von Linné's* "journeys" and other works about the rich and frequently beautiful environment in which human beings have their existence, to *The Seasons* (1726–1746) and other works by the Scottish poet James Thomson (1700–1748), and to various French and English contemporaries of Thomson, including Alexander Pope.

Not only an informed enthusiast about literature and music but also a master of the nuances of the Swedish language and of versification, Creutz contributed major poetry that can still be enjoyed: *Sommar-qväde* (1756; Summer Song), a delightful landscape poem in which he describes Swedish nature in its calm, sunlit moods; *Atis och Camilla* (1762, 1942) one of the most beautiful of modern pastorals with happiness of phrasing, musical flow of superbly constructed verse, and charmingly genuine nature descriptions; and shorter lyrics such as *Ode öfver ängslan* (1754; Ode about Anguish), *Elegie* (1754), and *Fråga* (1743; Question).

Creutz's poetry was widely read and appreciated for generations to come because of his presentation in verse of external nature, his revelation of the possibilities of the Swedish language for poetic expressions, and for his admirable mastery of poetic forms. Among his many admirers was Carl Michael Bellman,* the greatest of eighteenth-century Scandinavian poets.

FURTHER WORKS

Vitterhetsarbeten af Greutz och Gyllenborg, vol. 1 (1795); *Dikter* (1950).

REFERENCES

Breitholtz, Lennart, *Studier i frihetstidens litteratur* (Uppsala, 1956); Castrén, Gunnar, *Gustaf Philip Creutz* (Stockholm, 1917); Hultin, Arvid, *Gustaf Philip Creutz, hans levnad och vittra skrifter* (Helsinki, 1913); Johnson, Walter James, *Thomson's Influence on Swedish Literature in the Eighteenth Century* (Urbana, Ill., 1936); Lamm, Martin, *Upplysningstidens romantik* (Stockholm, 1918–1920).

Walter Johnson

Criticism. *See* Scandinavian Literary Criticism, History of.

D

Dagerman, Stig. Swedish novelist, dramatist, essayist, poet, and short story writer, b. 5 October 1923, Älvkarleby, d. 4 November 1954, Stockholm.

Dagerman was born into the working class and for a while studied literature and art at the university. His first marriage into a syndicalist family confirmed his political interests. In 1944 he was the cultural editor of the syndicalist newspaper *Arbetaren*.

Dagerman, one of the foremost writers of the 1940s, verbalized the anxiety and dread of the time with unusual force. His second novel, *De dömdas ö* (1946; The Island of the Condemned), portrays seven people isolated on an island full of repulsive animals. The perversions and narcissism of the characters, who are always ready to betray each other or themselves in misguided loyalties, reflect his views on contemporary political and social corruption. Also in erotic interaction Dagerman conveys a dark message. The theme of *Bränt barn* (1948; *A Burnt Child*, 1950) is betrayal. A son sleeps with his father's mistress while demanding chastity and purity from everyone but himself.

Dagerman's overriding theme of guilt and anxiety is apparent also in his dramas. *I skuggan av Mart* (1949; In Mart's Shadow) deals with a young man's attempt to live with his mother's daily glorification of his dead brother, who becomes more important in his false martyrdom than the living Mart.

In *Tysk höst* (1947; *German autumn*, 1951), Dagerman's journalistic writing captures the suffering of postwar Germany whose guilt he believes is shared by the West. And in his short and witty poetic commentaries on current events in *Dagsedlar* (1945; Comments of Daily Events) he can be both satirical and poetic.

A poetic tone is also found in his posthumously published *Tusen år hos Gud* (1954; A Thousand Years With God), presenting a God who walks away from his creation.

Dagerman's style is characterized by a mixture of the fantastic and realistic elements. The comic is blended with the grotesque in a narrative technique with forceful impact. Dagerman has masterfully captured the despair of his generation, and yet his writing has never become timebound and outdated. After five years of silence he committed suicide, a desperate end of the career of one of the most outstanding writers of his generation.

FURTHER WORKS

Ormen (1945); *Nattens lekar* (1947; *The Games of Night,* 1959), *Den dödsdömde* (1947; *The Condemned,* 1951); *Dramer om dömda* (1948); *Judasdramer* (1949); *Bröllopsbesvär* (1949); *Den yttersta dagen* (1952); *Vårt behov av tröst* (1955; *Our Need of Consolation,* 1958); *Föräldrabesvära* (1955); *Samlade skrifter* (1959); *Skrifter* I- (1983–).

FURTHER TRANSLATIONS

Delta 11 (1957); *Swedish Book Review,* Supplement: Dagerman (1984).

REFERENCES

Bergman, S. A., "Blinded by Darkness: A Study of the Novels and Plays of Stig Dagerman." *Delta: The Cambridge Literary Magazine* 11 (1957); Lagercrantz, Olof, *Stig Dagerman* (Stockholm, 1958); Sandberg, Hans, *Den politiske Stig Dagerman* (Stockholm, 1979); Sandberg, Hans, comp., *Stig Dagerman—Författare och journalist* (Stockholm, 1975); Sastamoinen, Armas, *Stig Dagerman och syndikalismen* (Stockholm, 1974); Thompson, L. A., "In Fear and Trembling: A Study of Stig Dagerman's Imagery," in *Erfahrung und Überlieferung. Festschrift for C. P. Magrill,* ed. H. Siefkar and A. Robinson (Cardiff, 1974); Thompson, L. A., *Stig Dagerman: Nattens lekar* (Hull, 1975); Thompson, L. A., "Stig Dagerman 1923–1954," in *Essays in Swedish Literature,* ed. Irene Scobbie (Aberdeen, 1978); Thompson, L. A., *Stig Dagerman* (Boston, 1983); Thompson, L. A., "Stig Dagerman's 'Vår nattliga badort': An Interpretation." *Scandinavica* 13.2 (1974); Thompson, L. A., "Stig Dagerman and Politics." *Scandinavica* 19.1 (1980).

Torborg Lundell

Dalin, Olof von. Swedish essayist, poet, and historian, b. 29 August 1708, Vinberg, d. 12 August 1763, Stockholm.

Though born a pastor's son, Dalin spent most of his adult life in aristocratic circles, beginning with his move to Stockholm as tutor to the Rålamb family. Of his personal life and character, we know little, but he apparently had considerable gifts as a wit that can be seen in his lifelong production of occasional verse, having especial success in two genres, the folk-song imitation and the then-popular pastoral.

Without question, Dalin's most successful writing appears in his newspaper *Then swänska Argus,* which appeared from December 1732 to December 1734. The *Argus* was one of a type of personal newspaper popular in Europe, imitative of, and sometimes a translation of, Joseph Addison and Sir Richard Steele's *The Tatler* and *The Spectator* (1709–1712). In the *Argus,* and elsewhere, Dalin introduced the personal essay and the social satire to Sweden, as well as the political allegory made popular by Jonathan Swift. In form, he began by copying Steele's use of a framing tale, set in a coffeehouse with recurring characters out of whose conversation the ideas in the essay develop. Dalin soon abandoned this structure. Though he continued to take material from abroad, he reworked it into his own personal style. That style brought a new fluidity to the language, and marks such a contrast with that which preceded it, that the linguistic development known as "younger new Swedish" is dated from this period. Indeed, the state of the language was an issue that deeply concerned Dalin, as we can see in his satire in *Argus* 45, where he rails against foreign borrowings and tarted-up speech in Swedish.

Dalin's life covered a period of great political development in Sweden, with the emergence of parties in a time of weak royal authority. Though a royalist, Dalin stayed in the middle ground between those who wanted a war of revenge against Russia and those who wanted to concentrate on internal problems. In the overheated atmosphere of 1740, Dalin published his splendid historical allegory, *Sagan om hästen* (The Tale of the Horse). Dealing with the Swedish people under their differing rulers, the allegory is seen by many as the artistic high point of Dalin's writing.

For the newly established national theater in Stockholm (1737), Dalin wrote two plays, both performed first in 1738, *Den afwundsjuke* (*Envy*, 1876), a comedy of character in the French manner, and *Brynhilda*, a tragedy in the French classical style.

Appointed tutor to the crown prince (later Gustaf III, 1746–1792) in 1750, ennobled in 1751, and given a series of high offices, Dalin's principal interest after 1743 was the writing of a new history of Sweden, which appeared in four volumes between 1747 and 1762. It was the first and, for a long time, the only such history to attempt to approach its subject in a dispassionate and scholarly manner.

Dalin's importance for the development of modern Swedish can hardly be overestimated, and his ironic passion makes his chief works readable today.

FURTHER WORKS

Witterhetsarbeten, 6 vols. (1767); *Poetiska arbeten*, 2 vols. (1782–1783); *Valda Skrifter* (1872).

Alan Swanson

Dass, Petter. Norwegian poet, b. 1647, Nord-Herøy, d. 1707, Alstahaug, Nordland.

Dass's father, Peiter Dundass, was a Scottish merchant who settled in Nordland; his mother was the daughter of a Norwegian tax collector. Dass was educated as a pastor in Copenhagen 1666–1669. After years of poverty in humble positions he was ultimately, in 1689, appointed to the parish of Alstahaug, where he lived the rest of his life. Owing to his fearless and generous personality, Dass grew to be a hero and a figure of legend among the people of northern Norway.

Socially and culturally Dass belonged to the small group of Dano-Norwegian officials and merchants. His occasional poetry, written in the elaborate style of the Baroque era, clearly reflects the conventions of his class. In any other respect, however, Dass differs from most of his contemporaries for the plain accuracy and common appeal of his style, especially in poems where he directly approaches his parishioners. None of his poems, except *Den Nordske Dale-Viise* (1683; The Norwegian Song of Valleys), was published during his lifetime; all were circulated in manuscript. Dass's songs were written in a swinging meter that made them easy to memorize. Some of them, particularly those from *Bibelske Viise-Bog* (1711; Biblical Song Book), were spread like folk songs all over the country. This traditional character of Dass's poetry may account for the great number of "religious" folk tunes that have been connected to his songs.

Dass's literary masterpiece, however, is his versified description of the land and people in northern Norway, *Nordlands Trompet* (1739; *The Trumpet of Nordland*, 1954). With humor, everyday nearness, and intimate knowledge, it depicts the general emotions of climate, animal life, agriculture, and fishing. And it describes in particular the topography, occupation, and inhabitants of the northernmost provinces. One characteristic quality of the poem is the emphasis the author puts on the near relation between physical resources and people's living conditions, which gives it a tinge of modern realism.

For a long time the literary circles of Norway showed little interest in Dass's works. But steadily the estimate of Dass's standing in Norwegian literature has become higher. In recent years the establishment of the University of Tromsø seems to have given a new impetus to the study of Dass's poetry.

FURTHER WORKS

D. Morten Luthers lille Katechismus, forfattet i begvemme Sange under føyelige Melodier (n.d.); *Evangelier sangviis, forfattet udi begvemme Melodeir* (1722); *Irende bibelske Bøger, nemlig: Ruths, Esthers og Judiths* (1723); *Om alle Land laa øde*, ed. Lars Roar Langslet (1984).

REFERENCES

Hjortsvang Isaacson, Lanae, "Petter Dass. Story-teller, Moralist and Student. The Changing Narrator of Nordlandstrompet." *Edda* 6 (1980); Jakobsen, Alfred, *Norskhet i språket hos Petter Dass* (Svorkmo, 1952); Midbøe, Hans, *Petter Dass* (Oslo, 1947); Muribø, Elias, *Petter Dass* (Trondheim, 1947); Welhaven, Johan Sebastian, *Digteren fra Alstahaug, Peder Dass* (Christiania, 1856).

Jostein Fet

Davið Stefánsson. *See* Stefánsson, Davið.

Delblanc, Sven Axel Herman. Swedish novelist and essayist, b. 26 May 1931, Swan River, Canada.

Failing to establish themselves in Canada, Delblanc's cosmopolitan family soon returned to Sweden and Sven Delblanc grew up in rural Sörmland. An academic by profession, Delblanc taught literature at the University of Uppsala until the early 1970s, when he became a full-time author.

Characteristic of Delblanc is his experimental approach to narration: even in realistic novels, his narrator frequently intrudes to comment not only on the story being told, but often on the art of storytelling in general. Delblanc's breakthrough came with *Prästkappan* (1963; The Cassock), a picaresque novel set in the Prussia of Frederick the Great; grotesquely comic and ironic, it has a pessimistic message about the nature of freedom and tyranny. Like most Swedish writers, Delblanc gave his works of the late 1960s a left-wing political message; notable among them is *Åsnebrygga* (1969; Donkey Bridge), a diary of a year spent as Guest Professor at Berkeley, California. Delblanc's most popular success in Sweden was undoubtedly the four Hedeby novels (1970–1976), rollicking chronicles that, on one level, depict the transformation of rural Sweden into a modern Social Democratic state. Delblanc's increasingly pessimistic view of the future is encapsulated in *Speranza* (1980; trans. 1983), named after a slave ship whose fate suggests that the outlook for individual freedom and humanity is bleak indeed. In the early 1980s Delblanc also achieved considerable success with his autobiographical tetralogy, beginning with *Samuels bok* (1981; Samuel's Book); in the last of the series, *Maria ensam* (1985; Maria Alone), the family returns from Canada to Hedeby, thus establishing a link with the earlier cycle.

Delblanc is also a considerable essayist, but he is primarily a novelist who delights in experimentation and possesses a great natural storytelling talent. Although influenced inevitably by current fashions, Delblanc is too much of an individualist to set literary trends; he distrusts both authority and human nature, and attracts extreme reactions, positive and negative.

FURTHER WORKS

Eremitkräftan (1962); *Ära och minne* (1965); *Homunculus* (1965; tr. 1969); *Nattresa* (1967); *Åminne* (1970); *Zahak* (1971); *Trampa vatten* (1972); *Stenfågel* (1973); *Primavera* (1973); *Vinteride* (1974); *Kastrater* (1975; *The Castrati*, 1979); *Stadsporten* (1976); *Grottmannen* (1977); *Morgonstjärnan* (1977); *Gunnar Emmanuel* (1978); *Kära farmor* (1979); *Stormhatten* (1979); *Treklöver* (1980); *Samuels döttrar* (1982); *Senecas död* (1982); *Jerusalems natt* (1983); *Kanaans land* (1984); *Maria ensam* (1985); *Moria land* (1987).

FURTHER TRANSLATIONS

Swedish Book Review 1 (1984).

REFERENCES

Fritzdorf, Britta, *Symbolstudier i Sven Delblancs Hedebysvit* (Stockholm, 1980); Keutermans, Lisette, ''Nagari Revealed: The Genesis of Nagari in Sven Delblanc's Novel *Homunculus*.'' *Scandinavica* 23.2 (1984); Orton, Gavin, ''The Swedish Novel Today.'' *Scandinavica* 15 (1976); Orton, Gavin, and Philip Holmes, ''The Novel since 1950,'' in *Essays in Swedish Literature*, ed. Irene Scobbie (Aberdeen, 1978); Robinson, Michael, *Sven Delblanc: Åminne* (Hull, 1981); Sjöberg, Leif, ''Delblanc's *Homunculus*: Some Magic Elements.'' *Germanic Review* 49 (1974); Sondrup, Steven P., ''Sven Delblanc's

Narrative Art.'' *Swedish Book Review* 1 (1984); Vowles, Richard B., ''Myth in Sweden: Sven Delblanc's *Homunculus.*'' *Books Abroad* 48.1 (1974).

Laurie Thompson

Diktonius, Elmer. Finland-Swedish poet, novelist, and critic, b. 20 January 1896, Helsinki, d. 23 September 1961, Helsinki.

Diktonius was unusual among the Finland-Swedish authors of his generation in that he came from modest circumstances (his father was a printing foreman) and was completely bilingual: although Swedish was spoken at home, he was sent to Finnish-language schools, and spent his summers in the Finnish-speaking section of northern Nyland (Uusimaa), from which his mother's family had migrated to the capital. (Yet his mother, to whom he remained deeply attached, had grown up as a Swedish speaker.) Fascinated by music—a heritage from his parents, both of whom liked to sing—he began violin lessons at an early age; this musical passion, and a desire to educate himself (he was a wide-ranging reader), led him to abandon formal schooling at the age of fourteen; however, he then entered the Helsinki Conservatory, with plans of becoming a composer. It was as a musician that he met the political activist Otto Ville Kuusinen (1881–1964), to whom he gave lessons in music theory; Kuusinen in turn attempted to instruct him in Marxism. During Finland's Civil War (1918), in which Kuusinen played a major role in the Red regime, Diktonius lay low, not enlisting in the Red Guard, despite his political sympathies; after the end of the conflict he spent a year, stationed in Karelia, as a draftee (an experience he later said he enjoyed) in Finland's new army. In 1920 he went abroad, ostensibly to study composition, but devoted himself instead to poetry of a radical political and formal bent, sending much of it to Kuusinen, now a refugee in Sweden; in Paris, Diktonius wrote his famous suite on revolutionary action, ''The Jaguar,'' which became the main display in his first book, *Min dikt* (1921; My Poem), together with some of his aphorisms. His subsequent experiences in London, where (he claimed) he came close to starvation, and on the Cornish coast were incorporated into *Hårda sånger* (1922; Hard Songs), in which he included ''The Jaguar'' again, together with autobiographical verse and the first of his many poems about storms. Returning to Finland, he helped to create the short-lived bilingual magazine *Ultra*, meant to open Finland's eyes to expressionism, and to the work of its own ''modernist,'' Edith Södergran.* A new volume of revolutionary poetry, *Taggiga lågor* (1924; Barbed Flames), was distinguished by its portrait poems on some of Diktonius's cultural idols, among them Friedrich Nietzsche, August Strindberg,* and Arnold Schönberg, and by its poems about children—considerably more innocent than the ''pansexual'' verse in *Hårda sånger* addressed to a six-year-old English girl. (It had shocked even friendly readers.)

Meanwhile, Diktonius proved himself to be a vigorous and unorthodox literary critic, assailing what he regarded as the Finland-Swedish literary establishment (for example, the work of Bertil Gripenberg,* Jarl Hemmer,* and Runar Schildt*) with boisterous humor; he was allowed these liberties by a new mentor, Axel Åhlström, the editor of the socialist paper *Arbetarbladet*, to which Diktonius contributed regularly until the late 1930s. Diktonius employed the same gusto in his prose idyll, *Onnela* (1924; The Happy Place), where his "expressionist" prose (shot through with jokes, Fennicisms, and musical and literary allusions) lightly concealed a deep-seated Finnish patriotism. A second trip abroad, to Paris in 1925–1927, led to disaster: divorce from his wife, the singer Meri Marttinen (who immediately married his cousin), a sense of failing poetic power, and a repetition of the paralyzing poverty of his London days; saved through the efforts of friends, in particular the poet Gunnar Björling,* he produced a powerful verse collection, *Stenkol* (1927; Coal), with its fine comical poem on "The Orchestra" (in fact, a farewell to his own musical ambitions), the "snapshots" of cultural idols (from Johann Sebastian Bach to Edgar Allan Poe and Edith Södergran) and *bêtes noires* (Pär Lagerkvist*), and its "Tightrope Walker," about the difficulty of poetic production, without the safety net of rhyme, regular rhythm, and traditional image. A second section of the book, devoted to "the workers' cause," is much weaker than the more personal part; a coda is formed by two long poems on an imaginary uprising, the one with a scene suggesting London, the other Paris—and both remarkably ambiguous in their attitude toward revolution. Diktonius's radical poetry then came to an end with the retrospective *Stark men mörk* (1930; Strong but Dark). "Red Eemili," the "ballad from 1918," recounting the brief and brutal life and death of a Finnish farm boy, is Diktonius's farewell, for the nonce, to the failed "Finnish revolution." Otherwise, music and nature and sometimes painful self-analysis shove revolutionary concerns from the center of his lyric stage.

Diktonius was rapidly becoming a figure of note in Finland's cultural life: the little magazine *Quosego* (1928–1929) displayed his experimental verse, he was given serious essayistic treatment by Professor Gunnar Castrén of Helsinki University, he was invited to lecture in Sweden. His second marriage was a happy one, he won friends and admirers in the establishment he had once scorned, and he became the regular music critic for the liberal journal *Nya Argus*; in 1933, he published a collection of his Shavian reviews as *Opus 12, musik* (Opus 12, Music). The year before, he had brought out his short novel "in woodcuts," with his own quasi-learned commentary, *Janne Kubik* (1932), another of his ambiguous statements about Finland's recent history and about himself; the lazy, unprincipled, and outright stupid Janne—sporadic dockworker, soldier in the Red Guard, bootlegger, and fascist gangster—may be an instrument for self-castigation and apology. A collection of short stories, *Medborgare i republiken Finland* (1935; Citizens in the Republic of Finland), a gallery of life's losers, variously loathsome or pathetic—a pedophiliac harmonium builder (who is, in fact, Janne's brother), a mad shoemaker, an orphan boy driven to suicide, a drunken peasant, a pious mother of a never-do-well son, a farmer dying of cancer. (Diktonius's concern with such figures can already be seen in the book of prose sketches, *Ingenting* [1928; Nothing], whose title is taken from a poem of Södergran; there, a boy—a traveling acrobat—almost kills himself at the insistence of a mob of drunken lumberjacks.) A sequel, *Medborgare II* (Citizens

II), came out in 1940, containing a Helsinki love story, "Josef and Sussan" (where the main characters are not Finns but a Jew, a half-Jew, and a Finland-Swedish girl), a legend about the transformation of a slaughterer into a saint, and a picture (one of Diktonius's favorite set-pieces) of a Finnish roofing bee that ends in a drunken dance. The line of Diktonius's prose closed with *Höstlig bastu* (1943; Autumnal Sauna), a potpourri of reflections on music, literature (Aleksis Kivi*), favorite Finnish landscapes, and political and linguistic toler-ance, all permeated by the tired melancholy becoming more and more charac-teristic of the sometime revolutionary. Diktonius was painfully aware of his premature aging; the book concludes with the wish to die alone, by the light of the sauna's lamp.

The "simple verse" subjoined to the "satisfied prose" of the innocuous sketchbook, *Mull och Moln* (1934; Clod and Cloud), had been disappointing. Diktonius had hoped that his lyric verse would someday return, but *Gräs och granit* (1936; Grass and Granite) is made up mostly of poems reprinted from earlier collections, *Jordisk ömhet* (1938; Earthly Gentleness) is brought to book length by translations of Finno-Ugric folk poetry, and *Varsel* (1942; Portents) by translations from Arthur Waley's versions of Chinese poetry. Nevertheless, the collections do have some gems, in those cases where Diktonius does not wax solemn or sentimental but rather, a Finnish equivalent of William Carlos Williams, brings his gifts for whimsical humor and startling observation to bear. See, for example, "Unhappy Bass Tuba" and "Salvation Guitar" (another swipe at Lagerkvist) in the book from 1936, the plain but subtle "Heart of the World, 1938" and the complexly comical and pacifistic "Villa Golicke" in the middle volume, the poems on Franz Peter Schubert and on "The Dictator's Grave" in the wartime collection.

In the Winter War (1939–1940), Diktonius traveled through Sweden, speaking against the Soviet Union (a country to which, less than a decade before, he had talked of moving); in the "Continuation War" of 1944–1945, he served very briefly as a writer of propaganda, and then, because of his declining health, re-turned to his free-lancer's existence. The armistice of 1944, and the sudden change in Finland's political climate, brought his leftist past to life again; and, in such poems as "The Red Rainbow" of *Annorlunda* (1948; Otherwise), he sought to excuse himself for his "defection." Nevertheless, the collection also included some nonpolitical poems destined to be classics of the Swedish lyric ("Unreally True," to the memory of his first wife, who died a suicide, and "Elegy," on age erotically confronted by youth), as well as the verse portrait of the drink-ridden Eino Leino* and the curious anthem, "Our Country Number Two." Critics were variously merciful or cruel to *Novembervår* (1952; November Spring), intimating that it should not have been printed; yet this swan song is fascinating because of the valor with which Diktonius, his mental powers swiftly fading, sought to find a new poetic style. The last years of his life were spent in sanatoriums.

Criticism has been most interested, poetically and politically, in the "revo-lutionary" works of the young Diktonius; however, his genuine contribution to

Swedish-language literature may lie in the poems where his idiosyncratic personality and his verbal invention have full play (as Rabbe Enckell* said, "there are many secrets here"), and in his narrative and critical prose. It has been argued that Diktonius's language is often "Finnish" in its essence, to the point of sheer uncorrectness; this charge was brought against his translations of Eino Leino (1930) and of Kivi's *Seven Brothers* (1948), and was leveled at his original books of prose as well; in fact, Diktonius did translate *Janne Kubik* into Finnish (1946), asserting that he was restoring the book to its "original language." But his many Fennicisms are a source of his vitality, like the Irishisms of a Sean O'Casey or a Sean O'Faolain.

FURTHER WORKS

Brödet och elden (1923); *Ringar i stubben*, ed. Jörn Donner (1954); *Dikter 1912–1942, Prosa 1925–43, Meningar 1921–43*, ed. Olof Enckell (1956–1957). *Samlade dikter* (1987).

TRANSLATIONS

Swedo-Finnish Short Stories, ed. George C. Schoolfield (1974); *The Prose Poem: An International Anthology*, ed. M. Benedikt (1976); *Books from Finland* 16.2 (1982).

REFERENCES

Enckell, Olof, *Den unge Diktonius* (Helsinki, 1946); Henrikson, Thomas, *Romantik och Marxism: Estetik och politik hos Otto Ville Kuusinen och Diktonius* (Helsinki, 1971); Petherick, Karin, "Four Finland-Swedish Prose Modernists: Aspects of the Work of Hagar Olsson, Henry Parland, Elmer Diktonius, and Rabbe Enckell." *Scandinavica* 15. Supplement (1976); Romefors, Bill, *Expressionisten Elmer Diktonius* (Helsinki, 1978); Schoolfield, George C., "Diktonius and the Art of Orchestration." *Scandinavian Studies* 53.2 (1981); Schoolfield, G. C., "Elmer Diktonius and Edgar Lee Masters," in *Studies in Scandinavian-American Interrelationships, Dedicated to Einar Haugen*, ed. S. Skard and H. Naess (Oslo, 1971); Schoolfield, George C., "Elmer Diktonius as a Music Critic." *Scandinavica* 15. Supplement (1976); Schoolfield, George C., *Elmer Diktonius* (Westport, Conn., 1985); Schoolfield, George C., "A Portrait of Elmer Diktonius." *Books from Finland* 16.2 (1982); Schoolfield, George C., "Strindberg and Diktonius: A Second Chapter," in *Structures of influence*, ed. M. H. Blackwell (Chapel Hill, 1981); Vainio, Matti, *Diktonius: Modernisti ja säveltäjä* (Helsinki, 1976); Willner, Sven, "Elmer Diktonius," in *Finländska gestalter*, vol. 6 (Ekenäs, 1967).

George C. Schoolfield

Dinesen, Isak (pseud. of Karen Blixen). Danish short story writer, b. 17 April 1885, Rungsted, d. 7 September 1962, Rungsted.

Dinesen used different pseudonyms for each of her literary personae, and others for the major languages in which her works were published. Dinesen's father was a romantic adventurer, writer, and politician; her mother came from a wealthy Copenhagen family of merchants and traders. Dinesen was educated at home in the tradition of previous centuries' aristocracy. After her father's suicide in 1895, Dinesen was raised by loving but strict female relatives. She studied painting in Copenhagen, Paris, and Rome, never taking these studies seriously. When Dinesen was twenty-nine, her need for freedom and adventure made her break loose from the puritanical restraints of home life to marry Bror von Blixen-Finecke, the second son of a Swedish baron. With the help of Dinesen's family, the couple settled in Kenya to run a coffee plantation. The marriage soon failed, but Dinesen remained in Africa until 1931. During these years she met and fell in love with the English nobleman Denys Finch-Hatton, a big game hunter, an intellectual, and a truly free spirit; and under his tutelage Dinesen gradually adopted the English language as her own. When after years of hazardous finances the plantation went bankrupt and Finch-Hatton died in the crash of his airplane, Dinesen was compelled to return to a bleak future in Denmark, with a broken spirit and suffering from advanced syphilis. Once again supported by her family, Dinesen began work on a collection of fantastic tales, some of which she had already composed while living in Africa. With the publication in 1934 in England and America of *Seven Gothic Tales (Syv fantastiske Fortællinger,* 1935), Dinesen established herself as one of the major writers of this century.

For Dinesen the dominant concerns of life and therefore of literature lay in man's unceasing existential quest—the quest to discover one's own identity, to discover God's design for mankind. Dinesen struggled in her personal life and in her writing to realize her identity as an artist and a woman, but also as a member of society. Her art, she considered, was something to be earned through courage and suffering, as a bargain with God or with Lucifer. She was a feminist who believed that the sexes were at once complementary and fundamentally and irreconcilably opposed. She was a primal mother who had only borrowed children. *Seven Gothic Tales* (which Dinesen said had too much of the author in it) contains "The Dreamers," Dinesen's most autobiographical story. The chief protagonist, Pellegrina Leoni ("The Wide-travelling Lioness"), an opera singer who has lost her voice, vows never again to be confined to any single role in life. She flees from each new identity and each new lover who tries to keep her, until her only escape is to jump off a cliff. Mira, the storyteller, (i.e., Dinesen herself), defines dreaming as "well-mannered people's way of committing suicide." Dreamers are those whose destiny has been bent like the taproot of certain coffee trees, so that the tree will never bear fruit but flowers more richly than others.

Seven Gothic Tales is set in the romantic past, usually the eighteenth and nineteenth centuries. Filtered through the unreality of Dinesen's artificial and fantastic setting, the essence of her characters emerges as if in silhouette. Rather than being psychological studies of individuals, they become symbolic variations of archetypes. In each of the seven stories the protagonists are confronted with their destinies, usually with a fatal outcome. *Seven Gothic Tales* embodies Dinesen's personal philosophy: "A man gets exactly the destiny he can hold, exactly the destiny he can bear.'' The African books, although mostly read as autobiography, clarify these views of the synthesis between nature and culture. The idealized wild animals and the natives of Africa, whose life is in accordance with their God-given nature, and who accept good and evil as two sides of the same principle, are contrasted with the domestic animals and the overly civilized bourgeoisie whose priority is comfort and security and who therefore have no destiny.

In *Winter's Tales*, her most Danish book, Dinesen continues her established themes of fate, courage, and pride. In ''Heloise'' the heroine, an exotic dancer, is granted Dinesen's ironic vision as she proudly sacrifices herself and thus fulfills her destiny by successfully feigning chastity. ''Sorrow Acre,'' one of Dinesen's most striking stories, based on a traditional Danish tale, opposes the true aristocrat and the true proletarian, who both act in accordance with their worldviews. Anne-Marie, the archetypal mother, embracing her fate, saves her son through a superhuman effort and dies maintaining universal order. *Winter's Tales*, written at the high point of her career, is the most polished of Dinesen's works.

Abroad Dinesen enjoyed the status of an international celebrity, and at home she figured prominently as a controversial figure in artistic and intellectual circles, participating in live public debates as well as on radio and television. During the war and postwar years, Dinesen also wrote essays, reviews, and stories for the periodical press. With Ole Wivel,* Bjørn Poulsen, and Thorkild Bjørnvig* she helped found the avant-garde literary journal *Heretica*, one of whose chief editorial aims was to introduce European modernism to Denmark, and which represented the first successful attempt since J. L. Heiberg,* one hundred years earlier, to create a Danish school of literature. Dinesen's greatest impact both as a writer and as a social critic is derived from the distance between her personal philosophy and the egalitarian spirit of her time. She was despised and adored for her excesses and her cosmopolitan, decadent artificiality, and for being an antithesis to the ''true'' Dane, described by Nikolaj Grundtvig* (in his patriotic anthems) as one who is best served by staying on level ground—the type of person and attitude toward life that Dinesen never tolerated. She was a mythmaker who herself became a myth. Dinesen is still an enigmatic, best-selling author more than a quarter century after her death.

FURTHER WORKS

Sandhedens Hævven (1936; *The Revenge of Truth*, 1971); *Den Afrikanske Farm* (1937; *Out of Africa*, 1937); *Gengældelsens Veje* (1944; *The Angelic Avengers*, 1946); ''Babett's Feast'' (1950; ''Babettes Gæstebud,'' 1952 and 1955 by Karen Blixen); ''Daguerreotypier'' (1951; *Daguerreotypes and Other Essays*, 1979); ''The Ghost-Horses'' (1951; ''Spøgelseshestene,'' 1955); *Sidste Fortællinger* (1957; *Last Tales*, 1957); *Skæbne-Anekdoter* (1958; *Anecdotes of Destiny*, 1958); *Skygger paa Græsset* (1960; *Shadows on the Grass*, 1960); *Osceola* (1962); *Ehrengard* (1963; trans. 1963); *Essays* (1965; *Daguerreotypes and Other Essays*, 1979); *Efterladte Fortællinger* (1975; *Carnival: Entertain-*

ments and Posthumous Tales, 1977); *Breve fra Afrika: 1914–1931* (1978; *Letters from Africa: 1914–1931*, 1981).

REFERENCES

Bjørnvig, Thorkild, *Pagten* (Copenhagen, 1974; *The Pact*, 1983); Hannah, Donald, *"Isak Dinesen" and Karen Blixen* (New York, 1971); Henriksen, Aage, *Det Guddommelige Barn og andre essays om Karen Blixen* (Copenhagen, 1971); Henriksen, Liselotte, *Isak Dinesen: A Bibliography* (Copenhagen, 1977); Johannesson, Eric O., *The World of Isak Dinesen* (Seattle, 1961); Juhl, Marianne, and Bo Hakon Jørgensen, *Dianas Hævn* (Odense, 1981); Langbaum, Robert, *The Gayety of Vision: Isak Dinesen's Art* (New York, 1965); Lasson, Frans, and Clara Svendsen, *The Life and Destiny of Isak Dinesen* (Chicago and London, 1970); Thurman, Judith, *Isak Dinesen: The Life of a Storyteller* (New York, 1982); Wamberg, Bodil, ed., *Out of Denmark*: (Copenhagen, 1985); Whissen, Thomas Reid, *Isak Dinesen's Aesthetics* (New York, 1973).

Wera Hildebrand

Ditlevsen, Tove. Danish poet, short story writer, and novelist, b. 14 December 1918, Copenhagen, d. 4 March 1976, Copenhagen.

Ditlevsen, who grew up in a working-class milieu in Copenhagen, represents in her works a continuation of earlier conventional lyric form and a limited range of motifs. Nevertheless, after the publication of her first work, *Pigesind* (1939; A Girl's Mind), she proved to be popular. There followed the publication of six novels, in the realistic mode, between 1941 and 1968, four volumes of novellas, two of essays, one of aphorisms, and eight further collections of poetry—one of which, *Kvindesind* (1955; A Woman's Mind), updates the experiences of the first collection. She has also written children's books and, drawing much renewed attention to herself, an autobiographical work, *Gift* (1971; Married, but "gift" in Danish also means "poison"), remarkable for its candor and honesty in treating the author's early loves, marriages, and addiction to narcotics; equally relentless is *Vilhelms Værelse* (1973, Wilhelm's Room), a mixture of novel and auto-biography, which in painful and painstaking detail reveals destructive tendencies within a marriage.

Ditlevsen may not be a writer of a wide scope, but she is forceful in her continuing dissection of Eros, her abiding love for children, and her tribute to the poor section of Copenhagen in which she was born and raised.

FURTHER WORKS

Man gjorde et barn fortræd (1941); *Lille verden* (1942); *Barndommens gade* (1943); *Den fulde frihed* (1944); *For barnets skyld* (1946); *Blinkende lygter* (1947); *Dommeren* (1948); *Kærlighedsdigte* (1949); *Paraplyen* (1952); *Vi har kun hinanden* (1954); *Forår* (1956); *Flugten fra opvasken* (1959); *Annelise—tretten år* (1959); *Hvad nu Annelise* (1960); *To som elsker hinanden* (1960); *Den hemmelige rude* (1961); *Den onde lykke* (1963); *Barndom* (1967); *Ungdom* (1967); *Ansigterne* (1968); *De voksne* (1969); *Min nekrolog og andre skumle tanker* (1973); *Det runde værelse* (1973); *Paranteser* (1973); *Tove Ditlevsen om sig selv* (1975); *En sibylles bekendelser* (1976).

TRANSLATIONS

Modern Danish Poems, ed. Knud K. Mogensen (1950); *The Other Voice: Twentieth-Century Women's Poetry in Translation* (1976); *Contemporary Danish Poetry,* ed. Line Jensen et al. (1977); *Orbis* 27/28 (1977); *The Penguin Book of Women Poets* (1978); *Complete Freedom and Other Stories* (1982); *Early Spring* (1985).

REFERENCES

Levy, Jette Lundbo, *De knuste spejle* (Copenhagen, 1976); Mogensen, Harald, ed., *Om Tove Ditlevsen* (Copenhagen, 1976); Petersen, Ove, "Kvinden, døden og Skriften," in *Analyser af moderne dansk lyrik,* ed. Per Olson (Copenhagen, 1976); Richard, Anne Birgitte, *Kvindelitteratur og Kvindesituation* (Copenhagen, 1976).

                                                                  Otto M. Sorensen

Donner, Jörn. Finnish novelist and journalist writing in Swedish, b. 5 February 1933, Helsinki.

Donner is nearly a cultural institution of his own in Finland and Sweden. His early breakaway from the conservative literary establishment earned him an enfant terrible label that has proven quite permanent.

Välsignade dag (1951; Blessed Day), marked Donner's debut, which was followed by a number of novels dealing with the generation growing up in postwar Helsinki. Here Donner attempts epic description in a realistic mode, already giving indications of keen perceptions of the forces of society, but the protagonists are central in a traditional narrative grip. *Jag, Erik Anders* (1955; I, Erik Anders) and *Bordet* (1957; The Table) are representative of this period in Donner's production.

Displeased with his reception, Donner turned to what has been termed journalistic writing, a genre in which he quickly received international acclaim with *Rapport från Berlin* (1958, 1966; *Report from Berlin,* 1961) and continued with *Rapport från Donau* (1962; Report from the Danube) and *Nya boken om vårt land* (1967; The New Book about Our Country). In this phase Donner further develops his already sensitive exposition of cultural dynamics.

When Donner returns to purely fictional writing in the 1970s, he presents a personal brand of the epic novel, one where the characters function as the backdrop to unfolding events. The Anders clan, about which these novels at first seem to deal, is actually a rather loose gallery whose purpose it is to mirror the dynamics of a society in development. The Anders series is best seen as a *Bildungsroman* for twentieth-century Finland; the perspective seems to be a refinement upon *Janne Kubik,* by Elmer Diktonius.*

Donner's reception at home continues to be cool; he is accused of being a poor stylist and incapable of presenting live characters. His aims are different, however, and he persists with a prolific production.

FURTHER WORKS

Slå dig inte till ro (1952); *Brev* (1954); *På ett sjukhus* (1960); *Helsingfors, Finlands ansikte* (1961); *Djävulens ansikte* (1962, rev. ed. 1965; *The Personal Vision of Ingmar*

Bergman, 1964, or *The Films of Ingmar Bergman*, 1972); *Världsboken* (1968); *Sommar av kärlek och sorg* (1971); *Marina Maria* (1972); *Jakob och friheten* (1973); *Sverigeboken* (1973); *Nu måste du* (1974); *Angelas krig* (1976); *Angela och kärleken* (1981); *Gabriels dag* (1982); *Far och son* (1985); *Hemåt i höstregn* (1985); *Presidenten* (1986); *År av kärlek och sorg* (1987); *Motströms* (1988).

REFERENCES

"Jörn Donner Writes 'for Adults'." *Books from Finland* 2.1 (1968).

Kim Nilsson

Dorothe Engelbretsdatter. *See* Engelbretsdatter, Dorothe.

Drachmann, Holger. Danish poet, novelist, playwright, and journalist, b. 9 October 1846, d. 14 January 1908, Hornbæk.

Born the son of a Copenhagen physician, Drachmann was little interested in formal schooling. He later entered the Academy of Art, became a landscape painter of some note, and began to write verse. In 1871 he journeyed to London, became acquainted with workers there and with refugees from the Paris Commune, whence he derived his initial revolutionary tendencies. He returned to Denmark, befriended Georg Brandes,* and published *Digte* (Poems) in 1872, in which his English experiences played a large role. Apparent already was the poet's sensitivity and power of imagination, and these first poems reflect his subjective approach to the world.

His later verse in this decade, *Sange ved havet* (1877; Poems by the Sea) and *Ranker og roser* (1879; Vines and Roses) shows a break with earlier nineteenth-century poetry. There is an irregular treatment of form with great stress on rhythmical flow. The sea here and in ensuing lyrics plays a significant role.

With his novel *Derovre fra grænsen* (1877; Beyond the Border) Drachmann adopted a nationalist position. This led to a break with the Brandes school in 1880. Thereafter, at least for a time, the poet joined the middle class and extolled the virtues of family, hearth, and home.

At the end of the 1880s he left his second wife and their four children and became involved with a popular Copenhagen songstress, Amanda Nilsson, whom he called "Edith" and whom he loved passionately even beyond their estrangement ten years later. "Edith" was the inspiration for two collections of verse, *Sangenes bog* (1889; Book of Songs) and *Unge viser* (1892; Young Songs). During this period he again moved to the left, readopted his anti-bourgeois attitude of the 1870s, and was reconciled with Brandes.

Drachmann wrote several plays, some of which were set to music by P. E. Lange-Müller and one of which, *Der var engang* (1885; Once upon a Time), continues to be played. Some of his lyrics, too, were set to music: *Du danske mand!* (You Danish Man) by Carl Nielsen, remains ever popular. In all, eleven of Drachmann's lyrics appear in the widely published two-volume work *Danmarks melodibog* (Danish Book of Melodies).

Two of Drachmann's novels, *En overkomplet* (1876; A Supernumerary) and *Forskrevet* (2 vols., 1890; Pledged), despite structural, stylistic, and logical deficiencies, are interesting from the autobiographical point of view. In each the author divides himself between the two main characters who embody, on the one hand, form, reason, and responsibility (and their corruption), and on the other, rebelliousness and impulsiveness—in other words a clash essentially between classic and romantic, an opposition Drachmann was never able to synthesize, either in his work or within himself.

He is remembered primarily as a lyricist who introduced new forms, rhythms, and vitality into Danish poetry. It is for this reason that he continued to have such strong influence on later generations of lyricists.

FURTHER WORKS

Samlede poetiske skrifter. Folkeudgave, 12 vols. (1906–1909); *Skrifter*, 10 vols. (1926); *Poetiske skrifter*, 10 vols. (1927); *Holger Drachmanns breve til hans fædrene hjem*, ed. Harriet Bentzon (1932).

TRANSLATIONS

The Cruise of the Wild Duck (1893); *Paul and Virginie of Northern Zone* (1895); *Daedalus* (1900); *Nanna, a Story of Danish Love* (1901); "Renaissance" (1908); *Robert Burns* (1925); *Book of Danish Verse*, comp. Oluf Friis (1922, 1976); *Byron in Homespun* (1928); *A Second Book of Danish Verse* (1947, 1968).

REFERENCES

Rubow, P. V., *Holger Drachmann*, 3 vols. (Copenhagen, 1940–1950); Ursin, Johannes, *Holger Drachmann* (Cophenhagen, 1954); Vedel, Valdemar, *Holger Drachmann* (Copenhagen, 1909).

Otto M. Sorensen

Duun, Olav. Norwegian novelist, b. 21 November 1876, Tosnes, Namdalen, d. 13 September 1939, Botne by Holmestrand.

Duun was born on an island off the coast of North Trøndelag, where his father was a farmer and fisherman. During his adolescence he worked as a farmer and fisherman as well, and didn't leave home until he was twenty-five years old. From 1901 to 1904 he attended teachers college in Levanger, a small town in the Trondheimsfjord. He married Emma Møller in 1908 and moved to Holmestrand, where he worked as a teacher until 1927. During this period he wrote a number of significant novels and stories, and he was awarded a writer's salary from the Norwegian government in 1923. He was a finalist for the Nobel Prize twice (1925 and 1926). Duun's fate as a writer is thought-provoking. He composed more than twenty-five volumes, and Sigrid Undset* referred to him as "Norway's greatest writer." Inside Norway his reputation has grown steadily. Yet elsewhere—unlike Henrik Ibsen,* Knut Hamsun,* and Undset herself—Duun is virtually unknown. One reason for this probably is his language, a highly subtle rendering of the Trønder dialect, with its understatements, ellipses, and humor. This language, the essence of Duun's writing, has misleadingly stamped his work as difficult, and few translators have undertaken the challenge.

Duun made his debut in 1907, the same year as Sigrid Undset. *Lønlege skruvar og anna folk* (1907; Queer Birds and Other Folk), a volume of short stories, was followed by a string of novels, *Marjane* (1908), *På tvert* (1909; Athwart), *Nøkksjølia* (1910; The Nøkksjø Meadow), *Gammal jord* (1911; Old Soil), *Hilderøya* (1912; The Hilder Island), and *Sigyn* (1913).

Between 1907 and 1938 Duun virtually published one book each year. His early novels describe people who appear to be life's losers, covering their vulnerability with a shell of defiance. In *På tvert* Danel is the crippled son of a dairy maid, and his life is a constant struggle with adversity. Danel foreshadows a string of negative male characters in Duun's work, most notably Lauris in *Juvikfolke* (1918–1923; *The People of Juvik*, 1930–1935), and above all, Didrik in *Medmenneske* (1929; Fellow Being). Nevertheless, the goal of Duun's writing was not to explore psychologically destructive elements in people, but rather to portray life-affirming characters, able to face the harshness of existence without losing their humanity. These characters have the ability to experience the richness of life as well, and reach out to others with great compassion. The two characters who come closest to fulfilling Duun's ideal are Odin in *Juvikfolke* and Ragnhild in the trilogy *Medmenneske, Ragnhild* (1931), and *Siste leveåre* (1933; Last Year of Life).

The central conflict in Duun's work is precisely the struggle between the humane and the inhumane, between good and evil, between the individual and nature. His most positive characters are lovers of life, "for life is surely the best we have," as Odin says in *Juvikfolke*. Duun's insistence that good must prevail in the end is not based on facile optimism, but on a refusal to accept defeat, a stubborn faith in what he considers the essence of being human, a confidence in the human spirit and the human heart.

The most dramatic acting out of the archetypal struggle between good and evil is the description of Odin and Lauris on the overturned keel of a small boat that was to take them across the stormy sea to get medical help for Lauris's wife, Astri. It immediately becomes evident that the keel can hold only one of the two men, and at first Odin was tempted to push the evil Lauris into the roaring waves. However, a keen realization that Lauris, in spite of his crooked ways, is nevertheless a human being, makes him change his mind, and instead he permits himself to slip into the water.

Unlike Odin, Ragnhild in the trilogy does kill her diabolical father-in-law, Didrik. She is compelled to commit the murder because she understands that if she does not act, her husband, Håkon, will. Nevertheless, Ragnhild knows that Håkon would be unable to carry the psychological burden of patricide through life. Therefore, she suffers exile, prison, and a painful homecoming, but Ragnhild never loses her open, harmonious, life-accepting personality.

The title of Duun's last novel, *Menneske og maktene* (1938; *Floodtide of Fate*, 1961), encapsulates the central theme in his entire production, the combat of the human spirit against depersonalized nature or evil. In *Menneske og maktene* we are informed in the very first chapter that the small island society that provides the setting for the novel will ultimately be swallowed up by the surrounding ocean. The inhabitants live in constant fear of the gigantic waves that will one day flood their island and possibly sweep them away. The final chapter of the book describes the fulfillment of the prophecy, the arrival of the long-awaited final assault of the sea against the island. While many perish, the catastrophe also helps eliminate old enmities, and by staying together, a small group of the island's inhabitants manage to survive the night, illustrating once again Duun's unwavering faith that the human spirit will survive even the most devastating struggle against the powers that are constantly threatening to destroy it.

FURTHER WORKS

Tre venner (1914); *Harald* (1915); *Det gode samvite* (1916; *Good Conscience*, 1928); *På Lyngsøya* (1917); *Blind-Anders* (1924; *The Blind Man*, 1931); *Straumen og evja* (1926; *The Trough of the Wave*, 1930); *Olsøygutane* (1927); *Carolus Magnus* (1928); *Gud smiler* (1935); *Samtid* (1936); *Vegar og Villstig* (1939); *Skrifter*, 12 vols. (1948–1949).

REFERENCES

Birkeland, Bjarte, "Olav Duun." *Scandinavica* 10 (1971); Dalen, Kari Johanne, *Olav Duuns 'Samtid'* (Oslo, 1971); Dalgard, Olav, ed., *Olav Duun* (Skien, 1976); Fetveit, Leif, *Juvikfolke og tradisjonen* (Oslo, 1979); Haakonsen, Daniel, *Olav Duun* (Oslo, 1958); Haukaas, Kaare, *Olav Duun og bøkene hans* (Oslo, 1954); Johnson, Pal Espolin, *Mennesket i motgang* (Oslo, 1973); Øverland, Arnulf, *Olav Duun* (Oslo, 1955); Schelderup, Alv G., *Dikteren Olav Duun* (Oslo, 1945); Svensen, Åsfrid, *Mellom Juvikfolke og Øyvære* (Oslo, 1978); Thesen, Rolf, ed., *Seks unge om Olav Duun* (Oslo, 1950; rev. ed., 1969); Thompson, Lawrence, "Olav Duun: 1876–1939." *Books Abroad* 14.2 (1940).

Randi Brox

E

Edfelt, Bo _Johannes_. Swedish poet, translator, and essayist, b. 12 December 1904, Kyrkefalla.

Edfelt began to publish poetry while studying at Uppsala University (from where he graduated in 1930): he was branded an "academic poet," compared with and to some extent overshadowed by Hjalmar Gullberg.* The inaccuracy of such judgments eventually became clear, but the ironic wit couched in a mixture of lyrical and colloquial language typical of the academic poets is prominent in *Högmässa* (1934; High Mass), the book that signaled his breakthrough. Edfelt's poems of the 1930s and 1940s are generally pessimistic, and his adherence to strict, rhymed verse forms gives an austere impression. Ecstatic love poems occasionally suggest glimmers of hope, although typically, the central physical experience is secondary to the metaphysical union of spirits.

Edfelt's pessimism and angst seemed justified by political developments, and he wrote a number of poems directly critical of the approaching and ongoing war. Edfelt is better, however, when he applies his melancholic irony to more general questions of human existence, as in *Bråddjupt eko* (1947; Echo from the Depths).

In his insistence on strict, traditional form, and a consistently gloomy message, Edfelt risked seeming stereotyped and monotonous. Perhaps sensing this, he writes his poems from the 1950s onward increasingly in poetic prose. The themes of death, aging, and the transience of all things human become ever more dominant.

Edfelt has translated prolifically from German, also from English and other languages; he is also a notable editor and critic. He has won most available prizes in Sweden for writing and translating, and entered the Swedish Academy in 1969. Edfelt's main influence was in the 1930s, but he continues to typify the ascetic poet, highly skilled at expressing with ruthless honesty a pessimistic worldview in strict form.

FURTHER WORKS

Gryningsröster (1923); *Unga dagar* (1925); *Ansikten* (1929); *Aftonunderhållning* (1932); *I denna natt* (1936); *Järnålder* (1937); *Vintern är lång* (1939); *Sång för reskamrater* (1941); *Elden och klyftan* (1943); *Hemliga slagfält* (1952); *Under Saturnus* (1956); *Insyn* (1962); *Ådernät* (1968); *Brev från en ateljé* (1976); *Dagar och nätter* (1983); *Ekolodning* (1986); *Broar* (1987).

TRANSLATIONS

Family Tree. Thirteen Prose Poems, ed. Robin Fulton (1981); *Swedish Book Review* 2 (1983).

REFERENCES

Carlson, S., and A. Liffner, eds., *En bok om Johannes Edfelt* (Stockholm, 1960); Eriksson, Erik, *Johannes Edfelt. En bibliografi* (Stockholm, 1975); Lagerroth, U.-B., and G. Löwendahl, eds., *Perspektiv på Johannes Edfelt* (Stockholm, 1969); Landgren, Bengt, *De fyra elementen* (Stockholm, 1979); Vowles, R. B., "Johannes Edfelt: A Man Confined." *World Literature Today* 55.2 (1981).

Laurie Thompson

Edgren, Anne Charlotte. *See* Leffler, Anne Charlotte.

Egill Skallagrímsson. *See* Skallagrímsson, Egill.

Ehrensvärd, Thomasine G. *See* Gyllembourg, Thomasine.

Einar Benediktsson. *See* Benediktsson, Einar.

Ekelöf, Gunnar. Swedish poet, b. 15 September 1907, Stockholm, d. 16 March 1968, Sigtuna.

Ekelöf grew up as an "outsider," according to his own claims, since his wealthy father had a mental breakdown when Ekelöf was still a boy. As a student, he lived in Uppsala, London, and Paris specializing in music and Oriental studies. He returned from Paris with his first collection of poems, *sent på jorden* (1932; *Late Arrival on Earth*, 1967). This collection began the illustrious career that was to end some three and a half decades later with Ekelöf established as one of the most important Swedish poets of the century. He had received an honorary doctorate from Uppsala University and was a member of the Swedish Royal Academy when he died. His rich and constantly changing poetry became a major influence on all Swedish poets to follow him.

What was it that made this shifting and changing poet so powerful? The revolutionary volume *sent på jorden* reflects some influences of the French surrealists, although Arthur Rimbaud and Stéphane Mallarmé may actually have been more important to Ekelöf's early writing. The originality of Ekelöf's first volume derives partly from his attempt to portray the process of human consciousness as well as the imagery that seems to rise from the unconscious. The opening line of the last poem in this collection, "Give me poison to die or dreams to live," suggests some of the themes that run throughout his work.

While his next volumes continue to show influences of romanticism, symbolism, and surrealism, Ekelöf's developing poetic strength appears most effectively in the war-related volume *Färjesång* (1941; Ferry Song). There the paradoxical nature of man and Ekelöf's own strong individualism are both given expression. In the poem "Eufori" (Euphoria), life and death unite in one beautiful moment of inner tranquillity. *Non serviam* (1945; I Will Not Serve) pushes Ekelöf's concern with the isolated individual even further. Some of his greatest poems, "Samothrake" and "Absentia animi," appear in this collection and reflect Ekelöf's desire to show mankind's place on a historical continuum as well as on an inner journey. The concept of "meaninglessness" takes on a mystical dimension in "Absentia animi," a sense in which people can reach into or beyond the limitations of humanity. This poem demonstrates Ekelöf's extraordinary ability to create a musical structure within language.

Continuing this sense of musical structure in his next volume, *Om hösten* (1951; In Autumn), Ekelöf reaffirms his own subconscious life. "Röster under jorden" (Voices under the Ground) presents Ekelöf's intimate sense of the past and the present united into a single fluid substance of time. In this substance, characters seem to be imprisoned, yet trying to reach and to communicate with one another.

The volume *Strountes* (1955; Nonsense) plays with the trivial and the nonsensical. As an absurdist and anti-poetical volume of poetry, it had a major influence on the next generation of Swedish poets. Ekelöf continued to write anti-poetic poetry in his next volume, but simultaneously he published another paradoxical and richly complex poem *En Mölna-elegi* (1960; *A Mölna Elegy*, 1984). *En Mölna-elegi* has a musical structure, yet combines pieces of Ekelöf's private past with allusions from literature and public events. The poet attempts to weave together, in a fashion not unlike that of Ezra Pound in the *Cantos*, thoughts and experiences that are comic, serious, nonsensical, obscene, and visionary, and all of which seem to be related to one summer day when he sat on the Mölna jetty outside of Stockholm.

During his career, Ekelöf wrote several collections of critical and autobiographical essays. These finely wrought prose works, written like short stories, provide additional insight into the sources of Ekelöf's inspiration. Although he was already established as one of the major Swedish poets of the twentieth century, his poetic career attained new heights in the trilogy that he wrote during the final years of his life.

The trilogy—*Dīwān över Fursten av Emgión* (1965, The Dīwān about the Prince of Emgión), *Sagan om Fatumeh* (1966; The Tale of Fatumeh), and *Vägvisare till underjorden* (1967; *Guide to the Underworld*, 1980)—constitutes a major poetic event in Swedish literature. The three volumes are based upon a mystical experience that Ekelöf had in Constantinople in 1965. He felt that the poems in the first volume, written in an intense burst of activity over a period of four weeks, were written by someone else, as if he were being used as a medium. The central character of the first collection is the hero of an eleventh-century Byzantine epic. The poems basically tell the sad story of the tortured and blinded Byzantine hero figure. The prince's story includes an earth-mother or goddess-like character who possesses qualities of the mystical "something else" sought by Ekelöf in his earlier poetry. *The Tale of Fatumeh* continues within the context of this Byzantine world, but now tells the story of a young girl whose tortuous life ranges from being a courtesan to the beloved of a prince. Finally, she becomes a deserted old woman, degraded, yet living on her visions and her memories. This powerful volume extends Ekelöf's search for unity within the realm of his own life and in the paradoxical and contradictory experiences of all human beings.

> Like fog lingering
> there remains a longing without purpose,
> and without anyone who still lacks someone.
> But such a fog can also signify the Shadow
> who lives without Sun and without Moon.
> She exists, he exists in the depth of an urn
> even if the urn were shattered.

> (Excerpt from "En prins vars namn bör
> vara onämnt," *Sagan om Fatumeh*.)

The final volume continues Ekelöf's effort to discover a harmony beyond the dualism of human experience. This unity may be related to death, but its ultimate representation as an almost cosmic union with the universe reflects the Eastern mysticism which so attracted Ekelöf. The combination of his own unique individualism and mysticism characterizes his writing from his first volume to his last.

That Ekelöf's poetry has been recognized throughout the world is attested by the numerous translations of his work published in the past twenty years. In the 1960s and 1970s major translations appeared by such poets as Muriel Rukeyser, W. H. Auden, both with Leif Sjöberg, and Robert Bly. More recently, excellent translations of Ekelöf's work have been published by Rika Lesser, and Leonard Nathan and James Larson. In Scandinavia, Ekelöf's influence permeates modern Swedish poetry, and the beauty and significance of his work continue to be discovered and rediscovered.

FURTHER WORKS

Dedikation (1934); *Sorgen och stjärnan* (1936); *Köp den blindes sång* (1938); *Promenader* (1941); *Utflykter* (1947); *Dikter*, 3 vols. (1949); *Dikter 1932–51* (1956); *Blandade kort* (1957); *Verklighetsflykt* (1958); *Opus incertum* (1959); *Valfrändskaper* (1960); *En natt i Otočac* (1961); *Sent på jorden med Appendix 1962 och En natt vid horisonten, 1930–32* (1962); *Dikter* (1965); *Glödande gator* (1966); *Vatten och sand* (1966); *Urval. Dikter 1928–68* (1969); *Lägga patience* (1969); *Partitur* (1969); *En självbiografi* (1971); *En röst* (1973); *Dikter 1965–68* (1976); *Variationer* (1986).

FURTHER TRANSLATIONS

Selected Poems of Gunnar Ekelöf (1967); *I Do Best Alone at Night* (1968); *Selected Poems by Gunnar Ekelöf* (1971); *Songs of Something Else* (1982).

REFERENCES

Ekner, Reidar, *Gunnar Ekelöf: En bibliografi* (Stockholm, 1970); Ekner, Reidar, "Gunnar Ekelöf: The Poet as a Trickster." *Scandinavian Studies* 42 (1970); Hellström, Pär, *Livskänsla och självutplåning* (Uppsala, 1976); Landgren, Bengt, *Ensamheten, döden och drömmarna* (Lund, 1971); Olsson, Anders, *Ekelöfs nej* (Stockholm, 1983); Perner, Conradin, *Gunnar Ekelöfs Nacht am Horizont und seine Begegnung mit Stepháne Mallarmé* (Basel, 1974); Shideler, Ross, "An Analysis of Gunnar Ekelöf's 'Röster under jorden.' " *Scandinavica* 9.2 (1970); Shideler, Ross, "A Functional Theory of Literature Applied to Poems by Paul Valéry and Gunnar Ekelöf." *Psycho Cultural Review* (Summer 1978); Shideler, Ross, "The Glass Clear Eye of Dreams in Twentieth-Century Swedish Poetry." *World Literature Today* 51.4 (1977); Shideler, Ross, *Voices Under the Ground* (Berkeley, 1973); Sjöberg, Leif, "The Later Poems of Gunnar Ekelöf: Dīwān and Fatumeh." *Mosaic* 2 (1970); Sjöberg, Leif, *A Reader's Guide to Gunnar Ekelöf's "A Mölna Elegy"* (New York, 1970); Sjöberg, Leif, "A Note on Poems by Ekelöf." *Scandinavian Studies* 39.2 (1967); Sjöberg, Leif, "Gunnar Ekelöf's 'Tag och Skriv.' A Readers Commentary." *Scandinavian Studies* 35.4 (1963); Thygesen, Erik G., *Gunnar Ekelöf's Open-Form Poem "A Mölna Elegy"* (Uppsala, 1985); Brita Wigforss, *Konstnärens hand. En symbol hos Gunnar Ekelöf* (Göteborg, 1983).

Ross Shideler

Ekelund, Vilhelm. Swedish poet, essayist, and aphorist, b. 14 October 1880, Stehag, d. 3 September 1949, Saltsjöbaden.

Ekelund was born and reared in Skåne and is strongly associated with that region. He enjoyed a happy childhood, but a certain disquietude and aggressiveness was apparent even in his youth. He studied at the University of Lund but never seriously pursued a degree. He began publishing at seventeen, and by the time he was twenty, he was determined to become a writer. His earliest poetic efforts sought to capture the changing moods of the lonely Scania landscapes and were inspired in substantial measure by the work of Ola Hansson.* His poetry gradually became more and more refined as he assimilated the influence of contemporary European masters. His career as a poet was a combination of triumphs and bitter disappointments. He received good reviews, but his books were published in small editions. Various grants allowed him to visit the Mediterranean countries and Germany, where he developed a special admiration for German culture. In 1908 he left Sweden in order to avoid the consequences of a minor legal infraction (he had been involved in a fight with a sheriff) and at the same time abandoned poetry in favor of the essay and aphorism. He spent four unhappy years in Berlin, after which he married and settled in Denmark. In 1921, twelve years after his original flight, Ekelund once again took up residence in Sweden. He had hoped that with his return he would become the spiritual leader of the younger generation but, to his disappointment, found himself isolated—and, to a degree, alienated—from the public. His writing became ever more inward, cryptic, and esoteric. A small but devoted group of followers has, nonetheless, remained loyal and seen to the publication of his works.

Among Ekelund's poems are a number that are counted among Sweden's most accomplished. His first two volumes are clearly the work of a sensitive and gifted poet and, while manifesting derivative and experimental elements, gave ample promise of what was to follow. In *Melodier i skymning* (1902; Twilight Melodies) the influence of Charles Baudelaire, Paul Verlaine, Richard Dehmel, Stefan George, and Hugo von Hofmannsthal can be observed in both a spontaneous lyricism and extreme artfulness reminiscent of the tradition of *poésie pure*. The moods move effortlessly from quiet reverence and devotion through gentle melancholy to subdued ecstasy. The themes and imagery of the poems are similar to those typically associated with the symbolist tradition while others are drawn from Ekelund's experience with the Swedish landscape. Ekelund's use of free verse is particularly fluid and well exploits the inherent possibilities of the language. In subsequent volumes, a more disciplined form is indicative of Ekelund's growing interest in the values and ideals of classical antiquity. *Dithyramber i aftonglans* (1906; Dithyrambs in Evening Splendor), frequently regarded as Ekelund's most distinguished work, was conceived and executed in this spirit. These drunken hymns of ecstatic exultation reveal at once the depth of his feeling and his mastery of passionate speech melodies.

When Ekelund first turned from poetry to essays and aphorisms, he drew much of his inspiration from Friedrich Nietzsche. His utter contempt for vapid halfheartedness stands in striking contrast to his celebration of fortitude and the struggle for harmony and wholeness. A serious illness and extended convalescence occasioned a shift in his spiritual allegiance from heroic and titanic figures to more moderate and humane models like Goethe and Ralph Waldo Emerson. *Veri similia* (1915–1916) and *Metron* (1918) are the most reasoned and eloquent representations of this position. His aphorisms unite a severity of thought with a remarkable linguistic flexibility in order to give direct and forceful expressions to his highly personal mode of being.

Although Ekelund never has enjoyed wide popularity, he was one of the most powerful influences in Swedish poetry from the early 1920s through the late 1940s and the point of departure for many later modernistic experiments.

FURTHER WORKS

Vårbris (1900); *Syner* (1901); *Elegier* (1903); *In candidum* (1905); *Grekisk bukett* (1906); *Hafvets stjärna* (1906); *Antikt ideal* (1909); *Böcker och vandringar* (1910); *Båge och lyra* (1912); *Tyska utsikter* (1913); *Nordiskt och klassiskt* (1914); *Attiskt i fågelperspektiv* (1919); *På hafsstranden* (1922); *Sak och sken* (1922); *Lefnadsstämning* (1925); *Väst-östligt* (1925); *Passioner emellan* (1927); *Lyra och Hades* (1930); *Spår och tecken* (1930); *Båge och lyra 1932* (1932); *Det andra ljuset* (1935; *The Second Light*, 1986); *Elpidi* (1939); *Concordia animi* (1942); *Atticism-humanism* (1943); *Plus salis* (1945); *Den ensammes stämningar*, ed. Jonas Ellerström (1985).

FURTHER TRANSLATIONS

Agenda (1976).

REFERENCES

Ekelund studier 1912–1976 (Lund, 1976); Ekman, Rolf, *Vilhelm Ekelunds estetik* (Lund, 1953); Ekman, Rolf, *Vilhelm Ekelund och Nietzsche* (Lund, 1951); Gustafson, Alrik, "Two Early Fröding Imitations: Vilhelm Ekelund's 'Skördefest' and 'I pilhäcken.' " *Journal of English and Germanic Philology* 35 (1936); Johannesson, Eric O., "Vilhelm Ekelund: Modernism and the Aesthetics of the Aphorism." *Scandinavian Studies* 56.3 (1984); Ljung, Per Erik, *Vilhelm Ekelund och den problematiska författarrollen* (Lund, 1980); Nært, Pierre, *Stilen i Vilhelm Ekelunds Essayer och Aforismer* (Lund, 1949); Stahl, Eva-Britta, *Vilhelm Ekelunds estetiska mysticism: En studie i hans lyrik 1900–1906* (Uppsala, 1984); Svensson, Karl, *Vilhelm Ekelund: Moralisten, Kulturkritikern* (Stockholm, 1946); Valdén, Nils G., *Inledning till Vilhelm Ekelund* (Lund, 1972); Werin, Algot, *Vilhelm Ekelund*, 3 vols. (Lund, 1960–1961).

                                                                        Steven P. Sondrup

Ekman, Kerstin. Swedish novelist, b. 27 August 1933, Risinge.

Ekman began her career as a writer and producer in the Swedish film industry. In the 1960s, she became known to a wider public for mystery stories of increasing complexity and psychological insights. Her literary breakthrough came in 1972 with a humorous tale about people in a village in northern Sweden who are trying to save their way of life, rather than move south in search of jobs, prosperity, and a warmer climate.

Since that time, Ekman has firmly established herself as one of Sweden's foremost writers through her tetralogy about people in a small town in central Sweden from the 1890s to the 1970s, beginning with *Häxringarna (The Witches' Circles,* 1983) in 1974 and ending with *En stad av ljus* (A Town of Lights) in 1983. In this series of novels the author depicts a society in change, from the backward, isolated Sweden of last century to the welfare state of today. In a language acclaimed for its richness of expression and its sparkling vitality, Ekman recreates a bygone world in all its manifestations and with an almost Proustian sense for minute details. Its heroes are the common people, those whom history usually forgets.

Ekman has been called the foremost social realist of the Swedish seventies, and she has often been compared to the great proletarian writers of the thirties in Sweden. But in contrast to them, with the exception of Helga Maria (Moa) Martinson,* Ekman writes about women and women's life: the backbreaking labor of women, and the caring and sharing in a woman's world. Everything is seen from a woman's perspective, something particularly noticeable in language and imagery.

In the course of these novels, Ekman's emphasis shifts as she moves between different levels of reality. In the first two volumes, with their welter of people and events, the world of external reality dominates the scene; only Konrad, the young communist in *Springkällan* (1976; Spring Fountain), articulates the communal dream of a better tomorrow and ponders the secrets of the world around him.

In *Änglahuset* (1979; The House of Angels) the action turns inward as the atmosphere darkens, dreams go unfulfilled, and disillusionment sets in. In Ekman's latest work, with its almost ironic title, the vision of a new society has turned into a nightmare, and the external reality, so overpowering at first, bears the stamp of almost unbearable sordidness. And yet, despite all indications to the contrary, when Ekman delves into the souls and selves of her characters, "the innermost chamber of existence," she sees beyond their limited consciousness a cosmic world of possibility that for all its teasing elusiveness is there to be discovered: "A city inside the real city, and a pattern underneath the pattern."

FURTHER WORKS

30 meter mord (1959); *Han rör på sig* (1960); *Kalla famnen* (1960); *De tre små mästarna* (1961); *Den brinnande ugnen* (1962); *Dödsklockan* (1963); *Pukehornet* (1967); *Menedarna* (1970); *Mörker och blåbärsris* (1972); *Hunden* (1986); *Rövarna i Skuleskogen* (1988).

FURTHER TRANSLATIONS

Scandinavian Review 68.4 (1980); *Swedish Book Review* 2 (1984).

REFERENCES

Forsås-Scott, Helena, "Women's Worlds." *Swedish Books* 2 (1979); Wright, Rochelle, "Kerstin Ekman: Voice of the Vulnerable." *World Literature Today* 55.2 (1981); Wright, Rochelle, "Kerstin Ekman's Crime Fiction, and the 'Crime' of Fiction: The Devil's Horn." *Swedish Book Review* 2 (1984).

Rose-Marie G. Oster

Elster, Kristian Mandrup (pseud. Peter Paal). Norwegian dramatist, critic, short story writer, and novelist, b. 4 March 1841, Namdalen, d. 11 April 1881, Trondheim.

Elster spent much of his short life trying to find his niche. Poor eyesight made him unable to become an officer, nervousness kept him from finishing school and becoming an actor, and his first dramas received poor reviews. Feeling a need to learn something practical, Elster succeeded in studying forestry and worked in Trondheim as assistant forester, continuing his literary endeavors. As theater and literary reviewer, Elster wrote about significant works (e.g John Stuart Mill's *The Subjection of Women*) and on contemporaries like Camilla Collett* and Magdalene Thoresen. He also translated Turgenev.

Elster was a western Norwegian at heart, despite only a few years' residency; his essay "Om Modsætningen mellom det vestlige og østlige Norge" (1872; On the Contrast between Western and Eastern Norway) was the first significant attempt to characterize nature and temperament in the two parts. Elster's few works go to the heart of social and class conflict. The novel *Tora Trondal* (1879) takes up tension between "the two cultures," the indigenous folk culture and the government officials. Conflicting views are personified in main characters, for example the debate concerning which currents will revitalize Norwegian culture. *Farlige folk* (1881; Dangerous People) has a large cast representing conflicting interests. The outsiders, Arne and Knut Holt, are dangerous people, radicals believing in the working classes. Knut has been abroad, seen large-scale class struggle, and opened his eyes to the inability of Norwegian class struggle to solve great social questions. Through love for Kornelia Vik, Knut resumes the fight, only to resign again.

A leading critic in the Modern Breakthrough of the 1870s, Elster was an important catalyzer for new ideas. At his untimely death Elster had not reached full maturity as an author. Though his works are flawed, Elster had a masterful hand in characterizing people undergoing development and maturing and in giving life to social and cultural debates of the day. His few works are a significant contribution to the rise of the Norwegian realistic novel and short story.

FURTHER WORKS

Samlede skrifter, 2 vols. (1898, 1903–1904); *Fra det moderne gjennombruds tid: litteraturkritikk og artikler 1868–1880* (1981).

REFERENCES

Dahl, Willy, *Kristian Elster: veien fra Grundtvig til Marx* (Oslo, 1977); Nilsson, Josef, *Kristian Elster 1841–1881* (Lund, 1942).

Nancy L. Coleman

Enckell, Rabbe. Finland-Swedish poet and critic, b. 3 March 1903, Tammela, d. 17 June 1974, Helsinki.

Enckell's debut book, *Dikter* (1923; Poems), depended on quick perceptions and small forms, and, even at this early stage, demonstrated Enckell's exquisite taste and his painter's eye. (Throughout his life, Enckell followed a second career as an artist in oils and watercolors.) His lucid laconicism continued in *Flöjtblåsarlycka* (1925; Flute-Player's Happiness) and *Vårens cistern* (1931; The Cistern of Spring); the last-named volume in particular—with its compressed views of the Acropolis, of a freight car, of "the calf Pirkko, dancing in heaven"—has become a favorite of anthologists searching for the best of Enckell's miniaturist poems. *Tonbrädet* (1935; The Sounding Board) provided another example of Enckell's "joy in sharpened senses," but his very sensitivity became a destructive force in the next years; *Valvet* (1937; The Vault), which critics have called Enckell's most powerful book, used classical myth to talk about a personal crisis (see "Toward Ithaca," the poem about the sleep of Odysseus, "likest unto death").

Political poetry was surely not to be expected from Enckell; instead, in his two lyric collections from the war years, *Lutad över brunnen* (1942; Inclined over the Well) and *Andedräkt av koppar* (1946; Breath of Copper), he indirectly commented upon the unhappy times through his awareness of the ironies surrounding the human condition, for which the poet has difficulty in finding accurate and honest words. In a poem from the later book, "Cervantes" says: "I wish I lived in some connection, / I wish the words / would find their way to me." He struggled with the problem again in what is the most famous of his poems, the elegy "Oh bridge of words-between." During the final third of his life, Enckell continued to produce verse, from *Sett och återbördat* (1950; Seen and Restored) to the posthumous *Flyende spegel* (1974; Fleeing Mirror). Enckell's old pleasure in his perception of nature and his love for the classical allusion (lightly applied, never learnedly) remain constant; but they are intermingled with an ever-increasing melancholy, sometimes taking almost querulous forms, at the brutal mechanization of existence.

Enckell's debut as a prose narrator came with *Tillblivelse* (1929; Origination), and he continued this line of production well into the 1930s; publishing his five small narratives together in 1958, he called them, rather disparagingly, "my youthful pieces." They are best when they turn into what might be called autobiographical observation, including the picture, *Ett porträtt* (1931; A Portrait), of his adored first wife; his attempts at direct storytelling, for the most part, are less successful. Every sentence is perfectly formed; there is a keen awareness of intellectual and emotional currents and cross-currents; yet the books—for example, the little novel about two friends, Vidrack and Blasius, *Landskapet med den dubbla skuggan* (1933; The Landscape with the Double Shadow)—suffer from that psychologizing bloodlessness and air of withdrawal so characteristic of Finland-Swedish narrative prose in the 1930s. Indeed, Enckell's apparent unwillingness to be concerned with the society around him made him an object of scorn for the angry young men of the 1960s. During the very years when he was accorded high literary honor—as resident in the Poet's House at Porvoo (Borgia), as a kind of Finland-Swedish *poeta laureatus*—he felt impelled to reply to the attacks he received; the situation may help to account for the sometimes haughty, sometimes complaining tone of the reflections in *Och sanning?* (1966; And Truth?) and *Tapetdörren* (1968; The Tapestried Door). He felt he had been the victim of a heavy-handed misapprehension of his life's work.

Enckell's poetic production also embraced another field. After a start with *Orfeus och Eurydike* (1938), he wrote a series of dramas on Greek themes, ending with *Alkman* (1959)—or, then, with *Dikt* (1963; Poem, a reprinting of *Iokasta* from 1939, accompanied by a new pendant, *Laios*). The plays had a certain success in radio performances; but, someday, they may be regarded as equivalents to Johan Ludvig Runeberg's* verse tragedy, *Kungarne på Salamis*—interesting but stillborn paralipomena to the central lyric work. Nonetheless, they comment obliquely on the trauma of their day—*Hekuba* (1952) on the lot of postwar refugees, *Mordet på Chiron* (1954; The Murder of Chiron) on the Korean War.

As a critic, Enckell is magisterial, speaking with a confidence reminiscent of T. S. Eliot's; the essays of almost three decades, collected in *Relation i det* *personliga* (1950; Connection to the Personal), are produced by an extremely stimulating literary and artistic mind, although they sometimes show (as in the essay on the baroque poet, Jakob Frese) a sublime indifference to the literary-historical context. Enckell's newspaper reviews deserve reprinting; he is full of insights and scrupulously fair, able to approach a poet so radically different from himself as Elmer Diktonius* with genuine understanding.

In part because there are almost no specifically "Finnish" elements in Enckell's work, it soon found devoted followers in Sweden, and was much admired there in the 1940s and 1950s, when Swedish poets applied his famous line, about "poets of the difficult school," to themselves—an enthusiasm that abated during the radicalized 1960s. In fact, Thomas Warburton has suggested that the "marble chill" emanating from the classical dramas and some of the later poetry will serve to drive future readers away. One may wonder if the verse of the early and middle years is not the essential part of his production.

FURTHER WORKS

Ljusdunkel (1930); *Herrar till natt och dag* (1937); *Nike flyr i vindens klädnad: Lyrik 1923–1946* (1947); *Agamemnon* (1949); *Skuggors lysen* (1953); *Traktat* (1953); *Dikter i urval* (1957); *Strån över backen* (1957); *Kärnor av ögonblick* (1959); *Essay om livets framfart* (1961); *Kalender i fragment* (1962); *Det är dags* (1965); *Resonören med fågelfoten* (1971).

TRANSLATIONS

"The Japanese Children," in *Swedo-Finnish Short Stories,* ed. G. C. Schoolfield (New York and Boston, 1974); *Modern Scandinavian Poetry*, ed. Martin S. Allwood et al. (New York, 1982).

REFERENCES

Enckell, Olof, *Rabbe Enckell i Borgå: En kommentar till hans sena diktning* (Helsinki, 1978); Ekelund, Louise, *Rabbe Enckell: Modernism och klassicism under tjugotal och trettital* (Helsinki, 1974); Ekelund, Louise, *Rabbe Enckell, lyriker av den svåra skolan: Studier i diktningen 1935–1946* (Helsinki, 1982); Petherick, Karin, "Four Finland-Swedish Prose Modernists: Aspects of the Work of Hagar Olsson, Henry Parland, Elmer Diktonius, and Rabbe Enckell." *Scandinavica* 15 Supplement (1976); Schoolfield, G. C., "Rabbe Enckell's 'Mot Itaka.' " *Germanic Notes* 7 (1976).

George C. Schoolfield

Engelbretsdatter, Dorothe. Norwegian hymnist, b. 16 January 1634, Bergen, d. 19 February 1716, Bergen.

With Engelbretsdatter's hymns Norwegian poetry gained prominence and eloquence. Her collection *Siælens Sang-Offer* (1678; The Soul's Song-Sacrifice) was reprinted six times before 1700, and fifteen during the next century. She was praised highly by her colleagues Thomas Kingo* and Petter Dass* and even by Ludvig Holberg* who called her "the greatest poetess who can be found in the Nordic countries." She lived to be eighty-two years old and survived all her eight children; thus, it is hardly surprising that she writes with intensity about the deprivations that a human being may easily experience in this world. She mastered the complex baroque techniques to perfection, and even if some of her lines or stanzas, like some of those by Kingo and Dass, may seem contrived today, she shares their talent for conjuring up mental states and for expressing the vanity of life and the perennial proximity of death. Unlike Kingo, whose hymns often are filled with torment, maybe even with doubt, Engelbretsdatter writes hymns that offer a more harmonious form of Christianity and much consolation to the fearful, penitent soul. The fact that her texts often are, or were, left out of Norwegian anthologies has undeservedly obscured her reputation.

FURTHER WORKS

Samlede skrifter, 2 vols. (1955–1956).

REFERENCES

Kvalbein, Laila Akslen, *Feminin barokk* (Oslo, 1970); Pettersen, Egil, *Norskhet i språket hos Dorothe Engelbretsdatter* (Bergen, 1957).

Niels Ingwersen

Engström, Albert. Swedish artist and short story writer, b. 12 May 1869, Lönneberga, d. 16 November 1940, Stockholm.

Engström's childhood in Småland set deeply into his being and eventually became, on one level, the major focus of his writing. It would be a mistake, however, to see him as just a regional writer. In writing about the people he knew best, Engström not only broadened the folk-types then current in Swedish popular literature, but also used them as instruments of his social criticism.

Engström's early career, after unfinished university studies in literature at Uppsala, centered around his drawing talent. He studied for one year under Carl Larsson in Gothenburg, whose favorite pupil he became, but moved to Stockholm in 1893 as cartoonist for *Söndags-Nisse,* a popular comic weekly. In 1897, he started his own paper, *Strix,* which he edited until 1924, and for which he also wrote and drew pictures. Much of Engström's work as a writer is associated with the drawings that often accompanied it. Both the drawings and the stories are firmly anchored in the international hobo/bohemian tradition of Mark Twain, Bret Harte, and their European counterparts, but viewed through the filter of Småland's forests and the Uppland archipelago.

Though he is counted as a humorist, such a term does not adequately cover Engström. Sharper than Twain, Engström's satirical attack on the upper classes is merciless and unrelenting, both verbally and pictorially. He saw the farmers and fisherfolk as survivors and, therefore, worth commemorating. It is surely no accident that Engström was especially popular among Swedish emigrants, who came chiefly from among these people.

Engström came to be taken seriously as a writer only later in his career, first in connection with *Genom mina guldbågade glasögon* (Through my gold-framed glasses) in 1911. Thereafter, his popularity increased considerably. He was elected to the Academy for the Free Arts in 1919, to the Swedish Academy in 1922, and became professor at the Academy of Art in 1925. From 1913 on, he also wrote travel books, of which that from 1926, *Gotska sandön* (Gotland Sand Island), is one of the best.

As a writer, Engström is a master of the laconic style. Some of his stories have no formal plot to them, dealing with moods and attitudes rather than events, though this does not lessen their satiric point. The typical situation will be a discussion among several old men, Engström's beloved *gubbar*, which may be in the style of Mark Twain's "Jumping Frog," as in *"Carl XII, Herkules, och Gustaf Matsson,"* from *Bläck och saltvatten* (1913; Ink and Salt-Water), or which may be a delineation of a character, as in "Skeppar Vesterbom" from *Hemma och på luffen* (1916; At Home and on the Road). Engström succeeds by keeping close to the earth and sea with which his characters are familiar.

FURTHER WORKS

Vänner och bekanta (1896); *En Gyldenne Bok* (1897); *Drufklasar och fikonkvistar* (1898); *En bok* (1905); *Riksdagsgubbar* (1906); *Mitt lif och lefverne* (1907); *Äfventyr och hugskott* (1908); *En bok till* (1909); *Min 5:te bok* (1910); *Kryss och landkänning* (1912); *Åt Häcklefjäll* (1913); *Samlade berättelser*, 24 vols. (1915–1935); *Medan det jäser* (1918); *Min 12:te bok* (1919); *Ränningehus* (1920); *Hemspånad och taggtråd* (1921); *Adel, präster, smugglare, bönder* (1923); *August Strindberg och jag* (1923); *Moskoviter* (1924); *En konstig blandning* (1925); *Agnarna och vetet* (1925); *Med penna och tallpipa* (1927); *Ur mina memoarer* (1927); *Anders Zorn* (1928); *Vid en milstolpe* (1929); *Bouppteckning* (1930); *Mot afton-glöden* (1932); *Naket o.s.v.* (1934); *Med Kaaparen till Afrika* (1937); *Läsebok för svenska folket* (1938); *Skrifter*, 28 vols. (1939–1941); *Siktat och sammalet* (1952); *En brevbok* (1952).

REFERENCE

Mårtenson, Gunnar, *En själ att dansa med: Essäer om svenskt och finskt* (Helsingfors, 1973).

Alan Swanson

Enquist, Per Olof. Swedish novelist, playwright, and journalist, b. 23 September 1934, Hjoggböle.

His father died when Enquist was a baby and he was raised by his mother. After Enquist finished high school, he left the religious and provincial forest region of northern Sweden to study at the University of Uppsala. A good high-jumper and a good student, Enquist completed his undergraduate and graduate degrees while writing his first novel. His breakthrough occurred with *Magnetisörens femte vinter* (1964; The Magnetizer's Fifth Winter). Based on the life of the famous hypnotist, F. A. Mesmer, this historical novel draws parallels between the past and the present.

In *Hess* (1966) Enquist utilizes techniques from the French "new novel" to explore the identity of Rudolf Hess, the deputy of Hitler who parachuted into England during World War II. The documentary novel *Legionärerna* (1968; *The Legionnaires*, 1973) depicts the story of Sweden's deportation of several hundred Baltic soldiers who fled from the German army at the end of World War II. Enquist received Scandinavia's most important literary prize for this much-debated novel. *Sekonden* (1971; The Second) combines sports and politics to weave together the puzzle of a dishonest athlete and his emotionally isolated son.

All of these novels force the reader to examine the past in order to see how the present and future might be changed. This theme continues in the highly successful play *Tribadernas natt* (1975; *The Night of the Tribades*, 1977). In it Enquist portrays the marital strife of August Strindberg* during the rehearsal of one of his plays. Enquist's next play retells in verse the myth of Phaedra, while the third in his "triptych" of plays, *Från regnormarnas liv* (1981; From the Lives of Earthworms) is based on the life of Hans Christian Andersen.*

In one of his finest novels, *Musikanternas uttåg* (1978; *The March of the Musicians*, 1984), Enquist describes the arduous life of northern Sweden's non-union laborers in the early 1900s. *Strindberg—Ett liv* (1984; Strindberg—A Life) was produced as a series by Swedish television. Enquist's ability to write in several genres and probe sensitive social issues within the framework of a documentary-style fiction has made him a controversial and central figure in contemporary Swedish literature.

FURTHER WORKS

Kristallögat (1961); *Färdvägen* (1963); *Katedralen i München och andra berättelser* (1972); *Berättelser från de inställda upprorens tid* (1974); *Chez Nous*, with A. Ehnmark (1976); *Mannen på trottoaren*, with A. Ehnmark (1979); *Till Fedra* (1980); *Doktor Mabuses Nya Testamente*, with A. Ehnmark (1982); *Nedstörtad ängel* (1985: *Downfall: A Love Story*, 1986).

FURTHER TRANSLATIONS

Box 749—A Magazine of the Printable Arts 2. 1 (1975); *Scandinavian Studies* 49.2 (1977); *Modern Swedish Prose in Translation*, ed. Karl Erik Lagerläf (1979); *Swedish Books* 3/4 (1980).

REFERENCES

Björksten, Ingmar, "The Monumental Seventies." *Sweden Now* 13.1 (1979); Gill, Brendan, "Fear of Women." *New Yorker*, 24 October 1977; Henningsen, Erik H., *Per Olov Enquist* (Copenhagen, 1975); Shideler, Ross, "The Swedish Short Story: Per Olov Enquist." *Scandinavian Studies* 49.2 (1977); Shideler, Ross, "Putting together the Puzzle in Per Olov Enquist's Sekonden." *Scandinavian Studies* 49.3 (1977); Shideler, Ross, "Strindberg: The Man and the Myth as Seen in the Mirror of Per Olov Enquist," in *Structures of Influence*, ed. Marilyn Johns Blackwell (Chapel Hill, 1981); Shideler, Ross, "Per Olov Enquist's Hess." *Scandinavica* 22.1 (1983); Shideler, Ross, *Per Olov Enquist:*

A Critical Study (Westport, Conn., 1984); Simon, John "Strindberg Agonistes." *New York Times* 31 October (1977); Stenkvist, Jan, *Flykt och motstånd* (Stockholm, 1978).

Ross Shideler

Erikson, Åke. *See* Gripenberg, Bertil.

Ericsson, Volter. *See* Kilpi, Volter Adalbert.

Erlingsson, Þorsteinn. Icelandic poet, b. 27 September 1858, South Iceland, d. 28 September 1914, Reykjavík.

After matriculation in 1883 Erlingsson went to Copenhagen to study law, but soon gave it up for Old Icelandic studies and literary pursuits, having caused a sensation with his celebrated and notorious poem on the centenary of the great Danish philologist Rasmus Christian Rask (1787–1832) in 1887. Erlingsson's thirteen years in Copenhagen were marked by a relentless struggle with poverty and ill health. In 1896 he returned to Iceland and became the editor of provincial journals, until in 1900 he settled in Reykjavík where he eked out a meager living by teaching.

Erlingsson's two principal works are the collection *Þyrnar* (Thorns), first published in 1897 and augmented in later editions, and a long narrative poem, *Eiðurinn* (1913; The Oath), the second part of which was never finished. In *Þyrnar* the two major strains of all Erlingsson's poetry are in evidence: on the one hand, beautifully cadenced and fervently romantic love and nature lyrics; on the other hand, scathing satirical poems attacking the ruling order, state and church, political oppression and religious hypocrisy. During his sojourn in Copenhagen Erlingsson came under the strong influence of Georg Brandes* and realism, but was never able to subdue his romantic leanings, so that his literary output is strangely extended between two opposing poles. In his later satirical poems there is a much lighter touch, probably inspired by Lord Byron, whom he revered next to Goethe. Erlingsson was also a great lover of animals and a pioneer in the field of animal protection. Many of his poems and short tales deal with such subjects in a provocative and endearing manner.

Erlingsson aspired to reach the common man with his poetry, an aspiration he largely achieved through his masterful and melodic use of folk meters, especially the quatrain. Many of his poems were composed to popular melodies and have been sung by the entire nation to this very day. He is also cherished as the first political radical among major Icelandic poets, having embraced socialism in Copenhagen a generation before it got a foothold in his native land.

FURTHER WORKS

Íslenskar sögur og sagnir (1906); *Sagan af Tuma þumli* (1913); *Tólf Þrautir Heraklesar* (1913); *Kvæði* (1918); *Málleysingjar* (1929); *Litli dýravinurinn* (1950); *ÞjóðsögurÞorsteins Erlingssonar* (1954); *Rit*, ed. Tómas Guðmundsson, 3 vols. (1958).

TRANSLATIONS

Ruins of the sagatime (1899).

REFERENCES

Benediktsson, Bjarni, frá Hofteigi, *Þorsteinn Erlingsson* (Reykjavík, 1958); Beck, Richard, *History of Icelandic Poets 1800–1940* (Ithaca, N.Y., 1950).

Sigurður A. Magnússon

Eskimo Literature. *See* Inuit Literature.

Eufemiavisor. Three Old Swedish verse romances from the early fourteenth century.

Eufemia was the German-born queen of the Norwegian king Hakon Magnusson. She may have been inspired to commission the Eufemiavisor by her relationship with the Swedish Duke Erik Magnusson, who visited the Norwegian court in 1302, became engaged to Princess Ingeborg in 1307, and married her in 1312. These dates correspond roughly to the dates indicated by the texts themselves for the three romances.

According to these dates, the earliest of the Eufemiavisor was *Herr Ivan* or *Ivan lejonriddaren* (Ivan, Knight of the Lion), a translation of *Yvain* by Chrétien de Troyes. The translator also used an earlier Norwegian prose translation, *Ívents saga*. *Hertig Fredrik af Normandie* (Duke Fredrik of Normandy) appears to have been the second translation. It followed a German translation of a French original, neither of which is extant. The final romance is *Flores och Blanzeflor*, the well-known story of Floire and Blanzeflur. Whether it was translated from Norwegian or French is unknown. The identity of the translator(s) of the three romances is also unknown.

Despite the varying languages and forms of the originals from which they were translated, the Eufemiavisor are all in the meter *knittel*—rhymed couplets with four stressed syllables and a varying number of unstressed syllables per line. This was a German form, and the Eufemiavisor show German influence also in the courtly ideal that animates them.

As the first verse romances in Scandinavia, the Eufemiavisor were influential, particularly in Sweden, where *knittel* remained an important meter. *Hertig Fredrik* is of broader interest, for it retains a Continental romance unknown elsewhere.

EDITIONS

Flores och Blanzeflor, ed. Emil Olsson (Skrifter utg. av Svenska Fornskriftssällskapet 46, 1921; 60, 1956); *Hertig Fredrik af Normandie*, ed. Erik Noreen (Skrifter utg. av Svenska Fornskriftssällskapet 49, 1927); *Herr Ivan*, ed. Erik Noreen (Skrifter utg. av Svenska Fornskriftssällskapet 50, 1930–1931).

REFERENCE

Jansson, Valter, *Eufemiavisorna* (Uppsala Universitets årsskrift, 1945).

John Lindow

Evander, Per Gunnar Henning. Swedish novelist and dramatist, b. 25 April 1933, Ovansjö.

Evander was brought up in the steel town of Sandviken, Gästrikland, where his father was a clerk. As a young man he worked as a laborer, then trained as an elementary school teacher of science before studying literature at Uppsala and teaching at folk high schools. In the 1960s he worked for Sveriges Radio as a dramatist and television producer.

His novels fall roughly into two periods. In the first, from 1966 to 1972, he produced complex experiments in style and technique in which he often examines the problem of art versus reality. His early work is influenced by Franz Kafka and Pär Lagerkvist,* but also by the behaviorist documentary method of P. O. Sundman,* and was regarded by the reading public as difficult. Evander frequently employs narrator disguises—confusingly, he also appears as a character in his own works—and delights in tantalizing the reader as to the value of the information he offers. Also among these disguises is a pseudo-documentary form used to depict men at work: brickmakers, metalworkers, and shift workers in heavy industry. The most accessible novel of this period is *Sista dagen i Valle Hedmans liv* (1971; The Last Day in the Life of Valle Hedman), in which he reconstructs in the form of an official investigation the last day, and thereby the world, of a self-employed craftsman before he falls to his death from a school roof.

In the second period, after 1972, Evander does not distance himself in the same way, but as an invisible author presents a series of more straightforward, realistic narratives, each centering on a main character with whom the reader may empathize. Several of these deal with a personal crisis from which the character gradually recovers with help from understanding friends. *Det sista äventyret* (1973; The Last Adventure) and *Måndagarna med Fanny* (1974; Mondays with Fanny) have been made into feature films. *Lungsnäckan* (1977; The Snail) (written under the pseudonym Lillemor Holm) and *Fallet Lillemor Holm* (1977; The Case of Lillemor Holm) caused a literary sensation.

Evander's characters are shaped by parents or siblings and have difficulty in forming relationships, but often succeed in turning their sense of guilt and anxiety into an enriching experience.

Evander's radio drama and television productions sketch relationships and situations, but incorporate strong elements of symbolism and mysticism.

Evander concentrates on the eternal existential problems, studiously ignoring politics, which sets him apart from many of his contemporaries and may explain his great popular success.

FURTHER WORKS

Tjocka Släkten (1965); *Det är söndagseftermiddag, min bror springer på åkern* (1966); *Smultrontrollet* (1967); *Bäste herr Evander* (1967, 1981); *Medan dagen svalnar* (1968); *Fysiklärarens sorgsna ögon* (1968); *Demonstranten* (1969); *Uppkomlingarna—en personundersökning* (1969); *I min ungdom speglade jag mig ofta* (1970); *Tegelmästare Lundin och stora världen* (1970); *Min farsa hade också en pokal* (1971); *En kärleksroman* (1971); *Det är redan mörkt, Horst Müller måste väckas* (1973); *Härlig är jorden* (1975); *Två komedier: Och alla mina levnads dagar, Guldfiskarna* (1976); *Judas Iskariots knutna händer* (1977); *Se mig i mitt friska öga* (1980); *Ängslans boningar* (1980); *Hundarnas himmel* (1982); *Orubbat bo* (1983); *Himmelriket är nära* (1986).

FURTHER TRANSLATIONS

Swedish Book Review 1 (1984).

REFERENCES

Hedlund, Tom, *Mitt i 70-talet: 15 yngre författare presenteras* (Stockholm, 1975); Lagerlöf, Karl Erik, "Per Gunnar Evander erövrar kärleken," in his *Strömkantringens år och andra essäer om den nya litteraturen* (Stockholm 1975); Nettervik, Ingrid, *Ängslans bilder: symbol och verkligheten i Pär Gunnar Evanders roman Uppkomlingarna* (Stockholm, 1984); Petherick, Karin, *Per Gunnar Evander* (Boston, 1982); Rying, Matts, "Fredagarna med hr Evander," in his *Tungomål: Samtal med diktaren* (Stockholm, 1979).

Philip Holmes

Evensmo, Sigurd. Norwegian novelist and journalist, b. 14 February 1912, Hamar, d. 17 October 1978, Oslo.

Evensmo's first novel, *Englandsfarere* (1945; *Boat for England*, 1947), was one of the most gripping accounts of the German occupation and the Resistance to appear in Norway at the end of World War II. Based largely on the author's personal experiences, it provides a realistic portrayal of how class differences were transcended and people were forced to question their basic assumptions in the desperate conflict.

The war and its causes also form the subject matter of Evensmo's next novel, *Oppbrudd etter midnatt* (1946; Departure after Midnight). Far more wide-ranging is Evensmo's most ambitious work, the trilogy *Grenseland* (1947; Border Country), *Flaggermusene* (1949; The Bats) and *Hjemover* (1951; Homewards). Through the medium of the central character Karl Martin, the trilogy depicts in broad social perspective the rise of the labor movement and the economic crisis of the 1920s, the strikes and emergent fascism of the 1930s, and finally the war with the occupation and its urgent demands. Here Evensmo successfully combines a sociohistorical study with a convincing portrait of a man whose early life, in a family and an environment hostile to warmth and joy, contains the seeds of his later betrayal, but who finds the strength to face what he has done and learn from it.

Evensmo was much more besides being a novelist; he was a journalist and newspaper editor; a writer of film manuscripts, travel descriptions, and science fiction; an essayist and polemicist deeply concerned with contemporary political and social issues. But it is undoubtedly the Karl Martin trilogy that will remain as his outstanding contribution to modern Norwegian literature.

FURTHER WORKS

Glassveggen (1954); *Trollspeilet* (1955); *Østenfor Vest og vestenfor Øst* (1956); *Gåten fra år null* (1957); *Femten døgn med Gordona* (1963); *Feider og finter* (1964); *Miraklet på Blindern* (1966); *Det store tivoli* (1967); *Vold i filmene* (1969); *Observasjoner* (1970); *Den nakne sannhet* (1971); *Gyldendal og gyldendøler* (1975); *Inn i din tid* (1976); *Ut i kulda* (1978).

REFERENCE

[Øyslebø], Olaf, *Etterkrigsprofiler* (Oslo, 1957).

Janet Garton

Ewald, Johannes. Danish lyric poet and dramatist, b. 18 November 1743, Copenhagen, d. 17 March 1781, Copenhagen.

Ewald's upbringing and education in a strict pietistic milieu, interrupted by service in the Austrian army 1759–1760, was concluded with a degree in theology in 1762. Ewald's experiences as a soldier ruined his health completely, and his unstable, bohemian life resulted in a breaking off of an engagement that marked him fatally for the rest of his life and led to alcoholism. These events are poetically re-created in his fragmentary autobiography *Levnet og Meeninger* (1804–1808; Life and Opinions) in which Ewald approaches the topics of adventure, women, and wine with imaginative flight reminiscent of Laurence Sterne's novels.

Ewald's fervent religiosity and sensitive self-consciousness point beyond the harmony of eighteenth-century classicism, and in Danish literature he is regarded as a connecting link between rationalism and romanticism. His debut drama, *Adam og Eva* (1769; Adam and Eve) is a psychological play about the fall of man written in traditional French classical style. His prose tragedy *Rolf Krage* (1770) is, however, a Shakespearean drama of action. The motif is taken from the Nordic legendary history by Saxo* Grammaticus and is utilized to illustrate the contemporary ideas of humanity and patriotism. The decisive break with the period's ideals takes place with the singspiel *Balders Død* (1775; *The Death of Balder*, 1889). The motif is again taken from Saxo: the story of the mythological demigod who falls in love with a mortal woman and therefore must die. But Ewald lets the title character experience his own resignation and weltschmerz—colored by the melancholy Ossianic poems—creating a timeless drama about the all-consuming power of erotic passion. His second singspiel, *Fiskerne* (1779; The Fishermen), based on an actual rescue operation off the Danish coast, marks a return to the ideas of Enlightenment in its glorification of the common people's heroic and virtuous behavior. Nevertheless, into the trivial plot Ewald has inserted some of his most exquisite poems, among others the Danish royal anthem "Kong Christian" (King Christian).

Ewald's absolute greatness emerges in his lyrical poetry, in particular in the form of the ode that he became acquainted with through his association with the circle around the German poet Friedrich Klopstock, who lived in Copenhagen from to 1751 to 1770. Under the guardianship of his mother, Ewald was periodically sent to the countryside to overcome his drinking. During his stay at Rungsted he wrote his famous ode "Rungsteds Lyksaligheder" (1773; The Joys of Rungsted). Taking its point of departure in concrete descriptions of the locality, the poem rises to an enthusiastic glorification of God, of whom nature is not solely a reflection but an integral part. Equally romantic is Ewald's accentuation of the significance of the artistic vocation as an intermediary between God and man. The concluding stanza expresses his gratitude toward his mother for giving him the opportunity to live at peaceful Rungsted. This stanza points to Ewald's great talent as a writer of occasional poetry. Through a combination of sensitivity and strict adherence to structure he was able to elevate this genre above similar contributions of the period. Particularly successful are his death poems, which focus on the painful sorrow of the bereaved, as well as a number of poems to friends and benefactors. One example is the ode "Til min Moltke" (1777; To My Moltke). In unrhymed, antique meters Ewald indirectly praises his own poetic genius and the purpose of his writings: to glorify God and the loftiest of human virtues. Ewald's last poetry was predominantly religious confession: in the ode "Poenitenten" (1777; Penance) the powers of darkness—gold, lust, and vanity—are rejected and with contrite heart the poet turns to his Savior, whom he ecstatically beholds in "Følelser ved den hellige Nadvere" (1777; Feelings at the Holy Communion). Ewald describes man's condition until he has placed his destiny in God's hands in "Til Sielen. En Ode" (1777; Ode to the Soul), the eighteenth-century's most grandiose Danish poem. The story of the fallen soul is symbolized in the disobedient young eagle that has fallen from its nest to the depths and helplessly strives toward the light until its mother comes to its rescue. This purely Christian confession stands in stark contrast to Ewald's former belief in the self-reliant power of the genius and points toward his last poem and only church hymn, "Udrust dig, Helt fra Golgatha" (1781; Gird thyself, Hero of Golgotha), the dying poet's fervent prayer for the grace of Christ.

Ewald also tried his hand as a writer of comedies with the satires *Pebersvendene*, (1771; Bachelors) and *Harlequin Patriot* (1772; Patriotic Harlequin), which, in spite of linguistic excellence, are devoid of dramatic qualities. As a prose writer Ewald had made his debut with the allegory *Lykkens Tempel* (1764; (Temple of Fortune), a dream vision of the perishableness of worldly happiness. Psychological realism, however, marks the later stories Ewald wrote for a journal he had hoped to establish. *Herr Panthakaks Historie* (1805; The Story of Mr. Panthakak), based on the idea that we must show total confidence in God, is modeled on Voltaire's philosophical stories but contrasts clearly with the French writer's pessimistic account of Candide. *Mester Synaals Fortælling* (1780; The Story of Master Sewing Needle) is a satiric Robinsonade, whereas *Den unge*

Herr von Frankhuysens Historie (1805; The Story of Young Mr. Frankhuysen), which includes elements from Ewald's own youth, tells of a young adventurer whose wantonness becomes fatal and emerges as an exceptionally brilliant psychological analysis of an individual temperament.

It is precisely this individualism in Ewald's writings that points beyond his own time. He focuses directly on the self, emphasizing the importance of the subjective experience in man's encounter with God Almighty. This experience is expressed with overwhelming poetic force that is kept in a tight rein by strict artistic discipline. It is in his lyric poetry and in the poetic parts of his prose and plays that Ewald emerges as a major figure, a renewer and pathfinder, in eighteenth-century Danish literature and, indeed, as one of its greatest authors.

FURTHER WORKS

Samtlige Skrifter, 4 vols. (1787–1814); *Samtlige Skrifter*, 8 vols. (1850–1855); *Samlede Skrifter,* 6 vols. (1914–1924; 2nd ed., 1969).

TRANSLATION

An Anthology of Scandinavian Literature, ed. Hallberg Hallmundsson (1965).

REFERENCES

Bobé, Louis, *Johannes Ewald* (Copenhagen, 1943); Brix, Hans, *Johannes Ewald* (Copenhagen, 1913); Eaton, J. W., *The German Influence in Danish Literature in the Eighteenth Century* (Cambridge, 1929); Jørgensen, A. D., *Johannes Ewald* (Copenhagen, 1888); Toldberg, Helge, *Det nordiske element i Johannes Ewalds Digtning* (Copenhagen, 1944); Zeruneith, Keld, *Soldigteren.* En biografi om Johannes Ewald (Copenhagen, 1985).

Sven H. Rossel

F

Fabricius, Sara *See* Sandel, Cora.

Faldbakken, Knut. Norwegian novelist, playwright, literary editor and reviewer, filmscript writer, b. 31 August 1941, Hamar.

Faldbakken is one of Norway's most widely read writers of the 1970s and 1980s. He began writing his psychologically oriented fiction in the late 1960s, precisely at the time when the writers in the mainstream demanded the politization of literature. Faldbakken followed his own course, however, writing primarily about individuals on a collision course with the restrictive behavioral norms of modern Western society. His debut novel, *Den grå regnbuen* (1967; The Grey Rainbow) did not make much of an impact, but his second novel, *Sin mors hus* (1969; His Mother's House) generated considerable discussion due to its theme of incest, and his fourth novel, *Insektsommer* (1972; Insect Summer), about a young boy's troubling rites of passage into adulthood, won Faldbakken a reading public that he has never lost. The latter two novels were both made into films. Faldbakken's tour de force to date is the two-volume *Uår* (1974 and 1976; The Lean Years), a modern Robinson Crusoe epic, which has been made into a film for Swedish television. Two of his later novels, *Adams dagbok* (1978; *Adam's Diary*, 1988) and *Bryllupsreisen* (1981; *The Honeymoon*, 1987), have been viewed as major contributions to the crucial debate in the 1970s and 1980s on the roles of men and women in our society. Faldbakken has also been active on other literary fronts. He has written plays and scripts for both film and television. He was editor of the literary periodical *Vinduet* from 1975 to 1980, and he is one of the chief literary reviewers for *Dagbladet*.

Though Faldbakken in general has been concerned with the crippling effects of repressive cultural norms—psychological, moral, sociological—on individuals, he in recent years has concentrated more and more on the plight of modern men in their roles as fathers, lovers, and sons. This is particularly true of *Adams dagbok* (1978) and *Bryllupsreisen* (1981), the first about three male personalities all tied to and wounded by the same woman, the second about a contemporary, seemingly liberated husband and father who suffers through the initial stages of a marital breakup. But whether Faldbakken is writing about men or women, his underlying thesis is the same, that is, our society corrupts our ability to feel, particularly in the case of men, leading to the perversion of our emotional lives. Faldbakken's tendency to date is to conclude that we stand little chance of reversing the process.

Faldbakken follows in the tradition of the major psychological realists of Norwegian fiction, Sigurd Hoel,* Johan Borgen,* and Agnar Mykle.* In recent years Faldbakken has captured the attention of the Norwegian reading public like few other writers, his books being some of the most successful of the best-sellers. In addition, Faldbakken's works have gained recognition in other countries, in particular, Denmark, Sweden, Germany, Eastern Europe, and the Soviet Union.

FURTHER WORKS

Eventyr (1970); *Maude danser* (1971); *Uår. Aftenlandet* (1974); *Uår. Sweetwater* (1975); *Tyren og jomfruen* (1976); *E 18* (1980); *To skuespill: Kort Opphold i Verona, Den siste landhandleren* (1981); *Glahn* (1985); *Livet med Marilyn* (1987); *Bad boy* (1988).

REFERENCES

Norseng, Mary Kay, "Faldbakken's Crippled Children." *Scandinavica* 22.2 (1983); Ødegaard, Bent, "Psykologi og samfunnskritikk. Linjer i Knut Faldbakkens forfatter-skap," in *Norsk litterær årbok*, ed. Leif Mæhle (Oslo, 1982); Ramberg, Mona Lyche, "Fanget av natur og samfunn," in *I diktningens brennpunkt*, ed. Rolf Nybo Nettum (Oslo, 1982).

Mary Kay Norseng

Falkberget, Johan. Norwegian novelist and short story writer, b. 30 September 1879, Rugeldalen, d. 5 April 1967, Røros.

Falkberget grew up in humble circumstances, the son of a miner and mountain farmer in Rugeldalen near Røros. He started out in his father's footsteps working in the mines from age seven to twenty-seven. In 1907, however, he took a position as an editor of a Labor party newspaper in western Norway, before moving to the Oslo region, where he worked as a newspaper editor, journalist and writer. Upon his mother's death (1922) he moved back to Rugeldalen, where he stayed with his family the rest of his life. He was a member of the Norwegian Parliament (Storting) 1930–1933.

Falkberget's first novels were cast in the mold of the semiromantic peasant tales of the nineteenth century (cf. Bjørnstjerne Bjørnson*), but the setting of his novels, the mining community, was new, and with *Svarte Fjelde* (1907; Black Mountains) he won critical acclaim as well. Almost all his novels have this same setting, similar to his native region. The most notable exceptions were *Eli Sjursdotter* (1913), a tale of love—which reflects a medieval ballad theme—

between a young Norwegian woman and a Swedish soldier during the time of the Great Nordic War in the early eighteenth century. *Lisbeth på Jarnfjeld* (1915; *Lisbeth of Jarnfjeld*, 1930), a grim psychological study of a strong woman of the mountains who, through fate's irrational blows, succumbs to the dark forces of the mind; and *Brændoffer* (1917; Burnt Offering), an equally grim study of human degradation, depicting how members of the lower classes of rural Norway, faced with the structural changes of the early twentieth century, were forced to move into the industrial centers and how they were destroyed in the process.

In his early years Falkberget was strongly influenced by utopian socialist thought, and by Maxim Gorky, and his lifelong commitment to the labor movement was marked by idealism and his strong Christian faith. Like the early Gorky, he could not accept the Marxist dogmas, but it is clear, as well, that the despair he had depicted in *Brændoffer* would not disappear through acts of idealism, a fact that undoubtedly led to his return to historical fiction, a genre in which he wrote all his later major works.

His first great historical novel, *Den fjerde nattevakt* (1923; *The Fourth Night Watch*, 1968), is set, with conspicuous attention to the historical detail, in early nineteenth-century Røros and depicts the arrival of a proud young clergyman and his family. The clergyman falls madly in love with a young married woman of his congregation, and in the ensuing battle between Eros and his Christian conscience he learns humility, but it has been a destructive battle for all involved. The novel has a modern psychological intensity that Falkberget never reached again. Two forces that Falkberget throughout his production depicted as the main positive elements in human life, the power of Eros and the ethics of Protestantism, are here pitted against each other in a destructive battle.

His next work, the trilogy *Christianus Sextus* (1927–1935; Christian VI—the title refers to the name of a copper mine), is considered his best novel by many critics. It depicts the life of a group of Swedish mine workers who, in the aftermath of the Great Nordic War, travel to Røros to look for work, and settle there. The life of the eighteenth-century mining community is portrayed with a vivid sense of the historical setting and with great narrative force. The novel is a tale of heroism and courage—it contains the most moving portrait of a child in Norwegian literature—in face of poverty, starvation, and brutality.

In his last great novel, *Nattens brød* (1940–1959; Bread of Night) Falkberget has re-created life in the community surrounding one of the smelters about thirty miles north of Røros during the latter half of the seventeenth-century. On the surface it is a historical novel with attention to customs, mores, and physical details of life, in a community in the throes of advancing industrialization and market economy. Above all, however, it is the story of An-Magritt, a girl and woman larger than life, strong, beautiful, and pure, who conquers all enemies with her strength and unyielding belief in the inherent goodness of man, and his ability to improve his material and spiritual lot. It is a novel with the power of a myth, convincing and moving, despite its air of unreality.

Although Falkberget's view of life was traditional, marked by his time and circumstances, his best works are imbued with poetry and mythic qualities that bridge time and literary movements. He remains one of the pivotal figures in twentieth-century Norwegian literature.

FURTHER WORKS

Mod lys og grav (1901); *Naar livskvelden kjem* (1902); *Bjarne* (1903); *Vaarsus* (1905); *Dovrefjeld* (1905); *Hauk Uglevatn* (1906); *Ved den evige sne* (1908); *Mineskud* (1908); *Urtidsnat* (1909); *Fakkelbrand* (1909); *Vargfjellet* (1910); *Nord i haugene* (1910); *Fimbulvinter* (1911); *En finnejentes kjærlighetshistorie* (1912); *Jutul-historier* (1913); *Av jarleatt* (1914); *Eventyrfjeld* (1916); *Helleristninger* (1916); *Sol* (1918); *Rott jer sammen!* (1918); *Barkebrødstider* (1919); *Vidden* (1919); *Bjørne-Skytten* (1919); *Bør Børson jr.* (1920); *Byd lykken haanden, eller da Johannes Mo løste rebusen* (1920); *Naglerne—eller Jernet fra Norden og andre fortellinger* (1921); *I nordenvindens land* (1924); *Vers fra Rugelsjøen* (1925); *Den nye Bør Børson* (1927); *Det høie fjeld* (1928); *I forbifarten* (1929); *Der stenene taler* (1933); *I vaktårnet* (1936); *I lyset fra min bergmannslampe* (1948); *Jeg så dem* (1963); *Vers fra Rugelsjøen og andre dikt* (1964).

REFERENCES

Barth Pettersen, T., ed., *Falkberget nå* (Oslo, 1980); Beck, R., "Johan Falkberget." *Scandinavian Studies* 16.8 (1941); Beck, R., "Johan Falkberget: A Great Social Novelist." *American-Scandinavian Review* 38.3 (1950); Falkberget, J., "Røros: The Copper Town of Norway." *American-Scandinavian Review* 13.9 (1925); Freding, T., "Johan Falkberget." *American-Scandinavian Review* 21.8–9 (1933); Kojen, J., "Grand Old Man of Literature: Johan Falkberget." *Norseman* 6 (1962); Kommandantvold, K. M., *Johan Falkbergets bergmannsverden*, 2 vols. (Oslo, 1971); Raastad, Ottar, "Johan Falkberget: An Appreciation." *American-Scandinavian Review* 58.2 (1970); Thesen, R., *Johan Falkberget og hans rike* (Oslo, 1959).

Kjetil Flatin

Fangen, Ronald. Norwegian novelist, dramatist, and essayist, b. 29 April 1895, Kragerø, d. 22 May 1946, Fornebu.

A lonely child of divorced parents, Fangen grew up a voracious reader and precocious writer. After raising hopes that he would renew the Norwegian drama, Fangen devoted himself from the late 1920s to an intellectual type of fiction indebted to Aldous Huxley and to Adlerian psychology.

Fangen's writing always deals with spiritual crisis. In his best novels, *Duel* (1932; *Duel*, 1934), *En kvinnes vei* (1933; A Woman's Way), and *Mannen som elsket rettferdigheten* (1934; The Man Who Loved Justice), the point of departure is the shattering of the characters' routine existences, an event that prompts a ruthless self-scrutiny. By means of a basically psychological plot, the layers of deception that have sustained the characters' social personalities are gradually stripped off, leaving Christian conversion or disaster, often suicide, as the only alternatives. *Duel*, widely translated, has been Fangen's most popular book, but *Mannen*, a Norwegian Book of Job, is artistically superior. In this novel, theme, setting, characterization, and style are perfectly blended, a rare occurrence in Fangen's fiction.

Fangen was a key figure in the interwar period as a champion of Christian humanism. His importance today, in the absence of a distinctive narrative talent and stylistic flair, rests chiefly on the spiritual passion with which he pursues perennially relevant themes like the disguises and perversions of love, the dark labyrinth of power, the elusiveness of personal identity. Endowed with a literary and intellectual culture of European format, Fangen brought to these themes the new knowledge of depth psychology as well as the accumulated wisdom of the Christian tradition.

FURTHER WORKS

De svake (1915); *Slægt føder slægt* (1916); *En roman* (1918); *Krise* (1919); *Streiftog i digtning og tænkning* (1919); *Syndefald* (1920); *Fienden* (1922); *Den forjættede dag* (1926); *Tegn og gjærninger* (1927); *Nogen unge mennesker* (1929); *Erik* (1931); *Dagen og veien* (1934); *Det nye liv* (1934); *En kristen verdensrevolusjon* (1935); *Som det kunde ha gått* (1935); *Paulus og vår egen tid* (1936); *På bar bunn* (1936); *Allerede nu* (1937); *Kristen enhet* (1937); *Kristendommen og vår tid* (1938); *Borgerfesten* (1939); *Krig og kristen tro* (1940); *Presten* (1946); *Nåderiket* (1947); *Om frihet, og andre essays* (1947); *Samlede verker*, 9 vols. (1948–1949); *Essays*, ed. Carl F. Engelstad (1965); *I nazistenes fengsel* (1975).

REFERENCES

Elseth, Egil Yngvar, *Ronald Fangen: Fra humanist til kristen* (Oslo, 1953); Engelstad, Carl F., *Ronald Fangen: En mann og hans samtid* (Oslo, 1946); Friese, W., *Nordische Literaturen im 20. Jahrhundert* (Stuttgart, 1971); Govig, S. D., "Ronald Fangen: A Christian Humanist." *American-Scandinavian Review* 49.2 (1961); Plomer, W., review of *Duel, Spectator*, 22 June 1934; Quennell, P., review of *Duel, TLS*, 28 June 1934; Strauss, H., review of *Duel, New York Times Book Review*, 17 June 1934; Thompson, Lawrence, "Ronald Fangen: 1895–1946." *Books Abroad* 20 (1946).

Sverre Lyngstad

Faroese Literature. Faroese literature began, properly speaking, with the medieval ballads, still considered to be the greatest Faroese literary treasure. Most famous is the great *Sjúrðarkvæði*, a version of the story of Sigurd the Dragon Slayer, related to the Nibelungen legends of Germany.

As Faroese only received its orthography in the nineteenth century, modern literature was late in making its appearance. Early poets such as Fríðrikur Petersen (1853–1917), Rasmus Effersöe (1857–1916), and Jóannes Patursson (1866–1946) were unpretentious romantics seeking to create the foundations for a modern Faroese literature in the nineteenth-century European tradition. The breakthrough came with the work of J.H.O. Djurhuus (1881–1948), who combined Greek and Nordic mythology into a splendid poetry of great vision and musicality. A little rhetorical for modern taste, he nevertheless stands as an outstanding example of Faroese literary creativity, by many considered the greatest Faroese poet.

His rival for this distinction is Christian Matras* (b. 1900), one of a group of writers born around the turn of the century. His work is profounder and less rhetorical, and Matras combines the linguistic skills of a philologist with those of a lyrical innovator. His near contemporary, Heðin Brú* (b. 1901), ranks as the father of Faroese prose, a stylist who has fashioned the language into a modern literary medium for his descriptions of village life. Another prose writer of this generation was Martin Joensen (1902–1966); his stylistic sense is less, but he depicts village mentality with great insight and understanding in two novels and numerous short stories. The two other writers born at the same time, completing what must be seen as the Faroese golden age, are William Heinesen* (b. 1900), and Jørgen-Frantz Jacobsen* (1900–1938), both of whom write in Danish. Jacobsen left one novel, *Barbara*, which has achieved worldwide fame, while Heinesen is now one of Scandinavia's leading novelists.

These men brought Faroese literature into the modern world, and have been succeeded by a younger generation that takes its literary position for granted. The leading novelist is Jens Pauli Heinesen (b. 1932), whose work ranges from the village sketch related to those of Heðin Brú and Martin Joensen, though in a more modern idiom, to lengthy and ambitious novels, one of which, *Frænir eitur ormurin*, seeks to translate the entire Sigurd myth from the ballad to modern surroundings.

Modernist poetry made its first appearance in the work of Karsten Hoydal (b. 1912), who writes under the influence of early modern poets from England and America, and has translated Edgar Lee Masters and Pablo Neruda into Faroese. The other important modernist of the older generation is Regin Dahl (b. 1918), who adopts the style, though not the religious content, of T. S. Eliot.

A more radical approach to modern poetry, clearly following the general Scandinavian trend, is the work of Steinbjörn Jacobsen (b. 1937), while Guðrið Helmsdal (b. 1941), the first woman poet in the Faroes, is influenced by Edith Södergran.* Of younger prose writers, mention should be made of Gunnar Hoydal (b. 1941) and Hanus Andriassen (b. 1942), both of whom write short stories with international as well as Faroese backgrounds.

Over the past century Faroese literature has progressed from a few, scattered beginnings to a literature conforming generally to the European pattern, but often very Faroese in spirit.

TRANSLATIONS

Faroese Short Stories, ed. Hedin Brønner (1972); *Faroese Folktales and Legends,* ed. John F. West (1980); *Rocky Shores,* ed. George Johnston (1981).

REFERENCES

Bandle, Oskar, "Moderne färöische Literatur." *Skandinavistik* 12.2 (1982); Bergström, Ejnar Fors, *Den färöiska boken* (Stockholm, 1974); Brønner, Hedin, *Three Faroese Novelists* (New York, 1973); Jacobsen, Ole, "Nyere digtning," in *Færøerne,* vol. 2 (Copenhagen, 1958); Jones, W. Glyn, *Faroe and Cosmos* (Newcastle upon Tyne, 1974); Jones, W. Glyn, "Types of Determinism in the Works of Heðin Brú and Martin Joensen."

Skandinavistik 14.1 (1984); West, John F., *Faroe: The Emergence of a Nation* (New York, 1972); *Faroe Isles Review* (Tórshavn, 1976–1978).

W. Glyn Jones

Ferlin, Nils Johan Einar. Swedish poet, b. 11 December 1898, Karlstad, d. 28 October 1961, Penningby.

Ferlin had a tragic childhood; his father drowned himself in 1909, and in youth in Filipstad, Värmland, Ferlin acquired a reputation as a drunkard and brawler. After working as a seaman, journalist, and actor he settled to writing popular songs for revues, cabaret and records. This last occupation has left its mark on his serious poetry, both in its simplicity and immediacy and in its rhythms and motifs. Ferlin was to become more popular with a broad public than his contemporaries Karin Maria Boye* and Hjalmar Gullberg,* partly because a number of his poems were brilliantly set to music. In the public mind he came to represent the classic figure of the world-weary bohemian poet.

His debut came in 1930 with *En döddansares visor* (Ballads of a Death-dancer), a darkly pessimistic collection revealing an obsession with death that appears in a variety of forms in his work, both startlingly original and clichéd, but the bitter hopelessness is tempered by the poignant music within the verse and by the poet's enormous compassion for the human condition.

Barfotabarn (1933; Barefoot Children) is more homogeneous, expressing the loneliness of the individual, the cruelty of those with power over us, and here Ferlin introduces both a personal and a religious element. With *Goggles* (1938) Ferlin reached the peak of his powers, using variations of his favorite motifs to complement one another. The collection includes topical satire and personal experiences.

The clown, fool, jester, and tramp are frequent representations of the artist in Ferlin's work. He was an anarchist with great love for the little people. Christ is regarded as an outsider like the poet himself, a joker even, but Ferlin sees him as the defender of the poor and weak. Ferlin's speculations on God imply no love of organized religion.

Ferlin stands apart from poetic modernism, keeping to traditional rhythmical and rhymed verse, though his rhymes are often daringly improvised. The characteristic features of Ferlin's work are his unerring selection of the apt word or expression, original and laden with meaning, his use of the banal in an elevated context, and his black humor and dark irony.

FURTHER WORKS

Tio stycken splitter nya visor, tryckta i år (1940); *Med många kulörta lyktor* (1944); *Kejsarens papegoja* (1951); *Från mitt ekorrhjul* (1957); *En gammal cylinderhatt* (1962); *Och jag funderade mycket* (1962).

TRANSLATION

With Plenty of Colored Lanterns: Selected Poems (1986).

REFERENCES

Björck, Staffan, "Det tomma tunet," in his *Lyriska läsövningar* (Lund, 1961); Eng, Uno, *Att umgås med Nils Ferlin* (Stockholm, 1962); Ferlin, Henny, *Nils. Ett försök till porträtt* (Stockholm, 1971); Lagerkrantz, Olof, "Den sorgsne Ferlin," and "På händerna för Ferlin," in his *Svenska lyriker* (Stockholm, 1961); Runnquist, Åke, *Poeten Nils Ferlin* (Stockholm, 1958); Vowles, Richard B., "Nils Ferlin: The Poet as Clown and Scapegoat." *Norseman* 12 (1954).

                                                                                                       Philip Holmes

Finnish Folklore. *See* Kalevala and Finnish Folklore.

Fløgstad, Kjartan (Pseud K. Villum). Norwegian novelist, b. 7 June 1944, Sauda.

Fløgstad worked in industry and as a sailor before becoming a writer. His sympathy with the working class is evident in all he writes, as is his intimate familiarity with their language and ways of thought. However, he is not first and foremost a political writer; his works are rich in fantasy and experiment, intellectual word-games and puzzles that tease the reader's understanding.

His early works, *Fangliner* (1972; Mooring Lines) and *Rasmus* (1974), are stories of industrial workers and seamen written from a position of complete solidarity, re-creating their daily life in the unpolished *nynorsk* (New Norwegian) of their own milieu. Fløgstad's literary breakthrough came with *Dalen Portland* (1977; *Dollar Road*, 1989), which was awarded the Scandinavian literary prize. Set in western Norway, it traces the evolution of a rural farming community into a modern industrial society, and the consequences for the social life and political awareness of its inhabitants. It combines the political with the fantastic; picaresque and comic episodes abound, making the novel richly entertaining at the same time it demonstrates the alienation and rootlessness that follow in the wake of "progress." Fløgstad's recent novels have also been critical successes. *Fyr og flamme* (1980; All Afire) is a many-faceted novel, with a large number of colorful characters involved in a series of loosely linked episodes ranging from the tragic to the grotesque, the whole couched in a richly allusive language. The central character of *U3* (1983) is a pilot with a working-class background who becomes slowly disillusioned by the political trickery and corruption of the cold war. It is a more directly political novel, yet also more personal, with less of the distancing effect of intellectual wordplay.

Fløgstad is one of the most exciting and innovative of contemporary Norwegian novelists.

FURTHER WORKS

Valfart (1968); *Seremoniar* (1969); *Den hemmelege jubel* (1970); *Døden ikke heller* (1975); *Ein for alle* (1976); *Loven vest for Pecos* (1981); *Ordlyden* (1983); *Det 7. klima* (1986); *Tyrannosaurus Text* (1988); *Portrett av eit magisk liv* (1988).

TRANSLATION

Stand 23.3 (1982).

REFERENCES

Garton, Janet, "New Directions in Norwegian Literature," in *Review of National Literatures: Norway,* ed. Sverre Lyngstad (New York, 1983); Petersen, Teddy, "Kjartan Fløgstads konfrontasjon med det verklege," in *Norsk litterær årbok,* ed. Leif Mæhle (Oslo, 1977); Stegane, Idar, "The New Norse Literary Tradition," in *Review of National Literatures: Norway,* ed. Sverre Lyngstad (New York, 1983); various articles in Norwegian on *Dalen Portland* in *Syn og Segn* 83.9 (1977).

Janet Garton

Fogelklou-Norlind, Emilia Maria. Swedish author, theologian, and lecturer, b. 20 July 1878, Simrishamn, d. 26 September 1972, Uppsala.

In 1909, at Uppsala University Fogelklou-Norlind became the first Swedish woman to earn a theological degree. Three years earlier, she had completed her undergraduate education at the same university, and in 1899, had obtained public school teaching certification. During her long life, Fogelklou-Norlind worked as a lecturer in many different capacities; until 1938, for example, she was a social psychologist at the Social Institute and University of Stockholm. Fogelklou-Norlind married Arnold Norlind in 1922 but was widowed seven years later. In 1932, she joined the Quaker Society of Friends and won a literary prize from *Samfundet De nio* (The Society of the Nine). Fogelklou-Norlind's scholarship in religious psychology was recognized in 1941 with an honorary doctorate in theology.

Fogelklou-Norlind affirmed that everyday experience should be a natural expression of the Christian religion. Believing that institutionalized distinctions between higher and lower realms have occurred at the expense of women's feelings of self-worth, she became one of the first feminist mystics of the century. Fogelklou-Norlind's study *Birgitta* (1919; Birgitta) explores the relationship between this Swedish saint's womanly consciousness and her spirituality. A later study, *Bortom Birgitta* (1941; Beyond Birgitta) makes the pioneering suggestion that Birgitta be viewed as a Christian representative for Magna Mater, the ancient Mother Goddess worshipped throughout the world in earlier eras. Fogelklou-Norlind's most well known literary works are her autobiographical novels, including *Barhuvad* (1950; Bareheaded), in which she describes her personal experience of Divinity.

In the past, Fogelklou-Norlind's major impact has been on other women writers such as Elin Wägner.* As patriarchal traditions continue to give way to more modern, humanist spiritualities, however, the general interest in Fogelklou-Norlind is increasing. She is remembered as much for her warmth and generosity toward other people and her dedicated service to women's causes as she is for her written achievements.

FURTHER WORKS

Allvarsstunder (1903, 1913); *Frans af Assissi* (1907); *Medan gräset gror*, 2 vols. (1911);
Förkunnare (1915); *Från längtans vägar* (1916); *Från hövdingen till den törnekrönte*
(1916); *Ur fromhetslivets svensk-historia* (1916); *Protestant och katolik* (1919); *Från
själens vägar* (1920); *Människoskolan* (1924); *Vila och arbete* (1924); *Befriaren i hög-
tidssägner och bilder* (1925); *Samhällstyper och medborgarideal* (1926); *Människan och
hennes arbete i psykologisk-historisk belysning* (1926); *Skolliv och själsliv* (1927); *Kväk-
aren James Nayler* (1929; *James Nayler, the Rebel Saint, 1618–1660*, 1931); *Samarbetets
psykologi och förvärvslivet* (1929); *Den allra vanligaste människan* (1931); *Vad man tror
och tänker inom svenska folkrörelser* (1934); *William Penn* (1935); *Arnold* (1944); *Ljus
finns ändå* (1948); *Helgon och häxor* (1952); *Resfärdig* (1954); *Form och strålning* (1958);
Minnesbilder och ärenden (1963); *Brev till vännerna/Emilia Fogelklou*, ed. GunnelVall-
quist et al. (1979).

TRANSLATIONS

Reality and Radiance, ed. Howard T. Lutz (1986).

REFERENCE

Wahlström, Lydia, *Glada givare* (Stockholm, 1929).

Laura M. Desertrain

Folklore. *See* Scandinavian Folklore.

Forssell, Lars. Swedish poet, playwright, essayist, and novelist, b. 14 January
1928, Stockholm.

Although deeply involved with the Swedish literary tradition, Forssell has
shown a decided inclination toward Anglo-Saxon influences, as indicated by his
translations of Ezra Pound and Lewis Carroll. His literary horizons are international.

Forssell first earned his literary reputation as a poet. His early poetry collections, especially *F. C. Tietjens* (1955), take issue with the reigning intelligentsia,
but gradually, his poetry adopts a more political cast. Forssell is interested in
questions of identity, displaying a fondness for role poems and masks. The poetic
ego in Forssell's poems fluidly changes in accommodation to the outside world.
His poems often possess a subaqueous quality; images are suddenly illuminated
only to sink from consciousness into the darkness, as in the case of the tigerlike
beast in "I natt när jag låg" (1968; *Last Night when I Lay*, 1969).

During the 1960s, Forssell came into his own as a playwright. His historical
drama *Galenpannan* (1964; *The Madcap*, 1973) depicts the story of Gustaf IV
Adolf and contains appropriate resonances from August Strindberg's* *Carl XII*.
The king is an idealist whose idealism slips into pathology, as he chooses to
disregard political and personal necessities. In his later theater, Forssell utilizes
dream-play techniques, as in *Christina Alexandra* (1968), and experiments with
aggressive political theater, as in *Show* (1971).

Forssell's single novel, *De rika* (1976; The Rich), masterfully exhibits an insight central to Forssell's authorship. The silent and oppressive codes of bourgeois behavior reveal themselves most clearly in the presence of aberrations. The novel portrays the uneasy responses of a wealthy Swedish family to its gentle daughter Jenny, who sees visions. Elsewhere in Forssell's authorship, figures like the Fool, Nijinskij, Gustav IV Adolf, Queen Christina, and Lenny Bruce expose the values of their society by upsetting them.

During his lengthy career, Forssell has been a highly visible figure in the cultural life of Sweden. His opinions on politics and culture, as expressed in his several essay collections, have inspired many a lively discussion. His distinctive poetic diction has been admired and imitated. Though not always well received, Forssell's theatrical venturesomeness has brought vitality to the Swedish stage.

FURTHER WORKS

Ryttaren (1949); *Narren* (1952); *Chaplin* (1953); *Cattus* (1955); *Kröningen* (1956); *Telegram* (1957); *Snurra min jord* (1958); *En kärleksdikt* (1960); *Prototyper* (1961); *Mary Lou* (1962); *Söndagspromenaden* (1963; *The Sunday Promenade*, 1969); *Torsten Andersson* (1963); *Röster* (1964); *Jack Uppskäraren och andra visor tryckta i år* (1966); *Upptåg* (1967); *Samtal vid Ganges* (1967); *Ändå* (1968); *Nedslag* (1969); *Borgaren och Marx* (1970); *Solen lyser på havet blå* (1971); *Oktoberdikter* (1971); *Sigfrid Siwertz* (1971); *Försök* (1972); *Visor svarta och röda* (1972); *Det möjliga* (1974); *En bok för alla människor* (1975); *Dikter* (1975); *Teater* (1977); *Haren och vråken* (1978); *Jag står här på ett torg* (1979); *Stenar* (1980); *Brokligheten* (1980); *Lasse i gatan eller Pirater* (1982); *Axplockerskan eller Den främmande kvinnan* (1984); *Ola med handklaveret* (1985); *Visa stenar* with Carl Fredrik Reuterswärd, (1987).

FURTHER TRANSLATIONS

The Sunday Promenade, in *The New Theatre of Europe*, ed. Robert Corrigan (1968); *Eight Swedish Poets*, ed. Frederic Fleisher (1969); *The Madcap*, in *Modern Nordic Plays: Sweden* (1973).

REFERENCES

Bäckström, Lars, *Under välfärdens yta* (Stockholm, 1958); Carlson, Harry, "Lars Forssell—Poet in the Theater." *Scandinavian Studies* 37.1 (1965); Franzén, Lars-Olof, *Omskrivningar* (Stockholm, 1968); Hagerfors, Lennart, *På väg in i femtiotalet* (Stockholm, 1979); McKnight, Christina, "Lars Forssell: The Jester as Conscience." *World Literature Today* 56.2 (1982); Printz-Påhlson, Göran, *Solen i spegeln* (Stockholm, 1958); Syréhn, Gunnar, *Osäkerhetens teater* (Uppsala, 1979); Syréhn, Gunnar, *Makten och ensamheten* (Stockholm, 1985); Törnqvist, Egil, *Svenska dramastrukturer* (Stockholm, 1973).

Susan Brantly

Franzén, Frans Michael. Finland-Swedish poet, b. 9 February 1772, Weåborg (Oulu), d. 14 August 1847, Härnösand.

The gifted son of a prosperous merchant, Franzén entered Åbo Academy (which at the time was Finland's university) at thirteen, and became a favorite student of Henrik Gabriel Porthan (1739–1804), a central figure in the awakening of Finnish cultural nationalism. Although Franzén was appointed docent at the academy in 1792, his interest lay more with literature than with learning, and in 1793, he attracted considerable attention when Johan Henric Kellgren* printed several of his poems in the newspaper *Stockholms Posten*. (A native Swede, Kellgren had spent some eight years at the academy, as a student, teacher, and disciple of Porthan.) Franzén's verse showed a clear enthusiasm for the proto-romantic currents emanating from Germany and Sweden, and, in "The Old Soldier," for Finland's history. After a trip through Finland in Porthan's company (1794), Franzén undertook a grand educational tour in 1795–1796, on the German leg of which he met Friedrich Gottlieb Klopstock (and wrote a poem to him), the Danish poet Jens Baggesen,* and Göttingen's great classical scholar, C. G. Heyne. An admirer of the French Revolution from afar, Franzén was shocked, during his stay in Paris, by what he learned about revolutionary excesses. In England he found a more congenial atmosphere, attracted as he was by the sentimentality he found in English letters, and the liberal strain in English political life. Thomas Gray's poetry in particular stands behind Franzén's major poem, a eulogy of the late, Finnish-born poet Gustaf Philip Creutz* (1731–1785). The "Song about Gustaf Philip Creutz" also served as a celebration of the two urges in Franzén's own work, toward classicism on the one hand and a kind of Nordic romanticism on the other. After the poem's submission to the Swedish Academy, it was subjected to numerous "anti-romantic" emendations, or mutilations, by the rationalist critic, Carl Gustaf Leopold* (1756–1829), and then was awarded the first prize.

In 1798, Franzén was named professor at Åbo Academy, where he remained until 1811; in the war of 1808–1809, Finland had been passed into Russia's hands, and Franzén left his homeland for a post as pastor at Kumla in Sweden, then (1824) in Stockholm, and finally, in 1834, as bishop in Härnösand. There is a marked change in Franzén's work after the death of his first wife (1805), his marriage (1807) to the widow of the poet Michael Choraeus (1774–1806), and his removal to Sweden; his later poetry—even his psalms and the Fanny poems of the early 1820s—is notably pale and abstract, while his epic poems and drama from the Swedish years are deadly dull. The veneration in which his sometime fellow countrymen continued to hold him, however, is demonstrated by the accolades he received upon his visit to Finland for the university's bi-centennial (1840), and by the words that Johan Ludvig Runeberg* (thinking not least of Franzén's early erotic poems to "Selma" and the convivial songs of his last decade in Åbo) addressed to him in a review. Runeberg had known his poems since youth, he said, but felt he "had made the true acquaintanceship of [these songs] for the first time," as a mature man. "I do not regard it child's play to read Franzén. . . . "

FURTHER WORKS

Emili eller En afton i Lappland (1802); *Gustaf Adolf i Tyskland* (1817–1818); *Julie de St. Julien eller Frihetsbilden* (1825); *Columbus eller Amerikas upptäckt* (1831); *Svante Sture eller Mötet vid Alvestra* (1832); *Audiensen eller Lappskan i Kungsträdgården* (1836); *Gustaf den tredje med de första Aderton af Svenska Akademien* (1836); *Drottning Ingierd eller Mordet på Eljarås* (1836); *Skaldestycken*, 7 vols. (1824–1861); *Samlade dikter*, 7 vols. (1867–1869); *Till min biografi: Självbiografiska anteckningar*, ed. Gösta Lundström (1945); *Frans Michael Franzéns Åbodiktning*, ed. Karin Allardt Ekelund (1969); *Resedagbok 1795–96*, ed. Anders Henmarck (1977).

REFERENCES

Andersson, Sven L., *En romantikens kyrkoman: Frans Michael Franzén och den andliga förnyelsen i Sverige under förra delen av 1800-talet* (Uppsala, 1977); Castrén, Gunnar, *Frans Michael Franzén i Finland* (Helsinki, 1902); Ek, Sverker, *Franzéns Åbodiktning* (Stockholm, 1916); Färnström, Emil, *I vänskapens spegel: Frans Michael Franzén och Fredrika Bremer* (Solna, 1971); Grellman, H., *Goethes Wirkung in Finnland von Porthan bis Lönnrots Tod* (Helsinki, 1948); Johnson, Walter, *James Thomson's Influence on Swedish Literature in the Eighteenth Century* (Urbana, Ill., 1936); Lundström, Gösta, *Frans Michael Franzén: Liv och dikt under Kumlatiden* (Göteborg, 1947); Nilsson, Albert, *Svensk romantik: Den platonska strömningen* (Lund, 1916); Schmalensee, Bo von, *Frans Michael Franzén och Johan Olof Wallin som förkunnare* (Norrköping, 1932); Spjut, Einar, *Frans Michael Franzén* (Uppsala, 1925).

George C. Schoolfield

Fridegård, Jan (Johan Fridolf). Swedish novelist and short story writer, b. 14 June 1897, Enköpings-Näs, d. 8 September 1968, Uppsala.

Fridegård, the son of a *statare* (farmhand paid largely in kind and tied to a large estate), grew up among the most impoverished of the rural proletariat. His education was scant. As a young man he was first an enlisted cavalryman, then a manual laborer in a series of odd jobs. Frequently unemployed, he was once confined to a work camp. His debut came relatively late, in 1931.

Like so many of the working-class writers of the 1930s, Fridegård drew frequently on his own experiences in his literary production. His first major work, the autobiographical trilogy *Jag Lars Hård* (1935; *I, Lars Hård*, (1983), *Tack för himlastegen* (1936; *Jacob's Ladder*, 1985), and *Barmhärtighet* (1936; *Mercy*, 1985), incorporates many details from Fridegård's difficult years in the 1920s and establishes one of his major themes, the individual versus the collective. Much of the work's tension derives from the fact that although Lars Hård rebels against a repressive class system, he also refuses to identify himself with his own social class, striving instead to become an intellectual aristocrat. That the author sees through the posturing of his fictional alter ego in no way undercuts the social indignation that imbues the text. The detached, bemused irony of the narrative voice, and in general the flexible, colloquial style, lend the work much of its appeal.

Autobiographical elements are also prominent in another series, *Lyktgubbarna* (1955; Night Watchmen), *Flyttfåglarna* (1956; Birds of Passage), and *Arvtagarna* (1957; The Inheritors). Set in the first decade of the century, the novels focus more on the author's parents and the now-vanished way of life they represent than on the author himself as a child. In an additional four volumes of memoirs,

Fridegård offers anecdotes and reflections about a wide variety of experiences and subjects, including the function of memory itself.

Fridegård had been interested in early Swedish history since childhood and was a skilled amateur archaeologist. His knowledge of customs and details of everyday life during the Viking period gives authenticity to the trilogy *Trägudars land* (1940; Land of the Wooden Gods), *Gryningsfolket* (1944; People of the Dawn), and *Offerrök* (1949; Sacrificial Smoke). Fridegård's protagonist, however, is not the stereotypical seafaring Viking who pillages and conquers, but the embittered, rebellious thrall Holme, whose temperament and situation demonstrate more than a passing parallel to those of Lars Hård. Fridegård's other major work of historical fiction is a five-volume series published between 1959 and 1963 about the lives of common soldiers and the families they left behind from the reign of Gustaf III through the Napoleonic Wars.

Fridegård may, broadly speaking, be classified as a realist. A lyrical, mystical strain nevertheless runs through many of his works and reaches its fullest expression in *Torntuppen* (1941; The Weathercock), the story of a soul after death. Fridegård differs from most autodidacts of his generation in that his production is not tied to any specific political or artistic program. He is sometimes identified with the *statare* school, and much of his fiction is set in the rural environment of his childhood and youth, but he remains an individualist, concerned at least as much with psychological questions of identity as with social issues. At his best he is unmatched as a stylist. His prose is energetic, incisive, deceptively simple, and displays an unfailing ear for the nuances of speech.

FURTHER WORKS

Den svarta lutan (1931); *En natt i juli* (1933); *Offer* (1937); *Äran och hjältarna* (1938); *Statister* (1939); *Här är min hand* (1942); *Kvarnbudet* (1944); *Fäderna* (1947); *Johan From, Lars Hård och andra* (1948); *Kvinnoträdet* (1950); *Lars Hård går vidare* (1951); *Johan Vallareman och andra sagor* (1952); *Porten kallas trång* (1952); *Vägen heter smal* (1953); *Sommarorgel* (1954); *Larsmässa* (1955); *From och Hård* (1956); *En bland eder* (1958); *Muren* (1959); *Soldathustrun* (1960); *De vilda jägarna* (1960); *Mot öster—soldat!* (1961); *Soldatens kärlek* (1962); *Hemkomsten* (1963); *Den gåtfulla vägen* (1963); *Fyra noveller* (1964); *På oxens horn* (1964); *Lättingen* (1965); *Det kortaste strået* (1966); *Tre stigar* (1967); *Hallonflickan* (1968); *Den blå dragonen* (1971).

FURTHER TRANSLATIONS

Scandinavian Review 68.2 (1980); *Malahat Review* 55 (1980).

REFERENCES

Gamby, Erik, *En bok om Jan Fridegård* (Uppsala, 1957); Gamby, Erik, *Jan Fridegård* (Stockholm, 1956); Graves, Peter, *Jan Fridegård: Lars Hård* (Hull, 1977); Graves, Peter, and Philip Holmes, "Jan Fridegård," in *Essays in Swedish Literature from 1880 to the Present Day*, ed. Irene Scobbie (Aberdeen, 1978); Lundkvist, Artur, and Lars Forssell, *Jan Fridegård och forntiden* (Uppsala, 1973); Schön, Ebbe, *Jan Fridegård: Proletär-*

diktaren och folkkulturen (Stockholm, 1978); *Svensk litteraturtidskrift* 33.4 (1970) (entire issue devoted to Fridegård).

Rochelle Wright

Fröding, Gustaf. Swedish poet, b. 22 August 1860, Alstern near Karlstad, d. 2 February 1911, Stockholm.

Fröding was born into a socially and intellectually distinguished family, but was exposed from infancy on to emotional and mental instability, pietistic emphasis on self-examination and self-condemnation, a rich cultural heritage, and rewarding knowledge of rural Värmland and its people. Because of his father's and other relatives' inability to deal realistically with financial and personal matters, the family existed in Fröding's childhood on the verge of financial disaster and in emotional distress. Notable results of all this were a hyperactive imagination, a tender and even sickly conscience, and an addiction to finding himself wanting. Yet in 1880 he passed "studentexamen," the comprehensive final examinations, and went on to the University of Uppsala to study political science.

When he came of age in the fall of 1881, he inherited tidy sums from his father, his paternal grandmother, and a maternal aunt. Within two years he had wasted the inheritance through irregular living, stemming from a desperate desire to enjoy life; he had, moreover, borrowed money from fellow students. The following years in the 1880s were marked by his failure to pursue his university studies, dependence on his sister Hedda and others for support, intermittent bouts of melancholy, and work as a journalist for a Karlstad paper.

An inheritance from a paternal aunt in 1889 enabled him to spend several months in a nerve clinic in Görlitz, Germany. While he was undergoing treatment there, he wrote most of his first anthology, *Guitarr och dragharmonika* (1891; Guitar and Accordion). From the fall of 1891 to the spring of 1894 he was a member of the staff of *Karlstads-Tidningen*, a daily in the provincial capital Karlstad. His major contributions to the paper were causeries about human concerns and articles about literature. These are still highly readable. In April 1894, he became mentally and emotionally seriously unbalanced: among other things, he suffered from hallucinations and illusions of sight and hearing, periods of complete apathy, and, on occasion, was tortured by uncontrollable movements of his limbs. From autumn 1894 to March 1896, he was a patient at the asylum Suttestad near Lillehammer, Norway. Before that Fröding had completed *Nya dikter* (1894; New Poems); in 1895 and 1897 two volumes were published, *Räggler å paschaser* (Tall Tales and Adventures) and *Stänk och flikar* (Splashes and Spray). The authorities in Stockholm objected to "En morgondröm" (A Morning Dream), a poem in the last-named collection, as pornographic and brought Fröding to trial in November 1896; although the jury acquitted him, he suffered from shame and at times remorse.

In 1897 Fröding published *Nytt och gammalt* (New and Old) and in 1898 *Gralstänk* (Splashes of Grail), *Om lifsmonader* (About Life's Monads) and *Grillfängerier* (Flights of Fancy). In 1896 he and his sister Cecilia moved to Uppsala, where he entered the asylum in 1898 and stayed until March 1905. He recovered enough to undertake a trip to Germany and Switzerland in 1905, but he then had to enter an asylum in Stockholm. There he met Signe Trotzig, the nurse who was to care for him for the rest of his days, particularly at Gröndal in Djurgården, a section of Stockholm.

Unsurpassed as a poet in a country unusually rich in lyric poetry, Fröding was one of the truly great poets. Unfortunately, many attempts to translate his poems into other languages have been extremely difficult and discouraging. Fröding himself was an accomplished translator of poems by Robert Burns, Lord Byron, Goethe, Heinrich Heine, and others.

As master of rhyme and rhythm and of versification in general and of detail, Fröding exploited the nuances of his native language, a highly musical tongue, as a means of interpreting life as he believed it should be and life as he believed it is. He had a vivid imagination, the ability to imitate other people and to caricature himself and others, ready identification with the unfortunate and insecure, a playful approach on occasion, and a good sense of humor. Fear of recurrent illness and its implications, a conviction that he could not adjust adequately to his environment, and concern about sexuality made him feel he was an outsider but also helped make him an unusually keen observer. As he says in one of his poems, he felt imprisoned within himself, looking out between the bars at a tantalizingly attractive world in which he could not be an active participant.

A large number of his poems are narrative lyrics (many of them are dramatic monologues) in which both regional types and individuals from his native province as well as types and individuals from both the past and his present elsewhere are memorable character studies. (Innumerable Swedes know them by heart). Take, for example, "Våran prost" (Our Dean), a delightful interpretation of a Church of Sweden pastor who can take religion and life comfortably, and "I bönhuset" (In the Chapel), a humorous account of a low-church dilemma. There are poems about neighbors at odds, the handicapped and the unfortunate, men's mistreatment of their fellowmen, generation gaps, hypocrisy, marriage and its problems, happiness and unhappiness, the pleasures and the sorrows of living—in short about almost every conceivable object of human concern: God, man, and the world. The poems range all the way from the cycle of poems about the sixteenth-century King Erik XIV and his commoner queen Karin to biblical characters such as Pontius Pilate, from landscape poems about Värmland to mock heroic poems, from extremely personal autobiographical reflective lyrics to visionary poems.

FURTHER WORKS

Samlade Skrifter, ed. Ruben G:son Berg, 16 vols. (1917–1922); *Brev till en ung flicka*, ed. O. Holmberg (1952); *Äventyr i Norge*, ed. G. Michanek (1963); *Återkomsten och andra okända dikter*, ed. G. Michanek (1964).

TRANSLATIONS

Stork, C. W., *Gustaf Fröding, Selected Poems* (1916); Locock, C. D., *Guitar and Concertina: Poems by Gustaf Fröding* (1925).

REFERENCES

Austin, Paul Britten, *Gustaf Fröding: His Life and Poetry* (Karlstad, 1986); Fleisher, Frederic, "Gustaf Fröding: 1860–1911." *American-Scandinavian Review* 42.4 (1954); Flygt, Sten G., "Gustaf Fröding's Conception of Eros." *Germanic Review* 25 (1950); Fröding, Cecilia, *Och minns du Ali Baba* (Stockholm, 1960); Johnson, Walter, "Fröding and the Dramatic Monologue." *Scandinavian Studies* 24.4 (1952); Landquist, John, *Gustaf Fröding* (Stockholm, 1956); Michanek, Germund, *En morgondröm* (Stockholm, 1962); Olsson, Henry, *Fröding: ett diktarporträtt* (Stockholm, 1950); Rosenblad, Ingvald, and Jan Szczepanski, *Gustaf Frödings bibliografi* (Karlstad, n.d.); Vickner, Edwin, "A Study in Fröding." *Scandinavian Studies* 21.2 (1949).

Walter Johnson

G

Garborg, Arne. Norwegian novelist, lyric poet, playwright, and critic, b. 25 January 1851, Time, d. 14 January 1924, Oslo.

Garborg came from a small farm in the Jæren district in southwestern Norway. The oldest son in the family, he had both a legal right and a moral obligation to take over the farm, but chose not to do so as he wanted an education and above all the opportunity to become a writer. This rejection became a contributing factor in his father's suicide when Garborg was still a young man, an event for which Garborg felt guilty all of his life.

After a stint as a rural schoolteacher Garborg made an uncertain living as a journalist and later worked in a government office. From the time of his marriage to Hulda Bergersen in 1887, however, he supported himself entirely by means of his writing. In his later years he enjoyed a continuing governmental stipend.

Garborg published his first successful novel in 1883. Titled *Bondestudentar* (1883; Students from the Country), the book was based on his own observations and experiences as a rural boy who had come to the city for an education and can be classed as an ironic *Bildungsroman*. Its hero, a young man named Daniel Braut, is progressively demoralized and finally marries for money and social status, whereas he ought to have used his education to champion the cause of his own class, the peasants. This positive approach to life is represented by a group of radical idealists centered around the character Fram.

The author's next novel, *Mannfolk* (1886; Men), constitutes his contribution to the great morality debate of the 1880s and caused Garborg to lose a poorly paid but secure position as a civil servant. An attempt to survey the possibilities for erotic happiness for both men and women that existed at the time, it presents a large number of case histories that together illustrate the ways sexuality is dealt with by society. The author especially criticizes the fact that most men of the upper classes were financially unable to marry until their late twenties or early thirties. This led them to both take advantage of the services offered by prostitutes and to try to seduce working-class girls who, after giving birth to an illegitimate child, would often have to turn to prostitution to support themselves. Their seducers would then marry women of their own class who had been brought up so strictly that they rarely had any capacity either to give or receive erotic happiness, for which reason their husbands would continue to frequent houses of prostitution. Garborg would remedy these social ills by permitting young people to marry earlier in their life and by allowing women the same sexual freedom as men.

The next novel, *Hjaa ho Mor* (1890; Living with Mama), explores similar questions. The protagonist, Fanny Holmsen, is being brought up in the manner of the bourgeois family, and Garborg portrays her development from early childhood to her mid-twenties, when her mother persuades her to marry an older man whom she does not love. The burden of this naturalistic novel is to show how parents use religious teachings to stifle the sound and healthy erotic tendencies of their daughters in order to preserve their virginity, which in turn will make it easier to marry them off to financially attractive men. Marriage thus becomes a form of prostitution. The author also demonstrates how divorce affects women and argues in favor of greater financial protection for them. Fanny's mother, who treats her daughter in such a reprehensible manner, is actually left with no other choice because of societal conditions over which she has no control.

These two novels have several characters in common. One of them is Gabriel Gram, who is in love with Fanny Holmsen, who loves him in return but does not marry him because she dares not accept herself as a sexual being. Gram is the protagonist in Garborg's next book, *Trætte Mænd* (1891; Weary Men), a diary novel that tells the story of the relationship between him and Fanny from the man's point of view. Gram is a typical victim of the male inability to marry early. Gram's longstanding use of prostitutes has by his late thirties deprived him of the capacity to physically love and socially honor the same woman. This split in his erotic life has also adversely affected other sides of his personality, and in the end he turns to religion for comfort. Garborg shows, however, that Gram is an unreliable narrator and that the book is to be read ironically. One of the author's main points is that an interest in religion is simply another manifestation of sexuality.

All of these four novels are set in the capital city of Kristiania. In *Fred* (1892; *Peace*, 1929) Garborg returned to his home district of Jæren and presented a naturalistic treatment of the relationship between religion and insanity. The main character, Enok Hove, is modeled on the author's own father, and like him he commits suicide as a result of long-term depression brought on and fueled by concern for his soul. The author admires certain aspects of Enok's religiosity, such as the manner in which he attempts to live according to Christian morality, and shows that it is the fundamentalist beliefs in sin, man's inherent depravity, and the tortures of Hell that prevent Enok from arriving at peace with his god and with himself. Garborg also sees that there is a strong connection between religious ideas and economic conditions in society, and shows that Enok's tragedy is in part the result of changing times.

Members of the Hove family figure in three more books, in which Garborg developed his own nondogmatic, nonsectarian, and quite radical religious views. The protagonist of the fine drama *Læraren* (1896; The Teacher), Enok's son Paulus, abandons pietism and views true Christianity as a social and spiritual revolution. In *Den burtkomne Faderen* (1899; *The Lost Father*, 1920), a diary novel narrated by Paulus's brother Gunnar, true Christianity has become the quiet life of work and everyday morality.

Garborg has had a deep impact on Norwegian literature. Writing primarily in *nynorsk* (New Norwegian*), a form of Norwegian emphasizing the dialects of the people rather than the speech patterns of the upper classes, he became one of the founders of a separate and rich literary tradition. Recognized as perhaps Norway's most intellectual writer, he is highly esteemed by both literary critics and the reading public.

FURTHER WORKS

Ein Fritenkjar (1879); *Uforsonlige* (1888); *Kolbotnbrev* (1890); *Haugtussa* (1895); *I Helheim* (1901); *Knudaheibrev* (1904); *Jesus Messias* (1906); *Den burtkomne Messias* (1907); *Heimkomin Son* (1908).

REFERENCES

Andersen, Thor M., *Garborgs skrifter* (Oslo, 1937–1945); Larsen, Hanna Astrup, "Arne Garborg." *American-Scandinavian Review* 12 (1924); Lillehei, Ingebrigt, "The Language and Main Ideas of Arne Garborg's Works." *Publications of the Society for the Advancement of Scandinavian Study* 3 (1916); Lillehei, Ingebrigt, "Some of the Earlier Writings of Garborg." *Publications of the Society for the Advancement of Scandinavian Study* 2 (1914–1915); Sjåvik, Jan, "Form and Theme in Arne Garborg's *Mannfolk* and *Hjaa ho Mor*." *Pacific Northwest Council on Foreign Languages*. Proceedings (1980); Wiehr, Josef, "Arne Garborg." *Scandinavian Studies and Notes* 5 (1919).

Jan Sjåvik

Geijer, Erik Gustaf. Swedish poet and historian, b. 12 January 1783, Ransäter, Värmland, d. 23 April 1847, Stockholm.

"Äreminne över Sten Sture," Geijer's first major work, won the Swedish Academy's grand prize in 1803. In his early critical writings, Geijer advocated increasing the role of imagination and religiosity in the creative process. While this insistence is in a sense conventional romanticism, it should be borne in mind that neoclassicism's most doctrinaire apologist, Carl Gustaf Leopold,* was critically active until his death in 1829, so Geijer's ideas were part of an active cultural debate. In 1811, Geijer with others founded the Gothic Society (Götiska förbundet), and in its journal *Iduna* he published five poems that outline principal themes in Swedish romanticism: "Manhem," "Den siste kämpen," "Den siste skalden," "Vikingen," and "Odalbonden" (all 1811), and the ballad imitation,

"Den lilla kolargossen" (1815). Geijer's translation of *Macbeth* in 1815 was the first uncut version of Shakespeare to be produced in Swedish.

Geijer's later production lay more in the area of historiography and less in formal literature, although he composed a fair amount of instrumental and vocal music. While his edition of Swedish folk songs was of great importance, his most memorable contribution to literature were his *Iduna* poems. In these poems, not only did Geijer express the basic polarities of Scandinavian Gothicism—the warrior and the poet, the Viking and the farmer—but he did so in eminently readable poetry, free from the egregious posturing characterizing previous medieval visions. In general, the vigor of his style and the clarity of his thought stand in considerable contrast to the penchant for melancholy obscurity of his romantic contemporaries.

FURTHER WORKS

Samlade Skrifter, 13 vols. (1849–1855, 1873–1882); *Minnen*, ed. F. Böök (1915, 1929); *Samlade Skrifter*, ed. J. Landquist, 13 vols. (1923–1931); *Arvet från Geijer*, ed. Greta Hedin (1942); *Den levande Geijer*, ed. A. Kjellén (1947); *Ur Erik Gustaf Geijers historiska föreläsningar*, ed. Anton Blanck (1947).

TRANSLATIONS

The History of the Swedes (1845); *Erik Gustaf Geijer: Impressions of England*, 1809–1847, ed. Anton Blanck (1932); *The Poor Laws and Their Bearing on Society* (1842); *Anthology of Swedish Lyrics from 1750 to 1925*, ed. C. W. Stork (1917; rev. ed., 1930); *Voice of the Spirit* (185?).

REFERENCES

Benson, A. B., *The Old Norse Element in Swedish Romanticism* (New York, 1914); Blanck, Anton, *Geijers Götiska diktning* (Stockholm, 1918); Greenway, John L., *The Golden Horns* (Athens, Ga., 1977); Henningsson, Bengt, *Geijer som historiker* (Stockholm, 1961); Landquist, John, "Erik Gustaf Geijer: Swedish Poet and Historian." *American-Scandinavian Review* 16.10 (1928); Landquist, John, *Geijer, en levnadsteckning* (Stockholm, 1954); Maury, Lucien, *L'Imagination scandinave* (Paris, 1929); Norberg, Elsa, *Geijers väg från romantik till realism* (Stockholm, 1944); Sponberg, Viola, *The Philosophy of Erik Gustaf Geijer* (Rock Island, Ill., 1945); Wallén, Erik, *Nordisk mytologi i svensk romantik* (Stockholm, 1918); Wallén, Erik, *Studier över romantisk mytologi i svensk litteratur* (Malmö, 1923)

John L. Greenway

Gelsted, Otto. Danish poet, journalist, and critic, b. 4 November 1888, Middelfart, d. 22 December 1968, Copenhagen.

Gelsted's years at a Catholic school strengthened his natural inclination for philosophy and logical reasoning and, contrary to its purpose, dislike of Christianity. The Greek antiquity as well as the Renaissance became his ideal. Whether in intellectual debates or lyrical creation, Gelsted was more or less directly advocating the classicist idea of harmony and unity.

Interested in Freud and contemporary painting, with a leftist orientation socially and culturally, Gelsted occupied a central role in the so-called *Kulturra-dikale* (cultural radical) movement in Denmark. He was an important contributor, as a poet, to the influential periodical at the time called *Klingen* (1917–1920)— primarily a magazine for Danish expressionist and cubist painters. Gelsted contributed to numerous periodicals and published his own journal, *Sirius* (1924–1925), in six issues. As a journalist for daily newspapers, he wrote for the liberal *Politiken* from 1923 and for the communist *Land og Folk* from 1945, having then joined the Danish Communist party.

The rise of nazism and the events in the 1930s and 1940s encouraged Gelsted to opt for communism with its theoretical promise of social equality and order. His communist allegiance brought with it its negative attitude toward artistic expression and especially toward modernism. However, Gelsted remained faithful to the communist ideology even if it created contradictions in his own stringent thinking and was counterproductive to his lyrical vein. Gelsted's communism was theoretical, first and foremost, tracing its roots to Kantian thinking; at heart Gelsted was a classicist humanist, and he tried to add this humanist element to his Marxism.

Gelsted's importance to Danish literature is in great part due to his role as critic and cultural mediator. Most notable are his works on the Danish writer Johannes V. Jensen,* his three volumes on Greek culture, his adaptation to Danish prose of the *Iliad* and the *Odyssey*, his translations of Sigmund Freud as well as of Walt Whitman, Bertolt Brecht, and Pablo Neruda.

WORKS

Johannes V. Jensen (1913); *Ekspressionisme* (1919); *De evige Ting* (1920); *Dansens Almagt* (1921); *Enetaler* (1922); *Jomfru Gloriant* (1923); *Lazarus' Opvækkelse* (1924); *Paa flugt* (1925); *Rejsen til Astrid* (1927); *Enehøje-Digte* (1929); *Henimod Klarhed* (1931); *Under Uvejret* (1934); *De danske Strande* (1940); *Hymne til Badstuestræde* (1940); *Solemærker* (1941); *Emigrantdigte* (1945); *Flygtninge i Huseby* (1945); *Frihedens Aar* (1947); *Sange under den kolde krig* (1952); *Døden i badekarret* (1955); *Guder og helte* (1956); *Græsk drama* (1957); *Den græske tanke* (1958); *Aldrig var dagen sa lys* (1959); *Digte fra en solkyst* (1961).

Charlotte Schiander Gray

Gestur Pálsson. *See* Pálsson, Gestur.

Gill, Claes. Norwegian poet, actor, and director, b. 13 October 1910, Odda, d. 10 June 1973.

While Gill is commonly remembered for his acting career in the 1950s and 1960s, literary historians see his greatest impact in the role his two slim volumes of poems played in the development of modernism in Norwegian poetry. A world traveler, who had been a sailor, whaler, and elevator operator in a New York skyscraper, Gill was an exotic figure when he debuted with a collection of esoteric poems, reflecting his contact with European and American literary trends. Influenced by T. S. Eliot and W. B. Yeats, Gill broke with the poetic traditions of his Norwegian forebears and became the center of a lively debate over the value of experimental poetry. Although many early critics scoffed at Gill's work, twenty years later the *Profil* group could trace their roots back to him, and Gill's poetry is now recognized as unique and central.

Gill's themes are universal—love, death, and the impermanence of life and art. What distinguishes his poetry is its form. His poems present a series of partial images that flow quickly into each other, re-creating a complex, yet often fragmentary collage of experience. Breaks with logical syntax are frequent. Gill's choice of language conflates the poetic and the prosaic, and he uses foreign expressions liberally. His rhyme schemes are intricate, his rhythms range from strict classical meters to irregular patterns that mimic human breathing.

Critics have paid special attention to Gill's longest poem, "Stone for a Tower," the portrait of a frustrated poet who longs to capture a complete vision of creation, but is bound by the impotence of words. The recognition that the artist can only temporarily transcend life's dichotomies and achieve such a vision may have silenced Gill as a poet and sent him onto the stage, where the living voice could have more impact than written words.

WORKS

Fragment av et magisk liv (1939); *Ord i jern* (1942); *Samlede dikt* (1967).

REFERENCES

Aarnes, Asbjørn, ed., *I store linjers riss* (Oslo, 1973); Fløgstad, Kjartan, *Portrett av eit magisk liv* (Oslo, 1988).

Frankie Shackelford

Gjellerup, Karl Adolph. Danish novelist and dramatist, b. 2 June 1857, Roholte, d. 11 November 1919, Klotzsche, Germany.

Both of Gjellerup's parents were descendents of clergy from the Danish countryside. He grew up in Copenhagen, where he received a degree in theology in 1878. Studies of Charles Darwin and Herbert Spencer as well as a strong influence from the radical ideas of the critic Georg Brandes* contributed to turning Gjellerup into a militant atheist. However, after returning from an educational journey to Germany, Greece, and Russia in 1882, Gjellerup broke with Brandesian naturalism and wrote a number of speculative and philosophical plays. After 1892 Gjellerup lived in Dresden, but in his last works he frequently returned to a Danish milieu as well as to traditional Christianity. In 1917 he shared the Nobel Prize in literature with Henrik Pontoppidan.*

Gjellerup's early novels, *En Idealist* (1878; An Idealist) and *Germanernes Lærling* (1882; The Teutons' Apprentice), portraying the main character's wavering between orthodoxy and atheism, marks the author's own revolt against Christianity and Danish romanticism in general. Less propagandistic, hence of greater artistic value, are the novels *Romulus* (1883) and *G-Dur* (1883; G Major), subdued love stories permeated with dreamlike and melancholy moods that point toward the second phase in Gjellerup's authorship. It opens with the tragedy *Brynhild* (1884), based on Old Norse mythology, with passionate lyrical exclamations and extensive epic passages making it totally unactable. It has, nevertheless, a grandiose, classical format and an elevated idealistic tone, which secures it a unique position in Danish literature. The same idealism permeates the novel *Minna* (1889; trans. 1913) set in Saxony. Its title character is a woman objecting to the Brandesian ideas of woman's liberation and sexual promiscuity. Gjellerup avoids any heavy-handed moralizing and succeeds in creating a poetic and suggestive love story of subdued beauty. Of similar artistic quality is the forceful, psychological novel *Møllen* (1896; The Mill), at the same time a realistic and a symbolic portrayal of a man striving beyond himself in his search for a religious experience.

Succeeding dramas from the 1890s have contemporary Danish settings but remain stilted and abstract in their depiction of Nietzschean superhumans fighting the trite and pragmatic views of morality and love in contemporary society. Of greater substance are Gjellerup's works influenced by the pessimistic views of Arthur Schopenhauer and Richard Wagner as well as Buddhist asceticism. The legendary drama *Offerildene* (1903; Sacrificial Fires) was successfully performed in Dresden and Copenhagen, and from this time on Gjellerup also belonged to German literature, having all of his following works translated. The novels *Pilgrimen Kamanita* (1906; *The Pilgrim Kamanita*, 1911) and *Verdensvandrerne* (1910; The World Wanderers) are both influenced by Eastern philosophy, the first describing a single soul's pilgrimage toward Nirvana in a totally abstract universe, the latter portraying a colorful, contemporary India. Both works are strongly didactic, as are the last novels from the third phase of Gjellerup's authorship. They, too, preach the message of self-denial, but on a Christian basis, and are set in either the Danish provinces as *Rudolph Stens Landpraksis* (1913; The Country Practice of Rudolph Sten) or based on themes from the Middle Ages as *Guds Venner* (1916; God's Friends) and the early church as *Den gyldne Gren* (1917; The Golden Bough).

These last works lack coherence and stylistic discipline and are, like most of Gjellerup's writings, rather immaterial, without substance and firm structure. However, the seriousness of Gjellerup's search for truth cannot be doubted—accusations of superficiality would be false—and when he was able to give his artistic intentions an adequate expression he succeeded in creating works that ought to save him from that oblivion to which he undeservedly has been consigned.

FURTHER WORKS

Det unge Danmark (1879); *Antigonos* (1880); *Rødtjørn* (1881); *Arvelighed og Moral* (1881); *En klassisk Maaned* (1884); *Vandreaaret* (1885); *St. Just* (1886); *Thamyris* (1887); *Hagbard og Signe* (1888); *Bryllupsgaven* (1888); *Min Kjærligheds Bog* (1889); *Herman Vandel* (1891); *Wuthorn* (1893); *Ti Kroner og andre Fortællinger* (1893); *Kong Hjarne Skjald* (1893); *Pastor Mors* (1894); *Hans Excellence* (1895); *Ved Grændsen* (1897);

Konvolutten (1897); *Gift og Modgift* (1898); *Fabler* (1898); *Tankelæserinden* (1901); *Elskovsprøven* (1906); *Den fuldendte Hustru* (1907); *Fra Vaar til Høst* (1910); *Villaen ved Havet* (1910); *Richard Wagner i hans Hovedværker* (1915).

FURTHER TRANSLATIONS

A Second Book of Danish Verse (1947, 1968).

REFERENCES

Bang, Herman, *Realisme og Realister* (Copenhagen, 1879); Buchreitz, Georg, "Karl Gjellerup." *Edda* 30 (1930); Fritz, Paul, "Gjellerup und die Aufwertung des Jugendstils." *Danske Studier* 66 (1971); Zberae, Nicolae, "Karl Gjellerup: A Master of Expression of Indian Thought." *Indo-Asian Culture* 19.1 (1970).

Sven H. Rossel

Goldschmidt, Meïr Aron. Danish journalist and novelist, b. 26 October 1819, Vordingborg, d. 15 August 1887, Copenhagen.

After initial studies at Copenhagen University Goldschmidt began a journalistic career in 1837, taking a radical stance in social and political matters. His major journalistic contribution was the satirical periodical *Corsaren,* now famous for its persecution of Søren Kierkegaard.* Subsequently Goldschmidt was active in the pan-Scandinavian movement and worked for the Danish cause in the border area between Denmark and Germany. An attempt to settle in England and become established as an English writer came to nothing.

Goldschmidt's novels and stories belong to the romantic-realist tradition, and in their portrayal of Jewish life in Copenhagen—an exotic aspect of Denmark to most Danes—they formed a parallel to Steen Steensen Blicher's* highly successful stories of Jutlandic peasants and gypsies. Goldschmidt is throughout very much aware of his Jewish background and of the position of Jews in nineteenth-century society; at the same time his work also reflects the influence of the liberal Christians—for example, Nikolaj Grundtvig* and Ole Lehman— with whom Goldschmidt associated. Thus, his first novel, *En Jøde* (1845; *Jacob Bendixen, the Jew*, 1852; *The Jew of Denmark*, 1952), is the account of a Jew who becomes engaged to a Christian girl, is forced to break with her because of cultural and social tensions, and ends his life as a disillusioned usurer.

The long novel *Hjemløs* (1853–1857; *Homeless*, 1861), the account of a man who lets down the girl he wants to marry, and spends the remainder of his life atoning for his mistake before finding peace with himself, is the first statement of the nemesis principle that now becomes the essential feature of Goldschmidt's work. It is clearly the basis of the last and probably best novel, *Ravnen* (1867; The Raven), in which the realism of his earlier work becomes fused with a more fantastic fairy-tale element, and also in the important short stories *Maser* (Tythes) and *Avromche Nattergal* (1871). In *Livs-Erindringer og Resultater* (1877; Memories and Accomplishments of Life) Goldschmidt vainly seeks a scientific analysis and defense of his belief.

Goldschmidt is the first major psychologist in Danish fiction, and the realism of his character studies goes hand in hand with his conviction that human actions are determined by some external force. One feature stemming from this conviction is the large number of apparent coincidences in otherwise realistic works.

FURTHER WORKS

Fortællinger (1846); *Fortællinger og Skildringer* (1863–1865); *Breve fra Choleratiden* (1865); *Dagbog fra en Reise paa Vestkysten af Vendsyssel og Thy* (1865); *Kjærlighedshistorier fra mange Lande* (1867); *En Hedereise i Viborgegnen* (1867); *Den Vægelsindede paa Graahede* (1867); *En Skavank* (1867); *Smaa Fortællinger* (1869); *Rabbien og Ridderen* (1869); *Fortællinger og Virkelighedsbilleder* (1877–1883); *Smaa Skildringer fra Fantasi og Virkelighed* (1887).

REFERENCES

Bredsdorff, Elias, *Corsaren, Goldschmidt og Kierkegaard* (Copenhagen, 1977); Brøndsted, Mogens, *Goldschmidts fortællekunst* (Copenhagen, 1967); Brøndsted, Mogens, *Meïr Goldschmidt* (Copenhagen, 1965); Kyrre, Hans, *Meïr Goldschmidt* (Copenhagen, 1919); Ober, Kenneth, *Meïr Goldschmidt* (Boston, 1976).

W. Glyn Jones

Greenlandic Literature. *See* Inuit Literature.

Grieg, Johan *Nordahl* Brun. Norwegian poet and dramatist, b. 1 November 1902, Bergen, d. 2 December 1943, Berlin.

Grieg felt compassion for all levels of society, especially seamen, whose rigorous life he shared aboard the *Henrik Ibsen*. The voyage resulted in a collection of poems, *Rundt Kap det gode haab* (1922; *Around the Cape of Good Hope*, 1979), and a naturalistic novel, *Skibet gaar videre* (1924; *But the Ship Goes On*, 1927).

Grieg's craving for education, adventure, and commitment frequently took him away from Norway; yet his love for his native land was intense. This patriotism was regarded skeptically for a time; however, when Norway was invaded, Grieg threw himself into dangerous missions and wrote poems that heartened his countrymen. While encouraging his fellow Norwegians to dream of peace, with a fatalistic compulsion Grieg volunteered to join a bombing mission over Berlin, where he was killed in 1943.

Grieg had warned of the spreading power of fascism and the corruption of big business. While in the Soviet Union (1932–1934), he learned about theatrical techniques and wrote with enthusiasm of the people's dedication and kindness. During the civil war in Spain Grieg observed the fighting from the front lines.

Profoundly stirred by World War I, members of Grieg's generation seemed to long to prove their own heroism. After writing *De unge døde* (1932; The Young Dead), a study of English poets, including some who fought in that war, Grieg became a spokesman for peace. Through the periodical *Veien Frem* (The Road Ahead), fiction, poetry, and drama, Grieg appealed to reason and human goodness, refusing to accept the instinct to wage war as a necessary element of human nature.

Although Grieg is not ranked with the dramatist he resembles, Bertolt Brecht, his plays are significant and stageworthy. *Vår ære og vår makt* (1935; *Our Power and Our Glory*, 1971) uses devices of cinema and epic theater to contrast representatives of Bergen society during World War I: endangered seamen, families waiting anxiously at home, businessmen profiting from the war. The theatrically innovative play ends with a sobering, stylized epilogue focused on the threat of a new war.

Nederlaget (1937; *The Defeat*, 1944) presents a panorama of the Paris commune. Grieg orchestrates a large cast of historic figures, along with representatives of all generations and social classes who suffer as government troops mercilessly restore order, destroying the idealistic comrades who believed they could reform society. Seen in vivid vignettes, characters are memorable, whether for their corruption and cynicism or for their courage and generosity. Although the play disappoints Marxist critics because of the abstract, romantic conclusion, its poetic beauty and dramatic vitality are impressive.

As a poet Grieg turned to Norwegian landscape, the open sea, and his own experiences for inspiration. He explored philosophical questions, paid tribute to valiant comrades, and drew upon an appreciation of nature. His stirring war poems expressed confidence in the Norwegian people and grief over the fallen, as on 17 May 1940:

> We are so few in this land;
> Each one who fell is our brother and friend.
> The dead will be with us
> The day we return.

Never a party member, Grieg was considered a communist; this may account for the mixed critical attention he has received. He is generally respected because of his legendary personality, literary achievement, and honorable commitment to peace and freedom.

FURTHER WORKS

Vers fra sjøen (1922); *Stene i strømmen* (1925); *Kinesiske dage* (1927); *En ung mands kjærlighet* (1927); *Barrabas* (1927); *Norge i våre hjerter* (1929); *Atlanterhavet* (1932); *Digte i utvalg* (1932); *Men imorgen—* (1936); *Spansk sommer* (1937); *Ung må verden ennu være* (1938); *Friheten* (1943; *All That is Mine Demand; War Poems* (1944); *Dikt i utvalg* (1944); *Flagget* (1945); *Håbet* (1946); *Veien frem*, ed. Odd Hølaas (1947); *Samlede verker*, 7 vols. (1947); *Skuespill* (1948); *Samlede dikt* (1950); *Græske breve* (1952); *Længselen* (1957); *Langveisfra* (1964); *Morgen over Finnmarksvidden* (1967); *Et varig vennskap: 46 brev fra Nordahl Grieg til Nils Lie* (1981).

FURTHER TRANSLATIONS

Anthology of Norwegian Lyrics, ed. Charles Wharton Stork (1942); *Modern Scandinavian Poetry: The Panorama of Poetry 1900–1975*, ed. Martin Allwood (1982).

REFERENCES

Dahlie, Hallvard, "On Nordahl Grieg's *The Ship Sails On.*" *International Fiction Review* 2 (1975); Fischer, Gerhard, "The Paris Commune on the Stage." Diss., State University of New York at Binghamton (1976); Grieg, Gerd, *Nordahl Grieg* (Oslo, 1957); Grieg, Harald, *Nordahl min bror* (Oslo, 1956); Haslund, Fredrik Juel, *Nordahl Grieg* (Oslo, 1962); Koht, Halvdan, "Nordahl Grieg." *American-Scandinavian Review* 30.1 (1942); Nag, Martin, *Streiflys* (Oslo, 1967); *Nordahl Grieg og vår tid* (Oslo, 1964); Weatherhead, I. A., and A. K. Weatherhead, "The Last Poems of Nordahl Grieg." *Twentieth Century Literature* 28.1 (1982).

Carla Waal

Grímsson, Stefán Hörður. Icelandic poet, b. 31 March 1920, Harnarfjörður, South Iceland.

After brief studies in a secondary school Grímsson went to sea for several years and has worked at various occupations, his poor health permitting, for instance as farmhand, swimming instructor, and night watchman.

Grímsson's poetry is characterized by intense lyricism, fertile imagination, startling associations, very sparse diction, and a sure sense of form and rhythm. The fishing village and the seaside are his favorite settings. Although his poems are starkly visual and tactile, he is greatly preoccupied by such abstract themes as love, loneliness, time, and distance. Some of his poems express a certain tedium of life, but they are usually enlivened by whimsical humor, vivid imagery, and a language rich in nuances and cadences. His books of poems have been few, slim, and far apart, and his poems are as a rule very short, but they are "loaded," and there is an uncanny and seducing presence in even his most obscure lines, something almost mystical, and they all shine with bright colors. It is as if the boundaries between mind and matter were spirited away: the poems often strike the reader as pure sensation. One is at times reminded of some master of modern painting, a Jean Arp or a Piet Mondrian.

Grímsson's impact on modern Icelandic poetry has been significant in that he has been instrumental in deflating traditional prosody, indicating how to use hidden resources of the language, how to renew words and give them more weight, but above all how to make strange or obscure lines sparkle with an intensity that resides in some hidden place between words and sentences. In spite of his very slender production, Grímsson is undoubtedly one of Iceland's three or four most effective living poets.

FURTHER WORKS

Glugginn snýr í norður (1946); *Svartálfadans* (1951; rev. ed., 1970); *Hliðin á sléttunni* (1970); *Farvegir* (1981); *Tengsl* (1987).

TRANSLATIONS

Modern Poetry in Translation 30 (1977); *The Postwar Poetry of Iceland*, ed. Sigurður Magnússon (1982); *Icelandic Writing Today*, ed. Sigurður A. Magnússon (1982); *Modern Scandinavian Poetry 1900–1975*, ed. Martin S. Allwood (1982).

REFERENCES

Höskuldsson, Sveinn Skorri, "The Triumph of Modernism in Icelandic Poetry, 1945–1970." *Scandinavica* 12 (1973); Magnússon, Sigurður A., *Northern Sphinx* (London, 1971); Magnússon, Sigurður A., "Postwar Literature in Iceland." *World Literature Today* 56. 1 (1982).

Sigurður A. Magnússon

Grímur Þorgrímsson Thomsen. *See* Thomsen, Grímur (Þorgrímsson).

Gripenberg, Bertil (pseud. Åke Erikson). Finland-Swedish poet, b. 10 September 1878, St. Petersburg, d. 5 May 1947, Sävsjö, Sweden.

The son of a high-ranking civil servant, Gripenberg was intended for a military career, but decided against it at the age of seventeen, becoming instead a tutor to rural aristocratic families before himself becoming a landowner. Despite his lack of success in the army, he became a poet who sang the praises of the old military virtues, a patriot of the old school, with decidedly conservative views.

Gripenberg's early poems, beginning with *Dikter* (1903; Poems), shows him to be related to the Swedish poetry of the 1890s, an aesthete with a clear sense of style, a technically gifted poet with a clear instinct for sound and image, a gifted writer of love poems. These early poems are colorful and energetic, expressive of a youthful zest for life. In a series of sonnets in the volume entitled *Gallergrinden* (1905; The Wrought Iron Gate), Gripenberg established himself firmly as a master of form, and revealed himself to be a writer who could utilize mood to the full. A disappointment in love subsequently added an element of disillusionment to his work.

As a tutor in Tavastland (Häme), Gripenberg came to love the Finnish countryside, which now became the essence of his poetry. His sense of affinity with it, and a newfound peace and resignation, are at the center of his poems after 1909, though something like relief at the thought of approaching death also makes itself felt.

The proclamation of Finnish independence and the Civil War changed Gripenberg's tone and called upon the patriotic sentiments and conservative sympathies that had been bred in him and fostered by his years among the rural gentry, and he now expresses his national sentiments in terms of a profound hatred of the Red cause. The Winter War brought about a renewal of Gripenberg's patriotic poetry.

As an archconservative Gripenberg expressed the sentiments of many of his Finland-Swedish compatriots earlier in the century, and thus he gained not only recognition as a highly skilled artist, but also great popularity as a poet who in clear, ringing tones gave unambiguous and inspiring—often rhetorical—expression to a national sentiment. In a changed climate, these same qualities have served to put him somewhat in the shade.

FURTHER WORKS

Vida vägar (1904); *Rosenstaden* (1907); *Svarta sonetter* (1908); *En dröm om folkviljan* (1908); *Vid mörkrets portar* (1909); *Drivsnö* (1909); *Det brinnande landet* (1910); *Skuggspel* (1912); *Spillror* (1917); *Under fanan* (1918); *Kanonernas röst* (1922); *Efter striden* (1923); *På Dianas vägar* (1925); *Skymmande land* (1925); *Den hemliga glöden* (1925); *Den stora tiden* (1928); *Vid gränsen* (1930); *Spökjagaren* (1933); *Livets eko* (1933); *Sista ronden* (1941); *Det var de tiderna* (1943); *Genom gallergrinden* (1947); *Dikter 1903–1904* (1948).

REFERENCES

Björkenheim, M., *Bertil Gripenberg och hans skaldskap* (Stockholm, 1950); Nordenstreng, R., *Bertil Gripenberg och hans skaldskap* (Stockholm, 1921).

W. Glyn Jones

Grønbech, Vilhelm Peter. Danish historian of religion and culture, b. 14 June 1873, Allinge, d. 21 April 1948, Elsinore.

After grammar school education in Copenhagen, Grønbech studied literature and language at the university with the great linguists Vilhelm Thomsen and Otto Jespersen. After a doctoral thesis on the phonology of the Turkish language, Grønbech switched his interests to the study of religion and culture. As a professor of the history of religion from 1911, Grønbech over the years published a number of original works on a wide range of subjects within the humanities, including studies of primitive religion and the culture of the Germanic people in the heroic age; four volumes on mysticism in Europe and India; monographs on William Blake, Friedrich Schlegel, and Goethe; a trilogy on early Christianity; as well as voluminous surveys of the age of Hellenism and of the religion and culture of Hellas. In these books, based on painstaking erudition, but unencumbered by all traditional scholarly apparatus, Grønbech attacks the arrogance of European civilization, which due to its spiritual inwardness, abstract speculation, and exploitatory materialism has become a moral threat to other ways of life and to nature. At the same time he points to the culture of so-called primitives, their reverence of nature, solidarity of kinship, and the vitality of their religious life confirmed in great cult festivals. Grønbech's empathic interpretations of his subjects lend to his books the quality of works of art. Grønbech's criticism of culture and insistence on the relevance of religious experience have made an impression on writers (e.g., J. Anker-Larsen, Martin A. Hansen,* and the *Heretica* group of poets) and on Danish religious life. Outside Denmark Grønbech's ideas and works have been noted in Sweden and Germany. Grønbech also published four volumes of poetry, a book of dialogues, and a novel.

WORKS

Forstudier til tyrkisk lydhistorie (1902); *Vor Folkeæt i Oldtiden*, 4 vols. (1909–1912); *Religionsskiftet i Norden* (1913); *Primitiv religion* (1915); *Religiøse strømninger i det nittende århundrede* (1922); *Mystikere i Europa og Indien*, vol. 1 (1925), vols. 2–4 (1932–1934); *Kampen om mennesket* (1930); *The Culture of the Teutons*, 3 vols. (1931;

rev. ed. of *Vor folkeæt i Oldtiden*); *William Blake, Kunstner. Digter. Mystiker* (1933); *Jesus menneskesønnen* (1935); *Friedrich Schlegel i årene 1791–1808* (1935); *Goethe*, 2 vols. (1935–1939); *Hellenismen*, 2 vols. (1940); *Sejersen fra Variager*, ed. V. Grønbech (1940); *Paulus, Jesu Kristi apostel* (1940); *Kristus, den opstandne frelser* (1941); *Solen har mange veje* (1941); *Hellas. Kultur og religion*, 4 vols. (1942–1945); *Sprogets musik* (1943); *Sangen om livet og døden* (1944); *Madonna og gøgleren* (1946); *Kampen for en ny sjæl* (1946); *Dostojefski og hans Rusland* (1948); *Philon* (1949); *Spillemænd og andre folk* (1949); *Den unge Friedrich Schlegel* (1949); *Lyset fra Akropolis* (1950); *Angst. Religion. To foredrag* (1951); *Livet er et fund* (1951); *Hellas. Supplement* (1953); *Atombomben og andre essays* (1957).

TRANSLATIONS

Religious Currents in the Nineteenth Century (1964, 1973).

REFERENCES

Hansen, Birgit Helene, *Omkring Heretica. Vilhelm Grønbechs forfatterskab som forudsætning for Hereticas første årgang* (Aarhus, 1970); Holst, Poul, *Vilhelm Grønbech. En bibliografi* (Copenhagen, 1948); Kemp, Torkil, *Vilhelm Grønbech* (Copenhagen, 1943); Mitchell, P. M., *Vilhelm Grønbech. En indføring* (Copenhagen, 1970); Mitchell, P. M., *Vilhelm Grønbech* (Boston, 1978); Riisgård, Ejvind, *Vilhelm Grønbechs kulturopgør*, 2 vols. (Copenhagen, 1974).

Niels Lyhne Jensen

Gröndal, Benedikt Sveinbjarnarson. Icelandic poet, novelist, essayist, translator, and scholar, b. 6 October 1826, Bessastaðir, d. 1907.

Born the son of one of Iceland's most prominent poets and scholars, Gröndal studied several academic disciplines at the university in Copenhagen before receiving a degree in Old Icelandic. A polyhistor as well as a writer, Gröndal believed that "true" poets were students of all forms of knowledge and that poetry was the highest expression of man's understanding and intuition. The task of the poet as universal mediator was to reveal the infinite and divine in art and to give symbolic representation to the primal cause of life through the beautiful in man and nature.

Like many of his contemporaries, Gröndal was dedicated to the revitalization of themes and forms from Icelandic antiquity, but he was also an advocate of poetic idealism. Beauty, peace, and harmony are the major themes of his poetry, while enchanting moonlit skies, blue flowers, maidens at water falls or mermaids emerging from the sea, and golden strings of harps glittering in eternal summer evenings make up the stock of the stereotyped metaphors Gröndal drew on with little variation throughout his life.

Gröndal's most important contributions to Icelandic literature are his verse parodies and mock-heroic burlesques in prose, in particular his novel *Sagan af Heljarslóðarorrustu* (1861; The Saga of the Battle of Hel's Field). Written shortly after Napoleon III's victory at Solferino, *Heljarslóðarorrusta* ridicules the fashions of nineteenth-century aristocracy and the greed for fame that led to the war between France and Austria. Cast in the setting of a medieval Icelandic romance of chivalry, the novel invests the aristocracy with bourgeois manners and satirizes social conventions in a narrative style that has brought this magnum opus permanent stature as one of the wittiest books in Icelandic literary history.

While Gröndal also gained considerable recognition for his scholarly and pedagogical achievements, his primary importance to Icelandic literature lies in his development of the literary burlesque.

FURTHER WORKS

Drápa um Örva-Odd (1851); *Kvæði og nokkrar greinar um skáldskap og fagrar menntir* (1853); *Kvæði* (1856); *Gandhreiðin* (1866); *Ragnarökkur* (1868); *Göngu-Hrólfsrímur* (1893); *Kvæðabók* (1900); *Dagrún* (1906); *Úrvalsljóð* (1938); *Ritsafn*, 5 vols. (1948–1954); *Gullregn úr ljóðum Benedikts Gröndals* (1960).

TRANSLATIONS

Icelandic Lyrics, ed. Richard Beck (1930).

REFERENCES

Einarsson, Stefán, "Benedikt Gröndal og *Heljarslóðarorrusta,*" in *Skáldaþing* (Reykjavík, 1948); Finnbogason, Guðmundur, "Um skáldskap Gröndals," in *Benedikt Gröndal áttræður* (Reykjavík, 1906); Stefánsson, Ingvar, *Gandreiðin: skopadeila Benedikts Sveinbjarnarsonar Gröndals ásamt ritgerð um verkið* (Reykjavík, 1973).

W. M. Senner

Grundtvig, Nikolaj Frederik Severin. Danish poet, mythologist, educational thinker, and churchman, b. 8 September 1783, Udby, d. 2 September 1872, Copenhagen.

Like his father Grundtvig studied divinity. His initiation as a poet came in 1805 when as a tutor at a manor house he fell unhappily in love. Now he understood the romantic vision, a glimpse of the Eternal in ancient Scandinavian poetry and legends. This inspiration made a lasting impression on his work and is particularly manifest in his early masterpiece, *Nordens Mytologi* (1808; Nordic Mythology). Here he shows himself as a pioneer of mythology, recognizing for the first time the Edda lays as the primary sources of Norse religion and advancing a poetic view of the ancient legends as reflecting a mythic drama about the glory, downfall, and rebirth of the gods.

Grundtvig's obsession with Norse heathendom soon passed as he moved on to an orthodox Christian standpoint, provocatively asserted in his probationary sermon in 1810. In 1811, after a religious and mental crisis, Grundtvig became convinced of his calling as a poet and preacher working toward a religious and national revival. Between 1812 and 1820 an enormous literary output issued from his pen: hymns, historical and biblical poems, books and articles on historical and philosophical themes, besides monumental translations of Saxo's* and Snorri Sturluson's* chronicles and of the Anglo-Saxon lay of Beowulf. Grundtvig's poetry is uneven, but a few poems of this decennium are profoundly original and powerful. An example is the dramatic poem *Paaske-Liljen* (1817; *The Easter-Lily*, 1919) with the Resurrection as its theme.

After a polemical bout in 1815 Grundtvig gave up the cloth. But in 1821 he accepted a position in a Zealand provincial town, exchanging it, however, a year later for the pulpit of a Copenhagen church. Years of writing and immersion in the past had sapped Grundtvig of vitality, and it was not until 1824 that he experienced his desired engagement in the life of the present that is expressed in the magnificent but obscure poem "Nyaars-Morgen" (1824; New Year's Morning). Here in the foil of a myth he looks back on his own development as he proclaims his hope for Christianity, Denmark, and himself. This new mood went with a rethinking about the essence of Christian faith. Moving away from his biblical orthodoxy, he now found a historical foundation of the Church in the Apostles' Creed, at baptism, and in the words spoken in Communion. Here was a living oral witness passed on from Christ and his Disciples to believers of succeeding ages. Finally Grundtvig emphasized the goodness of Creation and the positive value of human life in this world. He expounded his new Christian position in a pamphlet *Kirkens Gjenmæle* (1825; The Rejoinder of the Church), which was occasioned by a work of liberal theology claiming that the true word of God in the Bible was as established by scriptural scholarship. Grundtvig attacked this academic view of religious truth in the most violent terms. When a libel suit arising out of this polemic went against him and censorship was imposed upon him, Grundtvig resigned from his post.

During the following subdued period he turned again to scholarship. A grant from the king enabled him to visit England during three summers from 1829, where he studied Anglo-Saxon literature in manuscripts hitherto buried and neglected in libraries. By drawing attention to this literary heritage Grundtvig became a founder of Anglo-Saxon scholarship, but the all-important fruit of his visit to England is the impression he received of the dynamism of English society and its people. There he found the Norse heroic spirit at work that he wished to awaken in the stagnant Danish nation. In addition, Grundtvig's acquaintance with the colleges of Oxford and Cambridge made him recognize their residential system as an ideal forum for the human and intellectual development of youth. The effect of his stay in England is reflected in the entirely revised second edition of his mythology *Nordens Mytologi eller Sindbilled-Sprog* (1832; Nordic Mythology or Symbolic Language). In the introduction Grundtvig outlines his ideas for a modern form of learning and education, which was to be concerned with the heroic spirit of Greece and the North as found in mythology and combined with a Christian-Mosaic way of thinking. He thought such a synthesis should be taught in schools open to citizens from all social classes. One aim was to oust the traditional classical erudition in grammar schools that represented the elitist tyrannical spirit of Rome, tied to the dead letter and inimical to life. Grundtvig enlarged upon his educational ideas in a series of essays from the 1830s, one being *Skolen for livet* (1838; The School for Life). For the use in the schools he had in mind, he published *Haandbog i Verdens-Historien* (3 vols.,

1833, 1836, 1843; Handbook of World History). Abandoning the theocentric view of history of earlier works of 1812 and 1817, Grundtvig now wished to show the working of the respective national spirits of the major European nations in history and their universal historical roles. The series of lectures on contemporary history given in 1838 and published under the title *Mands Minde* (1877; Within Living Memory) are a sequel to this book.

The greatest achievement begun in the very active 1830s was the *Sang-Værk til den danske Kirke* (1837; Hymnary for the Danish Church), to which was added a belated second part in 1870. Other supplementary volumes appeared after Grundtvig's death. Including translations from Greek, Latin, Anglo-Saxon, English, and German as well as reworkings of hymns by other Danes, Grundtvig's hymns number some 1,400. As a hymnist he celebrates the Christian hope in redemption and immortality, the triumph of life over death. His reenactment of the great moments of his faith in his hymns are dramatized in settings he knows: the angels bring the good tidings of Holy Night in a snowy Nordic landscape, and the Pentecostal miracle coalesces with the balmy breeze stirring the foliage of a glorious Danish June morning. Grundtvig's poetry is marked by his use of a complex imagery drawn from mythology, folk beliefs, and the Bible; and central to it is the symbolism of light and radiance as well as elemental color contrasts. To Grundtvig, poetry was a medium of vision, not an art, and he wrote with sovereign disregard of poetic convention. Only readers with the experience of modern poetry will appreciate him as the great and original poet he is. In addition to his religious poetry there is a no less impressive body of secular poetry; it is similarly of varying merit, but includes some poems that rank among the finest in the poetic heritage of Denmark.

Grundtvig's active engagement in public life, begun in the 1830s, was continued until advanced old age. As an intermittent member of Parliament from 1849 to 1866, he was a champion of freedom, speaking up for legal, educational, and ecclesiastical reform. Once an isolated figure, Grundtvig became the spiritual head of a great popular movement, through which his ideas left a mark on the religious, intellectual, and political life of Denmark that is felt to this day.

FURTHER WORKS

Poetiske Skrifter, ed. Svend Grundtvig, C. J. Brandt and Georg Christensen, 10 vols. (1880–1930); *Udvalgte Skrifter,* ed. Holger Begtrup, 10 vols. (1904–1909); *Haandbog i N.F.S. Grundtvigs Skrifter,* ed. Ernst Borup and Frederik Schrøder, 3 vols. (1929–1931); *Værker i Udvalg,* ed. Georg Christensen and Hal Koch, 10 vols. (1940–1949); *N.F.S. Grundtvigs Sangværk,* ed. Th. Balslev et al., 5 vols., 2nd ed. (1982–1983); *Breve til og fra N. F. S. Grundtvig,* ed. Georg Christensen and Stener Grundtvig, 5 vols. (1924–1926); *Grundtvigs Erindringer og Erindringer om Grundtvig,* ed. Steen Johansen and Henning Høirup (1948); *Dag-og Udtogsbøger,* ed. Gustav Albeck, 2 vols. (1979); *Danne-Virke. Et Tids-Skrift,* 4 vols. (1983; repr. of Grundtvig's magazine); *Nordens Mytologi,* ed. Poul Engberg (1983, repr. of 3rd ed.) *N. F. S. Grundtvig Prædikener,* ed. Christian Thodberg, vol. 1– (1983–).

TRANSLATIONS

Selected Writings, ed. Johannes Knudsen (1976); *A Grundtvig Anthology*, ed. Niels Lyhne Jensen (1984).

REFERENCES

Allen, E. L., *Bishop Grundtvig* (London, 1947); Arden, G. Everett, *Four Northern Lights: Men Who Shaped Scandinavian Churches* (Minneapolis, 1964); Borup, Johan, *N.F.S. Grundtvig* (Copenhagen, 1948); Bugge, Knud E., *Skolen for Livet* (Copenhagen, 1964); Hansen, Uffe, *Grundtvigs Salmedigtning*, 2 vols. (Odense, 1937–1951); Høirup, Henning, *Grundtvigs Syn paa Tro og Erkendelse* (Copenhagen, 1948); Jørgensen, Aage, *Grundt- vig—litteratur 1969–81. En bibliografi* (Aarhus, 1986); Johansen, Steen, ed., *Bibliografi over N. F. S. Grundtvigs Skrifter*, 4 vols. (Copenhagen, 1948–1954); Knudsen, Johannes, *A Danish Rebel* (Philadelphia, 1955); Koch, Hal, *Grundtvig* (Yellow Spring, Ohio, 1952); Linhardt, P. G., *Grundtvig* (London, 1951); Lundgreen-Nielsen, Flemming, *Det han- dlende ord*, 3 vols. (Copenhagen, 1980); Mortensen, Enok, *Schools for Life* (Junction City, Oreg., 1977); Nielsen, Ernest D., *Grundtvig* (Rock Island, Ill., 1955); Sneen, Donald Jul, *The Hermeneutics of N. F. S. Grundtvig* (Ann Arbor, Mich., 1979); Thaning, Kaj, *Menneske først*, 3 vols. (Copenhagen, 1963); Thodberg, Christian, and Anders Pontoppidan Thyssen, eds., *N. F. S. Grundtvig* (Copenhagen, 1983); Toldberg, Helge, *Grundtvigs Symbolverden* (Copenhagen, 1950).

Niels Lyhne Jensen

Guðbergur Bergsson. *See* Bergsson, Guðbergur.

Guðjónsson, Halldór. *See* Laxness, Halldór Kiljan.

Guðmundsson, Kristmann. Icelandic novelist, b. 23 October 1901, Bor- garfjörður, d. 21 November 1983, Reykjavík.

After finishing studies at the Co-operative College in Reykjavík and publishing a book of poems, Guðmundsson settled in Norway in 1924 and wrote a significant part of his fiction in Norwegian, achieving an international reputation. In 1939 he returned to Iceland and wrote his later fiction in his native tongue, his Nor- wegian books having been turned into Icelandic by various translators.

Guðmundsson's first book in Norwegian, a collection of short stories, *Islandsk kjærlighet* (1926; Icelandic Love), was an instant success. There followed eleven novels in a highly romantic vein, which celebrate the spiritual and physical aspects of love between man and woman with a kind of pagan abandon. Of these novels, *Livets morgen* (1929; *Morning of Life*, 1936) was artistically the most successful, incarnating in the protagonists as it were, the age-old heroic ideals of the medieval sagas in a modern setting. After his return to Iceland, Guðmundsson wrote over a dozen novels in his native language, some of them treating historical and mystical subjects, but the erotic element is as a rule the center of gravity.

Evidently Guðmundsson's themes and mode of expression coincided with the prevailing mood of the period between the two world wars, when he was living in Norway, and he was able to imbue his adopted language with some kind of luster that endeared his novels to the Norwegian public and readers in some thirty other countries. However, his struggle with his own language, after his return, never produced the desired results, and translations of his Norwegian novels seem strangely dated, even though they all deal with Icelandic themes. His later production is marred by romantic excesses as well as by formal and linguistic flaws. For all that, he is reputed to be the second most widely translated Icelandic author of his century.

FURTHER WORKS

Rökkursöngvar (1922); *Brudekjolen* (1927; *The Bridal Gown*, 1931); *Armann og Vildis* (1928); *Sigmar* (1930); *Den blå kyst* (1931); *Det hellige fjell* (1932); *Den förste vår* (1933); *Hvide nætter* (1934); *Jordens barn* (1935); *Lampen* (1936); *Gudinnen og oksen* (1938; *Winged Citadel*, 1940); *Arma Ley* (1940); *Nátttröllið glottir* (1943); *Félagi kona* (1947); *Kvöld í Reykjavík* (1948); *Þokan rauða*, 2 vols. (1950–1952); *Höll Þyrnirósu* (1952); *Harmleikurinn í Austurbæ* (1955); *Kristmannskver* (1955); *Heimsbókmenntasaga*, 2 vols. (1955–1956); *Ferðin til stjarnanna* (1959); *Ævintýri í himingeimnum* (1959); *Ísold hin svarta* (1959); *Dægrin blá* (1960); *Loginn hvíti* (1961); *Ísold hin gullna* (1962); *Torgið* (1965); *Skammdegi* (1966); *Tilhuglíf* (1968); *Blábrá og fleiri sögur* (1968); *Smiðurinn mikli* (1969); *Sumar í Selavík* (1971; *Brosið* (1972); *Leikur að ljóðum* (1974); *Stjörnuskipið* (1975); *Skáldverk*, 8 vols. (1978); *Haustljóð* (1981).

REFERENCES

Einarsson, Stefán, "Five Icelandic Novelists." *Books Abroad* 16.3 (1942); Einarsson, Stefán, *History of Icelandic Prose Writers 1800–1940* (Ithaca, N.Y., 1950).

Sigurður A. Magnússon

Guðmundsson, Tómas. Icelandic poet and translator, b. 6 January 1901, Efri-Brú, Grímsnes, d. 14 November 1983, Reykjavík.

After early years spent in the south of Iceland Guðmundsson moved to Reykjavík and graduated from the university there with a law degree in 1926. A short, unsuccessful period in private practice was followed by employment in Iceland's Bureau of Statistics (1928–1943). From 1943–1946 and in 1954 he was a coeditor of the literary periodical *Helgafell,* and for many years he was involved with musical comedy in Reykjavík.

After Guðmundsson's first publication, *Við sundin blá* (1925; By the Blue Straits), a dreamy, romantic collection of well-crafted poems that remained largely unnoticed, eight years passed before his second effort, *Fagra veröld* (1933; Beautiful World), appeared in print. This time his poetry was an instant success, with three editions of the work being published in two years. The focus of his muse is the growing city of Reykjavík, and the pictures he paints furnish the setting for the nostalgic reminiscences of his earlier years there. While the poems range from the whimsical to the purely lyrical, all show Guðmundsson's facility of expression and mastery of form. In appreciation of his endeavors on its behalf, the city of Reykjavík sent him on a visit to the Mediterranean, a trip that resulted in *Stjörnur vorsins* (1940; Spring Stars). He sings songs of love to the historic and beautiful surroundings but also includes autobiographical poems displaying an unexpectedly successful blend of rich lyricism and delightful humor. World War II and the ensuing years forced sober concern on the effects of war in *Fljótið helga* (1950; The Holy River), and show an increasing tendency for the poet to brood on the transience of youth and beauty.

Guðmunsson published many of his poems in *Helgafell* and edited the works of the poet Stefán Sigurðsson in 1945 *(Ljóðmæli)*. He, in turn, was the subject of short sketches by the poets Sigurður Nordal in *Nordens Kalendar* (1935) and Sigurður Einarsson in *Yndi unaðsstunda* (1952).

FURTHER WORKS

Fljúgandi blóm (1952); *Ljóðasafn* (1953); *Ljóðasafn* (1961).

TRANSLATIONS

American-Scandinavian Review 32.2 (1944); *20th Century Scandinavian Poetry*, ed. Martin S. Allwood (1950); *American-Scandinavian Review* 48.1 (1960); *An Anthology of Icelandic Poetry*, ed. Eirikur Benedikz (1969).

REFERENCES

Andrésson, Kristinn, E., *Íslenzkar nútímabókmenntir: 1918–1948* (Reykjavík, 1949); Beck, Richard, *History of Icelandic Poets: 1800–1940* (Ithaca, N.Y., 1950); Ringler, Richard N., "The Poems of Tómas Guðmundsson." *Scandinavian Review* 63.2 (1975).

Peter A. Jorgensen

Guðmundur Böðvarsson. *See* Böðvarsson, Guðmundur.

Guðmundur Gíslason Hagalín. *See* Hagalín, Guðmundur Gíslason.

Guðmundur Kamban. *See* Kamban, Guðmundur.

Guðmundur Magnússon. *See* Magnússon, Guðmundur.

Gullberg, Hjalmar Robert. Swedish poet and translator, b. 30 May 1898, Malmö, d. 19 July 1961, Lake Yddingen near Malmö.

Gullberg studied classical languages and literary history in Lund. He was literary advisor to Stockholm's Royal Dramatic Theater (1934–1961), director of theater for Swedish Radio (1936–1950), and a member of the Swedish Academy. His studies in the classical humanities, as well as his participation in the traditional "studentspex" (parodistic comic reviews) and editorship of the satirical student publication *Lundegård,* left their stamp on his poetry, which displays both a mastery of classical form and an ironic humor that permeates even many of his more serious poems.

Gullberg's first collection of poems, *I en främmande stad* (1927; In a Foreign

City), introduces a motif repeated throughout his poetry: the individual's isolation in a misunderstanding world.

Gullberg gained recognition with *Andliga övningar* (1932; Spiritual Exercises), in which he juxtaposes Christian mysticism with modern skepticism in a clash of opposites characteristic of much of his poetry. In *Kärlek i tjugonde seklet* (1933; Love in the Twentieth Century), for example, erotic mysticism collides with an ironic, matter-of-fact attitude toward sensual love.

Growing international tension probably contributed to the tone of *Att övervinna världen* (1937; To Conquer the World), a collection of poems filled with pessimism, world denial, and mysticism. The atmosphere is even darker in *Fem kornbröd och två fiskar* (1942; Five Barley Loaves and Two Fishes), with its anti-Nazi protests, religious lyricism, and apocalyptic visions of the end of the world.

In addition to his own original work, Gullberg translated many literary classics into Swedish, including works of Aristophanes, Euripides, Sophocles, Molière, Pedro Calderón de la Barca, Federico García Lorca, and Gabriela Mistral.

Gullberg's work reveals a poet who was outwardly a suave, refined gentleman and inwardly an isolated artist, who had a touch of both the saint and the clown; who vacillated between reverence and revolt; and whose poems, even when deep and metaphysical, are light, graceful, and often playful—a poet considered one of the most important and influential of his day.

FURTHER WORKS

Sonat (1929); *Ensamstående bildad herre* (1935; *Gentleman, Single, Refined and Selected Poems 1937–1959*, 1979); *Dödsmask och lustgård* (1952); *Terziner i okonstens tid* (1958); *Ögon, läppar* (1959); *Dikter*, ed. Anders Palm (1985).

REFERENCES

Fehrman, Carl, *Hjalmar Gullberg* (Stockholm, 1958; rev. ed., 1967); Karlström, Lennart, *Hjalmar Gullberg, en bibliografi 1952–1979* (Stockholm, 1981); Landgren, Bengt, *Hjalmar Gullberg och beredskapslitteraturen* (Uppsala, 1975); Lesser, Rika, "Gunnar Ekelöf and Hjalmar Gullberg: 'But in Another Language.' " *American Poetry Review* (September-October 1981); Palm, Anders, *Kristet, indiskt och antikt i Hjalmar Gullbergs diktning* (Stockholm, 1976); Petherick, Karin, "Hjalmar Gullberg (1898–1961)," in *Essays on Swedish Literature from 1880 to the Present Day*, ed. Irene Scobbie (Aberdeen, 1978); Sjöberg, Leif, Foreword to *Gentleman, Single, Refined and Selected Poems* (Baton Rouge, La., 1979); Thavenius, Jan, *Konkordans till Hjalmar Gullbergs lyrik* (Stockholm, 1971); Vowles, Richard B., "Hjalmar Gullberg. An Ancient and a Modern." *Scandinavian Studies* 24.3 (1952).

Barbara Lide

Gunnar Gunnarsson. *See* Gunnarsson, Gunnar.

Gunnarsson, Gunnar. Icelandic novelist, author of short stories, plays, and three early volumes of poetry, b. 18 May 1889, Fljótsdalur, East Iceland, d. 21 November 1975, Reykjavík.

In 1907, at the age of eighteen, Gunnarsson moved to Denmark and became a student at the well-known folk high school Askov in Jutland. He married a Danish woman and lived in Denmark until 1939. Then, at the beginning of World War II, he went back to Iceland and settled as a farmer and writer in his native district. From 1948 to his death he lived in Reykjavík.

In Denmark, Gunnarsson entered his career as an author with extraordinary energy and went through some hard years of apprenticeship. In order to reach a wider public, and to be able to live by his pen, he wrote in Danish instead of Icelandic. His first literary success was a novel in four volumes, *Borgslægtens Historie* (1912–1914; *Guest the One-Eyed*, 1920, abr. trans.). In a long series of novels dealing with different epochs of Icelandic history, he consolidated his position as one of the most prominent Nordic prosaists of his generation. During the interwar years he made himself known as an eager spokesman for the unity of the Nordic countries and propagandist for their union into one state. After his return to Iceland in 1939 he continued writing, but now in his mother tongue.

At the head of Gunnarsson's writings stands the novel *Kirken paa Bjerget* (1923–1928; The Church on the Mountain). In its five volumes the principal character, Uggi Greipsson, relates his development, from his childhood and youth in Iceland to his breakthrough as an author in Denmark and his marriage with a Danish woman. The author himself wants to have the work regarded as pure fiction. But in fact he has so much in common with Uggi that it is hardly misleading to designate this novel as a slightly veiled autobiography.

The first two volumes, *Leg med Straa* (1923; Play with Straw) and *Skibe paa Himlen* (1925; *Ships in the Sky*, 1938, also comprising the preceding volume), deal with little Uggi's growing up in East Iceland, Gunnarsson's own native place. We enter an old-fashioned world, where the unrest of modern times has still not begun to ferment. Life passes by in the calm and irresistible rhythm of the seasons. Men and animals, nature and tools—everything appears as an animated whole. The characters around the boy are often originals and are described with a refreshing sense of humor.

The relation between Uggi and his mother has a deep and vibrating undertone. Her gentle nature gives even the weekday a dimension of sanctity and mysticism. When the seven-year-old's mother dies, an ashen light falls over the world. Her death overshadows also the third volume, *Natten og Drømmen* (1926; *The Night and the Dream*, 1938). With her the meaning of things has disappeared; the safety in life is lost. When Uggi at the age of seventeen makes his literary debut with two booklets of poetry, one of them is a cycle in memory of his mother— a close parallel to Gunnarsson himself.

In the two concluding volumes, *Den uerfarne Rejsende* (1927; The Inexperienced Traveler) and *Hugleik den Haardtsejlende* (1928; Hugleik the Hard-Sailing), the scene is Denmark. The story of Uggi's struggle for his success as a writer is interesting in itself. But it is perhaps too close to the author's personal experiences. We miss the artistic unity of the former volumes, where the distance in time and space, the longing for the far-off Saga Island of his childhood, has provided the author with the perspective for a great synthesis.

A masterpiece of a more limited size is *Advent*, (1937; *Advent*, 1939; *The Good Shepherd*, 1940). An aging shepherd, a simple and humble man, is struggling in a snowstorm to rescue sheep that have got lost in the mountains. In his endurance and sense of responsibility for men and animals he appears as a true representative of human ideals. *Advent* is a heroic poem as well as a legend.

Along with Halldór Laxness,* Gunnarsson is the leading Icelandic prose writer of our century. In his works he has created a monumental vision of his native country, its nature, history and people.

FURTHER WORKS

Móðurminning (1906); *Vorljóð* (1906); *Digte* (1911); *Sögur* (1912); *Livets Strand* (1915); *Smaa Historier* (1916); *Varg i Veum* (1916); *Drengen* (1917); *Smaa Skuespil* (1917); *Edbrødre* (1918; *The Sworn Brothers: A Tale of the Early Days of Iceland*, 1920); *Smaa Historier* (1918 new collection); *Salige er de enfoldige* (1920; *Seven Days' Darkness*, 1930); *Ringen* (1921); *Dyret med Glorien* (1922); *Den glade Gaard og andre Historier* (1923); *Det nordiske Rige* (1927); *En Dag tilovers og andre Historier* (1929); *Svartfugl* (1929; *The Black Cliffs*, 1967); *Jón Arason* (1930); *Rævepelsene eller Ærlighed varer længst* (1930); *Verdens Glæder: en Tylft Historier* (1931); *Vikivaki* (1932); *De Blindes Hus* (1933); *Jord* (1933); *Hvide-Krist* (1934); *Sagaøen* (1935); *Graamand* (1936); *Trylle og andet Smaakram* (1939; *Trylle and Other Small Fry*, 1947); *Heiðaharmur* (1940); *Sálumessa* (1952); *Brimhenda* (1954).

FURTHER TRANSLATIONS

Seven Icelandic Short Stories, ed. Ásgeir Pétursson (1960); *An Anthology of Scandinavian literature*, ed. Hallberg Hallmundsson (1965).

REFERENCES

Arvidsson, Stellan, *Gunnar Gunnarsson Islänningen* (Stockholm, 1960); Beck, Richard, "Gunnar Gunnarsson: Some Observations," in *Scandinavian Studies*, ed. Carl F. Bayerschmidt and Erik J. Friis (Seattle, 1965); Einarsson, Stefan, "Gunnar Gunnarsson: An Icelandic author," in *Jón Bjarnason Academy Yearbook* (Reykjavík, 1940); Elfelt, Kjeld, *Gunnar Gunnarsson, Et Essay* (Copenhagen, 1927); Gelsted, Otto, *Gunnar Gunnarsson* (Copenhagen, 1926); Magnússon, Sigurður A., "Gunnar Gunnarsson: Iceland's First International Novelist." *Atlantica and Iceland Review* 11.1 (1973); Sigurðsson, Haraldur, *Skrá um bækur Gunnars Gunnarssonar á íslensku og erlendum málum* (Reykjavík, 1963).

Peter Hallberg

Gustafsson, Lars. Swedish novelist, poet, and critic, b. 17 May 1936, Västerås.

Gustafsson's training in philosophy—he holds a Ph.D. from Uppsala—to a large extent accounts for his preoccupation with existential and epistemological questions. He is a sophisticated writer, technically accomplished, and fond of subtle intellectual distinctions.

His early novels tend to center around the exploration of an uncertain sense of identity, the impossibility of knowing reality, and the multiplicity of meaning that the world offers up to the inquiring mind. His later "essayistic" poems and novels strive to make the reader conscious of the social and historical forces that define what we know and who we are and attempt to find an outlook in which things are endowed with a lasting significance. At times he seems attracted to mysticism, which he however ultimately rejects, as he also rejects any definitive attitude to life; his reflections on existential dilemmas lead to a sense of being on the track of something indefinable, some kind of authentic being or ultimate reality, the nature of which is such, however, that it always will elude understanding. Like Tomas Tranströmer,* with whom he has much in common, he sees the world as mysterious and beyond rational explanation. But he is drawn to the uncanny in ways quite his own, to the arcane and the esoteric, to facts borrowed from the exact sciences or culled from the footnotes of intellectual history—from Jules Verne to alchemy—and to mechanical objects of a dated technology. Strange pieces of machinery are described with a precision of detail that tends to veer toward the fantastic while, at the same time, their very uselessness makes them seem wrenching and mysterious.

Gustafsson has participated vigorously in the cultural debate in Sweden, both as an editor of the influential and prestigious *BLM* magazine (*Bonniers Litterära Magasin*), 1962–1972, and as a prolific writer of articles and commentaries on contemporary social and cultural issues, often taking the outsider's point of view. He is read and appreciated abroad, especially in Germany, but also in the United States where several translations of his work have appeared.

WORKS

Vägvila (1957); *Poeten Brumbergs sista dagar och död* (1959); *Bröderna* (1960); *Nio brev om romanen*, with Lars Bäckström (1961); *Ballongfararna* (1962); *Följeslagarna* (1962); *En förmiddag i Sverige* (1963); *The Public Dialogue in Sweden* (1964); *En resa till jordens medelpunkt och andra dikter* (1966); *Den egentliga berättelsen om Herr Arenander* (1966); *Förberedelser till flykt och andra berättelser* (1967); *Bröderna Wright uppsöker Kitty Hawk* (1968); *Konsten att segla med drakar* (1969); *Utopier* (1969); *Kärleksförklaring till en sefardisk dam* (1970); *Två maktspel* (1970); *Herr Gustafsson själv* (1971); *Kommentarer* (1972); *Varma rum och kalla* (1972; *Warm Rooms and Cold*, 1975); *Den onödiga samtiden*, with Jan Myrdal (1973); *Världsdelar* (1975); *Familjefesten* (1975); *Sigismund* (1976; *Sigismund*, 1985); *Strandhugg i svensk poesi* (1976; *Forays into Swedish Poetry*, 1978); *Tennisspelarna* (1977; *The Tennis Players*, 1983); *Sonetter* (1977); *Den lilla världen* (1977); *En biodlares död* (1978; *The Death of a Beekeeper*, 1981); *Språk och lögn* (1978); *Kinesisk höst* (1978); *Filosofier* (1979); *Konfrontationer* (1979); *I mikroskopet* (1979); *Yllet* (1979); *Afrikanskt försök* (1980); *Artesiska brunnar*, *cartesianska drömmar* (1980); *För liberalismen* (1981); *Berättelser om lyckliga människor* (1981); *Ur Bild i Bild; Collected Poems 50–80* (1981); *Världens tystnad före Bach* (1982); *Sorgemusik för frimurare* (1983); *Sprickorna i muren* (1983); *Fåglarna* (1984); *Bilderna på Solstadens murar* (1985); *Bernard Foys tredje rockad* (1986); *Samlade berättelser* (1987).

FURTHER TRANSLATIONS

Selected Poems (1972); *Modern Swedish Prose in Translation*, ed. Karl Erik Lagerlöf (1979).

REFERENCES

Graves, Peter, "Poetry of the 1960's," in *Essays on Swedish Literature from 1880 to the Present Day*, ed. Irene Scobbie (Aberdeen, 1978); Gustafsson, Lars, "The Machines" (text of poem in English and analysis by the author). *American Review* 21 (1974); Hertz-Ohmes, Peter, "The Public Lie, the Truth of Fiction, and Herr Gustafsson Himself." *Pacific Coast Philology* 17 (1982); Sandström, Yvonne, "The Machine Theme in Some Poems by Lars Gustafsson." *Scandinavian Studies* 44.2 (1972); Sprinchorn, Evert, "Lars Gustafsson: The Public Dialogue in Sweden, Current Issues of Social, Aesthetic, and Moral Debate." *Scandinavica* 4.1 (1965).

Joanna Bankier

Gyllembourg (-Ehrensvärd), Thomasine. Danish short story writer, b. 9 November 1773, Copenhagen, d. 1 June 1856, Copenhagen.

The epoch-making events in Gyllembourg's life were her divorce from P. A. Heiberg and subsequent new marriage, both of which she wrote about in a nonscandalous manner. She began her writing career at the age of fifty-four. The central topic of her short stories is the woman's role in a bourgeois family. She developed an entertaining psychological prose in which she depicts complex emotions and inner conflicts, and the self-denying attitude imprinted on the minds of bourgeois girls already in adolescence.

Gyllembourg articulated a rebellion against the seemingly well integrated system of morality. The critical content tends to be neutralized, however, by the compositional structure of her stories, which conforms to the conventions of the eighteenth-century moralizing literature. As a result, her stories are characterized by a stylistic ambivalence typical of poetic realism and aesthetic idealism. She insisted on writing anonymously to the end of her career, calling herself "the author of everyday stories," from the title of *Hverdags-Historie* (1828), one of her central works. This need for anonymity appears to reflect her experience of the role conflict in being a woman and an author. Feminist critics in particular have shown interest in Gyllembourg's ambivalence.

FURTHER WORKS

Familien Polonius (1827); *Den magiske Nøgle* (1828); *Kong Hjort* (1830); *Slægtskab og Djævelskab* (1830); *Den lille Karen* (1830); *Sproglæreren* (1831); *Magt og List* (1831); *Fregatskibet Svanen* (1831); *Drøm og Virkelighed* (1833); *Mesalliance* (1833); *De Forlovede* (1834); *Findeløn* (1834); *De lyse Nætter* (1834); *Ægtestand* (1835); *En Episode* (1835); *Extremerne* (1835); *Jøden* (1836); *Hvidkappen* (1836); *Montanus den Yngre* (1837); *Nisida* (1837); *Maria* (1839); *Een i Alle* (1840); *Nær og fjern* (1841); *En Brevvexling* (1843); *Korsveien* (1844); *Castor og Pollux* (1844); *To Tidsaldre* (1845).

TRANSLATIONS

The Literature and Romance of Northern Europe, ed. William Howitt and Mary Howitt (1852).

REFERENCES

Broue, Anni, *Penge og kærlighed: religion og socialitet i Thomasine Gyllembourgs forfatterskab* (Odense, 1983); Hude, Elisabeth, *Thomasine Gyllembourg og Hverdags-historierne* (Copenhagen, 1951); Johansen, Jørgen Dines, "Vare og pris," in *Analyser af dansk kortprosa* I (Copenhagen, 1971).

Jørgen Egebak

Gyllenborg, Gustaf Fredrik. Swedish poet, b. 6 December 1731, Strömsbro near Linköping, d. 30 March 1808.

Count Gustaf Fredrik Gyllenborg belonged to one of the most powerful Swedish aristocratic families. He was, for example, a nephew of Carl Gyllenborg (1679–1746), who was not only the founder of the Hat party but also the author of *Swenska sprätthöken* (1737; The Swedish Fop) and other works.

Gyllenborg became a student at the University of Uppsala in 1747 and, from 1748 to 1750, at the University of Lund, where his father, Count Johan Gyllenborg (1682–1752), was chancellor. In 1751, Gyllenborg became a government employee in Stockholm; from 1756 to 1762, he was gentleman-in-waiting to Crown Prince Gustaf. In 1762 he became chancery secretary and in 1773 a member of the Academy of Belles Lettres (*Vitterhetsakademien*). In 1774, he became commissioner of revenue. He became one of the first eighteen members of the Swedish Academy when it was founded in April 1786. He had married Anna Margareta Gottsman in 1764 and became the father of a son and a daughter. He held various government positions until his death in 1808.

Gyllenborg's contributions to Swedish literature have been given a far more important place in Swedish history than his services to the royal family and the government. His interest in both poetry and prose can be traced to family traditions, wide reading in both native and foreign literature, and, most particularly, to his close friendship with the poet Count Gustaf Philip Creutz* and his membership in the literary society Tankebyggarorden, headed by the poet Hedvig Charlotta Nordenflycht.* Basically a neoclassicist who emphasized correctness in prosody, morality, and didacticism, Gyllenborg contributed a substantial number of odes, satires, and miscellaneous poems to the society's *Våra försök* (Our Attempts, 1753, 1754, 1756) and *Vitterhetsarbeten* (Literary Works, 1759, 1762).

Among his better works are odes, fables, satires, and nature poems. His satires—*Satir öfver mina vänner* (Satire of My Friends), *Verldsföraktaren* (Despirer of the World), *Menniskans nöjen* (Human Pleasures), and *Menniskans elände* (Human Misery)—rank among the best Swedish poetry of the eighteenth century along with some of his fables and odes, including *Ode öfver själens styrka* (Ode on the Strength of the Human Spirit). His dramas are dull and lifeless. But his autobiography, *Mitt lefverne 1731–1775* (1885), is anything but dull: it reveals him as a kindly, lovable human being with a good mind and high ideals.

As interesting as anything Gyllenborg ever wrote is his *Landtqväden öfver årstiderna* (1779; Country Songs about the Seasons). Inspired both by Carl von Linné* and by James Thomson and his school of poets, Gyllenborg appreciated the beauty of external nature, not least as revealed on his family estate Skenäs in Södermanland. *Vinterqväde* and *Vårqväde* (Winter and Spring) appeared in 1759, but the whole cycle was not completed until 1779 when *Sommar* (Summer), *Höst* (Autumn), and a unifying *Ode til naturen* (Ode to Nature) were published. The cycle is important not only because it is still readable but because it is one of several indications that his educated countrymen had become intensely aware of Swedish seasons and Swedish customs, Swedish practices and Swedish traditions, substantially, of course, because of Carl von Linné's inspiring investigation of Swedish nature and Swedish practices.

REFERENCES

Blanck, Anton, *Den nordiska renässansen* (Stockholm, 1911); Johnson, Walter, *James Thomson's Influence on Swedish Literature in the Eighteenth Century* (Urbana, Ill., 1936); Lamm, Martin, *Upplysningstidens romantik*, 2 vols. (Stockholm, 1918–1920); Levertin, Oskar, *Svenska gestalter* (Stockholm, 1903); Sahlberg, Gardar, *Gustaf Fredrik Gyllenborg: Hans liv och diktning under frihetstiden* (Stockholm, 1943).

Walter Johnson

Gyllensten, Lars. Swedish novelist and essayist, b. 12 November 1921, Stockholm.

Already as an adolescent Gyllensten familiarized himself with traditional and modern philosophy. At the same time he showed strong scientific interests and was torn between alternatives for his academic studies before settling for medicine. While at medical school he and a fellow student (Torgny Greitz) perpetrated a literary hoax with the publication of a collection of poetry, *Camera obscura* (1946), under the pseudonym Jan Wictor, in which the "incomprehensible" poetry of the 1940s was parodied. Gyllensten's studies and subsequent research at the Caroline Institute led to a doctorate in medicine and a professorship. Concurrently with his scientific work, he established himself as a major figure in Swedish literature. In 1973, having already earned international recognition for his scientific work, he left the Caroline Institute in favor of his literary pursuits. In 1966 he had been elected a member of the Swedish Academy. Since 1968 he has served on the Academy's Nobel Committee. In 1977 he was appointed permanent secretary of the Academy. In 1975 he was elected a member of the Royal Swedish Academy of Sciences.

Gyllensten's authorship has its point of departure in the ideological crisis in the wake of nazism and Hiroshima, what Gyllensten terms the "bankruptcy of naïveté." A profound skepticism of all dogmas and -isms and a recognition of the necessity of finding meaningful and creative modes of responding to an elusive reality form the basis of Gyllensten's activity as an author. Refusing the comforts of a religious commitment, he formulates his "nihilistic credo" and, in terms reminiscent of Albert Camus, he suggests a "meaningless resistance to meaninglessness." All his books are demonstrations of existential alternatives, offering examples of different attitudes toward life. Although each work can be read separately, the true scope of Gyllensten's undertaking can only be grasped through the totality and the dialectic interplay of individual works.

From the beginning Gyllensten rejected the concept of literary realism, which he viewed as an "art of illusionism" presupposing the existence of a fixed reality that could be described. With Immanuel Kant he bows to the impossibility of knowing reality "in itself," and with Arthur Schopenhauer he regards "the world as will and idea," a view that he found further confirmed by modern scientific theory that our experience of the world is delimited by our instruments of perception. In this context Gyllensten stresses the role of language as a major "organ of perception" determining our apprehension of reality. He denies the idea of "scientific objectivity"—scientific hypotheses are approximations, models to be tested and implemented as far as they are useful, only to be discarded and replaced by new models. With the American pragmatist Charles S. Peirce he sees this process as an "infinite inquiry," a concept he applies to his own activity as an author. The existential freedom that Gyllensten posits lies in man's option to *create* his own reality or realities. Gyllensten's books are demonstrations of such creations, or "artifacts."

The most pervasive influence behind Gyllensten's particular literary method is Søren Kierkegaard.* Gyllensten's early discovery of the Danish philosopher was to affect his whole future as a writer, in particular Kierkegaard's employment of pseudonyms to present different "stages" or attitudes, each put forward by the respective pseudonyms as persuasively as possible without authorial comment or judgment. In a similar way, Gyllensten's books are explorations of existential attitudes and possibilities, in which the author assumes different roles behind the constant pseudonym "Lars Gyllensten."

In addition to his fiction Gyllensten offers comments in articles and essays clarifying his own position. Here he advocates a watchful mobility to avoid too strict an adherence to any given tenets with the implied danger of dogmatism or fanaticism. Through newspaper articles he frequently takes unequivocal stands on social, political, or cultural issues.

Gyllensten's position in Swedish literature is unique. Intellectualism, irony, and passionate humanism are vital elements in his authorship, which also displays formidable stylistic and linguistic resources as he assumes the voices of his different "incarnations."

FURTHER WORKS

Moderna myter (1949); *Blå skeppet* (1950); *Barnabok* (1952); *Carnivora* (1953); *Senilia* (1956); *Senatorn* (1958); *Sokrates' död* (1960); *Desperados* (1962); *Kains memoarer* (1963; *The Testament of Cain*, 1967); *Nihilistiskt credo* (1964); *Juvenilia* (1965); *Lotus i Hades* (1966); *Diarium spirituale* (1968); *Palatset i parken* (1970); *Ur min offentliga sektor* (1971); *Mänskan, djuren, all naturen* (1971); *Grottan i öknen* (1973); *I skuggan av Don Juan* (1975); *Lapptäcken—Livstecken* (1976); *Baklängesminnen* (1978); *Klipp i 70-talet* (1979); *Huvudskallebok* (1981); *Rätt och slätt* (1983); *Skuggans återkomst eller Don Juan går igen* (1985); *Sju vise mästare om kärlek* (1986).

REFERENCES

Haack, Elsbeth G., "Semantic Detour: A Post-Structuralist Study of Lars Gyllensten's Text *Senilia.*" *Pacific Northwest Council on Foreign Languages.* Proceedings 30 (1979); Isaksson, Hans, *Lars Gyllensten* (Boston, 1978); Orton, Gavin, "A Swedenborgian Dream Book: Lars Gyllensten's *Palatset i parken.*" *Scandinavica* 23.1 (1984); Sjöberg, Leif, "Lars Gyllensten: Master of Arts and Science." *American-Scandinavian Review* 55.2 (1967); Warme, Lars G., "Lars Gyllensten's *Diarium spirituale*: The Creative Process as a Novel." *Scandinavica* 19.2 (1980).

Lars G. Warme

H

***

Haanpää, Pentti. Finnish short story writer, dramatist, and novelist, b. 14 October 1905, Piippola; d. 30 September 1955, Piippola.

The geographic perimeters of Haanpää's life were narrow; he never left the small, north Ostrobothnian village of Piippola. Only once did he venture abroad, in 1952 to Mainland China with a delegation of Finnish authors. Yet he had wanderlust in his blood. Every year when the snows melted and the roads opened, he took his bicycle and pedaled through the Finnish countryside. On these trips he lived the life of his fictional heroes, the lonely hoboes and backwoods lumberjacks, whose existence was unconstrained by social institutions and who lived close to nature, frequently pitching their strength against its might.

Haanpää came from an enlightened farming family. Both his father and grandfather had been involved in politics and were published authors. Although Haanpää's formal education ended with the compulsory school, he read extensively on his own and learned English through correspondence courses. This enabled him to read English literature in the original, and he thus became one of the first in Finland to discover and appreciate James Joyce. In his interest in Anglo-Saxon culture, as in many other instances, Haanpää moved against the current. Finland of the 1920s and 1930s belonged firmly in the sphere of German cultural influence. Nowhere was the old Prussian impact felt stronger than in the military, which also bore the brunt of Haanpää's criticism. His impressions of the military were largely based on his own experiences. To him the army stood for the ultimate deprivation of individual freedom, moral decay, and disrespect for human life. These sentiments were best expressed in the collection of short stories *Kenttä ja kasarmi* (1928; The Barracks and the Field), which was received with a bitter public outcry. Finland's independence, only ten years old, was still fragile, and anyone critical of the country's institutions was labeled unpatriotic and a communist. As a result, no publisher dared to touch Haanpää's works for the next seven years. He continued to write, however. *Noitaympyrä* (wr. 1931, pub. 1956; The Magic Circle), perhaps Haanpää's best novel, was written during this period. Its theme centers on the disillusionment with life in the contemporary society. Although nature offers here, as in many of Haanpää's works, peace and consolation, a retreat to the wilderness is not portrayed as a viable long-term solution. Neither is the protagonist's final straying into Soviet territory viewed as a positive resolution to his dilemma. Rather, it strikes as a resigned acknowledgment of the futility of continued struggle.

The masterful short stories of *Korpisota* (1940; War in the Wilderness), written at the close of the Finno-Russian Winter War, restored respect for Haanpää in the eyes of the educated. Where Haanpää earlier, in bitter irony, had lambasted the peacetime army as an institution, he now pays homage to the ordinary soldier but condemns war itself. In these unadorned stories, Haanpää laid the ground for the realistic war novel, a prolific genre in Finnish literature that culminated in Väinö Linna's* *Tuntematon sotilas*.

In spite of the mellower tone of the later Haanpää and a shift from sarcastic irony to humor, his pessimistic outlook on life never changed. He continued to speak for the little man and for individual integrity, but now the adversary was the ruthless capitalist society rather than the blind fate or unperturbed nature of his early works. Life was a game of hazards, and human relations destructive. The early hero, a rebel relentlessly struggling against all odds, was replaced by a trickster, who in the face of life's unfairness and futility tried to sneak through life while making the most of it. Haanpää's own drowning death in 1955 has been interpreted as a suicide.

Haanpää was the right person in the wrong place and at the wrong time. He lived and wrote about a lifestyle that has since disappeared. With him ended the long tradition in Finnish literature of peasant authors describing the life of the countryside. His social criticism was misconstrued, and during his lifetime he never received the appreciation due to him. Today he is recognized as the unsurpassed stylist of his generation, and his short stories are among the best ever written in Finnish.

FURTHER WORKS

Maantietä pitkin (1925); *Rikas mies* (wr. 1925, pub. 1956); *Kolmen töräpään tarina* (1927); *Tuuli käy heidän ylitseen* (1927); *Hota-Leenan poika* (1929); *Karavaani ja muita juttuja* (1930); *Ilmeitä isänmaan kasvoilla* (wr. 1933, pub. 1956); *Pojan paluu* (wr. 1933, pub. 1956); *Väljän taivaan alla* (wr. 1934, pub. 1956); *Isännät ja isäntien varjot* (1935); *Vääpeli Sadon tapaus* (wr. 1935, pub. 1956); *Lauma* (1937); *Syntyykö uusi suku eli Kaaleppi Köykkänän vanhuus* (1937); *Taivalvaaran näyttelijä* (1938); *Ihmiselon karvas ihanuus* (1939); *Nykyaikaa* (1942); *Yhdeksän miehen saappaat* (1945); *Heta Rahko korkeassa iässä* (1947); *Jauhot* (1949); *Atomintutkija ja muita juttuja* (1950); *Iisakki Vähäpuheinen* (1953); *Kiinalaiset jutut* (1954); *Kolme mestarijuttua* (1955); *Jutut* (1946;1966); *Valitut teokset* (1955); *Kertomuksia ja tarinoita* (1956); *Pentti Haanpään jälkeenjääneet teokset*, vols. 1–3; cont. as *Teokset*, vols. 4–10 (1956–1958); *Maa-ja metsäkyliltä*, ed. Eino Kauppinen (1968); *Juttuja*, ed. Helena Anhava (1969); *Valitut teokset* (1970); *Kirveeniskuja*, ed. Veikko Huovinen (1971); *Muistiinmerkintöjä vuosilta 1925–39* (1976); *Teokset*, 8 vols. (1976).

REFERENCE

Kauppinen, Eino, *Pentti Haanpää* (Keuruu, 1966).

Virpi Zuck

Haavardsholm, Espen. Norwegian novelist, essayist, and critic, b. 10 February 1945, Oslo.

Haavardsholm belongs to the so-called *Profil* Generation, a group of young writers who formed a kind of literary circle around the student magazine *Profil* in the mid–1960s. Like his fellow writers Haavardsholm was in severe opposition to the traditional psychological and critical realism, demanding a more visionary and symbolic form of writing.

The young Haavardsholm was strongly influenced by European modernism. His literary form was one of complex symbolic structure, and as a writer he expressed a rather fatalistic and pessimistic outlook on life and society. In his first books he is occupied with the possibilities of individual freedom and the structuring of the human Self. In *Munnene* (1968; The Mouths) he rejects the notion of an authentic, indivisible Self as an illusion. The individual is always in a process of change, subjected to the defining tyranny of the Other.

Man is basically unfree, but nevertheless always in search of freedom. This striving is expressed in the creating of utopias. Thus the making of utopias is the theme of *Den avskyelige snømannen* (1970; The Abominable Snowman). The dreams of his characters are doomed to fail because they never transcend the privacy of individual phantasies.

In the early 1970s Haavardsholm came under the influence of Marxist Leninism, and his political sympathies became apparent in all that he wrote. The modernist heritage is still perceptible in the literary form and structure of the texts in *Zink* (1971; Zinc), but later in the 1970s his commitment to the new social realism even breaks this formal bond with the past.

In *Drift* (1980; Drift) and even more in *Store Fri* (1983; The Long Break), Haavardsholm breaks away from his political and aesthetic dogmatism of the 1970s, although he does so reluctantly and ambivalently. Both books are political-psychological novels. Haavardsholm has played an important role in his generation's development from apolitical modernism to Marxist social realism. Moreover, his recent books have demonstrated his ability to adapt to "new" trends in Norwegian literature.

FURTHER WORKS

Tidevann (1966); *Kartskisser* (1969); *Grip dagen* (1973); *Historiens kraftlinjer* (1975); *Poesi, maktspråk* (1977); *Boka om Kalle og Reinert* (1978); *Svarte fugler over kornåkeren* (1981); *Roger, gult* (1986); *Mannen fra Jante. Et portrett av Aksel Sandemose* (1988).

TRANSLATIONS

Literary Review 22.2 (1968–1969).

REFERENCE

Rønning, Helge, "Ufrihet og frigjøring—linjer i Espen Haavardsholms forfatterskap," in his *Linjer i norsk prosa* (Oslo, 1977).

Øystein Rottem

Haavikko, Paavo. Finnish poet, playwright, and novelist, b. 25 January 1931, Helsinki.

Haavikko is the son of a businessman. After graduating from high school in 1951, he worked in real estate. He is now literary editor of a leading Finnish publishing company, and a director of a company publishing periodicals. In 1984 Haavikko was awarded the prestigious Neustadt Prize.

With his first volume of poetry in 1951, Haavikko was heralded as a leader of the new poetry. At first his major themes were poetry and language, love and death. His more recent poems have concentrated on history and power. The concept of impermanence is constantly present, contrasted with man's blind belief that he can control events and create something permanent. Those who symbolize power in Haavikko's poetry are emperors, ministers, and merchants. His experience in the business world has clearly influenced his ideas. Many of his plays for stage and radio, his novels and short stories, and his libretto for Aulis Sallinen's opera *Ratsumies* (1974; *The Horseman*, 1974) reflect similar preoccupations. In this opera and several of his poems and prose works, Haavikko shows a keen interest in the history and politics of his own country, and such problems as Finland's role in World War II, which he considers was wholly dictated by the realities of the time. His perhaps best-known short story, "Lumeton aika" (1964; "Snowless Time," 1980), is a study of what might happen to Finland after a takeover. But unlike many Finnish writers, Haavikko is able to see his country against wider perspectives; for him, Finland is only a microcosm representing a larger world.

Haavikko has been accused of skepticism, but he himself does not accept this description; he sees himself as the one-eyed man in the country of the blind. Sometimes his work suffers from obscurity, an oracular quality comparable with that of T. S. Eliot, with whom he is often compared. Nevertheless, after the publication of two large collected volumes of his poetry in 1975, he is now generally considered to be Finland's greatest living poet, a provocative and powerful playwright and novelist, and a major influence on the Finnish writing of his time.

FURTHER WORKS

Tiet etäisyyksiin (1951); *Tuuliöinä* (1953); *Synnyinmaa* (1955); *Lehdet lehtiä* (1958); *Talvipalatsi* (1959); *Munchhausen. Nuket* (1960); *Yksityisiä asioita* (1960); *Toinen taivas ja maa* (1961); *Runot 1951–1961* (1962); *Vuodet* (1962); *Lasi Claudius Civiliksen sala-*

liittolaisten pöydällä (1964); *Puut, kaikki heidän vihreytensä* (1966); *Ylilääkäri* (1968); *Agricola ja kettu* (1968); *Neljätoista hallitsijaa* (1970); *Puhua, vastata, opettaa* (1972); *Sulka* (1973); *Runoja matkalta salmen ylitse* (1973); *Kaksikymmentä ja yksi* (1974); *Harald Pitkäikäinen* (1974); *Runot 1949–1974* (1975); *Runoelmat* (1975); *Viiniä, kirjoituksia* (1976); *Kansakunnan linja* (1977); *Puolustuspuhe* (1977); *Näytelmät* (1978); *Soitannollinen ilta Viipurissa, 1918* (1978); *Romaanit ja novellit* (1981); *Viisi pientä draamallista tekstiä* (1981); *Ikuisen rauhan aika* (1981); *Rauta-aika* (1982); *Pimeys* (1984); *Wärtsilä 1843–1984* (1984); *Näkyväistä maailmaa*, ed. Tuomas Anhava (1985); *Vaella Helsingissä* (1986; *In Search of Helsinki*, 1986); *Viisi sarjaa nopeasti virtaavasta elämästä* (1987).

FURTHER TRANSLATIONS

Selected Poems of Paavo Haavikko and Tomas Tranströmer, ed. Anselm Hollo (1974); *Snow in May*, ed. Richard Dauenhauer and Philip Binham (1978); *Territorial Song: Contemporary Writing from Finland* (1980); *Modern Scandinavian Poetry*, ed. Martin Allwood et al. (1982); *Books from Finland* 18.2 (1984); *2 Plus 2: A Collection of International Writing* (1985).

REFERENCES

Ahokas, Jaakko, "Two Poets of Finland: Paavo Haavikko and Bo Carpelan." *Books Abroad* 46.1 (1972); Anhava, Tuomas, " 'Toivo': A Reading of Paavo Haavikko's novel *Private Affairs.*" *World Literature Today* 58.4 (1984); Binham, Philip, "The Writer's Dilemma." *Books from Finland* 18.2 (1984); Binham, Philip, "Dreams Each Within Each." *Books Abroad* 50.2 (1976); Binham, Philip, "Poet's Playground." *World Literature Today* 53.2 (1979); Dauenhauer, Richard, "The View from the Aspen Grove," in *Snow in May* (Cranbury, N.J., 1978); Haavikko, Paavo, "What Has the *Kalevala* Given Me?" *Books from Finland* 19.1 (1985); Hollo, Anselm, Introduction, in *Paavo Haavikko and Tomas Tranströmer* (London, 1974); Ivask, Ivar, "Paavo Haavikko, 1984 Laureate of the Neustadt International Prize for Literature." *World Literature Today* 58.2 (1984); Kinnunen, Aarne, *Syvä nauru* (Forssa, 1977); Kinnunen, Aarne, "An Interview with Paavo Haavikko." *Books from Finland* 3 (1977); Laitinen, Kai, "How Things Are." *Books Abroad* 43.1 (1969); Lomas, Herbert, "Haavikko and Saarikoski: Lyrical Strategies." *2 Plus 2*: (1985); Sihvo, Hannes, *Soutu Bysanttiin* (Joensuu, 1980); Tarkka, Pekka, "Haavikko, Money and History." *World Literature Today* 58.4 (1984).

Philip Binham

Haavio, Martti Henrikki. *See* Mustapää, P.

Hagalín, Guðmundur Gíslason. Icelandic novelist, short story writer, biographer, poet, critic, and playwright, b. 10 October 1898, Arnarfjörður.

Born in the harsh environs of Northwestern Iceland, Hagalín engaged in a variety of practical vocations as multifarious as the many pursuits of his literary career. As a sailor, newspaper reporter, town councillor, teacher, postal worker, librarian, public speaker, and secretary to the parliament, Hagalín secured the broad foundation that enabled him to popularize his social and moral ideas.

Amid early attempts at writing verse, a brief tenure as editor of a journal, and lectures on Icelandic culture in Norway, Hagalín quickly established himself as a major novelist of the 1920s and 1930s. Set against the rough and rugged landscape of Northwestern Iceland, his prose works deal with conflicts between generations *(Vestan úr fjörðum,* 1924; West From the Fjords), economic classes *(Brennumenn,* 1927; Firebrands), and between the individual and society *(Sturla í Vogum,* 1938). Although the themes of many of his novels and short stories derive from problems of social change and conflict, Hagalín focuses the critical thrust of his narrative skills on the psychological and irrational motives that give bone and sinew to his characters or prevent them from coming to grips with underlying political and social forces. Thus, the struggle between a powerful revenue officer and a rising labor organization over the control of economic productivity is reduced to a personal battle of hatred and revenge in *Brennumenn*.

Hagalín's characters are carved from primitive and simplistic stock. Rugged, power-bent individualists, as earthy and robust as the naturalistic language they speak, they struggle like the title character in *Kristrún í Hamravík* (1933) for existence with fearless perseverance and independence in a world that often makes their single-minded efforts seem much bigger than life.

Hagalín's short stories represent some of his finest efforts as a narrator, and in his numerous biographies he created a narrative form that retains the best aspects of his art of characterization and his naturalistic style.

Hagalín is one of modern Iceland's most prolific writers and maintains a solid position in Icelandic literature as a novelist of his native region.

FURTHER WORKS

Blindsker (1921); *Strandbúar* (1923); *Veður öll válynd* (1925); *Guð og lukkan* (1929); *Einn af postulunum og fleiri sögur* (1934); *Kristrún í Hamravík og himnafaðirinn* (1935); *Virkir dagar* (1936–1938); *Saga Eldeyjar-Hjalta* (1939); *Hagalín segir frá* (1939); *Barningsmenn* (1941); *Blítt lætur veröldin* (1943); *Förunautar* (1943); *Gróður og sandfok* (1943); *Konungurinn á Kálfskinni* (1945); *Móðir Ísland* (1945); *Ritsafn* (1948); *Við Maríumenn* (1950); *Ég veit ekki betur* (1951); *Á torgi lífsins* (1952); *Sjö voru sólir á lofti* (1952); *Úr blámóðu aldanna* (1952); *Ilmur liðinna daga (1953); Útilegubörnin í Fannadal* (1953); *Þrek í þrautum* (1953); *Blendnir menn og kjarnakonur* (1954); *Hér er kominn Hoffinn* (1954); *Konan í dalnum og dæturnar sjö* (1954); *Hrævareldar og himinljómi* (1955); *Í kili skal kjörviður* (1957); *Sól á náttmálum* (1957); *Þrettán sögur* (1958); *Fílabeinshöllin* (1959); *Í vesturvíking* (1960); *Mannleg náttúra* (1960); *Töfrar draumsins* (1961); *Það er engin þörf að kvarta* (1961); *Að duga eða drepast* (1962); *Margt býr í þokunni* (1962); *Í fararbroddi* (1964–1965); *Danskurinn í Bæ* (1966); *Márus á Valshamri og meistari Jón* (1967); *Íslendingur sögufróði* (1968); *Sonur bjargs og báru* (1968); *Eldur er beztur* (1970); *Úr Hamrafirði til Himinfjalla* (1971); *Stóð eg úti í tunglsljósi* (1973); *Þá var ég ungur* (1973); *Segið nú amen séra Pétur* (1975); *Ekki fæddur í gær* (1976); *Fornar dyggðir* (1977); *Hamingjan er ekki alltaf ótukt* (1977); *Guð og lukkan* (1978).

TRANSLATIONS

American-Scandinavian Review 43.3 (1955); *Seven Icelandic Short Stories,* ed. Asgeir Pétursson et al.(1960).

REFERENCES

Andrésson. Kristinn, "Milli skers og báru," in *Íslenzkar nútímabókmenntir: 1918–1948* (Reykjavík, 1949); Jóhannesson, Matthías, "Kristrún í Hamravík," in *Lesbók Morgunblaðsins* (1971); Nordal, Sigurður, "Saga Eldeyjar-Hjalta," in *Áfangar*, vol. 2 (Reykjavík, 1944).

W. M. Senner

Hagerup, Inger Halsør. Norwegian lyric poet, b. 12 April 1905, Oslo; d. 6 February 1985.

In the center of Hagerup's poetry stands the human being. The stage, whether provided by nature, the city, a specific situation, or an event, is secondary. Many of the poems directly address people she knows; others, figures from the present and the past she did not know, but felt mentally close to. Hagerup was keenly interested in human behavior, human reactions, and underlying psychological forces. Her main topic was love in all its aspects, ranging from love between man and woman to charity. Although the negative sides, the perversions, such as betrayal, envy, jealousy, and egotism, are often mentioned, the basic tone remains gentle and optimistic. Death is questioned, but nevertheless accepted in a sincere and refreshingly unpathetic manner. In some of her poetry she picked up topics important to her time; the war and the occupation especially had much impact. But the poems from those days do not exude generalities and common moral judgments; rather they deal with the tragedy of the individual.

Occasionally there are glimpses of humor, mainly evident in a surprising rhyme or in the way a line breaks. The form of Hagerup's poetry ranges from the sonnet to free verse. But she seems to have felt most comfortable with couplets or cross rhymes. It was this preoccupation with the simple form and her love for children that led her to write several collections of children's poems. Like most children's poetry, Hagerup's work assumes different and rewarding perspectives for adults. To the artist these provided a frame for the linguistic experiment, for toying with the absurd and for expressing truths that in other contexts would sound schoolmasterly or trite. In her later years Hagerup added a new dimension to her authorship: the writing of radio plays.

As far as her literary models are concerned, her artistic relationship to Arnulf Øverland* is rather obvious. But whereas the effect of Øverland's poetry is frequently based on the use of irony, Hagerup's poems excel in astute observations on human behavior, the ability to capture the spirit of the moment, changing moods and feelings, and in the inherent demonstration of the causes.

WORKS

Jeg gikk meg vill i skogene (1939); *Flukten til Amerika* (1942); *Videre* (1945); *Den syvende natt* (1947); *Sånn vil du ha meg* (1949); *Så rart. Barnevers* (1950); *Mitt skip seiler* (1951); *Hilsen fra Katarina. Tre hørespill* (1953); *Drømmeboken* (1955); *Strofe med vinden* (1958); *Lille Persille. Barnevers* (1961); *Fra hjertets krater* (1964); *Det kommer en pike gående* (1965); *Dikt i utvalg* (1965); *Hva skal du her nede?* (1966);

Trekkfuglene og skjæra (1967); *Ut å søke tjeneste* (1968); *Den sommeren* (1971); *Samlede dikt* (1976).

REFERENCES

Hagerup, Klaus, *Alt er så nær meg* (Oslo, 1988).

Fritz H. König

Halldór Guðjónsson. *See* Laxness, Halldór Kiljan.

Halldór Kiljan Laxness. *See* Laxness, Halldór Kiljan.

Hallgrímsson, Jónas. Iceland lyric poet, b. 16 November 1807, Hraun in Öxnadalur, North Iceland, d. 26 May 1845, Copenhagen.

Hallgrímsson graduated from the Latin School at Bessastaðir, Iceland, in 1829. He entered the University of Copenhagen in 1832, where he first studied law and subsequently natural sciences. Despite the lack of a formal academic degree, Hallgrímsson became a pioneer explorer and scientist in Iceland, where he did research in geology and other related fields from 1838 to 1842. Hallgrímsson was also a master of poetic form and one of the two pioneer romantic poets in nineteenth-century Iceland. In his poetry, Old Icelandic tradition in meter, metaphor, and diction assumed a new quality of refinement and directness. Here, Iceland, the country itself, is quite often presented in its romantic beauty, and even the starker features of geography are endowed with undertones of tenderness. In his poems Hallgrímsson pointed out that in medieval times, the country had been the home of enterprising heroes, maintaining also that the qualities of the land and the grandeur of an old civilization must serve as an incentive and an example for his countrymen. In his time, the political domination of a foreign colonial power had virtually drained the Icelanders of the very spirit and ambition that had led to the founding of the Old Icelandic Free State. Appraising the contemporary scene, Hallgrímsson therefore maintained that it was the Icelandic people themselves rather than their country who had diminished in quality in comparison with a remote past.

In the ordinary sense, Hallgrímsson was not a politician. Yet his poetry played a central role in a new cultural reawakening and, combined with political means provided by others, it sustained the Icelander's in their fight for increased autonomy and, generally speaking, improved living conditions. It was in accordance with this evolution that, in 1835, Hallgrímsson and three other Icelanders in Copenhagen founded *Fjölnir,* an annual in which Hallgrímsson's most iomportant works were published, that is, poems, short stories, translations into Icelandic, and articles on natural history. Through *Fjölnir* romanticism became an entrenched and enduring force in Icelandic literature, and as is the case with Hallgrímsson's own writings, an effective medium for the espousal of a new and progressive attitude based on faith in the country and its old language and culture. Hallgrímsson's best known poem "Ísland" (Iceland), published in the first volume of *Fjölnir* in 1835, is in form and content quite representative of his entire corpus of poetry. This poem is at once a patriotic confession of faith in Iceland and a challenge to action. Indeed it sounded a clarion call at the beginning of the Icelanders' long and arduous struggle for independence from Denmark. In it patriotism, love of nature, and sense of history form an indivisible whole that, through the years, has retained its appeal and relevance in a nation that sees its own identity in terms of language and literature. The poem "Gunnarshólmi" (Gunnar's Island) is also a revealing example in which Hallgrímsson gives a famous episode from the medieval Njál's Saga a new interpretation. In the saga, the tenth-century Icelandic hero, Gunnar, decides to remain on his farm despite a sentence of outlawry against him. Fate and principles of heroic conduct force him to make this choice, which he knows will cost him his life. In Hallgrímsson's poem it is patriotic love rather than fate or heroism that motivates the hero. According to the poem, love of his farmland and country not only survives the hero, but in the role of a guardian spirit, it continues to give protection against erosive forces. This example shows Hallgrímsson's ability to give medieval themes a new meaning and function in a nineteenth-century context.

On the level of form, as has been mentioned above, he gave old poetic patterns a new lyrical quality. He also introduced into Icelandic foreign meters, among them the sonnet, the terza rima, the strophe, and the meter of Heinrich Heine.

Hallgrímsson's narrative prose adds considerably to his pioneer role in the evolution of modern Icelandic literature. One may even say that, to a certain extent, nineteenth-century Icelandic prose literature had its beginnings in his short prose narratives *(Fjölnir,* 1847).

Special mention must be made of Hallgrímsson's Icelandic translation of *Stjörnufræði eftir Ursin* (1842; Astronomy by A. G. Ursin), in which there appeared a number of new coinages that subsequently became part of everyday Icelandic vocabulary. Hallgrímsson and his coeditors of *Fjölnir* successfully advocated linguistic purism in Iceland, which, first and foremost, meant the elimination of Danicism from the Icelandic language.

Some of the literary influences on Hallgrímsson may be traced to Old Icelandic and classical literature, Ossian and the German Romanticists, notably Heinrich Heine. To the Icelanders, Hallgrímsson's poetry is without parallel in lyrical beauty and is indeed one of the cornerstones of Icelandic nationhood.

FURTHER WORKS

Rit eftir Jónas Hallgrímsson, ed. Matthías Þorðarson, 5 vols. (1929–1936).

TRANSLATIONS

Icelandic Lyrics, ed. Richard Beck (1930); *An Anthology of Scandinavian Literature, from the Viking Period to the Twentieth Century,* ed. Hallberg Hallmundsson (1965).

REFERENCES

Finnbogason, Guðmundur, "Jónas Hallgrímsson." *Skírnir* (1907); Gíslason, Vilhjálmur
Þ., *Jónas Hallgrímsson og Fjölnir* (Reykjavík, 1980); Pétursson, Hannes,
Kvæðafylgsnium skáldskap (Reykjavík, 1979); Sveinsson, Einar Ölafur, "Um kveðskap
Jónasar Hallgrímssonar, Jónas Hallgrímsson og Heinrich Heine," A aldarártíð Jónasar
Hallgrímssonar in *Við uppspretturnar* (Reykjavík, 1956).

Haraldur Bessason

Hallgrímur Pétursson. *See* Pétursson, Hallgrímur.

Hamri,Þorsteinn frá. *See* Þorsteinn frá Hamri.

Hamsun, Knut (Pseud. of Knud Pedersen). Norwegian novelist, dramatist,
and poet, b. 8 August 1859, Lom, d. 19 February 1952, Grimstad.

When Hamsun was three, his family moved 600 miles north to Hamarøy in
Nordland County, where Hamsun grew up. The spectacular scenery and the
colorful dialects of Nordland left a deep impression on his writings. After years
of hardship in Norway and America (where he worked 1882–1884 and 1886–
1888 as a farmhand, secretary, and tramcar conductor), Hamsun finally gained
fame as a writer when, in 1888, he published a fragment of his novel *Sult*
(*Hunger*, 1899). The following two decades were years of restless travel—to
France, Finland, Russia, Denmark. In 1909, however, Hamsun moved with his
second wife to a farm in his original hometown of Hamarøy. In 1918 he bought
a large estate, Nørholm, near Grimstad in southern Norway, where he lived as
a farmer and writer until his death.

English arrogance (which he had experienced as an American immigrant) and
German appreciation of his work seem to have decided Hamsun's political sympathies: unlike most of his countrymen, who sided with the Allies, Hamsun
supported the Axis during World War I, and Hitler's Germany after 1933 and
during the German occupation of Norway 1940–1945, for which he had to pay
when the war was over. During the winter of 1946 he was examined by two
psychiatrists, who declared him to be "permanently mentally disabled," but
though the attorney general thereafter decided not to prosecute for treason,
Hamsun was later found guilty of economic collaboration with the enemy and
sentenced to pay a fine of $80,000, which left him destitute. The following
year—1949, in which Hamsun published his moving memoir *Paa gjengrodde
stier* (*On Overgrown Paths*, 1967)—marks the beginning rehabilitation of this
once very popular novelist. He is today considered the major prose writer of
Norwegian literature and, after Henrik Ibsen,* its most widely known literary
figure.

Hamsun in 1904 published an important collection of poetry, *Det vilde Kor*
(*The Wild Chorus*, 1904), and between 1895 and 1910 six plays, which at one
time enjoyed some popularity, particularly in Russia. Today he is remembered
first and foremost for his novels, which fall into three major groups: the early

romantic works from the 1890s; the social novels written before and during World War I; and the so-called vagabond trilogy from around 1930. His early works include his greatest novels—*Hunger* (1890), *Mysterier* (1892; *Mysteries*, 1927), *Pan* (1894; trans. 1920), and *Victoria* (1898; trans.1923)—all of which feature a Byronic hero, a tragic love story, and an emphasis on what Hamsun, in his essay "From the Unconscious Life of the Mind" (1890) called "the whisper of the blood," meaning, presumably, the strange psychology of exceptional people.

After a transitional period with books characterized either by folksy Nordland humor—*Sværmere* (1903; *Dreamers*, 1921), *Benoni* (1907; trans. 1925), *Rosa* (1908; trans. 1926)—or by lyric-melancholic self-portraiture—the *Vandreren* trilogy (1906–1912)—Hamsun in his next stage turned to large-scale social novels. These describe the development of a small town, where, in the spirit of Rousseau, the author praises the rural settlement, while ridiculing and condemning the urban experience. The old artist-hero is still present, but now reduced to a secondary character, whose comments often reflect Hamsun's own opinions. These novels include *Børn av Tiden* (1913; *Children of the Age*, 1924), *Segelfoss By* (1915; *Segelfoss Town*, 1925), and *Markens Grøde* (1917; *The Growth of the Soil*, 1921), for which, in 1920, Hamsun won the Nobel Prize. A curiously optimistic account of homesteading in the Nordland wilderness, it was followed by two of Hamsun's darkest novels, *Konerne ved Vandposten* (1920; *The Women at the Pump*, 1928) and *Siste Kapitel* (1923; *Chapter the Last*, 1929).

After a severe crisis and psychoanalytic treatment in the mid-twenties, Hamsun in 1927 produced his longest novel, *Landstrykere* (1927; *Vagabonds*, 1930), followed in 1930 and 1933 by *August* (trans. 1931) and *Men Livet lever* (*The Road Leads On*, 1934). In this popular trilogy from the last stage in Hamsun's writing career, the old artist-protagonist reemerges on a deromanticized level as August, a slightly ridiculous, but very human, charlatan. Hamsun's last novel, *Ringen sluttet* (1936; *The Ring is Closed*, 1937), though never completed, is one of his great books. In his portrait of Abel, Norwegian sailor and American hippie, Hamsun, in his seventy-eighth year, showed his ability to keep up with the newest trends in international fiction.

Hamsun's position in European literature receives its strength from two sources. One is his place in the development of literary modernism. His manic-depressive heroes, his elitism, his emphasis on the unconscious life of the mind, and his stream-of-consciousness techniques make him at the same time a disciple of Fyodor Dostoyevski and Friedrich Nietzsche, and a precursor of Franz Kafka and James Joyce. Very different is his popular appeal, resulting from the melodrama of his love stories and from the central place of nature in all his work: Hamsun insisted that, in the last resort, industry and materialism do not hold a promise for the future.

FURTHER WORKS

Den Gaadefulde (1877); *Bjørger* (1878); *Fra det moderne Amerikas Aandsliv* (1889; *The Intellectual Life of Modern America*, 1969); *Lars Oftedal* (1889); *Redaktor Lynge* (1893);

Ny jord (1893; *Shallow Soil*, 1914); *Ved rigets port* (1895); *Siesta* (1897); *Livets Spil* (1898); *Aftenrøde* (1898); *Munken Vendt* (1902); *I æventyrland* (1903); *Dronning Tamara* (1903); *Kratskog* (1903); *Stridende liv* (1905); *Under høststjernen* (1906; *Under the Autumn Star*, 1922); *En vandrer spiller med sordin* (1909; *A Wanderer plays on Muted Strings*, 1922); *Livet* (1910; *In the Grip of Life*, 1924); *Den siste glæde* (1912; *Look Back on Happiness*, 1940); *Dikte* (1921); *Samlede verker*, 17 vols. (1936); *Artikler, 1889– 1928* (1939); *Samlede verker*, 15 vols., 5th ed., (1954–1956); *Knut Hamsun som han var; et utvalg av hans brev*, ed. Tore Hamsun (1956); *Paa turne. Tre foredrag om litteratur* (1960); *Brev til Marie* (1970).

FURTHER TRANSLATIONS

Great Stories by Nobel Prize Winners, ed. Leo Hamalian and E. L. Volpe (1960); *On the Prairie*, ed. John Christianson (1961); *An Anthology of Scandinavian Literature, from the Viking Period to the Twentieth Century*, ed. Hallberg Hallmundsson (1965); *Norwegian-American Studies* 24 (1970); *Slaves of Love and Other Norwegian Short Stories*, ed. James McFarlane (1982).

REFERENCES

Ferguson, Robert, *Enigma. The Life of Knut Hamsun* (New York, 1987); Hansen, Thorkild, *Prosessen mot Hamsun* (Oslo, 1978); Kittang, Atle, *Luft, vind, ingenting* (Oslo, 1984); McFarlane, James, "The Whisper of the Blood." *PMLA* 71 (1956); Naess, Harald, *Knut Hamsun* (Boston, 1984); Nyboe Nettum, Rolf, *Konflikt og visjon* (Oslo, 1970); Østby, Arvid, *Knut Hamsun. En bibliografi* (Oslo, 1972); Popperwell, Ronald, "Critical Attitudes to Knut Hamsun 1890–1969." *Scandinavica* 9 (1970); Sehmsdorf, Henning, "Knut Hamsun's *Pan*: Myth and Symbol." *Edda* (1974); Simpson, Allen, *Knut Hamsun's Landstrykere* (Oslo, 1973).

Harald S. Naess

Hannes Sigfússon. *See* Sigfússon, Hannes.

Hannes Pétursson. *See* Pétursson, Hannes.

Hansen, Carl. Danish-American short story writer, journalist, teacher, and novelist, b. 28 May 1860, Holbæk, d. 31 October 1916, Seattle.

Hansen was born and educated in Denmark. He immigrated to the United States in 1885. After brief stays in Elk Horn, Iowa, and West Denmark, Wisconsin, he settled in Tyler, Minnesota, where he taught at the folk high school, became the town's postmaster, and established a pharmacy.

The primary theme of Hansen's fiction is the tension between economic prosperity and personal well-being, portrayed in an essentially optimistic view. In describing a pattern of the poor immigrant's moving from initial poverty, through difficult times, to a final position of material wealth, Hansen's works show the inevitable conflict between an individual immigrant's struggle to attain economic success and his ability to maintain a humanitarian concern for others. This progression of material development is typical for Hansen's protagonists, yet subtly underlying this model of economic success is Hansen's predominant interest in "Mennesket" (humanity), that is, the effects of material gain and poverty upon an individual's daily life and values.

In *Præriens Børn* (1895; Children of the Prairie), *Præriefolk* (1907; Prairie People), *Landsmænd* (1908; Countrymen), and *Fra Prærien* (1918; From the Prairie), the characters generally succeed to an economic degree beyond all reasonable expectation. They do achieve the American Dream, but in the process they also lose their social conscience. While the lives of the characters in Hansen's short stories are surely difficult and lonely, most show the inevitably deleterious effects of material well-being upon the ideals of brotherhood.

Hansen's only novel, *Præriefolk*, presents his most inclusive view of man and existence. The novel shows the impoverished origin of a Danish settlement in South Dakota, its successful economic development, and finally its ineluctable social dissension and spiritual anomie. For the area's farmers, who are the collective protagonist, the correlative to material prosperity is an individual tendency toward socially destructive action in order to increase personal economic gain. Most of Hansen's characters do not suffer serious doubts about their decision to leave Denmark, primarily because they succeed economically, yet they do suffer a loss of humanity.

As is characteristic of many first-generation immigrant writers, Hansen's works indicate the hope of a significantly better future for the next generation. Hansen is now regarded as one of the two or three best Danish-American writers who wrote in Danish.

FURTHER WORKS

Dansk Jul i Amerika (1909); *Nisqually* (1912).

REFERENCES

Jensen, Rudolf J., "A Comparative Study of Sophus Keith Winther and Carl Hansen." *Bridge* 1 (1978); Watkins, Donald K., "Carl Hansen, Prairie Iconoclast." *Bridge* 2 (1979).

Rudolf Jensen

Hansen, Jens Alfred Martin. *See* Hansen, Martin A.

Hansen, Martin A. (Jens Alfred Martin Hansen). Danish novelist, short story writer, poet, literary and cultural critic, amateur cultural historian, lecturer, and teacher, b. 20 August 1909, Stevns, d. 27 June 1955, Copenhagen.

Hansen spent his boyhood, from the age of nine, on a farm and later worked on neighboring farms. He attended Haslev Teachers' College, taught at Blaagard's Teachers' College Training School in Copenhagen, married Vera Louise Marie Jensen, and served five months in the Danish military. In Copenhagen, he taught by day and wrote by night. To combat exhaustion, he took stimulants, and yet blamed himself for having the kind of career that stole time and attention away from his family. In 1935, he decided to live by his pen and published the first of two Marxist-inspired "communal" novels about the crises-ridden farming community. When German troops occupied Denmark in 1940, Hansen began to write articles for the underground magazine *Folk og Frihed* (People and Freedom). He advocated action being taken against the nazis and their Danish collaborators, and after September 1944, he had to live in hiding. Although he had written that informers ought to be liquidated, he was devastated at war's end when he discovered that two of the young men inspired by his articles had lost their lives in the resistance movement.

Hansen not only recognized the moral responsibility of each individual to face evil, but also the power of the pen for good or ill. Hansen had abandoned social realism as his major mode of writing, and in 1941, he published the first work in which he treated the problem of being contaminated by evil while trying to oppose it. In the novel *Jonatans Rejse* (1941; Jonatan's Journey) Hansen used fairy-tale motifs to describe modern man's moral dilemma, and the tale's rousing humor renews and emphasizes those familiar themes. In 1946, *Tornebusken* (The Hawthorne Bush), three thematically linked short stories in increasingly experimental form, took up both the individual's and the individual author's relationship to evil. This metaliterary work undoubtedly established Hansen's credentials among those young writers who started the magazine *Heretica* (1948–1953), a forum for modernism. Hansen became its editor from 1950 to 1952. Since he wanted his works to be ethically significant, he found it increasingly difficult to share his contemporaries' view that an artist's primary responsibility was to art itself. The urge to experiment with symbols and form seemed to threaten a further dissolution of values, and Hansen, who—in an unpublished draft for a work to be called "Kains Alter" (finished January 1946; Cain's Altar)—had expressed his fears over the artist's destructive spiritual seduction of others through the demonic power of language, turned once again from the individualism of art to the ethical responsibility for humanity to be found in transmitting one's cultural heritage.

Storytelling became for Hansen a means of conjuring up the sustaining values of the past. From his work *Løgneren* (1950; *The Liar*, 1969), in which his protagonist makes a similar choice in lifestyle, to the end of his life, Hansen wrote few new works of fiction, but he wrote travel books on landscape and climate as evidenced in several cultures (Denmark, Iceland, Norway). He was frequently tired and ill during those last years of traveling and lecturing, and in April 1955, he was hospitalized. After an extremely painful period, during which he again turned to fiction, he died of uremia on 27 June 1955. A number of collections of his short stories and essays were published after his death.

Hansen wrote only a few novels, but beginning with *Jonatans Rejse*, they were brilliantly executed. Although his style varies from book to book, certain themes recur again and again, and one of the most important was the curative power of the old rural culture, which tamed the demonic inherent to the wilderness and combated the blight and eventual savagery produced by modern civilization. The smith Jonatan, a faithful representative of that old culture, braves evil (in the forms of prosperity, science, and politics) to protect home, king, and country. The seductive and manipulative are evil, and those "arts" are examined in *Lykkelige Kristoffer* (1945; *Lucky Kristoffer*, 1974), whose sly protagonist, the cleric Martin, proves to be not only a survivor of, but a profiteer from, the chaos of strife-torn Denmark during the civil wars of the 1500s. Finally, *Tornebusken* maintains that the evil of selfishness and indifference to human needs calls forth suffering in others, who—if they accept their suffering in a longing for the good—may find that suffering leads to their own rebirth and transforms evil itself. Like the symbol of the "hawthorne bush," the cyclic nature of existence seems to be suffering, death, and rebirth to new suffering. Good and evil seem indistinguishable, but in *Løgneren* the protagonist, Johannes Vig, chooses to sacrifice his desires, which are always demonically manipulative, in order to support cultural values, which are man's means of redemption, for they promise a meaningful rebirth of the generations. Finally, in *Orm og Tyr* (1956; Serpent and Bull) Hansen examined the gift of Christianity to the Nordic peoples: security and rest in death; the malignant spirits of the dead that had suffused nature in pagan times were at last laid to rest. Odin, the greatest god of the Nordic pantheon, was a god not just of death, but of poetry as well. Hansen felt that within himself he carried the seeds of both Christianity and the farming culture— the ethical—from his father and that of the pagan wilderness—the poetic—from his mother. Hansen was celebrated for his optimistic message and religious attitude, but his was a "willed" optimism, the conscious act of "an unbeliever who believes what he does not believe" (the words are Johannes Vig's; see *Løgneren* [Copenhagen: Gyldendal, 1950], p. 66). Hansen's deep existential interest and brilliant use of symbolism and experimental forms caused his imitators' works to seem merely mannered. With the waning of social realism Hansen's star should again be one of the twentieth-century's brightest.

FURTHER WORKS

Nu opgiver Han (1935); *Kolonien* (1937); *Agerhønen* (1947); *Tanker i en Skorsten* (1948); "Eneren og Massen" in *Mennesket i Tiden* (1950); *Leviathan* (1950); *Kringen* (1953); *Paradisæblerne og andre Historier* (1953); *Dansk Vejr* (1953); *Konkylien* (1955); *Gyldendals Julebog 1955* (1955); *Midsommerkrans* (1956); *Af Folkets Danmarkshistorie* (1957); *Martin A. Hansen Fortæller* (1958); *Efterslæt* (1959); *Ved Korsvejen* (1965); *Martsnat* (1965); *Verdens romanen* (1966); *Martin A. Hansen og Skolen* (1968); *Isen bryder* (1969).

FURTHER TRANSLATIONS

Against the Wind, ed. H. Wayne Schow (1979).

REFERENCES

Bjørnvig, Thorkild, *Kains Alter* (Copenhagen, 1964); Bredsdorff, Elias, Introduction to *The Liar* (New York, 1969); Ingwersen, Faith, "The Truthful Liars: A Comparative Analysis of Knut Hamsun's *Mysterier* and Martin A. Hansen's *Løgneren*" (Ph.D. diss., University of Chicago, 1974); Ingwersen, Faith, and Niels Ingwersen, *Martin A. Hansen*

(Boston, 1976); Ingwersen, Niels, Introduction to *Lucky Kristoffer* (New York, 1974);
Kettel, Henrik, *Martin A. Hansens forfatterskab. En Bibliografi* (Copenhagen, 1966);
Printz-Påhlson, Göran, *"The Liar*: The Paradox of Fictional Communication in Martin
A. Hansen." *Scandinavian Studies* 36.4 (1964) and rpt. in *Omkring Løgneren* (see below);
Vowles, Richard B., "Martin A. Hansen and the Uses of the Past."
American-Scandinavian Review 46.1 (1958); Wivel, Ole, *Martin A. Hansen*, 2 vols.
(Copenhagen, 1967–1969); Wivel, Ole, ed., *Omkring Løgneren* (Copenhagen, 1971).

Faith Ingwersen

Hansen, Thorkild. Danish writer of historical monographs, travel books,
and essays in criticism, b. 9 January 1927, Ordrup, d. 4 February 1989, France.

After studies in literature at Copenhagen University, Hansen worked as a
journalist and critic in Paris from 1947 to 1952. With two books of literary essays
to his credit Hansen, as a correspondent and critic with two Copenhagen dailies
during the following years, traveled widely and participated in archaeological expeditions to Kuwait and Nubia, recorded in his travel books from 1959, 1960, and
1961. Inspired by this experience, Hansen in his first major book, *Det lykkelige
Arabien* (1962; *Arabia Felix*, 1963), writes about the famous but ill-fated Danish
Oriental expedition of 1961–1967. Here he develops his gift of shaping a narrative
out of illuminative selections from sources and vivid descriptions of people and
places combined with ingenious conjectures and a knack of tracing the ironies of
the patterns of events. A skeptical existentialist view of life seems reflected in
Hansen's humorous and poetic style. An expedition to arctic Canada in 1964 provides material for *Jens Munk* (1965; *North West to Hudson Bay*, 1970; Am. ed.
The Way to Hudson Bay) where Hanson applies his art to the tragic career of a
famous Danish seventeenth-century navigator. With no less success he uses his
narrative skill in his trilogy on the Danish slave trade, *Slavernes kyst* (1967; The
Slave Beach), *Slavernes skibe* (1968; The Slave Ship), and *Slavernes øer* (1970;
The Slave Islands) to uncover a suppressed dimension of Danish history. In his
three volumes of *Processen mod Hamsun* (1978; The Hamsun Trial) Hansen examines Knut Hamsun's* pro-German stance in occupied Norway during World
War II and Hamsun's trial for high treason after the liberation. Hansen's sympathy
with the old writer of genius and his provocative critical attitude to the showdown
with Hamsun and other collaborators in Norwegian courts in the postwar period
roused a heated debate in the Scandinavian countries after the appearance of Hansen's gripping and penetrating analysis.

Hansen's combination of scholarship, intellectual acumen, and poetic sensibility makes him a very special figure in modern Danish letters. The epic proportions and sophisticated narrative art of his main works have made them classics
and secured for their author a prominent place among the prose writers of his
generation.

FURTHER WORKS

Minder svøbt i Vejr (1947); *Resten er Stilhed* (1953); *Pausesignaler* (1959); *Syv seglsten*
(1960); *En kvinde ved en flod* (1961); *Jens Munks Minde-ekspedition*, with Peter Seeberg

(1965); *Rejsedagbøger* (1969); *Vinterhavn* (1972); *De søde piger. Dagbog 1943–47* (1974); *Sidste sommer i Angmagsalik* (1978); *Samtale med dronning Margrethe* (1979); *Søforhør* (1979, 1982); *Kurs mod solnedgangen* (1982).

REFERENCES

Jensen, Niels Lyhne, "Thorkild Hansens forfatterskab." *Nordisk tidsskrift för vetenskap, konst och industri* 47 (1971); Franzén, Lars Olof, *Punktnedslag i dansk litteratur 1870–1970* (Stockholm, 1971); Schou, Søren, "Existentiel historieskrivning. Om Thorkild Hansens forfatterskab," in *Linjer i nordisk prosa. Danmark 1965–1975*, ed. Peter Madsen (Lund, 1977).

Niels Lyhne Jensen

Hansson, Ola. Swedish poet, novelist, short story writer, and essayist, b. 12 November, 1860, Hönsinge (Skåne), d. 26 September, 1925, Buyuktolere (near Istanbul), Turkey.

In 1882, Hansson took his degree at Lund, where he had been a warm adherent of the philosophy of Georg Brandes* that literature should deal with contemporary social problems. Two years later he published his first volume of poetry (*Dikter*, 1884; Poems), where social realism, naturalism, and nature poetry marked by strongly sensual and physical images were mingled with poems that were almost wholly atmospheric, poems as *paysages d'âmesr* in the spirit of Paul Verlaine. Hansson emphasized his departure from the Brandesian school in *Notturno* (1885), where landscapes become soulscapes, and the physical world becomes infused with human emotions of loneliness or bitterness.

The collection of stories entitled *Sensitiva amorosa* (1887) is Hansson's attempt to explore the many-faceted world of erotic experience (including the homoerotic), which caused the book to be viciously attacked by critics and moralists. *Parias* (1890; Pariahs) is an analysis, in subtle and sensitive subjective prose, of the nature of crime and the criminal psyche. Both *Sensitiva amorosa* and *Parias* come stylistically close to continental symbolism or decadence, as represented by authors like Paul Bourget, J.-K. Huysmans, and Edgar Allan Poe. Poe is the subject of an especially fine essay in *Kåserier i mystik* (1889–1897; Articles on Mysticism), which also contained some of the first essays in Sweden on Arnold Böcklin, Paul Bourget, and Guy de Maupassant.

Hansson left Sweden in 1890 and spent the rest of his life in self-imposed exile from a country that at first did not understand him and then gradually came to forget him. He continued to write (often in German) and produced fine work in a vigorously Nietzschean vein (e.g., *Ung Ofegs visor*, 1892; *Young Ofeg's Ditties*, 1893) that purged his work of its somewhat decadent strain. He remained fascinated with the darker sides of the soul, hypnotism, and the irrational. Hansson had provided the method for the technical transformation of Swedish poetry away from A. U. Bååth's lyrical realism toward Verner von Heidenstam's* aestheticism and the liberation of the imagination. Despite the eclipse of his reputation after his death, Hansson's importance in the evolution of modern Swedish verse—indeed, the modern Swedish consciousness—is paramount.

FURTHER WORKS

Alltagsfrauen (1891); *Kärlekens trångmål* (1892); *Fru Ester Bruce* (1893 in Danish); *Resan hem* (1895); *En uppfostrare* (1885); *Vägen till lifvet* (1896); *Det förlofvade landet* (1906); *Nya visor* (1907); *På hemmets altare* (1908); *Rustgården* (1910); *Samlade skrifter*, 17 vols. (1917–1922).

REFERENCES

Ahlström, Stellan, *Ola Hansson* (Stockholm, 1958); Borland, Harold H., *Nietzsche's Influence on Swedish Literature* (Göteborg, 1956); Ekelund, Erik, *Ola Hanssons ung-domsdiktning* (Helsingfors, 1930); Harrie, Ivar, "Europeen från Honsinge," in *Orientering* (Stockholm, 1932); Holm, Ingvar, *Ola Hansson, en studie i åttiotalets romantik* (Lund, 1957); Hume, David R., "The First Five Years of Ola Hansson's Literary Exile 1888–93," in *Facts of Scandinavian Literature*, Germanische Forschungsketten 2 (Lexington, Ky., 1974); Kassius, Torsten, *Idébakgrunden till Ung Ofegs visor* (Stockholm, 1939); Levander, Hans, *Sensitiva amorosa: Ola Hanssons ungdomsverk* (Stockholm, 1944).

Lars Emil Scott

Haslund, Ebba. Norwegian novelist, short story writer, dramatist, and critic, b. 12 August 1917, Seattle.

Having published a steady stream of popular fiction and criticism since 1945 and served as chairman of the Norwegian Writers' Association from 1971 to 1975, Haslund has both participated in and monitored the mainstream of postwar literary production in Norway.

Problems of marriage and family life provide the central themes for Haslund's writings. Many of her works revolve around the figure of a strong woman who undergoes an ordeal that shakes her confidence, but leaves her with the resolve to redefine her life and begin afresh. One of the best of these is *Det trange hjerte* (1965; The Closed Heart), in which the question "Am I my brother's keeper?" is posed amid the crisis brought on by a family's business scandal. Similarly, in *Bare et lite sammenbrudd* (1975; Just a Little Nervous Breakdown) the smooth surface of a homemaker's world is turned to temporary turmoil by the events surrounding her fiftieth birthday. The short stories in *Hver i sin verden* (1976; Each in His Own World) illustrate the impact of expectations on women's lives. Haslund's strength lies in the sensitive detail and mild irony with which she describes the lifestyle and mentality of her bourgeois protagonists. In contrast to the indignation and bitterness voiced by more radical feminists, Haslund proffers a message of resignation and basic optimism.

In her most complex novel, *Syndebukkens krets* (1968; The Tropic of the Scapegoat), Haslund joins Sigurd Hoel and others in examining the problem of collaboration with the Nazis during the occupation years. A woman writer confronts the dilemma of assigning guilt and exacting retribution faced by many Norwegians in the aftermath of the occupation. This work also affords some self-satirizing insight into the relationship between the writer and the public in Norway.

Haslund has also written radio plays and works for young readers. She has published several volumes of essays and the criminal novel *Skritt i mørke* (1982; Footsteps in Darkness).

FURTHER WORKS

Også vi (1945); *Siste halvår* (1946); *Det hendte ingenting* (1946; *Nothing Happened*, 1987); *Middag hos Molla* (1951); *Krise i august* (1954); *Drømmen om Nadja* (1956); *Hvor går du Vanda?* (1960); *Midlertidig stoppested* (1972); *Født til klovn* (1977); *Behag og bedrag* (1978); *Kvinner, fins de?* (1980); *Åfferdea* (1981); *Mor streiker* (1981); *Hønesvar til hanefar* (1983); *Døgnflues lengsel* (1984); *Spurv i hanedans* (1986); *Som plommen i egget* (1987).

Frankie Shackelford

Hauge, Alfred. Norwegian novelist, dramatist, lyric poet, and critic, b. 17 October 1915, Finnøy.

Hauge grew up in a pietistic environment on a small island in southwestern Norway. He then studied theology for a while, but decided that he would rather be a teacher. After a period of time in this vocation he joined a Stavanger daily, where he has remained as a cultural journalist.

The author's first important novels dealt with the tension between religious and artistic demands felt by the religious artist, but have been overshadowed by his later works. Hauge became internationally known for his trilogy *Cleng Peerson* (1961–1965; *Cleng Peerson*, 1975), which tells the story about the earliest Norwegian emigrants to America.

Hauge's major work is his Utstein Monastery cycle, which consists of the novels *Mysterium* (1967; Mystery) and *Legenden om Svein og Maria* (1968; The Legend of Svein and Maria), a collection of poetry titled *Det evige sekund* (1970; The Eternal Second), and an intended series of novels under the common title "Century." Two of these have so far appeared, namely *Perlemorstrand* (1974; A Shore Made of Mother-of-Pearl) and *Leviathan* (1979). The theme of these works is the question of how it is possible for human beings to endure suffering in such a manner that their humanity is preserved or even enhanced, and how people can be aided by others in enduring suffering. In the Utstein Monastery novels this central theme is given expression through the use of a sophisticated narrative technique. The author first skillfully creates an illusion of reality by solidly anchoring his narrative in a geographically and historically identifiable world, after which the illusion is broken down by numerous apostrophes directed at the reader. In this manner Hauge seeks to communicate with his readers both through their imagination and their reason. In addition, he makes use of a number of archetypal symbols through which he hopes to engage the reader's subconsciousness.

Hauge is regarded as one of the most important figures in contemporary Norwegian literature. Having demonstrated the ability to progress artistically at an age when most writers have their best work behind them, he has created an enduring place for himself in the literature of his country.

FURTHER WORKS

Septemberfrost (1941); *Tuntreet blør* (1942); *Storm over Siglarholmen* (1945); *Skyer i drift over vårgrønt land* (1945); *Ropet* (1946); *Vi har ingenting lært* (1947); *Året har ingen vår* (1948); *Fossen og bålet* (1949); *Vegen til det døde paradiset* (1951); *Ingen kjenner dagen* (1955); *Kvinner på Galgebakken* (1958); *Gå vest* (1963); *Cleng Peerson. Utvandring* (1968); *Legenden om Svein og Maria* (1968); *Barndom* (1975); *Morten Kruse* (1975); *Ungdom* (1977).

REFERENCES

Flatin, Kjetil A., "The Rising Sun and the Lark on the Quilt: Quest and Defiance in Alfred Hauge's *Cleng Peerson* Trilogy." *Pacific Northwest Council on Foreign Languages,* Proceedings (1976); Sjåvik, Jan, "Alfred Hauge's Utstein Monastery Cycle." *World Literature Today* 56.1 (1982).

Jan Sjåvik

Hauge, Olav Håkonson. Norwegian lyric poet, b. 18 August 1908, Ulvik.

Hauge does not write in any version of standard *nynorsk* (New Norwegian*), but rather in his own Vestlands dialect, a medium he handles with spectacular virtuosity. Although formally following the same road as many of his contemporaries—from strict meter and end rhyme to free verse—he is a master of any form. The imagery he uses varies widely. However, much of it centers around nature in western Norway where he grew up and still lives and around the traditions of the simple farm life he is familiar with. On the other hand, Hauge is well read, and subtle influences of poetry from the whole spectrum of world literature can be traced in many of his poems.

Hauge's early poetry may suffer occasionally from overpowering rhymes and alliteration. But many of his later poems are reduced to a bare minimum, eliminating any need for interpretation, often approaching in concept the aphorism. One of the best examples is:

December Moon 1969

He hides the steel
in a silver sheath
There is blood on the edge.

Hauge lives in total harmony with nature. Thus the point of departure for a poem is usually an aspect of nature or a certain situation in nature. Nature is secretive, powerful, and intertwined with human fate. The setting may comprise the mountains, the sky, and the sea, or it may simply be a man mowing:

The Scythe

I am so old
that I keep to the scythe.
Quietly it sings in the grass

allowing the thoughts to wander.
It doesn't hurt,
says the grass
to fall in under the scythe.

In almost every poem Hauge mulls over the basic problems of human life, the eternal questions that remain forever without answer, but need to be asked again in each generation. What makes the poems especially attractive is Hauge's quiet sense of humor, the ever-changing ocean of associations, and the frequent surprise.

WORKS

Glør i oska (1946); *Under bergfallet* (1951); *Seint rodnar skogen i djuvet* (1956); *På ørnetuva* (1961); *Dropar i austavind* (1966); *Spør i vinden* (1971).

TRANSLATIONS

Micromegas 4.3 (1971); *Lines Review* 55–56 (1976); *Scandinavian Review* 68.4 (1980); *2 Plus 2* (Spring/Summer 1984); *Don't Give Me the Whole Truth*.

REFERENCE

Stegane, Idar, *Olav H. Hauges diktning: fra Glør i oska til Dropar i austavind* (Oslo, 1974).

Fritz H. König

Heiberg, Gunnar Edvard Rode. Norwegian dramatist and essayist, b. 18 November 1857, Christiania, d. 22 February 1929, Oslo.

Heiberg grew up in a cultivated Christiania home where interest in theater and intellectual issues provided the foundation for his development and material for his plays. His association with the radical group known as the Bohème; contact with artists in Copenhagen, Paris, and Berlin; and the influence of authors such as Henrik Wergeland,* Lord Byron, Georg Brandes,* and Henrik Ibsen* all played a role in forming his literary style and ethical position. In addition to productivity as a creative writer, Heiberg deserves credit for achievements as journalist and stage director. His theater reviews and essays on political issues at home and abroad, such as the union with Sweden and the Dreyfus affair, were clever and challenging. His productions as artistic director of the theater in Bergen (1884–1888) were significant events in the breakthrough of realism and contemporary drama. With encouragement from the playwright Heiberg staged the world premieres of Ibsen's *Vildanden (The Wild Duck)* and *Rosmersholm*. After a controversy over artistic freedom in choice of repertory Heiberg left Bergen and never again held a full-time position with a theater, but was occasionally a guest director. Although he often viewed Norway from a geographic distance, Heiberg was deeply concerned about national and artistic issues and expressed his convictions with bold and biting wit.

Tante Ulrikke (1884; Aunt Ulrikke), Heiberg's first play, may be compared to Ibsen's and Bjørnstjerne Bjørnson's* social dramas. The socialist rally at which Ulrikke, modeled on Aasta Hansteen, a pioneer in the Norwegian women's movement, faces the taunts of the crowd and her niece Helene courageously steps forth as her ally in the struggle, symbolizes Heiberg's faith in the future. Effective when staged, the play is different in form and tone from the remainder of Heiberg's canon.

Two plays form a complementary pair: *Balkonen* (1894; *The Balcony*, 1922) and *Kjærlighetens tragedie* (1904; *The Tragedy of Love*, 1921). Lyrical and intense, they focus on a stunning, liberated woman representative of the 1890s. Both show the tension created by the heroine's obsession with passionate love and its destructiveness of those who find her fascinating. Early productions were sensational theatrical events, providing vehicles for leading Scandinavian actresses. *Balkonen* is concentrated, stylized, and abstract. *Kjærlighetens tragedie* presents more fully dimensioned characters and action encompassing several encounters and developments. Although Heiberg may have intended the latter as a statement of his philosophy, the play is of interest now as a psychological study of a tormented woman unreconciled to a way of life that does not accommodate her ecstatic vision of erotic love. Karen's husband, Erling, with his commitment to work and a generous, but rational, concern for her, is bewildered by her suicide. The mystical poet Hadeln, who resembles Sigbjørn Obstfelder,* functions as confidant and chorus, captivated by Karen's uncompromising exaltation of love. Although the play had its early champions, it evokes an atmosphere of melodrama and fin de siècle decadence.

During his lifetime Heiberg's reputation was controversial. To his younger contemporaries he represented the heroic assertion of individual freedom, a philosophy of egoism, and the championing of aesthetics above conventional morality. To the literary historians he is the link between the drama of Henrik Ibsen* and that of Helge Krog.* Einar Skavlan's biography (1950) expressed unconditional admiration for the author as dramatic craftsman and courageous champion of freedom and truth. Ragnvald Moe (1957) acknowledged Heiberg's imagination and lyricism, vigor and stylistic skill, but pointed out shortcomings in characterization, dramatic structure, and the ethical views derived from positivism. More recent assessments of Heiberg stress the intensity of emotions in his plays, the clear and witty expression of ideas in his essays, and his place in the romantic tradition.

FURTHER WORKS

Kong Midas (1890); *Kunstnere* (1893); *Gerts have* (1894); *Det store lod* (1895); *Folkeraadet* (1897); *Harald Svans mor* (1899); *Pariserbreve* (1900); *Kjærlighet til næsten* (1902); *Jeg vil værge mit land* (1912); *Paradesengen* (1913); *Set og hørt* (1917); *Samlede dramatiske verker*, 4 vols.(1917–1918); *Ibsen og Bjørnson på scenen* (1918); *Franske visitter* (1919); *Norsk teater* (1920); *1905* (1923); *Salt og sukker* (1924); *I frihetens bur* (1929); *Hugg og stikk* (1951); *Natscener* (1951); *Hans Majestæt* (1951); *Artikler om mange ting* (1972); *Artikler om teater og dramatikk* (1972).

FURTHER TRANSLATIONS

Kjærlighetens tragedie in *Chief Contemporary Dramatists*, ed. Thomas H. Dickinson, 2nd ser., (1921); *Balkonen*, in *Poet Lore* 33 (Winter 1922).

REFERENCES

Longum, Leif, *To kjærlighetsromantikere* (Oslo, 1960); Nygaard, Knut, *Gunnar Heiberg: Teatermannen* (Bergen, 1975); Skavlan, Einar, *Gunnar Heiberg* (Oslo, 1950).

Carla Waal

Heiberg, Johan Ludvig. Danish poet, dramatist, editor, and aesthetic theorist, b. 14 December 1791, Copenhagen, d. 25 August 1860, Bonderup near Ringsted.

Heiberg's parents were the authors P. A. Heiberg (expatriated in 1800 for revolutionary sympathies) and Thomasine Gyllembourg.* In 1817 he completed his doctorate, which focused on aesthetics in the drama of Pedro Calderón de la Barca. Shortly thereafter he lived with his father in Paris from 1818 to 1822, where his encounter with the French vaudeville and Augustin-Eugène Scribe's vaudeville comedy became of vital importance to his work as a dramatist. In 1824 Heiberg met Georg Wilhelm Friedrich Hegel in Berlin, whose dialectic thinking greatly influenced his aesthetic theories and poetic practice. Within the same year, thanks to a receptive mind and quick-working intelligence, Heiberg introduced Hegelian philosophy to Denmark with the publication of his treatise *Om den menneskelige frihed* (1824; On Human Freedom). Although he lived most of his life as an independent intellectual, from 1849 to 1856 he was general director of the Royal Theater, where his much younger wife, the exceptionally talented Johanne Louise Heiberg, was leading actress.

As a dramatist Heiberg's main achievement was the vaudevilles, which were performed with great success at the Royal Theater. In his treatise *Om Vaudevillen som dramatisk Digtart* (1826; On the Vaudeville as Dramatic Genre) Heiberg defines the genre as a unity of words and music, a series of situations in ''poetical-realistic'' style. Vaudeville contains stylized types, rather than more or less profound characters, a tinge of local life and social satire and, most important to Heiberg, the poetic element personified in the role of the ingenue. Songs are an integral part of the action. The most frequently performed of all plays in the history of the Royal Theater was Heiberg's *Elverhøj* (1828; The Elves' Hill, music by Friedrich Daniel Rudolph Kuhlau), a national and royalistic sort of musical with dialogue, music, and dance. After 1824 all of Heiberg's writing—dramatical, lyrical, critical, and theoretical—reflects, in varying degrees of mastery, Hegel's influence: the dialectic balance between free will and necessity, satirical realism and pure poetry, content and form. Primarily, and in a rather formalistic way, his esthetic-critical essays demand full harmonic correspondence between the technical aspect (criterion of genre) and the poetical aspect (the poet's intuitive handling of the subject matter). Consequently, a major element in Heiberg's aesthetic system is irony, that is, the poet's ability to distance himself from his work. As an editor of a series of periodicals Heiberg demonstrates his polemical ability in a clear, witty, and now and then reckless manner. The title of one of his papers is typical: *Intelligensblade* (1840; Papers of Intelligence). Here he writes about what he called "Æstetisk Moral" (Aesthetical Ethics), and criticizes the bigotry of society. In *Nye Digte* (1841; New Poems) Heiberg once more, from a rather aristocratic point of view, attacks the bourgeois society. Central to this collection is the satirical verse drama *En Sjæl efter Døden* (*A Soul after Death*, 1972) in which the deceased petty-bourgeois is called "a soul" because he actually lacks one. The "eternal values" must be found within the human personality. *Nye Digte* seems to be based on a Dante pattern, the central idea being that hell, purgatory, and heaven are mental possibilities, all to be experienced in this life. This cult of personality also makes its mark in his treatises on astronomy, especially in those on Tycho Brahe and his most learned sister Sophie Brahe. Heiberg always reveals his admiration for stars and purity in his writing.

There appears to be a contradiction in the works of this remarkable writer, one of the most influential in his own time. Although a man of refined manners and taste, of classical clarity and form in his writing, Heiberg provided a theater with broad popular appeal. He was abstract and ahistorical in his speculative-systematic thinking and concretizing in his poetry. Realistic critics and dramatists like Georg Brandes* and Henrik Ibsen* have acknowledged their debt to him.

FURTHER WORKS

Samlede skrifter. Prosaiske skrifter, 11 vols. (1861–1862); *Samlede skrifter. Poetiske skrifter,* 11 vols. (1862); *Breve og aktstykker vedrørende J. L. Heiberg,* ed. Morten Borup, 5 vols. (1947–1950).

FURTHER TRANSLATIONS

A Translation from the Danish of Three Plays by Johan Ludvig Heiberg, ed. D. E. Malmgren (Ph.D. diss., University of Denver, 1972).

REFERENCES

Borup, Morten, *Johan Ludvig Heiberg,* 3 vols.(Copenhagen, 1947–1949); Fenger, Henning, *The Heibergs* (Boston, 1971).

Tage Hind

Heidenstam, Carl Gustaf *Verner* **von.** Swedish poet and novelist, b. 6 July 1859, Olshammars gård, on Lake Vättern, d. 20 May 1940, Övralid, Östergötland.

The unquestioned leader of the neoromantic poetic renaissance of the 1890s, Heidenstam spent his childhood in the lap of aristocratic luxury. Largely privately educated, he decided to become a painter and left Sweden in 1876 on a protracted series of journeys that ultimately took him to Egypt, Syria, Greece, and the Holy Land before he settled in Rome to concentrate on art. By the early 1880s, he was in Paris, where his interests changed swiftly from painting to literature. There, he began to compose some of the poems later collected in his debut volume, *Vallfart och vandringsår* (1888; Pilgrimage and Wandering Years). He reacted strongly to the new realistic/naturalistic school of literature led by August Strindberg* (with whom Heidenstam had become very friendly in Switzerland, only to see their friendship turn gradually to the bitterest animosity). He was disturbed by what he perceived to be an increasing tendency toward "cobbler realism," a dreary Darwinistic determinism that stifled imagination, hope, and beauty.

To demonstrate what he thought poetry should be, he brought out *Vallfart och vandringsår* shortly after his return to Sweden. The volume was a tremendous public success, and Heidenstam became almost overnight the leader of a countermovement in Swedish letters, whose hallmarks were fantasy, exoticism, imagination, and a modern, heightened aestheticism. His own poetry was marked by a sensual abandon, richness of palette, and youthful vitality. His themes, too, were exotic, drawn from vivid recollections of his widely traveled youth. The following summer (1889), he published the essay that secured his status as leader of the neoromantic movement and gave it its remarkable character of rebirth: *Renässans* (1889; Renaissance), which stated forthrightly that the new literature would be based on national Swedish characteristics, an earthy realism, and a healthy respect for the freedoms that Strindberg (if not his followers) had won for art. Heidenstam was not yet prepared to distance himself totally from the Strindberg camp because he was still essentially philosophically, if not aesthetically, aligned with it.

However, throughout the 1890s, Heidenstam's ideals became more and more nationalistic and reactionary, driving him further and further from Strindberg and finally even from his own followers. What had begun as a daring blow struck for artistic freedom and poetic license gradually became a chauvinistic political campaign to revive lost virtues and patriotic zeal. The volume *Ett folk* (1902; One People) spelled out his new program in uncompromising terms: Sweden must heed the call of its mythic ancestors to regain its place under the sun. Unfortunately, the great power and undeniable splendor of much of *Ett folk* and other volumes—*Dikter* (1895; Poems) and *Nya dikter* (1915; New Poems)— is now lost because of the disturbingly aristocratic and authoritarian tone of the political poetry. But Heidenstam was still one of the greatest lyrical masters in late nineteenth-century Sweden. A poem like "Tiveden," which is a paean to the great primeval forest at the head of Lake Vättern where the poet was to spend most of his adult life, is among the finest works of its kind in Swedish. And his increasing absorption in Swedish history did result in some of the greatest works of historical fiction ever penned in Swedish. *Heliga Birgittas pilgrimsfärd* (1901; The Pilgrimage of St. Birgitta), *Folkungaträdet* (1907; *The Tree of the Folkungs*, 1925), *Svenskarna och deras hövdingar* (1908–1910; *The Swedes and Their Chieftains*, 1925) all attested to Heidenstam's almost mystical affinity with figures from Sweden's distant past. But it was his first novel, written in two parts between 1897 and 1898, that won him future generations of readers. *Karolinerna* (*The Charles Men*, 1933) was the story of Sweden's "hero king," Charles XII, and his tragic attempt to restore Swedish hegemony over the Baltic. While few readers today share Heidenstam's view of the doomed king and his loyal warriors, *Karolinerna* still has an undeniable appeal as a classic of neoromantic nationalism.

In 1910, Heidenstam became embroiled in a bitter public debate with his former friend and confidant, August Strindberg, over the essential political and aesthetic ideals of the neoromantic movement. The debate, which finally became known as "Strindbergsfejden" (the Strindberg feud), lasted nearly two years and was won by the Strindberg camp. Although Heidenstam was elected to the Swedish Academy in 1912 and was awarded the Nobel Prize for literature in 1916, his role as a national poet was definitely over. He lived until 1940, his last years marred by a premature senility that led him into a most troublesome flirtation with National Socialism. His last poetic work was the posthumous volume *Sista dikter* (1942; Last Poems).

FURTHER WORKS

Skissbok. Reseminnen 1876–77 (1939); *Samlade verk*, ed. Kate Bang and Fredrik Böök, 23 vols. (1943–1944); *Brev* (1949); *Fragment och aforismer* (1959); *Brev och dikter*, ed. H. Gullberg (1960).

FURTHER TRANSLATIONS

An Anthology of Swedish Lyrics, ed. C. W. Stork (1917); *The Soothsayer* (1919); *Sweden's Laureate. Selected Poems of Verner von Heidenstam* (1919); *The Birth of God* (1920); *Christmas Eve at Finnstad* (1950).

REFERENCES

Axberger, Gunnar, *Diktaren och elden* (Stockholm, 1959); Bang, Kate, *Vägen till Övralid* (Stockholm, 1945); Berg, Ruben G:son, "Verner von Heidenstam." *American-Scandinavian Review* 5.3 (1917); Björk, Staffan, *Heidenstam och sekelskiftets Sverige* (Stockholm, 1946); Böök, Fredrik, *Verner von Heidenstam*, 2 vols. (Stockholm, 1959); Gustafson, Alrik, "Nationalism Reinterpreted: Verner von Heidenstam," in his *Six Scandinavian Novelists* (New York, 1940); Kamras, Hugo, *Den unge Heidenstam* (Stockholm, 1942); Lundevall, Karl-Erik, *Från åttiotal till nittiotal: om åttiotalslitteraturen och Heidenstams debut och program* (Stockholm, 1953); Mortensen, Johan, *Från Röda rummet till sekelskiftet*, 2 vols. (Stockholm, 1918–1919); Schoolfield, George, "Charles XII Rides in Worpswede," *Modern Language Quarterly* 16 (1955).

Lars Emil Scott

Heikel, Karin Alice. *See* Vala, Katri.

Hein, Piet. Danish poet, designer, and scientist, b.16 December 1905, Copenhagen.

The multitalented Hein received a diversified education. After passing his university entrance examination in mathematics in 1924, he went to the Royal Academy of the Arts in Stockholm. In 1927 he returned to Copenhagen, where he studied philosophy and theoretical physics at the Niels Bohr Institute. In the following years, Hein was occupied with various design projects and technical inventions within the industrial arts; he invented, for example, the Polygon board game and the three-dimensional SOMA Cube puzzle. His most renowned achievement within industrial design is the so-called super-ellipse: a rectangular oval that he first designed for the city center of Stockholm.

Hein is also known internationally because of his "grooks" (he invented the Danish word "gruk"), which have been translated into many languages. The grooks are epigrammatic poems expressing a wisdom about life in a concentrated form. They are mostly humorous, based on paradoxical statements or puns; they are elegant rather than intricate, quick-witted rather than profound. Written under the pseudonym of Kumbel (Old Norse "kumbl" means a stone with inscription), the grooks are presented in a special print, with a specific layout preferably including a small sketch; the graphic impression is an integral part of the poem.

The cosmopolitan Hein has traveled all over the world, lived in many places, and received numerous international awards. He has been committed to the fostering of greater tolerance among nations and actively involved in a multitude of organizations such as World Federalism Government, Open Door International, and International P. E. N. Club. Hein's activities have in common his wish to harmonize: he tries to bridge the gap between the natural sciences and the humanities, just as he strives for better international understanding. This pursuit is facilitated by his eloquence and flair for coining a striking motto such as "coexistence or no existence."

WORKS

Gruk, vols. 1–10 (1940–1949); *Den tiende Muse* (1941); *Vers i Verdensrummet* (1941); *Kumbels Almanak* (1942); *Man skal gaa paa Jorden* (1944); *Vers af denne Verden* (1948); *Kumbels fødselsdagskalender* (1949); *Ord* (1949); *Selvom den er gloende* (1950); *Gruk*, vols. 11–20 (1954–1963); *Gruk fra alle årene* vol. 1 (1960); *Du skal plante et træ* (1960); *Vis Electrica* (1962); *Husk at elske* (1962); *Kilden og Krukken* (1963); *Gruk fra alle årene*, vol. 2 (1964); *Husk at leve* (1965); *Grooks*, vol. 1 (1966); *Lad os blive mennesker* (1967); *I Folkemunde* (1968); *Runaway Runes* (1968); *Grooks*, vol. 2 (1968); *Det Kraftens Ord* (1969); *Grooks*, vol. 3 (1970); *Gruk fra alle årene*, vol. 3 (1971); *Grooks in Music* (1971); *Grooks*, vol. 4 (1972); *Digte fra alle årene*, vol. 1 (1972); *Grooks*, vol. 5 (1973); *Grooks*, vol. 6 (1978); *Digte fra alle årene*, vol. 2 (1978); *Hjertets lyre—Kærlighedsdigte og -gruk* (1985); *Lars Løvetand—Gruk* (1985); *WordS* (1985).

REFERENCE

"Quality Translator Wanted." *Danish Foreign Office Journal* 47.33 (1964).

Charlotte Schiander Gray

Heinesen, William. Faroese novelist and poet, b. 15 January 1900, Tórshavn.

After an initial schooling in Tórshavn Heinesen went to study at the Copenhagen School of Commerce, with the intention of entering his father's business, but also worked for a time as a journalist. He settled in Tórshavn in 1932 and has since lived as an artist and writer, using Danish as his medium.

Heinesen's poetry from the 1920s echoes the symbolist and neoromantic Danish poetry of the turn of the century, influenced also by Johannes V. Jensen,* Thøger Larsen, and Otto Gelsted,* though with distinctive Faroese overtones. When he returned to writing poetry in 1961, his approach was more modernistic, and he used his poems as social criticism and as an ironical comment on modern civilization. His latest volume, *Panorama med regnbue* (1972; Panorama with Rainbow) contains satirical poems of this kind, but also represents a return to the reflective poetry of earlier years, though in a bolder, more modern idiom and without the elegiac qualities of the earlier work.

Heinesen's international reputation is principally based on his prose work. He is the author of seven novels, published between 1934 and 1976, and five collections of short stories, published between 1957 and 1980. His work is throughout informed by a dichotomy between social awareness and a philosophical examination of man's place and role in the universe, in which he gives expression to an almost religious reverence for life and for woman as the vehicle of life. These abstract elements are present even in Heinesen's first novel, *Blæsende Gry* (1934; Windswept Dawn), though the elements of the social novel, inspired by the Danish collective novel, predominate. The portrayal of Faroese village society on one of the outlying islands is on the one hand tempered by a warm respect for even the more eccentric manifestations of human life and on the other by early signs of the mythical content of the mature work.

With *De fortabte spillemænd* (1950; *The Lost Musicians*, 1972), Heinesen reaches the peak of the collective novel with a part humorous, part poetical portrayal of the struggle to achieve the complete prohibition of alcohol in the Faroes, in which the sectarian prohibitionists are confronted by the unsophisticated poor of Tórshavn. It can be read on more than one level, revealing a sense of conflict between life and anti-life forces, but showing them also to be divided socially and economically, thus also allowing a social interpretation. In *Moder Syvstjerne* (1952; *The Kingdom of the Earth*, 1973) Heinesen has moved a stage further into the realm of the myth and the symbol. *Det gode Håb* (1964; The Good Hope) is unique among his works, being a lengthy allegory of dictatorship and oppression inspired by a particularly difficult time in Faroese history.

The short stories, which predominate from 1957, show the same preoccupations, though these are now expanded by a series of stories reflecting the complexity of human nature—an important theme also in *Det gode Håb*—and by a series of portraits of the dawning erotic awareness of puberty. In his latest volume of stories, *Her skal danses* (1980; The Dance Shall Go On) he returns to the theme of sectarian belief and to obsession, but also, in the title story, presents the cultic significance of the Faroese dance as it raises the dancers above the symbols of death with which they are surrounded, and asserts life as the supreme force. It is the most intensely Faroese of all Heinesen's stories.

Heinesen is recognized as one of the leading novelists in twentieth-century

Scandinavia, a man of never-failing imagination and stylistic brilliance. Though placing his work almost entirely in a Faroese setting, he transcends it and creates a microcosm of it, addressing himself to an international public with no knowledge of his native islands.

FURTHER WORKS

Arktiske Elegier (1921); *Høbjergning ved havet* (1924); *Sange mod Vaardybet* (1927); *Ranafelli* (1929); *Stjernerne Vaagner* (1930); *Den dunkle Sol* (1936); *Noatun* (1938); *Niels Peter* (1939); *Den sorte Gryde* (1949); *Det fortryllede lys* (1957); *Det dyrebare liv* (1958); *Gamaliels besættelse* (1960); *Hymne og harmsang* (1961); *Kur mod onde ånder* (1967); *Don Juan fra Tranhuset* (1970); *Tårnet ved verdens ende* (1976; *The Tower at the Edge of the World*, 1981); *Laterna magica* (1985; trans. 1986); *Samlede digte* (1985).

FURTHER TRANSLATIONS

Contemporary Danish Poetry, ed. Line Jensen et al. (1977); *Arctis* (1980); *Rocky Shores*, ed. George Johnston (1981); *Modern Scandinavian Poetry*, ed. Martin Allwood et al. (1982); *The Winged Darkness* (1983).

REFERENCES

Andersen, Harry, *Tre Afhandlinger om William Heinesen* (Copenhagen, 1983); Brønner, Hedin, *Three Faroese Novelists* (New York, 1973); Brønner, Hedin, "William Heinesen: Faroese Voice—Danish Pen." *American-Scandinavian Review* 61.2 (1973); Jones, W. Glyn, *William Heinesen* (New York, 1974); Jones, W. Glyn, *Færø og kosmos* (Copenhagen, 1976); Jones, W. Glyn, "*Noatun* and the Collective Novel." *Scandinavian Studies* 42.3 (1969); Jones, W. Glyn, "William Heinesen and the Myth of Conflict." *Scandinavica* 9 (1970); Jones, W. Glyn, "William Heinesen's *De fortable spillemænd*" in *Den moderne roman og romanforskning i Norden* (Bergen, 1971); Jones, W. Glyn, "Tärnet ved verdens ende, a Restatement and an Extension." *Scandinavian Studies* 50.1 (1978); Ljungberg, Henrik, *Eros og samfund* (Copenhagen, 1976).

W. Glyn Jones

Helaakoski, Aaro. *See* Hellaakoski, Aaro.

Hellaakoski, Aaro (orig. Helaakoski). Finnish poet, pedagogue, scientist, b. 22 June 1893, Oulu, d. 23 November 1952, Helsinki.

Hellaakoski's father was a teacher of natural sciences who defended his doctoral thesis at the age of seventy-eight. As a young student Hellaakoski got his basic training in geology from his father, and he later became an outstanding doctor of geography whose geomorphological research on lakes was appearing in scientific publications by 1928. Hellaakoski had already previously published six volumes of poetry.

These six collections, the first entitled simply *Runoja* (1916; Poems), form the first period of his poetry. From the very beginning Hellaakoski's main themes were man's relationship with nature, and the individual whose self is liberated from its egocentricity by the elements of nature. His aim was to gain control over his verse. Hellaakoski was familiar with European expressionism and futurism, as well as Guillaume Apollinaire's innovative use of the typographic tradition in poetry. This tradition was a major influence on the experimental word patterns of Hellaakoski's last volume. Modernist poetry, besides experimenting typographically, intentionally broke with traditional metric schemes. Hellaakoski's style was reminiscent of cubism. He became known as a poet of the senses, and in the 1920s his poetry and that of Finnish modernist and poet-scholar P. Mustapää* won critical acclaim. Mustapää's poetic method used objective correlatives and relativity as structural principles that distinguishes his work from that of Hellaakoski.

From 1928 to 1941 Hellaakoski was silent as a poet. He was a teacher and docent of geography at the University of Helsinki. In 1940 his selected poems were well received, and he started to publish very open, humane volumes of poetry. He experienced a religious crisis, which gave rise to a new experimental collection, *Sarjoja* (1952; Series). This last book was his best work.

Hellaakoski's poetry is ambitious and learned and shows great technical virtuosity. The works inspired the modernists in the 1950s.

FURTHER WORKS

Nimettömiä lauluja (1918); *Maininki ja vaahtopää* (1920); *Me Kaksi* (1920, 1945); *Elegiasta oodiin* (1921); *Tyko Sallinen* (1921); *Suursaimaa* (1922); *Suljettujen ovien takana* (1923); *Iloinen yllätys* (1927); *Jääpeili* (1928); *Puulaan järviryhmän kehityshistoria* (1928); *On the Transportation of Materials in the Esker of Laitila* (1930); *Die Eisstausseen des Saimaa-Gebietes* (1934); *Das Alter des Vuoksi* (1936); *Zur Tiefenkarte des Saimaa-Sees* (1940); *Vartiossa* (1941); *Uusi runo* (1943); *Huojuvat keulat* (1946); *Hiljaisuus* (1949); *Kuuntelua* (1950); *Huomenna seestyvää* (1953); *Lumipalloja* (1955); *Niinkuin minä näin* (1959); *Runon historiaa* (1964).

TRANSLATIONS

Finnish Odyssey, ed. Robert Armstrong (1975); *Salt of Pleasure*, ed. Aili Jarvenpa (1983); *Books from Finland* 20.2 (1986).

REFERENCE

Laitinen, Kai, "Nature and Love—the Poems of Aaro Hellaakoski." *Books from Finland* 20.2 (1986).

Kalevi Lappalainen

Helle, Eeva. *See* Joenpelto, Eeva.

Hellström, Gustaf. Swedish novelist, short story writer, journalist, and playwright, b. 28 August 1882, Kristianstad, d. 27 February 1953, Stockholm.

Hellström was born into a middle-class family and studied at Lund University, where he developed strong social and political interests. After completing his education, he took a position as foreign correspondent for *Dagens Nyheter*, a Stockholm daily, partly because of those interests, partly out of necessity. His years in London (1907–1911), Paris (1911–1918), and New York (1918–1920) greatly influenced his work: he wrote both sociopolitical commentaries and novels about England, France, and America, and his work frequently benefits from the objectivity he gained abroad. After another sojourn (1927–1935) in London for another newspaper, Hellström returned to Sweden and lived in Stockholm until his death. He became a member of the Swedish Academy in 1942.

Hellström's literary output is considerable and even includes two plays, *Han träffas inte här* (1947; You Won't Find Him Here) and *Ung man gör visit* (1950; Young Man Pays a Visit), and a biography, *Adolf Hedin* (1948). But his major works are only three: *Snörmakare Lekholm får en idé* (1927; *Lacemaker Lekholm Has an Idea*, 1930), *Carl Heribert Malmros* (1931), and *Storm över Tjurö* (1935; Storm over Tjur Island). The first of these novels—Hellström's undisputed masterpiece—has become a classic genealogical novel in Swedish literature. By focusing on one family and examining the historical and social changes that affect it over a period of nearly a hundred years, Hellström analyzes the roots and development of modern Swedish society. The book is rich in historical detail and impressive for the range of personalities it depicts. In *Carl Heribert Malmros*, Hellström again brings his journalistic skills to bear, this time to examine the social and personal factors leading up to the main character's suicide: workers' rights to strike, an issue having its real-life counterpart in the famous Ådal strike of 1931, and the problem of alcoholism. Finally, in *Storm över Tjurö*, Hellström creates a microcosm of the world by describing life in the Stockholm archipelago. The evil and pettiness of the small society on Tjur Island reflect that of post–World War I and pre–World War II Europe.

Hellström is one of the most important novelists of his generation and has continued influence today through his novel *Lacemaker Lekholm Has an Idea*. His work is typically compared with that of Sigfrid Siwertz,* Ludvig Nordström, and Elin Wägner.*

FURTHER WORKS

Ungkarlar (1904); *När mannen vaknar* (1905); *Kaos* (1907); *Snödroppen* (1909); *Vid kaféfönstret* (1908); *Kuskar* (1910); *Kring en kvinna* (1914); *Vår tids ungdom* (1914); *Joffre, människan och härföraren* (1916); *Kulturfaktorn. Franska stämningar under världskriget* (1916); *Bengt Blancks sentimentala resa* (1917); *Förenta staterna och världsfreden* (1919); *Ett rekommendationsbrev* (1920); *En man utan humor* (1921–1925)— collective title of *Dagdrömmar* (1921), *En mycket ung man* (1923), and *Sex veckor i Arkadien* (1925); *Olsson går i land* (1924), *Mannen vid ratten* (1926); *Noveller* (1927); *Från redingot till kavajkostym* (1933); *Det tredje riket* (1933); *Vägen till paradiset* (1937); *Det var en tjusande idyll* (1938); *Kärlek och politik* (1942); *Gunnar Mascoll Silfverstolpe* (1942); *Den gången* (1944); *Personligt* (1953).

FURTHER TRANSLATIONS

Best Continental Short Stories of 1923–27, ed. Richard Eaton (1924); *Modern Swedish Short Stories* (1934, 1974).

REFERENCES

Ahlenius, Holger, *Gustaf Hellström* (Stockholm, 1934); Tomson, Bengt, *Gustaf Hellström och hans väg mot Snörmakare Lekholm får en idé* (Stockholm, 1961).

Robert E. Bjork

Hemmer, Jarl Robert. Finland-Swedish poet and novelist, b. 18 September 1893, Vasa (Vaasa), d. 6 December 1944, Borgå (Porvoo).

After studying at Helsinki University and graduating in Russian, Hemmer worked for a time as a secondary school teacher, but was financially independent.

Hemmer's early poetry contains a clear romantic element, and his optimistic love poems express an idealistic search for purity in love and a rejection of sensuality. Before long, however, the other pole in his writing, a profound pessimism, also makes itself felt, the two typifying the violent contrasts in mood that are characteristic of his work as a whole. World War I and the Civil War developed this dichotomy further, and brought to the surface Hemmer's intense ethical awareness.

Ethical considerations are at the center of the novel *Onni Kokko* (1920), the story of a fourteen-year-old boy who, after seeing his uncle being taken away to execution by the Reds, becomes a fanatical supporter of the White cause, unceasing in his pursuit of his Red adversaries, until he is finally shot in a vain attempt to save the life of a superior officer. The novel is fast-moving, but together with the action go a psychological insight and a preoccupation with the ethical problems arising from the Civil War. The questions of suffering and guilt are also present, while Onni Kokko's death touches on the theme of personal sacrifice, which, after the publication of some more optimistic poems, including the verse novel *Rågens rike* (1922; The Rye Kingdom), is further examined in Hemmer's later work.

The question of suffering and guilt is the essence of *Fattiggubbens brud* (1926; The Poorbox Bride), the symbolical story of a woman who overcomes the knowledge of her own guilt only to be confronted with the need to betray her own mother. She is finally killed, stoned to death, whereby she receives the mantle of martyrdom and becomes an object of veneration in the local community that has killed her in blind passion.

However, it is in the novel *En man och hans samvete* (1931; *A Fool and His Faith*, 1935) that Hemmer finally works out the problem to the full. He tells of the life of a pastor, Johannes Bro (a symbolical name meaning "bridge"), his experience of personal suffering and conscience, and his being unfrocked for his unorthodox religious views. Finally, as a jailer in Sveaborg, he is overcome by compassion, takes the place of one of the prisoners condemned to death, and is executed. The question is left open as to whether this sacrifice has any wider significance, as, indeed, it is at the end of *Onni Kokko*.

Hemmer's work is uneven, and at times suffers from too obvious a construction in its working out of the ethical theme. It is for the three major novels that he is chiefly remembered. The intensity of the central problem puts them in a category of their own, symbolizing an essential problem in a divided Finland in need of reconciliation.

FURTHER WORKS

Rösterna (1914); *Fantaster* (1915); *Pelaren* (1916); *Ett land i kamp* (1918); *Förvandlingar* (1918); *Prins Louis Ferdinand* (1919); *Över dunklet* (1919); *De skymda ljusen* (1921); *Väntan* (1922); *Med ödet ombord* (1924); *Skärseld;* (1925); *Budskap* (1928); *Helg* (1929); *Morgongåvan* (1934); *Brev till vänner* (1937); *Klockan i havet* (1939); *Du land* (1940).

REFERENCES

Ruin, Hans, *Jarl Hemmer* (Stockholm, 1946); Salminen, Johannes, *Jarl Hemmer, 1893–1931* (Helsinki, 1955).

W. Glyn Jones

Hermodsson, Elisabet. Swedish poet, essayist, novelist, visual artist, composer, and singer, b. September 1927, Gothenburg.

Remarkably versatile, highly imaginative, and independently spirited, Hermodsson has been characterized as a philosopher who expresses her ideas in a multiplicity of forms. She was trained as a visual artist, but also wrote poetry at an early age. She entered Swedish cultural life writing art criticism for *Upsala Nya Tidning* in the 1950s, and became engaged in the religious and political questions of the 1960s, especially the Christian-Marxist debate, as contributor to the magazine *Vår lösen.* Her literary debut is dated 1966, with the publication of *Dikt = ting* (Poem-Thing), which demonstrates her poetic and artistic talents. This was followed just two years later by a collection of poetry and an LP recording called *Mänskligt landskap, orättvist fördelat* (1968; Human Landscape, Unjustly Divided) and a book of essays entitled *Rit och revolution* (1968; Ritual and Revolution). She has continued to work in all these genres and, as recently as 1983, at age fifty-four, made a well-received debut as a novelist with *Samtal under tiden* (Conversation in the Meantime).

Regardless of the form it takes, the content of Hermodsson's work shows ideological consistency and commitment. Given a choice between religious faith and political activism, she chose both, deriving support from Latin American liberation theology, feminist theology, and religious ritual in pre-industrial societies. Central to her worldview is an affirmation of dialectical complexity, of the creative tension between opposite tendencies that she deems essential to artistic freedom. Hermodsson has been outspoken in her resistance to any dogmas that threaten to limit the cultural debate. She has aroused controversy with opposition to the scientific positivism underlying Sweden's advanced technology and its rational forms of social organization. All her works speak for a harmonious integration of human society with a serene natural order. Her most popular work, *Disa Nilssons visor* (1974; Disa Nilsson's Ballads), which she wrote, illustrated, composed, and recorded, especially plays on this theme. Presented as an homage to Birger Sjöberg* and the Swedish ballad tradition, it introduced a critical female subject into that tradition. The ballads are good-natured, ironic, linguistically clever, and melodic enough for a sing-along, but carry within them a passionately serious message: a society that isolates its dreamers and visionaries is ultimately self-destructive. This theme is picked up again in *Samtal under tiden*, but this time the threat comes from a doctrinaire Marxism that leaves no room for aesthetic sensibility. More and more since *Disa Nilssons visor*, Hermodsson has cast the opposition between technology and nature, reason and vision, science and art, dogmatism and paradox in male-female terms. Reviewers see in her feminism the influence of Elin Wägner* and theologian Emilia Fogelklou.*

For many years Hermodsson wrote and painted and sang as a provocateur on the margins of Swedish cultural life without much critical attention, due in part to her own skepticism about the dominant cultural trends of the 1960s and 1970s. As she has chosen more accessible genres and as feminism and environmentalism have aroused greater public interest in the issues her work addresses, Hermodsson herself has begun to win a critical acclaim and a readership to match her talent and versatility.

FURTHER WORKS

AB Svenskt själsliv (1970); *Kultur i botten* (1971); *Röster i mänskligt landskap*, LP record (1971); *Vad gör vi med sommaren, kamrater?*, songbook and LP record (1973); *Genom markens röda väst* (1975); *Ord i kvinnotid* (1979); *Gör dig synlig* (1980); *stenar, skärvor, skikt av jord* (1985).

REFERENCES

Bergom-Larsson, Maria, *Kvinnomedvetande* (Stockholm, 1976); Dahlström, Catherine, "Now Apollo I'm Your Sister." *Swedish Books* 1.4 (1980); Hedwall, Lennart, "Disa Nilsson—en modern Frida," in *Birger Sjöbergsällskapets årsbok* (1976); Ivarsson, Birgitta, "Woman and Man in God. An Interpretation of a Poem by Elisabet Hermodsson," in *Mothers—Saviours—Peacemakers*, ed. Karin Westman-Berg and Gabriella Åhmansson (Uppsala, 1983); Register, Cheri, "Winds of Change at Uppsala." *Scandinavian Review* 65.3 (1977).

Cheri Register

Hjálmarsson, Jóhann. Icelandic poet and critic, b. 2 July 1939, Reykjavík.

Hjálmarsson attracted attention at an early age with the collection of poems *Aungull í tímann* (1956; A Hook in Time). He followed in the footsteps of older poets who had blazed a trail for modernistic poetry in the fifties. Introspective and obscure poems of a philosophical nature with obvious influence from surrealism characterize his early writing. For a time he was on the editorial board of the periodical *Birtingur*, a platform for modernism between 1955 and 1968.

In the early seventies his poetry took a new direction. He turned from the language of modernism to a style that in some respects was an innovation in Icelandic poetry. In *Athvarf í himingeimnum* (1973; Refuge in Space), he uses everyday material in a concrete and intelligible manner, evoking the moods and incidents of immediate experience in a language based on ordinary speech. His object is to describe everyday life in terms so simple that the poem and daily reality merge. In *Myndin af langafa* (1975; Portrait of a Great-grandfather), he develops his poetic style even further. The descriptive technique is objective and documentary, combining recollections against a background of the socialist movement from the time of Stalin to the present day. In this poem, as in later works, the poet finds his subject matter in the peaceful world of family life contrasted with an outside world of chaos. In his judgment it is here that the values that matter most in an uncertain world are to be found. In some respects his poetry shows signs of a common tendency of the times: the flight into personal life.

In addition to composing poetry and a book on modern Icelandic poetry, Hjálmarsson has engaged in literary criticism and for a long time has been a prolific writer of reviews for the largest daily newspaper in Iceland.

FURTHER WORKS

Undarlegir fiskar (1958); *Malbikuð hjörtu* (1961); *Fljúgandi næturlest* (1961); *Mig hefur dreymt þetta áður* (1965); *Ný lauf, nýtt myrkur* (1967); *Hillingar á ströndinni* (1971); *Íslenzk nútímaljóðlist* (1971); *Dagbók borgaralegs skálds* (1976); *Frá Umsvölum* (1977); *Lífið er skáldlegt* (1978).

Matthías Viðar Sæmundsson

Hjartarson, Snorri. Icelandic poet, b. 22 April 1906, Hvanneyri, Borg, d. 27 December 1986.

Born of well-to-do parents, Hjartarson studied at the college preparatory school in Reykjavík until the onset of a lifelong struggle with ill health forced him to withdraw. After early attempts at writing poetry, Hjartarson interrupted his brief literary career to study art in Oslo (1931–1932) where he published a novel, *Høit flyver ravnen* (1934; High Flies the Raven), about an artist's search for untainted creativity and the rediscovery of his roots in Iceland, a theme that forms the basis for much of Hjartarson's lyrical poetry.

After Iceland had gained its political independence in 1944, Hjartarson realized that the traditional role of the poet as a leader of the people in their struggle for freedom and cultural rebirth had to change. For Hjartarson, the function of contemporary poetry was to cultivate compassionate feelings for the inseparable entities of the beautiful and the good and to lead the way against the commercial exploitation of human values and nature by external powers driven by greed. He cast these classical virtues in an aesthetic mold that brought forth a superbly polished style, a brilliant kaleidoscope of imagery, and finely honed verse forms that are innovative in the treatment of rhyme and meter, but not revolutionary to the point of lyrical distortion.

Formal innovation is particularly evident in the first two collections of his poetry, *Kvæði* (1944; Poems) and *Á Gnitaheiði* (1952; On Gnitaheath). In both collections, Hjartarson conjures up from his palette of color symbolism a mystical union of cosmic forces and objective nature. Thus, the rising silver of solitary peaks is transformed into bright stars, and the island of a moon immersed in an endless ocean becomes an iridescence of shades of blue on glittering shores. Life is presented as a journey in search of a time-suspended state of innocence; the journey begins at home, is fraught with extreme dangers in a dark and deathly cold world of suffering and distorted values that alienate man from nature, and ends, often in a fire of inner purification or in a flashing bolt of white wings, at home.

Hjartarson's last two works *Lauf og stjörnur* (1966; Leaves and Stars) and *Hauströkkrið yfir mér* (1979; The Autumn Mist above Me) draw on the repertoire of themes and motifs of his earlier writing with less color intensity and reliance on tradition but with renewed optimism and faith.

Although Hjartarson was not as prolific as his contemporaries, his well-wrought and mystically beautiful lyricism assures the continuity of a lyrical tradition initiated by Jónas Hallgrímsson* and perpetuated by Einar Benediktsson.*

FURTHER WORKS

Kvæði 1940–1952 (1960).

TRANSLATIONS

The Postwar Poetry of Iceland (1982); *Icelandic Canadian* (Spring 1987).

REFERENCES

Hjálmarsson, Jóhann, "Átthagar hvítra söngva," in *Íslenzk nútímaljóðlist* (Reykjavík, 1971); Kress, Helga, "Mannsbarn á myrkri heiðri." *Tímarit máls og menningar* 42 (1981); Pálsson, Hjörtur, "Hauströkkrið yfir mér." *Tímarit máls og menningar* 42 (1981).

W. M. Senner

Hoel, Sigurd. Norwegian novelist, short story writer, critic, editor, and translator, b. 14 December 1890, Sand, Nord-Odal, north of Oslo, d. 14 October 1960, Oslo.

A country boy turned urban intellectual, Hoel was well suited for the mission of cultural and literary mediation that he performed throughout his life. His best fiction derives from the tension between his rural provenance and the radical thought—of Karl Marx, Sigmund Freud, and others—that he absorbed as a lifelong resident of the capital.

While Hoel's novels reflect modern fragmentation, they also manifest a quest for coherence and meaning in human experience. The structure of the stories in his first collection, *Veien vi går* (1922; The Road We Walk), derives from the breakup of the established orders of meaning, whether Christian or bourgeois. Similarly, *Ingenting* (1929; Nothing), a novel in story form, presents traditional modes of meaning—religious, communal, or folkloric—as a background to disenchantment. In *Syvstjernen* (1925; The Seven-Pointed Star) and *Syndere i sommersol* (1927; Sinners in Summertime, 1930), both of uneven artistic quality, Hoel grapples with the specter of determinism, the paradigm of a human world without freedom and meaning. Like Aldous Huxley in the 1920s, Hoel in these books—one satiric, the other comic—shows the limitations of scientific rationalism.

With *En dag i oktober* (1931; *One Day in October*, 1932) Hoel reached maturity as a writer. A collective novel, *En dag i oktober* represents the first significant impact of modern Anglo-American literature in Norway. With its setting in an Oslo apartment house, the story juxtaposes the interior monologues of a number of tenants, whose most secret dreams, anxieties, and frustrations are activated by the tragic predicament (ending in violent death) of a lodger, Tordis Ravn, the estranged wife of a scientist. Despite Hoel's disclaimer, Freud's influence is evident in the character portrayal, as is that of Marx in the analysis of middle-class society. In *Fjorten dager før frostnettene* (1935; A Fortnight before the Nights of Frost) and *Møte ved milepelen* (1947; *Meeting at the Milestone*, 1951), Freud has yielded to Wilhelm Reich, with whom Hoel underwent analysis from 1934 to 1936 and whose sociopsychological synthesis of Marx and Freud was influential in Norway between the wars. Like Dr. Ravn in *October*, the main characters in these books, Dr. Holmen and the Blameless One, betray a fear of Eros which thwarts their development, poisons their marriages, and causes them to escape into careerism, epicureanism, and mystical philosophy. Hoel attributes this fear to a prohibitive morality instilled into them from the nursery on. The retrospective technique, use of dream symbolism, and the return of the repressed are in keeping with the psychoanalytic themes. Artistically these books are quite impressive. In *Fjorten dager før frostnettene*, free indirect discourse is brilliantly handled as a vehicle of narration; its nimbleness, varied pace, and capricious twists and turns render the rhythm of modern life as well as the main character's consciousness. In *Møte ved milepelen*, whose thematic range, moral urgency, and probing analysis of evil, including Nazism, are unprecedented in his previous work, Hoel uses an involuted Conradian technique of authenticated narration with superb skill. The movement of the plot resembles an infernal vortex: examining his life, the Blameless One is caught up in ever-narrowing circles and whirled around at increasingly faster speed until he is faced with the paralyzing revelation that he has fathered a Nazi. The novel is masterfully constructed, with internal as well as external suspense.

Veien til verdens ende (1933; The Road to the Ends of the Earth) and *Trollringen* (1958; The Troll Circle), Hoel's greatest achievements, have a rural setting; both were the product of a long period of gestation. *Veien til verdens ende*, an autobiographical development novel, sensitively explores the psychology of childhood, while informing the inward experience of one individual with universal significance through religious, folkloric, and mythic allusions. The many genre figures and inserted local stories evoke an idiosyncratic milieu. While classic in content, the novel invites psychoanalytic interpretation.

In *Trollringen*, a continuation of *Arvestålet* (1941; The Family Dagger) based on a local murder, Hoel uses a tragic form to express his psychoanalytically founded view of social conservatism. Håvard Viland, the hero, a pioneer who tries to introduce new methods of agriculture in a benighted east Norwegian hamlet, ends up as the community's scapegoat, charged with and innocently convicted for the death of his wife. In presenting Håvard's unhappy fate, Hoel has grafted a psychoanalytic perspective upon the folkloric stem of the story (given in *Arvestålet*). The presence of a number of vividly portrayed foil characters accents Håvard's nobility, but also casts an ironic light on his acceptance of a terrible death. One hesitates which qualities to single out for praise—the book's mordant social analysis, probing depth-psychological portrayals, Sophoclean terror, or masterly use of image and symbol. The chief symbol, the troll circle, significantly resembles the ouroboros (an emblematic serpent of ancient Egypt and Greece), chosen by Hoel as the emblem for his collected works.

Hoel's place in Norwegian literature is quite secure. Throughout his life he displayed an excess of intellectual energy and a fund of positive values indicative of a practical optimism—in conspicuous contrast to the pessimistic view of man reflected in his fiction. He was a formidable critic who, for several decades, shaped literary opinion in Norway. His most outstanding accomplishment as an editor at Gyldendal Publishers for nearly forty years was Den gule serie (The Yellow Series), a library of contemporary foreign fiction in translation. By choosing works that were politically advanced, intellectually challenging, and often novel in technique, Hoel served as a catalyst of change in Norwegian literature. Finally, he gave unstintingly of his time to help defend intellectual and artistic freedom wherever he felt it was being threatened.

While Hoel's gallery of characters is not overwhelmingly large, his range is still wide—from traditional to modernist fiction, from autobiographical novel to period satire, from breezy comedy to fate tragedy. Heir to the literary depth psychology of Henrik Ibsen* and Knut Hamsun,* he sharpened their focus through psychoanalytic study, creating characters of exceptional social and cultural resonance. His accomplished and varied artistry attracted disciples not only in Norway but also in other parts of Scandinavia. The important Danish novelist Leif Panduro* was one of them. If he had written in English, according to the poet André Bjerke, Hoel "would have had a world reputation" (*Dagbladet*, 14 October 1960).

FURTHER WORKS

En manns død . . ., with Finn Bø (1919); *Knut Hamsun* (1920); *Mot muren* (1930); *Don Juan*, with Helge Krog (1930); *Sesam sesam* (1938); *Prinsessen på glassberget* (1939); *Femti gule* (1939); *Tanker i mørketid* (1945); *Tanker fra mange tider* (1948); *Samlede romaner og fortellinger*, 12 vols. (1950–1958); *Jeg er blitt glad i en annen* (1951); *Norge: Glimt fra et stort lite land*, with K. W. Gullers (1951; *Norway: Where Yesterday Meets Tomorrow*, 1951); *Sprogkampen i Norge: En kriminalfortelling* (1951); *Mellom barken og veden* (1952); *Stevnemøte med glemte år* (1954); *Tanker om norsk diktning* (1955); *Ved foten av Babels tårn* (1956); *De siste 51 gule* (1959); *Essays i utvalg*, ed. Nils Lie (1962); *Ettertanker*, ed. Leif Longum (1980).

FURTHER TRANSLATIONS

Archer 2 (1928); *Norseman* 8.3 (1950); *Slaves of Love and Other Norwegian Short Stories*, ed. James McFarlane (1982).

REFERENCES

Bollvåg, Merete Andersen, *Kjærlighetsbegrepet i Sigurd Hoels forfatterskap* (Oslo, 1981); Egeland, Kjølv, *Skyld og skjebne* (Oslo, 1960); Eydoux, Eric, "Sigurd Hoel, le groupe et la revue *Mot Dag*," in *Le Groupe et la revue "Mot Dag," 1921–1925* (Caen, 1973); Haaland, Arild, *Hamsun og Hoel: To studier i kontakt* (Bergen, 1957); Inadomi, Masahiko, *Den plettfrie* (Oslo, 1968); Joos, Martin, "A Lecture on Sigurd Hoel," in *Festskrift til Sigurd Hoel på 60-årsdagen* (Oslo, 1950); Lyngstad, Sverre, *Sigurd Hoel* (Westport, Conn., 1984); Lyngstad, Sverre, "Sigurd Hoel: The Literary Critic." *Scandinavica* 22.2 (1983); Lyngstad, Sverre, "Sigurd Hoel and American Literature." *Edda* 4 (1984); Mylius, Johan E. de, *Sigurd Hoel—befrieren i fugleham* (Odense, 1972); Øyslebø, Olaf, *Sigurd Hoels fortellekunst* (Oslo, 1958); Stai, Arne, *Sigurd Hoel* (Oslo, 1955); Tiemroth, Jørgen E., *Panduro og tredivernes drøm* (Copenhagen, 1977); Tvinnereim, Audun, *Risens hjerte—en studie i Sigurd Hoels forfatterskap* (Oslo, 1975).

Sverre Lyngstad

Hoem, Edvard. Norwegian poet, novelist, and dramatist, b. 10 March 1949, Fræna.

Born on the west coast of Norway, Hoem has his roots in the geographical periphery, a fact that, especially in his early years, was central to his writing. The use of New Norwegian* as his language also attests to this attachment. He attended the university briefly before turning to writing and theater work. Although his first book was a volume of poetry, he soon switched to prose, where he has alternated between novels and dramas, in the 1980s mainly novels.

His first novels were received as renewals of the Norwegian local color writing, of which *Kjærleikens ferjereiser* (1974; Love's Ferrytrips) may still be considered his best artistic achievement. The use of Brechtian alienation techniques, especially the way in which the narrator functions, gives a special impact to the presentation of the theme. The novel is set in contemporary Norway, in a milieu marked by urbanization and the depopulation of rural areas. Several of Hoem's later books are very much in the tradition of the socialist realism of the 1970s. The two novels, out of a planned trilogy, *Gi meg de brennende hjerter* (1978–1980; Give Me the Burning Hearts) are not analytical but didactic, socialist novels in which the characters are described as representative of class and ideology. Many of Hoem's plays have historical settings, deal with social issues, and have the class struggle as their theme, as for instance *Musikken gjennom Gleng* (1977; The Music through Gleng). They are realistic in form, but the use of songs within this frame again shows the Brechtian influence. *God natt, Europa* (1982; Good Night, Europe) is a play that breaks with his earlier realism, using a dream-play technique that mixes realistic and symbolic elements in a description of contemporary Europe in the midst of the nuclear arms race.

The majority of Hoem's works are novels. With his plays though, which have been staged by several theaters, he has made a substantial contribution to the rather meager body of contemporary Norwegian drama. In the 1970s his works were strongly marked by the social realism of the times. Hoem's writings in the 1980s seem to take new directions, for example *Prøvetid* (1984; Rehearsal Time) shows a shift in theme from social relations to emphasis on the individual and his relation to love and art. His latest novel, *Ave Eva* (1987), dealing with social, cultural and existential aspects of man's life, is his major artistic achievement to date.

FURTHER WORKS

Som grønne musikantar (1969); *Landet av honning og aske* (1970); *Anna Lena* (1971); *Kvinnene langs fjorden* (1973); *Tusen fjordar, tusen fjell* (1977); *Der storbåra bryt* (1979); *Du er blitt glad i dette landet* (1982); *Lenins madam* (1983); *Heimlandet Barndom* (1985).

REFERENCES

Mork, Geir, "Eit romanprosjekt i samanbrot? Edvard Hoem: *Gi meg de brennende hjerter,*" in *Norsk Litterær Årbok* (Oslo, 1982); Tjora, Øvstein, "Sjølvinnsikt og politisk innsikt i Edvard Hoems romanar," in *Norsk Litterær Årbok* (Oslo, 1977); Tusvik, Sverre, " '—den er ikkje lett for folket, den tida vi lever i.' Edvard Hoems forfattarskap," in *Linjer i norsk prosa*, ed. Helge Rønning (Oslo, 1977).

Ingeborg Kongslien

Hofmo, Gunvor. Norwegian lyric poet, b. 30 June 1921, Oslo.

Hofmo was born in the aftermath of World War I, and World War II became one of the central experiences in her life, setting the stage for a sustained feeling of despair and loneliness. The title of her very first book, *Jeg vil hjem til menneskene* (1946; I Want to Go Home to People), suggests that she feels herself an outcast. However, her poetry is not necessarily self-centered; the message is that the individual finds himself in a desert, in a vacuum; there are no roads, no known markers—only chaos; what is left is a vague longing for a different world or, at least, for human understanding and spiritual company. Her second volume, *Fra en annen virkelighet* (1948; From Another Reality), caused Bjørn Nilsen, a fellow author, to comment that her poetry is "about human suffering as a phenomenon but also as a fertile possibility for a dignified human existence," something he considers to be very rare in Norwegian literature.

Whereas the first collection espoused the strict metric form, reminiscent of Arnulf Øverland's * poems, the second and all subsequent collections exhibit freer forms. For instance, the key poem in *Fra en annen virkelighet*, "Kollektivmennesket," is a prose poem. In it she finds another world behind the suffering and a mystic union with the divine. Through the religious experience (Christ's suffering is seen as parallel to her own), she finds her way back to society. The existential possibility she sees hinges on compassion and charity. Poetically, Hofmo's strongest work is probably *Blinde nattergaler* (1951; Blind Nightingales). It contains some very simple but enchanting nature poetry. Elements of nature echo her loneliness, but loneliness and suffering have become bearable because they break the way to new insights.

After two more volumes of poetry, in themes and form closely related to the previous ones, there is a hiatus in Hofmo's work of sixteen years, but renewed publishing activity (for a while almost one book of poetry per year) follows in the 1970s. These more recent poems frequently deal with personages out of world history, or they turn to current political and social issues. There is more variety, both in form and content, yet the tone set at the beginning of her authorship, the fear, suffering, and search for God, the existential struggle, never subsides.

FURTHER WORKS

I en våkenatt (1954); *Testamente til en evighet* (1955); *Samlede dikt* (1968); *Gjest på jorden* (1971); *November* (1972); *Veisperringer* (1973); *Mellomspill* (1974); *Hva fanger natter* (1976); *Det er ingen hverdag mer: dikt i utvalg*, ed. Odd Solumsmoen (1976); *Det er sent* (1978). *Stjernene og barndommen* (1986).

TRANSLATIONS

North American Review 257.1 (1972).

REFERENCE

Nilsen, Bjørn, "En annen virkelighet. Streiflys over Gunvor Hofmos diktning." *Samtiden* 76 (1967).

Fritz H. König

Holberg, Ludvig. Dano-Norwegian dramatist, essayist, and historian, b. 3 December 1684, Bergen, d. 28 January 1754, Copenhagen.

After attending the Bergen Grammar School and the University of Copenhagen, young Holberg gave way to his wanderlust, visiting Holland in 1704–1705, and in 1706–1708 England, where he studied in the Bodleian Library at Oxford and received lasting impressions of the English Enlightenment. He traveled to France and Italy in 1714–1716, a journey of great importance for his later development as a writer, and visited Paris again in 1725–1726. Following his stay in England, Holberg had settled in Copenhagen, where, after 1709, he was a fellow of Borch's Kollegium and where he completed his first book, a history of Europe. In 1717 he became a professor at the University of Copenhagen. His subject was metaphysics, which did not interest him and which, in 1720, he was happy to exchange for Latin literature. Not until 1730 did he receive a chair in his chosen field of history. From 1735 to 1736 he was rector of the University, and from 1737 to 1751, its bursar. A lifelong bachelor, Holberg was a lonely man whose chief enjoyment was his writing. He was also musical and played the flute and the violin. From his writings he gradually acquired considerable income, which he invested in landed property, and as an old man he enjoyed nothing so much as caring for his country estates. These in 1747 he willed to the newly reestablished Sorø Academy and as a result was made a nobleman: Holberg, who in his comedies had ridiculed all kinds of social ambition, ended his days as a baron.

It has been said that Holberg's anger at a colleague, whom he attacked in two Latin tracts, first made him aware of his own satiric gifts. In 1719 he published the first part of *Peder Paars* (*Peder Paars*, 1962), a mock heroic poem of more than 6,000 lines. This parody of Virgil's *Aeneid*, in which a modern day Aeneas, Peder Paars, and his servant Peder Ruus are driven off course and land in the island of Anholt, gives Holberg the opportunity not only to make fun of the pagan gods, but to ridicule university disputations in Copenhagen as well as the superstition and greed of his countrymen at Anholt. As in Cervantes's *Don Quixote*, the ridiculous in Holberg's "hero" is mixed with a certain wrongheaded idealism, and this ambivalence recurs later in his comedies. Several lines in the poem also indicate an interest in the women's cause, which is more clearly evident in a poem, "Zille Hansdotters Forsvarsskrift for Qvindekiønnet" (Zille Hansdotter's Defense of Womankind), from 1722. In that year a new Danish theater was opened in Copenhagen, and on 25 September, Holberg's play *Den politiske Kandestøber* (*The Political Tinker*, 1914) was performed there for the first time. During the next five years Holberg composed twenty-five comedies, most of which have belonged to the regular repertory of Danish and Norwegian theaters ever since. Many of Holberg's plays, like those of his admired model Molière, are dramatic portraits of a confused central character. The political tinker, with no education or experience of public service, wishes to become mayor of Hamburg. Jeppe of the Hill, in the comedy of that name, after drinking himself into a stupor believes he is dead and in heaven, where he proceeds to sentence his former superiors to death. In an epilogue to this play about the transformed peasant, the local baron philosophizes about the danger of giving power to the people. While on the surface these plays seem antidemocratic, their major characters have a certain dignity and facility with language that make them more than mere caricatures. In *Jean de France*, on the other hand, the ludicrous Francophile of the title role lacks any redeeming qualities and, like Tartuffe, is chased away rather than reformed, while Vielgeschrey of *Den stundesløse* (The Fussy Man) has again something of the idealist in him. This is also the case with Erasmus Montanus, a farmer's son recently returned from the university, who terrorizes parents, neighbors, and in-laws with his new learning. Though in himself a ridiculous character, his enforced Galileo-style recantation (he believes the Earth is round rather than flat) is not without tragic connotations, and this double vision in many Holberg comedies could be seen as blurring the contours of the genre. Some critics, however, have felt that Holberg, by adding "human" dimensions to his comic characters, actually improves upon the characterizations of his master Molière. In addition to his comedies of character, Holberg produced a number of plays that are better termed "comedies of intrigue," where the Italian commedia dell'arte rather than Molière seems to have been the inspiration. They are plays in which didactic content is less important than exciting plot or festive pageantry, as in *Henrik og Pernille* (Henry and Pernilla) or *Mascarade* (Masquerades), in which the cunning and wit of the servant pair (Henrik and Pernilla) are central features.

In 1727 the Danish theater in Copenhagen was closed, and Holberg entered the second stage of his writing career when he published a number of important historical works—about Norway and Denmark, the city of Bergen, the church, the Jews, and about heroes and heroines. As a historian Holberg was careful in his choice of sources. Always mindful of his readers' taste, he tried to emphasize the topical and presented his story in a lively and readable style.

After the satires and comedies (1720s) and historical works (1730s), the third stage in Holberg's writing career—from 1740 till his death—is taken up with his moral writings, namely, his Latin science fiction about Niels Klim *(Nicolai Klimii iter subterraneum,* 1741), his *Moralske Tanker* (1744; Moral Thoughts), and his five volumes of *Epistler* (1748–1754). In a cave near Bergen, Niels Klim falls through a hole into the interior of the Earth, where there is an ideal state, Potu (Utop/ia/backwards), whose inhabitants are slow-thinking but wise trees, and once more the female sex seems to be favored. In Europe *Nicolai Klimii* was Holberg's most popular book, being translated into several languages already during the author's lifetime. *Moralske Tanker* and *Epistler* consist of more than 600 essays in the manner of Montaigne. They include Holberg's amusing accounts and opinions of himself and in the past have been much used as a source by biographers and critics. Holberg also provided a colorful memoir of his life and works in three autobiographical ''letters,'' written in Latin and published, respectively, in 1728 and 1743 under the title *Epistola ad virum perillustrem* (Letter to a Person of Renown, translated as *Memoirs*).

Holberg is the most important man of letters in eighteenth-century Denmark-Norway and is often referred to as the father of Danish and Norwegian literature. Critical opinions of his production have varied: is it the work of a secret revolutionary living under a repressive system or of a faithful supporter of absolutism and the status quo? Also, to what extent does Holberg the artist depend on the moralist, and in what degree does he adhere to the classical genres? In many ways a child of the Enlightenment, Holberg probably saw tolerance and moderation as cardinal virtues. On the other hand, his radical views of educational reform, including education for women, and his preference for imagination over rules in literature (Epistles 347 and 435) show his complex personality. In the history of drama his greatest admirer was Henrik Ibsen,* who resembled the old master, not only in his satirical outlook and love of royal favors, but in his defense of women and his modern treatment of traditional dramatic genres.

FURTHER WORKS

Samlede Skrifter, ed. Carl S. Petersen, 18 vols. (1913–1963); *Festutgaven 1922,* eds. Francis Bull, Georg Christensen, Carl Roos, S. P. Thomas, and A. H. Winsnes, 6 vols. (1923–1925); *Værker i Tolv Bind,* ed. F. J. Billeskov Jansen, 12 vols. (1969–1971).

FURTHER TRANSLATIONS

Three Comedies (Henry and Pernilla, Captain Bombastes Thunderton, Scatterbrains) (1912); *Comedies by Holberg* (Jeppe of the Hill, The Political Tinker, Erasmus Montanus) (1915); *Four Plays by Holberg* (The Fussy Man, The Masked Ladies, The Weathercock, Masquerades) (1946); *Seven One-Act Plays by Holberg* (The Talkative Barber, The Arabian Powder, The Christmas Party, Diderich the Terrible, The Peasant in Pawn, Sganarel's Journey to the Land of the Philosophers, The Changed Bridegroom) (1950); *Selected Essays of Ludvig Holberg* (1955); *The Journey of Niels Klim to the World Underground* (1960); *Three Comedies* (The Transformed Peasant, The Arabian Powder, The Healing Spring) (1962); *Memoirs. An Eighteenth-Century Danish Contribution to International Understanding* (1970).

REFERENCES

Bull, Francis, *Holberg som historiker* (Oslo, 1913); Campbell, J., *The Comedies of Holberg* (Cambridge, 1914); Foss, Kåre, *Konge for en dag* (Oslo, 1960); Jansen, F. J. Billeskov, *Holberg som epigrammatiker og essayist*, 2 vols. (Copenhagen, 1938–1939); Jansen, F. J. Billeskov, *Ludvig Holberg* (New York, 1974); Kruuse, Jens, *Holbergs maske* (Copenhagen, 1964); Müller, Th. A., *Den unge Holberg* (Copenhagen, 1943; Thomsen, Ejnar, *Sfinxen, Streger til et Holberg-portræt* (Copenhagen, 1954).

Harald S. Naess

Holm, Lillemor. *See* Evander, Per Gunnar Henning.

Holm, Sven. Danish novelist, short story writer, and playwright, b. 13 April 1940, Copenhagen.

The dominant themes in Holm's extensive production are inner and outer violence, and the gradually more marked protests by self-willed characters, a type of anti-anti-heroes, or oftentimes, heroines. Holm's writing has as its point of departure the "fantastic" element of modernist prose. Feeling caught in the conflicts characteristic of the splintered Western civilization, the author seeks to find release through fantasy and art. In his later works Holm attempts to expose the ecological, social, technological, and political forces that inhibit collective longing as well as individual inner growth. The themes reappear in a slightly varied form in the experimental novels and prose poems. There the protest against erotic convenience is juxtaposed to limits set by society on individual freedom, and the feeling of alienation to the basic human necessity of some shared social values. Since the late 1970s Holm has in his works articulated the need for documentary research as well as for a reconciliation between one's existential yearnings and everyday life in today's society. This is particularly true of Holm's historical dramas. Although he thus revives interest in historical topics, he does not do so in a nostalgic manner.

Cleverly exploited aesthetic positions have time after time been staked by Holm when confronted with late modernist trends: metafiction, pop art, confessional literature. He has thereby demonstrated an unusual degree of open-mindedness and a willingness to experiment. It is ultimately this open-mindedness, although viewed by Holm with cold professionalism and even irony, that accounts for his productiveness and significance as a literary figure.

WORKS

Den store fjende (1961); *Nedstyrtningen* (1963); *Fra den nederste himmel* (1965); *Jomfrutur* (1966); *Termush, Atlanterhavskysten* (1967; *Termush,* 1969; *Min elskede, en skabelonroman* (1968); *Et spil om et lukket rum* (1969); *En ø næsten som et paradis* (1969); *Rex* (1969); *Møblerne* (1971); *Syv passioner* (1971); *Berøringer* (1972); *Syg og munter* (1972); *Det private liv* (1974); *Torvet i dit hjerte* (1975); *Golgatha 75* (1975); *Langt borte taler byen med min stemme* (1976); *ægteskabsleg* (1977); *Struensee var her* (1977); *Møbler er en sund baggrund* (1978); *Luftens temperament* (1978); *Hans Egede eller Guds ord for en halv tønde spæk* (1979); *Mænd og mensker* (1979); *Aja, hvor skøn!* (1980); *Een mand gør ingen vinter* (1980); *Koster det sol?* (1981); *Leonora* (1982); *Hummel af Danmark* (1982); *Heksehaven* (1983); *Peter von Scholten—en filmroman* (1987).

FURTHER TRANSLATIONS

Literary Review 8.1 (1952); *The Devil's Instrument, and Other Danish Stories,* comp. Sven Holm (1971); *Mundus Artium* 8.2 (1975); *Zone* (1980).

REFERENCES

Baggesen, Søren, "Magt og medler," in *Analyser af dansk kortprosa,* vol. 2 (Copenhagen, 1972); Brunse, Niels, "Den barnlige lyst, ungdommens oprør og det gamle samfund," in *Romanen som offentlighedsform,* ed. Jørgen Bonde Jensen and Karen Nicolajsen (Copenhagen, 1977); Christensen, Hans Jørn, *Tekstanalyse* (Copenhagen, 1977); Johansen, Jørgen Dines, "Novelle og roman," in his *Novelle og kontekst* (Copenhagen, 1972); Sørensen, Villy, "Sven Holm," in *En bog om inspirationen, Det danske Akademi 1974–1981* (Copenhagen, 1981).

Jørgen Egebak

Holstein, Ludvig Ditlef. Danish poet, b. 3 December 1864, Kallehave, d. 11 July 1943, Copenhagen.

The son of a count, Holstein grew up at his father's mansion and was financially independent throughout his life. He entered Copenhagen University in 1883, but spent only a short time studying. His life was spent mainly in Copenhagen, where from 1918 he worked as a publisher's reader for Gyldendal.

Holstein's link with the 1890s was his belief in something behind and above external reality. His early poems, love poems and nature poems, are more harmonious than those of his more introspective contemporaries. His first book, *Digte* (1895; Poems), reveals an uncomplicated delight in nature coupled with an elegant, but often quite humorous treatment of love. As a whole it mirrors a longing for happiness and only occasionally expresses any sign of anxiety, as in the poem "Uro" (Unease), in which Holstein urges his friends to appreciate their happiness. The same uncertainty is fundamental to "Far, hvor flyver Svanerne hen?" (Father, Whither Fly the Swans?), showing the swans, and by implication mankind, moving toward the unknown.

The harmony reflected in the early poetry was disturbed when Holstein underwent a personal crisis. Poems from this time are included in the later volume
entitled *Løv* (1915; Foliage). The next major volume of poems, *Mos og Muld*
(1917; Moss and Soil), is a close-knit cycle of poems reflecting the changes in
nature over the year, and echoing changes in the poet's mood. "Den hvide
Hyacinth" (The White Hyacinth) expresses a pantheistic belief in a life force
in nature and wonderment at the miracle of life emerging from the soil. Written
with deceptive simplicity, the poem proclaims naturalistic pantheism via Christian symbols.

The same ideas mark the great poem "Jehi" from 1925, in which Holstein
uses the biblical command for creation in a pagan, life-worshipping context. It
was included in a prose work, *Den grønne Mark* (1925; The Green Field), in
which Holstein expressed his belief in a life force and the fundamental unity of
all living things.

Many of Holstein's poems are well known and much loved in Denmark. He
is seen as representing the scientific belief in a life force, which has been a
feature of Danish poetry through much of the twentieth century.

FURTHER WORKS

Tove (1898); *Æbletid* (1920); *Jehi* (1929); *Spredte Blade* (1942).

REFERENCES

Andersen, Harry, *Ludvig Holsteins kunst* (Copenhagen, 1956); Andersen, Harry, *Ludvig Holstein i den litterære tradition* (Copenhagen, 1963); Balslev, Kjeld, *Ludvig Holstein og hans Lyrik* (Copenhagen, 1941); Frandsen, Ernst, *Ludvig Holstein* (Århus, 1931); Werner, Hans, *Ludvig Holstein* (Copenhagen, 1920).

W. Glyn Jones

Holt, Kåre. Norwegian novelist, b. 27 October 1917, Våle.

Holt was born and has lived most of his life in the southwestern part of
Norway. His working-class background led him to journalism within the labor
press, and has also strongly influenced his creative writings. The social theme
prevailing in his works is matched by an existential one.

Det store veiskillet (1949; At the Crossroads) marked his breakthrough as a
novelist; its theme of choice as well as the employment of a variety of rhetorical
devices within a realistic framework are typical of his writing. The story explores
the ethical implications of man's choices by giving three versions of the same
life story, the fate of a young man at the outbreak of World War II—as a
collaborator, a nazi, and a partisan. In three consecutive novels, beginning with
Det stolte nederlag (1956; The Proud Defeat), Holt gives a fictionalized story
of the Norwegian labor movement, with great richness of historical detail and
an understanding of the social struggle. Considered to be his main artistic achievement, the historical trilogy *Kongen* (3 vols., 1965–1969; The King) depicts the
entire life of the medieval King Sverre, from his youth and through his struggle

for power and the throne of Norway. The novels show intimate historical knowledge, and their style is influenced by the sagas, but they are modern both in composition and in their psychology and their theme of identity. During the 1970s, Holt wrote several books that might be labeled documentary novels, where he examines some Norwegian national heroes. These works aroused heated debates, for instance, *Kappløpet* (1974; *The Race*, 1976), a critical discussion of Roald Amundsen's expedition to the South Pole, which questions the kind of heroism he represented. The two latest books by Holt are memoirs, the first one with the appropriate title *Sannferdig beretning om mitt liv som løgner* (1982; True Story of My Life as a Liar). He has also written six children's books.

Holt is the great epic novelist of his generation; humanism, broad historical knowledge, and real narrative talent mark his work. He has won both critical acclaim and acquired a large reading public.

FURTHER WORKS

Tore Kramkar (1939); *Tore finner vei* (1940); *Spillemann og kjøgemester* (1941); *Udåden* (1945); *Hurra for han som innstifta da'n* (1945); *Demring* (1946); *Nattegjester* (1948); *Cleng Peerson og Nils med luggen* (1948); *Brødre* (1951); *Hevnen hører meg til* (1953); *Mennesker ved en grense* (1954); *Storm under morgenstjerne* (1958); *Rømlingen Oskar og Maria fra hulesjøen* (1959); *Opprørere ved havet* (1960); *Den gamle veien til Kierlighed* (1961); *Perlefiskeren* (1963); *Hest for alle pengene* (1970); *Kristina av Tunsberg* (1971); *Oppstandelsen* (1971); *Ansikter i sagaens halvlys* (1971); *Farvel til en kvinne* (1972); *Hilsen fra Rafnaberg* (1973); *Folket ved Svansjøen* (1973); *Sjøhelten* (1975); *De lange mil til paradiset* (1977); *Sønn av jord og himmel* (1978); *Gjester fra det ukjente* (1980); *Biter av et bilde* (1981); *Mørke smil* (1981); *Veien videre* (1983); *Skoggangsmann* (1984); *Budbringeren fra Tunsberg* (1985); *Vandringen* (1986).

REFERENCES

Dahl, Willy, "Kåre Holt—almuens historiker," in *Fra 40-tall til 70-tall* (Oslo, 1973); Larsen, Petter, *Holt* (Oslo, 1975); Thon, Jahn, "Kåre Holt—arbeiderdikteren i det evige borgerlige univers," in *Linjer i norsk prosa*, ed. Helge Rønning (Oslo, 1977).

Ingeborg Kongslien

Huldén, Lars. Finnish poet writing in Swedish, b. 5 February 1926, Jakobstad (Pietarsaari).

Huldén, the son of a noted poet, Evert Huldén, grew up in Ostrobothnia where verbal games are a part of folk tradition. His fascination with language most immediately led to an academic career and a professorship in Nordic languages at the University of Helsinki. As a scholar he has studied C. M. Bellman* and J. L. Runeberg*; both have influenced his poetry.

In many ways Huldén's poetry is anti-modernistic, reacting against the difficult and nebulous. His debut, *Dräpa näcken* (1958; Kill the Kelpie), and the immediately following works are often mundane in subject matter but comical in tone. The frivolous subsides in later works; with *Herr Varg!* (1969; Mr. Wolf), Huldén turns increasingly somber, and in the collection of epitaphs, *Läsning för vandrare* (1974; Reading for Wanderers) he can be downright morbid. A balance is attained in *Herdedikter* (1973; Shepherd Songs) with its alternating lyrical and commentary verses.

Ostrobothnian phrases occur frequently in Huldén's poetry, but in *Heim/Hem* (1977; Home), he presents a bilingual collection of poetry in his native dialect and standard Swedish. In these compassionate poems his themes and diction find a liberated resonance and often sublime elegance. As an Ostrobothnian Huldén strikes up a friendship with the spirit of Runeberg, similarly transplanted to Borgå in southern Finland, in *J. L. Runeberg och hans vänner* (1978; J. L. Runeberg and His Friends). Here Huldén excels in his mastery of the pastiche, while at the same time paying tribute to Runeberg.

Huldén is a versatile writer who produces abundant occasional poetry, chanteys and cabaret lyrics, and a hilarious collection of short stories in *Hus* (1979; Houses). His style is deceptively simple, turning on unobtrusive metaphoric imagery. Because it seems so effortless it may give an impression of being hasty. But the simplicity masks irony and a deep concern for mankind. In Swedish Finland Huldén's poetry is appreciated as a fresh alternative from a modernist idiom that has run its course.

FURTHER WORKS

Speletuss (1961); *Spöfågel* (1964); *Enrönnen* (1966); *Två raseborgsspel* (1974); *Island i december* (1976); *Visbok* (1976); *Dikter vid särskilda tillfällen* (1979); *Jag blir gammal kära du* (1982); *Judas Iskariot samfundets årsbok 1987* (1987).

TRANSLATIONS

Poetry East 6 (1981).

REFERENCE

Jones, W. G., "Lars Huldén." *Books from Finland* 11.2 (1977).

Kim Nilsson

Hvítadal, Stefán frá. *See* Sigurðsson, Stefán.

Hyry, Antti. Finnish short story writer and novelist, b. 20 October 1931, Kuivaniemi.

The northern Finnish village of Hyry's childhood was agricultural and insular. He took a degree in electrical engineering but has never practiced. Since his graduation he has been a writer. In his books Hyry offers no overt message to the reader. It becomes clear, however, that he disagrees with the world of modern technology.

The past, that which has been experienced and felt, is most important to Hyry's narrative method. His stories often deal with a boy's childhood, youth, and adulthood. His first novel *Kevättä ja syksyä* (1958; Spring and Autumn), which has as its main character a country boy, can be read as a religious book as well as social criticism. Hyry published a volume of short stories the same year. In these and later works the characters are involved in constructive activities, and images derive from everyday actuality. Hyry has sharp observational skill; his characters live in a world full of things, and Hyry tells us what is true for them. He gives concrete descriptions of ordinary things and names objects in meticulous detail. His stories are bare, the dialogue dry, but he manages to convey the characters with clarity.

Hyry's novel *Kotona* (1960; At Home), translated into German in 1980, is the first volume of a four-part novel. Hyry sensitively portrays the protagonist's development to early adulthood. The narration of this boy's life is simple, compact, and free from a conformist stance common to many learned men. Hyry uses a straightforward, objective, yet lyrical style.

Hyry's realistic, exacting prose style broke new ground for the fiction of the 1950s. His narrative style has had no followers among the younger generation of writers, but his works enjoy a widening scholarly attention.

FURTHER WORKS

Maantieltä hän lähti (1958); *Junamatkan kuvaus ja neljä muuta novellia* (1962); *Kesäkuu* (1963); *Alakoulu* (1965); *Maailman laita* (1967); *Suolla* (1967); *Leveitä lautoja* (1968); *Tupakeittiö* (1970); *Isä ja poika* (1971); *Lohivene* (1973); *Silta liikkuu* (1975); *Liippa* (1977); *Maatuuli* (1980); *Kertomus* (1986).

TRANSLATIONS

Odyssey Review 3.1 (1963); *Snow in May*, ed. Richard Dauenhauer and Philip Binham (1978); *Finnish Short Stories*, ed. Inkeri Väänänen-Jensen and K. Börje Vähämäki (1982); *Books from Finland* 16.2 (1983).

REFERENCES

Ahokas, Jaakko A., "The Short Story in Finnish Literature," in *Snow in May*, ed. Richard Dauenhauer and Philip Binham (Cranbury, N. J., Binham 1978).

Kalevi Lappalainen

I

Ibsen, Henrik Johan. Norwegian dramatist and poet, b. 20 March 1828, Skien, d. 23 May 1906, Christiania (now Oslo).

Ibsen was the second child of a prosperous businessman, whose profligacy and ultimate bankruptcy brought the family close to economic disaster and left a deep impression on the young boy. At the age of fifteen he was apprenticed to an apothecary in the provincial town of Grimstad, where he remained some six years. Here he studied for university entrance in what little spare time he had, and also found opportunity to try his hand at writing: lyric poems in the first instance, and then drama. *Catilina* (1850; *Catiline*, 1921), inspired in part by the Latin texts he was studying and also reflecting some of the revolutionary spirit of 1848, was his first published drama. In April 1850 he moved to Christiania, the capital city, where he was active in student journalism and completed his second play *Kjæmpehøjen* (*The Burial Mound*, 1921), which was given its first performance on 26 September 1850.

In 1851 he accepted an invitation to join the Norwegian theater in Bergen, recently established by Ole Bull. Here it was intended that he should assist the theater as "dramatic author," but he soon found himself also deeply engaged in the more practical side of the theater's operations as assistant producer and "regissør." A study tour of theaters in Denmark and Germany in 1852 contributed much to his understanding of the ways of the theater.

Ibsen's years in Bergen had great formative influence on his later life and work. He continued to write for the theater; and every year saw a new play from his pen performed on 2 January, the anniversary of the founding of the theater: in 1853 *Sancthansnatten* (first published 1909; *St. John's Night*, 1970); in 1854 a revised version of *Kjæmpehøjen* (first published 1854, *The Burial Mound*, 1921); in 1855 *Fru Inger til Østeraad* (published 1857; *Lady Inger of Østråt*, 1890); in 1856 *Gildet paa Solhoug* (1856; *The Feast at Solhoug*, 1908); and

1857 *Olaf Liljekrans* (1902; *Olaf Liljekrans*, 1921). One or two of these were near disasters; others were only qualified successes.

In the autumn of 1857 Ibsen moved to Christiania to take over the post of artistic director to the Norwegian theater there, taking with him the completed drama *Hærmændene paa Helgeland* (1858; *The Vikings at Helgeland*, 1890). He had become engaged to Suzannah Thoresen in 1856, but another two years were to elapse before they could afford to marry. Their son and only child, Sigurd, was born on 23 December 1859. The years that followed in Christiania were times of great material and spiritual hardship for Ibsen: his debts mounted, his depression deepened, and the public was often woundingly indifferent. The appearance of a verse comedy *Kjærlighedens Komedie* (1862; *Love's Comedy*, 1900), a work of wit and elegance, was nevertheless greeted by the public with a storm of disapproval. In 1863 there appeared his first unquestionably great work: *Kongsemnerne* (1863; *The Pretenders*, 1890), a large-scale historical drama with strong personal overtones.

In 1864 Ibsen was awarded a small traveling scholarship by the state, and in April of that year he left Norway for Italy. It was the start of a long period of self-imposed exile from Norway, which—briefly interrupted by visits back to his native country in 1874, 1885, and 1890—was to last until 1891. During these twenty-seven years he lived abroad, mainly in Rome, Dresden, and Munich.

The first fruits of his residence in Italy were the two complementary "dramatic poems" *Brand* (1866; *Brand*, 1891) and *Peer Gynt* (1867; *Peer Gynt*, 1892)— works that were immediate cultural and commercial successes. Ibsen was given a state award to allow him to continue to write; and from this time on there were changes in his manner, his dress, his physical appearance, and even his handwriting to bear witness to his newfound confidence. *Brand* marks Ibsen's stern repudiation of the values of national romanticism that had served as the basis of the greater part of his earlier work; and in its treatment of the concept of "mission" as a powerful motive force in life, it gives a portrait of a man in profound spiritual conflict. By contrast, *Peer Gynt* is a work of exuberant invention and wit, which nevertheless is sustained ultimately by the same values as *Brand*. Thereafter Ibsen abandoned verse as a dramatic medium. In 1868 he moved to Germany, first to Dresden and subsequently (in 1875) to Munich; in 1869 he also traveled to Egypt to attend the ceremonies attaching to the opening of the Suez Canal. These were the years that saw the publication of his first prose drama about modern life, *De unges Forbund* (1869; *The League of Youth*, 1890), followed by a volume of his collected poems, *Digte* (1871), and his huge "double drama" in prose, *Kejser og Galilæer* (1873; *Emperor and Galilean*, 1876)—the first of his dramas, incidentally, to be translated into English. Although ostensibly a historical drama set in a distant period of time, this dramatic treatment of the fateful clash between the old Hellenism and the new Christianity during the reign of Julian the Apostate in the fourth century A.D. had a deliberately contemporary message, and reflected many of the urgent issues of the 1870s.

There then began, in 1877, that series of "dramas of contemporary life," twelve in all, which finally established and consolidated Ibsen's international fame. First came *Samfundets Støtter* (1877; *Pillars of Society*, 1888), which focused on the hypocrisy that Ibsen detected in many aspects of public life; then *Et Dukkehjem* (1879; *A Doll's House*, 1880) examined the role of women inside the matrimonial home, and provoked widespread public debate; *Gengangere* (1881; *Ghosts*, 1885) roused even greater public outrage by its daring treatment of the tensions inherent within contemporary family living; and *En folkefiende* (1882; *An Enemy of the People*, 1888) traced the consequences of daring to bear witness to the truth in the context of a polluted society. All four of these "social" plays subjected contemporary patterns of living to merciless scrutiny, and by implication insisted strongly on the individual's right to self-realization.

Ibsen's next four plays—*Vildanden* (1884; *The Wild Duck*, 1890), *Rosmersholm* (1886; *Rosmersholm*, 1889), *Fruen fra havet* (1888; *The Lady from the Sea*, 1890), and *Hedda Gabler* (1890; *Hedda Gabler*, 1891)—reveal a certain shift of emphasis away from the mainly social to the individual and psychological, from the pressures of convention and received opinion to the conflict of mind with mind.

In 1891 Ibsen returned to Norway and took up residence in Christiania. The following year, on 11 October 1892, Ibsen's son Sigurd was married to Bergliot Bjørnson, daughter of Norway's other great author and playwright of these years. The same year there appeared *Bygmester Solness* (1892; *The Master Builder*, 1893), a play that examined the conflict of will and conscience across the generation gap. *Lille Eyolf* (1894; *Little Eyolf*, 1895) is a subtle and complex study of human relations at a number of levels: marital, sexual, family. *John Gabriel Borkman* (1896; *John Gabriel Borkman*, 1897) returned to a theme Ibsen had touched on several times earlier: the consequences of sacrificing the happiness of oneself and others in the pursuit of fame, power, and fortune. Finally, Ibsen's "dramatic epilogue" *Når vi døde vågner* (1899; *When We Dead Awaken*, 1900) asked remorsefully whether the claims of art should ever be allowed to prevail over simple human happiness.

A stroke in 1900 and another a year later left him an almost helpless invalid. He died in Christiania on 23 May 1906.

The more immediate impact that Ibsen had on the society of his own day came from the treatment of "problems" in his dramas. He had responded eagerly to those challenging phrases of Georg Brandes* in 1871: "What shows a literature to be a living thing today is the fact of its subjecting problems to debate." The principal commitment of the "problem drama" was to truth, which must be fearlessly recognized and boldly declared, however unpalatable or unexpected. Ibsen's achievement under this rubric is unique: never before or since has a dramatic author so dominated the European theater or monopolized public debate as did Ibsen in those years when (particularly) *Et Dukkehjem* and *Gengangere* were creating public outrage in most of the countries of Europe. Not only was it a social phenomenon without parallel, but from it there developed a continuing theatrical tradition wherein dramatists like Gerhart Hauptmann, George Bernard

Shaw, Frank Wedekind, Maxim Gorky, and Bertolt Brecht attempted (in the latter's phrase) to give the main problems of the age a dramatic structure.

Alongside these public polemics was another less conspicuous but in the longer term probably more significant achievement: Ibsen's abandonment of verse after *Peer Gynt*—a decision that is often and confidently claimed as the most important event in the history of modern drama—and his subsequent sustained attention to what he called "the far more difficult art" of writing prose drama. By his sensitivity to subtleties and profundities below the commonplace surface of everyday speech and his ability to communicate them in dramatic dialogue, Ibsen opened up new and previously unexpected dimensions in drama. Other European writers who were themselves greatly sensitive to nuance in language—Hugo von Hofmannsthal, Henry James, Anton Chekhov, and Maurice Maeterlinck in the 1890s, James Joyce and Rainer Maria Rilke later—were warm in their admiration for this aspect of Ibsen's achievement. Fascinated, Maeterlinck detected a second unspoken reality, a "dialogue du second degré," behind the seemingly bleak surface of the language; Rilke saw in Ibsen's authorship a tireless search for visible correlations of the *inwardly* seen.

Ibsen's consummate technical mastery, his profound insight into human character, and his creation of a new type of dramatic dialogue, a "poetry of the theatre" in prose, gave to twentieth-century drama a lead that is still very much alive and that places him among the world's greatest dramatists.

FURTHER WORKS

Norma, eller en politikers kjærlighed (1851; *Norma, or a Politician's Love*, 1970); *Breve fra Henrik Ibsen*, 2 vols. (1904); *Efterladte skrifter*, 3 vols. (1909); *Henrik Ibsens brev*, ed. Ø. Anker (1978).

FURTHER TRANSLATIONS

The Collected Works of Henrik Ibsen, ed. W. Archer, 12 vols. (1906–1912); *The Oxford Ibsen*, ed. J. W. McFarlane, 8 vols. (1960–1977); *Henrik Ibsen*, ed. Rolf Fjelde (1978). Selections from the letters include: *The Correspondence of Henrik Ibsen*, ed. Mary Morison (1905); *Ibsen: Letters and Speeches*, ed. Evert Sprinchorn (1964). See also *Lyrics and Poems from Ibsen*, ed. F. E. Garrett (1912).

REFERENCES

Beyer, Edvard, *Henrik Ibsen* (London, 1980); Downs, B. W., *A Study of Six Plays by Ibsen* (Cambridge, 1950); Koht, H., *The Life of Ibsen* (New York, 1971); McFarlane, James, *Henrik Ibsen: A Critical Anthology* (Harmondsworth, 1970); Meyer, M., *Henrik Ibsen*, 3 vols. (London, 1967–1971); Northam, John, *Ibsen, Dramatic Method* (London, 1953); Pettersen, H., *Henrik Ibsen bedømt af samtid og eftertid* (Oslo, 1928); Tedford, I., *Ibsen Bibliography 1928–57* (Oslo, 1961); Valency, M. J., *The Flower and the Castle* (New York, 1963); Weigand, H., *The Modern Ibsen* (New York, 1925).

James McFarlane

Icelandic Sagas. The Old Norse word *saga* (related to *segja*, 'say, tell') refers to the numerous novel-length prose narratives produced in medieval Iceland and Norway. Modern scholars have categorized these narratives according to content. The *Íslendingasögur* (Icelandic family sagas, sagas of Icelanders) are the quasi-historical accounts of leading citizens during and immediately after the period of settlement (A.D. 870–1050). The related *konungasögur* (kings' sagas) are political biographies of the Norwegian kings. Together these categories are sometimes referred to as the "classical" sagas. Somewhat shorter and more fabulous are the *fornaldarsögur* (legendary sagas, mythic-heroic sagas), which tell stories of the legendary past. Other sagas include translations, adaptations, or imitations of foreign romance, epic, hagiography, and the like. Twelfth- and thirteenth-century Icelandic events are chronicled in the *biskupa sögur* (sagas of Icelandic bishops) and the compilation known as *Sturlunga saga*.

Although the term "Icelandic sagas" is sometimes used broadly to refer to any or all of these categories, the bulk of which were used in Iceland by Icelanders, it serves more narrowly to designate the first: those accounts of the fortunes of prominent Icelanders during the Viking Age. These thirty-odd "family" sagas can in turn be divided into two groups: individual or biographical sagas, and collective or so-called district sagas. The main characters of the biographical sagas are typically men who distinguished themselves in the Viking Age not only as warriors and adventurers but also as poets (skalds). The poetry composed in the tenth century by the premier skald of early Scandinavia, Egill Skallagrímsson,* survived well enough in memorial tradition to be rendered in, and serve as backbone of, his saga (*Egils saga*). Other sagas with poet-heroes are *Kormáks saga, Gunnlaugs saga, Bjarnar saga Hítdoelakappa, Hallfreðar saga, Gísla saga, Grettis saga,* and *Fóstbræðra saga*. Such men tend to share more than poetic ability. They are also characteristically outsiders (by virtue of travel or outlawry or both), unpleasant in looks and social behavior, and prone to erotic entanglements. Sagas are otherwise notoriously short in their treatment of romantic matters; with the exception of the love story of Kjartan and Guðrún in *Laxdæla saga*, virtually every love story occurs in the skald sagas.

Although the collective or district sagas too have their share of memorable individuals—Njáll, Gunnarr, Guðrún, Snorri the Priest—their interest is primarily in the affairs of the community, above all in the processes of conflict and settlement. The paradigmatic feud saga has six phases: introduction (presenting characters and background), conflict (commonly arising from a minor irritation), climax (entailing the death of one of the protagonists), revenge and counterrevenge, reconciliation, and aftermath (remarking on the survivors and their descendents). The plan is not a rigid one: *Njáls saga* doubles it, *Heiðarvíga saga* greatly elaborates the conflict phase, *Ljósvetninga saga* distributes the middle stages over two generations, and so on. The conflict in *Bandamanna saga* is little more than a vehicle for class satire. Two sagas, *Eyrbyggja* saga and *Vatnsdæla saga*, constitute compilations of local traditions only loosely harnessed to the feud pattern. *Laxdœla saga* exhibits the scheme to perfection—even as it exhibits, also to perfection, a biographical structure organized around the life of Guðrún Ósvífrsdóttir. Among the purest feud narratives may be counted *Hœnsa-þóris saga* and *Hrafnkels saga*, though even here other preoccupations—concerning social hierarchy—are clearly evident.

The events of the sagas occurred in the tenth and eleventh centuries; the sagas in the form we have them appeared during the course of the thirteenth. Just what sort of development lies between these two points has long been a matter of debate. The inventionists (whether "bookprose" or "Icelandic school") have minimized the importance of oral tradition and maximized the artistic imagination of the well-read medieval authors. The traditionalists (whether "free prose" or "new formalist") argue for the decisive role of oral tradition in both matter and form. The evidence is indeed contradictory. On the inventionist side, one can point, here and there throughout the corpus, to loans from learned and other sources (Gregory's *Dialogues*, for example), Christian *topoi*, and the like. The digressive and interlaced composition of certain of the sagas smacks of medieval theory (rhetoric manuals) and practice (Latin historiography, French prose romance). The sheer length and complexity of many of the longer sagas would seem to mark them as a literary enterprise. Likewise, the nature and number of anachronistic elements (for example, certain legal and architectural details, or the echoes of Sturlung-age violence) would seem to indicate later literary mediation. On the traditionalist side, one can point to the fact that the sagas (unlike skaldic poetry and other Icelandic writings) are anonymous; that they are remarkably stereotyped in diction, structure, and theme; that their plain style is closely akin to that of the folktale; that their mixture of prose narrative and speech-verse has numerous analogues in oral traditions throughout the world; that the word *saga* itself implies a told story; and that, anachronisms notwithstanding, the sagas do preserve a massive amount of general and particular information from an earlier era. The prudent conclusion is that the sagas are both oral and literary: produced in a unique social forum by literate authors conversant with native oral traditions, and meant to be read as well as heard.

One model of development derives the family sagas from the slightly older kings' sagas, a genre known to have been written by Icelanders on the basis of both oral (skaldic) and written sources and under the influence of Latin biography and chronicle. Once established for kings, the long prose form was then extended to the kings' poets (hence the skald sagas) and from them to their Icelandic families (hence the collective sagas). This scheme suggests a neat shift in orientation from Norway to Iceland, from individual to community history, and from kings to citizens. The problem with it is that not every skald saga predates every collective saga: *Fóstbrœðra saga* (a saga dealing with royal poets) has recently been dated to the end of the saga-writing period, and *Reykdœla saga* (an emphatically collective saga) has been designated the oldest of all the sagas on Icelandic subjects. The impetus of the kings' sagas in the writing of family sagas must therefore have been secondary, not primary. Indeed, it may be that the kings' sagas emerged in the form they did precisely because the Icelanders who produced them had a prior tradition of saga telling on local subjects. In either case, the embedded verse was surely an integral element. Skaldic poetry was transmitted in memorized form, and one theory holds that the sagas evolved out of the increasingly elaborate explanations that necessarily accompanied the later recital of the poems. It should be noted, however, that some saga verse is inauthentic, fabricated, and attributed to specific poets after the fact, and further, that some of the collective sagas contain little or no verse.

Saga language is notoriously plain, relying on nouns and verbs and using adjectives only sparingly and in predicate position ("He had a horse; it was brown," not "he owned a brown horse"). Except for the occasional use of litotes ("he was not unhappy at the news") or the stray ominous detail ("two ravens flew with them all the way"), the narrative is unadorned; simile and metaphor have no place. Description is limited to the functional: weather, dress, topography, and architecture are mentioned only if they will figure specifically in the later action. Emotion is indicated by behavior (falling silent, flushing red, exiting abruptly) or in dialogue, seldom by authorial declaration. Women are on the whole more direct in their expression of grief and hostility; men tend to deflect emotion into mannered understatements, proverbs, or skaldic verse. The virtual absence of authorial intrusion in saga narrative gives it the look of objectivity. That objectivity is only apparent, however. Readers know to expect the worst of characters described as unpopular, overbearing, or ugly, and the best of the ones described as accomplished or handsome. Authorial judgment is commonly displaced onto the community at large: "people condemned the killing," "people doubted that she thought the news as good as she pretended." It is a measure of saga art that from such oblique and external indications can emerge characters of such complexity as Egill, by turns murderous, wistful, greedy, truculent, and lovelorn; Guðrún, who engineers the death of the man she most loves; Gísli and Þorkell, whose history together is a case study in fraternal ambivalence; and Hallgerðr, vicious author of the death of her third husband but loving and resourceful wife to her second. The same may be said of social issues. Again by oblique means the saga narrators condemn feud violence and those who pursue or urge revenge; society, we are to understand, might be better served by something like a hierarchical Christian state than the traditional system of clan government.

At the same time, there is a strong sense of nostalgia for times and champions past. Even as they criticize the system that results in an abundance of dead heroes and a shortage of live workers, the sagas commemorate those who, like Skarphéðinn and Grettir, lived and died in the grand old style. Another inheritance from the past is the sagas' supernatural element: the sorcerers, walking dead, prophetic dreams, and manifestations of luck and fate. If such matters were once a part of a coherent belief system, they do little more than add period color to the sagas we have. Nor is there a trace of divine machinery, pagan or Christian. Cause and effect are located squarely in the human world. The conflicts enumerated in the sagas are fully explicable in here-and-now terms: social violence follows from real people's actions, which in turn follow from flawed character or regrettable lapses or both. W. P. Ker considered such secular rationalism premature; it in any case sets the sagas apart from contemporary European literature.

Most of the Icelandic sagas were written down during a relatively short period of eighty years (1220–1300). Few can be assigned absolute dates, and scholars have had to content themselves with establishing a relative chronology. That chronology—it continues to be debated and adjusted—gives little evidence of formal evolution, a fact that traditionalists have taken to indicate an oral prehistory. Still, some broad generalizations can be made. The skald sagas tend to cluster in the beginning. There is an increasing tendency toward length: *Njáls saga* and *Grettis saga* are late. The sagas from the end of the period are less anchored in history and show strong affinities with the mythic-heroic and romance genres. It is precisely these latter genres—the *fornaldarsögur* and the *riddarasögur*—that displaced the Icelandic family sagas in popularity.

Just why the Icelanders ceased to write family sagas after this short burst is a matter of conjecture. It may be that the underlying traditions were exhausted. It may also be that with the loss of independence in 1262, Icelanders felt a decline of national impetus and a concomitant decline of interest in the "free state" past. The orientation toward Norway must also have had its impact on Icelandic literary tastes. For whatever reason, Icelanders gave up telling about their ancestral past and turned instead to tales of a timeless and fabulous elsewhere. The brilliant prose style appears to have been specific to historical narrative; it did not in any case survive the generic shift, and by the fourteenth century Icelandic literature yielded its special place in European letters.

REFERENCES

Andersson, Theodore M., *The Problem of Icelandic Saga Origins* (New Haven, 1964); Andersson, Theodore M., *The Icelandic Family Saga: An Analytic Reading* (Cambridge, 1967); Andersson, Theodore M., "The Icelandic Family Sagas," in *Heroic Epic and Saga*, ed. Felix J. Oinas (Bloomington, 1978); Clover, Carol J., *The Medieval Saga* (Ithaca, 1982); Clover, Carol J., "Icelandic Family Sagas," in *Old Norse-Icelandic Literature: A Critical Guide*, eds. Carol J. Clover and John Lindow (Ithaca, 1985), includes extensive bibliography; Clover, Carol J., "Icelandic Family Sagas," in *Dictionary of the Middle Ages*, vol. 4 (New York, 1984); Hallberg, Peter, *The Icelandic Saga* (Lincoln, 1962); Heusler, Andreas, "Die Anfänge der isländischen Saga," in *Abhandlungen der Königlich Preussischen Akademie der Wissenschaften* (1913), repr. in *Kleine Schriften*, ed. Stefan Sonderegger (Berlin, 1969); Knut, Liestøl, *The Origin of the Icelandic Family Saga* (Westport, Conn., 1930; repr. 1974); Lönnroth, Lars, "*Njáls Saga": A Critical Introduction* (Berkeley, 1976); Nordal, Sigurður, *Hrafnkels saga Freysgoða* (Cardiff, 1958); Nordal, Sigurður, "Sagalitteraturen," in *Nordisk kultur*, 8: B

(1953); Schach, Paul, Icelandic Sagas (Boston, 1984); Schier, Kurt, *Sagaliteratur* (Stuttgart, 1972).

Carol J. Clover

Immigrant Literature. *See* Scandinavian Immigrant Literature.

Indriði G. Þorsteinsson. *See* Þorsteinsson, Inðridi G.

Ingemann, Bernhard Severin. Danish poet and novelist, b. 28 May 1789, Torkildstrup, d. 24 February 1862, Sorø.

Ingemann never concluded his studies in theology at the University of Copenhagen but earned his living as a tutor for several years until he in 1822 received a teaching position at the Sorø Academy. This school was a rallying ground for a number of significant scholars and writers of the romantic era, and Ingemann stayed here until his death. He served as headmaster of the academy from 1843 to 1849.

Prior to a journey to Italy in 1818–1819, poetically described in *Reiselyren* (2 vols., 1820; Travel-Lyre), which brought about a turn toward greater realism, Ingemann wrote in the manner of sentimental and Gothic pre-romanticism. A large number of deaths in his family increased his awareness of the perishableness of everything and directed his thoughts at an early stage toward death. Ingemann's first poetry collections, *Digte* (2 vols., 1811–1812; Poems) and *Procne* (1813), consist partly of moralizing Gothic ballads, partly of allegories behind the best of which emerges a romantic longing for eternity. Allegorical also are the large epic poem *De sorte Riddere* (1814; The Black Knights) and the fairy-tale play *Reinald Underbarnet* (1816; Reinald the Wonder Child), which depict the battle between the forces of light and darkness. The fate dramas *Blanca* (1815) and *Masaniello* (1815) are, however, built up on purely external shock effects influenced by the period's strong fascination with Shakespeare.

A departure from Ingemann's youthful, idealistic, and abstract writing takes place with the historical cycle of poems *Waldemar den Store og hans Mænd* (1824; Waldemar the Great and His Men). A glorification of the Danish Middle Ages, its heroism and adherence to Christianity, the work was to serve as a counterweight to the defeatism after Denmark's defeat during the Napoleonic Wars. Ingemann's main source for this work and the succeeding historical novels, *Valdemar Seier* (1826, 1966; *Waldemar, the Victorious*, 1841). *Erik Menveds Barndom* (1828, 1966; *The Childhood of Erik Menved*, 1846, 1913), *Kong Erik og de Fredløse* (1833, 1966; *King Eric and the Outlaws*, 1843), and *Prinds Otto af Danmark* (1835, 1966; "Prince Otto of Denmark"), are Saxo Grammaticus* and medieval balladry, whereas Sir Walter Scott is the decisive artistic model. But in contrast to Scott, Ingemann lets the historical figures serve as the protagonists while the milieu becomes secondary and historically incorrect. The character delineation and dialogue might appear somewhat stereotyped, but the language is vivid and firm and the novels are filled with evocative and thrilling, though rather naïve, episodes that have guaranteed their great popularity into the twentieth century.

Naïveté became an integral artistic device in Ingemann's hymn writing, which, to a greater extent than his novels, will secure his name for posterity. Already in 1816 Ingemann had published some hymns that were permeated with German-influenced pantheistic religiosity; other hymns were published in 1822 and 1825, but Ingemann first emerged as the great master with the two collections *Morgensange for Børn* (1837; Morning Songs for Children) and *Syv Aftensange* (1838; Seven Evening Songs) written for the students at Sorø. The meter and phraseology of these hymns are simple and natural, qualities which make the hymns comprehensible to both children and adults: concealed behind the idyllic surface, however, are depth of thought and cosmic perspectives.

Ingemann's final works are dominated by the two major elements that are so typical of his entire authorship. A number of stories as well as the strongly underrated novel *Landsbybørnene* (1852; The Village Children) with their contemporary settings represent the realistic trend, the poem *Tankebreve fra en Afdød* (1855; Philosophical Letters from a Deceased), the account of the pilgrimage of a soul toward eternity, represents the idealistic and speculative trend. Ingemann's entire writings, however, including the historical novels that place him as one of Denmark's most prolific national romantics, are completely determined by a spiritual, Christian view of life. This philosophy is most exquisitely expressed in Ingemann's hymns, which exemplify the lasting qualities in his authorship: the melodious and intimate tone that was passed on to the Danish symbolist poets at the turn of the century.

FURTHER WORKS

Samlade skrifter, 40 vols. (1845–1865); *Breve til og fra B. S. Ingemann*, ed. V. Heise (1879); *Brevveksling mellem B. S. Ingemann og Fru I.C.v. Rosenørn*, ed. V. Heise (1881).

FURTHER TRANSLATIONS

Book of Danish Verse, comp. Oluf Friis (1922, 1976); *A Second Book of Verse* (1947, 1968); *A Harvest of Song*, ed. Johannes Knudsen (1953).

REFERENCES

Aaberg, J. C., *Hymns and Hymnwriters of Denmark* (Des Moines, 1945); Galster, Kjeld, *Ingemanns historiske Romaner og Digte* (Copenhagen, 1922); Galster, Kjeld, *Fra Ahasverus til Landsbybørnene* (Kolding, 1927); Langballe, Carl, *B. S. Ingemann* (Copenhagen, 1949); Nørregaard, Jens, *B. S. Ingemanns Digterstilling og Digterværd* (Copenhagen, 1886); Rønning, F., *B. S. Ingemanns Liv og Digtning* (Copenhagen, 1927); Schwanenflügel, H., *Ingemanns Liv og Digtning* (Copenhagen, 1886).

Sven H. Rossel

Inuit Literature. The Inuit (the Eskimos' preferred name for themselves), including those who settled in Greenland, 2600 B.C. onward, had no writing. After nearly four millennia, the Greenlandic Inuit finally came in contact with literate Europeans. Although the Norse were in West Greenland 983–1410 (?), all contacts were incidental or hostile, and the Inuit language was incomprehensible to the Norse. Similarly, the Inuit contacts with the English, Dutch, Bascayan, Danish-Norwegian explorers, whalers, and traders beginning in the fifteenth century resulted in only a few mutually mangled words useful for trade.

But on 3 July 1721, the Lutheran missionary Hans Egede and his family landed on a rock skerry outside Nuuk (Godthaab), Greenland, and began the processes that led to literacy. First came the making of adequate linguistic tools. Poul Egede compiled the first dictionary in 1750 *(Dictionarium Grönlandica-Danica-Latinum)* and the first grammar in 1760 *(Grammatica Grönlandica)*. The work started by the Egedes was continued by many such as Otto Fabricius (from 1768) and the nineteenth-century linguistic genius Samuel Kleinschmidt (from 1859).

Whatever its other effects, this literacy that was brought from the outside divides the Greenlandic compositions into the pre-literate oral and the written. In 1950, Professor William Thalbitzer, in the first substantial treatment of Greenlandic literature, labeled the three resulting periods: Heathen unwritten, Transition (1721–1905), and Modern. For students of literature, Greenlandic may be especially useful and interesting because it shows these divisions particularly clearly even to the slight overlapping, such as the oral after writing began.

PRE-LITERATE ORAL COMPOSITIONS

According to Finn Gad, the Inuit settled the vast perimeter of Greenland in six successive but not necessarily overlapping waves; thus: (1) Independence I (2600–1800 or 1000 B.C.), (2) Sarqaq (1000–500 B.C.), (3) Independence II (c. 700–400 B.C.), (4) Dorset (100 B.C. 700–900 A.D.), (5) Dorset-Thule (900–1000), and (6) Thule and Ingusuk (1200–1700). Of course all these Inuit groups must have had their oral literature to which they could add as desired, as, for instance, did Pôq, one of two Greenlanders sent to Denmark in 1724. On his return, he made and often sang a ballad about his trip. Those who lived after him continued to sing it.

Fortunately, much of this oral literature was saved by collectors such as Inspector H. J. Rink (1819–1893); Commander Gustav Holm (1847–1940); Professor William Thalbitzer (1873–1959); and greatest of all, the half-Greenlander, half-Dane Knud Rasmussen (1879–1933). Rasmussen spent much time collecting material in Greenland, but his finest collection came from his Fifth Thule Expedition (1921–1924), which resulted (among other things) in nearly 2,000 pages of stories and songs gathered from Thule, Greenland, to the Bering Sea. Even a glance at the tables of contents of these collections shows how remarkably homogeneous the compositions are in form and subject matter.

The eight groups of Inuit represented in the collection are Iglulik Caribou, Netsilik, Cooper, Mackenzie, Alaskan, East Greenlanders, and Polar. The chances for any appreciable additions are extremely slight because of the effects of modern culture on even the remotest areas.

In these eight groups, there are five common categories: (1) myths and legends, (2) epic, (3) views of nature, (4) killings and revenge, and (5) strange (unbelievable) stories. Special, but usually small, localized categories also occur in some of the groups; for example, although the category "meeting with strange tribes" does not seem to appear in Greenland, there are enough magical tales to be put into groups such as those about resuscitation, about people who have been abandoned, taboos and their effects, and tales about deranged people. The animal life that appears is generally the same throughout, for instance, the raven, bear, fox, louse, whale, caribou, and dog. The "characters" often have type names or one appropriate to humans; yet their characteristics are those of both animal and man. The astonishing shading from human to monster (superhuman) to nonhuman usually seems both subtle and convincing. All, of course, can speak (if speaking is involved) or can speak a mysterious language as with an *angákoq* (a shaman) in a trance. All show human emotions.

Both the compactness of characterization, often just a few syllables, and the brutality of the actions, especially in revenge, strike the non-Inuit as extreme yet sophisticated in their own way. Seldom does the audience fail to see the intended purposes even with tricks or actions gone awry. The savagery seems to match the lifestyles and conditions of the tellers.

However, Rasmussen has explained away some of the seeming strangeness. For instance, he differentiates between *oqalugtuat*—old myths that go back into the distant past of the original homeland(s)—and *oqaluatât*—legends about people who have lived within memory. Rasmussen in *East Greenland Myths and Legends* distinguishes four types of tales: epic, religious, humorous, and soporific. For the last he explains,

The soporific tales were merely intended for passing the time away and by means of sleep getting people through the long waiting of the winter months. In relating, the teller adopts a monotonous and lethargic form calculated to put his audience to sleep in a very short time. It is the highest form of praise if it can be said of such a narrator that no one has ever heard the end of his tales; his audience always falls asleep before he gets that far.

Unfortunately, one of Rasmussen's admonitions is difficult to observe, as when he says all the tales "are for oral use exclusively; really they should never be read." He adds that one must relive the events and feel the force of the narrator; but for that, one needs the drum, the gestures, the masks, and so on.

In any of the stories a reader can expect that actions will be exceptionally vicious; there will be no premium put on happy endings, and enormous strength and unemotional acceptance of any hardship will be admired. Women and children are praised for these same qualities even though they may have lesser strength.

The story of Kâgssagssuk is one of the most widely known and represents a typically brutal tale. However, in an illustrated 1967 trilingual edition (English, Danish, and Greenlandic), the truly savage wording is softened somewhat in

English and Danish, as when Kâgssagssuk asks for water and fondles two girls successively, whom he then squeezes to death. Their parents watch and excuse Kâgssagssuk. He himself is a viciously treated orphan (e.g., his teeth are always extracted so that he will not be able to gnaw bones or to eat). He is befriended by an old couple, is violently tormented by other children, goes to a mountain, calls on the Master of Strength, and a doglike magic figure gives him superhuman strength in two episodes. He returns to his tormentors, shows his great strength, and exacts truly terrible vengeance, but his benefactors he treats most generously. He then challenges any and all powerful champions until he is finally overcome in the north by a short man with superior superhuman power. He returns to the south and lives more or less normally from then on.

The pre-literate poetry is complicated and varied in genre and form. Thalbitzer found fifteen genres: (1) ceremonial invocations by an *anqákoq*, (2) dionysiacs, (3) lyrics of happiness, (4) many cultic hymns and dramatic dance songs such as strife and dueling songs (not used in reference to duels between "song cousins" who are the best of friends), (5) East Greenlandic epic-lyric without drums, (6) children's play songs, (7) lullabies, (8) magic songs, (9) kayakers' hunting and signal songs, (10) reports of hunting, (11) salesmen's vending (cries) songs, (12) elegies that sound like a dog howling, (13) a few erotic love songs (much in the European mode), (14) sport songs, and (15) lyrics praising one's home territory. Each of these may have special metrics.

As long as the poet is living, his poem belongs to him, but afterward it belongs to the people, who of course may make changes. Usually the poems are in short unrhymed verses and are sung or half-sung and framed by a melodic repetitive variant of the meaningless disyllable, *aja*. The short verse of spoken words contains the poet's motive and deeper meaning, but the relation to the *aja* -frame is very intricate. Even when the words are neither magical nor fragmentary, it is extremely difficult for a non-Inuit to fully grasp the meaning of this poetry.

Perhaps some of the native writers in the modern period may be able to translate and interpret old Inuit poetry adequately. At least the Tūkak' theater group (see below) is trying, but they are using dance, drums, masks, and mime.

THE TRANSITION PERIOD: FOREIGNERS' USE AND CONTROL OF LANGUAGE

It would be difficult to imagine a greater change in subject matter and manner of thinking than that that took place from the pre-literate use of language to the first written uses of Greenlandic. Of course, there is no way to measure to what extent the cultural biases of the Danes necessarily skewed the Greenlandic natural expressions. There had to be lexical changes for ideas and perceptions not known to the Greenlanders or not known to the Danes about them.

The above-mentioned, first scholars made remarkable progress especially considering the state of linguistics in the eighteenth and nineteenth centuries. By the nature of their purposes, most of those working with the language produced

only (1) religious works, psalms, and Bible translations in a "church language";
and (2) works of scholarly apparatus—dictionaries and grammars.

Some secular works did appear. For example, in 1810, Rasmus Brandt put
into Greenlandic short dialogues he had made up, some moral fables, and a
longer Danish novel, *Hanna von Ostheim*. Peter Kragh, a missionary, collected
and published these in 1839. In 1837, there appeared a Greenlandic version of
Hans Egede's life. In 1832, there had been a collection of current Danish romantic
songs, including drinking songs and a bloody Greenlandic "Lorelei." A first
play in Greenlandic was Kragh's translation of Bernhard Severin Ingemann's*
Johannes den Døber i Ørkenen (printed in 1874).

Hinrik J. Rink (1818–1893) made the first real move to the secular by founding
in 1860 the newspaper *Atuagagdliutit* with three Greenlanders in charge: Lars
Møller, Aron Kangeq, and Rasmus Berthelsen, editor until 1873. Møller took
over and was editor until 1922. Many articles, some literary, appeared. The
outstanding native author was Ungâralak. Other newspapers also were started.

During this period, writing of poetry (except for psalms) was slight. However,
the Moravian Carl Jul. Spindler (1838–1918), a German, wrote many psalms in
such admired Greenlandic that his style set the fashion for the next generation.
Also Rasmus Berthelsen's psalm, conceived in a dream, became a favorite
everywhere in Greenland. In *Atugagdliutit* Hanserâq (Johannes Hansen) from
Nanortalik published his diary concerning the so-called women's boat expedition
(1883–1885). Christian Rosing's *Tunuamiut* serves as a contrast to Hanserâq in
realism.

Although the total number of works by the Danes was large, there was little
of lasting value except for the hymns. The bulk of the 560 in the 1971 *Tugsiutit*
(hymnal) were produced in the period. Also there was another side to this Danish-
dominated period, as was shown in the first Greenlandic publications, which
included slender volumes heavily illustrated in often a near-comic manner. Examples would be the Pok-book (1857) and two books in 1858. One showed the
natives of the world, in this case Denmark, England, Russia, China, Spain, and
Turkey, plus three maps (the world in two hemispheres, Europe and the Holy
Land), all in just twenty sheets with very little text. The other book added a
Danish text beside the Greenlandic and in a dialogue "explained" war to the
Greenlanders. Perhaps the still mostly illiterate Greenlanders needed mainly
pictures (almost caricatures), but whatever the reason these works promised little
for secular writing. Thus one recognizes what Knud Rasmussen did by founding
with sixteen others in 1908 the Greenland Literary Society with the express
purpose of giving Greenlanders something to read besides the religious works
and the newspaper. In 1909, he published *Avángarnisalerssârutit* (130 pages),
a version of his *People of the Polar North* (1908 English 358-page translation
of his 1905 *Nye Mennsker* of 243 pages). In 1911 he and his sister Vilhelmine
translated from the Danish the *Grænlandinga Saga* and the Greenlandic section
of *Fóstbrœðra Saga*. The formidable title for this fifty-seven-page work was
K'avdlunâtsiait kalâtdlit nunâliarkârnermingnik oqalugtualiaisa ilait; the Dan-

ish title was *Erik den rødes Saga* [sic] *og Uddrag af Fostbrødresaga*. Other publications of the society were Frederick Lynge's *Hans Egedip inûneranik* [(life)] in 1915; Jakob Olsen's *Akilinermiulerssârut* (1927), his work on the Fifth Thule Expedition; Gustav Olsen's *Ivnânganermititdlune uvdlorsiutaisa ilait* (1923) on his work among the Cape York Polar Inuit. And thus was begun the modern age.

THE MODERN AGE

The modern age really began in 1914, the year Mathias Storch, a native Greenlander, published *Singnagtugaq,* a popular fifty-page novel of unique importance. Knud Rasmussen published a Danish translation *En Grønlænders Drøm* in 1915. A second Greenlandic edition appeared in 1959, less than a decade after Greenland was opened to outsiders and the effective moves toward home rule had begun. In 1974, one year after the adoption of the new orthography, a third edition came out, *Sinnattugaq*. And on the centenary of Storch's birth the eleven-chapter work was serialized (25 May–20 July 1983)—in original orthography in *Atuagagdliutit* (# 21–29).

In addition to its unique popularity, Storch's novel contains the seeds of many of the themes and much of the method of telling for the novels to date. Storch opens his novel with a shouting match, the antagonists representing Greenlander versus Dane, town versus country, and even the different generations and the important place of women. There are discussions of values—wisdom from the elderly, the retreat to nature to think, the bureaucratic difficulties in the settlement, the social problems of near-starvation, troubles with poorly trained teachers, and the struggle to get an education. Then there is a love story and traditional family prejudices, a disagreement over a dog and food allegedly stolen by the animal, only resolved by a brutal killing of and autopsy on the innocent dog. A lover becomes a runaway, a near-*qivitoq* (outcast), and decides to return only to fall through the ice and drown because of poor judgment. Later his body is found. The novel ends with the nationalistic dream about the development of Greenland—a theme taken up by modern poets and later novelists. Rasmussen's notes to his translation clarify Greenlandic details, especially the old ways such as kayakers' sickness, the different types of settlements, and prejudices about hunting. Later writers expand and incorporate these Greenlandic touches, for more is now known about the twentieth-century (European) tastes. Later novelists also make better transitions than Storch and feel particularly free to intrude themselves far more than Storch did.

But Storch's novel has held its place possibly because it is largely an autobiographical story of a Greenlander in transition. Its dramatic scenes have the desired realism especially as they raise problems. Without a happy ending and no pat solutions, the novel still expresses much about the Greenlandic situation even though Storch's dream about 2105 was modest and most of his goals had already been achieved, as Christian Berthelsen pointed out in 1962. In short,

Storch's themes and ideas have been better expressed and most often Europeanized. He is not, however, a forerunner of the rare detective novel, the novel about the Inuit past, and novels about expeditions. But one may try to see subsequent developments in Storchian terms or, in other words, to note the variations and changes with respect to the first novel.

The first full-length survey of Greenlandic literature appeared in 1983 in Christian Berthelsen's *Grønlandsk litteratur*, which in itself is a real achievement even though he had written in Danish several times before on the topic: articles in *Bogen om Grønland* in the five editions, the first three 1962, 1968, and 1970 with little change, and 1976 with the subtitle Review of the Last Fifteen Years, and 1978 Review of the Last Twenty Years. Generous excerpts in Danish accompany Berthelsen's brief evaluations in this first long critical work by a Greenlander.

Of course, it may be too early to assess with great accuracy the modern writers, but Berthelsen's last three groupings are very helpful: (1) new inspiration from the 1920s, (2) literary production inspired by the old Greenlandic huntersealer culture, and (3) the present day in poetry and prose. Following Thalbitzer and Berthelsen, one can outline the chief figures and their works.

The second Greenlandic novel was Augo Lynge's *Ukiut 300-ngornerat* (1931), 300 years after Egede's arrival, that is, 2021. In addition to seeing a vision of a finer (in the European sense) society, Lynge also adds gold discovery, murder, and detectives, but he is politically motivated, as was Storch.

The most prolific and versatile of the modern Greenlandic writers is Frederik Nielsen (b. 1905). He is the author of the third novel *Tuumarsi* (1934), a story about Thomas and his family in eighteenth-century Greenland. Nielsen translated this novel into Danish in 1980. He has also written poetry, translated from the Danish; published in 1970 a second novel, *Ilissi tassa nunassari* (This Is Your Land), about the Inuit wandering from Canada to Greenland; and in 1982 *Siulittuutip eqquunnera* (Prediction Come True), about the Viking times in Greenland. As chief of Radio Greenland, he gives numerous talks and has presented a radio play, *Oooroq angakkuagaq* (The Enchanted Valley).

The other writers in the post–1920 inspiration follow Nielsen's lead. Thus, Pavia Peterson (1904–1943) translated from the Danish; wrote a short play in (1934), *Ikinngutigiit* (Friends), a problem play about modern times, and two novels—in 1941 *Assaq ukiorlu—asanninnerlu* (Summer and Winter—and Love), and in 1944 *Niuvertorutsip pania* (The Outpost Manager's Daughter).

Hans Lynge (b. 1906) wrote *Ersinngitsup piumassa* (The Invisible Will) (typescript in 1938 but printed in 1967), a work in two parts from Rasmussen's Fifth Thule Expedition. Thalbitzer (p. 241) summarizes this work as describing the suffering and loneliness of a *qivitoq* (outcast) that produce the great shaman and bring together the fated, the passionate, and the sublime. Lynge also wrote poetry, plays about the Inuit past (e.g., *Kâgssagssuk* and *Sainak Sunai*, a play about the meeting of Thule Inuit and Christianity). In 1967 he published *Inugpait*

(Magnificent, Unmixed People), a report of a group in the Upernivik area, and in 1981 *Grønlands indre liv* (in Danish), memories of childhood.

Kristen Poulsen (1910–1951) published a collection of poetry with subjects from everyday life and in 1947 a novel *Angakkoq Papik* (Shaman Papik) about an East Greenlandic shaman who goes to West Greenland and is baptized.

The six authors in Berthelsen's second period add some variety to Greenlandic literature. Otto Rosing (1896–1965) wrote three biographies (of Carl Julius Spindler, Hans Henrik, and Samuel Kleinschmidt), polemics about Greenlandic youth, works about East and North Greenland, and in 1955 the novel *Taseralik*, about a summer place where north and south meet, and in 1968 *Gulunnguaq*, a novel taking place in Disko Bay in the early missionary days. His *Tikippog* in Danish is about the making of a priest.

Villads Villadsen (b. 1916) has written *Jense* (1958), about a catechist in East Greenland after World War I; *Nalusuunerup taarneerani* (In Heathendom's Darkness) in 1965; *Ikerasaamiut*, life in the Disko Bay area after 1700; in 1974, *Juulut* (Jørgen), life before modern times; in 1979 a story about life aboard the ship *Disko*; and in 1980, *Siivali* (Sigvard), a novel about the problems of today. He has also written many schoolbooks.

Otto Brandt (1918–1981) wrote a trilogy—*Oooqa* (1971), *Tuuluartoq* I and II (1973) about hunters in the eighteenth century—and *Ippiarsuup imai* (Contents of a Skinbag), fatalistic stories (1982).

Otto Sandgren (b. 1914) has written stories about a sled trip in North Greenland, about revenge, conversion, hunting, and a catechist's record of a catechist's work, and a novel (1980) about the original culture. He has also written other works about Greenland's cultural history.

Jens Røsing (b. 1924), an artist and author, has written poetry and prose in Danish. Incidentally, he introduced the tame reindeer from Finnmark and has made many expeditions to Greenland.

Writers in Berthelsen's final section are probably too recent to be judged, but poetry and prose are often political and about controversial matters, such as the Inuit problems, home rule, and so on. Berthelsen lists Amandus Petrussen (b. 1927); Jens Poulsen (b. 1929); Kristian Olsen, aaju (b. 1942)—his novel style is like that of an essayist and chronicler; Aqqaluk Lynge (b. 1947), Jens Geisler (b. 1951); Aqigssiaq Møller (b. 1939); Ole Korneliussen (b. 1947)—his poetry searches especially for "identity"; Hans Anthon Lynge (b. 1945), who produced the novel *Seqajuk* (The Useless or Indifferent) in 1976, the first real attempt to write social criticism in the form of a novel. Perhaps this last is the culmination of the seed sown by Storch.

One more influence on Greenlandic literature, but one difficult to evaluate, is translation. Some of the above authors have translated, but mostly from the Danish. But there are many translations by those who have composed no original works in Greenlandic. Berthelsen, in his 1978 article in *Bogen om Grønland* mentions translations of H. C. Andersen,* Johannes V. Jensen,* Bjørnstjerne

Bjørnson,* Selma Lagerlöf,* William Heinesen,* and Halldór Laxness* in Scandinavian literature and Nevil Shute, Howard Pyle, A. Maclean, David Howarth, and Lloyd Douglas among those from outside Scandinavia. But the non-Greenlander will notice that the works by these authors are often not their most important (as judged in their homelands), and they are often condensed or truncated, as was Rasmussen's translation of his own work. Of course, some of the translations are via the Danish. So far no pattern has developed as to the choice of works translated. Perhaps Greenlanders do prefer action to ideas, but there is no common "message" in the translated works. There has been no survey to show which works, by which authors, or what portions of which works are chosen.

Since 1971, as a final section in *Dansk Bogfortegnelse*, there has appeared *Grønlandsk Bogfortegnelse*, which cites translations. From 1971 through 1982, the following main translations have appeared (omitting Danish and children's and religious books): Laxness's *Gerpla*, Somerset Maugham's *The Trembling of a Leaf*, Nevil Shute's *Chequer Board*, Alexandre Dumas's *Count of Monte Cristo* (from Danish) in two volumes, Leon Uris's *Exodus* (four volumes), Harriet Beecher Stowe's *Uncle Tom's Cabin* (from a truncated Danish translation), Alistair Maclean's *Night Without End*, Jack London's *Story of Keesh* (from the Danish), Colin Forbes's *Target Five*, and S. E. Hinton's *The Outsiders*. None of the translators of these works are mentioned by Berthelsen, except for Pavia Petersen, who translated Dumas.

In summary, in 1942 Berthelsen, in his article "Hvad man læser i Grønland?" (in *Aarskrift Det Grønlandske Selskab*), calculated there were only about 5,700 pages all told in Greenlandic and that the number of Greenlandic books was growing at a rate of forty to fifty books a year. These totals have risen appreciably, even though bilingual and Danish books still outnumber those in Greenlandic alone.

Finally, there is the question, what is Greenlandic about Greenlandic literature. Of course, there is the language, which has such a compressed structure that a single syllable inserted in a word often requires a whole phrase in translation into an Indo-European language. Naturally the lexicon, despite borrowed words, can contain only Greenlandic forms. Rasmussen is quoted in the introduction to the trilingual *Kâgssagssuk* (p. 9); "This gift of rendering life and thoughts with a decidedly national colouring is disappearing now that the evolution has caused an entirely new civilization to be engrafted into the people." Thus, Greenlandic literature may become localistic and otherwise a pale but indistinct European imitation.

However, there is one group, the Tûkak' Theater, founded in 1975 in Holstebro, Denmark, and now based in Lemvig, Denmark. This group—through song, dance, drums, and (near) masks (including sticks in the mouth and paint on faces)—is trying to bridge the gap or mix both old and new. Especially their performances of *Inuit, Nattoralik* (The Eagle), and *Kattutta* (Let's Unite) exhibit merging of the oldest notions of the Inuit and the problems of the changing modern life. These performances have been enthusiastically received in Europe, Canada, and the United States, especially among Native Americans. Perhaps their programs and interpretations will help Greenlandic authors find a way to produce a truly distinctive literature incorporating pre-literary concepts and ways of thinking and yet to deal more than adequately with changes.

REFERENCES

Bergsland, Knut, *A Grammatical Outline of the Eskimo Language of West Greenland* (Oslo, 1955); Berthelsen, Christian, *Grønlands Litteratur. En kommentaret antologi* (Copenhagen, 1983); Berthelsen, Christian, "Grønlands litteratur"[title varies], in *Bogen om Grønland* (Copenhagen, 1962, 1968, 1970, 1976, 1978); Berthelsen, Christian, "Hvad Man Laeser i Grønland," in *Aarsskrift Det Grønlandske Selskab* (1942); Gad, Finn, *History of Greenland*, trans. Gordon C. Bowden, 2 vols. (Montreal, 1970, 1973); Holtved, Erik, *The Polar Eskimos' Language and Folklore*, in *Meddelelser om Grønland* (Copenhagen, 1951); Nielsen, Frederik, "Knud Rasmussen." *Grønland* 6, 7 (1970); Ostermann, H., ed., *Knud Rasmussen's Posthumous Notes on the Life and Doings of the East Greenlanders in Olden Times*, in *Meddelelser om Grønland* 109 (1936); *Report of the Fifth Thule Expedition, 1921–1924*, V; VII.1,2; VIII; IX.2,3 (Copenhagen, 1927–1952); Rosendahl, Philip, ed., *Kâgssagssuk* (Copenhagen, 1967); Schultz-Lorentzen, C. W., "The Intellectual Culture of the Greenlanders," in *Greenland*, ed. Kaj Birket-Smith et al., vol. 2 (Copenhagen, 1929); Thalbitzer, William, "Grønlandsk Litteraturhistorie," in *Grønlands Bogen*, ed. Kaj Birket-Smith et al. (Copenhagen, 1950).

John Allee

Isaksson, Ulla. Swedish novelist and playwright, b. 12 June 1916, Stockholm.

Isaksson began her literary career with a series of rather conventional religious novels. With *Ytterst i havet* (1950; Furthest Out on the Sea), a compassionate portrayal of a pastor who leaves his faith, she made a noted break with her literary and religious past. In this novel, Isaksson had already defined many of the major themes of her later works.

Isaksson's writing has often been compared to that of the novelist Lars Ahlin* for her attention to the problems of the "little people," her sensitivity, and the religious and moral tone of her work.

Isaksson's strength as the explorer of the minute surfaces of everyday reality and her ability to enter into the lives of her characters have been noted by many critics. She describes people in situations where, on the surface, rationality and respectability rule, from the summery island paradise of *Paradistorg* (1977; Paradise Square), the quintessence of Swedish summer with all its loving rituals, to the upper-class bourgeois surroundings of Christian Dettow in *De två saliga* (1962; *The Blessed*, 1970). Yet, behind the facade of this deceptively well ordered universe, momentous events take place; for many of Isaksson's protagonists are people who find themselves in extreme situations: in total spiritual emptiness, unable to give or receive love, shattered by mental illness, or tormented by an overpowering sense of guilt. Only rarely does Isaksson allow for the moment of grace.

Most of Isaksson's works have a clear woman's perspective, from *Kvinnohuset* (1952; House of Women), the story of a women's collective for which Isaksson won *Svenska Dagbladet's* literature prize in 1952, to *Paradistorg*. Her register spans such diverse characters as the aging beauty Helen in *Klänningen* (1959; The Dress), terrified at the emptiness that is engulfing her, to the emancipated woman physician Katha in *Paradistorg*, whose lifestyle for all its openness and tolerance freezes out the emotional resources that she needs to relate to her own child.

Through portrayals of mother-child relationships like those in *Paradistorg*, Isaksson illustrates what she sees as the dilemma of a society in which changing attitudes have led to the abandonment of old beliefs and family structures. According to the author herself, her works are not to be contributions on one side or the other in a political and social debate. She offers no suggestions for social remedies; instead she ponders the implications of such a change for the behavior of individuals and for basic human relationships.

FURTHER WORKS

Trädet (1940); *I denna natt* (1942); *Av krukmakarens hand* (1945); *Dödens faster* (1954); *Dit du icke vill* (1956); *Nära livet* (1958); *Jungfrukällan* (1959); *Våra torsdagar* (1964); *Klockan* (1966); *Amanda eller den blå spårvagnen* (1969); *Elin Wägner*, with Erik H. Linder, 2 vols. (1977–1980).

                                                                                       Rose-Marie G. Oster

REVIEWS

"Kvinnohuset," a review, *Books Abroad*, 28.1 (1954); "Dit du icke vill," a review, *Books Abroad* 31.4 (1957); "De två saliga," a review, *Books Abroad* 38.2 (1964).

J

Jacobsen, Jens Peter. Danish novelist and poet, b. 7 April 1847, Thisted, d. 30 April 1885, Thisted.

Jacobsen, who was the son of a prosperous Jutland merchant, was educated as a natural scientist. After a religious crisis in his youth, from which he emerged as an unbeliever, he fell under the influence of Charles Darwin's theory of evolution, and in the 1870s he translated Darwin's two main works into Danish. In histories of Danish literature Jacobsen is traditionally listed with Georg Brandes* and the writers of the Modern Breakthrough, a realistic-naturalistic movement in Scandinavian literature. The independent Jacobsen was not, however, a slavish follower of Brandes's initial literary program. In 1871 Brandes had urged Scandinavian writers to "take problems up for debate," and thereby prove that they were "modern," abreast of the new literary trends on the European continent. But this pragmatic approach to literature did not appeal to the lyrical-psychological Jacobsen. In a letter of 1880 he wrote: "I am too aesthetic in the good-bad sense of the word to be interested in the kind of literature where problems are said to be taken up for debate, while, in fact, they are only postulated to be solved; this applies both to the right and to the left."

In spite of his limited literary output, Jacobsen was one of the major writers in nineteenth-century Danish literature. He was a naturalist with a nostalgia for romanticism, a stylistic perfectionist who recalls Gustave Flaubert in France. His fame rests on two novels: *Marie Grubbe* (1876; *Marie Grubbe: A Lady of the Seventeenth Century*, 1917, 1952, 1975) and *Niels Lyhne* (1880; *Niels Lyhne*, 1919, 1967), six novellas, and a collection of highly original poetry. Both *Marie Grubbe* and *Niels Lyhne* are penetrating psychological novels, partly naturalistic, partly lyrical in style. Both show a "falling curve" kind of composition. *Marie Grubbe*, which is based loosely on historical facts, traces the gradual debasement of the young Danish noblewoman Marie Grubbe through a series of relationships with men who are unworthy of her. But at the end of the novel the strong-willed

Marie is not defeated by reality, but resigned to it. The style of this historical novel is highly ornate and synthetic in Jacobsen's ambitious attempt to reconstruct the language of the seventeenth century. In the pessimistic *Niels Lyhne*, on the other hand, Niels Lyhne, ineffectual dreamer and impotent poet, is defeated by reality. He is one of the many fantasts in Danish literature. He fails in everything he attempts: literary creativity, love relationships, idealistic atheism. At the end of the novel, when his child is dying, the freethinking Niels breaks down and prays to God for help, to no avail. After this philosophical defeat, as he considers it, he is a nonperson, a vegetable. He has lost his identity and escapes into the army where he is killed in the Dano-Prussian War of 1864. Although the style of *Niels Lyhne* today seems mannered and artificial in places, especially in some of the dialogues, the novel still impresses by frequent stylistic beauty and by Jacobsen's knowledge of female psychology. His women—Edele Lyhne, Bartholine Lyhne, Mrs. Boye, and Fennimore—are almost more interesting than the main character. What is particularly impressive is the variety in the portrayal of character. They all seem convincingly feminine, but they are very different from one another. Another feature in both *Marie Grubbe* and *Niels Lyhne* that still commands respect today is the author's intellectual honesty: he describes life as he sees it; he does not cheat.

The only one of Jacobsen's major works that ends happily is the novella *Mogens* (1872; *Mogens, and Other Stories*, 1926, 1972, 1977). The main reason for its optimism is probably the fact that it was written before the onset of Jacobsen's grave illness, tuberculosis, in 1873. His life from 1873 to his death in 1885 was a hopeless struggle against illness and despondency. Most of his major works were written during the last twelve years of his life, and most of them are pessimistic. Jacobsen's pessimism finds its most pregnant, philosophical expression in the celebrated poem "Arabesque" (1874; "Arabesque. For a sketch by Michelangelo," 1972). In an almost Schopenhauerian manner, human beings in this gloomy work are seen as helpless slaves to forces of nature over which they have no control. They are goaded on to continue a painful existence by blind passions that they cannot resist. The "will to life" is a mindless force that desires only one thing: more life. Since, according to Jacobsen, there is more pain than pleasure in life, the result is misery—from generation to generation, until time runs out. Several others of his best-known poems reveal a similar pessimism, as do such novellas as "Pesten i Bergamo" (1881; "The Plague in Bergamo," 1923, 1972) and "To Verdener" (1879; "Two Worlds," 1926). The novella "Fru Fønss" (1882; "Mrs. Fønss," 1928), Jacobsen's last completed work, takes a more balanced view of the pleasure-pain problem, in admitting that happiness, too, exists in life.

In the history of the Danish novel and in the development of Danish prose style, Jacobsen occupies an important position. With his scientific training and Darwinian orientation, he is the first naturalistic novelist in Danish literature. His philosophy is pessimistic, but the pessimism is tempered by compassion and tolerance. Jacobsen is a profoundly humane writer. His style is very sensuous, at times sensual, extremely sensitive in its descriptions of colors and scents. It is not without its mannerisms and pitfalls, especially in Jacobsen's occasionally excessive use of compound color adjectives. (In a review of *Niels Lyhne* Georg Brandes wrote: "There are five hundred adjectives too many in the book.") Nevertheless, no perceptive reader can help falling under the spell of the almost hypnotic style of *Marie Grubbe* and *Niels Lyhne*. In Denmark the style had a strong impact on such writers as Herman Bang,* Harald Kidde,* and Johannes Jørgensen,* in Norway on Tryggve Andersen*; in Sweden on Per Hallström and Hjalmar Söderberg.* In Germany, where Jacobsen is well known and greatly admired, Rainer Maria Rilke for many years led a regular cult to him. In the United States and Great Britain Jacobsen is known mainly by a small group of literati and college students taking courses on Scandinavian literature. He deserves to be better known in the English-speaking world.

FURTHER WORKS

Samlede Værker, ed. Fredrik Nielsen, 4 vols. (1972–1974).

FURTHER TRANSLATIONS

Book of Danish Verse, comp. Oluf Friis (1922, 1976); *A Second Book of Danish Verse,* trans. Charles W. Stork (1947, 1968); *Anthology of Danish Literature,* ed. P. M. Mitchell and F. J. Billeskov-Jansen (1972); *The Royal Guest,* ed. P. M. Mitchell and Kenneth H. Ober (1977).

REFERENCES

Arestad, Sverre, "J. P. Jacobsen's *Niels Lyhne,*" in *Scandinavian Studies,* ed. Carl F. Bayerschmidt and Erik J. Friis (Seattle, 1965); Gustafson, Alrik, "Toward Decadence: Jens Peter Jacobsen," in his *Six Scandinavian Novelists* (Princeton, N.J., 1940, 1968, 1969); Ingwersen, Niels, "Problematic Protagonists: *Marie Grubbe* and *Niels Lyhne,*" in *The Hero in Scandinavian Literature,* ed. John M. Weinstock and Robert T. Rovinsky (Austin, 1975); Jensen, Niels Lyhne, *Jens Peter Jacobsen* (Boston, 1980); Madsen, Børge Gedsø, "J. P. Jacobsen Reconsidered." *American-Scandinavian Review* 50.3 (1962); Nielsen, Frederik, *J. P. Jacobsen: Digteren og Mennesket* (Copenhagen, 1953); Vosmar, Jørgen, *J. P. Jacobsens Digtning* (Copenhagen, 1984).

Børge Gedsø Madsen

Jacobsen, Jørgen-Frantz. Faroese novelist and essayist, writing in Danish, b. 29 November 1900, Tórshavn, d. 24 March 1938, Vejlefjord.

At the age of sixteen Jacobsen went to study at Sorø Academy, then moved to Copenhagen to study history and French. In 1922 he developed tuberculosis, which led to his early death. Meanwhile, right from his student days he devoted his energies to working for a degree of Faroese independence, while employed as a journalist on the newspaper *Politiken.*

In 1927 Jacobsen published *Danmark og Færøerne* (Denmark and the Faroes), a political work analyzing the historical relationship between the two countries. The patriotism that inspired this book also lay behind his later *Færøerne, Natur* *og Folk* (1936; The Faroes, Countryside and People), a topographical and cultural description of the Faroes in which Jacobsen's journalistic gifts are transformed into poetry as well as information. A selection of his newspaper articles, edited by Christian Matras,* was published in 1953 under the title of *Nordiske Kronikker* (Nordic Features), the most famous of them being the intensely poetical "Den yderste kyst" (*The Farthest Shore*, 1965), an enchanted description of the north-ernmost point of the island of Streymoy, the inaccessible area around Sjeyndir, which is raised to the status of a symbol.

Jacobsen's fame is based principally on his one novel *Barbara* (1939; *Barbara*, 1948), which was published posthumously, with a few minor additions by William Heinesen* to put the unfinished manuscript into publishable form. Based on an eighteenth-century legend, "Beinta," about a woman who causes the death of her first two husbands and the downfall of the third, this is the poetical presentation of a woman of great charm and sweetness who attracts both devotion and resentment, and drives her third husband, the well-intentioned but naïve Pastor Poul, demented. She is incapable of constancy, devoid of any real ethical sense, and she follows her erotic impulses with no thought for their consequences and no understanding of what she causes. She has been said to represent im-mediacy, an untamed life force, a demonic urge. The setting of the novel is described with a historian's sense of accuracy as well as a novelist's insight.

Thanks to this novel, which contains a notable personal element, Jacobsen stands as one of the most internationally known Scandinavian writers of his generation, a central figure in the history of the novel in Denmark in the twentieth century, and a figure almost of veneration in the Faroe Islands.

REFERENCES

Brønner, Hedin, "Jørgen-Frantz Jacobsen and *Barbara.*" *American-Scandinavian Review* 61.1 (1973); Heinesen, William, *Det dyrebare liv. Jørgen-Frantz Jacobsen i strejflys af hans breve.* (Copenhagen, 1958); Heinesen, William, "Jørgen-Frantz Jacobsen," in *Danske digtere i det 20. århundrede*, vol. 2, ed. Frederik Nielsen and Ole Restrup (Copenhagen, 1966); Matras, Christian, "Jørgen-Frantz Jacobsen," in *Gyldendal's Julebog* (Copenhagen, 1941); Matras, Christian, "Jørgen-Frantz Jacobsen, Writer and Friend," in *Welcome to the Faroes* 9 (1975).

W. Glyn Jones

Jacobsen, Rolf. Norwegian poet, b. 8 March 1907, Oslo.

Although a city dweller most of his life, Jacobsen spent much of his childhood in rural Solør, and his poetry is above all an expression of the relationship between nature and urban civilization. Using the practical vocabulary of a mech-anized world, Jacobsen was initially hailed as the poet of modern technology. While the individual's sense of isolation amid the tumult of the city occasionally shines through, the poems of the 1930s fairly quiver with excitement about urban life. Turbines, asphalt, and neon signs are seen not in opposition to the organic world, but as a positive and natural expression of human potential.

After World War II Jacobsen becomes more skeptical of technology's promise. He often paints rich and unique portraits of nature quite apart from human culture in a conscious effort to obtain distance from the holocaust. Many poems from the 1950s and 1960s focus on small or forgotten things that take on symbolic significance, and an undertone of pessimism is heard. From *Stillheten etterpå* (1965; *Silence Afterwards*, 1985) and throughout the 1970s Jacobsen's poetry grows increasingly critical of all aspects of consumer society and a sense of hopelessness becomes pervasive. The poet's personal concern with aging and death is also a prominent theme in the later collections, culminating in *Tenk på noe annet* (1979; Think about Something Else). Here Jacobsen also presents impressions from his travels in the United States.

Stylistically, Jacobsen's development marks the progression from symbolism to New Simplicity. From the beginning many of his poems could be called "thing poems:" objects are personified with an empathy ranging from affection to abhorrence and on a scale of seriousness from pathos to playful humor and irony. Like other modernists, Jacobsen found traditional poetic language and forms incapable of expressing contemporary reality. He abandoned rhyme and classical meters and experimented with syntax and word associations. His main interest is in capturing images, though most of his poems contain a philosophical or political message as well.

Jacobsen's influence on young writers of the *Profil* generation contributed to his lasting popularity in Norway, and his poetry has been widely translated.

FURTHER WORKS

Jord og jern (1933); *Fjerntog* (1951); *Vrimmel* (1953); *Hemmelig liv* (1954); *Sommeren i gresset* (1956); *Brev til lyset* (1960); *Headlines* (1969); *Pass for dørene, dørene lukkes* (1972); *Samlede dikt* (1973); *Pusteøvelse* (1975); *Nattåpent* (1985).

TRANSLATIONS

Lines Review 55–56 (1976); *Twenty Poems* (1977); *Scandinavian Review* 69.4 (1981); *Scandinavian Review* 70.4 (1982); *South Dakota Review* 21.1 (1983).

REFERENCES

Bly, Robert, "What Norwegian Poetry Is Like." *Sixties* 10 (1968); Grinde, Olav, "Interview with Rolf Jacobsen." *South Dakota Review* 21.1 (1983); Naess, Harald, "The Poetry of Rolf Jacobsen." *American-Scandinavian Review* 62.3 (1974).

Frankie Shackelford

Jæger, Frank. Danish poet, novelist, short story writer, and essayist, b. 19 June 1926, Frederiksberg, d. 4 July 1977, Elsinore.

Jæger was educated as a librarian, but from 1950 he was able to live from writing. He briefly coedited the literary periodical *Heretica*. Jæger also translated numerous literary works into Danish, especially from French and German. He received some ten literary awards.

Jæger lived in Farum from 1948 until 1954, on Langeland from 1954 to 1970, and in Elsinore from 1970 until his death. The tenor of Jæger's works differs in each of these periods: in his Farum works, a more optimistic, lyric poetry and fantastic, surrealistic prose predominate; during his Langeland period, a somber, disquieting, and erotic mood settles over his poetry, and his prose grows more realistic; the Elsinore period is one of reflection, almost resignation, in which essays and shorter, realistic prose works prevail.

His most buoyant Farum-period poems appear in *Dydige digte* (1948; Virtuous Poems) and *De 5 aarstider* (1950; The Five Seasons). The poems of *Tyren* (1953; The Bull) and the autobiographical prose fantasy *Den unge Jægers lidelser* (1953; The Sufferings of Young Jæger) both flavored with a dash of the absurd, confront the themes of illusion versus reality and the power of the erotic. The novel *Iners* (1950; Iners) transcends the idyllic and explores the surreal, the grotesque, and the demonic.

The short stories of *Kapellanen og andre historier* (1957; The Curate and Other Stories) are grounded firmly in realism and contain some of Jæger's finest narrative prose. Those of *Danskere: Tre fortællinger af fædrelandets historie* (1966; Danes: Three Narratives from the History of the Fatherland) raise unsettling questions about the place of art in life and expose a dark and forbidding aspect of the erotic. Jæger's Langeland poetry is more brooding and more sensual than that of the Farum years. Symptomatic of this tendency is the title poem of *Idylia* (1967; Idylia) in which unrestrained eroticism threatens human existence.

The short novel *Døden i skoven* (1970; Death in the Forest) represents a transition to the Elsinore period. A realistic narrative, it articulates a crisis in human relationships and adumbrates the problems of the artist; yet it contains little of the angst of the works which immediately preceded it. *Døden i skoven* emanates a quiescent fatalism. Absent from the stories of *Provinser* (1972; Provinces) as well as from the stories and essays of *Udsigt til Kronborg* (1976; View of Kronborg), are the surrealism, the grotesqueness, and the undercurrent of despair that often suffuse Jæger's earlier works. In Jæger's last years, the uncomplicated aspects of life seemed to be most meaningful to the author. Jæger published only occasional poems in Elsinore.

Unlike many of his contemporaries, Jæger never became socially engaged. One of Denmark's most versatile writers, he chose to write in an individual instead of a societal context; his works assume a more personal idiom than those of most postwar Danish authors.

FURTHER WORKS

Morgenens trompet (1949); *Hverdagshistorier* (1951); *Tune* (1951); *19 Jægerviser* (1953); *Didrik* (1955); *Jomfruen fra Orleans. Jeanne d'Arc* (1955); *Havkarlens sange* (1956); *Til en følsom Veninde* (1957); *Hvilket postbud—en Due* (1958); *Velkommen Vinter* (1958); *Cinna, og andre digte* (1959); *Pastorale* (1963); *Pelsen* (1964); *Drømmen om en Sommerdag* (1965); *Naive rejser* (1968); *Der er en Verden også i Verona* (1969); *Alvilda* (1969); *Den, som ingen holder tilbage* (1970); *Provinser* (1972); *S* (1973); *J.A.P.* (1973); *Hvor er Ulla-Katrine?* (1974); *Miraklernes bog* (1977).

TRANSLATIONS

The Devil's Instrument, and Other Danish Stories, comp. S. Holm (1971); *Scandinavian Review* 64.3 (1976); *Contemporary Danish Poetry,* ed. Line Jensen et al. (1977); *Orbis* 27/28 (1977); *Mundus Artium* 14 (1984).

REFERENCES

Baggesen, Søren, "Om Frank Jægers Dit Land erobret," in *Analyser af moderne dansk lyrik,* vol. 1 (Copenhagen, 1976); Bjørnvig, Thorkild, *Virkeligheden er til* (Copenhagen, 1973); Brovst, Bjarne Nielsen, *Frank Jægers forfatterskab* (Copenhagen, 1977); Harvig, Steen, *Frank Jæger* (Copenhagen, 1974); Holm, Sven, "Frank Jæger," in *Danske digtere i det 20. århundrede,* vol. 3. ed. Torben Brostrøm and Mette Winge (Copenhagen, 1982); Hugus, Frank, "The Dilemma of the Artist in Selected Prose Works of Frank Jæger." *Scandinavian Studies* 47.1 (1975); Hugus, Frank, "Frank Jæger's Defeated Protagonists." *Scandinavian Studies* 54 (1982); Maelsaeke, Dirk van, *The Strange Essence of Things* (London, 1977); Paludan, Jakob, *Draabespil* (Copenhagen, 1971); Skou-Hansen, Tage, *Det midlertidige fællesskab* (Copenhagen, 1972).

Frank Hugus

Järnefelt, Arvid. Finnish novelist, b. 16 November 1861, Pulkova, Russia, d. 27 December 1932, Helsinki.

The Järnefelt family was highly gifted. Järnefelt's father was governor of the Finnish province of Kuopio, where the writer Minna Canth* was airing her advanced social views. Järnefelt's Russian mother gathered around her a salon of talented young writers, including the important novelist Juhani Aho.* One brother, Armas, became a distinguished conductor, another, Eero, a painter. Järnefelt's sister Aino married the composer Jean Sibelius.

Järnefelt became something of a classic with his first novel, *Isänmaa* (1893; The Fatherland), a realistic work about student life and the growth of Finnish nationalism at a time when Finland was restless under Russian rule. He did not, however, become a "national" writer. Instead, he became a convinced Tolstoyan, defending the exploited in social questions, and bitterly criticizing the then-powerful Lutheran church in Finland. Like Leo Tolstoy, some of whose works Järnefelt translated into Finnish, he carried his teachings into practical life, trying to earn his living as a cobbler, a smith, and a small farmer. He was often doubtful about the value of his literary work, feeling that it was only a subsidiary element in his life.

His novels and short stories are notable for their ethical quality, their depth, and their sincere and open self-searching. He became a kind of conscience for Finnish literature. In his old age, Järnefelt made an impressive comeback with two major novels. Of these, *Vanhempieni romaani* (3 vols., 1928–1930; The Novel of My Parents), which is partly memoirs, is the best remembered today.

Järnefelt's principle was truth. He believed that the artist must remain faithful to his inner vision, and must reject materialism. The fact that his selected works were republished in 1953 is in some measure proof that his teachings are not forgotten in Finland.

FURTHER WORKS

Heräämiseni (1894); *Ihmiskohtaloja* (1895); *Ateisti* (1895); *Puhtauden ihanne* (1897); *Maria* (1897); *Evankeliumin alku* (1898); *Matkaltani Venäjällä ja käynti Leo Tolstoin luona* (1899); *Samuel Croëll* (1899); *Veljekset* (1900); *Helena*, 2 vols. (1902); *Orjan oppi* (1902); *Kuolema* (1903); *Elämän meri* (1904); *Maaemon Lapsia* (1905); *Maa kuuluu kaikille* (1907); *Veneh'ojalaiset*, 2 vols. (1909); *Tiitus* (1910); *Manon Roland* (1913); *Hiljaisuudessa* (1913); *Kallun kestit* (1914); *Valtaset* (1915); *Onnelliset* (1917); *Kirkkopuheet* (1917); *Kirjeitä sukupuolikysymyksestä* (1924); *Greeta ja hänen herransa* (1925); *Teoksia*, 5 vols., (1925–1927); *Huligaani ynnä muita kertoelmia* (1926); *Kuolema* (1927); *Minun Marttani* (1927); *Lalli* (1933); *Valitut teokset* (1953).

REFERENCES

Häkli, Pekka, *Arvid Järnefelt ja hänen lähimaailmansa* (Porvoo, 1955); Kolehmainen, John I., "When Finland's Tolstoy Met His Russian Master." *American Slavic and East European Review* 16 (1957); Nokkala, A., *Tolstoilaisuus Suomessa* (Helsinki, 1958).

Philip Binham

Jakobsdóttir, Svava. Icelandic novelist, playwright, and short story writer, b. 4 October 1930, Neskaupsstaður. Member of the Icelandic Parliament 1971–1979.

Jakobsdóttir has published three collections of short stories, *12 konur* (1965; 12 Women), *Veizla undir grjótvegg* (1967; Party under a Stone Wall), and *Gefið hvort öðru* (1982; Each Given to the Other . . .), as well as the novel *Leigjandinn* (1969; The Roomer).

Woman and her role in society is the main theme in Jakobsdóttir's writings. Her heroine is often a middle-class housewife existing solely for her home and family, completely dependent on her husband, living in total isolation, and utterly lacking in self-realization or sense of identity. Her women often do not have names, and their interests and values are purely materialistic. "A Story for Children" ("Saga handa börnum"), from the collection *Veizla undir grjótvegg*, is a rather typical example of Jakobsdóttir's narrative style. Using both irony and satire, together with some rather grotesque effects, or black humor, it is reminiscent both of a Grimms' fairy tale and the chilling short stories of Villy Sørensen, although it speaks its powerful message with its own voice.

Five plays by Jakobsdóttir have been performed in Iceland, four on stage: *Hvað er í blýhólknum* (1970; What's in the Lead Pipe); *Friðsæl veröld* (1974; A Peaceful World), a one-act play about abortion; *Æskuvinir* (1976; Childhood Friends), about a woman in a man's world and a small nation against the whole world; and *Lokaæfing* (1983; Final Rehearsal), which had its premiere in the National Theater of the Faroe Islands. The fifth play was written for the radio *Í takt við tímana* (1980; In Step with Time) and deals with double standard in a modern marriage.

FURTHER WORKS

Smásögur (1987); *Gunnlaðar saga* (1987).

TRANSLATIONS

Sixty-five Degrees 2.4 (1968); *Atlantica and Iceland Review* 7.4 (1969); *Short Stories of Today*, comp. Alan Boucher (1972); *Icelandic Short Stories*, comp. Evelyn Scherabon Firchow (1974); *Scandinavian Review* 64.1 (1976); *Scandinavian Studies* 49.2 (1977); *Scandinavian Review* 68.4 (1980); *Women's Studies International* 4 (1984); *Icelandic Canadian* (Summer 1987).

REFERENCES

Firchow, Evelyn S., "Women's Predicament: Svava Jakobsdóttir Interviewed." *Icelandic Writing Today* (September, 1982); Magnússon, Sigurður A., "The Icelandic Short Story: Svava Jakobsdóttir," *Scandinavian Studies* 49.2 (1977).

Ingrid Claréus

Jakobsson, Jökull. Icelandic playwright and novelist, b. 14 September 1933, Neskaupsstaður, d. 25 April 1978, Reykjavík.

The son of a leading clergyman, who was also a writer, and brother of Svava Jakobsdóttir,* Jakobsson moved with his family to Canada. Back in Iceland, Jakobsson graduated from the Reykjavík Grammar school in 1953, studied theater and literature in Vienna, turned to journalism, and later lived exclusively by his writing; he was also a popular radio personality, and a translator of plays. During his short life Jakobsson was a prolific writer, leaving ten full dramas, several short radio plays, six television plays, six novels, a collection of short stories, and three travel memoirs from the Greek archipelago and the isles around Iceland.

As one of the youngest debutants in the history of Icelandic literature since Halldór Laxness,* Jakobsson wrote his first novel *Tæmdur Bikar* (1951; Bottoms Up) at age seventeen. By the age of twenty-six he had written four novels set in the 1950s about young people searching for meaning in life, intellectual as well as emotional. These novels had a mixed reception and are perhaps best viewed today as an earnest document of the uncertainty and rootlessness of those years. A collection of short stories, *Næturheimsókn* (1962; Night Visit), fared better. Here Jakobsson's mastery of style and language became apparent.

Jakobsson wrote a farce for the stage that showed some promise, but his breakthrough came with *Hart í bak* (1962; Hard a Port), a realistic as well as impressionistic play set in modern Reykjavík, describing a young man's break with the past and his surroundings, and search for a new approach to self-knowledge. Many think that the success of this play signals a new era in Icelandic playwriting; during the last twenty years a significant characteristic of Icelandic theater has been the success of new native plays.

Hart í bak was followed by a number of popular plays that established Jakobsson as a leading playwright. These dramas deal with people in different kinds of milieus in Reykjavík, torn between dream and reality, searching for identity. Since many of these pieces have only a few characters they can be labeled "chamber plays" (e.g., one of his best plays, *Dóminó*, 1972). With artistic playfulness the author toys with time, place, and roles, both sexual and social. Although Jakobsson admitted in an interview that Anton Chekhov and Harold Pinter were close to his heart, his dialogue has a very personal accent and color; he is a master of the subtext.

However, two of Jakobsson's plays reveal a different quality: *Kertalog* (1974; Candlelight), a grim, and yet very sensitive love story about youngsters in a lunatic asylum, and *Sonur skóarans og dóttir bakarans* (1978; The Song of Mylai), a committed play for a big cast, posing the big questions about personal conscience in a world that no longer knows any limits. Jakobsson died during the rehearsal of this last "major opus." Some works appeared posthumously: the novel *Skilaboð til Söndru* (1981; Message to Sandra, filmed in 1983), a television and chamber play *Í öruggri borg* (1980; In a Strong City), which combined the artistry of earlier chamber plays with the commitment of "Mylai," resulting in a condensed vision of a human race facing its own end.

Jakobsson's role in the new growth of Icelandic drama is most important, and his treatment of despair in lyrical and tender tones touches upon many of the most vital questions of modern man: his self-realization, his search for identity, his alienation, his insecurity in a complex world that is moving out of his reach. He is not an innovator of form for the sake of form, and the role changes in his plays are rooted in psychological or philosophical causes; that is, form is determined by content. His style is very personal, and his works have recently gained attention in other countries.

FURTHER WORKS

Ormar (1956); *Fjallið* (1958); *Dyr standa opnar* (1960); *Pókók* (1961); *Næturheimsókn* (1962); *Aðalfundur í jólasveinafélaginu* (1962); *Gullbrúðkaup* (1963); *Síðasta skip suður* (1964); *Knall* (1964); *Sjóleiðin til Bagdad* (1965; *The Seaway to Baghdad*, 1973); *Afmæli í kirkjugarðinum* (1965); *Tvö leikrit* (1965); *því miður, frú* (1966); *Dagbók frá Díafaní* (1967); *Suðaustan 14* (1967); *Herbergi til leigu* (1967); *Romm handa Rósalind* (1968); *Sumarið '37* (1968); *Frostrósir* (1970); *Nafnlaust leikrit* (1971); *Klukkustrengir* (1973); *Sálin í útlegð* (1974); *Herbergi 213, eða Pétur Mandólín* (1974); *Kalda borðið* (1974); *Hlæðu Magdalena hlæðu* (1975); *Feilnóta í fimmtu sinfóníunni* (1975); *Keramik* (1976); *Vandarhögg* (1980).

TRANSLATIONS

Short Stories of Today, comp. Alan Boucher (1972); *Modern Nordic Plays: Iceland,* ed. Erik J. Friis (1973).

Sveinn Einarsson

Jansson, Tove Maria. Finland-Swedish artist, novelist, and author of children's books, b. 9 August 1914, Helsinki.

The Moomintroll books and the Moomin comic strip became popular and widely translated after the birth of the Moomin world in 1945. In Jansson's best works, *Trollkarlens hatt* (1949; *Finn Family Moomintroll,* 1950), *Muminpappans bravader* (1950; *The Exploits of Moominpappa,* 1952), *Farlig midsommar* (1954; *Moominsummer Madness,* 1955), *Trollvinter* (1957; *Moominland Midwinter,*

1958), and the early comic strips, the text and black-and-white drawings form a carefully designed whole, similar to the blend of text and words in A. A. Milne's and Ernest H. Shepard's Winnie the Pooh books.

The species moomintroll look a little like graceful small white hippos and are in the center of the stories, represented by the bourgeois-bohemian Moomin family. Moominmamma with her voluminous black handbag is always ready to provide sandwiches for sudden expeditions to caves and mountains. Moominpappa's top hat signals his adventurous spirit, inherited by his only son Moomintroll. His best friend is Snufkin, a wanderer who turns south every winter when the moomintrolls turn in for their winter hibernation with their stomachs full of scratchy pine needles. Each book confronts a nature catastrophe, which the family and their many odd friends and acquaintances overcome through sheer luck and cooperation. The moomintrolls live in high, turretlike houses similar to the tiled fireplaces their ancestors once inhabited. The books are a humorous hymn to childhood and family life.

Since 1962 Jansson has resumed her painting, and furnished material for exploring the genesis of the moominworld in autobiographical short stories and essays. *Sommarboken* (1976; *The Summer Book*, 1977), about the friendship between a little girl and her very old grandmother, is an unsentimental description of the frailties of old age.

FURTHER WORKS

Småtrollen och den stora översvämningen (1945); *Kometjakten* (1946; *Comet in Moominland*, 1947); *Det osynliga barnet* (1962); *Solstaden* (1964; *Sun City*, 1977); *Pappan och havet* (1965; *Moominpappa at Sea*, 1977); *Bildhuggarens dotter* (1968; *The Sculptor's Daughter*, 1975); *Sent i november* (1970; *Moominvalley in November*, 1977); *Lyssnerskan* (1971); *Den farliga resan* (1977); *Dockskåpet och andra berättelser* (1978); *Skurken i Muminhuset* (1980); *Den ärliga bedragaren* (1982); *Stenåkern* (1984); *Resa med lätt bagage* (1987).

REFERENCES

Bargum, Marianne, "Tove Jansson: The Art of Travelling Light." *Books from Finland* 21.3 (1987); Fleisher, Frederic, and Boel Fleisher, "Tove Jansson and the Moomin Family," *American-Scandinavian Review* 51.1 (1963); Jones, W. Glyn, "Tove Jansson: My Books and Characters." *Books from Finland* 12.3 (1978); Jones, W. Glyn, *Tove Jansson* (Boston, 1984).

Margareta Mattsson

Jensen, Johannes Vilhelm. Danish poet and novelist, b. 20 January 1873, Farsø, d. 25 November 1950, Copenhagen.

Jensen studied medicine at the University of Copenhagen from 1893 to 1898. He traveled to the United States in 1896 and later, around the world in 1902–1903, to the Far East in 1912–1913, and to Egypt and Palestine in 1925–1926. Jensen was awarded the Nobel Prize in literature in 1944.

The balance between an extrovert, optimistic, and materialistic outlook determined by a Darwinian view of man as part of an evolutionary trend, and introvert, spiritual reflection that characterizes Jensen's major works, is not yet present in his youthful writings. The protagonists of *Danskere* (1896; Danes) and *Einar Elkær* (1898), two novels about students from the provinces and their confrontation with the modern metropolis, are obsessed by a paralyzing introspection that prevents them from establishing a healthy and instinctive rapport with life. Self-analysis remains a major problem in the two travelogues *Intermezzo* (1899) and *Skovene* (1904; The Woods) but is strongly rejected in *Den gotiske Renaissance* (1901; The Gothic Renaissance), an edited reprint of travel letters from Spain and the World Exhibit in Paris in 1900. This work glorifies the technological, expansive spirit of the Gothic, that is, Anglo-Saxon race, the fullest expression of which Jensen found in the American pragmatic way of life. The volume climaxes in Walt Whitman–inspired prose hymns to progress and technology.

It was Jensen's theory that the Gothic race had its origin in his home region, Himmerland. Its nature and people are portrayed in the short stories *Himmerlandsfolk* (1898; Himmerland People), and in the two collections *Himmerlandshistorier* (1904, 1910; Himmerland Stories). The early texts are marked by Jensen's preoccupation with the tragic meaninglessness of life and its end. Later stories containing masterful character studies rendered with satirical humor and irony, focus on man's stubborn fight against his sordid environment. This purely realistic trend is continued in the two novels *Madame D'Ora* (1904) and *Hjulet* (1905; The Wheel). These novels, set in the splendidly depicted milieus of New York and Chicago respectively, advocate modern scientific viewpoints as opposed to metaphysical speculation. They are, however, marred by stereotyped suspense effects and by grotesque character delineation based on Jensen's wish not to portray individuals but progressing stages in man's evolution. The United States also provides the setting for some of the stories in the three volumes *Singaporenoveller* (1907; Singapore Stories), *Lille Ahasverus* (1909; Little Ahasuerus), and *Olivia Marianne* (1915). However, most of these "exotic short stories" are localized to China and Java and owe their quality exclusively to the local setting and linguistic virtuosity. In their simplistic view of the life of the Europeans among the natives, they are an example of the strong influence Rudyard Kipling had on Jensen's early writings.

A renewal of Jensen's authorship had already taken place in 1900–1901 with the novel *Kongens Fald (The Fall of the King*, 1933), in which he manages to combine the extrovert and introvert elements into a mythic composition. The book can be read as a historical novel—the most significant in Danish literature—attacking the lack of power to act that Jensen perceived as a major component of Danish mentality. This passivity is exemplified by the Renaissance king Christian II and his companion, the mercenary Mikkel Thøgersen—like the protagonists of Jensen's first novels, unintegrated and thus barren personalities. But Jensen has departed from the traditional realistic novel form. He ignores both historical accuracy and psychological character delineation. Dream passages of exquisite beauty are blended with ruthlessly naturalistic scenes of violence and destruction into a magnificent, deeply pessimistic vision of man's inability to reach happiness; only death brings the desired peace.

This spiritual expansion of the perspective also characterizes Jensen's brief prose texts, *Myter* (Myths), which were published in eleven volumes between 1907 and 1944. In essays and sketches describing nature, animals, and journeys Jensen symbolically presents—usually with a concrete sense impression as his point of departure—his basic ideas: present reality is the source and final goal of all longing and a belief in the cyclic eternity of the revitalizing nature. All of Jensen's myths are based on his belief in the necessity of creating links to the most distant memories from the history of the human race in order to secure a harmonious development of man. Several of these myths laid the foundation for the six-volume novel *Den lange Rejse* (1908–1922; *The Long Journey*, 1923) that forms an evolutionary history of mankind and a scientific counterpart to the biblical legends. The challenge of nature is seen as the driving force of progress that brings about the transition from animal to man. A basic trait of the Nordic people—"the Gothic race"—is the dream about warmth and sun. This dream, which is Jensen's explanation of the religious sentiment, is expressed through a longing for distant places, for paradise, a longing that becomes embodied in the structures of the ship and the Gothic cathedral. The Viking migrations were a result of this longing, as was the voyage of the Goth, Columbus. His attempt to find legendary lands resulted, however, in the discovery of America, of reality, the possession of which is man's true task.

The contrast between longing and the firm belief in the bliss of the present moment also forms the major theme in Jensen's first poetry collection, *Digte* (1906; Poems; later enlarged eds. 1917, 1921, 1943, 1948), a milestone in the development of Danish lyric poetry. The most characteristic texts of the volume are a number of prose poems formed after Goethe's, Heinrich Heine's, and Walt Whitman's free verse but in their bold imagery linked to modern technology and the metropolis. Jensen's subsequent poetry collections are dominated by traditional verse meter or alliterating poems in the Old Norse style, praising the child, the woman as wife and mother, and Danish nature, sometimes in a most grandiose manner, sometimes with the deepest intimacy, melting together precise observation, vision, and reflection into a perfect artistic entity.

With the years Jensen's fictional writing decreased significantly. He turned to the feature article and the essay in order to popularize the Darwinian, evolutionary view of life. The content of the numerous essay collections, mainly about natural science, archeology, and anthropology, is often based on dubious scientific theories and deductions. Linguistically, Jensen turns from the lyrical expressiveness to a terse, matter-of-fact diction. But his stylistic mastery often breaks forth when he opens up for vast perspectives and unsuspected connections through his mythic technique.

Although insignificant as a scientist, Jensen was one of the greatest innovative spirits in Danish cultural life. The brilliantly captured and concisely sensed reportage in *Den gotiske Renaissance* became epoch-making for modern Danish journalism. This book was, on the whole, decisive in the turning away from French to Anglo-American culture that was characteristic of the first decades of the twentieth century in Denmark. Jensen was indeed unusually well informed about current events. His knowledge of American social and political conditions was unique. His familiarity with modern American literature made him the first to introduce Jack London, Frank Norris, and Ernest Hemingway in Scandinavia. In many respects Jensen marks a new direction in Danish literature: through his masculine but also fragile lyrical style, through his immensely precise power of observation as well as visionary perspectives, through his strong love for the microcosm in nature as well as dynamic international orientation, and finally through his ability to combine the present and eternity, reality and dream.

FURTHER WORKS

Myter og Jagter (1907); *Den ny Verden* (1907); *Nye Myter* (1910); *Myter* (1910); *Nordisk Aand* (1911); *Myter* (1912); *Rudyard Kipling* (1912); *Introduktion til vor Tidsalder* (1915); *Aarbog* (1916, 1917); *Johannes Larsen og hans Billeder* (1920); *Sangerinden* (1921); *Æstetik og Udvikling* (1923); *Aarstiderne* (1923); *Myter* (1924); *Hamlet* (1924); *Evolution og Moral* (1925); *Aarets Højtider* (1925); *Thorvaldsens Portrætbuster* (1926); *Verdens Lys* (1926); *Jørgine* (1926); *Dyrenes Forvandling* (1927); *Ved Livets Bred* (1928); *Aandens Stadier* (1928); *Retninger i Tiden* (1930); *Den jydske Blæst* (1931); *Form og Sjæl* (1931); *Paa danske Veje* (1931); *Pisangen* (1932); *Kornmarken* (1932); *Sælernes Ø* (1934); *Det Blivende* (1934); *Dr. Renaults Fristelser* (1935); *Gudrun* (1936); *Darduse* (1937); *Paaskebadet* (1937); *Jydske Folkelivsmalere* (1937); *Thorvaldsen* (1938); *Nordvejen* (1939); *Fra Fristaterne* (1939); *Gutenberg* (1939); *Mariehønen* (1940); *Mindets Tavle* (1941); *Vor Oprindelse* (1941); *Om Sproget og Undervisningen* (1942); *Kvinden i Sagatiden* (1942); *Folkeslagene i Østen* (1943); *Møllen* (1944); *Afrika* (1949); *Swift og Oehlenschläger* (1950); *Tilblivelsen* (1951).

FURTHER TRANSLATIONS

Book of Danish Verse, comp. Oluf Friis (1922, 1976); ; *The Waving Rye* (1958). *Denmark's Johannes V. Jensen*, ed. Marion L. Nielsen (1955); *Norseman* 16.6 (1958); *The Waving Rye* (1958).

REFERENCES

Andersen, Harry, *Studier i Johannes V. Jensens forfatterskab* (Copenhagen, 1972); Friis, Oluf, "Johannes V. Jensen." *Scandinavica* 1.2 (1962); Friis, Oluf, *Den unge Johannes V. Jensen*, 2 vols. (Copenhagen, 1974); Gelsted, Otto, *Johannes V. Jensen* (Copenhagen, 1938); Ingwersen, Niels, "America as Setting and Symbol in Johannes V. Jensen's Early Works." *Americana Norvegica* 3 (1971); Johannes, Frits, *Johannes V. Jensen. En bibliografi* (Copenhagen, 1933–1951); Marcus, Aage, "Johannes V. Jensen." *American-Scandinavian Review* 20.6–7 (1932); Nedergaard, Leif, *Johannes V. Jensen* (Copenhagen, 1968); Nielsen, Marion L., *Denmark's Johannes V. Jensen*, Utah Agricultural College Monograph Series 3 (1955); Rossel, Sven H., *Johannes V. Jensen* (Boston, 1984); Schiøttz-Christensen, Aage, *Om Sammenhængen i Johannes V. Jensens Forfatterskab*,

2nd. ed. (Copenhagen, 1969); Wamberg, N. B., *Johannes V. Jensen* (Copenhagen, 1961).

Sven H. Rossel

Jersild, Per Christian. Swedish novelist, b. 14 March 1935, Katrineholm.
Jersild grew up outside of Stockholm, began to write fiction as a teenager, but studied medicine and became a doctor in 1962. As assistant professor of social and preventive medicine and medical consultant to the National Government Employee Administration Board, Jersild absorbed information about hospitals and government bureaucracy to use in his fiction.

However, in his first novel, *Till varmare länder* (1961; To Warmer Lands), he uses letters to describe the one-sided love affair between an eccentric youth and his high school sweetheart. The sparse writing style and the quality of the fantastic in this novel typify some of Jersild's later writing. His breakthrough came with *Calvinols resa genom världen* (1965; Calvinol's Journey through the World), a novel that traverses time and history to tell the story of a charlatan.

More typical of Jersild's political and social satire is *Grisjakten* (1968; The Pig Hunt), in which we read the diary of a bureaucrat in charge of the extermination of a breed of pigs in a Swedish province. Jersild's fascination with bureaucratic language and its tendency to dehumanize individuals appears again in the military novel *Vi ses i song My* (1970; See You in Song My). The futuristic *Djurdoktorn* (1973; *The Animal Doctor*, 1975) shows a middle-aged female veterinarian trying, yet failing, to resist social and political pressures to conform. In *Barnens Ö* (1976; *Children's Island*, 1986), a young boy stays home alone one summer. He discovers the brutality and complexity of modern commercial society as he tries to support himself and keep his absence from summer camp hidden from his neighbors and his vacationing mother.

With *Babels hus* (1978; *The House of Babel*, 1987), a realistic description of one man's illness and death in a large modern hospital, Jersild became one of the most widely read authors in Swedish history. Turning again to the future and the fantastic, Jersild uses a brain in an aquarium as the narrator of *En levande själ* (1980; *A Living Soul*, 1988). Having its IQ increased for commercial purposes, the brain struggles to preserve its identity. This novel reaffirmed Jersild's concern with the relation between the individual and society, as does his next work, *Efter floden* (1982; *After the Flood*, 1986). In it, Jersild portrays the decimated and primitive society that might exist after a third world war and its resulting nuclear winter. This powerful and dark novel confirmed Jersild's position as one of Sweden's major contemporary authors.

FURTHER WORKS

Räknelära (1960); *Ledig lördag* (1963); *Prins Valiant och Konsum* (1966); *Drömpojken* (1970); *Uppror bland marsvinen* (1972); *Stumpen* (1973); *Den elektriska kaninen* (1974); *Gycklarnas Hamlet* (1980); *Professionella bekännelser* (1981); *Den femtionde frälsaren* (1984); *Geniernas återkomst* (1987).

FURTHER TRANSLATIONS

Modern Swedish Poetry in Translation, ed. Gunnar Harding and Anselm Hollo (1979); *Children's Literature* 9 (1981); *Swedish Book Review,* Suppl., special issue on P. C. Jersild (1983).

REFERENCES

Jersild, P. C., "Pro Patria." *Atlas—Magazine of the World Press* 2.4 (1961); Jersild, P. C., "My Bit of Sweden." *Sweden Now* 6.4 (1972); Lundquist, Åke, *Från Sextital till Åttital* (Stockholm, 1981); Nordwall-Ehrlow, Rut, *Människan som djur. En studie i PC Jersilds författarskap* (Lund, 1983); Shideler, Ross, "Dehumanization and the Bureaucracy in Novels by P. C. Jersild." *Scandinavica* 23.1 (1984); Shideler, Ross, "The Battle for the Self in P. C. Jersild's *En Levande Själ,*" *Scandinavian Studies* 56. 3 (1984); Shideler, Ross, Afterword, in P. C. Jersild, *Children's Island* (Lincoln, 1986); *Swedish Book Review,* Suppl. (1983) issue devoted to P. C. Jersild.

Ross Shideler

Jochumsson, Matthías. Icelandic poet, dramatist, translator, and journalist, b. 11 November 1835, Skógar in Þorskafjörður, d. 18 December 1920, Akureyri.

Jochumsson grew up as the son of a poor farmer in northwest Iceland, traveled to Copenhagen to learn about business, but studied languages as well as classical and modern literature under Steingrímur Thorsteinsson.* At the age of thirty he received his degree in theology in Reykjavík, and except for only a few years, he served as pastor in various churches around Iceland. In 1893 he traveled extensively in North America (one of eleven trips abroad), and from 1900 until his death his writing was supported by a pension from the Icelandic government.

Jochumsson's first literary success came in 1864 with the five-act play *Útilegumennirnir* (The Outlaws, revised as the even more popular *Skugga-Sveinn* in 1898). It treats a purely Icelandic situation and is rich in beautiful scenery and comic interludes, showing perhaps the influence of Friedrich Schiller's *Die Räuber* or similar stories fashionable in Denmark and Norway. Although Jochumsson wrote another five plays and produced fine translations of *Macbeth* (1874), *Hamlet* (1878), *Othello* (1882), and *Romeo and Juliet* (1887), it is as a lyric poet that he has made his lasting impact. The thematic breadth of Jochumsson's work is truly impressive. His lengthy narrative poem *Grettisljóð* (1897) displays his intimate familiarity with Icelandic literature and history, as do his historical eulogies (Snorri Sturluson,* Jón Arason, Hallgrímur Pétursson*). The numerous obituary pieces that Jochumsson has left behind show his rare ability to capture the individual personalities of his subjects (e.g., Guðbrandur Vigfússon), his nature poems paint large and majestic canvasses (e.g., "Hafísinn"), and his religious poems and hymns are often profound and inspired. His work is characterized by an uncommon mastery of the Icelandic language and originality of expression.

As a dramatist, Jochumsson is credited with having written the first romantic play in Iceland and helped to popularize the genre there. As a journalist, he influenced his countrymen as editor of the oldest Icelandic weekly (*Þjóðólfur*, 1874–1880) and of the biweekly, *Lýður* (1889–1891). As a poet, Jochumsson is considered by many as Iceland's finest in the second half of the nineteenth century. Few if any of his countrymen can match the quantity and versatility of his work, and as a hymnologist he ranks with Hallgrímur Pétursson as Iceland's greatest. His hymn "Ó, Guð vors lands" is known by all Icelanders today as their national anthem.

FURTHER WORKS

Ljóðmæli (1884); *Helgi hinn magri* (1890); *Chicago-för mín* (1893); *Hinn sanni þjóðvilji* (1898); *Vesturfararnir* (1898); *Jón Arason* (1900); *Aldamót* (1901); *Ljóðmæli*, 2 vols. (1902–1906); *Frá Danmörku* (1906); *Ferð um fornar stördvar* (1913); *Sögukaflar af sjálfum mér* (1922); *Bréf Matthíusar Jochumssonar* (1935); *Ljóðmæli* (1936).

TRANSLATIONS

Icelandic Lyrics, ed. Richard Beck (1930); *The North American Book of Icelandic Verse*, ed. Watson Kirkconnell (1930); *Icelandic Poems and Stories*, ed. Richard Beck (1943); *Northern Lights*, trans. Jakobina Johnson (1959); *An Anthology of Scandinavian Literature*, ed. Hallberg Hallmundsson (1965); *An Anthology of Icelandic Poetry*, ed. Eiríkur Benedikz (1969).

REFERENCES

Beck, Richard, *History of Icelandic Poets: 1800–1940* (Ithaca, 1950); Beck, Richard, "Matthías Jochumsson: Icelandic Poet and Translator." *Scandinavian Studies* 13 (1935).

Peter A. Jorgensen

Jökull Jakobsson. *See* Jakobsson, Jökull.

Jølsen, Ragnhild. Norwegian novelist, b. 28 March 1875, Enebakk, d. 28 January 1908, Enebakk.

Jølsen was the daughter of a landowner who lost the family estates through industrial speculation; her writings reflect both her affinity with deep-rooted traditions and her awareness of the problems of a new age. In her short and turbulent life she produced five works in as many years; works in which an intense romantic sensibility struggles with a harsh, sometimes cynical realism.

Jølsen's first three novels vividly evoke the demonic side of female sexuality; her heroines are torn between light and dark, between an acceptance of everyday reality and an urge toward a satanic eroticism. In *Ve's mor* (1903; Ve's Mother), faithful affection finally conquers enslavement to a sensual passion. However, darkness triumphs in *Rikka Gan* (1904), a Gothic novel set in 1800 in which the proud Rikka prostitutes herself for her family's sake—and throws away her own life. *Hollases krønike* (1906; Hollas's Chronicle) depicts an eighteenth-century village in which the fight between good and evil assumes mythical proportions, with Hollas as the devil himself. His opponent Angelica, defeated in love, yet finds the courage to start an independent life. Both humor and social criticism are more in evidence here, as they are in *Brukshistorier* (1908; Tales from Working Life), which portrays industrialization and its effect on the lives of the workers. Here mysticism has given way to a robust sympathy devoid of sentimentality.

Jølsen's works belong to the transitional period in Norwegian literature between the neoromanticism of the 1890s and the new realism of the 1900s; they reflect the changing literary climate as strongly as they do the conflicts in her own personality. Previously rather overlooked, she has recently been "rediscovered," and her importance as a turn-of-the-century figure and as a feminist writer has been reassessed.

FURTHER WORKS

Fernanda Mona (1905); *Efterladte arbeider* (1908).

TRANSLATIONS

Slaves of Love and Other Norwegian Short Stories, ed. James McFarlane (1982); *An Everyday Story*, ed. Katherine Hanson (1984).

REFERENCES

Nettum, Rolf Nyboe, "Romantikk og realisme i Ragnhild Jølsens forfatterskap." *Edda* 3 (1972); Tiberg, Antonie, *Ragnhild Jølsen i liv og digtning* (Kristiania, 1909).

Janet Garton

Joenpelto, Eeva (pseud. Autere, Eeva; Helle, Eeva). Finnish novelist, short story writer, and dramatist, b. 17 June 1921, Sammatti.

Joenpelto grew up in a middle-class family in the semi-rural town of Lohja, a prosperous industrial center in southwestern Finland with long historical traditions. After graduation from high school in 1940, Joenpelto studied at the College of Social Sciences. In addition to receiving numerous prestigious literary awards, she became a professor of the arts in 1980, and two years later in 1982, she was granted an honorary doctorate by the University of Helsinki.

Joenpelto displayed her great narrative talent already in her first novel, *Kaakerholman kaupunki* (1950; The Town of Kaakerholm), which describes the life of a working-class family in a small urban community. The initial impression was further confirmed by her second novel, *Veljen varjo* (1951; A Brother's Shadow), in which she examines the impact that the memory of a man who died in the war has on those that stood nearest him. It is, however, Joenpelto's next novel *Johannes vain* (1952; Just Johannes) that marks her real breakthrough. The novel focuses on the relationship between spiritual and material values. Johannes, a modest owner of a rural shop feels dissatisfied with his job and subsequently abandons it and his materialistic wife in order to live close to nature.

Similar conflicts of value and the question of how man's selfishness in various ways exacts its own revenge continue to occupy Joenpelto in her later works. In the related novels *Neito kulkee vetten päällä* (1955; A Maiden Walks on Waters) and *Kipinöivät vuodet* (1951; Sparkling Years), two of the most polished works of Joenpelto's early period, events take place in a farmhouse left between an expanding town and the receding countryside. The conflict of generations is often linked with the conflict between the old and new way of life in Joenpelto's works. Likewise, the contrast between the sexes is frequently present, her men being weak and the women strong and life-sustaining.

Alongside these works Joenpelto published a number of novels, among the best of which was a book about a dog, *Ralli* (1959). A new successful period in Joenpelto's career opened in 1974 with the novel *Vetää kaikista ovista* (A Draft from all the Doors). It was followed by three sequel volumes: *Kuin kekäle kädessä, Sataa suolaista vettä,* and *Eteisiin ja kynnyksille* (1976–1980; Like Holding a Red-Hot Coal, Raining Salt Water, and To the Doorsteps and the Porches). As in the previous novels, the story of this tetralogy unfolds in a community that is no longer rural nor yet truly urban. The events are set in the early years of Finnish independence and span most of the 1920s. The novel offers an accurate and historically documented cross section of the period and its problems. Each part of the sequel has its own focal point: the first one deals with the aftermath of the 1918 Civil War with its tension between the victorious and the defeated, in the second one the focus shifts to a description of the rapid economic recovery and the effects of the Prohibition (1919–1932), while the third volume depicts the activities and eventual dissolution of the underground communist movement. In the fourth volume, Joenpelto finally describes the Great Depression, which was felt strongly in Finland. The problems are never presented as abstract issues but in terms of concrete human relationships. Joenpelto's character sketches are convincing and individualized; so that even the most unexpected reactions and decisions by her characters seem justified. Her narrative is imbued with humor, particularly when she describes the local people's extreme reserve and reticence. Joenpelto's dialogue frequently employs a spoken language based on the Lohja dialect.

FURTHER WORKS

Seitsemän päivää (1946); *Tulee sittenkin päivä* (1950); *Kivi palaa* (1953); *Missä lintuset laulaa* (1957); *Syyskesä* (1961); *Naisten kesken* (1962); *Viisaat istuvat varjossa* (1964); *Ritari metsien pimennosta* (1966); *Liian suuria asioita* (1968); *Halusit tai et* (1969); *Vesissä toinen silmä* (1971); *Elämän rouva, rouva Glad* (1982); *Rikas ja kunniallinen* (1984); *Jottei varjos haalistu* (1986).

REFERENCES

Koskimies, Rafael, "Eeva Joenpelto: A Time of Reckoning." *Books from Finland* 11.3 (1977); Laitinen, Kai, "Eeva Joenpelto and Her Lohja Trilogy." *World Literature Today* 54.1 (1980); Lehtola, Erkka, "Eeva Joenpelto: Portraits of Change." *Books from Finland*

21.1 (1987); Niiniluoto, Marja, "A Literary Portrait: Eeva Joenpelto." *Books from Finland* 3.2 (1969).

Kai Laitinen

Jørgensen, Johannes. Danish poet, novelist, and hagiographer, b. 6 November 1866, Svendborg, d. 29 May 1956, Svendborg.

While only fifteen Jørgensen went to Copenhagen to go to school and university. He joined the radical cultural movement centered on Georg Brandes,* and worked as a journalist for a time. He gradually moved towards the neoromantic and symbolist movements, founding and editing the symbolist periodical *Taarnet* (The Tower). In 1896 he became a Roman Catholic, later moving to Italy, where he spent most of his remaining years. He returned to Denmark in 1953, and was made a citizen of honor in his native Svendborg.

The early work, revealing a restless nature, was much influenced by Brandesian ideas, and stylistically shows clear signs of Jens Peter Jacobsen.* Jørgensen sees himself as Ahasverus, as Faust, and expresses himself in ornate prose and verse with pantheistic overtones. By the 1890s, however, his work becomes informed by a tension between the bohemianism of his Copenhagen life and an awareness of the ethical ideals of his youth, and a movement toward Christianity becomes apparent. Poetically, this new orientation is linked to Charles Baudelaire and Paul Verlaine, who influence him both stylistically and philosophically. The volume of poems entitled *Bekendelse* (1894; Confession) clearly shows this progression, the first half depicting the movement toward a vague metaphysics; the second, concluding with a cycle of sonnets entitled "Chaldea" and the poem "Confiteor," pointing to the final acceptance of Christianity with obvious Catholic affinities. Later poetry shows a growing simplicity of style, at first tinged with a deep sense of sin, but finally reflecting peace and tranquility.

After his reception into the church, Jørgensen considered giving up writing, but he was persuaded to continue, the result being a series of travel books and lives of saints in which he combined his task, as he saw it, of writing on behalf of Catholicism with the artist's creative urge to express himself. This new artistic compromise is seen in *Pilgrimsbogen* (1904; *Pilgrim Walks in Franciscan Italy*, 1908), but emerges with full force in *Den hellige Frans af Assisi* (1907; *St. Francis of Assisi*, 1908), in which Jørgensen reflects his own spiritual struggle and final conversion through the story of the saint. He does not identify himself with him, but is aware of certain parallels in their early lives. Likewise, Saint Francis's insistence on obedience, discipline, and self-knowledge reflects Jørgensen's own ideals and the difficulty he had in achieving them. Thus, *Den hellige Frans af Assisi* becomes a unique combination of scholarship and creative writing, at once a serious study of a saint and a personal revelation.

Jørgensen continued this course, first in some shorter hagiographies, then, in 1915, in *Den hellige Katarina af Siena (St. Catherine of Siena*, 1938), in which the theme of self-knowledge is further explored, and *Den hellige Birgitta af Vadstena* (1941–1943; *St. Bridget of Sweden*, 1954), where the personal element in particular emerges through the depiction of the saint's being a Scandinavian who has chosen voluntary exile in Italy.

Between 1916 and 1928 Jørgensen published an autobiography in seven parts, *Mit Livs Legende (Jörgensen: An Autobiography*, 1928–1929), a work outstanding for its personal revelations, its portrayal of Danish intellectual life at the end of the nineteenth century, and the strains of religious conversion. Though it undoubtedly contains a good deal of conscious arrangement, Jørgensen makes no attempt to idealize himself.

Jørgensen thought his prose to be his most important work, but his reputation in Denmark rests rather on his poetry. He is remembered as one of the leading figures from the 1890s, and in particular as the man who formulated the program of the symbolist school in Denmark.

FURTHER WORKS

Vers (1887); *Foraarssagn* (1888); *En Fremmed* (1890); *Livets Træ* (1893); *Hjemvee* (1894); *Rejsebogen; Den yderste Dag* (1897); *Helvedfjender* (1898); *Digte 1894–98* (1898); *Vor Frue af Danmark* (1900); *Eva* (1901); *Romerske Mosaik* (1901); *Den hellige Ild* (1902); *Romerske Helgenbilleder* (1902); *Græs* (1904); *Blomster og Frugter* (1907); *Den yndigste Rose* (1907); *Af det Dybe* (1909); *Bag alle de blaa Bjerge* (1913); *Alvernerbjerget* (1920); *Der er en Brønd, som rinder* (1920); *Jorsalafærd* (1923); *Don Bosco* (1929; *Don Bosco*, 1934); *Efterslæt* (1931); *Charles de Foucauld* (1934); *Ti Digte* (1940); *Vers fra Vadstena* (1941); *Digte i Danmark* (1943); *Fyen og andre Digte* (1948).

FURTHER TRANSLATIONS

Book of Danish Verse, comp. Oluf Friis (1922, 1976).

REFERENCES

Frederiksen, Emil, *Johannes Jørgensens Ungdom* (Copenhagen, 1946); Jones, W. Glyn, *Johannes Jørgensens modne år* (Copenhagen, 1963); Jones, W. Glyn, *Johannes Jørgensen* (New York, 1969); Jones, W. Glyn, "Johannes Jørgensen and His Apologetics." *Scandinavian Studies* 32.1 (1960); Jones, W. Glyn, "Some Personal Aspects of Johannes Jørgensen's Prose Writings." *Modern Language Review* 55 (1960); Jones, W. Glyn, "The Early Novels of Jørgensen." *Scandinavian Studies* 36.2 (1964); Jones, W. Glyn, "Johannes Jørgensen in the Centenary of His Birth." *Scandinavica* 5.2 (1966); Nielsen, Bo, *Johannes Jørgensen og symbolismen* (Copenhagen, 1975); Nugent, Robert, "Jørgensen's Devotional Verse: A Contemporary Act of Faith." *Renascence* 15 (1963).

W. Glyn Jones

Jóhann Sigurjónsson. *See* Sigurjónsson, Jóhann.

Jóhann Hjálmarsson. *See* Hjálmarsson, Jóhann.

Jóhannes Bjarni Jónasson. *See* Jóhannes úr Kötlum.

Jóhannes úr Kötlum (pseud. of Jóhannes Bjarni Jónasson). Icelandic poet and novelist, b. 4 November 1899, Dalir, d. 27 April 1972, Reykjavík.

Jóhannes is one of Iceland's most prolific and versatile poets of the twentieth century. During a long and eventful career that spanned nearly fifty years and produced more than twenty volumes of verse, Jóhannes established himself as a master of intricate forms, both traditional and modern, as an idealistic spokesman for humanity and nature, and as a scathing critic of oppressive political institutions.

Jóhannes's first collections of poetry, *Bí bí og blaka* (1926; Sleep, Baby, Sleep) and *Álftirnar kvaka* (1929; The Swans Are Singing), continue the preoccupation of earlier generations with the heritage of verse forms from medieval and folk poetry. A reverent love of nature and the historical past provide the major sources for themes composed in a style that demonstrates a thorough control of language from all ages of Icelandic literature.

Abrupt changes in Jóhannes's poetry occur in his next books of verse, *Ég læt sem ég sofi* (1932; I Pretend I Am Sleeping) and *Samt mun ég vaka* (1935; Nevertheless, I Will Stay Awake), which reflect the political turmoil of the 1930s and the rising power of socialism. In these as well as in his later works, Jóhannes renounces traditional allegiances and attacks political and economic corruption with unrelenting and, occasionally, humorous optimism. His earlier adulation of great historical individuals yields to a compassionate sympathy for nameless heroes, ranging from Viking thralls to workers demonstrating in the streets of Reykjavík. From this point on, Jóhannes advocates the social function of poetry and the attendant necessity of truth in all literary expression.

During and after the war years, Jóhannes raised doubts about his political mission as a poet and experimented with free forms, which appeared alongside traditional forms in *Sjödægra* (1955; Seven Days), but to the end of his career he remained the compassionate champion of nameless humanity.

Although Jóhannes wrote some novels, children's books, and a play, his importance to modern Icelandic literature derives from his accomplishments as a political poet and as a versemaker of immense adaptability.

FURTHER WORKS

Jólin koma (1932); *Ömmusögur* (1933); *Árstíðirnar* (1934); *Og björgin klofnuðu* (1934); *Hrímhvíta móðir* (1937); *Fuglinn segir* (1938); *Hart er í heimi* (1939); *Eilífðar smáblóm* (1938); *Bakkabræður* (1941); *Verndarenglarnir* (1943); *Sól pér sortna* (1945); *Ljóðið um Labbakút* (1946); *Dauðsmannsey* (1949); *Siglingin mikla* (1950); *Frelsisálfan* (1951); *Sóleyjarkvæði* (1952); *Hlið hins himneska friðar* (1953); *Roðasteinninn og ritfrelsið* (1958); *Vísur Ingu Dóru* (1959); *Óljóð* (1962); *Tregaslagur* (1964); *Vinaspegill* (1965); *Mannssonurinn* (1966); *Ný og nið* (1970); *Ljóðasafn* (1972–1976).

TRANSLATIONS

Poems of Today, ed. Alan E. Boucher (1971).

REFERENCES

Andrésson, Kristinn, "Jóhannes úr Kötlum," in *Íslenzkar nútímabókmenntir: 1918–1948* (Reykjavík, 1949); Hjálmarsson, Jóhann, "Fyrirheitna landið," in *Íslenzk nútímaljóðlist*

(Reykjavík, 1971); Pálsson, Hermann, "Myth and Symbol in Jóhannes úr Kötlum's *Sjödægra,"* in *Skandinavische Lyrik der Gegenwart* (Glückstadt, 1972).

W. M. Senner

Johannesen, Georg. Norwegian poet, novelist, dramatist, and essayist, b. 22 February 1931, Bergen.

Like Bertolt Brecht, but in the more pessimistic mode of the atomic age, Johannesen is above all a bearer of historical awareness. In various genres he seeks to encourage skepticism of language by using it in such a pointedly metaphorical or shockingly concrete fashion that the reader is forced to stop and assess the relationship between the words and the world they represent. Between his literary efforts, socialist Johannesen has worked in more direct ways to transmit political consciousness—on the Oslo city council (1967–1971), in the classroom, and in journalism.

Johannesen's debut novel, *Høst i mars* (1957; Autumn in March), presents the struggle of two teenage lovers against the bourgeois backdrop of the early NATO years. The suppression of their love and the senseless act of terrorism with which the novel concludes express Johannesen's central theme of society's potential for self-destruction.

Dikt 1959 (1959; Poems 1959) is a confession of the postwar intellectual's sense of alienation, his fear of imminent catastrophe, and his feelings of political guilt vis-à-vis developing countries. Concrete images are counterbalanced by the use of symbol and metaphor as didactic devices requiring the reader's conscious effort to interpret, and subsequently alter, his historical situation.

Ars Moriendi eller de syv dødsmåter (1965; Ars Moriendi or the Seven Ways of Dying) is a series of forty-nine poems, one for each weekday for seven weeks. Each weekly cycle updates one of the seven deadly sins. These allegorical miniatures of modern man's escapism are intended to instruct, but readers often find them opaque, as the language is at once concrete and cloaked, like that of riddles.

The biblical style of Johannesen's "prophet books" also consciously builds on allegorical tradition. By using Old Testament language to decry current capitalist society, Johannesen hopes to shock the reader into insight and action.

FURTHER WORKS

Nye Dikt (1966); *Kassandra* (1967); *Bertolt Brecht: 100 dikt* (1968); *Tu Fu* (1968); *Om den norske tenkemåten* (1975); *Om "Norges litteraturhistorie"* (1978); *Tredje Kongebok* (1978); *Johannes bok* (1978) *Simons bok* (1980).

REFERENCES

Grøgaard, Johan, Kjell Heggelund, Jan Erik Vold, and Einar Orland, eds., *En bok om Georg Johannesen* (Oslo, 1981).

Frankie Shackelford

Jóhannessen, Matthías. Icelandic poet, essayist, and playwright, b. 3 January 1930, Reykjavík.

A prolific writer in both prose and verse, Jóhannessen has produced eleven volumes of poetry as well as interviews, biographies, collections of essays, plays, and short stories in the course of twenty-six years. He has also had considerable influence on Icelandic cultural affairs as editor of the country's largest daily newspaper since 1959. For several years he was engaged in Icelandic studies at the University of Iceland.

In his volumes of poetry Jóhannessen attempts to combine past with present; mythological themes and material from the ancient Icelandic literature are interwoven with modern symbolism in a manner reminiscent of the technique of T. S. Eliot. Such a combination, for example, is found in *Jörð úr ægi* (1961; Earth from Ocean), in which he brings the Eddic poem Völuspá up to date by fusing the ancient world of symbols with experiences of modern man. Jóhannessen's poetry is loaded with symbolism and symbolic references though it is seldom as obscure as the work of most Icelandic modernists. Nature is generally the basis of his imagery, but man and his experience dominate the foreground.

In his day Jóhannessen exploited modernist art, but in many respects he went his own way, cultivating a more "open" poetic style, often in extroverted rhetorical poems supported by an emotional pathos and susceptibility. His work has always evinced a strong religious bent. This appears clearly in the cycle "Sálmar á atómöld" (Hymns for an Atomic Age) from *Fagur er dalur* (1966; Fair Is the Dale)—a group of religious poems in which judgment of the present age accompanies affirmation of life and a conviction of its value, which is sustained by an obstinate conflict. Love, transience, and death are the themes that have occupied the poet from the beginning: the existential destiny of the individual. But this conflict alternates with the display of a sensitive social awareness. Jóhannessen's attitude is both conservative and humanistic. In his poems he frequently criticizes the forces of violence and destruction in a modern world.

FURTHER WORKS

Borgin hló, ljóð (1958); *Njála í íslenzkum skáldskap* (1958); *Í kompaní við allífið* (1959); *Hólmgönguljóð* (1960); *Svo kvað Tómas* (1960); *Hundaþúfan og hafið* (1961); *Sólmyrkvi* (1962); *Hugleiðingar og viðtöl* (1963); *Vor úr vetri* (1963); *Í dag skein sól* (1964); *Kjarvalskver* (1968; enl. ed., 1974); *Klofningur sjálfstæðisflokksins gamla* (1971); *Vísur um vötn* (1971); *Bókin um Ásmund* (1971; *Sculptor Asmundur Sveinsson an Edda in shapes and symbols*, 1974); *Skeggræður í gegnum tíðina* (1972); *Gunnlaugur Scheving* (1974); *Fjaðrafok og önnur leikrit* (1975); *Dagur ei meir* (1975); *Sverrir Haraldsson* (1977); *Samtöl*, 4 vols. (1977–1982); *Morgunn í maí* (1978); *Veður ræður akri* (1981); *Tveggja bakka veður* (1981); *Nítján smáþættir, smásögur* (1981); *Olafur Thors*, 2 vols. (1981); *Félagi orð, greinar, samtöl og ljóð* (1982); *Ferðarispur* (1983); *Flýgur örn yfir* (1984); *Bókmenntagreinar* (1985).

TRANSLATIONS

American-Scandinavian Review 52.1 (1964); Magnússon, Sigurður A., "Modern Icelandic Poetry." *Modern Poetry in Translation* 30 (1977).

                                                                Matthías Viðar Sæmundsson

Johansson, Lars. *See* Lucidor.

Johnson, Eyvind Olof Verner. Swedish novelist, b. 29 July 1900, Svartbjörnsbyn, Överluleå socken, Norrbotten, d. 25 August 1976, Stockholm.

A feeling of rootlessness was part of Johnson's earliest self-awareness. His father, a former railroad worker, was disabled with silicosis, and Johnson was adopted by relatives to help ease the provisional burden on his mother. After a few years of rudimentary schooling Johnson was on his own. He read whatever he could lay his hands on, held short-term jobs, and was politically active in the syndicalist movement and the local group of young socialists, for whom the Russian Revolution in 1917 was the answer to social injustice. In Stockholm in 1919, Johnson continued his political activity with contributions to the socialist magazine *Brand*. His friendship with the authors Gustav Hedenvind-Eriksson and Rudolf Värnlund was decisive for his own literary ambition. Two years later Johnson continued south, and except for a brief return, spent the 1920s in Germany and France.

Postwar depression on the Continent made existence precarious. Johnson barely managed to survive on poems and articles sent home for publication. But for his literary development these years were fundamental. In the political and intellectual melting pots of Berlin and Paris, Johnson met with avant-gardists, refugees, and wind-blown characters later to appear in his novels. The new experimental forms of Marcel Proust, André Gide, and James Joyce; Sigmund Freud's mapping of the subconscious; and Henri Bergson's philosophy provided stimulation and guidelines. Johnson abandoned, in 1924, his socialist affiliation but never his verbal struggle for human rights. In this struggle the question whether violence should be met with militant action was a central and recurrent dilemma.

Back in Sweden in the 1930s, Johnson's pessimism regarding the conventions and small-mindedness of a bourgeois, capitalist society was somewhat relieved by the primitivist movement in literature and the simplicity of functionalist design in architecture. During World War II Johnson was the editor of *Håndslag*, an underground paper smuggled into Nazi-occupied Norway. After the war he resumed his travels with Switzerland as a frequent place of residence for him and his family. A confederacy of European states seemed to Johnson a solution to Europe's predicament as a buffer zone for east-west tension. Among other honorary achievements, Johnson was a member of the Swedish Academy from 1957. Together with Harry Martinson,* he received the Nobel Prize in 1974.

Johnson's debut work, the short story collection *De fyra främlingarna* (1924; The Four Strangers), as well as his five novels of the 1920s are sociocritical with characters who see the remedies for social injustice but are unable to intervene. Alienation, action paralysis, dangerous repression of desires, and as a counterweight, the healing power of memory, are basic themes in *Kommentar till ett stjärnfall* (1929; Commentary to a Falling Star), the first Swedish novel to use the stream-of-consciousness technique. The wealth and bourgeois marriage of the fruit importer Stormdal are only deceptive signs of success. Stormdal is ashamed of his working-class origin, and his laborious attempts to deny his past eventually bring about a mental collapse, to which his wife Laura is a ready assistant. Stormdal recovers shortly before his death, when he is able to remember and accept the past. One of Stormdal's sons before his marriage, Magnus Lyck, is a typical Hamlet figure with insight but inability to take constructive action. His unhappy love affair is here, as elsewhere in Johnson's writing, a contributing cause.

The locked position of passivity and bitterness in *Kommentar till ett stjärnfall* was taken to task in *Avsked till Hamlet* (1930; Farewell to Hamlet). The protagonist, Mårten Torpare, overcomes his passivity, as he learns to understand and identify with his past. A cure had been found to the Hamlet dilemma, but the issue recurs in later novels. Mårten Torpare will also reappear in numerous texts as a reflector of ideas, a bystander, a note taker. His identity is transparently hidden in the names of Crofter Brace in *Lägg undan solen* (1951; Put Away the Sun), and Andreas Fermier in *Några steg mot tystnaden* (1973; Some Steps toward Silence).

After a short-lived experiment with primitivist ideas, the biting portrayal of capitalist society and its vulnerability to demonic power in *Bobinack* (1932; Bobinack), and the playful return to nature in *Regn i gryningen* (1933; Rain at Dawn), Johnson is ready for his autobiography. It was published in four parts, *Nu var det 1914* (1934; 1914, 1970), *Här har du ditt liv* (1935; Here You Have Your Life), *Se dig inte om* (1936; Don't Look Back), and *Slutspel i ungdomen* (1937; Finale in Youth). Since to Johnson the experience itself and the memory of that experience are necessarily different, the term *autobiography* is questionable. Johnson's emphasis is not on re-lived dates and events but on the teenager Olof's growing awareness of himself in relation to the surrounding world. Olof's maturing process is expressed in his discovery of words, their sensual and communicational force. Each part of the tetralogy contains a saga seemingly unconnected with the fictional world but an essential part of Johnson's narrative concern. Reality can only be apprehended in disguise, by means of detours, such as fairy tales, legends, and myth. Seeds of saga function and the use of a story within the story appear earlier in Johnson's texts, but they are now made as an explicit statement on the very making of a novel.

The voluminous, unwieldy Krilon trilogy, the climax of what Johnson termed his military service in words, consists of *Grupp Krilon* (1941; The Krilon Group), *Krilons resa* (1942; Krilon's Journey), and *Krilon själv* (1943; Krilon Himself). In this work the patient explorer can find most keys to Johnson's writing. The plot concerns business competition on the real estate market with decisive influence on the personal lives of Krilon and his friends. But the trilogy can also be read as an allegory of Western civilization threatened with extinction, or with immediate reference to World War II, of Western, and later Soviet, allies fighting against Hitler's onslaught. There is, in addition, a religious theme with Krilon as a Christ figure in the struggle of good versus evil. Johnson's humanist concern is particularly striking in this novel. The intricate compositional weave, the fusion of reality and fantasy, and the use of symbolic language are all recurrent aspects of Johnson's mythical-historical novels to come.

With *Strändernas svall* (1946; *Return to Ithaca*, 1952) Johnson realized a twenty-year-old dream to write about Ulysses's homecoming. Homer's epic provides a narrative frame and a perspective of man's universal predicament. Johnson's Ulysses is modern man, suffering from guilt and alienation, and plagued by nightmares and approaching old age. The question of justified bloodshed is raised when Ulysses kills the suitors to ensure lasting peace. The text offers no hope that such a peace is in view.

The demolition of walls is the literal and figurative issue raised in *Drömmar om rosor och eld* (1949; *Dreams of Roses and Fire*, 1984), set in seventeenth-century France. The outer walls are the Huguenot fortifications attacked by the Catholics. The inner walls are the defense mechanisms by which an individual suppresses unwanted desires. Propelling the action is the Jesuit priest, Grainier, who does not hesitate to live out his desires in love and politics. His self-confidence and freedom of spirit make him the ruler of sexual demons with which the nuns are afflicted, but also, with his execution, the victim of religious and political demons, represented by Richelieu. Of particular narrative concern is the ongoing dialogue between fictional characters and posterity mediated by the ironic narrator.

Alternating time levels and narrative voices become Johnson's trademark of composition. In *Hans nådes tid* (1960; *The Days of His Grace*, 1968), the three main narrators give their private and publicly censored testimony to Charlemagne's rise to the emperor's crown. A fascination with power, as well as a fear of its disastrous effects on individual lives, provides the tension of the narrative. The use of symbols and myth raises historical action to universal significance with man's capacity to survive oppression as a central concern.

Represented reality is increasingly elusive for Johnson. His last novel, *Några steg mot tystnaden* (1973, *A Few Steps Toward Silence*), contains gems of storytelling, for example, Colinet's tale of consolation to his fellow soldiers, but the intricate communicational games are of more interest to the student of narrative technique than to the reader who wants action. Nevertheless, *Några steg mot tystnaden* remains a worthy end station to a portal figure and innovator of Swedish fiction, and to a man whose humanist concern and self-taught erudition represent the core of Western civilization.

FURTHER WORKS

Timans och rättfärdigheten (1925); *Stad i mörker (1927); Stad i ljus* (1928); *Minnas* (1928); *Natten är här* (1932); *Än en gång, kapten* (1934); *Nattövning* (1938); *Soldatens återkomst* (1940); *Den trygga världen* (1940); *Pan mot Sparta* (1946); *Strändernas svall*, a play (1948); *Dagbok från Schweiz* (1949); *Lägg undan solen* (1951); *Romantisk berättelse* (1953); *Tidens gång* (1955); *Vinterresa i Norrbotten* (1955); *Molnen över Me-*

tapontion (1957); *Vägar över Metaponto* (1959); *Spår förbi Kolonos* (1961); *Livsdagen lång* (1964); *Stunder, vågor* (1965); *Favel ensam* (1968); *Olibrius och gestalterna* (1986).

REFERENCES

Bäckman, Stig, *Den tidlösa historien* (Stockholm, 1975); Bäckström, Lars, "Eyvind Johnson, Per Olof Sundman, and Sara Lidman: An Introduction." *Contemporary Literature* 12 (1971); Kårsnäs, Mona, *Eyvind Johnson och Djävulen* (Uppsala, 1984); Lindberger, Örjan, *Norrbottningen som blev europé* (Stockholm, 1986); Mazzarella, Merete, *Myt och verklighet* (Helsinki, 1981); Orton, Gavin, "Eyvind Johnson—An Introduction." *Scandinavica* 5.2 (1966); Orton, Gavin, *Eyvind Johnson: Nu var det 1914* (Hull, 1974); Schwartz, Nils, *Hamlet i klasskampen* (Lund, 1979); Sjöberg, Leif, "Eyvind Johnson." *American-Scandinavian Review* 56.4 (1968); Sjöberg, Leif, "The 1974 Nobel Prize in Literature: Eyvind Johnson and Harry Martinson." *Books Abroad* 49.3 (1975); Söderberg, Barbro, *Flykten mot stjärnorna* (Stockholm, 1980); Stenström, Thure, *Romantikern Eyvind Johnson* (Lund, 1978); Warme, Lars G., "Eyvind Johnson's *Några steg mot tystnaden*: An Apologia." *Scandinavian Studies* 49.4 (1977).

Monica Setterwall

Jón Trausti. *See* Magnússon, Guðmundur.

Jón úr Vör (pseud. of Jón Jónsson). Icelandic poet, b. 21 January 1917, Vatneyri on Patreksfjörður.

One of fourteen children of an impoverished village shoemaker, Jón grew up with equally poor foster parents and received little formal schooling as a youngster. He later, however, attended adult education classes in Reykjavík. In 1938, Jón went to Sweden for some further studies and afterward traveled on the European continent; this is evident in his *Stund milli stríða* (1942; A Moment between Wars). For some years after he returned home, he edited a small periodical, worked in a publishing house, and ran a secondhand bookstore in Reykjavík. He subsequently became a librarian in Kópavogur, a position from which he retired in 1976.

Jón began his literary career at twenty with a book of traditional verse, and his second volume was likewise filled with alliterated, rhymed poems, although his meters were light and open. But in *Þorpið* (1946; The Village), published during another stay in Sweden and influenced mainly by contemporary Swedish poets, he totally broke with tradition and gave Icelandic readers the first book of entirely free verse. Gone, too, was the romantic lyricism of his previous publications; instead, with simple, artless diction, he drew up a haunting picture of his native village with all its hardships and misery, yet without bitterness, extolling the basic goodness and decency of its hardworking people, while poking good-natured fun at their foibles. Although Jón has since published several fine volumes of poems, *Þorpið* remains his masterpiece; it is already a classic of modern Icelandic literature.

From the very beginning, Jón's strong points have been his human warmth, sincerity, and directness. Though a socialist by conviction, he has never let dogma overcome his humanity and always retained a healthy skepticism. Some disillusionment is evident in his later poems, and his tone has become somewhat darker, but his main concerns remain the same: the right of ordinary people to live their simple, everyday lives in peace and justice—a right he now sees gravely threatened by the nuclear superpowers with their capability for human extermination. In that context, Jón has also been an active opponent of U.S. military bases in Iceland, which he considers a threat to his nation.

FURTHER WORKS

Ég ber að dyrum (1937); *Með hljóðstaf* (1951); *Með örvalausum boga* (1951); *Vetrarmávar* (1960); *Maurildaskógur* (1965); *100 kvæði* (1967); *Mjallhvítarkistan* (1968); *Vinarhús* (1972); *Altarisbergið* (1978); *Regnbogastígur* (1981); *Gott er að lifa* (1984).

TRANSLATIONS

Iceland Review 4.2 (1966); *Poems of Today from Twenty-five Modern Icelandic Poets*, comp. Alan Boucher (1971); *Modern Poetry in Translation* 30 (1977); *The Postwar Poetry of Iceland*, trans. Sigurður A. Magnússon (1982).

REFERENCE

Höskuldsson, Sveinn Skorri, "Triumph of Modernism in Icelandic Poetry, 1945–1970." *Scandinavica* 12 (1973), Suppl.

Hallberg Hallmundsson

Jónas Hallgrímsson. *See* Hallgrímsson, Jónas.

Jónasson, Jóhannes Bjarni. *See* Jóhannes úr Kötlum.

Jónsson, Þórsteinn. *See* Þórsteinn frá Hamri.

Jónsson, Jón. *See* Jón úr Vör.

Jonsson, Tor. Norwegian poet and essayist, b. 14 May 1916, Lom, d. 14 January 1951, Oslo.

Jonsson was born in central rural Norway, where he experienced very strongly the contrast between the landowning class on the one hand and the cottagers on the other. Social injustices in general and poverty as an obstruction to spiritual growth in particular are recurrent themes in his prose writings and in a large part of his poetry.

Three collections of Jonsson's poetry were published during his own lifetime, while the fourth appeared posthumously. He is deeply steeped in the classical, realistic tradition of Norwegian poetry. His style can be characterized as disciplined and unembellished, but the frequent use of rhetorical devices, such as alliteration and antithetical constructions, give structure and feeling to his verse. Jonsson's use of New Norwegian* lends a richness as well as a substantiality of expression to his poetry. Nature symbols and abstract concepts, fundamental elements in his poetic vocabulary, are often presented as contrasts, like life/ death or light/darkness, and frequently provide his poetry with an air of proverbial expression. Jonsson's style corresponds to ideas in his poetry, such as contrasts in themes, the conflicts or opposites in his perception of man's existence. In the first three books social themes predominate, but underneath and closely connected are more personal themes, which become dominant in the last book of verse, *Ei dagbok for mitt hjarte* (1951; A Diary for My Heart). Here feelings of loneliness and despair, of wasted life, of ambivalent desire for life and death find expression. Jonsson's essays, published as *Nesler* (2 vols., 1950–1952; Nettles), provide a much broader social critique with ironic attacks on cultural conservatism and national romanticism, all forms of imperialism and suppression of man's potential.

In his essays Jonsson was an important spokesman for potential in human development. His poems, simple, yet full of meaning and emotion, concrete and well molded, are monuments to his belief in the power of the word.

FURTHER WORKS

Mogning i mørkret (1943); *Berg ved blått vatn* (1946); *Jarnnetter* (1948); *Dikt i samling*, ed. Helge Skaranger (1956); *Prosa i samling*, ed. Helge Skaranger (1960); *Og evig er ordet* (1970); *Tekster i samling*, ed. Inger Heiberg, 2 vols. (1973–1976).

REFERENCES

Hageberg, Otto, "Kjærleik og død—spenningsmønster i Tor Jonssons lyrikk," in *Fra Camilla Collett til Dag Solstad* (Oslo, 1980); Heiberg, Inger, *Drøm mot virkelighet* (Voss, 1984); Mæhle, Leif, "Einsemda ved grensa. Kontrastmønster i Tor Jonsson lyrikk," in *Fra bygda til verda* (Oslo, 1967); Olsen, Sparre, *Tor Jonsson-minne* (Oslo, 1968).

Ingeborg Kongslien

Jotuni, Maria Gustava (pseud. of Maria Tarkiainen). Finnish short story writer, playwright, and novelist, b. 9 April 1880, Kuopio, d. 30 September 1943, Helsinki.

The characters in Jotuni's works are often the fresh, quick-witted folk that her hometown Kuopio was known for. Jotuni left the world of the clever citizens of Kuopio and of her father's tinsmith shop to study history and literature at the University of Helsinki (1901–1905), where she was influenced by impressionism and naturalism, as well as by current attitudes such as Ellen Key's ideas about women.

The theme of Jotuni's first collection of short stories, *Suhteita* (1905; Relationships) is love from a woman's perspective: dream of true love leads in reality to disappointment and compromise. Disappointment leads to submission and ruin; compromise involves trading love for the comforts of life. The same motif reappears in her other short story collections, *Rakkautta* (1913; Love), *Kun on tunteet* (1918; When You Have Feelings), and *Tyttö ruusutarhassa* (1927; The Girl in the Rose Arbor).

Most of Jotuni's short stories are impressionistic "one minute stories," which rely for development on striking dialogue or monologue, a letter or a one-sided telephone conversation. Artistic and intellectual discipline, firmly sketched characters, and objectivity characterize Jotuni's short works as well as her longer short stories. *Jouluyö korvessa* (1947; Christmas Eve in the Wilderness) is the story of a tragic marriage in which raw malice opposes goodwill. The novella *Arkielämää* (1909; Everyday Life) portrays a day and night in the life of a rural community. It encompasses life in its entirety: birth and death, love and selfishness, insensibility and emotions so intense that they verge on the ridiculous.

In most of her plays, as in her short stories, Jotuni softens social criticism and the biting contrast between desire and reality with humor. In the comedy *Miehen kylkiluu* (1914; Adam's Rib) the theme involves the fallacy of finding Mr. Right. *Tohvelisankarin rouva* (1924; Henpecked Husband's Wife) is a satiric comedy about love and money.

Jotuni's short stories and plays have a prominent place among the classics of Finnish literature. *Miehen kylkiluu* and *Tohvelisankarin rouva* are contenders for the most popular play in Finland. The novella *Arkielämää* is considered one of the best portraits of Finnish people. Jotuni's multilayered prose, piercing character sketches, and unsparing humor make her a master of the short story.

FURTHER WORKS

Vanha koti (1910); *Martinin rikos* (1914); *Savu-uhri* (1915); *Musta härkä* (1915); *Kultainen vasikka* (1918); *Jussi ja Lassi* (1921); *Olen syyllinen* (1929); *Avonainen lipas* (1929); *Kootut teokset* (1930); *Kurdin prinssi* (1932); *Vaeltaja, Avonainen lipas*, vol. 2 (1933); *Klaus, Louhikon herra* (1946); *Norsunluinen laulu* (1947); *Jäähyväiset. Avonainen lipas*, vol. 3 (1949); *Valitut teokset* (1954); *Maria Jotunin aforismit* (1959); *Maria Jotunin ihmisiä* (1959); *Huojuva talo* (1963); *Neekeri tulee* (1963); *Äiti ja poika* (1965); *Novelleja ja muuta proosaa*, 2 vols. (1980); *Näytelmät* (1981).

FURTHER TRANSLATIONS

Books from Finland 14.1 (1980); *Finnish Short Stories*, ed. Inkeri Väänänen-Jensen and K. Börje Vähämäki (1982); *Prairie Schooner* (Spring 1982).

REFERENCES

Niemi, Irmeli, "Maria Jotunin pienproosan ääriviivoja," in Maria Jotuni, *Novelleja ja proosaa*, vol. 1 (Helsinki, 1980); Niemi, Irmeli, "Maria Jotunin näytelmätaiteen ääriviivoja," in Maria Jotuni, *Näytelmät* (Helsinki, 1981); Niemi, Irmeli, "Maria Jotuni: Money, Morals, and Love." *Books from Finland* 14.1 (1980); Sarajas, Annamari, "Maria Jotuni," in *Suomen kansalliskirjallisuus*, vol. 5 (Helsinki, 1965).

Terttu Hummasti

Juvonen, Helvi. Finnish poet, b. 5 November 1919, Iisalmi, d. 1 October 1959, Helsinki.

Juvonen worked as a language teacher, bank clerk, and translator and wrote all of her exquisite poems and prose pieces in the space of ten years. The distinguished critic Tuomas Anhava* called her the first of the new Finnish poets who reached full maturity.

Juvonen's groping for God and her mystical insights make her a writer through whom Finnish spirituality speaks with particular intensity. The tension out of which she created was partly due to the conflict between her Lutheran background and her own spiritual experiences. The reality she perceived through rational thought was as convincing to her as perception through mystic intuition.

Juvonen's preoccupation with Scripture led to poems in which she identifies completely with biblical personages, whose sufferings she understands out of the depth of her own soul. But even in distress, there is always a special positive note, hope that a miracle will occur, a great, deep waiting. In the nativity poem "Nights," the mysterious central happening appears as one small detail, embedded in the cosmic unity of terrestrial and heavenly life, small in its beginning, but of infinite reality.

Preoccupation with this cosmic unity led Juvonen to the study of German mystics, particularly Angelus Silesius. Her translations of some of his verse are so absolutely exact in wording, rhythm, and meaning that it could only have been achieved by a poet infinitely familiar with the experiences of her predecessor. Yet she was able to put herself outside the mystic experience and write a scholarly essay on Silesius.

Throughout her life Juvonen was waiting for the miracle of faith that would change man and his world. The expectation is expressed in the touching story *Pikku karhun talviunet* (1974; Little Bear's Winter Dreams), posthumously published by her friend, the poet Mirkka Rekola.*

FURTHER WORKS

Kääpiöpuu (1949); *Kuningas Kultatakki* (1950); *Pohjajäätä* (1952); *Päivästä päivään* (1954); *Kalliopohja* (1955); *Valikoima runoja* (1958); *Sanantuoja* (1959); *Kootut runot* (1960).

TRANSLATIONS

Thank You for These Illusions, ed. Anne Fried (1981).

REFERENCES

Anhava, Tuomas, "Helvi Juvonen, kehityksen piirteitä" in Helvi Juvonen, *Sanantuoja* (Porvoo, 1959); Kilpi, Mikko, "Helvi Juvonen, uudistuvan lyriikkamme klassikko," in Helvi Juvonen, *Kootut runot* (Porvoo, 1960); Koskenniemi, V. A., *Kootut teokset*, vol. 9 (Porvoo, 1955); Luojola, Yrjö, *Kristus ja ihminen* (Porvoo, 1967); Polkunen, Mirjam, "Helvi Juvonen," in *Suomen kirjallisuus*, vol. 6 (Helsinki, 1967); Vikstén, Vilho, *Runo ja tulkinta* (Porvoo, 1971).

Anne Fried

K

Kailas, Uuno (orig. Frans Uuno Salonen). Finnish poet, b. 29 March 1901, Heinola, d. 22 March 1933, Nice.

Kailas's childhood circumstances were difficult, and he was badly shell-shocked as a soldier at the age of eighteen at the front of Aunus in East Karelia in 1919. He suffered from feelings of inferiority and had a guilty conscience throughout his life. The times favored strict morals. In addition, Kailas saw the poet as an exceptional individual. His poetry, with introspection as its most important source, resulted in his ethically confessional style. Its main tendency of ethical rigor was one of the fundamental qualities of poetry written in Finnish between the world wars. Kailas, who was occupied with his inner self, committed his compact diction to that method. His writing provided him a means to search for the right way. His earliest books of poems emphasize the truth, and contrasting elements hold a balance. The imagery often used in the poems, like the sun and the sea, presented Kailas as a worshipper of life who also was inclined to glorify man's heroic fate. He translated a collection of poems by German expressionistic poets. His own poetry speaks for brotherhood and for the common man, and he feels empathy for the lonely.

From his third volume on, Kailas's poetic attitude was based on individualism. He was influenced by Charles Baudelaire's works. Kailas's poems depicted the growing conflicts between the ideal and the real, and in his important fourth book his diction became laconic, polished, and classical. He idealized beauty, as the postsymbolists had done earlier in Europe. His last volume, the fifth, includes patriotic poems, but his feelings of resignation ring painfully true throughout the volume. His struggle became a personal tragedy.

Kailas was the most prominent confessional poet between the world wars. His poetry of suffering had precarious elements. However, his conception of a poet as an individual rebel renders it valid, and his ethical rigor may challenge serious artists anytime.

WORKS

Tuuli ja tähkä (1924); *Purjehtijat* (1925); *Silmästä silmään* (1926); *Paljain jaloin* (1928); *Runoja* (1929); *Uni ja kuolema* (1931); *Runoja* (1932); *Punajuova* (1933); *Novelleja* (1936); *Valikoima runoja* (1938); *Isien tie* (1941); *Valikoima runoja* (1958); *Uuno Kailaan runoja* (1963).

TRANSLATIONS

Salt of Pleasure, ed. Aili Jarvenpa (1983).

REFERENCES

Niinistö, Maunu, *Uuno Kailas* (Helsinki, 1956).

Kalevi Lappalainen

Kalevala and Finnish Folklore. There are two editions of the *Kalevala*: the first published in 1835, comprising 12,978 lines of poetry arranged in thirty-two poems (the "Old *Kalevala*"), and that of 1849, which supersedes it, an enlarged and revised edition of 22,795 lines in fifty poems. The *Kalevala* was compiled by Elias Lönnrot (1802–1884), doctor of medicine and later professor of Finnish at Alexander's University in Helsinki. The name of the epic comprises two components: *Kaleva*, a male name, and *-la*, a locality suffix, hence "land of Kaleva." Lönnrot's reasons for using this name are obscure but probably refer to the notion of "an ancient land of heroes." Lönnrot compiled the epic largely from poems cast in trochaic, nonstrophic tetrameters, which he found as part of the oral tradition of the unlettered people in northeastern Finland and across the Finnish-Russian frontier in the neighboring areas of Archangel and Olonets Karelia, and in Ingria. Lönnrot acquired most of his materials on field expeditions between 1828 and 1846; poems published by earlier scholars also provided him with some of his materials, and he composed about 600 lines himself (a specimen of the text in English and Finnish is found at the end of this article).

The idea of compiling the *Kalevala* sprang from theories of nation and nationality current in various parts of Europe at the end of the eighteenth century and the beginning of the nineteenth century. National identity was understood in terms of a shared history, and a local language and culture; where such ideas took root, oral poetry, especially when cast in an epic mode, was seen as evidence of an ancient local culture and as the starting point for what was thought to be a revival of a national literature. Ideas of this kind were already common among intellectuals in late–eighteenth-century Finland; with the separation of Finland from Sweden in 1808–1809 and its incorporation in the Russian Empire as an autonomous grand duchy, the study of local history and the cultivation of a local language, literature, and culture became for many young scholars a patriotic imperative.

Those Finnish scholars who turned their attention to oral poetry found various sources for their work. Written records of a singular form of oral poetry cast in

trochaic tetrameters (hereafter referred to as "traditional Baltic-Finnish poetry"),
dated back to the sixteenth century when the Lutheran church set about stamping
out the performance of traditional Baltic-Finnish poetry as part of the long
struggle against paganism; in libraries and archives the materials of seventeenth-
and eighteenth-century historians and antiquarians who had studied what remained of the traditional poetry in search of clues about the past were eagerly
studied. But it was in the field that the richest sources were found as the search
for the living tradition led the young scholars across the frontier into Russian
Karelia, where they found that the performance of traditional Baltic-Finnish
poetry still survived, sung either solo or in chorus, sometimes to the accompaniment of the zitherlike *kantele*. The oral poetry that Lönnrot and his contemporaries heard was prolific in themes; rich in imagery, symbol, and metaphor;
and subtle in its associations. Its composition was governed by formal prosodic
conventions.

The collection of traditional Baltic-Finnish poetry, of which the *Kalevala* is
but one outcome, continues today. Several million lines of this poetry have been
recorded and deposited in archives in Finland, Estonia, and Russia. Analysis
and comparison of the distribution, form, function, and contents of these materials point to an oral poetry tradition of great age, once common throughout
the Baltic-Finnish region (i.e., the areas inhabited by the Estonians, Ingrians,
Karelians, and Finns). Scholars attribute this coherence of tradition to various
factors: an origin predating the division of the Baltic Finnish into their present-
day language groups (linguistic evidence points to a time as long ago as 2,500
years); possibly a common function as the oral accompaniment to ritual activity;
and common prosodic conventions ensuring a consistency of form and composition after division into separate language groups and migration in various
directions. To these reasons should be added the archaeological and historical
evidence that shows a high degree of mobility among the peoples of the Baltic-
Finnish region during the last two millennia; it may be that mobility of this kind
among peoples speaking closely related languages and dialects and sharing the
same prosodic structures and conventions in their oral poetry is a further reason
for the accumulation of common motifs and themes in this region.

Traditional Baltic-Finnish poetry falls into three main types, often with substantial overlapping of function: epic, lyric, and magic. A ritual function survives
in the performance of numerous spells, incantations, charms, and prayers with
which people sought to safeguard themselves against omnipresent danger, to
ensure the good health of man and beast, and to secure success in hunting,
fishing, and agriculture. Lyric materials convey mostly personal sentiments
through lullabies, laments, poems about love, longing, or loss, teasing and
propaedeutic poems, and eulogies. Some lyric themes also appear to have associations with ritual; in many propaedeutic lyric poems some scholars have
seen a connection with rites of passage performed to prepare members of the
community for their new status and responsibilities, especially in connection
with wedding ritual.

The themes and motifs of traditional Baltic-Finnish poetry have much in common with the oral poetry of preliterate peoples elsewhere in the world, the closest points of contact being with the native peoples of the Arctic regions of Eurasia and America. Myth poetry describes the creation of the cosmos and the ordering of the world at the beginning of time; etiological myths account for fertility and various other phenomena, animals and objects on which depends man's survival first as a hunter and later as a pastoralist. Gods, spirits of water, earth, forest, and the otherworld, and culture heroes all play a part in these events; prominent among them are Väinämöinen and Ilmarinen, frequently cast in the role of smiths. Man's perception of the spirit world finds expression in a substantial body of poetry about shamans; these poems tell of initiation, the ecstatic trance, the shaman's soul on its hazardous journey to the otherworld, the exercise of the powers thus acquired, and rivalry between shamans. Again it is around the characters of Väinämöinen and Lemminkäinen that much of this poetry crystallized.

Some scholars argue that the myth and shaman oral poetry represent an ancient corpus predating other forms of Baltic-Finnish epic poetry. Many of the motifs and themes in these poems also occur in reinterpreted forms in poems performed by successive generations of singers who have adapted the motifs and themes to new cultural conditions and linked them to new themes that were either created locally or borrowed from outside the local language area. Contacts with ancient Scandinavian cultures are evident in poems about Finnish Vikings who travel to distant lands in search of wives and plunder. A feature of this phase of accretion is the *sampo*, a mysterious object symbolizing wealth and power, originally forged in payment for a bride but subsequently the cause of strife between the land of Kaleva in the south, and the dark, evil Pohjola, in the far north.

Christianity introduced another rich phase of accretion and adaptation in Baltic-Finnish oral poetry. Archaeological, historical, and cultural evidence indicates that aspects of Christian thought first spread to the Baltic-Finnish area from the east during the early Middle Ages; evidence of this is found in poems about the life of the Messiah. Following the Swedish Crusade of 1155, the Church of Rome remained dominant in Finland until the Reformation, while Ingria and Karelia came under the Russian Orthodox church. Traditional poetry provided a vehicle for the clergy of both churches to communicate Christian doctrine and legends. The tension between Christian and pre-Christian tradition can be seen in a further phase of accretion with Väinämöinen variously depicted in the role of Jesus, Herod, and other stock figures of good and evil. Traditional poetry also assimilated popular European ballad themes, together with the structural characteristics of the ballad form; cultural features indicate borrowing both from Swedish and Russian sources. The most recent type of traditional Baltic-Finnish poetry dates from the early modern period. Its subject is warfare, often conflating various historical and mythical figures into a single character or event. A closely related poem type is the eighteenth- and nineteenth-century Ingrian and Karelian conscript songs performed as young men were taken away to military service.

Although Lönnrot had at his disposal only a small portion of the materials available to present-day scholars, his oeuvre shows that he was well aware of their typological and thematic differences. The companion volume to the *Kalevala*, the three-part *Kanteletar* (1840–1841), comprises for the most part lyric oral poetry; toward the end of his life Lönnrot completed the compilation of a collection of spell poems. The *Kalevala* itself is essentially a concatenation of epic poems, into which lyric and magic materials have been intercalated depending on motif, theme, and occasion.

In assembling his materials Lönnrot demonstrated a skillful command of the techniques by which his informants concatenated runs of poems into various narrative strings, often creating new plots, which were in turn concatenated into yet further plots. Lönnrot did not hesitate to follow the example of his informants and organized some of his materials into wholly new plots. The tragic characters of Aino and Kullervo, who are both driven to suicide (Poems 4–5, 31–36), owe their existence largely to Lönnrot's cultivation of this technique. Another feature attributable to Lönnrot is the language of the *Kalevala*. Lönnrot had to create his own system of standardizing the lexicon, grammar, and syntax of his materials, for most of his contemporaries would not have understood the various dialects in which he had recorded his materials, particularly those which had been heavily influenced by the Russian language and Russian Orthodox culture.

The purpose and criteria behind Lönnrot's approach to his task of compilation reflect the philosophy of the nationalist movement of his day. In his preface Lönnrot discussed how he had attempted in the *Kalevala* to offer a mythical history of the Finns from prehistory until the arrival of Christianity. He cast his materials in a form reminiscent both of classical and Scandinavian epic, and into this mythical recreation he implanted various levels of allegory consistent with the style of more recent literature. Very obvious is the allegory of "dark-evil" contrasting with "light-good" implicit in the strife between the Pohjola of Louhi and Väinämöinen's land of Kaleva. Less obvious to contemporary readers are the various levels of allusion to the strivings of Lönnrot's contemporaries to shape a nation-state.

The *Kalevala* begins with the myth of the creation of the world by Ilmatar, Spirit of the Air, and of how she gave birth to Väinämöinen, the first human, whose task was to clear and plant the land of Kaleva ready for his people (Poems 1–2). Once Väinämöinen has completed these primordial tasks, Lönnrot develops the narrative through a series of quests. The first series (Poems 4–5, 12–19) is the search for wives by Väinämöinen, the reckless Lemminkäinen (a composite character created by Lönnrot from shaman and Viking materials) and the primordial smith Ilmarinen. This brings the heroes of Kaleva into their first contact with Pohjola as each of them seeks to marry the wondrous daughter of Louhi, the Mistress of Pohjola. Associated with their various attempts, failures, and success is the need to perform magic tasks to prove their worth as suitors; they include the forging of the *sampo* (Poem 10), the catching of the Elk of the demon Hiisi, and the shooting of the swan of the Otherworld (*Tuonela*) River (Poems

13–14), and the plowing of a field of snakes (Poem 19). It is Ilmarinen whom Louhi's daughter finally agrees to marry. Several poems describe the preparations for and celebration of their wedding (Poems 20–25). The wedding sets in motion a new series of quests linked now to Lemminkäinen, the uninvited guest. Insulted, Lemminkäinen kills the Master of Pohjola in a duel, making it necessary for him to flee from his victim's avenging folk. In his travels Lemminkäinen engages in a succession of amorous adventures until, finally defeated by winter conditions at sea, he returns home, crestfallen but chastened (Poems 26–30).

The end of the Lemminkäinen quest marks a turning point in the *Kalevala*. The land of Kaleva is now thriving under the leadership of "Väinämöinen, old and steadfast," but its peace is disturbed by Kullervo, victim as an infant of fratricidal strife between his father and uncle and sold into serfdom by the latter. Purchased by Ilmarinen, he is set to herding. An evil trick played on Kullervo by Ilmarinen's wife leads to her violent death and Kullervo's flight. Having rediscovered his parents, long thought to be dead, he seduces a girl in the forest only to discover that she is his long-lost sister. Her suicide is followed by Kullervo's after he has taken murderous revenge on his uncle's family (Poems 31–36).

Ilmarinen's quest for a new wife brings the heroes of Kaleva once again into contact with Pohjola, when Ilmarinen travels there to woo Louhi's younger daughter. His suit refused, Ilmarinen abducts her, but on the journey home he responds to her insults by turning her into a seagull. On reaching home Ilmarinen persuades Väinämöinen and other heroes of Kaleva that they should take back from Pohjola the *sampo* Ilmarinen had forged as brideprice for his first wife, and themselves benefit from its magic power (Poems 37–39). As the heroes sail to Pohjola, their ship runs aground on the shoulders of a giant pike. It is from the jaws of this pike that Väinämöinen makes the first *kantele*, the bringer of harmony between man, beast, and the spirits (Poems 40–41). Väinämöinen and his men succeed in stealing the *sampo*, but in the ensuing sea fight the *sampo* and the *kantele* are both lost overboard; fragments of the *sampo* wash ashore on Kaleva, bringing fertility to the land and sea, but Väinämöinen has to make a new *kantele* from birchwood (Poems 42–44). The actions in the final poems of the *Kalevala* are shaped by Louhi's quest for vengeance. Lönnrot draws extensively on magic poetry to describe Louhi's assault on the land of Kaleva. First, she sends disease; second, a ravaging bear. Twice unsuccessful, at her third attempt to destroy her enemies she steals the sun and the moon and puts out all the fires in Kaleva. With the creation of a new sun and moon and the recovery of fire, Väinämöinen saves his people, triumphs over his enemies, and reaches the acme of his power; the prosperity of the land of Kaleva seems assured (Poems 45–49).

It is against this background that Lönnrot sets his adaptation of epic poems about the Messiah (in Baltic-Finnish tradition Jesus was conceived by the virgin Marjatta through eating a berry). When Väinämöinen refuses to baptize the fatherless child and sentences him to death, the infant speaks, condemning

Väinämöinen. Recognizing in this the act of a new leader, Väinämöinen relinquishes his power and departs forever. Into this concluding episode set at the beginning of the Christian era in Finland, Lönnrot inserts an allegorical message for his own day. The departing bard-leader, Väinämöinen, bequeaths to his people, as they enter a new phase in their history, two symbols that are in fact a typical clarion of nineteenth century national identity: music and oral poetry:

> Then the aged Väinämöinen
> went upon his journey singing,
> Sailing in his boat of copper,
> In his vessel made of copper,
> Sailed away to loftier regions,
> To the land beneath the heavens.
> There he rested with his vessel,
> Rested weary, with his vessel,
> But his kantele he left us,
> Left his charming harp in Suomi,
> For his people's lasting pleasure,
> Mighty songs for Suomi's children.
>
> (Poem 50, lines 501–12. Trans. W. F. Kirby, 1907)

EDITIONS

Kalevala (1849) and companion volume *Kanteletar* published by the Finnish Literature Society are kept in print.

TRANSLATIONS

Kalevala (1849 ed.), trans. John Martin Crawford (1888); *Kalevala. The Land of the Heroes*, trans. W. F. Kirby (1907; 1985); *The Kalevala or Poems of the Kaleva District*, trans. Francis Peabody Magoun, Jr. (1963); *The Old Kalevala and Certain Antecedents*, trans. Francis Peabody Magoun, Jr. (1969); *The Kalevala. Epic of the Finnish People*, trans. Eino Friberg, ed. George C. Schoolfield (1988).

REFERENCES

Abercromby, John, *The Pre- and Proto-historic Finns both Eastern and Western with the Magic Songs of the West Finns*, 2 vols. (London, 1898); Hautala, Jouko, *Finnish Folklore Research 1828–1918* (Helsinki, 1969); "Kalevala 1835–1985. The National Epic of Finland." *Books from Finland* 19.1 (1985)—entire issue devoted to *Kalevala*; Kolehmainen, John I., *Epic of the North* (New York Mills, Minn., 1973); Kuusi, Matti, et al., *Finnish Folk Poetry: Epic* (Helsinki, 1977); Wilson, William, *Folklore and Nationalism in Modern Finland* (Bloomington, Ind., 1976).

M. A. Branch

Kallas, Aino Julia Maria (pseud. Aino Suonio). Finnish novelist, short story writer, poet, and playwright, b. 2 August 1878, Viipuri, d. 9 November 1956, Helsinki.

As the wife of an Estonian diplomat, Kallas lived over twenty years in London

(1922–1934), St. Petersburg (1900–1903), and Stockholm (1944–1952). Despite her cosmopolitanism, she used Estonian peasant life and folktales as themes for her best works, which she wrote in archaic seventeenth century Finnish.

In her first notable collection of short stories, *Meren takaa* (2 vols., 1904–1905; From Beyond the Sea), Kallas uses impressionistic techniques and classic short story form to tell her tales: a lord of the manor exercises his "first-night" rights ("Häät"); a young shopkeeper's wife leaves off baking bread to follow a crowd to the coast at Tallinn, where a "white ship" that would bring them to freedom is expected. Five weeks later the smell of fresh bread brings her back to reality and she returns home ("The White Ship" in *The White Ship. Estonian Tales*, 1924).

Love so intense that it threatens the standards of society is the theme of Kallas's three important novels. *Barbara von Tiesenhusen* (1923; *Barbara von Tiesenhusen*, 1925, 1927, 1975) is the story of a young seventeenth century noblewoman, who runs away with her lover, a commoner. *Reigin pappi* (1926; *Clergyman of Reigi*, 1927, 1975) portrays the adultery between a pastor's wife and his assistant pastor. *Sudenmorsian* (1928; *The Wolf's Bride. A Tale from Estonia*, 1930, 1975) is a tale of the transformation of a forester's wife into a wolf. The setting for all these novels is the Estonian countryside of the sixteenth and seventeenth centuries. Here Kallas examines the conflict between all-consuming love and vital rules of society, the violation of which is punishable by death. The narrator in all three works supports these rules, thus allowing Kallas to suppress her natural sympathies, a technique she called "brain snake."

Kallas's clear intellectual style and her ability to portray the pain and ecstasy of the human mind are especially evident in her *Päiväkirja* (5 vols., 1952–1956; Diary), an honest examination of her soul, not intended for publication.

Perhaps better than any other Finnish writer, Kallas has examined the demonic forces of the human heart, especially of the female heart. With intelligence and a distinct technique of distancing herself from her characters, she portrays the power of love in a style not often equaled in Finnish or world literature.

FURTHER WORKS

Lauluja ja ballaadeja (1897); *Kuloa ja kevättä* (1899); *Kirsti* (1902); *Ants Raudjalg* (1907); *Lähtevien laivojen kaupunki* (1913); *Seitsemän* (1914); *Tähdenlento* (1915); *Suljettu puutarha* (1915); *Nuori Viro* (1918); *Musta raita* (1919); *Katinka Rabe* (1920); *Vieras Veri* (1921); *Novelleja* (1928); *Langatonta sähköä* (1928); *Pyhän joen kosto* (1929); *Marokon lumoissa* (1931); *Bathsheba Saarenmaalla* (1932; *Bath-Sheba of Saarenmaa*, 1934); *Talonpojan kunnia* (1936); *Valitut teokset*, 3 vols. (1938); *Kuoleman joutsen* (1942); *Kuun silta* (1943); *Löytöretkillä Lontoossa* (1944); *Polttoroviolla* (1945); *Mallen tunnustukset* (1945); *Kanssavaeltajia ja ohikulkijoita* (1945); *Uusia kanssavaeltajia ja ohikulkijoita* (1946); *Kolmas saattue kanssavaeltajia ja ohikulkijoita* (1947); *Seitsemän neitsyttä* (1948); *Virvatulia* (1949); *Rakkauden vangit* (1951); *Valitut teokset* (1954); *Vaeltava vieraskirja vuosilta 1946–1956* (1957); *Elämäntoveri* (1959); *Aino Kallaksen kauneimmat runot* (1959).

FURTHER TRANSLATIONS

Eros the Slayer: Two Estonian Tales (1927); *Three Novels* (1975).

REFERENCES

Krohn, Eino, *Surmaava Eros* (Helsinki, 1953); Laitinen, Kai, *Aino Kallas 1897–1921* (Helsinki, 1973); Laitinen, Kai, "Aino Kallas: Ambassador Extraordinary." *Books from Finland* 12.4 (1978).

Terttu Hummasti

Kamban, Guðmundur. Icelandic playwright, novelist, and film and theater director, b. 8 June 1888, Álftanes near Reykjavík, d. 5 May 1945, Copenhagen.

After attending Reykjavík Grammar School, Kamban went to Copenhagen in 1910 to study literature and philosophy at the University. Following the example of Jóhann Sigurjónsson* and Gunnar Gunnarsson,* he wanted to break through the isolation of his native language barrier to write in Danish and English as well. After a trip to the United States he decided to concentrate his efforts in Danish and Icelandic. However, two of his most powerful plays, *Marmari* (1918; Marble) and *Vér morðingjar* (1920; *We Murderers*, 1970), are set in New York, and describe an international milieu, as do some of his minor works; while his last play, the comedy *Grandezza* (1941), is based on an authentic Italian court case, with a theme similar to Jean Giraudoux's *Sigfried* and Jean Anouilh's *Voyageur sans bagage*. Kamban also lived in Germany for a while, but he spent most of his life in Copenhagen as a play director, among other things. He was the first Icelander to direct a film, based on his own novel *Det sovende hus* (1925; The Sleeping House), in 1925. He also directed some of his plays in Reykjavík. Kamban's life came to a tragic end when he was shot on the day of the Danish liberation after the war in 1945.

His first play, *Hadda Padda* (1914; trans. 1917), well received both in Reykjavík and Copenhagen, is a love story in the neoromantic vein of Jóhann Sigurjónsson that was later filmed. In his next play *Konungsglíman* (1917; Wrestling for the King), he takes up the dilemmas of modern urban society, a topic he continues to deal with in subsequent plays. In the 1930s he turned to Icelandic history for the subject matter of two major novels, *Skálholt* (4 vols., 1930–1935; *The Virgin of Skalholt*, 2 out of 4 vols., 1935) and *Vítt sé ég land og fagurt* (2 vols., 1936; *Wondrous Land*, 1938); the former, which is about the well-known historical adversaries Bishop Brynjólfur Sveinsson and his daughter RagnheiÐur, was later made into a popular play, while the latter tells of the discovery of North America around the year 1000. His first novel, however, *Ragnar Finnsson* (1952), which was partly written in the States, is an account of the conflict between a rural upbringing and tumultuous modern city life; the Icelandic hero ends up as a criminal in America.

Kamban's writing is moralistic, perceptive, and often witty. Without ever questioning the pillars of capitalistic society, he maintains a critical attitude. He deals with many moral-philosophical subjects with magnificent intellectual perceptiveness. Thus, for instance in *Marmari*, he questions the grounds on which the whole legislative system of Western countries regards crime and punishment. In *Vér morðingjar*, a well-made play about marital love and infidelity, the ethical question concerns responsibility: who is to blame, the individual who does the deed, or the one who provokes it? *Skálholt* describes the revolt of a young, strong-willed girl against the power of her patriarchical father and the church itself at a time when women's liberation was neglected.

Kamban's works have been translated into several European languages, and his plays were produced in all the Scandinavian countries and Germany during the 1920s. Today, his best plays count among the few classics of the Icelandic stage and are frequently performed although he is nearly forgotten in Denmark, his second home. His native popularity is due to free and bold thinking rather than stylistic and formal brilliance. The questions he asks and his often paradoxical conclusions still have validity for us today.

FURTHER WORKS

Úr dularheimum (1906); *Örkenens stjerner* (1925); *Sendiherrann frá Júpiter* (1927); *30. Generationen* (1933); *På Skalholt* (1934); *Jeg ser et stort skönt land* (1936); *Derfor skilles vi* (1939—rewritten from *De arabiske telte*, 1921); *Kvalitetsmennesket* (1941); *Komplekser* (1941); *Hvide falke* (1944); *De tusend mil* (wr. 1939, pub. in Icelandic as *Púsund mílur*, 1969).

REFERENCES

Einarsson, Stefán, "Five Icelandic Novelists." *Books Abroad* 16 (1942); Worster, W. W., "Four Icelandic Writers." *Edinburgh Review* 238 (1923).

                                                                                                      Sveinn Einarsson

Karlfeldt, Erik Axel. Swedish poet, b. 20 July 1864, Karlbo Village, Folkärna parish, Dalarna, d. 4 April 1931, Stockholm.

Although Karlfeldt was born into a family with strong ties to the soil—ties that Karlfeldt himself was later to articulate quite powerfully—his life was much more closely bound up with academics. Despite financial reverses, Karlfeldt took his student examination in 1885 and his doctorate in literary history and the English language in 1898. He served as a teacher in a folk high school, in various *gymnasia*, at the Royal Library, and as permanent secretary of the Swedish Academy.

Karlfeldt's first volume of poetry, *Vildmarks- och kärleksvisor* (1895; Songs of the Wilderness and of Love) was characterized by its neoromantic spirit, its technical skill, and the marked literary regionalism (*hembygdsdiktning*) of the many poems relating to Karlfeldt's native province, Dalarna. *Fridolins visor* (1898; Fridolin's Songs) introduced the title character (in part, Karlfeldt's alter ego), "a learned son of peasant stock, who had returned to the world of his forefathers because it appealed to him to dig in dirt, since most of his life he had dug in books." With *Fridolins lustgård* (1901; Fridolin's Pleasure Garden), Karlfeldt's identification as the singer of Dalarna was complete. His poetry grew in technical and thematic complexity, evincing a darker, erotic side that contrasted sharply with the spirit of robust innocence of the earlier volumes. This somber strain became even more evident in the postwar volume *Flora och Bellona* (1918; Flora and Bellona) and his final volume *Hösthorn* (1927; The Horn of Autumn). Karlfeldt's enormous popularity led, on the one hand, to his being awarded the Nobel Prize for literature posthumously in 1931 (the only person ever to have been posthumously honored) and, on the other, to Viktor Svanberg's warning of the "Karlfeldt danger" (an allusion to conservative, backward-looking unreflective idyllicism). With Karlfeldt, the neoromantic revival of the 1890s reached its zenith—nearly thirty years after its due time.

FURTHER WORKS

"Flora och Pomona" (1906); *Dalmålningar, utlagda på rim* (1920); *Samlade skrifter*, 5 vols. (1931).

TRANSLATIONS

Arcadia Borealis: Selected Poems of Erik Axel Karlfeldt, ed. C. W. Stork (1938).

REFERENCES

Fogelkvist, Torsten, *Erik Axel Karlfeldt: en minnesteckning* (Stockholm, rev. ed., 1941); Fridholm, Roland, *Sångmön av Pungmakarbo* (Stockholm, 1950); Hildeman, Karl Ivar, "The Evolution of 'Längtan heter min arvedel.' " *Scandinavian Studies* 31.2 (1959); Hildeman, Karl Ivar, '*Som en ort ur sin groningsgrund*': *anteckningar kring några Karlfeldtdikter* (Stockholm, 1965); Hildeman, Karl Ivar, *Sub luna och andra Karlfeldt essäer* (Stockholm, 1966); Hildeman, Karl Ivar, "Erik Axel Karlfeldt. An Evaluation." *Scandinavian Studies* 40.1 (1968); Larsson i By, Carl, "Erik Axel Karlfeldt: A Poet of Dalecarlia." *American-Scandinavian Review* 13.1 (1925); Mjöberg, Jöran, *Det folkliga och det förgångna i Karlfeldts lyrik* (Lund, 1945); Stork, C. W., *Arcadia Borealis: Selections from the Poetry of Erik Axel Karlfeldt* (Minneapolis, 1938); Stork, Charles W., "Erik Axel Karlfeldt." *American-Scandinavian Review* 19.10 (1931); Uppvall, A. J., "The Poetic Art of Erik Axel Karlfeldt." *Germanic Review* 2 (1927); Wennerberg, Klas, *Vårgiga och hösthorn* (Uppsala, 1944).

Lars Emil Scott

Keller, George. *See* Stenius, Göran Erik.

Kellgren, Johan Henric. Swedish poet and critic, b. 1 December 1751, Floby, d. 20 April 1795, Stockholm.

Kellgren was the foremost poet of the Gustavian period and a lifelong admirer of Voltaire. Kellgren's satiric "Mina löjen" (1777; My Laughter) established him as a poet and social critic of the first rank. Kellgren continued to develop his stylistic talents in his association with *Stockholms Posten* (1778–1795), which became Stockholm's leading paper largely due to his contributions as a critic, editor, and ultimately owner. Kellgren's contributions to *Stockholms Posten* provide an index to Enlightenment thought at its best, and stand in contrast to the sterile neoclassicism of Carl Gustaf Leopold.*

Kellgren's controversy with Thomas Thorild,* beginning in 1782, is of particular interest. Kellgren found Thorild's Ossian-inspired "Passionerna" (The Passions) offensive, formless, and rambling. Kellgren parodied Thorild in his "Nytt forsök till orimmad vers" (New Attempts at Unrhymed Verse). In a larger sense, Thorild became the focus for Kellgren's Pro Sensu Communi attack in 1787 on late-century emotionalism and general fuzzy-mindedness. In his "Man äger ej snille för det man är galen" (1787; One Isn't a Genius Just Because One Is Mad), Kellgren abandoned his early bantering satire in favor of genuine anger at stupidity and ignorance pretending to be creativity.

Kellgren's criticism of Thorild was not just a sterile defense of neoclassical rules. In "Mina löjen" he had criticized Carl Michael Bellman* for poor taste, but subsequently modified this position in 1790 with his preface to Bellman's "Fredman's Epistles." In the preface, Kellgren broke with conventional classical dicta and asserted the right of genius to create its own rules.

Unlike Leopold, Kellgren's tastes remained flexible and matured. The playful sensuality of "Sinnenas förening" (1778; The Union of the Senses) is an excellent example of Enlightenment eroticism. However, in "Den nya skapelsen eller inbillningens värld" (1789; The New Creation; or, The World of Imagination) Kellgren, under the influence of Jean-Jacques Rousseau, extends the cultivation of the senses into an idealized, Neoplatonic expression of love, where the object of the poet's love (in this case, Hedda Falk) becomes the animating force in nature.

In 1790, Kellgren changed the *Stockholms Posten* from a political to a cultural journal, in which he published not only "The New Creation," but "Dumboms lefverne" (The Numskull's Life) and "Ljusets fiender" (The Enemies of Light). While it is tempting to say that Kellgren changed with the times, abandoning his Enlightenment taste for freer romantic forms, he to the last eschewed directionless sentimentality in favor of a disciplined common sense. In this regard he must be considered the expression of Swedish Enlightenment thought at its best.

FURTHER WORKS

Samlade skrifter, 3 vols. (1796); *Samlade Skrifter*, 9 vols., ed. S. Ek, A. Sjöding, O. Sylwan (1923–   ).

FURTHER TRANSLATIONS

Anthology of Swedish Lyrics from 1750 to 1925, ed. C. W. Stork (1917; rev. ed., 1930).

REFERENCES

Bergh, Gunhild, *Litterär kritik i Sverige under 1600-och 1700-talen* (Stockholm, 1916); Ek, Sverker, "Den nya Skapelsen," in *Studier tillägnade Otto Sylwan* (Göteborg, 1924); Ek, Sverker, *Skämtare och allvarsmän i Stockholms Postens första årgångar* (Lund, 1952); Ek, Sverker, and Ingrid Ek, *Skalden och kulturkampen* (Stockholm, 1954); Lundgren, Tor, *Den ursprungliga versionen av Kellgrens "Mina löjen"* (Göteborg, 1954);

Sylwan, Otto, *Johan Henrik Kellgren* (Stockholm, rev. ed., 1939); Tigerstedt, E. N., *Johan Henric Kellgren* (Stockholm, 1954; rev. ed., 1966).

John L. Greenway

Kianto, Ilmari (orig. Calamnius). Finnish novelist, b. 7 May 1874, Pulkkila, d. 27 April 1970, Helsinki.

A pastor's son, Kianto completed his university education and began his career as a teacher of Russian. Later he worked as a journalist and finally turned to writing. His creative works focus on his home region Kainuu in northern Finland. They fall into four genres, beginning with poetry, then fiction, reports of travels, and memoirs. Kianto renounced his Lutheran heritage and voiced his views on this matter in *Vapaauskoisen psalttari* (1912; Freethinker's Psalter). He criticized the institution of marriage in his novel *Avioliitto* (1917; Marriage).

Two of Kianto's novels are particularly distinctive. *Punainen viiva* (1909; The Red Line) recounts Finland's, then a grand duchy of Russia, first parliamentary election campaign in 1907 and its impact on the poor peasantry of Kainuu. Full of hope they vote for the socialist candidate. Each ballot is marked with a red line, which will also be the mark of a fatal wound suffered by the hero in combat with a marauding bear. The tragic outcome suggests that not even free elections can bring salvation to the poverty-stricken crofters in their struggle for a better life. Kianto's novel later provided the basis for an opera by the same title, which has been performed with success in New York and elsewhere by the Finnish National Opera.

Kianto's second novel of distinction is *Ryysyrannan Jooseppi* (1924; Jooseppi Ragshores), a naturalistic portrayal of a shiftless peasant who resorts to moonshining to support his wretched family. The novel abounds with wry, folksy humor. It is reminiscent of *Tobacco Road* and another Finnish novel, *Putkinotko* (1919–1920; Weed Hollow), by Joel Lehtonen.*

Kianto's interest in the Karelian districts beyond the border had a political element as well. He was not free from the chauvinism familiar from the early, deceptively triumphant phase of the Continuation War in 1941. In 1918 Kianto published a book entitled *Suomi Suureksi, Viena Vapaaksi* (For a Greater Finland, and a Free Viena), Viena being the Finnish name for Russian Karelia. *Vienankävijän matkakuvia* (1954; Scenes from Travels in Viena-Karelia) is already written in a different vein. This report of a 1914 visit to the region is worth reading for its portrayal of an old *Kalevala* * singer.

Kianto will be remembered for his social criticism in *Punainen viiva* and *Ryysyrannan Jooseppi*. His sympathy for the downtrodden was obvious, although he may have exaggerated the sordid aspects of their existence. In the latter book he at times even seems to ridicule the peasant squalor. Yet this comic relief distinguished him from his contemporary F. E. Sillanpää,* whose sympathy for peasants seemed more genuine and complete.

FURTHER WORKS

Väärällä uralla (1896); *Soutajan lauluja* (1897); *Hiljaisina hetkinä* (1898); *Margareta* (1900); *Lauluja ja runoelmia* (1900); *Nuoria lauluja vanhasta säästöstä* (1902); *Kiannan rannoilta Kaspian poikki* (1903); *Nuoren miehen kädestä* (1904); *Isänmaallisia runoelmia* (1906); *Sieluja kevätyössä* (1907); *Auskultantin päiväkirja* (pseud. Antero Avomieli, 1907); *Nirvana* (1907); *Pyhä viha* (1908); *Pikku syntejä* (1909); *Kärsimys* (1909); *Pyhä rakkaus* (1910); *Kapinoitsija* (1910); *Orjantappuroita* (1911); *Metsäherran herjaaja* (1912); *Poro-kirja* (1913); *Talviretkiä Pohjolassa* (1915); *Vienan virroilta, Karjalan kankahilta* (1915); *Turjanlinnan satukirja* (1915); *Kiertävä kirjailija* (1916); *Kotoisten rantojen ikuinen kohina* (1916); *Vienan kansan kohtalo* (1917); *Hakkaa päälle!* (1918); *Vielä niitä honkia humisee . . .* (1919); *Vienan neitsyt* (1920); *Kolme hyvää juttua* (1920); *Vanha pappila* (1922); *Valitut teokset*, 4 vols. (1923); *Iloista kyytiä rajakomendan tin autossa* (1924); *Suloisessa Suomessamme* (1925); *K.H.P.V.* (1925); *Hallan jääkärit* (1927); *Kuhmon kulmilta* (1927); *Elämän ja kuoleman kentältä* (1928); *Papin poika* (1928); *Kertomuksia ja kuvauksia* (1930); *Nuori runoilijamaisteri* (1931); *Patruunan tytär* (1933); *Vanha postineiti* (1935); *Korpikirjailijan kirot* (1938); *Vienan Karjala—Kalevalan kehto* (1946); *Moskovan maisteri* (1946); *Poika maailman kylillä* (1946); *Omat koirat purivat* (1949); *Valitut teokset* (1954); *Iki-Kianto muistelee* (1954); *Mies on luotu liik-kuvaksi* (1957); *Salainen päiväkirja* (1980).

REFERENCES

Dauenhauer, Richard, and Philip Binham, eds., *Snow in May* (Cranbury, N.J., 1978); Nevala, Maria-Liisa, *Ilmari Kianto—anarkisti ja ihmisyyden puolustaja* (Helsinki, 1986).
                                                                                                   Reino Virtanen

Kidde, Harald. Danish novelist and short story writer, b. 14 August 1878, Vejle, d. 23 November 1918, Copenhagen.

The recurrent theme in Kidde's works consists of man's confrontation with modern industrial and urban reality, as well as an adolescent's confrontation with the demands of adult life. In the early works this dual conflict is closely associated with events in the author's own life; later on the distance between the author and his fiction grows.

Aage og Else (1902–1903), an intense novel, is one of Kidde's important early works. Influenced by contemporary psychiatry and late Ibsen-symbolism, Kidde varies the theme in *De blinde* (1906; The Blind Ones). After some phil-osophically reflective and less voluminous novels, Kidde undertook a study of Søren Kierkegaard.* Only then was he ready to write *Helten* (1912; The Hero), his only novel with wider popular appeal. The many references to concrete historical and geographical events and places, all described in detail, accrue mythological and psychological connotations as well. The novel advocates the development of a secular, ecological, and moral consciousness as a means of dealing with the conflicts occasioned by modern civilization.

The same conflicts are displayed even more fiercely in the novel *Jærnet* (1918; Iron), which was written during World War I. The reader experiences reality both in its relationship to the history of wars and industrial development and through the life of an adolescent boy in whose mind the novel unfolds. What makes this detailed and complicated work into a major contribution to the history of the twentieth-century novel is its vigor and the minute analysis of mental functions as products of the mind as well as in their relationship to the external world.

The essential issues in Kidde's works evolve around puberty problems and the author's persistent opposition to the glorified feats of physical strength of his day. His themes obtain, however, a paradigmatic validity through his historical studies, travels, and ingenious albeit demanding narrative technique.

FURTHER WORKS

Sindbilleder (1900); *Luftslotte* (1904); *Loven* (1908); *Den Anden* (1909); *De Salige* (1910).

TRANSLATIONS

Norseman 13.4 (1955); *Contemporary Danish Prose*, ed. Elias Bredsdorff (1958).

REFERENCES

Gad, Carl, *Omkring Kulturkrisen* (Copenhagen, 1929); Höger, Alfons, *Form und Gehalt der Romane und kleineren Erzählungen Harald Kiddes* (München, 1969); Kent, Charles, "Harald Kidde." *Edda* 11 (1919); Koch, Christian, "Harald Kidde," in *Danske digtere i det 20. århundrede*, vol. 1, ed. Torben Brostrøm and Mette Winge (Copenhagen, 1980); Kofoed, Niels, *Den nostalgiske dimension* (Copenhagen, 1980); Sørensen, Villy, "Erindringens digter: Harald Kidde," in his *Digtere og dæmoner* (Copenhagen, 1973).

Jørgen Egebak

Kielland, Alexander L. Norwegian novelist, short story writer, and playwright, b. 18 February 1840, Stavanger, d. 6 April 1906, Bergen.

Kielland was one of the three major realistic prose writers of the Modern Breakthrough in Norway, along with Bjørnstjerne Bjørnson* and Jonas Lie.* Born into one of Stavanger's oldest mercantile-political families, Kielland abstracted material for most of his writing from this patrician class for which he felt both sympathy and antipathy. According to one Kielland scholar, Johannes Lunde, Kielland inherited from his milieu a value system of Christian ethics, rationalistic and idealistic, according to which he judged others of all classes, though he reserved the harshest judgment for his own.

In 1872 Kielland married. That same year he bought the Malde Tile Works, which he ran for nine years. During that time he read the works of Charles Darwin, John Stuart Mill, Georg Brandes,* and very importantly, Søren Kierkegaard.* Kielland originally thought he would write moral-philosophical tracts, but when, during a half year stay in Paris in the late 1870s, he published several short stories and a play, his literary career was underway. The majority of his works were written during the 1880s, including his most important novels, *Garman & Worse* (1880; *Garman & Worse*, 1885), *Skipper Worse* (1881; *Skipper Worse*, 1885), and *Gift* (1883; Poison). In 1885 Kielland was involved in one of the more dramatic political clashes of the decade and one of the scandals of

Norwegian literary history. Bjørnson and Lie recommended him for the state-supported author's stipend, but the majority in Parliament, including the members of the Liberal party with which he had allied himself in his books, opposed the recommendation on the grounds that his authorship went contrary to the moral and religious precepts of the state. Though Kielland never participated directly in the debate, he was deeply hurt by the incident. In 1891, due to disappointments, personal problems, lack of money, and lack of sympathy for the new, lyrical literature of the fin de siècle, Kielland withdrew from literary life to become mayor of Stavanger; and in 1902 he became chief administrative officer (*amtmann*) of the district of Romsdal. During this time he wrote only nonfiction, including *Omkring Napoleon* (1905; *Napoleon's Men and Methods*, 1907). He died during a stay at Bergen Hospital and was buried in Stavanger.

Kielland achieved immediate success with the publication of two collections of short stories, *Novelletter* (1879; Short Stories) and *Nye Novelletter* (1880; New Short Stories). The stories showed traces of influence from Camilla Collett,* H. C. Andersen,* Charles Dickens, and Kierkegaard, but Kielland was already his own master, and the stories, in fact, struck the tone for all of his works to come. He wrote with a politically radical *tendens* that he had no intention of disguising, because, as he often said, his purpose was to awaken the public to social injustice. He was highly critical of social institutions, including the state church, the school system, and the government bureaucracy, at the same time as he was intensely sympathetic to society's oppressed. The obviousness of Kielland's message was countered by a sophistication in composition and style unmatched by any other Norwegian writer of the time.

Kielland's repeated theme is the lack of truth and justice in the private and public spheres of life. With satirical sharpness and disarming wit he exposes the unromantic truth about love, the superficiality of bourgeois liberalism, and the falseness of friendship. But Kielland's most persistent theme, accounting for some of the most powerful short stories in these volumes, is the great gulf between the rich and the poor.

Kielland's radicalism was suspect to a few, however, including his friend, Georg Brandes, who accused him of shooting sparrows with his scorn rather than beasts of prey. The question of Kielland's radicalism has been raised repeatedly by scholars and critics. Johannes Lunde argues that Kielland was more interested in "radically preserving" society than he was in "radically changing" it. His *tendens*, says Lunde, was ethical rather than political, closer to Kierkegaard than to Brandes (*A.L.K. Verdiarv og budskap*).

In 1880 Kielland published *Garman & Worse*. One of his best novels, it has become a classic of Norwegian literature. With Stavanger of the 1870s as its setting, the novel turns on the clash between the old patrician-patriarchal culture and the new, more democratic and more ruthless capitalistic culture, specifically as it affects the old mercantile house of Garman & Worse in its transition from sailing ships to steam. The novel has no central plot or protagonist, but the character in whom the opposing ages come together is Christian Frederik Garman. A good cut above all the others in wisdom, spirit, and class, he has Kielland's sympathy, but Kielland does not fail to make clear that C. F. Garman's way of life depends in good measure on the exploitation of the lower classes.

The novel is characterized by Kielland's compositional trademarks: a blatant but effective use of contrasts; a greater interest in the psychology of the group than the individual; a wide range of wit, humor, and satire in his characterizations; and an elegantly crafted prose.

In 1882 Kielland published *Skipper Worse*, returning to the house of Garman & Worse, but approximately a generation earlier in the Stavanger of the 1840s. Again Kielland describes a clash of cultures and value systems, but this time it is the old patrician world of Morten W. Garman (C. F. Garman's father), rooted in the Age of Enlightenment, versus the new world of merchants made up of petty-bourgeois businessmen and followers of a particular pietist sect (*Haugi-anere*) who exerted great influence in nineteenth-century Stavanger. Though Kielland portrays the pietists with remarkable objectivity, even sympathy, he shows them in their decline from true believers to all too worldly participants in society who use their religion as a weapon to gain power. One of the feistiest, most colorful representatives of the old culture falls prey to them. Jacob Worse, Garman's partner and the company's best sea captain, recovers his soul and his wits only in the last second of his life when he cries out, "Vi kommer sent, hr. Kunsul, men vi kommer godt!"

In 1883 Kielland published the third in his series of Stavanger novels, *Gift*, which fits chronologically in between the other two but which shares none of the same characters. *Gift* is primarily an attack on an authoritarian school system that stifles creativity, independence, and true learning in favor of discipline, rote learning, and a competitive, repressive grading system. At the center is Abraham Løvdahl, a self-portrait of sorts, caught between his father, Professor Løvdahl, a debilitating, paternalistic presence, and his honest, free-spirited, and tragic mother, Wenche. Ultimately her spirit does not have a strong enough hold on Abraham. Kielland follows his decline in *Fortuna* (1884; *Professor Lovdahl*, 1904), a novel about the corruptive forces of money.

Kielland, of course, wrote other works, among them *Arbeidsfolk* (1881; Working People), *Else* (1881; *Else*, 1894), *Sne* (1886; *Snow*, 1887), *Sankt Hans Fest* (1887; Midsummer Festival), and his last novel, *Jacob* (1891; Jacob). He claimed to detest plays, but he wrote *Tre Par* (1886; *Three Couples*, 1917), *Bettys Formynder* (1887; Betty's Guardian) and *Professoren* (1888; The Professor). But his greatest contribution to Norwegian literature remains the short stories and his three Stavanger novels, referred to by some as his *comédie humaine*. He was influenced by Kierkegaard, Collett, H. C. Andersen, Gustave Flaubert, the Goncourt brothers, and Alphonse Daudet; but from the beginning he was his own writer, combining a strong, social message with an elegant, witty, worldly style, and he became one of the pivotal figures of nineteenth-century Norwegian realism.

FURTHER WORKS

Samlede Digterværker, ed. Peter L. Stavnem and Andreas H. Winsnes, 5 vols. (1919); *Breve*, ed. Kielland's sons, 2 vols. (1907); *Breve til hans Datter* (1909); *Breve til hans*

Son (1910); *Brev*, ed. Francis Bull (1909); *Alexander L. Kielland, Brev, 1869–1906*, ed. Johannes Lunde (1978–1981).

FURTHER TRANSLATIONS

A Stork's Nest (1885); *Tales of Two Countries* (1891); *Norse Tales and Sketches* (1897); *Norway's Best Short Stories* (1927), ed. Hanna Astrup Larsen.

REFERENCES

Apeland, Owe, *A. L. Kiellands romaner* (Oslo, 1971); Brandes, Georg, "Alexander L. Kielland," in his *Samlede skrifter*, vol. 18 (Copenhagen, 1910); Bull, Francis, *Omkring Alexander Kielland* (Oslo, 1949); Dahl, Willy, *Garman & Worse i nærlys og perspektiv* (Bergen, 1973); Gran, Gerhard, *A. L. Kielland og hans samtid* (Stavanger, 1922); Lunde, Johannes, *A. L. Kielland. Verdiarv og budskap* (Oslo, 1970); Lunde, Johannes, *Liv og kunst i konflikt, A. L. Kielland; 1883–1906* (Oslo, 1975); Riis, Johan, *A. L. Kielland, mennesket bak dikteren* (Oslo, 1973); Storstein, Olav, *Kielland på ny* (Oslo, 1949); Sturtevant, Albert M., "Notes on Alexander Kielland." *Scandinavian Studies* 11 (1931); Sturtevant, Albert M., "*Skipper Worse and the Haugianere.*" *Scandinavian Studies* 11 (1931); Sturtevant, Albert M., "Regarding the Chronology of Events in Kielland's Novels." *Scandinavian Studies* 12 (1933).

Mary Kay Norseng

Kierkegaard, Søren. Danish philosopher and novelist, b. 5 May 1813, Copenhagen, d. 11 November 1855, Copenhagen.

Kierkegaard came from a pietistic home, with a domineering father, against whom he reacted briefly through a hedonistic rebellion. He was a brilliant student of theology, and in 1841 he received his doctorate for a dissertation on Socrates' concept of irony, *Om Begrebet Ironi* (1841; *The Concept of Irony*, 1966). The career seemingly cut out for him in academia or within the Lutheran church never materialized, for Kierkegaard staked out another path of rebellion. Outwardly his life may seem uneventful, but its inner drama is undeniable: in 1841, he was betrothed to Regine Olsen, but in spite of his love for her, he broke the engagement and fled to Berlin, where he started in earnest upon his writings. During the years 1842–1845, he wrote an impressive number of works that were a mixture of philosophical treatise, Christian sermon, and experimental fiction; most of them were published under clever pseudonyms, and Kierkegaard called them his aesthetic works (they all, in various ways, tell why he had to break with Regine). Although Kierkegaard was no recluse—he engaged eagerly in conversations with his contemporaries during his daily walks in the streets of Copenhagen—he became more and more isolated, particularly after he was cruelly attacked and caricatured in Meïr Aron Goldschmidt's* satirical magazine *Corsaren* (The Corsair) in 1846. It is telling that Kierkegaard brought that abuse upon himself and that he totally devoted his last year to an uncompromising attack on the institution of the Danish State Church. In a pamphlet from 1848, Kierkegaard had claimed that he aimed "to reintroduce Christianity into Christendom," and in 1854, he single-handedly started a magazine, *Øjeblikket* (The

Instant, trans. as *Kierkegaard's Attack upon 'Christendom'* 1854–1855, 1956), in which he lambasted the hypocrisy of the ministers. Kierkegaard never feared taking extreme positions, and during his last days in a hospital in Copenhagen, he unwaveringly refused to receive the last sacrament from a clergyman.

Kierkegaard's oeuvre has aroused awe; it is considered to be labyrinthine and immensely difficult. The latter part of that reputation may have disappointed Kierkegaard, for his aesthetic works are a concerted, pedagogic effort to meet an audience on its own level. Modern readers may partly find his works obscure because Kierkegaard devoted an inordinate amount of space at leveling scorn on the German philosopher G. W. Hegel. In Kierkegaard's reading of Hegel, the latter preposterously claimed that the human mind would eventually be capable of an objective understanding of existence. To Kierkegaard, Hegel represented "objective" thinking—a reductionist perception—that, like most other philosophical systems, did nothing to resolve the "single, solitary" individual's existential problems and that, thus, left that forlorn individual in a state of despair (Kierkegaard instead poses his idea of "subjective" truth). Fortunately, the ongoing battle with Hegel, mostly carried out indirectly and ironically, tended to sink into the subtext when Kierkegaard presented his ideas through fiction. Hence, newcomers to Kierkegaard may do themselves a favor by considering him to be an experimental novelist who tells stories without closure and about which readers thus make up their own minds. In fact, as readers move into Kierkegaard's fictional world, they are forced or seduced to discover that each of them—as single individuals—is the protagonist of the text: what really matters is how the reader reacts to the story told. Kierkegaard hopes that each reader will be so profoundly affected by his work that he or she will become—*choose* to become—a very different person. The concept of the existential choice that alters everything is at the core of Kierkegaard's philosophy.

The direction in which an individual can move through choices is suggested in *Enten-Eller* (1843; *Either/Or*, 1959), Kierkegaard's first puzzle-box novel, which he published under the pseudonym Victor Eremita (in allusion to his broken engagement). In the pages of the manuscript, which is supposedly found by Victor in a secret compartment of a desk, six different voices speak, and they embody various attitudes toward life—some very fashionable in 1843. The first part is filled with Byronic spleen, offered with the irony and melancholy that would appeal to a contemporary audience. The Byronic hero is Kierkegaard's *aesthete*, a hedonist who lives for pleasure alone, but who may discover that his life cannot only deprive him of pleasure, but also send him into a state of despair. Kierkegaard makes it very clear that the aesthete is demonic, for in his pursuit of pleasure he finds morals to be utterly ridiculous; that point is made elegantly and devilishly clear in the notorious "The Diary of a Seducer," in which the debonair aesthete plots a seduction in such a way as to provide him with as much intellectual pleasure as possible—and he does so without thought for the consequences for his victim. In part two of *Either/Or*, the aesthete's *ethical* opponent issues dire warnings against a hedonistic life, for it will eventually lead to a loss of identity and to self-destruction. He admonishes the despairing aesthete to choose, to use his free will, and to become an ethical person. The ethical man, a judge, outlines his harmonious, bourgeois life and indicates that, as a moral person, he experiences a kind of pleasure that the aesthete cannot obtain. Nevertheless, in an effort to penetrate the aesthete's armor, the ethical man finally lets a country parson speak and, thereby, suggests a third mode of life. *Either/Or* thus contains the essence of Kierkegaard's system, one that may be more fully delineated in *Stadier paa Livets Vei* (1845; *Stages on Life's Way*, 1940); the three stages are the aesthetic, the ethical, and the religious. That model for human development is, however, not a psychological one, which suggests a gradual process with an overlapping between the stages, but an existential one, which maintains that the individual "leaps" from one stage to a higher one in an instant of choice.

The works that followed *Either/Or* make it clear that the choice of the ethical is insufficient. The ethical person believes in objective truth (cf. Hegel) and will, consequently, discover that his private and public endeavors do not provide him with meaning in life. He will then look at his existence with a sense of irony, which—corresponding to the aesthete's despair—may foreshadow a choice of the religious. From the outset, Kierkegaard informs his readers that the choice of becoming truly religious is absurd; the individual chooses a subjective truth, for which no proof can be given. To live life as a truly religious person will entail many sacrifices and much suffering, for as Kierkegaard pointed out in *Opbyggelige Taler* (1843–1852; *Edifying Discourses*, 1943–1945), "purity of heart means to will one thing." In *Frygt og Bæven* (1843; *Fear and Trembling*, 1941), Kierkegaard offers an example of a truly religious person, the biblical Abraham, who, when called upon, gladly prepared to sacrifice his son. Only such a person—not one who has to rationalize such a sacrifice as being necessary for the common good—is "a knight of faith." For Kierkegaard there was a parallel between Abraham's willingness to sacrifice Isaac and his own decision to sacrifice his love for Regine. The consent to sacrifice, no matter how much suffering it exacts, is the mark of the person of fervent faith. That radical stance is one with which any student of Kierkegaard must come to terms.

Kierkegaard believes in salvation, but not that it is easily obtained. The nature of that salvation is suggested in the prolix and very penetrating study of religious psychology called *Begrebet Angest* (1844; *The Concept of Dread*, 1947). The cause of the individual's loss of purpose in life is angst, a concept that is defined as fear without an object and, thus, fear that is impossible to eliminate. The connection between angst and original sin must be skirted here, but the treatise intimates that only the religious person, as defined by Kierkegaard can endure or cope with angst. In fact, both the aesthete and the ethical person are haunted by angst, and it is that objectless fear that causes them to feel that their lives are becoming meaningless. Neither of these people, according to Kierkegaard, actually chooses himself, and thus their "selves" are abandoned for either empty pleasures or—in reality—equally empty duties (which have been deemed valuable by a bourgeois, hypocritical society). Angst ought—as Martin Heidegger has phrased it—to alert the human being to choose his or her own *self*. Kierkegaard's system, thus, is designed to prod the individual to make those choices that allow the self to emerge.

That idea of the self was a central concern of the nineteenth century, and it reflected a growing secularization of European culture. The term "self" was substituted for "soul," and thus the concept of the core of the human being became an object of debate. It seems, on the one hand, that Kierkegaard refused to participate in that debate by harking back to less reflective ages when Christianity was not doubted, but on the other hand, that he foreshadowed modern ontological relativity. Some Christians may see Kierkegaard as a radical pietist, who drew the most extreme consequence from the belief that all earthly pleasures are sinful, whereas others may find his Christianity to be inhumane and absurd (which Kierkegaard readily admitted). The non-Christian not only may realize that the old question of whether the ends justify the means returns with a vengeance in Kierkegaard's works, but may also find that idealism—commitment to a cause and willingness to sacrifice all—is called into question. It is hardly surprising that such major figures of the late nineteenth century as Henrik Ibsen,* Georg Brandes,* and August Strindberg* were profoundly influenced by Kierkegaard's thoughts.

Kierkegaard's impact on existentialism may initially seem curious, for such figures as Jean Paul Sartre, Simone de Beauvoir, or Albert Camus have had no use for Kierkegaard's third stage, the religious. Thus, Kierkegaard's thinking has been put to very selective use. But if, as Kierkegaard maintained, the higher truth is subjective, and if belief in a divinity is absurd, then to be truly religious is totally a matter of individual awareness. It must be noted that Kierkegaard did not preach about the flames of hell or the bliss of heaven, for the question of whether a person was damned or saved was one that the individual had to resolve in the here and now. That emphasis on individual responsibility has not only attracted those philosophers who inspired the existentialists, such as Martin Heidegger and Karl Jaspers, but also modern Protestant theologians, such as Karl Barth and Paul Tillich, and Jewish philosopher and theologian Martin Buber. Among American writers affected by Kierkegaard one can count John Updike, Walker Percy, and that comic poet of angst, Woody Allen. Kierkegaard scholarship is thriving today, much—if not most—of it outside Scandinavia.

FURTHER WORKS

Samlede Værker, 20 vols. (1963); *Papirer,* 9 vols. (1968–1970).

FURTHER TRANSLATIONS

Philosophical Fragments (1936); *Repetition* (1941); *The Sickness unto Death* (1941); *A Kierkegaard Anthology* (1946); *Concluding Unscientific Postscript* (1962); *The Point of View for My Work as an Author* (1962); *Søren Kierkegaard's Journals and Papers* (1967–1978); *Parables of Kierkegaard* (1978).

REFERENCES

Brandt, Frithiof, *Søren Kierkegaard 1813–1855* (Copenhagen, 1963); Elrod, John William, *Being and Existence in Kierkegaard's Pseudonymous Works* (Princeton, 1975); Himmelstrup, Jens, *Søren Kierkegaard: International Bibliography* (Copenhagen, 1962); Hohlenberg, Johannes, *Søren Kierkegaard* (New York, 1953); Jørgensen, Aage, *Søren Kierkegaard: An International Bibliography 1961–1970* (Århus, 1971); Lowrie, Walter, *A Short Life of Kierkegaard* (Garden City, 1961); Malantschuk, Gregor, *Kierkegaard's Thought* (Princeton, 1971); Stendahl, Brita, *Søren Kierkegaard* (Boston, 1976); Thompson, Josiah, *Kierkegaard* (New York, 1973); Veisland, Jørgen S., *Kierkegaard and the Dialectics of Modernism* (New York, 1985).

Niels Ingwersen

Kihlman, Christer. Finland-Swedish novelist, b. 14 June 1930, Helsinki.

Kihlman comes from a distinguished Finland-Swedish family: his great-grandfather, Alfred Kihlman, was a theologian, an active member of Finland's diet, a pedagogue, and an extraordinarily successful businessman, whose Helsinki mansion stands as a monument to his acumen and energy; his grandfather, Lorenzo Kihlman, was an important diplomat and jurist; an uncle, Erik Kihlman, was a major literary critic in the 1920s, and his father, Bertel Kihlman, an active novelist and translator; the Finnish side of the clan (called, from 1906 on, Kairamo) likewise produced important academicians and industrialists. It is against this background (and against the whole of Finland-Swedish "bourgeois" life) that Kihlman has rebelled in his work. Initial books of verse, *Rummen vid havet* (1951; Rooms by the Sea) and *Munkmonolog* (1953; Monk-monologue) were full of epigonic modernism; but an essay from 1955, "Svenskhetens Slagskugga" (The Shadow Cast By Swedishness), raised many hackles by its attack on the narrowness and hypocrisy of the Finland-Swedish establishment. Its promise was fulfilled with the novel, *Se upp salige!* (1960; Watch Out, Ye Blessed!), in which the numerous faults of the closed society were described (smallness of view, arrogance, and pettiness among them) against the background of a fictitious small town, Lexå—which many took to be Borgå (Finnish: Porvoo), "Finland's Weimar," the home of Johan Ludvig Runeberg.* The book was a sensation, both in Finland and in Sweden (where it confirmed the suspicions Swedes had long liked to entertain about their linguistic brothers to the east). It was followed by the novel that may be regarded as Kihlman's masterpiece, *Den blå modern* (1963; *The Blue Mother*, 1990)—the maritime title presents a reminder of Kihlman's strong interest in Richard Henry Dana's *Two Years Before the Mast*, and the brutal, all-masculine world that the American classic portrayed. Yet the events of the book take place on land, in Kihlman's familiar Finland-Swedish circles: the artistic and familial torments of one brother, Raf, are played off against the sadistic and homosexual phantasies of another, Benno. (Part of these phantasies, described with horrifying brilliance, take place in a German concentration camp; others, in the Helsinki boys' school of which Alfred Kihlman had once been the rector.) *Madeleine* (1965) continues the account from one side, describing the struggles of the gifted brother with his wife and with alcohol; although not of the intensity of *Den blå modern*, it has unforgettable pages concerning what Raf (and Kihlman) perceived as the killing isolation of Finland-Swedish existence. (In Kihlman's work of the time, there is an almost romantic belief that Finns are healthier and more vital than the members of the minority.) Shortly thereafter, Kihlman announced that he was abandoning his literary career because of the financial problems besetting a writer in a miniature culture; but, in 1971, he gave Finland (where his books, in fact, immediately were translated into Finnish) and Sweden a new shock with *Människan som skalv: Boken om det oväsentliga* (The Man Who Trembled: The Book about What's Unessential), a confession of Kihlman's own alcoholism and his bisexuality, as well as some particularly intimate details of his marital life.

Next, Kihlman brought out what was announced as the first volume of a chef d'oeuvre, *Dyre prins* (1976; *Sweet Prince*, 1981), an account of the fortunes of a distinguished Finland-Swedish family, the Blaadhs, and their chieftain, Donald, actually the offspring of a bastard branch, a ruthless self-made man. Somewhat misleadingly (the Blaadhs surely do not have the sense of propriety of Thomas Mann's famous Lübeck clan, nor do they appear in several generations), the book was called a " Finland-Swedish *Buddenbrooks*" by criticism. While traveling in South America in search of material for the suite's continuation (and for descendants of his own family), Kihlman then began the series of homosexual affairs with young men portrayed in *Alla mina söner* (1980; *All My Sons*, 1984), and *Livsdrömmen rena* (1982; Life's Pure Dream); here, Kihlman's stylistic magic is at its most effective—no writer in Swedish, save perhaps Harry Martinson,* has the same ability to capture the genius of tropical places—and Kihlman's belief in the rottenness of the bourgeoisie, set over against the nobility and vitality of the poor, is put on broad and persuasive display; at the same time, his middle-aged affection for tough and handsome youths leads to a mawkishness at which the reader (and perhaps the narrator himself) may smile.

There is no question about Kihlman's place as a leading force in contemporary Finnish letters; for all the apparent sensationalism of his themes (treated, however, with remarkable dignity), he can make—and repeatedly has made—a claim to be the spokesman of an essential morality, aiding others by means of his confessions.

FURTHER WORKS

Inblandningar, utmaningar (1966); *De nakna och de saliga*, with illus. by Henrik Tikkanen (1983); *På drift i förlustens landskap* (1986); *Gerdt Bladhs undergång* (1987).

REFERENCES

Sarajas, Annamari, "A Reading Experience: 'Man Who Tottered.' " *Books from Finland* 6.1 (1972); Schoolfield, G. C., "The Postwar Novel of Swedish Finland." *Scandinavian*

Studies 34.2 (1962); Svedberg, Ingmar, "Extending the Bounds of Reality: An Approach to the Work of Christer Kihlman." *Books from Finland* 10.1–2 (1976).

George C. Schoolfield

Kilpi, Eeva. Finnish short story writer, novelist, poet, and essayist, b. 18 February 1928, Hiitola.

Kilpi's early childhood was spent in Hiitola on the Karelian Isthmus. At the age of eleven, she and her family began a long journey of evacuation. The uprooting of the Karelians from their native soil during the last war, and their subsequent search for new homes and roots, is the theme of her novel *Elämän evakkona* (1983; The Evacuee of Life), one of many works with a strong autobiographical element. Kilpi was married from 1949–1966 and has three sons. The experience of divorce and its aftermath, and the love-hate relationship that can develop between a single parent and her growing children, especially while they are teenagers, are recurring themes in Kilpi. But Kilpi writes from multiple viewpoints, and her stories do not assign guilt to any one person or community. The wider contemporary world with its interlocking problems forms the broader context of her writing.

In her short story collection *Kesä ja keski-ikäinen nainen* (1970; Summer and the Middle-Aged Woman), Kilpi presents her focal character, the solitary middle-aged woman, in her many relationships, all of which demand growing insight into who she is, what her limitations are, and where she can find strength to sustain her new existence. When the nuclear family has collapsed, or when the demands of new love relationships prove too difficult, Kilpi's women find two sources of strength: they discover roots that connect them to their extended Karelian families and to nature. Her extended families are unmistakably Karelian in their capacity to grieve and rejoice together and to accept each other in spite of generation gaps and colliding convictions. Kilpi's characters find nature in the vast Finnish backwoods, where they join its battle to reconquer areas ravaged by modern technology. Nature also points a way to accepting life on its own tough conditions.

Kilpi is a thinker among contemporary Finnish storytellers. Her characters reflect more than they act. Their need to make at least provisional sense of existence keeps them in continual movement between despair and hope, solitude and human community.

FURTHER WORKS

Noidanlukko (1959); *Kukkivan maan rannat* (1960); *Nainen kuvastimessa* (1962); *Elämä edestakaisin* (1964); *Uudet jumalat* (1965); *Lapikkaita* (1966); *Rakkauden ja kuoleman pöytä* (1967); *Hyvän yön tarinoita* (1971); *Laulu rakkaudesta ja muita runoja* (1972); *Tamara* (1972; *trans.* 1978); *Häätanhu* (1973); *Ihmisen ääni* (1976); *Runoja 1972–1976* (1976); *Terveisin* (1976); *Naisen päiväkirja* (1978); *Se mitä ei koskaan sanota* (1979); *Ennen kuolemaa* (1982); *Kuolema ja nuori rakastaja* (1986); *Animalia* (1987); *Kootut novellit* (1987).

FURTHER TRANSLATIONS

Scandinavian Review 71.2 (1983); *Books from Finland* 18.3 (1984).

REFERENCES

Deschner, Margareta N., "Eeva Kilpi: Home and Solitude." *Books from Finland* 18.3 (1984); Kilpi, Eeva, "Summer and the Authoress." *Books from Finland* 5.1 (1971); Haavikko, Ritva, ed., *Miten kirjani ovat syntyneet*, vol. 2 (Helsinki, 1980); Savolainen, Erkki, "Eeva Kilpi and Her Erotical Novel." *Look at Finland* (1973).

Margareta Neovius Deschner

Kilpi, Volter Adalbert. (orig. Ericsson), Finnish novelist, short story writer, and essayist, b. 12 December 1874, Kustavi, d. 13 June 1939, Turku.

Kilpi came from a long line of seafaring men, captains and pilots from the southwest coast of Finland, and described them in his prose works. He took an academic degree and held all his life positions in university libraries, ending as head librarian of the Turku Finnish University. He suffered from progressive deafness, but had a basically robust, extroverted attitude toward life, although he could also describe human misery, dejection, and melancholy. He was a conservative, but established critics did not truly appreciate his art and it was a young radical, Elmer Diktonius,* who understood him best.

In his first works, Kilpi displayed a Nietzschean and aesthetic philosophy of life and art, fashionable at the time, for example, prose poems *Bathseba* (1900), *Parsifal* (1902), *Antinous* (1903); essays *Ihmisestä ja elämästä* (1902; About Man and Life), "Nykyajan taidepyrinnöistä" ("About Trends in Modern Art" in *Valvoja*, 1905). His philosophy is rather wordy and confused, but he had a keen eye for the visual arts and knew the works of contemporary European painters. He published his main works, the two-volume novel *Alastalon salissa* (In the Alastalo Hall) in 1933, the novel *Kirkolle* (To the Church) in 1937, and the short stories *Pitäjän pienempiä* (The Small People of the County) in 1934. They are about the near past in his home region, its inhabitants, captains and sailors, shipowners and fishers, farmers and small craftsmen, and represent an effort to catch, as he himself wrote, "the fleeting memory of a painful and rapturous moment." This effort leads him to describe in infinite detail his characters and their physical appearance; their actions, words, and thoughts; their surroundings and the objects they handle. This does not, however, result in a mere heaping of details, but grows into a coherent whole that gives what Kilpi himself called a "plastic," that is, sculptural, picture of a human group, its members, the bonds that unite or the contrasts that repel them. For his purposes, Kilpi created a language and style of his own—apart from the fact that he used elements from western dialects not found in standard Finnish—curiously combining his earlier aestheticism and his new realism; they remain close to the everyday reality of his characters, yet they describe a reality far deeper than that.

In his lifetime, Kilpi was much criticized for what was described as his oddities, and he can never be a popular writer—*Alastalon salissa* renders on 900 pages a six-hour discussion about building a ship—but his novels are now considered to be among the foremost in Finnish literature. They are the result of an immense and successful effort to give a full picture of a human situation and to create a language adequate to this attempt.

FURTHER WORKS

Kansallista itsetutkistelua (1917); *Tulevaisuuden edessä* (1918); *Suomenkielisen kirjallisuuden varhaispainokset vuoteen 1642* (1924); *Suljetuilla porteilla* (1933); *Gulliverin matka Fantomimian mantereelle*, unfinished (1944).

REFERENCES

Suomi, V., *Nuori Volter Kilpi* (Helsinki, 1952); Suomi, V., "Volter Kilven mestarivuodet," in *Juhlakirja Eino Kauppisen täyttäessä 60 vuotta* (Tampere, 1970).

Jaakko Ahokas

Kinck, Hans Ernst. Norwegian novelist, short story writer, dramatist, and essayist, b. 11 October 1865, Øksfjord in Finnmark, d. 13 October 1926, Oslo.

The son of a government physician, Kinck acquired wide knowledge of Norway's rural districts, people, and traditions. Decisive for his artistic development were years in Setesdal, an isolated valley rich in medieval lore, and Hardanger in the west. At the University of Oslo Kinck studied Greek, Latin, Old Norse, and philosophy and could have had an academic career; as a writer he drew widely on his studies. Kinck spent years abroad, first in Paris where he was inspired by painting, later in Italy where he encountered the Renaissance and baroque. Kinck was married to the author Minda Ramm.

Kinck was an enormously productive writer. His novels explore Western rural society, class and cultural tensions between natives and government officials, and people's longing for community, solidarity, and harmony. Considered best is *Fru Anny Porse* (1900; Mrs. Anny Porse). In *Ungt folk* (1893; *A Young People*, 1929) an uncouth social climber ruthlessly lays the community at his feet. Yet there is hope, an "ideal spark" in his character, promising vitality for the young Norwegian nation. Emigration to America, given impetus by the rootlessness of social upheaval, and longing, are the subject of *Emigranter* (1904; Emigrants) and the story "Den hvite lille dame" (1901; The Little White Lady). Of his many short story collections, *Flaggermus-vinger* (1895; Bat Wings), lyrical tales of "dusk people" influenced by painting and folklore, is perhaps the finest. Like Gjertrud in "Hvitsymre i utslaatten" ("White Anemones," 1982), who finds the essence of love, while her partner is locked in bourgeois notions of matrimony, the characters are at one with nature. *Driftekaren* (1908; The Drover), Kinck's best drama, illustrates the dilemma of modern man.

In his lifetime Kinck never achieved the stature many thought he deserved, but he has since gained a position alongside Knut Hamsun.* Kinck laid much groundwork for assimilation of dialect words into Dano-Norwegian and the use of dialect in dialogue, revitalizing Norwegian language. He experimented with form in the short story, novel and drama, drawing on other arts to create his special atmosphere. His stories are hardly surpassed; his novels and dramas may yet be too experimental to be fully appreciated.

FURTHER WORKS

Huldren (1892); *Eventyr vestfra* (1895); *Sus* (1896); *Fra hav til hei* (1897); *Hugormen* (1898); *Mellom togene* (1898); *Trækfugle og andre* (1899); *Vaarnætter* (1901); *Doktor Gabriel Jahr* (1902); *Naar kærlighed dør* (1903); *Italienere* (1904); *Præsten* (1905); *Livsaanderne* (1906); *Agilulf den vise* (1906); *Gammel jord* (1907); *Masker og mennesker* (1909); *Den siste gjest* (1910); *Bryllupet i Genua* (1911); *En penneknekt* (1911); *Spanske høstdøgn* (1912); *Paa Ekre'rnes gaard* (1913); *Mot karneval* (1915); *Renæssance- mennesker* (1916); *Kirken brænder* (1917); *Noveller i utvalg*, 2 vols. (1918); *Sneskavlen brast*, 3 vols. (1918–1919); *Stammens røst* (1919); *Guldalder* (1919); *Rormanden ov- erbord* (1920); *Lisabettas brødre* (1921); *Mange slags kunst* (1921); *Fra Fonneland til Svabergssveen* (1922); *Storhetstid* (1922); *Herman Ek* (1923; rev. ed. of *Sus* and *Hug- ormen*); *Steder og folk* (1924); *Paa Rindalslægret* (1925); *Foraaret i Mikropolis* (1926); *Italien og vi* (1926); *Kunst og kunstnere* (1928); *Torvet i Cirta* (1928); *Sagaenes ånd og skikkelser* (1951).

FURTHER TRANSLATIONS

Norway's Best Stories, ed. Hanna Astrup Larsen (1927); *Slaves of Love and Other Norwegian Short Stories*, ed. J. McFarlane (1982).

REFERENCES

Beyer, Edvard, *Hans E. Kinck,* 2 vols. (Oslo, 1956–1965); Bukdahl, Jørgen, "Hans E. Kinck." *American Scandinavian Review* 15.10 (1927); Coleman, Nancy L., *The Syn- thesizing Art: A Study of Hans E. Kinck's Short Stories* (Diss., Ann Arbor, 1975); Gierløff, Christian, *Hans E. Kinck* (Oslo, 1923); Lea, Dina, *Hans E. Kinck* (Oslo, 1941); Nettum, Rolf Nyboe, *En undersøkelse av Hans E. Kincks livssyn* (Oslo, 1949).

Nancy L. Coleman

Kingo, Thomas. Danish hymnist and poet, b. 15 December 1634, Slangerup, d. 10 April 1703, Odense.

Son of a weaver of Scottish origin, Kingo studied theology and became a successful servant of the Danish State Church; he was eventually appointed bishop during what was to be a century of strict Lutheran dogmatism. Some of his sensual and humorous poems are preserved, as well as the occasional poetry that he wrote throughout his life praising, in baroque hyperbole, the high and mighty of the realm, but his reputation rests on the multitude of hymns he composed. His *Aandelige Siungekoor* (2 vols., 1673, 1681; Spiritual Chorus) and *Vinterparten* (1689; The Winter Part) contain the culmination of baroque poetry in Denmark; they reveal Kingo's skill in utilizing baroque poetics: he knew how to employ the stylistic machinery of the time in such a way that the monotony that characterizes much of the baroque—at least in retrospect—was avoided. Like all baroque poets Kingo strove for an effect of emotional intensity, but in contrast to many of his colleagues, he achieved it.

In most of his texts a sense of antithesis dominates and captures the essence of life during the turbulent 1600s. During that century, which saw the establishment of an absolute monarchy in Denmark-Norway, commoners with education and ambition strove for power and wealth—Kingo must be counted among them—only to find that their success was often illusory, since their patrons let them down or lost their own positions of influence. Despite the age's being one of rigid dogmatism and strict social order, and thus a far cry from a Renaissance culture, one can detect in Scandinavian writings from the 1600s Renaissance impulses that stand in contrast to the official ideas of the age. That tension can be felt in many of Kingo's hymns: in some, Kingo admonishes the human being to accept his or her lot on this earth, since heaven will eventually offer the stability and order that this deceptive life cannot; in others, however, Kingo obviously refuses to convey that message of meek acceptance. In the famous "Far, Verden, Farvel" (Fare, World, Farewell) the voice speaking takes a radical stand by rejecting everything this-worldly as being mere vanity and yearns for the moment when the soul will rest in Abraham's bosom. Close analysis of the hymn will, curiously, show that the soul is deeply infatuated with the world thus being so harshly rejected and expects a grand spiritual reimbursement in paradise for its disappointments on this earth. Although Kingo often renders the human being as sinful, in this case the soul is someone who, nearly wronged, deserves the reward awaiting it.

The fluctuation in attitudes is bound to confuse the modern reader, and even though one can rationalize about the causes of that vacillation by assuming that Kingo intentionally created moods befitting the occasions for which he wrote (for example, the Passion and Resurrection during Easter), it is discernible that his vision grew darker with the passing of years. On the surface one finds in these hymns an expression of officialdom, but in the subtext, a lust for life. Kingo seems caught between the age's Lutheran dogmatism and the spirit of the Renaissance, and thus, he captures the essence of Danish baroque.

FURTHER WORKS

Samlede Skrifter, 7 vols. (Copenhagen, 1939–1975).

TRANSLATIONS

A Heritage in Song, ed. Johannes Knudsen (1978).

REFERENCES

Simonsen, Dag Finn, *Diktet og Makten* (Copenhagen, 1984); Simonsen, Johannes, *Thomas Kingo. Hofpoet og salmedigter* (Copenhagen, 1970); Thomsen, Ejnar, *Barokken i dansk digtning* (Copenhagen, 1971).

Niels Ingwersen

Kirk, Hans Rudolf. Danish novelist and critic, b. 11 January 1898, Hadsund, d. 16 June 1962, Copenhagen.

In his childhood Kirk experienced the strong social conflicts between rustic culture and the developing industrial and urban culture. He came from a radical family with a social consciousness, and he early learned the differences among social classes. An important theme in his writings, the conflict between the "Grundtvigianism" of the religious mainstream and "Indre Mission," is also based on the personal experience of his childhood and youth. In one of his major works, *Skyggespil* (1953; A Game of Shadows), a collection of memoirs, he has described his own social and cultural roots with remarkable realism and profound empathy.

Kirk earned a law degree from the University of Copenhagen in 1922, but his official career was brief. By the mid–1920s he had begun another career as journalist, critic, and author. He started out in the provincial press but soon became engaged in the radical and socialist circle in Copenhagen, where he became a leading figure. In 1931 he joined the Communist party, and from 1934 until his death he was the leading critic and cultural spokesman for the communist newspaper *Arbejderbladet* (after 1945, *Land og Folk*).

Although Kirk's authorship and line of thought are deeply influenced by Marxism and Freudianism, he is not a dogmatic or schematic writer. His novels are expressions of socialistic humanism and offer, in a vivid style, realistic portraits of both individual and social life. His most significant and popular works are the collective novels *Fiskerne* (1928; The Fishermen), *Daglejerne* (1936; The Day-Laborers), and its sequel, *De ny Tider* (1939; The New Era). They represent a new realistic tradition in Danish literature, a renewal of the Martin Andersen Nexø* tradition, portraying the breakthrough of the working class in Denmark and the birth of industrialized society.

After World War II Kirk's works became more satirical, philosophical, and allegorical. In the two historical novels *Slaven* (1948; The Slave) and *Vredens Søn* (1950; The Son of Wrath), he is not only describing the era of slave trading and the story of Jesus in social perspective, but he also discusses the problem of power and oppression in relation to his contemporaries and the experiences during the world war.

Kirk is a popular and much-read author in Denmark, and a prominent figure within the realistic tradition. His work as a critic and essayist is an important contribution to the development of a socialist and humanistic culture.

FURTHER WORKS

I Dyst for Livet (1930); *Borgmesteren gaar af* (1941); *Forvorpen Ungdom* (1941); *Kulturelle kommentarer* (1941); *Processen mod Scavenius* (1946); *Djævelens penge* (1952); *Klitgaard & sønner* (1952); *Præstens Søn* (1958); *Borgerlige noveller* (1958); *Danmarksrejsen* (1966); *Breve fra Horserød* (1967); *Det borgerlige frisinds endeligt* (1969); *Litteratur og tendens* (1974); *Jeppe og Nille og deres hund Tobias* (1977); *Godtfolk* (1980); *Hug til højre og venstre* (1981); *En plads i verden og andre fortællinger* (1987).

FURTHER TRANSLATIONS

Norseman 14.2 (1956); *Contemporary Danish Prose*, ed. Elias Bredsdorff (1958, 1974).

REFERENCES

Andersen, Jens Kr., and Leif Emerek, *Hans Kirks forfatterskab* (Copenhagen, 1971, 1974); Claudi, Jørgen, *Contemporary Danish Authors* (Copenhagen, 1952); Jensen, Carsten, *Folkelighed og utopi. Brydninger i Hans Kirks forfatterskab* (Copenhagen, 1981); Kristensen, Sven Møller, *Contemporary Danish Literature* (Copenhagen, 1956); Thierry, Werner, *Hans Kirk* (Copenhagen, 1977).

Ib Bondebjerg

Kivi, Aleksis (pseud. of Aleksis Stenvall). Finnish novelist, poet, and playwright, b. 10 October 1834, Palojoki (Nurmijärvi), d. 31 December 1872, Tuusula.

The son of a country tailor, Kivi suffered many privations during his studies but was able to register at Helsinki University. He did not subsequently take a degree, but read widely and soon started writing, encouraged in his efforts by a few well-known personalities, who secured him the prize of the Society for Finnish Literature for his tragedy *Kullervo* (1860), on a subject from the *Kalevala* epic, and the National Literary Award for the rural comedy *Nummisuutarit* (1865; Village Cobblers). His play *Lea*, on a biblical subject, was performed at the Finnish (later National) Theater in 1869, a date considered to mark the beginning of professional theater in Finland. He lived, however, always in straitened circumstances, for, in a country as sparsely populated as Finland was then and much later still, it was impossible for a writer to live on royalties, yet Kivi devoted himself entirely to writing. The happiest period of his life falls between 1863 and 1870, when he lived not far from Helsinki in the home of a woman several years older than he, who took motherly care of him. Kivi had the opportunity to write and to enjoy healthy outdoors life, but his dependent position irked him, and at times, he indulged in alcohol, which, together with the privations he had to suffer, contributed to ruin his health. His mental health suffered too, and when his great novel *Seitsemän veljestä* (1870; *Seven Brothers*, 1929; adapted for the stage, movies 1939, 1979 /animated film/) was the object of violently negative criticism, he had to be committed to a psychiatric clinic, from which he was released, but he never recovered and died at the home of his brother. It was not until the beginning of this century that his greatness was truly understood.

Kivi's only work of fiction, *Seitsemän veljestä*, has rather overshadowed the rest of his production, which, however, is not unimportant. *Nummisuutarit* is very popular and has been made into a movie (1923); *Kullervo* has been performed several times; and the broad farce *Olviretki Schleusingenissä* (1866), first considered too coarse and not staged until 1920, has been performed several times since. His other plays, the romantic tragedies *Karkurit* (1867; Escapees) and *Canzio* (1868), are seldom produced, *Karkurit* more often than *Canzio*, which has however quite recently had a number of successful performances. His poems, not written in the accepted forms of his time but in a meter developed by himself, were not truly appreciated until 1950 and after, although some of them are of the highest quality. They express an ethereal, dreamy love ("On-nelliset," "Sunnuntai"), or the relation of mother and child, happy as in "Lapsi" or "Kaunisnummella," or tragic, as in "Äiti ja lapsi," or visions of another world, dreamlike and far away, yet made of elements taken from a familiar Finnish nature ("Kesäyö," "Kaukametsä," "Lintukoto"). *Seven Brothers* also includes a few humorous songs sung by the characters. What most shocked Kivi's contemporaries were his descriptions of drunkenness and fighting, frank enough but very innocent when compared to what has been written later in Finland and elsewhere. Sex is almost totally absent in Kivi's works, or consists, outside the poems, in a young man asking for a young woman's hand, marrying her, and living happily ever after, as in *Seven Brothers*; or being rejected and ridiculed, as in the plays *Nummisuutarit* and *Kihlaus* (1866; Engagement).

Seven Brothers can be described as a moral story about seven young men who have inherited a substantial farm, but prefer to give it on lease and live free in the woods, hunting and fishing. However, after various incidents that end in a near tragedy, they come back to civilized life, marry, settle down, and live as industrious, law-abiding citizens. This side in the novel was earlier emphasized by well-meaning critics, who tried to defend Kivi against the charges of im-morality and brutality leveled at him, but the book is in fact much more than that, a broad and wide-ranging epic about the primeval activities of man in a savage and cultivated nature, his inner life and his relations to fellow men. It is realistic in the description of everyday work, building a house, clearing up ground for cultivation, plowing and sowing, fishing and hunting, but it also expresses the fundamental human meaning of such work. All human emotions, boisterous humor, violent and near-murderous hatred, dejection and terror due to alcohol—drunkenness is not only funny in Kivi—affection and comradeship are described in a simple and elemental yet penetrating manner through the reactions of the highly individual main characters.

The human breadth and depth of *Seven Brothers*, Kivi's undoubted master-piece, can be understood everywhere in the world, a fact that no doubt accounts for its being translated into at least thirteen languages, including Japanese, several times in some of them. His plays have a more limited appeal, and his poetry has remained practically unknown outside Finland, unjustly, though, considering its artistic level and wide range of subject as well as emotion.

FURTHER WORKS

Aino, lost (1860); *Vuoripeikot* (1864); *Kanervala* (1866); *Sankariteos*, lost (1867); *Leo ja Liina* (1867); *Yö ja päivä* (1867); *Alma*, unfinished (1869); *Selman juonet*, unfinished (1869); *Margareta* (1872); *Eriikka*, unfinished (n.d.); *Koto ja kahleet*, unfinished (n.d.); *Teokset* (1984).

FURTHER TRANSLATIONS

Voices from Finland, ed. Elli Tompuri (1947); *An Introduction to Finnish Literature*, ed. Ilmari Havu (1952); *Singing Finland*, ed. K. V. Ollilainen (1956).

REFERENCES

Castrén, G., *J. V. Snellmans kritik och Aleksis Kivi* (Helsinki, 1958); Elo, P., *Aleksis Kiven persoonallisuus* (Vaasa, 1950); Envall, Markku, *Aleksis Kiven maailmasta* (Helsinki, 1984); Haltsonen, S., *Aleksis Kivi. Bibliografinen opas Kiven maailmaan* (Helsinki, 1964); Kinnunen, A., *Aleksis Kiven näytelmät* (Porvoo, 1967); Kinnunen, A., *Tuli, aurinko ja seitsemän veljestä* (Helsinki, 1973); Laitinen, K., "Aleksis Kivi: The Man and His World." *American-Scandinavian Review* 50.4 (1962); Laitinen, K., "Aleksis Kivi 1834–1972—The Man and His Work." *Books from Finland* 18.3 (1984); Lounela, P., "The Stages of Aleksis Kivi." *Books from Finland* 18.3 (1984); Maury, L. "Aleksis Kivi," in *L'Imagination scandinave* (Paris, 1928); Nopsanen, A., "Aleksis Kivi—Master of Finnish Comedy." *Norseman* (1948); Tarkiainen, V., *Aleksis Kivi. Elämä ja teokset* (Porvoo, 1950), Viljanen, L., *Aleksis Kiven runomaailma* (Porvoo, 1953).

Jaakko Ahokas

Kjær, Nils. Norwegian essayist, critic, and dramatist, b. 11 November 1870, Holmestrand, d. 9 February 1924, Oslo.

Brought up in a middle-class home, Kjær early sympathized with political radicalism and even wrote in New Norwegian.* A subsequent about-face pitted him against social reforms and New Norwegian. Glorifying individual freedom, Kjær developed an anarchistic view of the state, eventually waging war on Marxism and communism and giving Italian fascism whole-hearted support.

Literature Kjær studied largely on his own. In his critical manifest he proclaims a program of writing "soul monographs" rather than cultural trends. He saw criticism as both science and art, writing himself impressionistic critiques. Kjær's best-known play is *Det lykkelige valg* (1913; The Fortunate Election), one of the most vital comedies in Norway. Lavinia, wife of the politician Celius, defeats him in election to Parliament. The irony aims at politicians' egocentrism and nonsense in politics, but also makes merciless fun of leftist issues, New Norwegian, and abstinence. The message is dubious, even reactionary; longevity is due to the comic situations and priceless dialogue. One of the strangest plays in Norwegian literature is the Strindbergian *Regnskapets Dag* (1902; Day of Reckoning) on the theme of guilt and suffering and final destruction. In this and two other plays, *Mimosas hjemkomst* (1907; Mimosa's Homecoming) and *For træet er det håp* (1917; Hope for the Tree), Kjær expounds on cultural decline and hollowness, finding religious salvation in the latter play.

Nicknamed "The Golden Pen," Kjær called himself a mere idler. He is regarded as one of the finest stylists in Dano-Norwegian literature. One of the founders of professional literary criticism, which grew up in the 1890s, Kjær was a leading essayist and man of letters in his day. He took up the art of epistle writing begun by Ludvig Holberg* and continued by Aasmund Vinje.* The salty humor, elegance, and irony of his language make his work live on. Because of his political views Kjær remains controversial.

FURTHER WORKS

Essays. Fremmede Forfattere (1895); *Bøger og Billeder* (1898); *I Forbigaaende* (1903); *De evige Savn* (1907); *Smaa Epistler* (1908); *Nye Epistler* (1912); *Svundne Somre* (1920); *Samlede Skrifter*, 5 vols. (1921–1922); *Siste Epistler* (1924).

REFERENCES

Kjær, Margrete, *Nils Kjær og hans samtidige* (Oslo, 1950); Noreng, Harald, *Nils Kjær. Fra radikal til reaksjonær* (Oslo, 1949).

Nancy L. Coleman

Knudsen, Erik. Danish poet, dramatist, essayist, and teacher, b. 27 March 1922, Slagelse.

Knudsen's attitude as a creative writer is strongly related to his role as a teacher and pedagogue. Closely connected with the Danish folk high school as a teacher for Krogerup High School from 1954 to 1982, Knudsen has furthermore been a diligent lecturer and participant in the ongoing public, cultural, and political debates. He was married to the writer Lise Sørensen in 1947 and was a member of the Danish Academy, 1966–1972.

Knudsen was attached to the literary periodical *Heretica* (1948–1953), reflecting his existentialist bend and postwar experience of crisis and bewilderment. His poetic debut—also inspired by the Swedish poets of the 1940s like Gunnar Ekelöf,* Erik Lindegren,* and Karl Vennberg*—is permeated by the outsider's feeling of unreality and desire to be engaged. The well-known, excellent collection of poems, *Blomsten og Sværdet* (1949; The Flower and the Sword), which vocalizes both fear and hope, draws its inspiration from the split between religious-poetic doubt and political commitment. Consequently, whereas Knudsen shared the anti-ideological humanism of *Heretica*, he came to dissociate himself from its self-centered, religiously colored tone. Knudsen left *Heretica* and became coeditor (together with Sven Møller Kristensen) of the socialist *Dialog*. Knudsen was in the forefront of the popular revolt that climaxed in the Vietnam antiwar movement in the 1960s and 1970s. He never became a doctrinaire Marxist; his standpoint was that of the ethically concerned humanist, as he states in his literary manifesto *Galileis kikkert* (1952; Galileo's Telescope).

Knudsen's early complex, metaphorical language underwent a change toward the straightforward, simple diction, and he has found successful new outlets for his social and moral messages such as the musical comedy and pamphlet poetry. Knudsen's commitment to humanitarian and political causes need not be a hindrance to poetic creativity; he will surely continue to find new ways of expression to prove this.

FURTHER WORKS

Dobbelte Dage (1945); *Til en ukendt Gud* (1947); *Fantomer* (1949); *Brændpunkt* (1953); *Friedleben* (1954); *Minotaurus* (1955); *Markedsanalyser* (1957); *Sensation og Stilhed*

(1958); *Digte 1945–58* (1958); *Taskenspil* (1960); *Frihed—det bedste guld* (1961); *Journal* (1963); *Det er ikke til at bære* (1963); *Læn Dem ikke ud* (1965); *Nik Nik Nikolaj* (1966); *Madman og hans verden* (1967); *Slap af* (1968); *Menneskebomben* (1968); *Anklagen Vietnam* (1969); *Tag parti* (1969); *Babylon marcherer* (1970); *Udvalgte digte* (1970); *Werner Holgersen* (1971); *Offervilje* (1972); *Vietnam* (1973); *Engang blir Danmark frit* (1974); *Snart dages det brødre* (1974); *Kommunister* (1976); *Hvem har bolden?* (1977); *Forsøg på at gå* (1978); *En oprørt folkelig modstand* (1981); *Ord fra Humlebæk* (1986).

FURTHER TRANSLATIONS

20th Century Scandinavian Poetry, ed. Martin S. Allwood (1950); *Contemporary Danish Poetry*, ed. Line Jensen et al. (1977); *Seventeen Danish Poets*, ed. Niels Ingwersen (1981).

Charlotte Schiander Gray

Knudsen, Jakob. Danish novelist and essayist, b. 14 September 1858, Rødding, d. 21 January 1917, Birkerød.

Knudsen's social background is the provincial vicarage, the rural culture with its attachment to the movement of Grundtvigianism and the folk high school. Knudsen was a student in 1877 in Copenhagen and was awarded a bachelor of divinity degree in 1881 from the University of Copenhagen. In this period he was also influenced by naturalism. Between 1881 and 1890 Knudsen worked as a teacher at the famous Askov Folk High School, and from 1890 to 1896 as vicar at Mellerup. But his divorce and remarriage to a young girl caused such a scandal in Grundtvigian circles that he had to leave his job and for the rest of his life live by his pen.

Knudsen's authorship bears witness to dramatic social and psychological conflicts, and his novels are heavily loaded with conflicting ideas and moral issues. A strong conservatism, austere morality, and religious tradition meet with an ecstatic mysticism and longing for freedom and love. This conflict between an old-fashioned, restricted view of life and a more modern feeling of expansion and development often results in drastic actions in his novels, in violence, killing, desperation and despair, or even insanity. Many of Knudsen's novels are suppressed pamphlets advocating authoritarian relationships between adult and child, man and woman, employer and worker; and his attacks on social and political reforms are many. In novels such as *Den gamle Præst* (1899; The Old Vicar), *Fremskridt* (1907; Progress), and *Lærer Urup* (1909; Urup the Teacher) he shows himself as a very reactionary author condemning the democratic tendencies at his time. More artistic strength and less tense ideological conflicts are to be found in his three major works, *Gjæring-Afklaring* (1902; Fermentation-Clarification), *Sind* (1903; Temper), and *Angst-Mod* (1912–1914; Fear-Courage). The first and last are novels describing a young man's development; the middle one is more like an Icelandic saga with its portrait of passion and feud among Jutlandish peasants. The two novels of development are attempts to understand and control those conflicts of authority and those religious and psychological contradictions that break up the universe of his authorship.

Knudsen also wrote a considerable number of philosophical and religious essays, and altogether his significance lies in his conservative and religious challenge to the Modern Breakthrough after Georg Brandes.*

FURTHER WORKS

Cromwells Datter (1891); *Christelige Foredrag* (1893); *Et Gjensyn* (1898); *For Livets Skyld* (1905); *Inger* (1906); *Varulven* (1908); *Livsfilosofi* (1908); *To slægter* (1910); *Rodfæstet* (1911); *En Ungdom* (1913); *Jyder*, 2 vols. (1915–1917); *Den Gang* (1916); *Digte* (1938); *Ide og Erindring* (1949); *At være sig selv* (1965).

FURTHER TRANSLATIONS

Contemporary Danish Prose, ed. Alexander Taylor et al. (1958, 1974).

REFERENCES

Andersen, Richard, *Jakob Knudsen* (Copenhagen, 1958); Begtrup, Holger, *Jakob Knudsen* (Copenhagen, 1918); Bredsdorff, Elias, *An Introduction to Scandinavian Literature* (Copenhagen, 1951); Jones, W. Glyn, "*Det forjættede Land* and *Fremskridt* as Social Novels: A Comparison." *Scandinavian Studies* 37.1 (1965); Roos, Carl, *Jakob Knudsen* (Copenhagen, 1954); Schmidt, Povl, *Drømmens dør. Læsninger i Jakob Knudsens forfatterskab*. (Odense, 1984).

Ib Bondebjerg

Koch, Martin. Swedish novelist, essayist, and poet, b. 23 December 1882, Stockholm, d. 22 June 1940, Hedemora.

Although Koch, together with Gustaf Hedenvind-Eriksson, is accounted the father of the proletarian novel in Sweden, his own background was petty-bourgeois and included several years of preparatory school. His identification with the urban working class nevertheless came early, largely through involvement with the temperance movement and its cultural and educational efforts. Koch's first novel, *Ellen* (1911), a love story about a factory girl who dies of tuberculosis, is saved from cliché by the detailed, realistic descriptions of the Stockholm working-class environment, among the first in Swedish literature. In the collective novel *Arbetare* (1912; Workers), a series of incidents typical of the period following the Great Strike of 1909, when the workers' movement was in disarray, reveals from the inside the conflicting approaches and attitudes their cause encompassed, from tactical, cautious social-democratic reform to fanatic idealism leading to anarchy.

Timmerdalen (1913; Timber Valley), about the industrialization of northern Sweden and in particular the plight of sawmill workers in coastal towns, is less the product of personal experience than the result of extensive research; it includes an analysis of both the Sundsvall strike of 1879—the first major labor conflict in Sweden—and a later, contemporaneous dispute. Koch's sympathies are obviously with the workers and his satire of those in power is broad, but the characterizations offer considerable psychological insight regardless of an individual's political persuasion.

Koch's masterpiece, *Guds vackra värld* (1916; God's Beautiful World), contrasts the old patriarchal agricultural system with the development of an impersonal capitalism, but is most memorable for its portrayal of the thief Frasse, who epitomizes the egocentricity that the author sees as the root of all evil. To Koch, political and social issues are not just matters of expediency but call for a moral stance, as the subtitle of the novel—*En historia om rätt och orätt* (A Story about Right and Wrong)—indicates. In his subsequent, primarily journalistic production, Koch continued to explore moral issues, for instance, in essays on the history of religion. His last novel, *Mauritz* (1939), gives a lively and unsentimental account of his childhood.

Koch belongs to the first generation of Swedish writers to describe working-class life with realism and from within. His novels are valuable documents of social history that often include considerable exposition of the theoretical issues of the workers' movement in light of broader moral concerns. Koch's sense of drama, his eye for everyday detail, and his ear for patterns of speech assure their survival as literature as well.

FURTHER WORKS

I Vattendroppen (1912); *Vargungarna* (1913); *Litterära storverk i västficksformat* (1913); *Februaridagarna 1914* (1914); *Blodet ropar* (1914); *Frihet och frihet* (1915); *Det glömda landet* (1915); *Romantiska brev* (1915); *Fromma människor* (1918); *Anteckningar på havet* (1918); *Upplösningstidens teologi* (1919); *Legend* (1920); *Proletärdiktning* (1929); *Dansvisor* (1929); *Svart på vitt* (1930); *Valda verk*, 7 vols. (1940–1941); *Brev från Martin Koch* (1957).

REFERENCES

Granlid, Hans O., *Martin Koch och arbetarskildringen* (Stockholm, 1957); Jonsson, Thorsten, *Martin Koch* (Stockholm, 1941); Lund(ström), Inge(borg), *Martin Koch* (Stockholm, 1945); Sundström, Erik, *Radikalism och religiositet* (Stockholm, 1961).

Rochelle Wright

Køltzow, Liv. Norwegian novelist, b. 14 January 1945, Oslo.

Øyet i treet (1970; The Eye in the Tree), Køltzow's first collection of short stories, provides minutely observed descriptions of the concrete physical detail of everyday experience. With her next book, however, she changes to a more straightforward, everyday narrative tone. *Hvem bestemmer over Bjørg og Unni?* (1972: Who Decides for Bjørg and Unni?) is a novel about the needs of the individual confronted by the faceless authority of a bureaucratic society. Two young women, Bjørg and Unni, faced with a council decision that will diminish the quality of their lives, decide to resist, and glimpse the way out of passive acceptance toward a more active control of their own lives. In *Historien om Eli* (1975; The Story of Eli), Køltzow returns to the form of the *Entwicklungsroman*, tracing the development of the girl Eli from early childhood until the age of twenty-eight. It is a story of self-discovery, in which Eli has to fight not only against social conventions and other people's expectations, but against forces in herself that precondition her into fatalistic acceptance of "the female role." By the end of the novel, however, she is taking her first tentative steps toward self-reliance and independent decision. With *Løp, mann* (1980; Run, Man), Køltzow moves on to the problems of a maturer age; here the focus is on a group of former young radical intellectuals who have settled down, had families, become "established." The novel explores the tensions between them as they try to reconcile their ideals with the compromises that maturity inevitably involves.

Køltzow is presumably still in the early stages of her literary career, but has already made a name for herself as a meticulous observer of people's (especially women's) habits of thought and conditions of life.

FURTHER WORKS

April/November (1983).

REFERENCES

Engelstad, Irene, "Kvinnespråk og kvinnelig bevissthet: om Liv Køltzows forfatterskap," in *Linjer i norsk prosa 1965–75,* ed. Helge Rønning (Oslo, 1977); Engelstad, Irene, and Irene Iversen, "Tre tilnærmingsmåter til kvinnelitteraturen," in *Et annet språk*, ed. Mai Bente Bonnevie et al. (Oslo, 1977); Rasmussen, Janet E., "Dreams and Discontent: The Female Voice in Norwegian Literature," in *Review of National Literatures: Norway*, ed. Sverre Lyngstad (New York, 1983).

Janet Garton

Kötlum, Jóhannes úr.   *See* Jóhannes úr Kötlum.

Koskenniemi, Veikko Antero.   Finnish poet, critic, essayist, translator, and writer of aphorisms, b. 8 July 1885, Turku, d. 4 August 1962, Turku.

Koskenniemi's debut collection *Runoja* (1906; Poems) began a poetic career that lasted over four decades and received both praise and belittlement. As a member of the Old Finnish party Koskenniemi was a rival of the Young Finnish Eino Leino.* Although cosmopolitan in his art, Koskenniemi was a nationalist in his political views and thus the exact opposite of Leino. From Leino's death in 1926 to the end of World War II, Koskenniemi ranked as the leading poet in Finland and was regarded as the semiofficial spokesperson for the nation's collective feelings. After the war his stature as a poet as well as a moral authority declined for poetic and political reasons alike; free verse was introduced, and the German orientation that Koskenniemi had advocated suffered defeat.

Koskenniemi's poetic prototypes can be found in the French *Les Parnassiens* school and in antiquity. Natural sciences, the materialistic monism of the turn of the century in particular, exerted an influence on the contents of Koskenniemi's rather philosophical poetry. Of basic concern in his pessimistic and impersonal poetry are the human condition and the fate of humans in a cold universe. Later on human destiny is viewed also in the light of tragic optimism. Modern readers feel alienated by the pathos of Koskenniemi's choral poetry and by his attempts to force antique meters upon the Finnish language, whereas his view of man's loneliness in a hostile world, akin to existentialist thinking, has met with understanding even among postwar generations.

Koskenniemi's official career was brilliant; in 1921 he became, by invitation, a professor of literature at the University of Turku and in 1948 a member of the Finnish Academy. He was influential and prolific as a critic, essayist, and scholar. His essays are erudite and perceptive even if at times invoking excessive pathos. The fact that Goethe, who was the primary focus of Koskenniemi's scholarly endeavors, was also his personal idol and role model did not detract from the scholarly quality of his monograph on Goethe (I, 1932; II, 1944). Koskenniemi also wrote biographies of Aleksis Kivi,* Maila Talvio, and Werner Söderström. Due to his three collections of aphorisms, Koskenniemi ranks among the best and most widely read aphorists in Finland. His extensive and multifaceted oeuvre also includes a novel, memoirs, travelogues, political writings, and epigrams.

Despite the fact that Koskenniemi's influence on the formal aspects of Finnish poetry ended after World War II, a similar break does not apply to his essays, his attitudes, or his aphorisms. The narrow-minded way of viewing Koskenniemi's poetry as if cast in a single mold has tended to depreciate his importance. Today's more variegated critical approach should, however, result in at least a partial "rehabilitation" of Koskenniemi's art.

FURTHER WORKS

Kootut teokset, 12 vols. (1955–1956).

REFERENCES

Luojola, Yrjö, *V. A. Koskenniemen totuudenetsijä-motiivi* (Porvoo, 1962); Luojola, Yrjö, *V. A. Koskenniemen uskonnollinen maailma* (Helsinki, 1977); Mattila, Pekka, *V. A. Koskenniemi lyyrillisenä taiteilijana* (Porvoo, 1954); Siltala, Touko, ed., *Kurkiauran varjo* (Helsinki, 1985); Viljanen, Lauri, *V. A. Koskenniemi* (Porvoo, 1935).

Markku Envall

Kristensen, Tom. Danish poet, novelist, and critic, b. 4 August 1893, d. 2 June 1974, Thurø.

As an important representative of the Danish avant-garde of the 1920s, Kristensen distanced himself from the petty-bourgeois milieu in which he grew up and which he never really left.

The stylistic range of Kristensen's poetry spans from philological-dadaistic wordplay via reflective verse to journalistic poems, always characterized by a highly developed sense of form. In many instances even his prose is lyrical.

The debut poems of *Fribytterdrømme* (1920; Dreams of a Freebooter) are partly expressionistic, lucid thematizations of a fragmented attitude to life. *Livets Arabesk* (1921; Arabesque of Life) is an experimental expressionistic novel, influenced by psychoanalysis, relativity theory, and cubist painting. It is a grotesque contemporary exposé of a revolution, presented with an almost nihilistic rejection of moral, religious, and political ideas.

An anxious search for a firmly defined attitude to life forms the recurring theme in most of Kristensen's works. On a study tour to China and Japan, the author with his persistent anguish was confronted with the calm composure of the Asians. The tour had a decisive impact on the collection of poems, *Paafuglefjeren* (1922; The Peacock Feather), in which Kristensen attempts to dissociate himself from the aestheticism of his earlier poems and deals in depth with the erotic-religious phenomena associated with death. Similar features characterize *En kavaler i Spanien* (1926; A Cavalier in Spain), a work where the author, under the guise of a travel book, describes a state of mind. It contains some of Kristensen's most important poems. The same relentless feeling of anguish is the motivating force in his next collection of poems, *Verdslige Sange* (1927; Worldly Songs). Gradually Kristensen's poems become stylistically less elaborate as in the journalistic verse in *Digte i Døgnet* (1940; Poems for All Hours), yet impressive as, for example, in the death poems for friends in *Mod den yderste Rand* (1936; Toward the Ultimate Brink).

Kristensen's most significant contribution to Danish literature is, however, to be found among his novels. Freudian influence, characteristic of European fictional prose between the wars, directs the stylistically traditional novel *En Anden* (1923; Another), in which the narrator through the juxtaposition of parallel episodes from childhood and adult life attempts to arrive at a psychological explanation for his lack of identity. Similar ideas are central to the structurally refined novel *Hærværk* (1930; *Havoc*, 1968), the culmination of Kristensen's writing career. The protagonist, an unproductive poet who makes his living by writing book reviews based on various "opinions," none of them his own, is confronted by a series of characters that symbolize his own repressed feelings. The conflict leads into an experimental process of self-destruction whereby the poet hopes to discover his true, inner identity. Instead, the process ends with total human disintegration. The novel presents an artistic and structurally disciplined incision through the intellectual circles of Copenhagen during the Roaring Twenties.

It can be argued whether *Hærværk* suggests political consciousness as a viable alternative to the anguish felt by Kristensen's fictional characters. That was the option advocated by Kristensen in his nonfictional writings but never carried out in his novels or poems. His lecture *Kunst-Økonomi-Politik* (1932; Art, Economy, Politics) rejects most of Danish literature in the 1920s, his own included, because of its sterile individualism and aestheticism. From the early 1930s to the Stalin Trials in 1936, Kristensen was attracted to Marxist-Freudian ideas. In the late 1930s his interest shifted to Christian concepts; but his artistic search was never limited to any one ideology. His openness, sensitivity, skeptical intellect, and refined sense of form account also for his importance as a literary critic in *Politiken*, a major Copenhagen daily, 1924–1927 and 1931–1963. Kristensen was, for instance, the first one to introduce James Joyce, William Faulkner, Ernest Hemingway, and Isak Dinesen* to Danish readers.

FURTHER WORKS

Mirakler (1922), *Bokserdrengen* (1925); *Sophus Claussen* (1929); *Vindrosen* (1934); *Hvad er Heta?* (1946); *Mellem Krigene* (1946); *En Omvej til Andorra* (1947); *Rejse i Italien* (1951); *Til Dags Dato* (1953); *Den sidste Lygte* (1954); *Det skabende øje* (1956); *Oplevelser med lyrik* (1957); *Den evige uro* (1958); *Hvad er Heta? og andre fortællinger* (1959); *Mord i Pantomimeteatret eller Harlekin Skelet* (1966); *I min tid* (1963); *Aabenhjertige fortielser* (1966); *Kritiker eller anmelder* (1966); *Fra Holger Drachmann til Benny Andersen* (1967); *Hvad var mit ærinde?* (1968); *Blandt københavnere* (1973).

FURTHER TRANSLATIONS

Modern Danish Authors, ed. Evelyn Heepe et al. (1946, 1974); *A Second Book of Danish Verse,* trans. Charles W. Stork (1947, 1968); *20th Century Scandinavian Poetry,* ed. Martin S. Allwood (1950); *Modern Danish Poems,* comp. Knud K. Mogensen (1951); *Norseman* 9.6 (1951); *Contemporary Danish Prose,* ed. Elias Bredsdorff (1958, 1974); *Contemporary Danish Poetry,* ed. Line Jensen (1977).

REFERENCES

Breitenstein, Jørgen, *Tom Kristensens udvikling* (Copenhagen, 1978); Byram, Michael, "The Reality of Tom Kristensen's 'Hærværk.' " *Scandinavica* 15.1 (1976); Byram, Michael, "Tom Kristensen's 'Livets Arabesk' Seen as a Political Gesture." *Scandinavica* 16.2 (1977); Byram, Michael, *Tom Kristensen* (Boston, 1982); Egebak, Niels, *Tom Kristensen* (Copenhagen, 1971); Jones, W. Glyn, "Tom Kristensen at Eighty." *Denmark* 164 (1973); Jørgensen, Aage, ed., *Omkring 'Hærværk'* (Copenhagen, 1969).

Jørgen Egebak

Kristmann Guðmundsson. *See* Guðmundsson, Kristmann.

Kristmundsson, Aðalsteinn. *See* Steinarr, Steinn.

Krog, Helge. Norwegian dramatist and critic, b. 9 February 1889, Oslo, d. 31 July 1962, Oslo.

The privileged social status and liberal intellectual atmosphere of Krog's childhood home were formative influences. Although Krog was sympathetic to the cause of labor and courageous in proclaiming his socialist views, he moved in aristocratic circles. He wrote excellent literary and theater criticism and numerous essays on political and social issues.

Krog's plays tend toward the abstract and psychological, but may be classified as problem plays. The attractive characters, representing intellectual concepts, engage in stimulating debates. The structure, style, and themes of his plays are reminiscent of works by playwrights he admired—Henrik Ibsen,* George Bernard Shaw, and Gunnar Heiberg.* Krog's first major play, *Det store vi* (1919; The Great We), was enjoyed by theater audiences, although it treated corruption in the newspaper world and the oppression of garment workers. *På solsiden*

(1927; *On Life's Sunny Side*, 1939) is his most charming comedy, with a delightful gallery of characters at a vacation home. Krog never again wrote in such a light, vivacious vein, for human relationships and the tensions of the era between the wars compelled a more serious approach.

Konkylien (1929; *Happily Ever After?*, 1934), *Underveis* (1931; *On the Way*, 1934), and *Opbrudd* (1936; *Break-up*, 1939) are usually discussed as a trilogy, although they are distinct in action and cast. They share a focus on a fascinating woman determined to be true to herself, even though going against society's norms and facing the world alone. Sonja in *Konkylien* is primitive and impulsive, faithful to her vision of a free and honest love. Cecilie, the heroine of *Underveis*, is named for Krog's mother, the first woman permitted to study at the university in Norway. In the preface Krog describes his mother's "smiling courage and a freedom of thought, much greater and stronger than what we usually call liberalism; she was, up until her death, 'on the way.' " Her namesake is a doctor who works with the poor and lives among radicals resembling those in the group Mot Dag, led by Erling Falk. Learning she is pregnant, Cecilie determines not to marry but to raise her child alone. When it becomes clear that she is estranged from her family and a liability to the radical group, Cecilie realizes how completely alone she will be. The play aroused a storm of controversy, both among the establishment and among the radicals, who found fault with Krog for using an upper-class woman as harbinger of the revolution.

Vibeke, the heroine of *Opbrudd*, is regarded as the most idealistic and appealing of Krog's heroines. Because the play is constructed retrospectively, it is called Krog's most Ibsenesque work. The action is tightly unified with Vibeke, her husband Ketil, and her lover Kåre caught in a crisis. Probing questioning reveals the shallowness of both men, who love Vibeke out of vanity and only conditionally. Ketil cannot tolerate the purity and intensity of her devotion. Vibeke, a descendent of Nora, decisively walks out of the home that has been a prison, determined to find a cause deserving of her zeal and energy.

Krog pointed out the injustices of a society established by men, who demand power and the privileges of polygamy. He saw women as stronger and nobler, capable of leading the restructuring of society. Although sometimes isolated and bitter, Krog was dedicated to intellectual freedom.

Krog's language, thought, and logic are simple and clear, sometimes as brilliant as "a flash of lightning through fog" (Sigurd Hoel, *Festskrift*, p. 7). He belongs to the succession of Norwegian writers in the radical tradition and among the masters of realistic drama.

FURTHER WORKS

Jarlshus (1923); *Blåpapiret* (1928); *Meninger om bøker og forfattere* (1929, 1971); *Meninger om mange ting* (1933); *Treklang* (1933; *Triad*, 1934); *Levende og døde* (1945); *6. kolonne—?* (1946); *Meninger: Litteratur, kristendom, politikk* (1947); *Kjærlighetens farce*, with Olaf Bull (1948); *Don Juan*, with Sigurd Hoel (1948); *Tankeleken* (1953);

Rent ut sagt (1954); *Sant å si* (1956); *Pasquino* (1963); *Meninger om religion og politikk* (1971); *Utvalgte skuespill* (1980).

FURTHER TRANSLATIONS

Scandinavian Plays of the Twentieth Century, 2nd ser. (1944).

REFERENCES

Arestad, Sverre, "Helge Krog and the Problem Play." *Scandinavian Studies* 37.4 (1965); Havrevold, Finn, *Helge Krog* (Oslo, 1959); Hoel, Sigurd, and Rolv Thesen, eds., *Festskrift til Helge Krog på sekstiårsdagen* (Oslo, 1949); Longum, Leif, *To kjærlighetsromantikere* (Oslo, 1960).

Carla Waal

Krusenstjerna, Agnes Julie Fredrika von. Swedish novelist, b. 9 October 1894, Växjö, d. 9 March 1940, Stockholm.

Krusenstjerna's father was an army colonel from the petty nobility. Through her mother's noble family Hamilton, Krusenstjerna was related to the great poet E. G. Geijer.* The conservative, high-bourgeois, economically spartan milieu of a small regimental town shaped Krusenstjerna's world. Family convention and a fragile constitution caused Krusenstjerna to receive only rudimentary formal schooling. An early erotic encounter precipitated her first psychiatric hospitalization, followed by many throughout her life. Against her family's wish Krusenstjerna in 1921 married the much older literary scholar and *littérateur manqué* David Sprengel, a specialist on Jean-Jacques Rousseau and French eighteenth century erotic literature. Sprengel made it his calling to further Krusenstjerna's writing. Always supportive during her long illnesses, he edited her texts, adding cultural and political touches.

Krusenstjerna's semiautobiographical trilogy about Tony is her most rounded work, lyrical, yet an almost clinical description of a girl's erotic awakening. Its nucleus was a brutally naked section about a psychiatric ward. Well received as a proper if daring work, it did not prepare the public and critics for her seven-volume cycle about the Misses von Pahlen, 1930–1935. A broad picture of depraved high society just before World War I, with numerous colorful characters, it is a bold and uneven attempt to map the entire range of sexual variation, on a scale from perfect intercourses to perverse orgies, from hymns in D. H. Lawrence's spirit to satire orchestrated by Sprengel's ironic hand. The fifth volume, *Älskande par* (1933; Loving Couples), literally the high point but also the most outspoken, led to the most fierce literary feud in Sweden since August Strindberg's* time, with crude personal attacks on Krusenstjerna and a heated debate of obscenity in literature lasting over two years. Krusenstjerna's final tetralogy *Fattigadel* (1935–1938; Poor Nobility) is a partly too personal revenge on family and society.

Krusenstjerna's style is lyrical and clear, though at times cloyingly romantic. Two aspects of her work are innovative in Swedish literature: her descriptions of the young woman's erotic awakening and of mental illness.

FURTHER WORKS

Ninas dagbok (1917); *Helenas första kärlek* (1918); *Tony växer upp* (1922); *En dag-driverskas anteckningar* (1923); *Tonys läroår* (1924); *Tonys sista läroår* (1926); *Den blå rullgardinen* (1930); *Kvinnogatan* (1930); *Höstens skuggor* (1931); *Porten vid Johannes* (1933); *Bröllop på Ekered* (1935); *Av samma blod* (1935); *Dunklet mellan träden* (1936); *Dessa lyckliga år* (1937); *I livets vår* (1938); *Samlade skrifter*, ed. J. Edfelt, 14 vols. (1944–1946).

REFERENCES

Jones, Llewellyn, "Agnes von Krusenstjerna: A Swedish Proust," *Books Abroad* 23.1 (1949); Lagercrantz, Olof, *Agnes von Krusenstjerna* (Stockholm, 1951; rev. ed. 1980); Svanberg, Birgitta, *Sanningen om kvinnorna. En tolkning av Agnes von Krusenstjernas Pahlen-serie* (Stockholm, 1987).

Margareta Mattsson

Kyrklund, Paul Wilhelm (Willy). Finland-Swedish novelist, short story writer, and dramatist, b. 27 February 1921, Helsinki.

Kyrklund studied law at Helsinki University, but made Sweden his permanent home after the war. He has a wide range of unusual knowledge, having read chemistry and Oriental languages in Stockholm, worked with computers, and studied mathematics; his erudition is frequently evident in his writings. Famed for his concise, sharp, ironic style, which is often compared with that of Hjalmar Söderberg,* Kyrklund tends to experiment with content and form. The angst-ridden atmosphere he conjures up is sometimes reminiscent of Franz Kafka and Jean Paul Sartre, with Sigmund Freud a constant background presence.

Kyrklund's early novels are characterized by irony often associated with dual narration, problems being examined from contrasting viewpoints. The technique is most highly developed in *Mästaren Ma* (1952; Ma, the Master), which features thoughts of the Chinese philosopher Ma, with comments and footnotes added by his wife, and his pedantic secretary.

Polyfem förvandlad (1964; Polyphemus Transformed) and *Den rätta känslan* (1974; The Right Feeling) are not so much novels as rhapsodic collages of anecdotes, sketches, fragments, and philosophical speculation, many with an Oriental or classical setting. (One chapter of the latter work is a learned commentary on a Sanskrit poem quoted in the original; another is a mathematical discourse.) The mood is pessimistic, but there is almost always sympathy for the humble and oppressed.

Similar themes and formal experiments characterize Kyrklund's short stories and plays. His latest closet drama, *Gudar och människor* (1978; Gods and Humans), mixes scientific language and blank verse, a parodied Greek chorus and an airplane.

Kyrklund is a very individual author who writes sparingly and concisely (his novels and plays are unusually short). The experimental nature of his work prevents him from being popular, but he ranks highly with critics and academics.

FURTHER WORKS

Vinkruset (1946); *Ångvälten* (1948); *Tvåsam* (1949); *Komedi för narr och ensemble* (1950); *Solange* (1951); *Hermelins död* (1954); *Den överdrivne älskaren* (1957); *Aigaion* (1957); *Till Tabbas* (1959); *Från bröllopet till Medea* (1976); *Zéb-un-nisá* (1978); *Elpenor* (1986).

REFERENCES

Arrias, Gunnar, *Jaget, friheten och tystnaden hos Willy Kyrklund* (Göteborg, 1981).

Laurie Thompson

Kyrklund, Willy. *See* Kyrklund, Paul Wilhelm.

L

La Cour, Paul. Danish poet, essayist, critic, and translator, b. 9 November 1902, Rislev, d. 20 September 1956, Roskilde.

As a young man la Cour tried his hand at various occupations; he was a painter and published some poems. In 1923 he left for France, where for seven years he made a living by taking any odd jobs. From France he sent home manuscripts for poems influenced by older writers such as Johannes V. Jensen* and Ludvig Holstein.* The prize-winning poems of *Den tredie dag* (1928; The Third Day), a breakthrough for la Cour, showed the openness and attention toward things that was to be his characteristic. His sense of color and light had been learned from Paul Cezanne and other painters. Two novels stand beside la Cour's work as secondary experiments; they have as common themes the destructive effect of childhood experiences.

In the 1930s the impact of French poetry shows itself in *Alt kræver jeg* (1938; All of It I Demand); these poems, moreover, bear the stamp of the crisis in Europe and the movement toward totalitarianism. La Cour, now working as a literary critic, could survey his own generation, which had had a "stumbling start," and relate the need for solidarity, for example, as described in "Hotellet" (The Hotel).

The series of theoretical reflections, *Fragmenter af en dagbog* (1948; Fragments of a Diary), about inspiration and the poetical work became the poetics and bible of many young writers. The profound impulse of this book was the almost religious aspiration to reach beyond the intellect. Some of la Cour's debate-provoking aphorisms were printed in *Heretica*, a literary periodical inspired by similar ideas and attacking the prewar social-ideological outlook on life. La Cour, however, broke with *Heretica* in order not to support one literary and political group.

In his postwar poems la Cour tried to carry out his new demands regarding poetry. He polished his language and responded to the symbols of the poets he translated, for example, Pierre Reverdy, Jorge Guillén, and Federico García Lorca. And he tried as an artist to jump through the intellect into a fundamental humbleness toward an almost metaphysical reality.

That la Cour was one of the finest critics is clearly demonstrated by *Solhøjde* (1959; Altitude of the Sun), a posthumous collection of essays, which is far more substantial than *Fragmenter*. With his spiritual incentive la Cour is able to make time-bound topics amazingly important even to modern readers.

FURTHER WORKS

Dagens alter (1922); *Arkadisk morgen* (1924); *Matissebogen* (1924); *Den galliske sommer* (1927); *Aske* (1929); *Leviathan* (1930); *Menneskets hjem* (1931); *Regn over verden* (1933); *Kramer bryder op* (1935); *Dette er vort liv* (1936); *Niels Lergaard* (1938); *De hundrede somre* (1940); *Axel Salto* (1941); *Mellem sværdene* (1942); *Astrid Noack* (1943); *Levende vande* (1946); *Mellem bark og ved* (1950); *Gør dig ikke skyldig i frygt* (1951); *Udvalgte digte 1928–51* (1951); *Efterladte digte* (1957); *De knuste sten* (1957); *Græske digte* (1958).

TRANSLATIONS

Contemporary Danish Poetry, ed. Line Jensen et al. (1977); *Literary Review* 8.1 (1964).

REFERENCES

Bjørnvig, Thorkild, "Paul la Cour," in his *Virkeligheden er til* (Copenhagen, 1973); Harder, Uffe, "Paul la Cour" in *Danske digtere i det 20. århundrede*, ed. Torben Brostrøm and Mette Winge, vol. 2 (Copenhagen, 1981); Schmidt, Povl, *Paul la Cour* (Copenhagen, 1971).

Svend Birke Espegård

Lagerkvist, Pär. Swedish poet, dramatist, short story writer, and novelist, b. 23 May 1891, Växjö, d. 11 July 1974, Stockholm.

Lagerkvist was born in the provincial town of Växjö in southern Sweden. In his basically autobiographical novel *Gäst hos verkligheten* (1925; *Guest of Reality*, 1936), Lagerkvist describes this childhood milieu and the pietistic religious faith of his parents as well as his own early sense of alienation and existential insecurity. As an adolescent Lagerkvist was introduced to the evolutionary theories of Charles Darwin and openly rebelled against the confining atmosphere of his home. He joined politically radical discussion groups and contributed revolutionary poems to socialist journals. Lagerkvist's early experience of "the two worlds," the secure world of religious acceptance of his parents and the other world of blind forces and cosmic infinitude as taught by the natural sciences, is at the root of his later works and metaphysical speculation.

After a brief sojourn at the Uppsala University Lagerkvist visited Paris in 1913 where he was confronted with the newest trends in the visual arts, especially the cubism of Pablo Picasso and Georges Braque. In a critical essay or manifesto, *Ordkonst och bildkonst* (1913), Lagerkvist rejects traditional realism in favor of a "literary cubism," disciplined, structured, and architectural, extracting from reality its artistic essence. He points to the monumental beauty and simplicity of such works as the Bible, the Avesta, and the Koran, and in the Scandinavian tradition the old Icelandic sagas and Eddic poems. Lagerkvist was to modify his rigorous demands in subsequent works, but certain elements remained constant throughout his career: the simplicity of expression and a predilection for stark contrasts and universal themes.

Lagerkvist's experimentation during the years of World War I placed him in the very vanguard of literary modernism in Sweden. The violent expressionism of his poetry collection *Ångest* (1916; Anguish) marks a defiant break with the more traditional poetry of the preceding era in its description of a metaphysical wasteland of anguish and despair, reflecting both the world situation and Lagerkvist's personal crisis. In a second literary manifesto, *Modern teater* (1918; Modern Theater), Lagerkvist is critical of the Henrik Ibsen* brand of naturalistic theater and points to the more revolutionary and liberating techniques of the late August Strindberg* of *A Dream Play* and the chamber plays as well as the morality and mystery plays of the Middle Ages. To Lagerkvist, the function of drama is to express and condense contemporary reality into effectively stylized images. He exemplified his own theories in a number of boldly experimental dramas in which the action is set in a limbo after death as in the three one-act plays *Den svåra stunden* (1918; *The Difficult Hour*, 1966) or staged on a rounded surface suggesting the globe as in *Himlens hemlighet* (1919; *The Secret of Heaven*, 1966).

Lagerkvist's production of the 1920s reveals a shift from the violent outbursts of an extreme subjectivity to a tenuous social and ethical awareness and a spirit of acceptance in an uneasy truce with existence in the poetry collection *Den lyckliges väg* (1921; The Path of the Happy One) or the play *Den osynlige* (1923; The Invisible). The short story collection *Onda sagor* (1924; Evil Tales) and the play *Han som fick leva om sitt liv* (1928; *The Man Who Lived His Life Over*, 1971) are informed by a basic pessimism about the human condition.

During his travels Lagerkvist gained first hand knowledge of Benito Mussolini's fascism and Adolf Hitler's nazism. Earlier than most writers of his generation, he was alert to the threat to civilization posed by these totalitarian regimes and took an unequivocal stand against these ideologies. The novella *Bödeln* (1933; *The Hangman*, 1936), which in 1934 was made into a successful play under the same title (1966), is set in a medieval tavern and in a contemporary nightclub in a totalitarian state. It explores the nature of evil and man's employment of its power as embodied in the figure of the hangman. In the Middle Ages he is viewed with awe and superstitious fear; in the more barbaric twentieth century he is ecstatically hailed as a glamorous hero of violence. A journey to Greece and Palestine resulted in the book *Den knutna näven* (1934; *Clenched Fist*, 1987), in which Lagerkvist returns to the sources of the humanistic tradition in our Greco-Judean heritage. He sees Greece as the birthplace of democracy, rationalism, and the spirit of free inquiry, and Palestine as the birthplace of man's metaphysical aspirations, forces that Lagerkvist now summons as a defense against encroaching barbarism. In the short story collection *I den tiden*

(1935; At That Time) he puts his Swiftian satirical gift in the service of his humanistic ideals.

With the novel *Dvärgen* (1944; *The Dwarf*, 1945), universally acclaimed as a masterpiece, Lagerkvist continued his investigation of the spirit of humanism as manifested at a princely court in Renaissance Italy. Events are viewed from the chilling perspective of the title figure. On the psychological level *Dvärgen* is the study of a stunted and sterile mind; on the symbolic level it explores the nature of evil and the destructive negation of all human values.

Lagerkvist's most widely translated novel, *Barabbas* (1950; trans., 1951), initiated a new phase in his authorship with a narrowed focus on man's metaphysical yearnings, his relationship with the divine, and his search for or escape from God. Lagerkvist, who liked to term himself a "religious atheist," reveals in *Barabbas* his own ambivalence before the Christian faith. Barabbas is a portrait of both an individual in a unique historical situation and of man in general condemned to existential freedom and despair. The novel's stark contrasts between light and darkness, good and evil, love and hate, unquestioning faith and rational doubt yield startling paradoxes and unsettling ambiguities. In a series of five loosely connected novels, the cycle forming a spiritual pilgrimage, Lagerkvist describes man's metaphysical hunger and offers variations on the relationship between God and man.

Lagerkvist is a major figure in twentieth-century Swedish literature. His unique contributions to all the major literary genres, his formal experimentations, and his treatment of what he himself termed "the universally human which rises above the narrowly individual" assures him a place in world literature. Lagerkvist was elected to the Swedish Academy in 1940, and he was awarded the Nobel Prize in 1951.

FURTHER WORKS

Människor (1912); *Två sagor om livet* (1913); *Motiv* (1914); *Järn och människor* (1915; *Iron and Men*, 1987); *Sista mänskan* (1917; *The Last Man*, 1987); *Kaos* (1919); *Det eviga leendet* (1920; *The Eternal Smile*, 1934); *Hjärtats sånger* (1926); *Det besegrade livet* (1927); *Kämpande ande* (1930); *Vid lägereld* (1932); *Konungen* (1932); *Mannen utan själ* (1937); *Genius* (1937); *Den befriade människan* (1939); *Seger i mörker* (1939); *Sång och strid* (1940); *Midsommardröm i fattighuset* (1941; *Midsummer Dream in the Workhouse*, 1953); *Hemmet och stjärnan* (1942); *De vises sten* (1947); *Låt människan leva* (1949); *Aftonland* (1953; *Evening Land*, 1975); *Sibyllan* (1956; *The Sibyl*, 1958); *Ahasverus död* (1960; *The Death of Ahasverus*, 1962); *Pilgrim på havet* (1962; *Pilgrim at Sea*, 1964); *Det heliga landet* (1964; *The Holy Land*, 1966); *Mariamne* (1967; *Herod and Mariamne*, 1968); *Antecknat* (1977); *Den svåra resan* (1985).

FURTHER TRANSLATIONS

Scandinavian Plays of the Twentieth Century (1941); *20th-Century Scandinavian Poetry*, ed. Martin S. Allwood (1950); *Scandinavian Plays of the Twentieth Century*, 3rd ser. (1951); *The Eternal Smile and Other Stories* (1954); *Seven Swedish Poets*, ed. Frederick Fleisher (1963); *Pär Lagerkvist: Modern Theatre; Seven Plays and an Essay* (1966); *Five*

Modern Scandinavian Plays (1971); *The Eternal Smile: Three Stories* (1971); *Five Early Works* (1987).

REFERENCES

Buckman, Thomas, "Pär Lagerkvist and the Swedish Theatre." *Tulane Drama Review* 6 (1961); Ellestad, Everett M., "Pär Lagerkvist and Cubism: A Study of His Theory and Practice." *Scandinavian Studies* 45.1 (1973); Gustafson, Walter, "The Patterns of Art of Pär Lagerkvist." *Edda* 41 (1954); Jackson, Naomi, "The Fragmented Mirror: Lagerkvist's *The Dwarf.*" *Discourse* 8 (1946); Johannesson, Eric O., "Pär Lagerkvist and the Art of Rebellion." *Scandinavian Studies* 30.1 (1958); Linnér, Sven, "Pär Lagerkvist's *The Eternal Smile* and *The Sibyl.*" *Scandinavian Studies* 37.2 (1965); Scobbie, Irene, *Pär Lagerkvist: An Introduction* (Stockholm, 1963); Sjöberg, Leif, *Pär Lagerkvist* (New York, 1976); Spector, Robert D., *Pär Lagerkvist* (New York, 1973); Weathers, Winston, *Pär Lagerkvist: A Critical Essay* (Grand Rapids, 1968).

Lars G. Warme

Lagerlöf, Selma Ottilia Lovisa. Swedish novelist, b. 20 November 1858, Mårbacka, Ö Ämtervik, Värmland, d. 16 March 1940, Mårbacka.

The local stories, legends, and fairy tales of Lagerlöf's childhood at Mårbacka became her lifelong source of inspiration. She was an avid reader of H C. Andersen,* Bjørnstjerne Bjørnson,* Thomas Carlyle, and Rudyard Kipling, among others, and decided early to make writing her career. But education was costly and academic training a dim prospect. Eventually, Lagerlöf was able to pursue her studies in Stockholm, 1882–1885. She then held a teaching position in Landskrona until 1895. The loss of Mårbacka, after her father's death, gave Lagerlöf the impetus to preserve this environment in memory. The result was her debut work, *Gösta Berlings saga* (1891; *The Story of Gösta Berling*, 1898). A grant in 1895 prompted her decision to devote all her time to writing. She made two longer journeys abroad, to Italy in 1896–1897, to Egypt and Palestine in 1899–1900. She also traveled widely in Sweden. In 1897, she settled down in Falun, a period of high creativity including important contributions to the suffragette movement. Lagerlöf's dream to return to Mårbacka was realized when she was able to buy back the house in 1907 and the estate in 1909. Lagerlöf was made honorary doctor of Uppsala University in 1907. She received the Swedish Academy gold medal in 1904, and the Nobel Prize in 1909. In 1914 she became the first woman elected a member of the Swedish Academy.

Gösta Berlings saga, an account of marvelous Värmland adventures of the past, participates uniquely in the literary credo of both the 1880s and 1890s. The powerful Margareta Celsing rules Ekeby, its land and iron works, where the pounding sledgehammer marks the obligations and rewards of everyday work. She gives room and board to twelve cavaliers of a motley past, allowing them to live out their artistic talents and eccentric whims. Among them is Gösta Berling, the defrocked priest, abundantly endowed with good looks, drinking capacity, eloquence, and charm over women. His uninhibited joy in life makes him receptive to demonic undercurrents, represented by Sintram, the evil squire and perhaps also the devil. Entering a bet with the devil, the cavaliers are promised the rule over Ekeby, if for one full year they can avoid work and womanly acts. The sledgehammer stops; life at Ekeby is now song and dance and wild adventure. At the end of the year comes the time of retribution and repentance over wasted resources and relationships. The sledgehammer starts up again, and the cavaliers break the power of the devil with their new insight that joyous life affirmation necessitates order and responsibility.

As a moral statement in praise of work and order, *Gösta Berlings saga* is true to the literary climate of the 1880s. In the glorification of the past, in the high-strung emotions and the nearness to the supernatural, the new aesthetics of the 1990s is evident. In addition, *Gösta Berlings saga* heralds a theme that will recur with variations in the stories to come: the presence in everyday life of vital forces of nature as threat and inspiration to human love and understanding.

In her shorter narratives Lagerlöf masters the stringency of form, which is sometimes found evasive in her longer novels. *En herrgårdssägen* (1899; *The Tale of a Manor and Other Sketches*, 1917) exemplifies the harmonious correspondence between the forces of nature and the power of human love. With deep psychological insight, and with a romantic adaptation of the folktale "The Beauty and the Beast," Lagerlöf shows how Ingrid's love for Gunnar Hede breaks through and cures his mental disorder.

Lagerlöf frequently used actual occurrences to develop her plot. A newspaper clipping about a group of farmers who emigrated from Dalarna to join a religious sect in Palestine was the inspiration for one of her best-loved novels, *Jerusalem*; volume 1 (1901; *Jerusalem*, 1915) and volume 2 (1902; *The Holy City*, 1918). Two main motifs are interrelated. The established order of the farming community, represented by the powerful Ingmarsson family, is disrupted by the arrival of a feverish evangelical movement from North America. Volume 1 centers on the painful breaking up of family relations, mingled with anticipation of missionary work in Palestine. Volume 2 is mainly set in Jerusalem with the harsh testing of the newcomers' religious faith.

With *Jerusalem* Lagerlöf was approaching the height of her fame. The conflict between loyalty to traditional beliefs and to affirmative acts of religious faith struck immediate chords of recognition in the readers. And yet opinions were divided as to Lagerlöf's own standpoint in the conflict. Did she support the evangelist movement or regard it as an unfortunate threat to the deep-rooted farming tradition? A clear-cut answer is not made easier with the next edition of 1909, where the beneficiary work of the missionaries is even more strongly emphasized.

A similar conflict, that of individual human love struggling with a superhuman power, underlies the short novel *Herr Arnes penningar* (1904; *Herr Arne's Hoard*, 1925) based on an actual occurrence: the brutal slaying of a priest and his household in the late 1500s. To this event Lagerlöf has added a supernatural motif. The dead seek revenge, and a ghost is sent out among the living to help the surviving Elsalil find the murderers. Complications arise, as Elsalil, who has not yet recognized the murderers, falls in love with their leader. As she realizes the truth, she is torn between loyalty to the dead and the wishes of her heart. But the dead insist on justice, and finally Elsalil takes her life in her attempt to prevent the murderers from escaping. This is no ordinary ghost story, however, for the dead are part of a higher order of retribution aligned with the forces of nature. The tension between individual love and a superhuman power strikes a discordant note with Elsalil's self-sacrifice.

Herr Arnes penningar points to Lagerlöf's growing preoccupation with spiritism and life after death, but equally strong was her societal concern. Her interest in children's education is best exemplified by *Nils Holgerssons underbara resa genom Sverige*, volume 1 (1906; *The Wonderful Adventures of Nils*, 1907) and volume 2 (1907; *Further Adventures of Nils*, 1911), written to order as a textbook on Swedish geography but in addition given the special Lagerlöf touch: a poetic novel of development about the fourteen-year-old Nils, who is punished for his maltreatment of animals. By a magic spell he is reduced in size, small enough to sit on the back of the wild goose Akka. With the flock of geese he flies over the Swedish landscape, matures in the process of many adventures, and in the end regains his normal size.

The outbreak of World War I had a dampening effect on Lagerlöf's creativity, certainly not for a lack of concern on her part, but perhaps her poetic mode of presentation was not an amenable receptacle to the immediacy of suffering around her. But her marvelous world of mingled reality and fantasy continues to attract new audiences. Several of her stories have been made into films. Translations today number around forty languages, a testimony to her versatility as an artist and to herself as a genuine, compassionate human being.

FURTHER WORKS

Osynliga länkar (1894; *Invisible Links*, 1899); *Antikrists mirakler* (1897; *The Miracles of Antichrist*, 1899); *Drottningar i Kungahälla* (1899; *The Queens of Kungahälla and Other Sketches*, 1917); *Kristuslegender* (1904; *Christ Legends, and Other Stories*, 1930; 1977); *Legender* (1904); *En saga om en saga och andra sagor* (1908); *Liljecronas hem* (1911; *Lilliecrona's Home*, 1913); *Körkarlen* (1912; *Thy Soul Shall Bear Witness*, 1921); *Kejsarn av Portugallien* (1914; *The Emperor of Portugallia*, 1917); *Troll och människor*, vol. 1 (1915); *Bannlyst* (1918; *The Outcast*, 1920); *Troll och människor*, vol. 2 (1921); *Mårbacka*, vol. 1 (1924); *Löwensköldska ringen* (1925; *The Ring of Löwenskölds*, 1931); *Mors porträtt och andra berättelser* (1930); *Mårbacka*, vol. 2 (1930; *Memories of My Childhood: Further Years at Mårbacka*, 1934); *Mårbacka*, vol. 3 (1932; *The Diary of Selma Lagerlöf*, 1936); *Höst* (1933).

FURTHER TRANSLATIONS

The Girl from the Marshcroft (1910); *Valda berättelser* (1913); *Our World* (1923); *Harvest* (1935); *Sister Kavin and Sister Sisla* (1986).

REFERENCES

Afzelius, Nils, "The Scandalous Selma Lagerlöf." *Scandinavica* 5.2 (1966); Berendsohn, Walter A., *Selma Lagerlöf: Her Life and Work* (Garden City, N.Y., 1932); De Vriezse,

F. S., *Fact and Fiction in the Autobiographical Works of Selma Lagerlöf* (Assen, Netherlands, 1958); Edström, Vivi, *Livets stigar* (Stockholm, 1950); Edström, Vivi, *Selma Lagerlöf* (Boston, 1984); Green, Brita, *Selma Lagerlöf: Herr Arnes penningar*, Studies in Swedish Literature 9 (Hull, 1977); Holm, Birgitta, *Selma Lagerlöf och ursprungets roman* (Stockholm, 1984); Lagerroth, Erland, "The Narrative Art of Selma Lagerlöf: Two Problems." *Scandinavian Studies* 33.1 (1961); Lagerroth, Erland, "Selma Lagerlöf Research 1900–1964: A Survey and an Orientation." *Scandinavian Studies* 37.1 (1965); Lagerroth, Ulla-Britta, "The Troll in Man: A Lagerlöf Motif." *Scandinavian Studies* 40.1 (1968); Toijer-Nilsson, Ying, *Naturens förbannelse* (Uppsala, 1955); Ulvenstam, Lars, "Selma Lagerlöf: Genius of Opposites." *American-Swedish Monthly* 12 (1958).

Monica Setterwall

Lange, Per. Danish poet, essayist, and translator, b. 30 August 1901, Hørsholm, outside Copenhagen.

As a son of the critic and writer Sven Lange (and related to the Danish poet Frederik Paludan-Müller*), Lange grew up in a milieu saturated with classical culture and literature, which turned out to be a decisive influence on him. After studying literature for some years, he spent 1923 in Austria and 1926–1927 in Italy, where he was influenced by Continental European culture and its roots in ancient Greek and Italian culture. The poetry of the young man and the essays of the mature one are dominated by these classical ideals, formally as well as in content.

The *poetical* body of his work consists of three collections of poems, dealing primarily with the schism between the chaotic, formless life and the impeccable, artistic vision, which, put forward with hard-won composure, demands agonized asceticism. The compensation is the purified poetry itself. Quite often the poems describe a rising curve toward the desired ideal, followed by a backsliding into reality. In Lange's aestheticism woman is brought to consciousness by man and is thus another artifact of the artist. But it is the artistic vision, not the earthly love, that is the organizing principle of life; thus the artist restlessly pursues the vision rather than the woman. Love is sublimated into art. Outside of his aesthetic vision the poet is lonely.

The *essays* of the mature Lange are among the most excellent in Danish literature; their subject is often the ideal world of art. They could be called memories from a life in art, with spiritual titles as *Spejlinger* (1943; Reflections), *Ved Musikkens Tærskel* (1957; On the Threshold of Music). When he is moving out into reality, he often seeks mythological places, such as Greece and Italy. He is a master of the short literary form, with its laconic, pinpointing aphorisms and precise dissections. The later essays are marked by a becomingly relaxed, self-ironical humor, which mitigates the author's tragic and aristocratic spirit.

With a consistent and exclusive corpus of works saturated with classical ideals and aesthetics, Lange is highly praised though little read.

FURTHER WORKS

Kaos og Stjærnen (1926); *Forvandlinger* (1929); *Orfeus* (1932); *Samtale med et Æsel* (1961); *Om Krig og Krigsmænd* (1966); *Dyrenes Maskerade* (1969).

FURTHER TRANSLATIONS

Modern Danish Writers, special issue of *Adam—International Review* (1948).

REFERENCES

Frederiksen, Emil, "Per Lange," in *Danske Digtere i det 20. Århundrede,* ed. Ernst Frandsen et al., vol. 2 (Copenhagen, 1951); Frederiksen, Emil, "Per Lange," in *Danske digtere i det 20. Århundrede,* vol. 2 (Copenhagen, 1963); Jensen, Lars-Henrik, "Per Lange," in *Danske digtere i det 20. Århundrede,* ed. Torben Brostrøm and Mette Winge, vol. 2 (Copenhagen, 1981).

Ole Wøide

Lapp Literature. *See* Sami Literature.

Larsen, Alf. Norwegian poet, essayist, and critic, b. 22 July 1885, Tjøme, d. 12 December 1967, Tjøme.

Larsen grew up in a humble fisherman's home in southern Norway. He settled in Denmark from 1903 to 1912, and his first collection of poems was written in Danish. In 1912 he moved back to Norway and bought a farm in Tjøme, where he lived for the rest of his life.

His first poems are in the fin de siècle style, influenced by Charles Baudelaire and the Belgian symbolist Emile Verhaeren. Nature, death, and the blindness of fate are predominant motifs, and the poems display deep pessimism. The poems from 1916 are more redeeming, marked by his love for his childhood landscape, especially the ocean and the waterfront.

In the mid–1920s Larsen came under the influence of the anthroposophist Rudolf Steiner, and there was a remarkable change in his literary production, to a metaphysical belief in the universality of life, nature, and the universe. From that time onward his religious belief was present in everything he wrote.

In the 1930s Larsen was busy as an essayist and critic. From 1933 to 1941 he edited and published his own magazine *Janus,* which attacked the materialism of the time in the name of anthroposophy. After the war he continued his essayistic writing side by side with his poetry.

His postwar poems deal mainly with man's relation to nature. The religious feeling shown in the poems is not expressed as a dualism between spirit and nature. Nature is also spiritualized, and man's plight is to realize and find his place in the totality of the spiritualized Nature and Universe.

Larsen has never been widely read in Norway, but his skill cannot be questioned. His essays are polemic, but well-informed, and written in the spirit of the anthroposophy Larsen adhered to.

FURTHER WORKS

Vinterlandet (1912); *Indgangen* (1915); *Billeder fra den gamle stue* (1916); *Digte* (1919); *I vindens sus* (1927); *Med vår under vingen* (1928); *Jordens drøm* (1930); *I jordens lys* (1946); *Den kongelige kunst* (1948); *Stemninger ved Okeanos bredder* (1949); *Ved Jo-*

hannes V. Jensens død (1951); *Nattetanker* (1951); *Høsthav* (1958); *En tangkrans* (1959); *I kunstens tjeneste* (1964); *Den jordiske vandringsmann* (1968); *Siste strofer* (1969).

REFERENCE

Werring, Henri, *Alf Larsen* (Oslo, 1977).

Øystein Rottem

Larsen, Marianne. Danish poet, translator, and prose writer, b. 1951 near Kalundborg.

Larsen studied literature and Chinese at the University of Copenhagen from 1970 to 1975, has worked as a laborer in factories and hospitals, and taken part in various left-wing activities.

Her first book, *Koncentrationer* (1971; Concentrations), and those immediately following are surrealistic descriptions of the loneliness and isolation of the powerless who live under the domination of the capitalistic power brokers who attempt to control even our language. From this early and accomplished surreal description of a nightmare world, Larsen's work moves through a structuralist phase to her key work, *Fællessprog* (1975; Common Language), where her language becomes more colloquial and less dreamlike, and her criticism of social oppression more direct and concrete, underscoring the general movement of her poetry from "isolation and loneliness to extroversion and community," as Asger Schnack comments in his introduction to Larsen's *Selected Poems* (1982). Though she describes the life of the oppressed in a simple language rich in metaphorical surprises in this and later work, the oppression is balanced by a faith in the awakening of the oppressed and a dream of community, so that her poetry expresses an essential optimism, as seen in the title of a recent collection: *Der er et haab i mit hoved* (1981; There Is a Hope in My Head). The speaker in the later poems is less nervous, less tense, and more sure of the source of individual despair and loneliness—the capitalistic system that invades every corner of our private lives, even our sexual relationships—and thus the speaker becomes aware of the need and possibility of revolution, of finding fellowship.

Larsen is the most important political poet in Denmark today. Her work is widely anthologized and is often used in Danish secondary school textbooks. The effectiveness of her attack on the male-dominated capitalistic system stems from the fact that it isn't simplistic or strident. In a quiet voice she describes the life of the downtrodden—sick women in the park, a girl working at a cash register—so concretely that the reader can come to only one conclusion. Furthermore, especially in the later verse, she emphasizes the underlying strength of those who, though fatigued, continue to resist being reduced to ciphers: "You Fatigued, learn from fatigue, be as strong as it."

FURTHER WORKS

21 digte (1972); *Ravage* (1973); *Noget tegnet syv gange* (1973); *Billedtekster* (1974); *Cinderella* (1974); *Sætninger* (1974); *Modsætninger* (1975); *Handlinger* (1976); *Det må siges enkelt* (1976); *Ukrudt: oversættelse af Lu Xun* (1976); *Aforismer* (1977); *Hvem er fjenden?* (1977); *Under jordskælvet i Argentina* (1978); *Opgørelse følger* (1978); *Det kunne være nu* (1979); *Hinandens kræfter* (1980); *At ville, jeg kan, vi gør!* (1981); *Bag om maskerne* (1982); *Jeg spørger bare* (1982); *Dagbogsleg 1958–83*, with Ib Hørlyck (1983); *I dag og i morgen* (1983); *Udvalgte digte 1969–82* (1983); *Direkte* (1984); *Hareungen uden frygt—og andre historier* (1984); *Kære levende* (1984); *Pludselig dette* (1985); *De andre, den anden* (1986); *Hr. Krone og fru Grøn* (1986); *Den lille natur og den store by* (1986); *Hvor du er* (1987); *I timer og udenfor* (1988).

FURTHER TRANSLATIONS

Contemporary Danish Poetry, ed. Line Jensen et al. (1977); *Scandinavian Review* 68.4 (1980); *Seventeen Danish Poets*, ed. Niels Ingwersen (1981); *Selected Poems* (1982).

REFERENCES

Barlby, Finn, *Og verden kan ikke erobres bagfra: en arbejdsbog om Marianne Larsen og hendes forfatterskab* (Copenhagen, 1982); Schnack, Asger, "Marianne Larsen: Drømmen om fællesskab," in his *Portræt* (Copenhagen, 1981); Skyum-Nielsen, Erik, "Marianne Larsen," in *Danske digtere i det 20. århundrede*, ed. Torben Brostrøm and Mette Winge, vol. 5 (Copenhagen, 1982).

Alexander Taylor

Lassila, Maiju. (pseud. of Algot Tietäväinen-Untola; alias Irmari Rantamala, J. I. Vatanen). Finnish novelist, journalist, and playwright, b. 28 November 1868, Tohmajärvi, d. 18 May 1918, Helsinki.

Lassila was a boy when his father died. He was forced to work as a farmhand, but managed to attend a normal school and be certified for teaching school. His final assignment was in Viipuri. In 1898 he left for St. Petersburg, where he engaged in the lumber business and had contact with revolutionary circles. In 1903 he married Thérèse Küstring. The marriage was apparently only a formality; the newlyweds separated before their wedding night. He soon returned to Finland.

Some of his experiences in Czarist Russia are reflected in his first novel. *Harhama*, with its sequel *Martva* (1909–1910), is a mixture of naturalism and religiosity. Eino Leino* criticized it for its sensationalism. Its messianic tone gives no promise of the comic talents that would blossom in his masterpiece, *Tulitikkuja lainaamassa* (1910; Borrowing Matches). *Harhama* bore the pseudonym Irmari Rantamala, but he took the name Maiju Lassila for his humorous tales. (Oddly enough, Maiju is a feminine name.) The setting for these stories is the northern Karelian countryside. Examples are *Pirttipohjalaiset* (1911; The Pirttipohja People), *Jussi Puranen* (1912), *Liika viisas* (1915; Too Much Wisdom). He also wrote several comedies in a light vein.

Lassila lived like a recluse during these years (1908–1917). Then the introvert changed into an extrovert. Lassila was involved in radical politics during the fateful period of Finnish history from 1917 to 1918. Again using the name Irmari Rantamala, he was editor of the socialist newspaper *Työmies* in Helsinki during the Civil War. He did not leave when the Whites occupied the city, and was arrested in April 1918. He was shot by his captors under obscure circumstances. Thus a life full of vicissitudes ended tragically. A movie entitled *Tulipää* (Flame-top) was shown in Cannes, France, in 1981, depicting his eventful existence.

Tulitikkuja lainaamassa is a classic of Finnish comic regionalism. The episodes develop in series like matches igniting each other at intervals. Antti Ihalainen sets out for a neighbor's farm to get matches, but is sidetracked when he meets his crony Jussi Vatanen. Antti gets entangled in his friend's marriage plans. His own errand slips from his mind; they get drunk and land in jail. Farfetched rumors spread through their village about their escapades. Lassila's humorous fancy is given a free rein. The dialogue is convincing, expressing the slow mental processes of the characters. Despite their caricatural features, the country folk Lassila knew as a boy come to life. Lassila belongs in the Aleksis Kivi* tradition, but his style is personal. Though he had read widely in non-Finnish literatures, Lassila leaves the impression of an untaught village genius. The author of *Harhama* has disappeared. Lassila remains.

FURTHER WORKS

Kun lesket lempivät (1911); *Pojat asialla* (1911); *Luonnon lapsia* (1912); *Nuori mylläri* (1912); *Rakkautta* (1912); *Elämän vaihteessa* (1912); *Pekka Puovalj* (1912); *Jussi Puranen* (1912); *Kun ruusut kukkivat* (1912); *Manasse Jäppinen* (1912; *Manasse Jäppinen*, 1983); *Kilpakosijat* (1913); *Avuttomia* (1913); *Israelitar* (1913); *Isä ja poika* (1914); *Iivana* (1915); *Kuoleman rajoilla* (1915); *Kuolleista herännyt* (1916); *Mimmi Paavilinna* (1916); *Mestari Nyke* (1917); *Turman talo* (1917); *Valitut teokset* (1945–1946, 1954); *Viimeiset Kirjoitukset*, ed. Ilpo Tiitinen and Auli Viikari (1977).

REFERENCES

Lindsten, Leo, *Maiju Lassila, Legenda jo eläessään* (Helsinki, 1979); Virtanen, Reino, "Review of Lindsten's *Maiju Lassila.*" *Scandinavian Studies* 52.1 (1980); Virtanen, Reino, "Review of *Viimeiset kirjoitukset.*" *Scandinavian Studies* 52.4 (1980).

                                                                            Reino Virtanen

Laxness, Halldór Kiljan (originally Halldór Guðjónsson, with the traditional and still firmly established Icelandic use of the patronymic; his father's name was Guðjón Helgi Helgason). Icelandic novelist, also a prolific author of short stories, plays, poetry, and essays, b. 23 April 1902, Reykjavík.

In 1905 Laxness's family moved to Laxnes, just northeast of the capital, where his father took up farming. After his father's death in 1919 Laxness, at the age of only seventeen, broke off his schooling in Reykjavík and went abroad. In the following years he traveled widely in postwar Europe, imbibing its problems, culture, and literary currents, with an intense desire for becoming a "modern man," in sharp contrast to the old-fashioned spirit of his native country. For some time he dwelt as a guest in a Benedictine monastery in the grand duchy of Luxembourg. He was baptized and confirmed in the Catholic faith. At his baptism he adopted the name of Kiljan, after an Irish saint, and at the same time the family name of Laxness, after his father's farm.

An interesting human document from this period of his life is the largely autobiographical novel *Vefarinn mikli frá Kasmír* (1927; The Great Weaver from Kashmir). It presents an impetuous and often paradoxical discussion of moral, social, and cultural ideas of the time. With its subjective and provocative style, it was a rather brusque breach with Icelandic narrative tradition, and an impressive literary breakthrough.

The next important phase in the author's career began with an long visit to the United States, from 1927 to 1929. He wanted to get to know and learn from this most advanced and modern country of the world. But his experience in these years of economic crisis and unemployment made him a vehement critic of capitalist society. He became a socialist, although in a very undogmatic vein. The negative aspects of the big country also kindled his feelings for Iceland and its peculiar traditions. Both socialism and nationalism leave their stamp on *Alþýðubókin* (1929; The Book of the People), a collection of essays, marking a decisive change in his interests from religious to social problems. It set the tone for his coming works of fiction.

In the thirties he created a series of novels, firmly rooted in Icelandic reality. *Þú vínviður hreini* (1931; O Thou Pure Vine, pub. as *Salka Valka*, 1936) and *Fuglinn í fjörunni* (1932; The Bird on the Beach, pub. as *Salka Valka*, 1936) tell the story of a typical fishing village in the beginning of our century, with its development from a patriarchal structure to a tentative opposition and organization among the fishermen. The main character is the fishergirl Salka Valka, instinctively taking sides with the poor and suffering. *Sjálfstætt fólk* (1934–1935; *Independent People*, 1945–1946) presents a small farmer in his relentless struggle for "independence" against a harsh nature and, not least, political and economic manipulation—before, during, and after World War I. A tetralogy (1937–1940), later known under the common title of *Heimsljós* (*World Light* 1969), deals with a parish pauper and folk poet, trying to vindicate his personal and mental freedom in oppressive surroundings.

The social criticism and satire of these novels are reckless, often utilizing well-known incidents from contemporary Iceland. However, they are far from any "social realism." Even the most "documentary" facts are transformed into a realm of fantasy and symbolic meaning. And Icelandic landscape and nature imbue the narrative with a lyrical quality.

To an increasing degree these works absorbed Icelandic tradition and literature. With the trilogy *Íslandsklukkan* (1943–1946; Iceland's Bell) the author picks up a historical topic, around the turn of the eighteenth century. With its skillful web of events and persons of the time, in a slightly archaic style, the novel gives an impressive picture of Icelandic tradition, mentality, and fight for independence. It is not by chance that it was composed around the year 1944, when Iceland after almost seven centuries regained full national sovereignty and became a republic.

The short novel *Atómstöðin* (1948; *The Atom Station*, 1961) takes us back to modern Iceland. In diary form a girl from a north Icelandic farm, serving as housemaid for a Reykjavík family, reports her experiences during a year in the capital. Through her honest mind the author aims a heavy blow at the machinations of Icelandic politicians around the demand by the United States for a permanent military base in Iceland. But on the whole the caustic satire has no single target. "The Atom Station," rather, is a symbol of wartime Reykjavík, with its hectic life and reevaluation of many old values.

Gerpla (1952; *The Happy Warriors*, 1958) again, returns to history. The novel is based on Old Icelandic sagas and adopts a personal variant of their style. But of course it has a message of its own. This "story of warriors" is a violent attack on war and hero worship, clearly inspired by the author's commitment to the peace movement of the postwar period. Somewhat paradoxically, however, it is at the same time an homage to the literary genius of those Old Icelandic writers.

In the decades after his Nobel Prize in 1955 Laxness published numerous novels, short stories, plays, and essays. They bear witness to decreasing political and social radicalism. His prose gets a tune of calm retrospection. Most of his novels from this period have a slightly documentary touch.

Brekkukotsannáll (1957; *The Fish Can Sing*, 1966), which takes place in Reykjavík at the turn of the century, is a profound discussion of central moral problems, of the ambiguity and vanity of an artist's fame, and of the importance of listening for the mystical One Tone, the only tone that matters. *Kristnihald undir Jökli* (1968; *Christianity at Glacier*, 1972) deals with the impossibility of reaching and rendering "reality" and "history." The truth ironically slips through our fingers, among rather irrelevant "facts" and "documents." 'We are left with the impenetrable mystery of man and life itself.

Beginning with *Í túninu heima* (1975; On the Farm at Home), the author has in four volumes presented charming recollections of his life from early childhood and youth until the age of twenty. The work is of great interest, both as an autobiography and as a vivid sketch of Icelandic culture in the first decades of our century.

In a quite unusual manner Laxness through his whole long career has been engaged in a fruitful dialogue with his people, not only in his fictional works but also, more directly, in his many articles and essays, covering almost every aspect of Icelandic culture. His vision of Iceland in brilliant dialectics combines a national with an international perspective, the outlook of "modern man" with a deep feeling for the values of his native country and its traditions. As a writer he has made his mother tongue a unique medium of literary art. Laxness has an important share in the development of twentieth-century Iceland.

FURTHER WORKS

Barn náttúrunnar (1919); *Nokkrar sögur* (1923); *Undir Helgahnúk* (1924); *Kapólsk viðhorf* (1925); *Kvæðakver* (1930); *Í Austurvegi* (1933); *Fótatak manna* (1933); *Straumrof* (1934); *Dagleið á fjöllum* (1937); *Ljós heimsins* (1937); *Gerska ævintýrið* (1938); *Höll sumarlandsins* (1938); *Hús skáldsins* (1939); *Fegurð himinsins* (1940); *Sjö töframenn*

(1942); *Vettvangur dagsins* (1942); *Hið ljósa man* (1944); *Eldur í Kaupinhafn* (1946); *Sjálfsagðir hlutir* (1946); *Reisubókarkorn* (1950); *Snæfríður Íslandssól* (1950); *Heiman eg fór* (1952; manuscript from 1924); *Silfurtúnglið* (1954); *Dagur í senn* (1955); *Gjörníngabók* (1959); *Paradísarheimt* (1960; *Paradise Reclaimed*, 1962); *Strompleikurinn* (1961); *Prjónastofan Sólin* (1962); *Skáldatími* (1963); *Sjöstafakverið* (1964; *A Quire of Seven*, 1974); *Upphaf mannúðarstefnu* (1965); *Dúfnaveislan* (1966; *The Pigeon Banquet*, 1973, in *Modern Nordic Plays*); *Islendíngaspjall* (1967); *Svavar Guðnason. Et udvalg af billeder med indledende tekst af Halldór Laxness* (1968); *Vínlandspúnktar* (1969); *Innansveitarkronika* (1970); *Úa* (1970); *Yfirskygðir staðir* (1971); *Guðsgjafaþula* (1972); *Norðanstúlkan* (1972); *Þjóðhátíðarrolla* (1974); *Úngur eg var* (1976); *Seiseijú, mikil ósköp* (1977); *Sjömeistarasagan* (1978); *Grikklandsárið* (1980); *Við heygarðshornið* (1981); *Og árin líða* (1984); *Dagar hjá múnkum* (1987).

FURTHER TRANSLATIONS

The Honour of the House (1959); *Seven Icelandic Short Stories*, ed. Asgeir Petúrsson and Steingrímur J.Þorsteinsson (1960); *An Anthology of Scandinavian Literature, from the Viking Period to the Twentieth Century*, ed. Hallberg Hallmundsson (1965).

REFERENCES

Eskeland, Ivar, *Halldór Kiljan Laxness* (Oslo, 1955); Hallberg, Peter, *Den store vävaren. En studie i Laxness' ungdomsdiktning* (Stockholm, 1954); Hallberg, Peter, *Skaldens hus. Laxness' diktning från Salka Valka till Gerpla* (Stockholm, 1956); Hallberg, Peter, *Halldór Laxness* (New York, 1971); Hallberg, Peter, "Halldór Laxness and the Icelandic Sagas." *Leeds Studies in English* 13 (1982); Höskuldsson, Sveinn Skorri, et al., *Sjö erindi um Halldór Laxness* (Reykjavík, 1973); Jónsson, Eiríkur, *Rætur Íslandsklukkunnar* (Reykjavík, 1981); Keel, Aldo, *Innovation und Restauration. Der Romancier Halldor Laxness seit dem zweiten Weltkrieg* (Basel/Frankfurt am Main, 1981); Kötz, Günter, *Das Problem Dichter und Gesellschaft im Werke von Halldór Kiljan Laxness* (Giessen, 1966); Kristjánsson, Gunnar, *Religiose Gestalten und christliche Motive im Romanwerk "Heimsljós" von Halldór Laxness* (Bochum, 1979); Sigurðsson, Haraldur, "Skrá un verk Halldórs Laxness á islensku og erlendum málum," in *Árbók Landsbókasafns Íslands* 28 (1971); Sigurjónsson, Árni, *Den politiske Laxness* (Stockholm, 1984); *Scandinavica* 11, Laxness issue, 1972; Sønderholm, Erik, *Halldór Laxness* (Copenhagen, 1981).

Peter Hallberg

Leffler, Anne Charlotte (also Anne Charlotte Edgren, duchessa di Cajanello). Swedish short story writer, novelist, and dramatist, b. 1 October 1842, Stockholm, d. 21 October 1892, Italy.

Leffler was born into an intellectual and gifted family, the only girl among the four children of Johan Olaf Leffler and Gustava Mittag-Leffler. At an early age, she had expressed literary aspirations, and in 1872, she attained her first major critical and popular success, the play *Skådespelerskan* (The Actress). However, Leffler was not to reach this same level of popularity until 1882, when at the urging of friend and feminist Ellen Key, she published a volume of short stories, *Ur lifvet*, volume 1 (From Life). In her short stories, novels, and plays Leffler explored various roles that woman can assume: mother, wife, lover, and/

or careerist. She posits the dilemma of how one can juggle these roles and still maintain personal and intellectual happiness and fulfillment. In her early works, Leffler stressed the need for reform in the social and economic position of women in Swedish society. She generally portrayed marriage as confining and morally and intellectually destructive for women. By 1885, Leffler's interest was turning away from tendential topics to the more personal side of woman's nature, especially the importance of passion in a woman's life.

Leffler was one of the leaders of the Modern Breakthrough in Sweden, a literary period that lasted from approximately 1879 until 1889. She was a member of many reform groups and led her own literary salon. However, as the Modern Breakthrough waned in popularity and critical support, Leffler's literary reputation also suffered. She began to have strong disagreements with the dominant, conservative Swedish women's movement on the nature of women. Leffler maintained that women could possess a desire for passionate relationships, a belief that was an anathema to the Swedish women's movement at that time.

Leffler's reputation today has remained overshadowed by that of her contemporary, August Strindberg.* Her influence and importance during the Modern Breakthrough is mentioned in the general literary histories, but her abilities as an author are dismissed as insignificant. However, she did write movingly and well about the concerns and problems of middle- and upper-middle-class Swedish women of the late nineteenth century.

FURTHER WORKS

Händelsevis (1869); *Pastorsadjunkten* (1876); *Under toffeln* (1876); *Elfvan* (1880); *Sanna kvinnor* (1883; *True Women*, 1919); *Ur lifvet*, 6 vols. (1882–93, 1950); *Hur man gör godt* (1885); *Kampen för lyckan* (1887); *Tre komedier* (1891); *Efterlämnade skrifter*, 2 vols. (1893); *En självbiografi*, ed. J. Gernandt and I. Essen (1922).

REFERENCES

Key, Ellen, *Anne Charlotte Leffler, Duchessa di Cajanello* (Stockholm, 1893); Lowe Shogren, Melissa, "The Search for Self-fulfillment" (Diss., Univ. of Washington, 1984); Sylvan, Maj, *Anne Charlotte Leffler: en kvinna finner sin väg* (Stockholm, 1984).

Melissa Lowe Shogren

Lehtonen, Joel. Finnish novelist, short story writer and a poet, b. 27 November 1881, Sääminki, near Savonlinna, d. 20 November 1934, Helsinki.

The son of an unknown father and a poor country woman, Lehtonen was farmed out, under the poor law, to a minister's widow who named him Lehtonen and took care of his education. After graduating from high school in Savonlinna, Lehtonen worked as a newspaperman in various small towns and then began a career in Helsinki as a free-lance writer, translator (i.e., Giovanni Boccaccio, Henrik Ibsen,* Stendhal, August Strindberg*), and critic. He learned several foreign languages, traveled widely and wrote about his experiences often by comparing provincial Finland with the great centers of Europe. His mind was torn by conflicting inclinations, reflected in his works. He suffered greatly from the violence and cruelty of his contemporary world, as well as from rheumatism, and eventually ended his various pains by committing suicide.

Lehtonen's first works reflect the vigorous and heroic romanticism of Friedrich Nietzsche, made known in Finland by Volter Kilpi,* and Maxim Gorky. The titles *Paholaisen viulu* (1904; The Devil's Fiddle) and *Villi* (1905; The Savage) are typical; *Mataleena* (1905; an allusion to the sinful Magdalen) is an indirect vindication of his mother. However, Lehtonen soon abandoned what one of the characters in the novel *Putkinotko* (1919–1920; Weedpatch, A Tale about a Lazy Moonshiner and a Foolish Gentleman) calls "heroic nonsense, humbug words" and embraced a broad, warm, tolerant, and humorous philosophy of life. This new attitude was due largely to his travels in southern Europe and the works of such great Renaissance writers as Miguel de Cervantes and François Rabelais. He then wrote a number of works depicting his home region of Savonlinna and a number of characters living there. His poems *Rakkaita muistoja* (1911; Dear Memories) and *Markkinoilta* (1912; From the Fair) provide boisterous scenes from popular life and also parodies of earlier idealized descriptions of country people, as, for example, in Johan Ludvig Runeberg*; the novel *Kerran kesällä* (1917, Once in Summer) as well as the short stories in *Kuolleet omenapuut* (1918; The Dead Appletrees) and *Korpi ja puutarha* (1923; The Wilderness and the Garden) have the same characters appearing in all of them (also in *Putkinotko*). There is much of the great Russian writers Nikolai Gogol and Anton Chekhov in the manner Lehtonen describes these characters; they are lazy, dirty, stupid, reckless, cunningly mean, or impractical in their idealism, but the author never assumes an attitude of contemptuous superiority toward them; the broad, tolerant human smile is always there. However, Lehtonen's inner conflicts prevented him from adopting a truly optimistic worldview. *Putkinotko*, his masterpiece, is an attempt to recapture in more than five hundred pages, the detailed events of one beautiful summer day in order to preserve them forever. From the very beginning, however, the narrative contains discordant, conflicting elements, and its end forebodes nothing good. Lehtonen wrote two additional novels, one in two parts, *Sorron lapset—Punainen mies* (1923–1925; The Oppressed and The Red Man), and *Henkien taistelu* (1933; The Struggle of the Spiritual Powers). Both include sharp criticism of contemporary society, as well as bitter and disillusioned observations of the weakness and futility of efforts to improve the world. Some of his works are lyrical meditations on nature that attempt to achieve inner harmony through spiritual communion with the religious experience of others, as, for example, St. Francis of Assisi, and not through established religion.

Lehtonen's works were not appreciated in the years following his death, but were rediscovered in the sixties and seventies. The wide variety in his works, from lyrical meditation to bitter sarcasm, from grotesque humor to portrayal of violence, as well as his interest in culture, art, and social questions, make him, along with Aleksis Kivi,* Volter Kilpi, and F. E. Sillanpää,* one of the great names in Finnish literature.

FURTHER WORKS

Perm (1904); *Tarulinna* (1906); *Ilvolan juttuja* (1910); *Myrtti ja alppiruusu* (1911); *Nuoruus* (1911); *Punainen mylly* (1913); *Munkkikammio* (1914); *Puolikuun alla* (1919); *Tähtimantteli* (1920); *Kevättä ja kesää* (1921); *Rakastunut rampa eli Sakris Kukkelman, Köyhä polseviikki* (1922); *Teokset*, 2 vols. (1923–1924); *Onnen poika* (1925); *Rai Jakkerintytär* (1927); *Sirkus ja pyhimys* (1927); *Lintukoto* (1929); *Kootut teokset*, 8 vols. (1931–1935); *Hyvästijättö Lintukodolle* (1934); *Valikoima kertomuksia* (1934); *Valitut teokset* (1954); *Keuruulainen impromptu* (1961); *Putkinotkon herra. Kirjeitä 1907–1920* (1969).

REFERENCES

Aalberg, Veikko, "The Suicide of a Finnish Writer. A Psychodynamic Study." *Psychiatria Fennica* (1972); Ahokas, Jaakko A., "Putkinotko—kadonnutta aikaa etsimässä," in *Joel Lehtonen-päivä Savonlinnassa 5.8, 1981*, ed., Pirjo Tuomi (Joensuu, 1982); Björkenheim, Magnus, *Joel Lehtosen Putkinotko* (Helsinki, 1955); Järvinen, Irma-Riitta, "Joel Lehtosen Tarulinnan kansansatulähteet." *Kirjallisuudentutkijain Seuran vuosikirja* 34 (1982); Nurminen, Antero, *Joel Lehtosen kirjallinen tuotanto* (Forssa, 1953); Suomi, Vilho, "Joel Lehtonen 1881–1934," *Ord och Bild* 68 (1959); Tarkka, Pekka, "Joel Lehtonen and Putkinotko." *Books from Finland* 11 (1977); Tarkka, Pekka, "Joel Lehtonen and His Alter Ego 1881–1934." *Books from Finland* 15.4 (1981).

Jaakko Ahokas

Leino, Eino (Armas Eino Leopold Lönnbohm). Finnish poet, critic, dramatist, novelist, and translator, b. 6 July 1878, Paltamo, d. 10 January 1926, Tuusula.

Leino was the first major Finnish poet and one of the greatest Finnish poets of all time. In fact, the first fifteen years of this century—a period of national romanticism in Finnish literature—are often referred to as the period of Leino. He was at the center of literary and other cultural activity during his prolific writing years. He belonged to the leading group of Finnish artists of the time, Jean Sibelius, Robert Kajanus, Otto Manninen,* Akseli Gallen-Kallela, and Emil Halonen among them, who were in close contact and greatly influenced each other's work.

Born as the youngest of ten children, Leino grew up absorbing the traditions of the Finnish countryside, and at the same time, through his educated older brothers and other relatives, he was also exposed to European culture. He was a precocious writer; at the age of eighteen he had already published his first collection of poetry *Maaliskuun lauluja* (1896; March Songs) when his older brother Kasimir Leino, a poet and critic, introduced him to the Helsinki literary circles. He soon became the center of attention and surpassed his brother in all genres of writing, just as he surpassed the other Finnish poets of the time. Leino wrote his best poetry in his twenties and thirties.

Leino was a prolific writer: he produced nearly thirty volumes of poetry, some twenty plays, and a great deal of fiction and other prose. As in his poetry, in his other writing Leino integrated the great European tradition with native Finnish culture. He was the leading verse translator of his time; he translated works by Zacharias Topelius* and Johan Ludvig Runeberg* and such classics of world literature as Dante's *Divina Commedia*, Racine's *Phèdre*, Corneille's *Le Cid*, Goethe's *Iphigeneia auf Tauris*, and Schiller's *Wilhelm Tell*. As a literary and drama critic, Leino acquainted the Finnish readership with cultural developments in Finland and abroad. Particularly in his early years, he was deeply involved in the political debates of the day, joining the Young Finland movement, which stressed the importance of Finnish language.

Leino's early poetry was filled with nature lyricism, often optimistic in tone. By the turn of the century, darker strains began to appear as he dealt with themes of life and death, good and evil. The influence of Goethe and Nietzsche became evident in his writing. The high point of Leino's early period, and perhaps his greatest masterpiece, was *Helkavirsiä* I (1903; *Whitsongs*, 1978), a collection of mythical poetry in the trochaic *Kalevala** meter. Leino drew on themes from myths, ballads, and legends, native and foreign, and he brilliantly combined them into a new creation. He has been called "the last great Kalevala singer" and in the words of Michael Branch, one whose "contribution to the two-thousand-year history of Kalevala poetry was to transform an elegant oral tradition into an elegant literary tradition" (*Whitsongs*, Introduction). *Helkavirsiä* II (1916; Whitsongs), also in trochaic meter, reflected Leino's inner turmoil and the sense of pessimism at the time of World War I.

Leino was a genius who gave Finnish poetry the tools with which it could become truly great. He masterfully moved from one poetic form to another, creating a synthesis of old and new, and of native and foreign elements. With his brilliant facility for language he created words that were all his own and yet accessible to his readers. Always present in his poetry are themes of life and death, good and evil, dream and fulfillment. He freely drew on a wide range of images: heroes of classical mythology, of old Finnish mythology, and the whole spectrum of nature: from birdsong to the stillness of the forest, from a calm summer night to the ice and snow of winter. Leino painted with images as he painted with sounds.

Leino's poetry has had a profound impact on those who have come after him. Each generation has to assess its literary forefathers; the poets of today readily acknowledge their indebtedness to Leino.

FURTHER WORKS

Tarina suuresta tammesta (1896); *Yökehrääjä* (1897); *Sata ja yksi laulua* (1898); *Tuonelan joutsen* (1898); *Ajan aalloilla* (1899); *Hiihtäjän virsiä* (1900); *Johan Wilhelm* (1900); *Sota valosta* (1900); *Kivesjärveläiset* (1901); *Pyhä kevät* (1901); *Kangastuksia* (1902); *Suomalainen näyttämötaide* (1902); *Päiväperhoja* (1903); *Kaunosielu* (1903); *Simo Hurtta* (1904, 1919); *Naamioita* (6 vols., 1905–1911); *Päivä Helsingissä* (1905); *Talvi-yö* (1905); *Runokirja* (1906); *Tuomas Vitikka* (1906); *Jaana Rönty* (1907); *Tervehdyssanoja* (1907); *Turjan loihtu* (1907); *Hall* (1908); *Luonnon luotteita* (1908); *Maailman kannel* (1908); *Naamioita* (1908); *Olli Suurpää* (1908); *Naamioita* (1909); *Phyä Martti* (1909); *Suom-*

alaisia kirjailijoita (1909); *Kuolemattomuuden toivo* (1910); *Nuori nainen* (1910); *Suomalaisen kirjallisuuden historia* (1910); *Kalevala näyttämöllä* (1911); *Työn orja* (1911); *Rahan orja* (1912); *Tähtitarha* (1912); *Juhlaruno* (1913); *Naisen orja* (1913); *Onnen orja* (1913); *Seikkailijatar* (1913); *Tienraivaajat* (1913); *Mesikämmen* (1914); *Painuva päivä* (1914); *Pankkiherroja* (1914); *Elämän koreus* (1915); *Paavo Kontio* (1915); *Musti* (1916); *Alla kasvon kaikkivallan* (1917); *Karjalan kuningas* (1917); *Leirivalkeat* (1917); *Ahven ja kultakalat* (1918); *Helsingin valloitus* (1918); *Kaarle Halme* (1918); *Vapauden kirja* (1918); *Vöyrin sotakoulu* (1918); *Bellerophon* (1919); *Elina* (1919); *Juhana herttuan ja Catharina Jagellonican lauluja* (1919); *Lemmen lauluja* (1919); *Tuulikannel* (1919); *Ajatar* (1920); *Kodin kukka ja uhrikuusi* (1920); *Meidät Moskova erotti* (1920); *Syreenien kukkiessa* (1920); *Sana Kalevalan päivänä* (1921); *Vanha pappi* (1921); *Pajarin poika* (1922); *Puolan paanit* (1922); *Shemeikan murhe* (1924); *Elämäni kuvakirja* (1925); *Kolme lähti, kaksi palasi* (1926); *Kootut teokset*, 16 vols. (1926–1930); *Runoja* (1928).

TRANSLATIONS

Krook, Anna, *Eight Swedish and Finnish Songs* (1909); *Finnish Odyssey*, ed. Robert Armstrong (1975); *Modern Scandinavian Poetry*, ed. Martin Allwood et al. (1982); *Salt of Pleasure: Twentieth-Century Finnish Poetry*, ed. Aili Jarvenpa (1983).

REFERENCES

Branch, Michael, "Introduction: Eino Leino," *Whitsongs* (London, 1978); Koskimies, Rafael, *Suomen kirjallisuus*, vol. 4 (Helsinki, 1965); Onerva, L., *Eino Leino* (Helsinki, 1979); Peltonen, Aarre M., *Eino Leinon varhaiskehitys ja-tuotanto* (Tampere, 1975); Peltonen, Aarre M., *Maan piiristä metafyysiseen* (Tampere, 1975); Riikonen, Hannu, "*Eino Leino, Hauptzüge der finnischen Literatur.*" *Jahrbuch für finnisch-deutsche Literaturbeziehungen* 14 (1980); Saarikoski, P., *Eino "Leino"* (Porvoo, 1974); Sakari, Aimo, "Litterature finlandaise," in *Profil litteraire de la France* 2 (1951); Sarajas, Annamari, "Eino Leino 1878–1926," *Books from Finland* 12.2 (1978); Tarkiainen, Viljo, *Eino Leinon runoudesta*, (Helsinki, 1954).

Aili Flint

Lenngren, Anna Maria. Swedish poet, b. 18 June 1754, Uppsala, d. 8 March 1817, Stockholm.

Lenngren grew up in Uppsala, where she received an extensive private education from her father, B. Malmstedt, who was a university instructor.

Lenngren's literary career was initially extremely active, beginning in 1774 with poetry and translations for the Swedish court of verse dramas and operas. In 1780 she obtained a permanent position on the Stockholm newspaper *Stockholms Posten* and married the newspaperman C. P. Lenngren. She was an active writer for the paper, contributing satirical poems, essays, and articles. After 1800 her literary production declined in quantity and quality.

Lenngren's poetry distinguishes itself from that of her contemporaries by its subject matter and style. Her best works, such as "Grevinnans besök" (The Countess's Visit) and "Några ord till min kära dotter" (A Few Words to My Dear Daughter) are filled with gently humorous observations of everyday life written in an almost colloquial style. Yet while casting a satirical eye upon almost all aspects and classes of Swedish society, she retains in her poetry a good-natured tolerance and understanding for the very institutions and people she satirizes. Because of her poetry, she is considered to be one of the major literary figures of the Swedish Enlightenment, and one of the few authors from this period who can still be read with enjoyment by twentieth-century readers.

WORKS

Skaldeförsök (1819); *Samlade Skrifter*, ed. T. Hjelmqvist and K. Warburg, 9 vols. (1916–1926).

TRANSLATIONS

Anna Maria Lenngren 1754–1817, ed. Philip K. Nelson (1984).

REFERENCES

Blanck, A., *Anna Maria Lenngren* (1961); Warburg, Karl, *Anna Maria Lenngren* (1917).

Melissa Lowe Shogren

Leonora Christina. Countess of Schleswig and Holstein. Danish writer, b. 8 July 1621 at Frederiksborg Castle, d. 16 March 1698, Maribo.

Leonora Christina was the daughter of King Christian IV by his second, morganatic spouse, Lady Kirsten Munk. After the estrangement of her parents in 1630 the king took charge of the education of his gifted and beloved daughter. At the age of fifteen Leonora Christina was married to a young nobleman, Corfitz Ulfeldt. In her French autobiography she has described her sometimes harsh upbringing, the Ulfeldts' eminence at the royal court, their downfall in 1651, exile in Sweden and Germany 1651–1660, imprisonment at Bornholm 1660–1661, and the couple's final separation at Bruges in 1663. Leonora Christina's further fate when, due to her husband's treacherous schemes against the Danish king, she was brought as a prisoner from London to Copenhagen and jailed in Christiansborg Castle from 1663 to 1685, is the subject of her main work, *Jammers-minde (Memoirs by Leonora Christina, Daughter of Christian IV of Denmark*, 1929). Pleading her innocence, Leonora Christina here gives a moving account of her trial and of the personal and religious crisis she undergoes before coming to terms with her fate. No less fascinating is the story of her struggle against the boredom of prison life when, deprived of all means of passing the time, she makes utensils for sewing, weaving, and writing from bits of rubbish. In Leonora Christina's description of her relationship with wardens and jailbirds her psychological insight, sense of humor, wit, and strength of character are reflected.

As a source of cultural and political history *Jammers-Minde* is invaluable; Leonora Christina's gift of narrative and the portrayal of her powerful and resilient personality make it one of the treasures of Danish literature and a work with few equals anywhere.

The French autobiography was completed in prison in 1673, whereas only the beginning of *Jammers-Minde* dates from those years; the major part of the work was written at Maribo in the 1690s. *Jammers-Minde* was unknown until 1868 when the manuscript, now at Frederiksborg Castle, was discovered in the archives of an Austrian noble family. Leonora Christina's personal manuscript for the French autobiography, known from variant copies, was considered lost until it turned up in a school library at Altona in 1962.

Besides her main autobiographies, Leonora Christina has left records in Danish of dramatic episodes in her life and a work of biography, *Hæltinners Pryd*.

FURTHER WORKS

Jammersminde, ed. S. Birket Smith (1869); *Leonora Christinas franske Levnedsskildring* (1673; facsimile ed., 1958); *Den fangne grevinde Leonora Christinas Jammers minde*, facsimile edition, ed. O. Andrup (1931); *Jammersminde og andre selvbiografiske skildringer*, ed. Johs. Brøndum Nielsen (1949; rev. ed., 1960); *Leonora Jammers Minde*, ed. Vagn Lundsgaard Simonsen (1980); *Hæltinners Pryd*, ed. Christopher Maaløe (1977).

REFERENCES

Bjørn, Hans, et al., *Leonora Christina,* in *Acta Jutlandica* 58, Hum Ser. 57 (Aarhus, 1983); Poulsen, Børge, *Træk af Leonora Christina og Corfitz Ulfeldts Levned,* 2 vols. (Kolding, 1979–1980); Smith, S. Birket, *Leonora Christinas grevinde Ulfeldts Historie,* 2 vols. (Copenhagen, 1879–1881).

Niels Lyhne Jensen

Leopold, Carl Gustaf. Swedish poet and critic, b. 26 March 1756, Stockholm, d. 9 November 1829, Stockholm.

Leopold's father was a customs official. The family originally spelled the name Leopoldt, but the poet dropped the *-t* sometime before 1790. When he was ennobled in 1809 he chose "af Leopold" as his new, noble name.

Leopold was educated in Uppsala and Greifswald, where he was appointed a professor in the history of knowledge. He was also librarian in Stralsund (both Greifswald and Stralsund were Swedish possessions at the time). In 1785 he was appointed librarian in Uppsala, and in the same year reached public notice with a collection of delightful love poems, entitled *Erotiska oder*. In 1786 Leopold was called to the court of Gustaf III, to assist the king in the production of court divertissements. His association with the king was close, productive, and positive.

Leopold was elected to the Swedish Academy in 1786, and became one of its most faithful workers, assisting in its new rules for correct spelling, its contributions to the new Freedom of Print regulations, and writing numerous reviews and poems. Throughout his production he attempted to defend the old, rococo style against the wave of romantic sentiment. His collected works were published from 1802 to 1807. Leopold withdrew from the public arena to care for his insane wife and to nurse his failing eyesight, but honors and titles continued to rain upon him. Until his death he remained a central figure in the Swedish world of letters.

Leopold's greatest impact on Swedish culture has come through his defense of French classicism and the ideas of the Enlightenment, and through his rhetorical style. Esaias Tegnér* was strongly influenced by Leopold and defended him vigorously against the romantics.

FURTHER WORKS

Samlade skrifter, rev. ed., vols. 1–3 (1814–1816); vols. 4–6 (1831–1833); new ed. 6 vols. (1911–1917).

REFERENCES

Holmberg, O., "Tegnér och Leopold," in *Esaias Tegnér, studier till hans person och verk*, ed. Olle Holmberg and Algot Werin (Lund, 1946); Holmberg, O., *Den unge Leopold* (1953); *Leopold och Gustaf III* (1954); *Leopold och Reuterholmska tiden* (1957); *Leopold under Gustaf IV Adolf* (1962); *Leopold och det nya riket* (1965).

Christina Söderhjelm McKnight

Levertin, Oscar Ivar. Swedish poet, critic, and scholar, b. 17 July 1862, Norrköping, d. 22 September 1906, Stockholm.

Levertin grew up in a highly cultured, aesthetic Jewish-Swedish milieu. He was an adherent of Georg Brandes's* programmatic "modern breakthrough" literature during his years at Uppsala and embraced the radical realism of August Strindberg.* His early prose works (e.g., *Småmynt*; 1883, Small Change) reflect the "shoemaker realism" against which, together with his new friend Verner von Heidenstam,* he was later to rebel. A brush with tuberculosis and the death of his young wife in 1889 inspired Levertin to throw off his pragmatic, socially conscious prose in favor of sensuous, highly charged lyrical verse. His first (and most characteristic) volume of poetry was *Legender och visor* (1891; Legends and Songs), which was typified by the twin themes of love and death. It owed a great debt to French models (Charles Baudelaire) and English sources (Dante Gabriel Rossetti and Algernon Charles Swinburne). Each of his subsequent volumes—*Nya dikter* (1894; New Poems), *Dikter* (1901; Poems), *Kung Salomo och Morolf* (1905; King Solomon and Morolf), and *Sista dikter* (1906; Last Poems)—strengthened his position as one of the leading neoromantic poets and champions of the new fantasy-filled, subjective literature of the 1890s.

Levertin's role as a critic, first for *Aftonbladet* (1885–1897) and then the reorganized *Svenska Dagbladet* (1897–1900), was probably more important than his role in the lyrical transformation of the national literature. The breadth of his reading, his cosmopolitanism, his elegant style, and his deep humanity combined to make him something of a national arbiter of literary taste. He was also a thoughtful scholar, having defended his dissertation as early as 1887. Later, when he was professor of literary history at the University of Stockholm, his lectures—especially on the French and Swedish eighteenth century—were extremely popular and well attended; most were later published. Levertin died suddenly under unusual circumstances in 1906, at the height of his poetic and critical career.

FURTHER WORKS

Konflikter (1885); *Teater och Drama under Gustaf III* (1887); *Pepitas bröllop*, with Verner von Heidenstam (1890); *Lifvets Fiender* (1891); *Från Gustaf III:s dagar* (1896); *Johan Wellander* (1897); *Diktare och drömmare* (1898); *Svenska gestalter* (1903); *Carl von Linné* (1906); *Samlade skrifter*, 23 vols. (1907–1911).

TRANSLATIONS

An Anthology of Swedish Lyrics from 1750 to 1925, ed. C. V. Stork (1917).

REFERENCES

Ahlenius, Holger, *Oscar Levertin: en studie i hans tankevärld* (Stockholm, 1934); Böök, Fredrik, *Oscar Levertin* (Stockholm, 1944), Fehrman, Carl, *Levertins lyrik* (Lund, 1944); Fehrman, Carl, *Oscar Levertin* (Stockholm, 1947); Julén, Björn, *Hjärtats landsflykt: en Levertin studie* (Stockholm, 1961); Levertin, Anna, *Den unge Levertin: minnen och brev* (Stockholm, 1947); Murdock, Eleanor E., "Oscar Levertin: Swedish Critic of French Realism." *Comparative Literature* 5 (1953); Rydén, Per, *En kritikers Väg*, (Lund, 1974); Rydén, Per, *En kritikers värderingar* (Lund, 1977); Söderhjelm, Werner, *Oscar Levertin: en minnesteckning*, 2 vols. (Stockholm, 1914–1917).

Lars Emil Scott

Library Resources for Scandinavian Literature.

A. LIBRARIES IN SCANDINAVIA

Finding literary resources in Scandinavian libraries can sometimes be complicated. Authors are not required to deposit personal papers anywhere, although most do go to the national libraries. Manuscript catalogs, particularly for modern authors, are inadequate, and one must resort to such sources as national biographies that frequently include location of personal papers. The following is intended to ease these problems by providing succinct information about major libraries specializing in literature in each country and suggesting appropriate bibliographic references, in particular library and collection guides and manuscript catalogs.

One library in each country is designated as the national library and assumes primary responsibility for its literature. Each acquires one copy of every new book published in the country, usually through a mandatory deposit law that may be 200 years old; collects pamphlets and minor works, for example, playbills, which are not listed in the national bibliography but maintained in special collections with their own catalogs; and seeks out works published elsewhere about the country, including translations of its literature, and sometimes publishes a list of them. All have manuscript collections with appropriate catalogs, such as letter recipients and writers, and maintain special collections of maps, prints, and photographs that are useful sources for pictures of authors and other illustrative material. Because of their similarities, this information is not repeated and must be assumed for each country.

REFERENCES

Encyclopedia of Library and Information Science (New York, 1971–1980), "Denmark" VI, "Finland" VIII, "Iceland" XI, "Norway" XX, "Sweden" XXIX; Esdaile, Arundell, *National Libraries of the World, Their History, Administration and Public Services*, 2nd rev. ed. (London, 1957); Harrison, K. C., *Libraries in Scandinavia*, 2nd rev. ed. (London, 1969); Welsch, Erwin K., Mariann Tiblin, and Dennis Hill, *Libraries and Archives in Scandinavia* (New York, 1985).

I. Denmark

The Royal Library (Kongelige Biblioteket) in Copenhagen, founded in 1660, is the country's largest (ca. 2,300,000 vols.), and the major library for Danish humanistic studies including literature. Due to a law mandating deposit of one copy of each book published in Denmark since 1697, it has a virtually complete collection of all books and pamphlets published in the kingdom. Among its famous collections are the Hielmstierne-Rosencrone Samling (Danish literature before 1800) and the Collinske Samling of manuscripts and books of Danish and Norwegian authors in the nineteenth century. Its manuscript holdings also include those of individual authors, for example, Georg Brandes,* as well as related materials such as the archives of major publishers, for example, Gyldendal. The library issues a large number of pamphlets, some of them in English and almost all of them free, describing its services and collections in a series entitled "Publikumsorienteringer." Number 1, "Salgsliste," is a frequently revised list of the titles in the series that also mentions other publications about the library's collections. It also issues a series of "Fagbibliografier," which are guides to doing research in selected parts of the library's holdings. A pamphlet issued in 1982, *The Royal Library Today,* provides basic information about its collections.

The University Library (Universitetsbiblioteket) is divided into two parts: humanistic studies in the first section (1. afdeling) and scientific in the second. In the mid-nineteenth century it ceded its humanistic and literary materials, and the responsibility for maintaining the central collection in the future, to the Royal Library. Today its humanities collections include theology, a substantial body of Danish literature (it is also a depository library), manuscripts relating to the university and its faculty, and responsibilities for the newspaper collection in Copenhagen. Its humanities books are dispersed among institute libraries, predominantly at the new campus on Amager, and the main building in the center of the city. Among its institute libraries is the Arnamagnæan Institute, which has original and microfilm copies of Old Norse and Icelandic materials.

The State Library (Statsbiblioteket) in Århus, founded in 1897, serves as the main library for the university in that city. It is also the central library in Denmark for the collection of Danish newspapers (Statens Avissamling) and has some literary manuscripts as well as a virtually complete collection of twentieth-century Danish literature due to its status as a depository library. Another notable library outside of Copenhagen is the Karen Brahes Bibliotek, located in the Landsarkiv for Fyn in Odense. It is a small but important library of early printed books and collections of "viser," as well as significant manuscript holdings.

REFERENCES

Arnamagnæanske Stiftelse. Katalog over de oldnorsk-islandske handskrifter i det Store kongelige bibliotek og i Universitetsbibliotek (Copenhagen, 1900); Behrend, C., *Katalog over det kongelige Bibliotekets haandskrifter vedrørende dansk personalhistorie* (Copenhagen, 1925–1927); *Biblioteksvejviser 1981* (Copenhagen, 1981), an annual list of all libraries in Denmark with brief indications of collecting emphases and special collections; *Fund og forskning i det kongelige biblioteks samlinger*, issued since 1954 featuring articles on the library's special collections; Krarup, Alf, *Katalog over Universitetsbibliotekets haandskrifter* (Copenhagen, 1929–1935); Linde, Helle, and Anker Olsen, *Manuskripter og arkivalier i danske samlinger* (Copenhagen, 1968); includes a useful bibliography; Nielsen, Lauritz, *Katalog over danske og norske digteres originalmanuskripter i det Kongelige Bibliotek* (Copenhagen, 1941–); Petersen, Carl S., *Det Kongelige bibliotekets haandskriftsamling* (Copenhagen, 1942), basic guide to earlier holdings; Sejr, Emanuel, *Statsbiblioteket i Århus, 1902–1952* (Århus, 1952); Vogelsang, H. C., "Fortegnelse over Haandskrifterne i Karen Brahes Bibliotek i Odense," in *Odense Cathedralskoles Indbydelsesskrift* (1857).

II. Finland

The oldest academic research library was founded at the University in Turku in the seventeenth century, and from the earliest years of the following century, it had deposit rights to one copy of each new Swedish book. Unfortunately, the collection was destroyed before it could be moved to the new capital of Helsinki in the nineteenth century, but important resources remain at both the 700,000-volume library of Turku University and the 750,000-volume Åbo Academy Library for Swedish Finland. Some of the newer university libraries (particularly Jyväskylä, which received some collections from the Finnish Literary Society) also have useful collections, but the center of library resources is now Helsinki.

The most important library in Finland is the Helsinki University Library (Helsingin yliopiston kirjasto), whose 1,500,000 volumes also serve as the national library. Among its five divisions, those most noteworthy for students of Finnish literature and humanities are the National Department (Kotimainenosasto), which includes the country's largest collection of Finnish literature (in a noncirculating collection), and the Manuscript Department (Käsikirjoituskokoelma), which includes major literary manuscripts as well as those of some literary organizations. The Finnish national bibliography (*Suomen kirjallisuus*), produced by the library since 1944, acts as a catalog of its Finnish collections, for there has been a national depository scheme since 1919 that provides one copy of each new book to the national library as well as to five other depository libraries elsewhere in the country. The library issues a series that includes bibliographies useful as resource guides. "Julkaisuja" (Publications) started in 1918 and has included a multipart guide to Finnish ballads and folk songs in the University Library, guides to medieval manuscripts, a volume on the history of medicine, etc. Recently the library started a new series of mimeographed publications, "Monistesarja," which features various holdings.

In addition to the university's central library there are more than 100 institute libraries whose holdings, including those in literature, are not represented in the central card catalog. There is also a 200,000-volume library at the university's Student Union (Helsingin yliopiston ylioppilaskunnan kirjasto) serving mostly undergraduate students.

Also in Helsinki is the Library of the Finnish Literature Society (Suomalaisen Kirjallisuuden Seuran kirjasto), which dates from 1878 and until 1944 produced the national bibliography. The 150,000-volume library now includes the Finnish Folklore Archive and is dedicated to collecting materials related to the Baltic Finns and Finno-Ugric philology.

REFERENCES

Ellsworth, Rudolf C., "Research Libraries in Finland." *Library Quarterly* 35 (1965); Hautala, Jouko, "The Folklore Archives of the Finnish Literature Society." *Studia Fennica* 7.2 (1957); Kauppi, Hilkka M., *Library and Information Services in Finland* (Helsinki, 1981); Lättilä, Leena, *Helsinki University Library Guide*, Helsinki University Library Occasional Papers 1 (1972); Nivanka, Eino, "The Library of the Finnish Literature Society." *Studia Fennica* 7.3 (1957); Nivanka, Eino, comp., *Suomen tieteellisten kirjastojen opas. Guide to the Research Libraries of Finland* (Helsinki, 1962), lists all libraries in a classified arrangement and includes for each information about holdings and a bibliography. There is also an abbreviated English-language version, Nivanka, Eino, comp., *Directory of Finnish Research Libraries* (Helsinki, 1962); Nohrström, Holger, *Helsingfors universitetsbiblioteks Fennica-Samling* (Helsingin Yliopiston Kirjaston Julkaisuja 1, 1918); *Suomen tieteellisten kirjastojen käsikirjoituskokoelmien yhteisluettelo* ("Catalog of Manuscript Collections in Scholarly Libraries in Finland") (Helsingin yliopiston kirjaston monistesarja 4, 1971); and its supplement *Käsikirjoituskokoelmien yhteisluettelo* (Helsingin yliopiston kirjaston monistesarja 6, 1972) are the best sources for locating literary manuscripts; Vuorela, Toivo, "The Finnish Literature Society." *Studia Fennica* 7.1 (1957).

III. Iceland

The National Library of Iceland (Landsbókasafn Íslands) was founded in the nineteenth century and as of 1980 had about 360,000 volumes and 13,000 volumes of manuscripts. This library will be integrated with the University Library in a single collection. It is responsible for collecting all books published in Iceland as well as works concerning the country. It has extensive manuscript collections, mostly recent, and either photocopies or originals of works produced abroad. The library maintains several specialized card catalogs and finding instruments for specialized parts of the collections such as an index to poems in the manuscript collections, as well as indexes to letters and specialized bibliographies of Icelandica held in foreign archives. The library's accession list (Ritaukaskrá) also served as the national bibliography from 1888 to 1943. Subsequently the Icelandic portion appeared in its yearbook (Árbók) from 1945 to 1974; the Icelandic National Bibliography (*Íslenzk Bókaskrá*) started with the volume published in 1975.

The University Library (Háskólabókasafn) was established in 1940 and currently has responsibilities for all areas of teaching and research in the university, but is now a research library only in the areas of science and technology. It has about eighteen branch or institute libraries. The University Library issues an annual report, *Árbók Háskóli Íslands* and has also published a brief guide *Leidarvísir* (Reykjavík, 1981).

The Arnamagnæan Institute in Iceland (Stofnun Árna Magnússonar á Islandi) is responsible for the preservation of the manuscripts transferred from the Arnamagnæan Institute in Copenhagen. It also sponsors research on all aspects of Icelandic literature and language. Its manuscripts are supplemented by a reference collection in the field. *Gripla,* published annually by the Institute, includes research articles.

REFERENCES

Hill, Dennis, "The National Library of Iceland: Its Development and Organization." *Journal of Library History* 17 (1982); *Skrá um handritasöfn Landsbókasafnsins* (Reykjavík, 1918–), the basic manuscript catalog first issued in three volumes between 1918 and 1937, with current supplements.

IV. Norway

The University Library in Oslo (Universitetsbiblioteket i Oslo), the largest in the country and the center for humanistic and literary research, was founded in 1811 and benefited in its early years by being the recipient of duplicates from the Danish Royal Library in Copenhagen. It has had a national depository plan since 1814, but it was interrupted from 1840 until 1882 when the library became the official bibliographic center and began issuing the national bibliography. Today the university is a decentralized system—the main library, with about 1,900,000 volumes, is near the center of the city, and an additional one million volumes are scattered among more than 100 institute libraries in Oslo and its suburbs. The Norwegian Department (Norske Avdeling) collects and preserves everything printed in Norway as well as books and articles about the country printed abroad. It has several notable literature collections including the Aure (Nynorsk literature) and a drama section (Teaterhistorisk Samling) created in 1957 to collect comprehensively materials, including clippings, playbills, and other ephemera, concerning the Norwegian stage. The Manuscript Section (Håndskriftsamlingen) contains manuscripts, largely from the nineteenth and twentieth centuries, on all aspects of Norwegian cultural life including literary archives of leading Norwegian authors such as Bjørnstjerne Bjørnson,* Ludvig Holberg,* and Henrik Ibsen.* In 1974 the library started publishing a bibliographic series, "Skrifter" (Writings), which includes information about its collections.

The public library in Oslo (Deichmanske bibliotek) dates from 1780, when Carl Deichman donated his library to the city. Although it is today similar in function to public libraries elsewhere, its older collections are still useful because they predate the establishment of a national library in Norway and include many older and rare books.

The second largest library (with ca. 900,000 volumes) is the Bergen University Library. Founded in 1825 as part of Bergens Museum, it became the university's library in 1948. It also has important works of Norwegian literature and several special collections such as those of Halvorsen (older Norwegian literature) and Ameln (Ibsen), as well as literary manuscripts related to authors from the Bergen area.

REFERENCES

Deichmanske bibliotek, *Katalog over Cancelliraad Carl Deichmans bibliotek: skjenket Christiania by 1780,* ed. Gunvor Rasmussen and Leiv Amundsen (Oslo, 1976–1977); Lie, Hallvard, *Norske og danske dikteres originalmanuskrifter* (Oslo, 1948); *Norske aviser 1763–1969. En bibliografi,* ed. Tom Arbo Høeg (Oslo, 1973–1974); *Norvegica: Minneskrift til femti-årsdagen for oprettelse af Universitetsbibliotekets Norske Avdeling* (Oslo, 1933), includes a description of the Norwegian collections; Privatarkiv kommisjonen, *Katalog over privatarkiver* (Oslo, 1976), a mimeographed list of 2,500 private archives; Riksbibliotekstjenesten, *Norske vitenskapelige og faglige biblioteker: en håndbok,* 4th ed. (Oslo, 1981), comprehensive guide with brief descriptions of holdings and a bibliography; Tunold, S., "Handskriftsamligen i Universitetsbiblioteket i Oslo," in *Norsk årbok for bibliotek og forskning* 3 (1954); *Universitetsbiblioteket i Bergen: en veileder* (Bergen, 1978?); *Universitetsbiblioteket i Oslo* (Oslo, 1983), explains the library and its functions and has a bibliography of guides to holdings; an earlier edition *The Royal University Library in Oslo* (Oslo, 1970) is available in English; Wiesener, A. M., "Katalog over Bergens Museums manuskriptsamling," in *Bergens Museums Aarbok* 5 (1913), continued in manuscript form in the library.

V. Sweden

The Royal Library (Kungliga Biblioteket) dates from the sixteenth century and is currently one of the largest in the country (1,600,000 volumes). Until 1977 it also served as the library of Stockholm University and collected the world of scholarship in general, but today it is the national library as well as the largest humanities library in Stockholm. Its collections of Swedish books include the Rålamb, Rosenadler, and Rosenhane collections of books printed before 1700. It has been the bibliographic center of Sweden since 1886, publishing the national bibliography (*Svensk bokförteckning*) and other bibliographic works. Collections of note include medieval manuscripts, important Swedish authors such as Carl Michael Bellman,* August Strindberg,* Selma Lagerlöf,* and others, and distinguished old Norse and Icelandic holdings. The Royal

Library's major bibliographic series, "Kungliga Bibliotekets handlingar," has been published since 1879.

In Sweden there are also unique collections in the university libraries of Lund and Uppsala which have benefited from a deposit law dating from the seventeenth century. Uppsala, the oldest library in Sweden and still, with 2,000,000 volumes and 40,000 manuscripts, one of the largest, has substantial collections of Swedish literature and history as well as Icelandic and other foreign materials. Lund, with about the same number of volumes and 12,000 manuscripts, is the main research library for southern Sweden and includes among its manuscript holdings the papers of the poet Esaias Tegnér.* The library at Gothenburg (Göteborgs universitets bibliotek—until 1961 called Göteborgs stadsbibliotek) dates from the late nineteenth century and with ca. 1,000,000 volumes is the smallest of the three. It has literary manuscripts of some Swedish authors, for example, A. Viktor Rydberg* and Hjalmar Söderberg,* and Danish and Norwegian literature are two areas of special collection emphasis. It also houses Kvinnohistoriska Samlingarna (women's historical archives). Each of these university libraries publishes a bibliographic series that includes information about holdings and special collections: *Acta Bibliothecae regiae Stockholmiensis* (1961–); *Skrifter utgivna från Lunds universitetsbibliotek* (1946–).

REFERENCES

Broome, Bertil, *Handskriftssamlarna och de svenska arkiven 1700–1950* (Acta Bibliothecae regiae Stockholmiensis 29, 1977), includes a bibliography of manuscript catalogs; Davidsson, Åke, *Litteratur om Uppsala universitetsbibliotek och dess samlingar, Bibliografisk förteckning* (Acta Bibliothecae R. Universitatis Upsaliensis 20, 1977), comprehensive bibliography of books and articles concerning all aspects of the library's operations and holdings; Fries, Carl-Thore, and Ulla Lövgren, eds., *Svensk biblioteksmatrikel 1955* (Stockholm, 1956), Gödel, V., *Katalog öfver Kongliga bibliotekets fornisländska och fornnorska handskrifter* (Kongliga bibliotekets handlingar 19–22, 1897–1900); Gödel, V., *Katalog öfver Upsala Universitets Biblioteks fornisländska och fornnorska handskrifter af Vilhelm Gödel* (Skrifter utgifna af Humanistiska Vetenskapssamfundet i Upsala 2.1, 1892); *Göteborgs stadsbibliotek, 1891–1941* (Acta Bibliothecae Universitatis Gothoburgensis 1, 1941), includes a survey of its manuscript holdings by J. V. Johansson; Idman, Christina, *Biblioteks-och informationstjänster i Sverige* (DFI publikationer 2, 1982); *Katalog der datierten Handschriften in lateinischer Schrift vor 1600 in Schweden* (Biblioteca Ekmaniana, a two-volume guide, each in 2 parts, 67: 1–2; 68: 1–2 (1977–1980); Ottervik, Gösta, Sigurd Möhlenbrock, and Ingvar Anderson, *Libraries and Archives in Sweden* (Stockholm, 1954); Ryberg, Anders, ed., *Bibliotek i Stor-Stockholm, Vägledning,* (Stockholm, 1969), Tegnér, Elof K., *Kongliga Bibliotekets samling af svenska brefvexlingar, öfversikt* (Kungliga bibliotekets Handlingar 2, 1880); *Uppsala universitets biblioteks minnesskrift* (Acta Bibliothecae R. Universitatis Upsaliensis 1, 1921), includes descriptions of various collections and manuscript holdings; *Uppsala University Library: Historical Notes* and *Guide to the Exhibits,* 3rd Eng. ed. (Uppsala, 1955).

B. COLLECTIONS IN AMERICAN LIBRARIES

There is no comprehensive survey of Scandinavian literature collections or collecting strengths in American libraries. In a survey completed a dozen years ago scholars ranked collections as "researchworthy." Their rankings are probably still reasonably accurate, but budget cuts and the impact of inflation during the 1970s together with increasing trends toward cooperative agreements may have significantly altered libraries' abilities and inclinations to keep up with current literatures beyond essential and basic purchases. Those libraries that are members of the Research Libraries Group in particular have changed responsibilities and collecting patterns. The top ten mentioned in 1971 were Minnesota, followed in order by Berkeley, Wisconsin, Harvard, the Library of Congress, Cornell, the University of California at Los Angeles (UCLA), Yale, the New York Public Library, and Chicago. But it is not possible to identify any single library as being the strongest in the country in Scandinavian literature or the one to which one would automatically turn for assistance or resources. Viewing holdings on a regional basis, one could conclude that the East Coast, despite some recent declines in support for Scandinavian literature, has the largest quantity. Since many of the university libraries were founded in the early years of the Republic, their collections also tend to be richer in early publications. Harvard, Yale, and Pennsylvania have sizable collections and have continued to add major new works, but Harvard is probably the only one still collecting in considerable depth. Cornell's Fiske Collection is unrivaled for Icelandic studies. The New York Public Library has a very strong collection of essential government publications and related materials as well as a large literature collection. Also in New York is the Swedish Information Service, which maintains a library but more importantly serves as a source of reference assistance for Swedish literature. The Library of Congress with its automatic acquisitions programs has become, for post–1945 Scandinavian literatures, probably the strongest collection in the country. Unfortunately, there has been a recent decision to downgrade cataloging of foreign literatures, and they are therefore not represented adequately in the usual finding tools such as the *National Union Catalog*.

In the South only two libraries stand out—Duke, with a strong program for acquiring contemporary Scandinavian literature, and Texas, which has also begun collecting in the field.

There are several distinguished collections in the Midwest, paralleling the rise of immigrant populations in those states and the presence of large Scandinavian Studies departments. Minnesota has a sound collection with notable strength in long runs of nineteenth-century periodicals rarely held elsewhere and a strong current acquisitions program (particularly Swedish literature). Wisconsin's collection is second in size and has benefited from the acquisition of several outstanding collections (e.g., Thordarson and Mimers Collections) as well as an active current acquisitions program (notably Danish and Norwegian literatures).

Illinois and Chicago, and to a lesser degree, Indiana, also have strong collections. In addition, there are resources at church- and immigrant-related colleges such as Dana (Danish); St. Olaf (Norwegian), Suomi (Finnish), Augustana (Swedish), and Luther (Norwegian).

Libraries on the West Coast started their collecting later but benefited from a period of tremendous growth in the 1960s. Berkeley acquired a number of important materials and quickly established itself as a major resource for Scandinavian literature. Washington has had a strong recent acquisitions program for Scandinavian (especially Danish) literatures. There are also collections at UCLA and the Claremont Colleges.

REFERENCES

Askey, Donald E., Gene G. Gage, and Robert T. Rovinsky, "Nordic Library Resources in the U.S. and Canada: A Preliminary Investigation." *Scandinavian Studies* 47.2 (1975).
                                                                                    Erwin K. Welsch

Lidman, Sara. Swedish novelist and essayist, b. 30 December 1921, Missenträsk.

Lidman grew up in Missenträsk, a village in the northern Swedish province of Västerbotten. She gained recognition with her first novel, *Tjärdalen* (1953; The Turf Pyre), a work that depicts her home region, its people, and its dialect, and also introduces her concern for moral questions and her interest in the confrontation between individuals and social forces.

In 1960, after having written three additional Västerbotten novels, Lidman made a journey to South Africa and Kenya that marked a turning point in her life and work. To the probings into psychological and behavioral aspects of human beings prevalent in her early work, she added the examination of international political and social problems, exemplified by her treatment of the schism between Africa's rich and poor and black and white in the novels *Jag och min son* (1961; My Son and I) and *Med fem diamanter* (1964; With Five Diamonds).

Spurred by indignation over U.S. involvement in Vietnam, Lidman traveled to North Vietnam and, renouncing fiction for reportage, wrote articles for Swedish newspapers, many of which later appeared in book form as *Samtal i Hanoi* (1966; Conversations in Hanoi) and *Fåglarna i Nam Dinh* (1972; The Birds of Nam Dinh) and established Lidman as one of Sweden's foremost politically engaged writers.

Lidman returned to writing fiction with *Din tjänare hör* (1977; Thy Servant Is Listening), first in a series of novels, including *Vredens barn* (1978; Anger's Child), *Nabots sten* (1981; Nabotn's Stone, 1989), *Den underbare mannen* (1983; The Miracle Man), and *Järnkronan* (1985; The Iron Crown), which form the chronicle of Lillvattnet, a rural parish in northern Sweden, from the 1870s until shortly before the inauguration of the railway in 1894. Lidman is presently planning to add more volumes to this northland epic.

An angry, compassionate writer with a strong sense of justice, Lidman also possesses a literary craftsmanship that has brought her widespread recognition as well as several literary awards.

FURTHER WORKS

Job Klockmakares dotter (1954); *Hjortronlandet* (1955); *Aina* (1956); *Regnspiran* (1958; *The Rain Bird*, 1962); *Bära mistel* (1960); *Gruva* (1968); *Vänner och u-vänner* (1969); *Marta, Marta* (1970); *Varje löv är ett öga* (1980).

TRANSLATIONS

Swedish Book Review 2 (1984).

REFERENCES

Bäckström, Lars, "Eyvind Johnson, Per Olof Sundman and Sara Lidman: An Introduction." *Contemporary Literature* 12 (1971); Borland, Harold, "Sara Lidman's Progress: A Critical Survey of Six Novels." *Scandinavian Studies* 39.2 (1967); Borland, Harold, "Sara Lidman, Novelist and Moralist," *Svensk Litteraturtidskrift* 36.1 (1973); Dembo, L. S., "An Interview with Sara Lidman." *Contemporary Literature* 12 (1971); Försås-Scott, Helena, "In Defense of People and Forests: Sara Lidman's Recent Novels." *World Literature Today* 58.1 (1984); Mawby, Janet, "The Inadequacy of Literature: Jan Myrdal and Sara Lidman," in her *Writers and Politics in Modern Scandinavia* (London, 1978); Wormuth, Diana W., "Sara Lidman's Chronicles of Norrland." *Swedish Book Review* 2 (1984).

Barbara Lide

Lie, Jonas. Norwegian novelist and short story writer, b. 6 November 1833, Hokksund, Eiker, near Drammen, d. 5 July 1908, Fleskum, Bærum, near Oslo.

Like Joseph Conrad, Lie had one career well behind him when he published his first novel, *Den Fremsynte (The Visionary*, 1894), in 1870. In the 1860s, while a lawyer in eastern Norway, Lie's speculations in timber values led to his virtual bankruptcy, burdening him with a debt of several hundred thousand Norwegian crowns. As with Conrad, his first career provided Lie with rich materials for his literary production.

Lie's exposure from childhood on to a variety of Norwegian landscapes and regional life may have sparked his ambition to mirror all of Norway in his work. In the process, Lie became the chief architect of the Norwegian novel, ironically enough while living as a self-exile in Paris (1882–1905), with summer sojourns at Berchtesgaden in the Austrian Alps. In this respect he closely resembles his friend and colleague Henrik Ibsen.* Lie's need of aesthetic distance bespeaks a basically contemplative mind whose subtle art of memory tended to merge with the imagination itself. With its aid, he was able to weave his personal experiences into a fabric that evoked a broad picture of nineteenth-century Norway.

Lie's fiction encompasses a considerable range. His first work, an initiation story of novelette length fraught with elements of the supernatural and the subconscious and set amid the fabulous landscape of Norway's arctic region, combines traits of spiritual autobiography with universal, tragic themes. *Lodsen og hans Hustru* (1874; *A Norse Love Story: The Pilot and His Wife*, 1876) is a novel of marriage in the guise of a tale of the sea. This hybrid form appears to better advantage in *Rutland* (1880), a book with a rich comic vein. *Gaa paa!* (1882; Go Ahead) grafts an apprenticeship novel upon the sea tale. *Thomas Ross* (1878) and *Adam Schrader* (1879), the former a not very successful *Künstlerroman*, the latter a novel of conversion, are notable for their greater strictness of form and for a strain of symbolic imagery—maelstrom (vortex), waterfall, rainbow, and trolls—that later is masterfully developed.

Lie's breakthrough came with *Livsslaven* (1883; *One of Life's Slaves*, 1895) and *Familien paa Gilje* (1883; *The Family at Gilje*, 1894). These novels, which mark the beginning of Lie's realistic phase, represent two variants on the tragic mode: the former, a proletarian apprenticeship novel in the spirit of naturalism, is tragedy pure and unrelieved; the latter, an "interior" set in the proximate past, tempers tragic disaster with spiritual renewal. Like *Familien paa Gilje*, Lie's subsequent bourgeois novels, *En Malstrøm* (1884; A Maelstrom), *Kommandørens Døttre* (1886; *The Commodore's Daughters*, 1892), *Et Samliv* (1887; A Marriage), and *Maisa Jons* (1888), focus on marriage and the family, the last-mentioned also on the relationship between the bourgeoisie and the lower classes. All are considerable artistic achievements, in which Lie, like Ibsen, scrutinizes the nature and dynamics of bourgeois society, in particular the abuse of parental and class-related power.

With *Onde Magter* (1890; Evil Powers), a new phase of Lie's creativity begins, marked by the return of the elements of fantasy and the supernatural seemingly repressed in his middle period. In *Onde Magter*, possibly influenced by Ibsen's *Rosmersholm* and August Strindberg's* *The Father*, a ruthless, power-hungry mill owner and town boss mentally tortures to death, half unconsciously, a weaker man, a friend of great spiritual nobility. *Niobe* (1893; trans. 1897), in some ways Lie's most impressive achievement, is a probing psychological novel about self-deception as well as a period novel dealing with such contemporary phenomena as militant feminism, decadence, and spiritualism; but it is classical myth that gives the book significant form and tragic élan. Lie's subsequent works, *Naar Sol gaar ned* (1895; When the Sun Goes Down), *Dyre Rein* (1896), and *Faste Forland* (1899), while presenting tragic situations, express an attitude of reconciliation. In these novels the dialectic of *Den Fremsynte* reemerges—love against alienation, social adjustment versus primordial angst, and affirmation of life despite foreknowledge of doom.

In his late sixties, Lie still had a couple of surprises up his sleeve. In *Naar Jernteppet Falder* (1901; When the Iron Curtain Falls), he reverts to the sea, using a contrapuntal form that enabled him to foreshadow central twentieth-century themes: the opaqueness of nature, the terror of finitude, cyclicalism, the absurdist perspective, a critique of secular utopias, and the existentialist emphasis of the self-motivated act. At the same time the plot, which hinges on a bomb scare aboard a transatlantic steamer and the consequent confrontation with death, captures the apocalyptic atmosphere of the historical moment. Lie's last novel, *Østenfor Sol, vestenfor Maane, og bagom Babylons Taarn* (1905; East of the Sun, West of the Moon, and Beyond the Tower of Babylon), is a renewed look at "evil powers" in a form that anticipates such classics of fictional modernism as Virginia Woolf's *The Waves* (1931) and Tarjei Vesaas'* *Isslottet* (1963; *The Ice Palace*, 1966). Some of the book's interludes in poetic prose show that Lie's mythopoeic imagination, demonstrated so superbly by the grotesque and fantastic tales in *Trold* (2 vols., 1891, 1892; partial trans. *Weird Tales from Northern Seas*, 1893), was as vivid as ever.

Lie's best work is impressionistic in method and style. His principal device of narration and characterization, *erlebte Rede*, or free indirect discourse, produces an effect of intense, living immediacy. Yet with all their surface movement and color, Lie's novels lack neither coherent structure nor symbolic resonance: they combine an impressionistic surface with archetypal imagery and an intuitive depth psychology. In some ways, Lie is akin to Ivan Turgenev and Henry James: he shares the former's blend of lyricism and objectivity, as well as his subtly evocative character portrayal and his scenic structure. As with James, Lie's technique developed simultaneously in two directions: toward consciousness-centered and toward dramatic narration.

Hailed by the younger naturalists of the mid–1880s, Lie was called by Herman Bang* "the grand master of the Nordic novel" (*Dagbladet*, 12 January 1889); one critic compared his importance in this respect to that of Ibsen in the drama (Ronald Fangen, *Dagen og veien* [1934], p. 218). Lie influenced regional writing, the literary treatment of marriage and the family, and the psychological novel of Herman Bang and Knut Hamsun.* Gustaf af Geijerstam and Strindberg were indebted to him. His influence on the strategies of fiction is ubiquitous in the Norwegian novel, which tends toward impressionism and is steeped in *erlebte Rede*. Finally, Thomas Mann used the family novels of Lie and Alexander L. Kielland* as models in planning his early masterwork, *Buddenbrooks*.

FURTHER WORKS

Digte (1866); *Fortællinger og skildringer fra Norge* (1872); *Tremasteren "Fremtiden" eller Liv Nordpaa* (1872; *The Barque Future, or Life in the Far North*, 1879); *Faustina Strozzi* (1875); *Grabows Kat* (1880); *Ole Bull* (1881); *Otte Fortællinger* (1885); *Digte* (1889); *Lystige Koner* (1894); *Lindelin* (1897); *Wulffie & Comp.* (1900); *Ulfvungerne* (1903); *Eventyr* (1909); *Samlede Digterverker*, ed. Paula Bergh, 10 vols. (1920).

FURTHER TRANSLATIONS

Little Grey, the Pony of Nordfjord (1873).

REFERENCES

Bache-Wiig, Harald, ed., *Sinn og samfunn: Fem artikler om Jonas Lies forfatterskap* (Oslo, 1983); Bergström, Carl Olof, *Jonas Lies väg till Gilje* (Örebro, 1949); Bjørnson, Bjørnstjerne, "Modern Norwegian Literature, II." *Forum* 21 (1896); Budd, John, comp., *Eight Scandinavian Novelists: Criticism and Reviews in English* (Westport, Conn., 1981);

Downs, Brian W., "Anglo-Norwegian Literary Relations, 1867–1900." *Modern Language Review* 47.4 (1952); Garborg, Arne, *Jonas Lie*, 3rd ed. (Oslo, 1925); Gustafson, Alrik, "Impressionistic Realism: Jonas Lie," in his *Six Scandinavian Novelists* (Princeton, N.J., 1940); Hauge, Ingard, *Jonas Lies diktning* (Oslo, 1970); Ingerslev, Frederik, *Jonas Lie: Et Personligheds- og Typebillede* (Copenhagen, 1939); Hiorth Lervik, Åse, *Ideal og virkelighet: Ekteskapet som motiv hos Jonas Lie* (Oslo, 1965); Lyngstad, Sverre, *Jonas Lie* (Boston, 1977); Lyngstad, Sverre, "The Vortex and Related Imagery in Jonas Lie's Fiction." *Scandinavian Studies* 51.3 (1979); Midbøe, Hans, *Dikteren og det primitive*, 4 vols. (Oslo, 1964–1966).

Sverre Lyngstad

Lindegren, Erik. Swedish lyric poet, librettist, and translator, b. 5 August 1910, Luleå, d. 30 May 1968, Stockholm.

Lindegren was born into an upper-class family, grew up in northern Lapland, and studied philosophy at the University of Stockholm. He made his literary debut with the rather conventional collection of poems *Posthum ungdom* (1935; Posthumous Youth). Shortly thereafter he came under the influence of Artur Lundkvist* and Finno-Swedish modernism and began work on his masterpiece, *mannen utan väg* (1942; *The Man Without a Way*, 1969). *Sviter* (1947; Suites), his next collection of poems, is more traditional in its evocation of erotic love but is at the same time full of occasionally obscure literary allusions. Lindegren's last collection of poems, *Vinteroffer* (1954; Winter Rites), continues this tendency in its oblique reference to Igor Stravinsky's *Sacre du printemps* and illustrates Lindegren's admiration for T. S. Eliot in its consideration of birth, sterility, and death in graphic mythic images drawn at least in part from *The Golden Bough*. During the late 1940s journalistic responsibilities brought him into contact with theater, ballet, painting, and music. As a result of these contacts, he wrote the scenarios for ballets and adapted two works—Harry Martinson's* *Aniara* (1956, *Aniara*, 1960) and Hj. Bergman's* *Herr von Hancken* (1965; Herr von Hancken)—as libretti for Karl Birger Blomdahl. Lindegren was elected to the Swedish Academy in 1962.

Lindegren's most notable work, *mannen utan väg* has been imitated by many younger Swedish poets but has never been equaled. The forty unrhymed, fourteen-line poems, often referred to as "exploded sonnets," consist of line upon line of anxiety-laden discordant images presented in explosive language and complex syntax. The poems were at first dismissed as mindless free association, but subsequent analysis has demonstrated that great effort was expanded in finding precisely the correct images with which to forge these surrealistic sequences that communicate the essence of the complicated and fragmentary modern world.

Lindegren is now universally regarded as one of the leading exponents of Swedish modernism. Throughout his career modernism meant the concrete expression of psychological reality and, thus, a break with history and externality. Art, of necessity, became a matter of thinking in images. Although he wrote relatively little, his impact on Swedish literature in terms of both theme and technique has been substantial.

FURTHER WORKS

Vinteroffer (1954); *Tangenter* (1974).

REFERENCES

Bäckström, Lars, *Erik Lindegren* (Stockholm, 1979); Ekner, Reidar, "The Artist in the Eye of a Needle." *Scandinavian Studies* 42.1 (1970); Hallind, Kristina, *Tavlor och deviser* (Lund, 1978); Hermelin, Carola, *Vinteroffer och Sisofys* (Uppsala, 1976); Sandgren, Folke, *Erik Lindegren: En bibliografi* (Stockholm, 1971); Steene, Birgitta, "Erik Lindegren: An Assessment." *Books Abroad* 49.1 (1975); Vowles, Richard B., "Sweden's Modern Muse: Exploded Sonnets and Panic Poetry." *Kentucky Foreign Language Quarterly* 2 (1955).

Steven P. Sondrup

Lindgren, Astrid (b. Ericsson). Swedish children's book author, b. 14 November 1907, Vimmerby.

Lindgren, the second of four children, was raised in a close-knit, happy family living on a farm in southern Sweden. The short biography *Samuel August från Sevdstorp och Hanna i Hult* (1975) portrays her parents. At age eighteen Lindgren bore a son whom her parents raised, while Lindgren left for secretarial work in Stockholm. In 1931 she married, adopted her son, and soon had a daughter. Her husband died in 1952.

Lindgren was thirty-seven years old when her first book *Britt-Mari lättar sitt hjärta* was published in 1944. It had won the second prize in a children's book contest organized by the publishing company Raben and Sjögren. It conformed in theme and style with the publisher's desire for a story that would promote "love of the home and of the family." Lindgren's real literary breakthrough came a year later with *Pippi Långstrump* (1945; *Pippi Longstocking*, 1954), which made her famous overnight. In it she breaks away from the moralistic tradition of children's stories and rails at the stifling rules and conventions of the narrow-minded adult world with boisterous humor and irony as her primary tools. Pippi, friendly, rich, and strong, free of everyday concerns and authorities, embodies the child's dream of omnipotence. The range of Lindgren's large production spans from fantasy to realism. Infectious humor and carefully observed everyday life fill the books about the children of Bullerbyn (1946) and Saltkrakan (1964) and other "easy readers" about children of city and country. *Mästerdetektiven Blomkvist* (1946; *Bill Bergson Master Detective*, 1951) is a small-town crime story. Lindgren's robust humor triumphs in *Emil på Lönneberga* (1968; *Emil in the Soup Tureen*, 1970) and its sequels about the pranks of a farmboy at the turn of the century. The Emil books also give insight into the working life of a farm in that period. The melancholy and beautiful *Mio min Mio* (1954; *Mio, My Son*, 1956), about an unloved foster child who finds his kingly father, and the fairy tales in *Sunnanäng* (1959; "Summer Meadow" in

Mio, My Son) represent a move toward the grim, colorful world of the folktale. The adventure *Bröderna Lejonhjärta* (1973; *The Brothers Lionheart*, 1975) attempts to deal with the death of a child. *Ronja Rövardotter* (1981; *Ronja Robber's Daughter*, 1983) is a boisterous and lyrical Romeo and Juliet set among two robber tribes in a troll-filled forest of long ago.

Lindgren's clear, supple style, wit, warmth, and humor have given her an influence and rank seldom bestowed on authors of children's books. In addition to her writing, Lindgren worked nearly thirty years for Raben and Sjögren, Sweden's largest publisher of children's books, and had therefore an opportunity to guide the development of Swedish children's literature in general.

FURTHER WORKS

Kerstin och jag (1945); *Pippi Långstrump går ombord* (1946; *Pippi Goes on Board*, 1957); *Alla vi barn i Bullerbyn* (1947; *Children of Noisy Village*, 1962); *Pippi Långstrump i Söderhavet* (1948; *Pippi in the South Seas*, 1959); *Mera om oss barn i Bullerbyn* (1949; *Christmas in Noisy Village*, 1981); *Nils Karlsson-Pyssling* (1949); *Kajsa Kavat* (1950); *Kati i Amerika* (1950); *Mästerdetektiven Blomkvist lever farligt* (1951; *Bill Bergson Lives Dangerously*, 1954); *Bara roligt i Bullerbyn* (1952); *Kati på Kaptensgatan* (1952; *Kati in Italy*, 1961); *Kalle Blomkvist och Rasmus* (1953; *Bill Bergson and the White Rose Rescue*, 1965); *Kati i Paris* (1954; *Kati in Paris*, 1961); *Lillebror och Karlsson på taket* (1955; *Karlsson-on-the-Roof*, 1971); *Rasmus på luffen* (1956; *Rasmus and the Vagabond*, 1960); *Rasmus, Pontus och Toker* (1957); *Barnen på Bråkmakargatan* (1958; *Children on Troublemaker Street*, 1964); *Madicken* (1960; trans. 1963); *Lotta på Bråkmakargatan* (1961; *Lotta of Troublemaker Street*, 1962); *Karlsson på taket flyger igen* (1962; *Karlsson Flies Again*, 1973); *Vi på Saltkråkan* (1964; *Seacrow Island*, 1968); *Nya hyss av Emil i Lönneberga* (1966; *Emil's Pranks*, 1971); *Karlsson på taket smyger igen* (1968; *The World's Best Karlsson*, 1980); *Än level Emil i Lönneberga* (1970; *Emil and His Clever Pig*, 1973); *Madicken och Junibackens Pims* (1976; *Mardie to the Rescue*, 1981); *Pippi Långstrump har julgransplundring* (1979); *När lilla Ida skulle göra hyss* (1984); *Emils hyss nr 325* (1985; *Emil's Sticky Problem*, 1986).

REFERENCES

Edström, Vivi, *Astrid Lindgren* (Uppsala, 1987); Slayton, Ralph, "The Love Story of Astrid Lindgren." *Scandinavian Review* 63.4 (1975); Strömstedt, Margaret, *Astrid Lindgren* (Kristianstad, 1977).

Margareta Mattsson

Linna, Väinö. Finnish novelist, b. 20 December 1920, Urjala.

The son of a butcher, Linna was born into the working class of young Finland. After working several jobs in the farm, forest, and mill industry, Linna settled in 1938 as a factory worker in Tampere, the industrial center of Finland. His tenure there, which lasted until he became a free-lance writer in 1955, was disrupted only for service in Finland's so-called Continuation War of 1941–1944. Linna has received several literary awards, for example, the state prize in literature in 1959, and again in 1960, as well as the Nordic prize in literature in 1963.

Linna's personal and literary development has been compared to that of several Scandinavian proletarian writers who had emerged out of the working class, who were largely autodidacts, and who had gained distance from and perspectives on their societies, perspectives that came from travels, in Linna's case the war experience.

Linna has gone from the extremely individualistic to the historically collective. His first novel *Päämäärä* (1947; The Goal) is pronouncedly autobiographical in its depiction of a materially and spiritually struggling youngster who aspires to become a writer. The next novel still represents the depth and power of individual passion. *Musta rakkaus* (1948; Black Love) is a tragedy of jealousy and destructive forces. The problem of passion, of ethical and religious conflicts, had occupied Linna's mind until 1952, when a crisis brought to an abrupt stop his work on a novel whose working title was "Messias" (Messiah). This crisis turned Linna's attitude and outlook around; his interest shifted from the individual to the socio-historical dimension of his characters.

Linna's national and international reputation rests on two works, *Tuntematon Sotilas* (1954; *The Unknown Soldier*, 1957) and the trilogy *Täällä Pohjantähden alla* (2 vols., 1959–1962; Here under the North Star). The novel *Tuntematon sotilas* is a dramatic rendition of a Finnish machine-gun platoon's experiences in the Continuation War. Although Linna set out to write a war novel with a message of humanism and pacifism, a goal he certainly attained, nationally the novel has become the definitive account of the Finn at war, and internationally a war novel read as an introduction to Finnish values and characteristics. The novel's all-encompassing representativeness is further added to by the variety of regional dialects the characters' speech reflects. The novel derives additional dimensions from humor and realistic detail. Ultimately, *Tuntematon sotilas* is a manifesto of humanism.

The extensive trilogy *Täällä Pohjantähden alla* brought to the fore another traumatic aspect of Finnish sociopolitical history: the tenant farmer situation of early twentieth-century Finland and the Civil War of 1918. Once again Linna lets a small collective, now the Koskela family of Pentinkulma, represent a whole segment of Finnish society. Linna himself says of the Pentinkulma trilogy that it portrays "a worldview projected onto history." He portrays history from the level of the ordinary Finn; the remote village is an inalienable part of national and international happenings and events. Linna combines unique skills in characterization and dialogue with an understanding of the philosophy of history. The result then is literature that leaves few readers cold; in fact, all of Linna's main works stirred up considerable public debate.

Since 1962 Linna has published a collection of essays but no fiction. Perhaps the therapeutic effect his writings have had on the general public of Finland— a fact reiterated often enough—also exhausted whatever source of creative energy he had drawn from. Linna is one of the most Finnish—if such a property can be measured—of Finland's writers, and truly one of the most relevant and significant ones as well.

FURTHER WORK

Oheisia (1967).

TRANSLATIONS

Scandinavian Review 69.4 (1981).

REFERENCES

Niemi, Juhani, "Väinö Linna. Introduction." *Books from Finland* 14.4 (1980); Storm-bom, Nils-Börje, *Väinö Linna* (Porvoo, 1963); Varpio, Yrjö, "Väinö Linna: A Classic in His Own Time." *Books from Finland* 11.4 (1977); Varpio, Yrjö, *Pentinkulma ja maailma* (Porvoo, 1979).

                                                                                    Börje Vähämäki

Linnankoski, Johannes (pseud. of Johannes Vihtori Peltonen). Finnish novelist, journalist, and playwright, b. 18 October 1869, Askola, d. 10 September 1913, Helsinki.

Linnankoski studied briefly at the Jyväskylä teachers college, but turned early to journalism, becoming editor of the periodical *Uusimaa,* named after the province. He strove to promote the spirit of nationalism. At age thirty he left the paper to devote himself to literature.

Linnankoski's first significant work was the drama *Ikuinen taistelu* (1903; The Eternal Struggle), appearing under his pseudonym. The theme is that of Cain and Abel. The play was in tune with the current neoromantic movement, but Linnankoski became widely known only with his novel *Laulu tulipunaisesta kukasta* (1905; *The Song of the Blood-Red Flower*, 1920). It enjoyed great popularity, was translated into many languages, and was adapted to the stage and film. With its rural setting it is not without autobiographical elements. The hero Olavi is a rustic Don Juan who eventually becomes a responsible member of society. Along with its lyrical and sentimental strains, it possesses certain epic qualities. Its fulsome, old-fashioned romanticism has lost much of its appeal with the passage of time.

Linnankoski's novel *Pakolaiset* (1908; Fugitives) shows greater maturity artistically. The title is allegorical and refers to those who seek to escape the dictates of conscience. The plot derives from a domestic tragedy that Linnankoski had observed when he lived in the province of Savo in 1902. Reminding us a little of Juhani Aho's* *Juha*, it recounts the life of another Juha, an old bachelor who ventures into marriage with a woman much younger than himself. Too late he realizes he has been hoodwinked, for she is already pregnant by another man. She has accepted Juha in order to save appearances. Linnankoski's achievement is his moving portrayal of Juha's spiritual torment and final victory over his urge for vengeance. He comes to accept his fate as retribution for his own misplaced pride.

In 1911 Linnankoski returned to biblical themes with the plays *Simson ja*

Delila and *Jeftan tytär* (Jephtha's Daughter). He was never to equal his success in his two novels. Illness ended his life only two years later.

Linnankoski is a typical if now neglected figure in Finland's neoromantic movement. Critics compared him with the Swedish novelist Selma Lagerlöf* as a portrayer of rural life in a somewhat idyllic style. His evolution toward realism coincided with the general trend of Finnish literature during that period.

FURTHER WORKS

Salon lapsia (1900); *Puhetaito* (1901); *Keksintöjen kirja*, 3 vols. (1907–1909); *Taistelu Heikkilän talosta* (1907); *Kirot* (1908); *Sirpaleita* (1913).

REFERENCES

Meyer, J. J., "Modern Finnish Cain." *Modern Philology* 7 (1909–1910); Söderhjelm, W., *Johannes Linnankoski* (Stockholm, 1918).

Reino Virtanen

Linné, Carl von. Swedish naturalist and writer, b. 23 May 1707, Stenbrohult (Småland), d. 10 January 1778, Hammarby (Uppland).

As a twenty-three-year-old student in Uppsala, Linné evolved the sexual system for the classification of plants that would make him Sweden's most renowned botanist. He then began a series of journeys to the Swedish provinces to study the flora, natural resources, and habits of the people. After being made professor in Uppsala, a position he filled with enormous success for thirty years, he continued his naturalist journeys. Besides his large production of scientific works in Latin, he left the *Iter Lapponicum* or *Lapplands resa* (1732; *A Tour in Lapland*, 1811) and descriptions of Dalarna, Öland and Gotland, Västergötland and Skåne, lectures, and philosophical essays. Linné's story is one of almost continual academic triumph. Certain later works, however, such as *Nemesis Divina* (1878) give vent to a pessimistic stoicism that stands in stark contrast to the enthusiastic writings of his youth.

When treating Linné's works as literature, one must make reservation with respect both to his goals and to the means used to transcribe his thought. In the travel books, his goal was to report, as factually and concisely as possible, on matters of interest to his government and to the scientific world. The free diary form precludes any overall literary plan or lengthy analysis of his findings, although a longer rhapsodic style is used in the lectures and in some portions of the travel books. But his short glimpses of nature and of human behavior, even in their unedited form, provide a fascinating picture both of Sweden in the eighteenth century and of the rationalist method of observation.

Much of the later work ascribed to Linné was not transcribed by the naturalist himself: his assistants took down his dictated observations at rest stops on the journeys, just as his students preserved his university lectures. Despite this—partially even because of it—Linné stands forth, in contrast to the rhetorical and often shallow literary paragons of his time, as personable and fresh as he must have been when he lived, an energetic, devout observer of a wild and unspoiled corner of Europe, a scientist who spared himself no toil to analyze and systematize what he saw, yet at the same time an enraptured nature lover who understood his world too well not to be awed by it.

FURTHER WORKS

Dalaresan (Iter Dalecarlium, 1734; printed 1889); *Carl Linnaei Öländska och Gothländska resa* (1745); *Carl Linnaei Wästgöta-resa* (1747); *Carl Linnaei Skånska resa* (1751); *Egenhändiga anteckningar af C. Linnaeus om sig sjelf*, ed. A. Afzelius (1823); *Carl von Linnés ungdomsskrifter*, ed. E. Ährling, 2 vols., (1888–1889); *Skrifter*, Kung. Svenska Vetenskapsakademien, 5 vols. (1905–1913); *Valda avhandlingar i översättning*, 3 vols. (1921).

REFERENCES

Blunt, W., *The Complete Naturalist* (London, 1971); Broberg, G., *Homo sapiens L.: Studier i Carl von Linnés naturuppfattning och människolära* (Stockholm, 1975); Dickinson, Alice, *Carl Linnaeus: Pioneer of Modern Botany* (London, 1967); Fries, S., ed., *Linnés språk och stil* (Stockholm, 1971); Fries, T., *Linné* (Uppsala, 1956); Hagberg, K., *Carl Linnaeus* (Stockholm, 1957); Larsson, J., *Reason and Experience: The Representation of Natural Order in the Work of Linné* (Berkeley, 1971); Silverstein, A., and V. Silverstein, *Carl Linnaeus* (New York, 1969); Wikman, K., *Lachesis and Nemesis: Four Chapters on the Human Condition in the Writings of Linnaeus* (Stockholm, 1970).

James Massengale

Literary Criticism. *See* Scandinavian Literary Criticism, History of.

Literary Journals. *See* Scandinavian Literary Journals.

Lönnbohm, Armas Eino Leopold. *See* Leino, Eino.

Løveid, Cecilie. Norwegian novelist and dramatist, born 21 August 1951, Mysen, eastern Norway, grew up in Bergen.

Both parents earned their living at sea, and Løveid spent most of her childhood and early youth with her maternal grandparents. From an early age she occupied herself with painting and writing, and her first story was published in an anthology in 1968. Her first novel, *Most* (1972), revealed a writer with a remarkable sensitivity to language, but was presented in a complicated, almost inaccessible form. In this novel, as in all later books, her main theme is the same, universal and common: the young woman fighting for self-realization caught between girlfriends, lovers, parents, and other family members—and in some books, with the added burden of being a single parent. Her handling of this theme rises above the ordinary because of her uncommon sensitivity to the effect of language, which she uses in an expressionistic form, with elements of the absurd. Her language is, paradoxically, filled with the unspoken. Through her poetic prose she tries to evoke feelings, sensations and understanding in order—as one of her protagonists says—"to bring in something new . . . reality itself." The protagonists in *Most* and *Tenk om isen skulle komme* (1974; What If the Ice Should Come) are women who seek freedom. In the first novel the protagonist is caught between several women and one man, in the latter between several men. In both novels the protagonist undergoes a process of growing awareness of the nature of human relationships and human liberation. The same process is described in the next two novels *Alltid skyer over Askøy* (1956; Always Clouds above Askøy) and *Sug* (1979; Pull) in which Løveid portrays the protagonist's, Kjersti's, fight for freedom and self-realization in a language that brings the expressionism of both August Strindberg* and Tarjei Vesaas* to mind. *Måkespisere* (1983; Sea Gull Eaters) contains, besides the title play, which won the coveted Prix Italia for radio plays in 1983, *Vinteren revner* (The Winter Is Torn), in which she has successfully transferred both the poetry of her language and its main themes to the stage.

Løveid is a writer who is rapidly gaining stature as one of Norway's most important writers of the younger generation. Her books are filled with eroticism, poetry, irony, and humor couched in a language of exceptional power.

FURTHER WORKS

Mørkets muligheter (1976); *Fanget villrose* (1977); *Fornuftige dyr* (1986); *En dobbel nytelse* (1988).

REFERENCES

Faldbakken, Knut, "Å være med i seg selv." *Vinduet* 31.1 (1977); Øverland, Janneken, "Frihet til å oppleve de merkligste eventyr." *Vinduet* 35.2 (1981).

Kjetil Flatin

Löwenhjelm, Harriet Augusta Dorotea. Swedish lyric poet and artist, b. 18 February 1887, Hälsingborg, d. 24 May 1918, Romanäs.

Löwenhjelm, originally aspiring to be an artist, studied at the Academy of Art in Stockholm and later at a private studio. She found early, however, that her poetic gifts matched her artistic ones. Her pictures and poems always interrelate and almost always reflect some aspect of her family background. Aristocratic and Christian, she led a protected life and formed a close relationship with her younger brother, Crispin. With him she constructed a fantasy world inhabited by "Klondyke" dolls, whose adventures mimicked events in the real world. An aristocratic attitude, religious themes, and a fanciful vein thus typify Löwenhjelm's work. She died of tuberculosis at age thirty-one.

Löwenhjelm's poetry, the earliest of which consists of limericks and nonsense verse, turns on various themes, including praise of indolence as a way of life. But religious themes and imagery dominate. Her struggles with God are revealed in the way she depicts him—a stern, inaccessible, Buddha-like figure patterned on the Yahweh of the Old Testament, a figure much influenced by Søren Kierkegaard.* Christ—feeble, accessible, but ultimately ineffectual—is set in opposition to God. This opposition forms part of a larger pattern of oppositions, encompassing man and woman, child and adult, earnest and game. For example, Löwenhjelm frequently takes on a male instead of female persona in her poems; she constantly struggles with her childlike yearning for simplicity, which must be set against harsh reality; and she characteristically plays with words and rhymes, even in her most serious poems. In addition to these oppositions is the implicit tension between her poems and drawings, each commenting upon the other.

Löwenhjelm can be considered a relatively minor figure in Swedish letters, though her work did command early attention. She was well thought of by authors of her day, and her poetry influenced writers such as Hjalmar Gullberg.* Her work was all posthumously published, although she and Crispin did handprint a few of her poems in their newspaper, *Midnattsolens land* (Land of the Midnight Sun). She also produced two lithographs, *De Smale och De Brede* (1906–1907; The Narrow and the Broad) and *Konsten att älska* (1913; The Art of Loving), and collected all her poems, together with illustrations, in her *Manuskriptboken* (Manuscript Book).

FURTHER WORKS

Dikter (1919, enl. eds., 1927, 1941); *Brev och dikter* (1952); *Harriet Löwenhjelms bönbok* (1963, in facs.); *Dikter, Bilder och brev* (1973).

TRANSLATIONS

A Selection from Modern Swedish Poetry, ed. C. D. Locock (1929).

REFERENCES

Björkman-Goldschmidt, Elsa, *Harriet Löwenhjelm* (Stockholm, 1947); Stenborg, Elisabeth, *Pierrot och pilgrim* (Stockholm, 1971).

                                                                                                        Robert E. Bjork

Lo-Johansson, Ivar. Swedish novelist, short story writer, essayist and social critic, b. 23 February 1901,Ösmo.

Lo-Johansson grew up among the rural proletariat in the province of Sörmland just south of Stockholm. Although he had little formal schooling, he was a voracious reader. As a young man he worked at various odd jobs in Stockholm and environs before leaving the country to embark on his first major socioliterary project, the attempt to describe life among the working classes in each of the countries of Europe. The enormous plan could understandably not be completed, but did result in several books of reportage that retain their immediacy today.

In the 1930s Lo-Johansson turned to fiction—although he has continued to write essays, newspaper articles, and books of reportage—and to an investigation of conditions in his own social class, the group of impoverished, landless farm workers called *statare*. *Godnatt, jord* (1933; Good Night, Earth), the first of the autobiographical novels by proletarian writers that dominate the literary profile of the 1930s in Sweden, ends with the author's alter ego leaving the land for the city, but it gives a sharply delineated portrait of the people and way of life he abandons. After *Kungsgatan* (1935; King's Street), which concerns the fate of two immigrants from the countryside caught up in the capital city's allure, Lo-Johansson's subject matter is again the rural poor. In keeping with his intent to write about the collective rather than the individual, the short stories in *Statarna* (2 vols., 1936–1937; The Statare) and *Jordproletärer* (1941; Proletarians of the Soil) illustrate the origins and entire history of this oppressed group. In *Bara en mor* (1939; Only a Mother), however, the focus is on an individual *statare* woman doomed to a life of drudgery not only by circumstances of birth but also by a narrow-minded community unwilling to forgive a youthful indiscretion. *Geniet* (1947; The Genius) expands on the theme of wasted human potential in a stultifying, unsympathetic environment, although it initially attracted attention primarily for its frank treatment of adolescent sexuality.

In the 1950s Lo-Johansson explores the development of the conflict within his own psyche between individualism and the collective—the desire to be different from and superior to others versus the longing for solidarity and identification with his roots—through eight autobiographical novels. Each book has its own flavor—*Gårdfarihandlaren* (1953; The Country Peddler), for instance, is notable for its burlesque humor—but they have in common a distancing effect in the narrative voice that creates an ironic tension between the narrator and his former self.

In the 1960s and 1970s the short story is once again Lo-Johansson's chosen genre in seven volumes, each investigating a given human passion: love, greed, martyrdom, careerism, and so forth. Some of these stories are among the finest in the Swedish language. Most recently Lo-Johansson has written memoirs in which the fictional mask is (largely) dropped.

Lo-Johansson's production is characterized by long-range planning, with many-volume series devoted to a specific subject matter, and by carefully thought out theoretical underpinnings. His literary efforts often have a clearly defined social as well as artistic goal; both in fiction and in reportage he is the champion of the underdog, the *statare*, gypsies, the aged and infirm. What is remarkable about his work is that *Tendenz* and artistic merit are rarely in conflict. This fact is due both to his psychological insight and to his consummately secure style. Lo-Johansson is no wooden social realist. His prose is concrete, sensory, understated, often ironic, and displays a wicked sense of humor and total lack of sentimentality. With respect to choice of subject matter he is among the most ambitious and far-ranging of the proletarian writers of the 1930s. With respect to literary quality, he has no superior.

FURTHER WORKS

Vagabondliv i Frankrike (1927); *Kolet i våld* (1928); *Ett lag historier* (1928); *Nederstigen i dödsriket* (1929); *Zigenare* (1929); *Mina städers ansikten* (1930); *Ur klyvnadens tid* (1931); *Jag tvivlar på idrotten* (1931); *Måna är död* (1932); *Statarklassen i Sverige* (1939); *Statarliv* (1941); *Traktorn* (1943); *Stad och land* (1945); *Stridsskrifter* (1946); *Monism* (1948); *Statarna i bild* (1948); *Ungdomsnoveller* (1948); *Vagabondliv* (1949);

Ålderdom (1949); *Romaner och noveller*, 14 vols. (1950–1951); *Analfabeten* (1951); *Ålderdoms-Sverige* (1952); *Okänt Paris* (1954); *Stockholmaren* (1954); *Zigenarväg* (1955); *Journalisten* (1956); *Att skriva en roman* (1957); *Författaren* (1957); *Socialisten* (1958); *Soldaten* (1959); *Proletärförfattaren* (1960); *Lyckan* (1962; *Bodies of Love*, 1971); *Statarnas liv och död* (1963); *Astronomens hus* (1966); *Elektra* (1967); *Passionerna: Älskog* (1968); *Martyrerna* (1968); *Girigbukarna* (1969); *Karriäristerna* (1969); *Vällus-tingarna* (1970); *Lögnhalsarna* (1971); *Vishetslärarna* (1972); *Statarskolan i litteraturen* (1972); *Ordets makt* (1973); *Folket och herrarna*, 2 vols. (1973); *Nunnan i Vadstena* (1973); *Furstarna* (1974); *Lastbara berättelser* (1974); *Dagbok från 20-talet* (1974); *Passionsnoveller*, 2 vols. (1974); *Dagar och dagsverkan* (1975); *Passioner i urval* (1976); *Under de gröna ekarna i Sörmland* (1976); *Den sociala fotobildboken* (1977); *En arbetares liv* (1977); *Pubertet* (1978); *Asfalt* (1979); *Att skriva en roman: en bok om författeri* (1981); *Tröskeln* (1982); *Frihet* (1985); *Till en författare* (1988).

REFERENCES

Edström, Mauritz, *Äran, kärleken, klassen* (Stockholm, 1976); Furuland, Lars, *Statarnas ombudsman i dikten* (Stockholm, 1976); Graves, Peter, and Philip Holmes, "Ivar Lo-Johansson," in *Essays on Swedish Literature from 1880 to the Present Day*, ed. Irene Scobbie (Aberdeen, 1978); Hansen, Hagmund, *Ivar Lo-Johansson: Statarnas diktare* (Stockholm, 1946); Holmgren, Ola, *Kärlek och ära: en studie i Ivar Lo-Johanssons Måna-romaner* (Stockholm, 1978); Oldberg, Ragnar, *Ivar Lo-Johansson: En monografi* (Stockholm, 1957); Oldberg; Ragnar, *Ivar Lo-Johansson: En bildbiografi* (Stockholm, 1964); Paulsson, Jan-Anders, "Ivar Lo-Johansson: Crusader for Social Justice." *American-Scandinavian Review* 59.1 (1971).

                                                                                                    Rochelle Wright

Lucidor (pseud. of Lars Johansson). Swedish baroque poet, b. 18 october 1638, Stockholm, d. 18 August 1674, Stockholm.

The biographical data on Lucidor is both imprecise and incomplete, but the legends surrounding his brief, bohemian existence are many and colorful, and have become an important element in his literary persona. Supposedly, Lucidor was born into a middle-class Swedish family in Stockholm and then orphaned at an early age. He studied in Germany at universities in Greifswald and Leipzig where his raucous, uninhibited behavior led to his expulsion. After sporadic studies he apparently traveled widely throughout Europe and did not permanently return to Stockholm until around 1669, five years before a dramatic death in a barroom brawl. During those five years Lucidor worked as a translator and tutor, and as a professional poet of occasional verse. It is through this verse—wedding and funeral poems, as well as erotic verse and drinking songs—that we know him. And it is the richness of this verse—ranging from the obscenely comical to the eloquently contemplative—that has prompted so much speculation as to the nature of his own life.

Lucidor's poetry is highly reflective of the baroque world in which he lived, not only in its choice of themes but also in the very fact that it existed at all. The seventeenth century witnessed the development of a prosperous bourgeoisie that was increasingly literate and that had increasing amounts of money to spend for the writing of poetry to accompany weddings and funerals and other occasions that dictated praise or celebration. Lucidor and others met this new demand for poetry, basing their work on imported conventions of the late Renaissance. Lucidor, however, was not confined by convention. He used language in daring, inventive ways. Moreover, he was acutely perceptive, both about the physical details of the temporal world and about the details of human nature in all its vanity, weakness, and fear. The brevity of life, the finality of death, and the eternity of hell—these are all major lines in Lucidor's poetry. They are perhaps nowhere more in evidence than in the famous poem "Oundwijklige Dödens öde" (Inevitable Death's Fortune). Paradoxically, it was precisely this sense of life's ephemerality, so typical of Lucidor and of baroque thinking in general, that lent an irresistible urgency and immediacy to his descriptions of life at its most festive moments. In his drinking songs and wedding poems, such as "Gilliare kvaal" (The Suitor's Agony), Lucidor is robust, bawdy, and witty. Defiantly he captures the moment and saves it from the vicissitudes of time. He celebrates life as death looks over his shoulder.

Lucidor was part of a tradition in Swedish poetry (including others such as Lars Wivallius* and Johan Runius) that culminated in the poetry and songs of Carl Michael Bellman.* Lucidor stands second only to Bellman in his use of language and powers of observation. Like Bellman, he wrote poetry that was directed toward a specific, contemporary audience. No known attempts were made to preserve his work during his short lifetime, and it was not before 1685 that it was published. In spite of this—and perhaps because of it—his poetry has retained a vitality and vividness that belie its age and make its closeness to life and death as contemporary as our own.

FURTHER WORKS

Samlade dikter, ed. F. Sandwall (1930).

REFERENCES

Hansson, Stina, *Bröllopslägrets skald och bårens. En Studie i Lucidors tillfällesdiktning* (Göteborg, 1975); Karlfeldt, Erik Axel, *Skalden Lucidor* (Stockholm, 1914); Linck, Josef, *Om Lars Johansson* (Stockholm, 1876); Olin, Lars, *Om Lars Johansson: Lucidor, hans levnad och andliga diktning* (Trelleborg, 1974).

Deborah Regula

Lundkvist, Artur. Swedish poet, novelist, and essayist, b. 3 March 1906, Hagstad.

Lundkvist was born into relatively humble surroundings and received only a modest formal education. He has, though, read widely—in Swedish as well as many other languages—and has traveled throughout the world. His earliest volumes of poetry celebrate life, energy, and power in robust imagery and vigorous free verse. By the mid–1930s, he came under the influence of the surrealists, although he never became a doctrinaire surrealist himself. He learned from their example, though, how mankind might liberate itself from its needless fears and anxieties. During World War II and the ensuing years of political tension, his sympathy for human suffering became more apparent in everything he wrote. Lundkvist has always carefully maintained his personal and aesthetic independence and in so doing has surprised many who reasoned that his background would necessarily assure a commitment to social realism and a loyalty to organized labor movements. Lundkvist was elected to the Swedish Academy in 1968.

Since the early 1960s, Lundkvist has made increasingly more extensive and effective use of prose. His prose poems are particularly notable in this regard. His mastery of the genre can be observed in the way the energizing power of antithetical relationships is fully exploited. Longer, more integrated narratives that approach the novel in scope have in recent years revealed his fascination with historical figures who break out of the social roles into which they were born to go on extended journeys that broaden their personal horizons. Lundkvist, an inveterate traveler himself, has also made especially effective use of the travel narrative. He has described his sojourns abroad not only to share impressions of exotic lands but also to suggest the range of human possibility.

Lundkvist's importance to Swedish literature is not to be assessed in terms of his intellectual depth or formal innovations but rather as a function of his aesthetic breadth and profoundly human concerns. His poetry and poetics are grounded in the world of daily experience heightened by the power of imagination and exist to expand and enhance man's fundamental commitment to humanity.

FURTHER WORKS

Glöd, (1928); *Naket liv* (1929); *Jordisk prosa* (1930); *Svart stad* (1930); *Atlantvind* (1932); *Vit man* (1932); *Negerkust* (1933); *Floderna flyter mot havet* (1934); *Himmelsfärd* (1935); *Drakblod* (1936); *Nattens broar* (1936); *Sirensång* (1937); *Eldtema* (1939); *Ikarus flykt* (1939); *Vandrarens träd* (1941); *Diktare och avslöjare i Amerikas nya litteratur* (1942); *Korsväg* (1942); *Dikter mellan djur och Gud* (1944); *Skinn över sten* (1947); *Fotspår i vattnet* (1949); *Negerland* (1949); *Indiabrand* (1950); *Vistelse på jorden* (1950); *Malinga* (1952); *Vallmor från Taschkent* (1952); *Spegel för dag och natt* (1953); *Darunga* (1954); *Liv som gräs* (1954); *Den förvandlade draken* (1955); *Vindrosor, moteld* (1955); *Vindingelvals* (1956); *Berget och svalorna* (1957); *Vulkanisk kontinent* (1957); *Ur en befolkad ensamhet* (1958); *Komedi i Hägerskog* (1959); *Utsikter över utländsk prosa* (1959); *Det talande trädet* (1960); *Orians upplevelser* (1960); *Agadir* (1961; trans., 1979); *Berättelser för vilsekomna* (1961); *Ögonblick och vågor* (1962); *Sida vid sida* (1962); *Drömmar i ovädrens tid* (1963); *Från utsiktstornet* (1963); *Hägringar i handen* (1964); *Texter i snön* (1964); *Sällskap för natten* (1965); *Så lever Kuba* (1965); *Självporträtt av en drömmare med öppna ögon* (1966); *Mörkskogen* (1967); *Brottställen* (1968); *Snapphanens liv och död* (1968); *Historier mellan åsarna* (1969); *Utflykter med utländska författare* (1969); *Besvärjelser till tröst* (1969); *Långt borta, mycket nära* (1970); *Himlens vilja* (1970); *Antipodien* (1971); *Tvivla, korsfarare!* (1972); *Läsefrukter* (1973); *Lustgårdens demoni* (1973); *Livsälskare, svartmålare* (1974); *Fantasins slott och vardagens stenar* (1974); *Världens härlighet* (1975); *Krigarens dikt* (1976); *Flykten och överlevandet* (1977); *Slavar för Särkland* (1978); *Sett i det strömmande vattnet* (1978); *Utvandring till paradiset* (1979); *Skrivet mot kvällen* (1980); *Babylon gudarnas sköka* (1981); *Sinnebilder* (1982); *Färdas i drömmen och föreställningen* (1984); *Sången om kvinnan*, ed. Maria Wine (1987).

FURTHER TRANSLATIONS

Scandinavian Review 68.4 (1980); *The Talking Tree* (1988).

REFERENCES

Espmark, Kjell, *Livsdyrkaren Artur Lundkvist: Studier i hans lyrik till och med Vit Man* (Stockholm, 1964); Miłosz, Czesław, "Reflections on Artur Lundkvist's *Agadir*." *World Literature Today* 54.3 (1980); Nordberg, Carl Eric, *Det skapande ögat* (Stockholm, 1981); Sjöberg, Leif, "An Interview with Artur Lundkvist." *Books Abroad* 50.2 (1967); Sondrup, Steven P., "Artur Lundkvist and Knowledge for Man's Sake." *World Literature Today* 55.2 (1981); Sondrup, Steven P., "Terms of Divergence: The Vocabularies of Pär Lagerkvist's *Ångest* and Artur Lundkvist's *Glöd*." *Scandinavian Studies* 58.1 (1986); Vowles, Richard B., "From Pan to Panic: The Poetry of Artur Lundkvist." *New Mexico Quarterly* 22 (1952); Vowles, Richard B., "Sweden's Modern Muse. Exploded Sonnets and Panic Poetry." *Kentucky Foreign Language Quarterly* 2 (1955).

Steven P. Sondrup

M

Magnússon, Guðmundur (pseud. Jón Trausti). Icelandic novelist and poet, b. 12 (or 22) February 1873, Rif, d. 18 November 1918, Reykjavík.

Magnússon was born into abject circumstances. Left fatherless at age five, he was forced to fend for himself. He had no formal education. In order to gain access to books, he undertook at age twenty to learn printing, a trade that he plied until his death. His apprenticeship took him to Reykjavík and to Copenhagen, where he also learned something of stagecraft. Back in Reykjavík, he published two volumes of poetry and a historical play, *Teitur* (1903), which won him a government travel grant. Negative reviews of these early works prompted Magnússon to adopt a pseudonym, Jón Trausti (Stalwart John).

Just as this pseudonym suggests the rugged individualism of his protagonists, beginning with the eponymic heroine of his first novel, *Halla* (1906), Magnússon's youthful experience of the harsh, famine-ridden northern Icelandic landscape and its struggling inhabitants inspired the settings of his best fiction. The cycle formed by *Halla* and *Heiðarbýlið* (4 vols., 1908–1911; The Heath Cot) is an Icelandic classic. Somewhat ambling at the outset, it is nevertheless rich in memorable characters. Halla, a peasant girl seduced by a married parson, weds an older cotter and moves to a remote cottage on the moor. Through the severe, lonely life she leads, in which she loses her children and husband, Halla assumes heroic proportions.

Magnússon favored representatives of the old ways in the midst of prevailing social change—the honest successor of the corrupt Danish trade monopoly against which new cooperatives fight in *Leysing* (1907; Spring Floods), the pastor of the old village church threatened by a new free congregation in *Borgir* (1909; Fortresses). Beginning in 1912 Magnússon turned increasingly from a realistic orientation to romantic fiction based on historical figures from the fourteenth to the eighteenth century.

Magnússon's strength lies in characterization and scope, not in style. His carefully crafted short stories are among his finest work.

FURTHER WORKS

Heima og erlendis (1899); *Íslandsvísur* (1903); *Ferðaminningar frá Þýzkalandi, Sviss, og Englandi* (1905); *Smásögur*, 2 vols. (1909–1912); *Sögur frá Skaftáreldi*, 2 vols. (1912– 1913); *Dóttir Faraós* (1914); *Góðir stofnar*, 4 vols. (1914–1915); *Tvær gamlar sögur* (1916); *Bessi gamli* (1918); *Samtíningur* (1920); *Kvæðabok* (1922); *Ferðasögur* (1930); *Ritsafn*, ed. Aðalsteinn Sigmundsson, introd. Stefán Einarsson, 8 vols. (1939–1946).

FURTHER TRANSLATIONS

American-Scandinavian Review 20.10/11 (1932); *Icelandic Poems and Stories*, ed. Richard Beck (1943); *Seven Icelandic Short Stories*, ed. Ásgeir Pétursson and Steingrímur J.Þorsteinsson (1960).

REFERENCES

Einarsson, Stefán, *History of Icelandic Prose Writers 1800–1940* (Ithaca, 1948).

George S. Tate

Manner, Eeva-Liisa. Finnish poet, prose writer, and playwright, b. 5 December 1921, Helsinki.

After finishing junior high school, Manner worked for a while for an insurance company, then for a publisher, settling eventually for the career of an independent author and translator (i.e., Herman Hesse, Franz Kafka, William Shakespeare). Shy and retiring, but no recluse, Manner, unmarried, has led an uneventful life in Tampere, traveling, however, at times, especially in Andalusia, a region appearing in her works. Although on a general human and poetic level, her works also have direct references to contemporary events, as, for example, to Francisco Franco's Spain in *Varokaa, voittajat* (1972; Victors, Beware) or the events of 1968 in Czechoslovakia, in *Jos suru savuaisi* (1968; If Smoke Would Rise out of Sorrow), ''mainly dedicated,'' says the author, ''to my friend and colleague Václav Havel in Prague.''

Manner's first works did not receive much notice, but when Finnish poetry was radically renewed by the modernists of the 1950s, she became, in the eyes of the public, one of their leading figures, on account of the collection of poems *Tämä matka* (1956; This Journey), which, it is said, made modernism acceptable to large audiences (modified by the author later on, with fifth edition, 1964). Manner contrasts often barren rationalism with the wisdom of the East, or, as she says, the magic order of childhood with the logical disorder of the adult world. She names the philosophers she is criticizing, Descartes, Spinoza, Wittgenstein, and the Devil, who, as she says, poured small cogwheels of logic into the ear of the world and said, ''now the hearing is good'' (*Fahrenheit 121*; 1968). However, Manner's poems are not the expression of an anarchic individualism; on the contrary, in an essay she writes that modern forms of expression taught her to discard self-centered lyrical feeling. ''Kambri'' (Cambrian), a cycle of poems subtitled ''Laulu merestä ja eläimistä'' (A Song About Animals and the Sea), in *Tämä matka*, does not voice any feelings, but, spanning geological ages, meditates on the fundamentally evil character of man, the sly animal with a heavy brain, who can stretch a string, not for music but for killing, and sharpen a stone to an arrowhead. Manner's poems, often pessimistic, are at times relieved by a humor both metaphysical and whimsical. Falling or dropping expresses an ontological change; emptiness, it is said, will drop whoever has the will of a poet into poetry. Whoever, the text goes on, sacrifices his most precious, his dream, will find himself in the midst of a wider, empty reality, without however dropping anymore, for, then, gravity will be dead, having died at 3:00 A.M. (*Fahrenheit 121*).

To pessimism, Manner opposes a Taoist type of philosophy and a communion with the stars, not mysterious although otherwordly. The lines of poetry in a book, for example, have a fine dust, shaken from the constellation of Lyra (*Fahrenheit 121*), the pulley of a well is fixed to the constellation of Cygnus (*Paetkaa, purret, kevein purjein*, 1971; Flee, Ships, with Light Sails), and, at the moment of death, one's head will be in the mirror world of the Wagoner, the constellation of Auriga (*Niin vaihtuivat vuoden ajat*, 1964; So the Seasons Changed). The more serene side of Manner's poetry is also expressed by references to music, often by Bach, or to Andalusia, the misery of that land being not hidden, but serving to emphasize the human warmth of its inhabitants and the cruelty of their oppressors; *Varokaa, voittajat*, a novel, mentions them directly at places. A few of Manner's works are directly humorous, as *Kamala kissa* (1976; A Horrible Cat) and *Kauhukakara ja Superkissa* (1982; Little Terror and Supercat). Manner has also written a few plays, unfrequently performed although appreciated, as, for example, the lyrical and mythic *Eros ja Psykhe* (1959; Eros and Psyche).

Manner is one of the few Finnish poets of her generation to have carried on her creative work without interruption to the present day. Different schools of poetry have appeared in the sixties and later, but the wide range of her vision, her deep and comprehensive understanding of the world, her human warmth, and her sympathy for small everyday matters, as well as her humor, make her one of the greatest poets, living or dead, in her country.

FURTHER WORKS

Mustaa ja punaista (1944); *Kuin tuuli ja pilvi* (1949); *Tyttö taivaan laiturilla* (1951); *Kävelymusiikkia* (1957); *Orfiset laulut* (1960); *Oliko murhaaja enkeli?* (pseud. Anna September, 1963); *Uuden vuoden yö* (1965); *Toukokuun lumi* (1966); *Kirjoitettu kivi* (1966); *Poltettu oranssi* (1968); *Varjoon jäänyt unien lähde* (1969); *Kuolleet vedet* (1977); *Viimeinen kesä* (1977); *Runoja 1956–1977* (1980); *Kamala kissa ja Katinperän lorut* (1985), *Santakujan Othello* (1987).

TRANSLATIONS

Modern Nordic Plays: Finland, ed. Erik J. Friis (1973); *The Penguin Book of Woman Poets*, ed. Carol Cosman, Joan Keefe, and Kathleen Weaver (1978); *Salt of Pleasure*, ed. Aili Jarvenpa (1983); *Woman Poets of the World*, ed. Joanne Bankier and Deirdre Lashgari (1983).

REFERENCES

Ahokas, Jaakko A., "Eeva-Liisa Manner: Dropping from Reality into Life." *Books Abroad* 47.1 (1973); Anhava, Tuomas, "Runon uudistumisesta," in *Suomen Sana*, vol. 1. (Porvoo, 1963); Hökkä, Tuula, *Maagisen ja loogisen ristiriidan teema Eeva-Liisa Mannerin runoudessa* (Oulu, 1975); Kinnunen, Aarne, "Eeva-Liisa Manner. Poems from *Kuolleet vedet*." *Books from Finland* 12.4 (1978); Sala, Kaarina, "Eeva-Liisa Manner. A Literary Portrait," in *Snow in May: An Anthology of Finnish Writing 1945–1972*, ed. Richard Dauenhauer and Philip Binham (Cranbury, N.J., 1978); Tarasti, Eero, "Strukturalistinen analyysi Eeva-Liisa Mannerin teoksesta 'Sanko kumahtaa syvyyteen' " in *Äidinkielen Opettajien Liiton vuosikirja* (1976).

Jaakko Ahokas

Manninen, Otto. Finnish poet and translator, b. 13 August 1872, Kangasniemi, d. 6 April 1950, Helsinki.

Manninen, who came from a farming family, moved to Helsinki to study at the university, received a master of arts degree, and worked until retirement as a lecturer of Finnish at the university. He became a professor *honoris causa* and was awarded an honorary doctorate by the theological and philosophical faculties.

Along with Eino Leino* and V. A. Koskenniemi,* Manninen was the leading lyric poet in Finnish-language literature at the beginning of the century. In terms of literary history, he belongs to the symbolist movement, although his poetic expression was strongly influenced by Finnish folk poetry, particularly *Kalevala*.* He published poetry over a long period of time but with intervals of some years between individual collections. The first volume of *Säkeitä* (Stanzas) appeared in 1905. It was followed by *Säkeitä II* (1910), *Virrantyven* (1925; Pools of a Stream), and *Matkamies* (1938; A Traveler). *Muistojen tie* (1951; A Road of Memories) was published posthumously.

As a lyricist Manninen is intellectual, often ironic, and concise. For a long time his poetry was considered abstruse. His language demands great concentration from the reader as well as an ability to read between the lines. Manninen's verse is not melodious. He views language as raw material and is fascinated by its potentialities. As a result, his poems are often syntactically complex, yet they possess, concurrently, a peculiarly timeless appeal. Manninen's attitude toward life is that of an onlooker who recognizes wretchedness and flaws, yet remains captivated by the primordial human emotions. As a translator Manninen is among the foremost in Finland. Both in terms of quantity and quality his translations remain unequaled. He translated primarily world classics such as the Homeric epics, Sophocles, Molière, Goethe, Heinrich Heine, Henrik Ibsen,* Johan Ludvig Runeberg,* and Sándor Petöfi. As a poet Manninen was not highly acclaimed when his collections first appeared, but after World War II his position has steadily solidified, and now he belongs unquestionably among the most respected classical writers of Finnish literature. In particular the modernists of the 1950s, who altered the concept of poetry and poetic expression in Finland and reordered the Finnish hierarchy of poets, stressed the significance of Manninen, while at the same time Koskenniemi's stature, for instance, was in decline.

FURTHER WORK

Runoja (1950).

REFERENCES

Fromm, Hans, *Otto Manninen. Ein finnischer Dichter* (Baden-Baden, 1952); Hellaakoski, Aaro, "Nainen ja vesi," in his *Kuuntelua* (Porvoo, 1950); Hollo, J. A., *Kohtaamiani* (Porvoo, 1953); Kupiainen, Unto, *Suomalainen lyriikka Juhani Siljosta Kaarlo Sarkiaan* (Porvoo, 1948); Kuusi, Matti, "Otto Manninen," in *Aleksis Kivestä Martti Merenmaahan* (Helsinki, 1954); Oinonen, Yrjö, "Otto Mannisen runous," in Otto Manninen, *Runot* (Porvoo, 1961); Tarkiainen, V., *O. Manninen runoilijana* (Porvoo, 1933); Viljanen, Lauri, "Kangasniemen viulu," in his *Ajan ulottuvuudet* (Porvoo, 1974); Sarajas, Annamari, *Elämän meri, tutkielmia uusromantiikan kirjallisista aatteista* (Helsinki, 1961).

Pertti Lassila

Martinson, Harry. Swedish poet, novelist, dramatist, and essayist, b. 6 May 1904, Jämshög, province of Blekinge, d. 11 February 1978, Gnesta.

Martinson's father died in 1910, and his mother departed for California the following year, leaving her children to public welfare. After some years as an ambulatory orphan, Martinson at the age of fourteen ran away from his guardians and later went to sea. Between 1920 and 1927 his travels took him to the major ports in Europe, India, and the Americas. Having acquired tuberculosis at sea, he was cured in Sweden and began vigorous literary activities. His debut was strongly influenced by Rudyard Kipling, Gustaf Fröding,* and Dan Andersson.* In 1929 Martinson married Moa Swartz (the proletarian writer, known later as Moa Martinson; *See* Martinson, Helga Maria); their marriage lasted eleven years, until 1941. His next books of poetry, *Nomad* (1931) and *Natur* (1934; Nature) established him as a poet in his own right, although he was heavily influenced by Rudyard Kipling, Walt Whitman, Carl Sandburg, Edgar Lee Masters, and their Swedish follower, Artur Lundkvist.* In 1939 Martinson volunteered his service on the Finnish side of the war between Finland and the Soviet Union. In 1942 he married Ingrid Lindcrantz; he had two daughters by her. In 1938 and 1962 he received the coveted prize of the Nine, in 1945, the literary prize of *Svenska Dagbladet*, and in 1947, the Fröding prize. Martinson became the first autodidact and worker to be elected to the Swedish Academy in 1949. He received an honorary doctorate from the University of Göteborg in 1954.

Martinson's "travelogues," *Resor utan mål* (1932; Travels without a Destination) and *Kap Farväl* (1933; *Cape Farewell*, 1934), mixing poetry and philosophy with exotic reportage, gave him great popular acclaim. He achieved even greater success through his thinly veiled autobiography, *Nässlorna blomma* (1935; *Flowering Nettle*, 1936), in which he described his life as an orphan. *Vägen ut* (1936; The Way Out) described his adolescence.

The "novel" *Vägen till Klockrike* (1948; *The Road*, 1955), about a tramp,

Bolle, and his philosophical vagrant companions, is neither an autobiography nor a novel proper. With it Martinson had created a genre of his own, in which his philosophical and poetic bents were allowed to play freely. A striking feature is the large number of new words Martinson himself coined. Remarkable as these books are, it is assumed in this context that Martinson will be remembered chiefly for two achievements: his nature poetry, and above all, his space poem, *Aniara* (1956; *Aniara: A Review of Man in Time and Space*, 1963), for which he received a (shared) Nobel Prize in 1974.

Of his many volumes of poetry, only one selection, *Wild Bouquet* (1985), is available in English. In an age of chromium, steel and speed, Martinson chose to write about butterflies, June bugs, harvest spiders, late-born swarms of flying beings, cuckoos, herons, swans, thrushes, roosters, and even hens. He wrote of the beach tussock, the dwarf juniper, the wild crabapple, the maple; peonies, cabbages, an earthworm, the brook and the leaf fall; the cutting of firewood in autumn, and a crumbling cottage as well. Robert Bly, who has translated Martinson, has written appreciatively on his poetry, as has David Ignatow, who in 1986 wrote that Martinson "writes with profound empathy, not simply identifying with the creatures of the woods, forests and waters, but with the very processes and thinking by which we too come to identify each as the creature it is, as it sees itself or as we are persuaded to believe by the extraordinary sympathy and insight of the poet."

"In the long history of American nature poetry, with Emily Dickinson as its most brilliant exponent, there is nothing quite so open and penetrating in expressing our identity with oneness, with the living processes of being as we find in *Wild Bouquet*," Ignatow states, and further mentions Walt Whitman and poets as remarkable as Robert Bly, William Stafford, Gary Snyder, Galway Kinnell, and others.

Martinson "allows himself time, and in return he *demands* time—his language meditates, broods on a marvellous secret, how long? a minute, an hour? . . . then, suddenly, the image, the metaphor, comes loose," writes Staffan Söderblom. Summer dominates Martinson's nature poems, and savage beasts or predators appear only infrequently; he looks for a measure of harmony until he finds it. And that is the good vision he wants to promulgate. But the other seasons are also represented, including winter.

Aniara (The Ship of Sorrow) recounts a tragedy brought about after "humans make evolution itself into a god, and do not allow time for the spirit to keep pace or even advance," as the poet wrote in program notes; Martinson has himself related how on a clear night in August 1953 he managed to sight the Andromeda nebula with his telescope. This experience may have given rise to *Aniara*. In a two-week period in October 1953, he wrote poems 1–29 of *Aniara* and completed the full 103 in 1956, when the book appeared, somewhat preceding the first sputnik.

The major portion of the poem is heavily rhymed, sometimes with triple- and quadruple-rhyme words, and written in an abundance of verse forms, which makes the translation from the Swedish a challenge. Although Martinson's language by and large is crystal clear, it is, in places, deliberately so ambiguous that it becomes opaque. The poet has, furthermore, ingeniously borrowed from modern scientific vocabulary with suggestive effect. But in many startling words, often of his own coinage, he has also created uncertainty in terms of meaning, and difficulties in rhythms.

Martinson's *Aniara* is set in a technologically incredibly advanced futuristic phase of the space age, when flights between the planets have become possible, indeed necessary, because the Earth (Dorisvale) has become uninhabitable. While the first phase of the space trip is uneventful: "A purely routine start / . . . Who could imagine that this very flight / was doomed to be a space flight, like to none / which was to sever us from Sun and Earth, from Mars and Venus and from Dorisvale." (Poem 2) "A swerve to keep clear of the Hondo asteroid / (herewith declared discovered) took us off course." With that swerve the fate of *Aniara* and its passengers is sealed. They now literally traverse "eternity," and their vehicle also serves as their sarcophagus. Realization of the enormity of their predicament leads to panic among the 8,000 space emigrants. On board the goldonder, fortunately, there is a clairvoyant technical wonder, Mima, who also possesses a soul and a conscience. Through her a measure of hope is restored.

A great consoler of the emigrants, Mima gradually acquires the status of a goddess. And a special cult is devoted entirely to her. But Mima loses her strength to live and serve and refuses to go on receiving the horrid images of Earth's destruction. After years of functioning beautifully and selflessly for these emigrants in their most precarious existential circumstances, Mima breaks down and dies, next to the last catastrophe in the world of *Aniara*.

Women dominate in *Aniara*. Apart from Mima and the female pilot, Isagel, there is also a remarkable set of seductive, erotic performers. But for variety the poet also employs highly individualized "voices," presenting the life stories of two noble women: the saintly Nobia, saving lives among the refugees, and the blind poetess, who manages to keep her faith by seeing an inner light, while those with full sight see nothing.

The concluding cantos stand apart from the rest of the work, since the poet speaks in his own voice: "I had hoped to make them an Edenic place / but once we left the one we had destroyed / our only hope was the night of empty space / where no god heard us in the endless void." (Poem 102) While Adam and Eve were expelled from Paradise, they had the prospect of man being saved by divine grace, but in *Aniara* that situation is not sustained, because "the god whom we had hoped for to the end / sat wounded and profaned in Doric glens" (102). The blame for the destruction of the Earth rests with man. In his greedy search for power, man finally distanced himself from God—losing the Paradise that had been destined to be his inheritance. Obviously cold scientific laws have replaced the pious beliefs of Dante's and Milton's religious worlds. The satanic forces are now victorious both in the world of humans and in infinite cosmos.

Martinson's incomparable vision of "the end of time"—to use the messianic words—is intricate in some respects and simple in others. Like a serious science fiction drama it moves, provokes, and enlightens, and it can be read for its "entertainment value" alone. In renewed readings its deeper significance will inevitably be felt, without the slightest lessening of the thrilling effect of the first or second reading. Is there a God? Is there a purpose to life? Is it reasonable to expect eternal life? Will the machine take over where man fails—in terms of efficiency and morals? Do we need more dreams to neutralize the combination of technology and greed? These are only some of the questions the poet touches upon in *Aniara*. If there is a lesson to be learned from it, it is a reminder of our responsibility and our obligation to cherish and defend all kinds of freedom and imagination. A veteran American poet, Stanley Kunitz, has said about *Aniara*: "it belongs to world literature." One must generally agree that had *Aniara* been written in English, it would undoubtedly have achieved the international recognition it deserves.

FURTHER WORKS

Spökskepp (1929); *Det enkla och det svåra* (1930); *Svärmare och harkrank* (1937); *Midsommardalen* (1938); *Verklighet till döds* (1940); *Den förlorade jaguaren* (1941); *Passad* (1945); *Cikada* (1953); *Gräsen i Thule* (1958); *Vagnen* (1960); *Utsikt från en grästuva* (1963); *Tre knivar från Wei* (1964); *Dikter om ljus och mörker* (1971); *Tuvor* (1973); *Längs ekots stigar* (1978); *Doriderna* (1980).

FURTHER TRANSLATIONS

Friends, You Drank Some Darkness: Three Swedish Poets, ed. Robert Bly (1975).

REFERENCES

Espmark, Kjell, *Harry Martinson erövrar sitt språk* (Stockholm, 1970); Hall, Tord, *Naturvetenskap och poesi* (Stockholm, 1981); Holm, Ingvar, *Harry Martinson. Myter, målningar, motiv* (Stockholm, 1960); Johannesson, Eric O., "*Aniara*: Poetry and the Poet in the Modern World." *Scandinavian Studies* 32.4 (1960); Sjöberg, Leif, "Harry Martinson." *American-Scandinavian Review* 60.4 (1972); Sjöberg, Leif, "Harry Martinson: From Vagabond to Space Explorer." *Books Abroad* 48.3 (1974); Steene, Birgitta, "The Role of the Mima: A Note on Martinson's *Aniara*," in *Scandinavian Studies. Essays Presented to Dr. Henry G. Leach,* ed. Carl F. Bayerschmidt and Erik J. Friis (Seattle, 1965); Tideström, Gunnar, "Harry Martinson's 'Aniara.' " *Scandinavica* 13.1 (1974); Tideström, Gunnar, *Ombord på Aniara* (Stockholm, 1975); Wrede, Johan, *Sången om Aniara* (Stockholm, 1965).

Leif Sjöberg

Martinson, Helga Maria (Moa), b. Swartz. Swedish novelist, short story writer, and poet, b. 2 November 1890, Norrköping, d. 5 August 1964, Södertälje.

Like her mother and the heroines of her fiction, Martinson grew up in poverty characterized by unreliable husbands, underpaid work, if any, raising children in constant struggle for survival. She was a political writer before she published her first novel, *Kvinnor och äppelträd* (1933; *Women and Appletrees*, 1985).

Her novels are set in city orr or country, each environment with its special form of misery. The city novels are best represented by *Mor gifter sig* (1936;

My Mother Gets Married, 1988) and *Kyrkbröllop* (1938; Church Wedding) about life in squalid rooms where the young teenager Mia lives with her thrifty and hardworking mother and her sloppy stepfather, often drunk and absent but basically kind. Mia learns early that true human value and life qualities exist not behind the facade that advertises them but in the essence of people like her mother and aunt, who bring a sense of comfort and even beauty to existence in spite of the dire realities.

In *Sallys söner* (1934; Sally's Sons) the country offers shreds of material comfort, but in *Hemligheten* (1959; The Secret) it contrasts sharply with the poverty of the characters. Still in the midst of poverty the women manage to save scraps of luxury, such as an embroidered towel, to maintain a sense of self-worth often defiled by men and ultimately the economic system. Her heroines stand strong and independent in their pursuit of what is morally right regardless of prejudices and neighborly pettiness.

Critical acclaim for Martinson's work is growing. She is one of the finest feminist writers and the only woman among the major "proletarian" writers. Her women show more strength through cooperation and moral support, especially between mother and daughter, than female characters in the bourgeois novel. Throughout her work she demonstrates the necessity of female bonding to defeat the ills created by a patriarchal and capitalist society.

Martinson's writing can occasionally seem unpolished, but she always conveys a deep conviction of the validity of her message as well as a sense of humor that makes her work eminently enjoyable and meaningful.

FURTHER WORKS

Rågvakt (1935); *Drottning Grågyllen* (1937); *Motsols* (1937); *Kungens rosor* (1939); *Vägen under stjärnorna* (1940); *Brandliljor* (1941); *Armén vid horisonten* (1942); *Den osynlige älskaren* (1943); *Bakom svenskvallen* (1944); *Kärlek mellan krigen* (1947); *Fem berättare* (1948); *Livets fest* (1949); *Jag möter en diktare* (1950); *Du är den enda* (1952); *Kvinnorna på Kummelsjö* (1955); *Klockor vid Sidenvägen* (1957); *Hemligheten* (1959).

TRANSLATIONS

Swedish Book Review 2 (1984).

REFERENCES

Boman, Glenn, ed., *Moa i brev och bilder* (Stockholm, 1978); Försås-Scott, Helena, "Moa Martinson." *Swedish Book Review* 2 (1984); Lehman, May-Brigitte, " Littérature ouvrière et féminism en Suède. L'Exemple de Moa Martinson, 1890–1964." *Études Germaniques* 34 (1979); Stiernstedt, Marika, *Moa Martinson* (Stockholm, 1946); Witt-Brattstrom, Ebba, *Moa Martinson* (Stockholm, 1988).

Torborg Lundell

Martinson, Moa. *See* Martinson, Helga Maria.

Matras, Christian. Faroese poet, b. 7 December 1900, Viðareiði, the northernmost village in the Faroe Islands, the landscape of which has marked his poetry throughout.

Matras went to school in Denmark and later studied at the University of Copenhagen, where in 1936 he began lecturing on Faroese language and literature. In 1952 he was given the personal title of Professor of Faroese, the only person so far to have achieved this distinction, and in 1965 he returned to his native Faroe Islands as Professor of Faroese in the newly established Faroese Academy. Matras has achieved great distinction and international recognition as a philologist, the compiler of the first Faroese-Danish dictionary, the principal editor of the monumental *Føroya Kvaeði, Corpus Carminum Færoensium,* the great collection of Faroese ballads, and the author of the first history of Faroese literature, *Føroysk bókmentasøga* (1935).

Matras's standing as a poet equals his reputation as a scholar. His poems exude a sense of the grandeur of Faroese nature, often with a cosmic perspective and coupled with a profound feeling for the Faroese past. To Matras, the present is the result of the labors of the unknown men of former times who trod the mountain paths and built the cairns to guide later generations. Their names are no longer known, but the present is the direct result of their labors. Matras's nature poetry is no mere superficial description, but an attempt to interpret nature as the visible but silent vehicle for the innermost nerve of the world.

The pattern was set in Matras's first collection of poems, *Grátt, kátt og hátt* (1926; Grey, Playful and Solemn), a volume containing poems written as early as 1917. His linguistic brilliance and his profound sensitivity to the Faroese landscape are already obvious in this collection, which contains his most famous poem, "Hitt blinda liðið" (The Company of the Blind), an allegorical portrayal of man as wandering blindly through life, enjoying brief insights into its nature, only to continue in his blindness.

These themes were developed and expanded in subsequent volumes. Matras emerged as a master of poetical form, not least in the complex metre of the great visionary poem, "Á hellu eg stóð." Many of his early poems are traditional in form, deeply inspired by the old Danish hymns (though without religious content), but he gradually moves toward a remarkable concentration and succinctness. In 1978 he published a new collection of poems, *Úr sjón og úr minni* (From Vision and Memory) in a new style, extremely short, pregnant poems, influenced by the haiku, expressing those momentary insights that have been the inspiration for much of his work. The shortest of them is only five words in length, a picture of a fowling tragedy which is at once intensely Faroese and yet presents the generally significant picture of human achievement, life, and death.

Not only is Matras a poet in his own right, but he is outstanding as a translator of both prose and poetry, and in particular associated with his sensitive renderings of Robert Burns. Writing in a language that only relatively recently became the medium for modern literature, Matras has seen it as one of his tasks to mold Faroese so that it can express the sophistication of modern poetical thought. He consequently stands in his native land as one of the creators of a Faroese literary language as well as one of his country's outstanding creative writers.

FURTHER WORKS

Heimur og Heima (1933); *Úr Leikum og Loyndum* (1940); *Yrkingar* (1965); *Á hellu eg stóð* (1972); *Leikur og loynd* (1975).

TRANSLATIONS

Rocky Shores, comp. and trans. George Johnston (1981).

REFERENCES

Johnston, George, comp. and trans. *Rocky Shores* (Paisley, 1981); Jones, W. Glyn, *Faroe and Cosmos* (Newcastle upon Tyne, 1974); Jones, W. Glyn, "From Kingo to Matras," in *Nordisk litteraturhistorie—en bog til Brønsted* (Odense, 1978); Jones, W. Glyn, "Nature and Man in Christian Matras' Poetry." *Scandinavica* 19.2 (1980).

W. Glyn Jones

Matthías Jochumsson. *See* Jochumsson, Matthías.

Matthías Jóhannessen. *See* Jóhannessen, Matthías.

Medieval Historical Writing.

ARI ÞORGILSSON THE LEARNED

Íslendingabók (The Book of the Icelanders, 1930)

In his prologue to Heimskringla from about 1220, Snorri Sturluson* states that the Icelandic historian Ari Þorgilsson (1068–1148) was the first man who wrote works of learning in the Norse language. There is no reason to doubt this, and two transcripts of his *Íslendingabók (The Book of the Icelanders)* have been preserved based on an original that Ari supposedly wrote some time in 1122–1132. This is a brief history of Iceland from the beginning to the year 1118. According to Ari's opening paragraph, the book is an abridgement of an earlier version that has been lost. *Íslendingabók* consists of the following chapters; Of the Settlement of Iceland; Of the Settlers and Legislation; Of the Establishment of the Althing; Of the Calendar; Of the Division into Quarters; Of the Settlement of Greenland; Of how Christianity came to Iceland; Of Foreign Bishops; Of Bishop Ísleifr; Of Bishop Gizurr. Finally, there is a Genealogical Appendix. Not only is *Íslendigabók* the most reliable source on the foundations and the development of medieval Icelandic society, but also the earliest source in the Norse language on the discovery and settlement of both Greenland and Vinland. Ari bases his book on oral accounts, and states the names of his informants whose knowledge and dependability he considers unquestionable. The way in which he verifies his statements has caused scholars to place unqualified credence in the historicity of his book. Yet one must remember that as an ordained priest, Ari gives his work some ecclesiastical overtones. In recent times, scholars have even pointed out the possibility that some of the most significant chapters in Ari's book may contain some literary motifs. Furthermore, it has been suggested that Ari's ultimate purpose was that of providing the Icelanders with examples worthy of emulation. The rule of law, peace, and Christianity are the three elements on which Ari places particular emphasis.

Landnámabók (The Book of Settlements, 1973)

In an epilogue to one of the extant versions of this book, Ari and Kolskeggr the Wise are said to have been the first to write about settlements in Iceland. Thus one may assume that Ari coauthored this book some time around 1140. The original is lost, but the work has survived in five different versions, only one of which is complete. Landnámabók lists the names of those who claimed land in Iceland during the Age of Settlements (ca. 870–930), beginning with an account of the discovery of Iceland and the arrival of the first permanent settler Ingólfr Arnarson, who made his home in Reykjavík. It then proceeds clockwise round the map of the country, gives a detailed account of the original settlements and states the names of the settlers themselves as well as of a number of their descendents.

Even though Landnámabók is a unique source on the origins of the Icelandic nation, its accuracy has been questioned. All five versions of the book differ considerably and cannot be accepted as faithful copies of the lost original. This problem is further complicated by the fact that their writers sometimes augmented their versions with materials from the Íslendingasögur (Icelandic Sagas). Conversely, it is generally recognized that the authors of the Family Sagas often derived some of their information from Landnámabók. Therefore, the relationship between the latter and the Family Sagas may be seen as reciprocal to some extent. Accordingly, circular borrowing has occurred, due to which versions of the original Landnámabók have been augmented with elements from Landnámabók's own derivatives. Yet it must be emphasized that in their analyses of Landnámabók, philologists have achieved notable success in distinguishing between original and secondary materials.

If one assumes that Ari, in addition to his two versions of The Book of the Icelanders, wrote at least a substantial part of Landnámabók, it becomes obvious why he is often referred to as the father of Icelandic history. One can in fact deduce from his extant Book of the Icelanders, and from references to its lost earlier version, that these two works were to some extent the forerunners of both the Kings' Sagas and the Lives of Bishops. If one also bears in mind that The Book of Settlements is, in a sense, a collection of miniature Icelandic Family Sagas, Ari's enduring influence on medieval saga writing becomes even more obvious.

KINGS' SAGAS

Most of the kings' sagas are the works of Icelandic authors and fall into three divisions: partly mythical sagas on prehistoric themes (i.e., Skjöldunga saga and Ynglinga saga), sagas about kings with reasonably firm foundations in past history, and sagas written by the kings' own contemporary biographers. The oldest kings' saga appears to have been written in Latin by Sæmundr Sigfússon the Learned (1056–1133) on the kings of Norway from Hálfdan the Black to Magnús the Good (d. 1047) in order to establish a reliable chronological sequence. Ari the Learned's writing on kings' lives in his lost version of *The Book of the Icelanders* appears, however, to have followed a somewhat different chronology.

The earliest contemporary saga is *Hryggjarstykki* (ca. 1170) (Bone Piece) by Eiríkr Oddsson from about the middle of the twelfth century. Although this saga is not extant as a separate entity, much of its content was incorporated into *Morkinskinna* (Rotten-Skinny), *Fagrskinna* (Fair-Skinny), and *Heimskringla* (*Heimskringla: History of the Kings of Norway*, 1964). This work, which centered on the life of Sigurðr Slembir, most certainly covered the period 1136–1139. Some scholars have suggested a much longer period, that is, 1130–1161. Nevertheless, it is not clear if there ever existed separate sagas about Norwegian kings reigning during the period 1140–1177. On the other hand, three separate kings' sagas were written in Norway during the last third of the twelfth century, two in Latin and one in Old Norse. The oldest of these is *Historia Norvegiae*, a synopsis of Norwegian history from King Haraldr Finehair to Saint Ólaf Haraldsson. This work appears to have been based on Latin sources, some oral tradition, and in all probability the works of Ari the Learned (see above). Next there is *Historia de antiquitate regum Norvagiensium* by Brother Theodoricus (Archbishop Þórir, 1206–1214, or Bishop Þórir at Hamarr, 1189–1196?), covering the period from King Haraldr Finehair to King Sigurðr Jórsalafari. The author quotes Icelandic informants and appears to have used both Icelandic and Latin source materials quite extensively. An Old Norse work *Ágrip* (Synopsis), written in Trondheim shortly after 1190, extends from King Hálfdan the Black up to the year 1177. This work, which is based on oral tradition, the previously mentioned work by Theodoricus, and in all probability *Historia Norvegiae*, has survived in the form of an incomplete Icelandic copy.

The first part of *Sverris Saga* (*Sverrissaga: The Saga of King Sverri of Norway*, 1899) was written at the request of King Sverrir Sigurðarson himself by Abbot Karl Jónsson of Þingeyrar during the latter's stay in Norway 1184–1188. This section of the work, which ends with either chapter 31 or 43, came to be called *Grýla* (the name of an ogress, a personification implying an unreal threat) and begins with King Sverrir's arrival in Norway in 1176. The second section of the saga is quite detailed and extends to the time of King Magnús Erlingsson's death in 1184. This portion appears to have been written by Abbot Karl Jónsson after his return to Iceland and is based on source materials he had previously collected in Norway. The last part of *Sverris Saga* was written after the king's death in 1202. *Sverris Saga* marks the beginning of new trends in the writing of kings' sagas in accordance with which the protagonist himself not only gave his biographer clear directives, but intended his saga to be a defense and vindication of certain political goals. *Böglunga sögur*, covering the period 1202–1217, may be seen as a direct continuation of *Sverris Saga*, and Sturla Þórðarson's sagas of

King Hákon Hákonarson and Magnús Hákonarson lagabætir also belong to the same category.

Toward the end of the twelfth century the Icelanders resumed their writing on the Norwegian past. Oddr Snorrason, a member of the Holy Brotherhood of Þingeyrar, wrote a saga around 1190 on King Ólaf Tryggvason that has been preserved in three different Icelandic redactions. Another member of the same monastery, Gunnlaugr Leifsson (d. 1218 or 1219), produced an expanded Latin version of Snorrason's work that has survived in a fragmentary Icelandic translation, the major part of which was incorporated into *The Longest Saga* of King Ólaf Tryggvason, written around 1300.

The Oldest Saga of King Saint Ólaf Haraldsson was written in Iceland about the end of the twelfth century and has survived only in fragments. Use was made of it in subsequent works on Saint Ólaf.

The affinity between *The Longest Saga* and the so-called *Helgisaga* (The Legendary Saga), also about Saint Ólaf, from the early thirteenth century and extant only in a Norwegian manuscript, is particularly strong.

OTHER SAGAS FROM THE EARLY THIRTEENTH CENTURY

Orkneyinga saga (trans. 1938, 1978) is related to the kings' sagas in that it tells of the Earls of Orkney from the ninth century up to about 1170. Although the original version of this saga has been lost, its extant redactions contain quite detailed accounts of twelfth-century events. The saga was one of Snorri Sturluson's sources for his *Heimskringla*. *Skjöldunga saga* (see above), an account of the ancient kings of Denmark, is extant only as a summary in Latin written by Arngrímur Jónsson the Learned toward the end of the sixteenth century. Mention must also be made of *Jómsvíkinga saga* (*The Saga of the Jómsvikings*, 1955, 1962), which describes the late tenth-century Battle of Hjörunga Bay (Hjörungavágr) in which the Jómsvíkings were defeated by the Norwegians. This saga, which has quite strong mythical-heroic overtones, was among the sources used in both *Fagrskinna* and *Heimskringla*. *Færeyinga saga* (*The Faroe Islanders' Saga*, 1975) is also from the same period. Even though it is to a large extent confined to the history of the Faroe Islands, it contains some significant accounts of both Earl Hákon of Hlaðir and King Ólaf Tryggvason. Some of the later kings' sagas make references to the *Saga of Earl Hákon of Hlaðir*, which has been lost, as is also the case with other kings' sagas, the existence of which scholars have postulated as sources used in later compilations. The oldest of such compilations is *Morkinskinna* from the first half of the thirteenth century.

Morkinskinna (see above), has survived in a late thirteenth-century manuscript of which the final portion is missing. It begins with accounts of King Magnús the Good and originally gave in all probability, a continuous account up to 1177. *Fagrskinna*, from about 1220, seems to have been written by an Icelander stationed in Norway. It extends from King Hálfdan the Black to the year 1177. In the fourth decade of the thirteenth century the writing of kings' sagas reached its climax in Snorri Sturluson's *Heimskringla*. To a considerable extent the mid–

thirteenth-century *Knýtlinga saga*, which contains sagas of the kings of Denmark from the middle of the tenth century up to the year 1187, was patterned after *Heimskringla*.

Sturlunga saga (trans. 1970–1974) is a compilation of sagas by Icelandic authors on their own contemporary scene in twelfth- and thirteenth-century Iceland. *Íslendinga saga* by Sturla Þórðarson (1214–1284) constitutes the main portion of this collection and appears to have been intended as a continuation of previous works on the history of Iceland such as *Landnámabók* (see above) and *Kristni saga* (The History of the Christianization of Iceland). *Sturlunga saga* is the chief source on the history of medieval Iceland.

Biskupa sögur (The Lives of the Bishops) are semihistorical accounts of Icelandic bishops from 1156 to ca. 1330. Although *Biskupa sögur* provide significant historical information, they adhere very strongly to the point of view of the medieval church. One of these, *Prestsaga Guðmundar Arasonar* (i.e., the first part of the Life of Bishop Guðmundur Arason the Good), was incorporated into the *Sturlunga saga* compilation (see above). The early thirteenth-century *Hungrvaka* (Appetizer), about the lives of the first five bishops of Skálholt, also falls into this category.

Finally, it must be noted that in varying degrees *Íslendinga sögur* (The Family Sagas) are based on historical facts.

EDITIONS

Biskupa sögur, 2 vols. (Copenhagen, 1858–1878); "Danakonunga sögur," ed. Bjarni Guðnason, in *Íslenzk fornrit*, vol. 35 (Reykjavík, 1982); "Heimskringla," ed. Bjarni Aðalbjarnarson, in *Íslenzk fornrit*, vols. 26–28 (Reykjavík, 1941–1951); "Landnámabók," ed. Jakob Benediktsson, in *Íslenzk fornrit*, vol. 1 (Reykjavík, 1969); *Sturlunga Saga*, ed. Jón Jóhannesson et al., 2 vols. (Reykjavík, 1946).

REFERENCES

Aðalbjarnarson, Bjarni, *Om de norske kongers sagœr* (Oslo, 1936); Clover, Carol, *The Medieval Saga* (Ithaca, 1982); Ellehøj, Sven, *Studier over den œldste norrøne historieskrivning*, in *Bibliotheca Arnamagnaaena* 26 (1965); Fry, Donald, *Norse Sagas Translated into English: A Bibliography* (New York, 1980); Glendinning, R. J., *Träume und Vorbedeutung in der Islendinga Saga Sturla Thordarsons: Eine Form- und Stiluntersuchung* (Bern, 1974); Guðnason, Bjarni, "Fyrsta sagan," in *Studia Islandica* 37 (1978); Guðnarson, Bjarni, *Um Skjöldungasögu* (Reykjavík, 1963); Jóhannesson, Jón, *Gerðir Landnámabókar* (Reykjavík, 1941); Jóhannesson, Jón, *A History of the Old Icelandic Commonwealth* (Winnipeg, 1974); Louis-Jensen, Jonna, *Kongesagastudier*, in *Bibliotheca Arnamagnaaena* 32 (1977); Rafnsson, Sveinbjörn, *Studier í Landnámabók* (Lund, 1974); Schach, Paul, *Icelandic Sagas* (Boston, 1984); Schach, Paul, "Norse Sagas in English Translation." *Yearbook of Comparative and General Literature* 33 (1984).

Haraldur Bessason

Mehren, Stein. Norwegian poet, novelist, and essayist, b. 16 May 1935, Oslo.

Mehren has studied philosophy, which has been of great importance to his writing. His poems are rich in pictures, musicality, and imaginative fantasy. At the same time there is a strong intellectual line in them. The central themes of his first three collections are alienation and existential fear. The problem of the relationship between language, reality, and cognition underlies these themes. This also holds true for the rest of his work.

From *Gobelin Europa* (1965) onward a new and more satirical tone is present in his poetry. The conflict between reflection and spontaneity is, however, the main issue. Throughout his whole work Mehren struggles with the problem of reconciling the intellectual meta-attitude toward life and the authenticity of emotional and metaphysical experience.

In *Aurora Det Niende Mørke* (1969; Aurora, The Ninth Darkness) his criticism of the modern technological way of thinking is contrasted with this striving to rebuild an authentic life. In the 1970s his preoccupation with the mythological aspects of life and modern philosophy to an increasing degree colors his work. The formal unity and the concentration of the pictorial structure of his poems become stronger, and his early pessimism is changed into a strong self-consciousness on behalf of the writer's task and importance.

Mehren has also been a very productive essayist. His early prose is collected in *Samtidsmuseet og andre tekster* (1966; The Contemporary Museum and Other Texts). *Kunstens vilkår og den nye puritanismen* (1974; The Conditions of Art and the New Puritanism) is among other things an attack upon the new ideology-ridden literature, and in *Myten og den irrasjonelle fornuft* (vol. 1, 1977; vol. 2, 1980; The Myth and the Irrational Reason) Mehren takes a stand against several trendy philosophies: Theodor Adorno's critical theory, the *Verfremdung* drama of Bertolt Brecht, the existentialism of Jean Paul Sartre. Mehren's alternative is a new philosophy of nature and a new picture of man that combine irrational mythological thinking and reason.

His two novels, *De utydelige* (1972; The Vague Ones) and *Titanene* (1974; The Titans), are slightly nihilistic, fictional pamphlets against political dogmatism. They illustrate his point of view that value conflicts of a society are integrated within the single individual.

Mehren has also written dramas. He has been nominated four times for the literary prize of the Nordic Council and ranks among the leading poets of Norwegian literature today.

FURTHER WORKS

Gjennom stillheten en natt (1960); *Hildring i speil* (1961); *Alene med en himmel* (1962); *Mot en verden av lys* (1963); *Tids Alder* (1966); *Vind Runer* (1967); *Narren og hans hertug* (1968); *Maskinen og menneskekroppen* (1970); *Kongespillet* (1971); *Den store frigjøringen* (1973); *Dikt for enhver som våger* (1973); *En rytter til fots* (1975); *Menneske bære ditt bilde frem* (1975); *Den store søndagsfrokosten* (1976); *Det trettende stjernebilde* (1977); *Vintersolhverv* (1979); *50 60 70 80* (1980); *Den usynlige regnbuen* (1981); *Timenes Time* (1983); *Corona* (1986); *Fortapt i verden* (1988).

REFERENCES

Andersen, Per Thomas, *Stein Mehren—en logos-dikter* (Oslo, 1982); Naess, Harald, "Stein Mehren: Dialectic Poet of Light and Dreams." *Books Abroad* 47.1 (1973).

Øystein Rottem

Meri, Veijo. Finnish novelist, dramatist, and poet, b. 31 December 1928, Viipuri.

Meri came upon the Finnish literary scene at a time when the epic realism of Väinö Linna* dominated taste and approval. Inevitably comparisons between the two writers were made, despite their quite different perspectives and aims. In part the comparison derives from the fact that both writers utilized army life as the arena where events unfolded. There, however, the similarity ends.

That Meri's earlier works were placed in a military setting is natural enough, since he grew up in garrisons, and came to the understanding that the absurdity of warring man is merely a magnification of life in general. Following a debut with *Ettei maa viheriöisi* (1954; Lest the Land Become Green), Meri broke through with *Manillaköysi* (1957; *The Manila Rope*, 1964), and affirmed his position with *Peiliin piirretty nainen* (1963; A Woman Drawn on a Mirror). His production has been extensive, ranging in genre from poetry to radio plays, though novels and short stories comprise the overwhelming bulk of his production and reputation.

In the view of Meri no detail or event is insignificant. The seemingly inconsequential, even absurd anecdotes interspersed in *Manillaköysi* and other works underscore a form of logical madness governing the world as it has been and continues to be. But the world is not an asylum of hopelessness; in spite of the apparent irrationality, everything goes on as if the irrational were an integral part of the grand design. Whether that design is good or bad, rational or not, it is one that must be accepted by those who live it. It is a stylistic figure of Meri to interrupt the principal story with anecdotes, usually bizarre, dovetailed into the overall narrative, thus expressing the view that despite incredible happenings the journey continues and nothing has really changed.

It would be easy to see pessimism in Meri's message, were it not for the circumstance that one rarely sees a hint of bias or condemnation of characters; there is neither joy nor sorrow in the peculiar and ever-present humor of Meri.

FURTHER WORKS

Irralliset (1959); *Vuoden 1918 tapahtumat* (1960, 1981); *Sujut* (1961); *Tilanteita* (1962); *Suomen paras näyttelijä* (1963); *Tukikohta* (1964); *Sotamies Jokisen vihkiloma* (1965; *Private Jokinen's Marriage Leave*, 1973); *Veijo Meren novellit* (1965); *Everstin autonkuljettaja* (1966, 1983); *Veijo Meren sotaromaanit*, 2 vols. (1966); *Yhden yön tarinoita* (1967); *Kaksitoista artikkelia* (1967); *Suku* (1968); *Veijo Meren romaanit* (1968); *Sata metriä korkeat kirjaimet* (1969); *Valitut teokset* (1969); *Veijo Meren näytelmiä* (1970); *Kersantin poika* (1971); *Leiri* (1972); *Morsiamen sisar ja muita novelleja* (1972); *Aleksis*

Stenvallin elämä (1973); *Aleksis Kivi* (1974); *Kuviteltu kuolema* (1974); *Keskeiset teokset*, 4 vols. (1975); *Mielen lähtölaskenta* (1976); *Kaksi komediaa* (1978); *Toinen sydän* (1978); *Goethen tammi* (1978); *Jääkiekkoilijan kesä* (1980); *Ylimpänä pieni höyhen* (1980); *Tuusulan rantatie* (1981); *Sanojen synty* (1982); *Runoilijan kuolema* (1985); *Yhdessä ja yksin* (1986); *Kevät kuin aamu* (1987).

FURTHER TRANSLATIONS

Modern Nordic Plays: Finland, ed. Erik J. Friis (1973); *Snow in May*, ed. Richard Dauenhauer and Philip Binham (1978); *Books from Finland* 15.3 (1981); *Poetry East* 6 (1981); *Finnish Short Stories*, ed. Inkeri Väänänen-Jensen with K. Börje Vähämäki (1982); *Salt of Pleasure: Twentieth-Century Finnish Poetry*, ed. Aili Jarvenpa (1983).

REFERENCES

Haikara, Kalevi, *Se oli se kultamaa* (Helsinki, 1969); Laitinen, Kai, "Väinö Linna and Veijo Meri: Two Aspects of War." *Books Abroad* 36.4 (1962); Stormbom, N. B., "Veijo Meri and the New Finnish Novel." *American-Scandinavian Review* 55.3 (1967).

Kim Nilsson

Meriluoto, Aila. Finnish poet and translator, b. 10 January 1924, Pieksämäki.

Meriluoto was born into an educated family, passed her matriculation examinations in 1943, and studied at the University of Helsinki and in Switzerland. She was married to the Finnish poet Lauri Viita* from 1948 to 1956, she lived in Sweden from 1962 to 1974, and currently resides in Espoo, Finland. Meriluoto gained sudden fame, when at the age of twenty-two she published her first collection of poetry in 1946. The collection, *Lasimaalaus* (Stained Glass), became a literary sensation, praised by critics, young and old alike, and was received enthusiastically by the general public. In a short time, 25,000 copies were sold.

The critics hailed her as a significant modern lyric poet. Readers recognized in her the voice of the generation that had grown up during the war and that now had to face the postwar world. The poem "Kivinen Jumala" (The Stone God) was frequently quoted at the time; it seemed to speak for many with its image of rebelling against a god who permits the horrors of war. The influence of Rainer Maria Rilke, whom Meriluoto has translated, is particularly clear in her collections *Sairas tyttö tanssii* (1952; The Sick Girl Dances) and in *Pahat unet* (1959; Bad Dreams).

In *Lasimaalaus*, Meriluoto demonstrated her command of traditional poetic forms. In her later collections, she turned more and more to free verse and often employed cosmic, physiological, and biological images in her poems. In her collections *Elämästä* (1972; About Life) and *Varokaa putoilevia enkeleitä* (1977; Beware of Falling Angels) she used a lighter, almost humorous tone. *Talvikaupunki* (1980; Winter City), her tenth collection of poetry, is particularly rich in imagery.

Meriluoto is the author of the biography of the poet Lauri Viita. She is the translator of Harry Martinson's* *Aniara*, among many other works. She received the state prize for her poetry in 1946 and 1962 and for her translations in 1974.

Meriluoto's early promise established her as one of the most important Finnish postwar modernists. She has confirmed her place among the leading Finnish poets by the quality of her subsequent works.

FURTHER WORKS

Pommorommo (1956); *Valikoima runoja* (1958); *Portaat* (1961); *Asumattomiin* (1963); *Ateljee Katariina* (1965); *Tuoddaris* (1965); *Meidän linna* (1968); *Silmämitta* (1969); *Peter-Peter* (1971); *Lauri Viita. Legenda jo eläessään* (1974); *Kootut runot* (1976); *Kotimaa kuin mies* (1977); *Sisar vesi, veli tuli* (1979); *Lasimaalauksen läpi* (1986); *Ruusujen sota* (1988).

TRANSLATIONS

Snow in May, ed. Richard Dauenhauer and Philip Binham (1978); *Salt of Pleasure,* ed. Aili Jarvenpa (1983).

REFERENCES

Binham, Philip, Review of *Lauri Viita. Legenda jo eläessään. Books Abroad* 49.3 (1975); Binham, Philip, Review of *Kootut runot. World Literature Today* 51.1 (1977); Vähämäki, K. B., Review of *Varokaa putoilevia enkeleitä. World Literature Today* 52.2 (1978).

Aili Flint

Moberg, Carl Artur *Vilhelm.* Swedish novelist and dramatist, b. 20 August 1898, Algutsboda, d. 8 August 1973, Väddö.

Moberg came of peasant stock; his father was a soldier-crofter in southern Småland, which, with its rugged terrain and hardy inhabitants, forms the basis for much of his work. Largely self-educated, he followed a classic path for the 1930s working-class generation of Swedish writers, via folk high school, socialism and provincial journalism.

In *Raskens* (1927) he records for posterity a rural peasant culture then vanishing and in a tragic plot reminiscent of Thomas Hardy establishes stock figures recurring in his works—the strong, self-reliant individualist and his loyal and pious wife. Moberg's 1930s novels deal with social change, urbanization and industrialization and the problem these entail for a rural culture unchanged for centuries. The trilogy about Knut Toring (1935–1939) is in part autobiographical. *Mans kvinna* (1933; Man's Woman) shows the influence of primitivism on Moberg.

Rid i natt! (1941; *Ride this Night*, 1943) marks the culmination of Moberg's contribution to *beredskapslitteratur*. Events in Småland in the 1650s parallel the difficult political situation of Sweden in the early war years—Moberg was actively pro-Allies. *Soldat med brutet gevär* (1944; *When I Was a Child*, 1956), a massive novel, is part autobiographical, part historical—tracing the democratization of Sweden in the period 1900–1920—and part allegorical—bitterly critical of the government's appeasement of the nazis.

The Emigration tetralogy also reflects Moberg's background—Småland was a major area of emigration—and in this meticulously researched account of the resettlement of sixteen peasants in Minnesota Moberg provides a dramatization of a neglected historical process while creating unforgettable characters and producing some of his best writing. The work was a best-seller and has been made into two feature films by Jan Troell.

Later novels are slighter, but Moberg turned to history proper with two volumes of a planned popular guide to Swedish history.

Moberg's weaknesses as a novelist of ideas are compensated for by his strengths as an epic realist storyteller and by his pure prose style, rooted in his own dialect and the rhythms of medieval, often biblical texts.

Moberg also made a major contribution to Swedish drama, especially with folk comedies like *Marknadsafton* (1930; Market Eve) and social dramas like *Våld* (1933; Violence). He dramatized several of his novels and was a pioneer of radio drama in the 1930s.

Moberg was an outsider, an uncompromising idealist, and a scourge of the Establishment who fought long battles against injustice but won great popular acclaim.

FURTHER WORKS

Raskens (1927); *Långt från landsvägen* (1929); *Hustrun* (1929); *Bröllopssalut* (1929); *De knutna händerna* (1930); *A. P. Rosell, bankdirektör* (1932); *Bönder emellan* (1933); *Sänkt sedebetyg* (1935; *Memory of Youth*, 1937); *Sänkt sedebetyg/Sömnlös/Giv oss jorden!* (1935; The Earth Is Ours!, 1940); *Sömnlös* (1937); *Giv oss jorden!* (1939); *Kyskhet* (1937); *De knutna händerna*, play (1939); *Änkeman Jarl* (1940); *En löskekarl* (1941); *Svensk strävan* (1941); *Rid i Natt!* (1942); *Sanningen kryper fram* (1943); *Segerstedtstriden* (1945); *Vår ofödde son* (1945); *Brudarnas källa* (1946); *Utvandrarna* (1949; The Emigrants, 1951); *Den okända släkten* (1950); *Fallet Krukmakaregatan* (1951); *Invandrarna* (1952; Unto a Good Land, 1957); *Mans kvinna* (1953; Fulfillment, 1953); *Att övervaka överheten* (1953); *Jungfru Maria på fattiggårn* (1954); *Gudens hustru* (1954); *Lea och Rakel* (1954); *Därför är jag republikan* (1955); *Komplotterna* (1956); *Nybyggarna* (1956); *Sista brevet till Sverige* (1959); *Nybyggarna/Sista brevet till Sverige* (1956 ed. and trans., The Last Letter Home, 1961); *Domaren* (1957); *Nattkyparen* (1961); *Sagoprinsen* (1962); *Din stund på jorden* (1962; A Time on Earth, 1965); *Kvinnas man* (1965); *Bondeåret* (1966); *Förrädarland* (1967); *Din stund på jorden*, Play (1967); *Berättelser ur min levnad* (1968); *Min svenska historia*, 2 vols. (1970–1971; A History of the Swedish People, 2 vols. 1972–1973); *I skrivande stund* (1973); *Otrons artiklar* (1973); *I egen sak: obekväma inlägg i det offentliga samtalet* (1984).

REFERENCES

Alexis, Gerhard T., "Moberg's Immigrant Trilogy: A Dubious Conclusion." *Scandinavian Studies* 38.1 (1966); Eidevall, Gunnar, *Berättaren Vilhelm Moberg* (Stockholm, 1976); Eidevall, Gunnar, *Vilhelm Mobergs emigrantepos: Studier i verkets tillkomsthistoria, dokumentära bakgrund och konstnärliga gestaltning* (Stockholm, 1974); Holmes,

Philip, *Vilhelm Moberg* (Boston, 1980); Holmes, Philip, *Vilhelm Moberg: Utvandrarna* (Hull, 1976); Johnson, Walter, "Moberg's *Emigrants* and the Naturalistic Tradition." *Scandinavian Studies* 25 (1953); Lagerroth, Erland, and Ulla-Britta Lagerroth, eds., *Perspektiv på Utvandrarromanen* (Stockholm, 1971); Mårtenson, Sigvard, *En bok om Vilhelm Moberg: En handledning till radioteaterns pjässerie spelåret 1953–54* (Stockholm, 1953); Mårtenson, Sigvard, *Vilhelm Moberg: en biografi* (Stockholm, 1956); Orton, Gavin, and Philip Holmes, "Memoirs of an Idealist: Vilhelm Moberg's *Soldat med brutet gevär.*" *Scandinavian Studies* 48 (1976); Winther, Sophus K., "Moberg and a New Genre for the Emigrant Novel." *Scandinavian Studies* 34.3 (1962).

Philip Holmes

Møller, Poul Martin. Danish author, philosopher, and critic, b. 21 March 1794, Uldum, d. 13 March 1838, Copenhagen.

Møller earned a bachelor of divinity degree from the University of Copenhagen in 1816, worked as a teacher at the metropolitan school in Copenhagen from 1822 to 1826 and as a professor of philosophy at the University of Christiania, Norway, from 1828 to 1831, and at the University of Copenhagen from 1831. In his short lifetime Møller published only a very few things, among them reviews and philosophical articles in several leading magazines and newspapers. His articles made him a spokesman for the reconciliation between the dominant idealism of the period and the new realistic tendencies in art. He also published a number of poems, among which the famous "Kunstneren mellem Oprørerne" (1823; "The Master among the Rioters," 1922) reflects the conflict between the bourgeois, revolutionary ideas and the idealistic conception of art. Møller both defends the idealistic artist and at the same time shows the collapse of idealism.

Møller was a leading figure in the liberal student circles in Copenhagen from 1820. Here a new concept of romanticism and idealism emerged and was transformed into so-called poetic realism. Møller's unfinished major work *En dansk Students Eventyr* (1824; The Adventures of a Danish Student) is an expression of this new trend. The poetic realism had a new interest for everyday reality, the trivial, and a satirical dimension toward affected behavior and the exaggerated worship of the bombastic and eccentric that characterized the romantic period.

Møller's prose is fragmentary and unfinished but represents a new tendency in its new style and its psychological understanding of the human personality. The same can be said about Møller's poetry, especially the collection of poems later known as *Scener i Rosenborg Slotshave* (1819–1821; Scenes from the Garden of Rosenborg Castle), where his poetic realism finds its lyrical expression. The poems reflect a bourgeois reality, an idyllic portrait of everyday life, but with a sometimes sharper light on reality than seen before.

Though small in proportions, Møller's authorship is an influential gateway from the idealistic and romantic period to early realism. His importance increased when, after his death, his total production was published in three volumes from 1839–1843.

FURTHER WORKS

Efterladte Skrifter, 3 vols. (1839–1843); *Skrifter i udvalg*, 2 vols. (1930); *En Dansk Students Eventyr og Lægdsgaarden i Ølseby-Magle* (1964); *Filosofiske essays og Strø-tanker* (1965).

FURTHER TRANSLATIONS

Book of Danish Verse, comp. Oluf Friis (1922, 1976); *A Second Book of Danish Verse*, trans. Charles W. Stork (1947, 1968); Keigwin, Richard P., *In Denmark I was Born . . . A Little Book of Danish Verse* (1950).

REFERENCES

Andersen, Wilhelm, *Poul Møller* (Copenhagen, 1894, 1944); Andreasen, Uffe, *Poul Møller og romantismen* (Copenhagen, 1973); Jones, W. Glyn, "Søren Kierkegaard and Poul Martin Møller." *Modern Language Review* 60 (1965); Thielst, Peter, "Poul Martin Møller (1794–1838): Scattered Thoughts, Analysis of Affectation, Combat with Nihilism." *Danish Yearbook of Philosophy* 13 (1976).

Ib Bondebjerg

Mørch, Dea Trier. *See* Trier Mørch, Dea.

Mørck, Paal. *See* Rølvaag, Ole E.

Mörne, Arvid. Finland-Swedish poet, b. 6 May 1876, Kuopio, d. 15 June 1946, Grankulla.

The son of a civil servant, Mörne grew up with a sense of loyalty to the Finland-Swedish culture that, as a result of his early work as a popular educator, was supplemented by a profound sympathy for the poverty-stricken rural population. Consequently, he joined the folk high school movement for a time, and was also politically active. The Civil War brought an end to his idealistic visions, and he withdrew from active political life, apart from a brief period in the 1930s. He was a lecturer in literature at Helsinki University from 1913–1943.

Mörne was one of the outstanding poets of his generation. His first publications, *Rytm och rim* (1899; Rhythm and Rhymes) and *Nya sånger* (1901; New Songs), consisted mainly of poems inspired by the Finnish coastline, though he also expresses his faith in the human spirit. In *Döda år* (1910; Dead Years) Mörne moved into a more introspective and pessimistic phase that was intensified by World War I. In the 1920s he published various prose works, including the novel *Kristina Bjur* (1922) reflecting his growing sense of isolation and resignation.

Mörne's finest poetry was written after this. His sense of isolation persists, expressed in well-formed poems, some reflecting the influence of modernism, which reveal something of the character of his earlier nature poetry, though his principal motifs are now used in a symbolic, subjective fashion to reflect his own moods and predicament. Not all are dark in tone, however. The advent of fascism in the 1930s, and World War II, brought a new active element into Mörne's poetry as he saw a renewed threat to his youthful ideals and sensed the general threat to mankind.

Mörne's pessimistic introspection has prevented him from becoming a widely popular poet, though some of his lyrical poems have indeed achieved widespread popularity. On the other hand, he has a following that has appreciated his integrity and understood the stylistically impressive manner in which he expressed the tension between idealism and disillusionment that is at the center of his work.

FURTHER WORKS

Ny tid (1903); *Skärgårdens vår* (1913); *De sex orden* (1914); *Den svenska jorden* (1915); *Sommarnatten* (1916); *Lotsarnas kamp* (1917); *Från fjärdarna* (1917); *Den röda våren* (1917); *Fädernearvet* (1918); *Offer och segrar* (1918); *Höstlig dikt* (1919); *Solens återkomst* (1920); *Inför havets anlete* (1921); *Klas-Kristians julnatt* (1923); *Vandringen och vägen* (1924); *Ett liv* (1925); *Mörkret och lågan* (1926); *Någon går förbi på vägen* (1928); *Morgonstjärnan* (1928); *Den förborgade källan* (1930); *Det ringer kväll* (1931); *Under vintergatan* (1934); *Hjärtat och svärdet* (1935); *Atlantisk bränning* (1937); *Över havet brann Mars* (1939); *Lyriker och berättare* (1939); *Sånger i världsskymning* (1941); *Det övergivne samvetet* (1943); *Sfinxen och Pyramiden* (1944); *Det förlorade landet* (1945).

REFERENCES

Barck, P. O., *Arvid Mörne och sekelskiftets Finland* (Helsinki, 1953); Hedlund, T., *Poeten Arvid Mörne* (Helsinki, 1974); Ruin, H., *Arvid Mörne* (Stockholm, 1946)); Wrede, J., *Arvid Mörnes lyrik* (Helsinki, 1968).

W. Glyn Jones

Moren, Halldis Vesaas. *See* Vesaas, Halldis Moren.

Mortensen, Enok. Danish-American novelist, minister, educator, and historian, b. 31 July 1902, Copenhagen, d. 14 December 1984, Solvang, California.

Mortensen immigrated with his family to Cedar Falls, Iowa, in 1919. He was an ordained Lutheran minister who served congregations between 1929 and 1967 in Chicago, Illinois; Salinas, California; Tyler, Minnesota; and Des Moines, Iowa. The dominant influence in Mortensen's life, and on his writing, is Grundtvigianism, that is, a happy Christianity with humanitarian and proletarian orientation.

The collection of short stories in *Mit Folk* (1932; My People) portrays the Danish immigrant between 1880 and 1920 as a virtually powerless victim of a socioeconomic system in which material gain was the foremost goal, and individual health and well-being were generally disregarded. Six stories are set in Chicago and three in the rural Midwest. The protagonists are poor Danish immigrants, often beggars or hoboes. All are first-generation immigrants who came to America expecting to quickly become rich and then return to the Old Country. Usually they do neither.

Saaledes Blev Jeg Hjemløs (1934; Thus I Became Homeless) and *Jeg Vælger*

et Land (1936; I Choose a Country) optimistically show the epic quest of Niels
Nord for the American immigrant dream of socioeconomic success and a new
national identity. Even though Niels Nord came to America as a Danish-
apprenticed carpenter and as the son of a comparatively wealthy farmer in South
Jutland, he is a have-not in the new country. In fact, he becomes an urban
proletarian, both economically and personally, subject to the cyclical patterns
of economic boom and bust typical of early twentieth-century America. After
an abortive one-year stay in Denmark, Niels knows he is neither a Dane nor a
farmer. He returns to marry a second-generation Dane and to continue the quest
to discover what it means to be a Danish-American. The two novels portray a
vicious American chauvinism during World War I, a continuous identity problem
for the first generation, the second generation's language conflict, as well as
economic exploitation and political graft. However, there remains the pervasive
sense of optimism, as among all immigrant groups, for a better life in a pluralistic
but egalitarian country, especially for their children.

The dominant theme of Mortensen's fiction is the identity problem faced by
the first-generation immigrant in the United States. The majority of his characters,
and those for whom he shows the most understanding and sympathy, are the
lower classes. Indeed, those in the lower socioeconomic class, both employed
and unemployed, might well be considered the collective protagonist in Mortensen's fiction. These people may lead a physically marginal existence, but they
are also more conscious than their better-off countrymen of the conflicts inherent
in their situation as first-generation immigrants. Family life is the most important
value in their lives.

Mortensen's nonfiction documents unique Danish-American institutions—the
Danish-American church and the folk high school. Among scholars of Scandinavian-American history and literature, Mortensen generally is considered to be
the most knowledgeable individual on the nature of the Danish-American experience.

FURTHER WORKS

Livets Lykke (1933); *Danish-American Letters* (1945); *The Danish-American Immigrant*
(1950); *Stories from Our Church: A Popular History of the Danish Evangelical Lutheran
Church of America* (1952); *75 Years at Danebod* (1961); *The Danish Lutheran Church
in America: The History and Heritage of the American Evangelical Lutheran Church*
(1967); *Schools for Life: A Danish-American Experiment in Adult Education* (1977); *A
Danish Boyhood* (1981); *Den lange plovfure* (1984).

REFERENCE

Skårdal, Dorothy Burton, "A Danish Dream of America." *Melus* 8 (1981).

Rudolf Jensen

Munch-Petersen, Gustaf. Danish poet and novelist, b. 18 February 1912,
Copenhagen, d. 28 March 1938, Spain.

Munch-Petersen, the son of a Danish father and Swedish mother, was born into an academic milieu. He began university studies in philosophy and psychology, but quit them in 1932 to live in Greenland as a laborer for a year. Then he wandered rather aimlessly through Europe, until 1935 when he settled on Bornholm to live as a fisherman. In 1937 he joined the People's Front in the Spanish civil war and was killed in action the following year.

Munch-Petersen's restless life is mirrored in his written works, which include four collections of poems, a novel published independently, and a collection of poems in English, *Black God's Stone,* and one in Swedish, *Solen finns,* both published in *Samlede skrifter* (1959; Collected Writings). His debut piece, *Det nøgne menneske* (1932; The Naked Man), describes a young man's revolt against social norms and traditions. Like the two collections of poetry that follow, it focuses on freedom and personal release from all restraints. He develops subconscious images in a style that is spontaneous and experimental. Munch-Petersen was part of the surrealist movement. He had close contacts with avantgarde Danish painters and was a painter himself. Significant inspiration also came from the modernistic Swedish and Finno-Swedish poets (Artur Lundkvist*, Harry Martinson,* Elmer Diktonius,* Edith Södergran*). Munch-Petersen's poetry reflects his life in its ceaseless searching. His last poems, *Nitten digte* (1937; Nineteen Poems), reveal a definite contrast to the previous collections. The style is simple and concrete and the subject involves an individual's psychological environment. Shortly after engaging in this new approach to reality, Munch-Petersen began his struggle against fascism. His attitude toward life as well as poetry was that of uncompromising involvement and commitment.

Munch-Petersen is the most outstanding Danish modernist poet of the 1930s although he remained unappreciated in his lifetime, aside from a narrow circle of like-minded cultural revolutionists. Post–World War II poets greatly concerned with existentialism, poetic theory, and the important periodical *Heretica* were the first to recognize Munch-Petersen as a pioneer. Their interest was reinforced by the modernists of the 1960s.

FURTHER WORKS

simon beqynder (1933); *det underste land* (1933); *mod jerusalem* (1934); *Samlede Skrifter,* 2 vols. (1959).

FURTHER TRANSLATIONS

Modern Danish Poems, ed. Knud K. Mogensen (1949); *Twentieth Century Scandinavian Poetry,* ed. Martin S. Allwood (1950); *Literary Review* 8 (1964); *Contemporary Danish Poetry,* ed. Line Jensen et al. (1977).

REFERENCES

Jensen, Thorkild Borup, "Gustaf Munch-Petersen," in *Danske digtere i det 20. år-*

hundrede, vol. 2 (Copenhagen, 1981); Loesch, Lise, *Tamme fugle længes—vilde flyver* (Copenhagen, 1980); Mitchell, P. M., "The English Poetry of Gustaf Munch-Petersen." *Orbis Litterarum* 22 (1967).

Preben Meulengracht Sørensen

Munk, Kaj. Danish playwright, b. 13 January 1898, Maribo, d. 4 January 1944, Silkeborg.

Munk grew up in a modest and religious country home. From the age of ten the weakly boy wrote poems in the romantic style of Adam Oehlenschläger* and a nationalist "novel" prophesying Denmark as a future great power. After completing his divinity degree in 1923, Munk worked as a vicar in Vedersø until his death.

Munk's early plays already portray an antagonistic lack of reconciliation between a belief in God and prayer and a fanatical worship of the romantic hero, the virile man of action. They also demonstrate Munk's extraordinary sense of drama, which made him the most popular Danish playwright of the 1930s and a leading figure in the rejection of naturalistic theater.

Munk's so-called Dictator-plays attracted special attention. *En Idealist* (1928; *Herod the King*, 1953) brought the message that an ideal goal and its means are inseparable. Munk highly admired Mussolini and Hitler, as *Diktatorinden* (1938; The Dictator), *Sejren* (1936; The Victory), and his version of Shakespeare's *Hamlet* reveal. In *Han sidder ved smeltediglen* (1938; *He Sits at the Melting Pot*, 1953) Munk did criticize the nazi persecution of Jews, but still worshipped the virile, almost godlike Führer.

Less dynamic but more prominent in his entire production were Munk's early so-called religious plays. *Ordet* (1932; *The Word*, 1953) and *Kærlighed* (1935; Love) in particular present precise religious peasants' tableaux and consider the power of faith in modern time.

When Germany occupied Denmark in 1940, Munk protested against the national offense, without comprehending the connection between Hitler the conqueror and Hitler the Führer. Not until *Før Cannae* (1943; *Before Cannae*, 1953) does Munk imply a faint distrust in the Führer and then mild humanity prevails. The author's personal martyrdom could be viewed as a drama staged by himself; in spite of censorship he often condemned the occupation openly. On 4 January 1944 the German Gestapo arrested him in his home and killed him near Silkeborg. Although Munk became a national hero, most of his plays lost their topicality after the war and declined in number of performances.

FURTHER WORKS

Pilatus (wr. 1917; 1937); *Samson* (wr. 1917; 1949); *Operationen* (wr. 1919; 1942); *I brændingen* (wr. 1926; 1929); *Fra tidehvervet* (wr. 1928; 1948); *Kardinalen og kongen* (wr. 1929; 1948); *Havet og menneskene* (wr. 1929; 1948); *Cant* (1931; trans., 1953); *De udvalgte* (1933); *Vedersø-Jerusalem retur* (1934); *—os bærer den himmelske glæde* (1934); *Døden* (1936); *Knaldperler* (1936); *Liv og glade dage* (1936); *Himmel og jord* (1938); *Puslespil* (wr. 1938; 1949); *Fugl Fønix* (1939); *Egelykke* (1940; 1954); *Atterdag* (wr. 1940; 1949); *Navigare necesse* (1941); *Kongen* (1941); *Sværg det, drenge* (1941); *Ved Babylons floder* (1941); *Foråret så sagte kommer* (1942); *Det unge Nord* (1942); *Niels Ebbesen* (1942); *De Herrer Dommere* (1942); *Med ordets sværd* (1942); *Med sol og megen glæde* (1942); *Ewalds død* (1943); *Danmark, lidt om folk og fædreland, fortalt de kæreste af mine landsmænd, børnene* (1943); *Tre prædikener* (1943); *Den skæbne ej til os* (1944); *Saml dig Norden* (1945); *I Guds bismer* (1946); *Et norsk digt om Norge* (1946); *Så fast en borg* (1946); *Tre tusinde kroner* (1946); *Alverdens-urostifterne* (1947); *Ansigter* (1947); *Landlige interiører i lollandsk bondemål* (1948); *Naturens egne drenge* (1948); *Mindeudgave*, 9 vols. (1948–1949); *Det onde liv og den gode gud* (1951); *Vers om syndefaldet* (1951); *En dreng på Lolland* (1952); *Julevers fra Landets Kirke på Lolland* (1956).

FURTHER TRANSLATIONS

Second Book of Danish Verse, trans. Charles W. Stork (1947, 1968); *Five Plays*, ed. R. O. Keigwin (1953); *Modern Scandinavian Plays* (1954); *Contemporary Danish Plays*, ed. Elias Bredsdorff (1955; 1970); *Anthology of Danish Literature*, ed F. J. Billeskov Jansen and P. M. Mitchell (1972).

REFERENCES

Arestad, Sverre, "Kaj Munk as a Dramatist." *Scandinavian Studies* 26 (1954); Brovst, Bjarne Nielsen, *Kaj Munk—liv og død* (Viby, Jylland, 1984); Dorset, Rolf, "Kaj Munk," in *Danske digtere i det 20. århundrede*, vol. 3 (Copenhagen, 1981); Eisenberg, Christian, *Die politische Predigt Kaj Munks* (Frankfurt am Main, 1980); Fausing, Bent, "Kaj Munk og offentligheden i mellemkrigstiden," in *Litteratur og samfund i mellemkrigstiden* (Copenhagen, 1979); Harcourt, Melville, "Kaj Munk," in *Portraits of Destiny* (New York, 1966); Madsen, Børge Gedsø, "Bjørnstjerne Bjørnson's *Beyond Human Power* and Kaj Munk's *The Word.*" *Modern Drama* 3 (1960); Nøjgaard, Niels, *Ordets dyst og dåd* (Copenhagen, 1946); Schwede, Alfred Otto, *Verankert im Unsichtbaren* (Berlin, 1971); Thomas, David, "Dansk drama i skyggen af magtpolitikken," in *Tilbageblik på 30'erne*, vol. 1 (Copenhagen, 1967).

Svend Birke Espegård

Mustapää, P. (pseud. of Martti Henrikki Haavio). Finnish poet, b. 22 January 1899, Temmes, d. 4 February 1973, Helsinki.

Mustapää, the son of a minister of the Finnish Lutheran Church in western Finland, a region at times reflected in his works and his language, took a degree in folklore at Helsinki University and became a widely respected authority in his field, a professor at Helsinki University, and a member of the Academy of Finland and of numerous learned societies abroad. His scholarly works are numerous, including English (*Väinämöinen Eternal Sage*, 1952) and French (*Essais Folkloriques*, 1959) translations of some of them.

They reflect his interest in ancient Finnish myths and religion, as, for example, *Karjalan jumalat* (1959; The Gods of Karelia) or *Kuolemattonten lehdot* (1961; The Groves of the Immortal), whereas his poems are often inspired by recent folk songs of western Finland, including their typical rhythms. Ghosts and other supernatural beings appear in them, but there is mostly a slight twist in the text to indicate that they are not to be taken quite seriously. In fact, the poet seems to have a yearning for the times of myth and legend, yet he is also gently ironic about this yearning. In the first two collections, *Laulu ihanista silmistä* (1925; A Song about the Wonderful Eyes), *Laulu vaakalinnusta* (1927; A Song about the Bird Rukh), some of the poems, with a touch of the Gothic tale in them, have no variation of tone, but some others show also a lighter element.

Not all of Mustapää's poems have mythological elements in them; in some of them, small animals, a frog, a squirrel, or a grasshopper, illustrate a happy, simple way of life, as in the collection *Jäähyväiset Arkadialle* (1945; A Farewell to Arcadia), and, in others, half-humorously, half-seriously drawn characters from the Finnish countryside represent the elemental joys and sorrows of humanity. The most tragic tunes in Mustapää's works are rendered by elements from classical mythology, as in the collection *Ei rantaa ole, oi Thetis* (1948; There Is No Shore, O Thetis), where they express the futility of human effort and a longing for an unattainable beauty. One of his poems is directly called "Runon synty" (The Birth of a Poem), in *Ei rantaa ole, oi Thetis*, and the same motif is also treated in "Burjaattilainen rukous" (A Buryat Prayer), in *Linnustaja* (1952; The Fowler) and in "Lehvähiukset eli Apollonin syntymä" (Leafy Hair or the Birth of Apollo), in *Tuuli Airistolta* (1969; A Wind from Airisto), where the evanescent quality of poetry is rendered by images in which it is never directly mentioned: "She [Daphne] is a shadow / a mist only / . . . a ripple she is / a wind in the tree."

Mustapää, who, as Martti Haavio, devoted himself exclusively to scholarly research from 1927 to 1945, was rather forgotten when he began publishing again. His art was not in the spirit of the young Finnish poets of the 1950s, who brought about a thoroughgoing change in the poetry of their country, but being absolutely individual, it was also unlike the officially approved poetry of the thirties and forties and was admired by the younger generation, mostly of course for its intrinsic values, a wide emotional and intellectual appeal, a vast learning always, however, subservient to art, and a penetrating sense of humor and tragedy at the same time, all qualities that make him a truly great poet.

FURTHER WORKS

Koiruoho, ruusunkukka (1947); *Valitut runot* (1958); *Kootut runot*, 4th ed. (1973).

TRANSLATIONS

Tompuri, Elli, *Voices from Finland* (1947); *Twentieth Century Scandinavian Poetry*, ed. Martin S. Allwood (1950); Ollilainen, K. V., *Singing Finland* (1956).

REFERENCES

Ahokas, Jaakko A., "No Serious Songs: P. Mustapää, Poet and Professor." *World Literature Today* 54.1 (1980).

Jaakko Ahokas

Mykle, Agnar. Norwegian novelist and short story writer, b. 8 August 1915, Trondheim.

Mykle grew up in a bourgeois home, and received his university degree in business administration. His first book, *Taustigen* (1948; The Rope Ladder), a collection of short stories, revealed an unusual narrative talent; in a warm, sensitive prose and with the true story writer's sense of economy of style and the well-turned point, he depicted the pain of entering manhood—the themes were loneliness, guilt, and despair. One of Mykle's main theses was that the torments of adolescence were inflicted by a restrictive, taboo-ridden bourgeois society that through its false values, prejudices, and hypocrisy, destroyed all potential for openness, love, and warmth. His first novel, *Tyven, tyven, skal du hete* (1951; *The Hotel Room*, 1963) attempts to illustrate this theme, but although written with passion and flair, the novel fails to convince the reader that the young protagonist's rampant narcissism, and corresponding contempt of others, should be attributed to social causes and therefore excused. In this novel, as in the two that were to follow, *Lasso rundt fru Luna* (1954; *Lasso Round the Moon*, 1960) and *Sangen om den røde rubin* (1956; *The Song of the Red Ruby*, 1961), the outstanding feature of the protagonist's search for contact seems to be his relentless pursuit of women. In the latter novels, however, the young man's loneliness and desperation is real and near, and depicted with intensity and passion. The story of Ask Burlefot is at once an *Entwicklungsroman*, a roman à clef, and an erotic novel, and the latter two aspects of the novel led to a public discussion and a much-publicized trial for pornography (1957). Both the author and his publisher were acquitted, but Mykle's growth as a writer seemed to have been stunted in the process, and only two minor works have been published since then.

With the exception of Knut Hamsun* and Sigrid Undset,* no other Norwegian writer has reached as great an international audience as Mykle. He is a writer of uncommon talent and with a narrative vigor that is unparalleled in Norwegian literature.

FURTHER WORKS

Jeg er like glad, sa gutten (1952); *Kors på halsen* (1958); *Rubicon* (1965); *Largo* (1967).

FURTHER TRANSLATIONS

Scandinavian Review 68.4 (1980).

REFERENCES

Houm, Philip, *Ask Burlefot og vi* (Oslo, 1957); Sandborn, T. Ystaas, *Mannsrolle og kvinnesyn hjå Agnar Mykle* (Oslo, 1972).

Kjetil Flatin

Myrdal, Jan. Swedish novelist, journalist, and playwright, b. 17 July 1927, Stockholm.

Myrdal made his literary debut in the 1950s with a series of novels and plays that, however traditional in form, were nonetheless marked by the acute perceptivity, intensity, and stridency that characterize Myrdal. He is an outspoken Marxist, a writer filled with indignation, and in the 1950s his works took an increasingly critical stance toward Swedish society and the hypocrisy of its "folkhem" ideal. By the 1960s Myrdal's personal political engagement was demanding new forms of literary expression and new subject matter. His travels to the Third World catalyzed such changes in direction. In *Kulturers korsväg. Resa i Afghanistan* (1960; The Crossroads of Culture. Journey to Afghanistan) he abandons the traditional novel and through an objective discussion of history, geography, and the political situation allows the reader to see the land as if from the eyes of its inhabitants. It is a technique he would continue to develop.

Rapport från kinesisk by (1963; *Report from a Chinese Village*, 1965) is a result of such development. With its publication came both his critical recognition and his international reputation. Myrdal's search for new ways in which to handle his new subject matter—to objectively describe the *actual* life of peasants and not a Western myth—led him to adopt anthropological methods of observation. As a result, the work is based primarily upon interviews with the villagers themselves—a technique that was highly innovative at the time. *Samtida bekännelser av en europeisk intellektuell* (1964; *Confessions of a Disloyal European*, 1968), another of his most influential works, does not, however, lay any claim to objectivity and instead is written in an intensely personal, reflective style that Myrdal has also developed in autobiographical works such as *Rescontra* (1962; Journey Through) and *Barndom* (1983; Childhood). Perhaps because it gives range for both his reportorial and literary instincts, Myrdal has turned increasingly to the essay and his production in this area has been prolific, *Skriftställningar* (13 vols., 1968–1983; Writings).

With indefatigable energy, Myrdal has questioned prescribed definitions of society and of literature. Consciously overstepping the boundaries of genre, he has fused the novel, reportage, and the personal essay in an attempt to depict reality and his own time as clearly and closely as possible. He has not done it without being controversial and at times caustic. In this regard, however, he sees a worthy prototype in August Strindberg,* who like himself, through prolific production and determined engagement in social issues, contributed significantly to a continued redefinition of society and literature.

FURTHER WORKS

Folkets hus (1953); *Hemkomst* (1954); *Jubelvår* (1955); *Att bli och vara* (1956); *Badrumskranen* (1957); *Bortom berg och öknar* (1962); *Söndagsmorgon* (1965); *Turkmenistan* (1966); *Kinesisk resa* (1966); *Fallet myglaren* (1967); *Moraliteter* (1967); *Ansikte av sten* (1968); *Hjälparen* (1968); *Garderingar* (1969); *Albansk utmaning* (1970; *Albania defiant*, 1976); *Kina, revolutionen går vidare* (1970; *China: The Revolution Continued*, 1970); *Tal om hjälp* (1971); *B. Olsen löper livet ut* (1972); *Ett femtiotal* (1972); *Den onödiga samtiden*, with Lars Gustafsson (1974); *Lag utan ordning* (1975); *Karriär* (1975); *Avgörande år: svenska frågor 1975–1977* (1977); *Sidenvägen* (1977); *Indien väntar* (1980); *Strindberg och Balzac: essayer kring realismens problem* (1981); *Kinesisk by tjugo år senare: rapport med frågetecken* (1983); *En annan värld* (1984); *Ord och avsikt* (1985).

REFERENCES

Granberg, Nils, ''Ett barns funderingar återskapade med hallucinatorisk realism.'' *Folket i Bild* 15 (1982); Thygesen, Marianne, *Jan Myrdal og Sara Lidman* (Grenå, 1971).

                                                                    Deborah Regula

N

Nedreaas, Torborg. Norwegian novelist and short story writer, b. 13 November 1906, Bergen.

As a youth, Nedreaas proved an eager and accomplished piano student. For a while she was employed as a music teacher. During World War II, she and her family kept a low profile due to their Jewish ties. They moved from the city and managed a largely hand-to-mouth existence. By this time Nedreaas was divorced, with two young sons, and for income had begun submitting stories to weekly magazines. Success with this popular mode encouraged her to develop her expressive talent. In 1945 her first collection of mature short stories appeared; *Bak skapet står øksen* (Behind the Closet Stands the Axe) is concerned with the problems of ordinary people in an occupied country and is noteworthy for its nuanced picture of human responses to violence and betrayal. Since 1947, Nedreaas has made her home near Oslo.

Best known of Nedreaas's works are the three volumes about Herdis and her passage from child to young adult. The first book, *Trylleglasset* (1950; The Magic Glass), presents the children of a Bergen neighborhood, just prior to the outbreak of World War I; serving to unify the stories is the presence of Herdis, the little girl with the unruly red hair. We follow Herdis through the war years and the divorce of her parents in the fine novel *Musikk fra en blå brønn* (1960; *Music from a Blue Well*, 1988). In response to the shattered world around her, Herdis cultivates a fantasy realm, symbolized by the seductive music that calls to her from the blue well. The blue well is a source of aesthetic inspiration, but it also represents dangerous personal isolation. Herdis must fight her way, both literally and figuratively, up into the world from within the well. The story continues in *Ved neste nymåne* (1971; At the Next New Moon) with Herdis entering puberty and struggling for independence. Her sense of uniqueness and her rebellion linger as a promise of things to come at the close of the novel. The Herdis books offer a picture of female maturation that is strongly realistic, enveloped by tangible emotions, and interwoven with sensitively conceived symbols.

Nedreaas's other major novel, *Av måneskinn gror det ingenting* (1947; *Nothing Grows by Moonlight*, 1987), is the wrenching account of a woman who has been broken, both physically and psychologically. Repeated abortions, poverty, and a destructive love relationship emerge as factors that crippled her potential even as a teenager. The details unfold during an all-night conversation with a compassionate stranger. In her short stories, too, Nedreaas addresses questions of human relationships and understanding. Some of the most successful stories may be found in the collection *Stoppested* (1953; Stopping Place). Nedreaas has also written commentaries and plays for Norwegian radio.

In describing her focus as a writer, Nedreaas has commented: "Literature has its richest sources in people's everyday lives. Everyday life is our whole life. It contains flashes of powerful joys and tragedies. . . . Even death belongs to our everyday" (*Nordens svale*, p. 114). Through her prose she seeks to communicate in a direct, sensual fashion, to reach readers through their pores, in the way that music does. Powerful emotions flow from her pen, but these are carefully sculpted and do not approach sentimentality. An avowed communist, Nedreaas usually relegates political views to the undercurrent of her narratives. She writes principally of love and its demands, labeling compassion and solidarity as central virtues. Her most comfortable form has been the short story; even the novels tend to be structured as a series of brief episodes. Nedreaas has earned an excellent reputation in Scandinavia. Now that her major works are starting to appear in English translation, her international reputation will no doubt grow accordingly.

FURTHER WORKS

Før det ringer tredje gang (1945); *De varme hendene* (1952); *Den siste polka* (1965); *Noveller i utvalg* (1966); *Ytringer i det blå* (1967); *Det dumme hjertet* (1976).

FURTHER TRANSLATIONS

Norseman 3 (1948); *Literary Review* 12.2 (1969); *Scandinavian Review* 69.4 (1981); *Slaves of Love and other Norwegian Short Stories*, ed. James McFarlane (1982); *An Everyday Story*, ed., Katherine Hanson (1984).

REFERENCES

Eriksen, Helge, *Nedreaas* (Oslo, 1979); Modal, Bitten, ed., *Nordens svale* (Oslo, 1976); Nedreaas, Torborg, "On the Short Story." *Kenyon Review* 31.4 (1969).

Janet Rasmussen

New Norwegian. Since 1929 *nynorsk* (New Norwegian) has been the official name of one of the two forms of written Norwegian, the other being *bokmål* (Book Norwegian). As a result of Norway's long union with Denmark, Danish remained the sole written language in Norway even after the 1814 dissolution of the union. Spurred by romantic, democratic, pedagogical, and social ideas, a strong interest in a written Norwegian language developed around 1850. After a thorough collection and study of Norwegian dialects (the results of which appeared in two important works: *Det norske Folkesprogs Grammatik* (1848; Grammar of Spoken Norwegian) and *Ordbog over det norske Folkesprog* (1850; Dictionary of Spoken Norwegian), Ivar Aasen* presented a new norm for written Norwegian in 1850. Until 1929 this norm was called *landsmål* (language of the country). Aasen based the new language on the common features found in the Norwegian dialects, with particular attention given to the archaic traits in the dialects of western Norway and the mountain regions. In the collection of texts entitled *Prøver af Landsmaalet i Norge* (1853; Specimens of *Landsmål* in Norway) Aasen gave the new language concrete form, and in a series of popular poems (collected in the book *Symra*, 1863) he presented literature in the new language. He was soon to be followed by such writers as A. O. Vinje* (1808–1870) and Arne Garborg* (1852–1924), who used *landsmål* in poetry, essays, and fiction.

In 1885 it was established by law that the two language forms were to be officially equal, and since 1892 parents have been free to choose their children's language of instruction in schools. Today about 17 percent of Norwegian schoolchildren use *nynorsk* as their primary language.

Through a series of spelling reforms during the 1900s, numerous features from East Norwegian and Trøndelag dialects have been incorporated into the standard *nynorsk*, and a gradual rapprochement between *nynorsk* and *bokmål* has taken place.

The 1900s have witnessed a remarkable growth in the amount of poetry and fiction written in *nynorsk* by such novelists as Olav Duun,* Kristofer Uppdal,* Tarjei Vesaas,* Edvard Hoem,* and Kjartan Fløgstad,* and poets like Olav Aukrust,* Olav Nygard, Tore Ørjasæter,* Halldis Moren Vesaas,* Aslaug Vaa,* Tor Jonsson,* and Olav H. Hauge,* to mention a few. Literature in *nynorsk* shares certain features, one of which is that the majority of the authors have their roots in the countryside. While *nynorsk* prose has strong ties with ordinary working life in the country, much of the lyric is associated with folk poetry and nature, with such central themes as national tradition and philosophical and religious experiences. In epic writing, drama, and poetry, *nynorsk* literature has preserved traditional poetic forms but also shown itself to be quite open to modern forms of expression and renewal, particularly during the past decade. However, within literary history it is not customary to treat *nynorsk* and *bokmål* literatures as two separate categories.

REFERENCES

Dale, Johannes, *Nynorsk dramatikk i hundre år* (Oslo, 1964); Fet, Jostein, ed., *New Norse Literature in English Translation 1880–1982* (Volda, 1985).

Leif Mæhle

Nexø, Martin Andersen (assumed name of Martin Andersen). Danish novelist, short story writer, poet, essayist, and public speaker, b. 26 June 1869, Copenhagen, d. 1 June 1954, Dresden.

Nexø, who was born into the poorest of the proletariat, spent his boyhood in the town of Nexø on the island of Bornholm, where his father was a stonecutter and where, after serving as a herdsboy on farms, Nexø became an apprentice cobbler in the town of Rønne. He attended the island's folk high school and then Askov Folk High School on the Jutland peninsula. After beginning to teach, he fell ill and received monetary help to visit Southern Europe to regain his health. After some time in Italy and Spain he returned to Denmark, where—under the assumed name of Nexø—he published stories from Bornholm and from his travels in Spain. In Spain Nexø's sympathy for the proletariat was solidified, and his admiration for those anarchists who longed for revolution against their "capitalist oppressors" was awakened. In the years preceding World War I he hoped that the workers of the world would unite to keep the peace. In the meantime, Nexø, who tried to make his works as timely as possible, often waited to see political developments before finishing a work in progress. His deep political involvement led him to sympathize, in turn, with anarchists, syndicalists, social democrats, and communists. The new Soviet Republic became his ideal, and he judged countries, parties, groups, works, and men according to the attitude they expressed toward the Russian experiment. Nexø came to be considered an unpatriotic propagandist. Between world wars, he married for the third time, lived briefly in Germany, tried to contribute to the establishment there of a publishing company for proletarian works, traveled in Russia, and generally became an unofficial spokesman for disaffected or unemployed workers. When he openly championed the Russian cause against the Finns in the Winter War, his works fell into further disrepute. During his arrest, release, and escape from internment during the Nazi occupation of Denmark, public admiration for him grew. At war's end he returned to a hero's welcome but soon again offended his countrymen's sensibilities. His last years were spent in East Germany.

The philosophy Nexø reflected in his early short stories and novels fluctuated between the decadence of the fin de siècle (e.g., the novel *Dryss*[1902; Waste]) and the crassest realism (e.g., the tragicomic novel *Familien Frank* [1901; The Frank Family] or one of his first famous tales "Lotterisvendsken" [1898; The Lottery-Swede, from *Skygger* (Shadows)]). In an attempt to portray the struggle taking place between the various factions of the proletariat and their employers in the industrialized cities and to express the hopes of the common people, Nexø wrote *Pelle Erobreren* (1906–1910; *Pelle the Conqueror*, 1913–1916), about a leader from Nexø's own background who leads the people in attaining their rights as workers. Nexø describes Pelle as an early social democrat, suffering through the labor strife that leads to the unionization of the urban proletariat and its first gains in wages, unemployment compensation, and limitation of the workday. The book ends with Pelle's advocating that labor's problems be mediated, cooperatives be widely instituted, and workmen live in "garden-cities."

Nexø's next major work, *Ditte Menneskebarn* (1917–1921; *Ditte*, 1920–1922), appeared in five volumes. Ditte, an illegitimate child, is brought up "to serve" others. She is a part of the rural proletariat but ends her work-worn days at the age of twenty-five in the abject poverty of Copenhagen's slums. The realism with which Pelle's and Ditte's lives are treated is offset by the use of fairy-tale motifs, biblical allusions, and even myth; and Ditte comes to represent the "divinely self-sacrificing" in the caring spirit of the poor.

Although Nexø's own early years had much of the fairy tale about them, he stressed in his *Erindringer* (1932–1939; Memoirs) the very real hardships, but unabated hopefulness, of his childhood, youth, and early manhood—all those years formative for him as a budding author. Finally, Nexø continued the tale of labor's struggles and the story of his life in fictionalized form in the three-volume work *Morten hin Røde* (1945–1957; Morten the Red). Unfortunately, Nexø no longer used the fairy tale of youthful hopes and dreams to enliven his tale, and his lack of differentiation between major crises and minor details in the ups and downs of political life, both at home and abroad, actually deadens the narrative. The book lacks spirit and optimism, and Nexø died before it could be completed. The last volume was edited for publication after his death.

Later, Nexø's many letters and speeches were also published. They, together with his fiction, travel descriptions of Spain and Russia, his one play, and his poetry, ensure his recognition as one of the most prolific and widely known of modern writers—*Pelle* appears in twenty-one languages. Nexø's works constitute a record of the lives of the Danish proletariat from feudalism to capitalistic industrialization to "revisionist" socialism. Nexø's works evince his ambiguity about the materialistic joys of the bourgeoisie and about the desirability of having women as equal partners within the labor movement. He was suspicious of the freedoms demanded both sexually and intellectually by modern women and preferred in women—as in countries—the quality of motherliness above all others. When describing the utopia he envisioned for the industrial worker, he portrayed cooperatives and suburbs, but made inconsistent declarations about the necessity of using violence in attaining those material goals. Actually, he longed for international brotherhood, prosperity, and peace. Through his alter ego, Morten, Nexø portrayed the role of a true author as that of a lamp guiding the proletariat to the altar of communism—whose blessing was admittance to the Promised Land. That age-old dream of living "happily ever after" is the golden promise of the fairy tale, and Nexø, who is receiving growing critical attention, remains widely and affectionately read.

FURTHER WORKS

Det Bødes der for— (1899); *En Moder* (1900); *Muldskud* (1900, 1905); *Soldage* (1903; Days in the Sun, 1929); *Af Dybets Lovsang* (1908); *Barndommens Kyst* (1911); *Bornholmer Noveller* (1913); *Folkene paa Dangaarden* (1915); *Under Himlen den Blaa* (1915); *Dybhavsfisk* (1918); *Undervejs* (1919); *De tomme Pladsers Passagerer* (1921); *Muldskud*, 3 vols. (1922, 1924, 1926; or *Samlede Fortællinger*, 1926); *Mod Dagningen* (1923); *Digte* (1926; rev. ed., 1951); *Midt i en Jærntid* (1929; *In God's Land*, 1933); *De sorte Fugle* (1930; extracts in *Under the Open Sky*, 1938); *To Verdener* (1934); *Mod Lyset*

(1938); *Breve til en Landsmand* (1945); *De tomme Pladsers Passagerer* (1946); *Taler og Artikler*, ed. Børge Houmann, 3 vols. (1954–1955); *Ungdom og andre Fortællinger* (1954); *Lykken og andre Fortællinger* (1955); *Breve fra Martin Andersen Nexø*, ed. Børge Houmann, 3 vols. (1969–1972); *Vejen mod Lyset*, ed. Jørgen Aabenhus (1979).

FURTHER TRANSLATIONS

American-Scandinavian Review 11.6 (1923); *Denmark's Best Stories*, comp. Hanna Astrup Larsen (1928); *American-Scandinavian Review* 18.8 (1930); *Great Love Stories of All Nations*, ed. Robert Lynd (1932); *Modern Danish Authors*, ed. E. Heepe and N. Heitberg (1946); *Modern Danish Writers*, issue of *Adam—International Review* 16.183 (1948); *Contemporary Danish Prose*, ed. Elias Bredsdorff (1958); *An Anthology of Scandinavian Literature from the Viking Period to the Twentieth Century*, ed. Hallberg Hallmundson (1965); *Anthology of Danish Literature*, ed. F. J. Billeskov Jansen and P. M. Mitchell (1972).

REFERENCES

Gemzøe, Anker, *Pelle Erobreren* (Copenhagen, 1975); Houmann, Børge, *Martin Andersen Nexø bibliografi*, 2 vols. (Odense, 1961–1967); Houmann, Børge, *Martin Andersen Nexø og hans samtid*, 2 vols. (Copenhagen, 1981–1982); Ingwersen, Faith, and Niels Ingwersen, *Quests for a Promised Land* (Westport, Conn., 1984); Johanson, Joel M., "Pelle, the Conqueror." *Sewanee Review Quarterly* 27 (1919); Le Bras-Barret, Jacqueline, *Martin Andersen Nexø—écrivain du prolétariat* (Paris, 1969); Madsen, Clara, "The Social Philosophy of Martin Andersen Nexø." *Scandinavian Studies and Notes* 12 (1932); "Martin Andersen Nexø: A Symposium." *Scandinavica* 8.2 (1969); Slochower, Harry, "On Martin Andersen Nexø's *Pelle the Conqueror*," in his *Mythopoesis: Myth Patterns in the Literary Classics* (Detroit, 1970); Slochower, Harry, "Socialist Humanism: Martin Andersen Nexø's *Pelle the Conqueror*," in his *Three Ways of Modern Man* (New York, 1937).

Faith Ingwersen

Nielsen, Hans-Jørgen. Danish journalist and editor, essayist and critic, novelist, and poet, b. 23 June 1941, Herlufmagle.

Nielsen belongs to the 1968 generation whose youth coincided with the economic boom in the West with its abundant possibilities for education and jobs, its cornucopia of commodities and, not the least, cultural activities and entertainment. The open and receptive Nielsen reflects this as he became personally involved in language, literature, art, music (especially rock), philosophy, psychology, sociology, sports (especially soccer), and politics.

Nielsen began his career of writing and cultural activities with the study of and experimentation with language—its properties and relation to the world. In connection with his reproduction into Danish of Japanese haiku, he emphasized their worldliness in contrast to the traditional self-centeredness of Danish poetry. The pursuit of this objective line led Nielsen to concretist poetry with its technical, even mechanical (for example, computer produced) approach to language that regards language as an autonomous entity separate from the world in which it functions. This view of language is, of course, influenced by the revolutionary development of the technical means of communication.

Nielsen has written extensively for the daily newspaper *Information* and the literary magazine *Vindrosen*, and he was editor of the avant-garde publication *Ta '*. In the 1970s, his increased essayistic production included contributions to the periodicals *Mak* and *Hug*, and he became editor of *Politisk Revy*. His writing, which came to include psychological aspects and current Marxist thinking, is distinguished by his ability to interrelate various subjects and to view them in a larger context—especially his essays on mass culture, popular music, and sport.

Fodboldenglen (1979; The Soccer Angel) is an important novel as it synthesizes the experiences of the 1968 generation who can identify with the characters' hard-won knowledge about manhood, sexual roles, and friendship. The good times have come to an end, but the matured self-reflection of the author and his generation will prove a fruitful asset for the future.

FURTHER WORKS

Haiku (1963); *at det at* (1965); *Konstateringer* (1966); *"Output"* (1967); *"Nielsen"* og *den hvide verden* (1968); *fra luften i munden*. (1968); *Diletariatets prokatur eller Overdadaens utrolige gerninger* (1969); *"Den mand der kalder sig Alvard"* (1970); *Modersmålets pris* (1972); *Oprøret i Kronstadt*, with Niels Brunse (1973); *Billeder fra en verden i bevægelse* (1980); *Hælen* (1981); *Efter den fjerde whisky trak han pistolen* (1982).

TRANSLATIONS

Contemporary Danish Poetry, ed. Line Jensen et al. (1977).

Charlotte Schiander Gray

Nordbrandt, Henrik. Danish poet, b. 21 March 1945, Copenhagen.

Nordbrandt studied Oriental languages at the University of Copenhagen and has adapted Turkish poems and tales into Danish. In the last fifteen years he has lived much of his time in Turkey, Greece, and Italy.

His first book, *Digte* (1966; Poems), won Hvedekorn Jubilæum's Prize. Since that time he has produced a steady stream of poetry of the highest quality and has received numerous grants, awards, and prizes that have enabled him to devote himself full-time to his writing. In 1980 he was awarded the Grand Prize of the Danish Academy.

Nordbrandt's early poems in the modernist-surrealist tradition are skillfully and tightly written, but it was with *Opbrud og ankomster* (1974; Departures and Arrivals) that he came fully into the highly distinctive voice and style that has made him one of Denmark's most original poets; one might say the most original anti-Danish poet, as he rejects the cold rationality of the North for the mysticism and sensuosity of Greece and Turkey. He is an admirer of Constantine Cavafy, one of the strongest individual voices in modern Greek literature, and Ymus Emre, the mystical Turkish poet of the Middle Ages, and though he is in no way imitative of either poet, he utilizes the strengths of both—an idiomatic, muscular speaking voice, and a blend of the concrete and the mystical in a poetry that often evokes unusual moods and startling psychic directions, often making us see definitively the indefinability of experience. His references to Athens, Ithaca, and Byzantium are not literary references or symbols but actual places encountered by a traveler who is seeking something that even he himself does not fully understand: "No matter where we go, we always arrive too late / to experience what we left to find" (*Selected Poems*, p. 24). There is an element of nihilism in Nordbrandt's poetry for which the poem becomes a frame and a repudiation, turning nothingness into a startling window on the world. As early as *Syvsoverne* (1969; The Late Sleepers) Nordbrandt quotes chapter 11 of the *Tao Te Ching*: Doors and windows are set into a house, / and the space makes us able to use it. / Thus we gain *something*. / But it is nothing that makes us able to use it.

No discussion of Nordbrandt's work would be complete without mentioning his love poetry. He has written some of the most interesting, most lyrical, and most modern love poems of our time. Poems such as "Now I Can No Longer Use You" (*Selected Poems*, p. 77) express with wit and originality a profoundly felt love that recognizes the essential otherness and integrity of the beloved: Now I can no longer use you / as a rose in my love poems: / you are much too large, much too beautiful / and much, too much yourself.

Nordbrandt is now generally recognized in Denmark as the most accomplished poet of his generation.

FURTHER WORKS

Miniaturer (1967); *Omgivelser* (1972); *Ode til blæksprutten og andre kærlighedsdigte* (1975); *Glas* (1976); *Guds hus* (1977; *God's House*, 1979); *Istid* (1977); *Breve fra en ottoman* (1978); *Spøgelseslege* (1979); *Rosen fra Lesbos* (1979); *Forsvar for vinden under døren* (1980); *Udvalgte digte* (1981); *Armenia* (1982; *Armenia*, 1984); *Finckelsteins blodige bazar* (1984); *84 Digte* (1985); *Violinbyggernes by* (1985); *Håndens skælven i november* (1986); *Under mausolæet* (1987).

FURTHER TRANSLATIONS

Selected Poems (1978); *Scandinavian Review* 69.4 (1981); *Seventeen Danish Poets*, ed. Niels Ingwersen (1981).

REFERENCES

Schnack, Asger, "Henrik Nordbrandt" in his *Portræt* (Copenhagen, 1981); Söderberg, Lasse, "Henrik Nordbrandt," in *Danske digtere i det 20. Århundrede*, vol. 5 (Copenhagen, 1982).

Alexander Taylor

Nordenflycht, Hedvig Charlotta. Swedish poet, b. 28 November 1718, Stockholm, d. 29 June 1763, Skolandet.

Like most girls of the new Swedish nobility, Nordenflycht received no formal training, although she was a precocious and avid reader. But she was fortunate enough to attach herself to men who guided her reading and acted as her mentors. Widowed in her twenties, she settled in the capital, and soon became one of its leading literary figures.

Nordenflycht wrote occasional poems to wealthy patrons, epic poems to celebrate historical events, moral and satiric treatises in verse, and a defense of women in response to Jean-Jacques Rousseau. She was, as Henrik Schück points out, Sweden's first feminist, and Oscar Ivar Levertin* said about her: "With Nordenflycht the Swedish woman enters into the national literature . . . [hers] is the first voice among many mute ones." Her writings reflect the shift in ideas and literary sensibility that took place in the middle of the eighteenth century. On the one hand, her keen passion for knowledge led her to embrace the rationalistic and progressive ideas of the philosophers of the Enlightenment. On the other hand, she was by temperament drawn to the pietistic, sentimental strains in late eighteenth-century culture. Independently of Rousseau, she expressed a cultural pessimism that we have become accustomed to associate with his name. Nordenflycht was sensitive and impulsive, animated by strong feelings that give a tone of urgency and sincerity to her lyrics. Her reputation has varied over the years: while her contemporaries admired her intellectual, philosophical, and poetic accomplishments, the nineteenth century was often critical of her emotionalism. Feminists see in her a foremother and admire her honesty and her refusal to divorce rational thought from her emotions and her experience. Her ardent lyric poems, however, with their simple diction and sincerity of feeling have always been, and still are, universally appreciated.

FURTHER WORKS

Samlade Skrifter, 2 vols. (1924–1938); *Den sörjande turturduvan. Poesi och prosa i urval*, ed. Torkel Stålmark (1963).

REFERENCES

Axelsson, Sun, "Hedvig Charlotta Nordenflycht," in *Författarnas litteraturhistoria*, vol. 1 (Stockholm, 1977); Bergom-Larsson, Maria, "En själ som fint och starkt och ömt och häftigt känner," in *Kvinnornas litteraturhistoria*, ed. Marie Louise Ramnefalk and Anna Westberg (Stockholm, 1981); Borelius, Hilma, *Hedvig Charlotta Nordenflycht* (Stockholm, 1921); Heyman, Viveka, "Fru Nordenflycht, sökerskan," in *Kvinnornas litteraturhistoria* (Stockholm, 1981); Levertin, Oscar, *Svenska gestalter* (Stockholm, 1907).

                                                                    Joanna Bankier

Numers, Lorenz Torbjörn Gustaf Gunnar von. Finland-Swedish poet, essayist, and novelist, b. 25 January 1913, Åbo (Turku).

Even while studying at Helsinki University von Numers was writing for the newspaper *Nyland,* moving later to the Finlandia Press Agency. He worked as a journalist in Stockholm from 1946 to 1959, since when he has spent most of his time in France as cultural attaché and press counsellor.

Von Numers's sense of style was obvious even in his first poems, *Svart harnesk* (1934; Black Armor) and *Porträtt med blomma* (1936; Portrait with Flower).

Subsequently, he turned to the prose for which he is now best known. As an essayist he has shown a penchant for the "curios of cultural history," and he has established himself as an erudite stylist, well versed in European history. All his work bears witness to a painstaking attention to detail in an attempt to make his writing, including his fiction, as historically authentic as possible. On this basis he published in 1946 a novel on the life of François Villon, *Snäckans bröder* (The Brothers of the Helix), followed in 1948 by a novel of the crusades, *Spel med fyra knektar* (Game with Four Knaves).

In recent years, von Numers's erudition and familiarity with history have led him to develop his historical fiction into historical studies that read like novels. Thus, in 1980, he published *De hemliga rummen* (The Secret Rooms), a suite of essays dominated by a lengthy study of Pontus de la Gardie, the son of a French merchant who entered Swedish service and played a hand in establishing Sweden as a major power in the sixteenth century. The following year came *Paschan i onåd* (1981; The Pascha in Disgrace), a biography of an equally unusual and colorful personality, the eighteenth-century Turkish politician Ahmut Pascha, who was also French by birth, and who likewise played a part in Swedish history through his links with Charles XII.

Between these two phases, von Numers, whose sense of humor had established itself in his essays, showed himself to be a master of the satirical novel, writing on the basis of a lively ethical awareness.

Von Numers's readership is not large, perhaps because of the intricacy of his style at times, but thanks to his elegance, his learning, and his delight in using it, he occupies a position of considerable respect in Finland-Swedish letters.

FURTHER WORKS

Havslyktan (1942); *Tveskäggs krumelurer* (1943); *Vinet som kaniken drack och andra essäer* (1943); *Ordkynne* (1945); *Konungariket Mallocra* (1951); *Månen är en säl* (1952); *Basturesan* (1953); *Lara* (1954); *Den druckna myran* (1959); *Drottningens handelsmän* (1964); *Lansarna vid Jordan* (1964); *Oting* (1968); *Valda dikter* (1977).

W. Glyn Jones

Nynorsk. *See* New Norwegian.

Nyquist, Arild. Norwegian poet and novelist, b. 6 March 1937, Oslo.

Nyquist attended the College of Art and Handicraft in Oslo and for many years lived and taught as a junior high school teacher in Stamsund, Lofoten. He has written extensively in many genres, his work being a blend of poetry and prose, naivism and surrealism, satire and baroque comedy. He continuously fights the prejudices and narrow-mindedness of Norwegian private and public life, without ever turning into an overtly political writer.

His maiden work is a rather traditional portrait of childhood. In his next three books, however, Nyquist gives his imagination free rein. The fantasies in the first one are rather private and hermetic, but the second is very sarcastic and funny and the third wildly surrealistic.

In *Blæsch og andre historier* (1974; Blæsch and Other Stories) the funny stories of Nyquist's own everyday life appear for the first time in his writing, a genre that he cultivates in the collection of epistles, called *Kollvikabrev* (1978; Letters from Kollvika). His own childhood forms, moreover, the scene of some of the stories, several of which have been reprinted in the autobiographical *Barndom* (1876; Childhood).

In *R. Fortellinger for nordmenn* (1977; R. Stories for Norwegians) and *Skalden Odvar og andre svingslag* (1980; Odvar the Bard and Other Swing Blows) the author's mixture of surrealistic and satirical devices is once more the main focus of interest. Ecological values are overtly discernible in *Abborfiske i Norge* (1981; Perch Fishing in Norway), where the fact that "Abborfiske" is one of the main characters of the plot takes the reader by surprise. A new and darker mood comes to the surface in some of the stories in *På Geilo, sa Tom* (1982; At Geilo, Tom Said).

Nyquist is an imaginative and peculiar poet and storyteller who has gradually developed and refined his own original style and found his own sphere of interest, outside the mainstream of contemporary Norwegian poetry and fiction. More-over, he is one of the great humorists of the last twenty years. He has also written children's books and written and performed as a rock poet.

FURTHER WORKS

Ringer i et sommervann (1963); *Dexter & Dotater* (1970); *Frakken tegner og forteller* (1971); *Nå er det jul igjen! og andre dikt* (1972); *Abel XIV* (1973); *Eplehøst* (1974); *Fra "Feriehuset September"* (1975); *Da onkel Krokodille og fetter Bamse drog til byen* (1978); *Snekkerne kommer* (1979); *Kelner!* (1979); *Epleslang/Tomme bord* (1981); *I avisen* (1981); *Flyvende fru Rosenkranz* (1983); *Havet* (1985).

Øystein Rottem

O

Obrestad, Tor. Norwegian lyric poet and novelist, b. 12 February 1938, Nærbrø.

Obrestad writes *nynorsk* (*see* New Norwegian). He is known above all for his poetry. His first collection *Kollisjon* (Collision) appeared in 1966. He has published a new volume of poetry nearly every other year. The poetry in *Kollisjon* is rather homogeneous; the basic elements of nature, landscape reduced to its essentials interspersed with biblical and mythical connotations, prevail as far as topics and imagery are concerned. The human being is captive to those surroundings that shape him and are in turn being shaped by human impact, most of the time in a very negative manner. Already in this first collection of poetry there is much social comment and much social commitment, a trend that becomes stronger in the second book of poetry, *Vårt daglige brød* (1968; Our Daily Bread) and culminates in the third volume, *Den norske løve* (1970; The Norwegian Lion), where the poems focus entirely on the political scene in Norway, attacking the capitalistic industrial society from a Marxist point of view. The predictable happens: many of these poems, since they comment on political issues in the late sixties, are tendentious, with limited life spans. On the other hand, *Vårt daglige brød* contains some very strong poems. In the poem "Den gamle" (The Old One), the ninety-year-old grandfather lives totally in harmony with nature; his approaching death is actually described as an assimilation into nature. The existential and political problem is obvious: the simple life, the road back to nature, cannot be the solution for a very complex set of social problems. What is needed is revolution, a point Obrestad tries to make in the two collections *Sauda og Shanghai* (1973) and *Stå saman* (1974; Stand Together). Clearly those poems are best in which his Jæren background is brought to bear in convincing unromantic nature imagery. Not only does Obrestad write poetry, but he is also a very good translator of poems by such leaders of the revolution as Mao and Ho Chi Minh.

His two novella collections, *Vind* (1968; Wind) and *Tolken* (1975; The Interpreter), are symbolic, sometimes satirical visions of cultivated landscapes (Jæren the first, China and Albania the second). The first novel, *Marionettar* (1969; Puppets), describes, eloquently and lyrically, human powerlessness and dependence in today's society. The two more recent novels, *Sauda! Streik!* (1973; Sauda! Strike!) and *Stå på!* (1976; Go On), represent the author's open engagement in labor conflicts and social issues.

FURTHER WORKS

Songar: dikt i utval 1966–1978 (1978); *Vinterdikt* (1979); *Misteltein* (1987).

TRANSLATIONS

Micromegas 4.3 (1971).

Fritz H. König

Obstfelder, Sigbjørn. Norwegian lyric poet, prose writer, and playwright, b. 21 November 1866, Stavanger, d. 29 July 1900, Copenhagen.

Obstfelder was Norway's poet par excellence of the fin de siècle. He grew up in Stavanger in a family oppressed by poverty, illness, insanity, and early death, all of which immeasurably influenced his poetry of angst and unease. He completed his *gymnasium* studies in Stavanger in 1884, but then seemed unable to commit himself to any one pursuit. First he took up philology at the university in Christiania in 1886, then engineering at Christiania Technical College in 1888, and then in 1890, without completing his exams due to a nervous condition, went to Milwaukee, Wisconsin, to join his brother and to find work as an engineer. While in the United States, Obstfelder grew increasingly emotionally unstable. When he returned to Norway in August 1891, he had a complete nervous breakdown and was hospitalized for several months. His breakdown too profoundly affected his work, as he consciously used the hallucinations and nightmares he suffered then as the raw material of his later writing. He had written serious poems already in the spring of 1890, but he did not devote himself entirely to writing as a profession until after his recovery from mental illness in 1892. His major works are confined to the 1890s, and relatively speaking, they are few: a collection of poems in verse and a collection of prose poems, two short stories, a novella, three plays, a novel, and several essays and articles. Himself the personification of the alienated poet about whom he persistently wrote, Obstfelder had no permanent home, moving restlessly between the cities of the Continent and Scandinavia. He married Ingeborg Weeke, a Danish actress, in 1898, and he died at the age of thirty-three on 29 July 1900.

Obstfelder is primarily and rightly known as a lyric poet, though he discontentedly searched for the perfect literary form to express what he called "the inexpressible." His debut volume, *Digte* (1893; *Poems*, 1920), the only volume of poetry to be published in his lifetime, was hailed as "the year's biggest literary event" (*Dagbladet*, 10 December 1893). Experimental in form, its dominant themes were those that would preoccupy Obstfelder throughout his life, erotic obsession and modern alienation. The poem "Jeg ser" (I See), now the classic expression of modern alienation in Scandinavian literature, is contained in this small volume of aesthetically revolutionary poems.

The lyric subgenre that Obstfelder mastered most completely, however, was the prose poem, perfected and popularized by the French symbolists. Though only twenty-five or so in number and never published as a group until Solveig Tunold's scholarly edition of Obstfelder's *Samlede Skrifter* (1950; Collected Works), the prose poems comprise a superior part of his writings. Their free, short form was well suited to his talent and artistic aims, allowing him to use more freely the deceptively simple language that had already become his hallmark in *Digte*. The moods of the prose poems are many, but those that predominate are dark, brooding, and melancholy, the haunted visions of a lonely man.

Obstfelder also wrote short fiction, his best-known works being the short stories "Liv" (1894; Liv) and "Sletten" (1895; "The Plain," 1982), published together as *To novelletter* (1895; Two Short Stories), the novella *Korset* (1896; The Cross), and the diary novel *En prests dagbok* (1900; *A Priest's Diary*, 1987). Though their forms vary somewhat, the emphasis in all these stories is the same. Epic development is submerged in favor of a seemingly random probing of the emotional depths of the sensitive outsider who is searching for a spiritual home in a hostile world. This persona became inextricably confused with Obstfelder himself during his lifetime. To his fellow artists such as Edvard Munch, Gustav Vigeland, and Rainer Maria Rilke, who used him as a model for their works, he became a legend, a personification of the sensitive man-child both terrified and in awe of life.

Obstfelder also wrote three plays in the tradition of Maurice Maeterlinck's symbolist dramas in which dramatic action was replaced by suggestion and mood, like the fiction, favoring the unconscious life of the protagonist. *De røde dråber* (1897; The Red Drops), written with the Norwegian actress Johanne Dybwad in mind, is his most important play, though none of the plays is remarkable.

Obstfelder's short life and small production are in direct inverse proportion to his importance in Norwegian literature. He was a pioneer in the poetry of the "soul," which attempted to explore the unconscious. One of the very few Scandinavian poets who can legitimately be called a symbolist in the European tradition, he stands irrefutably as Norway's major poet of the 1890s and one of the most significant precursors of Scandinavian modernism. His works, in particular his poetry, remain relevant, speaking softly to contemporary readers of the unease of their emotional lives.

FURTHER WORKS

Esther (1899); *Efterladte Arbeider*, ed. Viggo Stuckenberg (1903); *Samlede skrifter*, ed. Carl Nærup, 2 vols. (1917); *Samlede skrifter*, ed. Solveig Tunold, 3 vols. (1950); "Seks prosastykker og et dikt," ed. Reidar Ekner, in *Basar* 1 (1978).

FURTHER TRANSLATIONS

Anthology of Norwegian Lyrics, ed. C. W. Stork (1942); *Slaves of Love and Other Norwegian Short Stories,* ed. James McFarlane (1982)

REFERENCES

Bjørnsen, Johan Faltin, *Sigbjørn Obstfelder* (Oslo, 1959); Ekner, Reidar, *En sällsam gemenskap* (Stockholm, 1967); Hannevik, Arne, *Obstfelder og mystikken* (Oslo, 1960); McFarlane, James, "Sigbjørn Obstfelder," in his *Ibsen and the Temper of Norwegian Literature* (London, 1960); Norseng, Mary Kay, "Obstfelder's Prose Poem in General and in Particular." *Scandinavian Studies* 50.2 (1978); Norseng, Mary Kay, *Sigbjørn Obstfelder* (Boston, 1982); Schoolfield, George, "Sigbjørn Obstfelder: A Study in Idealism." *Edda* 57 (1957).

Mary Kay Norseng

Oehlenschläger, Adam. Danish poet and dramatist, b. 14 November 1779, Copenhagen, d. 20 January 1850, Copenhagen.

Oehlenschläger grew up at Frederiksberg Castle where his father was a steward. His studies of law, Scandinavian history, and mythology at the University of Copenhagen were disrupted shortly after 1800. From 1805 to 1809 he traveled extensively in Germany, France, and Italy, meeting with Goethe and a number of significant romanticists. In 1809 he was appointed professor of aesthetics and in 1829 crowned with laurels in the Cathedral of Lund by the Swedish poet Esaias Tegnér* as "the Nordic prince of poets."

Introduced to German romantic philosophy and views of art by the Dano-German philosopher and scientist Henrich Steffens, Oehlenschläger abandoned working on a number of projects based on topics from Nordic antiquity. Instead, he created a new poetry collection, *Digte* (1803; Poems), which marks the first manifestation of romanticism in Danish literature. The volume contains three sections: an epic, a lyrical, and a dramatic part, mingling the genres according to the romantic concept of *Universalpoesie.* The metric ingenuity, glowing colors, and plastic lucidity of Oehlenschläger's style emerges in particular in his free re-creations of medieval ballads. The romantic element is especially noticeable in his descriptions of nature, which is perceived with a hitherto unseen freshness and spontaneity. In the best-known poem of the collection, "Guldhornene" (The Golden Horns), romanticism is expressed through a longing for the past and a glorification of the poetic genius. The pantheistic idea that all things are spiritually interrelated forms the basis for "Sancthansaftenspil" (Midsummer Night's Play). While attacking eighteenth-century bourgeois rationalism, this hilarious, poetic mixture of fantasy and parody, period picture and philosophy also stresses the three major themes of Danish romanticism: love, nature, and history as the three most valuable ways of divine expression.

In 1805 Oehlenschläger further strengthened his fame with *Poetiske Skrifter,* (Poetic Works, 2 vols.). In addition to two cycles of poems, the intention of

which is "to display nature as an annually reoccuring myth of the Divine Redeemer," the volumes contain the prose story "Vaulundurs Saga" (The Saga
of Vaulundur) and the fairy tale play "Aladdin" (Eng. trs. 1857, 1968), both
texts portraying young men in full harmony with nature and themselves. Whereas
the first work is based on Old Norse material, the forceful language of which is
magnificently rendered by Oehlenschläger, the sources of the second are the
Arabian Nights and German romantic drama. The latter provides the model for
the major contrast in Oehlenschläger's play between the petty-bourgeoisie and
the supernatural world behind which stands the basic antithesis: the battle between
good and evil, light and darkness represented by Aladdin and the sorcerer Nou-
reddin respectively. Their efforts to conquer the magic lamp, symbol of fortune
and recognizable only to the creative genius, conclude with the victory of
Aladdin, matured by adversity. The Shakespearean blank verse of the dialogue
is interspersed with a multitude of varying, brilliantly executed metrical forms,
and contributes to the sparkling life of this drama, the major work of Danish
romanticism.

During his European journey Oehlenschläger wrote *Nordiske Digte* (1807;
Nordic Poems), in which he turns from a universal to a national, Nordic romanticism. "Thors Reise" (Thor's Journey) is a mock-heroic poem based on
Snorri's *Edda* and Homer. Similarly inspired by Greek models is the fate drama
about "Baldur hin Gode" (Baldur the Good), the pious god who is destroyed
by the giants. Friedrich Schiller's dramas, however, provide the inspiration for
the tragedy "Hakon Jarl hin Rige" (*Earl Hakon the Mighty*, 1857, 1874, 1905).
In this work two opposite worldviews clash as Oehlenschläger, with striking
dramatic force, lets Hakon, the pagan chief, fight against Olaf, the future Christian king. And as in Schiller the title hero succumbs disgracefully, but he is not
struck blamelessly by fate since he invites his defeat by abuse of power and by
the rejection of humanity as represented by Olaf. Here as well as in the related
drama *Palnatoke* (1809; tr. 1855) Oehlenschläger treats his historical material
with supreme liberty in order to build up a firm dramatic plot. This time his
model is Schiller's drama of liberty, *Wilhelm Tell*. Again Oehlenschläger focuses
on a monumental clash between two major antagonists, but now it is the upright
heathen who defeats the corrupt, Christian king. In *Axel og Valborg* (1810; *Axel
and Valborg*, 1851, 1873, 1906), a drama of love, Oehlenschläger, on the other
hand, follows the unity and simplicity of structure of French classical theater,
in which the hero has to make a choice between duty and inclination. The entire
action takes place in the Cathedral of Trondheim in order to illustrate the basic
idea: the church controls the destiny of the two lovers; it separates them in life
but unites them in death.

The artist's tragedy *Corregio* (1811; tr. 1846, 1854) projects a basic problem:
the fear of audience indifference that reflects Oehlenschläger's own sentiment.
Even though external recognition was generous after his return to Copenhagen
in 1809, he was increasingly criticized by colleagues such as Jens Baggesen*
and J. L. Heiberg* for lacking dramatic force and aesthetic discipline. The quality

of Oehlenschläger's writings now became highly uneven, indeed often marred by Gothic effects and sentimentality. However, with his trilogy *Helge* (1814), the prose story *Hroars Saga* (1817; The Saga of Hroar), and the epic poem *Hrolf Krake* (1828), Oehlenschläger won a convincing victory. *Helge*, in particular, is of superb quality. It consists of two poetry cycles that provide the introduction to the Sophocles-inspired fate drama "Yrsa," which concludes the volume. The Viking hero, Helge, incurs guilt by murdering his uncle and is subsequently punished when he unintentionally marries his own daughter, Yrsa. In the following two works Oehlenschläger tells of Yrsa and her child, Hrolf, who as a representative of the humanitarian ideas of a new epoch fights barbarity but himself falls victim to evil and treason, thereby atoning for the guilt of his family.

Here as well as in the two volumes *Digtninge* (1811–1813; Works) and in the poetic summary of the *Edda, Nordens Guder* (1819; *The Gods of the North*, 1845), it becomes evident that Oehlenschläger's artistic strength lies in the realm of poetic expression. The large number of national dramas that followed with motifs from Danish history are all weakened by his urge to harmonize and mediate the dramatic conflict—a trend that evidences the increasing impact that Goethe, the classicist, had on him. Not until Oehlenschläger attempted to follow the contemporary direction in Danish literature toward a more complex, individualized character delineation did he succeed in creating two valuable works, the tragedies *Dina* (1842) and *Kjartan og Gudrun* (1848; Kjartan and Gudrun), studies of passionate female mentalties executed with considerable psychological finesse.

For the two tragedies Oehlenschläger again received that recognition that he was entitled to as the renewer of Danish literature after the Age of Rationalism and as the poet who, with Johannes Ewald* as the solitary predecessor, aroused the feeling for the national tradition. Not only did he rejuvenate or create a number of genres—the tragedy, the lyrical cycle, and the narrative poem—but he also experimented with metrical forms and rhythms, renewing poetic imagery and adding to Danish literature a vigor, fantasy, and inspiration that made him the Danish writer who has had the greatest impact on posterity.

FURTHER WORKS

Oehlenschlägers tragødier, 10 vols. (1849), 4 vols. (1879); *Oehlenschlägers digterværker og prosaiske skrifter*, 26 vols. (1851–1854, Supplement vol., 1854); *Oehlenschlägers poetiske skrifter*, ed. F. L. Liebenberg, 32 vols. (1857–1962); *Poetiske skrifter i udvalg*, 7 vols. (1896–1899); *Udvalgte Digterværker*, 7 vols. (1914); *Poetiske skrifter*, ed. H. Topsøe-Jensen, 5 vols. (1926–1930); *Breve fra og til Adam Oehlenschläger*, January 1798–November 1809, ed. H. A. Paludan et al., 5 vols. (1945–1950), November 1809–October 1829, ed. Daniels Preisz (1953–   ); *Oehlenschlägers erindringer*, 2 vols. (1950–1951).

FURTHER TRANSLATIONS

The Shepherd Boy (1828); *Aladdin or the Wonderful Lamp* (1857, 1863); *The Gold Horns* (1913); *Book of Danish Verse*, ed. Oluf Friis (1922, 1976); *A Second Book of Danish*

Verse, trans. Charles W. Stork (1947, 1968); *In Denmark I Was Born . . . A Little Book of Danish Verse*, comp. Richard P. Keigwin (1950).

REFERENCES

Andersen, Vilhelm, *Adam Oehlenschläger*, 3 vols. (Copenhagen, 1899–1900); Arentzen, Kr., *Adam Oehlenschläger* (Copenhagen, 1879); Arentzen, Kr., *Baggesen og Oehlenschläger*, 8 vols. (Copenhagen, 1870–1878); Falbe-Hansen, Ida, *Oehlenschlägers nordiske Digtning* (Copenhagen, 1921); Ingerslev-Jensen, Povl, *Den unge Oehlenschläger* (Copenhagen, 1972); Ingwersen, Niels, "The Tragic Moment in Oehlenschläger's 'Hakon Jarl Hin Rige.' " *Scandinavica* 9.1 (1970); Jørgensen, Aage V. C., *Oehlenschlägerlitteraturen 1850–1966* (Copenhagen, 1966).

Sven H. Rossel

Økland, Einar. Norwegian poet, novelist, essayist, and critic, b. 17 January 1940, Sveio.

Økland studied psychology and philology. In the mid–1960s he was a member of the group connected with the magazine *Profil*. When several of the other *Profil* members turned to Social Realism in the 1970s, Økland stubbornly followed his own modernist tracks.

He is outspokenly skeptical of literature as a medium of political propaganda. According to Økland, the task of the author is to look for what he calls the "blind spots" of existence, phenomena that cannot be fitted into any ideological and political system of thinking. His point of departure is the subjective experience of fear, isolation, and lack of freedom in modern society. But at the same time he is thematically rooted in Norwegian reality, in the life of the countryside of the west coast where he was born and raised.

His first major work, *Amatør-album* (1969; An Amateur's Album), is a mixture of lyrics, reflective prose, and authentic documents, a tearing down of the traditional genre barriers. He calls it himself a "lyrical landscape novel." Here he studies the effect of the changing landscape, environment, and nature upon the young boy's experience of his own identity. The web of themes, genres, and literary forms is even more intricate and mixed in *Gull-alder* (1972; A Golden Age), in which the same landscape of his childhood constitutes a kind of unity. In the burlesque novel *Galskap* (1971; Madness) he rewrites the myth of Hamlet, putting the hero in a modern and typical West Norwegian setting.

The three collections of poems *Bronsehesten* (1975; The Bronze Horse), *Romantikk* (1979; Nostalgia), *Blå roser* (1985; Blue Roses), with the common subtitle *Folkeminne*, treat existential as well as metapoetic themes. The underlying attitude is all the way ironical, disrespectful, ludicrous, anti-romantic and anti-political.

The assiduous essayist Økland can be studied in two solid volumes: *Skrivefrukter* (1979; Fruits of Writing) and *Nå igjen* (1982; Once More). In the 1970s he played an important role in the literary magazine *Bazar*. He has also written extensively for children, for which he has been awarded several prizes. True to his modernist, skeptical, and experimental starting point, Økland ranks among the most original writers of contemporary Norwegian literature.

FURTHER WORKS

Ein gul dag (1963); *Mandragora* (1966); *Svart i det grøne* (1967); *Vandreduene* (1968); *Georg: sit du godt?* (1968); *Aberfan* (1969); *Du er så rar* (1973); *Stille stunder* (1974); *Det blir alvor* (1974); *Den blå ringen* (1975); *Slik er det* (1975); *Kven veit?* (1976); *Ingenting meir* (1976); *Snakk med dr. Ost* (1977); *Sikk-sakk* (1978); *På frifot* (1978); *Ein god dag* (1979); *Ei ny tid* (1981); *Snøsteinen* (1982); *Her er ingen papegøye* (1984).

REFERENCE

'' 'Carry on crow—' Hovuddrag ved Einar Øklands prosa,'' in *Linjer i norsk prosa,* ed. Helge Rønning (Oslo, 1977).

Øystein Rottem

Ørjasæter, Tore. Norwegian poet and playwright, b. 8 March 1886, Sjåk, d. 1968.

Ørjasæter's earliest intention was to farm the land in the valley in which he was born and raised. A lengthy illness forced him to abandon his ambition to be a farmer. Ørjasæter attended teacher's college for a time until he devoted himself entirely to his writing. He made his debut as a poet in 1908 with the collection *Ættararv* (Heritage), followed by *I dalom* (In the Valley) in 1910. Although deeply bound to his rural roots, Ørjasæter was by no means isolated from or afraid of new impulses and ideas.

In 1913, *Gudbrand Langleite*, the first volume of an epic lyric, was published, followed in 1920 by *Bru-millom* (The Bridge Between), and in 1927 by *Skuggen* (The Shadow). Ørjasæter rewrote this trilogy, which is generally accepted as his most important work, and the new edition was published in 1941 under the single title *Gudbrand Langleite*. In it, Gudbrand must wrestle with the conflict between his roots in the land and the old traditions and his artistic spirit and new ways of life. Although it is an epic in form, *Gudbrand Langleite* also contains some of Ørjasæter's finest nature lyrics. Ørjasæter wrote four plays, of which *Christophoros*, completed in 1948, is the most important both dramatically and artistically. This work is concerned with a theme similiar to his earlier dramatic works, that of the individual's struggle for self-realization versus his feelings of responsibility to others. The central philosophical problem which appears throughout Ørjasæter's artistic work is the basic conflict between will and destiny. For Ørjasæter, there was value in the struggle itself, and he maintained an underlying optimistic belief that the will and the spirit could provide the strength to overcome destiny.

Ørjasæter's work as a poet and as a dramatist has earned him a place among the foremost writers in New Norwegian of this century.

FURTHER WORKS

Mannskvæde (1915); *Jo Gjende* (1917); *Fararen* (1922); *Eldringen* (1924); *Skiringsgangen* (1925); *Ann paa Torp* (1930); *Elvesong* (1930); *Uppheimen paa Sandnes* (1933); *Jonsokbrev* (1936); *Livet skal vinne* (1939); *Livsens tre* (1945); *Viljen og lagnaden* (1946); *Den lange bryllaupsreisa* (1949); *Svein Kvittingen* (1950); *Ettersommar* (1953); *Brudekrona* (1956); *Klårhaust* (1963); *Den lange leid* (1966).

REFERENCES

Eds. Dale, Johannes A., and Rolv Thesen, *Festskrift til Tore Ørjasæter paa 70 aarsdagen* (Oslo, 1956); Thesen, Rolv, *Tore Ørjasæter: Ei innforing i diktinga hans* (Oslo, 1935).

Torild M. Homstad

Österling, Anders Johan. Swedish poet, critic, essayist, and translator, b. 13 April 1884, Hälsingborg, d. 13 December 1981, Stockholm.

Österling's first books of poetry were published while he was studying at Lund University; they were enthusiastically received, and in 1919 Österling became a member of the Swedish Academy. Two years later he joined its Nobel Committee, and was permanent secretary to the Swedish Academy 1941–1964.

The somewhat precious aestheticism of Österling's early poetry represented the first manifestation of symbolism in Sweden, a phase that soon passed. Visits to Italy helped to strengthen the appeal that country retained for Österling throughout his long life, but *Årets visor* (1907; Songs of the Year), the work he called his "second debut," demonstrated his main strength: the ability to capture in gentle, thoughtful, and realistic verse the atmosphere of the Scanian countryside.

Some uncharacteristically turbulent verse in the following decade was due partly to Österling's horrified reaction to World War I, partly to some unhappy love affairs. He returned to what he could do best, however, in *Idyllernas bok* (1917; The Book of Idylls), which contains some of his best-known poems. His verse continued along familiar lines in the 1920s and 1930s at the same time as he was establishing a formidable reputation as a literary and drama critic in *Svenska Dagbladet*, and a translator of prose and poetry from German, French, English, Italian, and Danish. Österling's late poetry is characterized by worries concerning the future of culture, and resignation as he accepts the proximity of death and reviews a long and productive life.

Österling was for many years an influential figure in Swedish literary circles, but will be remembered as a skilled lyricist who was happiest depicting his beloved Scania in idylls which place him alongside Carl Michael Bellman* and Erik Axel Karlfeldt* as a leading exponent of the form in Swedish.

FURTHER WORKS

Preludier (1904); *Offerkransar* (1905); *Nattens röster* (1906); *Hälsningar* (1907); *Döden inkognito* (1908); *Norrlandsresan* (1908); *Bäckahästen* (1909); *Blommande träd* (1910); *Människor och landskap* (1910); *Minuter och sekunder* (1912); *Facklor i stormen* (1913); *Tidsstämningar* (1916); *Sånger i krig* (1917); *Dagens gärning*, 3 vols. (1917–1931); *De sju strängarna* (1922); *Jordens heder* (1927); *Tonen från havet* (1933); *Horisonter* (1939);

Livets värde (1940); *Årens flykt* (1947); *Vårens löv och höstens* (1955); *Dikten och livet* (1961); *Minnets vägar* (1967); *Sent i livet* (1970); *Sena dikter* (1971); *Ögonblick* (1978).

TRANSLATIONS

Mortensson, Jeffery, "Poets of Two Vintages: Anders Österling and Lars Norén." *Swedish Books* 3 (1979).

REFERENCES

Engdahl, S., *Anders Österlings ungdomslyrik* (Stockholm, 1942); Schoolfield, George, "Anders Österling: A Life for Literature." *World Literature Today* 55.2 (1981); Willers, Uno, *Anders Österling. En bibliografi 1964–1974* (Stockholm, 1974).

Laurie Thompson

Øverland, Arnulf. Norwegian poet, b. 27 April 1889, Kristiansund, d. 25 March 1968, Oslo.

Øverland's father, a ship's engineer, died early, leaving his widow in narrow circumstances; she was, however, able to support her son through school. Later he began a study of philology, which he gave up in order to devote himself to his writing. He read extensively in Scandinavian authors, being influenced especially by August Strindberg.* He was a painter as well as a poet; and in 1911, the year his first volume appeared, he exhibited his work. Volumes of poems continued to appear up until the mid-sixties, with an interval during World War II when, for his consistent attacks on Nazism, he was confined in the concentration camp at Sachsenhausen. He maintained throughout his ordeal and for the rest of his life a fervent love of the Norwegian land and its people and a belief in the strength of the Norwegian character. He was chairman of students' and authors' groups, and from 1938 he was supported by a state grant. After the war, newly married, he was granted tenancy of the Grotto, the house in Oslo which the state has made available to honor its artists.

In *Den ensomme fest* (1911; The Lonely Feast), *De hundrede fioliner* (1912; The Hundred Violins), and other volumes before World War I, Øverland's poetry is characterized by acid complaints against the vanity of life and a romantic concern with death, hunger, loss, and loneliness. In "De hundrede fioliner," which has been set to music by Eyvind Alnæs, poverty, darkness, and pain become spring, stars, and music. From the beginning, though his work may use biblical allusions, it shows simplicity and economy and a signal absence of rhetoric; he was never to accept modernist techniques that impaired clarity of statement. After World War I, *Brød og vin* (1919; Bread and Wine) manifests despair and a longing for death even more strongly than before. Øverland, however, had been angry at the Treaty of Versailles and had become a committed socialist, and in the enlarged edition (1924) his poetry takes on social concerns and attacks the church, capitalism, the use of force, and, in general, the petty bourgeoisie and its values. He was strongly opposed to Christianity. But in *Hustavler* (1929; Laws of Living), which in its clear classic beauty has been considered to contain the height of his lyrical reach, Øverland is profoundly concerned with love for fellow human beings. In the thirties the poetry takes on a sterner tone: Øverland begins to utter his grave warnings against Nazism in volumes such as *Den røde front* (1937; The Red Front), in which appeared the celebrated "You must not sleep," with its references to Nazi horrors, its terrible warnings, and its judgment: "Forgive them not; they do know what they do." When he returned from the concentration camp, Øverland published his *Vi overlever alt!* (1945; We Survive It All), which collected the poems he had issued secretly during World War II, calling on the Norwegians to resist the enemy. After the war, in *Tilbake til livet* (1946; Back to Life), his poems turned away from socialism toward metaphysical interests. His last volumes, except for an occasional outcry against political events and some dark predictions for the human race, contain the peaceful reflections of an aging man. In "Jeg går omkring" (I Walk Around) he touches things to which memories and affection are attached—a pipe, a candlestick, a blue bailing vessel, a chair, and finally, with inexpressible feelings, the hair of his wife and children. In addition to his poetry Øverland wrote two plays and, more successful than the plays, three short story collections published between 1916 and 1931, which dwelt on romantic moods of loneliness and anxiety. Among his many articles were polemics against Christianity and, in spite of his support for the Labor party, arguments favoring *riksmål* in the debate about language, attacking the proposition that the language of Oslo workers should become standard Norwegian. After the war he expressed his opposition to Russian politics.

FURTHER WORKS

Advent (1915); *Den harde fred* (1916); *Venner* (1917); *Deilig er jorden* (1923); *Samlede dikt*, 2 vols. (1924); *Berget det blå* (1927); *Gi meg ditt hjerte* (1930); *Gud plantet en have* (1931); *Jeg besverger deg* (1934); *Riket er ditt* (1934); *Samlede dikt*, enl. ed. (1936); *Noveller i utvalg* (1939); *Ord i alvor til det norske folk* (1940); *Er vort sprog avskaffet* (1940); *Utvalgte dikt*, 3 vols. (1947); *Bokmålet—et avstumpet landsmål* (1949); *Fiskeren og hans sjel* (1950); *Sverdet bak døren* (1956); *Riksmål, landsmål og slagsmål* (1956); *Den rykende tande* (1960); *På Nebo bjerg* (1962); *Livets minutter* (1965); *Samlede dikt 1911–1940* (1979); *Samlede dikt, 1945–1965* (1979).

TRANSLATIONS

American-Scandinavian Review 29.4 (1941); *Anthology of Norwegian Lyrics* (1942); Gathorne-Hardy, G. M., *The Spirit of Norway* (1944); *Scandinavian Review* 37.3 (1949); *Modern Norwegian Poems*, comp. Allwood, Inga Wilhelmsen (1949); *Twentieth Century Scandinavian Poetry*, ed. Martin S. Allwood (1950); *Life & Letters* 65.153 (1950).

REFERENCES

Bjerke, Andre, *Arnulf Øverland, vårt sprogs konservator og fornyer* (Oslo, 1965); Eide, Ann Kristin, *En bibliografi* (Oslo, 1979); Gelsted, Otto, *Arnulf Øverland* (Copenhagen, 1946); Gill, Claes, *Minnetale over Arnulf Øverland* (Oslo, 1974); Grunt, Olav P., "The Poet and the World: The Case of Arnulf Øverland." *American-Scandinavian Review* 33.3 (1945); Haakonsen, Daniel, *Arnulf Øverland og den etiske realisme 1905–40* (Oslo,

1966); Hambro, Carl, *Arnulf Øverland* (Oslo, 1984); Houm, Philip, "Arnulf Øverland." *American-Scandinavian Review* 61.3 (1973); Houm, Philip, ed., *Om bøker og forfattere* (Oslo, 1972); Longum, Leif, *Drømmen om det frie menneske* (Oslo, 1986).

Ingrid Weatherhead

Ólafur Jóhann Sigurðsson. *See* Sigurðsson, Ólafur Jóhann.

Olavus Petri. Swedish Lutheran reformer, historian, and religious writer, b. 6 January 1493, Örebro, d. 19 February 1552, Stockholm.

Olavus's father was a smith in Örebro. Both Olavus and his brother Laurentius, also a cultural figure of renown, studied at the cathedral school in Örebro. Olavus completed his studies in Wittenberg, where Martin Luther was his professor. Upon his return to Sweden, Olavus assisted Gustavus Vasa in his Protestant reforms of the Catholic church. From 1524 Olavus was the secretary for the City of Stockholm for seven years, while preaching in the City Church. He was most active in the translation of the New Testament into Swedish, published in 1526. From 1528, when he preached at the coronation of Gustavus Vasa, to 1531, when he was appointed chancellor to the king, was his most productive period. In various pamphlets he develops the idea of the Protestant church in simple, clear, and rich language.

In 1533 he incurred the wrath of the king, and left the chancellor's position. Now he devoted himself to a translation of the Old Testament, and to his most important work, *En Swensk Crönika* (A Chronicle of Sweden).

Due to Olavus's perspective on tyranny and despotism, King Gustavus did not allow the printing of this work. It circulated in handwritten copies only, and was not printed until 1818, in the annals of *Scriptores rerum Suecicarum medii aeva*.

The conflict with the king broke into the open at the meeting of the Lords of the Realm in 1540, when both Olavus and his immediate superior, Laurentius Andreae, were accused of high treason, and sentenced to death. The sentences were commuted to a severe fine, which was paid for Olavus by the burghers of Stockholm. The king tried to smooth relations by appointing Olavus inspector of the School of Stockholm in 1542, and in 1543, Olavus was appointed as vicar of Storkyrkan, where he is buried.

Olavus's strongest influence has been in history research and writing. He was the first Swedish historian to distinguish clearly between fact and fiction, between myth and historicity. Even though his major work was not published for a long time, it had profound influence through its spirit of scientific inquiry and its refusal to accept hearsay and superstition as the basis of history. Olavus's perspective was also that of the common folk, not that of the ruling class, which of course is the reason for the conflict with Gustavus Vasa. Olavus refused to accept the idea that "might makes right," and defended both in his religious writings and his historical works the right of individuals to peace and freedom from tyranny.

Among his most important religious writings are *Een handbock paa swensko* (1529); *Een lijten postilla* (1530), which contains "Een lijten catechismus"; and ahymnal, *Swenske songer eller wijsor*, probably from 1526, but extant in a reprint from 1530. The dating of his *Domareregler* is uncertain, but they were probably written during his time as city secretary. These rules for how judges should approach their duties are still reprinted in the preambles to the Swedish and Finnish Law Codes. Although Olavus's participation and contributions to the translations of the New and Old Testaments are still debated, there is no doubt of his immense importance to the formation of a Swedish language suitable for literary expression. He made it possible to write clear, honest, strong Swedish.

FURTHER WORKS

Samlade skrifter av Olavus Petri, 4 vols. (1914–1917); *Skrifter i urval*, ed. G. T. Westin (1968).

REFERENCES

Murray, R., *Olavus Petri* (Stockholm, 1952); Schück, H., *Olavus Petri* (Stockholm, 1906).

Christina Söderhjelm McKnight

Old Norse Hagiography. Throughout the Middle Ages narratives of saints' lives played an important role throughout Europe, both as vehicles for inspiring piety and as entertainment. There was generally little historical accuracy in them, filled as they were with exciting events and marvelous happenings, often with hideous tortures and bloody executions. The monotony of the stereotyped miracles, which do not vary much from saint to saint, is often relieved by folklore elements and realistic details.

Saints can be divided into martyrs (such as Saint Catherine or Saint Sebastian), whose executions are the focal points of their stories, and confessors (such as Saint Nicholas or Saint Anthony), whose pious lives and numerous miracles are described. The central figure in many narratives, the basis for which can be found in the New Testament Apocrypha, is Jesus, the Virgin Mary, or one of the Apostles. The lives of early Eastern saints (such as Saint Blasius and Saint Anthony) tend to be marked by extreme contempt for the world, while the accounts of later saints' lives tend more to stress piety and good works or proselytizing zeal. All of these types were known in Scandinavia in the Middle Ages, and as monasticism spread, many were translated from Latin into the vernacular. The lives of Scandinavia's native saints were also related, although as a rule with fewer supernatural events and less spectacular miracles.

The most important collection of saints' lives in Danish, preserved in a manuscript from around 1400, is known as *Hellige kvinder* (Holy Women). It consists of fourteen narratives, most of them about women saints, such as the Virgin Mary, Margaret, Christine, and Catherine of Alexandria. The Mariager manuscript, written in 1488, contains a Danish translation of the lives of Catherine of Siena and Saint Jerome. There are also a number of Latin accounts of Danish saints, such as King Knud (Canute), Knud Lavard, and Erik Plovpenning.

The many foreign saints' lives translated into Swedish in the fifteenth century indicate a concerted attempt to disseminate this literature among the laity. The *Fornsvenska legendariet* (Old Swedish Legendarium) was a popular collection of short saints' lives to be read on commemorative occasions. It is derived mostly from the *Legenda aurea* of Jacobus de Voragine, a thirteenth-century Italian Dominican.

Latin lives of the early Swedish saints (Botvid, Sigfrid, Erik, Bishop Henrik of Finland) are brief and simple, but those of later saints, such as Birgitta* and Nikolaus Hermansson, are longer and much more detailed. A number of them were translated into Swedish and included in late manuscripts of the *Fornsvenska legendariet*. Swedish versions of the lives of Birgitta and Katarina are found in several manuscripts.

Over a hundred saints' lives are extant in Old Norwegian or Old Icelandic, some of the favorites being those of Maria, the Apostles, Barlaam and Josaphat, Martin, Nicholas and Thomas à Becket. The earliest Norwegian vernacular manuscript, from around 1150, contains the lives of Blasius, Eustacius, and Matthew. Saints' lives continued to be translated into Icelandic from Latin and Low German until the time of the Reformation (1540).

Norwegian and Icelandic saints' lives are also extant in Norse. The favorite is Saint Olaf, about whose life a number of accounts were written, including fragments of one in the 1150 codex mentioned above. There are also sagas of each of the three Icelandic saints, Jón helgi Ögmundarson, Þorlákr, and Guð-mundr hinn góði Arason.

G. Turville-Petre contended that the early religious literature had a decisive effect upon secular saga style. While it is true that the earliest saints' lives are written in clear, simple prose much reminiscent of classic saga style, when we consider how little they are affected by Latin grammar and Latin diction, it is conceivable that they were influenced by oral saga style. Many of the later saints' lives, such as those of John the Baptist and Saint Guðmundr, were written in a more ornate style, often with interpretations derived from homiletic works, but the simple style continued to be practiced.

EDITIONS

Latin: *Bibliotheca Hagiographica latina antiquae et mediae aetatis,* ed. Socii Bollandiani, 2 vols. (Brussels, 1898–1901), Supplement (1911); *Evangelia apocrypha,* ed. C. Tischendorf, 2nd ed. (Leipzig, 1876); Voragine, Jacobus de, *Legenda aurea,* ed. Th. Graesse, 3rd ed. (Breslau, 1890); Voragine, Jacobus de, *The Golden Legend,* 2 vols. (London, 1941); *Vitae sanctorum danorum,* ed. M. C. Gertz (Copenhagen, 1907).

Danish: *De hellige Kvinder, en Legende-Samling,* ed. C. J. Brandt (Copenhagen, 1859); *Mariager Legende-Haandskrift,* ed. G. Knudsen (Copenhagen, 1917–1930).

Swedish: *Ett forn-svenskt legendarium,* ed. George Stephens and F. A. Dahlgren, 3 vols. (Stockholm, 1847–1874); *Heliga Birgittas uppenbarelser,* ed. G. E. Klemming, 5 vols. (Stockholm, 1857–1884); *Helige Mäns lefverne,* ed. R. Geete (Stockholm 1902);

Jöns Buddes bok, ed. O. F. Hultman, (Stockholm, 1895); *Klosterläsning*, ed. G. E. Klemming (Stockholm, 1877–1878).

Norwegian-Icelandic: *AM, 623, 40*. *Helgensagaer*, ed. Finnur Jónsson (Copenhagen, 1927); *Biskupa sögur*, ed. Jón Sigurðsson and Guðbrandur Vigfússon, 2 vols. (Copenhagen, 1858–1878); *Heilagra manna sögur*, ed. C. R. Unger, 2 vols. (Christiania, 1877); *Isländska handskriften No 6450 i den Arnamagnæanska samlingen*, ed Ludvig Larsson (Lund, 1885); *Íslendzk Æventyri*, ed. Hugo Gering, 2 vols. (Halle, 1882–1884); *Maríu saga*, ed. C. R. Unger, 2 vols. (Christiania, 1871); *Postola sögur*, ed. C. R. Unger (Christiania, 1874).

REFERENCES

Bekker-Nielsen, Hans, "Legender—Helgensagaer," in *Norrøn fortællekunst* (Copenhagen, 1965); Bekker-Nielsen, Hans, "On a Handlist of Saints' Lives in Old Norse." *Mediaeval Studies* 24 (1962); Brix, Hans, "Oldtidens og middelalderens litteratur i Danmark," in *Litteratur-historie A: Danmark, Finland og Sverige*, ed. Sigurður Nordal, Nordisk Kultur, vol. 8, pt. A (Stockholm, 1943); Delahaye, H., *Les légendes hagiographiques*, 4th ed. (Brussels, 1955); Gad, Tue, *Legenden i dansk middelalder* (Copenhagen, 1961); Jónsson, Finnur, *Den oldnorske og oldislandske litteraturs historie*, 2nd ed., vol. 2 (Copenhagen, 1923); *Kulturhistorisk leksikon for nordisk middelalder* (Copenhagen, 1956–1978); Lehmann, Paul, *Skandinaviens Anteil an der lateinischen Literatur und Wissenschaft des Mittelalters* (Munich, 1936–1937); Lundén, Tryggve, "Medeltidens religiösa litteratur," *Ny illustrerad svensk litteraturhistoria*, ed. E. N. Tigerstedt, vol. 1 (Stockholm, 1955); Paasche, Fredrik, *Norges og Islands litteratur inntil utgangen av middelalderen*, 2nd rev. ed. (Oslo, 1957); Pipping, Rolf, "Den fornsvenska litteraturen," *Litteraturhistorie A* (see Brix); Rosenfeld, Hellmut, *Legende* (Stuttgart, 1961); Schier, Kurt, *Sagaliteratur* (Stuttgart, 1970); Turville-Petre, Gabriel, *Origins of Icelandic Literature* (Oxford, 1953); Widding, Ole, "Jærtegn og Maríu saga. Eventyr," in *Norrøn fortællekunst* (Copenhagen, 1965); Widding, Ole, Hans Bekker-Nielsen, and L. K. Shook, "The Lives of the Saints in Old Norse Prose. A Handlist." *Mediaeval Studies* 25 (1963).

Henry Kratz

Old Norse Poetry. Old Norse poetry was, with few exceptions, recorded in Iceland during the thirteenth and fourteenth centuries, with oral antecedents stretching back as far as several centuries. Division into two sorts—eddic and skaldic—is conventional despite lack of medieval evidence for such classification. Both eddic and skaldic verse share such formal features as division into strophes and structural use of alliteration and stress rather then metrical feet, and both rely on features of diction employing replacement of nouns (i.e., kennings) and tend toward scenic presentation of their material. However, some meters are typically eddic and some skaldic; skaldic poems are transmitted with poets' names, whereas eddic poems are anonymous; and skaldic poems tend to be occasional, whereas eddic poems tell timeless narratives. Single occasional verses are in skaldic form in family sagas and kings' sagas but in eddic form in legendary sagas (*fornaldarsögur*).

The term *eddic* is a misnomer. It dates from the modern discovery of the main manuscript of eddic poetry, now called "Codex Regius," by the Icelandic bishop Brynjólfur Sveinsson in 1643. He attributed the book to Sæmundr Sigfússon the Learned, the eleventh-century founder of Icelandic historiography, and called it Sæmundr's *edda* because of superficial similarity to the *Edda* of Snorri Sturluson* (ca. 1225). Although neither the attribution nor the comparison is justifiable, the work is still sometimes called *Sæmundar edda* (Sæmundr's Edda) or the "Elder Edda" (i.e., older than Snorri's). "Poetic Edda" is a more accurate designation, although the manuscript does contain some prose.

Codex Regius of the Poetic Edda contains twenty-nine poems about gods and heroes. It dates from the latter part of the thirteenth century and appears to be a copy of a manuscript from the middle of that century. The existence of another manuscript containing all or part of eight poems in a more random order suggests that Codex Regius is the result of a conscious redaction. Besides these two manuscripts, a few others contain similar poems, and related poetry is frequently embedded in legendary sagas.

Each eddic poem has its own textual history. Guesses at dating eddic poems range from the period of Germanic migrations (fourth to sixth centuries A.D.) to the thirteenth century, and scholars have localized various eddic poems to areas as geographically remote as Greenland and Sweden. A consensus would put the origin of most poems to the end of the Viking Age in Norway or Iceland.

Codex Regius begins with the greatest poem of the Norse Middle Ages, *Vǫluspa* (The Sibyl's Prophecy), in which a sibyl recounts the history of the gods and the cosmos, from beginning to end (Ragnarǫk) and subsequent rebirth. Odin, the chief of the Norse mythic pantheon, is the central character of the next poems. *Hávamál* (Words of the High One) appears to be an amalgamation of gnomic verse with several myths of Odin, including his acquisition of the mead of poetry and his self-sacrifice; and *Vafþrúðnismál* (Lay of Vafthrudnir) and *Grímnismál* (Lay of Grimnir) pit Odin in verbal duel with a giant and a human king respectively. These poems catalog much mythic lore. *Fǫr Skírnis* (Skírnir's Journey) details Skírnir's expedition to giantland to woo a giantess for his master, Freyr. *Hárbarðsljóð* (Song of Harbard) presents a verbal duel between Odin and the god Thor, but in the following poem, *Hymiskviða* (Lay of Hymir), Thor plays a more customary role by obtaining a huge cauldron for the gods and killing its giant owner. The same theme is played out in the obviously young poem *Þrymskviða* (Lay of Thrym), an amusing account of Thor's expedition to giantland, disguised as the goddess Freyja, to regain his hammer. In *Alvíssmál* (Words of All-Wise) Thor is again involved in a verbal duel, in this case with a dwarf who desires Thor's daughter in marriage. The trickster-god Loki is the main character of *Lokasenna* (Loki's Flyting), in which he reviles and tells home truths about the assembled gods. Among these mythological poems is *Vǫlundarkviða* (Lay of Volund), an account of Wayland the smith's cruel vengeance against King Niðuðr.

Roughly the second half of Codex Regius is given over to eighteen heroic poems, like the mythic poems gathered in cycles. As the mythic poems tell of the family of gods called *aesir*, so the heroic poems are all linked to a single family, the Volsungs, and the heroic cycles are therefore joined. The first three poems, *Helgakviða Hundingsbana* (2 vols., Lays of Helgi Hunding's Slayer) and *Helgakviða Hjorvarðssonar* (Lay of Helgi Hjorvardsson) make up the first cycle, after which the hero Sigurd dominates. *Grípisspá* (Grípir's Prophecy) predicts his fortune; *Reginsmál* (Words of Regin), *Fáfnismál* (Words of Fafnir), and *Sigrdrifumál* (Words of Sigrdrifa) tell of his youth and heroic exploits, and *Brot af Sigurðarkviðo* is a fragment of a more summary lay of Sigurd. Between *Sigrdrifumál* and *Brot* a gathering of eight leaves has been lost. Comparison with *Volsunga saga*, which paraphrases Codex Regius at this point, makes it possible to reconstruct the contents of this section; it summarized Sigurd's career, but the actual poetic form of the poem(s) lost remains a matter of conjecture. Following Sigurd's demise, the poems turn to his ladies, Brynhild and Gudrun. The latter is the focus of *Gudrúnarkviða*, 2 vols., three "lays of Gudrun," and she is a main character in *Atlakviða* and *Atlamál*, which recount the fall of the Burgundians Gunnarr and Hǫgni and Gudrun's murder of her husband Atli (Attila the Hun). The last two poems, *Guðrúnarhvǫt* and *Hamðismál*, play out the final vengeance taken by her sons on Jǫrmundrekkr (Ermanaric).

The so-called *Eddica Minora* (the title derives from the edition by Andreas Heusler and Wilhelm Ranisch) are also heroic: poems embedded in legendary sagas. At least in their present form these sagas are late, but many of the poems are thought to be much older. Among the most interesting of the *Eddica Minora* are the "Battle of the Goths and Huns," which seems to present very old Germanic tradition; the *Bjarkamál*, said to have been recited before battle to incite warriors to great deeds; "Heiðrek's riddles," the only verse riddles in Norse; and the *Tryggðamál*, quasi-legal verse. These give some idea of the variety of purposes that eddic verse might serve.

In its subject matter heroic eddic poetry, at least, has analogues in other older Germanic languages. The principal eddic meter, *fornyrðislag* (ancient meter), is a direct descendent of the common Germanic meter that may be reconstructed through comparison of these older poetries. The chief feature of this meter was alliteration, which linked into one long line two half-lines divided by a caesura. Only stressed syllables bore this alliteration; unstressed syllables and syllables before the first stressed syllable of the half-line were metrically irrelevant. Each half-line had two stressed syllables, and the first stressed syllable of the second half-line ordinarily bore alliteration, as did at least one stressed syllable in the first half-line. The following is an example of the eddic realization of this system:

Hljóðs bið ec *all*ar   **Helg**ar *kind*ir
meiri ok **minn**i   **mǫg**u *Heim*dalar.

Stressed syllables with alliteration appear here in bold face; other stressed syllables are in italic.

Fornyrðislag stanzas contain four long lines. In the middle of each stanza there is usually a sense pause. Division into stanzas is a Norse innovation.

The other important eddic meter, *ljóðaháttr* (chant meter), is also a Norse innovation. Here an ordinary long line is followed by a truncated long line with only three stresses and no caesura. Here is an example:

Deyr *fé*,   **dey**ja *froendr*,
    deyr **sialfr** it **sam**a.

Two such couplets make up a strophe.

As noted above, a number of features distinguish skaldic poetry from eddic poetry. Skaldic meters count all syllables, not just stressed syllables, and they keep careful track not only of alliteration but also of internal rhyme and assonance and of each half-line's cadence. Here is half of a skaldic stanza in the classic meter, *dróttkvætt*, or court meter (set, as is customary, by half-line rather than full line).

Fulloflug let **fjall**a
framm haf-Sleipni þramma
Hilldr; en **Hropts** of gildar
hjalmelda mar felldu.

Here again bold face indicates the alliteration; but note too the internal rhyme—assonance in the odd lines (e.g., *full-fjall*), full rhyme in the even lines (e.g., *framm-þramm*). Also characteristic is the trochaic cadence at the end of each line.

A literal translation of the passage, although nearly incomprehensible, will give some notion of the complex word order typical of skaldic poetry: " [The] full-powerful caused of-the-mountains forth [the] sea-Sleipnir to surge Hildr; but Hroptr's wielders of-helmet-flames [the] horse felled." The context is as follows: the poet describes the launching of the ship Hringhorni at Baldr's funeral by a giantess. She had arrived riding a wolf, which Odin's retainers killed. In more normal English, the stanza says: "the mighty Hildr' [valkyrie] of the mountains [i.e., giantess] caused the Sleipnir [famous horse] of the sea [i.e., ship] to surge forward; Hroptr [Odin]'s wielders of helmet-fire [battle] [i.e., warriors], killed the horse [i.e., wolf].

Inspection of the translation will reveal the most important aspect of skaldic diction, the substitution for a noun of another noun or noun phrase. Examples of the former include *Hildr*—the name of a valkyrie—here to be understood simply as "woman," and *mar*, "horse," for "wolf." The noun-phrase substitutions are called *kennings*. This passage exhibits three: "valkyrie of the mountains" [giantess]; "horse of the sea" [ship]; and "wielders of helmet-fire" [warriors]. The last is actually a three-part kenning: fire of helmets is battle, and wielders of battle are warriors. Kennings of up to six parts are attested, and substitution (such as *Hildr* for "woman") can occur at any point.

Skaldic poems are traditionally divided between *drápur* (sing. *drápa*) and *flokkar* (sing. *flokkr*). The *drápa* is a poem of a certain length, ornamented with one or more *stef* (refrains), formulas repeated within the strophe (unlike, say, ballad refrains). The less ornate *flokkr* lacked the *stef* and was essentially just a group of strophes on the same subject.

Clearly this verse remains at a considerable distance from reality. Its images operate not so much on a principle of similarity as of discordance. Noun substitutions occur, to be sure, within a limited range of semantic fields—man, woman, weapon, and so forth—and kennings fall into relatively predictable patterns, but the verse draws attention away from its immediate subject rather than toward it. The phenomenon seems comparable or parallel to Viking Age plastic art, which transformed zoomorphic forms into elaborate and ornate patterns of lines very far from direct representation. Gripping beasts and skaldic poems suggest a highly intellectual view of art, although some observers have sought the origins of kennings in religious language or other taboos.

Producing skaldic verse was obviously a craft, although we have little indication that skalds underwent formal training. It would seem likely, too, that appreciation of skaldic verse may also have involved some kind of practice or even training. Thirteenth-century Icelandic sagas contain a few incidents turning on someone's inability to understand a skaldic poem, but mostly they take for granted audiences' perception. Sagas also show skalds producing single occasional stanzas on the spur of the moment; these "loose" stanzas (*lausavísur*) make up a significant part of the corpus.

Longer poems, too, were for the most part occasional. There are poems in praise of living monarchs' deeds and newly departed ones' lives, and other poems retell the stories behind scenes carved on shields or other decorations. After the conversion to Christianity, poets composed devotional verse in skaldic forms, and the occasional nature of the genre began to fade. Besides Christ, the Virgin Mary, many saints, and some Icelandic bishops were celebrated in skaldic poems.

The transmission of authors' names with many skaldic poems makes it possible to date and localize them. The earliest known skald is Bragi the Old, who lived during the middle of the ninth century. He was among the retinue of a king Bjǫrn, whose seat has been placed anywhere between Norway and Russia. Bragi's nationality is unknown, but other early skalds were almost certainly Norwegian, and the form flourished in Norway during paganism. It became, however, an increasingly and finally wholly Icelandic phenomenon. Snorri Sturluson may have revived skaldic verse during the early thirteenth century in Iceland, and its final fluorescence occurred there in the great religious *drápur* of the fourteenth century.

Skaldic poetry therefore enjoyed at least as long a life as did eddic poetry, if not a longer one; and certain skaldic features were retained in the popular Icelandic *rímur*, a form in use into this century. It has never been conclusively demonstrated that skaldic and eddic poetry appealed to different social classes or that the same poets could not compose in both forms. For obvious reasons, however, skaldic poetry has not been as widely known outside Scandinavia as eddic poetry. Romantic poets like Thomas Gray and Johann Gottfried von Herder translated eddic poems, and the number of accomplished poets essaying such translation has grown. The latest addition to their number is W. H. Auden.

EDITIONS

Boer, R. C., *Die Edda mit historisch-kritischem Commentar*, 2 vols. (Haarlem, 1922); Bugge, Sophus, *Norrœn fornkvædi: Islandsk samling af folkelige oldtidsdigte om nordens guder og heroer almindelig kaldet Sæmundar Edda hins fróða* (Oslo, 1867; repr. 1965); Detter, Ferdinand, and Richard Heinzel, *Sæmundar Edda mit einem Anhang herausgegeben und erklärt*, 2 vols. (Leipzig, 1903); Dronke, Ursula, *The Poetic Edda*, vol. 1: *Heroic Poems* (Oxford, 1969); Helgason, Jón, *Eddadigte*, Nordisk filologi A4. 7–8, 3 vols. (Copenhagen, 1951–1952); Heusler, Andreas, and Wilhelm Ranisch, *Eddica Minora: Dichtungen eddischer Art aus den Fornaldarsögur und anderen Prosawerken* (Dortmund, 1903); Jónsson, Finnur, *Den norsk-islandske skjaldedigtning*, 4 vols. (Copenhagen, 1912–1915); Kock, Ernst A., *Den norsk-isländska skaldediktningen*, 2 vols. (Lund, 1946–1949); Kuhn, Hans, *Die Lieder des Codex Regius nebst verwandten Denkmäler*, vol. 1: *Text*, 5th ed. (Heidelberg, 1983; 1st ed. Gustav Neckel); Sijmons, B., and Hugo Gering, *Die Lieder der Edda*, Germanistische Handbibliothek 7. 1–5, 3 vols. (Halle/Saale, 1903–1931).

TRANSLATIONS

Bellows, Henry Adams, *The Poetic Edda, with Introduction and Notes*, 2 vols. (1923, 1969); Hollander, Lee M., *The Skalds: A Selection of Their Poems, with Introduction and Notes* (1945; repr. 1968); Hollander, Lee M., *The Poetic Edda, with Introduction and Explanatory Notes*, 2nd ed. (1962); Taylor, Paul B., and W. H. Auden, *The Elder Edda: A Selection* (New York, 1969; repr. 1970); Terry, Patricia, *Poems of the Vikings: The Elder Edda* (1969).

REFERENCES

Frank, Roberta, *Old Norse Court Poetry: The Drottkvætt Stanza*, Islandica 42 (Ithaca, 1978); Frank, Roberta, "Skaldic Poetry," in *Old Norse-Icelandic Literature: A Critical Guide*, ed. Carol J. Clover and John Lindow; Hallberg, Peter, *Old Icelandic Poetry* (Lincoln and London, 1975); Helgason, Jón, "Norges og Islands digtning," in *Litteraturhistorie: Norge og Island*, ed. Sigurður Nordal, Nordisk kultur, vol. 8B (Copenhagen, 1953); Heusler, Andreas, *Die altgermanische Dichtung*, 2nd ed. (Darmstadt, 1957); Harris, Joseph, "Eddic Poetry," in *Old Norse-Icelandic Literature: A Critical Guide*, ed. Carol J. Clover and John Lindow, Islandica, vol. 45 (Ithaca, 1985); See, Klaus von, *Skaldendichtung: Eine Einführung* (Munich and Zurich, 1980); Turville-Petre, Gabriel, *Skaldic Poetry* (Oxford, 1976).

John Lindow

Olofsson, Georg. *See* Stiernhielm, Georg.

Olsson, Hagar. Finland-Swedish critic, novelist, essayist, and dramatist, b. 15 March 1893, Kustavi, d. 21 February 1978, Helsinki.

A daughter of a Lutheran minister, Olsson grew up in rural vicarages, first in the Åland Islands and from 1906 in Räisälä on the Karelian Isthmus. After a student examination in 1913, Olsson moved to Helsinki to pursue studies at the university. Driven by an insatiable intellectual curiosity, she had read widely, albeit unsystematically, ever since her teenage years. As the leading literary critic from 1918 of the Swedish-language daily *Dagens Press* (and later of *Svenska Pressen*), she had an opportunity to keep abreast of the most recent intellectual and literary trends at home and abroad. Even more importantly, her position enabled her to influence the domestic literary scene.

Like many of her generation, Olsson rejoiced in the fast-paced intellectual tempo of the times and looked forward to a promising future with eager anticipation. Within art these sentiments were most adequately communicated by the Russian futurists and the German expressionists. Olsson became the chief spokesperson and theorist for these schools of thought in Finland. She was among the founding members of the two short-lived but important literary periodicals *Ultra* (1922) and *Quosego* (1928–1929), whose contributors included Elmer Diktonius,* Edith Södergran,* Rabbe Enckell,* and Gunnar Björling,* all names that have later become synonymous with Finland-Swedish modernism. The most significant of Olsson's protégés was Edith Södergran. Because of poverty and illness the young poet had lived in virtual isolation in the Karelian village of Raivola since the Russian Revolution in 1917. Until Södergran's death in 1923, Olsson was virtually her sole link with the outside world. Their intense correspondence, published by Olsson in 1955, gives a vivid illustration of the intellectual atmosphere of the period.

Although the emotional intensity of literary expressionism and emphasis on the universal rather than the individual appealed to Olsson, she never espoused the cynicism of some of the movement's practitioners. Her debut novel, *Lars Thorman och döden* (1916; Lars Thorman and Death), already exhibited a definite mystical quality, and Olsson remained preoccupied with the mystery of death and the search for a collective human soul throughout her life. In her dramas she was among the first in Swedish-language literature to experiment with expressionistic techniques, for example, in *Hjärtats pantomin* (wr. 1927, pub. 1962; Heart's Pantomine). Olsson regarded art as an essential element of social discussion; it was to take a stand on the issues of the day. As the most urgent of these issues she regarded the growing threat of war in the late 1920s and woman's role in society. Frequently, the two concerns merge in her works. In the 1928 drama *S.O.S.* the protagonist, a young woman, finds her calling in life by joining the pacifist cause championed by a scientist who has invented the ultimate poison gas. After a change of heart, the man destroys the coveted chemical formula and is subsequently sought by the authorities as a traitor of the fatherland. In *Lumisota* (Snowball Fight), Olsson's only Finnish-language drama, her reading of the political pulse assumes prophetic proportions. Written during the spring and summer of 1939, some six months before the outbreak of the Finno-Russian Winter War, *Lumisota* correctly identifies the dilemma of a small neutral nation squeezed between the demands of two superpowers and ominously predicts the land requests that were soon to be made by the Soviet Union. In the fall of 1939 the rehearsals were stopped by direct governmental intervention, and the play wasn't staged until 1958.

The most noteworthy of Olsson's novels is the partly autobiographical *Chitambo* (1933), which charts the maturing process of a young woman, Vega Maria, in the pre–World War I years from childhood via a failed love relationship to her final embracement of David Livingstone's words, "I shall open the way to the inner parts or perish," which to the protagonist signify the necessity for an individual, motivated by a collective love for humanity, to transcend personal desires in an effort to assist mankind. The modernist element in the novel consists of the interplay between two time levels with the frame story assessing past events as they are reported in the enclosed main narrative. As her name indicates, Vega Maria is a battleground for conflicting desires: her mother's meek Mary-nature and her father's bold dreams of adventure and discoveries, which, her father later claims, are inappropriate for a girl. Although Olsson deplores woman's powerless position, she goes beyond traditional feminist demands for equality just as she in her adoption of the Livingstone words had transcended a search for personal happiness.

Olsson's work as a literary critic and mentor of young modernists constitutes her lasting contribution to posterity. Her sharp intellect, clear vision, and astute assessment of older writers as well as of contemporary colleagues render many of her essays classic. Feminist literary critics of the 1970s and 1980s have paid homage to her perceptive articles about a number of notable women, for example, Queen Christina, Cora Sandel,* and Victoria Benedictsson.* In 1969 Olsson was granted an honorary doctorate in philosophy by the University of Helsinki.

FURTHER WORKS

Själarnas ansikten (1917); *Kvinnan och nåden* (1919); *Ny generation* (1925); *Mr. Jeremias söker en illusion* (1926); *På Kanaanexpressen* (1929); *Det blåser upp till storm* (1930); *Det blåa undret* (1932); *Arbetare i natten* (1935); *Träsnidaren och döden* (1940; *Woodcarver and Death,* 1965); *Rövaren och jungfrun* (1944); *Jag lever* (1948); *Kinesisk utflykt* (1949); *Kärlekens död* (1952); *Tidiga fanfarer och annan dagskritik* (1953); *Hemkomst* (1961); *Tidig dramatik* (1962); *Tidig prosa* (1963); *Möte med kära gestalter* (1963); *Drömmar* (1966); *Ridturen och andra berättelser* (1968).

REFERENCES

Enckell, O., *Den unga Hagar Olsson* (Stockholm, 1949); Fridell, Lena, *Hagar Olsson och den nya teatern* (Göteborg, 1973); "Hagar Olsson: 1893–1978," *Books from Finland* 12.1 (1978); Petherick, Karin, "Four Finland-Swedish Prose Modernists." *Scandinavica* 15. Supplement (1976); Schoolfield, George C., "Hagar Olsson's *Chitambo*: Anniversary Thoughts on Names and Structure." *Scandinavian Studies* 45.3 (1973); Stormbom, Nils-Börje, "Inward Journey: The Works of Hagar Olsson." *American-Scandinavian Review* 52.3 (1964); Törnqvist, Egil, "Hagar Olsson's First Play." *Scandinavica* 15. Supplement (1976); Varpio, Yrjö, *Hagar Olssonin näytelmä S.O.S. (1928) ja sen suhde ekspressionismiin* (Tampere, 1975).

Virpi Zuck

P

Paal, Peter. *See* Elster, Kristian Mandrup.

Pakkala, Teuvo. Finnish novelist, short story writer, playwright, editor, and translator, b. 9 April 1862, Oulu, d. 7 May 1925, Kuopio.

Although Pakkala was born into the old Frosterus family, which included the eighteenth-century churchman and early shaper of the Finnish language Juhana Frosterus, his early childhood was spent in poverty-stricken surroundings. He was accepted into the *lyseo* (senior high school), but spent his summers and youthful years in hard manual labor, keeping company with log-rafters, tar-burners, and other backwoods people, absorbing the details of their lives and the patterns of their speech. During his university years he came under the influence of the Norwegian writers Henrik Ibsen,* Bjørnstjerne Bjørnson,* Alexander Kielland,* and Jonas Lie.* During this time he published some translations and also his own first book. At the end of the 1800s he did editorial work for two newspapers and more translations, until precarious finances led him to a job as a traveling rope salesman. He finally accepted a job teaching Finnish and French. His varied experiences provided rich material for his writing, which ranged from early realistic works portraying working people, to musical comedy, to short stories about children, to experimental psychological works.

Pakkala's early works exhibit a keen ear for and appreciation of the folk dialects he heard during his stints of physical labor, and the themes of these works handle the problems of working-class people, in the impassioned social realistic style of the early Minna Canth.* Gradually Pakkala turned from strict social realism to a psychological approach, realized most successfully in his short stories about children. He understands and skillfully portrays the behavior and the underlying emotions and thought processes of children, unweakened by sentimentality or value judgments. Themes in Pakkala's works anticipate the psychological theories of Sigmund Freud, at a time when little or nothing was known of his work in Finland. The story "Veli" (Brother) is still considered one of the finest short stories in Finnish.

FURTHER WORKS

Lapsuuteni muistoja (1885); *Oulua soutamassa* (1885); *Vaaralla* (1891); *Elsa* (1894); *Lapsia* (1895); *Tukkijoella* (1896); *Pieni elämäntarina* (1903); *Pikku ihmisiä* (1913); *Kirjeet 1882–1925*, ed. Maija-Liisa Bäckström (Helsinki, 1983); *Väliaita ja muita kadonneita kertomuksia*, ed. Maija-Liisa Bäckström (1986).

TRANSLATIONS

Finnish Short Stories, ed. Inkeri Väänänen-Jensen and K. Börje Vähämäki (1982).

REFERENCES

Sarajas, Annamari, "Joel Lehtosesta Antti Hyryyn," in *Suomen Kirjallisuus*, vol. 5 (Helsinki, 1965); Tarkka, Pekka, *Suomalaisia nykykirjailijoita* (Helsinki, 1980).

Donna Palomäki

Palm, Göran. Swedish poet, novelist, and social critic, b. 3 February 1931, Uppsala.

Palm began his literary career with an irreverent attack on the modernist poetry of the preceding generation. He was instrumental in ushering in the so-called New Simplicity school, which advocated a poetry that would reflect the realities of society and quotidian existence by means of a language that could be understood by as many people as possible. Literary conventions stood in the way of communication of raw experience and had to be demystified, as they were in Palm's programmatic poem "The Sea":

> I stand in front of the sea.
> There it is.
> There is the sea.
> I'm looking at it.
> The sea. Well, yes. It's like at the Louvre.

The avowed purpose of the new poetry was to overcome the feeling of isolation that threatens the artist, who operates within modernist literary conventions and communicates only with an elite, in order to allow him to make contact with the outside world and with the larger community.

An important figure in Swedish radicalism of the 1960s, he reached a large audience through his books of social criticism. His critique of the hidden middle-class ideology in the Swedish welfare state, and of the ingenousness with which the West exploits the Third World, was widely influential. His account of the year he spent being employed as an ordinary worker at L. M. Ericsson, the Swedish phone company, was also an important and controversial document.

In the 1970s Palm devoted himself mainly to political journalism. However, in a volume of poetry published in 1971, his preoccupation with the irrational side of existence indicates that along with social indignation, he also has a fine ear for the complexities of the human psyche and its irrationality, which makes him a unique figure among the radicalized poets and critics of the 1960s. The book is a collection of notes, reflections, fragments, sallies, and miniature essays, exploring the unconscious and half-conscious in obvious disappointment over the purism of the left that had found in Palm one of its most combative and intelligent champions.

WORKS

Hundens besök (1961); *Världen ser dig* (1964); *En orättvis betraktelse* (1966; *As Others See Us*, 1968); *Indoktrineringen i Sverige* (1968); *Vad kan man göra?* (1969); *Grädd-vargen*, with Siw Wideberg (1970); *Varför har nätterna inga namn?* (1971); *Ett år på LM* (1972); *Bokslut för LM* (1974); *En by i Turkiet*, with Lüfti Özhök (1975); *Dikter på vers och prosa* (1976); *Kritik av kulturen* (1978).

FURTHER TRANSLATIONS

Two Swedish Poets, Gösta Friberg, Göran Palm (1974); *The Flight from Work*, abridgement of *Ett år på LM* and *Bokslut för LM* (1977).

REFERENCES

Hagefors, Lennart, "Göran Palm och verkligheten: Några synpunkter på dikter på vers och prosa." *Bonniers Litterära Magasin* 46 (1977); Platen, Magnus von, et al., "Göran Palms dikt 'Havet' och de sju uttolkarna." *Svensk Litteraturtidskrift* 36 (1974); Stark, Ulf, "Mystik och klartext." *Ord och Bild* 71.4 (1962); Stendahl, Brita K., "In Sweden Everybody Reads the Bulletin." *Books Abroad* 42.2 (1968).

Joanna Bankier

Pálsson, Gestur. Icelandic short story writer, poet, and journalist, b. 25 September 1852, Miðhús, d. 19 August 1891, Winnipeg.

After attending the Latin School in Reykjavík, during which time he wrote romantic poems and stories, few of which have ever been printed, Pálsson left for Copenhagen to study theology. There he came under the influence of Brandesian realism and, together with three other Icelanders, responded by publishing the journal *Verðandi* (1882). Returning to Iceland, he founded the newspaper *Suðri* (1883–1886) in which he argued both the social and literary aspects of the realist cause, appealing for educational reform, printing his own stories, and acknowledging through essays and translations his debt to Georg Brandes,* Alexander Kielland,* and Ivan Turgenev. Disheartened by his country's self-satisfaction, which he attacked in sharply critical lectures, Pálsson left for Winnipeg in 1890, the year before his death at thirty-eight, to edit the newspaper *Heimskringla*.

Pálsson's first published story, "Kærleiksheimilið" (1882; "Home of Charity," 1902), the finest original piece in *Verðandi*, shows him already to be a master of realism. Set in rural Iceland, the story depicts a home without charity in which a self-righteous matron in collusion with a hypocritical pastor forces her son to abandon the girl who is carrying his child—an act that leads to the girl's suicide and clarifies the moral weakness and religious pretense of the principals. As in Pálsson's later fiction, the style is reportorial, and the characters essentially types. The energy lies in the poignancy of situation, the penetrating social criticism, and the shrewd irony. In 1888, Pálsson published his only separate volume of stories, *Prjár sögur* (Three Stories), which contains two of his finest novellas: " Tilhugalíf" (Engagement), an urbane reworking of the motifs of "Kærleiksheimilið," and "Vordraumur" (Spring Dream), the fullest statement of Pálsson's ideals in his fiction.

Pálsson is Iceland's foremost proponent of realism, whose journalism and fiction, which is generally stronger than his poetry, are thoroughly complementary. Both are informed by ardent social criticism and increasingly bleak pessimism.

FURTHER WORKS

"Hans Vöggur," in *Suðri* (1883); "Uppreistnin á Brekku," in *Suðri* (1883); "Skjóni," in *Suðri* (1884); "Sveitsæla," in *Suðri* (1885); "Sagan af Sigurði formanni," in *Iðunn* (1887; "The Tale of Sigurður the Fisherman," in *Icelandic Poems and Stories*, ed. R. Beck, 1943); *Lifið i Reykjavík* (1888); *Menntunarástandið á Íslandi* (1889–1890). No edition of Pálsson's works is complete. The standard is *Ritsafn*, 2 vols. (1952); the best edition of the stories is *Sögur*, ed. Sveinn S. Höskuldsson (1970).

FURTHER TRANSLATIONS

Weekly Free Press (Winnipeg) 8 and 15 (January 1902).

REFERENCES

Einarsson, Stefán, *History of Icelandic Prose Writers 1800–1940* (Ithaca, 1948); Höskuldsson, Sveinn Skorri, *Gestur Pálsson: Ævi og Verk*, 2 vols. (Reykjavík, 1965).

George S. Tate

Paludan, Jacob. Danish novelist and essayist, b. 7 February 1896, Copenhagen, d. 26 September 1975, Copenhagen.

Paludan was the son of the literary historian Julius Paludan. He completed training as a pharmacist in 1918. An early collection of verse confirmed for him that poetry was not his forte. A journey to Ecuador and the United States in 1920–1921 and his stay in New York resulted in a rejection of Americanism, that is, materialism. In this respect Paludan perceived the New World with its influence on Europe in the manner of Knut Hamsun,* the earlier Thomas Mann (*Bekentnisse eines Unpolitischen*), and Hermann Hesse. It was a European phenomenon and it ran directly counter to Johannes V. Jensen's* affirmation of American vitalism a generation earlier (*Hjulet*, 1905).

Paludan's conservative stance is reflected (with one exception) in his ensuing novels, in *De vestlige veje* (1922; The Western Ways), with its direct attack on America, and in *Søgelys* (1923; Searchlight), where scorn is heaped on Danish conditions, to wit the shoddy press, women's emancipation, and current literature. *En vinter lang* (1924; Winter Long), with its psychological analysis of its characters, retreats from topical criticism. But the attack returns in two later novels, in *Fugle omkring fyret* (1925; Birds around the Lighthouse), which pits technology, progress, and greed for profit on the one hand against nature and man inclined to caution on the other. *Markerne modnes* (The Earth Is Ripening) of 1927 revives the rejection of modern woman and plumps for the gentle and yielding woman of former times.

Paludan's final novel and his major work is *Jørgen Stein* (1932–1933; tr., 1966), a generational novel. The new generation accepts the ensuing chaos and abandons all sense of responsibility. The central character, Jørgen, however, remains caught between old and new: he knows the old ideals are gone forever, yet he refuses to go along with the new cynicism and materialism. He remains an individualist and seeks succor in marriage and individual responsibility.

After 1933 Paludan abandoned the writing of novels and concentrated on the production of essays and aphorisms.

FURTHER WORKS

Urolige sange (1923); *Feodor Jansens Jeremiader* (1927); *Landet forude* (1928); *Aaret rundt* (1929); *Tanker om bagtanker* (1937); *Som om Intet var hændt* (1938); *Fra Amerika til Danmark* (1943); *Søgende aander* (1943); *Landluft* (1944); *"Mit kaktusvindu"; Mandens blads satiriske kavalkade* (1944); *Bøger paa min Vej* (1946); *Orfeus i bogverdenen* (1946); *Prosa* (1946); *Facetter* (1947); *Han gik ture* (1949); *Skribenter paa yderposter* (1949); *Retur til barndommen* (1951); *Fremad til nutiden* (1953); *Smaa aproposer* (1953); *Bøger, poeter og stilister* (1954); *Sagt i korthed 1929–1954* (1954); *Litterært selskab* (1956); *Den lille bog om de gode glæder*, ed. (1956); *Prosa* (1956); *Flere gode glæder*, ed. (1957); *Skribent at være* (1957); *Glæde over Danmark*, ed. (1958); *Røgringe* (1959); *En kunstsamlers meditationer* (1960); *Landveje og tankeveje* (1963); *Under regnbuen* (1964); *Mørkeblaat og sort* (1965); *Oluf Høst* (1966); *Siden De spørger—og andre Omkredsninger* (1968); *Her omkring Hjørnet her blæser det mindre* (1969); *Draabespil* (1971); *Skrivebord og stjernehimmel* (1972); *I høstens manefase* (1973); *Sløret Sandhed* (1974); *Vink fra fjern virkelighed* (1975); *Låsens klik: lidt af en livsregister* (1976).

REFERENCES

Frederiksen, Emil, *Jacob Paludan* (Copenhagen, 1966); Heltberg, Niels, "Jacob Paludan." *American-Scandinavian Review* 40.2 (1952).

Otto M. Sorensen

Paludan-Müller, Frederik. Danish poet, b. 7 February 1809, Kerteminde, d. 28 December 1876, Copenhagen.

Paludan-Müller studied law at Copenhagen University, but never entered the legal profession, turning to writing as early as 1831. In 1833 Paludan-Müller published his first major work, the verse novel *Danserinden* (The Dancer), in which he established himself as a realist writing in a romantic verse form. The work won considerable public acclaim for its portrayal of a charming but weak-willed central character. Even in his early works Paludan-Müller showed a preoccupation with death, and this theme became more significant in the principal works of his manhood, all written after a serious illness.

From an early period Paludan-Müller showed an interest in mythological themes, first *Amor og Psyche* (1834; Cupid and Psyche) and then *Venus* (1841), *Tithon* (1844), and *Dryadens Bryllup* (1844; The Wedding of the Dryad). In *Venus* he emerges as a moralist condemning sensual love, at the same time showing a realist's ability to portray precisely that; the preoccupation with death is further developed, and the work expresses a certain sense of fatalism. The same themes are taken up again and further expanded in *Tithon*.

Paludan-Müller's most important work was the verse novel *Adam Homo* (1841–1849; *Adam Homo*, 1981), written entirely in the ottava rima that he had used in *Danserinden*—with which it also shows a thematic affinity in its portrayal of a weak character. *Adam Homo* depicts the life of a man who deserts his own innate ideals and rises materially while falling morally. The main female figure is Alma, whom he deserts, but who achieves harmony through suffering and becomes the vehicle of Paludan-Müller's moral thesis that real happiness is achieved only through renunciation. She is ultimately the instrument of Adam's salvation after death. Despite a close link with the Copenhagen of Paludan-Müller's day, *Adam Homo* has a general significance that has maintained its place as one of the Danish masterpieces of the nineteenth century.

In his late work Paludan-Müller returned to the mythological themes, further developing his idea of the rejection of sensual pleasure and the need to sacrifice and renounce. The theme is fully worked out in *Ivar Lykkes Historie* (1866–1873; The Story of Ivar Lykke), which depicts a life opposite to that of Adam Homo, in which the central figure gains in moral stature as he fails on the material plane.

Paludan-Müller now stands as one of the great writers of the Johan Ludvig Heiberg* school, a man with a profound sense of form, whose undoubted moralizing is accompanied by a personal conviction born of personal trial. *Adam Homo* still belongs to the best-known Danish classics, though the moral element does tend to overshadow the starkly realistic traits that the novel also contains.

FURTHER WORKS

Raab til Polen (1831); *Kjærlighed ved Hoffet* (1832); *Fire romanzer* (1832); *Zuleimas Flugt* (1835); *Poesier* (1836–1838); *Trochæer og Jamber* (1837); *Abels Død* (1845); *Luftskipperen og Atheisten* (1853); *Tre Digte* (1854); *Nye Digte* (1861); *Paradiset* (1862); *Ungdomskilden* (1865; *The Fountain of Youth*, 1867); *Tiderne Skifte* (1874); *Adonis* (1874).

FURTHER TRANSLATIONS

Book of Danish Verse, ed. Oluf Friis (1922, 1976).

REFERENCES

Brandes, Georg, *Samlede Skrifter,* vol. 2 (Copenhagen, 1899); Haugsted, Mogens, "Frederik Paludan-Müllers prosaiske arbejder." *Studier fra Sprog- og Oldtidsforsking* 49.182

(1940); Kristensen, Sven Møller, *Digtning og livssyn* (Copenhagen, 1959); Jansen, F. J. Billeskov, *Poetik*, vol. 2 (1964).

W. Glyn Jones

Panduro, Leif. Danish novelist and television dramatist, b. 18 April 1923, Copenhagen, d. 16 January 1977, Asserbo.

Panduro was reared by relatives. His mother was mentally ill. His father was executed as a nazi sympathizer by the Resistance. A Resistance member himself, Panduro was accidentally shot on the day of Danish liberation. Suffering from neuroses, he underwent psychoanalysis and wrote as therapy. Many of his works deal with rejection, insanity, identity, and the Danish experience during World War II. Panduro practiced dentistry until 1962 when he abandoned the profession to devote his full energies to literature.

Neither Panduro's first novel, *Av, min guldtand* (1957; Ow, My Gold Tooth), light-hearted vignettes about life in the Danish provinces, nor his second, *Rend mig i traditionerne* (1958; *Kick Me in the Traditions*, 1961), a humorous narrative about the tribulations of adolescence, prepared the public for the direction his later works were to take. *De uanstændige* (1960; Those Who are Indecent), a disturbing novel that grapples with the weighty issues of right versus wrong as well as with the more elusive questions of normal versus abnormal, represents Panduro's breakthrough as a socially concerned writer. Central to this work as well as to his later novels is the confrontation of the "normal" and the "abnormal" elements in society: the former are often either shallow opportunists or cynical villains, and the latter, natural, guileless innocents. Panduro's novels and short stories frequently have an aura of unreality, as if one were dealing more with "types" than with actual human beings.

In his television dramas Panduro deftly interweaves realistic character portrayal with contemporary social issues. *Farvel Thomas* (1968; Goodbye, Thomas) records the psychological disintegration of the middle-aged male divorcé. *Bertram og Lisa* (1974; Bertram and Lisa) silhouettes the professional success of unambitious Bertram against the background of small-town politics and marital crises.

Many of Panduro's figures are outsiders, either having been rejected by others or having voluntarily placed themselves at the periphery of society. The former are often driven to despair while trying to establish human ties. The latter observe the world's "drama" as detached spectators. When they become active participants in life, however, they suffer discomfiting reverses.

Panduro wished not to condemn but rather to understand human obsessions and excesses; consequently, even his most unrepentant or unprepossessing characters are treated sympathetically.

Because of his ability to write clearly and unpretentiously both about social problems and the human psyche, Panduro was accessible to all segments of Danish society.

FURTHER WORKS

Øgledage (1961); *Fern fra Danmark* (1963); *Fejltagelsen* (1964); *Den gale mand* (1965); *Vejen til Jylland* (1966; *One of Our Millionaires Is Missing*, 1967); *Lollipop og andre spil* (1966); *Jul i landsbyen—en svinehøring* (1967); *Fortsættelses-sagoen eller Jul i den blandede landhandel* (1968); *Daniels anden verden* (1970); *Bella og et godt liv* (1971); *Vinduerne* (1971); *Amatørerne* (1972); *Selma, William og Benny* (1972); *Den ubetænksomme elsker* (1973); *Den store bandit* (1973); *Den bedste af alle verdener* (1974); *I Adams verden og Farvel, Thomas* (1974); *Høfeber* (1975); *Louises hus: Et TV-spil* (1977); *Hvilken virkelighed* (1977); *Bare det hele var anderledes* (1987).

FURTHER TRANSLATIONS

The Devil's Instrument, and Other Danish Stories, ed. S. Holm (1971).

REFERENCES

Bredsdorff, Thomas, *Sære Fortællere* (Copenhagen, 1968); Hammerich, Paul, ed., *Panduros verden* (Copenhagen, 1977); Hesselaa, Birgitte, *Leif Panduro* (Copenhagen, 1976); Holmgaard, Jørgen, "Det indeklemte oprør: Om Leif Panduros romaner," in *Linjer i nordisk prosa: Danmark 1965–1975* (Lund, 1975); Hugus, Frank, "The King's New Clothes: The Irreverent Portrayal of Royalty in the Works of Leif Panduro and Finn Søeborg." *Scandinavian Studies* 51.2 (1979); Jørgensen, John Chr., *Leif Panduro. Radio. Film. Theater. TV* (Copenhagen, 1973); Kampmann, Christian, "A Popular Social Critic." *Danish Journal* 72 (1972); Lundbo, Orla, *Panduro* (Copenhagen, 1973); Møllehave, Johanes, "Leif Panduro," in *Danske digtere i det 20. århundrede* IV (Copenhagen, 1982); Tiemroth, Jørgen E., *Panduro og tredivernes drøm* (Copenhagen, 1977); Wamberg, Bodil, *Den gale kærlighed: Motiver i Leif Panduros forfatterskab* (Copenhagen, 1978).

Alexander Taylor

Parland, Henry. Finnish poet writing in Swedish, b. 29 July 1908, Viborg (Viipuri), d. 10 November 1930, Kaunas.

Parland, the eldest of three gifted writer-brothers, lived his childhood in Russia, spoke German at home, and entered a Swedish school in Finland at age fourteen. Three years later he was writing fictional prose in Swedish. Befriended by Gunnar Björling,* he found a haven from an alienating intellectual climate in the circle of writers centered around the journal *Quosego*.

Parland's literary impulses came to a considerable extent from Russian literature; in prose he admired Aleksandr Pushkin and Nikolai Gogol, in poetry, Vladimir Mayakovski. He also had an interest in Russian formalist theory. His orientation was by no means exclusively Russian; F. Scott Fitzgerald and Marcel Proust also provided impulses.

Parland began and ended his brief career in prose, but upon the perhaps misguided advice of Björling, he turned to poetry. Parland's poetry is cynical, coldly humorous, and objectifying. It gives a first impression of nonchalance and superfluity, and in the end unmasks its own dispassion.

Having moved to Lithuania in 1929, and away from Björling's negative evaluation of his prose, Parland discovered Proust and promptly returned to narrative writing. The result, principally the novella *Sönder* (Apart), is perhaps the finest testament to Parland's talent. *Sönder* is a coldly objective account of a relationship, the objectivity underscored by the protagonist's preoccupation with photographic technique. As the latent image is developed, so the processing of mnemonic images reveals the truth of the relationship.

Most of Parland's prose work is posthumously edited and published by his brother Oscar in the volumes *Den stora Dagenefter* (1966; The Great Hangover) and *Säginteannat* (1970; So Much for that). It is a slight production, often unpolished. Parland's reputation continues to be that of a never fully realized genius. That is undoubtedly true, but it is also true that Parland indicated directions that later writers were either slow or disinterested in pursuing. Among the modernists in Finland, Parland was surely the most modern of them all.

FURTHER WORKS

Idealrealisation (1929); *Återsken* (1932); *Hamlet sade det vackrare*, ed. Oscar Parland (1964).

Kim Nilsson

Pedersen, Knud. *See* Hamsun, Knut.

Pekkanen, Toivo. Finnish novelist and poet, b. 10 September 1902, Kotka, d. 30 May 1957, Copenhagen.

Pekkanen was born in the small but important industrial town of Kotka, the son of a poor working-class father. After early years of unassuming physical labor, he began at age twenty-five a career as free-lance writer with a volume of promising short stories. After the publication of his first novel, *Tehtaan varjossa* (1932; In the Shadow of the Factory), he was recognized as a new writer of importance. He established himself with this work as the first Finnish working-class writer, equally interested in the position of men and women in the world of work. Even this early work revealed the outstanding traits of his literary personality. Though fully conscious of the restrictive class structure of Finnish society and determined to show all the hardships of the lower classes that he knew only too well from personal experience, he never became aggressively militant. All his writings distinguish themselves through the combination of acute realistic observations with a tender, often poetic sensitivity. He was deeply interested in individual developments and in the impact made upon them by social conditions.

The finest example of his insight into man's—particularly children's—inner life is the short story "Kaukainen Saari" (The Far-off Island), in which wish-dream and harsh reality meet in impressive fashion.

Dreams, fantasies, even Kafka-like mystic themes are as characteristic for Pekkanen's work as his accounts of Finland's industrialization. As Annamari Sarajas has pointed out, Pekkanen did not belong to any particular school of

thought, but he is nevertheless considered one of the most important representatives of Finnish realism. His conviction of the necessity of that which he had
to say, is perhaps documented by the fact that he continued his work even after
suffering a brain stroke. Though his great documentary on the industrial development of Kotka could not be completed, it is an important contribution to the
social history of Finland.

Pekkanen's achievements were fully honored during his lifetime. He was
accorded many literary prizes and was one of the earliest members of the Finnish
Academy.

FURTHER WORKS

Rautaiset kädet (1927); *Satama ja meri* (1929); *Tientekijät* (1930); *Kuolemattomat* (1931);
Sisarukset (1933); *Kauppiaiden lapset* (1934); *Ihmisten kevät* (1935); *Takaisin Australiaan*
(1936); *Isänmaan ranta* (1937); *Ukkosen tuomio* (1937); *Levottomuus* (1938); *Maantie
meillä ja muualla* (1939); *Musta hurmio* (1939); *Demooni* (1939–1940); *Ne menneet
vuodet* (1940); *Raja merellä* (1941); *Rakkaus ja raha* (1941–1942); *Ajan kasvot* (1942);
Tie Eedeniin (1942); *Vihollislentäjä* (1942); *Hämärtyvä horisontti* (1944); *Elämän ja
kuoleman pidot* (1945); *Jumalan myllyt* (1946); *Nuorin veli* (1946); *Aamuhämärä* (1948);
Toverukset (1948); *Mies ja punapartaiset herrat* (1950); *Täyttyneiden toiveiden maa*
(1951); *Lapsuuteni* (1953; *My Childhood*, 1966); *Lähtö matkalle* (1955); *Täyttyneiden
toiveiden maa*, comp. Ahti Sonninen (1955–1956); *Totuuden ja kirkkauden tiellä* (1957);
Teokset, 7 vols. (1957–1958); *Toivo Pekkasen ajatuksia*, ed. Antero Pekkanen (1962).

FURTHER TRANSLATIONS

Finnish Short Stories, ed. Inkeri Väänänen-Jensen and K. Börje Vähämäki (1982).

REFERENCES

Ahti, Keijo, "Literary Portrait: Toivo Pekkanen." *Books Abroad* 2 (1968); Kare, Kauko,
Toivo Pekkanen (Porvoo, 1952); Koskimies, Rafael, "Toivo Pekkanen," in *Elävä kan-
salliskirjallisuus* (Helsinki, 1949); Kupiainen, U., *Toivo Pekkanen runoilija* (1955);
Kurjensaari, Matti, "Naapuriportaan akateemikko," in his *Veljeni merellä myrskyävällä*
(Helsinki, 1966); Laitinen, Kai, "Toivo Pekkanen," in *Suomen Kirjallisuus,* ed. Matti
Kuusi, vol. 5 (Helsinki, 1965); Sarajas, Annamari, " 'Onnellisten saari' Toivo Pekkasen
tuotannossa," in her *Viimeiset romantikot* (Porvoo, 1962); Sarajas, Annamari, "Työ-
väestön kirjailijan 'naturalismi.' Pekkanen, Siippainen, Viita, Linna," in her *Viimeiset
romantikot* (Porvoo, 1962).

Anne Fried

Peltonen, Johannes Vihtori. *See* Linnankoski, Johannes.

Pennanen, Eila. Finnish novelist, short story writer, essayist, translator, and
critic, b. 8 February 1916, Tampere.

As a translator, essayist, and critic, Pennanen has been one of the most active
and versatile literary figures in Finland during the past forty years. Her first six
novels, published between 1942 and 1951, were dominated by her interest in
the exceptional individual, often a woman or a child whose inner reality comes

into conflict with the pragmatism of the masculine world. In her historical novels, *Pyhä Birgitta* (1954; Saint Birgitta) and *Valon lapset* (1958; The Children of Light), Pennanen is concerned with the relationship between religious experience and economic activity. In the 1960s she experimented with contemporary social satire, but her greatest popular success came with the cycle of Tampere novels (1971–1973, 1986, 1988), which are set in the early years of this century when Finland's development toward a modern industrialized society was just beginning. This time it is the socialists instead of the Quakers as in *Valon lapset* that engage Pennanen's interest. She succeeds even better, however, in portraying the well-to-do shopkeeper class from which she herself springs—a group that remained largely outside class conflicts and was therefore able to develop a style of living marked by some degree of taste and refinement.

The best of Pennanen can be found in the five collections of short stories (1952–1980); which contain examples of the genre that must rank among the finest that Finland has produced. In the stories written during the 1950s one can recognize the influence of Anglo-Saxon models such as D. H. Lawrence and Katherine Mansfield, whose sensualism and virtuosity clearly fascinated Pennanen. But by the end of the 1960s she was moving away from the conventions of the traditional short story and developing a very original type of structure in which the patterns of popular fiction are used as the vehicle for her mocking satire. Pennanen has stated that at the core of a good story lies "a rift in reality," that is, a clash between the artificial rationality of the "adequate person" and the unexpectedness of life itself.

FURTHER WORKS

Ennen sotaa oli nuoruus (1942); *Kaadetut pihlajat* (1944); *Proomu lähtee yöllä* (1945); *Pilvet vyöryvät* (1947); *Leda ja joutsen* (1948); *Kattoparveke* (1951); *Tornitalo* (1952); *Tunnustelua* (1955); *Tunnussana ystävyys* (1956); *Pasianssi* (1957); *Kaksin* (1961); *Mutta* (1963); *Mongolit* (1966); *Aurinkomatka* (1967); *Tilapää* (1968); *Pientä rakkautta* (1969); *Kiitos harhaluuloista* (1970); *Himmun rakkaudet* (1971); *Koreuden tähden* (1972); *Ruusuköynnös* (1973); *Valitut novellit* (1973); *Naisen kunnia* (1975); *Kapakoitten maa* (1977) *Lapsuuden lupaus* (1979); *Äiti ja poika* (1979); *See pieni ääni* (1980); *Kirjailijatar ja hänen miehensä* (1982); *Naivistit* (1982); *Santalahden aika* (1986); *Kulmatalon perhe* (1988).

TRANSLATIONS

Snow in May, ed. Richard Dauenhauer and Philip Binham (1978); *Thank You for These Illusions*, ed. Anne Fried (1981); *Books from Finland* 16.3 (1982); *Finnish Short Stories*, ed. Inkeri Väänänen-Jensen and K. Börje Vähämäki (1982).

REFERENCES

Niemi, Juhani, "Eila Pennanen's 'Mutta,' " in *Romaani ja tulkinta*, ed. Mirjam Polkunen (Keuruu, 1973); Pennanen, Eila, "Eila Pennanen," in *Miten kirjani ovat syntyneet*, ed. Ritva Haavikko, vol. 1 (Porvoo, 1969); Pennanen, Eila, "Tulkinta novellista 'Kaksin,' " in *Novelli ja tulkinta*, ed. Mirjam Polkunen and Pekka Tarkka (Tapiola, 1969); Tarkka,

Pekka, "Eila Pennanen—Reality versus Morality." *Books from Finland* 16.3 (1982); Viljanen, Aulimaija, "Woman and the Chains of Chance." *Books from Finland* 4.3 (1970).

Pekka Tarkka

Petersen, Nis. Danish novelist and poet, b. 22 January 1897, Vamdrup, d. 9 March 1943, Laven.

Petersen was orphaned early and raised by his maternal grandmother in Herning. A mediocre pupil at first, he developed rapidly in his later years of formal schooling. Thereafter he worked as an apprentice in an apothecary in Nakskov (Lolland) and later as a journalist in Holbæk (Sjælland) and in Copenhagen. Then he joined the ranks of the outcasts in the capital and continued this life during two journeys to northern Sweden. *Nattens pibere* (*Whistlers in the Night*, 1983), his first collection of verse, appeared in 1926, and with the publication of his first novel, *Sandalmagernes gade* (*The Street of the Sandalmakers*, 1933) in 1931, which is set in the chaotic Rome of Marcus Aurelius but reflects conditions in contemporary Western Europe, he became immediately famous. The novel was quickly translated into ten languages. A second novel, *Spildt mælk* (*Spilt Milk*, 1935) of 1934, which treats the Irish rebellion in the early 1920s, did not meet with the success of its predecessor.

Further collections of poetry include *En drift vers* (1933; A Drove of Verse), *Til en dronning* (1935; To a Queen), *Stykgods* (1940; Mixed Cargo), and the posthumously published *Stynede popler* (1943; Pollarded Poplars). *For tromme og kastagnet* (For Drum and Castanet), a collection of early poems, was published in 1951, and the author's *Lyrisk efterladenskab* (Lyrical Remains) appears in his *Samlede digte* (1949; Collected Poems), edited by Hans Brix. In his later years Petersen published three volumes of short stories of varied quality: *Engle blæser paa trompet* (1937; Angels Blow the Trumpet), *Dagtyve* (1941; Day Thief), and *Muleposen* (1942; The Nose Bag).

Petersen has been termed a nihilist, and this would seem to be true if one were to read only his "Dødens nat" (Night of Death) from *Stynede popler*, where death overrides all, including any hope for salvation through Christ's birth, and a few other poems where the influence of Friedrich Nietzsche is apparent. But many poems, in which he extols his love for women and children and for nature, and where he sets forth his often-asserted imperative to be true to himself, run counter to this claim. Many of his lyrics possess an incredible beauty, and they strongly influenced young poets in the 1940s and into the 1950s.

Petersen paid for his artistic creativity with eventual physical and spiritual debility. He was a driven man, hopelessly addicted to alcohol during most of his adult life. The effects were apparent in his last few years, when his powers waned. Despite his early demise he is considered one of Denmark's major poets in this century.

FURTHER WORKS

Bemærkninger (1936); *Brændende Europa* (1947); *Aftenbønnen* (1947); *Da seeren tav* (1947); *Memoiren: "Lad os leve i nuet"* (1948); *Mindeudgave*, 8 vols. (1962).

TRANSLATIONS

Twentieth Century Scandinavian Poetry, ed. Martin S. Allwood (1950); *Whistlers in the Night and Other Verse*, trans. Otto M. Sorensen (1983).

REFERENCES

Andersen, Jørgen, *Nis Petersen* (Copenhagen, 1957); Johansen, Frits, *Nis Petersen bibliografi* (Copenhagen, 1953); Petersen, Annalise Nis, *Mod hæld* (Copenhagen, 1948).

Otto M. Sorensen

Petri, Olavus. *See* Olavus Petri.

Pétursson, Hallgrímur. Icelandic poet, b. 1614 in or near Hólar, d. 27 October 1674, Ferstikla.

Pétursson was the son of a sexton at the cathedral in Hólar and a relative of the bishop there, the famous Bible translator and hymnologist Guðbrandur Þorláksson. Evidently expelled from school because of his derisive verses, Pétursson ran away to Copenhagen where he became a blacksmith's apprentice. At the instigation of Brynjólfur Sveinsson, the future bishop of Skálholt, his education continued in Copenhagen for almost four years (1632–1636). He left for Iceland after a woman, for whose religious instruction he had been responsible, bore a child fathered by him. From 1637 to 1644 Pétursson worked as a laborer and fisherman until his patron, Bishop Brynjólfur, once again came to his aid and appointed him pastor at Hvalsnes. From 1651 until leprosy forced his retirement in 1669, Pétursson lived in financial security as pastor at Saurbær on Hvalfjörður, and he died a blind man five years later.

Although Pétursson first produced a variety of secular poetry, it forms only about a quarter of his oeuvre and is not confined to the time prior to his holding religious office. His three *rímur* cycles (Króka-Refur, Lykla-Pétur, Flóres og Leó) display great formal skill and their heroes have been given a human touch not common in contemporary representatives of the genre. Pétursson also wrote "dance-songs" (*vikivakar,*) a drinking song, and the longer poem *Aldaháttur*, which in leonine hexameter and rich diction compares Saga Iceland (about which he was considered an expert by contemporaries) with his own time. However, it was as a hymnologist that Pétursson made his contribution to literature, and the influence of German writers (e.g., Paul Gerhardt, Martin Möller) is discernible. Pétursson's work culminated in the *Passíussálmar*, fifty Passion hymns intended to be sung to known religious melodies of the day. Written in 1659 and first distributed in manuscript to friends, these hymns spoke plainly to the hearts of the people and constituted a sharp break with the religious poetry of Scandinavia after the advent of Lutheranism.

Pétursson is regarded as one of the premier poets of seventeenth-century Iceland and as one of the great Lutheran hymn writers of all time. His work has had an effect on the lives of the Icelandic people and on their writers down to the present day.

FURTHER WORKS

Fimmtíu Passíu Sálmar (1666); *Sjö Guðrækilegar Umþenkingar* (1677; with additions, 1688); *Diarium Christianum* (1680); *Rímur af Króka-Ref* (1945); *Rímur af Lykla-Pétri og Megellónu* (1956); *Rímur af Flóres og Leó* (1956).

TRANSLATIONS

Translations from the Icelandic, ed. W. C. Green (1908); *The Passion Hymns of Iceland*, ed. C. Venn Pilcher (1913); *Meditations on the Cross from Iceland's Poet of the Passion*, ed. C Venn Pilcher (1921); *Icelandic Meditations on the Passion*, ed. C. Venn Pilcher (1923); *Kirjulög*, ed. Jon Leifs (1933); *Icelandic Christian Classics*, ed. C. Venn Pilcher (1950); *Hymns of the Passion: Meditations on the Passion of Christ*, ed. Arthur C. Gook (1966); *An Anthology of Icelandic Poetry*, ed. Eirikur Benedikz (1969).

REFERENCES

Guðmundsson, Gils, "Útgáfur Passíusálma Hallgríms Péturssonar," in *Andvari* 89 (1964); Jónsson, Magnús, *Hallgrímur Pétursson,ævi hans og starf*, 2 vols. (Reykjavík, 1947); Ólason, Páll Eggert, *Saga Íslendinga*, vol. 5 (Reykjavík, 1942); Poestion, J. C., *Isländische Dichter der Neuzeit* (Leipzig, 1897).

Peter A. Jorgensen

Pétursson, Hannes. Icelandic poet and scholar, b. 6 December 1931, Sauðarkrók.

After studying philology and literature at the universities in Reykjavík, Cologne, and Heidelberg, Pétursson made his debut as a poet in the anthology *Ljóð ungra skálda* (1954; Songs of Young Poets) at the age of twenty-three. In *Ljóð* and in his first collection of poetry, *Kvæðabók* (1955; Book of Poems) he established himself as a mature poet who combines a profound sensitivity for themes from history and folk literature and an independent respect for traditional forms with a discursive style of detached circumspection. *Kvæðabók* also reveals Pétursson as a poet of startling paradox, as an intellectual who reflects on man's estrangement from nature and attempts to distill the essence of reality in a poetic process that assimilates the seemingly dissimilar. Thus, a beloved is likened to a dark house in winter, caresses become winds gusting against an ice-covered door, and the life-giving power of poetry resides in a decrepit cotter.

A problematic desideratum in all of Pétursson's works is the attainment of poetic creativity itself. As he shows in his next work, *Í sumardölum* (1959; In Summer Valleys), a poet alienated from nature cannot write until, like the magical "leaf-green harp" of a tree in leaf, he finds within himself the creative power that unites nature and the cosmos. To a large extent, *Í sumardölum* expresses Pétursson's preoccupation with contemporary events of the world and with the celebration of momentary joys. Paradox remains a driving thrust, however, in his affirmation of the fearful experience of ultimate oblivion.

After two literary prizes and extended sojourns abroad, Pétursson returned to Iceland and to a rejuvenating rediscovery of his native land and youthful past which he gave expression to in *Innlönd* (1968; Interior Lands). In ironic juxtaposition to the dark fears of *Kvæðabók*, the poetic journey into the dark unknown now is lighted by an inner beam of hope.

Many of the themes from Pétursson's earlier works are reforged with a new, passionate intensity in *Heimskynni við sjó* (1980; Home at the Sea). Here the poet discovers the creative power of nature that becomes a mirror of the poet's imagination and a model for man in his reaffirmed isolation and self-limitation.

Pétursson's growing stature in Icelandic literature has been enhanced by his achievements as a translator (Franz Kafka and Rainer Maria Rilke) and as a distinguished scholar of Icelandic literature with outstanding interpretations of the works of Steingrímur Thorsteinsson* (1964) and Jónas Hallgrímsson* (1979).

FURTHER WORKS

Sögur að norðan (1961); *Stund og staðir* (1962); *Eyjarnar átján* (1965); *Tvær gönguferðir* (1966); *Á faraldsfæti* (1967); *Rímblöð* (1971); *Ljóðabréf* (1973); *Rauðamyrkur* (1973); *Sögur um Ísland* (1974); *Úr hugskoti* (1976); *Af Pétru Eyjólfsyni og herskipum* (1976); *Kvæðasafn 1951–1976* (1977); *36 ljóð* (1984).

TRANSLATIONS

The Postwar Poetry of Iceland, trans. Sigurður A. Magnússon (1982).

REFERENCES

Hjálmarsson, Jóhann, "Inn í hjörtu mannanna," in *Íslenzk nútímaljóðlist* (Reykjavík, 1971); Jónsson, Erlend, "Ljóðskáld skrifa sögur," in *Íslenzk skáldsagnaritun 1940–1970* (Reykjavík, 1971); Karlsson, Kristján, "Hannes Pétursson." *Helgafell* (1959).

W. M. Senner

Pontoppidan, Henrik. Danish novelist and short story writer, b. 24 July 1857, Frederecia, d. 21 August 1943, Charlottenlund.

Pontoppidan was one of sixteen children born to the Reverend Dines Pontoppidan and his wife. His childhood was characterized by the modest economic circumstances of the family, the poor health of his ailing parents and, most of all, the strict puritanism of his conservative, Lutheran father. Playing and hiking in nature became the young Pontoppidan's escape from this restrictive background; however, when he was sixteen, he obtained his father's reluctant permission to move to Copenhagen to prepare for the entrance exam to the polytechnical institute. He studied engineering from 1874 to 1879, when he withdrew before his final exam in order to make the break irrevocable. A sojourn in the Alps in 1876 seems to have brought forth Pontoppidan's growing disenchantment with engineering as well as his latent desire for creative writing.

In order to make a living, Pontoppidan joined a folk high school in 1879 that had been started by one of his brothers in accordance with the ideas of N.F.S. Grundtvig (1783–1872). Pontoppidan became a teacher of practical subjects, but as he could not reconcile himself with its Christian overtones, he decided to live from his pen alone. This became feasible when he published his first short story, "Et Endeligt" (1881; The End of a Life), in the journal *Ude og Hjemme*.

Pontoppidan's early short stories predominantly take place in the countryside: either in nature or, more specifically, in a village. Some are stories about love, others deal with the social conditions of the poor. Pontoppidan is a perspicacious narrator of love affairs, of the relationship between man and woman, and of the power of irrational passion. However, perhaps more known today are his social descriptions, such as his exposures of village life in the collection of short stories *Landsbybilleder* (1883; Village Sketches) and *Fra Hytterne* (1887; From the Huts). Although Pontoppidan felt attracted to country life and believed in being close to nature (he married a farmer's daughter and settled in the country himself), he had a keen eye for the shortcomings of social life in the countryside. His criticism is distinct in that it always embraces at least two points of view on any question, as when, for example, he describes economic disparity and the hypocrisy of the well-to-do farmers as well as the connivance and the lack of vision on the part of the poor; he does not align himself permanently with one side or one issue.

In the collection of short stories *Skyer* (1890; Clouds), it is the political situation that Pontoppidan castigates. At the end of the 1870s and during the 1880s, Denmark was governed not by parliamentary procedures but by series of provisional decrees issued by Prime Minister J. B. S. Estrup. During that period Denmark was, in fact, ruled as a dictatorship. The anti-authoritarian Pontoppidan strongly opposed Estrup, but as in the case with the social descriptions, he criticizes one side as much as the other. A well-known example of this is his scathingly ironical story "Den første Gendarm" (The First Gendarme).

The vacillation between different issues and moods in his short stories reflects an ongoing inner debate that in the second half of the 1880s turned into a real crisis in Pontoppidan's life. This culminated in Pontoppidan's move alone back to Copenhagen and change of pseudonym—which he used when writing in journals—from Rusticus (the man from the country) to Urbanus (the man from the city). He was eventually divorced and married the daughter of a Copenhagen civil servant. In Copenhagen he came in closer contact with the leading literary circles and the eminent literary critic Georg Brandes* (1842–1927), who spearheaded the so-called Modern Breakthrough.

Pontoppidan's major works are his three great panoramic novels that are both chronicles of fifty years of Danish history and social development as well as psychological portrayals of individuals in social interaction. *Det forjættede land* (1891–1895; *The Promised Land*, 1896) deals with country life and the many religious movements at the time. Emmanuel is a religious idealist whose "return to nature" becomes a failure. He does not learn from experience but pursues his messianism to the point of madness. Pontoppidan's view on his protagonist is ambivalent: Emanuel is portrayed as unrealistic; on the other hand, he receives sympathy for the perseverance of his conviction.

Lykke-Per (1898–1904; Lucky Per) is the archetypal story about the son who rebels against his authoritarian father. But Per's rise in society as an engineer (without a degree), in defiance of his father's otherworldliness, is paralleled with a growing inner shallowness.

It takes him a lifetime and a journey through various stages of Danish society before he understands about himself and his roots. The explicit goal in this individualistic novel is to "know thyself," but a social awareness is indicated by Per's donation to his ex-fiancée's home for orphans.

The movement from outer to inner is continued in *De Dødes Rige* (1912–1916; The Realm of the Dead) where "erratic" characters are rushing for some chimera or other. This novel may be termed a collective novel, whereas *Lykke-Per* is a *Bildungsroman*. It has a group of protagonists whose lives interrelate to form a final overall pattern indicating that all lives are predetermined. The metaphysical message is that the humans should relinquish their senseless struggles and accept their fate irrespective of its content. Although gloomy and almost destructive in its underlying idea, *De Dødes Rige* is a novel of great power and beauty, and the pessimism is not unwarranted as the novel was written in the days before World War I.

Pontoppidan today holds the position as the great classical realist in Danish literature due to his choice and range of subject matter as well as his style, which is a model of clarity and conciseness. But his love and concern for the Danish country and its people were often expressed through satire if not chastisement; maybe that is why he had to share the Nobel Prize for literature with Karl Gjellerup* (1857–1919) in 1917.

FURTHER WORKS

Stækkede Vinger (1881); *Sandinge Menighed* (1883); *Ung Elskov* (1885); *Mimoser* (1886); *Spøgelser* (1888); *Reisebilder aus Dänemark* (1890); *Natur* (1890); *Krøniker* (1890); *Minder* (1893); *Nattevagt* (1894); *Den gamle Adam* (1894); *Højsang* (1896); *Kirkeskuden* (1897); *Lille Rødhætte* (1900); *Det ideale Hjem* (1900); *De vilde Fugle* (1902); *Borgmester Hoeck og Hustru* (1905); *Asgaardsrejsen* (1906); *Det store Spøgelse* (1907); *Hans Kvast og Melusine* (1907); *Den kongelige Gæst* (1908); *Et Kærlighedseventyr* (1918); *En Vinterrejse* (1920); *Mands Himmerig* (1927); *Drengeår* (1933); *Hamskifte* (1936); *Arv og Gæld* (1938); *Familjeliv* (1940); *Undervejs til mig selv* (1943).

FURTHER TRANSLATIONS

The Apothecary's Daughters (1890); *Emanuel or Children of the Soil* (1896); *American-Scandinavian Review* 15.8 (1927); *American-Scandinavian Review* 17.9 (1929); *Anthology of Danish Literature*, ed. I. J. Billeskov Jansen and P. M. Mitchell (1971); *The Royal Guest*, ed. P. M. Mitchell and Kenneth H. Ober (1977).

REFERENCES

Ahnlund, Knut, *Henrik Pontoppidan* (Stockholm, 1956); Andersen, Poul Carit, *Henrik Pontoppidan* (Copenhagen, 1934); Ekman, Ernst, "Henrik Pontoppidan as a Critic of

Modern Danish Society." *Scandinavian Studies* 29.4 (1957); Geismar, Oscar, "Henrik Pontoppidan." *American-Scandinavian Review* 21.1 (1933); Gray, Charlotte S., "From Opposition to Identification: Social and Psychological Structure behind Henrik Pontoppidan's Literary Development." *Scandinavian Studies* 51.3 (1979); Jones, W. Glyn, "Henrik Pontoppidan 1857–1943." *Modern Language Review* 52, (1957); Jones, W. Glyn, "Henrik Pontoppidan, the Church and Christianity after 1900." *Scandinavian Studies* 30.4 (1958); Jones, W. Glyn, " 'Det forjættede Land' and 'Fremskridt' as Social Novels." *Scandinavian Studies* 37.1 (1965); Larsen, Hanna Astrup, "Pontoppidan of Denmark." *American-Scandinavian Review* 31.3 (1943); Madsen, Børge Gedsø, "Henrik Pontoppidan's Emanuel Hansted and Per Sidenius," in *Scandinavian Studies*, ed. Carl F. Bayerschmidt and Erik J. Friis (Seattle, 1965); Mitchell, P. M., *Henrik Pontoppidan* (Boston, 1979).

Charlotte Schiander Gray

Portaas, Herman Theodor. *See* Wildenvey, Herman Theodor.

Prøysen, Alf. Norwegian balladist, short story writer, and novelist, b. 23 July 1914, Ringsaker, d. 23 November 1970, Oslo.

Born and raised on a tenant farm in the country of Hedmark, Prøysen was destined to record in satirical and humorous ballads and stories a form of life that has gradually been dying out in Norway. In 1865 there were 65,000 tenant farmers in Norway, but by 1928, during Prøysen's childhood, there were only 6,000 left. Prøysen wrote about all sorts of rural people: men, women, cooks, carpenters, masters, servants, house workers, field workers, young and old, and his peasant background shines through in all his works. For the most part, he wrote in his native Hedmark dialect.

Prøysen's three ballad collections of 1948 and 1949 soon became immensely popular. After only two years they had sold 245,000 copies. Subsequent collections achieved similar success. Usually, his ballads and short stories were heard on the radio during the "Children's Hour" before being published in written form. Prøysen was enormously popular with children; the recordings of his stories in his special voice and Ringsaker dialect can still be heard often on the Norwegian radio.

Prøysen's stories for adults are almost all humorous anecdotes from Hedmark. Especially popular are the "Teskjekjerring" stories about a woman who becomes as small as a teaspoon and in spite of seemingly insuperable odds always manages to achieve her goals.

Prøysen's only novel, *Trost i Taklampa* (1950; Thrush in the Ceiling Light), was his greatest success. It is a biting satire on rural society with its class consciousness, discrimination, and oppression. Gone is the romanticism many writers had found in rural life. Prøysen even sympathizes with those who leave the farm for the city. The novel was dramatized and filmed.

Beyond compare, Prøysen has been the most popular writer in Norway since World War II. There is a timelessness in his stories and songs that make them seem somehow familiar and applicable to many other places than just to the

Norwegian tenant farm. Clearly there is a socialist tendency in his works, although he was not a doctrinaire socialist. He spoke for the little people everywhere, and his ability to portray suffering and still not lose his sense of humor and balance has endeared him to his people.

FURTHER WORKS

Dørstokken heme (1945); *Drengstu' viser* (1948); *Musevisa* (1949); *Lillebrors viser* (1949); *Teddybjørnen og andre viser* (1951); *Viser i tusmørke* (1951); *Fløttardag* (1952); *Skøyerviser* (1952); *Ut på livets vei* (1952); *Rim og regler fra barnetimen* (1954); *Matja Madonna* (1955); *Geitekillingen som kunne telle til ti* (1957); *Julekveldsviser* (1957); *Kjerringa som ble så lita som ei teskje* (1957); *Kjaerlighet på rundpinne* (1958); *Alle tiders gullhøne* (1959); *Muntre minner fra Hedemarken* (1959); *Teskjekjerringa på nye eventyr* (1960); *Mikkelsen og Monsen* (1961); *Halvmeter'n* (1962); *Sirkus Mikkelikski* (1963); *Den grønne votten* (1964); *12 viser på villstrå* (1964); *Teskjekjerringa i eventyskauen* (1965); *Fra Hompetitten til Bakvendtland* (1966); *Teskjekjerringa på camping* (1967); *"Så seiler vi på Mjøsa" og andre viser* (1969); *Teskjekjerringa* (1969); *Teskjekjerringa på julehandel* (1970); *Det var da, det, og itte nå* (1971); *Snekker Andersen og julenissen* (1971); *Jinter je har møtt* (1972); *Teskjekjerringa og Kvitebjørn Kong Valemon* (1972); *Finn et strå og træ dom på. Alf Prøysens blomster og planter i dikt og bilder*, ed. Klaus Høiland (1986).

FURTHER TRANSLATIONS

Little Old Mrs. Pepperpot (1959); *The Goat That Learned to Count* (1961); *Mrs. Pepperpot Again* (1961); *The Town That Forgot It Was Christmas* (1961); *Mrs. Pepperpot to the Rescue* (1963); *Down the Mouse Hole* (1964); *Mrs. Pepperpot's Year* (1973).

REFERENCES

Engen, Kari Marie, *Individ og fellesskap. Samfunnskritik og etiske holdninger i Alf Prøysens prosa* (Oslo, 1972); Fjeld, Svein-Erik, *Trost i taklampa—fra roman til skuespill* (Bergen, 1976); Viken, Torhild, *Alf Prøysen; et forfatterbilde i forandring?* (Oslo, 1978).

Walter D. Morris

R

Rantamala, Irmari. *See* Lassila, Maiju.

Rasmussen, Halfdan. Danish lyric poet, b. 29 January 1915, Copenhagen.

Rasmussen was born in a humble district of the Danish capital. His early years seemed quite hopeless; he had various minor jobs but was unemployed and poverty-stricken for years. His working-class background, his study of proletarian literature while attending folk high schools, and the years of economic crisis and war in the 1930s and 1940s were the growing conditions of Rasmussen's earlier writings.

During the German occupation his poetic struggle against social injustice was naturally extended to a struggle against political and military dehumanization. Typical is that his first collection of poems was called *Soldat eller menneske* (1941; Soldier or Human), and that he was the most published underground lyric poet in Denmark during the war.

His writings from and about this period were brought to a conclusion in the collection *Korte skygger* (1946; Short Shadows), which at the same time heralds an increased artistic maturity and refinement. Rasmussen's conscientious feeling for man's struggle for life becomes a feeling for life itself in the shadow of the bomb. Life proves fragile and constantly overshadowed by fear and doubt and death. But its fragility only makes it more deeply appreciated, as suggested by his next title *Paa knæ for livet* (1948; Kneeling Down before Life).

Rasmussen is in favor of intimate contact with the basics of life—nature and children—and alien to artificial philosophy. Approaching tradition is his way to come up to new circumstances and in touch with new generations. His many children's books and collections of nonsense and nursery rhymes may well be read in continuation of his more serious works. And so may his books and poems about Greece, Greenland, and Vietnam be viewed as extensions of his (ab)original social and political involvement. He is a studious traveler whose horizonhas become worldwide without moving its center from the backstreets of Copenhagen.

Rasmussen is not a great modernistic innovator of Danish literature. But he is loved by readers of all ages for his naïve charm and respected by many for his genuine expressions of human and social concerns. He is a great minor classic.

FURTHER WORKS

Kejser Næsegrus og Kæmpesmeden (1942); *Det lukkede ansigt* (1943); *Min barndom var en by* (1945); *Digte under besættelsen* (1945); *De afsindige* (1948); *Fem smaa troldebørn* (1948); *Gaden* (1948); *Den som har set september* (1949); *Tullerulle Tappenstreg* (1949); *Aftenland* (1950); *Lange Peter Madsen* (1950); *Livet i vold* (1951); *Forventning* (1951); *Tosserier*, 7 vols. (1951–1957); *Den lille frække Frederik* (1951); *Skoven* (1954); *Kasper Himmelspjæt* (1955); *Hemmeligt forår* (1956); *I mørket* (1956); *Torso* (1957); *Himpegimpe og andre børnerim* (1957); *Lyriske installationer* (1958); *Pumpegris og andre børnerim* (1959); *Stilheden* (1962); *Med solen i ryggen* (1963); *Børnerim* (1964); *Julekalender for voksne* (1965); *Mørke over Akropolis* (1967); *Halfdans ABC* (1967); *Hokus Pokus og andre børnerim* (1969; *Hocus Pocus. Nonsense Rhymes*, 1973); *Og det var det—* (1977); *Fremtiden er forbi* (1985); *Tante Andante* (1985).

FURTHER TRANSLATIONS

Halfdane's Nonsense and Nursery Rhymes (1973); *Hundreds of Hens and Other Poems for Children by Halfdan Rasmussen* (1983).

REFERENCE

Clausen, Ernst, ed., *Hilsen til Halfdan* (Copenhagen, 1965).

Poul Houe

Reich, Ebbe Kløvedal. Danish writer, editor, and agitator, b. 7 March 1940, Odense.

Originally a student of history—especially modern and Eastern—Reich became a journalist in 1965; he was editor of *Politisk Revy,* 1965–1967. Always politically engaged, Reich took keen part in the counterculture of the 1960s in the demonstrations against the Vietnam War, and in the resistance to Denmark's entry into the Common Market (editor of the anti–Common Market publication *Notat* since 1973). Politically, Reich has been associated with "det radikale venstre" (the Radical Left), a liberal party, as well as "venstre socialisterne" (the Left Socialists), being too nonconformist for the former and less dogmatic than the latter.

A true representative of his times, Reich has been, consecutively or concomitantly, a flower child (took part in the hashish and LSD subculture), a Christian, a liberal (with models like Henry George, about whom he wrote a biography), a declared Marxist, an anarchist (wrote a book about Errico Malatesta), and a mysticist. He adopted a middle name, Kløvedal (from J.R.R. Tolkien), as did all members of his collective, which settled in "Maos lyst" (Mao's Delight) in a wealthy suburb of Copenhagen. Contradictions notwithstanding, there is a basic attitude and a unifying theme throughout this diversity: a belief in personal freedom and creativity combined with social awareness and egalitarianism nationally and internationally.

Reich's most original contribution to Danish literature—he has also written poetry and professional works—are his "historiske krøniker" (historical chronicles), where historical facts are mixed with fiction in order to create a kind of history of ideas where the old distinction between specialist literature and fiction or creative writing has been obliterated. His "method of analogy" serves to show how past times and events are analogous to contemporary ones. Related to the historical chronicle is his biographical chronicle and contemporary chronicle. In all of these, the fusion of rational and irrational approaches to the subject naturally leads to the breakdown of conventional definitions of style and genre.

Reich is a kind of modern romantic who unifies traditionally separate elements into one. As a visionary populist, he is undeniably original as well as sincere, but an assessment of his lasting impact on the Danish literary scene can only be made in retrospect.

WORKS

Vietnam (1965); *Kina—den ideologiske stormagt* (1967); *Billedalmanak* (1967); *Retning til venstre* (1968); *Svampens tid* (1969); *Hvem var Malatesta?* (1969); *Holger Danske* (1970); *Eventyret om Alexander 666* (1970); *Frederik* (1972); *Langelands-manifestet* (1972); *Svampen og korset* (1973); *Du danske svamp* (1974); *Rejsen til Messias*, 3 vols. (1974); *Henry George* (1976); *Til forsvar for masselinien og den rette tro* (1976); *Fæ og frænde* (1977); *Svaneøglen* (1978); *Festen for Cæcilie* (1979); *Mediesvampen* (1980); *Viljen til Hanstholm* (1981); *De første* (1981); *Ploven og de to sværd* (1982); *Den bærende magt* (1983); *Kong Skildpadde* (1985); *Nissen fra Nürnberg* (1985); *David—slægtens konge* (1985); *Bibelen* (1986).

Charlotte Schiander Gray

Reiss-Andersen, Gunnar. Norwegian poet, b. 21 August 1896, Larvik, d. 29 July 1964, Arendal.

After having been to sea at an early age, Reiss-Andersen had a great wish to become a painter, but his application to the Art Academy in Oslo in 1916 was refused. He then went to Copenhagen and later to Paris on his own to study and to paint. In his poetic debut, *Innvielsens år* (1921; Years of Initiation), his elegant and witty verse reveals the influence of Olaf Bull* and Herman Theodor Wildenvey.* Reiss-Andersen's early poetry expresses a loneliness and a longing to recapture his lost youth. His desire to paint is seen in his extensive pictures of seasonal landscapes.

A growing social awareness is evident in *Vitnesbyrd* (1936; Testimony). Reiss-Andersen reacted strongly to the rise of the nazis in Germany, the war in Spain, and unemployment at home. When World War II broke out, he fled to Sweden after having distributed illegal poetry in Norway. In Sweden he wrote war poems that remind one of Arnulf Øverland* and Nordahl Grieg* in their excellent portrayal of Norwegian character, but they also reveal much self-criticism in their descriptions of a fugitive's feelings.

After the war, Reiss-Andersen wrote some of his best poems and was received with more unreserved admiration than ever before. Modernism had its influence on him, causing him to use freer forms, and visionary ideas led him to see a more permanent world behind the one of our senses. His later poems also show greater resignation and more pleasure in simple things near at hand.

Reiss-Andersen was an artist who loved verse for its own sake. He is still widely read; in 1980, the Norwegian Book of the Month Club offered a selection of his work. Particularly popular are his timeless sea poems about voyages, wind, storms, and seasons, and his beautiful love poems. One poem that all Norwegians know or have at least heard is "Til hjertene" (To the Hearts), about the ideal love one carries in one's heart but has never met. The last verse runs,

> Never forget her
> For she alone
> Is what you love
> in the one you love.

FURTHER WORKS

Mellem Løven og Venus (1923); *Solregn* (1924); *Nyt liv* (1925); *Kongesønnens bryllup* (1926); *Himmelskrift* (1928); *Lykkens prøve* (1931); *Spansk farver og annen kulør* (1933); *Horisont* (1934); *Sensommerdagene* (1940); *Kampdikt fra Norge* (1943); *Norsk røst* (1944); *Dikt fra krigstiden* (1945); *Prinsen av Isola* (1949); *Det smilende alvor* (1954).

REFERENCES

Aarnes, Asbjørn, "Gunnar Reiss-Andersen," in his *Den poetiske fenomen* (Oslo, 1963); Krog, Helge, "Gunnar Reiss-Andersen," in his *Meninger om mange ting* (Oslo, 1933).

Walter D. Morris

Rekola, Mirkka. Finnish poet and translator, b. 26 June 1931, Tampere.

Rekola made her debut with the collection *Vedessä palaa* (1954; Burning in the Water). These poems are relatively traditional in form, with rhyme and fixed meter. Soon, however, she adopted modernism. A significant predecessor for Rekola, about whom she has written a personal essay in *Suomalaisia Kirjailijoita*, was Helvi Juvonen.* Characteristic of Rekola's poetry are a highly concentrated form and visual and intellectual sharpness of imagery. Although extremely condensed, the poems possess an explosive quality of multiple interpretations. They seem to expand the boundaries of language and reality by means of paradox. Many have called Rekola a mystic whose dialectics of unity and separateness resemble medieval mystic thought. The concrete and the mystical exist concentrically in Rekola's poems. An individual's experience of oneness with the world and his or her fundamental feeling of community with others present themselves as a counterpoise to the other field of energy created by man's sense of loneliness and isolation. In her poetry Rekola has created a philosophy of life that is both all-encompassing and seemingly finalized yet simultaneously open-ended. In this respect her poetry possesses a unity matched only by a few representatives of the 1950s modernistic verse.

Rekola's significance as one of the most important postwar lyric poets in Finland was soon recognized and her long career of over thirty years has already ensured her a position among the classic writers of Finnish lyric poetry. It was at the very latest with the publication of *Runoja 1954–1978* (Poems) in 1979 that Rekola's significance became generally acknowledged. The following characterization captures the essence of her poetry: "Through the decisively concise diction and a thought process that speeds forward by means of paradoxes, we are taken to a world which focuses on the dizzying event itself rather than on the end results." Rekola has also been active as a translator, having rendered Shakespeare's *Othello* in Finnish, for instance.

FURTHER WORKS

Tunnit (1957); *Syksy muuttaa linnut* (1961); *Ilo ja epäsymmetria* (1965); *Anna päivän olla kaikki* (1968); *Muistikirja* (1969); *Minä rakastan sinua, minä sanon sen kaikille* (1972); *Tuulen viime vuosi* (1974); *Kohtaamispaikka vuosi* (1977); *Maailmat lumen vesistöissä* (1978); *Runot 1954–1978* (1979); *Kuutamourakka* (1981); *Puun syleilemällä* (1983); *Silmän kantama* (1984); *Maskuja* (1987); *Tuoreessa muistissa kevät* (1987).

TRANSLATIONS

Books from Finland 12.2 (1978); *Thank You for These Illusions*, ed. Anne Fried (1981); *Salt of Pleasure*, ed. Aili Jarvenpa (1983).

REFERENCES

Krohn, Leena "Niin kuin hiljainen jota me etsimme," in *Suomalaisia kirjailijoita—kirjailijat kirjailijoista,* ed. Mirjam Polkunen (Helsinki, 1982); Polkunen, Mirjam, "Mirkka Rekola." *Books from Finland* 12.2 (1978); Tarkka, Pekka, ed., *Suomalaisia nykykirjailijoita* (Helsinki, 1980).

Pertti Lassila

Rifbjerg, Klaus. Danish poet, novelist, dramatist, journalist, and critic, b. 15 December 1931, Copenhagen.

Rifbjerg comes from an academic home—his parents were both teachers—and he began to study literature as a matter of course at the University of Copenhagen. After some years, in 1955, he broke off his studies in order to work as a film director and journalist. He made his poetic debut in 1959 but continued as a journalist until 1966. Rifbjerg became coeditor of the literary periodical *Vindrosen* with Villy Sørensen* from 1959 to 1963. Rifbjerg has received numerous literary awards and was made a member of the Danish Academy in 1967.

The vast production of the prolific Rifbjerg embraces numerous genres and media. Rifbjerg played a central role in the modernism of the 1960s. As a dramatist, he innovated the Danish drama with his revues, which were satirical (political) dramas with music and songs. In addition, he has written other kinds of drama, radio plays, television plays, and even a so-called listeners' novel in cooperation with his readers. But also in the largest part of his production—novels and short stories—Rifbjerg has been truly creative and has revitalized the genres. Again the lyrical quality is apparent in his novels, which usually are I-centered with a frequent use of stream of consciousness. However, each novel distinguishes itself from the others by its unique approach to genre, structure, and tone: from individualistic novel to larger social portrayal, from travelogue to science fiction. Likewise, the atmosphere ranges from the tragic to the satirical, from the idyllic to the humorous or even hilarious. In short, Rifbjerg is a self-conscious artist who experiments with the media and who is therefore, not surprisingly, also an astute critic and cultural commentator. In 1984 he became literary manager of Gyldendal Publishing House.

Many Danish critics consider Rifbjerg's poetry—especially *Konfrontation* (1960; Confrontation) and *Camouflage* (1961; Camouflage)—to be his most significant contribution to Danish literature. If the former represents a "confrontation" with the modern, concrete, and very technical world, the latter is the artistic outcome of a dive into the subconscious: all the way down to primeval layers. *Konfrontation* emphasizes the "now" in rich physical imagery revealing the borderland areas of consciousness and submerged sexuality—a process that evokes guilt feelings. If *Konfrontation* is powerful through its choice and juxtaposition of the word, *Camouflage* is intriguing in its attempt to go beyond the word, and together the two works signify a major literary and cognitive conquest. Of the many succeeding collections of poems, *Amagerdigte* (1965; Amager Poems) stands out in its simple diction and everyday realism.

Rifbjerg's novels deal with contemporary life—always close to Rifbjerg's own—which is experienced through the biological and psychological development of the protagonist as it is often disclosed through a stage of crisis. *Den kroniske uskyld* (1958; The Chronic Innocence) is a puberty novel focusing on the problem of conveying some of the prepuberty innocence (immediacy) into adulthood. *Operaelskeren* (1966; *The Opera Lover*, 1970) represents a later stage of crisis, that of the middle-aged man. The professor has lost contact with the intuitive part of his unconscious—represented by his mistress, the opera singer. A continuous theme in Rifbjerg's writing is the latent danger of the unrecognized irrational as also portrayed in *Arkivet* (1967; The Archives), a masterly description of everyday banality where routine and traditions serve to stall irrational impulses and fear. Anna in *Anna (jeg) Anna* (1969; *Anna (I) Anna*, 1982) is the female counterpart to the opera lover. However, her repression has social overtones: her "betrayal" of her humble social origin emerges as a pathological desire to kill her little daughter.

All of Rifbjerg's works together constitute one large oeuvre where the separate entities represent various creative approaches to a thematically coherent unity. The originality of this large puzzle will ensure Rifbjerg a lasting, outstanding position in Danish literature.

FURTHER WORKS

Under vejr med mig selv (1956); *Efterkrig* (1957); *Voliere* (1962); *Weekend* (1962); *Hva' ska vi lave* (1963); *Portræt* (1963); *Boi-i-ing '64* (1964); *Og andre historier* (1964); *Diskret ophold* (1965); *Udviklinger* (1965); *Hvad en mand har brug for* (1966); *Der var engang en krig* (1966); *Rif* (1967); *Fædrelandssange* (1967); *Voks* (1968); *Lonni og Karl* (1968); *Rejsende* (1969); *I medgang og modgang* (1970); *I skyttens tegn* (1970); *År* (1970); *Mytologi* (1970); *Marts 1970* (1970); *Narrene* (1971); *Leif den Lykkelige jun.* (1971); *Til Spanien* (1971); *Lena Jørgensen, Klintevej 4, 2650 Hvidovre* (1971); *Svaret blæser i vinden* (1971) *Dengang det var før* (1972); *Rifbjergs lytterroman* (1972); *Den syende jomfru og andre noveller* (1972); *Brevet til Gerda* (1972); *R. R.* (1972); *Spinatfuglene* (1973); *Dilettanterne* (1973); *Scener fra det daglige liv* (1973); *Du skal ikke være ked af det Amalia* (1974); *Privatlivets fred* (1974); *Sommer* (1974); *En hugorm i solen* (1974); *25 desperate digte* (1974); *Vejen ad hvilken* (1975); *Den søndag* (1975); *Tak for turen* (1975); *De beskedne, 4 vols.* (1975–1976); *Stranden* (1976); *Kiks* (1976); *Det korte af det lange* (1976); *Twist* (1976); *Et bortvendt ansigt* (1977); *Drengene* (1977); *Dobbeltgænger eller Den korte, inderlige men fuldstændig sande beretning om Klaus Rifbjerg's liv* (1978); *Tango eller Syv osmotiske fortællinger* (1978); *Livsfrisen* (1979); *Joker* (1979); *Voksdugshjertet* (1979); *Det sorte hul* (1980); *Vores år, 2 vols.* (1980); *Odysseus fra Amager* (1981); *De hellige aber* (1981); *Spansk motiv* (1981); *Kesses krig* (1982); *Landet Atlantis* (1982); *Mænd og kvinder* (1982); *Hvad sker der i kvarteret?* (1983); *Patience eller kortene på bordet* (1983); *Det svævende træ* (1983); *Intet nyt fra køkkenfronten* (1984); *Falsk forår* (1984); *Udenfor har vinden lagt sig* (1984); *Harlekin skelet* (1985); *Borte tit* (1986); *Som man behager* (1986); *Digte af Klaus Rifbjerg*, ed. Asger Schnack (1986); *Engel* (1987); *Byens tvelys* (1987).

FURTHER TRANSLATIONS

Literary Review 8.1 (1964); *Modern Poetry in Translation* (London) 15 (1973); *Selected Poems*, ed. Nadja Christensen and Alexander Taylor (1976); *Contemporary Danish Poetry*, ed. Alexander Taylor et al. (1977); *Seventeen Danish Poets*, ed. Niels Ingwersen (1981).

REFERENCES

Borum, Poul, *Danish Literature* (Copenhagen, 1979); Brostrøm, Torben, *Klaus Rifbjerg* (Copenhagen, 1970); Glienke, Bernhard, "Anna, Balthazar und die Deutschen. Ein Aspect zweir neuer dänischer Romane." *Skandinavistik* (1970); Gray, Charlotte S., "Klaus Rifbjerg: A Contemporary Writer." *Books Abroad* 51.1 (1977); Gray, Charlotte Schiander, *Klaus Rifbjerg* (Westport, Conn., 1986); Dines Johansen, Jørgen, *Hvalerne venter* (Odense, 1981); Kistrup, Jens, "Klaus Rifbjerg—the Latest Phase." *Danish Journal* 59 (1967).

Charlotte Schiander Gray

Rintala, Paavo. Finnish novelist, b. 20 September 1930, Viipuri.

Rintala lost his father in World War II, and was for a time a student of theology: both facts have left their mark on his books, in which war and religion are recurring themes. Sometimes he has incorporated biblical happenings into accounts of events in modern Finland, as in his realistic novel *Rikas ja köyhä*

(1955; Rich and Poor). The trilogy *Mummoni ja Mannerheim* (1960–1962; My Granny and Mannerheim) sets side by side the story of the artistocratic field marshal and that of a poor countrywoman, a device that leaves the reader in no doubt as to his Tolstoyan "populist" leanings. The novel *Sissiluutnantti* (1963; *The Long Distance Patrol*, 1967), in which he depicts a commando lieutenant as the agent of demonic forces, evoked a lengthy controversy and brought down upon his head the concerted rage of forty retired Finnish generals. Subsequently Rintala turned to documentary methods of presenting the history of Finland's wars, compiling scrapbooks from the letters, diaries, and tape-recorded reminiscences of former soldiers. The most noteworthy of these compilations is *Sotilaiden äänet* (1966; Soldiers' Voices). The central character of *Nahkapeitturien linjalla* (1976–1979; On the Tanners' Line) is an elderly theologian who looks at war from the standpoint of Christian ethics.

Rintala has always believed in playing his part in public life. He was a supporter of Urho Kekkonen's policies, and from 1969 onwards took part (as a representative of the Liberals) in the activities of the communist-inspired peace organization. His novel, *Valehtelijan muistelmat* (1982; The Memoirs of a Liar), is strongly critical of his earlier political stances. In all Rintala has written over thirty prose works. They are uneven in quality, but in the best of them the "message" fuses effectively with a vivid and highly readable narrative style.

FURTHER WORKS

Kuolleiden evankeliumi (1954); *Lakko* (1956); *Pojat* (1958); *Jumala on kauneus* (1959); *Pikkuvirkamiehen kuolema* (1959); *Mummon ja marskin tarinat* (1962); *Kunnianosoitus Johann Sebastian Bachille* (1963); *Palvelijat hevosten selässä* (1964); *Keskusteluja lasten kanssa* (1965); *Sukeltaja* (1965); *Sodan ja rauhan äänet* (1967); *Leningradin kohtalonsinfonia* (1968); *Napapiirin äänet* (1969); *Paasikiven aika* (1969); *Kekkosen aika* (1970); *Vietnamin kurjet* (1970); *Valitut teokset* (1970); *Viapori 1906* (1971); *Paavalin matkat* (1972); *Uu ja poikanen* (1972); *Kesäkuu 44* (1974); *Romeo ja Julia häränvuonna* (1974); *Se toinen Lili Marlen* (1975); *Maatyömies ja kuu* (1983); *Eläinten rauhanliike* (1984); *Porvari punaisella torilla* (1984); *Vänrikin muistot* (1985); *Carossa ja Anna* (1986); *St. Petersburgin salakuljetus* (1987).

REFERENCES

Tarkka, Pekka, *Paavo Rintalan saarna ja seurakunta* (Helsinki, 1966); Tarkka, Pekka, *En roman och dess publik* (Stockholm, 1970); Tarkka, Pekka, "Paavo Rintala: A Literary Portrait." *Books from Finland* 3.1 (1969).

Pekka Tarkka

Rode, Helge. Danish poet, b. 16 October 1870, Copenhagen, d. 23 March 1937, Copenhagen.

As a small child Rode moved with his mother to Norway. In 1891 he underwent a powerful spiritual experience, in which he felt his soul detach itself from his body, and as a result he adopted a religious view of life akin to theosophy. Most of his poetry bears the stamp of this and rejects intellectualism, occupying itself with the mysteries of life and death.

Rode's poetry, in which silence and whiteness are characteristic features, is very intense, and even the simpler poems such as "Sne" (Snow) are intended to awaken the reader to the depths of his own being. Rode sees himself, his soul, as part of the eternal soul of the universe, as he clearly says in "Ariels Sang" (Ariel's Song), where he talks of his mission on earth and his longing for spiritual things.

The poles of human experience are reflected in two of Rode's major poems, "Fødslen" (The Birth) and "Den Druknede" (The Drowned Man). The first of them is a poem ranging from the humorous to the dithyrambic, a portrayal of all the events surrounding the birth of a baby, the intensity of experience and the miracle of a new life emerging. In the second the opposite is depicted in a chilling presentation of the atmosphere surrounding a drowning accident, a reflection on the inexplicability of the transition from life to death. Both poems reflect a preoccupation with the borderline between life and death, time and eternity, and with wonderment at the prospect of eternity.

Rode wrote a number of outstanding memorial poems; best known are those to the Norwegian poet Sigbjørn Obstfelder,* with whom he felt a close affinity, to the Danish novelist Herman Bang,* and to the poet's own mother and father.

In his opposition to materialism and intellectualism, and as a statement of his own unorthodox religious views, Rode wrote both essays and plays centered round the mysteries of life and death. He is nevertheless mainly remembered for his poetry and stands as a champion of a new form of spirituality combating the irreligious tendencies in modern Danish intellectual life.

FURTHER WORKS

Styrke (1891); *Hvide Blomster* (1892); *Digte* (1896); *Kongesønner* (1896); *Sommereventyr* (1897); *Dansen gaar* (1898); *Den Rejsende* (1900); *Kampene i Stefan Borgs Hjem* (1901); *Solsagn* (1904); *Komedier* (1905); *Digte, gamle og nye* (1906); *Morbus Tellermann* (1907); *Italien* (1909); *Flugten* (1909); *Grev Bonde og hans Hus* (1912); *Ariel* (1914); *Krig og Aand* (1917); *Det store Forlis* (1917); *En Mand gik ned fra Jerusalem* (1920); *Moderen* (1920); *Den stille Have* (1922); *Regenerationen i vort Aandsliv* (1923); *Pladsen med de grønne Træer* (1924); *Det store Ja* (1926); *Det sjælelige Gennembrud* (1928); *Den vilde Rose* (1931).

REFERENCES

Hansen, Henrik Juul, *Dramatikeren Helge Rode* (Copenhagen, 1948).

W. Glyn Jones

Rølvaag, Ole E. (pseud. Paal Mørck). Norwegian-American novelist, b. 22 April 1876, Dønna, d. 5 November 1931, Northfield, Minnesota.

Rølvaag grew up in a poor fisherman's family in northern Norway. After confirmation, he sailed with the fishing fleet to Lofoten until he emigrated to the United States in 1896. After several years of menial farm labor, described in his first novel, *Amerika-Breve* (1912; *The Third Life of Per Smevik*, 1971), he entered Augustana Academy in Canton, South Dakota, in 1898. He then attended St. Olaf College, graduating in 1905. As a student, Rølvaag began to write seriously, contributing articles to the student newspaper and completing the manuscript of a novel. He spent one year as a graduate student at the University of Oslo, and was then offered a teaching position at St. Olaf College, where he remained until his death in 1931. His experiences during these early years helped form the philosophy that is conveyed in his books, his essentially tragic vision of immigration, and his belief in the importance of maintaining cultural traditions.

Rølvaag's masterpeice was published in two volumes in Norway under the titles *I de Dage* and *Riket grundlægges* (1924–1925; *Giants in the Earth*, 1927). Rølvaag's great novel is epic in scope, depicting both the promise and the cost of the great westward movement. It can be characterized as a psychological interpretation of the pioneer and immigrant experience. The cost in human terms is represented by the two main characters, Per Hansa and his wife, Beret. Per Hansa has all the forward-looking, unquenchable optimism of the model pioneer, building his kingdom on the prairie. However, he also has a fatal flaw, an overabundance of pride and self-confidence. Beret cannot give up her traditions, and her fear of the unknown and her sensitivity lead her temporarily into madness. However, in spite of the power of the plains that "drink the blood of Christian men," a community springs up, paid for in both human suffering and human lives. Though Per Hansa loses his battle with nature, the final scene of *Riket grundlægges* is one of hope and optimism, as his body is found in the spring, with his eyes firmly fixed toward the West. *Peder Seier* (1928; *Peder Victorious*, 1929) takes up the story of Per Hansa and Beret's son, Peder, though Beret remains a central figure. The main theme is Peder's conflict with his mother's values as he tries to break with his Norwegian past and become fully Americanized. In this novel the conflict is no longer the grand and at times mythic struggle against nature and against inner demons; instead, it portrays the social and cultural conflict of an immigrant community trying to establish its own norms and sense of identity. Rølvaag's last novel, *Den signede dag* (1931; *Their Father's God*, 1931), continues the story of Peder and his marriage to the culturally and intellectually incompatible Irish Catholic girl, Susie Doheney. Again, Beret emerges a central figure. She is perhaps Rølvaag's alter ego, embodying both the tragic spiritual loss entailed in immigration, as well as the promise America held out for material and intellectual betterment. Although the price is high, perhaps incalculably so, a new community does spring up, the prairie is conquered, Beret's farm does prosper, and in the end, we feel that Peder is groping his way toward an understanding and acceptance of his cultural heritage. Rølvaag's artistic vision presents us not only with a great epic of the American frontier, but also with a penetrating insight into the universal human condition.

FURTHER WORKS

Paa glemte veie (1914); *To tullinger* (1920; *Pure Gold*, 1930); *Omkring fædrearven* (1922); *Længselens baat* (1920; *The Boat of Longing*, 1933); *Fortællinger og skildringer* (1932).

REFERENCES

Eckstein, Neil T., "The Social Criticism of Ole Edvart Rølvaag." *Norwegian-American Studies* 24 (1970); Eckstein, Neil T., "*Giants in the Earth* as Saga," in *Where the West Begins*, ed. A. Huseboe and C. Geyer (Sioux Falls, S. D., 1978); Gvåle, Gudrun Hovde, *Ole Edvart Rølvaag: nordmann og amerikanar* (Oslo, 1962); Haugen, Einar, "O. E. Rølvaag: Norwegian-American." *Norwegian-American Studies and Records* 7 (1933); Jorgenson, Theodore, and Nora O. Solum, *Ole Edvart Rølvaag: A Biography* (New York, 1939); Paulson, Kristoffer, "Berdahl Family History and Rølvaag's Immigrant History." *Norwegian-American Studies* 27 (1927); Reaske, Hubert E., *Rølvaag's "Giants in the Earth"* (New York, 1965); Reigstad, Paul, *Rølvaag: His Life and Art* (Lincoln, 1972); Simonson, Harold P., *Prairies Within* (Seattle, 1987); Simonsen, Harold P., "Rølvaag and Kierkegaard." *Scandinavian Studies* 49 (1977); Thorson, Gerald, ed., *Ole Rølvaag: Artist and Cultural Leader* (Northfield, Minn., 1975).

Solveig Zempel

Runeberg, Johan Ludvig. Finnish poet, playwright, short story writer, and critic (writing in Swedish), b. 5 February 1804, Jakobstad (Pietarsaari), d. 6 May 1877 Borgå (Porvoo).

Runeberg went to school in Uleåborg (Oulu) and Vasa (Vaasa), passed his matriculation examinations in 1822, studied at the Åbo Academy, worked as a tutor from December 1823 to January 1825 in the Finnish interior (Saarijarvi and Ruovesi), and received a master of arts degree in 1827. In 1830 Runeberg became an assistant professor of rhetoric at the university which, following a disastrous fire in Turku (Åbo) in 1827, had been located in Helsinki (Helsingfors). Between 1832 and 1837 Runeberg worked also as the editor of *Helsingfors Morgonblad,* but moved to Borgå in 1837 to assume a job in a high school, teaching Roman and Greek literature. Runeberg lived in Borgå for the rest of his life. He traveled abroad only once, in Sweden in 1851. He was married to Fredrika Tengström, also an interesting literary figure and an author of a number of novels. In December 1863 Runeberg suffered a stroke that caused the end of his writing career.

Runeberg was first and foremost a lyricist and an epic poet in the classical tradition but wrote also dramas and short stories. As a literary critic of *Helsingfors Morgonblad* he displayed a clearly defined attitude to literature and was, for instance, very critical of the dominant contemporary Swedish literary trends.

Runeberg made his debut with the collection *Dikter* (1830; Poems) and published two more collections of lyric poetry in 1833 and 1843. In his early poetry he stands on traditional ground; one may note the influence of Frans Michael Franzén* and Carl Michael Bellman,* both of whom he praises in his critical articles. Of great importance to Runeberg's own poetry was his encounter with a collection of Serbian folk songs in German translation. His Swedish translation of them appeared in 1830. The cycle of poems "Idyll och epigram" (*Lyrical Songs. Idylls and Epigrams*, 1878), which contains perhaps his best lyric poems, at least the most original ones, was strongly influenced by the folk songs. This influence is displayed in the form, for example, the trochaic, unrhymed meter, as well as in the subject matter, for example, the succession of events and the use of dialogue. Idylls are rarely strictly tied to a specific milieu but rather reflect universal human concerns ("In the arms of her fiancé a maiden cried"). On the other hand, some of them are characterized by the national idealism to which Runeberg was to devote himself and to which so many others, because of him, have been devoted. The best-known example is the poem "Bonden Pavo" (1830; The Peasant Paavo). Its realistic background derives from the familiarity with Finnish peasant life that Runeberg acquired during his time as tutor in the Finnish interior. When Paavo after years of toil has succeeded in draining his own lands so that frost can no longer destroy his crops, his wife looks forward to a better life. But Paavo asks her to continue mixing bark into the bread "because our neighbor's field remains frozen."

Woman's role in Runeberg's poetry is interesting. In the love poems it is usually the woman that speaks. In principle Runeberg avoids personal allusions; if there are any, they are attributed to others. Nature, preferably Finnish summer nature, is a recurrent theme, with potential for symbolism that, however, rarely becomes obtrusive.

Many of Runeberg's lyric poems were set to music and quickly became popular, such as the still frequently sung *Svanen* (1830; The Swan) and *Vid en källa* (1833; At a Fountain), which were set to the music of F. A. Ehrström. Runeberg's exceptionally keen sense of rhythm renders his poems very melodious.

Nevertheless, it was Runeberg's epic poems that made him a pioneer within Swedish literature. The first one of them is *Elgskyttarne* (1832; The Moose Hunters), written in hexameters, a description of the milieu, people, and events of a moose hunt in the Finnish interior. With its many keenly observed ethnographical details the poem introduces a new realism while at the same time giving an idealized image of the nation, an image that was in force for decades to come. The epic poems *Hanna* (1836) and *Julqvällen* (1841; Christmas Eve) had a similar effect. On the very eve of Christmas the old soldier Pistol learns that his only son has been killed in the Turkish War. When the owner of the estate invites Pistol to come to live with him, Pistol declines, gratefully, and returns to his cabin.

In *Kung Fjalar* (1844; *King Fjalar*, 1904, 1912) Runeberg chooses an entirely new form, a stanzaic one with features from Old Norse skaldic poetry. It is a tragedy of fate that takes place among the ancient Scandinavians and in Scotland. The king is stern in manner and trustful in his ability to govern his own fate. When he hears about the prediction that his daughter and son are to fall in illicit love with each other, he has the daughter thrown into water. Fate spins on! What was to happen, happens and king Fjalar takes his own life.

Runeberg had already attained the position of Finland's leading poet, when the first part of his most read and most widely distributed work appeared, *Fänrik Ståls sägner* (2 vols., 1848, 1860; *The Tales by Ensign Stål*, 1925, 1938, 1952). The tales can be described as a collection of ballads (many of them have been set to music) with motifs from the war of 1808–1809 that marked Finland's separation from Sweden, to which it had belonged for centuries, and its becoming a Grand Duchy of Imperial Russia. From an aesthetic standpoint the tales are of varying quality, but that has in no way prevented them from assuming the role of a patriotic song of songs in Finland (and in Sweden). The introductory poem "Vårt land" (1846; Our Country) became Finland's national anthem.

As a dramatist Runeberg does not attain the same stature as in the rest of his production. His comedies are insignificant, some compositional details being almost painfully simple. The first comedy from 1834 was destroyed by Runeberg himself (a few copies escaped his attention)—perhaps with an awareness of his future role. *Kungarne på Salamis* (1863; The Kings of Salamis) has, however, been considered a powerful drama. Here as in *Kung Fjalar* man stands in opposition to his fate. Father and son belong to opposing camps. The father ends up killing his son, who has exchanged attire with his brother-in-arms. The drama is clearly structured in accordance with Greek patterns. The verse is unrhymed, iambic trimeter. It is hard to adapt to Swedish; as a result, the word order sounds unnatural in many places. Although the work is probably impossible to stage today, it contains passages of great lyric beauty. It was Runeberg's last work and although it was published shortly before he fell ill, he had started working on it as early as in the mid–1840s.

During the 1850s Runeberg was asked to participate in the creation of a new hymnbook for Finland's Evangelical Lutheran church. Many of his hymns still remain in the hymnal that is currently in use.

When Runeberg, for instance in *Kung Fjalar*, depicts fate's grim game with human beings and shows how time after time it destroys those that dare to challenge it, he was not merely following a classical tradition. Occasionally his own feelings got him involved in situations of conflict that only time could resolve. It is these personal storms that sweep over the Old Norse and classical Greek grounds.

Runeberg's significance within the history of Finland has been greater than that of any other poet, and of such greatness that it can hardly be matched even by poets in other countries. Since its infancy Finland's conception of national identity has been wrapped in phrases from Runeberg's works; and for the country's struggle for independence both before and after the 1917 declaration of independence, Runeberg's poetry has meant possibly more than all weapons.

Runeberg's significance in today's Finland is hard to assess. For most people he is perhaps just a name. Yet in the beginning of the 1980s an illustrated reprint edition of *Fänrik Ståls sägner* became a great sales success. And the clichéd image of Finland, based on Runeberg's work, as a poor land of wilderness has been amazingly long-lived. Among those of Runeberg's works that survive by virtue of their literary quality, the poems in the "Idyll och epigram" rank possibly highest.

FURTHER WORKS

Samlade Arbeten, 6 vols. (1861–1864); *Efterlämnade Skrifter*, 2 vols. (1878, 1879); *Samlade skrifter*, 2 vols. (1886); *Samlade Arbeten. Normalupplaga*, 8 vols. (1899–1902); *Samlade skriffer*, ed. G. Castrén and M. Lamm; G. Tideström and C. E. Thors; C. E. Thors and T. Wretö; J. Wrede and T. Wretö, 18 vols. (1933–   ); *Skrifter i urval*, 4 vols. (1960).

FURTHER TRANSLATIONS

Anthology of Swedish Lyrics from 1750 to 1915, trans. Charles W. Stork (1917); *Swedo-Finnish Short Stories*, ed. George C. Schoolfield (1974); *Books from Finland* 19.4 (1985).

REFERENCES

Brydolf, Ernst, *Runeberg och Sverige,* 2 vols. (Helsinki, 1943, 1966); Estlander, Carl Gustaf, *Uppsatser om Johan Ludvig Runeberg*, in his *Skrifter*, vol. 1 (Helsinki, 1914); Hedvall, Ruth, *Johan Ludvig Runeberg*, 2nd rev. ed. (Stockholm, 1931); Hirn, Yrjö, *Runebergskulten* (Helsinki, 1935); Hirn, Yrjö, *Runeberggestalten* (Helsinki, 1942); Hornborg, Eirik, *Fänrik Ståls sägner och verkligheten* (Helsinki, 1954); Jones, W. Glyn, "Introduction." *Books from Finland* 2.2 (1977); Nilsson, Kim, "J. L. Runeberg as a Modern Writer: The Evidence of 'Julqvällen.' " *Scandinavian Studies* 58.1 (1986); Runeberg, Fredrik, *Anteckningar om Runeberg* (Helsinki, 1946); Schoolfield, George C., "Poetry and Patriotism: Johan Ludvig Runeberg." *Books from Finland* 19.4 (1985); Söderhjelm, Werner, *Johan Ludvig Runeberg: Hans liv och hans diktning*, 2 vols. (Helsinki, 1904–1906; 2nd rev. ed., 1929); Tideström, Gunnar, *Runeberg som estetiker* (Helsinki, 1941); Viljanen, Lauri, *Runeberg och hans diktning*, 2 vols. (Lund, 1947, 1969); Wrede, Johan, *Jag såg ett folk . . . : Runeberg, Fänrik Stål och nationen* (Helsinki, 1988); Wretö, Tore, *J. L. Runeberg* (Boston, 1980).

Lars Huldén

Rydberg, Abraham *Viktor*. Swedish novelist, scholar, and poet, b. 18 December 1828, Jönköping, d. 21 September 1895, Stockholm.

Rydberg's childhood was impoverished and his education spotty, but he managed to pass his student examination and secure a position as a journalist, first on *Jönköpingsbladet,* then on the liberal—even radical—*Göteborgs Handels-och Sjöfartstidning*. Its editors, Johan Sandwall and his successor S. A. Hedlund, encouraged Rydberg's aesthetic and political development by publishing his articles and, ultimately, his novels in the pages of *Göteborgs Handels- och Sjöfartstidning*. Rydberg's first success came with *Fribrytaren på Östersjön* (1857; *The Freebooter of the Baltic*, 1891), a historical novel set in the seventeenth century, but with a clearly tendentious attack on the forces of reaction, especially religious fanaticism and intolerance. *Singoalla* (1858; rev. ed. 1965; new rev. ed. 1903) was a medieval romantic tale about a Swedish knight and a gypsy girl, filled with speculations about hypnosis and the darker aspects of the life of the spirit.

Rydberg's breakthrough as a novelist came with *Den siste Atenaren* (1859; *The Last Athenian*, 1869), a huge novel about Emperor Julian the Apostate's vain attempt to reintroduce paganism (which, for Rydberg, represented the ideal synthesis of logic, sensuality, and humanism) in the face of fanatical, world-denying Christianity. In 1862, Rydberg published a highly controversial pamphlet, *Bibelns lära om Kristus* (The Teachings of the Bible about Christ), which argued that the Trinity and the dual nature (divine/human) of Christ have no scriptural basis. In later years, Rydberg turned his attention to ancient Scandinavian culture in *Undersökningar i germansk mytologi* (1886–1889; first volume only as *Teutonic Mythology*, 1889). He was, during a long period of depression, also interested in Platonism and the works of Gottfried Wilhelm Leibniz, Johann Gottlieb Fichte, and Immanuel Kant. As a poet, Rydberg's greatest works came in the 1880s, with *Dikter, andra samlingen* (1891; Poems, Second Collection), in which he continues his attack on materialism, lack of piety, and dogmatic institutions that inhibit intellectual freedom, an attack he continued in his last historical novel, *Vapensmeden* (1891; The Armorer). He became a member of the Swedish Academy in 1877, and a professor, first of cultural history, and then of the history and theory of the fine arts at the University of Stockholm until his death in 1895.

FURTHER WORKS

Skrifter, ed. K. Warburg, 14 vols. (1896–1899); *Filosofiska föreläsningar*, 4 vols. (1899–1901); *Kulturhistoriska föreläsningar*, 6 vols. (1903–1906); *Brev*, 3 vols. (1923–1926); *Skrifter*, ed. I. Wizelius, 12 vols. (1945–1946).

FURTHER TRANSLATIONS

An Anthology of Swedish Lyrics from 1750–1925, ed. C. W. Stork (1917).

REFERENCES

Ek, Sverker, *Möten med Runeberg, Rydberg och Fröding* (Lund, 1949); Forsström, Axel, *Viktor Rydberg, Barndom och ungdom, 1818–1855* (Lund, 1960); Hegerfors, Torsten, *Viktor Rydbergs utveckling till religiös reformator* (Göteborg, 1960); Holmberg, Olle, *Viktor Rydbergs lyrik* (Stockholm, 1935); Krook, Isak, *Viktor Rydbergs lära om Kristus* (Stockholm, 1935); Lindberger, Örjan, *Prometeustanken hos Viktor Rydberg*, 2 vols. (Stockholm, 1938); Svanberg, Victor, *Novantiken i Den siste Atenaren* (Uppsala, 1928); Svanberg, Victor, *Rydbergs Singoalla* (Uppsala, 1923); Warburg, Karl, *Viktor Rydberg, en lefnadsteckning* (Stockholm, 1900).

Lars Emil Scott

S

Saarikoski, Pentti. Finnish poet, translator, and prose writer, b. 2 September 1937, Impilahti, d. 24 August 1983, Kajaani.

Even in his childhood home Saarikoski was surrounded by books. He was drawn to classical literature and languages early on at school, and pursued this interest at the university where he studied Greek for two years. His first collection of poetry appeared in 1958.

Saarikoski's poetry of the 1950s was not unlike that of his modernist contemporaries. His lyrical voice at the time was somewhat effete, and the well-crafted poems in the three volumes of this first period contained classical references. He emphasized the clarity of imagery, but by using everyday speech together with classical idioms, he created a new and special effect in his poems.

During the 1960s Saarikoski became the most prominent of the Finnish modernist poets; he was seen as a polemical and aware individual, whose classical mode of reasoning informed his seemingly carefree diction. He often used parody, which offended many readers. In addition to his artistic achievements, he was known to the public for his bohemian ways and his political activities. In rebellion against his middle-class background, Saarikoski joined the Communist party for a short period of time, contributed to its publications, and even stood as the party's candidate for Parliament. His most influential collection of the early 1960s was *Mitä tapahtuu todella* (1962; What Actually Happens). In it the poet combines political commentary with everyday speech in an intriguing mesh of the trivial and the lofty. The result was confusing, yet immediate and real. Another notable collection from this period is *Kuljen missä kuljen* (1965; I Wander Here and There), in which he vents his feelings of disillusionment and dejection but also makes an effort to overcome them.

Equal in importance to Saarikoski's original poetry are his numerous translations—approximately forty-five books in all—ranging from James Joyce's *Ulysses*, Homer's *Odyssey*, and Saul Bellow's *Herzog* to Arthur Miller, Allen

Ginsberg, and Philip Roth. These writers no doubt contributed to Saarikoski's own stylistic development. Among his Finnish predecessors, Saarikoski identified himself most closely with Eino Leino* from the early part of the century. In a lyric essay bearing the older poet's name, *Eino Leino* (1974), Saarikoski combines elements from Leino's life with a perceptive probing of his own poetic identity.

In 1975, partly due to frustration with politics, Saarikoski settled in Sweden. Concern with nature and mythical-ecological issues transcended day-to-day political questions. From the 1970s date a collection of love lyrics and several autobiographical prose works. In Sweden, Saarikoski continued to publish and translate world literature into Finnish. Together with his Swedish wife, Mia Berner, he wrote the collection *Ja meille jäi kiireetön ilta/Kvällen gör sig ingen brådska* (1975; The Evening That Knows No Rush). His last volumes, a trilogy, show increased optimism and precision in style.

Through his poetry, permeated by the modernist sensibility, Saarikoski revised the Finnish poetic tradition. His translations have also been acclaimed a masterly achievement.

FURTHER WORKS

Runoja (1958); *Toisia runoja* (1958); *Runot ja Hipponaksin runot* (1959); *Nenän pakinoita* (1960); *Maailmasta* (1961); *Ovat muistojemme lehdet kuolleet* (1964); *Runoja, 1958– 1962* (1964); *Punaiset liput* (1966); *Ääneen* (1966); *Laulu laululta pois* (1966); *Aika Prahassa* (1967); *En soisi sen päättyvän* (1968); *Kirje vaimolleni* (1968); *Katselen Stalinin pään yli ulos* (1969); *Onnen aika* (1971); *Alue* (1973); *Valitut runot* (1974); *Tanssilattia vuorella* (1977); *Tähänastiset runot* (1978); *Asiaa tai ei* (1980); *Tanssiinkutsu* (1980); *Hämärän tanssit* (1983); *Nuoruuden päiväkirjat*, ed. Pekka Tarkka (1984); *Köyhyyden filosofia* (1986).

TRANSLATIONS

Helsinki, trans. Anselm Hollo (1962, 1967); *Finnish Odyssey*, ed. Robert Armstrong (1975); *Snow in May*, ed. Richard Dauenhauer et al. (1978); *Scandinavian Review* 68.4 (1980); *Scandinavian Review* 70.4 (1982); *Poems 1958–1980*, ed. Anselm Hollo (1983).

REFERENCES

Berner, Mia, *PS* (Stockholm, 1985); Hollo, Anselm, "On His Way Home: The Poems of Pentti Saarikoski." *Scandinavian Review* 72.2 (1984); Laitinen, Kai, *Suomen kirjallisuus 1917–1967* (Helsinki, 1967); Leitch, Vincent B., "The Postmodern Poetry and Poetics of Pentti Saarikoski." *Scandinavian Review* 70.4 (1982); Simonsuuri, Kirsti, "Myth and Material in the Poetry of Pentti Saarikoski since 1958." *World Literature Today* 54.1 (1980); Tarkka, Pekka, "The Death of a Poet." *Books from Finland* 17.4 (1983); Tarkka, Pekka, "An Introduction to the Poetry of Pentti Saarikoski." *Books from Finland* 11.4 (1977).

Kalevi Lappalainen

Salama, Hannu. Finnish novelist, b. 6 October 1936, Kouvola.

Salama left school early and went to work, first as an agricultural laborer and later as an electrician. He was, nevertheless, an avid reader, and steeped himself in the works of Fyodor Dostoyevski, Friedrich Nietzsche, and Albert Camus. His first novel, *Se tavallinen tarina* (1961; The Same Old Story) at once brought him to the attention of the reading public. In it he describes the onset of a schizophrenic illness. In *Juhannustanssit* (1964; Midsummer Dance), a "well-made" and dramatic novel, he described a pagan midsummer orgy with a tragic end. Many readers, including the archbishop of Finland, were offended by his language, and certain expressions put into the mouth of Jesus led to a prosecution for blasphemy: Salama was given a suspended sentence. The novel *Minä, Olli ja Orvokki* (1967; Olli, Orvokki and Me) can be seen as his riposte to a hypocritical public: its characters are outcasts from society, demonstrating their depravity in the struggle for money, women and fame.

Salama's most important work to date is *Siinä näkijä missä tekijä* (1972; No Crime Without a Witness), a multi dimensional novel about the communists in Finland, who found themselves in a difficult position when the Finns were fighting on Hilter's side against the Soviet Union. The book is a study of conflicting personal relationships, bringing out, in particular, the mental factors that led some communists to support the "hard" line while others favored revisionism. It is not, however, purely a political novel: Salama's main interest is concentrated on the people who live on the fringes of the party and its activities: small-time rural crooks, double agents, the rebel destroyed by his own existential defiance; the insulted and the injured whose road to freedom is beset with guilt, suffering, and death. Although the novel is made up of several parallel narrations by different characters, and thus makes considerable demands upon the reader, it has pleased both the public and the critics, and was awarded the literature prize of the Nordic Council in 1975.

Since then, however, Salama's reputation as the best Finnish novelist of his generation has been somewhat shaken by the mixed reaction accorded to the five-part series of novels to which he has given the ironical title of *Finlandia* (*Kosti Herhiläisen perunkirjoitus*, 1976; *Kolera on raju bändi*, 1977; *Pasi Harvalan tarina*, 2 vols., 1981–1983; *Kaivo kellarissa*, 1983); and which defies every known literary convention. It is an unwieldly, rather formless work—parts of it can only be described as chaotic—about seven authors who destroy everyone around them, and each other.

FURTHER WORKS

Lomapäivä (1962); *Puu balladin haudalla* (1963); *Kenttäläinen käy talossa* (1967); *Joulukuun kuudes* (1968); *Kesäleski* (1969); *Tapausten kulku* (1969); *Lokakuun päiviä* (1971); *Villanpehmee, taskunlämmin* (1971); *Tienviitta ja muita novelleja* (1974); *Runot* (1975); *Pentti Saarikoski, legenda jo eläessään* (1975); *Ihmisen ääni* (1978); *Kolme sukupolvea* (1978); *Vuosi elämästäni* (1979); *Itäväylä* (1980); *Runoja* (1984); *Punajuova* (1985); *Romaanit*, 4 vols. (1986), *Amos ja saarelaiset* (1987); *Näkymä kuivaushuoneen ikkunasta* (1988).

FURTHER TRANSLATIONS

Snow in May, ed. Richard Dauenhauer and Philip Binham (1978); *Finnish Short Stories,* ed. Inkeri Väänänen-Jensen and K. Börje Vähämäki (1982).

REFERENCES

Tarkka, Pekka, *Hannu Salama* (Helsinki, 1973; Uddevalla, 1976); Tarkka, Pekka, "Hannu Salama: A Writer between the Social Classes." *World Literature Today* 54.1 (1980); Tarkka, Pekka, "Writer, Church and Party." *Index on Censorship* 2 (1982).

Pekka Tarkka

Salonen, Frans Uuno. *See* Kailas, Uuno.

Sami Literature. The Samis constitute a small group of ethnically and linguistically related people without a national state of their own. They live in four different countries—the northern parts of Norway, Sweden, Finland, and on the Kola isthmus of the USSR.

Although the Samis comprise the native population of these regions, they have never been granted political rights as a separate people with a language and culture of their own. Throughout history the Sami areas have been occupied by the four national states and subjugated to their jurisdiction. The Samis showed little resistance because the colonization occurred gradually and precipitated an early collapse of the Samis' own internal system of government. For a long time the Samis have been oppressed, especially in terms of culture, by the powerful societies that surround them. For instance, their language has been repressed and nearly eliminated since its usage is prohibited in education. Consequently, the language situation has been rather precarious in certain areas, but for the Sami population as a whole, language remains vigorous and is one of the most important carriers of culture. Also the unique Sami music, the *joik,* which was to some extent linked to the Sami religion, was forbidden by the missionaries. But it was not possible in the long run to eliminate either the *joik* or the language, and today both are experiencing a renaissance together with Sami visual arts and handicrafts.

The oldest Sami poetry that has been recorded can be found in Johannes Schefferus's work *Lapponia* from 1673, to which the Sami student Olaus Sirma has contributed two traditional song (*joik*) texts. These two lyrical love poems were later translated into a number of other languages and included, for example, in J. G. Herder's book *Stimmen der Völker in Liedern* (1807).

In the 1820s while Jacob Fellman was a minister on the Finnish side of the Tana river in the northernmost part of Finland, he recorded a number of *joiks* of both epic and lyric quality, whose content encompasses everything from shamanism to animal *joik* (perhaps derived from exorcisms or hunting magic) and songs in a freer form recounting various events in the life of the Sami people. Some of these old texts can also be read as a firsthand Sami commentary on the colonization process and as such they are early examples of internal Sami mobilization against oppression from outside. But the actual folk epic that tells, for instance, about the origin of the Sami people, is a work that the Sami minister Anders Fjellner (1795–1876) recorded from a man named Leuhnje in the mid–1800s. It must be assumed that this epic about the "Daughters of the Sun" and

"Sons of the Sun" had been greatly abridged so that Fjellner's version (which incidentally is reproduced in Swedish in Gustav von Düben's *Lappland och lapperna* [1873]) contains only the most central sections. Although the poems resemble other folk epics in terms of structure and form, they do not conflict with the traditions of Sami poetry. Thus it is possible to regard them as genuine Sami poetry. Among the Samis, oral tradition has always been stronger than the written, and good storytellers have seen to it that legends and folktales have been passed on from generation to generation. Yet we must assume that much has been lost, particularly such songs and *joik* texts that formed part of the old Sami religious practices.

Joik poetry in all its great variety has always had a strong position among the Sami people. It includes short and witty proverb-like sayings as well as longer narrative stories. And even if only a select few had learned and could perform the longer epic poems, all who created *joiks* must be regarded as poets in their own right. Most of the singers added words that briefly described the intention of their particular *joik*. This tradition remains alive in today's Sami lyric poetry. In general, Sami poetry shows a clear awareness of tradition, which in itself is rather surprising considering that the schools have not offered any instruction in the subject. For example in 1932–1933, H. A. Guttorm wrote an epic (published in 1983) that in form and imagery is strongly reminiscent of Fjellner's *Beaivi bártnit* ("Solsønene"), while he at the same time refers in his poems to both Olaus Sirma's nature lyrics and Jacob Fellman's *joik*-like poetry.

The first books in Sami language were religious writings, hymns as well as sermons, both translations and original texts. In 1910 the first book by a Sami was published. This book, *Muittalus sámiid birra (Turi's Book of Lappland*, 1931) recounts aspects of ordinary life among the Sami. The author was a reindeer herder by the name of Johan Turi. The book was published simultaneously in a Danish translation by Emilie Demart, who had originally encouraged Turi to write his account. Later Turi's work was translated into Swedish, German, and English. His narrative is a realistic and dramatic story about the life of Sami reindeer herders with an added dimension; it adopts a clear stand on the colonization of Sami territory. The book also contains much traditional material about Sami folklore, customs, and folk medicine and provides historical background for some of the legends, such as the one about the robbers in Samiland.

Only two years after the publication of Turi's book, the first novel in Sami language appeared. It was written by Anders Larsen (1870–1949). Entitled *Beaivi-álgo* (Day Break), it portrays a Sami youth's development from childhood to adult awareness. The protagonist, Ábo, is always painfully aware of the difficulties in being a Sami, both at home and within the larger Norwegian society. Through a tragic love story, he matures to understand that if the Sami people are to improve their condition, they must become more aware of themselves just as outsiders must improve their knowledge of the Samis. The book is characterized both by romantic and social trends that are realistic and offer a clear ethnic message. Anders Larsen himself was very active within Sami politics in the early part of this century and edited among other things a newspaper, *Sagai Maîttalægje*, in which he introduced Isak Saba, the person who later was to be elected to the Norwegian parliament as the first Sami representative.

Pedar Jalvi's (1888–1916) *Muohta' calmit* (1915; Snow Flakes) is a small collection of five poems and seven short stories. It is a low-key book in which one can sense an underlying strength and a careful optimism on behalf of the Sami people that characterizes for example the sections that deal with children.

After the publication of these three books, over twenty years passed before anything was published again in Sami. Yet, another Sami author, a contemporary of Turi, Larsen, and Jalvi, wrote a number of books in Norwegian. Matti Aikio chose to support the Norwegianization and assimilation of the Sami people. This he accomplished both in his articles and books, apart from the last work in which he presented a somewhat more varied picture that seems to advocate a pluralistic society. It was Aikio's decision to write in Norwegian, whereas today many Sami authors are forced to write in one of the majority languages since they have had no chance for formal training in their own mother tongue.

During the period between the two world wars the efforts to create one homogenous Norwegian population were intensified even further, and this in turn rendered the Samis' political activity difficult. Consequently, no literature in the Sami languages was published in Norway during this time, aside from an important work collected and edited by a scholar: J. K. Qvigstad's *Lappiske eventyr og sagn* (Lappish Legends and Tales). The work comprises four volumes and includes 600 stories with parallel texts in Norwegian and Sami. In Sweden two books in Sami were published, both dealing with the reindeer-herding milieu; the one written by Anta Pirak (1937) and the other written and illustrated by Nils Nilsson Skum (1938). In Finland Hans Aslak Guttorm made a debut in 1940 with the poetry and short story collection *Koccam spalli* (Arousing Wind). He had been writing for a long time prior to this, but the manuscripts remained in his desk drawers until 1983. Now, however, a series of his poems, short stories, and novels are being printed by a Sami publishing house. Guttorm in many ways provides the link between old traditions and the Sami authors who are today establishing themselves even though several decades passed before the younger generation started publishing.

Another source of inspiration for the new authors is Paulus Utsi. By profession he was a reindeer herder, a skilled handicrafter, teacher, and poet. In his poetry he used language both to reveal and to be revealed. But it served also as a trap to capture his understanding of reality. Paulus was preoccupied with the fate of the Sami people, oppressed by society at large; he witnessed much suffering and was somewhat pessimistic regarding the future of the individual, but he believed in the Sami people as an active and fighting whole. In order to illustrate this optimism he often used the image of firewood. If only we provide enough fuel for the fire, no wind or storm can extinguish it. Unfortunately, he died young and had published only two collections of poetry, which have since won international acclaim.

The 1970s experienced an enormous blossoming of Sami authors, a development that has continued. Today there are more active Sami writers than ever before. During this period women authors finally have begun to participate in the shaping of future trends. Most of the authors continue to write in Sami, but there are some, in poetry as well as in prose, who have made a name for themselves in one of the national languages. To give a brief characterization of today's generation of Sami authors and at the same time do full justice to the authors is of course impossible, but one can sum up by saying that today's Sami literature strives to show the strength of the Sami people. More than ever before there is an awareness of the Sami minority position and of the oppression under which they have struggled and continue to struggle. Therefore, the authors consider it their duty to prove the independence of Sami culture in order to eliminate any feeling of inferiority and resignation among their people. They also consider it important to compare themselves to other native populations in similar situations so that through common ethnic awareness they can more readily resist external threats. Modern Sami poets address personal and social conflicts regarding cultural identity. Of course they also write about general human conditions as do all authors in the world. Important names among the younger writers include Eino Guttorm, Kirsti Paltto, Nils Aslak Valkeapää, Rauni Lukkari, Synnöve Persen, Ellen-Marie Vars, Johan Gustavsen, and Ailo Gaup. In addition, it is necessary to mention Sami authors of children's books who consider it their mission to create original Sami reading materials for the young. Old legends and stories often form the starting point for a story that also has validity for today's society. Marry Ailonieida Somby is the first Sami author in the genre.

A number of Sami biographies and much factual literature have also been published during the past few years.

TRANSLATIONS

Valkeapää, Nils Aslak, "Poems from *Giða ijat čuov' gadat* ('The light nights of spring')." *Books from Finland* 11.2 (1977); Valkeapää, Nils Aslak, *Greetings from Lappland* (1983); Valkeapää, Nils Aslak, *The Flute of Ice* (1984).

REFERENCES

Eidheim, Harald, *Aspects of the Lappish Minority Situation* (Oslo, 1974); Gaski, Harald, *Med ord skal tyvene fordrives, om samernes episk poetiske diktning* (Karasjok, 1987); Jahreskog, Birgitta, ed., *The Sami National Minority in Sweden* (Stockholm, 1982); Lundmark, Bo, *Anders Fjellner—Samernas Homeros* (Umeå, 1979); Nickul, Karl, *The Lappish Nation*, Indiana University Publications 122 (Bloomington, 1977); Ruong, Israel, *The Lapps in Sweden* (Stockholm, 1967); Siuruainen, E., and P. Aikio, *The Lapps in Finland* (Helsinki, 1977); Wicklund, K. B., *Lapparnas sång och poesi* (Uppsala, 1906).
                                                                    Harald Gaski

Sandel, Cora (pseud. of Sara Fabricius). Norwegian novelist, b. 20 December 1880, Kristiania, d. 3 April 1974, Uppsala.

Sandel's early ambition was to be a painter; her literary debut did not come until she was forty-six, with the first part of the trilogy that many consider her finest achievement: *Alberte og Jakob* (1926; *Alberta and Jacob*, 1962); *Alberte og friheten* (1931; *Alberta and Freedom*, 1963); and *Bare Alberte* (1939; *Alberta Alone*, 1965). These novels describe the slow and painful maturing—both as an artist and as a woman—of the central character, Alberte. She grows up in a small North Norwegian town, frozen in body and spirit; not until she comes to Paris as a young woman does her talent begin to emerge from her passive conditioning. Her struggles are thrown into sharp relief by descriptions of other women's acceptance of or revolt against the female roles imposed on them by society. Characters and milieu are observed with a sharp eye for the telling detail, and a warm sympathy for those whose dreams end in bitterness.

These traits are also in evidence in Sandel's short stories, collected in *En blå sofa* (1927; A Blue Sofa), *Carmen og Maja* (1932; Carmen and Maja), and *Mange takk, doktor* (1935; Thank You, Doctor). Here too the central character is often a talented and sensitive woman whose desperate attempts to realize her own potential are thwarted by petty social convention or a cold and domineering family. The novel *Kranes konditori* (1945; *Krane's Café*, 1967) presents another tragic female fate; the wretchedness of the misused Katinka Stordal is presented through the medium of spiteful small-town gossip and outraged scandalmongering, in such a way that she is made to seem doubly alone.

Sandel's Alberte trilogy has long been recognized as a central work of modern literature, an *Entwicklungsroman* on a par with the contemporary *Kristin Lavransdatter* by Sigrid Undset.* However, it is not until recently that much critical attention has been devoted to her works, and she has taken her place as a leading twentieth-century author.

FURTHER WORKS

Dyr jeg har kjent (1945); *Figurer på mørk bunn* (1949); *Kjøp ikke Dondi* (1958; *The Leech*, 1960).

FURTHER TRANSLATIONS

Slaves of Love, ed. J. McFarlane (1982); *An Everyday Story*, ed. Katherine Hanson (1984); *Cora Sandel: Selected Short Stories*, trans. Barbara Wilson (1985); *The Silken Thread*, trans. Elizabeth Rokkan (1986).

REFERENCES

Gimnes, Steinar, *Cora Sandel* (Oslo, 1982); Lervik, Åse Hiorth, *Menneske og miljø i Cora Sandels diktning* (Oslo, 1977); Nettum, Rolf Nyboe, "A Tempestuous Era: Norwegian Literature between the Wars," in *Review of National Literatures: Norway*, ed. Sverre Lyngstad (New York, 1983); Øverland, Janneken, *Cora Sandel om seg selv* (Oslo, 1983); Ryen Mangset, Berit, *Alberte—fra et kvinnesynspunkt* (Oslo, 1977); Solumsmoen, Odd, *Cora Sandel* (Oslo, 1957); Wilson, Barbara, "To Possess both Children and Work." *Backbone* 3 (1981); Zuck, Virpi, "Cora Sandel, a Norwegian Feminist." *Edda* 1 (1981).

Janet Garton

Sandemose, Aksel. Norwegian novelist, b. 19 March 1899, Nykøbing Mors, Denmark, d. 6 August 1965, Copenhagen.

Sandemose was born on an island off the northern coast of Jutland, the eighth in a family of nine children. His father was a socialist blacksmith and model worker; his mother, a Norwegian immigrant, spent her life in a perpetual struggle to feed her large family. Aksel's ambivalent relationship with his parents and siblings is in significant ways at the root of Sandemose's fiction. As a young man Sandemose went to sea, but jumped ship at Fogo and spent a few months working in lumber camps in Newfoundland. In 1930 he settled permanently in Norway.

Most of Sandemose's protagonists are proletarians, and the author describes the life of small-town workers in early twentieth-century Denmark as a living hell. It is an environment from which the protagonist will attempt to escape at any cost, but to which he at the same time is curiously tied. He confronts the problem most directly in his path-breaking novel, *En flyktning krysser sitt spor* (1933; *A Fugitive Crosses His Tracks*, 1936), where he sets down the ten commandments for his celebrated Jante law:

1. You shall not believe you *are* something.

2. You shall not believe that you are as much as *we* are.

3. You shall not believe that you are wiser than *we* are.

4. You shall not imagine that you are better than *we* are.

5. You shall not believe that you know more than *we* do.

6. You shall not believe that you are more than *we* are.

7. You shall not believe that *you* are good for anything.

8. You shall not laugh at *us*.

9. You shall not believe that anybody cares for *you*.

10. You shall not believe that you can teach *us* anything.

The repetitious, negative clauses of the Jante law all serve the same purpose, namely to pit the individual against the collective, *you* against *we*. The individual of Jante is oppressor and oppressed at the same time. Individual growth is discouraged, dreams are ridiculed. The Jante child quickly loses his spontaneity and becomes as petty, cruel, and miserable as the adults. Any sign of revolt is efficiently crushed by scorn and ridicule. Everyone is keeping everyone else down, and all are equally miserable.

Sandemose's work can be read as a desperate quest for alternative lifestyles, different modes of living that will permit the child to escape from Jante and grow into a happy, healthy adult. In spite of their apparent diversity, a close reading of these works reveals a striking cohesiveness. The same anguished voice is speaking through the various narrators from *Fortællinger fra Labrador* (1923; Tales from Labrador) through *En flyktning krysser sitt spor*, *Det svundne er en drøm* (1946; The Past Is a Dream), *Alice Atkinson og hennes elskere* (1949; Alice Atkinson and Her Lovers), to *Varulven* (1958; *The Werewolf*, 1966) and *Felicias bryllup* (1961; Felicia's Wedding). Only toward the end of the author's life, after he had abandoned fiction in favor of autobiography, did this voice lose its bitter tone. *Murene rundt Jeriko* (1960; The Walls around Jericho) is the work of a human being who has accepted his fate and is finally at peace with the world. Before reaching this point, however, Sandemose's narrators are desperately trying to understand their past and their present, and hopefully perceive glimpses of what the future may have in store. What is at the root of war and violence? What is the relationship between warfare among nations and the little battles that individuals are constantly fighting with each other? Is it possible either to sublimate our destructive energy or else turn it into a positive force, which might be utilized to construct a truly free, humane society? These are questions that Sandemose's protagonists are constantly posing and that each of them answers in a slightly different way.

FURTHER WORKS

Storme ved jævndøgn (1924); *Ungdomssynd* (1924); *Mænd fra Atlanteren* (1924); *Klabavtermanden* (1927); *Ross Dane* (1928); *En sjømann går i land* (1931); *Fesjå*, 4 vols. (1934–1936); *Vi pynter oss med horn* (1936; *Horns for Our Adornment*, 1938); *Sandemose forteller* (1937); *Der stod en benk i haven* (1937); *Brudulje* (1938); *September* (1939); *Fortellinger fra andre tider* (1940); *Det gångna är en dröm* (Swed. ed., 1944); *Tjærehandleren* (1945) *Eventyret fra kong Rhascall den syttendes tid om en palmegrønn øy* (1950); *Årstidene*, 13 vols. (1951–1955) *Rejsen til Kjørkelvik* (1954); *En flyktning krysser sitt spor. Espen Arnakkes kommentarer til Janteloven* (1955); *Mytteriet på barken Zuidersee* (1963; *Mutiny on the Barque Zuidersee*, 1970); *Dans, dans, Roselill* (1965); *Verker i utvalg*, 8 vols. (1965–1966); *Som et neshorn med hjernebetennelse* (1972); *Dikteren og temaet* (1973); *Epistler og moralske tanker* (1973); *Brev fra Kjørkelvik* (1974); *Minner fra andre dager* (1975).

REFERENCES

Aarbakke, Jorunn Hareide, *Høit på en vinget hest* (Oslo, 1976); Birn, Randi, *Aksel Sandemose* (Westport, Conn., 1984); Dupont, Bent, et al., *Atlanten har så mange mil streiflys over Sandemose og hans forfatterskab* (Jylland, 1986); Nordberg, Carl-Eric, *Sandemose. En biografi* (Oslo, 1967); Vaeth, Johannes, *Aksel Sandemose og Jante* (Oslo, 1965); Vaeth, Johannes, *På Sporet af Sandemose* (Nykøbing Mors, 1975); Vaeth, Johannes, ed., *Om Sandemose—en rapport fra Jante* (Nykøbing Mors, 1974); Vaeth, Johannes, and Frits Johansen, *Aksel Sandemose og Skandinavia* (Oslo, 1969); Vogt, Johan, *Aksel Sandemose. Minner, brev, betraktninger* (Oslo, 1973); Wamberg, Niels Birger, ed., *Sandemoses ansikter* (Oslo, 1969),

Randi Brox

Sarkia, Kaarlo. Finnish poet and translator, b. 11 May 1902, Kiikka, d. 16 November 1945, Sysmä.

Sarkia grew up under humble circumstances and was orphaned early in life. After taking his matriculation examinations, he enrolled at the University of Turku. There he came in contact with V. A. Koskenniemi,* who was a teacher at the university. In Koskenniemi's literary circle Sarkia's interest in Swedish and French lyric poetry was kindled. He translated Italian and French poetry, for example, Arthur Rimbaud's *Le bateau ivre*, into Finnish. Another French poet that Sarkia felt affinity with was Charles Baudelaire. Particularly in his early poetry Sarkia is a romantic who favors heavily ornamented and colorful imagery. He is a master of rhythm and rhyme. At times, his facility with rhyme led him to solutions that strike the modern reader as unintentionally comic, especially in his later years. The central themes of the early volumes include self-contemplation, the dualism of the ugly and the beautiful, and a concept of love that has been considered platonic.

In his later collections Sarkia transcends the conflicts of the ego to focus on concerns that stress the interdependence and fraternity of people. These ideas become clearly discernible in his last volume of verse, *Kohtalon vaaka* (1943; The Scale of Destiny), which is also characterized by strong antiwar sentiments. Here the worship of beauty, so peculiar to Sarkia's earlier collections, is augmented by declamatory pathos. Generally, Sarkia gained great success and popularity with his collections at the time of their publication, 1929–1943. However, during the era of change after World War II when the modernists were reshaping the concept of poetry, Sarkia's ranking as a poet came under harsher scrutiny than that of many others. Seen from today's perspective, his poetic expression seems outmoded. Neither the thematic nor the intellectual impetus of Sarkia's poetry has proven sufficient to compensate for its loss of stylistic appeal.

FURTHER WORKS

Kahlittu (1929); *Velka elämälle* (1931); *Unen kaivo* (1936); *Runot* (1944); *Valikoima runoja* (1958); *Kaarlo Sarkian runoja* (1966).

REFERENCES

Björkenheim, Magnus, *Kaarlo Sarkia* (Porvoo, 1952); Hiisku, Aune, *Kaarlo Sarkia, uneksija-kilvoittelija* (Porvoo, 1972); Koskenniemi, V. A., "Kaksi runoilijakutsumusta," in his *Runousoppia ja runoilijoita*, vol. 6 (Porvoo, 1967); Kupiainen, Eino, *Suomalainen lyriikka Juhani Siljosta Kaarlo Sarkiaan* (Porvoo, 1948); Marjanen, Kaarlo, "Kaarlo Sarkian runouden kehitysviivoja," in Kaarlo Sarkia, *Runot* (Porvoo, 1959); Viljanen, Lauri, "Kaarlo Sarkia lapsuuden runoilija," in his *Lyyrillinen minä ja muita kirjallisuustutkielmia* (Porvoo, 1959).

Pertti Lassila

Sarvig, Ole. Danish lyric poet, essayist, and novelist, b. 27 November 1921, Copenhagen, d. 4 December 1981, Copenhagen.

From 1943 through 1948 Sarvig wrote a poem cycle in five volumes, and through 1954 he was an extensive European traveler and an inspired art critic in press, television, and books. From 1954 through 1963, when he mostly lived in Spain, Sarvig wrote a series of four novels, also accompanied by art critique. Now followed a critical period of fifteen years in which he produced a variety of texts, including a fifth novel. Then, in 1978, he had a new breakthrough with the first novel of a planned trilogy; it was succeeded in 1981 by a collection of hymns, allegedly inspired by the tragic death of his wife. A year after his wife's death, Sarvig took his own life.

Sarvig's choice of genres obviously is deliberate, and his novels, as well as his poems, seem to form a cycle. However, this overall impression of compositional necessity does not prevent his genres from interacting. Their locations are often the same, and so are their travel motifs. They share a significant poetic imagery (expounded in Sarvig's art criticism), and what they share within this imagery is the very theme of interaction and meeting. Sarvig's vision is the synthesis of an "outlook" (a philosophy of life and art), an "inlook" (a perception of something not actually visible), and a "look" (a perception of visible reality).

Within the poem cycle, *Grønne Digte* (1943; Green Poems) articulates creation; *Mangfoldighed* (1945; Multiplicity), growth; *Jeghuset* (1944; The House of Self), the ego-identification; and *Legende* (1946; Legend), a dream of redemption anticipating the real redemption in *Menneske* (1948; Man), a book about the meeting with You, or the ego-identification fulfilled as self-realization. A consequent but most dramatic tour de force through the crisis of Western civilization to a temporary ethical solution, even further dramatized by the way in which the following series of novels seems to reverse the process, the ultimate result being that everything and nothing has happened, that confidentiality (nature) and alienation (city) have been separated only to prove inseparable.

Never were Sarvig's meetings more captivating than in his last two books. *De rejsende* (1978; The Travelers) is the beginning of a modern divine comedy in prose, and *Salmer og begyndelser til 1980' erne* (1981; Hymns and Beginnings of the 1980s) is a comparable synthesis of religious tradition and modernity. Sarvig's notion of our time may be obsolete, but as an artistic reality it is second to none.

FURTHER WORKS

Digte (1945); *Et Foredrag om Abstrakt Kunst* (1945); *Bondegaarden* (1945); *Edvard Munchs grafik* (1948); *Tre elegier* (1948); *Krisens billedbog* (1950); *Midtvejs i det 20. aarhundrede* (1950); *Nattevagten* (1951); *Min Kærlighed* (1952); *Evangeliernes billeder belyst af denne tid* (1953); *Stenrosen* (1955); *I forstaden* (1956); *Glimt* (1956); *De sovende* (1958); *Havet under mit vindue* (1960); *Limbo* (1963); *Palle Nielsen* (1964); *Stedet som ikke er* (1966); *Efterskrift* (1966); *Poèmes Germes* (1968); *Rekviem* (1968); *Stemmer. I mørket* (1970); *Glem ikke* (1972); *Forstadsdigte* (1974); *Jantzens sommer* (1974); *I lampen* (1974); *Sejlads* (1974); *Igår—om lidt* (1976); *Jydske essays* (1976).

FURTHER TRANSLATIONS

Twentieth Century Scandinavian Poetry, ed. Martin S. Allwood (1950); *Late Day* (1976); *Contemporary Danish Poetry*, ed. Line Jensen et al. (1977).

REFERENCES

Andersen, Preben Skovgaard, *Omkring Ole Sarvigs kristusdigte* (Holstebro, 1979); Borum, Poul, *Samtale med Ole Sarvig* (Copenhagen, 1969); Holk, Iben, ed., *Tidstegn: En bog ome Ole Sarvigs forfatterskab* (Århus, 1982); Jørgensen, Carl Martin Frovin, *Ole*

Sarvigs lyrik (Copenhagen, 1971); Rossel, Sven H., "Crisis and Redemption: An Introduction to Danish Writer Ole Sarvig." *World Literature Today* 53.4 (1979).

Poul Houe

Saxo Grammaticus ("the grammarian"). Danish historian of the late twelfth and early thirteenth centuries, author of *Gesta Danorum*.

The little that is known about Saxo himself derives from the preface to *Gesta Danorum* and a few other medieval references. He was one of Bishop Absalon's men (*comites*), a clerk (*clericus*), and a colleague (*contubernalis*) of the older historian Sven Aggesen. His father and grandfather were in royal military service.

According to common opinion, Saxo was at work on *Gesta Danorum* during the years around 1200. The full text is established from Christiern Pedersen's printed edition of 1514, but earlier manuscript fragments exist, one of which may be an autograph antedating the final redaction.

In the prologue, Saxo describes his principal sources as ancient poems that he has translated, the tales of diligent Icelanders, and the oral accounts of Absalon. In the opening lines of book 1, however, he cites a written authority (Dudo of St. Quentin), and scholars have identified many other written sources.

Gesta Danorum is a history of Denmark, focusing on her kings, from prehistoric times through Knut VI (ca. 1185). Possible models include such national histories as that of Bede for the English and Paul the Deacon for the Langobards. Saxo probably also followed more classical models (e.g., Virgil), and he wrote ornate Latin prose in imitation of the so-called silver age and translated his verse sources into classical meters. The work consists of sixteen books, of which the first nine concern prehistory and the remaining seven known history. It has been noted that books 1–4 treat the period before the birth of Christ, book 5 the peace of Frodi—a presumed parallel to the peace of Augustus, books 6–8 the remaining period of Christianity's approach to Denmark, 9–12 the introduction of Christianity, and 13–16 the years following the institution of the archbishopric at Lund. The focus, however, is always Danish.

Saxo's is the oldest known Danish history and probably the greatest literary monument of the Danish Middle Ages.

FURTHER WORKS

Saxonis Gesta Danorum, ed. J. Olrik and H. Ræder (1931).

TRANSLATIONS

The First Nine Books of the Danish History of Saxo Grammaticus, trans. Oliver Elton (1894); *Saxo Grammaticus: The History of the Danes,* trans. Peter Fisher, 2 vols. (1979–1980).

REFERENCES

Dollerup, Cay, *Denmark, Hamlet and Shakespeare,* 2 vols. (Salzburg, 1975); Friis-Jensen, Karsten, ed., *Saxo Grammaticus.* Engl. summary (Copenhagen, 1981); Herrmann, Paul, *Erläuterungen zu den ersten neun Büchern der dänischen Geschichte des Saxo*

Grammaticus, 2 vols. (Leipzig, 1901–1922); Johannesson, Kurt, *Saxo Grammaticus* (Stockholm, 1978). Kroman, E., *Saxo og overleveringen af hans værk* (Copenhagen, 1971).

John Lindow

Scandinavian Folklore. Folklore comprises the (usually unwritten) traditions of a given group or people, such as beliefs and practices, as well as narrative materials. In Scandinavia, much of the older literature reflects or reveals aspects of folklore, particularly folk belief. The oldest known Scandinavian literary manifestations—rhythmic runic inscriptions, the earliest eddic poetry—reveal something of the folk belief of their times, as do the medieval sagas and chronicles, the ballads, romantic poetry, and neoromantic dramas and prose. Although we see little of traditional folk belief in a modern poet like Edith Södergran,* for example, by contrast Erik Axel Karlfeldt* relied often on motifs from folk belief and folk culture.

Folk belief manifests itself in narratives called legends (*sagn, sägner*). Although they vary greatly, most legends are short, almost-anecdotal accounts of interesting events that are purported to have taken place within the community or a world recognizable to the community, with characters either known to the community or in some way recognizable within it. Some legends are very close to narratives of personal experience, while others approach fairy tales in their use of fantasy.

Much of the technical scholarship on legends has been done in Scandinavia. The Swedish scholar C. W. von Sydow coined many generic terms, including *memorate* for a firsthand account of an experience and *fabulate* for a legend controlled by imagination. Other categories that folklorists sometimes use include the "historical legend," which is concerned with a historical person or event; "local legend," which is fixed to a definite place and lacks the means or ability to be transmitted elsewhere; and "migratory legend," a legend collected in many places and thus presumed to have been transmitted in space as well as time.

Until recently most Scandinavian folklorists have concentrated their interests in legends involving the supernatural and supernatural beings, who assuredly were an empirical phenomenon for the rural peasantry who told legends about them. These supernatural beings included giants (the race who lived long ago and formed the environment); creatures of the uninhabited areas—mountain, forest, sea, and watercourse; household beings; and anti-Christian demons. The actual terminology varies greatly, particularly for the nature beings who people the uninhabited areas. Common designations for them include *troll* (adapted in English in the mid–nineteenth century under the influence of Norwegian and Old Norse usage), *rå* (perhaps "those who control"), and "hidden people." For the most part these people look like ordinary humans, although they may also have hollowed-out backs or tails, and the major difference between them and humans is that they are not Christian. They are, however, quite capable of interaction with humans, and that forms the subject of many legends (relatively few tell only of supernatural beings). Contact between humans and supernatural beings is by the conventions of this narrative tradition dangerous, and some legends do tell of humans now living, contentedly or otherwise, not in the human but the supernatural world. There a kind of reversal is common: all is gold and riches according to some stories, but it is revealed in many others to be nothing but dung and toads.

Humans enter the supernatural world, or are threatened with such entry, most frequently through kidnapping or sexual contact. Kidnapping takes two forms: changing, in which a supernatural mother substitutes her brat for a human child, and outright kidnapping, often called "mountain-taking." Most folklorists accept that stories of changelings may have functioned as explanation for sick or retarded children and stories of mountain-taking as explanation for persons lost in the woods. Since stories of erotic contact with supernatural beings often have human protagonists in lonely, stressful situations (looking after cattle at a mountain shieling, burning charcoal deep in the forest), many folklorists are inclined to view the stories as projections of sexual frustrations or fantasy.

There is, however, a strong didactic slant to legends. They punish those who actually do succumb to supernatural beings' erotic charms by depriving them of happiness or wit—a possible warning against unsanctioned promiscuity in general; and notions of changelings and mountain-taking would appear to advise caution with small children and on solitary ventures into the wilderness. The household beings seem nearly wholly didactic creatures, who swiftly punish any breakdown in smooth operating procedures on the farm; and demons, witches, and the devil are just as quick to punish, in their own way, doctrinal deviation.

Because of their essentially local focus, Scandinavian legends have not been widely known outside of Scandinavia. By contrast, the vivid style of Peter Christen Asbjørnsen and Jørgen Moe's tales and the wit of H. C. Andersen's* literary imitations of folktales are world-famous. The oral genre behind these tales (called *eventyr* in Danish and Norwegian, *saga* in Swedish) is the "fairy tale," or *Märchen* as it is known to folklorists. Unlike legends, these tales are multi-episodic and set in a fantasy world, where time may be suspended and where the fantastic is taken for granted. The characters may have fantastic names and certainly are not known directly to members of the community (although all the members of the community may know them in tales). Heroes may be of low social class, but royal characters appear, and villains are not necessarily those of folk belief. Where these tales differ most from legends, however, is in the social dynamics of the plot. In a typical legend, some action changes or threatens to change the status quo, but the threat is countered and the danger averted, and the status quo remains unchanged (example: a supernatural being attempts to seduce a girl at the shieling, but her dog races back to the village and summons her fiancé, who scares off the trolls). In a *Märchen*, on the other hand, a poor boy may kill a supernatural being who threatened a princess and marry her himself, thus succeeding to the kingdom. This elevation in social status would be out of place in a legend.

Other material not fitting the definition of legend is also classified with the *Märchen*. This includes tales in which all the characters are animals; tales about foolish men and women; nonsacred anecdotes about saints; and so forth. What all these and the classical *Märchen* share is a one-dimensional view of the world, a willing suspension of causal reality.

Like legends, *Märchen* are found all over Europe, but because *Märchen* lack legends' association with the local community, there is little about them that is peculiarly Scandinavian. Asbjørnsen and Moe made Askeladden, the Norwegian form of the cinder-lad, into a kind of national icon; and the Scandinavian *Märchen* sometimes offer trolls where *Märchen* of other traditions have other supernatural beings; but in general *Märchen* belong more to international than national tradition.

Although Old Norse literature and medieval Latin records frequently reflect legends and *Märchen*, the oldest genre to be recorded in something like verbatim form is the ballad. During the sixteenth and seventeenth centuries it became fashionable among the upper classes to include ballads in private manuscripts of lyric poetry, and these poetry books are the oldest Scandinavian recordings of ballads. Later, chapbooks and recordings from oral tradition of the rural peasantry came to complement the earlier manuscript records and to suggest a continuation and adaptation of the genre over several centuries.

Ballads (Danish and Norwegian *folkeviser*, Swedish *folkvisor* or the more technical term *ballader*) are relatively short verse narratives that frequently include dialogue and ordinarily focus on the dramatic high points of a story. The form is strophic, with couplets said to be characteristic originally at least of East Scandinavia (Denmark and Sweden), quatrains of West Scandinavia (Norway, the Faroes, and Iceland). Incremental repetition (alternation over several strophes of repeated phrases and new ones), a typical ballad feature, tends to retard the narrative pace. In oral tradition, ballads are sung, in earlier times as the accompaniment to a ring-dance or chain-dance—a tradition still surviving in the Faroes. Many but not all ballads are transmitted with a fixed refrain, which occurs between strophes and sometimes interlinearly within the strophes as well. In dance situations, a lead singer sang the verses and was joined by the chorus of dancers for the refrain. Some ballads begin with one or more lyric, apothegmatic stanzas (Danish *stevstamme*, Norwegian *stevstomn*, Swedish *omkvädesstam*), a peculiarly Scandinavian feature.

Scandinavian ballads have since A. I. Arwidsson been divided by content into various categories, systematized by Svend Grundtvig in his great Danish ballad edition, *Danmarks gamle folkeviser* (the model for F. J. Child's *English and Scottish Popular Ballads*), and these categories have been followed in the type-index of B. R. Jonsson, S. Svalheim; and E. Danielsson (1978). The categories, and number of known types, are as follows: "ballads of the supernatural" (75), "legendary ballads" (37), "historical ballads" (41), "ballads of chivalry" (441), "heroic ballads" (167), and "jocular ballads" (77).

For most ballads, a medieval, chivalric setting is typical, but the supernatural intrudes freely, and historical characters may be no more than names. However, the late medieval setting, the references to historical personages, and above all the archaic language of the ballads point to their presence in Scandinavia by the thirteenth century at the latest. The place of ultimate origin seems to have been France. Even for the nobles who wrote down ballads in the sixteenth and seventeenth centuries, the stories were set in the past and not in their own milieu. For the later peasantry from whose lips ballads were collected, the characters and settings were no doubt exotic. A possible hint of their creators' attitude toward ballads may, however, be found in the apparently political, propagandistic aim of some of the "historical" ballads.

Tragedies of love are common, but some ballads, particularly the typically West Scandinavian heroic ballads, stress combat. The legendary ballads tell religious stories piously, whereas other secular ballads—those termed "jocular" by scholars—may be quite ribald. It is therefore difficult to generalize about the use of ballads in Scandinavian culture. The history of collection, however, suggests an upper-class phenomenon becoming part of mass culture, spread through chapbooks for a reading public and via oral tradition among the peasantry. Anthropologists able to study recent ballad dancing in the Faroe Islands have concluded that there, at least in certain contexts, ballad dancing promotes feelings of large group solidarity in situations where mixing of smaller groups under charged circumstances is potentially disruptive.

The Norwegian *Draumkvæde*, or dream ballad, assumes a special position for its beauty and subject matter. Approximately seventy fragments recorded in Telemark from the 1840s onward suggest a long vision poem now known in reconstructed form. It reports the dreams of one Olav Åsteson, who slept through the twelve days of Christmas and saw Heaven, Hell, and the Last Judgment. The vivid imagery is primarily that of medieval Christianity, although some elements echo Old Norse tradition. The popularity of such vision literature during the late Middle Ages has led most scholars to postulate medieval origin, although the argument is necessarily circumstantial, and most folklorists would now be more interested in the context of performance of the fragments in nineteenth-century Telemark. The reconstituted text, even so, remains a powerful and effective poem.

Nordic scholars have contributed much to international folkloristics. Kaarle Krohn was among the originators of the historic-geographic or "Finnish" method, which through comparison of as complete a collection as possible of variants of an item of folklore seeks to reconstruct an archetype and a path of diffusion of the item over time and space. Krohn's student Antti Aarne compiled the first edition of the folktale type-index, still a tool of fundamental importance, and Axel Olrik's "epic laws" are still in use. The contributions of von Sydow and others in legend study and the recent ballad type-index have already been mentioned, and countless other contributions could also be noted.

In modern literature, folklore was particularly important in the works of romantic poets and of such neoromantic writers as Bjørnstjerne Bjørnson* and

Jonas Lie.* Many other authors have relied on folk tradition in their poetry and fiction.

EDITIONS

Editions of Scandinavian folklore are virtually numberless; those included here are either standard in some way or are modern and include useful commentary or bibliography.

Denmark: Grundtvig, Svend, et al., *Danmarks gamle folkeviser*, 12 vols. (Copenhagen, 1853–1976); Kristensen, Evald Tang, *Danske sagn som de har lydt i folkemunde*, 6 vols. (1892–1901), new series, 6 vols. and index (Copenhagen, 1928–1939).

Faroe Islands: Jakobsen, Jakob, *Færøiske folkesagn og aeventyr*, Samfund til udgivelse af gammel nordisk litteratur 27, 3, vols. (Copenhagen, 1898–1901; repr. Tórshavn, 1961–1973); Grundtvig, Svend, and Jørgen Bloch, *Corpus Carminum Færoensium*, ed. Chr. Matras, 6 vols. (Copenhagen, 1944–1972).

Iceland: Árnason, Jón, *Íslenzkar þjóðsögur og ævintýri* (Leipzig, 1862–1864; new ed. by Árni Böðvarsson and Bjarni Vilhjálmsson, 6 vols., Reykjavík, 1956–1961); Helgason, Jón, *Íslenzk fornkvæði*, 7 vols., Editiones Arnamagnæanæ, B10–16 (Copenhagen, 1962–1970).

Norway: Asbjørnsen, Peter Chr., and Jørgen Moe, *Samlede eventyr*, 3 vols. (Oslo, 1936); *Norsk folkediktning*, 7 vols. (Oslo, 1957–1963); *Norsk eventyrbibliotek*, 1– . (Oslo, 1967–); Blom, Ådel Gjøstein, *Norske mellomaldersballadar*, 1– . (Oslo, 1983–).

Sweden: *Svenska sagor och sägner*, 12 vols. (Stockholm, 1953–1961); Liungman, Waldemar, *Sveriges samtliga sägner i ord och bild*, 6 vols. (Stockholm, 1949–1964); Arwidsson, A. I., *Ballader*, ed. Swedish Folksong Archives, 1– . (Stockholm, 1983–).

TRANSLATIONS

Olrik, Axel, *A Book of Danish Ballads* (1926); *Norwegian Folk Tales: From the Collection of Peter Christen Asbjørnsen and Jørgen Moe* (1960; repr. 1982); Dal, Erik, *Danish Ballads and Folksongs* (1962); Christiansen, Reidar Th., *Folktales of Norway* (1964); Simpson, Jacqueline, *Icelandic Folktales and Legends* (1972); Lindow, John, *Swedish Legends and Folktales* (1978); West, John F., *Faroese Folk-Tales and Legends* (1981).

REFERENCES

Aarne, Antti, and Stith Thompson, *The Types of the Folktale*, 2nd rev. ed., Folklore Fellows Communications, 184 (Helsinki, 1961); Christiansen, Reidar Th., *The Migratory Legends*, Folklore Fellows Communications, 175 (Helsinki, 1958); Jonsson, Bengt R., Svale Solheim, and Eva Danielson, *The Types of the Medieval Scandinavian Ballad* (Oslo, 1978); Krohn, Kaarle, *Folklore Methodology* (Austin, 1971; Germ. orig. 1926); Liungman, Waldemar, *Die schwedischen Völksmärchen*, Veröffentlichungen des Instituts für deutsche Volkskunde, 20 (Berlin, 1961); Ólason, Vésteinn, *The Traditional Ballads of Iceland*, Stofnun Árna Magnússonar á Íslandi, rit 22 (Reykjavík, 1982); Olrik, Axel, "Folk Narrative," in *The Study of Folklore*, ed. Alan Dundes (Englewood Cliffs, N.J., 1965); Strömbäck, Dag, ed., *Leading Folklorists of the North* (Oslo, 1971); Sydow,

C. W. von, *Selected Papers on Folklore* (Copenhagen, 1948); Wylie, Jonathan, and David Margolin, *The Ring of Dancers* (Philadelphia, 1976).

John Lindow

Scandinavian Immigrant Literature. Between 1840 and 1920, approximately 1,105,000 Swedes, 800,000 Norwegians, and 310,000 Danes immigrated to the United States. These numbers represent the percentages of the respective indigenous populations: 21 percent, 33 percent, and 12 percent. Even so, the total number of Scandinavians arriving in the United States made up less than 5 percent of all immigration during this period. Broadly speaking, immigrants from Sweden and Norway arrived in the United States earlier and in larger numbers than did immigrants from Denmark. Swedish and Norwegian immigrants also tended to establish tightly knit nationality communities, and this pattern can be further illustrated by comparing the numbers of prepaid tickets among the three groups. The percentages of immigrants who came to America on tickets paid for by a friend or relative in this country were: Swedes—80 percent, Norwegians—40 percent, and Danes—25 percent.

Scandinavians settled primarily in the middle western states of Illinois, Wisconsin, Minnesota, Iowa, and Nebraska. Family units dominated the initial immigration period, while by the 1890s most Scandinavian immigrants were young single men and women. It is also important to recognize that most Scandinavian immigrants were in their prime working years, that is, fifteen to thirty-nine, and most were also poor and unskilled, but literate. Norwegian communities tended to be rural, Swedish communities were the most urban, and Danish communities tended to be less well defined. One final and significant factor among Scandinavian Americans was religion. Both Danish and Norwegian Americans had two separate Lutheran churches: the high church and low church, with the latter being more pietistic.

In this general situation Scandinavian-American literature was written, published, and read. This process began in the 1870s and lasted until the 1940s, and thus, as a distinctive genre, Scandinavian-American literature can be considered time-specific. The definition of the genre formulated by Dorothy Burton Skårdal (*The Divided Heart,* 1974) includes authors writing out of their own experience and most commonly in their Scandinavian language. The central theme of immigrant literature is the identity problem—both for the individual and for the group. The sociocultural transition from the values and norms of the old country to those of the new one informs the genre and is shown in its hyphenated title. A related theme was the continual doubt about the wisdom of deciding to leave the old country. This conflict is often represented in fiction as between husband and wife, with the husband being future-oriented and the wife being past-oriented. Ole Rølvaag,* Enok Mortensen,* and Sophus Winther* portray this theme.

The Scandinavian-language newspapers were the earliest sources for authors of poetry, short stories, and even novels. *Nordlyset, Dannevirke, Skandinavia,*

Decorah-Posten, Emigranten, Hemlandet, Nordstjernen, Bien, and *Den Danske Pioneer* were all newspapers that regularly published fictional works. Often, immigrant papers would periodically publish literary supplements. However, because the number of Danish immigrants was comparatively smaller, more of their fiction and poetry was published in newspapers and periodicals. The general pattern of Scandinavian-American literature indicates a peak period between 1890 and 1940, after which the number of native speakers radically declined. In fact, the ebb in the production of immigrant literature can be seen in a tendency for later publications to be written in English.

Major authors of Swedish-American literature include Magnus Elmblad, Vilhelm Berger, Peter A. Lindberg, Gustav Malm, and Anna Olsson. Significant Norwegian-American authors include Waldemar Ager, Hjalmar H. Boyesen, O. A. Buslett, J. A. Erickson, Hans A. Foss, Kristofer Janson, Dorthea Dahl, Einar Lund, Jon Norstog, Peer Strömme, Johannes B. Wist, James A. Peterson, Lars Hellesnes, Simon Johnson, and Ole Rølvaag. Major Danish-American authors were Adam Dan, Sophus K. Winther, E. M. Faurholdt (Canadian), Carl Hansen, Kristian Østergaard, M. Sørensen, and Enok Mortensen.

In conclusion, it might be noted that as a group the Scandinavian Americans were prolific producers of literature, particularly if one includes publication in newspapers and periodicals. A comprehensive summary of immigrant literary themes reflects the major problems of moving from one culture to another culture that was significantly more heterogeneous than the original. Themes include doubt about emigration, bitter religious conflict—both within the church and in the community, cultural tension, native language maintenance, intergenerational conflict, material success as destructive of spiritual and communal values, isolation of the immigrant—particularly the wife—in the vastness of America, natural disasters, and conjugal conflict. Scandinavian-American literature is representative of the immigrant genre, but it possesses a distinctive Scandinavian quality. This can perhaps be explained by the essential cultural similarity of the three countries from which they emigrated, as well as by their common languages. Scandinavian-American literature is distinctly different from American literature written during this period. As is true of any genre, its quality varies; some is extremely poor and some is excellent, with the works of Ole E. Rølvaag generally considered to be the best. Some is highly optimistic and some is devastatingly pessimistic. While the majority of Scandinavian-American literature has a rural setting, reflecting the rural nature of their settlement, a few works have an urban setting. Its central theme, the quest for identity, is as old as humankind, but in Scandinavian-American literature this quest is both culture-specific and time-specific.

REFERENCES

Christiansen, J. R., *Scandinavians in America: Literary Life* (Decorah, Iowa, 1985); Mortensen, Enok, and Johannes Knudsen, *The Danish-American Immigrant: Phases of His Religion and Culture* (Des Moines, Iowa, 1950); Skårdal, Dorothy Burton, *The*

Divided Heart: The Scandinavian Immigrant Experience through Literary Sources (Oslo, 1974).

Rudolf Jensen

Scandinavian Literary Criticism, History of. Scandinavian literary criticism can be said to start auspiciously, for its first entry is that of the Icelander Snorri Sturluson.* His *Edda* (ca. 1225), a poetics that he created as an artist in his own right, seems highly original when compared to those textbooks produced on the Continent for training priests-to-be in the scholastic version of rhetoric and poetics; in Sweden, works survive of just such a textbook scribe, Mattias ("testa nucis," a fragment of his rhetoric, and his *Poetria*, ca. 1318). Also the Dane Peder Laale's collection of proverbs (1300s) served didactically as a textbook in Latin.

Although the Reformation was a profound reorientation, the teaching of the humanists continued to stress the learning of classical skills: students demonstrated their understanding of the classical authors by expressing themselves in the same fashion; thus, grammar, rhetoric, and metrics remained crafts to be mastered at the centers of learning. It was also during the 1500s, the century of Reformation, that an antiquarian interest resulted in the preservation of older texts and of what is now considered to be folklore. The Norwegian Peder Clausson (1545–1614) translated Snorri Sturluson's *Heimskringla*, and the Dane Andersen Sørensen Vedel published a surprisingly early anthology of Danish ballads (1591).

The collection and publication of older texts, often with a commentary, continued in the 1600s. Ole Worm (1588–1654) initiated the study of runes and advocated gathering and preserving the Icelandic manuscripts. That task was undertaken by the Icelander Tormod Torfæus (1639–1719) and continued by his countryman Arni Magnússon (1663–1730). The Dane Peder Syv (1631–1702) issued a collection of proverbs and continued Vedel's work (he enlarged the 1591 edition by another hundred texts).

During the 1600s, normative Continental aesthetics entered Scandinavia, and poetry became regulated by Renaissance rules. The Swede Lars Fornelius (1606–1673), who served as professor of poetry (a chair that was established at Uppsala University in 1626), wrote mainly his *Poetica Tripartita* (1643) for authors who composed in Latin, but Peder Syv in *Nogle betænkninger om det cimbriske sprog* (1663; Reflections on the Cimbrian Language), advocated, as did some of his contemporaries, that his native language be enriched and cleansed (of dialects), a process that would elevate it above ordinary language. That refined, expressive diction would prove that the Nordic languages could compete in eloquence and beauty with the classical and Romance languages. Owing to the work of such language patriots—following in German footsteps—Latin was gradually abandoned; quantitative meter, that is, a meter based on the length of the syllable, was replaced by the strong stress meter. The Danes Søren Poulsen Gotlænder (1599–1688) and Hans Mikkelsen Ravn (1610–1643) and the Swede Andreas

Arvidi (1620–1673), all disciples of Martin Opitz, published guides for poets that advocated metrical reform and combined respect for classical poetics with Baroque taste.

In the second half of the 1600s, neoclassical aesthetics, a reaction against the excesses of Baroque, arrived in Scandinavia. The Swedes Samuel Columbus (1642–1679) and especially Petrus Lagerlöf (1648–1699), professor in Uppsala, as well as the Dane Thøger Reenberg (1656–1742), advocated Nicolas Boileau's strict neoclassicism. A more relaxed attitude toward those French inspired rules and regulations was assumed by the Dano-Norwegian Ludvig Holberg* in the next century; his critical essays on drama suggested that a modern sense of historicity was entering Scandinavian criticism. Holberg was a neoclassicist, but first and foremost a rationalist, and he shared that movement's sense of historical process; thus, the authority of the classics was weakened. That modernity is also expressed in Sweden in the works of Jens Schelderup Sneedorff (1724–1764) and, significantly, by Olof Dalin,* who in *Den swenska Argus* (1732–1734), the first Scandinavian moral weekly—patterned on English models—expressed the spirit of rationalism. His demand for clarity and elegance in language had a profound impact on Swedish diction. Both Holberg's and Dalin's works make demands on the human being; that is, they are moral and introduce that social *Bildungs* ideal that was imparted in the spirit of the Age of Reason and that later became quite prominent, albeit in somewhat changed form.

The second half of the 1700s was the age of a flowering of literary societies and salons that vowed to be the arbiters of proper taste. The most significant was to be *Svenska vitterheten*, renamed in 1786 *Svenska akademien* (the Swedish Academy that today administers the Nobel Prize in literature), a powerful organization that for years was under the firm guidance of the quite rigid neoclassicist Carl Gustaf Leopold* (1756–1829). During those years the reading public was growing rapidly, and there came into existence a bourgeois audience for magazines and newspapers and mass-produced fiction. Consequently, the reviewer emerged, and in Norway the appearance of the reviewer marked the start of Norwegian criticism. In the Iceland of the 1790s, the energetic Magnus Stephensen (1762–1833) promoted rationalistic ideals through the literary society *Landsuppfræðingarfélagið* (the Society for the Enlightenment of the Country). In Finland, the beginnings of criticism may be traced to the establishment of literary societies, for example, Lauantaiseura Society (Saturday Society) and to such Finnish-language journals as *Kanava* and *Suometar*, both established in the 1840s, and to the Swedish *Litteraturblad*.

When romantic aesthetics began to sift into Scandinavia in the last third of the 1700s, the protectors of neoclassicism tried to stem the tide, for the experimentation and subjectivity of both romantic philosophy and literature seemed to the old guard to spell barbarism and chaos. Figures like the Swede Johan Henrik Kellgren* and the Norwegians Christian Tullin (1728–1765) and Claus Fasting (1756–1791) and the Dane Knud Lyhne Rahbek (1760–1830) were transitional critics, but during the second decade of the 1800s, romantic taste emerged victorious. In Denmark, the Norwegian philosopher Henrik Steffens (1773–1845), who was profoundly influenced by Friedrich Schelling, exerted a good deal of influence on a generation of young poets. In Sweden the romantic movement was foreshadowed in the programmatic writings of Thomas Thorild* (1759–1808) and became ensconced with the publication of the Uppsala-based magazine *Phosphorus* (1810–1813) and the founding of Götiska förbundet (1811; The Gothic Society). Among the members of the Uppsala group were Lorenzo Hammarsköld (1785–1827) and Vilhelm Frederik Palmblad (1788–1852), both of whom were to be overshadowed by Per Amadeus Atterbom,* poet, critic, and eventually professor (from 1835 on, in aesthetics). He followed Johann Gottfried von Herder's call for literary histories and wrote the impressive five-volume *Svenska Siare och Skalder* (1841–1855; Swedish Seers and Poets) in which he tendentiously viewed Swedish literature as a preparation for romanticism, but in which some approaches can be found that are still used in the field. Atterbom offers a historical perspective, examines biographical matters, and—influenced by Charles-Augustin Sainte-Beuve—attempts to give psychological portrayals. There had been earlier attempts at writing literary histories. The Dane Johannes Møller had issued *Cimbria Litterata* in 1745, an atomistic list of authors offered without any sense of that historical continuity in which the modernity in Atterbom's work consists. The Danish professor Lyhne Rahbek started in 1800 his *Bidrag til den danske digtekunst* (5 vols., 1800–1808; Contributions to Danish Literary Art).

The most significant Danish critic in the first half of the nineteenth century was Johan Ludvig Heiberg,* who—like Atterbom—was an accomplished poet in his own right. As a young man he came under the influence of Georg Wilhelm Friedrich Hegel, and in *Vaudevillen som dramatisk digtart* (1826; Vaudeville as a Dramatic Form), he developed a highly normative system that rigidly ordered the various genres within a hierarchy. Heiberg's systematization may be seen as a reaction against the subjectivity and emotionalism of romanticism, and one may detect in it an affinity with neoclassical taste. Heiberg's position was very prominent; he published a successive number of magazines and for a period was the director of the Royal Theater. His influence could be felt in Norway, the capital of which became embroiled in the 1830s in a heated debate between the adherents of Johan Welhaven* and of Henrik Wergeland.* The former, following Heiberg's taste, insisted that art should reflect the ideal and refrain from engaging in the arbitrary matters of everyday life, whereas the latter maintained that the poet should commit himself politically and speak up for social causes.

The same polarization, if fraught with less vindictiveness, appeared in Sweden, where liberal forces expressed themselves in the newspaper *Aftonbladet* (The Evening Paper). Carl Frederik Bergstedt (1817–1903) and Johan Peter Theorell (1791–1861) actually advocated realism as a needed substitute for lofty, abstract romanticism.

Critics often managed, however, to merge the old and the new tastes, hence, a term like "poetic realism," of which Peter Jonas Collett (1813–1851) and

Marcus Jacob Monrad (1816–1897), both Norwegians, were proponents, came into use: reality should be depicted realistically, but from an idealistic orientation. The same idea is reflected in the nonfictional writings of a Finn, Johan Ludvig Runeberg.* One of the most common critiques leveled at artists who tried their hand at realistic depictions of social problems was that they lacked "idealitet."

Although a realistic current was apparent in Denmark, liberal critics were not prominent. Heiberg's dominance may partly explain that phenomenon, but some liberals found a home in Meïr Aron Goldschmidt's* Corsaren (1840–1846; The Corsair), now best known for its attacks on Søren Kierkegaard.* The author of those notorious entries was Peder Ludvig Møller (1814–1865). He was critical of the esoteric idealism of his time (thus his displeasure with Kierkegaard) and attempted—as many a twentieth-century new critic would do later—to approach a text without any preconceived notion of what ought to constitute beauty. His approach was thus the exact opposite of Heiberg's. Like Atterbom, he was influenced by Sainte-Beuve and wrote psychological-biographical studies. His younger colleague Clemens Petersen (1834–1918), who emerged as the most powerful Danish critic in the 1860s, also opposed Heiberg by emphasizing the need for criticism to be ethical in nature. Nevertheless, no matter how liberal those critics were, none of them could quite shrug off romantic ideology. The notion of "the ideal" continued to take preeminence over "the real." It should be kept in mind that those Scandinavian critics as a rule belonged to a small group of educated people and promoted their culture as the correct one; in Norway that culture was tellingly called "embedsmandskulturen" (the civil-servant culture).

During the romantic period, however, other cultures were finally taken seriously. The romantic interest in the folk led to the collecting of folklore. Peter Christen Asbjørnsen and Jørgen Moe gathered together an impressive bulk of folktales, as did the Dane Evald Tang Kristensen (1843–1929), while Svend Grundtvig (1824–1883) and Arvid August Afzelius (1785–1871) started publishing editions of, respectively, Danish and Swedish ballads. It should be noted that Grundtvig's Danmarks Gamle Folkeviser (1853–1976; Denmark's Old Folk Ballads) was the model for Francis James Child's edition of English and Scottish Popular Ballads (1882–1898). On Iceland Jón Árnason (1819–1888), who had more respect for the storytellers' delivery than most of the other Scandinavian collectors, except Tang Kristensen, gathered Icelandic folklore and published a modest volume Íslenzk ævintyri (1852; Icelandic Tales). In Finland Elias Lönnrot (1802–1884) compiled Kalevala* and thus demonstrated how powerful a role art—the concept of a folk epic—can play in the minds of a people of a nation to be. Lönnrot's effort was foreshadowed by Henrik Gabriel Porthan (1739–1804), who, with his De poesi Fennica (1766–1778), first examined folk poetry systematically.

In midcentury a few voices questioned the ideology of the ruling classes. In Denmark young Frederik Dreier (1827–1853), a declared socialist, denied the dogma of the autonomy of art with more fervor than did any of the earlier protestors against the abstract, aesthetic nature of romantic writing. Dreier died young, but he foreshadowed, as did Aasmund Olausson Vinje* in Norway, the social commitment that was to become a part of criticism. Vinje criticized the young Bjørnstjerne Bjørnson* and Henrik Ibsen* for not writing realistically enough; the characters they created were abstract constructions, not living people. Poetic realism was about to give way to realism/naturalism.

Scandinavian literary histories have tended to take a quite dramatic turn when Georg Brandes* enters upon the stage. The term "The Modern Breakthrough," which is commonly used throughout Scandinavia, suggests the abruptness and the power of the example set by that one person. With Brandes, literature was used to debate social issues—and narrative prose turned technically a good deal more sophisticated—but, as indicated, both realism and social debate had been foreshadowed. The reorientation, one that had already taken place elsewhere on the Continent and in England, would undoubtedly have happened without Brandes, but it cannot be denied that both his lectures in 1871 and his publications were a catalyst and that during the next thirty years he set his mark on literature and criticism in Scandinavia and even beyond the perimeters of his own culture. No other Scandinavian critic has enjoyed the same recognition or power. Brandes's writings may seem slanted—after all he took up causes—but he wrote eminently well, and although much romantic criticism now reads poorly, some of Brandes's works are tantalizingly alive. Brandes's power over minds is suggested by the fury of his detractors; the works of the Norwegian Christian Collin (1857–1926) suggest the unease with which the educated establishment saw their world change and recognized Brandes as one of the instigators of that change. In the Dane Harald Nielsen (1879–1957), a particularly astute critic of the literature of the 1890s, that unease is replaced by wrath against Brandes, an anger that even today is to be found among conservatives in Denmark.

A number of critics, forming a common front against bourgeois romanticism, naturally emulated Brandes. Among them was Edvard Brandes (1847–1931), who tended to be much more doctrinaire than his brother. In Sweden A. W. Ahnfelt (1845–1890) was a mouthpiece of the authors of the 1880s, and in Norway Kristian Elster* (1841–1881) was an advocate not only of realism, but of a narrative technique that demoted the omniscient author. In Denmark, Herman Bang* became the major proponent for a realistic "impressionism" that likewise undermined the authority of narrative omniscience. In Finland Werner Söderhjelm (1859–1931) advocated that Swedish speakers pay attention to the achievement of the Finnish language, and Vilhelm Snellman* (1806–1881), in elegant Swedish, did his best to convince the country's Swedish-speaking educated elite to adopt Finnish as its first language. The best-known academic critic was the comparatist, Professor Viljo Tarkiainen (1879–1951).

Brandes had translated John Stuart Mill's *The Subjection of Women* (in 1869), and the issue of "women's emancipation" had become prominent in the cultural debate. The significant women authors during the romantic period had been early realists and had discussed the sex roles found in their bourgeois society, and some female critics spoke out forcefully in behalf of their sex. In Norway, Camilla Collett* addressed the issue of needed liberation, and Amalie Skram,* before she became a major novelist, wrote for a daily and issued warnings against literature that creates illusions and thus obscures life.

About 1890 new signals suggested once again a reorientation, and Brandes himself, with an article on Friedrich Nietzsche, partly set the tone. Political engagement was left behind for an anti-positivism that lacked the power to unite disparate temperaments. Little connects ideas and practice in the work of the Danes Johannes Jørgensen* and Valdemar Vedel (1865–1940), the Swedish Oscar Levertin* (1862–1906), or the Norwegian reviewers Carl Nærup (1864–1931) and Nils Kjær* (1870–1924). Constituting some common ground for them were French symbolism, Nietzscheanism, and attempts to define *Zeitgeist* (especially Vedel tried to capture the spirit of the literature of the 1890s), but—as was the case with Scandinavian literature at that time—the ideological homogeneity had been lost.

By that point the teaching of national literatures at the universities and the high schools was a long-established tradition, and since there were few universities in Scandinavia and very few chairs, the appointments to those chairs attracted much attention. The scholar who was successful in getting such a position would have a good deal of say on how young people were taught literature. Institutional authorities provided those voluminous literary histories that for decades became the canon. In Sweden Professor Henrik Schück (1855–1947) began his project of creating a modern Swedish literary history in 1890. Eventually a revised edition, *Illustrerad svensk litteraturhistoria* (Illustrated Swedish Literary History), comprising seven volumes, was published 1926–1932; parts of it were written by Karl Warburg, and the Finnish scholar Gunnar Castrén authored volume 7. Schück was a historicist who had little use for romantic idealism, gushy language, or aesthetic judgments. He offered facts and gave empirical background; and although he was influenced by Hippolyte Taine, he avoided the cultural determinism that could cloud the judgment of the positivist. In fact, even though Schück, unlike Atterbom or Brandes, was not overtly tendentious, one is left with the impression that his engaging picture of Swedish literature expresses the cultural optimism of a humanist, one who was firmly rooted in the bourgeois *Bildungs* tradition of the 1800s.

In Denmark, a counterpart called *Illustreret dansk litteraturhistorie* (4 vols., 1916–1934) was produced by Professor Vilhelm Andersen (1864–1953), with Carl Petersen, who wrote volume 1. Andersen may be more subjective and less positivistic than Schück, but the work can nevertheless be seen as an expression of the humanistic tradition, and it is remarkable how many later literary histories, no matter what their level, read like a condensation of Andersen's accomplishment. His concern for national and regional characteristics—as well as some of his rather cryptic readings—may no longer attract attention, but his periodization and his way of presenting authors (his emphasis is on temperament rather than works) have shown a remarkable ability to survive.

Norway's counterpart to Schück's and Andersen's achievements is *Norsk litteraturhistorie* (6 vols., 1926–1937; vol. 6, written by Philip Houm, appeared in 1955); it was written mainly by Francis Bull (1887–1974) and Johan Fredrik Paasche (1886–1943). Slightly earlier, Kristian Elster, Jr. (1881–1947) had published another literary history, which, however, never gained the prominence of "Bull and Paasche"—as the work is affectionately called by Norwegian students of literature. "Bull and Paasche" is very useful, it offers innumerable facts, sociocultural information on the various periods, and—of course—much biographical information; but it shares the limitations of its Swedish and Danish counterparts: instead of offering something more than a rudimentary analysis of texts, it offers a commentary that is often bound to disappoint the inquisitive student. Analyses that are, or pretend to be, exhaustive are, of course, a later phenomenon, and thus those three monumental works should not be chided for lacking what their authors did not intend to offer and what their audiences very likely did not demand. Revealing the norms of their day, none of the works attempts to generalize or summarize for the sake of drawing larger perspectives; for example, the changing forms of the novel may be merely mentioned briefly in the comments on a specific author, or the changing point of view from omniscient author to unreliable narrator will be mentioned, if at all, only in passing. Theory or methodology was of no interest and was simply not an issue. Thus, in spite of presenting a sweeping historical development, the presentation of the national literatures nevertheless remains atomistic. The modern reader, who certainly can find much information in these learned pages, will also be struck by the absence of many now recognized women writers, by the neglect of workers' literature, and by the short shrift given to folk narratives (with the exception of the ballad).

As mentioned earlier, a well-educated, quite small class in the 1900s had—or felt it had—a monopoly on what was considered to be the proper and valid culture. The school systems, as they were revised and redevised, were meant to promote certain norms and values, so that any and all, no matter what their social standing, would emulate that culture. And those three famous literary histories, however different they may be from one another, all instill a *Bildungs* ideal and a bourgeois humanistic tradition that have set their mark on the vast majority of literary histories written since, even on some very recent ones.

Perhaps it was the dominance of that humanistic tradition that for long prevented any theoretical or methodological discussion in Scandinavia (as it did elsewhere in fairly similar cultures). With the Modern Breakthrough it was acknowledged that more stringent methods were warranted, and with naturalism critics were prodded to engage in postivistic research, but even if, with the Breakthrough, they reacted against cultural and political conservatism, they were brought by it to strive for an enlightened humanism. Brandes's ideal was the *citoyen*, the "source" for a humanistic culture.

Many solid studies were written in the late 1800s and in the first half of the 1900s, but they were often composed in the spirit of the ruling professors, and very little in them can be called innovative. It is telling that one contribution that aroused international attention was a paper given, not by a literary scholar, but by the Danish folklorist Axel Olrik (1864–1917). At an international conference held in Berlin (1906), he delivered a paper, "Episke love i folkedigtningen" ("The Epic Laws of Folk Narrative," in Alan Dundes, ed., *The Study of Folklore*, 1965) that foreshadowed Vladimir Propp's ground-breaking study of the structure of the magic tale in *The Morphology of the Folktale* (1928; trans. into English, 1958). The literary scholars had no such goals.

In Finland, however, major advances in folklore had taken place. Julius Krohn (1835–1888) had devised the later so famous historical-geographical approach to folklore, and his son Kaarle Krohn (1863–1935), who further developed the method, became the first professor in folklore in the world. Together with Olrik he founded the society of *Folklore Fellows* in 1907 (the society's publication *Folklore Fellows Communications* is definitely one of the field's major journals). In 1910, Antti Aarne (1867–1925) suggested a typology of the folktales, which later was further developed by the American scholar Stith Thompson in *The Types of the Folktale* (1928, rev. 1961). The Norwegian Reidar Th. Christiansen (1886–1971) used the same method to establish an index for migratory legends in *The Migratory Legend* (1958).

As this sketch progresses into the twentieth century, outlining becomes a necessity, and it must be confined largely to trends and only rarely to the names of scholars. The historical, biographical approach—positivism in the service of a humanistic tradition—tended very nearly to dominate during the first sixty years of the century, and homage ought to be paid to those scrupulously prepared scholarly editions, soberly and meticulously annotated, that have appeared in all the countries; one particularly outstanding example is *Íslenzk fornrit* (1932-   ). Biographies, monographs, studies of style, and period studies—all expanding on the knowledge given in the great literary histories—were published in every Scandinavian country. Occasionally such a work could challenge and revise scholarly opinion; one striking example was offered by the Icelander Sigurður Nordal (1886–1974), whose *Hrafnkatla* (1944; *Hrafnkel's Saga*, 1958) created a ruckus among Old Norse scholars when he argued that the sagas were historical fiction, rather than history. Other major Icelandic contributions to the study of medieval Iceland are discussed elsewhere in this volume. (*See* Icelandic Sagas; Medieval Historical Writing; Old Norse Poetry.)

Of course, some alternatives did appear. In Finland what now would be called modernist criticism appeared in some short-lived little avant-garde magazines, for example, *Quosego* (1928–1929); a later development was once again foreshadowed. Psychoanalysis made some inroads into critical practice, especially in Norway where Trygve Braatøy (1904–1953) published his *Livets cirkel* (1929; The Circle of Life), but it was hardly until the structuralists and neo-Marxists in the 1970s reread Sigmund Freud, often through the eyes of Jacques Lacan, that a psychoanalytical criticism became a trend in Scandinavia.

Marxist approaches were tested in the 1930s, and some criticism took a more sociological turn, but the surge of neo-Marxism did not occur until the quiet 1960s suddenly became quite turbulent, with protest movements among both students and academic teachers that severely questioned the existential and social validity of the humanistic tradition.

Formalist approaches have tended to surface repeatedly in attempts to make criticism more objective and more scientific, springing from an urge often felt by literary scholars; some of those approaches resulted in stylistic studies that have not tried to draw conclusions as to meaning or value, but others have gone beyond such atomism to making genre surveys that can be quite profitably read today. Paul V. Rubow (1896–1972) shed new light on the shorter forms that Hans Christian Andersen* used in his *H. C. Andersen's Eventyr* (1929; The Tales of Hans Christian Andersen), and Staffan Björk dealt with in detail with the techniques of the novel in *Romanens formvärld* (1953; The Form World of the Novel), but both these works—like many others—may strike the modern reader as curiously lacking a conclusion.

A reaction against the limitations of the ruling criticism emerged most strongly and most visibly in Norway, when Peter Rokseth (1891–1945) defended his doctoral dissertation (such events are major ones in Scandinavia and were in Rokseth's days and are today covered by the national press) on *Den franske tragedie* (1929; The French Tragedy). Rokseth, who was immediately appointed professor of French, had studied Benedetto Croce, who had addressed the aesthetic issues that a critic must face. Moreover, Rokseth was uneasy about the ruling tradition, which he felt was becoming increasingly bourgeois, and he expressed viewpoints quite similar to those that the New Critics voiced in America. In a sense, both they and he reintroduced an idealistic, metaphysical view of art, by maintaining that a higher, spiritual reality is expressed through art. Francis Bull, who was one of Rokseth's public opponents, took strong issue with this anti-positivism; sparks flew between what became two quite distinct camps, and in Norway one may still operate with the Bull and Rokseth division in criticism. In the terminology used by René Wellek and Austin Warren in their *Theory of Literature* (1949), the followers of Bull can generally be viewed as the representatives of extrinsic methods, whereas those in the Rokseth camp favor intrinsic approaches. It was to Rokseth's credit that he maintained it to be the critic's job to bring out the individuality of a work—the uniqueness that distinguishes it from other texts.

Other critics now also gave close textual readings a higher priority, but New Criticism did not become a trend, as such, until the early 1960s. Although in recent years shifts in criticism have been abrupt and, at times, even violent in Scandinavian academia, that surge was foreshadowed by such eminent close readers as the Danish professor Hans Brix (1870–1961) and the Swede Gunnar Tideström, who actually advocated the use of New Criticism as early as the 1950s. In the 1960s a stream of new critical analyses poured from academia, and their effects were strongly felt in the high schools. For many, that reorientation, which was followed by a number of theoretical works—not the least of which were textbooks—was felt as a liberation from shouldering a lot of increasingly heavy learned baggage.

At the same time the learned tradition reasserted itself, not by insisting on the positivistic accumulation of data, but by advocating, once again, the validity of the *Bildungs* ideal, of humanistic ideas and ideals that retained their connection to past ages. Since the arrival of New Criticism, partly through the influence of the Dane Johan Fjord Jensen's paperback *Den ny kritik* (1962; The New Criticism), created a special fervor in Denmark, the humanistic reaction there has apparently also been more fervent, the evidence for which lies in the circle that formed around Professor Aage Henriksen. The early issues of the journal *Kritik* (1966–   ), which at the time was co-edited by Fjord Jensen and Henriksen, reflect that duality.

The fact that New Criticism has difficulty in dealing well with either longer texts or diacronic views suggests that a stricter formalism was needed. In the late 1960s the solution to that problem was structuralism, with its search for narrative grammars, general paradigms, and a strict terminology. Structuralist anthologies suddenly became the academic fashion of the day, for example, the Swedish *Form och struktur* (1971; Form and Structure), edited by Kurt Aspelin. Soon, however, the structuralists, awakened by the events of 1968, became neo-Marxists, and thus the barely concealed enmity between structuralists and Marxists that was to be found elsewhere on the European continent did not exist to any measurable extent in Scandinavia.

What followed in the 1970s was a flood of Marxist analyses, the sophistication of which was not initially impressive—seemingly, their purpose was to show that the humanistic tradition and its literature contained repressive ideologies; hence, the term *ideologikritik* began to be used about those studies. Literary criticism became a cultural fight that was intended to change society. Needless to say, valuable studies undertaken by Marxists did cause some revisions of past perceptions. That was especially so in the case of feminist criticism, which became both highly visible and often very sophisticated, for example, Pil Dahlerup followed up Brandes's *Det moderne gennembruds mænd* (1883; The Men of the Modern Breakthrough) with her *Det moderne gennembruds kvinder* (1983; The Women of the Modern Breakthrough).

In the 1980s Scandinavian criticism has turned quite pluralistic. The battles that often took vicious form with regard to the correct orientation for critic and author alike have now subsided, even if various critics and journals continue to adopt and discuss those postmodernist methods or stances from abroad that claim to offer new insights into the critical act. Recently, *Kritik* has started to voice deconstructionist opinions, and the venerable *Edda* has turned to a methodological debate of literature. Nevertheless, the age of myopic critical pietism seems to have passed, a point that was recently made implicit by an impressive, if uneven, *Dansk litteraturhistorie* (1983–1985; Danish Literary History) written by members of the 1968 generation. The Marxist orientation still shows, but extrinsic and intrinsic views alternate, and most chapters evince little dogmatism.

Today's students of Scandinavian literature are treated to a plethora of approaches.

REFERENCES

Aarnes, Sigurd Aa., ed., *Norsk litteraturkritikk fra Tullin til A. H. Winsnes* (Bergen, 1970); Andersen, Frank Egholm, and John Weinstock, eds., *The Nordic Mind* (Austin, 1986); Borup Jensen, Thorkild, ed., *Digterne om digtningen i det 20. århundrede*, 2 vols. (Copenhagen, 1970); Christofferson, Birger, *Svenska litteraturkritiker* (Stockholm, 1970); Elbek, Jørgen, ed., *Dansk litterær Kritik fra Anders Sørensen Vedel til Sophus Claussen* (Copenhagen, 1964); Fehrman, Carl, *Forskning i Förvandling. Män och metoder i svensk litteraturvetenskap* (Stockholm, 1972); Fjord Jensen, Johan, *Den ny kritik* (Copenhagen, 1962); Hannevik, Arne, ed., *Norsk litteraturkritikk 1890–1914* (Oslo, 1973); Rydén, Per, *Domedagar. Svensk litteraturkritik efter 1880* (Lund, 1987); Skard, Sigmund, ed., *Norsk litteraturvitenskab i det 20. århundre* (Oslo, 1957); Varpio, Yrjö, ed., *Kirjallisuuskritiikki Suomessa* (Helsinki, 1982).

Niels Ingwersen

Scandinavian Literary Journals. The literary journals of all five Scandinavian countries experienced their breakthrough during the Age of Enlightenment when the essay in the manner of Joseph Addison and Sir Richard Steele in their *Tatler* and *Spectator* papers appeared. The journals are significant for the immediate picture they give of times past, the influence they exert on their own times, and the forum they provide for discussion and debate. Many Scandinavian authors have begun their literary careers by writing in such journals.

To be included in the following list a journal must contain literary selections and criticism and/or play a role in the literary world. No attempt has been made to be all-inclusive. Criteria for selection have rather been that a journal has had a certain prominence in its country, and that it has carried significant literary debuts and debates. They are the journals that a student of Scandinavian literature is likely to encounter.

DENMARK

Currently Existing Journals

Hvedekorn (1920–), published by Borgens Forlag, was started as *Klinte* (1920–1921) by a group of students including Tom Kristensen, whose poetry often appeared there. *Klinte* reorganized in 1925 with a new editor, Viggo F. Møller, and the name changed first to *Ung dansk Litteratur*, then to *Vild Hvede*, and finally to *Hvedekorn* in 1950. Both new and seasoned authors have contributed, among them Tove Ditlevsen* and Harald H. Lund.

Kritik (1967–), edited by Poul Behrendt, Johs. H. Christensen, and Klaus P. Mortensen, was founded by Johan Fjord Jensen and Aage Henriksen. It is Denmark's only centrally literary cultural journal with a broad readership. Its main content is devoted to a discussion of text analysis illustrated with specific examples. The journal rejects modernism, finding its view of life empty and formalized.

Kultur og Klasse (1977–   ), formerly *Poetik* (1967–1977), is sponsored by the State Humanities Research Council. It publishes articles analyzing cultural phenomena, especially literature, within an historical context.

Important Journals of the Past

Kiøbenhavnske lærde Efterretninger (1720–1836) was founded by Joachim Wielandt under the name *Nye Tidender om lærde Sager* with the aim of reviewing newly appearing literature and carrying news from the scholarly world. After 1811 it appeared under the name *Dansk Litteraturtidende* with P. E. Müller as editor.

Minerva (1785–1808), a monthly edited by C. Pram and Knud Lyhne Rahbek, was an all-sided cultural journal that provided an excellent organ for orientation and debate. The leading people of the times wrote for it including numerous poets and literary figures. More specifically literary in focus was *Den danske Tilskuer* (1791–1806), also edited by K. L. Rahbek, the greatest name in Danish periodicals during this period, being as well the editor of several other general cultural and literary journals. *Athene* (1813–1817) was edited by the other great name in Danish periodicals, C. Molbech. It was the cultural organ of the romantic movement and attracted writers like C. Hauch, J. L. Heiberg,* B. S. Ingemann,* and Adam Oehlenschläger.* It was succeeded by *Nordisk Tidsskrift for Historie, Litteratur og Konst* (1827–1839). J. L. Heiberg also edited his own journal, *Den flyvende Post* (1827–1829; 1834–1837), which was chiefly an organ for his own aesthetic ideas. It was influential in giving a more modern character to Danish journals.

Maanedskrift for Litteratur (1829–1838) was founded by a group of fourteen scholars with the aim of orienting an interested public in the developments within art and scholarship.

Chiefly remembered today for its long-lasting campaign against Søren Kierkegaard* is the satirical journal *Corsaren* (1840–1846), edited by M. A. Goldschmidt.*

For Idé og Virkelighed (1869–1873) was founded by Clemens Petersen and Rasmus Nielsen, the university philosopher who had the greatest impact on the times, urging that empirical knowledge and religious faith rather than being mutually exclusive *must* coexist. Bjørnstjerne Bjørnson* was an active contributor to the journal, which opposed the positivism of Georg Brandes* and his followers.

By contrast, both *Nyt dansk Maanedskrift* (1870–1874), edited by Vilhelm Møller, and *Det nittende Aarhundrede* (1874–1877), edited by Edvard and Georg Brandes, led the discussion of new ideas including those of Charles Darwin (presented in the former by J. P. Jacobsen*), the German freethinkers, Hippolyte Taine, John Stuart Mill, and Ivan Turgenev. The latter especially featured reviews and examples of the realistic problem literature that Brandes had called for.

Tilskueren (1884–1939) played an important role because of its articles by Johannes Jørgensen* about the foreign authors (Edgar Allan Poe, Charles Baudelaire, Paul Verlaine, and Joris-Karl Huysmans) who were models for the coming Danish ones. Jørgensen later edited the journal *Taarnet* (1893–1894) as a forum for the symbolistic revolt against naturalism.

Heretica (1948–1953) was a journal written by poets, among them Martin A. Hansen,* who sought to orient themselves in a new reality, questioning accepted ideas whether Christian, humanistic, or communistic. In opposition to it, *Athenæum* (1945–1950) and its continuation *Dialog* (1950–1962), edited by Erik Knudsen* and Sven Møller Kristensen, presented a consistently Marxist view.

Vindrosen (1954–1974), edited by Tage Skou-Hansen and Peter R. Rohde, was a literary and political journal taken over in 1959 by Klaus Rifbjerg* and Villy Sørensen* and made a stronghold for modernism and the new radicalism.

FINLAND

Currently Existing Journals

Finsk Tidskrift (1876–   ), founded by C. G. Estlander and currently edited by Krister Ståhlberg, is the voice of the Swedish-speaking minority in Finland. Its editorial policy has been dictated by leading Finland-Swedish cultural personalities. In 1940 publication was taken over by an association from Åbo Akademi called Granskaren, with their periodical (*Granskaren*) being incorporated into the present journal. Politically liberal in outlook, it has published literature from all over Scandinavia and carries articles on new directions in art and culture.

Nya Argus (1908–   ), edited by Ingmar Svedberg, though politically nonaligned, is also essentially liberal and radical in its cultural view. In the 1930s it strongly criticized the extreme right in Finnish politics, and in the 1940s it avidly supported Finland's new foreign policy. More recently it has urged the development of a more open and unprejudiced society. It follows events in literature, drama, and cultural affairs.

Kanava (1932–   ) was first published under the name of *Suomalainen Suomi* (1932–1969), then as *Aika* (1970–1972). It has appeared since 1973 under the current title and is a general cultural and current affairs magazine without a declared editorial policy, containing reviews and articles on the subjects of art, politics, economics, and literature.

Parnasso (1951–   ), edited by Juhani Salokannel, is Finland's only Finnish-language literary magazine. It provides a comprehensive picture of Finnish and foreign literature, publishing poetry, short stories, essays, and articles about literature. Special sections are devoted to theater, cinema, and records.

Horisont (1954–   ) is a Swedish-language magazine edited in Ostrobothnia by Christer Lauren. It contains essays and articles on Finland-Swedish, Finnish, Scandinavian, and other literature as well as original works of prose and poetry.

Kulttuurivihkot (1972–   ) is a general cultural magazine edited by Anssi Sinnemäki attempting to develop the tradition of Marxist aesthetic and cultural criticism. Contents include essays, artist interviews, photodocumentaries, and evaluations of cultural policy as well as much prose and poetry.

Näköpiiri (1978–   ), founded by an association of 200 Finns and edited by Eero Taivalsaari, attempts to provide an objective picture of today's world in the fields of art and society. Its editorial policy stresses democracy, equality, national culture, and international communication.

Important Journals of the Past

Litteraturblad för allmän medborgerlig bildning (1847–1863), a journal of popular enlightenment, was founded by J. V. Snellman,* the philosopher who was the leading spirit in Finland's national awakening. It became the country's most important forum for discussion.

Kirjallinen Kuukausilehti (1866–1880) was a literary monthly and the organ for the Finnish nationalist segment of the population. Also supportive of this group and specifically the Finnish language movement were *Valvoja*, founded in 1881, and *Aika*, founded in 1907. *Aika* appeared until 1922 and then joined with *Valvoja* to become *Valvoja-Aika* (1923–1943). After 1944 the journal continued to appear as *Valvoja* through 1968, merging in 1969 with *Suomalainen Suomi*. This alliance lasted only until 1970, after which *Suomalainen Suomi* resumed its independent existence under the title of *Aika*, which was changed to *Kanava* in 1973. (See above.)

During the fall of 1922 seven issues of *Ultra*, a "journal for new art and culture," were published in Helsinki. Edited by Lauri Haarla and Hagar Olsson,* it attracted the active collaboration of Edith Södergran,* Gunnar Björling,* Elmer Diktonius,* and Henry Blomberg. Confidently attacking established cultural views, *Ultra* announced the beginnings of a new literary direction, now known as Finland-Swedish modernism. Both it and its successor, *Quosego*, managed to arouse violent opposition in more conservative circles, and succeeded in playing a significant role in debate despite their short life spans. *Quosego* appeared for a total of only four issues during 1928–1929. Dubbing itself "The journal for a new generation," it was edited by Cid Erik Tallqvist. Its most active contributors were the prominent Finland-Swedish modernists, Gunnar Björling, Elmer Diktonius, Rabbe Enckell,* and Henry Parland.*

ICELAND

Currently Existing Journals

Skírnir (1827–   ) is the journal of the Icelandic Literary Society, founded in Copenhagen in 1816 by Rasmus Chr. Rask with the purpose of securing and strengthening the Icelandic language and literature. It had two branches, Copenhagen and Reykjavík; the former produced a newsletter called *Islenzk Sag-*

nablöð (1817–1826) which changed its name to *Skírnir* in 1827. Publication was taken over in 1890 by the Reykjavík branch, which was already publishing *Tímarit Hins Íslenzka Bókmenntafélags* (The Journal of the Icelandic Literary Society), and in 1904 the two journals merged, continuing as *Skírnir*. The Literary Society has been one of the most significant factors in the intellectual life of Iceland, about which the journal's articles give an excellent orientation. It is currently edited by Ólafur Jónsson.

Andvari (Copenhagen and Reykjavik, 1874–   ) is the journal of the Cultural Fund and Friends of the Nation (Tímarit Bókautgáfu Menningarsjóðs og þjó-ðvinafélagsins), a state-sponsored literary society.

Eimreiðin (Copenhagen and Reykjavik, 1895–   ) was founded by Valtýr Guðmundsson as an outlet for his writings about social and political matters. In the editorial policy he stated that both Icelandic and foreign literature would have priority in the journal because they were of interest to everyone but most neglected in other journals. The current editor is Magnús Gunnarssen.

Along with *Skírnir* the most significant and widely read literary journal is *Tímarit Máls og Menningar* (1940–   ). It provides a thorough orientation to the cultural scene and has published works by many of the nation's best-known authors. While not belonging to any political party, it has a radical view of both society and literary matters. First edited by Kristinn E. Andrésson (editor of *Rauðir Pennar*), its current editor is Þorleifur Hauksson.

Important Journals of the Past

Fjölnir (1835–1839) was founded by Icelanders in Copenhagen (Tómas Sæmundsson, Konráð Gíslason, Brynjólfur Pétursson, and Jónas Hallgrímsson*) to reach their countrymen at home with their ideas and those of the outside world. Aiming to encourage Icelanders to take greater pride in their country and urging the publication of new literary works, it had a rapid and decisive influence on the language and literature of the country. The reviews excelled any that had previously appeared in Iceland, and its poetry, written by Jónas Hallgrímsson, set new standards.

An important predecessor of the current journal *Tímarit Máls og Menningar* was *Rauðir Pennar* (1935–1938), edited by Kristinn E. Andrésson and published by the Society of Revolutionary Authors. It contained short stories, poems, and articles written from a Marxist viewpoint.

The forties and fifties saw the production of several journals that were outlets for young writers and artists. These include *Helgafell* (1942–1946; 1953–1955), edited by Magnús Ásgeirsson and Tómas Guðmundsson*; *Líf og List* (1950–1953), edited by Stengrímur Sigurðsson and Gunnar Bergmann; and *Birtingur* (1955–1968), edited by Einar Bragi Sigurðsson, a widely read journal, the longest lasting and most respected of these three.

NORWAY

Currently Existing Journals

Samtiden (1890–   ), the oldest cultural periodical still being published, was founded by Gerhard Gran and edited by him until 1918. Current editors are Helge Rønning, Simen Skjønsberg, and Mariken Vaa. Through the years it has maintained the liberal and unprejudiced editorial policy established by Gran. It treats political, literary, and social issues, and annually publishes an overview of the year's Norwegian literary works. A *nynorsk* (New Norwegian) counterpart of *Samtiden* is *Syn og Segn* (1894–   ), started by Det norske Samlaget with Rasmus Flo as editor. Other prominent editors have been Halvdan Koht (1901–1908) and Olav Midttun (1908–1955). Also begun in 1894 was *Kirke og Kultur*, a journal of liberal Christian culture founded by Eivind Berggrav and currently edited by Inge Lønning. It contains book reviews and articles about literature as well as religious matters.

A journal entirely devoted to Scandinavian literary research is *Edda* (1914–   ), founded by Gerhard Gran, later edited by Francis Bull and currently by Asbjørn Aarseth. It is sponsored by the Norwegian Research Council and Aschehoug Publishers, with the goal of communicating the findings of professional research to the public at large. The more recently founded *Vinduet* (1947–   ) is published by Gyldendal and edited by Jan Kjærstad. The first journal to focus on contemporary Norwegian literature, it has been an important stimulus to literary activity and includes original creative works as well as articles, essays, and reviews.

Important Journals of the Past

Typical of the Age of Enlightenment were P. F. Suhm's *Trondhjemske Samlinger* (1761–1765) and Claus Fasting's *Provinzialblade* (1778–1781). During the romantic period *Almindeligt norsk Maanedskrivt* (1830–1832), edited by Jonas Anton Hjem, was the journal of the Patriot's party and contained many poems by Henrik Wergeland,* along with sympathetic reviews of his work. It was opposed by *(Intelligents) Vidar* (1832–1834), edited by P. A. Munch, A. Schweigaard, and J. S. Welhaven* for the Intelligence party, and prominently featured Welhaven's poetry.

One of the most outstanding journals of the 1800s was *Norsk Tidsskrift for Videnskab og Litteratur* (1847–1855), edited by Chr. A. Lange and embodying the spirit of the Modern Breakthrough. With the aim of guiding an enlightened public in the selection of reading material, it consisted of a literary overview combined with scholarly articles describing the collection activities and intellectual endeavors for which this period is noted.

In 1851 Paul Botten-Hansen, Henrik Ibsen,* and A. O. Vinje* collaborated on the satirical journal *Andhrimmer*. In 1855 Paul Botten-Hansen became the editor of *Illustreret Nyhedsblad* (1851–1866) and went on to create a significant cultural organ by drawing to it the contributions of just about every contemporary writer and scholar. It featured the best literary criticism seen in Norway until that time, along with original works by Ibsen, Bjørnson, and Jonas Lie.* A. O. Vinje produced the personal journal *Dølen* (1858–1870), in which he demonstrated the suitability of *nynorsk* as a journalistic medium.

The journals of the 1870s and 1880s reflect the political division of the times in which virtually every issue became characterized as either liberal or conservative. *Norsk Tidsskrift for Litteratur* (1876–1878), edited by K. A. Winterhjelm, sought like Lange's journal to provide a general overview and guide to literature of all types, but was rather conservative in tone and literary taste. Far more radical were the journals with which the historian J. E. Sars was associated. In both *Nyt norsk Tidsskrift* (1877–1878) (with Jens Daniel C. Lieblein) and *Nyt Tidsskrift* (1882–1887) (with Olav Skavlan) he aimed to familiarize Norway with the new social and political ideas currently being hotly debated in the rest of Europe. These journals were opposed by the conservative ones, *Norsk Maanedskrift* (1884–1885), edited by Ditmar Mejdell, and *Vidar* (1887–1889), edited by L. L. Daae and Yngvar Nielsen. In response to the latter Sars produced (with Sigurd Ibsen, Chr. Collin, and Arne Løchen) a new series of *Nyt Tidsskrift* (1892–1895), this time featuring the literary works and theories of neoromanticism. Even more radical than Sars's journal was *Impressionisten* (1886–1890), edited by Chr. Krohg and Hans Jæger as an organ for the Bohème circle.

Typical of the radicalization of the young academic milieu that took place during the 1920s was the influential communist organization and journal *Mot Dag* (1921–1939), edited by Erling Falk and Sigurd Hoel.* To oppose it Ronald Fangen* and Henrik Groth founded *Vor Verden* (1923–1931), which became part of *Samtiden* in 1932.

Magasinet for alle (1927–1970) appeared under the name of *Arbeidermagasinet* until 1940. It was founded by Birgir Madsen as a proletariat propaganda organ, but under the editorship of Nils Johan Rud (1932–1970) it developed into a widely read, quality-conscious forum especially for young and new writers in which many prominent authors made their debut. Two authors who produced personal journals during this period were Nordahl Grieg* (*Veien Frem*, 1936–1937) and Aksel Sandemose* (*Fesjå*, 1930s, and *Årstidene*, 1951–1955).

Perhaps the most significant journalistic phenomenon in recent years was the appearance of the February 1966 issue of *Profil*, the student literary journal founded in 1942 under the title of *Filologen* (until 1958). In this revolutionary issue authors like Tor Obrestad,* Espen Haavardsholm,* and Dag Solstad* proclaimed that they felt no obligation to any literary tradition other than the one they would create themselves, and they introduced Norway to modernism.

SWEDEN

Currently Existing Journals

Ord och bild (1892–   ) was founded by Karl Wåhlin, whose affection for neoromanticism is evident in the first issues, which overflow with names like Gustaf Fröding,* Verner von Heidenstam,* Erik Axel Karlfeldt,* Selma Lagerlöf,* Oscar Ivar Levertin,* and Hjalmar Söderberg.* Authors of different schools and generations have succeeded each other, and the journal features a broad range of cultural coverage with a Scandinavian orientation.

Bonniers Litterära Magasin (1932–   ) is principally literary in focus, providing examples of original creative work as well as critical essays and reviews. Under Georg Svensson's leadership (1932–1961) it gave a thorough reflection of literary development in Sweden. Under Lars Gustafsson* (1966–1972) it became a forum for heated debate representing a Marxist orientation.

Important Journals of the Past

Then swänska Argus (1732–1734) was authored by Olof Dalin* and is typical of the Age of Enlightenment, containing essays parodying the follies and vices of the times.

Of the profusion of journals that appeared during the romantic period, *Polyfem* (1809) and *Phosphorus* (1810–1813) were the most militant in proclaiming the views of the new school. The latter featured the poetry of Per Daniel Amadeus Atterbom.* The poet Erik Gustaf Geijer* was editor of *Iduna* (1811–1824), an organ of opinion for the Gothic Society, which had the goal of rebuilding Swedish national morale after the loss of Finland.

The journal *Revy i literära och sociala frågor* (1885–1886), edited by Gustaf af Geijerstam, reflected the Young Sweden group of authors interested in creating a modern realistic problem literature.

The vigorous cultural debate of the 1930s produced three journals: *Spektrum* (1931–1933), an organ of radical social and political opinion on which Karin Boye* collaborated, was one of Sweden's foremost avant-garde cultural journals. It introduced Sweden to new currents of international literature while also featuring many of the most prominent young Swedish authors. *Fönstret* (1930–1936) characterized itself as an organ for free debate and defended the primitivism and poetic experiments of the "fem unga" group. *Fronten* (1931–1932) attracted young radical writers and featured heated literary, cultural, and political polemics against the other two journals.

Bonniers published several generational literary journals for young writers: *40-tal* (1944–1947), *Utsikt* (1948–1950), *Femtiotal* (1951–1952), and *Upptakt* (1955–1958). Like the journals of the 1930s, *Perspektiv* (1950–1964) had the goal of encouraging debate. Founded by E. A. Bjelle and edited by Ragnar Oldberg, it covered current developments in literature in brief articles and re-

views. It featured a long series of Swedish authors, including Gunnar Ekelöf*
and Karl Vennberg,* but never became a forum for young authors.

REFERENCES

Avis og bladlista (previously entitled *Fortegnelse over blad og tidsskrifter som utkommer i Norge*) (Oslo, 1978–   ); Bull, Francis, "Fra Samtidens anegalleri." *Samtiden* 16 (1915); *Dansk tidsskriftfortegnelse* (Ballerup, 1949–1971; continued as *Dansk periodicaforteg-nelse*, 1977–1980); Gjønnes, Svein Tore, *Current Norwegian Serials*, 2nd rev. ed. (Oslo, 1970); Häkli, Esko, "Cultural Journals in Finland." *Books from Finland* 14.3 (1980); Hannula, Risto, et al., eds., *Akkaväestä ytimeen* (Helsinki, 1985); Heidreksdottir, Ragn-heiður, "Timarit um bókmenntir eftir 1874." *Skírnir* 150 (1976); Hermansson, Halldor, "The Periodical Literature of Iceland down to Year 1874." *Islandica* 11 (1918); Holm-berg, Claes-Göran, *Litterära tidskrifter i Sverige 1900–1970* (Lund, 1975); Jørgensen, Harald, *Tidsskriftspressen i Danmark indtil 1848* (Copenhagen, 1961); Kurikka Jussi and Marketta Takala, eds., *Suomen aikakauslehdistön bibliografia 1782–1955* (Helsinki, 1983); Lundstedt, Bernhard Wilhelm, *Sveriges periodiska litteratur 1645–1899. Biblio-grafi*, 2 vols. (Stockholm, 1895–1902); Runnquist, Åke, *Litterära tidskrifter 1920–1960* (Stockholm, 1964); *Svensk tidskriftsförteckning* (Stockholm, 1967/68–   ).

Kathleen Stokker

Scandinavian Studies in North America and Britain. In America, the
study of the Scandinavian languages was originally an extension of Old World
instruction in the mother tongue, which continued to be practiced in the church
academies, colleges, and seminaries established after 1860. Early efforts to create
university positions in Scandinavian studies—as in other foreign languages and
literatures—are known from Columbia (1858) and Cornell (1874) universities,
but a movement was not created until Rasmus B. Anderson of Wisconsin, in
1869, began arguing for the establishment of Scandinavian chairs in the Midwest.
By 1914 Scandinavian languages were taught at twenty-five colleges and universities, including Bryn Mawr, Chicago, Columbia, Cornell, Harvard, Johns
Hopkins, Northwestern, Princeton, Yale, and the state universities of California,
Colorado, Illinois, Indiana, Minnesota, Nebraska, Kansas, North Dakota, Oregon, South Dakota, Washington, and Wisconsin. By this time, too, there were
already four Scandinavian *departments,* with one or more full-time Scandinavianists: Wisconsin, founded in 1875, Minnesota (1883), North Dakota (1891),
and Washington (1910). Enrollments were largest in Old Icelandic language,
followed by Norwegian, Swedish, and Danish. Sixty years later, according to
the Askey-Gage-Rovinsky report of 1975, courses in Scandinavian subjects were
offered at forty-two universities and ten colleges, with language enrollments as
follows: Swedish 1,074, Norwegian 1,031, Old Norse 232, Danish 135, Finnish
83, and Modern Icelandic 21. In addition to the four universities with Scandinavian departments mentioned above, the University of California at Berkeley
established a Scandinavian department in 1946; it was also the first of the state
universities to introduce a doctoral program in Scandinavian studies. At the
present, Minnesota, Washington, and Wisconsin have the largest programs in

the country. These centers of Scandinavian study offer advanced instruction in all Scandinavian languages and Finnish, in medieval and modern literature, as well as in area studies (geography, history, political science, sociology, economics, art history, music, etc.). A great variety of Scandinavian language and literature courses are furthermore offered by the departments of Germanic Languages and Literatures at Texas and the University of California at Los Angeles (UCLA) (the latter has a separate and autonomous "Scandinavian Section"), while smaller programs exist at Kansas and Massachusetts, and at Chicago, Harvard, Illinois, and Yale. All of these institutions offer doctoral degrees in either Scandinavian Studies or Germanic Languages and Literatures. Most of them also have impressive library collections, notably Minnesota, Berkeley, Wisconsin, Harvard, and Cornell (the last known for its famous Fiske Library of Old Norse and Icelandic literature). Important among the old church colleges with Scandinavian programs are, for Swedish, Augustana, Illinois (1860) and Gustavus Adolphus (1862); for Norwegian, Luther (1861), Augsburg (1869), and St. Olaf (1874); for Danish, Dana College (1884); and for Finnish, Suomi College (1896). A center for Icelandic studies—besides the Fiske collection at Cornell—is the University of Manitoba, Canada, where a chair in Icelandic has existed since 1972. The Askey-Gage-Rovinsky report lists instruction in Scandinavian language and/or literature at the following Canadian universities: British Columbia, Calgary, and Toronto. To these should be added, at least, the University of Alberta, Edmonton.

In May of 1911 a number of American scholars from the Midwest met in Chicago to form the Society for the Advancement of Scandinavian Study. Eight papers were read and discussed, and a publication series was initiated, later known as *Scandinavian Studies*, a quarterly journal of articles and reviews. Now in its seventy-third year, it is the oldest scholarly journal devoted to Scandinavian studies anywhere outside the Nordic countries. From the beginning, the editors emphasized the study of Scandinavian languages and literatures, though in recent years—as also reflected in a change of the society's constitution (1971)—the importance of social sciences has been recognized. At the society's annual meetings in the 1980s, between seventy and eighty papers have been presented, with approximately one-fifth devoted to Scandinavian history and politics. Scholars working in the field of Scandinavian immigration studies have an outlet also in the journals and other publications of the various historical societies, such as the Norwegian-American Historical Association (1925) and the Swedish Pioneer Historical Society (1948). Somewhat more general in nature are the articles and reviews appearing in the *Scandinavian Review*, an illustrated journal published since 1913 by the American-Scandinavian Foundation (1910). On the other hand, the foundation's various publications series—in all some 150 volumes—have been very important for the teaching of Scandinavian studies in the United States, with its classical texts, literary histories, etc., in English translation. Similarly important in recent years have been the numerous studies of Scandinavian writers in Twayne's World Author Series. Also in this connection can be mentioned the

Scandinavian series—literature in translation, history, criticism, etc.—put out by Wisconsin, Minnesota, Nebraska, and other university presses. In Canada, an Icelandic Studies series has been published by the University of Manitoba Press. WITS (Wisconsin Introductions to Scandinavia) is a pamphlet series published since 1981 by the Department of Scandinavian Studies at Wisconsin and consists of an Essay series (WITS I) and a Text series (WITS II). A retrospective listing of American scholarship in the field of Scandinavian studies can be found in *Index Nordicus*, published by the American-Scandinavian Foundation in 1980. Current bibliographies are included in the *MLA International Bibliography* (language, literature, folklore) and in *Scandinavia in English* (humanities and social sciences), originally published periodically as an article in *Scandinavian Studies* and later (1975–   ) in book form (available from the University of Minnesota Library). Since 1982, Canadian Scandinavianists have had their own professional organization, the Association for the Advancement of Scandinavian Studies in Canada (AASSC).

In Britain, regular instruction in Scandinavian studies began with W. A. Craigie's appointment as Taylorian Lecturer in Scandinavian Languages at Oxford in 1904. The languages taught were Old and Modern Icelandic, and the tradition of medieval Scandinavian language and literature has continued at Oxford under O. G. Turville-Petre. The first program in modern "continental" Scandinavian languages and literatures was instituted in 1918 at University College, London, with W. P. Ker, professor of English, as director, and native lecturers from Denmark, Norway, and Sweden. Not until 1963 was a full-time Scandinavianist appointed to the directorship (Peter Foote, professor of Old Scandinavian). The present program, under Michael Barnes, emphasizes the study of Scandinavian linguistics. At Cambridge a Scandinavian program was begun in the later 1920s and formally constituted as a Scandinavian Department in 1950, with B. W. Downs as professor and director, and with lecturers in Danish, Norwegian, and Swedish. Following the retirement of Professor Downs in 1960, Elias Bredsdorff served as reader and director until his retirement in 1976. After World War II a very active Scandinavian program was built up within the Department of German at the University of Newcastle by D. M. Mennie and his staff of seven British and Scandinavian teachers. By the year 1973 a separate Scandinavian department was created, with Glyn Jones as professor and director. The fourth fully developed Scandinavian program in Britain was set up by the dean of European studies at East Anglia, J. W. McFarlane (formerly of Newcastle). This program, in addition to offering courses in the languages and literatures of Denmark, Norway, and Sweden, includes instruction in Scandinavian history by a professional historian. Scandinavian departments on a somewhat smaller scale exist at Aberdeen and at Hull, while language instruction in either Swedish (S) or Norwegian (N) is provided at the universities of Aberystwith (S), Bangor (N), Belfast (S), Cardiff (S), Glasgow (N), and Surrey (S). Icelandic is taught at Edinburgh, where Hermann Palsson holds the position of reader. British Scandinavianists have been active in bibliography, in translation and text edition, as well as in literary history and criticism. Examples of their work are the many volumes of *The Year's Work in Modern Language Studies*, the Penguin translations of Icelandic sagas, the eight-volume English *Oxford Ibsen*, with notes, drafts and scholarly introductions and commentaries, as well as critical contributions on Scandinavian writers from Hans Christian Andersen* to Knut Hamsun.* In 1962 the first issue appeared of *Scandinavica*, a scholarly journal devoted to modern Scandinavian literature, with articles, reviews, and bibliographical information. Unlike the American *Scandinavian Studies*, which is published by a society and aims to provide an outlet for the scholarly activities of the society's members, *Scandinavica* is an international journal, whose editorial board represents nineteen different nations and whose contributors are Scandinavianists from all over the world. Articles and reviews are written mostly in English, but occasionally in French and frequently in German. The first conference of what is now known as the International Association for Scandinavian Studies (IASS) was held 1956 in England, with the Cambridge Scandinavian Department serving as hosts and initiators. The conference, which has been held every second year since that time, has attracted scholars from all parts of Europe and beyond. Thus, in 1980, the conference was held in Greifswald in the German Democratic Republic, and in 1984 it was hosted by the Scandinavian Department, University of Washington. Regular instruction in Scandinavian languages and/or literatures is now offered by more than thirty different nations of the world, including Australia and New Zealand.

REFERENCES

Askey, Donald E., Gene G. Gage, and Robert T. Rovinsky, "Nordic Area Studies in North America." *Scandinavian Studies* 47.2 (1975); Bothne, Gisle, "Nordiske studier ved amerikanske universiteter," in *Norsk-Amerikanernes Festskrift* (Decorah, Iowa, 1914); Flom, George T., "A Sketch of Scandinavian Study in American Universities." *Scandinavian Studies* 1 (1911); Kvavik, Robert B, ed. *A Directory of Scandinavian Studies in North America* (Madison, Wis. 1990); Mennie, Duncan M., "Modern Scandinavian Studies in Britain: An Historical Introduction." *Scandinavica* 14.2 (1975). For a survey of worldwide instruction in Scandinavian studies, write the embassies of each of the five Scandinavian countries.

                                                                    Harald S. Naess

Scandinavian Theater. *See* Theater in Scandinavia.

Schack, Hans Egede. Danish novelist and statesman, b. 2 February 1820, Sengeløse, d. 20 July 1858, Schlangenbad at Frankfurt am Main.

Schack, the son of a minister, grew up in the countryside and later lived in Copenhagen, where he received his education as a jurist. Through his marriage he came in contact with influential members of the official class. Soon Schack became interested in liberalism and Scandinavianism and wrote several political articles on these subjects. He took part in the War of 1848, at which time he was also a member of the constituent assembly. From 1850 to 1853 he was a member of the Danish parliament, although not a party liner. His political ideal was the freedom of the individual, which was not always compatible with actual politics in the young Danish democracy.

His ideal of individualism is also the main theme of the only novel Schack published, *Phantasterne* (The Fantasts) from 1857. It traces the development of three boys in establishing their positions in life. Although the novel is a *Bildungsroman*, its real subject is the psychological analysis of the three characters, that is, the analysis of fantasy and realism. The story is told by Conrad, one of the three boys, who is also the main character. In their youth Christian and he dream about fame and honor, while the third companion, Thomas, represents stolid skepticism. Later Conrad's intellect is directed toward erotic fantasies. The novel focuses on man's personal search for balance between reality and dream. Conrad succeeds while Christian loses himself in fantasy that finally leads to schizophrenia. For Thomas, the world of dreams prepares the way to a better social position. Along with psychological exposure the novel also provides a picture of a social contrast between traditional feudalism and modern liberalism, the first related to dreams, the second to reality.

Schack's work on a second novel, *Sandhed med Modification* (Truth with Modification) was terminated with his death.

Thus *Phantasterne* alone has placed Schack in the history of Danish literature as a forerunner of realism in the 1870s. The novel's presentation of human character is still fascinating for the modern reader.

REFERENCES

Andersen, Jens Kr., *Feudalistisk fantasteri og liberalistisk virkelighed* (Copenhagen, 1978); Hertel, Hans, ed., *Omkring Phantasterne* (Copenhagen, 1969); Jørgensen, Aage, "On 'Phantasterne,' the Novel by Hans Egede Schack.' " *Scandinavica* 5.1 (1966); Jørgensen, John Chr., *Den sande kunst* (Copenhagen, 1980); Madsen, Børge Gedsø, "Hans Egede Schack's 'Phantasterne.' " *Scandinavian Studies* 35 (1966).

                                                          Preben Meulengracht Sørensen

Scherfig, Hans. Danish painter, novelist, short story writer, and essayist, b. 8 April 1905, Copenhagen, d. 28 January 1979, Copenhagen.

Scion of an upper-middle-class family, Scherfig early turned to communism. The rigidities of the elite Metropolitanerskole (which he attended) and its faculty, as well as a fateful sojourn in New York City during the depression, contributed to his conversion. As a communist, Scherfig was interned briefly during World War II.

Scherfig studied zoology, Danish, literature, and German at the University of Copenhagen without taking a degree. Convinced of his calling as a visual artist, he began exhibiting his paintings in 1928. During his career he decorated numerous public buildings with murals and even painted advertisements. He was a frequent contributor (of both artwork and articles) to leftist periodicals. He often illustrated his own books.

His first novel was the mystery *Den døde mand* (1937; The Dead Man), and was set appropriately in an artistic milieu. It contains much of the humor and irony found in vintage Scherfig but is not as critical of the bourgeois establishment as his later works. His second novel, *Den forsvundne Fuldmægtig* (1938; *The Missing Bureaucrat*, 1988), depicts the hollow existence of the midlevel bureaucrat. Together with *Det forsømte Foraar* (1940; *Stolen Spring*; 1986), it is a scathing, if often humorous, indictment of a society that has allowed its educational system to blight the lives of its most gifted children.

Scherfig's novel *Idealister* (Swedish edition 1942, first Danish printing 1945; *The Idealists*, 1949) portrays the turbulent 1930s both as a period of a plethora of (frequently grotesque and hypocritical) ideals and as an ominous prelude to World War II. Its sequel, *Frydenholm* (1962; Frydenholm), recounts, at times movingly, how one fictitious rural community fared during the German occupation. It is a worthy epitaph to Scharfig's fallen comrades.

In his later years, Scherfig turned increasingly to his essays and travel books, writing mostly about communist lands and ideals.

Because of his humor and straightforward style, Scherfig was one of Denmark's most widely read contemporary authors. His works enjoyed a renaissance during the 1970s, less because of their political message than their ability to hold the imagination and to entertain.

FURTHER WORKS

Hvad lærer vi i skolen? (1933); *Litografi* (1947); *Danmark i Lys og Skygge* (1947); *Hellas* (1949); *På vej ind i vandmanden* (1951); *Rejse i Sovjetunionen* (1951); *Skorpionen* (1953); *Det befriede Rumænien* (1953); *Dammen* (1958); *Den gloende drage over Roskilde* (1959); *Krigs-ABC* (1961); *Holbergs Niels Klim* (1961); *Tre digtere* (1963); *Den fortabte abe* (1964); *Naturens uorden* (1965); *Hos kirgiserne* (1965); *Rumænsk Billedbog* (1967); *Morgonrødens land* (1971); *Den fattige mands bil* (1971); *Månen og Trediveårskrigen* (1972); *Butleren og andre historier* (1973); *Holberg og andre forfattere* (1973); *Det borgerlige samfund og dets institutioner* (1974); *Marxisme, rationalisme, humanisme* (1974); *Journalistik fra 30'rne* (1975); *En rænkefuld prælat* (1977); *Den kolde krig i Danmarks Radio* (1986).

REFERENCES

Andersen, Jens Kr., and Leif Emerek, *Hans Scherfigs forfatterskab* (Copenhagen, 1973); Berg, Arngeir, and Espen Haavardsholm, *Partiskhed* (Oslo, 1975); Bredsdorff, Elias, *Fra Andersen til Scherfig* (Copenhagen, 1978); Clante, Carsten, *Normale mennesker. Hans Scherfig og hans romaner* (Copenhagen, 1975); Clante, Carsten, and Nils Frederiksen, eds., *Omkring Det forsømte forår* (Copenhagen, 1974); Jansen, F. J. Billeskov, "Hans Scherfig," in *Det Danske Akademi* (Copenhagen, 1974); Joost, Vilhelm, *Scherfig* (Copenhagen, 1974); Kristensen, Sven Møller, "How to Castigate Your Public—and Write Best Sellers." *Danish Journal* 76 (1973); Mayfarth, Antje, "Antifascistischer Widerstandskampf als geschichtliche Aufgabe. Zum Hans Scherfigs weltanschaulich-künstlerischer Konzeption." *Nordeuropa* 12 (1979); Moestrup, Jørgen, *Hans Scherfig*

(Copenhagen, 1977); Nielsen, Hans-Jørgen, "Hans Scherfig," in *Danske digtere i det 20. århundrede*, ed. Torben Brostrøm and Mette Winge, vol. 3 (Copenhagen, 1981).

Frank Hugus

Schildt, Ernst *Runar*. Finland-Swedish short story writer and dramatist, b. 26 October 1888, Helsinki, d. 27 September 1925, Helsinki.

Through his father's family Schildt belonged to the nobility, but had contact through his mother with another social milieu in the coastal Swedish countryside. Schildt studied literature at the University of Helsinki and received a master of arts degree in 1910. In subsequent years he worked as director of the domestic section of the Swedish Theater in Helsinki, as editor in his cousin's publishing house, and from 1924 as co-owner and manager of a bookstore in Borgå (Porvoo).

The young Schildt is associated with the *dagdrivare* (idler) group of upper-class intellectuals who, disillusioned with life, looked with gloom toward the future. As members of the privileged social and linguistic minority, they perceived a threat in the country's Finnish-speaking majority, in the rising social democratic movement, and the Russification efforts of Czarist Russia. Theirs was a cult of the fleeting moment, of stylish appearance, of the cafés and boulevards of Helsinki, and their jargon was full of wit and cynicism. Within literature, Schildt became the most outstanding representative of the *dagdrivare* generation.

The concise prose, quick humor, and vivid rendering of the *dagdrivare* atmosphere in Schildt's debut collection, *Den segrande Eros och andra berättelser* (Victorious Eros and Other Stories) in 1912, won him immediate critical acclaim. Schildt was compared to Hjalmar Söderberg* and hailed as the author who would write the long-awaited novel about Helsinki.

Despite his insider position among the *dagdrivare*, Schildt never lost the keen and critical eye of an outsider. Behind the elegant surface and anecdotal twists of plot one detects a darker streak, an empathy with the loner and the underdog, a theme that was to dominate in Schildt's later works. For the typical protagonist, membership in the *dagdrivare* group was only provisional and often bought at a high price. Also Schildt, the artist, soon felt a need to expand his horizons. *Regnbågen* (1916; The Rainbow) and *Rönnbruden och andra noveller* (1918; The Rowan Tree Bride and Other Short Stories) are set in a country village. The events unfold back in time, the narrative pace has slackened, and an unmistakable quality of oral storytelling prevails. As if to dispel the *dagdrivare* fears of rootlessness, Schildt now treads on a soil, rich in local traditions and folklore, that had for centuries been inhabited by Swedish speakers.

In the collection *Perdita och andra noveller* (1918) Schildt conquers yet another milieu, the lower bourgeoisie of Helsinki, a social group that until then had been virtually ignored by Finland-Swedish writers. A theme alluded to in *Regnbågen* is developed further in the short story "Den Svagare" (The Weaker), one of Schildt's best. Blomqvist, a humble shop clerk, is rendered weak and spineless out of love for his young and beautiful wife. Faced with the truth of his wife's blatant marital betrayal, Blomqvist becomes first furious, then rebels, and finally resigns himself to the fact that he cannot live without his wife. This thoroughly honest man stands prepared to sacrifice his own moral principles in an effort to win back his wife. The author's sympathy with the weak individual is mingled with an awareness of the potentially perilous consequences of such weakness. The same psychological syndrome emerges in the collection *Hemkomsten och andra noveller* (1919; Homecoming and Other Short Stories) as an explanation for the socialist, Red element in the Finnish Civil War of 1918. Particularly noteworthy is the collections's title novella, "Hemkomsten."

Schildt was increasingly bothered by bouts of severe depression, attributable at least in part to his fear of losing his creativity. In the exquisite novella "Häxskogen" (1921; Witchwood) in a collection by the same name, he bares his innermost self. The protagonist, an author spending his summer vacation at the estate of his successful relatives, has reached the eighth chapter of his book when inspiration fails him. While the robust relatives live life to its fullest, the author has always stood on the sidelines as an observer. That he cannot be productive even within art, his realm of "reality," leaves him with a feeling of futility and self-loathing. Finally, after being rejected by his beloved, the last tie to ordinary happiness thus severed, the paralyzing spell is broken and the eighth chapter finished. But even at this successful moment, the author questions the value of a written page, the very justification of his existence.

Schildt's last works consist of three dramas, *Galgmannen* (1922; *The Gallows Man*, 1944), a short one-act play celebrating the power of woman's love; *Den stora rollen* (1923; The Great Role), set at the time of the Civil War; and *Lyckoriddaren* (1923; The Fortune Hunter). The first two proved successful and extended Schildt's fame beyond the borders of Finland. Not long after, in September 1925, Schildt took his own life.

Although Schildt never produced the great Helsinki epic about which the critics had prophesied, his short stories have retained their freshness and have secured him a place among the finest prose writers of Swedish Finland. A number of his works have been filmed. In addition, the story "Hemkomsten" was dramatized in 1973 by Johan Bargum, and in 1975 a new adaptation of *Lyckoriddaren* was staged in Helsinki.

FURTHER WORKS

Asmodeus och de tretton själarna samt tre noveller (1915); *Armas Fager* (1920); *Några blad* (1926); *Noveller*, 2 vols. (1955); *Från Rönnbruden till Häxskogen*, ed. Göran Schildt (1974); *Från Regnbågen till Galgmannen*, ed. Göran Schildt, 2 vols. (1988).

FURTHER TRANSLATIONS

Swedo-Finnish Short Stories, ed. George C. Schoolfield (1974); *Scandinavian Studies* 49.2 (1977).

REFERENCES

Castrén, Gunnar, *Runar Schildt* (Helsinki, 1927); Cederlöf, Henrik, *Stilstudier i Runar Schildts novellistik* (Helsinki, 1967); Schoolfield, George C., "The Post-War Novel of

Swedish Finland." *Scandinavian Studies* 34.2 (1962); Schoolfield, George, C., "Runar Schildt and Swedish Finland." *Scandinavian Studies* 32.1 (1960); Zuck, Virpi, *Runar Schildt and His Tradition: An Approach through Genre* (Helsinki, 1983).

Virpi Zuck

Schoultz, Solveig von. Finland-Swedish poet, short story writer, and novelist, b. 5 August 1907, Borgå (Porvoo).

Home background has influenced Schoultz in a dual way. Her father, a minister and teacher of religion, set definite ethical standards for his large family. Schoultz distanced herself from the "conscience-building" norms of her youth by creating a literary world of acceptance and compassion. The deeper her psychological probing cuts, the more evident becomes the insufficiency of one limiting viewpoint. Yet the biography of her painter mother, Hanna Frosterus-Segerstråle, *Porträtt av Hanna* (1978; Portrait of Hanna), demonstrates how much she has learned from her mother's strict artistic discipline, and also how much her writing reflects the whole and secure world of her childhood.

Schoultz claims that the line between a poem and a story is fluid, and her poems and short stories do have much in common in their themes and technique. In her poetry she creates "portraits of life," vignettes of human existence, caught in a fleeting, often dreamlike moment, as in "Tre systrar" (Three Sisters), where through a technique of transparency she gives threefold depth to a single human gesture. Nature in Schoultz's work not only interacts with the author's mood, but suggests multiple metaphorical dimensions, as in "Siesta." Schoultz can be seen more as younger friend than as heir of the Finland-Swedish modernists. Her language, though unconventional and suggestive in a novel way, has found a simplicity and lucidity all its own. This language has undergone an increasingly strict condensation in Schoultz's short stories and corresponds to the frugality with which she pries open whole human destinies through seemingly insignificant everyday events. The collection *Somliga mornar* (1976; Some Mornings) gives glimpses of complex human relationships: a mother thinking of her child while waiting for her lover, or an aging husband and wife, as cunning in their last power struggle as in their cautiously expressed tenderness for each other.

The measure of Schoultz's literary vitality is demonstrated by her capacity to recast the Finland-Swedish cultural heritage into contemporary themes through post-modernist literary forms of her own creation.

FURTHER WORKS

Petra och silverapan (1932); *December* (1937); *Min timme* (1940); *De sju dagarna* (1942); *Den bortvända glädjen* (1943); *Nalleresan* (1944); *Eko av ett rop* (1945); *Ingenting ovanligt* (1947); *Nattlig äng* (1949); *Luftombyte* (1950); *Låt inte Kåstad göra er illa* (1951); *Närmare någon* (1951); *Allt sker nu* (1952); *Gökungen* (1953); *Mosses resa* (1953); *Råttans namnsdag* (1953); *Vänta* (1953); *Ansa och samvetet* (1954); *Nätet* (1956); *Tessi kan vänta* (1956); *Den blomstertid* (1958); *Terrassen* (1959); *Passgångaren* (1960); *Millaskolan* (1961); *Parkbänk* (1961–1962); *Strumpan X* (1963); *Sänk ditt ljus* (1963); *Halv sex en morgon* (1965); *Även dina kameler* (1965); *Javisst, kära du* (1967); *Situationen*

(1967); *Klippbok* (1968); *Pulli* (1968); *Nästa dörr* (1969); *Besöket* (1970); *En ängel går genom rummet* (1970); *Rymdbruden* (1970); *Amaryllis* (1971); *Ett rum för natten* (1972); *Där står du* (1973); *Weekend i oktober* (1973); *De fyra flöjtspelarna* (1975); *Ostkupan* (1975); *Bortom träden hörs havet* (1980); *Katri* (1980); *En enda minut* (1981); *Kolteckning, ofullbordad* (1983); *Ingen dag förgäves* (1984); *Vattenhjulet* (1986).

TRANSLATIONS

Swedo-Finnish Short Stories, ed. George C. Schoolfield (1974); *Poems 1940–80,* trans. Jeremy Parsons (1982); *New Jersey Poetry Journal* 2 (1983); *Sequoia* 27 (1983); *Books from Finland* 21.2 (1987).

REFERENCES

Haavikko, Ritva, ed., *Miten kirjani ovat syntyneet,* vol. 2 (Helsinki, 1980); Warburton, Thomas, "Solveig von Schoultz," in *Kirjallisuudentutkijain Seuran vuosikirja* 18 (1965).

Margareta Neovius Deschner

Seeberg, Peter. Danish novelist, playwright, essayist, and director of Viborg Museum, b. 22 June 1925, Skrydstrup.

In addition to four novels, plays, and many short stories, Seeberg has written on a wide range of nonfictional subjects, including Friedrich Nietzsche and Ludwig Josef Johan Wittgenstein, philosophers who have influenced Seeberg's worldview.

Seeberg's first novel, *Bipersonerne* (1956; The Extras) placed Seeberg among the foremost contemporary Danish writers. The themes of alienation, detachment from reality, and the loss of self, which permeate Seeberg's writings, are all presented in *Bipersonerne*. Based on Seeberg's own experience as a volunteer worker during the war, the novel is set in Berlin in 1943. The cast consists of displaced persons, deported from occupied countries to assist in the production of an imaginary German propaganda film. Isolated from any reality and without any moral or ideological engagement in the war, the extras live a "shadow existance." Seeberg observes his characters as if through a camera lens and describes them in a terse, objective language, so that the narrative takes on a sense of the absurd. Seeberg maintains that because modern man has lost the ability to perceive things realistically, an exact description of reality will produce a symbolic effect.

In *Fugls føde* (1957; *The Impostor,* 1990), Seeberg continues his exploration of contemporary nihilism; but whereas Sim in *Bipersonerne* has no true existence, except inside himself, Tom, the protagonist of Seeberg's second novel, does achieve a kind of self-realization. In the end he can declare: "I am here."

Seeberg's succeeding works also deal with the experience of loss. One man's body is replaced piece by piece by artificial parts. Another man loses the use of his limbs, his identity, and his life. When the king in "Yndlingsglasset" (The Favorite Glass) in *Argumenter for benådning* (1967; Points in Favor of a Reprieve) loses his glass, he loses the meaning of life itself, and is left with a yearning void that becomes his eternity.

A true member of the silent generation of the 1950s, Seeberg is a modernist whose ironies only recount, never explain. The final interpretation is up to the reader.

In Seeberg's recent works humanism and optimism seem to have won out, and Seeberg appears to have gained confidence in man's ability not only to survive but to overcome.

FURTHER WORKS

Eftersøgningen og andre noveller (1962); *Ferai* (1970); *Hyrder* (1970); *Dinosaurens sene eftermiddag* (1974); television version of St. Blicher's *En Landsbydegns Dagbog* (1975); *Erobringen af Fyn* (1975); *Efter middagsluren* (1976); *En lille musebog* (1977); *At se på VIBORG at være i* (1978); *Ved havet* (1978); *På selve dagen* (1979); *Hovedrengøring* (1979); *Om fjorten dage* (1981); *Uden et navn* (1985); *Værkfører Thomsens endelige hengivelse* (1986); *Roland kommer til verden* (1986).

TRANSLATIONS

Literary Review 8.1 (1964); *Boundary, A Journal of Postmodern Literature* 1.3 (1973).

REFERENCES

Bondebjerg, Ib, *Peter Seeberg: En ideologikritisk analyse* (Aalborg, 1972); Rossel, Sven H., "The Search for Reality: A Study in Peter Seeberg's Prose Writings." *Proceedings: Pacific Northwest Conference on Foreign Languages* 27 (1976); Thule, Vagn, *Peter Seeberg* (Copenhagen, 1972).

Wera Hildebrand

Sigfússon, Hannes. Icelandic poet, novelist, and translator, b. 2 March 1922, Reykjavík.

Sigfússon has pursued various occupations; presently, he works as a librarian in Norway, where he has lived for a long time. He belongs to the group of Icelandic poets who have made the most radical break with conventions and traditional forms in bringing Icelandic poetry into the modern age.

His first published work, *Dymbilvaka* (1949; Holy Week), was composed under strong influence from *The Waste Land* of T. S. Eliot. Like *Imbrudagar* (1951; Ember Days), *Dymbilvaka* constitutes a mapping of new areas of human consciousness, as well as the rejection of a petrified poetic tradition. Like many other poets of his generation, he was conditioned by the recent terrors of war and the tensions of the postwar years; the cold war, doubts regarding communism, and the fear of the atom bomb threw a long shadow on his view of life and poetry. In his earlier volumes the foreground is occupied by an existential dilemma; his attitude is introspective and characterized by confusion, pessimism, and despair. The poetry belongs to a twilight world between dream and waking, inspired rather than conceived, obscure, and chaotic. The imagery is surrealistic and evokes features both of a disordered world and a divided being. In 1955 Sigfússon produced the novel *Strandið* (The Stranding), inspired by a tragic sea disaster of which the author was witness. For several years he contributed to the production of *Birtingur*, a periodical that provided a literary platform for Icelandic modernists, 1955–1968.

Around 1960 Sigfússon's poetry took a new direction. His diction became more formal and logical, the poems less diffuse and obscure. This change was partly due to a new outlook in the poet toward the end of the fifties, when he became a socialist. He then stressed the poet's moral and political responsibility and tried to write unambiguously, embracing socialist dialectic in his writing. In the volumes *Sprek á eldinn* (1961; Kindling) and *Jarteikn* (1968; Signs), poems of political involvement are prominent.

FURTHER WORKS

Norrœn ljóð 1939–69 (1972); *Örvamœlir* (1978); *Flökkulíf* (1981); *Ljóðasafn* (1982).

REFERENCES

Carleton, Peter, "Dymbilvaka, skáldið i vitanum." *Tímarit Máls og menningar*, vol. 1 (1979); Hjálmarsson, Johann, *Íslenzk nútímaljóðlist* (Reykjavík, 1971); Þorvaldsson, Eysteinn, *Atómskáldin. Aðdragandi og upphaf módernisma í íslenskri ljóðagerð* (Reykjavík, 1980).

                                                                                    Matthías Viðar Sæmundsson

Sigurðsson, Ólafur Jóhann. Icelandic poet and novelist, b. 26 September 1918, Hlíð, Gullbringu district.

From the age of six, Sigurðsson grew up, a farm boy, in one of the most beautiful districts of southern Iceland, and though he moved to Reykjavík at fifteen, determined to become a writer, his mind remained in southern Iceland. In the capital, he worked at odd jobs, but aside from some studies in Copenhagen (1936–1937) and in New York (with Manuel Komroff, 1943–1944), he is largely self-educated.

Sigurðsson grew to maturity in a Reykjavík that he knew first as a depression-worn small town of scarce employment and often violent labor disputes, and later, during World War II, as a boom city of opportunists enriching themselves by pandering to foreign occupation forces. It was a time of great upheaval, when old values crumbled and social, economic, and moral conditions were in a state of extreme fluidity. All this is reflected in his works, which, reduced to their essence, always deal with standards of ethics, judgment of values.

Sigurðsson published his first book, a collection of children's stories, when he was only sixteen, and that volume, as well as his first novel, published two years later, was set in the countryside. By 1940, however, in his second novel, the country boy had embraced the radical viewpoint of urban socialism, focusing on the harsh life in the city where the poverty and squalor of ordinary working people contrasted with the more affluent but, in his view, empty and superficial existence of the so-called better citizens. Sigurðsson's later novels have alternated between rural and urban settings, his major works being *Fjallið og draumurinn* (1944; The Mountain and the Dream) and its sequel *Vorköld jörð* (1951; The

Cold Earth of Spring), and the trilogy *Gangvirkið* (1955; The Clockwork), *Seiður og hélog* (1977; Magic and Mirage), and *Drekar og smáfuglar* (1983; Dragons and Sparrows). He has also written several volumes of short fiction and ranks among the top Icelandic writers in that form; two of his novellas, *Litbrigði jarðarinnar* (1947; *The Changing Earth*, 1979) and *Bréf séra Böðvars* (1965; *Pastor Böðvar's Letter*, 1985) have already become classics.

Sigurðsson's style is one of meticulous clarity, twined with a strong strand of lyricism and colored by humor, which may turn into sharp satire. From time to time, his lyrical nature has gained the upper hand, resulting, so far, in four volumes of poetry. It was for two of these that he was awarded the literary prize of the Nordic Council in 1976, the first Icelander to be so honored.

FURTHER WORKS

Við Álftavatn (1934); *Velkomnir Færeyingar* (1934); *Um sumarkvöld* (1935); *Skuggarnir af bænum* (1936); *Liggur vegurinn þangað?* (1940); *Kvistir í altarinu* (1942); *Teningar í tafli* (1945); *Speglar og fiðrildi* (1947); *Nokkrar vísur um veðrið og fleira* (1952); *Á vegamótum* (1955); *Ljósir dagar* (1959); *Spói* (1962); *Leynt og ljóst* (1965); *Glerbrotið* (1970); *Hreiðrið* (1972); *Seint á ferð* (1972); *Að laufferjum* (1972); *Að brunnum* (1974); *Að laufferjum og brunnum* (1976); *Virki og vötn* (1978).

FURTHER TRANSLATIONS

Childhood Education 20 (1944); *American-Scandinavian Review* 33.1 (1945); *American-Scandinavian Review* 35.4 (1947); *American-Scandinavian Review* 36.4 (1949); *Short Stories of Today by Twelve Modern Icelandic Authors*, trans. Alan Boucher (1972); *Poetry* 128.3 (1976); *Icelandic Canadian* 35.3 (1977); *The Changing Earth and Selected Poems*, trans. Alan Boucher (1979); *The Postwar Poetry of Iceland*, trans. Sigurður A. Magnússon (1982).

Hallberg Hallmundsson

Sigurðsson, Stefán (Stefán frá Hvítadal). Icelandic poet, b. 11 October 1887, Hólmavík, d. 7 March 1933, Saurbær, Dalasýsla.

Sigurðsson spent his youth on a farm at Hvítadal in northwestern Iceland and became a printer's apprentice in 1905, but he was unable to continue this work after an infection necessitated the amputation of his foot. In 1912 he sailed to Norway, where he traveled extensively and worked at shipbuilding in Bergen, but serious illness forced him to enter a sanatorium. After returning to Iceland, he married, raised a large family, and just barely managed to earn a living as a farmer in his native district. Sigurðsson was a member of the *Unuhús* group of poets, and, like fellow member Halldór Kiljan Laxness,* converted to Catholicism in 1923.

Sigurðsson burst upon the literary scene in Iceland with his first book of poems, *Söngvar förumannsins* (Wanderer's Songs), in 1918. His work was marked by a new and intensely personal quality as well as by uncommon verse forms. Although the thematic and formal influence of Herman Theodor Wildenvey,* Henrik Ibsen,* and Per Sivle is apparent, Sigurðsson transforms his models into an emotional blend of joy in sadness that is truly his own. Although in his second collection, *Óður einyrkjans* (1921; Song of the Lone Farmer), these earlier themes lack some of their freshness and originality, the losses are replaced by a greater thematic range, often inspired by folklore and fairy tale. Unique for the work as a whole is the mutually exclusive interplay between the earlier, dreamy wanderer and the contemporary, earthbound farmer. After a deeply emotional eulogy to the Catholic church, *Heilög kirkja* (1924; Holy Church), written in medieval verse form, Sigurðsson mixed poems on religious and secular themes three years later in *Helsingjar* (1927; People of Helsing). The former seem rooted in Sigurðsson's lifelong bout with ill health and often deal with suffering as a means to the attainment of the soul's purity, while the latter display his increasing interest in the past. Among the most notable of the poems of Sigurðsson's final years is *Anno domini 1930* (1933), written to commemorate the millennium of Iceland's parliament.

Sigurðsson was the spokesman for an entire generation of Icelandic poets and occasioned numerous imitations of his metrical skills, his diction, and his personal mixture of melancholy and hope. Especially with his earlier poems, but also with the finest of his later efforts, Sigurðsson still has a place among Iceland's contemporary poets.

FURTHER WORKS

Ljóðmæli, ed. Tómas Guðmundsson (1945).

TRANSLATIONS

Fimm einsöngslög. Five Icelandic Songs, ed. Sigurður Þórðarson (1944); *An Anthology of Icelandic Poetry,* comp. Eiríkur Benedikz (1969).

REFERENCES

Beck, Richard, *History of Icelandic Poets: 1800–1940* (Ithaca, 1950); Laxness, Halldór Kiljan, ''Stefán frá Hvítadal.'' *Iðunn* 18 (1934).

Peter A. Jorgensen

Sigurjónsson, Jóhann. Icelandic dramatist and poet, b. 19 June 1880, Laxamýri, Þingeyjarsýsla, d. 30 August 1919, Copenhagen.

Poet, writer of tales and aphorisms, but most famous as a dramatist, Sigurjónsson was born on the farm Laxamýri near Húsavík in northern Iceland. He was the son of a prosperous farmer, and after a year of studying with the minister at Sauðárkrókur, he enrolled in the Latin school in Reykjavík. Like many of his countrymen around the turn of the century who wanted to become writers, Sigurjónsson traveled to Copenhagen in 1899 to continue his education, but broke off his studies in veterinary medicine three years later to devote himself to writing. With the exception of four subsequent visits to Iceland, he made his permanent home in Denmark. Before leaving Iceland he had become a free-thinker, and his works show also influences from writers such as Henrik Ibsen,*

Holger Drachmann,* Friedrich Nietzsche, August Strindberg,* Fyodor Dostoyevski, and William Butler Yeats.

Sigurjónsson began writing poetry in the late 1890s and continued to do so both in Icelandic and Danish until his death in 1919. Both his verse and his tales are drawn from his personal life and frequently make use of the images of the sun and the sea. His plays, many of which exist in both Icelandic and Danish versions, often with variant texts, may be divided into three categories: those that have modern, European themes such as *Dr. Rung* (1905; Dr. Rung), the saga plays like *Løgneren* (1917; The Liar) based on *Njál's Saga*, and the Icelandic plays. The latter are his best known works, especially *Fjalla-Eyvindur* (1912; *Eyvindur of the Mountains*, 1961.) This is about a famous outlaw who lived in the barren interior of Iceland for many years during the eighteenth century and the power of the love between him and his wife, who gave up a comfortable life on her farm to share his exile with him.

Sigurjónsson projected himself into his dramatic characters, and the less detailed and rigidly constructed his source material was, the better he was able to mold theme and subject matter for his own purposes. Through his Icelandic dramas he wished to give Danes a picture of what life in Iceland was like and to show that the people there had an active and productive culture. In doing this, he established the modern drama as a genre in Iceland and won the affection of his countrymen. His writings accordingly have enjoyed a prominent place in Icelandic as well as Danish literature.

FURTHER WORKS

Bóndinn á Hrauni (1908; *The Hraun Farm*, 1916); *Galdra-Loftur* (1915; *The Wish*, 1967); *Smaadigte* (1920); *Rit*, 2 vols. (1940–1942).

REFERENCES

Leach, H. G., " 'Eyvind of the Hills'/Outlaws." *American-Scandinavian Review* 4.6 (1916); Magoun, Francis P., Jr., "Jóhann Sigurjónsson's Fjalla-Eyvindur: Source, Chronology, and Geography." *Publications of the Modern Language Association* 61.1 (1946); Sigurjónsson, Ingeborg, *Mindernes Besøg* (Copenhagen 1932); Toldberg, Helge, *Jóhann Sigurjónsson* (Copenhagen, 1965).

Christopher Hale

Sillanpää, Frans Eemil. Finnish novelist, b. 16 September 1888, Hämeenkyrö, d. 3 June 1964, Helsinki.

Of humble rural origins, Sillanpää entered the University of Helsinki in 1908. He studied biology with a view to medicine, but withdrew in 1913, and returned home to find his way to a writing career. He married Sigrid Salomäki in Hämeenkyrö in 1916.

His subjects would always be the farmers, farmhands, and hired girls of his home region. He rarely chose urban settings. Sillanpää's first book was *Elämä ja aurinko* (1916; Life and the Sun), a rustic romance. Its meditative style recalls the early works of Knut Hamsun.* Next appeared a collection of short stories, entitled *Ihmislapsia elämän saatossa* (1917; The Procession of Life).

Sillanpää's first great success was the naturalistic *Hurskas kurjuus* (1919; *Meek Heritage*, 1938). It portrays a poor tenant farmer named Juha Toivola who is caught up in the Civil War of 1917 on the side of the Reds. Sillanpää presents his nonhero with pity but with a detachment bordering on distaste. Juha has little will of his own and not much intelligence. Sillanpää's ambiguous stance is indicated in one passage referring to "the thoughts of one secretly outside of it all and careful not to disclose himself." He was not in complete sympathy with the repression of the vanquished by the victors.

Sillanpää next published several collections of short stories, notably *Maan tasalta* (1924; On the Ground Level) and *Töllinmäki* (1925; The Hill with Cabin). A good sample is "Juhannusvieraat" (Midsummer Guests) from *Maan tasalta*, an ironic account of a family from the city imposing on country relatives during the Midsummer holiday. Its pointed humor reminds one of Guy de Maupassant.

Sillanpää gained broad approval with *Nuorena nukkunut* (1931; *Fallen Asleep While Young*, also *The Maid Silja*, 1933). A young girl is forced by growing poverty at home to go into domestic service. She has a love affair, is left alone, and eventually dies of consumption, a fate she accepts with resignation. Sillanpää distilled from Silja's surrender to destiny a delicate poetry that the reader finds subtly toxic. Sillanpää may have been influenced by Maurice Maeterlinck's mysticism, for he translated some of the Belgian's work. Incidentally, a girl resembling Silja had been depicted in an earlier story in *Töllinmäki*.

Sillanpää's later novels do not end with the death of the main character. *Miehen tie* (1932, The Way of a Man) is more epical than *The Maid Silja*, though less poetic. A night in summer indirectly links various human destinies in *Ihmiset suviyössä* (1934; *People in the Summer Night*, 1966). Here Sillanpää is more interested in exploring inner motives than in recounting external events.

In much of his work, the place given to dialogue is minor, and indirect discourse is common. The characters are creatures of instinct with little insight into their own motives. Their passivity is related to the author's biological mysticism. The major themes are sex, treated without grossness, and death, treated almost as something to be welcomed. Sillanpää's aim is to portray the poor of his world with understanding. His manner is usually quiet and undramatic, now and then warming to a lyrical glow. Sillanpää's descriptions of nature have been much admired.

When Sillanpää was awarded the Nobel Prize for literature in 1939, his chief accomplishments were long in the past. His wife died in 1938. His second marriage was not a happy one (1939–1941). The war years were difficult for him. His health broke down, and some works were left unfinished. After the war, Sillanpää produced several books of reminiscences going back to his childhood. In his old age, he blossomed into a popular radio *raconteur*. He is remembered as the outstanding Finnish writer of the period between the world wars.

FURTHER WORKS

Rakas Isänmaani (1919); *Hiltu ja Ragnar* (1923); *Enkelten suojatit* (1923); *Rippi* (1928); *Kiitos hetkistä, Herra . . .* (1930); *Virran pohjalta* (1933); *Viidestoista* (1936); *Elokuu* (1941); *Kootut teokset*, 12 vols. (1942–1950); *Ihmiselon ihanuus ja kurjuus* (1945); *Erään elämän satoa* (1947); *Kerron ja kuvailen* (1954); *Valitut teokset* (1954, 1969); *Päivä korkeimmillaan* (1956); *Ajatelmia ja luonnehdintoja* (1960); *Novellit*, 2 vols. (1961).

FURTHER TRANSLATIONS

Finnish Short Stories, ed. Inkeri Väänänen-Jensen and K. Börje Vähämäki (1982).

REFERENCES

Johnson, Edgar, "Nobel Prizeman: 1939." *New Republic*, 29 November 1939; Laurila, Aarne, *F. E. Sillanpää vuosina 1888–1958* (Helsinki, 1958); Laurila, Aarne, *F. E. Sillanpään Romaanitaide* (Helsinki, 1979); Rajala, Panu, *F. E. Sillanpää vuosina 1888–1923* (Helsinki, 1983).

Reino Virtanen

Siwertz, Per *Sigfrid*. Swedish poet, dramatist, and prose writer, b. 24 November 1882, Stockholm, d. 26 November 1970, Stockholm. Member of the Swedish Academy from 1932.

Siwertz's early work revealed a weary air of pessimism associated with Hjalmar Söderberg* and other fin de siècle writers, but after attending Henri Bergson's lectures in Paris in 1907, Siwertz developed an interest in man's will and ability to act. In his adventure story *Mälarpirater* (1911; Pirates of Mälare) his lonely passive anti-hero is superseded by active young boys who form true friendships and shape their own destiny. Siwertz's ensuing short stories and plays deal realistically with modern society while apparently sustaining a belief in free will, which caused him to be grouped with "tiotalisterna," that is, the middle-class realistic prose writers of the 1910s. This was reinforced with his acknowledged masterpiece, *Selambs* (1920; *Downstream*, 1923), a psychological and social novel that, in tracing the five Selamb children's development over five decades, shows how heredity and adverse social conditions can lead to sterile egoism. Man's will is again demonstrated, but now it is the will to do evil. The novel's many deterministic traits prove that Siwertz never wholly escaped his earlier pessimism, but instead of passivity Siwertz's ferocious indignation at capitalistic excesses and unscrupulous wartime profiteering shines clearly through the controlled irony.

Such involvement by Siwertz is rare. A most prolific, fluent, and entertaining writer, he was nevertheless reluctant to commit himself. A lack of depth and his tendency to take up current events (Ramsay McDonald's break with his own party in *En hederlig man* [1933; An Honourable Man] and Kreuger's crash in *Spel på havet* [1938; Gambling at Sea]) have dated much of his work. Apart from *Selambs*, Siwertz is best remembered for some elegant collections of short stories and his charming, candid memoirs *Att vara ung* (1949; On Being Young).

FURTHER WORKS

Gatans drömmar (1905); *Margot* (1906); *Den unga lönnen* (1906); *Cirkeln* (1907); *Indiansommar* (1908); *De gamla* (1909); *Hamn och haf* (1911); *Visdomständerna* (1911); *Åmbetsmän på äfventyr* (1912); *En strid på Defvensö* (1913); *En flanör* (1914); *De stora barnen* (1915); *Eldens återsken* (1916); *Lördagskvällar* (1917); *Noveller* (1918); *Storm i vattenglas* (1918); *Vindros* (1919); *Dikter* (1920); *Ställverket* (1921); *En handfull dun* (1922); *Hem från Babylon* (1923); *Taklagsölet* (1923); *Lata latituder* (1924); *Vattenvärlden* (1925); *En färd till Abessinien* (1926); *Det stora varuhuset* (1926; *Goldman's* 1926); *Jonas och draken* (1928); *Reskamraterna* (1929); *Ekotemplet* (1930); *Det stora bygget* (1930); *Trions bröllop* (1930); *Jag har varit en tjuv* (1931); *Saltsjöpirater* (1931); *Änkleken och andra berättelser* (1931); *Minne av Tor Hedberg* (1932); *Lågan* (1932); *Två tidsdramer* (1933); *Sista äventyr* (1935); *Jorden min hobby* (1936); *Minnas* (1937); *Skönhet* (1937); *Ett brott* (1938); *Det stora bullret* (1938); *Jag fattig syndig* (1939); *Medelålders herre* (1940); *Mer än skuggor* (1940); *Brutus* (1942); *Sex fribiljetter* (1943); *Renässanssängen* (1944); *Djami och vattenandarna* (1945); *Förtroenden* (1945); *Spegel med amoriner* (1947); *Slottstappning* (1949); *Slottsfinal* (1950); *Glasberget* (1952); *Pagoden* (1954); *Liten herre i grå kostym* (1955); *Den goda trätan* (1956); *Trådar i en väv* (1957); *Korsade spår* (1958); *Enhörningen och andra noveller* (1958); *Fåfäng gå— Minnen, vandringar, utkast* (1959); *Det skedde i Liechtenstein* (1961); *Adolf Törneros* (1961); *Minnets kapriser* (1963); *Trappan och Eurydike* (1966); *Nils Personne* (1967); *Episodernas hus* (1968).

REFERENCES

Soivio, Iris, *Symbolerna i Sigfrid Siwertz' prosa* (Åbo, 1966); Stolpe, Sven, *Sigfrid Siwertz* (Stockholm, 1933); Svanberg, Nils, *Studier i Sigfrid Siwertz' prosa* (Stockholm, 1941).

Irene Scobbie

Sjöberg, Birger. Swedish poet and novelist, b. 6 December 1885, Vänersborg, d. 30 April 1929, Växjö.

Sjöberg was an autodidact, a trait that made him one of the most original poets of his time. He left school at fourteen and tried his hand at various professions until he received a position at the newspaper *Helsingborgs-Posten*. During this time, his most important literary discovery was Carl Michael Bellman.* Like Bellman, Sjöberg set his own poems to music and performed them for friends with virtuosity.

His first work, *Fridas bok* (1922; Frida's Book), met with wide popular success. The legacy of Bellman, Gustaf Fröding,* and Johan Ludvig Runeberg* is clear, but like a true artist, Sjöberg does not merely imitate the masters. Instead, he gives new life to old forms and makes them his own. The poems of *Fridas bok* are set in a small Swedish town referred to as Lilla Paris (Little Paris) and often consist of dialogue between a self-educated shop assistant and his beloved, practical Frida. As the inspired shop assistant holds forth on nature, death, and the universe, Frida listens and interjects an occasional comment or protest. The effusions of the shop assistant and the life of Lilla Paris are treated with humor and irony, but never condescension. Each of the poems has been set to original music by the author.

After *Fridas bok*, Sjöberg surprised his public with a change of genre. *Kvartetten som sprängdes* (1924; The Quartet that Burst) is a lengthy work that does not easily fit into any of the subcategories of the novel, though one might detect the influence of Charles Dickens and Alexandre Dumas. The novel presents a dizzying parade of events and a rich cast of characters. Once again the action is set in a small Swedish town. The destinies of the individual members of the quartet weave their way through erotic adventures and economic disaster. A central theme is that of quixotic artistry domesticated by love and financial necessity, an issue already present in *Fridas bok*. Though humor sets the dominant tone in the novel, an undercurrent of bitterness and disillusionment periodically rears its head.

If Sjöberg's public was surprised by *Kvartetten som sprängdes*, they were even more astonished by his next poetry collection, *Kriser och kransar* (1926; Crises and Laurels). Here Sjöberg drops the mask of irony and embarks on an odyssey of drastic social commentary and self-criticism. His poetic style is masterful and disciplined, drawing on the monologues of Shakespeare for inspiration. Abstract ideas are personified; formal language alternates strikingly with everyday speech; the tone is dark and, at times, brutal. *Kriser och kransar* is a deeply personal and profoundly original work.

Sjöberg's production is marked by a distancing of the poet from his audience through masks and cryptic utterances. He distrusted the popularity of his first two works and was crushed by the critical reception of *Kriser och kransar*. When he died in 1929 of double pneumonia, he left behind him over 3,000 unpublished poems, many of which have been subsequently published in posthumous collections. Sjöberg's authorship bears witness to enormous talent and versatility. He was a great stylistic innovator, and as such, he has exerted a substantial influence on modern Swedish poetry.

FURTHER WORKS

Fridas andra bok (1929); *Skrifter*, 5 vols. (1929); *Minnen från jorden* (1940); *Samlade dikter* (1946); *Syntaxupproret* (1955); *Fridas tredje bok* (1956).

TRANSLATIONS

Scandinavian Review 69.4 (1981).

REFERENCES

Abenius, Margit, *Kontakter* (Stockholm, 1944); Axberger, Gunnar, *Lilla Paris' undergång* (Stockholm, 1960); Delblanc, Sven, *Treklöver* (Stockholm, 1980); Edfelt, Johannes, *Birger Sjöberg* (Stockholm, 1971); Hallström, Anders, *Lilla Paris' kulisser* (Lund, 1955); Nilsson, Gustaf-Adolf, *Birger Sjöberg och Frida* (Stockholm, 1943); Peterson, August, *Birger Sjöberg den okände* (Stockholm, 1944); Tunving, Lars Helge, ed., *Synpunkter på Birger Sjöberg* (Stockholm, 1966). Since 1962, the Birger Sjöberg Society has annually published a series of writings on Birger Sjöberg.

Susan Brantly

Skallagrímsson, Egill. Icelandic poet and warrior, b. ca. 910 at Borg in Southwest Iceland, d. ca. 990 at Mosfell in South Iceland.

One of the major Icelandic family sagas, *Egils Saga,* is essentially Skallagrímsson's biography, written (possibly by Snorri Sturluson*) about 1220. The saga is in part based on Skallagrímsson's poetry, which he is said to have begun to compose at the age of three and then continued to the end of his life. Not only is Skallagrímsson the greatest Viking about whom a separate saga was written but also the one who excelled in the art of skaldic poetry.

In *Egils Saga* about fifty stanzas attributed to Skallagrímsson have been preserved as well as three poems, "Höfuðlausn" (Head Ransom), "Sonatorrek" (Revenge Denied), and "Arinbjarnarkviða" (In Praise of Arinbjörn). Even though Skallagrímsson made his home on an Icelandic farm, his Viking expeditions took him far afield, both in the northern regions of the European continent and in England. In keeping with his Viking temperament and heroic attributes, Skallagrímsson, in his saga, makes both friends and enemies, and fights in single combat and as a valued member of contingents. On other occasions he makes appearances as a professional *skáld* (court poet) and is said to have declaimed poems at the courts of both King Eiríkr Bloodaxe of Norway and King Athalstan of England.

Although Skallagrímsson himself has strong and unquestionable historical foundations, his saga has distinct overtones of mythology. In the first chapter of the saga one reads, for example, about Skallagrímsson's grandfather whose conduct after sunset in the evening reminds one of the legendary werewolf, and Skallagrímsson's father has similar attributes that he then passes on to his son who, on a number of occasions, behaves like a true berserker. Therefore, one may say that in *Egils Saga* different levels of existence can be easily identified. One must, for example, recognize that when Skallagrímsson goes berserk in his saga, he no longer belongs to the realm of ordinary mortals but has reached the level of the supreme god Odin and joined the god's warriors. Skallagrímsson, according to his own testimony, worshipped Odin, and in some way his career appears to have resembled that of his god. In the saga Skallagrímsson has to face and overcome a number of obstacles that may be seen as tests of endurance designed to give the heroic poet increased mental and physical strength. At the age of three, Skallagrímsson not only rises to a difficult occasion that required him to go against his father's wishes but celebrates the same event in verse of intricate meter and diction. At the age of six, having killed an adversary older than himself and thus earned praise from his mother for his unmistakable Viking traits, Skallagrímsson, paraphrases his mother's comments in verse. To Skallagrímsson, the art of poetry and the warrior's skill are gifts from Odin. In the first part of the saga these two are quite distinct, but gradually, as Skallagrímsson's accomplishments keep growing in their impact, the two divine gifts become almost an indivisible whole. Skallagrímsson's rare abilities make him sought after by foreign chiefs and kings and, at the same time, get him into many a close corner that he consistently describes in his stanzas. Irrespective of odds, Skallagrímsson defeats his enemies easily as long as they are fairly ordinary mortals. His difficulties, however, grow in intensity when the enemies are none other than King Eiríkr Bloodaxe and his evil Queen Gunnhildr. On this occasion the warrior-poet escapes death by composing a poem of praise about the king. Appropriately, the poem is called Head Ransom ("Höfuðlausn"). Having redeemed his head at the court of King Eiríkr, Skallagrímsson defeats an obnoxious berserker in single combat, an event attested by certain stanzas Skallagrímsson is said to have composed and recited during combat, but his most severe trial awaits him in Iceland, where one of his sons dies from natural causes and another son is drowned. The poet holds the divine powers responsible for his loss but acknowledges, at the same time, his inability to take revenge on them. Having made an abortive attempt to starve himself to death as a result of his sons' deaths, Skallagrímsson composes the poem "Sonatorrek" (Revenge Denied) in memory of his two sons, the first poem in Norse literature in which an author known by name analyzes his own psychological dilemma. In it genuine lament blends with the poet's efforts to make honorable peace with the gods. Whereas "Höfuðlausn" (Head Ransom) saves Skallagrímsson from being defeated by an overpowering external enemy force, "Sonatorrek" becomes his salvation from destructive inner forces. In his saga these two poems therefore form a very important equilibrium. The last samples of Skallagrímsson's poetry, included in the final part of his saga, are in response to jeering remarks made by some maidservants on his frail physical condition. In his old age the celebrated warrior can no longer challenge berserkers or divine beings but stumbles about plagued by impaired vision. Thus one is reminded that despite Skallagrímsson's superhuman achievements, he must eventually succumb just as any other mortal. His poetry shows him to have been the greatest master of the skaldic craft in pre-Christian times.

WORKS

Egils saga Skalla-Grímssonar, in *Íslenzk fornrit,* vol. 2 (1933; repr. 1955, 1979).

TRANSLATIONS

Egil's Saga, trans. Glyn Jones (1960; repr. 1970); *Egil's Saga,* trans. Christine Fell and Johan Lucas (1975); *Egil's Saga,* trans. Hermann Pálsson and Paul Edwards (1976).

Haraldur Bessason

Skram, Amalie. Norwegian novelist, b. 22 August 1846, Bergen, d. 15 March 1905, Copenhagen.

Skram spent her childhood and youth in Bergen. The commercial life, people, and dialect of this bustling port were later masterfully re-created in several of her novels. Her parents, Mons and Ingeborg Alver, had ambitions of rising from their humble origins. They sent Skram to the city's best schools and groomed her striking beauty. A marriage proposal by ship captain Bernt Ulrik August Müller was viewed as socially attractive, and Skram felt obliged to accept the older Müller, in particular given her father's bankruptcy. They married in 1864, when Skram was eighteen. Together she and Müller sailed to many exotic destinations throughout the world, including the Caribbean and Australia. The marriage produced two sons but underwent numerous crises, finally ending in divorce in 1882. She married Danish author Erik Skram in 1884 and moved to Copenhagen. This union proved more compatible and loving, but in 1899 it, too, was dissolved. A daughter, Johanne, was born in 1889.

Although she made a late debut, Skram's career was a productive one. With her twelve novels and assorted stories she made a major contribution to the Scandinavian literary scene between 1885 and 1905. Her portraits of unhappy marriages were deemed shockingly explicit and these, coupled with her divorce and radical opinions, made her the object of controversy. Animosity toward the Norwegian critics, whose evaluations she found insulting, ultimately led her to renounce her homeland and to declare herself a "Danish author." In recent years Skram has experienced a critical renaissance throughout Scandinavia, coinciding with the rise of contemporary feminism.

In *Constance Ring* (1885; trans. 1988) Skram explored themes to which she frequently returned. Constance, a young and naïve wife, is ill-prepared for sexual intimacy, the double standard, and the subordinate role to which she is relegated. Her family and clergyman urge that she resign herself; but for Constance, conventional marriage has been unmasked as an immoral institution. Successive relationships reinforce the negative experiences from this first marriage. Disillusioned by the age of thirty, Constance takes her own life. The novel has certain technical weaknesses, but it is a genuinely moving story and sets the stage for novels like *Lucie* (1888) and *Forraadt* (1892; *Betrayed*, 1987), where the conflict between husband and wife is examined in greater detail. Unlike Constance, Lucie is knowledgeable in sexual matters when she marries her lawyer-lover; yet their marriage becomes an ugly power struggle, as Gerner attempts to erase the marks of his wife's "plebeian" upbringing. Ory, in *Forraadt*, is an innocent bride so revolted by her husband's sexual past that she develops a fanatical obsession with the details of his erotic adventures, hounding the sea captain until he jumps to his death. *Forraadt* ranks as one of Skram's best efforts, in part because the narrative is tight and effectively controlled.

In these novels Skram displays a fine grasp of the ideological inconsistencies that surround love, sex, and marriage. Both men and women are shown to be victims of the prevailing social code, and a strong current of passion is woven into the texts. Her characters react with desperation, but the grotesque aspects of their behavior (frigidity, suicide, obsessive jealousy) are psychologically grounded. Skram examines these issues further in *Fru Inés* (1891) and in the powerful short story collection *Sommer* (1899; Summer).

Hellemyrsfolket (The People of Hellemyr) is Skram's most ambitious and impressive work. Four volumes make up this naturalistic masterpiece: *Sjur Gabriel* (1887), *To Venner* (1887; Two Friends), *S. G. Myre* (1890), and *Afkom* (1898; Offspring). Here Skram drew upon her intimate knowledge of Bergen and of the Bergen dialect to illustrate social hypocrisy and the demoralizing effects of poverty and alchohol abuse. Four generations of the family from Hellemyr farm are presented, with drunken grandmother Oline serving as the graphic reminder of their fate. Grandson Sivert attempts to escape the family influence; his experiences aboard the ship *To Venner* provide a vivid portrayal of life at sea. But Sivert returns to Bergen and plays out the inevitable path of suffering and depravity. *Hellemyrsfolket* offers telling examples of family conflict, especially the relationships between children and their parents. Skram's skill at depicting children's situations is also apparent in the collection *Børnefortællinger* (1890; Stories of Children).

Skram was drawn to the plight of the vulnerable and powerless, be they women, children, or the poor. In two novels from 1895, *Professor Hieronimus* (*Professor Hieronimus*, 1899) and *På St. Jørgen* (At St. Jørgen's), she examined the highly vulnerable position of a female mental patient. Skram's own bouts of nervous depression brought her into contact with the medical establishment; incensed by her experiences in 1894 under the care of a renowned Copenhagen specialist, she prepared these thinly veiled fictional accounts. While obviously autobiographical, the books display good artistic control and present important social themes. The protagonist, Else Kant, is a painter whose breakdown is traceable to the enormous conflict she feels between her role as artist and her role as wife and mother. The passivity and obedience that is forced upon Else by her male doctor is counterbalanced by the affection and concern of the female nurses. Eventually, Else Kant is allowed to leave the hospital. Her story is an exception to the usually tragic pattern of Skram's works.

Skram approached her writing as an opportunity to tell the truth. She stated emphatically that what she wrote was "true" and that the people she described were people she had met. Her intention was clearly to awaken compassion for those who suffered and a great sense of anguish runs through much of her prose. Skram tried her hand at drama and in her last books moved away from a pure social realism. Yet it is her naturalistic novels that have earned her a central place in the history of the Modern Breakthrough, alongside such contemporaries as Arne Garborg* and Alexander Kielland.* That her influence has been a lasting one is seen, for example, in the writings of Torborg Nedreaas* and in the warm response of readers and critics in the 1970s and 1980s.

FURTHER WORKS

Om Albertine (1887); *Fjældmennesker*, with Erik Skram (1889); *Kjærlighed i Nord og Syd* (1891); *Agnete* (1893); *Julehelg* (1900); *Landsforrædere* (1901); *Mennesker* (1905); *Mellom slagene*, ed. Eugenia Kielland (1955); *Og nu vil jeg tale ut*, ed. Øyvind Anker and Edvard Beyer (1982).

FURTHER TRANSLATIONS

Told in Norway (also pub. as *Norway's Best Stories*), ed. Hanna Astrup Larsen (1927); *Slaves of Love and Other Norwegian Short Stories*, ed. James McFarlane (1982); *An Everyday Story*, ed. Katherine Hanson (1984).

REFERENCES

Engelstad, Irene, *Amalie Skram* (Oslo, 1978); Engelstad, Irene, *Amalie Skram om seg selv* (Oslo, 1981); Engelstad, Irene, *Sammenbrudd og gjennombrudd* (Oslo, 1984); Krane, Borghild, *Amalie Skram og kvinnens problem* (Oslo, 1951); Krane, Borghild, *Amalie Skrams diktning* (Oslo, 1961); Rasmussen, Janet E., "Amalie Skram as Literary Critic." *Edda* 1 (1981); Tiberg, Antonie, *Amalie Skram som kunstner og menneske* (Kristiania, 1910).

Janet Rasmussen

Snellman, Johan Vilhelm. Finnish philosopher, journalist, politician, and prose writer, b. 12 May 1806, Stockholm, d. 4 July 1881, Kirkkonummi.

Snellman studied philosophy at the University of Helsinki, where Hegelianism had an exceptionally strong foothold at the beginning of the nineteenth century. He was an active member of a literary Saturday Society that was founded to promote national culture, especially in literature. As docent of philosophy Snellman came in serious conflict with the inflexible bureaucracy of the university, which led to his exile. In 1839–1842 he traveled in Sweden and Germany, where he met several prominent liberals, developed his Hegelian philosophy in numerous books, and outlined a semiliberal political program of his own. Like Georg Wilhelm Friedrich Hegel, Snellman emphasized the importance of the state in his philosophy, but he also stressed the role of national spirit and consciousness.

Due to his works, young Snellman was considered an ideological leader of the radical student groups associated with the Finnish nationalist movement. After returning to Finland he was forced to leave Helsinki and become a teacher in the remote town of Kuopio. Soon he became famous throughout the country as a newspaper publisher. He started editing a Finnish newspaper, *Maamiehen Ystävä* (1844; Farmer's Friend), for Finnish-speaking peasantry. More important was Swedish *Saima* (1844–1846), Finland's first political newspaper. In *Saima* Snellman advocated an immediate nationalistically inspired reform program. He demanded that Swedish-speaking intelligentsia adopt Finnish language and identity. Since the reactionary government of the Grand Duchy of Finland couldn't accept the liberal reforms that Snellman demanded in *Saima*, the dangerous newspaper was suppressed. Snellman continued editing *Litteraturblad* (1847–1849, 1855–1862; Magazine for Literature) for a few years.

FURTHER WORKS

Samlade arbeten, 10 vols. (1894–1898); *J. J. Tengströms och J. V. Snellmans brefväxling 1843–1849* (1906); *J. V. Snellmans och hans hustrus brevväxling* (1928); *Snellman i urval,* ed. Johannes Salminen (1981).

REFERENCES

Havu, Ilmari, *Snellmaniana* (Keuruu, 1970); Lehmusto, Heikki, *Kansallisfilosofimme aatemaailma* (Hämeenlinna, 1953); Karkama, Pertti, *Snellman kertojana* (Helsinki, 1985); Rein, Th., *J. V. Snellmanin elämä ja filosofia* (Helsinki, 1944); Snellman-Borenius, Clara, *Isoisäni J. V. Snellman* (Porvoo, 1968); Tenkku, J., "J. V. Snellman as an Ethical Relativist." *Ajatus* 35 (1973); Wilenius, Reijo, *Snellmanin linja* (Jyväskylä, 1978).

Matti Kinnunen

Snoilsky, Carl. Swedish poet, b. 4 September 1881, Stockholm, d. 19 May 1903, Stockholm.

Count Snoilsky, although born into the Swedish aristocracy, ultimately became practically the only writer of his social class to empathize, or at least sympathize, with the great movements for social reform of his day. He began his literary career at Uppsala while he was a member of the Namnlösa sällskapet (Nameless society), or Signaturerna (Signature poets), which published Snoilsky's *Italienska bilder* (Italian Pictures) in 1865. Snoilsky's political views were markedly liberal: he defended Denmark and Poland against the Prussians, and was influenced by Lord Byron and Heinrich Heine. In *Italienska bilder* he painted a glowingly sensuous view of southern Europe, filled with the joy of youth, *joie de vivre*, and written with sophistication and poetic virtuosity. However, he soon abandoned his youthful exuberance and dutifully settled down to the diplomatic career that his rank necessitated. In nearly a decade, he published only one volume of sonnets (1871) in which the coolly objective form-consciousness of the French Parnassian school is the strongest single influence.

Then, in 1879, Snoilsky shocked Swedish society by abruptly resigning his post, divorcing his wife, remarrying, and settling in Dresden. Now began the final, and most important, period in Snoilsky's literary career. He began a series of poems based on events in Swedish history, some of which were inevitably related from his own aristocratic point of view but others of which reflected a strong desire to identify with the common man and the economically and socially oppressed. Other poems reflected clearly a desire to speak with a liberal voice for new social, political, and economic reforms, to become, in fact, the spokesman for the oppressed. His own aesthetic ideals, however, plus the circumstances of his birth and career, never allowed him to be accepted by those for whom he strove to speak. He was a member of the Swedish Academy for nearly thirty years and head of the Royal Library from 1890 until his death.

FURTHER WORKS

Samlade dikter, 5 vols. (1903–1904).

TRANSLATIONS

An Anthology of Swedish Lyrics from 1750 to 1915, ed. C. W. Stork (1917).

REFERENCES

Gosse, Edmund, "Carl Snoilsky and Some Recent Swedish Poetry," in *Portraits and Sketches* (New York, 1912); Olsson, Henry, *Den unge Snoilsky* (Stockholm, 1941); Warburg, Karl, *Carl Snoilsky: hans lefnad och skaldskap* (Stockholm, 1905).

Lars Emil Scott

Snorri Hjartarson. *See* Hjartarson, Snorri.

Snorri Sturluson. *See* Sturluson, Snorri.

Söderberg, Hjalmar. Swedish short story writer, novelist, playwright, and polemicist, b. 2 July 1869, Stockholm, d. 14 October 1941, Copenhagen.

Provincial regionalism strongly characterizes Swedish letters of the 1890s, and Söderberg emerges in this context as the quintessential observer and depicter of fin de siècle Stockholm. While the horizons of his imagined world infrequently extend south of Södermalm or north of Vasastan, his artistic and intellectual forebears are more exclusively Continental than native. They include Voltaire for his skepticism and anticlericalism, Heinrich Heine for his cynicism and irony, Anatole France for his elegant irreverence, and Jens Peter Jacobsen* and Herman Bang* for their subdued disillusionment.

One formidable Swedish writer did exert lasting influence on Söderberg. Stylistic and intellectual continuity extends from the realistic, vitriolic, and satiric young August Strindberg* of *Röda rummet* (1879) and *Det nya riket* (1882) to virtually the whole of Söderberg's literary production. The "confessionless Christianity" of the mature, post-Inferno Strindberg remained, however, far removed from Söderberg's thoroughgoing skeptical position. Whatever faith he had was consistently and firmly determined by reason and empiricism.

The best structure for Söderberg's analytic precision and critical insight remains the highly charged prose sketch brought to stylistic perfection in *Historietter* (1898; *Selected Short Stories*, 1935, 1987), whether his target be the mechanical behavior of the huddled masses as in "Vox populi" and "Gycklaren" (The Joker) or the comic or tragic implications of his own self-irony as in "En kopp te" (A Cup of Tea) and "Syndens lön" (The Wages of Sin). His four short novels are also eminently readable. Among them, *Martin Bircks ungdom* (1901; *Martin Birck's Youth*, 1930) is notable for one of the most sensitive portrayals in Swedish letters of the vulnerability of childhood. It also contains depressingly gray stretches describing the central character's coming to terms with "det stora, tomma hålet, som kallas världen" (the void that is called the world). The erotic love by means of which Martin Birck ultimately is able to transcend this emptiness becomes the cruelest of all illusions in Söderberg's most mature works, the play *Gertrud* (1906) and the semidocumentary novel *Den allvarsamma leken* (1912; The Serious Game).

During middle and old age, Söderberg largely abandoned prose fiction—except for his renderings in Swedish of such congenial writers as Guy de Maupassant and Alfred de Musset—and devoted himself all the more obsessively to studies of the history of religion. A series of anti-Christian polemics resulted from these studies.

"En smal men klar stråle" (a narrow but clear ray of light): Söderberg's modest assessment of his own literary achievement is characteristically penetrating and accurate. Nowise the most protean writer in Swedish literature, he may well be, all the same, its most consistently readable prose stylist.

FURTHER WORKS

Förvillelser (1895); *Främlingarna* (1902); *Doktor Glas* (1905; *Doctor Glas*, 1963); *Det mörknar över vägen* (1907); *Valda sidor* (1908); *Hjärtats oro* (1909); *Aftonstjärnan* (1912); *Den talangfulla draken* (1913); *Jahves eld* (1918); *Skrifter*, 10 vols. (1919–1921); *Ödestimmen* (1922); *Jesus Barabbas* (1928); *Resan till Rom* (1929); *Den förvandlade Messias* (1932); *Sista boken* (1942); *Samlade verk*, 10 vols. (1943); *Makten, visheten och kvinnan* (1946); *Hjalmar Söderbergs skrifter*, 9 vols. (1977–1978).

FURTHER TRANSLATIONS

Short Stories, trans. Carl Lofmark (1987).

REFERENCES

Bergman, Bo, *Hjalmar Söderberg* (Stockholm, 1951); Cassirer, Peter, *Stilen i Hjalmar Söderbergs Historietter* (Göteborg, 1970); Holmbäck, Bure, *Det lekfulla allvaret* (Stockholm, 1969); Rein, Sten, *Hjalmar Söderbergs Gertrud* (Stockholm, 1962); Söderberg, Eugenie, "Hjalmar Söderberg." *American-Scandinavian Review* 29.4 (1941); Sundberg, Björn, *Sanningen, myterna och intressenas spel* (Uppsala, 1981); Wästberg, Per, ed., *Kära Hjalle, Kära Bo* (Stockholm, 1969).

Raymond Jarvi

Södergran, Edith. Finland-Swedish poet, b. 4 April 1892, St. Petersburg, d. 24. June 1923, Raivola.

Södergran's life offered the stuff of which legends are made. Her father came from Ostrobothnian peasant stock, received a technical training of sorts, and took employment with the firm of Alfred Nobel in Russia; her mother was a second-generation member of the Finland-Swedish colony in St. Petersburg, who—thanks to parental success in small industry—had received an excellent education. Their marriage took place rather late in their lives; Matts Södergran had lost his first Russian wife to tuberculosis, while Helena Holmroos had borne an illegitimate child (who died shortly thereafter) some six years before her marriage to the "engineer." After the birth of Edith, the union's only child, the couple moved out to Raivola, on the Karelian Isthmus, where Matts Södergran became the director of a sawmill, and where Helena Södergran's devoted father had purchased a villa for his daughter and granddaughter. The Finnish-Russian community was known for its great larch forest, planted by Peter the Great; it provided the scene for much of Södergran's poetry. A small irony in the career of Södergran, one of the major poets in the Swedish language, is that she visited

Sweden only in transit, and, save for visits to Helsinki and sojourns in the sanatorium at Nummela, never lived in what could be called a Finland-Swedish milieu. Her mother was her prinicpal "Swedish informant."

Södergan's linguistic background was complicated still more by the fact that, like her mother before her, she was enrolled (1902) in a girls' school at St. Petersburg whose language of instruction was German. The result was that, as she pointed out in later life, her "best language" was German; the question of Teutonisms in her Swedish poems remains to be closely analyzed by scholarship. Throughout the school term, mother and daughter lived in the Russian capital, going to Raivola in the summers. In October 1907, Matts Södergran died of tuberculosis, and a little more than a year later, Edith Södergran was diagnosed as suffering from the same disease; immediately, she was sent off for the first of her several stays at Nummela, where her father had been a patient.

Happily, mother and daughter were in comfortable circumstances, because of an inheritance; in 1911, they went to Arosa in Switzerland and, in 1912, changed to Davos-Dorf; there, Södergran came under the care of Dr. Ludwig von Muralt, of whom she became enamored. The "Magic Mountain" days in Switzerland (which had the side effect of giving her access to contemporary European cultural currents) ended in 1914, when the little family returned to Raivola; the village remained Södergran's home for the rest of her life. The October Revolution of 1917 wrought a disastrous change; the family fortune, deposited in Russian banks, disappeared, and the once affluent pair was reduced to poverty. During the Finnish Civil War of 1918, their home was behind Red lines until liberation by the Whites in April; subsequently, Raivola remained in a restricted military area, to which travel was difficult. The villa was sold, and mother and daughter moved to an ill-heated summer house; it is generally conceded that sheer deprivation contributed to Södergran's death on Midsummer's Day, 1923. The home became the object of pilgrimages by Swedish and Finland-Swedish poets in the 1930s; the actual sites of Södergran's life and poetry were then destroyed in the course of the two Finno-Russian wars of 1939–1940 and 1941–1944. Now Raivola—Russian: Rodzino—lies inside the Soviet Union.

Not surprisingly, Södergran's poetic career began in German, with verses set down in a notebook, from January 1907 until the time of her first hospitalization; the influence of Heinrich Heine is palpable, and her subjects are many—her fascination with St. Petersburg; her dislike of the czarist regime; her infatuation with her French teacher, Henri Cottier, and with various schoolmistresses and classmates; and her deep affection for her country home. In the notebook (which also had a few poems in French and Russian), German was slowly replaced by Swedish, and regular meters and rhymes gave way to rhymeless strophic blocks. It is assumed that some verse written during the Swiss years was taken into her first printed collection, *Dikter* (1916; *Poems*, 1980, 1984); however, a main impetus for that book was an unhappy love affair with a Russian physician, at the nearby seaside resort of Terijoki, during 1914–1915. The materials making up the book are several: the willowy maidens, quiet ponds, and enchanted gardens of the German *Jugendstil* lyric; the vaguely sinister fairy-tale world created by Maurice Maeterlinck in *Serres chaudes* (1889) and *Douze chansons* (1896); the resentment of the deserted girl (who saw herself as a kind of Ariadne) against her lover (on whom poetic revenge is repeatedly taken); the sensation of an overwhelming loneliness—all set against the background of a Raivola given, at times, an almost tropical lushness. The press the book received was mixed, and the unfriendly reviews seem to have caused a nervous crisis in the sensitive girl; however, the argument that the reception was unsparingly brutal—proposed later on by some cultists—is not supported by the evidence.

The crushing blow was reserved for her next and far more original collection, *Septemberlyran* (1918; *September Lyre*, 1980, 1984); an arrogant preface, the unexpected imagery of the verse itself, and a prideful (and illogical) open letter to a newspaper made her the object of a campaign of ridicule. However, this very campaign got her the friendship of the critic and author Hagar Olsson* (1893–1978), leading to the correspondence that forms a major source of knowledge about the last years of her life; as well, it brought other writers to her defense—among them Jarl Hemmer* and Runar Schildt.* (Schildt, a reader at the publishing house of his cousin, Holger Schildt, became the patient editor of her manuscripts.) *Septemberlyran* is distinguished by Södergran's altogether surprising reactions to the Civil War, her burgeoning Nietzscheanism, her often fey wit, and her sometimes quite untranslatable puns. The volume also contains, near its end, the "Fragment" describing a dream St. Petersburg and the "storm" of revolution, one of the great visionary poems in a Nordic literature.

In *Rosenaltaret* (1919; *The Rose-Altar*, 1980, 1984), the self-stylization (and the self-importance of the isolated genius) grow stronger; the persona of the poems is transformed from a fairy tale princess into a prophetess, a wanderer through the solar systems (with echoes of the German cosmic poet Alfred Mombert), a martyr of beauty; the book's second section, "Fantastique," is a little novella, in lyric outbursts, about Södergran's love for her "sister," Olsson. The book's remarkable finale takes up where *Septemberlyran* left off, with poems about "Dionysos," placing the capstone on her retelling of the Ariadne myth; "Fragment of a Mood," a memoir of her Swiss days and a farewell to the late Muralt; and "Scherzo," in which a "tired dancer," amidst the stars, is lured toward the embrace of a mysterious sea-king. A pamphlet of aphorisms from the same year, *Brokiga iakttagelser* (*Motley Observations*, 1984), containing a good many self-evident details and attacks on critics, ends with a salute to "strong men," who "come, see, and conquer." This no doubt compensatory admiration for the mighty ruler, beyond good and evil, gets a full poetic statement in the opening part of *Framtidens skugga* (1920; *The Shadow of the Future*, 1980, 1984); a more appealing tone appears in the book's latter pages, where Södergran confesses her sense of homelessness ("Where is my home? Is it distant Finland, strewn with stars?"), her vague hope of a "pan-erotic" salvation, and her sexual fantasies (which, in "The Elf-Queen's Wand," become unwitting pornography); at the same time, she is tormented by the thought of personal annihilation

("Materialism," "Hamlet"), and tries to find solace in a Goethean "dying-and-becoming" ("The Hyacinth").

In March 1922 Södergran was visited by Elmer Diktonius,* whom her mother entrusted, after Södergran's death, with the publication of her uncollected poems. These appeared as *Landet som icke är* (1925; *The Land Which Is Not*, 1980, 1984); thanks to the scholarly work of Gunnar Tideström, a reader can now approach them in the proper chronology. Among the early lyrics are the bald statement about the debasement that sexual passion can bring ("To Eros"), the disturbing "Sick Days," and the unforgettable "Nothing"—an enjoinder to "love life's long hours of illness / and narrow years of longing / as the brief moments when the desert blooms." The later poems in the posthumous volume include the title verses (about yearning for a nonexistent realm), together with lyrics about a return to the Raivola world of her childhood summers, about death, feared and yet desired, and, finally, "Arrival in Hades"—with its effective scenery so starkly reminiscent of Arnold Böcklin's "Isle of the Dead," and its pathetically rudimentary rhymes. Toward the end of her life, abandoning Nietzsche, Södergran—filled with her characteristic enthusiasm—threw herself into a study of the anthropomorphism of Rudolf Steiner, and then the message of the New Testament; the question of a Steinerian or a fundamentalist Christian impact upon Södergran's final verse continues to fascinate some commentators. Just so, more recently, feminist criticism has made her work a hunting ground.

Indeed, Södergran can be used, or misused, by many sorts of believers, who overlook the circumstance that she was not a systematic or tenacious thinker, but rather the reporter (and sometimes the victim) of her own quick impressions and reactions. In her poetry, there is much that is turgid and vague; her passions, and her special rhetoric, may sweep her away—surely, she is not "a poet of ideas." Yet, in the direct and intense description of emotional states, she has no equal in Swedish or in the whole of Nordic letters.

FURTHER WORKS

Samlade dikter, ed. Gunnar Tideström (1947); *Ediths brev*, ed. Hagar Olsson (1955); *Dikter 1907–1909*, ed. Olof Enckell, 2 vols. (1961).

FURTHER TRANSLATIONS

Eight Swedish Poets, trans. Frederic Fleisher (1969); *We Women*, trans. Samuel Charters (1977); *Collected Poems*, trans. Martin S. Allwood (1980); *Love and Solitude, Selected Poems*, trans. Stina Katchadourian (1981); *Poetry East* 6 (Fall 1981); *Scandinavian Review* 69.4 (1981); *Complete Poems*, trans. David McDuff (1984).

REFERENCES

Brunner, Ernst, *Till fots genom solsystemen; En studie i Edith Södergrans Expressionism* (Stockholm, 1984); Enckell, Olof, *Esteticism och nietzscheanism i Edith Södergrans lyrik* (Helsinki, 1949); Fages, Loup de, *Edith Södergran* (Paris, 1970); Hird, Gladys, "Edith Södergran: A Pioneer of Finland-Swedish Modernism." *Books from Finland* 12.1 (1978); Jänicke, Gisbert, *Edith Södergran: Diktare på två språk* (Helsinki, 1984); Schoolfield,

G. C., "Edith Södergran's *Wallensteinprofil*," in *Scandinavian Studies*, ed. Carl F. Bayerschmidt and Erik J. Friis (New York, 1965); Schoolfield, G. C., *Edith Södergran: Modernist Poet in Finland* (Westport, Conn., 1984); Schoolfield, G. C., "A Life on the Edge." *Books from Finland* 17.3 (1983); Tideström, Gunnar, *Edith Södergran* (Stockholm, 1949).

George C. Schoolfield

Sørensen, Villy. Danish short story writer, social and literary critic, b. 13 January 1929, Frederiksberg.

Sørensen studied philosophy and languages first at the University of Copenhagen and then in Freiburg, West Germany (1952–1953). He is a former editor (1959–1963, with Klaus Rifbjerg*) of the literary journal *Vindrosen*, member of the Danish Academy, and recipient of numerous literary prizes. Sørensen, who has lived abroad for brief periods, is particularly well versed in German philosophy and deeply committed to European culture. He has translated Seneca (1976), Erasmus of Rotterdam (1979), Franz Kafka (1960), and Hermann Broch (1960, 1966–67); written introductions to Friedrich Nietzsche (1963) and Arthur Schopenhauer (1969); written on Kafka (*Kafkas digtning*, 1968; Kafka's Art) and *Seneca* (1976; *Seneca*, 1984); and edited Søren Kierkegaard's* *The Concept of Dread* (*Begrebet Angst* [1844], ed. 1960), Kafka's collected tales (1967–1968), and anthologies of Karl Marx (1962) and Richard Wagner (1983). Sørensen has been influenced not only by Broch, Kafka, and Kierkegaard, but by Thomas Mann, Robert Musil, and Martin A. Hansen* as well. Sørensen has published six volumes of essays and coauthored (with Niels I. Meyer and Helveg Petersen) both a work on achieving a more utopian modern political system (*Oprør fra midten*, 1978; *Revolt from the Center*, 1981) and an answer to its critics (*Røret om oprøret*, 1982; Roar about the Uproar). Finally, Sørensen has retold the story of "Aladdin and His Wonderful Lamp" (*Aladdin og hans vidunderlige lampe*, 1981) and the tales of the Nordic gods, as they inevitably brought about their own doom (*Ragnarok*, 1982; *The Downfall of the Gods*, 1989). In 1979, Sørensen received an honorary doctorate from the University of Copenhagen on the occasion of that institution's 500th anniversary.

Sørensen, who is often called a philosopher-poet and Denmark's sage, combines the preeminent stylistic abilities of a Hans Christian Andersen* with the ethical conundrums of a Kierkegaard. Though easily read, Sørensen's stories can be only uneasily resolved. He stresses the human being's many-sided and sometimes—through alienation—even divisive nature. A great many stories treat periods of transition—puberty, betrothal, etc.—in which an initially harmonic period must give way to new impulses. Not allowing such impulses succeeds only in limiting the good and thus creating a division: good versus evil, the beautiful versus the horrible. Although in the story "Duo" (from *Ufarlige historier*, 1955; Harmless Stories) Sørensen has the perfect half of a double character say that truth is the love between people, the horribly imperfect half, rejected by his fellows, seems to suggest that love can also divide and destroy. As the story "Fjenden" (also from *Ufarlige historier*; "The Enemy," 1955) shows, hate brings about destruction and eventually seeks self-destruction, for death is its goal and love. In *Formynderfortællinger* (1964; *Tutelary Tales*, 1988), Sørensen examines the recurrent problem of a rebellion against authority for a freedom that becomes itself repressive. In *Digtere og dæmoner* (1959; Poets and Demons), Sørensen points out the importance of art in learning to face future problems. Once the demonic is captured and depicted it loses something of its power to harm; thus, art becomes a form of exorcism. In some measure Sørensen and his coauthors in *Oprør fra midten* have also captured and pinned down the problems to be faced in modern Denmark and have tried to assess the country's possibilities of achieving desired goals and thus reduce its obstacles to a handleable size. In *Ragnarok* Sørensen wittily describes the unreflective old Norse gods' headlong plunge into the almost total annihilation of the world—the fate of those who have no past to learn from and only weapons to resort to. Sørensen continues to take up the wisdom of the past and to show its ethical relevance to a twentieth-century audience.

FURTHER WORKS

Sære historier (1953; *Strange Stories*, 1956; also as *Tiger in the Kitchen and Other Strange Stories*, 1957, 1969); *Hverken-eller* (1961); *Friedrich Nietzsche* (1963; 2nd ed., *Nietzsche*, 1982); *Mellem fortid og fremtid* (1969); *Schopenhauer* (1969); *Uden mal—og med* (1973); *Den gyldne middelvej* (1979); *Vejrdage* (1980); *De mange og de enkelte* (1987).

FURTHER TRANSLATIONS

Literary Review 8.1 (1964); *American-Scandinavian Review* 52.4 (1964); *Danish Journal* 65 (1969); *The Devil's Instrument and Other Danish Stories*, ed. Sven Holm (1971); *The Soldier's Christmas Eve* (1973); *Scandinavian Review* 69.4 (1981).

REFERENCES

Jensen, Jørgen Bonde, *Litterær arkæologi* (Copenhagen, 1978); Sønderriis, Ebbe, *Villy Sørensen* (Aarhus, 1972).

                                                                Faith Ingwersen

Solstad, Dag. Norwegian novelist, short story writer, and playwright, b. 16 July 1941, Sandefjord.

Solstad's authorship shows a steady development from his early experimental fiction to the documentary novels that have made him the best known writer of his generation. Solstad moves from a psychologistic, Kafkaesque preoccupation with subjective experience toward a documentary realism he regards as an instrument of Marxist-Leninist politics. His most recent novel marks a return to a (politically self-conscious) psychological realism.

While the short stories of *Spiraler* (1965; Spirals) address the experiences of the isolated consciousness, the prose texts of *Svingstol* (1967; Swivel Chair) already demonstrate a shift of emphasis to the external everyday world. In the novel *Irr! Grønt!* (1969; Copper Rust! Green!), Solstad analyzes the objective structures, rooted in social reality, that form and contain subjective attitudes. In *Arild Asnes 1970* (1970), Solstad virtually announces his political conversion to a revolutionary communism inspired by the pedagogy of Mao Zedong. This is the turning point of the authorship; Solstad has rejected the "bourgeois" psychological novel in favor of a nondogmatic socialist realism, an analytical and hortatory political literature.

25. septemberplassen (1974; 25. September Square) and the trilogy on World War II—*Svik. Førkrigsår* (1977; Betrayal, Pre-War Years), *Krig. 1940* (1978; The War. 1940), and *Brød og vapen* (1980; Bread and Weapons)—are successful examples of the new documentary style. The first analyzes the new prosperity, and disappointments, of the Norwegian working class in a postwar society the Norwegian Labor party (Det norske Arbeiderparti or DNA) has done much to shape. Using individualized, but socially representative, characters and a class-conscious analysis of social conditions, Solstad explores the social origins of failed lives. In a similar vein, the war trilogy evokes hitherto unrecorded dimensions of the German occupation of Norway (1940–1945), in particular the sufferings and moral dilemmas of Oslo's working class.

Solstad's most recent novel examines, and appears to retract (though not without humor), the Marxist-Leninist commitment that underlies his documentary fiction.

FURTHER WORKS

Georg: Sit du godt?, with Einar Økland (1968); *Kamerat Stalin, eller familien Nordby* (1975); *Tilbake til Pelle Erobreren?* (1977); *Artikler om litteratur 1966–1981; Gymnastlærer Pedersens beretning om den store politiske vekkelsen som har hjemsøkt vårt land* (1982).

REFERENCES

Bache-Wiig, Harald, "Dag Solstad—spiral, sirkel og tangent," in *Linjer i norsk prosa,* ed. Helge Rønning (Lund, 1977); *For og imot. En samling av pressens anmeldelser og omtaler* (Oslo, 1975); Sehmsdorf, Henning K., "From Individualism to Communism: The Political and Esthetic Transformation of Dag Solstad's Authorship." *Proceedings of the Pacific Northwest Conference on Foreign Languages* 27 (1976).

John M. Hoberman

Sonne, Jørgen. Danish poet, novelist, and translator, b. 15 October 1925, Copenhagen.

When he graduated with a master of arts degree in history and English in 1951, Sonne had already made his debut as a translator and poet. As a skilled linguist, he has always shown his faculty for combining specific details and pictures in a mosaic vision of the world, and as a historian he has drawn on many different documents of human experience and social structure. Sonne's translations are expeditions into history and culture, from Arthur Rimbaud, William Shakespeare, and Ezra Pound to Cuban and African poetry.

Two main phases appear in Sonne's works. With his selection of older poems in År (1965; Years), Sonne has himself taken stock of the first phase: the Ego has familiarized itself with the world, has had its erotic and political experiences, and has traveled in history and modern civilization. A central work is *Krese* (1963; Circles), in which the Ego and the historian circle, move backwards into family and to the saurians of prehistory, where the dynamics of the world is found to be dialectical, both destructive and creative, hungry and satiated. Finally, they move forward again from the border between life and death toward psychical growth and change—to the meeting of man and woman, to the child— all described in "Foldemændene" (The Fold-out Men).

In his second phase, beginning in the late 1960s, Sonne seeks out "the foreign" in order, as he says, to surpass his own habituation. His global engagement reaches a climax in the poems of *Nærvær* (1980; Presence). In four movements he touches on politics, travels, history, and the "darkness"—the barrier against one's fellowman and the world—and finally points out the disastrous contrast between the poverty of the developing countries and the wealth of industrialized ones. This political theme is elaborated even more in Sonne's novels, especially in *Natten i Rom* (1983; The Night in Rome), a colorful historical novel. For a long time Sonne has been appreciated as a distinctive linguist; he is also a sublime narrator.

FURTHER WORKS

Korte digte (1950); *Delfiner i skoven* (1951); *I en levende tid* (1952); *Italiensk suite* (1954); *Midtvejs* (1960); *Blå turist* (1971); *Norsk time* (1971); *Rejsekoncert* (1972); *Horisonter* (1973); *Thai noter* (1974); *Huset* (1976); *Eroterne* (1977); *Deruda. 25 år gennem Danmark* (1979); *Elskovs grønne ø* (1985); *Tid* (1985); *Nul* (1987).

TRANSLATIONS

Contemporary Danish Poetry, ed. Line Jensen et al. (1977); *Orbis* 27/28 (1977); *Flights* (1982).

REFERENCES

Brostrøm, Torben, "Jørgen Sonne," in *En bog om inspirationen, Det danske Akademi 1974–1981* (Copenhagen, 1981); Pedersen, Orla, "Jørgen Sonne," in *Danske digtere i det 20. århundrede*, ed. Torben Broström and Mette Winge (Copenhagen, 1982).

Svend Birke Espegård

Sonnevi, Göran. Swedish lyric poet, b. 3 October 1939, Lund.

As a high school student Sonnevi was keenly interested in chemistry and jazz, and as a university student he engrossed himself in Swedish and European modernistic poetry. Scientific, musical, and linguistic principles were to remain a major concern in his own lyrical production, although his definitive breakthrough in the late 1960s as one of Sweden's foremost lyrical poets was probably due to an alignment of these matters with the Vietnam War and other political issues.

Sonnevi's first book, *Outfört* (1961; Unperformed), subscribes to a well-known modernistic notion of reality. But the poetic attitude is defensive, if not reluctant, and it relegates traditional correspondences between soul, language, and reality to the sphere of bad performances, or *abstractions*. A landscape is not the image of the soul; a language is merely its prisonhouse. The structures of reality are just alienating, and a sort of mystical dream of direct contact between self and reality, both liberated from structural confinement, comes to the fore.

In Sonnevi's next collection, *Abstrakta dikter* (1963; Abstract Poems) the abstractions are still conceived of as impediments but at least accredited for their crystal clear representation of nothingness and emptiness. Sonnevi is almost ready to even associate them with political reality and to recognize at least some of them as a necessary evil or as instruments for poetic cognition, as suggested by his next title *ingrepp—modeller* (1965; Intervention—Models). A political repertory is being touched upon, but still within a linguistic frame of reference.

In *och nu!* (1967; And now!) this challenge eventually causes a determined political response. Linguistic structures are viewed as indicative of societal structures that can be alternated by political action, for example, modeled on alternative scientific structures. *Det måste gå* (1970; It Has to Work) is an assertive vote of confidence in the outcome of this insight, whereas *Det oavslutade språket* (1972; The Unfinished Language) depicts how language free from finish may contribute to mankind's liberation from the straitjacket of the present society. The historical process is contradictory, and the liberating potentials of language lie entirely within the contradictions of that process, in the cracks of it.

The growing complexity of Sonnevi's poetry has incorporated Noam Chomsky as well as Karl Marx and has approached *Det omöjliga* (1975; The Impossible). The first part of this monumental volume of poetry is an extension of *Det oavslutade språket* and includes a large section of "Mozart Variations," or a musical vision of Sonnevi's powerful revolt against petrifying structures. In his later big collection of poems *Språk; Verktyg; Eld* (1979; Language; Tool; Fire) Sonnevi elaborates on his language as a tool that hits both ways—by transgressing artistic and political possibilities at the same time. It is a passionate and controlled language, judgmental and self-critical, abstract and concrete, impossible and yet convincing.

FURTHER WORKS

Det gäller oss (1969); *Dikter 1959–73* (1974); *Små klanger: En röst* (1981); *Dikter utan ordning* (1983); *Oavslutade dikter* (1987).

TRANSLATIONS

The Economy Spinning Faster and Faster (1982); *Swedish Books* 1 (1982).

Poul Houe

Soya, Carl Erik Martin. Danish dramatist, novelist, and critic, b. 30 October 1896, Copenhagen, d. 10 November 1983, Rudkøbing.

Soya's father was a painter and professor at the Academy of Art in Copenhagen. His debut, the short story "De, der skammer sig" (1918; They Who Are Ashamed), demonstrates two of the main themes that appear in his later writings: his preoccupation with Freud and his offensive use of taboo words. Soya's dramatic works, about twenty longish plays, often experimental in form and satirical in content, are uneven in quality. His first play, *Parasitterne* (1926; The Parasites), is typical of his social-realistic style. It is a roughly naturalistic unmasking of a parasitic and hypocritical petty-bourgeois. *Umbabumba skifter Forfatning* (1934; Umbabumba's New Constitution) is an early, politically conscious assault on "muhism" (mu = Mussolini, hi = Hitler) and on the Danish social democratic government as well. The government's banning of his play for political reasons indicated that his criticism was justified.

Among the more experimental and Freudian plays are *Hvem er jeg?* (1931; Who Am I?) and *Det nye Spil om Enhver* (1938; The New Play about Everyone), symbolic dramatizations of the psychic fight between instinctive desire (id) and the socialized I (super-ego). Soya is a moralist who condemns as a sinner everyone who represses his instincts, although at the same time he requires the individual not to hurt anyone. During the German occupation Soya was imprisoned for publishing *En Gæst* (1941; A Visitor). In this allegorical fable a Danish family is visited by an earwig, which they find in their butter dish but which grows as large as the father and eats them out of house and home. In the end a young friend of the family (the resistance movement) kills the beast. In a style Soya called neorealistic he wrote the dramatic tetralogy *Blindebuk eller sådan kan det gå* (1940–1947; Blindman's Buff or How It May Happen). Here Soya is concerned with a philosophical question: do the events of life form a pattern of destiny, or is everything purely accidental?

To Soya, the world was a mirror-room; he was a solitaire in Danish literature.

FURTHER WORKS

Fire Komedier, 2 vols. (1946); *Udvalgte Værker,* 6 vols. (1956).

TRANSLATIONS

Seventeen: A Novel of Puberty (1961, 1969, 1974); *The Rites of Spring* (1962); *Farmor's House* (1964); *Grandmother's House* (1966); *Bedroom Mazurka: Seven Erotic Stories* (1971); *Five Modern Scandinavian Plays* (1971).

REFERENCES

Bræmme, E., *Soyas sociale budskab* (Copenhagen, 1981); Gress, Elsa, *Dramatikeren Soya* (Copenhagen, 1976); Wamberg, N. B., *Soya* (Copenhagen, 1966); Woel, Cai M., *Bibliografisk fortegnelse over Soyas arbejder, 1917–46* (Copenhagen, 1946).

Tage Hind

Staffeldt, Adolph Wilhelm *Schack* von. Danish poet, b. 28 March 1769, Rügen, d. 26 December 1826, Slesvig.

Staffeldt published the first poetry in Danish to be influenced by German romantic theory. While in Göttingen in the 1790s, he read extensively in Johann

Gottfried von Herder and Friedrich Schiller, and published some poetry in the *Musenalmanach*. One sees his view of nature as organic and dynamic in "Til den vendelige Natur" (To Friendly Nature) and "Til den Helliganede" (To the Holy-longing'd). In "Menneskehedens Bane," Staffeldt traces the development of mankind, asserting that the poet is the highest stage of evolution. In these poems one can see both Staffeldt's strength and his weakness: he assimilates a theoretical vision, but his poetic talent is at best pedestrian. In 1795, Staffeldt received a grant to travel more widely and kept an interesting journal in German of his travels to Vienna, Venice, and Florence, showing the influence of Immanuel Kant over Herder and also including some poems in Danish that he was to publish later.

Staffeldt returned to Denmark in 1800, bringing the ideas of Friedrich Schelling with him. In 1802 he publicized Schelling's gospel, before Henrich Steffens's more famous lectures. When Adam Oehlenschläger* published his *Digte 1803* (1803; Poems), Staffeldt followed suit, though using *Digte 1804* (1803; Poems) on his title page. He included in this collection "Indvielsen" (The Initiation), a virtual index of romantic Neoplatonic motifs. The "romances" in the collection, however, brought Staffeldt some notoriety. While Staffeldt brought conventional criticism to bear against rationalism, he also criticized Oehlenschläger. Unfortunately, several of Staffeldt's romances bore more than coincidental resemblances to those of Oehlenschläger, causing Staffeldt some embarrassment.

From Kiel, Staffeldt published his *Nye Digte 1808* (1808; New Poems), containing poems from his earlier travels and some new works. Poems such as "Forvandlingerne" (The Metamorphoses), while still poetic renderings of abstract philosophy, betray some maturity. Unfortunately, Staffeldt fell victim to his own melancholy and hypochondria, and his significance must be counted historically, as a forerunner and intermediary.

FURTHER WORKS

Skrifter, 4 vols. (1843–1851).

REFERENCES

Brandes, Georg, *Mennesker og Værker i nyere europæisk Literatur* (Copenhagen, 1883); Molbech, Christian, *Digteren Adolph Vilhelm Schack Staffeldt* (Copenhagen, 1940), Stangerup, Hakon, *A. W. Schack Staffeldt* (Copenhagen, 1940); Vedel, Valdemar, *Studier over Guldalderen i dansk Digtning* (Copenhagen, 1890).

John L. Greenway

Stagnelius, Erik Johan. Swedish poet, b. 14 October 1793, Gårdslösa (Öland), d. 3 April 1823, Stockholm.

Almost nothing is known of the private life of this, Sweden's most quintessentially romantic poet. He grew up in the parsonage of the parish of Gårdslösa on Öland and, after 1810, on the mainland in Kalmar, where his father, Magnus Stagnelius, had been made bishop. Stagnelius attended universities both in Lund and Uppsala briefly before taking a position as copyist at the ministry of education in Stockholm, a poor-paying job that the poet loathed and worked at as little as possible.

His first work, published anonymously, was *Vladimir den store* (1817; Vladimir the Great), an epic poem in hexameters that praised Czar Alexander, the conqueror of Finland. (Stagnelius had hoped to find employment at the Imperial Chancellery in Åbo.) A year later, Stagnelius's poem "Sång till kvinnorna i Norden" won second prize in the Swedish Academy competition. But 1821 must be reckoned as his breakthrough year for it was then that his most remarkable volume, *Liljor i Saron* (Lilies of Sharon), appeared. It also contained (in the third, augmented, edition) Stagnelius's poetic drama *Martyrerna* (1821; The Martyrs). The only other work to appear before his death was the classical drama *Bacchanterna eller Fanatismen* (1822; The Bacchantes, or Fanaticism).

Liljor i Saron is a remarkable blend of philosophical speculation and dazzling poetic virtuosity. Stagnelius's *Weltanschauung* was a strange mixture of platonism, Swedenborgianism, and most importantly, Gnosticism, with frequent references to Pythagorean, alchemical, cabalistic, and astrological systems. His powerful erotic drive became transformed into a spiritual or metaphysical passion, but the transformation was an ambiguous one: Stagnelius's intensely personal, private, and unrequited love could easily revert to the physical plane. The so-called Amanda poems reflect Stagnelius's desire for sensual gratification as well as his ecstatic yearning for a mystical Gnostic reunion with the Godhead.

Stagnelius's several dramatic and epic works—nearly half of his total production—chronicle his religious and erotic struggle quite as clearly as the more famous lyric poetry. *Bacchanterna* (like the earlier drama *Martyrerna*) can be seen as a kind of reconciliation with the world: Orpheus represents the calmly accepting, even forgiving, spirit of classical legend infused with Christian idealism. As a result, Stagnelius is today regarded as the most exquisite Swedish exponent of romantic passions at their most intense.

FURTHER WORKS

Samlade skrifter, 3 vols. (1824–1826); 5 vols. (1911–1919); 4 vols. (1957).

TRANSLATIONS

An Anthology of Swedish Lyrics, ed. C. V. Stork (1917).

REFERENCES

Andreæ, Daniel, *Erik Johan Stagnelius* (Stockholm, 1919); Böök, Fredrik, *Kreaturens suckan och andra Stagneliusstudier* (Malmö, 1957); Böök, Fredrik, *Stagnelius än en gång* (Stockholm, 1942); Böök, Fredrik, *Erik Johan Stagnelius* (Stockholm, 1924); Böök, Fredrik, *Stagnelius och hans omgivning* (Stockholm, 1936); Cederblad, Sven T., *Studies i Stagnelii romantik* (Stockholm and Uppsala, 1923); Nilsson, Albert, *Svensk romantik* (Lund, 1924); Nilsson, Albert, *Kronologien i Stagnelius' diktning* (Uppsala, 1926).

Lars Emil Scott

Stefán Hörður Grímsson. *See* Grímsson, Stefán Hörður.

Stefán frá Hvítadal. *See* Sigurðsson, Stefán.

Stefán Sigurðsson. *See* Sigurðsson, Stefán.

Stefánsson, Davíd. Icelandic poet, playwright, and novelist, b. 21 January 1895, Fagriskógur, Eyjafjörður district, d. 1 March 1964, Akureyri.

Born into a well-to-do family of farmers, his father a member of the Althing, Stefánsson grew up in a cultured home. He attended secondary school in Akureyri, but his education was then interrupted by an illness that he barely survived. Later, he resumed his training at the gymnasium in Reykjavík and at the University of Iceland. He subsequently traveled in Scandinavia and in Central and Southern Europe. From 1925 to 1951, Stefánsson was a librarian in Akureyri, but he made several other journeys abroad, including one to the Soviet Union in 1928; foreign themes are prominent in some of his books, especially *Kveðjur* (1924; Greetings) and *Ný kvæði* (1929; New Poems).

Stefánsson's first volume, *Svartar fjaðrir* (1919; Black Feathers), which at once established him as a leading neoromanticist in Iceland, became so popular that it was literally "read to pieces," and his subsequent publications did nothing to diminish that popularity. Though he adhered to the Icelandic tradition of alliterative verse, his forms were light—frequently ballad and similar meters—and he wrote of the simple pleasures of life, praising freedom, love, joy, and kindness. On the other hand, there was also a deep note of pain and sadness in his verse (an echo from his years of illness?) and he was much concerned with the poor, the social outcasts, the sinners, the eccentrics, and the loners. One of the latter was the protagonist of his only novel, the two-volume *Sólon Íslandus* (1940), a beautifully written story of a nineteenth century Icelandic vagabond, famous for his self-important tall tales. Stefánsson also wrote four plays, one of which, *Gullna hliðið* (1941; *The Golden Gate*, 1967), based on a well-known folk story, is a perennial favorite of Icelandic audiences.

Although an anti-clerical strain could be found in some of his early poems, Stefánsson did not scorn faith, and as he grew older he became more religiously inclined, his tone more philosophical. His last poems revealed a deep apprehension of nuclear armaments and tensions in the world. Probably the most beloved Icelandic poet of this century, whose own readings of his works were immensely popular, Stefánsson, along with such poets as Stefán frá Hvítadal (*See* Sigurðsson, Stefán) and others, formed a bridge between the tradition-bound verse of the nineteenth century and the "atom poetry" of the post–World War II era.

FURTHER WORKS

Kvæði (1922); *Munkarnir á Möðruvöllum* (1925); *Kvæðasafn*, 2 vols. (1930); *Í byggðum* (1933); *Að norðan* (1936); *Kvæðasafn*, 3 vols. (1943); *Vopn guðanna* (1944); *Ný kvæðabók* (1947); *Landið gleymda* (1956); *Ljóð frá liðnu sumri* (1956); *Tvær greinar* (1959); *Í dögun* (1960); *Mælt mál* (1963); *Síðustu ljóð* (1966).

FURTHER TRANSLATIONS

Icelandic Lyrics, ed. Richard Beck (1930); *20th Century Scandinavian Poetry*, ed. Martin S. Allwood (1950); *Icelandic Canadian* 15.4 (1957); *Northern Lights*, trans. Jakobína Johnson (1959); *More Echoes*, trans. Paul Bjarnason (1962); Soya, Carl Erik, et al., *Five Modern Scandinavian Plays* (1971).

REFERENCES

Einarsson, Stefán, "Davíð Stefánsson." *American-Scandinavian Review* 55.1 (1967); Haugen, Einar, Introduction to *The Golden Gate,* in *Fire and Ice*, comp. Einar Haugen (Madison, 1967).

Hallberg Hallmundsson

Steinarr, Steinn (pseud. Aðalsteinn Kristmundsson). Icelandic poet, b. 13 October 1908, Nauteyrarhreppur, North Iceland, d. 25 May 1958, Reykjavík.

Steinarr, who grew up in a foster home in the countryside, moved to Reykjavík at the age of twenty. Physically frail and with a lame arm, he was little fit for earning his living by bodily labor, and lacked means of entering higher education. Leading a bohemian life in a time of crisis and unemployment, he joined politically radical circles and assumed a critical attitude to bourgeois society. His first collection of poems, *Rauður loginn brann* (1934; "The Red Flame Was Ablaze," a refrain from a well-known medieval ballad), is characterized by some caustic social satire and revolutionary strains, but also by a kind of metaphysical pessimism. Artistically he is already on his way to a terse and carefully chiseled form, avoiding the rhetoric of an older poetic trend, but using the time-honored alliteration of Icelandic tradition.

Steinarr's three following collections, *Ljóð* (1938; Poems), *Spor í sandi* (1940; Footsteps in the Sand), and *Ferð án fyrirheits* (1942; Aimless Journey), sharpen his characteristic diction. The pessimism is now deeper, in poems under such significant headings as "Ekkert" (Nothing), "Myrkur" (Darkness), and "Dimmur hlátur" (Dark Laughter) with the refrain:

> Heigh-ho!
> I am the man,
> the eternal man
> without goal and purpose.

But also an ingenious humor and irony, and even tenderness, make themselves felt in concentrated pictures of men and nature.

With Steinarr's fifth and last collection, *Tíminn og vatnið* (1948, enl. ed. 1974; Time and Water), his poetry takes a radically new turn. The motto of this cycle of poems is Archibald MacLeish's famous words "A poem should not mean, / but be." The diction is as terse as ever, but it now points to a rather mystic experience, molded into a cryptic imagery. Impressions from modern art reveal themselves in a refined use of colours.

Steinarr is an impressive poet of pronounced originality, a central figure in the development of Icelandic poetry in our century.

FURTHER WORKS

Við opinn glugga (1961); collected works in *Kvæðasafn og greinar* (1964).

TRANSLATIONS

Modern Poetry in Translation 30 (1977); *Atlantica and Iceland Review* 16.4 (1978).

REFERENCES

Hjálmarsson, Jóhann, "Án takmarks og tilgangs," in *Íslenzk nútímaljóðlist* (Reykjavík, 1971); Höskuldsson, Sveinn Skorri, "The Triumph of Modernism in Icelandic Poetry." *Scandinavica* 12 Supplement (1973).

Peter Hallberg

Steingrímur Thorsteinsson. *See* Thorsteinsson, Steingrímur.

Steinn Steinarr. *See* Steinarr, Steinn.

Stenius, Göran Erik (pseud. Georg Keller). Finland-Swedish novelist and poet, b. 9 July 1909, Viborg (Viipuri).

Stenius studied at Helsinki University, and then worked as a journalist before joining the Finnish diplomatic service. Posted originally to Stockholm, he also spent lengthy periods in the Vatican (1942–1951) and London (1969–1973).

Stenius's work spans more than one genre: fiction, poetry, cultural and historical studies, and a biography of Giuseppe Gioachino Belli entitled *Den romerska komedin* (1967; The Roman Comedy). He is nevertheless mainly known as a novelist.

Stenius's religious and ethical preoccupations were apparent in his first published work, the novel *Det okända helgonets kloster* (1934; The Monastery of the Unknown Saint), in which in symbolical form and in a Russian Orthodox setting he examines the need for faith and reflects on the limits of human autonomy. The theme was taken up again on a larger scale in the major novel *Klockorna i Rom* (1955; *The Bells of Rome*, 1961), in which Stenius trades the conversion of a young Finn and his subsequent hesitation between a career in the Curia and the work of a poor parish priest. He chooses the latter, and the novel ends on a highly charged note of poetry and mysticism. The perspective is broadened yet again in the novels *Bronspojken från Ostia* (1974; The Bronze

Boy from Ostia), though this time the work is concerned less with religious mysticism than a general acceptance of monotheism in a world of doubtful values.

Alongside these novels with their metaphysical and philosophical preoccupation go three others, enacted against a more realistic Finnish background, though through family names linked to *Klockorna i Rom*. These are *Hungergropen* (1944; The Hunger Pit), *Fästningen* (1945; The Fortress), and *Brödet och stenarna* (1959; The Bread and the Stones), which in fictitious form trace the cultural history of Karelia and of Stenius's home town of Viborg up to about 1860.

Stenius has been called anti-intellectual, but in fact his novels have been intellectually demanding from the start. He does, however, always leave room for elements which defy a rational, nonmetaphysical explanation. His particular range of problems has ensured him a limited but faithful following in Finland, while abroad, especially in Germany, his religious novels have been widely acclaimed.

FURTHER WORKS

Femte akten (1937); *Mannen som uppfann vädret* (1937); *Fiskens tecken* (1940); *Vatikanen* (1947); *Avhopparen* (1957); *Från Rom til Rom* (1963).

REFERENCES

Jones, W. Glyn, "Göran Stenius' Philosophical Novels." *Scandinavica* 17.2 (1977); Jones, W. Glyn, "For Keller Read Stenius." *Scandinavian Studies* 53 (1981).

W. Glyn Jones

Stenvall, Aleksis. *See* Kivi, Aleksis.

Stephan G. Stephansson. *See* Stephansson, Stephan G.

Stephansson, Stephan G. Icelandic poet, b. 3 October 1853, Kirkjuhóll, Skagafjarðarsýsla, d. 10 August 1927, Markerville, Alberta, Canada.

Stephansson was the first of two children born into the family of a tenant farmer. Educated in the family home, he proved to be an avid reader at an early age. He immigrated to the United States with his family in 1873, and after sixteen years in Icelandic settlements in Wisconsin and North Dakota, moved with his wife and children to a homestead near Markerville, Alberta, where he spent the rest of his life. Stephansson began writing poetry even before leaving Iceland, became active in Icelandic literary societies in his new homeland, and carried on an extensive correspondence with prominent Icelanders both in North America and his mother country. Eventually he became an agnostic through his readings of Robert Ingersoll, Herbert Spencer, and Charles Darwin. He always believed in the possibility of the betterment of mankind, and during World War I his supporting the pacifist cause created some friction with the community where he lived.

In his poetry Stephansson used both traditional Icelandic and contemporary verse forms, showing his mastery of the Icelandic language. His best known work is the six volumes of poems entitled *Andvökur* (3 vols., 1909–1910; Wakeful Nights), most of which he composed during the late hours of the night after he had finished his farm chores. This collection is quite varied, consisting of meditations, epic poems in the tradition of the Eddas, sagas and *rímur*, political verse, and odes to both Iceland and Canada with striking descriptions of nature. Especially poignant is the famous elegy *Gestur*, composed to the memory of his son who was struck and killed by lightning.

In Iceland, Stephansson was recognized as a leading poet already in his lifetime, but only recently has this recognition been extended to Canada, probably because his total output was in the Icelandic language. Many contemporary Nordic scholars regard him as the greatest Icelandic poet since the Middle Ages.

FURTHER WORKS

Úti á víðavangi (1894); *Á ferð og flugi* (1900); *Kolbeinslag* (1914); *Heimleiðis* (1917); *Vígslóði* (1921); *Jökulgöngur* (1921); *Bréf og ritgerðir*, 4 vols. (1938–1948).

FURTHER TRANSLATIONS

Icelandic lyrics, ed. Richard Beck (1930); *Odes and echoes*, ed. Paul Bjarnason (1954); *An Anthology of Scandinavian Literature*, ed. Hallberg Hallmundsson (1965); *Selected Translations from Andvökur*, trans. Paul Bjarnason et al. (1982).

REFERENCES

Crawley, F. S., "The Greatest Poet of the Western World: Stephen G. Stephansson." *Scandinavian Studies and Notes* 15 (1938–1939); Kirkconnell, W., "Canada's Leading Poet." *University of Toronto Quarterly* 5 (1936); McCracken, Jane W., *Stephan G. Stephansson: The Poet of the Rocky Mountains* (Alberta, 1982); Nordal, Sigurður, *Andvökur, urval* (Reykjavík, 1939); Nordal, Sigurður, *Stephen G. Stephansson* (Reykjavík, 1959).

Christopher Hale

Stiernhielm, Georg (orig. Georg Olofsson). Swedish poet and scholar, b. 7 August 1598, Vika, Dalarna, d. 22 April 1672, Stockholm.

Known since Per Daniel Amadeus Atterbom's* day as "den svenska skaldekonstens fader" (the father of Swedish poetry), Stiernhielm remains one of the few authentically Renaissance figures in Swedish culture. His scholarship was encyclopedic, embracing jurisprudence, history, mathematics, natural science, philology, and philosophy. His lasting contributions, however, have emanated from his establishment of a humanistic tradition in Swedish letters. Stiernhielm is the fountainhead of such latter-day Swedish writers and thinkers as Johan Henric Kellgren,* Esaias Tegnér,* Johan Ludvig Runeberg,* Abraham Viktor Rydberg,* and Pär Lagerkvist.*

Stiernhielm made his literary debut with laudatory verses to Queen Christina in the early 1640s. His adaptations of pre-existing French ballet libretti such as

Then fångna Cupido (1649; Cupid Captured) and *Parnassus Triumphans* (1651; The Triumph of Parnassus) are landmarks in the history of Swedish prosody. In these works, he demonstrated the adaptability and suitability of the Swedish language to a wide range of standard metrical lines and verse forms (sapphic, anacreontic, and others).

Stiernhielm's own literary achievement was determined by the aspirations of the late Renaissance. In his allegorical, didactic epic *Hercules* (written ca. 1647, published 1658), he succeeded in introducing to Swedish literature not only the classical line of the hexameter but also the tone and spirit of the great stoical poems of antiquity. The theme, an inexperienced nobleman's confrontation with vice and virtue, is treated with originality and power; the diction is earthy and robust; the imagery is vivid and exuberant; and the construction is flawless. *Hercules* is not only the high-water mark of seventeenth-century Swedish letters but also a greatly influential work on the development of Swedish poetry.

FURTHER WORKS

Gambla Swea-och Göta-Måles fatebvr (1643); *Fredz-Afl* (1649); *Lycksalighetens ähre-pracht* (1650); *Virtutes repertae* (1651); *Musae Suethizantes* (1668).

REFERENCES

Friberg, Axel, *Den svenske Herkules* (Lund, 1945); Lindroth, Hjalmar Axel, *Stiernhielms Hercules* (Lund, 1913); Swartling, Birger, *Georg Stiernhielm* (Uppsala, 1909); Wiesel-gren, Per, *Georg Stiernhielm* (Stockholm, 1948).

Raymond Jarvi

Stigen, Terje. Norwegian novelist and dramatist, b. 26 June 1922, Magerøy.

Stigen is one of the more varied and prolific of modern Norwegian novelists. Although he was brought up in Oslo and received a university degree there, he has written mainly about northern Norway. In his early writings, the influence of Knut Hamsun* is discernible, but gradually he freed himself of this and other influences and developed his own style, which is simple, unaffected, and somewhat ironical. But his subject matter is almost always serious.

In his early novels, beginning with *To døgn* (1950; Forty-eight Hours), Stigen dealt with dreamers who are psychologically unfit for life and society and who seek escape as drunkards and tramps. His breakthrough came in 1956 with *Vindstille underveis* (*An Interrupted Passage*, 1973) in which four people on a train tell each other stories that all blend together in the same pattern. At the same time, Stigen began writing historical novels that gave him more opportunity for free fantasy. He has dealt with all historical epochs from the Vikings to the Renaissance to the twentieth century. His most famous historical novel is *Det flyktige hjerte* (1967; The Hasty Heart), which is written partially in diary form. It deals with a drunkard priest who comes from Copenhagen to minister to the people in the small seacoast towns of northern Norway.

In 1970, Stigen returned to modern times to write the psychological novel

Besettelse (Obsession), a powerful story about a forty-four-year-old school-teacher who falls in love with one of his fifteen-year-old pupils. From the beginning the two are tormented by a society that will not accept them, but the real difficulty is the young girl's inability to bridge the gap in experience between herself and her lover. Other social themes Stigen has treated include love among the handicapped and conflicts between the sexes.

Stigen is important for the richness and variety of his production, but also, and more importantly, for his close, passionate relationship to northern Norway. His best books bear witness to this fascination. Stigen has also distinguished himself as a writer of radio plays, six of which were published in 1974 under the title *Den røde sommerfugl* (The Red Bird of Summer).

FURTHER WORKS

Skygger på mitt hjerte (1952); *Nøkkel til ukjent rom* (1953); *Før solnedgang* (1954); *Frode Budbæreren* (1957); *Åsmund Armodsons saga* (1958); *Stjernøy* (1959); *Elskere* (1960); *Kjærlighet* (1962); *Glasskulen* (1963; *The Crystal Ball*, 1971); *Til ytterste skjær* (1964); *Krystallstjernen* (1965); *Timer i grenseland* (1966); *De tente lys* (1968); *Det siste paradiset* (1969); *Kains merke* (1971); *Norsk rapsodi* (1972); *Min Marion* (1972); *Skum-søylene* (1973); *Peter Johannes Lookhas* (1974); *De faste lys* (1975); *Forliset* (1976); *En hekto kandis* (1977); *Avikfjord* (1979); *Huset og byen* (1978); *Rekviem over en sommer* (1979); *Øgler i Avikfjord* (1980); *Blindgjengeren* (1981); *Bak våre masker* (1983); *Ved foten av kunnskapens tre* (1986); *Monolitten* (1988).

REFERENCES

Longum, Leif, "Den poetiske sannhet," in his *Et speil for oss selv* (Olso, 1968); Morris, Walter D., review of *Besettelse* in *Books Abroad* 45.4 (1971); Øyslebø, Olav, *Etter-krigsprofiler* (Oslo, 1957).

Walter D. Morris

Strindberg, Johan *August*. Swedish playwright, novelist, short story writer, and poet, b. 22 January 1849, Stockholm, d. 14 May 1912, Stockholm.

Strindberg was the son of steamship agent Carl Oscar Strindberg and his wife, former waitress Ulrica Eleonora Norling. Strindberg was trained by a strict father, a pietistic mother, and a pietistic stepmother; a Church of Sweden that emphasized a strict code of moral behavior; and schools that insisted on discipline, moral as well as intellectual. Self-scrutiny, self-judgment, self-justification and/or self-condemnation led to his lifelong concern with himself, the individual, the family, society, and the world and whatever force or being that created and controls it.

He remembered his childhood as an unhappy period of fluctuating economic fortunes, strained relationships, awareness of his mother's social inferiority, inadequate parental affection, stern discipline in and out of the home, and a strong feeling of isolation and fear.

He attended public and private schools from 1854 to 1867 when he passed *studenten* (the comprehensives), which admitted him to the University of Uppsala. In 1864 he had been confirmed in the Church of Sweden. He remembered both school and church as institutions more given to torturing the young than as institutions preparing them for living. But both served him well by stimulating his intellectual curiosity and imagination so that he extended his interest in both the humanities and the sciences into what became a lifelong habit of reading widely and examining and speculating about everything and everyone in the world about him. Few other laymen, for example, can have known the Bible and much other religious literature as well as Strindberg. But his reading and study were not restricted to literature, profane as well as religious; it was as if he had, as Francis Bacon said, "taken all knowledge for his province."

Although Strindberg did not take a degree at the university, he benefited from his intermittent stays there largely through associating with fellow students and acquiring vast sources of material for his future writing. He served as a substitute teacher in Stockholm, and as a tutor for the sons of a Stockholm doctor, who for a time directed his studies in medicine. He tried out as an actor and failed. He wrote plays of the kind then popular on the Stockholm stage: *En namnsdagsgåva* (1860; A Namesday Gift); *Fritänkaren* (1870; The Freethinker); *Hermione* (1869), a historical tragedy; *I Rom* (1879; In Rome), a historical proverb or situation in one scene; and *Den fredlöse* (1871; *The Outlaw*, 1969), a one-act historical tragedy with a Scandinavian theme. Although only the last two were staged, these exercises in dramatic composition convinced Strindberg that he could write plays.

His creative breakthrough came with his next play, *Mäster Olof* (1872; *Master Olof*, 1959), a prose masterpiece that was not produced until 1881 in spite of being superior to every Swedish play written before 1872. The play has now been accepted by Swedes, theater people, and the public as the very good realistic drama it is. But from 1872 until 1878 Strindberg spent much time revising it with the hope of its acceptance. There are two stageworthy versions: *Mellanspelet* (1875; The Middle Version) and the verse *Mäster Olof* (1876) as well as *Efterspelet* (1873; The Epilogue).

Mäster Olof was, moreover, one factor that led to Strindberg's first marriage, the most important of his three marriages. Siri von Essen (1850–1912), the wife of Baron Carl Gustaf Wrangel, had, in spite of her aristocratic origins, ambitions for a career on the stage. Her initial interest in Strindberg centered substantially in his being a dramatist. Her divorce in 1876 was followed by marriage to Strindberg very late in 1877, a marriage that lasted until 1892 and that provided him not only with happiness and unhappiness but with a spur to his creative activity and his work in journalism. He served as a librarian in the Royal Library (1874–1882). The marriage even led to his writing two conventional plays— *Gillets hemlighet* (1880; The Secret of the Guild) and *Herr Bengts hustru* (1882; Sir Bengt's Wife)—to provide Siri with roles in her stage career (1876–1883).

From 1877 on Strindberg established his claims to high rank as a writer of prose fiction, as a popular rather than scholarly social and cultural historian, as a poet, and as a social and political satirist. His early prose fiction includes the short stories in *Från Fjärdingen och Svartbäcken* (1877; From Town and Gown);

the highly popular novel *Röda rummet* (1879; *The Red Room*, 1913); the long narratives *Svenska öden och äventyr* (1882–1892; Swedish Destinies and Adventures) in four volumes; and short stories in *Giftas* (1884, 1886; *Getting Married*, 1972), *Utopier i verkligheten* (1885; Actual Utopias), and *Kvarstadsresan* (1885; Journey into Detention). His cultural and social historical volumes were *Gamla Stockholm* (1880; Old Stockholm), in collaboration with Claes Lundin; *Svenska folket* (1882; The Swedish People); and the satire *Nya riket* (1882; The New Nation). In 1883 and 1884 respectively appeared his books of poetry, *Dikter på vers och prose* (Poems in Verse and Prose) and *Sömngångar-nätter* (1884; Nights of Sleepwalking).

Important as all of these are to Swedish literature, two of them are especially significant for world literature: *Giftas* and *Kvarstadsresan*. In 1884, while Strindberg was living in Switzerland, he was brought home to Stockholm to be tried for blasphemy in one of the short stories in *Giftas* I, the actual primary objection to which was a frank treatment of socially enforced premarital abstinence from sex. *Kvarstadsresan* is an autobiographical account in letter form of the journey to face trial.

Although he was acquitted, the trial had both unhappy and happy effects on Strindberg. Albeit traumatic (the experience helped to lead to the collapse of his first marriage), it also helped lead to his first period of creative writing that raised him to world significance; the writing of the first four volumes of his autobiography *Tjänstekvinnans son* (1886; *The Son of a Servant*, 1913); great naturalistic-realistic plays, *Fadren* (1887; *The Father*, 1907), *Fröken Julie* (1888; *Lady Julie*, 1913), *Fordringsägare* (1889; *Creditors*, 1910); several one-act "cynical" plays (1889–1892); volumes of psychological narrative essays, *Vivisektioner* (1887–1890; Vivisections), including "The Battle of the Brains" and "Psychic Murder," both of which treat highly important matters in his plays and novels. Among the latter are *Le plaidoyer d'un fou* (1887; *En dåres försvarstal*, 1895; *A Madman's Defence*, 1967), a fictional account of his first marriage; *Hemsö-borna* (1887; *The People of Hemsö*, 1965), a delightful novel about the country people on Kymmendö, his favorite island in the Stockholm archipelago; *Skär-karlsliv* (1888; Life in the Skerries); and *I havsbandet* (1890; *By the Open Sea*, 1913, 1984).

After his divorce from Siri in 1892, Strindberg moved to Berlin, where he met the Austrian journalist Frida Uhl (1872–1943); their marriage in 1893 ended the next year although the divorce did not become final until 1897. "The Quarantine Master's Second Story" in *Fagervik och Skamsund* (1902; Fairhaven and Foulstrand) is an account of his second marriage.

From 1894 to 1897 Strindberg lived through what he called Inferno crisis. Physically ill and mentally disturbed, he kept a detailed account of his "occult" and other experiences, carried on "scientific" studies including attempts at making gold, wrote several scientific and pseudoscientific works, and was converted from freethinking (atheism) to Strindbergian syncretism. He kept his *Ockulta dagboken* (1963; Occult Diary) from 21 February 1896 to 11 July 1908, and wrote his autobiographcial novel *Inferno* (1897; trans. 1913) and its sequels *Legender* (1898; Legends) and *Jakob brottas* (1898; Jacob Wrestles).

His recovery was followed by *Ensam* (1903; *Alone*, 1968), a self-portrait, and an outburst of creative writing in drama, prose fiction, verse, essays, religious, historical and philological studies, and contributions to national debate.

Strindberg provided Sweden with a cycle of historical plays comparable to Shakespeare's: *Folkungasagan* (1899; *The Saga of the Folkungs*, 1959), *Gustav Vasa* (1899; trans. 1916), *Erik XIV* (1899; trans. 1931), *Gustav Adolf* (1900; trans. 1957), *Carl XII* (1901; *Charles XII*, 1964), *Engelbrekt* (1901; trans. 1949), *Kristina* (1901; *Queen Christina*, 1955), *Gustav III* (1902; trans. 1955), *Siste riddaren* (1908; *The Last of the Knights*, 1956), *Riksföreståndaren* (1908; *The Regent*, 1956), *Bjälbojarlen* (1908; *Earl of Bjälbo*, 1956) as well as less stageworthy historical plays: *Näktergalen i Wittenberg* (1903; *The Nightingale of Wittenberg*, 1970), *Moses* (1903), *Socrates* (1903), and *Kristus* (1903; Christ). *Erik XIV* and *Kristina* have had very successful productions abroad.

In 1898 he began to write plays that were to affect the development of world drama and theater: the autobiographical trilogy of confession, *Till Damaskus* (vols. 1–2, 1898; vol. 3, 1901; *To Damascus*, 2 vols., 1933); *Advent* (1898; trans. 1912), *Brott och brott* (1899; *Crimes and Crimes*, 1960), *Påsk* (1900; *Easter*, 1912), *Dödsdansen* (2 vols., 1900; *The Dance of Death*, 1912), *Ett drömspel* (1901; *A Dream Play*, 1912); the chamber plays: *Oväder, Brända tomten, Spöksonaten, Pelikanen* (1907; *Thunderstorm*, 1913; *The House That Burned; The Ghost Sonata*, 1916; *The Pelican*, 1962), *Svarta handsken* (1909; The Black Glove), and his self-defense *Stora landsvägen* (1909; *The Great Highway*, 1965).

His marriage to the gifted, ambitious actress Harriet Bosse (1878–1961) on 6 May 1901 was again a marriage to a woman who wanted a career other than that of homemaker. Her role in his life was twofold: stimulant and irritant. Much of the material in the occult diary and his letters deal with a usually stormy relationship that did not end with their divorce in 1904 but continued at intervals until her remarriage in 1908. Substantial proof of her influence on his creative writing is to be found particularly in his folk dramas *Kronbruden* (1901; *The Bridal Crown*, 1916, 1981) and *Svanevit* (1901; *Swanwhite*, 1914), in the diary, and in his letters.

Strindberg's novels, short stories, *novellen*, satires, and poetry have been highly important in twentieth-century Swedish and other Scandinavian literature. They include post-Inferno *Fagervik och Skamsund* (1902), a volume of prose narratives and verse; *Sagor* (1903; Tales), *Götiska rummen* (1904; The Gothic Rooms), *Svarta Fanor* (1904; Black Banners), *Taklagsöl* (1905; *The Roofing Ceremony*, 1987), *Historiska miniatyrer* (1905; Historical Miniatures), *Syndabocken* (1907; *The Scapegoat*, 1967). They have influenced Swedish prose fiction both in form and substance: in emphasis on psychological insight, extension of its imagery and its vocabulary, and the elimination of many artificialities in style. His *Öppna brev till Intima teatern* (1908; *Open Letters to the Intimate Theater*,

1966), his major contribution to dramatic theory and criticism, deals with the highly influential Intiman (the theater devoted to Strindberg's plays, 1907–1910) and contains the gist of his thinking about drama and theater.

His importance in world literature lies in his autobiographical works and in his contributions to drama and theater. Written in his naturalistic-realistic pre-Inferno period, *Tjänstekvinnans son* is essentially, as indicated by its subtitles (The Development of a Human Being, 1849–1967; Time of Ferment, 1868–1872; In the Red Room, 1872–1875; and The Author, 1877–1887), a study of his development as he saw it in terms of the naturalistic emphasis on heredity, environment, time, and chance. *Le Plaidoyer d'un fou* belongs to this phase of his autobiographical works. While his pre-Inferno autobiographical volumes are based primarily on what his five senses provided him, his post-Inferno volumes (*Inferno, Legender, Jakob brottas, Till Damaskus, Ockulta dagboken, Ensam,* and *Stora landsvägen*) go far beyond what his five senses could offer him to such sources as the unconscious, dreams, hallucinations, intuitions and the like as sources for self-understanding.

His autobiographical works and his major plays (*Fadren, Fröken Julie, Fordringsägare,* and his "cynical" plays in the pre-Inferno period and his post-Inferno Damascus trilogy, *Brott och brott, Påsk, Dödsdansen, Ett drömspel,* and the chamber plays—particularly *Spöksonaten* and *Stora landsvägen*) have fascinated dramatists and other writers, psychologists and psychiatrists, other intellectuals and a host of other readers.

As a dramatists' dramatist, Strindberg contributed to the naturalistic-realistic theater through his concept of the characterless character (as explained in the preface to *Fröken Julie*), his structural compression of segments of life, his close analytic scrutiny of human relationships, and verisimilitude of staging. Through his dream plays and other related post-Inferno dramas, he provided expressionists, impressionists, surrealists, and absurdists with matter to probe and forms to exploit: the synthetic examination of inner life against the backdrop of outer actuality, with staging controlled less by the five senses than by distortion provided by the imagination and the unconscious.

FURTHER WORKS

Det sjunkande Hellas (1869); *Den fredlöse* (1871; trans. 1913); *Anno fyrtioåtta* (1876); *Lycko-Pers resa* (1882; *Lucky Pehr*, 1912; *Lycko Per's Journey*, 1965); *Jäsningstiden* (1886; *The Growth of a Soul*, 1914); *I röda rummet* (1886); *Författaren* (1886); *Marodören* (1887); *Kamraterna* (1887; *Comrades*, 1919); *Tschandala* (1888); *Paria* (1889; *Pariah*, 1913); *Samum* (1889; *Simoon*, 1969); *Bland franska bönder* (1889); *Den starkare* (1889; *The Stronger*, 1964); *Första varningen* (1892; *The First Warning*, 1969); *Debet och kredit* (1892; *Debit and Credit*, 1969); *Inför döden* (1892; *In the Face of Death*, 1969); *Moderkärlek* (1892; *Mother Love*, 1969); *Leka med elden* (1892; *Playing with Fire*, 1969); *Himmelrikets nycklar* (1892; *The Keys of Heaven*, 1965); *Bandet* (1892; *The Bond*, 1960); *Midsommar* (1900; *Midsummertide*, 1912); *Kaspers fet-tisdag* (1900); *Holländarn* (1902); *Världshistoriens mystik* (1903; *World Historical Plays*, 1970); *Ordalek och småkonst* (1905); *Hövdingaminnen* (1906); *Nya svenska öden* (1906); *Toten-Insel* (1907); *Blå boken,*

4 vols. (1907–1912; *Zones of the Spirit*, 1913); *Abu Cassems tofflor* (1908); *Fabler* (1909); *Religiös renässans* (1910); *Samlade skrifter*, 55 vols. (1912–1920); *Samlade otryckta skrifter*, 5 vols. (1918–1921); *Skrifter*, 14 vols. (1946); *Strindbergs ungdomsjournalistik* (1946); *Från Fjärden till blå tornet* (1947); *Brev*, 15 vols. (1948–1976); *Brev till min dotter Kerstin* (1961); *Nationalupplagan av August Strindbergs samlade verk*, 75 vols. (1981–1997).

FURTHER TRANSLATIONS

The Washington Strindberg, Walter Johnson, trans. (1955–1983); *Five Plays* (1960); *Seven Plays* (1960); *Chamber Plays* (1962); *Selected Plays and Prose* (1964); *Eight Expressionistic Plays* (1965); *Inferno, Alone, and Other Writings* (1968); *The Strindberg Reader* (1968); *Strindberg's One-Act Plays* (1975); *The Plays of Strindberg* (1976); *Five Plays* (1983); *Plays from the Cynical Life* (1983).

REFERENCES

Brandell, Gunnar, *Strindberg in Inferno* (Cambridge, 1974); Brandell, Gunnar, *Strindberg—ett författarliv*, vol. 1 (Stockholm, 1987); Carlson, Harry G., *Strindberg and the Poetry of Myth* (Berkeley, 1982); Dahlström, Carl, *Strindberg's Dramatic Expressionism* (New York, 1930, 1965); Johannesson, Eric, *The Novels of August Strindberg* (Berkeley, 1968); Johns Blackwell, Marilyn, ed., *Structures of Influence* (Chapel Hill, 1981); Johnson, Walter, *Strindberg and the Historical Drama* (Seattle, 1963); Johnson, Walter, *August Strindberg* (Boston, 1976); Lamm, Martin, *August Strindberg* (New York, 1971); Lagercrantz, Olof, *August Strindberg* (New York, 1980); Meyer, Michael, *Strindberg* (New York, 1985); Sprinchorn, Evert, *Strindberg as Dramatist* (New Haven, 1982); Steene, Birgitta, *Strindberg: An Introduction to His Major Works* (Stockholm, 1982); *Swedish Book Review* 2 (1986), Strindberg supplement; Törnqvist, Egil, *Strindbergian Drama* (Stockholm, 1982).

Walter Johnson

Stub, Ambrosius. Danish poet, b. 17 May 1705, Gummerup, d. 15 July 1758, Ribe.

After his university entrance examinations in 1725, Stub studied theology for ten years at the University of Copenhagen without taking any degree. Subsequently he earned his living as a secretary and social companion in various aristocratic circles. In 1752 he had to give up this type of livelihood due to sickness and increasing alcoholism and spent the rest of his life in Ribe as the principal of a boys' school.

The basis for Stub's writing is his musicality. He modeled his philosophical and religious poems on meters from contemporary worldly song, the rococo arias. Best known—and Stub's two masterpieces—are the arias "Du deylig Rosen-Knop" (Thou Beautiful Rosebud), in which female beauty is compared with that of the perishable rose, and "Den kiedsom Vinter gik sin Gang" (The Tiresome Winter Went Its Course). This poem is one of the first in Danish literature to be based on a direct observation of nature. The scenery, however, is personalized, and the poem turns into a symbol of the course of life. Behind each stanza is the sense of the Divine Creator, who guides everything for the best. This belief in Providence also permeates Stub's philosophical songs in which the poet confesses to a moderation of joy: "Jeg lever jævnt fornøyet" (I Live in Modest Joy).

In Ribe, where Stub was under the influence of the hymn writer H. A. Brorson,* he wrote his religious poetry. He composed his hymns to "Christi syv Ord paa Korset" (The Seven Words of Christ on the Cross) and a number of pietistic penitential hymns. Employing a popular baroque emblem, "Livet som en Seylads" (Life as a Voyage), Stub renders a grandiose demonstration of Divine Providence as man's sole salvation.

Stub was a master of playful improvisation, and some of his most popular poems are occasional poetry and drinking songs. Only a few of these texts were printed during his lifetime. A collected edition of his poetry was not published until 1771. Here Stub finally emerges as a significant religious poet who in an elegant form manages to express the transience of life—"Lykke veltes op og under; Graved ned, i Mulden giemmes" (Happiness Is Found and Lost; Buried, Hidden in the Dust)—balanced by an acceptance of this destiny as expressed in the hymn "Jeg er fornøyet med min Gud" (I Am Content with My God).

FURTHER WORKS

Arier og andre poetiske Stykker (1771); *Samlede Digte* (1852, 1961); *Digte*, 2 vols. (1972).

REFERENCES

Brix, Hans, *Ambrosius Stub* (Copenhagen, 1960).

Sven H. Rossel

Sturluson, Snorri. Icelandic statesman, historian, and mythologist, b. 1178 at Hvammur in West Iceland, d. 1241 at Reykjaholt in southwest Iceland.

Snorri Sturluson was the son of an influential chieftain, Sturla Þórðarson, whose descendants became so prominent in Icelandic politics that the last decades of the Icelandic Freestate, which came to an end in 1262, are often identified with them and called the *Age of the Sturlungs*. Although Sturluson became one of the wealthiest and most powerful men in Iceland in his time and accepted high honors from Earl Skúli Bárðarson of Norway, he got caught in a steadily intensifying struggle between the two countries and was, as a result of this, murdered in 1241. This aspect of Sturluson's life does not fall within our terms of reference. Therefore, attention must be drawn to his writings, which established him as Iceland's most outstanding man of letters in the Middle Ages. *Snorra-Edda* (The Prose Edda or The Younger Edda) Sturluson most likely completed about 1220. In the main, it deals with mythology and poetics and has been preserved in four reasonably complete manuscripts and a few fragmentary ones. Of these *Codex Regius*, from the first part of the fourteenth century, is generally regarded as the most accurate version of a lost original. *Snorra-Edda* falls into four quite independent divisions: "Prologus," "Gylfaginning" (The

Beguiling of Gylfi), "Skáldskaparmál" (The Language of Poetry), and "Háttatal" (A Catalog of Meters). "Prologus" describes the creation of the world from a Christian point of view, the Flood, the world's religions, ideas on the composition of mother nature and the positioning of the continents. The family of the Norse gods is traced back to the champions of Troy and mention is made of Óðinn's journey into the north to take up residence there. "Gylfaginning" consists of myths told in Ásgarðr by three divine characters, Hárr, Jafnhárr, and Þriði (no doubt three different manifestations of Óðinn himself) in reply to questions posed by a royal visitor from Sweden named Gylfi. Gradually, one realizes that all the events staged in this section have had their origins in optical illusions, an element Sturluson may have added to satisfy the ecclesiastical authorities of his day that the purpose of his book was not to advocate the adoption of the old heathen faith. "Skáldskaparmál" describes a drinking feast where Bragi, the god of poetry, uses the opportunity to teach his fellow god Ægir about poetic metaphor and diction (*kenningar* and *heiti*), their origins and usage. In imparting this knowledge, the god uses myths for explanatory purposes and makes a number of references to skaldic verse. About 350 stanzas by sixty different poets (skalds) are quoted in this section. "Háttatal" is Sturluson's own poem of praise about King Hákon Hákonarson and Earl Skúli Bárðarson of Norway designed to provide examples of skaldic meters.

From the above it can be seen that *Snorra-Edda* is primarily a textbook on poetry intended, as Sturluson himself states in his text, for young poets. Indeed it was to ensure continued interest in the production of skaldic poetry, the very literary genre that had its beginning in mid–ninth-century Norway, was later monopolized by Icelandic skalds and had almost run its course at the time Sturluson wrote his *Edda* (ca. 1220). Although Sturluson failed in his attempt to revive the skaldic art, his *Edda* has remained one of our most valuable sources on Norse mythology and poetics. From the purely literary point of view, it is one of the masterpieces of medieval Scandinavian writing.

In compiling and writing his *Edda*, Sturluson drew heavily on older mythological and heroic poems, many of which have been preserved in the *Codex Regius* of *Sæmundar Edda* (The Elder Edda or The Poetic Edda). In addition, he is likely to have derived much from oral tradition. Third, he seems to have drawn on some of the Latin works that were part of medieval school curricula.

In considering Sturluson's educational background, it is important to remember that he was brought up at Oddi, one of the most highly renowned seats of learning in medieval Iceland. His mentor and guardian there was Jón Loftsson who, on his father's side, was the grandson of Sæmundr Sigfússon the Learned, Iceland's first historian and a man who had been educated in France. On his mother's side he was the grandson of King Magnús Barefoot of Norway.

Jón Loftsson was a powerful lay chieftain and had also received clerical education. Although direct information is lacking, one may assume that the school curriculum at Oddi reflected a balance between native Icelandic culture and classical European education. Pride in family ties with Norwegian royalty is furthermore likely to have inspired interest on the part of Jón Loftsson and his kinsfolk in the history of the kings of Norway. The study of this history required knowledge in the field of court poetry (skaldic poetry) because all the significant episodes in the kings' lives were embedded in poems their own court poets had composed about them. Some of these poems had apparently survived in the oral tradition for three to four centuries before they were finally put down in writing.

Even though the foregoing reflections on Sturluson's educational background are somewhat hypothetical, they are worthy of consideration in the present context. His *Edda* not only attests to its author's command of medieval Scandinavian learning, it has unmistakable links with classical works and shows, in addition, an overwhelming command of skaldic poetry and the ability to analyze its form and interpret its meaning. It is significant here that not only is skaldic poetry fraught with mythological images and allusions, but the royal houses of Scandinavia were indeed believed to have originated on the mythological plane. As a result, one may say that the boundary line between mythology and skaldic poetry is often blurred. If one then views these two fields as an almost indivisible area of study with a close connection with the lives of kings, it becomes obvious why Sturluson's upbringing and education, coupled with his various connections with Norwegian leaders, made him well qualified to write about their forefathers. Then it must be repeated that he had already produced his *Edda* when he began to write medieval Scandinavia's greatest historical work, *Heimskringla* (Orbis Terrarum), that is, the history of the kings of Norway from their remote mythological beginnings until the year 1177.

To come back to the connection already mentioned between *Snorra-Edda* and *Heimskringla*, it is of particular interest to note that the latter begins with the prehistoric *Ynglinga Saga*, which, owing to the source materials available to its author, is of a highly mythological or legendary nature. In fact, Sturluson himself discusses this problem in a very enlightening "Prologue" to his *Heimskringla*. Also, it does not escape the reader's attention that throughout the entire *Heimskringla* sequence skaldic poetry is quoted as a primary source.

The writing of *Heimskringla* seems to have come about in the following manner: Between 1220 and 1230 Sturluson wrote a separate saga about Saint Ólaf King of Norway, that is, *Ólafssaga helga hin sérstaka*, using among other things several older and quite legendary sagas about Saint Olaf as his sources. Although Sturluson found these older sagas useful, he realized that, from the scholarly point of view, they were quite inadequate. Thus he decided to produce a new version based on a more critical examination of source materials and with a stronger logical coherence. Having succeeded in this undertaking, Sturluson wrote sagas about all the Norwegian kings, prehistorical and historical, who had preceded Saint Olaf, adding those also who had succeeded him until the year 1177, that is, to the beginning of the reign of King Sverrir Sigurðarson, whose saga had already been written in Sturluson's time by the king's private biographer and on his own initiative. Having written these sagas of kings before and after

Saint Olaf and applied the same scholarly methods as were mentioned above, he inserted a revised version of his *Ólafssaga helga hin sérstaka* to complete his sequence, which later came to be known as *Heimskringla*. A correct understanding of the evolution of this work helps explain why *Ólafssaga*, which covers only about fifteen years of Norwegian history, constitutes in length about one-third of the entire sequence.

Several scholars have maintained that Sturluson must have written *Egils saga* (*see* Skallagrímsson, Egill). Nevertheless, a conclusive proof of his authorship has not yet been found.

Sturluson's political career, which ended with his murder, can be assessed only in the context of the political turmoil that prevailed in both Norway and Iceland during the last decades before the collapse of the Icelandic Commonwealth shortly after the middle of the thirteenth century.

EDITIONS

Heimskringla, ed. Bjarni Aðalbjarnarson, 3 vols. in *Íslenzk fornrit,* vols. 26–28 (1941–1951).

TRANSLATIONS

Heimskringla: History of the Kings of Norway, trans. L. M. Hollander (1964); *King Harald's Saga,* trans. Magnús Magnússonar and Hermann Pálsson (1966); *Heimskringla: Sagas of the Norse Kings,* trans. Samuel Laing, rev. Peter Foote (1979).

REFERENCES

Ciklamini, Marlene, *Snorri Sturluson* (Boston, 1978); Dronke, Ursula, and Peter Dronke, *The Prologue of the Prose Edda: Exploration of a Latin Background* in *Sjötíu ritgerðir* helgaðar Jakobi Benediktssyni 20. Juli 1977 (Reykjavík, 1977); Faulkes, Anthony, ''Pagan Sympathy: Attitudes to Heathendom in the Prologue to Snorra Edda,'' in *Edda, A Collection of Essays* (Winnipeg, 1983); Hallberg, Peter, ''Snorri Sturluson och Egils saga Skallagrímssonar,'' in *Studia Islandica* 20 (1962); Halldórsson, Halldór, *Old Icelandic Heiti: A Terminological Discussion* (Reykjavík, 1975); Nordal, Sigurður, *Snorri Sturluson* (Reykjavík, 1920; rev. ed., 1973); *Snorri atla alda Minning* (Reykjavík, 1979).

Haraldur Bessason

Sundman, Per Olof. Swedish novelist and short story writer, b. 4 September 1922, Vaxholm.

Although Sundman spent most of his childhood and formative years in Stockholm, it was in the desolate areas of Norrland that he found his literary domain and style. In 1949 he moved to Jämtland, one of Sweden's northernmost provinces, as the owner of a tourist hotel. For the next fourteen years he involved himself actively in local politics and followed the transformation of his adopted region through the construction of monumental power plants. His observations provided material for his short stories and novels set in Norrland. Back in Stockholm, he continued his political activities as a member of the Center party and won a seat in the Swedish Parliament (1969–1979). In 1975 he was elected a member of the Swedish Academy.

From the very beginning Sundman was recognized as a major writer whose literary technique attracted critical attention. In his cultivation of extreme economy he wielded his personal literary style, patterned on the rigorous discipline of the Icelandic sagas. Subscribing to a behaviorist theory, he refrains from psychological explanations and restricts himself to surface observations. Through a masterful use of silences his descriptions convey a sense of concrete immediacy and suggestive space.

In the broadest sense of the term, Sundman is a political writer, whose concern is to investigate man as a social being. The early short stories show individuals, often outsiders, in interaction with other individuals or groups and describe the social impulses emanating from either direction in terms of "hunting" and "seeking." The Norrland novels extend the investigations to the larger social units and lay bare the structures and mechanisms behind a community. With the two "expedition novels," dealing with H. M. Stanley's relief expedition through the Congo and S. A. Andrée's ill-starred attempt to reach the North Pole by balloon respectively, Sundman makes a major contribution to the documentary genre of the 1960s. These novels also contain a critical view of some basic Western attitudes and assumptions that have contributed to shaping our present world.

WORKS

Jägarna (1957); *Undersökningen* (1958); *Skytten* (1960); *Expeditionen* (1962; *The Expedition*, 1967); *Sökarna* (1963); *Två dagar, två nätter* (1965; *Two Days, Two Nights*, 1969); *Människor vid hav* (1966); *Ingenjör Andrées luftfärd* (1967; *The Flight of the Eagle*, 1970); *Ett år* (1967); *Ingen fruktan, intet hopp* (1968); *Lofoten, sommar* (1973); *Berättelsen om Såm* (1977); *Ishav* (1982); *Norrlands-berättelser* (1984).

REFERENCES

Jenkins, David, "A Rugged Individual." *Sweden Now* 5 (1971); Reynolds, Stanley, "Black Comedy." *New Statesman*, 1 December 1967; Sjöberg, Leif, "Per Olof Sundman and the Uses of Reality." *American-Scandinavian Review* 59.2 (1971); Sjöberg, Leif, "The Writer as a Reasonably Unbiased Observer." *Books Abroad* 47.2 (1973); Stendahl, Brita, "Per Olof Sundman on the Expedition of Truthtelling." *World Literature Today* 55.2 (1981); Warme, Lars G., "The Quests in the Works of Per Olof Sundman." *Proceedings of the Pacific Northwest Conference on Foreign Languages* 28 (1977); Warme, Lars G., "Per Olof Sundman and the French New Novel: Influence or Coincidence." *Scandinavian Studies* 50 (1978); Warme, Lars G., *Per Olof Sundman: Writer of the North* (Westport, Conn., 1984).

Lars G. Warme

Suonio, Aino. *See* Kallas, Aino Julia Maria.

Svava Jakobsdóttir. *See* Jakobsdóttir, Svava.

Swartz, Helga Maria. *See* Martinson, Helga Maria.

Swedenborg, Emanuel. Swedish scientist, philosopher, and theologian, b. 29 January 1688, Stockholm, d. 29 March 1772, London.

The second son of the popular although controversial bishop Jesper Swedberg,

Swedenborg received his surname when his family was ennobled in 1719. He devoted the first thirty years of his remarkable career to a many-faceted inquiry into the emerging natural sciences of the day, contributing to such far-ranging disciplines as mathematics, astronomy, optics, metallurgy, physics, chemistry, mechanics, and geology. In the 1730s, he turned to anatomical and physiological studies in an attempt to understand the human soul. These studies and this aim led to a bizarre and harrowing series of visions, hallucinations, and dreams methodically recorded but never published by Swedenborg himself. Resolution of this psychic crisis occurred in London in April of 1745; Swedenborg claimed that he came face to face with the Lord God, the world's creator and redeemer, and that his spiritual sight was opened, giving him access to the heavenly and hellish realms that correspond with states of being in the material world. He retired from public life—although he nowise became a hermit—and produced a long series of exegetical and theological works that had to be published in London or Amsterdam because of Swedish censorship. In 1787 his British disciples founded the Church of the New Jerusalem, an enterprise that Swedenborg consistently had discouraged during his lifetime.

Readers of Swedenborg's visionary works have had to cope with their exceedingly dry, pedantic, and academic style. Few Swedish writers, nevertheless, have exerted such pervasive influence on world literature; Swedenborg's influence can be discerned in the works of such seminal figures as William Blake, the young Goethe, Honoré de Balzac, Charles Baudelaire, Ralph Waldo Emerson, Henry James, Sr., William Butler Yeats, and Jorge Luis Borges. Although a vast majority of Swedes habitually have shared Johan Henric Kellgren's* assessment of Swedenberg as a deranged person, his impact on Swedish literature is readily apparent in the works of such outsiders as Carl Jonas Love Almqvist,* August Strindberg,* and Vilhelm Ekelund*—and in such eminently modern writers as Gunnar Ekelöf* and Lars Gyllensten.*

WORKS

Religiösa skrifter i urval, ed. M. Lamm (1925).

TRANSLATIONS

The Principia, 2 vols. (1846); *The Animal Kingdom,* 2 vols. (1843–1844); *Chemistry* (1847); *Miscellaneous Observations* (1847); *Motion and Position of the Earths and Planets* (1900); *The Infinite and the Final Cause of Creation* (1908); *The Worship and Love of God* (1925); *The True Christian Religion* (1933); *Heaven and Its Wonders and Hell* (1938); *Marital Love* (1938); *The Economy of the Animal Kingdom,* 2 vols. (1945–1946); *The Earths in the Universe* (1951); *The Intercourse of the Soul and the Body* (1951); *The New Jerusalem and Its Heavenly Doctrine* (1951); *The Heavenly Arcana,* 12 vols. (1951–1956); *A Brief Exposition of the Doctrine of the New Church* (1952); *Concerning the Last Judgment* (1961); *A Continuation of the Last Judgment* (1961); *Angelic Wisdom about Divine Providence* (1963); *Angelic Wisdom Concerning Divine Love and Wisdom* (1965); *The Apocalypse Revealed* (1968).

REFERENCES

Dingwall, E. J., *Very Peculiar People* (New York, 1962); Emerson, Ralph Waldo, *Representative Men* (Boston, 1850); Hyde, James, *A Bibliography of the Works of Emanuel Swedenborg* (London, 1906); Jonsson, Inge, *Emanuel Swedenborg* (New York, 1971); Lamm, Martin, *Swedenborg* (Stockholm, 1915); Sigstedt, Cyriel Odhner, *The Swedenborg Epic* (New York, 1952); Stroh, A. H., and Greta Ekelöf, *Kronologisk förteckning över Emanuel Swedenborgs skrifter* (1910; Holmberg, A., *Supplement*, 1937); Toksvig, Signe, *Emanuel Swedenborg* (New Haven, 1948); Trobridge, George, *Swedenborg*, 4th ed. (New York, 1962).

Raymond Jarvi

T

Takvam, Marie. Norwegian lyric poet, b. 6 December 1926, Örsta.

Takvam is one of the first Norwegian poets who, rather consistently, analyzes the city, the people living in the city, the quality of life in Norway seen through the eyes of a city dweller, a view spreading outward from Oslo like concentric ripples in the water. There are not only critical views of Norway, but also of Scandinavia, of Europe—the world.

In one of her central poems, "Norway," that nation is seen as a marginal and originally frugal country on the outskirts of Europe. Norwegian nature, in a very decisive and innovative step, is translated through imagery into the "Age of Aquarius." It is too cosmic, too overpowering, too divine, negating any possibility of close human relationship and identification, constituting a very cold backdrop for human dwellings and human life. People are mass-produced like chickens, and the quality of human life is correspondingly low. Urban life in its present form is clearly seen as the undoing of Norwegian civilization.

Yet people seek this life by their own ruinous volition, only to find themselves adrift in various stages of loneliness, desperate and occasionally rebellious. Often, as in the poem "The Day," life does not seem to be really lived, but is depicted as a totally unreflecting and unreflected experience, very much akin to the mindless watching of mindless television programs, suggesting that life is an endlessly repeated routine and overpowering familiarity with surroundings, a familiarity that proves to be destructive. There is little contact, almost no impact of human beings on each other. Death lures at every corner; the colors in the poems are forever fading. When death does occur, even when closely witnessed, it still passes almost unnoticed.

What makes the poems bearable, despite their bleak setting, is Takvam's precise language, the astute and often startling observation, the frequent irony, and the typical sarcastic endings.

In her last collection, *Falle og reise seg att* (1980; To Fall and to Rise Again), the tone of Takvam's poetry is changing; there is more acceptance of life, of reality, however harsh it may be, and perhaps the hope of coming to terms with it.

FURTHER WORKS

Dåp under stjerner (1952); *Syngjande kjelder* (1954); *Signal* (1959); *Merke etter liv* (1962); *Mosaikk i lys* (1965); *Idun* (1966); *Brød og tran* (1969); *Auger—hender* (1975); *Dikt i utval* (1976).

TRANSLATIONS

Micromegas 4.3 (1971); König, Fritz H., "The Woman's Voice in Modern Norwegian Poetry." *North American Review* 257.1 (1972).

Fritz H. König

Tarkiainen, Maria. *See* Jotuni, Maria Gustava.

Tavaststjerna, Karl August. Finland-Swedish poet and novelist, b. 13 May 1860, St. Michel (Mikkeli), d. 20 March 1898, Björneborg (Pori).

Tavaststjerna came from the Finland-Swedish upper class (his father was an estate owner and a retired major-general in the Russian army); but Tavaststjerna's own life was marked by a sense of rootlessness, evidently caused in part by his mother's death during the famine of 1868 (from typhus contracted while nursing refugees from the north of Finland, an event retold in Tavaststjerna's novel about the disaster, *Hårda tider* [1891; Hard Times]), and by his father's remarriage. During studies at the new Polytechnical Institute at Helsinki, Tavaststjerna became fascinated by literature, urged on by his friend, the critic Hjalmar Neiglick (1860–1889), making his debut with *För morgonbris* (1883; With the Morning Breeze), a collection both giving a new vigor to Finland's Swedish verse and a new field of observation—the sea. Nonetheless, Tavaststjerna employed a dying literary form, inherited from Johan Ludvig Runeberg, the verse-tale, in the epyllia of *Nya vers* (1885; New Verses); Runeberg would have been surprised, though, at the frankness and psychological awareness of these novellas-in-poetry.

With the Helsinki novel, *Barndomsvänner* (1896; Childhood Friends), Tavaststjerna established himself as Finland's representative in the description of a type just then popular in the rest of Nordic letters, the ineffectual dreamer, of whom the Dane J. P. Jacobsen* had given a classic formulation in *Niels Lyhne* (1880); in the title tale of the collection *En inföding* (1887; A Native), Tavaststjerna portrayed Neiglick as the cosmopolitan and himself as the clumsy "aborigine." In 1896, Tavaststjerna published a new volume of verse, *Dikter i väntan* (Poems While Waiting), a demonstration of his close interest in problems besetting Finland at the time—for example, in the poem, "On Swedish Ground," a contrasting of Sweden's calm with Finland's troubles (but not to Finland's disfavor). The patriotic Tavaststjerna became a central figure in the wave of protest arising in reaction to growing political pressure from St. Petersburg: see the story "A Misunderstanding" in *I Förbindelser* (1888; In Connections), in which a harmless Finn is unintentionally killed by a Cossack recruit, and "The Kiss of Spring" in *Marin och genre* (1890; Marine and Genre Paintings), a lyric tale in which springtime, personified, awakens the cynical poet to Finland's beauties and perils. However, that same cynicism was renewed in *Hårda tider*, in which the author's spokesman admires the self-sacrifice of "Fru von Blume" but thinks it has been useless, and in *Kvinnoregemente* (1894; Women's Rule), scarcely an idealized view of the Finnish peasant—the novel's main figure is brutally disabused of his romantic notions about the nation's pristine soul. In *En patriot utan fosterland* (1896; A Patriot without a Homeland), Tavaststjerna expresses some sympathy for those Finlanders whom circumstances have turned into servants of the Russians, and in the programmatic poem, "Finnbacka Finne" from *Dikter* (1896; Poems), Tavaststjerna, who had once held a moderate and conciliatory position in the language struggle between Finnish and Swedish, gave vent to his anger at what he believed was Finnish ingratitude and short-sightedness.

Tavaststjerna's growing embitterment, and the desire to reach a larger audience, led him to begin a long trip abroad late in 1892; and after stays in Switzerland and Italy, he briefly joined the circle around August Strindberg* in Berlin. Although the trip was in many respects unhappy, because of Tavaststjerna's growing deafness and the fascination of his wife, an actress, with the Swedish dramatist, he became interested in new continental paraliterary fashions—decadence, Nietzscheanism, spiritualism—and produced the fascinating, if artistically unsuccessful, novel *I förbund med döden* (1893; In Union with Death), and the long verse novella "Laureatus" (in the volume of the same name from 1897), whose lonely genius of a hero and Alpine scenery are reminiscent of *Also sprach Zarathustra*. After a sojourn in Sweden, Tavaststjerna returned to Finland in September 1895, taking work as a provincial newspaper editor, first in Hangö (Hanko), then in Pori; his ever-darkening mood led to the most famous of his poems, "Homeward in Autumn Rain" and "Bells Ring for a Funeral" (both in *Dikter*) and to the sonnet cycle "Diana" in *Laureatus*, with its "antique" imagery influenced by the paintings of Arnold Böcklin and its identification of Aline Borgström, the wife of a friend, with the goddess, and Tavaststjerna himself with Endymion. Finally, returning once again to thoughts of his childhood, he wrote the quasi-memoir, *Lille Karl* (1897; Little Karl). His death was grotesque; in hospital with pneumonia, he was given Lysol, instead of medicine, by an inattentive nurse.

Of all Finland's authors in the later nineteenth century, Tavaststjerna—thanks not least to the efforts of his German translator, Ernst Brausewetter—had the greatest international reputation, a reputation his works, in their intellectual strength and the variety of their thematics, fully deserved. Unhappily, he never found a style, in prose or verse, adequate to his needs.

FURTHER WORKS

Afffärer (1890); *Unga år* (1892); *Uramo torp* (1892); *Korta brev från en lång bröllopsresa* (1893); *Heder och ära* (1894); *Kapten Tärnberg* (1894); *Finska vikens hemlighet* (1895);

Brev till Nixe, ed. *Gabrielle Tavaststjerna* (1923); *Samlade skrifter*, 10 vols. (1924); *Brev till Diane*, ed. Greta von Frenckell-Thesleff (1966).

TRANSLATIONS

Swedo-Finnish Short Stories, ed. G. C. Schoolfield (1974).

REFERENCES

Ekelund, Erik, *Tavaststjerna och hans diktning* (Helsinki, 1950); Kihlman, Erik, *Karl August Tavaststjernas diktning* (Helsinki, 1926); Söderhjelm, Werner, *Karl August Tavaststjerna* (Helsinki, 1924, 1900, 1913).

George C. Schoolfield

Tegnér, Esaias. Swedish poet, b. 13 November 1782, Kyrkerud, Värmland, d. 2 November 1846, Östrabo, near Växjö, Småland.

As the youngest of six children in the modest circumstances of a parish minister's family, Tegnér was not initially encouraged to follow the studious path of his brothers Lars Gustaf and Elof. Upon the early (1792) death of his father, however, Tegnér was allowed to join his brother at the home of the rich proprietor, Chr. Myhrman. The genial surrogate father and the large classical library in his home were of decisive importance for the young Tegnér. A chance to study for a lower exam at Lund University in 1799 became a second springboard for the precocious youth, and his enormous facility in the classical literatures was soon discovered by the philosopher L. P. Munthe and others. Soon it was evident that Tegnér would join his instructors as a colleague at Lund.

Tegnér's early poetry is clearly a product of his classical and philosophical studies. He scattered a few fresh lyrical pieces about in his circle of friends, but turned his reading of Immanuel Kant and Johann Gottlieb Fichte into larger topical historical-philosophical poetic essays, with which he entered, and eventually won, the prize competition given by the Swedish Academy (with "Svea," composed 1811). Established as the center of a "southern wing" of the Swedish romantic movement, Tegnér contributed to Götiska förbundet's publication *Iduna,* rather than to *Phosphorus* or other mouthpieces of Per Daniel Amadeus Atterbom's* group in Uppsala. A rivalry with the latter group sprang up, and it became at times bitterly antagonistic during the 1810s. Tegnér was labeled— to some extent unjustly—a political reactionary, and he was apparently driven to the right by the literary polemics. Actually equally skeptical of the eighteenth century's "heartless enlightenment" and the "mindless ecstasy" of the nineteenth, Tegnér attempted to hold his own polemic on the line of the passionate intellectual search for truth and its poetic expression, or what he called "den manliga, den svenska sång" ("the manly, Swedish song," in "Sången," 1819). In the excitable 1810s it was a difficult position to defend. A melancholy trait, which would eventually take on misanthropic and manic-depressive attributes, appeared in the character of the otherwise witty and sociable Tegnér. Economic problems in his personal life and Sweden's politics played their role as well.

Tegnér's rise in the Lund University hierarchy (to professor in 1812, the year he also received the title of vicar) was not followed immediately by commensurate raises in salary. In his family life he was probably happy initially, married since 1806 to Anna Myhrman, the daughter of his patron.

As a poet, however, he only gained increasing fame. He received substantial recognition for his philosophical poems, being chosen into the Swedish Academy in 1819; but it was the Nordic epic poem *Frithiofs saga* (1820–1825) that secured his place at the pinnacle of the Swedish Parnassus of his time. Early translations of the work into German and English established Tegnér as the first truly internationally recognized Swedish poet. After this success, however, Tegnér's depressive traits reappeared, together with problems in his married life. Named to yet another promotion as Bishop of Växjö, he took up the task of provincial church authority with the same energy and intelligence with which he had acquitted himself as professor. But the inner story is better recounted in the poem "Mjeltsjukan" ("Spleen," publ. 1828), and plans for further epics with the sweep of *Frithiofs saga* were never realized. An apoplectic stroke in 1840 contributed to a mental condition from which Tegnér never fully recovered.

From the simple but masterly lyric "Det eviga" (1810; The Eternal Truths) to the elegiac "Den döde" (1834; The Dead Man), Tegnér maintained a unique and singular voice in Swedish literature. To his didactic poems he brought a comprehensive classical training that was unsurpassed in his eighteenth-century forebears. But to this training he added a meticulous care and an insight for choosing the right expression, the most moving turn of phrase and the most absolute clarity of thought. In his poems "Nyåret 1816" (The New Year 1816), "Epilog vid magisterpromotionen i Lund 1820" (Epilog at the Commencement Ceremony in Lund, 1820), "Sång den 5 April 1836" (Song on the Fifth of April 1836), and many others, the occasional or topical event is lifted from its ceremonial place and given truly eternal values. Phrases such as "Der låg ett skimmer öfver Gustafs dagar" (There lay a shimmer over the days of King Gustaf); "Väl formar den starke med svärdet sin verld" (Though the strong man forms the world by his sword); and most characteristically, "det dunkelt sagda är det dunkelt tänkta" (that which is said unclearly is unclearly thought out) still have their place in the Swedish consciousness as if they had been parts of a national anthem.

Frithiofs saga is, nonetheless, Tegnér's undisputed masterpiece. The epic, divided into twenty-four cantos of widely varied meters, builds on a minor *fornaldarsaga* about a Viking who wins his bride by seducing her, gaining riches, proving his nobility of spirit, and then defeating the woman's two unpleasant brothers. It is in its Old Norse form an archetype for the "happy end" saga, the rise of a young man in society. Tegnér transforms the story into a poetic vehicle with metrical virtuosity, using pastiches of Old Norse and ballad meter, classical verse form and newly created atrophic types. But in addition, he superimposes a noticeably Swedish bias in the hero—a persistent guilt complex and a religious struggle—and manages thereby to interweave Neoplatonic ideas from German neoromanticism, Christian ideals and Old Norse mythology with seeming ease and apparent unanimity of purpose. While partially derived in its design from Adam Oehlenschläger's* epic *Helge* (1814), *Frithiofs Saga* has attained a far more prominent place in Scandinavian literature than has the Danish work.

Tegnér's political views have not aged as well: the twentieth century has tended to shrug both at the "liberal" Napoleonism of his youth and at the clearly conservative tendencies that gradually pervaded his later development. It is rather Tegnér's precision and beauty of expression—his lyrical rhetoric, in the best sense of that word—that can be most inspiring to the modern reader.

FURTHER WORKS

Samlade skrifter, ed. E. Wrangel and F. Böök, 10 vols. (1918–1925), *Esais Tegnérs brev*, ed. N. Palmborg, 11 vols. (1953–1976).

TRANSLATIONS

Of the many translations of *Frithiofs saga* W. Strong's early one (1933) and Ida Mauch's recent one (1960) deserve mention; "Axel and Svea," trans. O. Baker (1840); *Specimens of Swedish and German Poetry* (1848); *Poems by Tegnér*, trans. H. W. Longfellow and W. L. Blackley (1930); *Swedish Books* 2 (1986).

REFERENCES

Appelmann, A., "The Relation of Longfellow's Evangeline to Tegnér's Frithiofs Saga" *Scandinavian Studies* 2.3 (1915); Bohman, Svante, *Esaias Tegnérs tänkesätt och idéer* (Uppsala, 1933); Böök, Fr., *Esaias Tegnér: En levnadsteckning* (Stockholm 1946); Brandes, Georg, *Creative Spirits of the Nineteenth Century* (New York, 1923); Hedin, Greta, *Tegnérs uppfattning av klassiskt och romantiskt* (Göteborg, 1936); Hedin, Greta, et al., *Tegnérs Fritjofs saga: Fyra studier* (Stockholm, 1931); Nordell, O., "Concerning English Translations from the Swedish Poem Frithiof's Saga: A Critique." *Scandinavian Studies* 13.4 (1934); Sondén, Torsten, *Tegnérs psykiska ohälsa* (Lund, 1946); Sturtevant, A. M., "A Study of Tegnér's Personality and Views as Revealed in His Skoltal." *Scandinavian Studies* 15.6 (1939); Werin, Algot, *Esaias Tegnér: från Det eviga till Mjältsjukan* (Lund, 1934); Wrangel, Ewert, *Tegnér i Lund* (Stockholm 1932).

James Massengale

Tervapää, Juhani. *See* Wuolijoki, Hella.

Theater in Scandinavia. In its more established forms, theater in Scandinavia is at once an old and a young phenomenon, old with regard to the kingdoms of Denmark and Sweden, young with regard to Norway and the republics of Finland and Iceland.

Our knowledge of theater conditions during the Middle Ages is limited due to scarcity of material. Yet, just as the plays preserved (mystery plays, miracle plays, morality plays, farces) belong to a general European tradition, we may safely assume that the staging of these plays did not essentially differ from that in other parts of Europe. In Scandinavia, too, theater seems to have originated in the liturgical ceremonies inside the Catholic churches. Outside, in market-places and churchyards, full-scale productions were staged during the warm season. The life of man or the life of particular men (Jesus, the Saints) was depicted in its parabolic aspect according to the principle of simultaneous staging. The productions, witnessed by an audience familiar with the "spectacles" of public torture and execution, were often characterized by gory realism and technical inventiveness, for which the *maître de secrets* was responsible.

With the advent of the Reformation, the medieval religious plays were replaced by school dramas, the purpose of which was to educate the young to high morals and good manners. Works by Plautus and Terence in Latin or in translation, as well as adaptations and original dramas in the vernacular, were performed in much the same way as during the preceding era: polyscenic staging by means of mansions. Musical and choreographic passages would sometimes further enhance the epic nature of humanist drama. Along with plays adhering to the classical genres of tragedy and comedy, heroic and historical plays (Messenius) were written and performed. Both at the Danish and at the Swedish court, student players were invited to stage dramas in the humanist tradition.

As the two countries, notably Sweden, expanded into major European powers, more spectacular festivities were called for. At the courts of Christian IV and Frederik III of Denmark and Queen Christina of Sweden, regal processions (*trionfi*) and splendid *ballets de cour* were introduced.

Of importance for the further development of the Scandinavian theater is the impact of strolling players from England, Germany, Holland, and France visiting Denmark and Sweden in the seventeenth and eighteenth centuries. The foundation in 1722 of the first permanent national playhouse in Scandinavia—the Copenhagen theater in Lille Grønnegade connected with Ludvig Holberg*—is the direct result of the activities of one such visiting company, that headed by René Magnon de Montaigu. Significantly, this theater opened with a play by Molière, followed by Holberg's *Political Tinker*. During the first eighteen months of its existence, it produced no less than fifteen new Holberg comedies.

By making a strong plea for localized comedy, Holberg could turn his characters into recognizable counterparts of the audience, despite his predilection for exaggerated characterization. Although character delineation stands central in his work, Holberg's plays make ample use of comic stage business, derived from the *lazzi* of commedia dell'arte, visual display, and even dance and music.

During the reign of the pietistic Christian VI, Danish theater dwindled, while in Sweden a national theater, the Royal Swedish Stage, opened in the refurbished tennis court, the Bollhus, in 1737. Eleven years later, the Danish Royal Theater, today one of the oldest functioning playhouses in Europe, opened on Kongens Nytorv, where it has been located ever since. The first Scandinavian actors and actresses of renown now made their appearance.

In Sweden Queen Lovisa Ulrika, dissatisfied with the commonness of the Swedish plays performed at the Bollhuset, transformed Drottningholm, the eighteenth-century summer palace, into a center for theatrical entertainments.

After the first Drottningholm Theater had burned down, a second and larger playhouse, now world-famous as the best preserved eighteenth-century court theater in existence, opened in 1766. The 350-seat auditorium was designed, in rococo style, to blend with the equally large stage to form a single harmonious whole. The machinery and technical devices are still to be seen in actual use in the summer season when operas are staged in eighteenth-century fashion.

During the 1770s, the theater entered a new era in Scandinavia. The Danish national theater began to cultivate the new *Singspiel* and the drama of sensibility. In Norway a first vague attempt at the establishment of a native professional company was made. In Sweden, the succession of Gustav III to the Swedish throne marked the beginning of one of the most luminous periods in the history of the Scandinavian theater.

More directly than earlier monarchs, Gustav III demonstrated a lasting passion for the stage. Not only did he himself write some of the most successful plays of the period, he also took an interest in all aspects pertaining to stage production. It was under the aegis of this actor-king, devoted to the staged glorification of Swedish history, that a native drama, theater, and opera were called into being. The famous Carlo Bibiena was invited to design the stage settings for Gustav's first historical play. A more permanent relationship was established with Louis Jean Deprez, whose stage designs, anticipating the atmospheric settings of the romantic period, represent a high point in contemporary European theater. After the symptomatic death of Gustav III in 1792—he was mortally wounded at a *bal masqué* in the opera house—a cultural Iron Age followed in Sweden, affecting also the theater.

In the new century, the Danish Royal Theater, housing resident companies for opera, drama, and ballet under one roof, became the center of Scandinavian theater culture. An unexcelled company of actors and actresses, with Johanne Luise Heiberg as prima donna, turned the Royal Theater into one of the leading playhouses of Europe around midcentury. The new romantic ideals that, nourished by the introduction of Shakespeare on the Scandinavian stage, permeated Scandinavian (verse) drama in the early 1800s (Adam Oehlenschläger,* Johannes Ewald,* Carl Jonas Love Almqvist*) had its repercussions in the Gothic atmosphere re-created in the stage settings of the period. The architect of the neoclassical theater gave way to the landscape painter of the romantic one, the side wings of the former to the backcloth of the latter. Scene shifts were gradually facilitated, and in 1829 August Bournonville introduced the box set of the modern theater in one of his ballets. Due to the technical development, stage lighting could be utilized in a more varying way. Thus candles and tallow lamps were gradually replaced by more flexible Argand lamps, and colored lighting was introduced. Eventually gas lighting, with its increased possibilities of visualizing romantic moods, was installed. The style of acting adhered to Goethe's demand for a combination of truth and beauty, of what is natural with what is ideal.

As romanticism turned into bourgeois realism, tragedy gave way to comedy and vaudeville (Johan Ludvig Heiberg,* Henrik Hertz, Jens Christian Hostrup,

August Blanche). Especially popular was Heiberg's *Elverhøj* (Elves' Hill), a folksong-inspired romantic piece that, partly due to Friedrich Daniel Rudolph Kuhlau's music, has become Denmark's most frequently performed play.

It was in Bergen's Norwegian Theater, initiated by the violinist-composer Ole Bull,* that Henrik Ibsen* and Bjørnstjerne Bjørnson* acquired their experience in stage production. Their active involvement in the theater undoubtedly had a definite impact on their dramatic writing; we need only think of the suggestive interplay between verbal and visual elements (setting, props, costumes, lighting) in Ibsenite drama.

Like Ibsen and Bjørnson, August Strindberg* was actively involved in play production, although he never functioned as a director in the usual sense. Failing to launch a Scandinavian Experimental Theater devoted to performances of his own (short) plays, he finally succeeded, with the assistance of the young director August Falck, in establishing the Intimate Theater in Stockholm (1907–1910), for which he wrote his *Open Letters* and his chamber plays. In his preface to *Miss Julie* Strindberg succinctly formulated a program for the naturalistic theater. While he here tends to conform to current Zolaesque ideas, in his later so-called dream plays he calls for a dematerialization that could only be re-created with technical means developed in the twentieth century.

With the introduction of the revolving stage, the cyclorama, modern lighting, projection and sound techniques, a "New Stagecraft" (Adolphe Appia, Gordon Craig) has evolved, which has affected twentieth-century playwrights in their way of writing. New media—radio, television—have had a similar effect, resulting in a great number of Scandinavian radio and television plays. On the other hand, no Scandinavian playwright of this century has been of truly international stature. A list of the most prominent names would include Kaj Munk,* Kjeld Abell,* and Leif Panduro* from Denmark; Pär Lagerkvist,* Hjalmar Bergman,* Stig Dagerman,* and Lars Forssell* from Sweden; Helge Krog* and Nordahl Grieg* from Norway; Walentin Chorell* and Paavo Haavikko* from Finland; Guðmundur Kamban* and Halldór Laxness* from Iceland.

More impressive, perhaps, in an international perspective, is the list of prominent directors: Per Lindberg, Johannes Poulsen, Olof Molander, Per Knutzon, Holger Gabrielsen, Alf Sjöberg, and Ingmar Bergman.* The high level of the scenography is indicated by names like Svend Gade, Knut Ström, Isaac Grünewald, Helge Refn, and Sven Erixson, while the acting of Clara Pontoppidan, Poul Reumert, Bodil Ipsen, Gösta Ekman, Lars Hanson, Erik Lindström, Max von Sydow, and Liv Ullman has fascinated generations of theatergoers far outside Scandinavia.

In addition to the national stages—the Finnish Theater (1872) and the National Theater of Iceland (1950) being late additions—a number of regional and state touring theaters have been established in the course of this century. The number of commercial playhouses has been drastically diminished, while small experimental theaters like the Studio Theater (Oslo), the Violin Theater (Copenhagen), and the Pistol Theater (Stockholm) have usually led an intense but brief existence.

In the 1960s new ideologies resulted in a reaction against the established forms of theater production and in a changed attitude to the audience. The final rehearsals became open to the public, which was also invited to discuss the productions with director and actors. Independent theater movements were organized, catering to "underpriviliged groups" (children, immigrants, handicapped people, people in rural areas). Instead of always expecting the audience to come to the playhouse, actors often went in search of their audience (visiting theater), tried to make it partake actively in the performance (happenings) or to affect it emotionally (Antonin Artaud) or rationally (Bertolt Brecht). The hierarchical director's theater was replaced by an ideologically homogeneous group theater, most convincingly at the Gothenburg City Theater (Kent Andersson, Lennart Hjulström). At the Odin Theater in Holstebro, Denmark, Jerzy Marïan Grotowski's ideas were put into practice by Eugenio Barba.

The vitality characterizing Scandinavian theater in the politically tinted 1960s and early 1970s has been followed by a period marked by very varied forms of production and repertoire but rather lacking in truly remarkable performances. Many talented directors and actors have died, some have gone abroad, and the independent theater groups have lost some of their original enthusiasm, whether because of a changed political-cultural climate, a failing audience (cf. the rapid expansion of the video industry), reduced subsidies, or for some other reason, future theater historians will have to make out. However, an internationally renowned playwright like Lars Norén, a new generation of directors, including Klaus Hoffmeyer, Kjetil Bang-Hansen, Ralf Långbacka, and Peter Oskarsson, and a number of talented scenographers, actors, and actresses indicate that the Scandinavian Thalis is "a large, well-developed, gorgeous female figure with generous contours" (Ingmar Bergman), who will continue to play a central role in Scandinavian culture.

REFERENCES

Anker, Øyvind, *Scenekunsten i Norge fra fortid til nutid* (Oslo, 1968); Ansteinsson, Eli, *Teater i Norge. Dansk scenkunst 1813–1863* (Oslo, 1968); Arpe, Verner, *Das schwedische Theater* (Stockholm, 1969); Beijer, Agne, *Dramatik och teater* (Lund, 1966); Bergman, Gösta M., *Den moderna teaterns genombrott 1890–1925* (Stockholm, 1966); Bergman, Gösta M., et al., *Svensk teater. Strukturförändringar och organisation* 1900–1970 (Stockholm, 1970); Bjurström, Per, *Teaterdekoration i Sverige* (Stockholm, 1964); Brandes, Edvard, *Dansk Skuespilkunst* (Copenhagen, 1880); Einarsson, Sveinn, *The Reykjavík Theatre Company* (Reykjavík, 1972); Engel, P. G., and Leif Janzon, *Sju decennier. Svensk teater under 1900-talet* (Stockholm, 1974); Fjeldstad, Anton, et al., *Gruppeteater i Norden* (Copenhagen, 1981); Flakes, Susan, "The Norwegian Theater: A Theater in Debate." *Scandinavian Review* 72.3 (1984); Fridell, Lena, ed., *Children's Theater in Sweden* (Stockholm, 1979); Friðþjólfsdóttir, Aðalheiður, et al., *Theatre in Iceland 1971–75* (Reykjavík, 1982); Frisvold, Øivind, *Teatret i norsk kulturpolitikk* (Oslo, 1980); Gran, Ulf, and Ulla-Britta Lagerroth, eds., *Perspektiv på teater* (Stockholm, 1971); Hallingberg, Gunnar, *Radiodramat. Svensk hörspelsdiktningem bakgrund, utveckling och formvärld* (Stockholm, 1967); Heiberg, Gunnar, *Norsk teater* (Kristiania, 1920); Heikkilä, Ritva, ed., *Suomen Kansallisteatteri. The Finnish National Theatre* (Porvoo, 1962); Hilleström, Gustaf, *Drottningholmsteatern förr och nu* (with English text) (Stockholm, 1980); Holmarsson, Sverrir, ed., *Theatre in Iceland 1975–80* (Reykjavík, 1982); Holm-Hansen, H., et al., *Skuespil, opera og ballet i Danmark* (Copenhagen, 1970); Hoogland, Claes, and Gösta Kjellin, eds., *Bilder ur svensk teaterhistoria* (Stockholm, 1970); Jensen, Stig Jarl, et al., eds., *Dansk teater i 60-erne og 70-erne* (Copenhagen, 1983); Just, Carl, *Litteratur om norsk teater. Bibliografi* (Oslo, 1953); Krogh, Torben, *Studier over de sceniske Opførelser af Holbergs Komedier* (Copenhagen, 1929); Kvam, Kela, et al., eds., *Holberg på scenen* (Copenhagen, 1984); Marker, Frederick J., and Lise-Lone Marker, *The Scandinavian Theatre* (Oxford, 1975); Marker, Lise-Lone, and Frederick J. Marker, *Ingmar Bergman: Four Decades in the Theater* (Cambridge, 1982); Rønneberg, Anton, *Nationaltheatret 1949–1974* (Oslo, 1984); Sauter, Willmar, et al., *Teaterögon. Publiken möter föreställningen* (Stockholm, 1986); Savutie, Maija, "Die spezifischen Charakterzüge des finnischen Theaters." *Ausblick* 33.1–2 (1983); Savutie, Maija, *Finnish Theatre* (Helsinki, 1980); Sjögren, Henrik, *Stage and Society in Sweden* (Stockholm, 1979); *Theater in the Five Scandinavian Countries* (Stockholm, 1971); Tiusanen, Timo, *Teatterimme hahmottuu* (Helsinki, 1969); Törnqvist, Egil, and Arthur Sonnen, eds., *Niet alleen Strindberg, Sweden op de planken / Not Only Strindberg. Sweden on Stage* (Amsterdam, 1985); Veltheim, Katri, and Ilona Tainio, eds., *Finnish Theatre Today* (Helsinki, 1971); Wirmark, Margareta, *Nuteater. Dokument från och analys av 70-talets gruppteater* (Stockholm, 1976); Wrede, Johan, et al., eds., *20th Century Drama in Scandinavia* (Helsinki, 1979).

Egil Törnqvist

Thomsen, Grímur (Þorgrímsson). Icelandic poet and literary historian, b. 6 May 1820, Bessastaðir, d. 27 November 1896, Bessastaðir.

Thomsen's legacy to the history of modern Iceland is divided between his numerous contributions to lyrical poetry and his lifelong service to politics.

He entered the university in Copenhagen as a student of law in 1837, but soon devoted himself to philosophy and literature and obtained a doctoral degree for his thesis on the English poet Lord Byron. During his early years, he published several Icelandic poems and essays on French and Scandinavian literature in scattered periodicals, but in 1848 he interrupted his literary career and entered the Danish foreign service. In 1867 he retired to Iceland to become a gentleman farmer and an active member of the Icelandic parliament.

Although the quantity of Thomsen's lyrical writing was limited, his poetry in general represents the most cosmopolitan repertoire of themes and sources in nineteenth-century Iceland. His poems and translations draw on themes and motifs from Icelandic, Greek, and Roman antiquity as well as from every major contemporary European literature. Like many of his contemporaries, he sought to revitalize medieval Icelandic literature with modernized and dramatic versions of heroic figures from the sagas and folklore.

His most outstanding creations are his ballads and romances, which in form, thematic structure, and imagery resemble Icelandic folk ballads. In his early works, Thomsen made frequent use of romantic motifs from Continental balladry, but the most characteristic element of his style is his dramatic use of ancient phrases and metaphors to intensify the emotional impact of the narrative and to create associate moods.

During the later and quantitatively most productive years of his life, Thomsen turned more to the writing of occasional poetry, political satire, and the translation of ancient Greek verse.

In spite of occasional technical flaws in his work, Thomsen maintains his place in Icelandic literary history as a poet who was able to cultivate and disseminate world literature and at the same time revitalize native medieval verse and folk poetry.

FURTHER WORKS

Ljóðmæli (1880); *Ljóðmæli* (1895); *Rímur af Búa Andríðssyni og Fríði Dofradóttur* (1906); *Ljóðmæli*, 2 vols. (1934); *Úrvalsljóð* (1941); *Gull úr ljóðum Gríms Thomsens* (1957); *Ljóðmæli* (1969).

TRANSLATIONS

Icelandic lyrics, ed. Richard Beck (1930).

REFERENCES

Björnsson, Andrés, "Frá Grími Thomsen og Norðmönnum," in *Minjar og menntir: Afmælisrit helgað Kristjáni Eldjárn* (Reykjavík, 1976); Björnsson, Andrés, "Skáldið á Bessastöðum, dr. Grímur Thomsen," in *Lesbók Morgunblaðsins* (1954); Nordal, Sigurður, "Grímur Thomsen," in his *Áfangar*, vol. 2 (Reykjavík, 1944).

W. M. Senner

Thor Vilhjálmsson. *See* Vilhjálmsson, Thor.

Thorarensen, Bjarni (Vigfússon). Icelandic poet, b. 30 December 1787, Brautarholt, d. 24 August 1841, Möðruvellir.

Born of a wealthy and prominent family, Thorarensen showed early promise by graduating in law in Copenhagen at age twenty-one. He returned to Iceland in 1811 to become a justice in the supreme court in Reykjavík, where he remained until 1833 when he was named governor of North and East Iceland. A powerful and devoted state official, Thorarensen struggled throughout his life with the conflicting desiderata of public service and writing poetry. As a man of stern ethics, he stoically accepted the severity of his personal fate and allowed himself little time for his muse.

Although Thorarensen published only a few poems in journals and produced just one volume of poetry, he gained very early recognition and popularity as a writer of patriotic songs that combined an adulation of Icelandic antiquity with invigorating enthusiasm and a sublime vision of man and nature. He drew on traditional forms and meters and breathed new life into medieval Eddic meters with an explosive and dynamic imagery that infuses traditional metaphors with a dialectic spirit of dramatic tension.

Thorarensen's most outstanding works are his love poems with their ethereal and spiritual sublimity and his funeral elegies. In his elegies, Thorarensen presents not just celebrities, but individuals at odds with society, misfits and outcasts who struggle to overcome the undermining forces of life by taking refuge in the transcendental world of the imagination.

Thorarensen's poetry represents the beginning of a new, nationalistic movement in the nineteenth century, and his personification of Iceland as a woman has become a permanent fixture in the heritage of Icelandic literature.

WORKS

Kvæði (1847); *Kvæði* (1884); *Úrvalsljóð* (1934); *Ljóðmæli*, 2 vols. (1935, crit. ed.); *Kvæði* (1954); *Gullregn úr ljóðum Bjarna Thorarensen* (1955).

TRANSLATIONS

Icelandic lyrics, ed. Richard Beck (1930).

REFERENCES

Beck, Richard, "Bjarni Thorarensen: Iceland's Pioneer Romanticist." *American-Scandinavian Review* 15.3 (1938); Bjarnason, Páll, *Ástakveðskapur Bjarna Thorarensens og Jónasar Hallgrímssonar*, Studia Islandica 28 (Reykjavík, 1946); Guðmundsson, Sigurður, "Læknakviður Bjarna Thorarensens," in *Samtíð og saga*, vol. 3 (Reykjavík, 1946); Guðmundsson, Sigurður, "Líðan og ljóðagèrð Bjarna Thorarensens á Móðruvöllum," in *Samtíð og saga*, vol. 3 (Reykjavík, 1946); Guðnason, Bjarni, "Bjarni Thorarensen og Montesquieu," in *Afmælisrit Jóns Helgasonar* (Reykjavík, 1969); Hauksson, Þorleifur, *Endurteknar myndir í kveðskap Bjarna Thorarensens*, Studia Islandica 27 (Reykjavík, 1968); Nordal, Sigurður, "Bjarni Thorarensen," in *Áfangar*, vol. 2 (Reykjavík, 1944).

W. M. Senner

Þórbergur Þórðarson. *See* Þórðarson, Þórbergur.

Thorén, Thomas. *See* Thorild, Thomas.

Þorgrímsson, Grímur Thomsen. *See* Thomsen, Grímur, Þorgrímsson.

Þórðarson, Agnar. Icelandic playwright and novelist, b. 11 September 1917, Reykjavík.

Þórðarson, a graduate in Icelandic literature from the University of Iceland, pursued his studies in France, England, and the United States. Since 1957 he has been a librarian at the Icelandic State Library.

He had a promising start as novelist with *Haninn galar tvisvar* (1949; The Rooster Crows Twice), a story about a young man in search of intellectual and political belief in modern Reykjavík. Then followed *Ef sverð þitt er stutt* (1953; *The Sword*, 1970), one of the major Reykjavík-novels of the fifties. The hero is a young man who, after his father's death, feels Hamlet-like that something is rotten, not only in his father's firm and his mother's house, but in the whole state of Iceland. But "conscience makes cowards of us all."

He turned to play writing the same year, and after some exercises for radio, he made his stage debut with *Þeir koma í haust* (1955; They Come in the Fall), a powerful vision set in fifteenth-century Greenland, when the Norse settlement came to a tragic end. The play was enthusiastically received, as Þórðarson was the first young author to turn to theater in twelve years. Icelandic drama was at a very low ebb, and new plays were a kind of sidestep by elderly lyric poets and novelists.

The following year came *Kjarnorka og kvenhylli* (1956; "Atoms and Madams," 1967), a satirical comedy of manners, which to this day has remained Þórðarson's most popular work and is often revived. He consequently wrote four full-length stage plays, another comedy, *Spretthlauparinn* (1959; The Runner), and three which we could call "drames des mæurs." His one-act play *Kona* (1978; The Woman), billed with an earlier radio play *Sandur* (1974; Sand), on the little stage of the National Theater, was a new peak in his career as a playwright; *Kona* was later filmed for television.

In the meantime Þórðarson had gained popularity as a prolific writer of radio plays, among which are three series in many episodes. One of these, *Hæstráðandi til sjós og lands* (King of Sea and Land), he later turned into a full-length play titled *Hundadagakónungurinn* (King of Three Days): its hero is the Danish seafarer Jörgen Jörgensen who went to Iceland on an English ship during the Napoleonic War and made himself king and reigned for a few weeks in the summer of 1809. Two other leading playwrights have also written about this strange revolution, Indriði Einarsson (1936) and Jónas Árnason (1970).

Another of the radio series, *Ekið fyrir stapann* (1960; Drive Around the Peninsula), Þórðarson later turned into a novel titled *Hjartað í borði* (1968; A Medal of Distinction, 1984), describing the mentality of those who lost their roots and sense of values during the war years of wealth and prosperity and have been living above standard ever since. The critics hailed this novel as one of his best. Þórðarson has also written short stories, television plays, a travel book from Russia, and most recently the novel *Komnir aftur* (1983; Returned), about the loves and lives in the shadow of volcanic eruption in the Westman Islands in 1973.

Þórðarson's style in his best prose is subtle and ingenious; as a playwright he is a good craftsman, without being an innovator. It could be said that the realistic well-made modern American play has been his main influence.

FURTHER WORKS

Förin til Brasilíu (1953); *Andri* (1955); *Tónsnillingurinn* (1955); *Víxlar med afföllum* (1958); *Goðorðamálið* (1959); *Sannleikur í gifsi* (1965); *Mangi grásleppa* (1969); *Baráttusætið* (1970); *Lausnargjaldið* (1973); *Ungur maður með skegg* (1977); *Jarðarberin* (1980); *Úlfaldinn* (1980); *Þyrnirós vaknar* (1981).

TRANSLATIONS

"Atoms and Madams," in *Fire and Ice,* ed. Einar Haugen (1967); *Iceland Review* (1984).

Sveinn Einarsson

Þórðarson, Þórbergur. Icelandic essayist, poet, biographer, and polemicist, b. 12 March 1889, Hali, East Skaftafells district, d. 12 November 1974, Reykjavík.

Born in a remote farming district, Þórðarson did not have much schooling in his childhood. He left for Reykjavík when still in his teens and worked as a cook on a fishing boat, a day laborer, and in various other jobs while trying to obtain an education. This he did partly in a private school, partly in the teachers college, and finally (1913–1918) as an irregular student at the University of Iceland. He later became a teacher in Reykjavík, but after the mid–1930s writing was his sole profession.

Þórðarson's first book was a slim volume of verse, *Hálfir skósólar* (1914; Half Soles), written under a pseudonym. Humor was its most prominent element. It revealed at once his great gifts as a parodist and his captivating ability to poke fun at himself, both of which remained salient features of his writings. But not taking himself too seriously did not mean that Þórðarson was not serious; he was. And if espousing such diverse concepts as communism and spiritualism, theosophy and scientific precision—in addition to yoga, Esperanto, and an unshakable belief in elves and ghosts—may seem contradictory to some, it did not to Þórðarson: his keen intellect would find perfectly logical arguments to support his superstitions.

The book that established Þórðarson as a writer of first rank was *Bréf til Láru* (1924; A Letter to Laura), a series of essays, autobiographical ruminations, anecdotes, and polemical and imaginative sketches in an epistolary form. Shocking to some because of its radical views, liberating to others because of its freshness of style and irreverent humor, the book was arguably more influential in Icelandic literary circles than any other until that time. There is no doubt, for instance, about its impact on Halldór Laxness.*

Þórðarson later wrote many autobiographical and biographical works. Central in the former category are *Íslenzkur aðall* (1938; Icelandic Aristocracy; partial tr. *In Search of My Beloved*, 1967) and *Ofvitinn*, 2 vols. (1940–1941; The Alltoo-Wise), in which the author honed his talent for self-mockery to perfection. When Þórðarson subsequently teamed up with the Reverend Árni Þórarinsson, an old country pastor of considerable puckish wit, to write his biography, the wags termed it a collaboration of the greatest liar and the most gullible writer in the country. The outcome was an extraordinary six-volume work (1945–1950) that wove lore and legend, superstition, tall tales, folkways, and humor into a superbly colorful tapestry.

Þórðarson's remaining years were mostly occupied with other memoirs, both his own and others'; his last book was published posthumously. Two volumes of his letters and a book of diaries and early essays have also been printed since his death. Þórðarson's writings are unique in Icelandic literature, and his place beside Gunnar Gunnarsson* and Halldór Laxness as one of the country's three foremost modern prose writers is beyond question. Some consider him the most accomplished of the three.

FURTHER WORKS

Spaks manns spjarir (1915); *Hvítir hrafnar* (1922); *Leiðarvísir um orðasöfnun* (1922); *Heimspeki eymdarinnar* (1927); *Alþjóðamál og málleysur* (1933); *Pistilinn skrifaði . . .* (1933); *Rauða hættan* (1935); *Esperanto*, I-II, IV (1937–1939); *Refskák auðvaldsins* (1940); *Edda Þórbergs Þórðarsonar* (1941); *Indriði miðill* (1942); *Viðfjarðarundrin* (1943); *Fagurt mannlíf* (1945); *Í sálarháska* (1946); *Hjá vondu fólki* (1947); *Á Snæfellsnesi* (1948); *Með eilífðarverum* (1949); *Að æfilokum* (1950); *Sálmurinn um blómið*, 2 vols. (1954–1955); *Steinarnir tala* (1956); *Um lönd og lýði* (1957); *Rökkuróperan* (1958); *Ritgerðir 1924–1959*, 2 vols. (1960); *Í Unuhúsi* (1962); *Marsinn til Kreml* (1962); *Fagurt er í Eyjum* (1967); *Fagur fiskur í sjó* (1968); *Fagurt galaði fuglinn sá* (1971); *Frásagnir* (1972); *Fjórða bók* (1975); *Bréfin hans Þórbergs til Lillu Heggu og Biddu systur* (1982); *Bréf til Sólu* (1983); *Ljóri sálar minnar*, ed. Helgi M. Sigurðsson (1986); *Mitt rómantiska æði*, ed. Helgi M. Sigurðsson (1987).

TRANSLATIONS

20th Century Scandinavian Poetry, ed. Martin S. Allwood (1950); *An Anthology of Scandinavian Literature*, ed. Hallberg Hallmundsson (1966).

REFERENCES

Einarsson, Stefán, *Þórbergur Þórðarson fimmtugur* (Reykjavík, 1939); Johannessen, Matthías, *Í kompaní við allífið* (Reykjavík, 1959); Karlsson, Kristján, Introduction to Þórbergur Þórðarson's *In Search of My Beloved* (New York, 1967).

                                                                                    Hallberg Hallmundsson

Thorén, Thomas. *See* Thorild, Thomas.

Thorild, Thomas. Swedish poet, essayist, and critic, b. 18 April 1759, Svarteborg, Bohuslän, d. 10 October 1808, Greifswald. Until 1785 he called himself Thorén, and then took the name "Thor's Fire" = Thorild.

Thorild's father was a country bailiff in Bohuslän, and Thorild was, as so many other poor, bright boys, educated through the help of patrons. He studied at Lund and Uppsala, and ended his life in exile as professor and librarian at Greifswald (which was at the time a Swedish possession).

Thorild brought into Swedish poetry and debate the Sturm und Drang of the young Goethe. He also introduced and championed Ossian, Shakespeare, Milton, and Friedrich Gottlieb Klopstock. In Greifswald he fought on the side of Johann Gottfried von Herder against the German idealistic philosophy.

In the Swedish world of letters he was the rabble-rouser, the agitator, the representative of the crude people attacking the old order. He supported the French Revolution with great enthusiasm. By many he was thought to be insane. In 1792 he was arrested for political agitation, and exiled for four years. The trial became well known across intellectual and political Europe, and Thorild was hailed as a martyr to the cause of Liberty. His writings have survived with less grace than his personality. Parts of his *En critik övfer critiker* (1791–1792; Criticism of Critics) and *Rätt eller alla samhällens eviga lag* (1794; Justice or the Eternal Law of All Societies), in which he advocates a democratic government, are readable. Two of his works were published in English, "The Sermon of Sermons" (1789) and "True Heavenly Religion" (1790), but caused only ridicule.

Thorild's main importance lies not in his writings, although he shows the way to greater personal freedom in style and content, but in his personality and the scandals and debates he caused within the rather staid Swedish world of letters.

He introduced the idea of "The People" as a suitable topic of literature, and his influence has been felt by Erik Gustaf Geijer* and Johan Ludvig Runeberg* in particular.

FURTHER WORKS

Samlade skrifter, ed. E. G. Geijer (1819–1835) and ed. P. Hanselli (1874); *Samlade skrifter,* ed. Stellan Arvidson (1932–1968); *Brev,* ed. Lauritz Weibull, vols. 1–3 (1899) and ed. Anders Karitz, vol. 4 (1942); *Brev till C. F. Cramer,* ed. Martin Lamm (1907).

REFERENCES

Cassirer, Ernst von, *Thorilds Stellung in der Geistesgeschichte des achtzehnten Jahrhunderts* (Stockholm, 1941); Lamm, M., *Upplysningstidens romantik* (Stockholm, 1918–1920).

Christina Söderhjelm McKnight

Þorsteinn Erlingsson. *See* Erlingsson, Þorsteinn.

Þorsteinn frá Hamri (pseud. of Þorsteinn Jónsson). Icelandic poet and novelist, b. 5 March 1938, Borgarfjörður, West Iceland.

Upon giving up his studies at the Teacher Training College of Iceland, Þorsteinn published his first book of poems at twenty and very soon became the leading poet of his generation. Thematically, Þorsteinn's poetry is deeply rooted in old traditions, but he has gradually evolved a highly personal style, combining modern sensibilities with a rather traditional diction and imagery. Many of his poems express an inner struggle, contrasting his original rural and new urban milieus. He is introspective, his tone questioning, slightly ambiguous, characterized by doubt and circumspection, imbued with quiet irony and satirical, sometimes scathing, comment on the modern predicament. Few modern poets have been so successful in extracting from old Icelandic lore new and significant meaning and message.

In his three novels Þorsteinn has used a similar technique with even more startling results, weaving together ancient heroic tales, folklore, and the very latest gossip or headline stuff, making an exotic, but always meaningful and up-to-date tapestry out of the very dissimilar strands. In this endeavor his very considerable linguistic gifts stand him in good stead: his prose is somehow elevated and made significantly translucent in all its meanderings and apparent incongruities.

Þorsteinn has been of great importance to modern Icelandic letters, not only as a low-voiced but insistent soothsayer and jealous guardian of the nation's most delicate and precious treasures, but also as a model and yardstick for the proper use of an ancient and fragile language trying against heavy odds to survive and renew itself in an eroding international context.

WORKS

Í svörtum kufli (1958); *Tannfé handa nýjum heimi* (1960); *Lifandi manna land* (1962); *Skuldaskil* (1963); *Lagnætti á Kaldadal* (1964); *Jórvík* (1967); *Himinbjargarsaga eða Skórgardraumur* (1969); *Veðrahjálmur* (1972); *Möttull konúngur eða Caterpillar* (1974); *Fiðrið úr sæng Danadrottningar* (1977); *Haust í Skírisskógi* (1980); *Spjótalög á spegil* (1982); *Ljóðasafn* (1984); *Ný ljóð* (1985).

TRANSLATIONS

Modern Poetry in Translation 30 (1977); *Icelandic Writing Today*, ed. Sigurður A. Magnússon (1982); *Modern Scandinavian Poetry*, ed. Martin S. Allwood (1982); *The Postwar Poetry of Iceland*, trans. and ed. Sigurður A. Magnússon (1982).

REFERENCES

Magnússon, Sigurður A., *Northern Sphinx* (London, 1977); Magnússon, Sigurður A., "Postwar Literature in Iceland." *World Literature Today* 56.1 (1982).

                                                                        Sigurður A. Magnússon

Þorsteinn Jónsson. *See* Þorsteinn frá Hamri.

Þorsteinsson, Indriði G. Icelandic novelist, poet, and biographer, b. 18 April 1926, Gilshagi, Skagafjörður district.

A farmer's son, Þorsteinsson attended primary school in his home district and secondary school at Laugarvatn, graduating in 1943. He subsequently worked at various jobs—salesman, road gang laborer, truck and taxi driver—all of which he has drawn on for his fiction. Later, he became a journalist and was, at different times, editor of two Reykjavík dailies. He has traveled widely in Europe, the Soviet Union, China, and America—a fact reflected especially in his poetry. Since 1974, he has made writing his sole profession.

Þorsteinsson burst upon the literary scene in 1951 with a sensuous and—by the standard of that time—sensational short story that won first prize in a contest. His first book of short fiction, published later that year, revealed an already accomplished writer, who had evidently learned a good deal from American contemporary authors. Thus, he had looked to Ernest Hemingway to make his prose lean and sparse and to Erskine Caldwell for his earthy touch of ordinary people and the smell of the soil. But the soil out of which his characters grew was unmistakably Icelandic, for the hallmark of his writing has always been the intimate knowledge of the land and the people who work it. His unerring sense of time and place has resulted in an atmosphere in his stories that is almost palpable in its authenticity.

Þorsteinsson has, so far, published three other collections of short stories, but his main work is a series of novels depicting Icelandic society in flux before, during, and after World War II. Three of these novels were reissued in 1978 under the common title *Tímar í lífi þjóðar* (Times in the Life of a Nation).

As the years have passed, Þorsteinsson's style has grown away from his American models and, while retaining its lean, unsentimental quality, has become more mellow, lyrical, and infused with humor. At the same time, Þorsteinsson has increasingly championed the freedoms of the individual and his role as a master of his own destiny, even in the face of violence and death.

FURTHER WORKS

Sæluvika (1951); *Sjötíu og níu af stöðinni* (1955; *Seventy-nine from the Station*, 1960); *Þeir sem guðirnir elska* (1957); *Land og synir* (1963); *Mannþing* (1965); *Þjófur í Paradís* (1967); *Norðan við stríð* (1971; *North of War*, 1981); *Dagbók um veginn* (1973); *Áfram veginn* (1975); *Samtöl við Jónas* (1977); *Unglingsvetur* (1979); *Útlaginn* (1981); *Fimmtán gírar áfram* (1981); *Finnur Jónsson*, with Frank Ponzi (1983); *Vafurlogar* (1984); *Jóhannes Sveinsson Kjarval*, 2 vols. (1985); *Átján sögur úr álfheimum* (1986); *Þjóðhátíðin 1974* (1986).

FURTHER TRANSLATIONS

Icelandic Review 4.4 (1966); *Vagabond* 1.3 (1966); *American-Scandinavian Review* 57.1 (1969); *Short Stories of Today by Twelve Modern Icelandic Authors*, trans. Alan Boucher (1972); *Icelandic Short Stories*, ed. E. S. Firchow (1974); *Icelandic Writing Today*, ed. Sigurður A. Magnússon (1982).

REFERENCES

Hallmundsson, May, and Hallberg Hallmundsson, ''Introducing the Author,'' in Indriði G. Þorsteinsson, *North of War* (Reykjavík, 1981).

Hallberg Hallmundsson

Thorsteinsson, Steingrímur. Icelandic poet, translator, and educator, b. 19 May 1831, Arnarstapi, Snæfellsnes, d. 21 August 1913, Reykjavík.

The son of a governor and a daughter of one of Iceland's most renowned and literary bishops, Thorsteinsson was exposed to educational opportunities that gave immutable direction to his career. After his studies at the Latin school in Reykjavík, Thorsteinsson enrolled in the university in Copenhagen, first to study law, but ultimately to devote himself to classical philology and modern languages. Following postgraduate research in Norse antiquities and participation in the national emancipation movement, Thorsteinsson returned to Iceland to become a lecturer and, later, the rector of the Latin school he had graduated from.

Thorsteinsson's early poetry bears the unmistakable signs of the rejuvenating patriotism that captured the imagination of his contemporaries during the middle decades of the nineteenth century. Unlike predecessors such as Bjarni Thorarensen* and Jónas Hallgrímsson,* however, Thorsteinsson did not adulate Iceland's heroic past but advocated the virtues of undaunted determination, industry, and an idealistic vision of the future as the panacea for oppression and bondage.

In Thorsteinsson's later years the theme of staunch patriotism yielded to a lasting preoccupation with concepts of love and idealized nature and the struggle between the transcendental and the corrupting influence of civilization. For Thorsteinsson nature was the source of innocence and beauty, the teleological revelation of transcendental being, and in his poetry he sought to awaken in his readers a love for his own image of Icelandic nature with its gentle sun, white sheep in green meadows, waterfalls roaring down gorges, and bright glaciers silhouetted against a peaceful blue sea.

Thorsteinsson was profoundly aware that he lacked the lyrical finesse and free-flowing spontaneity he admired in the many foreign literatures he studied. In his view, good poetry was the product of arduous craftsmanship and deliberative editing, skills he utilized well as one of Iceland's foremost translators. To gain a complete understanding of Thorsteinsson's muse, it is necessary to consider his immense contributions to Icelandic literary culture as a translator of works from over fifteen literatures, modern and ancient.

Although increasingly at odds with the aesthetic views of younger generations of poets, Thorsteinsson's philosophically oriented lyricism and his role as a mediator of cultural values assures him a durable place in the evolution of modern Icelandic literature.

WORKS

Svava (1860); *Gilsbakkaljóð* (1877); *Ljóðmæli* (1881); *Úrvalskvæði* (1914); *Úrvalsljóð* (1939); *Ljóðmæli*, 5th ed. (1958); *Gullregn úr ljóðum Steingríms Thorsteinssonar* (1962); *Ljóðmæli* (1973).

TRANSLATIONS

Icelandic lyrics, ed. Richard Beck (1930).

REFERENCES

Beck, Richard, "Steingrímur Thorsteinsson—Lyric Poet and Master Translator." *Scandinavian Studies* 20.2 (1948); Blöndal, Sigfús, "Steingrímur Thorsteinsson. 1831–1931." *Nordisk Tidskrift* 7 (1931); Guðmundsson, Sigurður, "Steingrímur Thorsteinsson," in *Heiðnar hugvekjur og mannaminni* (Akureyri, 1946); Laxness, Halldór, *Skáld tveggja svana: upphaf mannúðarstefnu* (Reykjavík, 1965); Pétursson, Hannes, *Steingrímur Thorsteinsson: líf hans og list* (Reykjavík, 1964); Poestion, J. C., *Steingrímur Thorsteinsson, ein isländischer Dichter und Kulturbringer* (München, 1912).

W. M. Senner

Thorup, Kirsten. Danish poet, novelist, and television playwright, b. 9 February 1942, Gelsted.

Thorup comes from a provincial petty-bourgeois milieu; her father was a bookseller and owned a kiosk. She was the only member of her family to go to gymnasium but felt an outsider in her new academic surroundings, at the same time becoming estranged from her old, nonliterary background. Her own early poetry naturally focused on the theme of alienation, lack of identity, and difficulty of communication.

Thorup's poetic debut in 1967 was already technically sophisticated with her aesthetic approach, her particular cutting technique—also used in some of her many television plays—and cool distance from the subject. Thorup's modernist interest also led her to French absurdism as well as to modern psychology (R. D. Laing) as reflected in *Love from Trieste* (1969; *Love from Trieste*, 1980).

Although widely read herself, Thorup's fiction almost exclusively embraces the nonliterary world as in her novel *Baby* (1973; *Baby*, 1980), which describes the lower-class urban milieu. The characters in *Baby* are without many resources in all senses of the word, and their "stripped" existence manifests itself through the dominating physical aspect of life as well as in an "attitudinal relativism" underscored technically by the frequent use of the coordinating "and."

After the portrayal of the jungle life in the city, Thorup returned to the simple provincial milieu of her own childhood Funen with the Jonna books. Her novel, *Himmel og helvede* (1982; Heaven and Hell), is a broad social and psychological epic involving many characters and fates. Again the focus is on the outsiders of the social mainstream who seem to differ from the more staid bourgeoisie in their greater mobility. The implicit dream of a better society lies with these more open, less conforming people. The descriptions are realistic and full of vivid details, but the plot is also constructed to allow the unlikely incident: it is an epic of possibilities.

Although Thorup is already a renowned author with a distinct physiognomy on the Danish literary scene, she—like her fictional outsiders—is open for new impulses; her literary image is still in its promising development.

FURTHER WORKS

Indeni—udenfor (1967); *I dagens anledning* (1968); *Idag er det Daisy* (1971); *Lille Jonna* (1977); *Den lange sommer* (1979); *Romantica* (1983); *Den yderste grænse* (1987).

REFERENCES

Brostrøm, Torben, "It's Thorup Today," in *Out of Denmark,* ed. Bodil Wamberg (Copenhagen, 1985); Hardwick, Elizabeth, "Thoughts about Kirsten Thorup's *Baby*." *Denmarkings* (1982).

Charlotte Schiander Gray

Tietäväinen, Algot. *See* Lassila, Maiju.

Tietäväinen-Untola, Algot. *See* Lassila, Maiju.

Tikkanen, Henrik. Finland-Swedish poet, novelist, and artist, b. 9 September 1924, Helsinki, d. 19 May 1984, Helsinki.

Tikkanen was of the upper middle class by birth. His father was an architect and was of a family of considerable prestige. In 1963 Tikkanen married Märta Tikkanen,* who is also a Finland-Swedish author of note. Tikkanen worked as an artist and columnist for *Hufvudstadsbladet*, the leading Swedish-language newspaper in Finland, from 1947 to 1967; from 1967 until his death he served as artistic director for *Helsingin Sanomat*, Finland's largest newspaper. He held several art exhibits after 1967 and received the state prize in literature in 1975.

Tikkanen was an unusually versatile genius, witty in aphoristic formulation, incredibly prolific, restlessly energetic, yet sensitive and subtle. His intellectual curiosity, his skepticism in general, and his all-encompassing humanism and universal peace concerns make Tikkanen a significant voice in Finnish literature and Finnish society. Ironically enough, he got his literary breakthrough with his forty-eighth book. Following a series of causeries, travelogues, collections of drawings, and some unpublished plays for television and radio, Tikkanen published the novel *Brändövägen 8 Brändö Tel. 35* (1975; *A Winter's Day*, 1980), the first of what would become an autobiographical "address trilogy." The other two volumes were *Bävervägen II Hertonäs Tel. 78035* (1976; *Snob's Island*, 1980) and *Mariegatan 26 Kronohagen* (1977; 26 Mary Street, Kronohagen). These satirical revelations, labeled scandal chronicles by many, raised havoc in Finland-Swedish cultural circles. Tikkanen describes the degeneration and inevitable demise of an anachronistic family, his own. The instruments of this defeat are alcohol and money. From the devastations of the war on the human spirit to the relentless revelations of his alcoholism, his possessiveness in marriage and insatiable sex drive, Tikkanen treats his life's experiences with merciless search for truth.

Tikkanen repeatedly returned to the theme of pacifism and the absurdity of war. Particularly the two novels *30-åriga kriget* (1977; *The 30 Years' War*, 1987) and *Efter hjältedöden* (1979; After the Death of the Hero) combine witty humor with sincere concerns for human values and peace.

Tikkanen will be remembered in Finnish literature as a philosophical, witty master of aphoristic writing. His satire, his scorn and aggression, will be seen as serving his larger purpose, peace and humanism. He will, I am sure, be reassessed, from a writer of scandalous irresponsibility to one of serious humanity.

FURTHER WORKS

Mr. Gogo kommer till Europa (1946); *Satu pojasta, joka sai itse valita onnensa* (1951); *Kär i Stockholm* (1955) *Bilbiten* (1956); *Brinnande ord* (1957); *Ett sommarbarn* (1957); *Paddys land* (1957); *Portföljen* (1957); *Bedragen* (1958); *De fega* (1958); *Missat möte* (1959); *Över fjärden är himlen hög* (1959); *Texas* (1960); *Till sista droppen* (1960); *Hjältarna är döda* (1961); *Med bil och barn i Jugoslavien* (1961); *Murhakopla* (1961); *Bröllopsdagen* (1962); *Henrik tiger inte* (1962); *På väg* (1962); *Buren* (1963); *Den stora skandalen* (1963); *Jääkaappivarkaat* (1963); *Murha kantapöydässä* (1963); *Tähtiryöstö* (1963); *Viheliäinen vapaus* (1963); *Kring ett frånfälle* (1964); *Kansikuvapoika* (1965); *Gapa snällt* (1965); *Ödlorna* (1965); *Försnillaren* (1967); *Jag Borrman* (1967); *Koulukaverit* (1967); *På jakt efter etrusker* (1967); *Fyllhunden* (1968); *Min älskade skärgård*

(1968); *Vanhojen ystävä* (1968); *Vapenvägraren* (1968); *I Sovjet* (1969); *Klovni* (1969); *På botten av tingen* (1969); *Häng med om du kan, älskade* (1970); *Tankstrejk* (1970); *Mitt Helsingfors* (1972); *Dödens Venedig* (1973); *Unohdettu sotilas* (1974); *Ihmisen ääni* (1978); *Georgsgatan* (1980); *Henriksgatan* (1982); *Renault, mon amour* (1983).

REFERENCES

Envall, Markku, "Henrik Tikkanen: Master of Satire." *Books from Finland* 15.1 (1981)

Börje Vähämäki

Tikkanen, Märta. Finland-Swedish novelist, playwright, and poet, b. 3 April 1935, Helsinki.

Tikkanen's first two novels *nu i morron* (1970; Now Tomorrow) and *Ingenmansland* (1972; No Man's Land) are contributions to the debate on the role conflicts of woman, her revolt and liberation, responsibility and solidarity. In 1975 she published the novel *Män kan inte våldtas* (*Man Rape*, 1980) which deals with a woman's reaction after having been raped. Fighting her sense of humiliation and degradation, the woman finds strength in herself to go out and find the rapist and get her revenge. The same topic is discussed in the play *Våldsam kärlek* (1979; Violent Love).

Tikkanen's most famous book so far is, however, her collection of poems called *Århundradets kärlekssaga* (1978; *The Love Story of the Century*, 1984). For this book she was chosen to receive the alternative Nordic prize for literature, established by women writers in Scandinavia. The title is ironic, since the "love story" is about the hell in which the wife and children of an alcoholic husband and father are living day and night. It is a marriage where the husband is dependent on the wife, especially during his drinking bouts; it is the story of a love-hate relationship that neither of the two people involved has the strength or wish to dissolve. Some of these poems have successfully been performed on the stage.

Mörkret som ger glädjen djup (1981; Darkness That Gives Depth to Joy) is a collection of poems in two parts: the first is about Ulrika Sofia Wecksell, who lived 1811–1879 in Finland and was the mother of Josef Julius Wecksell,* author of the play *Daniel Hjort* and mentally ill since an early age. The second part deals with the same problem of a contemporary mother and her relationship to her mentally disturbed son. Although the subject matter is touchingly dealt with in this poetical description of the two mothers, it does not reach the same height as a work of art as *Århundradets kärlekssaga*.

FURTHER WORKS

Sofias egen bok (1984); *Rödluvan* (1986); *Önskans träd* (1987).

FURTHER TRANSLATIONS

The International Portland Review, ed. Cindy Ragland (1980); *Scandinavian Review* 68.4 (1980); *Swedish Books* 2/4 (1980).

REFERENCES

Hird, Gladys, "Märta Tikkanen: Confessions in Verse." *Swedish Books* 2/4 (1980).
                                                                        Ingrid Claréus

Tómas Guðmundsson. *See* Guðmundsson, Tómas.

Topelius, Zacharias (Zachris). Finland-Swedish poet, novelist, journalist,
and dramatist, b. 14 January 1818, Nykarleby (Uusikaarlepyy), d. 12 March
1898, Björkudden.

Topelius came from a cultured home in Ostrobothnia; his father, Zacharias
Topelius the elder (1781–1831), a physician who had received an unusually
extensive training, was a collector of Finnish folk songs, acknowledged by Elias
Lönnrot (1802–1884), the compiler of the *Kalevala** and *Kanteletar*, as the most
important of his predecessors. Topelius was sent to school in Uleåborg (Oulu)
and then, after his father's long illness and death, to Helsinki, where he boarded
for a time at the home of Johan Ludvig Runeberg,* a fellow Ostrobothnian. His
studies at the University of Helsinki appear not to have been carried on ener-
getically; an omnivorous reader, Topelius could not concentrate upon a single
field of learning, and he was also fascinated by the world around him—his diaries
(1832–1840) give a fascinating picture of Helsinki life. (He received his master's
in 1840 and his doctorate in 1847.) The breadth of his interests made him an
ideal editor for G. A. Wasenius's newspaper, *Helsingfors Tidningar*, a post he
held from 1841 to 1862 (the paper survived his resignation by only six years),
capturing the public by means of his causeries, the *Leopoldinerbrev* (1843–1854;
Leopoldine Letters), a feigned correspondence with a Finnish lieutenant on Russian service in the Caucasus, and, in fact, a witty report on events in Finland.
In the newspaper, he also began to publish the melodious poetry for which he
rapidly became known throughout Finland and Sweden; it was then issued in
pamphlets called *Ljungblommor* (1844, 1850, 1854; *Heather Blossoms*, 1902
[selection]), to be followed by the later collections, *Nya blad* (1870; New Leaves)
and *Ljung* (1889; Heather). His verse—often produced too facilely—appealed
to his contemporaries by its sentimental or even saccharine sides, in such poems
(quickly set to music) as "On Roine's Strand," "Karin Månsdotter's Cradle
Song," "Run, Swift Reindeer," and "Little Lasse"; contemporary readers will
be more interested by the numerous poems where Topelius comments trenchantly
on Finland or Europe, such as "The Break-up of the Ice in Oulu River" (about
the growth of Finnish national feeling) and "Communism's Cradle." (In both
the "Leopoldine Letters" and in later columns for the newspaper *Finland* [1885–
1892], Topelius showed an unusual awareness of social problems.)

Another of his major contributions to *Helsingfors Tidningar* lay in the historical
tales that appeared in the paper; the best known is surely *Fältskärns berättelser*
(1853–1867; *The Surgeon's Stories*, 1883–1884), the first part of which came

out in serial form in 1850. Like Runeberg in *Fänrik Stål*, Topelius chose a veteran of the Russian-Swedish War of 1808–1809 to tell his tales; but, while Stål speaks of events he has experienced, Topelius's narrator devotes himself to episodes from Finland's history during the seventeenth and eighteenth centuries. Of the five cycles, in whose pages Topelius repeatedly shows himself to be an attentive student of Sir Walter Scott, the earliest—dealing with the Thirty Years' War—is the liveliest, and most read today. Gustaf Adolf himself is the founder of the family whose fates are followed through the five cycles: the wealthy Finnish peasant Bertila sends his daughter to Stockholm for an education; there, she becomes the mother of Gustaf Adolf's love-child, who—grown up—is ennobled by the Swedish lion and given the sobriquet "Bertelskiöld." The tales also have a parallel family, the Larssons, whose interest concentrates less on military than on pacific and mercantile pursuits. Topelius's strength as a craftsman of historical fiction lies in re-creating the atmosphere of a time or place; his characterizations are frequently flat or sometimes simplistic, as in the case of the villainous Jesuit, Father Hieronymus, in the first cycle. The books, however, became enormously popular, and included among their admirers Selma Lagerlöf,* who (in 1920) published a melodramatic account of Topelius's childhood, youth, and early manhood.

Feverishly productive, Topelius also turned out many other pieces of narrative prose, working almost always with the novella or novella cycle. Sometimes, he used "modern" settings, as in the tales recalling the old Gustavians he had known in his first Helsinki years, *Gamla baron på Rautakylä* (1849; The Old Baron at Rautakylä), and then his own student days, *Vincent Vågbrytare* (1860; Vincent Breakwater); *Tant Mirabeau* (1863; Aunt Mirabeau) describes a trip with the new railroad from Helsinki to Hämeenlinna. Others were "historical," for example, *Hertiginnan av Finland* (1850; The Duchess of Finland), *Gröna kammarn i Linnais gård* (1859; The Green Chamber at Linnais Estate), *Kungens handske* (1863; The King's Gauntlet), and a belated prelude to the surgeon's tales, *Ungdomsdrömmar* (1879; Dreams of Youth). These tales and more were then included in the large collection *Winterkvällar* (1880–1897; Winter Evenings). From 1854 to 1878, Topelius served as professor of history at Helsinki, an appointment causing some wags to remember that he had once, in a lecture of 1843, attracted public attention by his negative answer to the question, "Do the Finnish People Have a History?" Retiring from the professorship, Topelius abandoned himself to historical tales with fresh devotion, and in the first part of the "novel" (in fact, another cycle) called *Planeternas skyddslingar* (1886–1889; The Planets' Protégés, then redubbed *Stjärnornas kungabarn*, The Royal Children of the Stars), he gave a memorable account of the turbulence in Finland at the close of the Civil War between supporters of King Sigismund and Duke Karl (later, Charles IX); here the central figure is the poet and polyhistor Sigfridus Aronus Forsius (1550–1642), inaccurately but winningly portrayed. Near the end of his life, Topelius returned to a project begun in the 1860s, *Ljungars saga* (1896; The Tale of Ljungars), a chronicle of the age of Arvid Kurck (1464–1522), the last of Finland's Catholic bishops.

An awareness that Finland needed a theatrical culture of its own led to Topelius's dramatizations of two of his tales; the first was *Efter femtio år* (1851; Fifty Years Later), taken from *Gamla baron på Rautakylä*. Its popularity encouraged Topelius to write *Regina von Emmeritz* (1853), based on a highly romantic episode in the first cycle of the field-surgeon's tales, about a German Catholic girl, almost persuaded by Father Hieronymus to assassinate Gustaf Adolf, in a reenactment of Judith's deed at Bethulia. Instead, Regina falls in love with the virile monarch. For the composer Fredrik Pacius (1809–1891), Topelius wrote the libretto of the opera *Kung Karls jakt* (1852; King Karl's Hunt), a story of a royal visit to Finland affording Pacius the opportunity to imitate the orchestral and vocal effects of Carl Maria von Weber's *Der Freischütz*; a second opera was *Prinsessan av Cypern* (1860; The Princess of Cyprus), in which Topelius made an attempt to wed Kalevala material with Greek antiquity. Thus Topelius holds an important position in the history of early Finnish theater and opera; he was also a perceptive drama critic, and a collection of his reviews appeared in 1917 as *Om teater i Finland* (Concerning Theater in Finland). Entertaining no illusions about his gifts as a playwright, Topelius abandoned his efforts for the stage once his pioneer work was done, referring to the 1850s with some irony as his "dramatic decade."

Even more swiftly than Runeberg, Topelius got a place in the consciousness of his nation's Finnish-speaking majority, and his avuncular image among Finland's elementary-school pupils was strengthened by his readers, *Naturens bok* (1859; The Book of Nature) and *Boken om vårt land* (1875; The Book about Our Country), a depiction of Finland's geography, ethnography, and history in short lessons, meant to appeal to—and to be remembered by—young minds. Of course, his name was already familiar to children both at home and in Sweden; in 1847, imitating H. C. Andersen,* he had published a little volume of *Sagor* (Fairy Tales); later, he collected these tales (most of which originally appeared in juvenile papers) as *Läsning för barn* (1865–1896; Stories for Children, 1907–1916). Topelius's tales are less ambivalent than Andersen's, and avoid the peculiarly erotic and blackly pessimistic notes to be detected in the Dane; Topelius's forte lies in a quiet humor, as in his story about the proud weathervane, and in an exuberant fantasy, seen in the tales with Oriental or Lappland settings. His emphasis upon kindness, honesty, modesty, and a truly democratic frame of mind may have had an effect upon generations of Finnish children; however, the stories sometimes betray a certain anti-intellectualism and, unhappily, contain flashes of anti-Semitism.

Topelius's role in Finland's literary history is not readily assessed; he was neither a careful thinker nor (save in his journalism) a brilliant stylist, his work does not have the tension lying beneath Runeberg's classic calm, and his incessant moralizing makes him seem the Finnish Victorian par excellence: he objected to the "filth" in August Strindberg's* first novel, *The Red Room*. Yet, because of the range of his concerns, his vivacity, and (save on "moral" issues) his genuine liberalism, he remains an attractive and refreshing figure in Finland's letters.

FURTHER WORKS

Samlade skrifter, 34 vols. (1899–1907, new ed. 1920–1927); *Evangelium för barn* (1893); *Blad ur min tankebok* (1898); *Dagböcker*, ed. Paul Nyberg, 4 vols. (1918–1922); *Självbiografiska anteckningar* (1922); *Fästmansbrev*, ed. Paul Nyberg (1948); *Konstnärsbrev*, ed. Paul Nyberg (1956–1960); *Anteckningar om det Helsingfors som gått* (1968); *120 dikter*, ed. Olof Enckell (1970).

FURTHER TRANSLATIONS

Poet Lore 28 (1917); *Swedo-Finnish Short Stories*, ed. G. C. Schoolfield (1974); *Books from Finland* 18.1 (1984).

REFERENCES

Granér, Martin, *Zachris Topelius' kärlekslyrik* (Helsinki, 1946); Laurent, Kaarina, *Topelius saturunoilijana* (Helsinki, 1947); Lunelund-Grönroos, Birgit, *Zachris Topelius' tryckta skrifter. Bibliografisk förteckning* (Helsinki, 1954); Nyberg, Paul, *Zachris Topelius: En biografisk skildring* (Helsinki, 1954); Schoolfield, G. C., "Fairy Tales of a Journalist." *Books from Finland* 18.1 (1984); Suhonen, Pekka, "The Pit of Star-Eye." *Books from Finland* 18 (1984); Vasenius, Valfrid, *Zachris Topelius: Hans lif och skaldegärning*, 6 vols. (Stockholm and Helsinki, 1912–1930).

George C. Schoolfield

Tornborg, Rita. Swedish novelist, b. 13 December 1930, South Africa.

Tornborg was born in South Africa and spent her adolescent years in Poland before settling in Sweden during World War II. This cultural and linguistic diversity in her background has no doubt influenced her work, both as to subject matter and style. Since her debut in 1970 with *Paukes gerilla,* she has published six novels and a short story and has gained increasing recognition as a writer. Tornborg's works, with their elements of mysticism and magic, revealing the author's joy at storytelling, in a unique prose style full of linguistic surprises, ironic turns of fate, and sensual descriptions of unknown worlds, have often been compared to those of Isaac Singer, and her uses of imagery have reminded reviewers of Marc Chagall paintings.

Tornborg's novels of the late 1970s are colorful tapestries, spanning several centuries and countries, as in *Friedmans hus* (1976; The House of Friedman), or depicting a multinational microcosmos in *Salomos namnsdag* (1979; Salomo's Nameday), Tornborg's widely praised novel about people living together in an old building in Stockholm in the 1970s. In her latest work, *Systrarna* (1982; The Sisters), leaner in style and more somber in mood and characterized as her most "Swedish" novel, she explores the secrets of childhood among four sisters growing up in Sweden in the thirties.

Tornborg's protagonists are often people who through the vagaries of fate find themselves as refugees in an alien country—contemporary Sweden: Jews, foreign workers, and, in her last novel, vestigial survivors of the bourgeois world of Sweden's yesteryear. In such environments the fabulous and the magical elements serve a definite purpose: to confront those irreparably stuck in a set pattern of living with a model for creative irrationality and to allow those who are living under unbearable circumstances the ability to transcend the limits of their everyday world.

Tornborg's novels are tragicomedies: a lady postal clerk dancing in the air before her startled inhibited Swedish lover in *Hansson and Goldman* (1974) is the comic counterpart to the novel's tragic theme.

Tornborg writes from a moral perspective. Her works are allegories about fundamental moral responsibility and basic human rights. She herself has characterized her writing as a "method of defending the three sources of human happiness, namely, freedom, pity, and laughter. Life without freedom is an inferno, love without pity is monstrous, and a world without laughter is a desert" (pamphlet, "Author Profile," Swedish Institute, Spring, 1983).

FURTHER WORKS

Docent Åke Ternvall ser en syn (1972); *Requiem för en liten flicka* (1979).

REFERENCES

"Docent Åke Ternvall ser en syn," a review by Ingrid Camerini, *Books Abroad* 47.3 (1973); "Hansson och Goldman," a review by Ingrid Camerini, *Books Abroad* 49.4 (1975); "Salomos namnsdag," a review by Anne S. Lundquist, *World Literature Today* 55.1 (1981); "Systrarna," a review by Ingrid Claréus, *World Literature Today* 57.3 (1983).

Rose-Marie G. Oster

Tranströmer, Tomas. Swedish poet, b. 15 April 1931, Stockholm.

Tranströmer grew up in a stimulating environment. His mother, a schoolteacher, encouraged his early interests in zoology, books, and music. An accomplished pianist, he has remained deeply involved with music. While still in high school, he became a member of a sophisticated literary coterie, and he published his first book of poems at twenty-three. It was received as a major literary event, and within a few years he had become one of the most influential poets of his generation. Since 1961 he has divided his time between his job as a practicing psychologist and his poetry. He is the only Swedish poet to have acquired a large following in the United States; his poems are widely translated and taught in creative writing courses.

While his early work combined surrealist boldness of metaphor with traditional forms—Sapphic and blank verse—his later poems are more personal, freer, some with long Whitmanesque lines and an artlessly plain diction. He has retained a certain affinity with the great modernists, especially T. S. Eliot, but his own style is both more precise and less monumental. His delight in and precise observation of nature places him in a Swedish tradition that reaches back to August Strindberg* and Carl von Linné.* Nature, time, history, memory, and experience are recurrent themes often expressed in images of archetypal resonance that seem to rise effortlessly from the unconscious. The world of his poetry is built, to a large extent, on or around epiphanies, momentary visions of a different temporal dimension. Often, as in a dream, the strange and the uncanny lie embedded in a deceptively plain surface. Unusual perspectives make the ordinary appear in a new light. Daring leaps of association draw the reader into the vortex of a mystery. The poet seems to position himself on the frontier between the known and the unknown where everyday reality, seen with photographic exactitude, becomes charged with meaning and larger metaphysical issues appear urgent and near at hand.

FURTHER WORKS

17 Dikter (1954); *Heligheter på vägen* (1958); *Den halvfärdiga himlen* (1962); *Klanger och spår* (1966); *Kvartett* (1967); *Mörkerseende* (1970; *Night Vision*, 1971); *Stigar* (1973); *Östersjöar* (1974; *Baltics*, 1975); *Sanningsbarriären* (1978; *Truthbarriers*, 1980); *Dikter 1954–1978* (1980); *Det vilda torget* (1983; *The Wild Marketplace*, 1985).

FURTHER TRANSLATIONS

Three Poems (1966); *New Directions* 19 (1966); *Twenty Poems* (1971); *Windows and Stones, Selected Poems* (1971); *Elegy, Some October Notes* (1973); *Friends, You Drank Some Darkness*, ed. Robert Bly (1973); *Selected Poems of Paavo Haavikko and Tomas Tranströmer* (1974); *Contemporary Swedish Poetry*, ed. Göran Printz-Påhlson and John Matthias (1980); *How the Late Autumn Night Novel Begins* (1980); *Selected Poems* (1981); *Collected Poems*, trans. Robin Fulton (1987).

REFERENCES

Espmark, Kjell, *Resans Formler: En studie i Tomas Tranströmers poesi* (Stockholm, 1983); Gustafsson, Lars, "Tomas Tranströmer," in *Forays into Swedish Poetry*, ed. Robert Rovinsky (Austin, 1978); *Ironwood* 13 (1979), a special Tranströmer issue; Julén, Björn, "Tomas Tranströmer: Hemligheter på vägen," in *Tjugo diktanalyser från Södergran till Tranströmer* (Stockholm, 1962); *Lyrikvännen* 5 (1981), a Tranströmer issue; Sellin, Eric, "Tomas Tranströmer, Trafficker in Miracles." *Books Abroad* 46.1 (1972); Vowles, Richard B., "Post-War Swedish Poetry: The Other Side of Anguish," *Western Humanities Review* 15 (1961); Wigforss, Brita, "Med händerna i Haydnfickor," in *Femtiotalet i backspegeln*, ed. K.-E. Lagerlöf (Stockholm, 1968).

Joanna Bankier

Trausti, Jón. *See* Magnússon, Guðmundur.

Trier Mørch, Dea. Danish novelist, essayist, and graphic artist, b. 9 December 1941, Copenhagen.

Trier Mørch grew up in central Copenhagen, daughter of an unmarried architect. When she started school, it was discovered that she was dyslexic, and she worked very hard to overcome this handicap, turning at an early age to drawing to express herself. In 1957 she was accepted by the Academy of Fine Arts and in 1961 she was debuted at the Artists' Autumn Exhibition. From 1965 to 1967, she studied in Poland, Yugoslavia, the Soviet Union, and Czechoslovakia. She was impressed by the poster art she saw throughout Eastern Europe and especially by Polish experimental theater. These three years were instrumental in her rejection of abstract art and her orientation toward a social realistic art form.

Upon her return to Denmark, she helped start the artists' collective "Røde Mor" (Red Mother); its aim was to create a political art relevant to modern life. Trier Mørch worked with graphics and poster art and she illustrated books by Pablo Neruda, Karl Marx and Friedrich Engels, and Ivan Malinowski, among others.

After her three children were born, Trier Mørch found that she could better combine writing with childrearing, although she continued to illustrate her own books. Her first books were travel narratives in which she shares her observations of daily life in the Soviet Union and Poland. In her next six books, she concentrates on basic human experiences in modern society—pregnancy and birth, illness and death, love and divorce, the everyday conflicts and joys in a politically active or artistic family.

In 1977, Trier Mørch was elected Danish Author of the Year for the novel *Vinterbørn* (1976; *Winter's Child*, 1986). This collective novel takes place in the maternity ward of the National Hospital and follows the pregnancies, labor, and deliveries of about eighteen women who come from different social classes and backgrounds. Dressed in their hospital gowns, the women make no class distinctions but convey a feeling of solidarity and warmth.

In her novels, Trier Mørch portrays the events of everyday people in everyday lives. With her novels, she has contributed much to the depiction of modern experience and therefore has a greater audience than most social realistic authors in Denmark. Her books are total works of art with her expressive graphics illustrating the pathos of Trier Mørch's modern milieu.

FURTHER WORKS

Sorgmunter socialisme. Sovjetiske raderinger (1968); *Polen* (1970); *En trekant* (1977); *Ind i verden* (1977); *Kastaniealleen* (1978); *Den indre by* (1980); *Aftenstjernen* (1982; *Evening Star*, 1988); *Morgengaven* (1984); *Da jeg opdagede Amerika* (1986).

REFERENCES

Vagn Jensen, Erik, "A Journey in the Soul," in *Out of Denmark,* ed. Bodil Wamberg (Copenhagen, 1985).

                                                                      Janis E. Granger

Trotzig, Birgitta. Swedish poet, novelist, and essayist, b. 11 September 1929, Gothenburg.

Trotzig grew up in Kristianstad, where her family moved when she was still a child. From 1954 to 1969 she lived in France with her artist husband, Ulf Trotzig, and their young children. This was an important period in her development as a person and writer. Her intimate knowledge of the art world, her continuing interest in world affairs, and her identification with the poor and oppressed of the world were intensified throughout this period of expatriation. It was also at this time that Trotzig came in contact with the vigorous progressive Catholic movements of the 1950s and joined the Catholic church.

Her first novel, *Ur de älskandes liv* (1951; From the Life of the Loving Ones), was well received in Sweden, but it was *De utsatta* (1957; The Exposed) that established her reputation as a gifted and profound writer. This major novel, as well as *En berättelse från kusten* (1961; A Tale from the Coast), is set in a remote historical period in rural Scania, whereas the later works, *Sveket* (1966; The Betrayal), *Sjukdomen* (1972; The Illness), and *Dykungens dotter* (1984; The March King's Daughter), are set in more recent times.

The Scanian landscape, with its icy desolation and its warm softness, is the background against which her characters are usually drawn. The plains of Scania provide a suitable background that keeps in view the metaphysical dimensions of the novels. A direct sense of self and rootedness in the world of nature distinguishes the major characters in Trotzig's fiction. The realism in all her novels is that of the visionary artist. The patterns of vivid images of landscape, characters, and events carry a particular moral force because they cannot be separated from a broader view of human life. The novels transcend the time and space that they depict so vividly.

The events of *Sjukdomen* are significantly framed by the two world wars. It is the tragic story of the retarded and mentally ill Elje Ström, who is cared for by his father, a lonely, poor, and religiously fanatic laborer. Elje's illness and the psychological drama of father and son are intertwined with the social conditions of rural Sweden and the political events in wartime Poland.

Dykungens dotter can be read as a sequel to *Sjukdomen*. It transposes the theme so that a young man's search for his mother becomes a young woman's search for her father and her lost child. The novel retells the Hans Christian Andersen* fairy tale whose title it bears, but it is also a new tale whose mythological dimensions are immediately evident. The prevailing imagery in *Dykungens dotter* is that of the pulsating, teeming, creative life of the marsh. Opposed to it is the "cage"—any of the man-made structures that confine the ever-creative force of the organic world. Humankind is one with the interwoven and interconnected parts of the universe of nature. The novel brings together the Christian and pagan worlds of body and spirit that are set apart in Andersen's "Marsh King's Daughter."

Trotzig's shorter prose narratives include novellas, short stories, and a collection of allegorical tales. Her versatility, her religious sensibility, and her breadth of vision have been widely recognized. It is, however, the intensity of her language and the purity and lyricism of her prose works as well as her poetry that make her one of the most important and original of Sweden's contemporary writers.

FURTHER WORKS

Bilder (1954); *Ett landskap* (1959); *Utkast och förslag* (1962); *Levande och döda* (1964); *Ordgränser* (1968); *I kejsarens tid* (1975); *Berättelser* (1977); *Jaget och världen* (1977); *Anima* (1982).

FURTHER TRANSLATIONS

Swedish Book Review (1983); *Cross Currents* 35.2–3 (1985).

REFERENCES

Boyer, Regis, *Job mitt ibland oss* (Stockholm, 1978); d'Heurle, Adma, "Introducing Birgitta Trotzig," *Swedish Book Review*, 1 (1983); Wrede, Gösta, *Livet, döden och meningen* (Lund, 1978).

Adma d'Heurle

Tunström, Göran. Swedish poet and novelist, b. 14 May 1937, Karlstad.

A clergyman's son, Tunström spent his boyhood in a parsonage in Sunne, a small community in western Sweden. The sorrow caused by his father's premature death and his family's subsequent expulsion from the parsonage is expressed in much of Tunström's work, with its dominant themes of overcoming sorrow and restoring a lost idyllic existence.

Tunström's deep interest in the complexity of human relationships, particularly those between the sexes, is also reflected in his work, especially in his two most significant volumes of poetry, *Svartsjukans sånger* (1975; Songs of Jealousy) and *Sandro Botticellis dikter* (1976; The Poems of Sandro Botticelli).

Tunström's poems contain vivid, rhythmic language and highly imaginative— even visionary—qualities that also are characteristic of his novels, several of which belong to the genre called "fantastic realism." The workings of Tunström's fantasy are especially evident in *Ökenbrevet* (1979; Letter from the Desert), an imaginary autobiography of Christ.

Tunström's most highly regarded novel to date is *Juloratoriet* (1983; The Christmas Oratorio), the fourth in a series of novels including *De heliga geograferna* (1973; The Holy Geographers), *Guddöttrarna* (1975; The Goddaughters), and *Prästungen* (1976; The Pastor's Son), in which Tunström—a widely traveled writer who has lived in places as remote from Sweden as Greece and India—returns home to Sunne and to the past, in order to gain insight into the present. Though serious works, these novels are filled with humor, warmth, and optimism; their protagonists, some patterned after Tunström's father are good human beings—idealistic, courageous, and admirable. The Sunne novels represent Tunström's own maturation process, both as a man and as a writer. With *Juloratoriet*, he achieves the mastery of his craft that brought him the major literature prizes of both the Nordic Council and the Association for Swedish

Literature, as well as recognition as one of Sweden's foremost contemporary writers.

FURTHER WORKS

Inringning (1958); *Två vindar* (1960); *Karantän* (1961); *Maskrosbollen* (1962); *Nymålat* (1962); *Familjeliv* (1964); *Om förtröstan* (1965); *De andra, de till hälften synliga* (1966); *Samtal med marken* (1969); *Stormunnens bön* (1974); *Dikter till Lena* (1978); *Sorgesånger* (1980); *Indien—en vinterresa* (1984); *Tjuven* (1986); *Chang Eng och andra pjäser* (1987).

REFERENCES

Andersson, Lars, "Juloratoriet," in his *Begynnelse bokstäver* (Stockholm, 1984); Frick, Lennart, "Göran Tunström," in his *Något annat* (Stockholm, 1979).

Barbara Lide

U

Undset, Sigrid. Norwegian novelist, b. 20 May 1882, Kalundborg, Denmark, d. 10 June 1949, Lillehammer, Norway.

The daughter of a well-known archaeologist, Undset experienced a childhood steeped in myth and history. Her father died when Sigrid was only eleven years old, and at sixteen the girl was forced to relinquish her dream of becoming a painter in order to earn a living as a secretary. During the following decade she observed the quest for identity of women in menial jobs at the turn of the century. In her spare time she was reading the literature and history of the Middle Ages. In 1912 she married the painter A. C. Svarstad, but the marriage was dissolved in 1922.

The most significant female writer in Norwegian literature, Undset's first novels and short stories deal with the fates of poor and middle-class women— *Fru Marta Oulie* (1907; Mrs. Marta Oulie), *Den lykkelige alder* (1908; The Happy Age), *Jenny* (1911; *Jenny*, 1921), *Fattige skjæbner* (1912; tr. in part *Four Stories*, 1959), *Vaaren* (1914; Spring), *Splinten av troldspeilet* (1917; *Images in a Mirror*, 1938), *De kloge jomfruer* (1918; The Wise Virgins). The women in Undset's early works are spiritually adrift, and marriage and family become the anchors that lend stability to their lives. The dream of happiness, which Undset's fictional women almost always associate with the ability to lose oneself in a total, unquestioning love, cannot be fulfilled in what the author sees as the emotionally sterile environment of the twentieth century. The best known of Undset's protagonists from this period is Jenny, who is unable to accept herself as a talented, independent artist because she has lost the ability to experience a deep, passionate love. Jenny, then, will drift from one mediocre erotic experience to another, until she in the end decides to take control of her own fate by committing suicide. The child to whom Jenny gives birth in the course of the novel dies, a symbol of failure and lack of confidence in the future.

Because of its realistic descriptions of eroticism, the novel was the object of vigorous debates in the contemporary Norwegian press.

Undset's pessimism concerning twentieth-century society, coupled with a belief in the timeless quality of the human soul, made her turn toward the past, most notably the Norwegian Middle Ages. From 1920 to 1922 she wrote the trilogy *Kristin Lavransdatter*, set in the beginning of the fourteenth century. This work gained her international fame. The obverse of Jenny, Kristin is a woman who centers her existence on love. The first volume, *Kransen* (1920; *The Bridal Wreath*, 1923), is the story of Kristin's all-consuming passion for the weak, charming Erlend, and her stubborn revolt against her father, Lavrans. The second and third volumes, *Husfrue* (1921; *The Mistress of Husaby*, 1925) and *Korset* (1922; *The Cross*, 1927), describe her marriage to Erlend, her guilt and punishment, and finally her self-sacrificing dedication to the victims of the Black Death. The trilogy was followed by the profoundly psychological historical novels about Olav Audunssøn, *Olav Audunssøn i Hestviken* (1925) and *Olav Audunssøn og hans børn* (1927, *The Master of Hestviken*, 1934), also set in the Middle Ages. Undset received the Nobel Prize for literature in 1928.

Even in some of her early fiction, as in *De kloge jomfruer*, Undset proposed religious faith as the solution to the dilemma of human existence. In *Kristin Lavransdatter* and *Olav Audunssøn* the religious motif becomes more prevalent, and Undset's conversion to Catholicism was a natural consequence of the development of her thought. In the Catholic religion Undset saw a counterweight to twentieth-century materialism. She discusses her ideas in a series of essays, *Katolsk propaganda* (1927; Catholic Propaganda), *Etapper* (1929; *Stages on the Road*, 1934), *Etapper. Ny række* (1933; Stages on the Road. New Series), and *Norske helgener* (1937; *Saga of Saints*, 1934 [sic]). Her Catholicism, moreover, was an integral part of the novels she wrote during this period: *Gymnadenia* (1929; *The Wild Orchid*, 1931), *Den brændende busk* (1930; *The Burning Bush*, 1932), *Ida Elisabeth* (1932; *Ida Elisabeth*, 1933), and *Den trofaste hustru* (1936; *The Faithful Wife*, 1937). In these works she turns away from the medieval past of Norway in order once more to concentrate on the triviality of contemporary life. Undset's later women characters are no longer possessed by a dream of romantic passion, but by the yearning for divine love and redemption. The biography *Caterina av Siena* (Catherine of Siena) was published posthumously in 1951.

All of Undset's fiction conveys her deep interest in the lives of women. Her women are strong and independent, always ready to fight for what they believe in. Once Kristin has met Erlend and decides that she loves him, her passion becomes the controlling force in her life to which all other loyalties must be subordinated. Undset was self-sufficient from the age of sixteen, and her own life certainly could provide a model for modern women. She is not a feminist in the conventional sense. A firm believer in hierarchical order, she professes faith in a unique female fate. Her women can find fulfillment only through loyalty to man, home, and children. This fits well into the system of her ethical thought in general, where the most significant human quality in fact is a powerful sense of commitment to family, society, and God.

During the 1930s Undset was an uncompromising adversary of totalitarianism, and in 1940 she had to flee Norway. She spent the war years in the United States, where she continued to write and speak against nazism. Her most important publications from this period are *Return to the Future* (1942; Norwegian ed., *Tilbake til fremtiden*, 1949) and *Happy Days in Norway* (1942; Norwegian ed., *Lykkelige dager*, 1947). A collection of her essays and speeches, *Artikler og taler fra krigstiden* (1952; Articles and Speeches from the War Years) was published posthumously.

FURTHER WORKS

Fortællingen om Viga-Ljot og Vigdis (1909; *Gunnar's Daughter*, 1936); *Ungdom* (1910); *Fortællinger om kong Artur og ridderne av det runde bord* (1915); *Et kvinde-synspunkt* (1919); *Elleve aar* (1934; *The Longest Years*, 1935); *Madame Dorthea* (1939; tr. 1940).

REFERENCES

Bayerschmidt, Carl F., *Sigrid Undset* (New York, 1950); Bliksrud, Liv, *Natur og normer hos Sigrid Undset* (Oslo, 1988); Brøgger, Niels Chr., *Korset og rosen* (Oslo, 1952); Brunsdale, Mitzi, *Sigrid Undset: Chronicler of Norway* (New York, 1988); Deschamps, Nicole, *Sigrid Undset ou la morale du la passion* (Montreal, 1966); Dunn, Margaret Mary, "The Master of Hestviken: A New Reading." *Scandinavian Studies* 38.4 (1966) and 40.3 (1968); Engelstad, Carl Fredrik, *Mennesker og makter* (Oslo, 1940); Gustafson, Alrik, "Christian Ethics in a Pagan World: Sigrid Undset," in his *Six Scandinavian Novelists* (Minneapolis, 1968); Heltoft, Bente, *Livssyn og digtning* (Oslo, 1985); McCarthy, Colman J., "Sigrid Undset." *Critic* 32 (1974); Monroe, Elizabeth N., "Art and Idea in Sigrid Undset," in *The Novel and Society* (Chapel Hill, 1941); Packness, Ida, *Sigrid Undset bibliografi* (Oslo, 1963); Vinde, Victor, *Sigrid Undset* (Seattle, 1930); Winsness, A. H., *Sigrid Undset: A Study in Christian Realism* (London, 1953).

Randi Brox

Uppdal, Kristofer. Norwegian poet, novelist, essayist, and critic, b. 19 February 1878, Beitstad, d. 26 December 1961, Oppdal.

Uppdal was the eldest son and thus heir to a farm (*odelsgard*) in Trøndelag. Bankruptcy forced his father to move to town to find work there. From the age of nine Uppdal had to support himself as a shepherd boy and farmhand. He endured hardship and poverty. For ten to twelve years he worked as a *rallar* (migrant worker) in different parts of the country. From 1910 he lived as an author.

Uppdal's major work is the ten-volume novel cycle *Dansen gjenom skugge-heimen* (1919–1924; The Dance through the Shadow Land). The cycle depicts the creation and growth of the working class—sociologically, ideologically, and psychologically. The plot spans the period from 1870 to 1915, and the main emphasis is put on the conditions of the *rallar*, but Uppdal describes the tensions building up within the organized labor movement as well.

The conflict between the indigenous farmer and the migrant *rallar* is also a main theme. Moreover, the erotic motives are dominant in several of the volumes.

Uppdal is torn between stubborn individualism, a Nietzche-inspired worship of the superman, and an urge for solidarity, between the traditional values of the old farming society and the new socialist, proletarian moral and political standards. His attempt at realism even hides a vitalism and a mystique of nature that stand in strong opposition to the rationalism of the socialist ideology.

His poetry shows the same signs of vitalism that in part turn into cosmic visions. This is particularly evident in his last trilogy, *Kulten* (1947; The Cult), which is obscure, but rich in metaphors and poetic skill.

Both in prose and poetry Uppdal's style and language are highly original. His ten-volume novel cycle is the masterpiece of Norwegian proletarian literature although the cycle as a whole varies in quality. Uppdal was also productive as a critic and essayist, and played an important part in the development of *nynorsk* (New Norwegian) as a literary language.

FURTHER WORKS

Kvæde (1905); *Ung sorg* (1905); *Sol-laug* (1908); *Villfuglar* (1909); *Vandringa* (1910; rev. *Ved Akerselva*, 1923); *Trolldom i lufta* (1912; rev. 1922); *Fjellskjeringa* (1913; rev. *Bas-Ola Storbas og laget hans*, 1924); *Røysingfolket* (1914; rev. 1923); *Snørim* (1915); *Uversskyer* (1917); *Andedrag* (1918); *Solbløding* (1918); *Elskhug* (1919); *Stigeren* (1919); *Kongen* (1920); *Domkyrkjebyggjaren* (1921); *I skiftet* (1922); *Herdsla* (1924); *Jotun-brunnen* (1925); *Galgberget* (1930); *Hagamannen* (1939); *Hestane mine* (1963); *Om diktning og diktarar* (1965).

REFERENCES

Dalgard, Olav, *Kristofer Uppdal* (Oslo, 1978); Solumsmoen, Odd, *Kristofer Uppdal, domkirkebyggeren* (Oslo, 1959); Ystad, Vigdis, *Kristofer Uppdals lyrikk* (Oslo, 1978).

Øystein Rottem

V

Vaa, Aslaug. Norwegian poet and dramatist, b. 25 August 1889, Rauland, d. 28 November 1965, Oslo.

Vaa grew up in a village milieu that was rich in old folk traditions. In 1909 she studied literature, philosophy, art histroy, and theater at universities in Paris and Berlin. For a while she worked as a teacher and journalist. She has based literary expression on *nynorsk* (New Norwegian), rich in dialect, ever since her debut collection, *Nord i leite* (1934; In the North Horizon), which she published when she was forty-five years old. During the following thirty years she published six more collections of poetry, the best of which were her last three collections: *Fotefar* (1947; Footsteps), *Skjenkarsveinens visur* (1954; The Innkeeper's Songs), and *Bustader* (1963; Living Quarters). In terms of form and tone, her lyric is influenced by folk poetry (ballads and popular sayings), classical poetry, and modern lyric trends. A dramatic-poetic undertone characterizes her four plays, which deal with strong emotional conflicts within and between people, and culture collisions.

Prevalent themes, particularly in the poetry, are a search for context and meaning, for contact among people, and for experiencing basic human values. At times this search leads to a critical cultural perspective in light of certain aspects of modern technology and civilization. This is particularly apparent in some of her newspaper essays that criticize modern times.

Her best literary achievement is poetry, distinguished by a language rich in imagery, a powerful register of emotion, intense experience of nature, and a broad perspective of human life.

FURTHER WORKS

Skuggen og strendan (1935); *Villarkonn* (1936); *Steinguden* (1938); *På vegakanten* (1938); *Tjugendagen* (1947); *Dikt i utval* (1964); *Honningfuglen og leoparden* (1965); *Munke-klokka* (1966).

TRANSLATIONS

Modern Scandinavian Poetry, ed. Martin S. Allwood (1982).

REFERENCES

Hamre, Kari, "Aslaug Vaa og dramaet." *Vinduet* (1954); Larsen, John Ludvig, "Fra samfunn til diktning. En studie i Aslaug Vaas artikkelforfatterskap," in *Norsk Litterær Arbok* (1979); Mæhle, Leif, "Det lydde eit bod—. Om Aslaug Vaa og diktinga hennar," in *Frå bygda til verda* (Oslo, 1967).

Leif Mæhle

Vala, Katri (pseud. Karin Alice Heikel, née Wadenström). Finnish poet, b. 11 September 1901, Muonio, d. 28 May 1944, Eksjö.

Vala was born in Lapland, a daughter of a forester. Her father's death when she was still young left the family impoverished. She majored in education, and became an elementary school teacher, teaching in many schools in the inland region of the country.

Vala's first two volumes of poetry established her as an important poet of her generation. She wrote highly romantic and exotic poems, characteristically using experimental free verse. The main poetic elements of the earliest poems were exultation and the celebration of light and life. Vala was a member of the radical writer's group Tulenkantajat (Torchbearers), whose bold and youthful manifesto expressed the poets' fearless optimism in change. The group fostered an aesthetic idealism, and it admired distant lands and the exotic. Vala fell victim to tuberculosis around the time her second book of poems was published. The Tulenkantajat dispersed shortly thereafter; exoticism and free verse went out of style among poets.

In the early 1930s Vala wrote for a new *Tulenkantajat* publication, published by a leftist political group. She was a social critic; her poetry, however, never became revolutionary. Instead it became tragic. Her theme was justice; concern for humanity was what she fought for. She wrote poems for the common man. In her last works her tone had tragic force.

Vala's exotic and exultant free verse reflected best the original ideals of the Tulenkantajat. Based on the symbol of light she often praised, her poetic feelings ranged between intense states of happiness and sorrow. Her social poetry was given only superficial acknowledgement outside the circle of her socially and politically aware fellow poets. Since the 1960s her work has been seen as a strong personal statement befitting our times.

FURTHER WORKS

Kaukainen puutarha (1924); *Sininen ovi* (1926); *Maan laiturilla* (1930); *Paluu* (1934); *Pesäpuu palaa* (1942); *Henki ja aine* (1945); *Kootut runot* (1945).

TRANSLATIONS

Twentieth Century Scandinavian Poetry, ed. Martin S. Allwood (1950); *Finnish Odyssey,* ed. Robert Armstrong (1975); *Salt of Pleasure,* ed. Aili Jarvenpa (1983).

REFERENCES

Paavolainen, Olavi, *Katri Vala—tulipatsas* (Helsinki, 1946); Saarenheimo, Kerttu, "Katri Vala," in Vala's *Kootut runot* (Helsinki, 1977); Savutie, Maija, "Katri Vala," in *Suomen kirjallisuus*, vol. 6 (Helsinki, 1967).

Kalevi Lappalainen

Vartio, Marja-Liisa. Finnish poet and novelist, b. 9 November 1924, Sääminki, d. 17 June 1966, Savonlinna.

Vartio, daughter of a schoolteacher and wife of poet Paavo Haavikko,* first published as a poet. Her poetry collections, *Häät* (1952, Wedding) and *Seppele* (1953; Wreath), are characterized by rich and dense imagery and mythological themes from Finland's past, taking form in dream and vision poems.

Some of the mythological and visionary emphasis remained with her after her transition to prose, particularly in the short story "Vatikaani," from the collection *Maan ja veden välillä* (1955; Between the Land and the Water). Dreamlike as elements of the story may be, Vartio grounds it with the use of Karelian local color and cultural-historical detail.

Concrete images and details characterize the four novels that follow: *Se on sitten kevät* (1957; And Then It Is Spring), *Mies kuin mies, tyttö kuin tyttö* (1958; A Man Like a Man, a Girl Like a Girl), *Kaikki naiset näkevät unia* (1962; All Women Dream Dreams), and *Tunteet* (1962; Feelings). These works consider human relationships, such as the effect of the death of a woman on the man who loved her, the situation of a young unwed mother, the financial difficulties of a small family, and courtship and marriage. Imagery and detail anchor the stories (with the possible exception of *Mies kuin mies*, which is generally considered thinner than the other works), which are narrated in a detached style that confines itself to describing actions and reactions and leaves judgments up to the reader.

As highly regarded as some of her earlier works are (Vartio received national literary awards in 1953 and in 1957), her posthumously published novel *Hänen olivat linnut* (1967; His Were the Birds) can be considered her best. The story of a slightly crazed rector's widow, her irritable servant, and the collection of stuffed birds that comes to symbolize all the people that they know and their relationships, it is told with a streak of humor that borders on the grotesque. This effective combination of humor and symbolism, along with simultaneous irony and sympathy for her characters, has created a style that has had some influence on later writers such as Anu Kaipainen.

FURTHER WORKS

Mikko Hovi (1960); "Sakki" (1964); "Saara" (1966); *Runot ja proosarunot* (1966).

TRANSLATIONS

Finnish Short Stories, ed. Inkeri Väänänen-Jensen and K. Börje Vähämäki (1982); *Books from Finland* 20.3 (1986).

REFERENCES

Alhoniemi, Pirkko, "Marja-Liisa Vartio: Hänen olivat linnut," in *Romaani ja tulkinta* (Helsinki, 1973); Alhoniemi, Pirkko, "Marja-Liisa Vartion *Kaikki naiset näkevät unia* ja Paavo Haavikon *Toinen taivas ja maa* rinnakkain," in *Kirjallisuudentutkijain seuran vuosikirja* (1973); Sarajas, Annamari, "Marja-Liisa Vartio," in *Suomen kirjallisuus*, vol. 5 (Helsinki, 1965); Särkilahti, Sirkka-Liisa, *Marja-Liisa Vartion kertomataide* (Tampere, 1973); Tarkka, Pekka, *Suomalaisia nykykirjailijoita* (Helsinki, 1980).

Donna Palomäki

Vatanen, J. I. *See* Lassila, Maiju.

Vennberg, Karl Gunnar. Swedish poet, critic, essayist, translator, and journalist, b. 11 April 1910, Blädinge.

Vennberg attended high school in Lund, where he described himself as "a religious communist": he has continued to alternate between acceptance and rejection of Christianity, but his political views have been consistently socialistic. He moved to Stockholm in 1932, mixing university studies with journalism. Vennberg's journalistic career has flourished ever since, his specialties being cultural criticism and lively polemic.

Together with Erik Lindegren,* Vennberg became leader of the young writers who emerged in the 1940s known as *fyrtiotalister* (writers of the forties): his collection of poems *Halmfackla* (1944; Straw Torch) helped set the tone of contemporary Swedish literature with its bleak pessimism expressed ironically in generally rhymeless, "modern" verse. Subsequent poetry confirmed his seminal role, as did his successful efforts to introduce Franz Kafka into Sweden and his leading part in the current debate on pessimism. The despair and occasional bitterness expressed in Vennberg's poems of the late 1940s and early 1950s spilled over into his political activities, and Vennberg was a leading figure in the debate advocating *tredje ståndpunkten* (the third point of view), that is, strict Swedish neutrality as the cold war intensified.

Vennberg was relatively inactive as a poet from 1955 until the late 1970s, when he seems to have been rejuvenated. The characteristic cool, intellectual analysis of the contemporary world is as sharp as ever; and the air of resignation that accompanies his increasing age is occasionally enlivened by intense love poems.

The late flowering of Vennberg's poetry might eventually necessitate a reassessment of his place in Swedish literature, which currently rates him as a key figure of the 1940s. His break with tradition, his insistence on a penetrating intellectual examination of contemporary life, his refusal to accept received wisdom without question, and his socialist leanings made him a natural leader of the postwar generation of Swedish writers.

FURTHER WORKS

Hymn och hunger (1937); *Tideräkning* (1945); *Fiskefärd* (1949); *Gatukorsning* (1952), *Dikter 1944–49* (1953); *Vårövning* (1953); *Synfält* (1954); *Vid det röda trädet* (1955);

Tillskrift (1960); *Dikter 1944–1960* (1962); *Sju ord på tunnelbanan* (1971); *Du måste värja ditt liv* (1975); *Vägen till Spånga folkan* (1976); *Visa solen ditt ansikte* (1978); *Bilder I–XXVI*, (1981); *Dikter kring noll* (1983); *Längtan till Egypten* (1987); *På mitt samvete*, ed. Björn Håkanson (1987).

REFERENCES

Lagerlöf, K. E., *Den unge Karl Vennberg* (Stockholm, 1967); Printz-Påhlson, Göran, *Solen i spegeln* (Stockholm, 1958); Thompson, Laurie, "Karl Vennberg," in *Essays on Swedish Literature*, ed. Irene Scobbie (Aberdeen, 1978); Vowles, R. B., "Postwar Swedish Poetry: The Other Side of Anguish." *Western Humanities Review* 15 (1961).

Laurie Thompson

Vesaas, Halldis Moren. Norwegian lyric poet, b. 18 November 1907, Trysil.

Vesaas is long established as a major poet; her production spans more than fifty years. Her poetry might be characterized as nature poetry; but nature poetry in the sense of tamed nature: there are fields and meadows, gardens and lonely mountain farms, but no majestic snowcapped mountains, abysmal gorges, churning seas, and ragnarok-like storms. The areas of imagery, then, are well defined and change rarely. However, Vesaas never turns into a symbolist in the Stéphane Mallarmé tradition; her poetry is no *poésie pure* that sees life from a distance. On the contrary, her poetry is life-sustaining matter, animated and moved by the mind of the reader.

The images usually are the light, the sun, the bright day, occasionally fire expressing the goodness and the joy of life, happiness and hope. Darkness, night, dark clouds often equal death, fear of death, and threats. Dusk and dawn, then, are border areas, but more often than not, they have a positive meaning. The earth, the soil, the fields, and the farm animals are friendly forces. The wind usually is gentle, a symbol of fertility. The beach and the sea provide aspects of eternity. Children are catalysts of life, demonstrating unknown potential. Finally, there are plants, flowers and, above all, trees. In at least fifteen poems the tree or parts of it provide the central image. One of the collections is entitled *Treet* (1947; The Tree) and another is called *I ein annan skog* (1955; In Another Forest). Vesaas seems fascinated with trees: they are exposed to relentless elements, but they weather the storms and grow old with dignity. They also bear seeds and are life-giving. In this image Vesaas finds most of the elements that interest and concern her. In one poem, she even shows the human relationship of a couple in love by depicting two trees in the forest that, leaning on each other, survive and age. Thus Vesaas manages to show delicate human interactions by using rather elementary nature imagery. Her poetry is very homogeneous, using strict metrical patterns and end rhyme.

Vesaas is also known as an accomplished writer of contemplative prose. There is a collection of essays on a wide range of topics and reminiscences about her father, Sven Moren, and her life with her husband, Tarjei Vesaas,* one of the leading Norwegian novelists of the twentieth century.

FURTHER WORKS

Harpe og dolk (1929); *Morgonen* (1930); *Strender* (1933); *Du får gjera det, du* (1935); *Lykkelege hender* (1936); *Den grøne hatten* (1938); *Hildegunn* (1942); *Tung tids tale* (1945); *Tidleg på våren* (1949); *Sven Moren og heimen hans* (1951); *Utvalde dikt* (1957); *Sett og levd* (1967); *Gudefjellet* (1970); *Utvalde dikt* (1974); *I Midtbøs bakkar* (1974); *Båten om dagen* (1976); *Dikt i samling* (1977).

TRANSLATIONS

König, Fritz H. "The Woman's Voice in Modern Norwegian Poetry." *North American Review* 257.1 (1972); König, Fritz H., guest editor, *Micromegas* 4.3 (1971).

Fritz H. König

Vesaas, Tarjei. Norwegian novelist and poet, b. 20 August 1897, Vinje, d. 15 March 1970.

Tarjei Vesaas was born in Vinje in Telemark in 1897. He attended Voss Folk High School during the winter of 1917–1918, but decided to return to Vinje and settle there for the rest of his life. Nevertheless, while Vesaas's writings reflect the vision of a person with strong roots in his native soil, they are by no means provincial. While Vinje provided him with a stable spatial center throughout his entire existence, he at the same time understood the value of extensive exposure to different places and different cultures. Vesaas traveled widely. In 1925–1926 he visited Sweden, Denmark, France, and Italy on a government scholarship. In 1927–1928 he spent several months in Munich and visited Belgium, Italy, and France. In 1932–1933 he traveled in Czechoslovakia, Germany, Switzerland, France, Austria, and Denmark. It was during this latter trip that he met the poet Halldis Moren, whom he married in 1934 (*see* Halldis Moren Vesaas). The couple had two children, a son, Olav, and a daughter, Guri.

Prior to the outbreak of World War II Vesaas's work was realistic. The novel *Dei svarte hestane* (1928; The Black Horses) is the story of an isolated youth, Kjell, whose perception of the adult world is portrayed with sensitivity and insight. Ultimately Kjell will break out of his solitude and find a place within the human community. The conflict between isolation and communion runs like a thread through Vesaas's entire corpus.

Vesaas's most ambitious work from the prewar period, the *Dyregodt* tetralogy (1930–1938), conveys the author's anguish concerning the political situation in Europe in the 1930s and advocates the individual's responsibility in preventing a catastrophe. The two novels about Per Bufast, *Det store spelet* (1934; *The Great Cycle*, 1967) and *Kvinnor ropar heim* (1935; The Women Call Home), reveal how Per Bufast learns to accept and even love both his native soil and his place within the life cycle. The Bufast novels are books about friendship, love, and fertility, about work, anxiety, and responsibility. They advocate, as the highest goal in life, an accepting, contented attitude toward the human condition.

Vesaas considers his novel *Kimen* (1940; *The Seed*, 1964) to represent a crossroads in his evolution as a writer. The outbreak of war in Europe and the German occupation of Norway were events so shocking to his sensibility that they produced a totally new way of writing. *Kimen* is about catastrophe and violence, illustrating the transformation of humans into beasts once they forget their individuality and melt into a mob. The characters take on an abstract and generalized form, representative of Vesaas's later novels. Like Aksel Sandemose's* *Det svundne er en drøm* (1946; The Past Is a Dream), *Kimen* is about the struggle between destructive and constructive forces within the human personality. In both novels the positive forces, "the seed," will survive and grow, confirming the continuation of the cycle of life. It is, however, the stylistic changes in *Kimen* that are most striking. Breaking with the realistic style of *Det store spelet, Kimen* is written in a concise, symbolic manner that will characterize Vesaas's later works.

An even more direct analogy to the Nazi occupation of Norway during World War II is *Huset i mørkret* (1945; *The House in the Dark*, 1976), which describes the work of the Norwegian Resistance. While working toward a collective goal, each character must ultimately face the catastrophe in his own way and choose the course of action that appears right to him.

In *Bleikeplassen* (1946; The Bleaching Yard) Vesaas once again shows the struggle between the dark, destructive forces of the mind and the longing for purification. A desperate quest for human kindness cannot prevent the violent death of the protagonist, Johan Tander, but it crystallizes the situation for the people surrounding his body, and at the end of the novel a spirit of acceptance and forgiveness prevails.

While Vesaas had always been interested in poetry and poems often are included in his novels, his first collection, *Kildane* (The Springs), was not published until 1946. It was followed by *Leiken og lynet* (1947; The Game and the Lightning), *Lykka for ferdesmenn* (1949; The Happiness of Travelers), *Løynde eldars land* (1953; *Land of Hidden Fires*, 1973), and *Ver ny, vår draum* (1956; May Our Dream Stay New). The themes of Vesaas's poetry are closely related to those of his novels, and there is a constant blurring between poetry and prose in his work. Vesaas has also written several plays and numerous short stories. The collection *Vindane* (1952; The Winds) was awarded the Venice prize in 1953.

Nevertheless, it is likely as a novelist that Vesaas will be remembered. Several important novels were published in the 1950s and 1960s; for instance, *Vårnatt* (1954; *Spring Night*, 1954), *Fuglane* (1957; *The Birds*, 1968), *Is-slottet* (1963; *The Ice Palace*, 1963), and *Bruene* (1966; *The Bridges*, 1969). All of these books describe the isolation of individuals and their attempts to construct bridges of communication. Particularly moving is the story of the retarded Mattis in *Fuglane*. While Mattis is never able fully to grasp the language of the so-called smart people, he possesses a keen sense of communication with the world of nature, especially with birds. Mattis himself is, in fact, compared to a strange, rare bird. The questions Vesaas asks in *Fuglane* are, what is communication?

who are the retarded ones? whose life is richer, that of ordinary, competent people, who are able to handle themselves in ordinary, daily life situations, or that of Mattis the half-wit, who is living closely in touch with the mystery of life itself. As in *Fuglane*, in *Is-slottet* isolation leads to death. In the later novel, however, Vesaas takes a clear stand in favor of human communciation, when Unn, at the end of the book, tears herself away from the ice palace where her friend, Siss, had entered and died several months earlier. The longing for human communication reaches its culmination in *Bruene*, which was to become Vesaas's last novel. His final, partly autobiographical work, *Båten om kvelden* (1968; *The Boat in the Evening*, 1972), consists of a series of imagistic fragments evoking themes and motifs from the author's earlier works, dealing with life and death, dreams, and human communication. Vesaas died two years later, at the age of seventy-three.

FURTHER WORKS

Menneskebonn (1923); *Sendemann Huskuld* (1924); *Grindegard, Morgonen* (1925); *Grinde-kveld eller Den gode engelen* (1926); *Klokka i haugen* (1929); *Sandeltreet* (1933); *Ultimatum* (1934); *Leiren og hjulet* (1936); *Tårnet* (1948); *Signalet* (1950); *Ein vakker dag* (1959); *Brannen* (1961).

FURTHER TRANSLATIONS

30 Poems, trans. Kenneth G. Chapman (1971); *Selected Poems*, trans. Anthony Barnett (1988).

REFERENCES

Beyer, Edward, "Tarjei Vesaas." *Scandinavica* 3.2 (1964); Chapman, Kenneth G., *Tarjei Vesaas* (New York, 1970); Dale, Johannes, "Tarjei Vesaas." *American-Scandinavian Review* 54.4 (1966); McFarlane, James W., "Tarjei Vesaas," in *Ibsen and the Temper of Norwegian Literature* (London, 1960); Mæhle, Leif, ed., *Ei bok om Tarjei Vesaas* (Oslo, 1964); Skrede, Ragnvald, *Tarjei Vesaas* (Oslo, 1964); Vesaas, Halldis Moren, *I Midtbøs bakkar* (Oslo, 1974); *Tarjei Vesaas, 1897—20. August—1967* (Oslo, 1967).

Randi Brox

Vigfússon, Bjarni. *See* Thorarensen, Bjarni.

Viita, Lauri Arvi. Finnish poet and novelist, b. 17 December 1916, Pirkkala, d. 22 December 1965, Helsinki.

Viita came from a working-class home near the industrial city of Tampere. He worked for some years as a carpenter, later devoting himself to writing. He was married to the poet Aila Meriluoto,* who has written a biography of her husband. In later life he suffered from schizophrenia, and he was under hospital treatment for many years.

Viita's early volume of poetry, *Betonimylläri* (1947; Mixer of Concrete), aroused considerable attention. A man who earned his living as a worker had taken traditional Finnish poetic style and molded it into something that looked quite new. In fact, his verse is technically traditional, with regular meter and ingenious rhyme. Later he incorporated elements of Finnish folk poetry. His originality is in his ability to give his poetry the quality and pace of natural speech. At the same time, Viita challenged the atmosphere of depression and uncertainty following World War II. In his work, hardships are there to be overcome; life is for the living.

The note of confidence is there again in Viita's novel *Moreeni* (1950; Moraine). It describes simple builders who carry life forward. In slightly altered form it is the story of his family and his own spiritual growth. It combines a picture of the common folk with proletarian ideas. In this novel, as in Viita's poetry, the language leaps and crackles with life, but sometimes there is an overintensity foreshadowing his later breakdown.

As a poet, Viita was so original that he has no direct followers. As a prose writer he has influenced a band of realistic working-class writers, including the foremost living Finnish novelist Väinö Linna,* from his hometown of Tampere. From Viita they have inherited some of the energy and self-confidence, the elemental force that radiates from his work.

FURTHER WORKS

Kukunor (1949); *Käppyräinen* (1950); *Suutarikin, suuri viisas* (1961); *Entäs sitten Leevi* (1965); *Kootut runot* (1966).

REFERENCES

Marjanen, Kaarlo, "Lauri Viita," in *Suomen kirjallisuus,* vol. 6 (Keuruu, 1967); Meriluoto, Aila, *Lauri Viita* (Porvoo, 1974); Varpio, Yrjö, *Lauri Viita* (Porvoo, 1973).

Philip Binham

Vik, Bjørg. Norwegian writer, b. 11 September 1935, Oslo.

Vik's adolescence in Oslo, journalistic career in Porsgrunn, family life, and participation in the new feminist movement are reflected in her work. In fiction and drama Vik explores the tensions of big-city loneliness, suburban materialism, and small-town tedium. Her characters are of all ages—some restless with unfulfilled longings, some haunted by disturbing dreams, some learning courage and generosity. The male-female relationship, childhood experiences, pressure of social boundaries, and insights of maturity are frequent themes. Using natural dialogue and situations evocative of reality, Vik polishes the form of her works, concentrating and refining until the surface is pulled taut over an undercurrent of frustration and the placid rhythm of daily life is syncopated by outbursts of accusation and despair. There has been progression in Vik's work from self-realization through rebellion to tolerance and hope. Positive resolutions often take place in settings of natural beauty, with insights expressed in images of trees, water, animals, and light.

To akter for fem kvinner (1974; Two Acts for Five Women), a witty and moving drama, brings together former schoolfriends for an evening of nostalgia and self-discovery. Disappointments and the injustice of social pressure are probed as Vik sets the women at the threshold of freedom and self-reliance. The play was produced widely throughout Scandinavia, in Germany, and in New York (as *Wine Untouched*).

The short story "Enkene" (1979; "The Widows," 1980) reveals Vik's compassion for the lonely and aging. Bereavement brings a solitary, critical old lady to reach out for new friends, in scenes with typical clarity of detail, set in the warmth of a cluttered kitchen and in the bright afternoon sunlight on an apartment stairwell.

Praised for her command of language, precise observation of contemporary life, and craftsmanship as a short story writer, Vik is considered one of Norway's foremost authors.

FURTHER WORKS

Søndag ettermiddag (1963); *Nødrop fra en myk sofa* (1966); *Det grådige hjerte* (1968); *Gråt, elskede mann* (1970); *Kvinne-akvariet* (1972; *An Aquarium of Women*, 1987); *Hurra, det ble en pike!* (1974); *Fortellinger om frihet* (1975); *Gutten som sådde tiøringer* (1976); *Sorgenfri* (1978); *En håndfull lengsel* (1979; *Out of Season*, 1983); *Det trassige håp* (1981); *Snart er det høst* (1982); *Fribillett til Soria Moria* (1984); *En gjenglemt petunia* (1985); *Når en pike sier ja* (1985); *Jørgen Bombasta* (1987); *Små nøkler store rom* (1988).

FURTHER TRANSLATIONS

Scandinavian Studies 49.2 (1977); *Scandinavian Review* 58.4 (1980); *Side by Side and Other Tales* (1980); *Stand* 23.3 (1982); *Slaves of Love and Other Norwegian Short Stories*, ed. James McFarlane (1982); *Out of Season and Other Stories* (1983); *An Everyday Story*, ed. Katherine Hanson (1984); *Norseman* 26.5 (1986); *View from the Window*, trans. Elizabeth Rokkan and Ingrid Weatherhead (1987).

REFERENCE

Waal, Carla, "The Norwegian Short Story." *Scandinavian Studies* 49.2 (1977).

Carla Waal

Vilhjálmsson, Thor. Icelandic novelist and essayist, b. 12 August 1925, Edinburgh.

After his high school examination in Reykjavík in 1944, Vilhjálmsson pursued his studies both at the University of Iceland and abroad, in England and Paris. For some years he was librarian at the National Library in Reykjavík.

Vilhjálmsson, who has among other things translated works by John Osborne, Eugene O'Neill, Thornton Wilder, Françoise Sagan, and Umberto Eco into Icelandic, is a traveled person and has a broad international orientation. In several collections of essays—for instance, *Undir gervitungli* (1959; Under an Artificial Moon), *Svipir dagsins, og nótt* (1961; Shapes of the Day, and Night), and *Fiskur í sjó, fugl úr beini* (1974; Fish in the Sea, Bird of Bone)—he gives fresh impressions from his journeys in many countries. He is a well-informed and stimulating guide in modern literature, painting, and cinematics, and has been of great importance as a mediator of international cultural influences to his fellow countrymen.

Vilhjálmsson's novels—for instance, *Fljótt, fljótt sagði fuglinn* (1968; Quick, Quick, Said the Bird, a title alluding to a phrase in the first of T. S. Eliot's *Four Quartets*), *Óp bjöllunnar* (1970; The Cry of the Beetle), and *Mánasigð* (1976; Crescent Moon)—deal with modern man and problems of our time. Their scene of action is usually Southern Europe. The first of the above-mentioned novels is a characteristic specimen. It takes place in modern Italy, yet, all the time periods seem to be present simultaneously; now and then intermingle. The principal character, "the man," sees himself as being under the spell of an ancient Roman fertility rite, and selected for the next sacrifice. In his hectic and apparently aimless flight from place to place he may be regarded as representative of man's alienation in our age. The dark outlook, however, is brightened by frequent touches of humor.

Vilhjálmsson's style is highly artistic and sophisticated, showing some influences from William Faulkner and the French nouveau roman. In *Folda* (1972; Native Soil) he gives the rein to his unusual stylistic versatility by parodying the popular genre of Icelandic travel reports.

Vilhjálmsson is a pioneering and leading figure in Icelandic prose writing after World War II.

FURTHER WORKS

Maðurinn er alltaf einn (1950); *Dagar mannsins* (1954); *Andlit í spegli dropans* (1957; Faces Reflected in a Drop, 1966); *Regn á rykið* (1960); *Ætlar blessuð manneskjan að gefa upp andann?* (1963); *Kjarval* (1964); *Hvað er San Marino?* (1973); *Fuglaskottís* (1975); *Skuggar af skyjum* (1977); *Faldafeykir* (1979); *Turnleikhusið* (1979); *Grámosínn glóir* (1986); *Náttvíg* (1989).

REFERENCE

Hallberg, Peter, "The One Who Sees: The Icelandic Writer Thor Vilhjálmsson." *Books Abroad* 47.1 (1973).

Peter Hallberg

Villum, K. *See* Fløgstad, Kjartan.

Vinje, Aasmund Olavsson. Norwegian lyric poet, essayist, and journalist, b. 6 April 1818, Vinje, d. 30 July 1870, Gran at Hadeland.

Vinje was born the son of a poor tenant farmer, and it had great effect on him that he came from a despised and subjected social class. He regarded education as a means of escaping these unfavorable circumstances, and became a rural schoolmaster at the age of eighteen. Further teacher training enabled him to teach the lower levels of secondary school at the same time as he was a pupil in the higher grades. In 1848 he enrolled in a famous college preparatory school commonly referred to as Heltberg's Student Factory, and two years later he passed his matriculation examinations and earned the right to study at the university. Vinje received a law degree in 1856, but never used it to practice law.

From 1851 to 1858, while a student in the capital city of Christiania, Vinje also wrote for a provincial newspaper and edited a satirical periodical together with Paul Botten-Hansen and Henrik Ibsen.* His engaging and witty journalism attracted considerable notice. In 1858 he founded his own weekly, called *Dølen* (The Dalesman), which lasted with interruptions until Vinje's death.

Vinje's articles and essays from these years show both that he had a sharp intellect and that he was continually in the process of developing. Vinje believed truth to be relative, and he therefore never tired at looking for alternative ways of regarding the issues of the day. He cultivated this attitude, to which he referred as his "double vision," to the point where it was difficult to determine what he really stood for regarding various social and political issues. The one issue where he never wavered, however, was the language question, for he early saw the need to liberate Norway from the cultural and linguistic hegemony of Danish. To this end Vinje created his own written form of Norwegian based on the principles advocated by the linguist Ivar Aasen.* Having his own periodical enabled him to regularly place before the reading public his views, expressed in this form of the language, and he thus became one of the founders of *nynorsk* (New Norwegian) literature.

Vinje's major prose work is his first book, titled *Ferdaminni fraa Sumaren 1860* (1861; Travel Memories from the Summer of 1860), which was the result of a jouney through the mountains to the city of Trondheim to witness the crowning of Charles XV. Vinje, whose literary heritage was essentially a romantic one, here expresses a realistic view of one of the chief objects of admiration of the Norwegian romantics, namely the native farmers.

It is his poetry, however, that is Vinje's greatest literary achievement. His best poems are deeply personal, and many of them are inspired by nature. There are also a series of philosophical poems that reveal a profound concern with ethical questions. His imagery is simple and clear, but his metric and stanzaic patterns are often very complex. Many of his best poems are found in *Diktsamling* (1864; Poetry Collection).

One of Vinje's most original books is *A Norseman's View of Britain and the British* (1863), written in English after a journey to Great Britain. Vinje hoped that this book would attract the attention of British men of letters, but the sales were disappointingly low both in England and in Norway.

Today Vinje is remembered as one of Norway's finest lyrical poets and as a pioneer of *nynorsk* literature. Although he has never attracted much attention abroad, he is considered a classic in his native land.

FURTHER WORKS

Storegut (1866).

TRANSLATIONS

Edvard Grieg Vocal Album, vol. 4 (1899); Knudsen, Dina, ed., *58 of the Best Known Scandinavian Songs* (n.d.); *Anthology of Norwegian Lyrics* ed. Charles W. Stork (1942); Midttun, Olav, *A. D. Vinje* (Oslo, 1966).

Jan Sjåvik

Vör, Jón úr. *See* Jón úr Vör.

Vold, Jan Erik. Norwegian poet, b. 18 October 1939, Oslo.

Vold's first poems were published around the time of the upsurge of modernist writing in the mid–1960s, centered around the magazine *Profil*. Vold was one of the leaders of this movement, and his poetry is correspondingly experimental, strongly influenced by contemporary American poetry and European modernism. He was one of the first in Norway to experiment with the look of the page, using varying typography and layout to help convey his meaning. *mellom speil og speil* (1965; between mirror and mirror) expresses both in content and form an oppressive feeling of confinement, of being locked up with one's own image; *blikket* (1966; the glance) consists of five words combined in a variety of ways, until they become either a game or a conflict.

Vold is a well-known reader of his own poetry, often accompanied by jazz. Particularly successful is his reading of *Mor Godhjertas glade versjon. Ja* (1968; Mother Goodheart's Happy Version. Yes), his most popular collection, where the poet, in an extroverted and chatty mood, celebrates his allegiance to the good and simple things of life. Expressed in colloquial language, with the rhythms of everyday speech, this collection is clearly influenced by the American poet William Carlos Williams, whom Vold has also translated extensively.

In recent years Vold has preferred more disciplined and concentrated poetic forms. *spor, snø* (1970; track, snow) contains miniature poems modeled on the three-line Japanese haiku. *Bok 8: LIV* (1973; Book 8: LIV) also consists of short poems, many with themes reminiscent of the philosophy of Zen Buddhism. Vold has been active throughout his career as a translator, editor, and polemicist; in 1980 he was a central figure in the heated debate about the deplorable state of Norwegian poetry (see *Det norske syndromet*, 1980; The Norwegian Syndrome).

FURTHER WORKS

fra rom til rom SAD & CRAZY (1967); *kykelipi* (1969); *Her. Her i denne verden* (1974); *Entusiastiske essays—Klippbok 1960–75* (1976); *BusteR brenneR* (1976); *S* (1978); *Sirkel, sirkel* (1976); *En som het Abel Ek* (1988).

TRANSLATIONS

Stand 23.3 (1982); *Modern Scandinavian Poetry*, ed. Martin Allwood (1982).

REFERENCES

Fjeldstad, Anton, "Jan Erik Volds dikt," in *Norsk litterær årbok 1973,* ed. Leif Mæhle (Oslo, 1973); Garton, Janet, "New Directions in Norwegian Literature," in *Review of National Literatures: Norway*, ed. Sverre Lyngstad (New York, 1983).

Janet Garton

W

Wadenström, Karin Alice. *See* Vala, Katri.

Wägner, Elin. Swedish novelist and journalist, b. 16 May 1882, Lund, d. 7 January 1949, Rösås.

Starting out as a journalist on the local paper of her home town of Hälsingborg, Wägner moved on to the woman's magazine *Idun* in 1905 and free-lanced at the daily *Dagens Nyheter*. One of the founders and editors of the weekly feminist paper *Tidevarvet* (1922–1936), Wägner became a radical pacifist, inspired by Mahatma Gandhi.

After Wägner's debut in 1907 with a collection of short stories, *Från det jordiska museet* (From Our Earthly Museum), her breakthrough came with the novel *Norrtullsligan* (1908; The Norrtull Gang). First published as a serial in *Dagens Nyheter*, it is a novel in the form of a diary written by Elisabeth, a young office worker living in a collective on Norrtullsgatan in Stockholm. Although a tender and humorous description of the life of young women clerical workers, it is also a strong criticism of the miserable economic and social conditions, under which they are living.

Wägner's next novel *Pennskaftet* (1910; The Penholder) is about her own situation as a journalist actively engaged in the suffragist movement. But it is also a plea for a new sexual ethics, against the double standard.

Wägner's pacifism is reflected in several short stories and novels like *Släkten Jerneplogs framgång* (1916; The Success of the Family Ironplow), *Den förödda vingården* (1920; The Ruined Vineyard), and *Från Seine, Rhen och Ruhr* (1923; From Seine, Rhine and Ruhr).

In two semi-autobiographical novels, *Genomskådad* (1937; Unmasked) and *Hemlighetsfull* (1938; Mysterious) Wägner gives the history of the women's liberation movement in Sweden as she herself has experienced it.

With her work *Väckarklocka* (1941; Alarm Clock) Wägner makes an urgent plea for a radical change of our society with its destructive patriarchal system. Her vision for a future society is one where there would be a dialogue between man and woman, maybe even a kind of matriarchal system.

Not always understood or well received by her contemporaries, Wägner has been the model for the new feminist movement in Sweden.

FURTHER WORKS

Åsa-Hanna (1918); *Den namnlösa* (1922); *Svalorna flyga högt* (1929); *Dialogen fortsätter* (1932); *Vinden vände bladen* (1947); *Tusen år i Småland* (1937); *Selma Lagerlöf* (1942–1943).

REFERENCES

Death, Sarah, "Sexual Politics and the Defeat of Sisterhood in Elin Wägner's *Släkten Jerneploogs framgång*," in *Mothers—Saviors—Peacemakers*, ed. Cheri Register et al. (Uppsala, 1983); Death, Sarah, "*Tidevarvet*: A Radical Weekly Magazine of the Inter-War Years." *Swedish Book Review* 1 (1986); Forsås-Scott, Helena, " 'En kvinnas självbiografi' Om Elin Wägners romankonst." (Eng. summary) *Kvinnovetenskaplig tidskrift* 6.3 (1985); Isaksson, Ulla, and Erik Hjalmar Linder, *Elin Wägner 1882–1922* (Stockholm, 1977); Isaksson, Ulla, and Erik Hjalmar Linder, *Elin Wägner 1922–1949* (Stockholm, 1980).

Ingrid Claréus

Wästberg, Per. Swedish novelist, essayist, poet, and editor, b. 20 November 1933, Stockholm.

Wästberg was born into an upper-middle-class family and enjoyed a good education that included undergraduate work at Harvard and graduate study at Uppsala. His literary career began when he was fifteen with the publication of his first novel and continued with more fiction as well as numerous articles recording his various experiences with notable maturity and sophistication. Thanks to a Rotary grant that he received in the late 1950s, he was able to spend time in Africa observing social and economic conditions. He was deeply struck by the injustices and suffering caused by white supremacy rule throughout much of the continent and, as a result, became a powerful advocate of social justice in the region. He has devoted much effort, moreover, to introducing and interpreting monuments of black culture to European and American audiences. As cultural editor and then editor-in-chief of *Dagens Nyheter* and an active member of the international PEN club, Wästberg has played a prominent role in Swedish life and letters.

Wästberg's most widely read work is the trilogy consisting of *Vattenslottet* (1968; The Water Castle), *Luftburen* (1969; *The Air Cage*, 1973), and *Jordmånen* (1972; *Love's Gravity*, 1977). The novels discuss passion, abundance, and human potential and suggest the need for complete sexual and personal freedom. Although the love scenes abound in joyous sensuality, Wästberg's principal concern is the representation of enlightened love as fulfilling interaction of individuals and society unrestrained by norms and conventions.

Wästberg enjoys broad appeal as a many-sided and highly disciplined writer. His fiction, poetry, and reportage all attest in different ways to his fundamental concern with human dignity and wholeness. His social commitments, though, do not remain airy abstractions, but are expressed with great power, sophistication, and subtlety.

FURTHER WORKS

Pojke med såpbubblor (1949); *Enskilt arbete* (1952); *Ett gammalt skuggspel* (1952); *Halva kungariket* (1955); *Klara* (1957); *Arvtagaren* (1958); *Förbjudet område* (1960); *På svarta listan* (1960); *Angola-Mozainbique*, with Anders Ehnmark (1962; *Angola and Mozambique: The Case against Portugal*, 1963); *Östermalm* (1962); *Tio atmosfärer* (1963); *Ernst och Mimi* (1964); *En dag på världsmarknaden* (1967); *Afrikas moderna litteratur* (1969); *Röda huset; Ett spel i Stockholm*, with Anna-Lena Westberg (1970); *Sommaröarna: En bok om Stockholmarnas skärgård* (1975); *Africa, ett uppdrag: Reflexioner, beskrivningar, gissningar* (1976); *Ett Hörntorn vid Riddargatan och andra Stockholmsskildringar* (1980); *Obestämda artiklar* (1981); *En avlägsen likhet* (1983); *Bergets källa* (1987).

REFERENCES

Ryberg, Anders, *Per Wästbergs skrifter: En bibliografi* (Stockholm, 1973).

Steven P. Sondrup

Waltari, Mika Toimi (various pseudonyms). Finnish novelist, short story writer, and playwright, b. 19 September 1908, Helsinki, d. 26 August 1979, Helsinki.

Graduating from high school at age eighteen, Waltari had published his first volume of poetry at seventeen, his first novel the next year, and a volume of short stories the next. He took a master of arts degree at Helsinki University and pursued his writing career. It was his second novel, *Suuri illusioni* (1928; The Great Illusion, before Jean Renoir's famous movie), that made him known, and up to 1949, he had published an average of more than three texts of various kinds every year, a total of eighty, mostly novels and other prose (forty), plays and radio plays (twenty-four), and translations (fifteen). He had a few journalistic jobs but worked mostly as one of the very few free-lance writers of his time in Finland. Especially the works he wrote after World War II earned him the reputation of a serious writer; he was elected to the Finnish Academy in 1957 and awarded a doctorate *honoris causa* in 1970.

Waltari's production falls into three periods. The first is devoted to the exciting modern life of the twenties in Helsinki, as for example, in the novel *Appelsiininsiemen* (1931; The Orange Seed). Waltari's descriptions of it appear now rather youthfully naïve (prohibition, 1919–1931, made alcohol sinful). During the second, he wrote, in accordance with the serious moral climate of the thirties, a trilogy, *Mies ja haave* (1933; A Man and a Dream), *Sielu ja liekki* (1934, The Soul and the Flame) and *Palava nuoruus* (1935; Burning Youth), later reduced to one volume, *Isästä poikaan* (1942; From Father to Son), depicting the growth of Helsinki from 1870 to 1935; a novel about destructive passions in a rural setting, *Vieras mies tuli taloon* (1937; *A Stranger Came to the Farm*, 1960); and two others on patriotic motifs, *Antero ei enää palaa* (1940; Antero Won't Come Back) and *Rakkaus vainoaikaan* (1943; Love in Times of War), in addition to detective stories, comedies, and war propaganda commissioned by the government. After the war he published the huge historical novels that made him known abroad, *Sinuhe* (1945; *Sinuhe the Egyptian*, 1949; also *The Egyptian*; movie in the United States by Michael Curtiz, 1954); *Mikael Karvajalka* (1948; *Michael the Finn*, 1950; also *The Adventurer*) and its sequel *Mikael Hakim* (1949; *The Sultan's Renegade*, 1951, also *The Wanderer*), *Johannes Angelos* (1952; *The Dark Angel*, 1953), and *Turms, kuolematon* (1955; *The Etruscan*, 1956), all published in many editions and translated into several languages. Some of his short novels, written in the thirties but rejected by the publisher as immoral (according to the very narrow standards then prevailing in Finland), were also printed at that time, as *Neljä päivänlaskua* (1949; *A Nail Merchant at Nightfall*, 1954), *Kuun maisema* (1953; *Moonscape and Other Stories*, 1954), and *Koiranheisipuu ja kolme muuta pienoisromaania* (1961; *The Tree of Dreams and Other Stories*, 1965). The same type of character appears in many of Waltari's novels from the beginning: a man, not always young, idealistic, shy and uncouth, who can't succeed in a harsh world and keeps yearning for happy relations with the other sex, but is always fooled by scheming and ruthless women, a motif that becomes repetitious after a while. His historical novels present a superficially tragic philosophy of life, the purport of which is that peace, freedom, and democracy are empty words, the world being ruled by the strong and the ruthless and history an endless series of wars and catastrophes. Religious problems appear in *Feliks onnellinen* (1958; *The Tongue of Fire*, 1959), set in modern times, and in *Valtakunnan salaisuus* (1959; *The Secret of the Kingdom*, 1960) with its sequal *Ihmiskunnan viholliset* (1964; *The Roman*, 1966), which describe the times immediately following the death of Christ.

Waltari's plays are mostly light comedies with a hint at serious problems, except for *Akhnaton, auringosta syntynyt* (1937; Akhena, Born of the Sun), in which his interest in ancient Egypt first appears, and *Paracelsus Baselissa* (1943; Paracelsus in Balse). Descriptions of his travels, a few poems, and filmscripts also appear among his works.

Waltari is greatly admired in his own country, but in spite of the translations of his works in numerous languages, he has not attained the status of a great writer, being, in fact, a skillful producer of serious entertainment. In Finland, he has not had any followers, his style and his choice of subjects belonging by now to the past.

FURTHER WORKS

Jumalaa paossa (1925); *Kuolleet silmät* (pseud. Kristian Korppi, 1926); *Dshinnistanin prinssi* (1927); *Sinun ristisi juureen* (1927); *Valtatiet*, with O. Paavolainen (1928); *Muukalaislegioona* (1929); *Yksinäisen miehen juna* (1929); *Jättiläiset ovat kuolleet* (1930);

Keisarin tekohampaat (pseud. Leo Rainio, with A. J. Pulla, 1931); *Kiinalainen kissa* (1931); *Siellä, missä miehiä tehdään* (1931); *Punainen madonna* (pseud. Leo Rainio, with A. J. Pulla, 1932); *Älkää ampuko pianistia* (pseud. Leo Rainio, with A. J. Pulla, 1932); texts to comic strip *Kieku ja Kaiku* (1933–1975); *Yö yli Euroopan* (1933); *Aiotko kirjailijaksi?* (1935); *Juudean yö* (1936); *Suomalainen lauantaiehtoo* (1936); *Surun ja ilon kaupunki* (1936); *Helsinki kautta vuosisatojen* (1937); *Kuriton sukupolvi* (1937); *Mies rakasti vaimoaan* (1937); *Toimittaja rakastaa* (1937); *Ihmeellinen Joosef* (1938); *Ihmeellinen Joosef eli elämä on seikkailu* (pseud. M. Ritvala, 1938); *Fine van Brooklyn* (1939); *Hämeenlinnan kaunotar* (1939); *Jälkinäytös* (1939); *Kuka murhasi rouva Skrofin?* (1939); *Sellaista ei tapahdu* (1939); *Komisario Palmun erehdys* (1940); *Hankala kosinta* (1941); *Kotikaupunkimme Helsinki*, with A. Blomberg (1941); *Maa on ikuinen* (1941); *Totuus Latviasta ja Liettuasta* (pseud. Nauticus, 1941); *Tulevaisuuden tiellä* (1941); *Yövuorossa* (1941); *Ei koskaan huomispäivää* (1942); *Hyvin harkittu—puoliksi tehty* (1942); *Kaarina Maununtytär* (1942); *Neuvostovakoilun varjossa* (1942); *Rakennustaide ja standardi* (1942); *Novelleja* (1943); *Yövieras* (1943); *Jokin ihmisessä* (1944); *Tanssi yli hautojen* (1944); *Unohduksen pyörre* (pseud. Leo Arne, 1944); *Gabriel, tule takaisin* (1945); *Runoja 1925–1945* (1945); *Jäinen saari* (1946); *Rakas lurjus* (1946); *Elämän rikkaus* (1947); *Noita palaa elämään* (1947); *Omena putoaa* (1947); *Oy Weilin & Göös Aktiebolag 1872–1947*, with N. Hentola (1947); *Pariisilaissolmio* (1947); *Portti pimeään* (1947); *Kultakutri* (1948); *Kutsumaton* (1948); *Lähdin Istanbuliin* (1948); *Myöhästynyt hääyö* (1948); *Huhtikuu tulee* (1949); *Leikkaus* (1952); *Vallaton Waltari* (1957); *Miljoonavaillinki* (1959); *Tähdet kertovat, komisario Palmu* (1962); *Keisari ja senaattori* (1963); *Pienoisromaanit* (1966); *Kirjailijan muistelmat*, ed. Ritva Haavikko (1980); *Nuori Johannes* (1981); *Joulutarinoita* (1985).

REFERENCES

Heino, Aarne, *Huomioita eräiden Waltarin pienoisromaanien kertojista* (Tampere, 1970); Hoek, K. van, "Waltari of Finland." *John O'London's Weekly* 40 (1951); Laitinen, Kai, "The Human Voice." *Books from Finland* 13.3 (1979); Musikka, Sirkka, "Mika Waltarin tuotanto," in *Mika Waltarin juhlakirja* (Porvoo, 1968); Randel, W., "This Man Waltari." *Books Abroad* 30.2 (1956); "Mika Waltari." *Saturday Review of Literature* 32 (20 Aug. 1949); Tanttu, Juha, "Mika Waltari Has Always Been with Us." *Look at Finland* 1 (1979); Vainionpää, Marja-Leena, "Mika Waltari ja modernismi," in her *Esseitä*, vol. 3 (Tampere, 1979); Vallinkoski, J., and A. Juurinen, eds. *Mika Waltari ulkomailla. Käännösten bibliografia* (Helsinki, 1978).

Jaakko Ahokas

Wecksell, Josef Julius. Finland-Swedish poet and dramatist, b. 19 March 1838, Åbo (Turku), d. 9 August 1907, Helsinki.

The son of a prosperous hatter, Wecksell showed literary talent very early; some of his schoolboy verse was included in his *Valda ungdomsdikter* (1860; Selected Poems of Youth), and the gifted if unstable youth seemed to be the great hope of Swedish-language literature in Finland, destined to assume the mantle of Johan Ludvig Runeberg.* Often, his poems have clear thematic and stylistic influences from Lord Byron, Heinrich Heine, and Runeberg himself, as well as from Zacharias Topelius*; however, the lyrics written during Wecksell's university years in Helsinki strike notes distinctly his own, both in their frank statements of guilt-ridden eroticism and in their subtle psychological insight. ("Don Juan's Departure from Life" and the "Almqvist Monologue," about the Swedish novelist Carl Jonas Love Almqvist's* plans to commit murder, are two of Scandinavian literature's finest examples of the dramatic monologue.) Wecksell's dramatic talent was also demonstrated in his historical play, *Daniel Hjort* (first performed on 26 November 1862), about an episode from the siege of Turku Castle in 1597, an exploration of the nature and causes of treason; it has been called the best tragedy in Swedish before August Strindberg's* *Master Olof*, despite the tortured quality of its blank verse.

The title of a centennial poem by Elmer Diktonius,* "So Quickly You Burned" (1938), sums up Wecksell's unhappy fate; afflicted, like his contemporary, Aleksis Kivi,* with emotional illness, Wecksell was unable to comprehend his own drama at its premiere, and after a sojourn in an institution at Endenich in the Rhineland (the site of Robert Schumann's confinement and death, the previous decade), he was sent to the mental hospital at Helsinki in 1865, remaining there the rest of his long life. (Some fascinating poems composed during his collapse survive; one of these, the confessional "I, Son of Midnight," published in his *Samlade dikter* [Collected Poems] in 1868, provides an overture to the surviving fragments from his asylum-days—for example, "I stood on clouds," first printed by Arvid Mörne* in 1909.) Wecksell's poetry has obtained some international currency through its settings by Jean Sibelius ("Was It a Dream?" and "The Diamond on March Snow"); and *Daniel Hjort* has kept a place in the repertoire of Finland's theaters, both in the original (sometimes recast into prose) and in translation. Recently, Märta Tikkanen* has treated the relationship between Wecksell's mother and her gifted son in the first section of her book-length poem, *Mörkret som ger glädjen djup* (1981; The Darkness That Gives Depth to Joy).

FURTHER WORKS

Samlade dikter, 5th ed., with introduction by Gunnar Castrén (1919); *Samlade Dikter*, with introduction by Karin Allardt Ekelund (1962).

TRANSLATIONS

"Josef Julius Wecksell," in Gustafsson, Lars. *Forays into Swedish Poetry* (1977).

REFERENCES

Enckell, Mikael, *Över stumhetens gräns* (Helsinki, 1972); Hird, Gladys, "Daniel Hjort: Classic or Outdated Naturalist Drama." *Scandinavian Studies* 54.2 (1982); Mörne, Arvid, *Josef Julius Wecksell: En studi* (Helsinki; 1909); Mörne, Arvid, *Nya Wecksellstudier* (Helsinki, 1920); Schoolfield, G. C., "J. J. Wecksell and Finland's Swedish Lyric." *Scandinavian Studies* 36.1 (1964).

George C. Schoolfield

Welhaven, Johann Sebastian Cammermeyer. Norwegian poet and literary critic, b. 22 December 1807, Bergen, d. 21 October 1873, Oslo.

Welhaven's father was a clergyman at the leper hospital in Bergen. On his mother's side Welhaven was related to the Danish critic J. L. Heiberg,* whose aesthetics had a formative influence on the young poet. The untimely death of his father in 1825 forced Welhaven to abandon his studies in theology and make a living as a private tutor.

In Christiania (now Oslo), Welhaven became the leader for a circle of young academicians, variously called the "Intelligence Party" or "Danophiles," in opposition to the party of the "Patriots" lead by the poet Henrik Wergeland.* Since 1814, when Norway had declared itself independent of Denmark, of which it had been a province for nearly 400 years, one urgent problem on the minds of the intellectual elite concerned the future of a national, Norwegian culture. Welhaven and his followers were convinced that cutting the intellectual ties to Denmark spelled cultural suicide for Norway. In his first major work, *Norges Dæmring* (1834; Norway's Dawn), a polemical poem, Welhaven inveighs against the limitations of a "homespun" culture and pleads for solidarity with the Danish, to be "grafted on the tree [of Norway's] wild forest nature."

The conflict between Welhaven and Wergeland was exacerbated by the fact that the two men took different views of the nature and function of poetry. Like Friedrich Schiller, Welhaven identified the task of the poet with self-control and ethical commitment. From Heiberg, who in a series of articles in 1827–1830 had castigated romantic formlessness and arbitrariness, Welhaven learned to appreciate the classicist demand for clarity, good taste, and respect for the established genres. Like William Wordsworth, he emphasized the role of reflection in the poetic process. Through detachment and thought, "raw" experience must be transformed into the expression of "essential humanity." Wergeland, on the other hand, shared Friedrich Schlegel's view that the creative imagination is analogous to that of God. The divine speaks through the poet of genius, who therefore is not bound by norms or rules, either in his art or in his life. Romantic poetry freely blends all genres, poetry, prose, criticism, life and art.

To Welhaven such a view was unacceptable, and he expressed his impatience with Wergeland's luxuriant and undisciplined youthful poetry in a number of major critical pieces, among them notably *Henrik Wergelands Digtekunst og Polemik ved Akstykker oplyste* (1832; Henrik Wergeland's Poetry and Polemics Documented) and *Tre Dosin Complimenter til Henrik Wergeland* (1832; Three Dozen Compliments to Henrik Wergeland).

While Welhaven was a classicist in form, his poetry nevertheless reveals important romantic themes and ideas. In "Digtets Aand" (1844; The Spirit of the Poem), a kind of versified poetics, Welhaven expresses the view that truth and reality cannot be stated in discursive, conceptual language, but can be evoked poetically through rhythm, metaphor, and symbol. Poetry expresses the "unsayable" through an intuitive synthesis of form and content that speaks directly to the imagination.

Welhaven also wrote numerous national-romantic romances and ballads, drawing on myth and history, folk belief, legend, folk life, and nature. In form these poems are often based on folk ballad and song, on the meters of the Old Norse *Edda*, and on folk dance rhythms.

Besides these, Welhaven composed memorable poems on classical themes, occasional poems on social issues of the day, as well as many nature and love poems occasioned by his unsuccessful relationship to Camilla Wergeland (Henrik's sister) and by Ida Kierulf (sister of the composer), to whom Welhaven was secretly engaged for several years. By the time an appointment as university lecturer in philosophy in 1839 made it possible for Welhaven to marry, Ida was on her deathbed, and a few weeks later she passed away from tuberculosis.

Today Welhaven is remembered mostly as the antipode of his greater rival, Henrik Wergeland, and as the champion of classical balance and form during the romantic period in Norway. At its best, his poetry conveys a harmonious, inward musicality. A good number of Welhaven's poems have in fact been set to music, along with others by Halfdan Kierulf and Edvard Grieg.

FURTHER WORKS

Samlede Skrifter, 8 vols. (1867–1868); *Samlede Digterverker*, 4 vols. (1907); *Welhavens kjærlighetsbrev til Ida Kierulf*, ed. O. H. Mohn (1945); *Metaphysik i 100 paragrafer*, ed. A. Aarnes and E. A. Wyller (1965).

REFERENCES

Aarnes, Asbjørn, *J. S. Welhaven—kritikeren og dikteren* (Oslo, 1955); Andersen-Næss, Reidar, *J. S. Welhaven—Mennesket og dikteren* (Oslo, 1959); Hauge, Ingard, *Tanker og tro i Welhavens poesie* (Oslo, 1955).

Henning Sehmsdorf

Wergeland, Henrik. Norwegian journalist, poet, and dramatist, b. 17 June 1808, Kristiansand, d. 12 July 1845, Oslo.

Wergeland's father, Nikolai Wergeland, was a clergyman and radical patriot. In 1814 the elder Wergeland was a member of the the the national assembly on Eidsvoll, which in three months drafted and adopted the constitution on the basis of which Norway declared itself independent of Denmark.

Wergeland studied theology, history, botany, and later, medicine at the university of Christiania (now Oslo) and took a degree in theology in 1829. His youthful love affairs became the inspiration for his earliest, ecstatic poetry in which he creates the mythic image of Stella, woman of flesh and blood, but no less an all-encompassing, cosmic spirit (*Digte. Første Ring,* 1829; Poems. First Cycle).

From his father Wergeland inherited the passionate commitment to human freedom, and to this day he is considered one of the most progressive social and political pioneers of Norway. Wergeland represents the liberal aspects of European romanticism on the background of the French Revolution. He hailed the revolutionary events in France, Belgium, and Poland during the early 1830s as the dawn of a new political order and in 1831 traveled to England and France, to inform himself about the socialist vision of Henri de Rouvroy de Saint-Simon.

In his own country, Wergeland supported the rise of the farmers in political power and in general championed the cause of common people and the disfranchised in society. His attacks on the "bloodsucking" bourgeoisie involved him in a number of suits for libel.

Convinced that the battle for social equality had to be won not only in the political arena but also by education, Wergeland in 1830 traveled widely in Norway on behalf of *Selskabet for Norges Vel* (Society for Norway's Welfare), lecturing, distributing books, and establishing lending libraries. In Kristiania he opened his own book collection to the poor, and he started two journals, *For Almuen* (For the Common People), which he edited from 1830 to 1839, *For Arbeiderklassen* (For the Working Class), which he edited from 1839 to his death, and in 1835 became the editor of the *Statsborgeren* (The Citizen), representing the liberal opposition. During the 1830s Wergeland became the leader of *Patrioterne* (The Patriots), a circle of students and academicians in Christiania championing the cultural independence of Norway from Denmark, in opposition to the poet J. S. Welhaven,* who led the party of the "Danophiles." A central issue in this battle concerned the future of Norwegian as a written, literary language. During the 400 years that Norway had been a province of Denmark, Danish had replaced the native tongue as the language spoken and written by the cultural elite. In *Om norsk Sprogreformation* (1835; Norwegian Language Reform), Wergeland argues that the cultural and political identity of a nation are inseparable from the language the people speak and write. Early on Wergeland introduced many Norwegian terms and expressions both in his literary and journalistic writing, thus anticipating the efforts of Knud Knudsen and especially Ivar Aasen.* In 1842 Wergeland published a volume of poems actually composed in the dialect of the East Norwegian valleys.

Another issue to which Wergeland devoted much energy concerned the status of Jews in Norway and the question of religious freedom in general. As editor of *Statsborgeren* Wergeland pleaded for a constitutional change to allow Jews to settle in Norway, and in 1839 he introduced a bill in parliament to that effect. He took his case to the public in several polemical pieces as well as two major poetic cycles (1841–1844). The proposed constitutional change was heatedly discussed in the press and in parliament, but when finally voted on fell short of the necessary two-thirds majority. However, six years after Wergeland's untimely death in 1845, the matter was taken up once more, and that time it passed.

In Wergeland's poetry we can trace the Judeo-Christian heritage, Greek humanism, Platonic and Neoplatonic mysticism, as well as the influence of Jean-Jacques Rousseau, Friedrich Schelling, Friedrich Schlegel, Henrich Steffens, Lord Byron and others. Wergeland was a poet of ecstasy, deeply religious, but his faith was pantheistic-animistic rather than orthodox. Like other romantic poets, Wergeland embraced the idea of a spiritual evolution from so-called inanimate nature to absolute spirit. In bold imagery he suggests that in the moment of poetic intoxication the poet's soul leaves the body and is merged with the universe. The poet has little control over the creative process; the poem as it were comes into being of itself.

During his short life of only thirty-seven years Wergeland published some twenty volumes of lyrical and narrative poetry, songs, occasional poems and political verse, folk and sailors' songs. The 700-page dramatic poem *Skabelsen, Mennesket og Messias* (1830; Creation, Man and Messiah) is an early synthesis of Wergeland's mystical and sociopolitical ideas. Another high point is *Jan van Huysums Blomsterstykke* (1840; Jan van Huysum's Flowerpiece), in which Wergeland combines the rarefied atmosphere of the fairy tale with precise botanical description, philosophical reflections on the nature of art, lyricism, drama, and storytelling in depicting a certain painting he had seen in Christiania. In this large-scale piece the poet perfects the so-called Wergeland-trochee that he had first used in his early poems to Stella. Like Friedric Gottlieb Klopstock and Johannes Ewald,* Wergeland experimented with the unrhymed ode based on various biblical and classical models, but his closest forerunner was the trochaic-dactylic "sapphic" ode of Horace. Consisting mostly of four-footed lines combined to long unrhymed sequences, the Wergeland-trochee is superbly suited to capture the flow of visions rising to an ecstatic climax.

Wergeland also was a rather productive dramatist although few, if any, of his twenty-seven plays have stood the test of time. About half are topical farces reflecting various political and cultural battles of the day. The balance of his dramatic production consists of full-length melodramas, historical plays, musical comedies, and even an opera. He experimented with various metric forms in his plays; the action is usually quite loose in structure, the characterization sketchy.

In 1844 the poet fell ill with tuberculosis. During the last year of his life, although bedridden, he continued his work as archivist, journalist, and editor. He also completed a major new work, the epic-lyrical cycle *Den engelske Lods* (1844; The English Pilot), and wrote some of his most memorable poems in which he returns to his preferred themes, nature, especially flowers, the round of the seasons, and the transcendence of life over death, through love.

Wergeland's contemporaries, among them notably Johann Welhaven, tended to disparage Wergeland's luxuriant experiments with poetic metaphor, metric form, and genre as undisciplined and chaotic, but today there is general agreement that not only the depth and scope of Wergeland's poetic vision, but also his genius for innovation is quite unparalleled in Norwegian literature.

FURTHER WORKS

Samlede Skrifter, ed. H. Lassen, 9 vols. (1852–1857); *Samlede Skrifter,* critical ed., H. Jæger and D. A. Seip, 23 vols. (1918–1940); *Brev til Henrik Wergeland,* ed. Leiv Amundsen (1956).

TRANSLATIONS

Henrik Wergeland, the Norwegian Poet, trans. I. Grøndahl (1919); *Wergeland, the Prophet*, trans. Elias Gordon (1938); *Poems*, ed. G. H. Gathorne-Hardy, I. Sithell, and I. Grøndahl, 2nd ed. (1970).

REFERENCES

Beyer, Harald, *Henrik Wergeland* (Oslo, 1946); Heiberg, Hans, *Så stort et hjerte* (Oslo, 1973); Koht, Halvdan, *Henrik Wergeland i strid for bonde og arbeider* (Oslo, 1939); Michaelsen, A. G., *Den gyldne lenke: norsk litteraturutvikling og det harmoniske imperativ* (Oslo, 1977); Ustvedt, Yngvar, *Henrik Wergeland* (Oslo, 1975).

Henning Sehmsdorf

Wessel, Johann Herman. Norwegian poet and dramatist, b. 6 October 1742, Vestby, d. 29 December 1785, Copenhagen.

A minister's son, Wessel grew up in a small community near Oslo and became a student in Copenhagen in 1765, where he stayed until the end of his brief life. Wessel never took a university degree, eked out a meager income as a private tutor, while trying his hand at writing drama, translating French plays for the stage in Copenhagen, and composing verse.

In 1772 Wessel made a name for himself with *Kierlighed uden Strømper* (Love Without Socks), a parody on neoclassical tragedy. An immediate success with the audience for its wit and lyrical virtuosity, the play has remained a favored staple of Danish and Norwegian theaters until today. The play has been variously interpreted as an attack on French tragedy or on its Dano-Norwegian imitations; inversely, the Danish literary historian and critic, Billeskov Jansen, has seen it as a "classicist's mocking play with classicism." Less successful were Wessel's *Lykken bedre end Forstanden* (1776; More Luck Than Wit), a comedy of intrigue in the tradition of Ludvig Holberg;* and *Anno 7603*, also a comedy that has never been performed, but was published posthumously (1785).

In 1774 Wessel, together with other Norwegian poets and intellectuals residing in Copenhagen, founded Det Norske Selskab (The Norwegian Society), thus providing a forum for Wessel's lyrical talent and satirical wit. In the spirit of Voltaire and neoclassic aesthetics, the members of the society rejected the cult of feeling and sensibility of their pre-romantic contemporaries, notably the German poet F. G. Klopstock (1724–1803) and his Danish follower Johannes Ewald* (1743–1771). The three collections of verse published by the society between 1775 and 1795 contained the bulk of Wessel's poetic oeuvre, ranging from epigrams, occasional poems, drinking songs, and love poems to versified, humorous narratives in which the poet pokes fun at the customs and morals of his day and at human nature in general. A good many of Wessel's humorous narrative poems enjoy continued popularity today, and they have left their mark on his successors in the genre, especially the well-known Norwegian poet Herman Wildenvey* (1886–1959).

In 1785, Wessel was stricken by a nervous disorder. He died as he had lived, in poverty, leaving behind a wife and a son, age four.

FURTHER WORKS

Samtlige Skrivter, 2 vols. (1787); *Samlede Digte*, ed. L. Levin (1862); *Digte*, 2 vols. (1918).

REFERENCES

Langberg, Harald, *Den store satire. J. H. Wessel og Kærlighed uden Strømper* (Copenhagen, 1973); Sommerfeldt, W. P., ed., *Johan Herman Wessel og Norge* (Oslo, 1942).

Henning Sehmsdorf

Wied, Gustav. Danish dramatist and novelist, b. 6 March 1858, Holmegaard at Nakskov, d. 24 October 1914, Roskilde.

Wied's outward life was rather uneventful. The son of a prosperous farmer, he grew up in a rural milieu characterized by provincial culture. For several years, he worked as a private tutor, tried his fortune as an actor, and finally found his calling as an author in the 1880s. He eventually settled in Roskilde near Copenhagen in the provincial surroundings that provide the background for most of his works.

Victorian respectability was Wied's favorite subject and aversion. He questioned the official morality of his time, and the disclosure of hypocrisy and the double standard is a major theme in his authorship. However, this approach to society did not lead Wied to formulate a political or ethical point of view. Since he was not able to transform his criticism and skepticism into a positive view of life, his approach became that of irony and satire. On the one hand, he was deeply influenced by the naturalistic concept of man, yet on the other he was unable to accept it. After all he was a disappointed moralist attracted by the idyll he constantly exposed as swindle. He saw man as an animal governed by instinct and low ambition, but also in search of something better and higher that did not exist. The solution to this tragic disintegration was humor. In Wied's works life is most often depicted as a comedy.

Wied wrote a number of plays for the traditional theater, but his most original dramatic contribution was the "Satyrplay." They were not intended for the stage, although some of them have been and still are performed. They represent a capacious genre whose extensive stage directions and commentaries are of no less significance than the dialogue. Some of them, especially the long *Dansemus* (1905; Dancing Mice), mirroring contemporary Denmark, resemble Wied's novels, which are known for their dramatic qualities. The most popular of these is *Livsens Ondskab* (1899; Life's Malice), a comedy with unforgettable exponents of hypocrisy and skepticism. *Slægten* (1893; Kin) is one of Wied's few serious works. It gives a pessimistic picture of degeneration, power, and sexuality.

Wied is one of the greatest humorists in Danish literature, whose satirical disclosure of human nature has kept his works topical. During recent years several of them have been staged for television.

FURTHER WORKS

Nogle Aforismer i Anledning af Interprellationen i Storeheddinge og dens Følger af Peter Idealist (1887); *Silhuetter* (1891); *En Bryllupsnat* (1892); *Barnlige Sjæle* (1893); *Ung-domshistorier* (1895); *Lystige Historier* (1896); *Adel, Gejstlighed, Borger og Bonde* (1897); *Første Violin* (1898); *Det svage Køn* (1900); *Skærmydsler* (1901); *Thummelumsen* (1901); *Knagsted* (1902); *Hendes gamle Naade* (1904); *Ranke Viljer* (1906); *Fædrene æde Druer* (1908); *Pastor Sørensen & Co.* (1913); *Digt og Virkelighed* (1915).

TRANSLATIONS

American-Scandinavian Review 3.5 (1915); *Autumn Fires. A comedy*, trans. Benjamin F. Glazer, in *Fifty Contemporary One-Act Plays*, ed. by Frank Shay and Pierre Loving (1920); *2 x 2 = 5; a comedy in four acts*, trans. Ernest Boyd and Holger Koppel (1923); *American-Scandinavian Review* 32.1 (1944).

REFERENCES

Ahnlund, Knut, *Den unge Gustav Wied* (Copenhagen, 1964); Neergaard, Ebbe, *Dommen og drømmen* (Copenhagen, 1951); Nielsen, Axel, *Parentesen, der voksede* (Copenhagen, 1948); Salicath, Eddie, *Omkring Gustav Wied* (Copenhagen, 1946).

Preben Meulengracht Sørensen

Wildenvey, Herman Theodor (orig. Herman Theodor Portaas). Norwegian poet and novelist, b. 20 July 1886, Nedre Eiker; d. 27 September 1959, Larvik. Wildenvey was married to the Norwegian novelist Gisken Wildenvey, b. 1895.

Wildenvey was one of the few survivors of the emigrant steamer *Norge,* which was wrecked at Rockall in 1904 on her voyage to America with 600 passengers. After three years of odd jobs and sporadic studies in the United States, he returned to Norway where he published *Nyinger* (1907; Fires in the Open), a collection of poems that was very successful with its strolling rhythms, surprising imagery, and charming humor. Wildenvey became one of the beloved poets of his country during the following two to three decades.

Subjectivity, opposition to conventions, and a sort of nonchalant arrogance are the most striking features of Wildenvey's first lyric works. During the 1920s and 1930s Wildenvey overcame his propensity for mannerism and poetic clowning and approached subjects of existential import. The superficiality of his love poems yielded to a strain of melancholy. Even though love is a form of eternal life energy, man's ability to accept it is weak and easily ended. This motif is closely connected to Wildenvey's conception of time. The intense experience of the moment lends insight into eternity, ''the eternal infinitive.'' Even the most worldly experience lacks borders of space and time.

The idea that any total perception of reality is unattainable becomes increasingly predominant in Wildenvey's later poetry. But in among the writer's cosmic fantasies are songs in lines of simple syntax and popular vocabulary that praise Wildenvey's native Nedre Eiker. After World War II, Wildenvey published four volumes of poetry. Despite their obvious weaknesses, they received favorable criticism. As a novelist and short story writer Wildenvey was a failure. His autobiographical works, however, acquired a wide circle of readers.

Wildenvey's impact on Norwegian literature is best measured in terms of his audience. More than any other Norwegian poet he influenced the poetic taste, for better or worse, of young readers between 1910 and 1940.

FURTHER WORKS

Campanula (1903); *Ringsang* (1910); *Digte* (1911); *Prismer* (1911); *Årets eventyr* (1913); *Lys over land* (1913); *Brændende hjerter* (1915); *Kjærtegn* (1916); *Flygtninger* (1917); *Alle slags vers* (1919); *Hemmeligheter* (1919); *Den glemte have* (1920); *Trold i Ord* (1920); *Nedfaldsfrugt* (1921); *Kjærlighetsdigte* (1922); *Ildorkestret* (1923); *Fiken av tistler* (1925); *Det falder stjerner* (1926); *Et herrens år* (1928); *Dagenes sang* (1930); *Høstens lyre* (1931); *På ville veier* (1932); *Stjernenes speil* (1935); *En ung manns flukt* (1936); *Vingehesten og verden* (1937); *Den nye rytmen* (1938); *En lykkelig tid* (1940); *Samlede dikt*, 6 vols. (1945–1952); *Filomele* (1946); *Ved sangens kilder* (1947); *En lykkelig tid* (1949); *Polyhymnia* (1952); *Ugler til Athen* (1953); *Soluret* (1956); *Samlede dikt*, 2 vols. (1957).

TRANSLATIONS

Owls to Athens (1935).

REFERENCES

Bjerke, Andre, *I syklonens sentrum* (1970); Elster, Kristian, "Three Lyric Poets of Norway." *American-Scandinavian Review* 13.11 (1925); Haave, Kristoffer, *Herman Wildenvey, Poeten—kunstneren* (Oslo, 1952); *Og alle fugle sjunge, festskrift til Herman Wildenvey 1957* (Oslo, 1957).

                                                                                     Jostein Fet

Willumsen, Dorrit. Danish short story writer and novelist, b. 31 August 1940, Copenhagen.

Willumsen's father, who was an opera singer, left the family, and Willumsen lived with her mother's parents. Although her grandparents were loving, she nevertheless grew up with a feeling of loss. This feeling clearly influenced her writing, which contains many descriptions of children who are neglected and grown-ups who are, consequently, unable and afraid to love.

Willumsen's early and fundamental experience of loneliness and absurdity predisposed her for modernism with its atomistic worldview and inclusion of the fantastic. Her style is unique in its brevity and abrupt compactness which reflect both disconnectedness and absence. However, this kind of narrative, where the accumulation of things replaces emotions, reads like a prose poem of distinct beauty; human content has been replaced by aestheticism.

A predominant symbol in this alienated world is the doll: the child's projection onto his or her doll or the stunted adult who resembles or even turns into a robot or doll. (One novel embraces a whole wax museum.) A central short story is "Modellen Coppelia," about a mannequin who constantly changes roles partly in search of identity, and partly as escape from it. Neither able to love, nor wanting to, she refuses to be wife, mother, and, finally, woman; she ends up as a sexless doll, a neuter, in narcissistic self-reflection in front of her many mirrors.

Willumsen has been considered a feminist due to her incisive descriptions of woman and her lot. But as she demonstrates with her objectively balanced book *Manden som påskud* (1980; The Man as an Excuse), the modern male is likewise without individuality and his problem inextricably connected to that of the woman; it brings woman nowhere to use the man as an excuse. There are no easy ways out in Willumsen's thematically concentrated and powerful writings, but there is a wealth of insight that indirectly brings hope.

FURTHER WORKS

Knagen (1965); *Stranden* (1966); *Da* (1968); *the, krydderi, acryl, salær, græshopper* (1970); *Modellen Coppelia* (1973); *En værtindes smil* (1974); *Kontakter* (1976); *Neonhaven* (1976); *Hvis det virkelig var en film* (1978; *If it Really Were A Film*, 1982); *Programmeret til Kærlighed* (1981); *Marie. En roman om Madame Tussauds liv* (1983); *Suk hjerte* (1986).

FURTHER TRANSLATIONS

No Man's Land, ed. Annegret Heitmann (1987).

REFERENCE

Wamberg, Bodil, "I Am Only Afraid of Pure Angels," in *Out of Denmark,* ed. Bodil Wamberg (Copenhagen, 1985).

Charlotte Schiander Gray

Winther, Sophus Keith. Danish-American novelist and English professor at the University of Washington, b. 24 June 1893, Søby, d. 1983, Seattle.

Winther immigrated in 1895, with his family, to Weeping Water, Nebraska, where he grew up. The family later moved to Eugene, Oregon, and Winther received his doctorate in English from the University of Washington in 1927. He taught at Washington, with a professional interest in Eugene O'Neill, until 1963.

Winther's trilogy of novels, *Take All to Nebraska* (1936), *Mortgage Your Heart* (1937), and *This Passion Never Dies* (1938), shows the basic conflict of the first-generation rural immigrant, that is, their doubts about the decision to leave their home in Denmark for an indeterminate future in a strange country. Yet in the story of the Grimsen family, this tension of identity is gradually resolved as they are forced by the economic realities of their new environment to either forget or sublimate their dreams of the old country in order even to survive.

In the late nineteenth century the Grimsen family settled in an area of the country where they had to rent-farm, and this economic situation determined their fate of material failure and familial tension. Their initial poverty, combined with land and crop speculation by big business, and with the capriciousness of nature, undermined any hope of material success. It made no difference that Peter planned well and worked hard; he simply had no chance for individual success. Still, while Peter's impoverished economic situation had always determined his view of life, his obsession for work, which may well have alienated his sons, did have as its goal the survival of his family as a social unit.

Eventually, the Grimsens lose their farm and Peter dies. Yet both he and Meta, the first-generation immigrants, implore their children to look to the future for a better life. Peter and Meta failed in their struggle for a free and independent existence in the "Promised Land," but they did believe that the next generation would succeed—economically *and* as good people.

In Winther's trilogy, one observes the tension between the ideals of material success and human understanding. It shows a family that suffers economic failure and only partial success in enduring as a social unit. The human values inherent in the Grimsen family are certainly positive indications of hope. However, the primary theme of the trilogy is failure—the failure of the isolated and unknowledgeable immigrant in his struggle against large-scale social and economic institutions in the United States.

Winther's trilogy is the best existing portrayal of Danish-American rural life currently available in English.

FURTHER WORKS

The Realistic War Novel (1930); *Eugene O'Neill: A Critical Study* (1934); *Beyond the Garden Gate* (1938).

REFERENCES

Bansen, Norman C., "The Danes in Winther's Trilogy." *Bridge* 1 (1978); Jensen, Rudolf J., "A Comparative Study of Sophus Keith Winther and Carl Hansen." *Bridge* 2 (1978).
                                                                                        Rudolf Jensen

Wivallius, Lars. Swedish poet and adventurer, b. 1604 or 1605, Wivalla farmstead, Längbro parish, Närke, d. 6 April 1669, Stockholm.

The precocious son of a bailiff, Wivallius matriculated at Uppsala University in 1623 but abandoned his studies to pursue a life of brash opportunism on the Continent. In 1629 he overreached himself by wedding the Scanian noblewoman Gertrud Grijp, who believed she had married Baron Erik Gyllenstierna. The ruse discovered, Wivallius fled to Sweden, where he was captured and imprisoned first in Stockholm and from 1634 to 1641 at Kajaneborg, northeastern Finland. He spent his last twenty-eight years mainly in Stockholm as a shyster lawyer. His widow had to seek charity to get him decently buried.

Wivallius emerges as a poet in spite of himself—the first authentic lyrical poet in Swedish literature. Almost all of his writings stem from his lengthy incarcerations: his prose writings are outlandish and pathetic apologies that found little favor with the judicial authorities, but his poetry, only a handful of works, is of high literary quality. While he turned out verses in German and Latin, he struck deep and resounding chords in his Swedish *visor*, songs rooted in the traditions of the medieval ballad and the Reformation lyric.

Of these, two are noteworthy, "Ach libertas, tu ädla tingh" (written ca. 1632; Ah, Liberty, Thou Noble Thing) and "Warer nu glad, mina fiender all!" (printed 1634; Be Glad Now, All My Enemies); and one remains an enduring masterpiece, "Klage-Wijsa, Öfwer thenna Torra och Kalla Wåhr" (printed 1642; Dirge over This Dry and Cold Spring). In reading these poems, one still can respond to their artless simplicity as lyrical ballads, their keenly felt longing for freedom and liberty, and—especially in the case of the "Klage-Wijsa"—a splendid re-creation of nature in all of its beauty, fullness, and restorative purity. Wivallius's all-embracing love of the Nordic land itself enabled him here to give unforgettable expression to one of the inexhaustible themes of Swedish letters.

WORKS

Lars Wivallius: Hans lif och dikter, ed. Henrik Schück, 2 vols. (1893–1895).

REFERENCES

Ahnlund, Nils, *Kring Gustav Adolf* (Stockholm, 1930); Sverker, Ek, *Lars Wivallius' visdiktning* (Stockholm, 1930); Sverker, Ek, *Studier i Wivalliusvisornas kronologi* (Uppsala, 1921).

Raymond Jarvi

Wivel, Ole. Danish poet, publisher, and essayist, b. 29 September 1921, Copenhagen.

Wivel's upper-class background determined the cultural ideals of his first poetry, until he was confronted with the tragedies of war in 1944 while working for the Red Cross. In 1945 Wivel established Wivels Forlag, which published *Heretica,* an important periodical, which from 1948 to 1953 espoused the conviction that art was the only valid response to postwar political and scientific problems. With his lyrical breakthrough, *I fiskens tegn* (1948; In the Sign of the Fish), Wivel more clearly than any other poet of the period expressed—in a symbolic and pathetic language—a foreboding of the Second Coming. The continuing poems of *Jævndøgnselegier* (1949; Equinoctial Elegies) contain a powerful contrast between the hopeless, modern civilization—for example, in the T. S. Eliot–inspired "Flyvepladsen" (The Airport) an early modernist poem—and a nostalgic childhood filled with hope.

From 1951 to 1953 a teacher at Askov Folk High School, Wivel became acquainted with other social classes that stimulated his growing social and ethical engagement. *Nike* (1958) contained open, surrealistic, critical poems; the title poem referred both to the Greek goddess of victory and to a rocket of that name.

Wivel was the codirector of Gyldendal Publishing House from 1954 to 1964 and again from 1971 to 1981. From 1964 Wivel has been a member of the Danish Academy. With regard to politics, he was active in the protest movement against the American war in Vietnam and criticized the capitalist and industrial world. The articles of *Poesi og protest* (1971; Poetry and Protest) reflect his development since *Heretica*. Wivel's latest poetry also shows his constant reconditioning. By virtue of his many-faceted talent, energy, and openness toward new concepts, Wivel has functioned as a dynamic contributor to Danish culture.

FURTHER WORKS

Digte (1940); *Udvalgte digte* (1942); *Den hvide rose* (1942); *Digte*, 2 vols. (1943–1944); *Den skjulte gud* (1952); *Månen* (1952); *Poesi og eksistens* (1953); *Jævndøgn* (1956); *Digte 1948–1958* (1960); *Templet for Kybele* (1961); *Kunsten og krigen* (1965); *Martin A. Hansen, fra barndommen til krigens år* (1967); *Martin A. Hansen, fra krigens år til døden* (1969); *Gravskrifter* (1970); *Romance for valdhorn* (1972); *Trio i nr. 3* (1973); *Tranedans* (1975); *Rejsen til Skagen* (1977); *Danmark ligger her endnu* (1979); *Skabelsen* (1981); *Guder i forårslys* (1983); *Sansning og symbol* (1985); *Til de fattige præster* (1985), *Musikken kommer fra væggene* (1986).

TRANSLATIONS

Contemporary Danish Poetry, ed. Line Jensen et al. (1977); *Seventeen Danish Poets*, ed. Niels Ingwersen (1981).

REFERENCES

Hansen, Birgit Helene, *Omkring Heretica* (Århus, 1968); Jeppesen, Bent Haugaard, "Ole Wivel," in *Danske digtere i det 20. århundrede*, ed. Torben Brostrøm and Mette Winge, vol. 3 (Copenhagen, 1981); Mjöberg, Jöran, "Poeten Ole Wivel." *Samtiden* 71 (1962).

Svend Birke Espegård

Women's Literature. Before the 1970s, it was accepted practice for Scandinavian literary histories and anthologies of prose and poetry to limit their coverage to male authors, with just a few exceptions such as Selma Lagerlöf* and Sigrid Undset,* award-winning writers whose works had been widely translated. Literature by women would, at best, be included under a subheading at the end of each chapter and treated as though whatever characterized the women's authorship was due to their biological gender. Disparaging remarks about the writers' personalities and behavior were not uncommon. For example, the eighteenth-century poet Hedvig Charlotta Nordenflycht,* who composed the first lyric poetry in the Swedish language, outraged her contemporaries by writing candidly about her unrequited love for a younger man. The ridicule she encountered so colored her reputation that even E. N. Tigerstedt's authoritative, multivolume literary history text includes this caption beneath a stylized portrait typical of Nordenflycht's time: "The antique lyre is ill suited to the Sunday-dressed matron's bourgeois corpulence." This caption prompted Karin Westman Berg, a pioneer in the field of women's studies, to ask, "What did Goethe look like when he, at eighty, was writing his last love poems to a young girl? Did he have a pot belly? Was he bald? Why are we not informed?'' In the same vein, the tragic fates of novelists Victoria Benedictsson* and Amalie Skram* have received scrutiny from critics and biographers of a psychoanalytic persuasion, while their novels have remained untranslated and been allowed to go out of print.

In retrospect, the exclusion of women from the canon of Scandinavian literature is shockingly discriminatory, but it took a gradual shift in public consciousness and a great deal of effort on the part of concerned scholars and critics to bring about a reappraisal of the works of female writers. Nearly all the scholars and critics have been women, and many have pursued this goal at considerable risk to their professional careers. What has come to be known as *kvinnolitteratur-forskning,* to use the Swedish variant of a compound term that translates literally as womanliteratureresearch, is clearly a by-product of the most recent phase of the women's movement, which began in Scandinavia, as in the United States and elsewhere in Europe, in the late 1960s. Attention to *kvinnolitteratur* has by no means been limited to academe. Some of the most provocative reassessments have appeared on the culture pages of daily newspapers or originated in informal reading circles. In fact, institutions of higher learning in Scandinavia have been quite reluctant to integrate *kvinnolitteraturforskning* into their curricula. Courses in women's literature have had temporary, quasi-official status, and doctoral candidates have often done their research without benefit of qualified advising.

The term *kvinnolitteraturforskning* has some semantic advantages over its usual English translation, ''research into women's literature'' or the more frequent counterpart ''feminist literary criticism.'' The ambiguity of *kvinnolitteratur* suggests literature by women, for women, or about women, or literature written from a particularly female perspective. The growing canon of *kvinnolitteratur* shows a preference for works that are all of these at once. A novel, for example, in which a female author writes about the condition of women from the perspective of her experience as a woman in language and imagery that female readers find familiar is more likely to receive attention than a work that conforms to the standards of the predominant male genre of its time, no matter how successfully. Thus Mathilde Fibiger's *Clara Raphael. Tolv Breve* (1851; Clara Raphael. Twelve Letters), Camilla Collett's* *Amtmandens Døttre* (1854; The Sheriff's Daughters), and Fredrika Bremer's* *Hertha* (1856) were obvious choices for a reevaluation, since each is regarded as the first female novel of protest in its national literature.

The first task of this new research was to rectify the critical mistreatment of those few women whose works received at least passing mention in the literary histories. New readings of Selma Lagerlöf, for example, underscore the moral complexity of her vision, adding dimension to her previous reputation as a clever recounter of folktales. New analyses of Sigrid Undset's and Karen Blixen's (*see* Isak Dinesen) perceptions of women have offered a more profound interpretation of their seemingly antifeminist public stance. One of the most dramatic revisions involves Anna Maria Lenngren's* poem "Några ord till min kära dotter ifall jag hade någon" (Some Words to My Dear Daughter if I Had One). For generations, male critics had taken its diatribe against learned women at face value and overlooked the irony in it, even though Lenngren was most renowned as a satirist.

The rediscovery of neglected women writers has been another important goal. New editions of works long out of print have appeared, some with lengthy critical introductions. Bibliographies and anthologies have been compiled to introduce previously obscure authors, as well as some first attempts at historical surveys. These publications are part of a campaign to educate readers about the conditions under which women have written—including overt discrimination in the literary marketplace and more subtle taboos against creative expression—and the kinds of life experiences that women have drawn on for literary material. The new readings of resurrected women's literature have rarely been strictly formalist, but rather examine the work in its social context. Thus the question, "But is this really good literature?" has not been the most compelling concern. Rather, the value of literature as cultural document has been emphasized. While women were long excluded from government, diplomacy, religious leadership, and the other areas of endeavor from which history is generally made, they *did* write fiction, poetry, and drama, as well as letters, diaries, and memoirs. Thus literature is one of the major sources for reconstructing women's history.

It became apparent fairly early that the traditional notion of periodization used to trace the development of literary styles and genres in Scandinavia is not always sufficient to explain trends in women's literature. For example, literary historians examining the romantic period in the early nineteenth century have perhaps been justified in excluding women. A search for lost female romantics might all too easily support the opinion voiced by Per Daniel Amadeus Atterbom*: "Sometimes nature itself makes exceptions and puts positive, masculine genius in a female body. From this anomaly come educated women, artists and heroines, of whom three or four have justifiably won the world's admiration. Their lot, however, is not to be desired. They must surrender all claim to feminine happiness." The appropriate question to ask is "What *were* women writing in the romantic period?" The answer is, domestic realism on the model of the British novel. In the preface to her anonymously published *Hverdagshistorier* (1828; Everyday Stories), the Danish prose writer Thomasine Gyllembourg* issued a justification that became a rallying call for several generations of female writers: "All my stories are true everyday stories. They bear the imprint of the earth from which they spring. They are fruits of life, not of learning and profound study. Domestic and social life, individual relationships and intrigues are the sphere from which they are taken, and I honestly admit that I assign these daily, domestic circumstances a great importance. That is, for all humans, the most intimate thing, the source from which their happiness and unhappiness spring." Neither the great novels of protest of the 1850s nor the indictments of marriage of the 1880s could have been written without this grounding in daily reality.

"Romanticism" for women writers is not a harking back to the classical period nor even the Viking Age, but to a pre-industrial Golden Age when women presumably held sway over large agrarian households. If there are any female romantics, they can be found exalting women's maternal qualities and peaceful natures in novels and poems that appeared in the 1920s and 1930s. Elin Wägner,* for example, adopted the *nyckelknippa*, the housewife's ring of keys that opened larders and linen closets, as a logo for the covers of her novels.

A group of writers of particular interest to scholars of women's literature is the women who wrote during the Modern Breakthrough of the 1880s, a period in which the emancipation of women was a popular subject for fiction and drama, even for male authors. Novelists Victoria Benedictsson and Amalie Skram, dramatist Alfhild Agrell, and others lesser known wrote excruciatingly realistic accounts of marital oppression. The tone of their works is more despondent than that of their male contemporaries, an observation that was sometimes used to belittle their literary quality. They were less inclined to follow Henrik Ibsen's* lead in exalting women as the embodiment of moral courage, and they placed little hope in free sexuality as a promise of liberation. When read against factual information about the condition of women in the late nineteenth century, these works clearly fulfill the expectations of naturalism, the reigning literary ideology of the time. Danish critic Anne Birgitte Richard maintains that the female writers of the Modern Breakthrough can be read "as models for the type of questions that the reading of women's literature of later periods also raises, about women in the literary marketplace, about a female aesthetic and literary trends, about women's thematizing of the conflicts between their identities as sexual, motherly, working, and creating human beings, about the women's movement and women's literature, about criteria of evaluation and methods of analysis." Another group that lends itself to such a study is the female proletarian writers of the first half of the twentieth century. A circle of independent scholars in Stockholm has begun to examine proletarian literature to see whether generalizations made on the basis of reading the men's works really hold true for the women's, as well.

An admirable attempt to reconstruct the history of women's literature on its own, more appropriate terms has been made by Stig Dalager and Anne-Marie Mai in the two-volume *Danske kvindelige forfattere* (1982; Danish Female Writers). They use a developmental scheme devised by the American feminist critic Elaine Showalter in her study of British novelists, *A Literature of Their Own*, to make the claim that there is a continuity and consistency to women's literature, a distinct female literary tradition. They show that women writing often look to a female heritage for models and do not necessarily try to conform to the masculine standards by which the compilers of literary histories judge whether they are worthy of inclusion.

The latest development in this female literary heritage is a heightened group consciousness among Scandinavian women writing today. Knowledge about the conditions under which their foremothers wrote has motivated them to join together to better the conditions for their own work. There have been several pan-Scandinavian seminars for female writers, organized by women's caucuses that have formed in the national writers' unions. These caucuses have looked into such matters as the receptivity of publishing companies to women's manuscripts, the efforts to promote and distribute women's books, the frequency with which women's books are reviewed, and the share of authors' stipends and literary prizes awarded to women. In addition, they provide a forum where women can read and discuss writing currently underway. There has been some cooperation between writers and literary scholars, again in the form of seminars. A coincidence worthy of mention is that by 1980, a major literary journal in each of the three larger countries was edited by a woman committed to making women's literature more visible: *Ord och Bild* in Sweden (Eva Adolfsson), *Vinduet* in Norway (Janneken Øverland), and *Vindrosen* in Denmark (Pil Dahlerup). The multilingual, international journal of Scandinavian literature, *Edda*, under Åse Hiorth Lervik's editorship, became an invaluable forum for new work on female writers.

Selecting a few outstanding scholars to be identified here would be difficult and arbitrary. There are, however, people in each country who stand at the center of a network of *kvinnolitteraturforskning*, who serve as liaisons and even mentors for others, as well as doing their own research and teaching. Karin Westman Berg began conducting informal reading groups as early as the 1950s and has, since the mid–1960s, led a seminar through the extension department at the University of Uppsala where participants present their new research into women's literature. More recently, she obtained government funding for a women's literature project, under the aegis of which several important books and articles, as well as a serial publication, have come to be. Pil Dahlerup and Jette Lundbo Levy were the first to apply a feminist critical perspective to the women of the Modern Breakthrough. In her courses at the University of Copenhagen, Dahlerup has adapted the methods of Marxist and structuralist criticism to elicit fresh readings of women's works. She is now at work on an all-inclusive compendium of Danish women writers. Besides encouraging younger scholars to venture publication of their findings in *Edda*, Åse Hiorth Lervik has compiled a two-volume anthology of literary criticism written by women from 1880 on called *Gjennom Kvinneøyne* (1980–1982, Through Women's Eyes), which shows what standards female critics have set for women's literature. Helga Kress, even while teaching at the University of Bergen, has focused on the women's literature of her native Iceland. In Finland, Karin Allardt Ekelund is respected by a younger generation of scholars for paying serious attention to Fredrika Runeberg's authorship, though her work predates this phase of *kvinnolitteraturforskning* and is somewhat different in perspective.

ANTHOLOGIES

Bankier, Joanna, et al., eds., *The Other Voice* (New York, 1976); Fried, Anne, ed., *Thank You for These Illusions: Poems by Finnish Women Writers* (Helsinki, 1981); Hanson, Katherine, ed., *An Everyday Story: Norwegian Women's Fiction* (Seattle, 1984); Heitmann, Annegret, ed., *No Man's Land: An Anthology of Modern Danish Women's*

Literature (1987); *Swedish Books* 1/4 (1980), special number devoted to writing by women.

REFERENCES

Adolfsson, Eva, et al., *Vardagsslit och drömmars språk: Svensk a proletärförfattarinnor från Maria Sandel till Mary Andersson* (Enskede, 1981); Bergom-Larsson, Maria, *Kvinnomedvetande* (Stockholm, 1976): Bonnevie, Mai Bente, et al, *Et annet språk* (Oslo, 1977); Dahlerup, Pil, *Det moderne gennembruds kvinder* (Copenhagen, 1983); Dalager, Stig, and Anne-Marie Mai, *Danske kvindelige forfattere*, 2 vols. (Copenhagen, 1982); Engelstad, Irene, and Janneken Øverland, *Frihet til å skrive* (Oslo, 1981); Hermelin, Carola, et al., *Kvinnliga författare 1893–1899: Biobibliografi över svensk och finlandssvensk skönlitteratur* (Uppsala, 1982); Jörgensen, Aage, *Kvindeforskning og Kvindelitteratur* (Aalborg, 1979); *Kvinnenes kulturhistorie*, 2 vols. (Oslo, 1985); Koch, Nynne, and Annie Winther, *Kvindeforskning: Women's Studies* (Copenhagen, 1981); *Kvinner og bøker: Festskrift til Ellisiv Steen* (Oslo, 1978); *Kvinnornas litteraturhistoria*, 2 vols. (Stockholm, 1981, 1983); Lervik, Åse Hiorth, *Gjennom kvinneøyne. Norske kvinners litteraturkritik*, 2 vols. (Oslo, 1981–1982); Levy, Jette Lundbo, *De knuste spejle* (Oslo, 1976); Malmström, Rosa, *Kvinnor och kvinnohistoria i Sverige* (Göteborg, 1981); Mazzarella, Merete, *Från Fredrika Runeberg till Märta Tikkanen* (Helsinki, 1985); *Norsk kvinnelitteraturhistorie*, 3 vols. (Oslo, 1988–); *Ny litteratur om kvinnor. En bibliografi* (Göteborg, 1980–); Paget, Birgitta, et al., eds., *Kvinnor och skapande* (Stockholm, 1983); Rasmussen, Janet, "Dreams and Discontent: The Female Voice in Norwegian Literature," in *Review of National Literatures: Norway*, ed. Sverre Lyngstad (New York, 1983); Rasmussen, Janet, "Kvinner og norsk litteratur. En bibliografi over forskning 1955–1980," in *Gjennom kvinneøyne*, ed. Åse Hiorth Lervik; Register, Cheri, *Kvinnokamp och litteratur i USA och Sverige* (Stockholm, 1977); Richard, Anne Birgitte, *Kvindelitteratur og kvindesituation* (Copenhagen, 1976); Richard, Anne Birgitte, *Kvindeoffentlighed 1968–75* (Cophenhagen, 1978); Wamberg, Bodil, ed., *Out of Denmark* (Copenhagen: 1985); Westman Berg, Karin, ed., *Könsdiskriminering förr och nu* (Stockholm, 1972); Westman Berg, Karin, *Textanalys från könsrollssynpunkt* (Stockholm, 1976); Westman Berg, Karin, *Könsroller i litteraturen från antiken till 1960-talet* (Stockholm, 1968); Westman Berg, Karin, and Gabriella Åhmansson, eds., *Kvinnolitteraturforskning*, 4 vols. (Uppsala, 1979–1983).

Cheri Register

Wuolijoki, Hella (pseud. Juhani Tervapää). Finnish playwright, novelist, and essayist, b. 22 July 1886, Helme, Estonia, d. 2 February 1954, Helsinki.

Estonian nationalism was part of the ethos of Wuolijoki's home in Helme and the decisive influence on her school years in Tartu (Dorpat). Enrolled later at the University of Helsinki, Wuolijoki studied Estonian and Finnish folklore. But after participation in the 1905 General Strike, her loyalties belonged to cosmopolitan leftist causes, and her success as a businesswoman of international stature created an ideological conflict that left its mark upon her literary work. Her political involvement during the Finno-Russian War (1939–1944) brought her first recognition, then imprisonment (1943–1944). After the war, she was executive director of the Finnish National Radio (1945–1949) and member of the Finnish Parliament (1946–1948). Wuolijoki's five autobiographical works portray—in a mixture of "poetry and truth"—a life full of conflict and adventure against the cultural and political background of Estonia's and Finland's struggle for independence in the larger context of the Russian Revolution. These works reveal Wuolijoki, in Bertolt Brecht's words, as an "enchanting storyteller." Brecht's stay as Wuolijoki's guest in 1940 resulted in two plays, Brecht's *Herr Puntila* and Wuolijoki's *Iso-Heikkilän isäntä ja hänen renkinsä Kalle* (1946; The Landlord of Iso-Heikkilä and His Servant Kalle), both rooted in an earlier Wuolijoki play.

Wuolijoki is best known as a dramatist. Three basic elements are constant in her work: love of nature and respect for the country people of Häme, humorous contempt for the shallow world of big business and the newly rich as represented by city slickers, and sharp political criticism as circumstances allowed. Her most performed and translated works belong to the five-volume *Niskavuori* cycle, which portrays generations of conflict at a large Häme estate. The strong Niskavuori women are Wuolijoki's best delineated characters. In repeated conflict between individual happiness and duty toward the land, these women ultimately choose Niskavuori and the solid country values it embodies.

Wuolijoki's plays carry on the late nineteenth-century tradition of idealistic realism with an added strong psychological element. But she also recasts the Finnish folk play into a more serious drama of ideological conflict.

FURTHER WORKS

Udutagused (1914); *Talulapsed* (1921); *Laki ja järjestys* (1933); *Ministeri ja kommunisti* (1933); *Udutaguste Leeni Tartus* (1933); *Kulkurivalssi* (1935); *Koidula* (1936); *Niskavuoren naiset* (1936); *Palava maa (1936); Vastamyrkky* (1936); *Justiina* (1937); *Juurakon Hulda* (1937); *Naiset ja naamarit* (1937); *Vihreä kulta* (1938); *Niskavuoren leipä* (1939); *Niskavuoren nuori emäntä* (1940); *Parlamentin tytär* (1941); *Enkä ollut vanki* (1944); *Häijynpuoleisia pikkunäytelmiä* (1945); *Koulutyttönä Tartossa* (1945); *Kuningas hovinarrina* (1945); *Tuntematon tuomari* (1945); *Ylioppilasvuodet Helsingissä* (1945); *Kummituksia ja kajavia* (1947); *Hetamuorin pitkä reissu* (1948); *Oppinut kissa kultaisessa ketjussa* (1949); *Työmiehen perhe* (1949–1950); *Ei se ollut rakkautta* (1950); *Omalla ajalla* (1950); *Salaperäinen sulhanen* (1950); *Niskavuoren Heta* (1950–1951); *Kallen kalossit eli korvapuusti* (1951); *Kuunsilta* (1951); *Entäs nyt, Niskavuori* (1953); *Minusta tuli liikenainen* (1953); *Sahanpuruprinsessa* (1965); *Työmiehen perhe* (1970); *Niskavuoren tarina* (1979).

REFERENCES

Ammondt, Jukka, *Niskavuoren talosta Juurakon torppaan* (Jyväskylä, 1980); Deschner, Margareta Neovius, "Wuolijoki's and Brecht's Politization of the Volksstück," in *Bertolt Brecht: Political Theory and Literary Practice*, ed. S. N. Weber and H. Heinen (Athens, Georgia, 1980); Lassila, Pertti, "Hella Wuolijoki: A Versatile Talent." *Books from Finland* 20.2 (1986); Lounela, Pekka, *Hella Wuolijoki, legenda jo eläessään* (Helsinki, 1979); Lounela, Pekka, "Hella Wuolijoki: A Woman of Contrasts." *Books from Finland* 13.3 (1979).

Margareta Neovius Deschner

Chronology

YEAR	SCANDINAVIA	OTHER COUNTRIES	
400–	Runic Writing		
850–1050	Viking Period		
	Eddic Poetry		
	Skaldic Poetry		
1000	Iceland adopts Christianity		
1122–33	Ari Þorgilsson: *Book of Icelanders*	Crusades begin	c. 1100
c. 1200	Saxo Grammaticus: *Gesta Danorum*		
1200–1300	Icelandic sagas		
1220–30	Snorri Sturluson: *Heimskringla*	*Magna carta*	1215
c. 1255	*King's Mirror*		
1262	Iceland united with Norway	Marco Polo's journeys	1271–95
		Dante: *Divine Comedy*	1307–21
1323	Finland a province under Sweden		
c. 1348	The Black Death	Boccaccio: *Decameron*	1348–53
1350–1550	Scandinavian ballads		
1380–1814	Norway united with Denmark		
1397–1520	Kalmar Union	Chaucer: *Canterbury Tales*	1387–1400
		Joan of Arc burned	1431
		Gutenberg prints *Constance Mass Book*	1450
		Leonardo da Vinci born	1452
		Michelangelo born	1475
1477, 1479	Universities of Uppsala, Copenhagen		
		Columbus discovers the West Indies	1492
		Copernicus: *Commentariolus*	1512
		Luther's posts his 95 Theses	1517

YEAR	SCANDINAVIA	OTHER COUNTRIES	
1524, 1526	Danish, Swedish Bible translations		
1536–44	Reformation in Scandinavia	Henry VIII establishes Anglican Church	1534
		Elizabeth I	1558–1603
		Shakespeare: *Romeo and Juliet*	1594
		Cervantes: *Don Quixote*	1605–15
1610–1718	Sweden enjoys great power status	Thirty Years' War	1618–48
		Landing of the *Mayflower*	1620
c. 1630	Arrebo: *Hexaemeron*	Galileo abjures theories of Copernicus	1633
		Corneille: *Le Cid*	1636
		Descartes: *Geometry*	1637
1640	University in Turku (Åbo)	Molière: *The Misanthrope*	1666
1658	Stiernhielm: *Hercules*	Milton: *Paradise Lost*	1667–74
		Pascal: *Thoughts*	1670
1673–74	Leonora Christina: *Jammersminde*	Racine: *Phèdre*	1677
1674, 1681	Kingo: *Aandeligt Sjungekor*		
1678–1700	Dass: *Nordlands Trompet*		
1679	Rudbeck: *Atlantica*		
1688	Lucidor: *Helicons blomster*	Newton: *Principles*	*1687*
		Peter the Great Czar of Russia	*1689–1730*
1700–21	*Great Nordic War*		
		Defoe: Robinson Crusoe	*1719*
		Montesquieu: *Persian Letters*	1721
1723–25	Holberg: *Comedies* I–III	Swift: *Gulliver's Travels*	1726
		Gay: *Beggar's Opera*	1728
1732	Linné: *Lapplands resa*		
1732–34	Dalin: *Then swenska Argus*		
1739	Brorson: *Troens rare Klenodie*	Bach: Mass in B Minor	1738
		Handel: *The Messiah*	1741
		Fielding: *Tom Jones*	1749
		Lisbon Earthquake	1755
		Voltaire: *Candide*	1759
1761	Creutz: *Atis och Camilla*		
		Catherine the Great of Russia	1762–96
		Rousseau: *Social Contract*	1762
1772	Wessel: *Kierlighed uden strømper*		
		Goethe: *Sorrows of Young Werther*	1774
		American War of Independence	1775–83
1775	Ewald: *Balders død*		
		Kant: *Critique of Pure Reason*	1781
		Schiller: *The Robbers*	
		Mozart: *The Marriage of Figaro*	1786

YEAR	SCANDINAVIA	OTHER COUNTRIES	
1789	Kellgren: "Den nya skapelsen"	French Revolution	1789
1790	Bellman: *Fredmans epistlar*		
1802	Oehlenschläger: *Digte*		
1803	Staffeldt: *Digte*	Napoleon proclaimed emperor	1804
		Hegel: *Phenomenology*	1807
1809	Sweden cedes Finland to Russia		
	Grundtvig: *Optrin av Nordens kæmpeliv*		
1811	Geijer: "Vikingen"	The brothers Grimm: *Fairy Tales*	1812
1814	Denmark cedes Norway to Sweden	Scott: *Waverley*	1814
1814–16	Afzelius: *Svenska folkvisor*	The Battle of Waterloo	1815
		Byron: *Don Juan*	1818–23
		Schopenhauer: *The World as Will and Representation*	1819
1821–22	Stagnelius: *Liljor i Saron*	Shelley: *Prometheus Unbound*	1820
		Greek War of Liberation	1821–29
1824	Ingemann: *Valdemar den Store*	First passenger railroad	1825
	Blicher: *En Landsbydegns dagbog*		
1824–27	Atterbom: *Lycksalighetens ö*		
1825	Tegner: *Frithiofs saga*	Cooper: *The Last of the Mohicans*	1826
		Heine: *Book of Songs*	1827
1828	Gyllembourg: *En hverdagshistorie*		
	Bremer: *Teckningar utur hvardagslifvet*		
1830	Wergeland: *Skabelsen*	Stendhal: *The Red and the Black*	1830
		Hugo: *Notre Dame of Paris*	1831
		Balzac: *Eugénie Grandet*	1833
1834–40	Almquist: *Törnrosens bok*		
1834	Paludan-Müller: *Amor og Psyche*		
	Welhaven: *Norges dæmring*		
1835	Andersen: *Eventyr fortalte for børn*		
1835–36	Lönnrot: *Kalevala*		
		Carlyle: *Sartor Resartus*	1836
		Victoria Queen of Great Britain	1837–1901
		Dickens: *Pickwick Papers* serialized	1837
		Poe: *Fall of the House of Usher*	1839
1841	Asbjørnsen & Moe: *Eventyr*		
1843	Kierkegaard: *Enten-eller*		
		Thackeray: *Vanity Fair*	1847–48
		February Revolution	1848
1848	Runeberg: *Fänrik Ståls sägner*	Marx & Engels: *Communist Manifesto*	
		Hawthorne: *The Scarlet Letter*	1850

YEAR	SCANDINAVIA	OTHER COUNTRIES	
1851–66	Topelius: *Fältskärns berättelser*	Melville: *Moby Dick*	1851
1853	Aasen: *Prøver af Landsmaalet*		
1855	Collett: *Amtmandens døttre*	Whitman: *Leaves of Grass*	1855
1857	Schack: *Phantasterne*	Flaubert: *Madame Bovary*	1856–57
	Bjørnson: *Synnøve Solbakken*	Baudelaire: *Flowers of Evil*	1857
1858–70	Periodical *Dølen*		
1859	Rydberg: *Den sista athenaren*	Darwin: *Origin of Species*	1859
1861	Vinje: *Ferdaminni*	American Civil War	1861–65
		Turgeniev: *Fathers and Sons*	1862
		Tolstoy: *War and Peace*	1864–69
		Pasteur invents pasteurization	1864
		Dostoevsky: *Crime and Punishment*	1866
1867	Ibsen: *Peer Gynt*		
		Mill: *On the Subjection of Women*	1869
1870	Kivi: *Seitsemän veljestä*	Franco-Prussian War	1870–71
1871	Brandes: *Hovedstrømninger*	Zola: the *Rougon-Macquart* series	1871–93
1872	Drachmann: *Digte*	Telephone and Electric Light	1876–80
1876	Jacobsen: *Fru Marie Grubbe*		
1880	Kielland: *Garman & Worse*		
	Bang: *Haabløse slægter*		
		Wagner: *Parsifal*	1882
1883	Lie: *Familjen paa Gilje*	Nietzsche: *Thus Spoke Zarathustra*	1883
	Garborg: *Bondestudentar*	Mark Twain: *Huckleberry Finn*	1884
1885	Skram: *Constance Ring*		
	Benedictsson: *Pengar*		
	Canth: *Työmiehen vaimo*		
1887	Strindberg: *Fadren*		
	Hansson: *Sensitiva amorosa*		
1890	Periodical *Samtiden*		
	Hamsun: *Sult*		
	Heiberg: *Kong Midas*		
1891	Fröding: *Gitarr och dragharmonika*	Doyle: *Adventures of Sherlock Holmes*	1891
	Lagerlöf: *Gösta Berlings saga*		
1891–95	Pontoppidan: *Det forjættede land*		
		Shaw: *Mrs. Warren's Profession*	1892
1893	Aho: *Papin rouva*		
	Periodical *Taarnet*		
		Kipling: *The Jungle Book*	1894
1895	Heidenstam: *Dikter*		
	Kinck: *Flaggermus-vinger*		
		Bergson: *Matter and Memory*	1896
		Pierre and Marie Curie discover radium	1898

YEAR	SCANDINAVIA	OTHER COUNTRIES	
1898	Karlfeldt: *Fridolins visor*		
1899	Claussen: *Pilefløjter*	Boer War	1899–1901
	Knudsen: *Den gamle præst*		
	Wied: *Livsens ondskab*		
1900	Jensen: *Kongens fald*	Freud: *The Interpretation of*	
		Dreams	1900
1901	Söderberg: *Martin Bircks*	Mann: *Buddenbrooks*	1901
	ungdom	Chekhov: *Three Sisters*	1902
1903–16	Leino: *Helkavirsiä*	Russo-Japanese War	1904–5
		Einstein's Special theory of	
		relativity	1905
1906–10	Nexø: *Pelle Erobreren*		
	Ekelund: *Dithyramber i*		
	aftonglans		
1907	Wildenvey: *Nyinger*		
1908	Linnankoski: *Pakolaiset*		
1909	Bull: *Digte*		
1910–24	Uppdal: *Dansen gjenom*		
	skuggeheimen		
1911	Undset: *Jenny*		
	Øverland: *Den ensomme fest*		
1913	Kjær: *Den lykkelige valg*	Proust: *Remembrance of Things*	
		Past	1913–27
	Ørjasæter: *Gudbrand Langleite*	Stravinsky: *The Rites of Spring*	1913
		Lawrence: *Sons and Lovers*	
		Chaplin: First movies	
		World War I	1914–18
1916	Aukrust: *Himmelvarden*		
		Russian Revolution	1917
		Jung: *Psychology of the*	
		Unconscious	
1918	Södergran: *Septemberlyran*		
1918–23	Duun: *Juvikfolke*	Bauhaus founded by Walter	
		Gropius	1919
1919	Bergman: *Markurells i*		
	Wadköping		
1920	Schildt: *Häxskogen*		
	Lagerkvist: *Det eviga leendet*		
1921–36	Periodical *Mot Dag*	Pirandello: *Six Characters in*	
		Search of an Author	1921
1922	Sjöberg: *Fridas bok*	Mussolini forms Fascist	
		government	1922
		Brecht: *Baal*	
		Eliot: *The Waste Land*	
		Joyce: *Ulysses*	
1923	Falkberget: *Den fjerde nattevakt*		
		Hitler publishes vol. 1 of *My*	
		Struggle	1925
		Kafka: *The Trial*	
1926	Sandel: *Alberte og Jacob*		
1927	Diktonius: *Stenkol*	Woolf: *To the Lighthouse*	1927

YEAR	SCANDINAVIA	OTHER COUNTRIES	
1928–29	Periodical *Quosego*	Weill/Brecht: *Three Penny Opera*	1928
		Faulkner: *The Sound and the Fury*	1929
		Hemingway: *A Farewell to Arms*	
		Remarque: *All Quiet on the Western Front*	
1930	Kristensen: *Hærværk*		
1931	Sillanpää: *Nuorena nukkunut*		
	Hoel: *En dag i oktober*		
1931–32	Laxness: *Salka Valka*		
1932	Ekelöf: *Sent på jorden*	Huxley: *Brave New World*	1932
	Paludan: *Jørgen Stein*	Roosevelt elected President of	
	Martinson: *Resor utan mål*	the U.S.	1932
1933	Sandemose: *En flyktning krysser sitt spor*		
	Jacobsen: *Jord og jern*		
1934	Vesaas: *Det store spelet*	Miller: *Tropic of Cancer*	1934
1935	Blixen: *Syv fantastiske fortællinger*		
	Lo-Johansson: *Kungsgatan*		
	Grieg: *Vår ære og vår makt*		
1936	Krog: *Opbrudd*	Spanish Civil War	1936–39
		Moscow Trials	1937–38
		Sartre: *The Nausea*	1937
		Picasso: *Guernica*	
1939	Abell: *Anna Sophie Hedvig*	World War II	1939–45
		Koestler: *Darkness at Noon*	1940
1941–43	Johnson: *Krilon*	Japanese bomb Pearl Harbor	1941
1942	Lindegren: *mannen utan väg*	Camus: *The Stranger*	1942
		Penicillin (1928) used successfully	1943
1944	Branner: *To minutters stilhed*		
1945	Waltari: *Sinuhe, egyptiläinen*	U.S. drops atomic bomb on Hiroshima	1945
		U.N. founded	
		Orwell: *Animal Farm*	
		Rosselini: *Rome, Open City*	1945
1948	Dagerman: *Bränt barn*	Gandhi assassinated	1948
1948–53	Periodical *Heretica*	Jewish state of Israel established	
		Kinsey Report	
1949–59	Moberg: *Utvandrarna*	NATO	1949
1950	Hansen: *Løgneren*	Mao Zedong leader of China	
	Nedreaas: *Trylleglasset*	Beauvoir: *The Second Sex*	
	Heinesen: *De fortabte spillemænd*	Korean War	1950–53
		Beckett: *Waiting for Godot*	1952
1953	Lidman: *Tjärdalen*	Stalin dies	1953
1954	Mykle: *Lasso rundt fru Luna*		
	Linna: *Tuntematon sotilas*		
1955	Bjørneboe: *Jonas*	Nabokov: *Lolita*	1955

YEAR	SCANDINAVIA	OTHER COUNTRIES	
1955–57	Borgen: *Lillelord trilogy*		
		Hungarian Uprising	1956
1957	Meri: *Manillaköysi*	U.S.S.R. launches Sputnik I	
	Ahlin: *Natt i marknadstältet*	and II	1957
	Seeberg: *Fugls føde*		
1958	Rifbjerg: *Den kroniske uskyld*		
1959	Periodical *Profil*	Ionesco: *The Rhinoceros*	1959
1960	Gyllensten: *Sokrates död*		
		Berlin Wall constructed	1961
		Cuban Missile Crisis	1962
		Albee: *Who's Afraid of Virginia Woolf*	
		Solzhenitsyn: *One Day in the Life of Ivan Denisovich*	
		Bellow: *Herzog*	1964
		Vietnam War	1965–73
		Marcuse: *Culture and Society*	1965
1968	Enquist: *Legionärerna*	Student riots in Europe and America	1968
1970	Tranströmer: *Mörkerseende*	U.S. Apollo II lands on Moon	1969
1971	Solstad: *Arild Asnes 1970*		
		Böll awarded Nobel Prize for Literature	1972
		President Nixon resigns over Watergate	1974
1978	Tikkanen: *Århundradets kärlekssaga*	Singer awarded Nobel Prize for Literature	1978
	Fløgstad Nordic Prize for Literature	Thatcher Prime Minister of the UK	1979
		U.S.S.R. invasion of Afghanistan	1980
		Reagan elected President of the U.S.	1980
		Miłosz Nobel Prize for Literature	1980
1981	Hjartarson Nordic Prize		
1982	Delblanc Nordic Prize	Marquez Nobel Prize for Literature	1982
1985	Tuuri Nordic Prize	Gorbachev Head of USSR Communist Party	1985

Bibliographical Sources

SCANDINAVIA

I. Bibliographies

A. In English

Budd, John, ed., *Eight Scandinavian Novelists*. Criticism and Reviews in English (West-
port, Conn., 1981).
Haugen, Eva L. *A Bibliography of Scandinavian Dictionaries* (White Plains, N.Y., 1984).
Kvamme, Janet, ed. *Index Nordicus*. A cumulative index to English-language articles in
periodicals on Scandinavian Studies (Boston, 1980).
*MLA International Bibliography of Books and Articles on the Modern Languages and
Literatures* (New York, 1921–   ). Annual.
Munch-Petersen, Erland, ed. *Guide to Nordic Bibliography* (Copenhagen, 1984).
Ng, Maria, and Michael S. Batts. *Scandinavian Literature in English Translation 1928–
1977* (Vancouver, B.C., 1978).
Scandinavia: A Bibliographic Survey of Literature (Washington, D.C., 1975).
Tiblin, Mariann. *Scandinavia in English. A Bibliography of Books, Articles, and Book
Reviews. Scandinavian Studies* 47.4 (1975), Suppl. Continued by the following
Tiblin entry.
Tiblin, Mariann, and Susan Larson-Fleming. *Scandinavia in English: An Annual Bibli-
ography of Humanities and Social Sciences 1978* (Minneapolis, 1980).
The Year's Work in Modern Language Studies (London, 1929/1930–).

B. In Scandinavian Languages

*Oversettelse til engelsk av nordisk skjønnlitteratur. Innstilling fra Nordisk kulturkom-
misjon angående Nordisk råds rekommandasjon* (Oslo, 1960).

II. Literary Journals and Annuals in English

Edda (Oslo, 1914–   ). Bimonthly. Includes articles in English.
Mediaeval Scandinavia (Odense, 1968–   ). Annual.

Scandinavian Review (New York, 1913–   ). Monthly. Title until 1975: *American-Scandinavian Review*.
Scandinavian Studies (1911–   ). Quarterly. Place of publication varies.
Scandinavica (London, 1962–   ). Biannual.
World Literature Today (Norman, Oklahoma, 1927–   ). Quarterly. Previous title: *Books Abroad*. Carries regularly reviews of Scandinavian literature.

III. Literary Histories

A. In English

Blankner, Frederika, et al. *The History of the Scandinavian Literatures* (New York, 1966; repr. of 1938).
Bredsdorff, Elias, et al. *An Introduction to Scandinavian Literature from the Earliest Time to Our Day* (Westport, Conn., 1970; repr. of 1951).
Höskuldsson, Sveinn Skorri. *Ideas and Ideologies in Scandinavian Literature since the First World War* (Reykjavík, 1975).
Rossel, Sven H. *A History of Scandinavian Literature, 1870–1980* (Minneapolis, 1982).
Topsøe-Jensen, H. G. *Scandinavian Literature from Brandes to Our Day* (New York, 1929).
Vowles, Richard B. "A Half Century of Scandinavian Drama." *Drama Survey* 1.2 (1961).
Winkel Horn, Frederik. *History of the Literature of the Scandinavian North* (Chicago, 1901).

B. In Scandinavian Languages

Brøndsted, Mogens, ed. *Nordens litteratur.* 2 vols. (Copenhagen, 1972).
Bukdahl, Jørgen. *Nordisk digtning fra oldtiden til vore dage* (Odense, 1956).
Fonsmark, Henning B., ed. *Nordisk litteratur før 1914.* 5th ed. (Copenhagen, 1975).
Runnquist, Åke. *Moderna nordiska författare* (Stockholm, 1966).

IV. Anthologies in English

Allwood, Martin S., ed. *Twentieth Century Scandinavian Poetry: The Development of Poetry in Iceland, Denmark, Norway, Sweden and Finland, 1900–1950* (Copenhagen, 1950).
―――, ed. *Modern Scandinavian Poetry: The Panorama of Poetry 1900–1975* (New York, 1982).
Allwood, Martin S., and Lindsay Lafford. *Scandinavian Songs and Ballads*, 4th ed. (Mullsjö, 1957).
Bannisher, Estrid. *Scandinavian Short Stories: A Selection of Swedish, Norwegian and Danish Stories* (Harmondsworth, 1943).
Canadian Overtones: An Anthology of Canadian Poetry Written Originally in Icelandic, Swedish, Norwegian, Hungarian, Greek and Ukrainian (Winnipeg, 1935).
Creekmore, Hubert, ed. *A Little Treasury of World Poetry: Translations from the Great Poets of Other Languages 2600 B.C. to 1950* (New York, 1952).
Gosse, Edmund, and W. A. Craigie. *The Oxford Book of Scandinavian Verse, 17th Century–20th Century* (Oxford, 1925).
Hallmundsson, Hallberg. *An Anthology of Scandinavian Literature from the Viking Period to the Twentieth Century* (New York, 1965).

The International Portland Review 1980, ed. Cindy Ragland (Portland, Ore., 1980). Includes poetry by Scandinavian authors.

Krook, Anna Sofia. *Songs of the North: A Collection of Poems* (Helsinki, 1926).

Leach, Henry Goddard, ed. *A Pageant of Old Scandinavia* (New York, 1968).

Modern Scandinavian Plays (New York, 1954).

New World Writing 15 (1959). Scandinavian issue.

Radio Plays from Denmark, Finland, Norway, Sweden, Awarded Prizes in the Scandinavian Radio Contest Held in 1969 (Stockholm, 1971).

Rossel, Sven. *Scandinavian Ballads* (Madison, Wis., 1982).

Scandinavian Plays of the Twentieth Century, 3 vols. (Princeton, 1944–1951).

Scandinavian Review. Literary Issue, 68.4 (1980); 69.4 (1981); 70.4 (1982).

Sprinchorn, Evert. *The Genius of Scandinavian Theatre* (New York, 1964).

Soya, Carl Erik, et al. *Five Modern Scandinavian Plays* (New York, 1971).

Corrigan, Robert Willoughby, ed. *Masterpieces of the Modern Scandinavian Theatre* (New York, 1967).

Writ 14 (1982). Translation issue: European languages.

V. Biography

Dictionary of Scandinavian Biography, 2nd ed. (Cambridge, England, 1976).

SWEDEN

I. Bibliographies

A. In English

Du Rietz, Rolf E. *Sweden Imprints 1731–1833*. A Retrospective National Bibliography, 27 vols. (Uppsala, 1977–   ).

Geddes, Tom. *Sweden: Books in English 1963–1978* (London, 1979).

Holmbäck, Bure, et al., eds. *About Sweden, 1900–1963: A Bibliographical Outline* (Stockholm, 1968; repr. from *Sweden Illustrated* 15 [1968]).

Larson-Fleming, Susan. *Books on Sweden in English. In-Print as of Jan. 1, 1983* (New York, 1983).

Sather, Leland B., and Alan Swanson, eds. *Sweden*. World Bibliographical Series, 80. (Oxford, 1987).

Suecana Extranea. Books on Sweden and Swedish Literature in Foreign Languages, 1963–   . Annual (Stockholm, 1969–   ).

Swedish Plays in English Translation from Strindberg to the Present. 3rd ed. (Stockholm, 1985).

B. In Swedish

Andersson, Per. *Pseudonymregister* (Lund, 1967).

Bygdén, Leonard. *Svenskt anonym-och pseudonymlexikon* (Stockholm, 1974; repr. of 1898–1915). *Corrections and Additions and Index of Authors' Names and Pseudonyms* (Stockholm, 1979).

Collijn, Isak. *Sveriges bibliografi intill år 1600*. 3 vols. (Uppsala, 1927–1938).

———. *Sveriges bibliografi. 1600-talet*. 2 vols. (Uppsala, 1942–1946).

Dahlbäck, Lars, and Kerstin Dahlbäck. *Bibliografisk vägledning i svensk litteraturvetenskap* (Stockholm, 1971).

Gren, Anders. *Litteratur om barns och ungdoms läsning* (Linköping, 1980).

Hagström, Tore, ed. *Svensk litteraturhistorisk bibliografi intill år 1900* (Uppsala, 1964–).

Hermelin, Carola, et al., eds. *Kvinnliga författare 1893—1899. Bibliografi över svensk och finlandssvensk skönlitteratur* (Uppsala, 1982).

Holmberg, Claes-Göran, ed. *Litterära tidskrifter i Sverige 1900–1970: en kommenterad bibliografi*. Press och Litteratur, 8 (Lund, 1975).

Leijonhufvud, Sigrid, and Sigrid Brithelli, ed. *Kvinnan inom svenska litteraturen intill år 1893: en bibliografi* (Stockholm, 1978; repr. of 1893).

Lundstedt, Bernhard, ed. *Svenska tidningar och tidskrifter utgifna inom Nord-Amerikas förenta stater* (Stockholm, 1979; repr. of 1886).

Malmström, Rosa, ed. *Svensk festskriftsbibliografi 1936–1960* (Stockholm, 1967). See Taube.

Ottervik, Gösta. *Bibliografier*. 3rd rev. ed. (Lund, 1971).

Samzelius, Jonas L:son, ed. *Svensk litteraturhistorisk bibliografi 1900–1935*. A cumulation of the bibliography in *Samlaren* (Uppsala, 1939–1950).

Svenska tidningsartiklar (Lund, 1953–). Through 1960 entitled *Svensk tidningsindex*.

Svenska tidskriftsartiklar. Swedish periodical articles, Index. (Lund, 1952–). Until 1960 entitled *Svensk tidskriftsindex*.

Svensk bokförteckning. Årskatalog. The Swedish National Bibliography (Stockholm, 1913–).

Svensk bokkatalog, 1866/75- (Stockholm, 1878–).

Svensk litteraturhistorisk bibliografi, in *Samlaren: tidskrift för svensk litteraturhistorisk forskning* (Uppsala, 1880–).

Svenskt pressregister. Index to Swedish newspaper articles from 1880– . (Lund, 1967–).

Taube, Gurli, ed. *Svensk festskriftsbibliografi åren 1891–1925* (Stockholm, 1954).

II. Literary Journals in English

Swedish Book Review (London, 1983–). Two regular yearly issues and a special supplement.

Swedish Books (Göteborg, 1979–1982).

III. Literary Histories and Handbooks

A. In English

Algulin, Ingemar. *Contemporary Swedish Prose* (Uppsala, 1983).

Gustafson, Alrik. *History of Swedish Literature* (Minneapolis, 1961).

Hilleström, Gustaf. *Swedish Theater during Five Decades* (Stockholm, 1968).

Scobbie, Irene, ed. *Aspects of Modern Swedish Literature* (Norwich, England, 1988).

Vowles, Richard B. "Post-War Swedish Poetry: The Other Side of Anguish." *Western Humanities Review* 15 (1961).

Wizelius, Ingemar. *Swedish Literature 1956–60* (Stockholm, 1960).

B. In Swedish

Ardelius, Lars, and Ebba Witt-Brattström, eds. *Författarnas litteraturhistoria*. 3 vols. (Stockholm, 1977–1984).

Björck, Staffan, et al. *Litteraturhistoria i fickformat. Svensk diktning från 80-tal till 70-tal* (Stockholm, 1966).

Brandell, Gunnar. *Svensk litteratur 1900–1950*. 2nd ed. (Stockholm, 1967).
Brandell, Gunnar, and Jan Stenkvist. *Svensk litteratur 1870–1970*. 3 vols. (Stockholm, 1974–1975).
Broström, Torben. *Modern svensk litteratur 1940–1972* (Stockholm, 1974).
Engman, Bo, et al., eds. *Litteraturlexikon: svensk litteratur under 100 år* (Stockholm, 1974).
Hedlund, Tom. *Mitt i 70-talet. 15 yngre svenska författare presenteras* (Stockholm, 1975).
Holmquist, Ingrid, et al., eds. *Kvinnornas litteraturhistoria*. 2 vols. (Lund, 1981–1983).
Lagerlöf, Karl-Erik. *Strömkantringens år och andra essäer om den nya litteraturen* (Stockholm, 1975).
Linder, Erik Hjalmar. *Fem decennier av nittonhundratalet*. 2 vols. (Stockholm, 1965–1966). (Vol. [5] of *Ny illustrerad svensk litteraturhistoria*.)
Lönnroth, Lars, and Sven Delblanc, eds. *Den svenska litteraturen* (Stockholm, 1987–).
Ny illustrerad svensk litteraturhistoria. 5 vols. (Stockholm, 1965–1967, vol. 1, 1967).
Olsson, Bernt, and Ingemar Algulin, *Litteraturens historia i Sverige*. 2nd ed. (Stockholm, 1987).
Runnquist, Åke. *Moderna svenska författare*. 2nd ed. (Stockholm, 1967).
Schück, Henrik, and Karl Warburg. *Illustrerad svensk litteraturhistoria*. 8 vols. (Stockholm, 1926–1949).
Svenskt Litteraturlexikon (Lund, 1970).
Tigerstedt, E. N. *Svensk litteraturhistoria* (Stockholm, 1969).

IV. Anthologies in English

Ahlberg, Fred. *Masterpieces of Swedish Poetry* (Tujunga, Calif., 1952).
Allwood, Martin S., et al., eds. *Modern Swedish Poems* (Rock Island, Ill., 1948).
Allwood, Martin S., and Lindsay Lafford. *Swedish Songs and Ballads* (New York, 1950).
Bäckstrom, Lars, and Göran Palm, eds. *Sweden Writes: Contemporary Poetry and Prose, Views on Art, Literature and Society* (Stockholm, 1965).
Brandberg, Paul, and R. J. McClean, eds. *A Swedish Reader* (London, 1953).
Fleisher, Frederic, ed. *Eight Swedish Poets* (Malmö, 1969).
———. *Seven Swedish Poets* (Malmö, 1963).
Friis, Erik J., ed. *Modern Nordic Plays: Sweden* (New York, 1973).
Fulton, Robert, trans. and comp. *Five Swedish Poets* (New York, 1972).
Gustafsson, Lars. *Forays into Swedish Poetry* (Austin, Texas, 1977).
Hannay, Carolyn, and J. M. Nosworthy, trans. *Some Swedish Poems* (Stockholm, 1958).
Harding, Gunnar, and Anselm Hollo, eds. *Modern Swedish Poetry in Translation* (Minneapolis, 1979).
Lagerlöf, Karl-Erik, ed. *Modern Swedish Prose in Translation* (Minneapolis, 1979).
Larsen, Hanna Astrup, ed. *Sweden's Best Stories* (New York, 1928).
Literary Review 9.2 (1965–1966).
Locock, Charles D., trans. *Modern Swedish Poetry* (London, 1936).
———. *A Selection from Modern Swedish Poetry* (London, 1929, 1930).
Matthias, John, and Göran Printz-Påhlson, trans. *Contemporary Swedish Poetry* (Chicago, 1980).
McClean, Reginald J., ed. *A Book of Swedish Verse* (London, 1968).
Modern Swedish Short Stories (Plainview, N.Y., 1974; repr. of 1934).
Mundus Artium 6.1 (Pittsburgh, Penn., 1973).

Poetry East. vol. 1 (New York, 1980).
Ragland, Cindy, ed. *The International Portland Review* (1980).
Stork, Charles W., trans. *Anthology of Swedish Lyrics from 1750 to 1925*. 2nd ed. (New York, 1930).
————, ed. *Modern Swedish Masterpieces* (New York, 1923).
Wästberg, Per, ed. *An Anthology of Modern Swedish Literature* (New York, 1979).
World Literature Today (Norman, Okla.) 55.2 (1981).

V. Biography

Åhlén, Bengt, ed. *Svenskt författarlexikon 1900–1940*, 3 vols. (Stockholm, 1942); *1941–1950* (Stockholm, 1953); *1951–1955* (Stockholm, 1959); *Register 1941–1955* (Stockholm, 1959).
Diehl, Barbro, and Gabriella Strömberg. *Lexikon över invandrarförfattare i Sverige* (Borås, 1977).
Harnesk, Paul, ed. *Svenskt författarlexikon 1956–1960* (Stockholm, 1963).
Lundblad, Bengt, ed. *Svenskt författarlexikon 1961–65* (Stockholm, 1968); *1966–1970*, ed. Bengt Lundblad and Torsten Lönegren (Stockholm, 1975); *1971–1975* (Stockholm, 1981).
Palmqvist, Arne, and Odd Grandin. *Svenska författare* (Stockholm, 1967).

NORWAY

I. Bibliographies

A. In English

Fet, Jostein. *New Norse Literature in English Translation 1880–1982* (Volda, 1985).
Grønland, Erling. *Norway in English: Books on Norway and by Norwegians in English 1936–1959. A Bibliography, Including a Survey of Norwegian Literature in English Translation from 1742 to 1959* (Oslo, 1961).
————, comp. "Some Norwegian Novels, Poems, and Plays Translated into English, 1959–1974," in *Norway Information*. UDA 424/74 (Oslo, 1974).
Naess, Harald S. *Norwegian Literary Bibliography 1956–70: Norsk litteraturhistorisk bibliografi 1956–70* (Oslo, 1975).
Norwegian Scholarly Books 1825–1967 (Oslo, 1968).
Sather, Leland B., comp. *Norway*. World Bibliographic Series, 67 (Santa Barbara, Calif., 1986).
Welsch, Erwin K., et al., comp. *Norwegian Literature since 1945 in the Memorial Library. University of Wisconsin–Madison* (Madison, 1984).

B. In Norwegian

Andresen, Harald. *Norsk tidsskriftindeks. Forfatterregister 1941–1950* (Oslo, 1964).
Aure, Anton, ed. *Nynorsk boklista, skrifter i bokform paa norsk bygdemaal og landsmaal 1646–1935*. 4 vols. (Oslo, 1916–1942).
Forfatterregister til Norsk tidsskriftindex 1931–1940 (Oslo, 1942).
Kolstad, Stener. *Norsk anonym- of pseudonymleksikon* (Oslo, 1981).
Martens, Johanne, and Gerhard Munthe, eds. *Håndbok over norsk bibliografi. Bibliografisk litteratur i utvalg. De humanistiske fag* (Oslo, 1965).
Norsk bokfortegnelse. The Norwegian National Bibliography, 1941– (Oslo, 1948–).

Norske tidsskriftartikler (Oslo, 1980–). Quarterly.

Norsk litterær årbok. Annual. (Oslo, 1966–). Includes a yearly bibliography, *Bibliografi over norsk litteraturforskning*, until 1975 entitled *Bibliografi til norsk litteratur.*

Norsk tidsskriftsindeks, 1918–1965. 40 vols. (Oslo, 1919–1971).

Øksnevad, Reidar. *Norsk litteraturhistorisk bibliografi 1900–1945* (Oslo, 1951); *1946–1955* (Oslo, 1958).

Pettersen, Hjalmar. *Norsk anonym- og pseudonym-lexikon* (Kristiania, 1924).

———, ed. *Bibliotheca Norvegica*, 4 vols. (Copenhagen, 1973–1974; repr. of 1899–1924).

Raabe, Gustav E., comp. *Norsk litteratur og bøker om Norge trykt i utlandet 1926–1930. Norwegian Literature and Books on Norway Printed Abroad* (Oslo, 1935); *1931–1935* (Oslo, 1941).

Tveterås, Harald L., ed. *Humaniora Norvegica.* 6 vols. (1954–1962).

II. Literary Journals in English

News from the Top of the World (Oslo, 1988–).
Norseman. Bimonthly. (London, 1943–1958; Oslo, 1960–).

III. Literary Histories and Handbooks

A. In English

Beyer, Harald. *A History of Norwegian Literature* (New York, 1952).
Downs, Brian W. *Modern Norwegian Literature 1860–1918* (Cambridge, 1966).
Grøndahl, Ingebright C. *Chapters in Norwegian Literature* (London, 1923).
Jorgenson, Theodore. *History of Norwegian Literature* (New York, 1970; repr. of 1933).
Lyngstad, Sverre, ed. *Review of National Literature: Norway* (Whitestone, N.Y., 1984).
McFarlane, James W. *Ibsen and the Temper of Norwegian Literature* (London, 1960).
Skard, Sigmund. *Classical Tradition in Norway: An Introduction with Bibliography* (Oslo, 1980).
Støverud, Torbjørn. *Milestones of Norwegian Literature* (Oslo, 1967).

B. In Norwegian

Aarnes, Asbjørn, ed. *Litterært leksikon* (Oslo, 1967).
Beyer, Edvard, ed. *Norges litteraturhistorie.* 6 vols. (Oslo, 1974–1975).
Beyer, Harald, and Edvard Beyer. *Norsk litteraturhistorie.* 4th ed. (Oslo, 1978).
Bull, Francis, et al., eds. *Norsk litteraturhistorie.* 2nd ed. 6 vols. (Oslo, 1957–1963).
Dahl, Willy. *Fra 40-tal til 70-tal. Norsk prosa gjennom et kvart århundres etterkrigstid.* 2nd ed. (Oslo, 1973).
———. *Norges litteratur.* 3 vols. (Oslo, 1981–).
———. *Stil og struktur: utviklingslinjer i norsk prosa gjennom 150 år.* 2nd rev. ed. (Oslo, 1969).
Elster, Kristian. *Illustrert norsk litteraturhistorie.* 2nd ed. 6 vols. (Oslo, 1934–1935).
Houm, Philip. *Norges litteratur, fra 1914 til 1950-årene.* 2nd ed. (Oslo, 1976). (Vol. 6 of Bull, above.)
Rønning, H., ed. *Linjer i norsk prosa 1965–1975* (Oslo, 1977).

IV. Anthologies in English

Allwood, Inga Wilhelmsen. *Modern Norwegian Poems* (New York, 1949).
Art and Poetry Today. Norwegian number (Winter/Spring 1979).
Friis, Erik J., ed. *Modern Nordic Plays: Norway* (New York, 1974).
Gathorne-Hardy, G. M. *The Spirit of Norway: Norwegian War Poems* (London, 1944).
Grøndahl, Carl Henrik, et al. *The Literary Masters of Norway with Samples of Their Work* (Oslo, 1978).
Hanson, Katherine, ed. *An Everyday Story: Norwegian Women's Fiction* (Seattle, 1984).
Jorgenson, Theodore, ed. *The Trumpet of Nordland and Other Masterpieces of Norwegian Poetry from the Period 1250–1700* (Northfield, Minn., 1954).
Johanssen, Terje, ed. *20 Contemporary Norwegian Poets* (Oslo, 1984).
Larsen, Hanna Astrup, ed. *Norway's Best Stories: An Introduction to Modern Norwegian Fiction*. Also published under the title *Told in Norway* (Freeport, N.Y., 1971; repr. of 1927).
Larsen, Hanna Astrup, ed. *Told in Norway* (Freeport, N.Y., 1971).
Life and Letters 65.153 (London, 1950). Norwegian writing.
Lines Review: Five Norwegian Poets 55–56 (Edinburgh, Scotland, 1976).
Literary Review 12.2 (Cranbury, N.J., 1968–1969).
McFarlane, James. *Slaves of Love and Other Norwegian Short Stories* (Oxford, 1982).
Micromegas 4.3 (Iowa City, Iowa, 1971). Norwegian issue.
Ragland, Cindy, ed. *International Portland Review* (1980).
Rokkan, Elizabeth, and Ingrid Weatherhead, eds. *View from the Window: Norwegian Short Stories* (Oslo, 1987).
Sehmsdorf, Henning, ed. *Short Stories from Norway* (Madison, Wis., 1986).
Stand 23.3 (1982). Modern Norwegian writing.
Stork, Charles W., ed. *Anthology of Norwegian Lyrics* (Freeport, N.Y., 1968; repr. of 1942).

V. Biography

A. In English

McDuff, David, ed. *Contemporary Norwegian Prose Writers* (Oslo, 1982).

B. In Norwegian

Anker, Øyvind and Bjarte Kaldhol, eds. *Norsk biografisk leksikon* (Oslo, 1921–1983).
Anker, Peter, et al., eds. *Norske Klassikere* (Oslo, 1985).
Dahl, Willy, ed. *Nytt norsk forfatterleksikon* (Oslo, 1971).
Ehrencron-Müller, H. *Forfatterlexikon omfattende Danmark, Norge og Island indtil 1814*, 12 vols. (Copenhagen, 1924–1939).
Halvdan, Hulde et al., eds. *Hvem skrev hva i de siste 25 år* (Oslo, 1950).
Halvorsen, Jens Braage. *Norsk Forfatter-Lexicon, 1814–1880*. 6 vols. (Kristiania, 1885–1908); vol. 5 and 6 by Halvdan Koht.

DENMARK

I. Bibliographies

A. In English and French

Bredsdorff, Elias. *Danish Literature in English Translation* (Westport, Conn., 1973; repr. of 1950).
Danish Children's Books (Copenhagen, 1971).
Dania Polyglotta. Literature on Denmark in Languages Other Than Danish (Copenhagen, 1945–). Annual.
Denmark. Literature, Language, History, Society, Arts. A Select Bibliography (Copenhagen, 1966).
Jørgensen, Aage. *Contributions in Foreign Languages to Danish Literary History, 1961– 81* (Aarhus, 1982).
Miller, Kenneth E., ed. *Denmark*. World Bibliographical Series, 83. (Oxford, 1987).
Mitchell, P. M. *A Bibliographical Guide to Danish Literature* (Copenhagen, 1951).
Munch-Petersen, Erland. *A Guide to Danish Bibliography* (Copenhagen, 1965).
Ober, Kenneth H. *Contributions in Dutch, English, Faroese, German, Icelandic, Italian, and Slavic Languages to Danish Literary History 1925–1970. A Provisional Bibliography* (Copenhagen, 1976).
Schmidt-Phiseldeck, K., ed. *Dania Polyglotta*. Répertoire bibliographique des ouvrages, études, articles, etc., en langues étrangère parus en Danemark de 1901 à 1944. 3 vols. (Copenhagen, 1947–1950).
Schroeder, Carol L. *A Bibliography of Danish Literature in English Translation 1950– 1980* (Copenhagen, 1982).
Thorning, Ebba. *Danish Plays in English Translation* (Copenhagen, 1965).
Welsch, Erwin K., et al., comp. *A Checklist of Danish literature after 1945*. Based on the Holdings of the Memorial Library, University of Wisconsin–Madison. 2nd ed. (Madison, 1986).

B. In Danish

Andersen, Axel. *Håndbøgernes håndbog* (Copenhagen, 1979).
Avis kronik index, 1940–1978 (Ballerup, 1940–1979).
Bruun, Christian V., ed. *Bibliotheca Danica, Systematisk fortegnelse over den danske Litteratur fra 1482–1830*. 4 vols. (Copenhagen, 1961–1963). Supplement 1831– 1840 (1948).
Dansk anmeldelsesindeks 1979– (Ballerup, 1979–). Annual. Continues indexing of reviews in *Avis kronik index*.
Dansk artikelindeks. Aviser og tidsskrifter, 1979– (Ballerup, 1979–). Continues *Dansk tidsskrift index* and *Avis kronik index*.
Dansk bogfortegnelse (Copenhagen, 1841–). Annual.
Dansk tidsskrift index 1915–1978. 64 vols. (Copenhagen, 1916–1980).
Jørgensen, Aage. *Dansk litteraturhistorisk bibliografi 1967–74*. 8 vols. (Copenhagen, 1968–1975).
Lindtner, Niels Chr. *Danske klassikere* (Copenhagen, 1976).
Munch-Petersen, Erland. *Kilder til litteratursøgning*. 2nd rev. ed. (Copenhagen, 1979).

II. Literary Histories

A. In English

Borum, Poul. *Danish literature* (Copenhagen, 1979).
Claudi, Jørgen. *Contemporary Danish Authors, with a Brief Outline of Danish Literature* (Copenhagen, 1952).
Mitchell, P. M. *A History of Danish Literature*. 2nd rev. ed. (New York, 1971).

B. In Danish

Brandt, Jørgen Gustava. *Præsentation. 40 danske digtere efter krigen* (Copenhagen, 1964).
Brøndsted, Mogens, and Sven Møller Kristensen. *Danmarks litteratur*. 3rd ed. (Copenhagen, 1975).
Brostrøm, Torben, and Mette Winge, eds. *Danske digtere i det 20. århundrede*, 5 vols. (Copenhagen, 1980–1982).
Dalager, Stig, and Anne-Marie Mai. *Danske kvindelige forfattere*, vols. 1–2 (Copenhagen, 1982).
Dansk litteraturhistorie. 9 vols. (Copenhagen, 1983–1985).
Friis, Oluf. *Den danske litteraturs historie* (Copenhagen, 1975; repr. of 1945). *Bibliografisk supplement til Oluf Friis: Den danske litteraturs historie*, ed. Thorkil Damsgaard Olsen et al. (Copenhagen, 1977).
Møller Kristensen, Sven. *Dansk litteratur 1918–52*. 7th ed. Supplement 1952–64 (Copenhagen, 1965).
Petersen, Carl S., and Vilhelm Andersen. *Illustreret dansk litteraturhistorie*. 4 vols. (Copenhagen, 1916–1934).
Ravn, Ole. *Dansk litteratur 1920–75*. 2 vols. (Copenhagen, 1976).
Thomsen, Ejnar. *Dansk litteratur efter 1870 med sideblik til det øvrige Norden* (Copenhagen, 1965; repr. of 1935).
Traustedt, P. H., ed. *Dansk litteraturhistorie*. 2nd rev. ed. 2 vols. (Copenhagen, 1976–1977).

III. Anthologies in English

Abrahamsen, Povl, ed. *The Heart Book: The Tradition of the Danish Ballad* (Copenhagen, 1965).
Bredsdorff, Elias. *Contemporary Danish Plays* (Freeport, N.Y., 1960; repr. of 1955).
———. *Contemporary Danish Prose* (Westport, Conn., 1974; repr. of 1958).
Dal, Erik, ed. *Danish Ballads and Folk Songs* (New York, 1967).
Five Danish Poets (Loanhead, Scotland, 1973).
Friis, Erik J., ed. *Modern Nordic Plays: Denmark* (New York, 1974).
Friis, Oluf. *A Book of Danish Verse* (New York, 1976; repr. of 1922).
Gray, Alexander. *Historical Ballads of Denmark* (Edinburgh, Scotland, 1958).
———, ed. *Four and Forty. A Selection of Danish Ballads Presented in Scots* (Chicago, 1954).
Heepe, Evelyn. *Swans of the North and Short Stories by Modern Danish Authors* (Copenhagen, 1953).
Heepe, Evelyn, and Niels Heltberg, eds. *Modern Danish Authors* (Folcroft, Pa., 1974; repr. of 1946).
Heitmann, Annegret, ed. *No Man's Land: An Anthology of Modern Danish Women's Literature* (Norwich, 1987).
Holm, Sven. *The Devil's Instrument and Other Danish Stories* (London, 1971).
Ingwersen, Niels, ed. *Seventeen Danish Poets: A Bilingual Anthology of Contemporary Danish Poetry* (Lincoln, Nebr., 1981).
Jensen, Line, et al. *Contemporary Danish Poetry* (Boston, 1977).
Keigwin, Richard P. *The Jutland Wind and Other Verse from the Danish Peninsula* (Oxford, 1944).

————. *In Denmark I Was Born: A Little Book of Danish Verse* (Copenhagen, 1948).

Knudsen, Johannes, ed. *A Heritage in Song* (Askov, Minn., 1978).

Koefoed, H. A. *Modern Danish Prose* (Copenhagen, 1955).

Larsen, Hanna Astrup. *Denmark's Best Stories* (New York, 1928).

Literary Review 8.1 (1964). Denmark number.

Mitchell, P. M., and Billeskov Jansen, F. J., eds. *Anthology of Danish Literature*. 2 vols. (Carbondale, Ill., 1971).

Mitchell, P. M., and Kenneth H. Ober. *The Royal Guest and Other Classical Danish Narrative* (Chicago, 1977).

Modern Danish Writers. Special issue of *Adam—International Review*. June 1948.

Mogensen, Knud K. *Modern Danish Poems* (New York, 1949).

Olrik, Axel. *A Book of Danish Ballads* (New York, 1976; repr. of 1922).

Rodholm, S. D. *A Harvest of Song: Translations and Original Lyrics* (Des Moines, Iowa, 1953).

Stork, Charles W., trans. *A Second Book of Danish Verse* (Freeport, N.Y., 1968; repr. of 1947).

IV. Biography

Bricka, C. F., ed. *Dansk biografisk leksikon*. 14 vols. (Copenhagen, 1887–1905).

Cedergreen Bech, Sv., ed. *Dansk biografisk Leksikon*. 16 vols. (Copenhagen, 1979–1984).

Dahl, Svend, and Poul Engelstoft, eds. *Dansk biografisk Haandleksikon*. 3 vols. (Copenhagen, 1920–1926).

Dahl, Svend, and Poul Engelstoft, eds. *Dansk skønlitterært Forfatterleksikon 1900–1950*. 3 vols. (Copenhagen, 1959–1964).

Ehrencron-Müller, H. *Forfatterlexikon omfattende Danmark, Norge og Island indtil 1814*, 12 vols.; Supplement, 2 vols. (Copenhagen, 1924–1939).

Engelstoft, Poul, and Svend Dahl, eds. *Dansk biografisk Leksikon*. 27 vols. (Copenhagen, 1933–1944).

Erslew, Thomas Hansen. *Almindeligt Forfatter-Lexicon for Kongeriget Danmark med tilhørende Bilande, fra 1814 til 1840*. 3 vols. (Copenhagen, 1843–1858). Supplement, 3 vols. (1962–1965; repr. of 1858–1868).

Hamilton-Nunnally, Tiina. *Kvindelige danske forfattere*. Bibliografi over prosa i bogform 1820–1910 (Ballerup, 1979).

Sønshagen, Kari. *Danske børnebogsforfattere siden 1970* (Copenhagen, 1983).

FINLAND

I. Bibliographies

A. In English

Aaltonen, Hilkka. *Books in English on Finland* (Turku, 1964).

Screen, J. O., comp. *Finland*. World Bibliographical Series, 31 (Oxford, 1981).

B. In Finnish and Swedish

Ellilä, E. J., ed. *Kirjallisia salanimiä ja nimimerkkejä* (Literary pseudonyms and signatures). 2nd ed. (Helsinki, 1966).

Elmgren, Sven Gabriel. *Öfversigt af Finlands litteratur ifrån år 1542 till 1770* (Helsingfors, 1861); *1771–1863* (Helsingfors, 1865).
Finsk Tidskrifts bok-katalog 1878–1885 (Helsinki, 1879–1886).
Grönroos, Henrik. *Finlands bibliografiska litteratur.* Annotated (Ekenäs, 1975).
Kaarna, Väinö, and Kaarina Winter. *Suomen sanomalehdistön bibliografia 1771–1963* (Helsinki, 1965).
Kallio, V. J. *Fennica-kirjallisuuden salanimiä ja nimimerkkejä vuoteen 1885* (Pseudonyms and signatures in Finnish literature through 1885). (Helsinki, 1939).
Katalog över den svenska litteraturen i Finland, 1886– (Helsinki, 1892–1938); *Katalog över den svenska litteraturen i Finland, samt arbeten utgivna på främmande språk i Finland och av finländska författare på svenska och främmande språk i utlandet, 1926–1932,* ed. Dolly Ölander, 2 vols. (Helsinki, 1974–1977); *Katalog över den svenska litteraturen i Finland och arbeten utgivna av finländska författare på svenska i utlandet, 1933–1938,* ed. Dolly Ölander, 2 vols, (Helsinki, 1982–1983).
Koski, Pirkko, and Kari Salosaari, eds. *Suomalaisen näytelmän- ja teatterintutkimuksen bibliografia vuoteen 1974* (Bibliography of Finnish Drama and Theatre Studies up to 1974). (Tampere, 1976).
Kurikka, Jussi, and Marketta Takkala, eds. *Suomen aikakauslehdistön bibliografia 1782– 1955* (Helsinki, 1983).
Luettelo suomalaisista kirjallisuudentutkimuksista, 1901–70 (List of Finnish research on literature). (Helsinki, 1936, 1939, 1954, 1959, 1963, 1975).
Palperi, Maija, ed. *Suomen aikakauslehti-indeksi 1803–1863. Index to Finnish Periodicals* (Turku, 1974).
Suomalaisia aikakauslehtiartikkeleita. Uutuusindeksi (Helsinki, 1982–). Quarterly.
Suomen aikakauslehti-indeksi (Turku, 1959–). Annual.
Suomen kirjallisuus. Finlands litteratur. The Finnish national bibliography, 1544– . Annual. (Helsinki, 1877–).
Suomessa ilmestyneen kirjallisuuden aineenmukainen uutuusluettelo. Systematisk katalog över i Finland utkommen litteratur (Helsinki, 1945–1946). Continued as *Suomessa ilmestyneen kirjallisuuden luettelo* (Helsinki, 1947–1971).
Takkala, Marketta, et al., eds. *Suomen aikakauslehdistön bibliografia 1956–1977* (Helsinki, 1986).

II. Literary Journals in English

Books from Finland (Helsinki, 1967–). Quarterly.
Kirjallisuudentutkijain Seuran vuosikirja. Annuaire des Historiens de la Litterature. (Helsinki, 1947–). Annual. Published in Finnish, summaries in French 1–30, in English 30– .
World Literature Today (Norman, Okla., 1927–). Quarterly. Carries reviews of Finnish books.

III. Literary Histories

A. In English

Ahokas, Jaakko. *A History of Finnish Literature* (Bloomington, Ind., 1973).
Finnish and Baltic History and Literatures (Cambridge, Mass., 1972).
Laitinen, Kai. *Literature of Finland: An Outline* (Helsinki, 1985).
Rantavaara, Irma. ''A Nation in Search of Identity: Finnish Literature 1830–1917,'' in

Literature and Western Civilization, vol. 5: *The Modern World. II. Realities*, ed. David Daiches and Anthony Thorlby (London, 1972).

B. In Finnish and Swedish

Författare om författare. 24 finlandssvenska diktarporträtt (Borgå, 1980).
Havu, Ilmari, and Thomas Warburton. *Finlands litteratur 1900–1950.* 2 vols. (Örnkrona, 1958).
Holmqvist, Bengt. *Modern finlandssvensk litteratur* (Stockholm, 1951).
Huldén, Lars, et al. *Finlands svenska litteratur*, vol. 1–(Helsinki, 1968–   ).
Laitinen, Kai. *Finlands litteratur* (Helsinki, 1988).
————. *Suomen kirjallisuuden historia* (Helsinki, 1981).
————. *Suomen kirjallisuus 1917–1967*. Ääriviivoja, päälinjoja, saavutuksia (Keuruu, 1967).
Lindström, Hans. *Finlandssvensk nittonhundratalslitteratur* (Stockholm, 1965).
Suomen kirjallisuus. 8 vols. (Helsinki, 1963–1970).
Tarkiainen, V., and E. Kauppinen. *Suomalaisen kirjallisuuden historia.* 4th ed. (Helsinki, 1967).
Warburton, Thomas. *Åttio år finlandssvensk litteratur* (Helsinki, 1984).

IV. Anthologies in English

Allwood, Martin S., ed. *Twentieth Century Scandinavian Poetry: The Development of Poetry in Iceland, Denmark, Norway, Sweden and Finland, 1900–1950* (Copenhagen, 1950).
Armstrong, Robert, ed. *Finnish Odyssey: Poetry and Folk Songs of Finland in Translation* (London, 1975).
Dauenhauer, Richard, and Philip Binham, eds. *Snow in May: An Anthology of Finnish Writing, 1945–72* (Cranbury, N.J., 1978).
Fried, Anne, ed. *Thank You for These Illusions: Poems by Finnish Women Writers* (Porvoo, 1981).
Friis, Erik J., ed. *Modern Nordic Plays: Finland* (New York, 1973).
Hollo, Anselm. *Word from the North: New Poems from Finland* (London, 1965).
Jarvenpa, Aili, ed. *Salt of Pleasure: Twentieth-Century Finnish Poetry* (St. Paul, Minn., 1983).
Kuusi, Matti, et al. *Finnish Folk Poetry: Epic* (Helsinki, 1977).
Literary Review 14.1 (1970).
Lomas, Herbert, ed. *Territorial Song: New Writing in Finland* (London, 1982).
Poetry East 6 (New York, 1981).
Ragland, Cindy, ed. *The International Portland Review* (Portland, Ore., 1980).
Scandinavian Review 75.4 (1987). Issue on Finland.
Schoolfield, George C., ed. *Swedo-Finnish Short Stories* (New York, 1974).
2 Plus 2: A Collection of International Writing (1985).
Väänänen-Jensen, Inkeri, and K. Börje Vähämaki, trans. *Finnish Short Stories* (St. Paul, Minn., 1982).
World Literature Today 54.1 (1980); 58.4 (1984).

V. Biography

Kuka kukin oli - Who was who in Finland. Henkilötietoja 1900-luvulla kuolleista julkisuuden suomalaisista (Keuruu, 1961).

Kuka kukin on (Aikalaiskirja). Who's who in Finland. Henkilötietoja nykypolven suomalaisista (Helsinki, 1920–).
Suomen kirjailijat. Finlands författare 1917. Writers in Finland 1917–1944 (Helsinki, 1981).
Suomen kirjailijat 1945–1980 (Helsinki, 1985).
Tarkka, Pekka. *Suomalaisia nykykirjailijoita* (Helsinki, 1967, 1968, 1980).
Tarkka, Pekka, et al. *Författare i Finland* (Helsinki, 1983).
Vem och vad? Uppslagsbok över samtida finländare—biografisk handbok (Helsinki, 1920–).

ICELAND AND THE FAROE ISLANDS

I. Bibliographies

A. In English

Clover, Carol, and John Lindow, eds. *Old Norse–Icelandic Literature: A Critical Guide. Islandica,* vol. 45 (Ithaca, N.Y., 1985).
Fry, Donald K. *Norse Sagas Translated into English: A Bibliography* (New York, 1980).
Hermansson, Halldór, comp. *Catalogue of the Icelandic Collection Bequeathed by Williard Fiske* (New York, 1914). Additions 1913–1926 (Ithaca, 1927); Additions 1927–1942 (Ithaca, 1943).
Hollander, L. M. *A Bibliography of Skaldic Studies* (Copenhagen, 1958).
Horton, John J. *Iceland.* World Bibliographical Series, 37. (Oxford, 1983).
Islandica: An Annual Relating to Iceland and the Fiske Icelandic Collection (Ithaca, N.Y., 1908–).
Josepsson, Bragi. *Icelandic Culture and Education: An Annotated Bibliography.* Western Kentucky University Research Bulletin, 1 (Bowling Green, 1968).
Mitchell, P. M., and Kenneth H. Ober. *Bibliography of Modern Icelandic Literature in Translation. Including Works Written by Icelanders in Other Languages. Islandica,* vol. 40 (Ithaca, N.Y., 1975).

B. In Scandinavian Languages

Árbók landsbókasafns Íslands. 1944– (Reykjavík, 1945–).
Færøsk bogfortegnelse 1841— (Copenhagen, 1861–).
Fors Bergström, Ejnar. *Den färöiska boken. En nordisk kulturinsats: språket och litteraturen, en översikt.* Dokumentation och data, 6. (Stockholm, 1974).
Islandsk bogfortegnelse 1897–1934 (Copenhagen, 1897–1934).
Íslenzk bókaskrá. The Icelandic National Bibliography, 1974– (Reykjavík, 1975–)
Kvaran, Böðvar, and Einar Sigurðsson, eds., *Skrá um íslenzk blöð og tímarit frá upphafi til 1966* (Reykjavík, 1970).
Pétursson, Einar Gunnar, and Ólafur F. Hjartar. *Íslensk bókfræði. Helstu heimildir um íslenskar bækur og handrit.* 2nd ed. (Reykjavík, 1981).
Sigurðsson, Einar, ed. *Bókmenntaskrá Skírnis* (1969–). Annual.
Sigurðsson, Einar, ed. *Skrá um efni tímaritum Bókmenntafélagsins.* (Reykjavík, 1966).

II. Literary Journals in English

Iceland Review (Reykjavík, 1963–). Quarterly. Title 1968–1984, *Atlantica and Iceland Review.*

Icelandic Canadian (Winnipeg, 1942–). Quarterly.
Magnússon, Siguður, ed. *Icelandic Writing Today* (Reykjavík, 1982).
Saga-Book (London, 1985–). Irregular.
65: The Reader's Quarterly on Contemporary Icelandic Life and Thought (Reykjavík, 1967–1970).

III. Literary Histories

A. In English

Beck, Richard. *History of Icelandic Poets 1800–1940. Islandica,* vol. 34. (Ithaca, N.Y., 1950).
Brønner, Hedin. *Three Faroese Novelists* (New York, 1973).
Chapman, Kenneth G. "From Edda to Atom: A Brief Look at Contemporary Icelandic Poetry." *Books Abroad* 38 (1964).
Einarsson, Stefán. *A History of Icelandic Literature* (New York, 1957).
———. *History of Icelandic Prose Writers 1800–1940. Islandica,* vols. 32–33. (Ithaca, N.Y., 1948).
Magnússon, Sigurður A. "Icelandic Literature: Preserver of National Culture." *Mosaic* 1 (1968).
———. "The Modern Icelandic Novel: From Isolation to Political Awareness." *Mosaic* 4 (1970).
———. "Postwar Literature in Iceland." *World Literature Today* 18–23 (1982).
Turville-Petre, G. *Origins of Icelandic Literature* (Oxford, 1953).

B. In Scandinavian Languages

Andrésson, Kristinn E. *Íslenzkar nútímabókmenntir 1918–1948* (Reykjavík, 1949).
Andrésson, Kristinn E. *Um Íslenzhar bókmenntir.* 2 vols. (Reykjavík, 1979).
Einarsson, Stefán. *Islensk bókmenntasaga, 874–1960* (Reykjavík, 1961).
Gíslason, Bjarni M. *Islands litteratur efter sagatiden, ca 1400–1948* (Copenhagen, 1949).
Helgason, Jón. "Norges og Islands digtning i middelalderen," in *Nordisk Kultur* vol. 8, pt. B (Stockholm, 1953).
Hjálmarsson, Jóhann. *Íslenzk nútimaljóðlist* (Reykjavík, 1971).
Jónsson, Erlendur. *Íslensk bókmenntasaga 1550–1950.* 5th ed. (Reykjavík, 1977).
Matras, Christian. *Føroysk bokmentasøga* (Copenhagen, 1935).
Nordal, Sigurður. *Utsikt over Islands litteratur i det 19. og 20. århundre* (Oslo, 1927).
Pálsson, Heimir. *Straumar og stefnur í íslenskum bókmenntum frá 1550* (Reykjavík, 1978).

IV. Anthologies in English

Beck, Richard. *Icelandic Poems and Stories; Translations from Modern Icelandic Literature* (Freeport, N.Y., 1968; repr. of 1943).
———, ed. *Icelandic Lyrics: Originals and Translation* (Reykjavík, 1930).
Benedikz, Eiríkur, ed. *An Anthology of Modern Icelandic Literature* (Reykjavík, 1959).
Bjarnason, Loftur, ed. *Anthology of Modern Icelandic Literature.* 2 vols. (Berkeley, 1961).
Bjarnason, Paul. *More Echoes: Being Translations Mainly from the Icelandic* (Vancouver, B.C., Canada, 1962).
———. *Odes and Echoes* (Vancouver, Canada, 1954).

Boucher, Alan E., trans. *Northern Voices: Five Contemporary Icelandic Poets* (Paisley, Scotland, 1984).
Brement, Marshall, trans. *Three Modern Icelandic Poets: Selected Poems of Steinn Steinarr, Jón úr Vör and Matthías Johannessen* (Reykjavík, 1985).
Brønner, Hedin. *Faroese Short Stories* (New York, 1972).
Firchow, Evelyn S. *Icelandic Short Stories* (Boston, 1975).
Friis, Erik J., ed. *Modern Nordic Plays: Iceland* (New York, 1973).
Haugen, Einar, ed. *Fire and Ice: Three Icelandic Plays* (Madison, Wis., 1967).
Johnson, Jakobina, trans. *Northern Lights: Icelandic Poems* (Reykjavík, 1959).
Kirconnell, Watson. *Centennial Tales and Selected Poems* (Toronto, 1965).
————. *The North American Book of Icelandic Verse* (New York, 1930).
Magnússon, Sigurður, trans. *Postwar Poetry of Iceland* (Iowa City, Iowa, 1984).
Micromegas 7.3 (1977). Icelandic issue.
Modern Poetry in Translation 30 (Spring 1977).
Pétursson, Ásgeir, and Steingrímur J. Þorsteinsson. *Seven Icelandic Short Stories* (Reykjavík, 1960).

VI. Biography

A. In English

Hermansson, Halldór. *Icelandic Authors of Today. Islandica*, vol. 6 (Ithaca, N.Y., 1913).

B. In Scandinavian Languages

Jónsson, Torfi, ed. *Æviskrár samtíðarmanna*, 3 vols. (Skuggsjá, 1982–1984).
Merkir íslendingar, ed. Þorkell Jóhannesson, 6 vols. (Reykjavík, 1947–1957); ed. Jón Guðnason, 6 vols. (Reykjavík, 1962–1967).
Pétursson, Hannes, and Helgi Sæmundsson, *Islenzkt skáldatal*, 2 vols. (Reykjavík, 1973–1976).
Skrá yfir bækur, ritaðar af konum 1800–1956, in *Kvenréttindafélag Islands. Afmælissýning. 25. jan. - 3. feb., 1957* (Reykjavík, 1957).

Index

The index includes references to names or pseudonyms of writers, artists, musicians, and film directors, and other cultural, historical, or political figures; literary works, in the original as well as in English translation, names of poems or stories that have been mentioned in the text; literary academies, major libraries, and literary prizes; journals, newspapers, and periodicals. Literary characters have, for the most part, been omitted, as have general literary periods, movements, or genres. If a proper name appears in an adjectival form in the text, for example, Zolaesque, a reference to it can be found under the name, in other words, Zola, Emile. No information from the bibliographies is cited, only what appears in the text proper, the preface included. Numbers in *italic* indicate the main discussion of a topic.

Contributors

AHOKAS, JAAKKO, University of Turku

ALLEE, JOHN, George Washington University[†]

BANKIER, JOANNA, Independent Scholar, Berkeley, California

BESSASON, HARALDUR, University of Manitoba

BINHAM, PHILIP, Helsinki School of Economics

BROX, RANDI, University of Oregon

BJORK, ROBERT E., Arizona State University

BONDEBJERG, IB, University of Copenhagen

BRANCH, M. A., University of London

BRANTLY, SUSAN, University of Wisconsin, Madison

CLARÉUS, INGRID, University of Wisconsin, Madison

CLOVER, CAROL J., University of California, Berkeley

COLEMAN, NANCY L., Ajer Videregående Skole, Hamar

D'HEURLE, ADMA, Mercy College

DESCHNER, MARGARETA NEOVIUS, Southern Methodist University

DESERTRAIN, LAURA M., Independent Scholar, Oakland, California

EGEBAK, JØRGEN, University of Copenhagen

EINARSSON, SVEINN, Ministry of Culture, Iceland

ENVALL, MARKKU, University of Helsinki

ESPEGÅRD, SVEND BIRKE, Risskov Amtsgymnasium, Århus

FET, JOSTEIN, Møre og Romsdal distriktshøgskule

FLATIN, KJETIL, University of Oslo

[†] Indicates that contributor is deceased.

FLINT, AILI, Columbia University

FRIED, ANNE, Independent Scholar, Helsinki, Finland

GARTON, JANET, University of East Anglia

GASKI, HARALD, University of Tromsø

GRANGER, JANIS E., Denmark's International Study Program, Copenhagen

GRAY, CHARLOTTE SCHIANDER, Independent Scholar, Berkeley, California

GREENWAY, JOHN L., University of Kentucky

HALE, CHRISTOPHER, University of Alberta

HALLBERG, PETER, University of Gothenburg

HALLMUNDSSON, HALLBERG, Independent Scholar, New York

HILDEBRAND, WERA, Harvard University

HIND, TAGE, University of Copenhagen

HOBERMAN, JOHN M., University of Texas, Austin

HOLMES, PHILIP, University of Hull

HOMSTAD, TORILD M., University of Minnesota

HOUE, POUL, University of Minnesota

HUGUS, FRANK, University of Massachusetts

HULDÉN, LARS, University of Helsinki

HUMMASTI, TERTTU, Independent Scholar

INGWERSEN, FAITH, University of Wisconsin, Madison

INGWERSEN, NIELS, University of Wisconsin, Madison

JARVI, RAYMOND, North Park College

JENSEN, JODY, University of California, Berkeley

JENSEN, NIELS LYHNE, Aarhus University

JENSEN, RUDOLF, Grand View College

JOHNSON, WALTER, University of Washington[†]

JONES, W. GLYN, University of East Anglia

JORGENSEN, PETER A., University of Georgia

KINNUNEN, MATTI, Helsingin Sanomat, Finland

KONGSLIEN, INGEBORG, University of Oslo

KÖNIG, FRITZ H., University of Northern Iowa

KRATZ, HENRY, University of Tennessee

LAITINEN, KAI, University of Helsinki

LAPPALAINEN, KALEVI, Independent Scholar, Poet, Emporia, Kansas

LASSILA, PERTTI, University of Helsinki

LESSER, RIKA, Translator, New York City

LIDE, BARBARA, Michigan Technological University

LINDOW, JOHN, University of California, Berkeley

LUNDELL, TORBORG, University of California, Santa Barbara

LYNGSTAD, SVERRE, New Jersey Institute of Technology

MCFARLANE, JAMES, University of East Anglia

MCKNIGHT, CHRISTINA SÖDERHJELM, University of California, Berkeley

MADSEN, BØRGE GEDSØ, University of California, Berkeley[†]

MÆHLE, LEIF, University of Oslo

MAGNÚSSON, SIGURÐUR A., Writer, Reykjavík

MARX, LEONIE, University of Kansas

MASSENGALE, JAMES, University of California, Los Angeles

MATTSSON, MARGARETA, University of Virginia

MORRIS, WALTER D., Iowa State University

NAESS, HARALD S., University of Wisconsin, Madison

NILSSON, KIM, University of Wisconsin, Madison

NORSENG, MARY KAY, University of California, Los Angeles

OSTER, ROSE-MARIE G., University of Maryland, College Park

PALOMÄKI, DONNA, University of Wisconsin, Madison

PARENTE, JAMES A., JR., Institute for Advanced Study, School of Historical Studies, Princeton, New Jersey

RASMUSSEN, JANET, Pacific Lutheran University

REGISTER, CHERI, Independent Scholar, Minneapolis, Minnesota

REGULA, DEBORAH, University of Minnesota

ROSSEL, SVEN H., University of Washington

ROTTEM, ØYSTEIN, University of Copenhagen

SÆMUNDSSON, MATTHÍAS VIÐAR, University of Iceland

SCHOOLFIELD, GEORGE C., Yale University

SCOBBIE, IRENE, University of Aberdeen

SCOTT, LARS EMIL, Augustana College

SEHMSDORF, HENNING, University of Washington

SENNER, W. M., Arizona State University

SETTERWALL, MONICA, Independent Scholar, Stockholm, Sweden

SHACKELFORD, FRANKIE, University of Wisconsin, Madison

SHIDELER, ROSS, University of California, Los Angeles

SHOGREN, MELISSA LOWE, Washington State University

SJÖBERG, LEIF, State University of New York, Stony Brook

SJÅVIK, JAN, University of Washington

SONDRUP, STEVEN P., Brigham Young University

SORENSEN, OTTO M., Macalester College

SØRENSEN, PREBEN MEULENGRACHT, Aarhus University

STEENE, BIRGITTA, University of Washington

STOKKER, KATHLEEN, Luther College

SWANSON, ALAN, Brigham Young University

TARKKA, PEKKA, Helsingin Sanomat, Finland

TATE, GEORGE S., Brigham Young University

TAYLOR, ALEXANDER, Eastern Connecticut State University

THOMPSON, LAURIE, St. David's University College, Lampeter, Wales

TÖRNQVIST, EGIL, University of Amsterdam

VÄHÄMÄKI, BÖRJE, University of Minnesota

VIRTANEN, REINO, University of Nebraska[†]

WAAL, CARLA, University of Missouri-Columbia

WARME, LARS G., University of Washington

WEATHERHEAD, INGRID, University of Oregon

WELSCH, ERWIN K., University of Wisconsin

WØIDE, OLE, Aarhus University

WRIGHT, ROCHELLE, University of Illinois

ZEMPEL, SOLVEIG, St. Olaf College

ZUCK, VIRPI, University of Oregon